Charles Walter Stansby Williams, Collection novels

In this ebook:
All Hallows' Eve, 1948
Descent into Hell, 1937
The Greater Trumps, 1932
Many Dimensions, 1930
The Place of the Lion, 1931
War in Heaven, 1930

Charles Walter Stansby Williams (1886 – 1945) was a British poet, novelist, theologian, literary critic, and member of the Inklings. Although Williams attracted the attention and admiration of some of the most notable writers of his day, including T. S. Eliot and W. H. Auden, his greatest admirer was probably C. S. Lewis, whose novel That Hideous Strength was at the time regarded as entirely inspired by Williams's novels.

In this book:

All Hallows' Eve…………………..…………Pag. 3
Descent into Hell………...……...…………Pag. 88
The Greater Trumps…………………..Pag. 165
Many Dimensions………………………Pag. 247
The Place of the Lion…………..………Pag. 343
War in Heaven…………………………Pag. 415

All Hallows' Eve

Chapter One

THE NEW LIFE

She was standing on Westminster Bridge. It was twilight, but the City was no longer dark. The street lamps along the Embankment were still dimmed, but in the buildings shutters and blinds and curtains had been removed or left undrawn, and the lights were coming out there like the first faint stars above. Those lights were the peace. It was true that formal peace was not yet in being; all that had happened was that fighting had ceased. The enemy, as enemy, no longer existed, and one more crisis of agony was done. Labour, intelligence, patience—much need for these; and much certainty of boredom and suffering and misery, but no longer the sick vigils and daily despair.

Lester Furnival stood and looked at the City while the twilight deepened. The devastated areas were hidden; much was to be done but could be. In the distance she could hear an occasional plane. Its sound gave her a greater sense of relief than the silence. It was precisely not dangerous; it promised a truer safety than all the squadrons of fighters and bombers had held. Something was ended, and those remote engines told her so. The moon was not yet risen; the river was dark below. She put her hand on the parapet and looked at it; it should make no more bandages if she could help it. It was not a bad hand, though it was neither so clean nor so smooth as it had been years ago, before the war. It was twenty-five now, and to her that seemed a great age. She went on looking at it for a long while, in the silence and the peace, until it occurred to her that the silence was very prolonged, except for that recurrent solitary plane. No one, all the time she had been standing there, had crossed the bridge; no voice, no step, no car had sounded in the deepening night.

She took her hand off the wall, and turned. The bridge was as empty as the river; no vehicles or pedestrians here, no craft there. In all that City she might have been the only living thing. She had been so impressed by the sense of security and peace while she had been looking down at the river that only now did she begin to try and remember why she was there on the bridge. There was a confused sense in her mind that she was on her way somewhere; she was either going to or coming from her own flat. It might have been to meet Richard, though she had an idea that Richard, or someone with Richard, had told her not to come. But she could not think of anyone, except Richard, who was at all likely to do so, and anyhow she knew she had been determined to come. It was all mixed up with that crash which had put everything out of her head; and as she lifted her eyes, she saw beyond the Houses and the Abbey the cause of the crash, the plane lying half in the river and half on the Embankment. She looked at it with a sense of its importance to her, but she could not tell why it should seem so important. Her only immediate concern with it seemed to be that it might have blocked the direct road home to her flat, which lay beyond Millbank and was where Richard was or would be and her own chief affairs. She thought of it with pleasure; it was reasonably new and fresh, and they had been lucky to get it when Richard and she had been married yesterday. At least—yesterday? well, not yesterday but not very much longer than yesterday, only the other day. It had been the other day. The word for a moment worried her; it had been indeed another, a separate, day. She felt as if she had almost lost her memory of it, yet she knew she had not. She had been married, and to Richard.

The plane, in the thickening darkness, was now but a thicker darkness, and distinguishable only because her eyes were still fixed on it. If she moved she would lose it. If she lost it, she would be left in the midst of this—this *lull*. She knew the sudden London lulls well enough, but this lull was lasting absurdly long. All the lulls she had ever known were not as deep as this, in which there seemed no movement at all, if the gentle agitation of the now visible stars were less than movement, or the steady flow of the river beneath her; she had at least seen that flowing—or had she? was that also still? She was alone with this night in the City—a night of peace and lights and stars, and of bridges and streets she knew, but all in a silence she did not know, so that if she yielded to the silence she would not know those other things, and the whole place would be different and dreadful.

She stood up from the parapet against which she had been leaning, and shook herself impatiently. "I'm moithering," she said in a word she had picked up from a Red Cross companion, and took a step forward. If she could not get directly along Millbank, she must go round. Fortunately the City was at least partially lit now. The lights in the houses shone out, and by them she could see more clearly than in the bad old days. Also she could see into them; and somewhere in her there was a small desire to see someone—a woman reading, children playing, a man listening to the wireless; something of that humanity which must be near, but of which on that lonely bridge she could feel nothing. She turned her face towards Westminster and began to walk.

She had hardly taken a dozen steps when she stopped. In the first moment, she thought it was only the echo of her own steps that she heard, but immediately she knew it was not. Someone else, at last, was there; someone else was coming, and coming quickly. Her heart leapt and subsided; the sound at once delighted and frightened her. But she grew angry with this sort of dallying, this over-consciousness of sensation. It was more like Richard than herself. Richard could be aware of sensation so and yet take it in its stride; it was apt to distract her. She had admired him for it, and still did; only now she was a little envious and irritated. She blamed Richard for her own incapacity. She had paused, and before she could go on she knew the steps. They were his. Six months of marriage had not dulled the recognition; she knew the true time of it at once. It was Richard himself coming. She went quickly on.

In a few moments she saw him; her eyes as well as her ears recognized him. Her relief increased her anger. Why had he let her in for this inconvenience? had they arranged to meet? if so, why had he not been there? why had she been kept waiting? and what had she been doing while she had been kept? The lingering lack of memory drove her on and increased her irritation. He was coming. His fair bare head shone dark-gold under a farther street lamp; under the nearer they came face to face.

He stopped dead as he saw her, and his face went white. Then he sprang towards her. She threw up her hand as if to keep him off. She said, with a coldness against her deeper will, but she could not help it: "Where have you been? what have you been doing? I've been waiting."

He said: "How did you get out? what do you mean—waiting?"

The question startled her. She stared at him. His own gaze was troubled and almost inimical; there was something in him which scared her more. She wondered if she were going to faint, for he seemed almost to float before her in the air and to be far away. She said: "What do *you* mean? Where are you going? Richard!"

For he was going—in another sense. Her hand still raised, in that repelling gesture, she saw him move backwards, uncertainly, out of the range of that dimmed light. She went after him; he should not evade her. She was almost up to him, and she saw him throw out his hands towards her. She caught them; she knew she caught them, for she could see them in her own, but she could not feel them. They were terrifying, and he was terrifying. She brought her hands against her breast, and they grew fixed there, as, wide-eyed with anger and fear, she watched him disappearing before her. As if he were a ghost he faded; and with him faded all the pleasant human sounds—feet, voices, bells, engines, wheels—which now she knew that, while she had talked to him, she had again clearly heard. He had gone; all was silent. She choked on his name; it did not recall him. He had vanished, and she stood once more alone.

She could not tell how long she stood there, shocked and impotent to move. Her fear was at first part of her rage, but presently it separated itself, and was cold in her, and became a single definite thought. When at last she could move, could step again to the parapet and lean against it and rest her hands on it, the thought possessed her with its desolation. It dominated everything—anger and perplexity and the silence; it was in a word—"Dead," she thought, "dead." He could not otherwise have gone; never in all their quarrels had he gone or she; that certainty had allowed them a licence they dared not otherwise have risked. She began to cry—unusually, helplessly, stupidly. She felt the tears on her face and peered at the parapet for her handbag and a handkerchief, since now she could not—O despair!—borrow his, as with her most blasting taunts she had sometimes done. It was not on the parapet. She took a step or two away, brushed with her hand the tears from her eyes, and looked about the pavement. It was not on the pavement. She was crying in the street and she had neither handkerchief nor powder. This was what happened when Richard was gone, was dead. He must be dead; how else could he be gone? how else could she be there, and so?

Dead, and she had done it once too often. Dead, and this had been their parting. Dead; her misery swamped her penitence. They had told each other it made no difference, and now it had made this. They had reassured each other in their reconciliations, for though they had been fools and quick-tempered, high egotists and bitter of tongue, they had been much in love and they had been but fighting their way. But she felt her own inner mind had always foreboded this. Dead; separate; for ever separate. It did not, in that separation, much matter who was dead. If it had been she——

She. On the instant she knew it. The word still meant to her so much only this separation that the knowledge did not at first surprise her. One of them was; she was. Very well; she was. But then—she was. On that apparent bridge, beneath those apparent stars, she stood up and knew it. Her tears stopped and dried; she felt the stiffness and the stains on her apparent flesh. She did not now doubt the fact and was still not surprised. She remembered what had happened—herself setting out to meet Evelyn at the Tube, and instead coming across her just over there, and their stopping. And then the sudden loud noise, the shrieks, the violent pain. The plane had crashed on them. She had then, or very soon after, become what she now was.

She was no longer crying; her misery had frozen. The separation she endured was deeper than even she had believed. She had seen Richard for the last time, for now she herself was away, away beyond him. She was entirely cut off; she was dead. It was now a more foreign word than it had ever been, and it meant this. She could perhaps, if it was he who had been dead, have gone to him; now she could not. She could never get back to him, and he would never come to her. He could not: she had thrown him away. It was all quite proper; quite inevitable. She had pushed him away, and there was an end to Richard. But there was no end to her.

Never in her life had she contemplated so final an end which was no end. All change had carried on some kind of memory which was encouragement. She had not always supposed it to be so; she had told herself, when she left school, when she was married, that she was facing a new life. But she had, on the whole, been fortunate in her passage, and some pleasantness in her past had always offered her a promise in the future. This however was a quite new life. Her good fortune had preserved her from any experience of that state which is—almost adequately—called "death-in-life"; it had consequently little prepared her for this life-in-death. Her heart had not fallen—ever, ever—through an unfathomed emptiness, supported only on the fluttering wings of every-day life; and not even realizing that it was so supported. She was a quite ordinary, and rather lucky, girl, and she was dead.

Only the City lay silently around her; only the river flowed below, and the stars flickered above, and in the houses lights shone. It occurred to her presently to wonder vaguely—as in hopeless affliction men do wonder—why the lights were shining. If the City were as empty as it seemed, if there were no companion anywhere, why the lights? She gazed at them, and the wonder flickered and went away, and after a while returned and presently went away again, and so on for a long time. She remained standing there, for though she had been a reasonably intelligent and forceful creature, she had never in fact had to display any initiative—much less such initiative as was needed here. She had never much thought about death; she had never prepared for it; she had never related anything to it. She had nothing whatever to do with it, or (therefore) in it. As it seemed to have nothing to offer her except this wide prospect of London, she remained helpless. She knew it was a wide prospect, for after she had remained for a great while in the dark it had grown slowly light again. A kind of pale October day had dawned, and the lights in the apparent houses had gone out; and then it had once more grown dark, and they had shone—and so on—twenty or thirty times. There had been no sun. During the day she saw the River and the City; during the night, the stars. Nothing else.

Why at last she began to move she could not have said. She was not hungry or thirsty or cold or tired—well, perhaps a little cold and tired, but only a little, and certainly not hungry or thirsty. But if Richard, in this new sense, were not coming, it presently seemed to her useless to wait. But besides Richard, the only thing in which she had been interested had been the apparatus of mortal life; not people—she had not cared for people particularly, except perhaps Evelyn; she was sincerely used to Evelyn, whom she had known at school and since; but apart from Evelyn, not people—only the things they used and lived in, houses, dresses, furniture, gadgets of all kinds. That was what she had liked, and (if she wanted it now) that was what she had got. She did not, of course, know this, and she could not know that it was the sincerity of her interest that procured her this relaxation in the void. If Richard had died, this would have remained vivid to her. Since she was dead, it remained also, though not (stripped of all forms of men and women) particularly vivid.

She began to walk. It did not much matter which way. Her first conscious movement—and even that was hardly a movement of volition—was to look over her shoulder in the seeming daylight to see if the plane were there. It was, though dimmer and smaller, as if it were fading. Would the whole City gradually fade and leave her to emptiness? Or would she too fade? She did not really attempt to grapple with the problem of her seeming body; death did not offer her problems of that sort. Her body in life had never been a problem; she had accepted it, inconveniences and all, as a thing that simply was. Her pride—and she had a good deal of pride, especially sexual—had kept her from commitments except with Richard. It was her willingness to commit herself with Richard that made her believe she (as she called it) loved Richard, though in her bad moments she definitely wished Richard, in that sense, to love her more than she loved him. But her bad moments were not many. She really did want, need, and (so far) love Richard. Her lack and longing and despair and self-blame were sincere enough, and they did not surprise her. It had been plain honest passion, and plain honest passion it remained. But now the passion more and more took the form of one thought; she had done it again, she had done it once too often, and this was the unalterable result.

She began to walk. She went up northward. That was instinct; she at least knew that part of London. Up from the bridge, up Whitehall—no-one. Into Trafalgar Square—no-one. In the shops, in the offices—no-one.

They were all full and furnished with everything but man. At moments, as she walked, a horrible fancy took her that those at which she was not, at the moment, looking were completely empty; that everything was but a façade, with nothing at all behind it; that if she had walked straight through one of those shops, she would come out into entire nothing. It was a creeping sensation of the void; she herself could not have put it into words. But there the suspicion was.

She came to the bottom of Charing Cross Road, and began to go up it. In front of her she saw the curtains of brick that hid the entrances to Leicester Square Tube Station. By one of them, on the opposite side of the road, someone was standing. She was still not conscious of any shock of surprise or of fear or even of relief. Her emotions were not in action. There had been no-one; there was now someone. It was not Richard; it was another young woman. She crossed the road towards the unknown; it seemed the thing to do. Unknown? not unknown. It was—and now she did feel a faint surprise—it was Evelyn. In the sudden recollection of having arranged to meet Evelyn there, she almost forgot that she was dead. But then she remembered that their actual meeting had been accidental. They had both happened to be on their way to their appointed place. As she remembered, she felt a sudden renewal of the pain and of the oblivion. It did not remain. There was nothing to do but go on. She went on.

The figure of Evelyn moved and came towards her. The sound of her heels was at first hideously loud on the pavement as she came, but after a step or two it dwindled to almost nothing. Lester hardly noticed the noise at the time or its diminution; her sense was in her eyes. She absorbed the approaching form as it neared her with a growing intensity which caused her almost to forget Richard. The second-best was now the only best. As they drew together, she could not find anything to say beyond what she had said a hundred times— dull and careless: "O hallo, Evelyn!" The sound of the words scared her, but much more the immediate intolerable anxiety about the reply: would it come? It did come. The shape of her friend said in a shaking voice: "O hallo, Lester!"

They stopped and looked at each other. Lester could not find it possible to speak of their present state. Evelyn stood before her, a little shorter than she, with her rather pinched face and quick glancing black eyes. Her black hair was covered by a small green hat. She wore a green coat; and her hands were fidgeting with each other. Lester saw at once that she also was without a handbag. This lack of what, for both of them, was almost, if not quite, part of their very dress, something without which they were never seen in public; this loss of handkerchief, compact, keys, money, letters, left them peculiarly desolate. They had nothing but themselves and what they wore—no property, no convenience. Lester felt nervous of the loss of her dress itself; she clutched it defensively. Without her handbag she was doubly forlorn in this empty City. But Evelyn was there, and Evelyn was something. They could, each of them, whatever was to happen, meet it with something human close by. Poor deserted vagrants as they were, they could at least be companions in their wanderings.

She said: "So you're here!" and felt a little cheered. Perhaps soon she would be able to utter the word *death*. Lester had no lack of courage. She had always been willing, as it is called, "to face facts"; indeed, her chief danger had been that, in a life with no particular crisis and no particular meaning, she would invent for herself facts to face. She had the common, vague idea of her age that if your sexual life was all right you were all right, and she had the common vague idea of all ages that if you (and your sexual life) were not all right, it was probably someone else's fault—perhaps undeliberate, but still their fault. Her irritation with her husband had been much more the result of power seeking material than mere fretfulness. Her courage and her power, when she saw Evelyn, stirred; she half-prepared a part for them to play— frankness, exploration, daring. Oh if it could but have been with Richard!

Evelyn was speaking. Her quick and yet inaccurate voice rippled in words and slurred them. She said: "You *have* been a long time. I quite thought you wouldn't be coming. I've been waiting—you can't think how long. Let's go into the Park and sit down."

Lester was about to answer when she was appalled by the mere flat ordinariness of the words. She had been gripping to herself so long her final loss of Richard that she had gripped also the new state in which they were. This talk of sitting down in the Park came over her like a nightmare, with a nightmare's horror of unreality become actual. She saw before her the entrance to the station, and she remembered they had meant to go somewhere by Tube. She began, with an equal idiocy, to say: "But weren't we——" when Evelyn gripped her arm. Lester disliked being held; she disliked Evelyn holding her; now she disliked it more than ever. Her flesh shrank. Her eyes were on the station entrance, and the repulsion of her flesh spread. There was the entrance; they had meant to go—yes, but there could not now be any Tube below; or it would be as empty as the street. A medieval would have feared other things in such a moment—the way perhaps to the *città dolente*, or the people of it, smooth or hairy, tusked or clawed, malicious or lustful, creeping and clambering up from the lower depths. She did not think of that, but she did think of the spaces and what might fill them; what but the dead? Perhaps—in a flash she saw them—perhaps there the people, the dead people, of this empty City were; perhaps that was where the whole population had been lying, waiting for her too, the entrance waiting and all below the entrance. There were things her courage could not face. Evelyn's clutch on her arm was light, light out of all proportion to the fear in Evelyn's eyes, but in her own fear she yielded to it. She allowed herself to be led away.

They went into the Park; they found a seat; they sat down. Evelyn had begun to talk, and now she went on. Lester had always known Evelyn talked a good deal, but she had never listened to more than she chose. Now she could not help listening, and she had never before heard Evelyn gabble like this. The voice was small and thin as it usually was, but it was speedier and much more continuous. It was like a river; no, it was like something thrown about on a river, twisted and tossed. It had no pressure; it had no weight. But it went on. She was saying—"that we wouldn't go to see it to-day, after all. I mean, there aren't many people about, and I do hate an empty theatre, don't you? Even a cinema. It always seems different. I hate not being with people. Should we go and see Betty? I know you don't much care for Betty, or her mother. I don't like her mother myself, though of course with Betty she must have had a very difficult time. I wish I could have done more for her, but I did try. I'm really very fond of Betty, and I've always said that there was some simple explanation for that odd business with the little German refugee a year or two ago. Naturally I never said anything to her about it, because she's almost morbidly shy, isn't she? I did hear that that painter had been there several times lately; what's his name? Drayton; he's a friend of your husband, isn't he? but I shouldn't think he——"

Lester said—if she said; she was not certain, but she seemed to say: "Be quiet, Evelyn."

The voice stopped. Lester knew that she had stopped it. She could not herself say more. The stillness of the City was immediately present again, and for a moment she almost regretted her words. But of the two she knew she preferred the immense, the inimical stillness to that insensate babble. Death as death was preferable to death mimicking a foolish life. She sat, almost defiantly, silent; they both sat silent. Presently Lester heard by her side a small and curious noise. She looked round. Evelyn was sitting there crying as Lester had cried, the tears running down her face, and the small noise came from her mouth. She was shaking all over, and her teeth were knocking together. That was the noise.

Lester looked at her. Once she would have been impatient or sympathetic. She felt that, even now, she might be either, but in fact she was neither. There was Evelyn, crying and chattering; well, there was Evelyn crying and chattering. It was not a matter that seemed relevant. She looked away again. They went on sitting.

The first shadow of another night was in the sky. There was never any sun, so it could not sink. There was a moon, but a moon of some difference, for it gave no light. It was large and bright and cold, and it hung in the sky, but there was no moonlight on the ground. The lights in the houses would come on, and then go out. It was certainly growing darker. By her side the chattering went on; the crying became more full of despair. Lester dimly remembered that she would once have been as irritated by it as all but the truly compassionate always are by misery. Now she was not. She said nothing; she did nothing. She could not help being aware of Evelyn, and a slow recollection of her past with Evelyn forced itself on her mind. She knew she had never really liked Evelyn, but Evelyn had been a habit, almost a drug, with which she filled spare hours. Evelyn usually did what Lester wanted. She would talk gossip which Lester did not quite like to talk, but did rather like to hear talked, because she could then listen to it while despising it. She kept Lester up to date in all her less decent curiosities. She came because she was invited and stayed because she was needed. They went out together because it suited them; they had been going out that afternoon because it suited them; and now they were dead and sitting in the Park because it had suited someone or something else—someone who had let a weakness into the plane or had not been able to manage the plane, or perhaps this City of façades which in a mere magnetic emptiness had drawn them to be there, just there.

Still motionlessly gazing across the darkening Park, Lester thought again of Richard. If Richard had been in distress by her side—not, of course, crying and chattering, more likely dumb and rigid—would she have done anything? She thought probably not. But she might, she certainly might, have cried to him. She would have expected him to help her. But she could not think of it; the pang took her too quickly; he was not there and could not be. Well … the pang continued, but she was growing used to it. She knew she would have to get used to it.

The voice by her side spoke again. It said, through its sobs, the sobs catching and interrupting it: "Lester! Lester, I'm so frightened." And then again: "Lester, why won't you let me talk?"

Lester began: "Why——" and had to pause, for in the shadow her voice was dreadful to her. It did not sound like a voice; only like an echo. In the apparent daylight, it had not been so bad, but in this twilight it seemed only like something that, if it was happening at all, was happening elsewhere. It could not hold any meaning, for all meaning had been left behind; in her flat perhaps which she would never occupy again; or

7

perhaps with the other dead in the tunnels of the Tube; or perhaps farther away yet, with whatever it was that had drawn them there and would draw them farther; this was only a little way—Oh what else remained to know?

She paused, but she would not be defeated. She forced herself to speak; she could and would dare that at least. She said: "Why…. Why do you want to talk *now*?"

The other voice said: "I can't help it. It's getting so dark. Let's go on talking. We can't do anything else."

Lester felt again the small weak hand on her arm, and now she had time to feel it; nothing else intervened. She hated the contact. Evelyn's hand might have been the hand of some pleading lover whose touch made her flesh creep. She had, once or twice in her proud life, been caught like that; once in a taxi—the present touch brought sharply back that other clasp, in this very Park on a summer evening. She had only just not snapped into irritation and resentment then; but in some ways she had liked the unfortunate man, and they had been dining pleasantly enough. She had remained kind; she had endured the fingers feeling up her wrist, her whole body loathing them, until she could with sufficient decency disengage herself. It was her first conscious recollection of an incident in her past—that act of pure courtesy, though she did not then recognize it either as recollection or as a courtesy. Only for a moment she thought she saw a taxi race through the Park away before her, and then she thought it could not be and was not. But she stiffened herself now against her instinctive shrinking, and let her arm lie still, while the feeble hand clutched and pawed at her.

Her apprehension quickened as she did so. To be what she was, to be in this state of death, was bad enough, but at the same time to feel the dead, to endure the clinging of the dead, being dead to know the dead—the live man in the taxi was far better than this, this that was Evelyn, the gabbling voice, the chattering teeth, the helpless sobs, the crawling fingers. But she had gone out with Evelyn much more than with the man in the taxi; her heart acknowledged a debt. She continued to sit still. She said in a voice touched by pity if not by compassion: "It's no good talking, especially like that. Don't you understand?"

Evelyn answered, resentfully choking, but still holding on: "I was only telling you about Betty, and it's all quite true. And no-one can hear me except you, so it doesn't matter."

No-one could hear; it was true enough—unless indeed the City heard, unless the distant façades, and the nearer façade of trees and grass, were listening, unless they had in them just that reality at least, a capacity to overhear and oversee. The thin nothingness could perhaps hear and know. Lester felt all about her a strange attention, and Evelyn herself, as if frightened by her own words, gave a hasty look round, and then burst again into a hysterical monologue: "Isn't it funny—we're all alone? We never thought we'd be alone like this, did we? But I only said what was quite true, even if I do hate Betty. I hate everyone except you; of course I don't hate you; I'm very fond of you. You won't go away, will you? It's nearly dark again, and I hate it when it's dark. You don't know what the dark was like before you came. Why are we here like this? I haven't done anything. I haven't; I tell you I haven't. I haven't done *anything*."

The last word rose like a wail in the night, almost (as in the old tales) as if a protesting ghost was loosed and fled, in a cry as thin as its own tenuous wisp of existence, through the irresponsive air of a dark world, where its own justification was its only, and worst, accusation. So high and shrill was the wail that Lester felt as though Evelyn herself must have been torn away and have vanished, but it was not so. The fingers still clutched her wrist, and Evelyn still sat there, crying and ejaculating, without strength to cry louder: "I haven't done anything, anything. I haven't done anything at all."

And what then could be done now? If neither Evelyn nor she herself had ever of old done anything, what could or should they do now—with nothing and no-one about them? with only the shell of a City, and they themselves but shell, and perhaps not even true shell? only a faint memory and a pang worse than memory? It was too much to bear. As if provoked by an ancient impetuosity of rage, Lester sprang to her feet; shell or body, she sprang up, and the motion tore her from the hand that held her. She took a step away. Better go alone then sit so companioned; and then as her foot moved to the second step she paused. Evelyn had wailed again: "Oh don't go! don't go!" Lester felt herself again thrusting Richard away, and she paused. She looked back over her shoulder; half in anger and half in pity, in fear and scorn and tenderness, she looked back. She saw Evelyn, Evelyn instead of Richard. She stared down at the other girl, and she exclaimed aloud: "Oh my God!"

It was the kind of casual exclamation she and Richard had been in the habit of throwing about all over the place. It meant nothing; when they were seriously aggressive or aggrieved, they used language borrowed from bestiality or hell. She had never thought it meant anything. But in this air every word meant something, meant itself; and this curious new exactitude of speech hung there like a strange language, as if she had sworn in Spanish or Pushtu, and the oath had echoed into an invocation. Nothing now happened; no-one came; not a quiver disturbed the night, but for a moment she felt as if someone might come, or perhaps not even that—no more than a sudden sense that she was listening as if to hear if it was raining. She was

8

becoming strange to herself; her words, even her intonations, were foreign. In a foreign land she was speaking a foreign tongue; she spoke and did not know what she said. Her mouth was uttering its own habits, but the meaning of those habits was not her own. She did not recognize what she used. "I haven't done anything…. Oh my God!" This was how they talked, and it was a great precise prehistoric language forming itself out of the noises their mouths made. She articulated the speech of Adam or Seth or Noah, and only dimly recognized the intelligibility of it. She exclaimed again, despairingly: "Richard!" and that word she did know. It was the only word common to her and the City in which she stood. As she spoke, she almost saw his face, himself saying something, and she thought she would have understood that meaning, for his face was part of the meaning, as it always had been, and she had lived with that meaning—loved, desired, denounced it. Something intelligible and great loomed and was gone. She was silent. She turned; she said, more gently than she had spoken before: "Evelyn, let's do something now."

"But I haven't done *anything*," Evelyn sobbed again. The precise words sounded round them, and Lester answered their meaning.

"No," she said, "I know. Nor have I—much." She had for six months kept house for Richard and herself and meant it. She *had* meant it; quarrels and bickerings could not alter that; even the throwing it away could not alter it. She lifted her head; it was as certain as any of the stars now above her in the sky. For the second time she felt—apart from Evelyn—her past present with her. The first had been in the sense of that shadowy taxi racing through the Park, but this was stronger and more fixed. She lived more easily for that moment. She said again: "Not very much. Let's go."

"But where can we go?" Evelyn cried. "Where are we? It's so *horrible*."

Lester looked round her. She saw the stars; she saw the lights; she saw dim shapes of houses and trees in a landscape which was less familiar through being so familiar. She could not even yet manage to enunciate to her companion the word *death*. The landscape of death lay round them; the future of death awaited them. Let them go to it; let them do something. She thought of her own flat and of Richard—no. She did not wish to take this other Evelyn there; besides, she herself would be, if anything at all, only a dim shadow to Richard, a hallucination or a troubling apparition. She could not bear that, if it could be avoided; she could not bear to be only a terrifying dream. No; they must go elsewhere. She wondered if Evelyn felt in the same way about her own home. She knew that Evelyn had continuously snubbed and suppressed her mother, with whom she lived; once or twice she had herself meant to say something, if only out of an indifferent superiority. But the indifference had beaten the superiority. It was now for Evelyn to choose.

She said: "Shall we go to your place?"

Evelyn said shrilly: "No; no. I won't see Mother. I hate Mother."

Lester shrugged. One way and another, they did seem to be rather vagrants, unfortunate and helpless creatures, with no purpose and no use. She said: "Well … let's go." Evelyn looked up at her. Lester, with an effort at companionship, tried to smile at her. She did not very well succeed, but at least Evelyn, slowly and reluctantly, got to her feet. The lights in the houses had gone out, but a faint clarity was in the air—perhaps (though it had come quickly) the first suggestion of the day. Lester knew exactly what she had better do, and with an effort she did it. She took Evelyn's arm. The two dead girls went together slowly out of the Park.

Chapter Two

THE BEETLES

It was a month or so since Lester Furnival had been buried. The plane crash had been explained and regretted by the authorities. Apologies and condolences had been sent to Mrs. Furnival's husband and Miss Mercer's mother. A correspondence on the possibility and propriety of compensation had taken place in the Press, and a question or two had been asked in the House. It was explained that nothing could be done, but that a whole set of new instructions had been issued to everyone connected with flying, from Air Marshals to factory hands.

The publicity of this discussion was almost a greater shock to Richard Furnival than his wife's death; or, at least, the one confused the other. He was just enough to see that, for the sake of the poor, the Crown ought always at such times to be challenged to extend as a grace what it refused as a claim. He was even conscious that Lester, if the circumstances had been reversed, might properly have had no difficulty in taking what he would have rejected; not that she was less fastidious or less passionate than he, but it would have seemed to her natural and proper to spoil those whom he was content to ignore.

The Foreign Office in which through the war he had been serving, pressed on him prolonged leave. He had been half-inclined to refuse, for he guessed that, after the first shock, it was not now that his distress would begin. The most lasting quality of loss is its unexpectedness. No doubt he would know his own loss in the expected places and times—in streets and stations, in restaurants and theatres, in their own home. He expected that. What he also expected, and yet knew he could not by its nature expect, was his seizure by his own loss in places uniquely his—in his office while he read Norwegian minutes, in the Tube while he read the morning paper, at a bar while he drank with a friend. These habits had existed before he had known Lester, but they could not escape her. She had, remotely but certainly, and without her own knowledge, overruled all. Her entrance into all was absolute, and lacking her the entrance of the pain.

He went away; he returned. He went away to spare his office-companions the slight embarrassment of the sight of him. He returned because he could not bear to be away. He had not yet taken up his work; in a few days he would. Meanwhile he determined unexpectedly one afternoon to call on Jonathan Drayton.

He had know him for a number of years, long before Jonathan became a well-known painter. He was also a very good painter, though there were critics who disapproved of him; they said his colour was too shrill. But he had been appointed one of the official war-artists, and two of his paintings—*Submarine Submerging and Night Fighters over Paris*—were among the remarkable artistic achievements of the war. He also had been for some time on leave, in preparation (it was understood) for the grand meetings after the peace, when he would be expected to produce historic records of historic occasions. He had been once or twice, a little before the accident, at the Furnivals' flat, but he had then gone to Scotland and written to Richard from there. A later postcard had announced his return.

Richard had come across the card accidentally on this particular afternoon, and had suddenly made up his mind to go round. Jonathan had been living, or rather had left his things while he was away, on the top floor of a building in the City, not far from St. Paul's, one room of which was sufficiently well-lit to be used as a studio. It was to the studio that he took Richard after a warm welcome. He was shorter and stockier than his friend, and he had a general habit of leaving Richard the most comfortable chair and himself sitting on the table. He settled himself there, and went on: "I've got several things to tell you; at least, I've got one to tell you and two to show you. If I tell you first … the fact is I'm practically engaged."

"Splendid!" said Richard. Such things were unlikely to distress him, as Jonathan guessed; one could not altogether say what might, but not that. He was quite simply pleased. He said: "Do I know her? and what do you mean by 'practically'?"

"I don't know if you know her," Jonathan said. "She's Betty Wallingford, the daughter of the Air Marshal. She and her mother are coming here presently."

"I remember hearing her name," Richard said. "She was a friend of Lester's—or rather not a friend, but they knew each other some time ago. But I rather gathered she was ill or something, and her mother didn't let her go out much."

"That's true enough," Jonathan answered. "It was the Air Marshal who asked me to dine one night after I'd painted him. He's a nice creature, though not interesting to paint. Lady Wallingford keeps Betty rather close, and why I say 'practically' is because, when things came to a head with Betty the other day, she didn't seem very keen. She didn't exactly refuse, but she didn't encourage. They're both coming here presently. Don't go, whatever you do. I've a particular reason for asking you to stay."

"Have you?" Richard said. "What is it?"

Jonathan nodded at an easel on which was a canvas covered by a cloth. "That," he said, and looked at his watch. "We've an hour before they come, and I'd like you to see it first. No; it's not a painting of Betty, or of her mother. It's something quite different, but it may—I don't know, but it just may—be a little awkward with Lady Wallingford. However, there's something else for you to see first—d'you mind? If you hadn't come along, I was going to ring you up. I'm never quite happy about a thing till you've seen it."

This, as Richard knew, was a little extreme. But it had a basis of truth; when Jonathan exaggerated, he exaggerated in the grand style. He never said the same thing to two people; something similar perhaps, but always distinguished, though occasionally hardly anyone but he could distinguish the distinction. Richard answered: "I've never known you take much notice of anything I said. But show it to me all the same, whatever it is."

"Over here," Jonathan said, and took his friend round to the other side of the room. A second easel was standing back to back with the first, also holding a canvas, but this uncovered. Richard set himself to look at it.

It was of a part of London after a raid—he thought, of the City proper, for a shape on the right reminded him dimly of St. Paul's. At the back were a few houses, but the rest of the painting was of a wide stretch of desolation. The time was late dawn; the sky was clear; the light came, it seemed at first, from the yet unrisen sun behind the single group of houses. The light was the most outstanding thing in the painting; presently, as Richard looked, it seemed to stand out from the painting, and almost to dominate the room itself. At least it so governed the painting that all other details and elements were contained within it. They floated in that imaginary light as the earth does in the sun's. The colours were so heightened that they were almost at odds. Richard saw again what the critics meant when they said that Jonathan Drayton's paintings "were shrill" or "shrieked", but he saw also that what prevented this was a certain massiveness. The usual slight distinction between shape and hue seemed wholly to have vanished. Colour was more intensely image than it can usually manage to be, even in that art. A beam of wood painted amber was more than that; it was light which had become amber in order to become wood. All that massiveness of colour was led, by delicate gradations almost like the vibrations of light itself, towards the hidden sun; the eye encountered the gradations in their outward passage and moved inwards towards their source. It was then that the style of the painting came fully into its own. The spectator became convinced that the source of that light was not only in that hidden sun; as, localized, it certainly was. "Here lies the east; does not the day break here?" The day did, but the light did not. The eye, nearing that particular day, realized that it was leaving the whole fullness of the light behind. It was everywhere in the painting—concealed in houses and in their projected shadows, lying in ambush in the cathedral, opening in the rubble, vivid in the vividness of the sky. It would everywhere have burst through, had it not chosen rather to be shaped into forms, and to restrain and change its greatness in the colours of those lesser limits. It was universal, and lived.

Richard said at last: "I wish you could have shown the sun."

"Yes?" said Jonathan. "Why?"

"Because then I might have known whether the light's in the sun or the sun's in the light. For the life of me, I can't be certain. It rather looks as though, if one could see the sun, it would be a kind of container … no, as if it would be made of the light as well as everything else."

"And very agreeable criticism," Jonathan said. "I admit you imply a whole lot of what I only hope are correct comments on the rest of it. You approve?"

"It's far and away the best thing you've done," Richard answered. "It's almost the *only* thing you've done—now you've done it. It's like a modern Creation of the World, or at least a Creation of London. How did you come to do it?"

"Sir Joshua Reynolds," said Jonathan, "once alluded to 'common observation and a plain understanding' as the source of all art. I should like to think I agreed with Sir Joshua here."

Richard still contemplated the painting. He said slowly: "You've always been good at light. I remember how you did the moon in that other thing—*Doves on a Roof*, and there was something of it in the *Planes* and the *Submarine*. Of course one rather expects light effects in the sea and the air, and perhaps one's more startled when the earth becomes like the sea or the air. But I don't think that counts much. The odd thing is that you don't at any time lose weight. No-one can say your mass isn't massive."

"I should hope they couldn't," said Jonathan. "I've no notion of losing one thing because I've put in another. Now to paint the massiveness of light——"

"What do you call this?" Richard asked.

"A compromise, I fear," Jonathan answered. "A necessary momentary compromise, I allow. Richard, you really are a blasted nuisance. I do wish you wouldn't always be telling me what I ought to do next before I've been let enjoy what I've done. This, I now see, is compromising with light by turning it into things. Remains to leave out the things and get into the light."

Richard smiled. "What about the immediate future?" he asked. "Do you propose to turn Churchill into a series of vibrations in pure light?"

Jonathan hummed a little. "At that——" he began and stopped. "No; I'm babbling. Come and see the other thing, which is different."

He led the way back round the easels. He said: "Have you ever heard of Father Simon?"

"Have I not?" said Richard. "Is he or is he not in all the papers, almost as much as the Peace? The Foreign Office has been taking a mild concern in all these new prophets, including this one. Then there's the Russian one and the Chinese. You get them at times like these. But they all seem, from our point of view, quite innocuous. I've not been very interested myself."

"Nor was I," said Jonathan, "till I met Lady Wallingford. Since then I have read of him, listened to him, met him, and now painted him. Lady Wallingford came across him in America when she was there soon after the last war, and I gather fell for him then. During this war he became one of their great religious

11

leaders, and when he came over she was one of—or rather she was—his reception committee. She's devoted to him; Betty—not so much, but she goes with her mother." He paused frowning, as if he were about to make a further remark about Betty and her mother, but he changed his mind and went on: "Lady Wallingford thought it would be a privilege for me to paint the Prophet."

Richard said: "Is that what they call him?"

His hand on the covering of the canvas, Jonathan hesitated. "No," he said, "I don't want to be unfair. No. What she actually calls him is the Father. I asked her if he was a priest, but she took no notice. He's got a quite enormous following in America, though here, in spite of the papers, he's kept himself rather quiet. It's been suggested that he's the only man to evangelize Germany. It's also been suggested that he and his opposite numbers in Russia and China shall make a threefold World Leadership. But so far he's not done or said anything about it. He may be just waiting. Well, I did the best I could. Here's the result."

He threw the covering back and Richard was confronted with the painting. It was, at first glance, that of a man preaching. The congregation, of which there seemed a vast number, had their backs to the spectator. They were all a little inclined forward, as if (Richard supposed) in the act of listening, so that they were a mass of slightly curved backs. They were not in a church; they were not in a room; it was difficult to see where they were, and Richard did not particularly mind. It was in an open space somewhere; what he could see of the ground was not unlike the devastation in the other picture, though more rock-like, more in the nature of a wilderness than a City. Beyond them, in a kind of rock pulpit against a great cliff, was the preacher. He seemed to be a tallish dark man of late middle age, in a habit of some sort. His face, clean-shaven, heavy, emaciated, was bent a little downward towards his audience. One hand was stretched out towards them, also a little downward, but the hand was open and turned palm upward. Behind him his shadow was thrown on the rock; above, the sky was full of heavy and rushing cloud.

Richard began to speak, and checked himself. He looked more closely at the preaching figure, especially at the face. Though the canvas was large the face inevitably was small, but it was done with care, and as Richard studied it, the little painted oval began to loom out of the picture till its downward-leaning weight seemed to dominate and press on the audience below, and to make all—clouds and crowds and rock-pulpit— greyer and less determined around it. If it was a pulpit; Richard was not clear whether the figure was casting a shadow on the rock or emerging from a cleft in the rock. But the face—it was almost as if the figure had lowered his face to avoid some expression being caught by the painter, and had failed, for Jonathan had caught it too soon. But what exactly had Jonathan caught? and why had Jonathan chosen to create precisely that effect of attempted escape and capture?

Richard said at last: "It's a wonderful effect—especially the colour of the face. I don't know how you got that dark deadness. But what——" He stopped.

"Richard," Jonathan said accusingly, "you were going to ask what it *meant*."

"I don't think I was," Richard answered. "I may have been going to ask what *he* meant. I feel as if there was something in him I hadn't grasped. He's…" and again he paused.

"Go on!" Jonathan said. "The ladies won't be here just yet, and you may now have got a general idea of why I'd like you to be here when they do come. Anyhow, go on; say anything that occurs to you."

Richard obediently renewed his study and his reverie. They had done this together on a number of occasions before a new painting. Richard did not mind sounding foolish before his friend, and Jonathan did not mind being denigrated by his friend; in fact, he always swore that one soliloquy of this kind was worth a great deal of judicious criticism. Painting was the only art, he maintained, about which it could be done; one couldn't hear a poem or a symphony as one could look at a painting; in time one could never get the whole at once, but one could in space—or all but; there was bound perhaps to be a very small time-lag even there. Except for that, all the aural arts aspired to escape from recollection into the immediate condition of the visual.

Richard said: "The skin looks almost as if it were painted; I mean—as if you were painting a painted effect. Very dark and very dull. Yet it's a sort of massive dullness—much like your mass *and* light; only the opposite. But what I don't get is the expression. At first he seems to be just a preacher driving his point home—convicting them of sin or something. Only, though that mass makes him effective enough—even his hand seems to be pressing down on them, though it is back downwards; it might almost be pulling the sky down on them by a kind of magic—a sort of Samson and the pillars of cloud—yet the more I look at what I can see of the face, the more I think that it doesn't mean anything. It seems to be as near plain bewilderment as anything I ever saw."

"Ho!" said Jonathan, getting off the table to which he had retired. "Ho! You're a genius, Richard. I thought that too. But I've looked at it so often that I can't make out now who's bewildered—him or me."

Richard looked a question.

"I began painting the damned fellow, as one does," Jonathan went on, pacing up and down the room and frowning at the floor; "of course, he wasn't sitting for me, so I had to do the best I could from one meeting at Sir Bartholomew's, a couple of orations, seven photographs in *Picture Post*, a dozen daily papers, and other oddments. Lady Wallingford says he won't sit because of his reserve, which may of course be true. But at a pinch I can manage to get something out of such a general hodge-podge fairly well, tiresome as the whole business always is, and this time I took particular notice. I wasn't trying to paint his soul or anything: I just wanted to get him done well enough to please Betty's mother. And when I'd done it I stared at it and I thought: 'Either I don't know *what* he is or he doesn't know *where* he is.' But a fellow who's put it over all America and bits of England is likely to know where he is, I suppose, so I must just have got him completely wrong. It's odd, all the same. I generally manage to make something more or less definite. This man looks as if he were being frightfully definite and completely indefinite at the same moment—an absolute master and a lost loony at once."

"Perhaps he is," said Richard doubtfully.

Jonathan came to a stop by the easel and sighed drearily. "No," he said, "no. I'm afraid not. In fact, I'm afraid it's a complete give-away for me. The main point is—do you think Lady Wallingford will notice it? And what will she say if she does?"

"I shouldn't think she would," said Richard. "After all, I only just did myself and I'm far more used to your style than she is."

"She may not be used to me, but she's extremely used to him," Jonathan said gloomily. "She's one of the real inner circle. Betty and I will have a much more difficult time if there's any trouble. Otherwise, I shouldn't mind in the least. What *do* you people know about him, Richard?"

"We know," said Richard, "that his name is Simon Leclerc—sometimes called Father Simon and sometimes Simon the Clerk. We gather he's a Jew by descent, though born in France, and brought up in America. We know that he has a great power of oratory—at least, over there; he hasn't tried it much here so far—and that it's said he's performed a number of very remarkable cures, which I don't suppose we've checked. We know that quite intelligent people are attached to him—and that's about all we do know; at least, it's all I know. But, as I told you, I've not been particularly interested. You say you've heard him preach; what does he preach?"

"Love," said Jonathan, more gloomily than ever as he looked at his watch. "They'll be here in a minute. Love, so far as I can gather, but I was more looking at him than listening to him, and it's almost impossible for me really to do both at once. I could sort of feel his effect going on all round. But it was mostly Love, with a hint of some secret behind, which Love no doubt could find out. He sometimes gives private interviews, I know, but I really felt it'd be too embarrassing to go to one. So I can only generalize from the bits I caught while I was staring. Love, and something else."

There was a ring at the front door bell. Jonathan threw the cover again over the painting, and said: "Richard, if you go now, I'll never forgive you. And if you don't say the right thing, I'll never listen to a word of yours again." He went hastily out.

He was back so soon that Richard had hardly time to do more than feel at a distance within him that full and recollected life which, whenever it did show itself, threatened to overthrow all other present experiences. It was his first experience of such a nature, of "another" life. Almost, as he too turned from the easel, he saw Lester's dead face, as he had seen it, floating, dim and ill-defined, before his eyes; and the two women who came into the room, though more spectacular, were more empty and shell-like than she.

They were not unlike, with thirty years between. They were both smallish. Lady Wallingford was grey and thin, and had something almost of arrogance in her manner. Betty was fair and thinner than, at her age, one would have thought she ought to be. She looked tired and rather wan. Her eyes, as she entered, were turned on Jonathan, and Richard thought he saw her hand drop from his. Jonathan presented him. Lady Wallingford took him, so to speak, for granted—so granted as to be unnecessary. Betty gave him a quick little glance of interest, which for the moment he did not quite understand; having forgotten that she was supposed to have known Lester. He bowed twice, and stepped back a pace. Jonathan said: "You'll have some tea first, Lady Wallingford? It's not too warm to-day."

Lady Wallingford said: "We'll look at the picture first. I'm anxious to see it."

"I'm very cold, Mother," Betty said—a little nervously, Richard thought. "Couldn't we have tea?"

Lady Wallingford entirely ignored this. She said: "Is that covered thing it? Let me see it."

Jonathan, with the faintest shrug, obeyed. He went to the easel; he said, over his shoulder: "You'll understand that this is rather an impression than a portrait," and he pulled aside the covering. There was a silence, concentrated on the painting. Richard, discreetly in the background, waited for its first quiver.

The first he observed was in Betty. She was just behind her mother, and he saw her yield to a faint shudder. Jonathan saw it too; he almost made a movement towards her, and checked it before Lady Wallingford's immobility. After what seemed like minutes, she said: "What is our Father coming out of, Mr. Drayton?"

Jonathan pinched his lip, glanced at Betty, and answered: "What you choose, Lady Wallingford."

Lady Wallingford said: "You must have some idea. What is he standing on? rock?"

"Oh yes, rock," said Jonathan readily; and then, as if reluctantly truthful, added: "At least, you might as well call it rock."

The private view was not going very well. Betty sat down, as if her power had failed. Lady Wallingford said: "*Is* he standing on it?"

Jonathan answered: "It doesn't much matter, perhaps." He glanced rather anxiously at Richard. Richard took a step forward, and said, as engagingly as he could: "It's the whole impression that counts, don't you think?"

It was quite certainly the wrong remark. Lady Wallingford took no notice of it. She went on, still addressing herself to Jonathan, "And why are the people so much like insects?"

Betty made an inarticulate sound. Jonathan and Richard both stared at the painting. It had not occurred to either of them—not even apparently to Jonathan—that the whole mass of inclined backs could be seen almost as a ranked mass of beetles, their oval backs dully reflecting a distant light. Once the word had been spoken, the painting became suddenly sinister. Jonathan broke out, but his voice was unconvincing: "They're not … they weren't meant … they don't look like beetles."

"They look exactly like beetles," Lady Wallingford said. "They are not human beings at all. And Father Simon's face is exactly the same shape."

Richard saw that there at least she was right. The oval shape of the face differed only in its features and its downward inclination from the innumerable backs, and in the fact that it reflected no light. It was this lack of reflection which gave it its peculiar deadness; the backs had that dim reflection, but this face none. But now he saw it as so similar in shape that it seemed to him for half a second not a face at all, but another back; but this eyed and mouthed as if the living human form ended in a gruesomeness, and had a huge beetle for its head, only a beetle that looked out backward through its coat and had a wide speaking mouth there also; a speaking beetle, an orating beetle, but also a dead and watching beetle. He forgot the aesthetic remark he had been about to make.

Jonathan was saying: "I think that's rather reading things into it." It was not, for him, a particularly intelligent remark; but he was distracted by the thought of Betty, and yet his voice was as cold as Lady Wallingford's own. He could manage his words but not his tone.

Lady Wallingford moved her head a little more forward. Richard saw the movement, and suddenly, as she stood in front of him, she too took on the shape of an overgrown insect. Outside the painting her back repeated the shapes in the painting. Richard suddenly found himself believing in the painting. This then was what the hearers of Father Simon looked like. He glanced at the face again, but he supposed he had lost that special angle of sight; it was now more like a face, though of that dead artificiality he had remarked before. Lady Wallingford leaned towards the picture, as if she were feeling for it with invisible tentacles. But she was feeling with a hideous and almost dangerous accuracy. She now said, and her voice was more than cold; it was indignant: "Why have you painted our Father as an imbecile?"

Here however Jonathan was driven to protest more strongly. He turned his back on the painting, and he said with some passion: "No, really, Lady Wallingford, I have not. I can see what you mean by complaining of the shapes, though honestly I never thought of anything of the sort, and I'll do something…. I mean, I'll paint something different somehow. But I never had the slightest intention of painting Father Simon in any displeasing way…."

Lady Wallingford said: "You intended…. Look at it!" Jonathan stopped speaking; he looked at the woman; then he looked beyond her at Betty. She looked back despairingly. Richard observed the exchange of their eyes, and the full crisis became clear to him. He felt, as they did, Betty swept away on Lady Wallingford's receding anger; he saw her throw out a hand towards Jonathan, and he saw Jonathan immediately respond. He saw him move away from the painting and go across to Betty, take her hands, and lift her from her chair so that she stood against him. His arm round her, he turned again towards the painting. And again Richard's eyes went with his.

It was as he had last seen it. Or was it? Was the face not quite so down-turned? was it more lifted and already contemplating the room? Had he misjudged the angle? of course, he must have misjudged the angle. But to say it was "contemplating" was too much; it was not contemplating but only staring. What he had called bewilderment was now plain lack of meaning. Jonathan's phrase—"an absolute master and a lost loony at the same time"—recurred to him. The extended hand was no longer a motion of exposition or of convincing energy, holding the congregation attentive, but rather drawing the congregation after it, a summons and a physical enchantment. It drew them towards the figure, and behind the figure itself perhaps to more; for the shadow of the figure on the cliff behind was not now a shadow, but the darkness of a cleft, which ran back very deeply, almost infinitely deep, a corridor between two walls of rock. Into that corridor the figure, hovering on its shadowy platform, was about to recede; and below it all those inclined backs were on the point of similar movement. A crowd of winged beetles, their wings yet folded but at the very instant of loosing, was about to rise into the air and disappear into that crevice and away down the prolonged corridor. And the staring emaciated face that looked out at them and over them was the face of an imbecile. Richard said impatiently to himself: "This is all that old woman talking," because, though one did get different angles on paintings, one did not usually so soon see on the same canvas what was practically a different painting. Blatant and blank in the grey twilight, where only a reflection of the sun shone from the beetles' coats, the face hung receding; blank and blatant, the thousand insects rose towards it; and beyond them the narrow corridor hinted some extreme distance towards which the whole congregation and their master were on the point of unchecked flight. And yet the face was not a true face at all; it was not a mockery, but the hither side of something which was hidden and looking away, a face as much stranger than the face they saw as that—face or back—from the other insect backs below it.

They had all been silent; suddenly they all began to speak. Richard said recklessly: "At least the colouring's superb." Betty said: "Oh Jon, *need* you?" Jonathan said: "It's a trick of this light. Don't cry, Betty. I'll do something else." Lady Wallingford said: "We won't keep you, Mr. Drayton. If that's serious, we have very little in common. If it's not serious, I didn't expect to be insulted. We'll go, Betty. My daughter will write to you, Mr. Drayton."

"This is quite absurd," Jonathan said. "Ask Mr. Furnival, and he'll tell you that it wasn't in the least like that until you talked us into believing it. I'm extremely sorry you don't like it, and I'll do something different. But you can't think that I meant to show you a painting of a madman and a mass of beetles as a portrait of your Father Simon. Especially when I know what you think about him. Is it likely?"

"It appears to be a fact," said Lady Wallingford. She had turned her back on the canvas, and was looking bitterly at Jonathan. "If we are nothing more than vermin to you—Betty!"

Betty was still holding on to Jonathan. It seemed to give her some strength, for she lifted her head and said: "But, Mother, Jonathan is going to alter it."

"Alter it!" said Lady Wallingford. "He will alter it to something still more like himself. You will have nothing more to do with him. Come."

Jonathan interrupted. "Lady Wallingford," he said, "I've apologized for something I never thought or intended. But Betty's engagement to me is another matter. I shan't accept any attempt to interfere with that."

"No?" Lady Wallingford said. "Betty will do what I tell her, and I have other plans. This pretended engagement was always a ridiculous idea, and now it is finished."

"Mother——" Betty began. Lady Wallingford, who had been looking at Jonathan, turned her eyes slowly to her daughter. The slight movement of her head was so deliberate that it concentrated a power not felt in that room till then. Her eyes held Betty as in the painting behind her the outstretched hand held the attentive congregation; they summoned as that summoned. Jonathan was thwarted, enraged, and abandoned. He stood, helpless and alone, at the side of an exchange of messages which he could not follow; he felt Betty flag in his arm and his arm was useless to her. He tightened it, but she seemed to fall through it as a hurt dove through the air by which it should be supported. Richard, as he saw that slow movement, was reminded suddenly of Lester's way of throwing up her hand; the physical action held something even greater than the purpose which caused it. It was not only more than itself in its exhibition of the mind behind it, but it was in itself more than the mind. So killing, though it may express hate, is an utterly different thing from hate. There was hate in the room, but that particular act was not so much hate as killing, as pure deliberate murder. As a man weak from illness might try to wrestle with a murderer and fail, he thought he heard himself saying sillily: "Lady Wallingford, if I may speak, wouldn't it be better if we talked about this another time? There's no need to murder the girl at once, is there? I mean, if Jonathan did something different, perhaps we could avoid it? or we might look at it—at the portrait—in a different light? and then you might see her in a different light? Sometimes a little attention…."

He was not quite sure how much of this he had actually said, but he stopped because Jonathan was speaking. Jonathan was speaking very angrily and very quickly, and he was talking of Betty's father the Air Marshal, and of his own aunt who would put Betty up for a few days, and how they would get married almost to-morrow, and how all the paintings and all the parents and all the prophets under heaven could not interfere. He spoke close above Betty's ear, and several times he tried to get her to turn and look at him. But she did not; she had gone even paler than she had been before, and as Lady Wallingford took the first step towards the door she too began to turn towards it. She twisted herself suddenly out of Jonathan's arm, and she said nothing in reply to the entreaties, persuasions, and commands which he continued to address to her. Richard thought her face as she did so was very like another face he had seen; the identification of that other troubled him for a moment, and then was suddenly present—it was Lester's when he had last seen it, Lester's when she was dead. The common likeness of the dead was greater than any difference between their living faces; they were both citizens of a remoter town than this London, and the other town was in this room. He saw beyond Betty Lady Wallingford, who had walked across the room and was looking back at Betty from the door, and her face, though it was not that of the dead, was like a hard cliff in the world of the dead, or like a building, if the dead had buildings, a house or a temple of some different and disastrous stone. The whole ordinary room became only an imitation of a room; Jonathan and he were ghosts in a ghostly chamber, the realities were the man in the cleft of the rock and the rising beetles, and the dead face of Betty, and the living face—but in what way living?—of her tyrant. Even while he shivered in a sudden bleakness, Betty had disengaged herself from Jonathan and gone over to her mother. Lady Wallingford opened the door. She said to Betty: "We will go to Holborn." She motioned her daughter before her; they went out. The two men heard the shutting of the outer door.

They looked at each other. With that departure, the room became again a room, and no more the outskirts of another world. Richard drew a breath, and glanced again at the painting. It seemed to him now impossible to miss its actuality. Seen as human beings, those shapes had been motionless; seen as beetles, they were already in motion and on the point of flight. The painting lived, as the *Mona Lisa* does, in the moment of beginning, in the mathematical exactitude of beginning. Yet now Richard uncertainly felt more; there was an ambiguity in it, for the shapes might be either. That was its great, apparently unexpected, and certainly unwanted, success: men who were beetles, beetles who were men; insects who had just been men, men who had just become insects. Metamorphosis was still in them. But could he then, he wondered, still gazing, think of them the other way, insects who had just become men, men who had just been insects? why not? Could humanity be living out of them?—some miracle in process? animality made newly rational? and their motion the rising into erect man? and the stretched arm the sign and power that called them?

He looked along the arm; his eyes rose to the face that ruled and called them? He saw it was impossible. That blank face could never work miracles; or if it could, then only miracles of lowering and loss. He could not persuade himself that it was growing into power; the metempsychosis there, if any had been, was done. The distance in the cleft behind, which he now clearly saw, as if the walls of it palely shone with their own light, held no promise of a lordlier change. There was no life there but that of rock—"*tutto di pietra di color ferrigno*—all iron-hued stone". What other life that stone might hold in itself, the life in the woman's face by the door, the life that had seemed to impinge on the room, could not be known by a face that had lost understanding. And then he remembered that this was but the backward-looking, the false, the devised face. What might the true face be that looked away down the cleft, between the walls, to the end of the corridor, if there was an end? That indeed might know more, much and very terribly more.

He made an effort and turned his eyes away. Jonathan was moving towards him; he said as he came, "What a mother!"

"But didn't you guess anything of this?" Richard asked, almost with curiosity.

"Oh I don't know," Jonathan answered irritably. "I thought perhaps while I was doing it that there was something odd about it, and then I thought there wasn't and that I was imagining things. One gets confused and can't judge. And I certainly thought she wouldn't notice it, or want to notice it. Nor would she, but she doesn't mean me to marry Betty."

Richard said: "But supposing to destroy it was the only way? Suppose Miss Wallingford asked you to?"

"Well, she hasn't," said Jonathan. "It'll be time enough, when she does. I don't know—probably I should. It'd be tiresome, but if it eased things…. She doesn't care for this Simon herself; she only goes because her mother makes her."

"I'd like to see him for myself," Richard said. "Where is he? What was that remark about Holborn?"

"You go," said Jonathan. "It's a place just between Holborn and Red Lion Square—you'll easily find it. Go and hear him speak. He doesn't do it often, but you'll find out when he's going to. Go and see, and tell me the result."

"Well, I think I will," said Richard. "To-morrow. I'm very sorry about all this. What do you think you'll do?"

"Just think first," Jonathan answered. "Shall I stick out or shall I try and come to terms? I don't believe Sir Bartholomew'll be much good, even when he does get back from Moscow, but at least I could see him, and it's going to be damned difficult to keep in touch with Betty. She might be a novice or a nun, the way her mother keeps her. I believe she even reads her letters, and I'm sure she watches her telephone calls. Come round to-morrow, will you, if it's not a bother? I shall want to talk to you."

Richard promised and left. He came out into the London streets about the time when everyone else was also going home, and after a glance at the crowded transport he determined to walk. There was about the general hubbub something that eased and pleased him. He relaxed his spirit a little as he moved among them. He thought of Jonathan and Betty, and he thought also: "I wish Lester were here; she'd know what to do, and she knows Betty." It would be very convenient now if Lester could call on Betty; he wished for Jonathan's sake that she could. A little of Lester's energy and Lester's style and even Lester's temper might be of a good deal of use to Betty now.

It occurred to him, with a light surprise, that he was thinking quite naturally of Lester. He was sincerely sorry, for Jonathan's sake, that her strong femininity was lost—for Jonathan's sake, not at that moment for his own. It was what she was that was needed. What she was—not what she was to him. It occurred to him then that he had on the whole been in the habit of thinking of Lester only in relation to himself. He saw suddenly in her the power that waited for use, and he saw also that he had not taken any trouble about that power; that he had, in fact, been vaguely content to suppose it was adequately used in attending to him. He said, almost aloud: "Darling, did I neglect you?" It was no ordinary neglect that he meant; of that certainly he had not been guilty—and of this other perhaps she had been as guilty as he. No—not as guilty; she knew more of him in himself than he had ever troubled to know of her in herself. It was why her comments on him, in gaiety or rage, always had such a tang of truth; whereas his were generally more like either cultured jesting or mere abuse. The infinite accuracy of a wife's intelligence stared out at him. He acknowledged what, in all his sincere passion, he had been unwilling to acknowledge, that she was often simply right, and the admission bound him to her the closer, dead though she might be. He thought how many chances he had missed of delighting in her entire veracity, instead of excusing, protesting, denying. The glowing splendour of her beauty rose, and it was a beauty charged with knowledge. It was that, among much else, that he had neglected. And now they all needed her, and she was not there.

She was. It was along Holborn that he was walking, for he had half-thought of going that night to look for Simon's hall or house or whatever it was. And there, on the very pavement, the other side of a crossing, she stood. He thought for the first second that there was someone with her. He was held by the appearance as motionless as in their early days he had thought he must be—though in fact in those early days he had never actually stopped. Now he did. It was as if that shock of her had at last compelled him to acknowledge it outwardly—at last, but as he had always almost believed he did, perhaps more in those days at the beginning when the strangeness was greater and the dear familiarity less. But the strangeness, for all the familiarity, had never quite gone, nor was it absent now; it was indeed, he felt, the greater, as well it might be. They stood on either side that Holborn by-way, and gazed.

He felt, as he gazed, more like a wraith than a man; against her vigour of existence he hung like a ghost, and was fixed by it. He did not then remember the past hour in Jonathan's room, nor the tomb-like image of Lady Wallingford. Had he done so, he would have felt Lester's to be as much stronger than that woman's as hers had seemed stronger than his own. Lester was not smiling any recognition; the recognition was in her stillness. The passionate mouth was serious and the eyes deep with wonder and knowledge: of him? certainly of him. He thought almost he saw her suspire with a relief beyond joy. Never, never again would he neglect. The broken oaths renewed themselves in him. One hand of hers was raised and still almost as if it rested on some other arm, but the other had flown to her breast where it lay as if in some way it held him there. They made, for those few seconds, no movement, but their stillness was natural and not strange; it was not because she was a ghost but because she was she that he could not stir. This was their thousandth meeting, but yet more their first, a new first and yet the only first. More stable than rock, more transient in herself than rivers, more distant-bright than stars, more comfortable than happy sleep, more pleasant than wind, more dangerous than fire—all known things similes of her; and beyond all known things the unknown power of her. He could perhaps in a little have spoken; but before he could, she had passed. She left with him precisely the sensation of seeing her go on; past him? no; up the by-way? no; but it was not disappearance or vanishing, for she had gone, as a hundred times she had, on her proper occasions, gone, kissing, laughing, waving. Now she neither kissed nor laughed nor waved, but that which was in all three lingered with him as he saw she was no longer there.

Lights were coming out in the houses; the confused sound of the City was in his ears. He was giddy with too much apprehension; he waited to recover; then he crossed the by-way, and he too went on.

———————————

17

Chapter Three

CLERK SIMON

Jonathan spent the rest of the day in the abandoned studio. After the first hour he made three efforts to ring up Betty. He gave his own name the first time, but was told that Miss Wallingford was not in. The second time he gave Richard's name, and for the third he invented a flight lieutenant. But neither was more successful. It was, of course, possible at first that the ladies had not returned from Holborn, but by half-past ten it seemed more likely that Lady Wallingford had simply secluded her daughter. He knew that if she had given orders that Miss Betty was not to be disturbed, it was very unlikely that anybody would disturb her. Between his two later calls he put in another. He knew that Sir Bartholomew had some small property in Hampshire, just as Lady Wallingford owned a house somewhere in Yorkshire, and he claimed to be speaking on behalf of the Hampshire County Council on some business of reconstruction. He asked if Sir Bartholomew had returned from Moscow or if not, when he was likely to return. The answer was that nothing could be said of Sir Bartholomew's movements. He suggested that Lady Wallingford might be asked. The answer was that that would be useless; instructions had been issued that no other answer could be given. Jonathan at last gave up the telephone, and sat down to write letters.

He wrote to Betty; he wrote to Lady Wallingford. He offered, after a slight struggle with his admiration of himself, to suppress the picture; the admiration just managed to substitute "suppress" for "destroy". It was still worth while trying to save Betty and the picture too. But he knew that if he were driven far enough, he would consent to its destruction; though he could not quite avoid envisaging another picture in which something much more drastic should be deliberately done about Father Simon. He succeeded, however, in keeping this on the outskirts of his mind and even in mentioning to himself the word "dishonesty". His virtue, with some difficulty, maintained itself in the uncertain centre of his mind. He told Betty he would be in his flat all the next day, in case she could ring up or indeed come. He proposed an aunt's house in Tunbridge Wells as a shelter for her. He told her that he would write to Sir Bartholomew through the War Office. He was perfectly well aware that Lady Wallingford would read the letter, but it told her nothing she could not have guessed, and it would at least make clear that he had other channels of communication with the Air Marshal.

He put off going to the post with these letters until almost midnight, in case by any wild chance Betty should ring up. But at last he gave up hope, took the letters, went to the door, and as he opened it switched out the light. At that moment the front door bell rang. He caught his breath and almost ran to it. He opened it; it was not she. In the dim light of the landing he saw a tall figure, apparently wrapped in some, kind of cloak, and in his fierce disappointment he almost banged the door shut. But as his hand tightened on it, a voice said: "Mr. Drayton?"

"Yes?" Jonathan said morosely. The voice was urbane, a little husky, and had the very slightest foreign accent which Jonathan did not at once recognize. He peered forward a little to see the face, but it was not easy, even though the caller wore no hat. The voice continued: "Lady Wallingford has been with me to-night to tell me of a painting. I am Simon the Clerk."

"Oh!" said Jonathan; "yes. I see…. Look, won't you come in?" He had been quite unprepared for this, and as he ushered his visitor into the studio, his only feeling was one of extreme gratitude that in a moment of peevishness he had flung the covering again over the canvas. It would have been awkward to show Simon straight in at it. He could not quite think why he had come. It must, of course, be about the painting, but unless to see if he agreed with Lady Wallingford … and it would be odd to be as urgent as all that, especially as he disliked being painted. Still, it would come out. He was very much on his guard, but as he closed the door he said, as friendlily as he could: "Do sit down. Have a drink?"

"No, thank you," Simon answered. He remained standing with his eyes on the covered canvas. He was a tall man, with a smooth mass of grey—almost white—hair; his head was large; his face thin, almost emaciated. The face had about it a hint of the Jew—no more; so little indeed that Jonathan wondered if it were only Richard's account that caused him to think he saw it. But, considering more carefully, he saw it was there. The skin was dark and Jonathan saw with a thrill of satisfaction that he had got in his painting almost the exact kind of dead hue which it in fact possessed. The eyes were more deeply set than he had thought; otherwise he had been pretty accurate in detail. The only thing in which he had been wrong was in producing any appearance of bewilderment or imbecility. There was nothing at all of either in the Clerk's gaze. It was not exactly a noble face, nor a prophetic; priestly, rather. A remote sacerdotalism lived in it; the

Clerk might have been some lonely hierarch out of a waste desert. He stood perfectly still, and Jonathan observed that he was indeed as near perfectly still as a man could be. There was no slightest visible motion, no faintest sound of breath. He was so quiet that quietness seemed to emanate from him. Jonathan felt his own disturbance quelled. It was in a softer voice than his usual one that he said, making what was almost an effort to move and speak at all: "Are you sure you won't have a drink?… Well, I think I will, if you'll excuse me." The other had very slightly shaken his head. Outside the room, the bells of the City began to chime midnight. Jonathan said to himself, as he had made a habit of doing since he had first met Betty whenever he was awake at midnight, as he often was: "Benedicta sit, et benedicti omnes parvuli Tui." He turned away and poured out his drink. With the glass in his hand, he came back. The hour was striking, near and far, wherever bells were still capable of sound, all over the wide reaches of London. Jonathan heard it through the new quiet. He said: "And now, Father Simon, Lady Wallingford?"

"Lady Wallingford was distressed about this painting," Simon answered.

"Distressed?" Jonathan said nastily. "Exhilarated was more the word, I should have thought." Then the sense of the quiet and of the other's presence made him ashamed of his petulance. He went on: "I beg your pardon. But I can't think she was altogether unhappy. She was very angry."

"Show it to me," the Clerk said. It was not perhaps quite a command, but very nearly; it almost sounded like a Marshal of the Air speaking to an official artist who ranked as a regular officer. Obedience was enforceable, though unenforced. Jonathan hesitated. If Simon took Lady Wallingford's view, he would be in a worse state than he was now. Was it possible that Simon would not take Lady Wallingford's view? In that case he might be very useful indeed; possibly he might persuade Lady Wallingford to alter her own. It was a great risk. The other saw the hesitation. The husky urbane voice said: "Come; you must not think I see things as she does."

"No," said Jonathan doubtfully. "Only … I mean she *has* talked to you. I don't know what she's told you, but she's so damned convinced and convincing that she'd even persuade me that a smudge of umber was a vermilion blot. Mind you, I think she'd made up her mind to find something wrong with it, in order to interfere with Betty and me, so she wasn't disinterested."

"It doesn't matter what she told me," the other said. "I never see things with other people's eyes. If she's wrong—I might be of use."

"Yes," said Jonathan, moving to the easel. "If you could convince her, of course."

"She will think what I say," the Clerk said, and there was such a sudden contempt in his voice that Jonathan looked round.

"I say, you are sure of her!" he said.

"I'm quite sure of her," the Clerk answered, and waited. All this time he had not moved. The room itself, and it was large and by no means over-furnished, seemed almost full and busy beside him. Jonathan, as he threw back the cover, began to feel a warm attraction towards this unmoving figure, which had the entire power to direct Lady Wallingford what to think. He determined, if by any chance Simon should pass this painting as harmless, to do him another about which there should be no doubt whatever. He stepped aside, and for the third time that day the picture was exposed to study.

As Jonathan looked at it, he became extremely uneasy. The beetles, the blank gaze, the receding corridor, had not grown less striking since he had seen them last. If this was the Father, he could not think the Father would like himself. He wished again with all his heart that he had never begun to paint it. He knew exactly how he could have avoided it; he could have said he wasn't worthy. It would have been a lie, for being worthy was not a thing that came in with painting; painting had nothing to do with your personal merit. You could do it or you couldn't. But it would have been a convenient—and to that woman an easily credible—lie, and he wished he had told it, however difficult it would have been to say it convincingly. Betty, after all…. He rather wondered if he could say now that he realized he wasn't worthy. But the Father did not look the sort of person who was taken in like that—anyhow, at the present stage, when he obviously had thought himself worthy. No; if things went wrong, he must argue again. By now he loathed and hated the entire painting; he would have cut it up or given it to the nation, if the nation had wanted it. He looked round.

Simon was still standing at gaze. The chimes rang a quarter-past twelve; otherwise the City was silent. Outside the large window beyond Simon the moon was high and cold. Her October chill interpenetrated the room. Jonathan shivered; something was colder—the atmosphere or his heart. Betty was far away, gone as lovers and wives do go, as Richard's wife had gone, gone to her deathbed. Betty's own bed was cold, even like her chastity. I would I were where Betty lies; no wedding-garment except this fear, in the quiet, in the quiet, in the quiet, where a figure of another world stood. All things rose fluttering round it; beetles? too light for beetles: moths, bright light moths round a flame-formed dark; the cloak of the dark and the hunger in the dark. The high moon a moth, and he; only not Betty, Betty dead like Richard's wife, dead women in the streets of the City under the moon.

A distant husky voice, with a strange accent, broke the silence. It said: "That is I." Jonathan came to himself to see the Clerk staring. His head was a little forward; his eyes were fixed. He was so gratified that his voice let fall the words and ceased. The shock of them and of relief was so great that Jonathan felt a little light-headed. He took a step or two back to get his vision into focus. He began to say something, but Simon was so clearly not listening that he gave it up and wandered away towards the window. But even as he did so he listened for what else that other should say which might give him hope, hope of Betty, hope of his work. He looked out into the moonlight, he saw in it, below him, on the other side of the road, two girls walking— they the only living in the night; and as his eyes took them in he heard again the voice behind him saying, but now in more than gratification, in low triumph: "That is I."

Jonathan turned. He said: "You like it?"

The other answered: "No-one has painted me so well for a hundred years. Everything's there."

Jonathan went back. He did not quite see how to carry on the conversation; the allusion to "a hundred years" baffled him. At last he said doubtfully: "And Lady Wallingford?"

The Clerk slowly looked round at him, as if he were recalled. He said, and his face twitched slightly, "Lady Wallingford? What has she to do with it?"

"She was rather annoyed with it," said Jonathan. "In fact, she talked, as no doubt she told you, about insects and imbeciles."

The Clerk, still looking at him, said: "They aren't insects; they are something less. But insects is the nearest you can get. And as for imbecile, haven't you read *Sapientia adepti stultitia mundi*? That is why your work is so wonderful."

"Oh!" said Jonathan.

"That," the Clerk went on, turning his head again, "is what I am to these creatures, and Lady Wallingford (as you call her) is one of them. She thinks herself someone, but presently she'll find out. It's quite good for them to be hypnotized; they're much happier. But you—you are different; you are a genius. You must paint me often. Now you have shown me as I am to them and to myself, you must paint me often as I am in myself."

The chill sense of death was receding from Jonathan's heart. He began to feel that life was still possible, even life with Betty. He also wondered what his own painting of the face was like. He had first thought it was an ordinary portrait; then he had been uneasy about the bewilderment that seemed to show in it. Richard had agreed. Lady Wallingford had spoken of imbecility. Now Simon seemed to see something else beyond that, something that was hidden in that and yet contradicted it. He might perhaps tell Lady Wallingford; he might make everything clear for him and Betty. In a second of silence Jonathan had married Betty, set up a house, painted Father Simon a stupendous portrait of himself without the beetles, painted several other shattering successes at the Peace Conferences and after, made a lot of money, become a father and an immortal at once, and was back again in the studio with the immediate necessity of explaining to Simon how all this was to be brought about. Better not go into farther details of the painting; better get on with the main job.

He began: "Then you'll speak to——" but the other was already speaking. He was saying: "You must come with me, Mr. Drayton. I must have one or two people with me who are something more than these other creatures. The Doctrine is good for them; one gets nowhere by fighting it. All your books have it—the Koran, the New Testament, the Law. Hitler fought it; where is Hitler? There is nothing better, for those who need it. But you are an exception. You belong to yourself—and to me. Great art is apostolic. You must not lessen yourself. You are to be a master. I can do something to help you, but then you must have courage to paint the right things."

Jonathan listened to this with a certain warmth. He was a little shaken by great art being apostolic, but there was no doubt a sense in which it was true, though Sir Joshua's "common observation and plain understanding" pleased him better. He did think he was a remarkable painter, and he did not care how often he was told so. But he did not lose sight of his main point. As soon as Simon paused, he said: "Then you'll speak to Lady Wallingford?"

Simon's voice had seemed to be closer and clearer. It receded again and grew huskier as he said: "What do you so want with Lady Wallingford?"

"I want to marry her daughter," Jonathan said.

The Clerk dropped his eyes to the ground. He said, after a moment: "I am not sure that you're wise. But it shall be as you like. I will talk to her—yes, in a few days, if you still wish. You shall have the girl, if you want her. Show me something else."

20

"I haven't much here," Jonathan said. "The war-paintings———"

"Oh the war!" the Clerk said. "The war, like Hitler, was a foolery. I am the one who is to come, not Hitler. Not the war; something else."

"Well, there's this thing of London," Jonathan said. "Wait; I'll turn it for you." He went round to the other easel, to the canvas on which he had not looked since the early afternoon, because of all that had since happened, but now he did, and saw it as he had seen it with Richard. He knew the validity of his own work—yet he knew also that he might so easily be wrong, as innumerable unfortunate bad painters had been. There was no way of being certain. But at least he believed that painting could be valid, could hold an experience related to the actuality of the world, and in itself valuable to mind and heart. He hoped this painting might be that; more he could not say. He saw beyond it the figure of the Clerk looming, and the window behind him, and it seemed almost as if he were now looking at the other painting made actual and released from canvas. The figure was there; the blank window behind; he could not at this distance and in this light see through it; it was but an opening into bleakness. And he himself the only other being there. He looked at the Clerk's face, and it too hung blank as the window, empty of meaning. "I am being a fool," he thought, and looked, as he stepped back after turning the easel again, at the light on the canvas. He said, with the least flash of arrogance in his voice: "There! What do you think of that?"

The Clerk looked, and flinched. Jonathan saw a quiver go through him; he shut his eyes and opened them. He said: "No, no; it's too bright. I can't see it properly. Move it."

Jonathan said coldly: "I'm sorry you don't like it. Myself, I think it's better than the other."

The Clerk said: "That is because you do not quite understand the meaning of your own work. This is a dream; that other is a fact. It is simply I who have come. I shall give all these little people peace because they believe in me. But these fancies of light would distract them. There is only one art, and that is to show them their master. You had better—well, I know how you painters love even your mistakes and I will not say you should destroy it. But hide it for a year, and come with me, and then look at it again, and you will see it as I do."

Jonathan said cautiously: "Well, I'll see what Betty says. Anyhow I shan't have much time for views of the City during the next year or so." The words, and the tone, of mastery did not seem altogether unsuitable to the towering form; he himself was on the defensive. The very hint that there was much more in the other picture than he had supposed, that he painted more greatly than he knew, subtly soothed him. He was the more ready to owe Betty to a man who saw so deeply. He added: "You won't forget to speak to Lady Wallingford?"

"Presently," the Clerk said. "But you must remember that you have a great work to do. When I am in union again, you shall paint me as I shall be. Soon."

Jonathan murmured something. The conversation was getting beyond him. He wished his visitor would go away, before he said the wrong thing. The Clerk, almost as if he too felt that all had been said, turned. He said: "I'll come to you again, or else I'll send for you."

"I may be moved about," Jonathan said. "We of the Services, you know———"

"Your service is with me," the other answered. "I or—or Betty will let you know." His eyes stared out through the blank window. "What you shall paint! Trust me. I will make you … never mind. But put the other thing away. The colour is wrong."

He gave Jonathan no opportunity for a reply. He went towards the door, and Jonathan followed. At parting he raised his hand a little. He came out into the street and the moonlight, and began to walk.

He went towards Highgate, and he went easily though at great speed, and as he went the City seemed to dwindle around him. His mind was very earnestly set on himself. As he went the Jewish quality in his face seemed to deepen; the occasional policemen whom he passed thought they saw a Jew walking by night. Indeed that august race had reached in this being its second climax. Two thousand years of its history were drawing to a close; until this thing had happened it could not be free. Its priesthood—the priesthood of a nation—had been since Abraham determined to one End. But when, after other terrible wars had shaken the Roman peace, and armies had moved over Europe, and Caesar (being all that Caesar could be) had been stabbed in his own central place, when then that End had been born, they were not aware of that End. It had been proposed that their lofty tradition should be made almost unbearably august; that they should be made the blood-companions of their Maker, the own peculiar house and family of its Incarnacy—no more than the Gentiles in the free equality of souls, but much more in the single hierarchy of kindred flesh. But deception had taken them; they had, bidding a scaffold for the blasphemer, destroyed their predestined conclusion, and the race which had been set for the salvation of the world became a judgment and even a curse to the world and to themselves. Yet the oaths sworn in heaven remained. It had been a Jewish girl who, at the command of the Voice which sounded in her ears, in her heart, along her blood, and through the central cells of her body, had uttered everywhere in herself the perfect Tetragrammaton. What the high priest vicariously spoke among the secluded mysteries of the Temple, she substantially pronounced to God. Redeemed from all division in herself, whole and identical in body and soul and spirit, she uttered the Word and the Word became flesh in her. Could It have been received by her own people, the grand Judaean gate would have been opened for all peoples. It could not. They remained alien—to It and to all, and all to them and—too much!—to It. The Gentiles, summoned by that other Jew of Tarsus, could not bear their vicarious office. Bragging themselves to be the new Israel, they slandered and slew the old, and the old despised and hated the bragging new. Till at last there rose in Europe something which was neither, and set itself to destroy both.

And when that had been thwarted, this also which was to happen had at last happened. Jew and Christian alike had waited for the man who now walked through the empty London streets. He had been born in Paris, in one of those hiding-places of necromancy which all the energy of the Fourteenth Louis had not quite stamped out. He was a child of the nobility, but he was hardly yet a boy when the Revolution had broken out. His family had moved safely through it, protected by wealth and cunning and in extremes by another kind of cunning learned in very ancient schools. His father had been to the world a scholar as well as a nobleman, one of the early philologists, but to a different circle and to his son his philology had been quite other. He knew sounds and the roots of sounds, almost the beginnings of sounds; the vibrations that overthrew and the vibrations that built up. The son followed his father.

He remembered now, as he walked, how he had come to know himself. It was not often he permitted himself the indulgence of memory, but that painted face which Jonathan had supposed to be blank of meaning yet in which he had read all he wished to read, seeing it full of power and portent—that artificiality had opened up recollection within him. He remembered how he had seen the crowds in Paris, their poverty, their need, their rage, and (so small as he was) understood how men need both comfort and control. And he had seen Napoleon rise and fall, but before that mastery was done his childish dreams of being king or emperor had been better instructed. He had learnt three things from that small college of which his father was president—that there was another power to use, that there were ways of directing it, that many men would pay much to learn them. Could they be sold! but they could not be. They were private to those who had the right by nature, as all art is, but these especially to the high-priestly race. Only a Jew could utter the Jewish, which was the final, word of power.

There were not in the circles where he grew up any of the mere obscenities of magic—no spectacular outrages of the Black Mass or profane sensualities of the Sabbath. There were certain bloody disciplines to test the postulant—it was all. The mass of men were at once despised and pitied by the chaste sorcerers. He learnt to shelter, to feed, to console them, but at the same time that he was separate from them. He had watched a man starve, but he was not cruel; it was in his training. He was not lustful; only once in all his life had he lain with a woman, and that for a rational purpose. He had not been kept from talk with holy Rabbis and charitable priests; if he had chosen their way no-one would have interfered with him unless he had become inconvenient to the great work. He did not so choose; he preferred his own.

He was not, in fact, much different from any man, but the possibilities slowly opened to him were more rare. There shaped itself gradually in his mind a fame beyond any poet's and a domination beyond any king's. But it was fame and domination that he desired, as they did. That his magical art extended where theirs could never reach was his luck. The understanding of his reach had come when he first assisted at a necromantic operation. As the dead body stood and spoke he felt the lordship of that other half of the world. Once, as he had learnt the tale, the attempt at domination had been made and failed. The sorcerer who had attempted it had also been a Jew, a descendant of the house of David, who clothed in angelic brilliance had compelled a woman of the same house to utter the Name, and something more than mortal had been born. But in the end the operation had failed. Of the end of the sorcerer himself there were no records; Joseph ben David had vanished. The living thing that had been born of his feminine counterpart had perished miserably. It had been two thousand years before anyone had dared to risk the attempt again.

He came up towards Highgate, and as he came he let his memories fade. He put away the recollection of the painting; the time for his spiritual enthronement was not quite come. But he felt the City lessen—not only London, but all bodies and souls of men. He lifted his head; his face was lean and hungry under the moon. He felt himself walking alone among tiny houses among which men and women ran about under his protection and by his will. There waited him, in the house to which he was going, the means of another operation than his coming empery in this world; of which his child was the instrument. For a moment he thought of Jonathan and Jonathan's love. He smiled—or rather a sudden convulsion passed across his face, a kind of muscular spasm rather than a smile. It was not meant to be unkind; he did not dislike Jonathan, and he wished his genius to thrive and paint the grand master even more intensely. But Betty was for another purpose. Nor was he even aware that what had once been a smile was now a mere constriction. One cannot smile at no-one, and there was no-one at whom he could smile. He was alone. He went on, ignorantly grimacing.

Chapter Four

THE DREAM

In the house at Highgate Betty Wallingford was lying awake. She was wholly wretched. Her mother, after they had returned from that secret conversation in Holborn, in which she had not been allowed to take part, had sent her to bed. She had wished to protest; she had wished to ring up Jonathan. But it would have been quite useless. She could not remember a time when it would not have been useless. If she had been Lady Wallingford's real daughter, she might have had a better chance, or so sometimes she thought. But since, years ago, Lady Wallingford had spoken of her adoption, she had always felt at a disadvantage. No allusion was ever made to it now. She had tried, once or twice, to ask Lady Wallingford about her real parents, but her adopted mother had only said: "We will not talk of that, Betty," and so of course they did not. As for Sir Bartholomew, she had been forbidden to mention it to him, and anyhow he was hardly ever at home, and was only interested in air matters. So she only knew she was not what everyone thought she was.

Everyone in London, that is. There was in the north, in Yorkshire, a small house where she and Lady Wallingford sometimes went. They always went by themselves, and when they got there she was not even treated as a daughter. She was, purely and simply, the servant. It was supposed to be training for her, in case (as might happen, Lady Wallingford said) she ever had to earn her own living. She did the work; she showed in the Vicar or any other local visitor, and then she went back to her nice bright kitchen, where she had that morning's *Daily Sketch* (which Lady Wallingford took in for her) and her radio on which she was only allowed to listen to the most popular music (because, Lady Wallingford said, that was what girls of that class liked). She was called Bettina there. "Ridiculous names these girls have nowadays!" Lady Wallingford had once said to the Vicar as he was leaving; and the Vicar had said: "Not at all ridiculous! a very good name." But he had not looked very attentive, and Lady Wallingford never let her go out alone; so there was no help there. And anyhow there was no need for help; what was there to help?

It had been going on for a long time, even before she had left school. She had always been in terror lest any of the other girls should pass and see her from a car. Or even, quite impossibly, call. She had tried to think what she would say, and to practise saying it. There would be nothing unusual in her mother and herself being there, but to be treated as a housemaid.... She knew they would never believe anything she could say, and still more certainly that she could never say it. She used to lie awake by night thinking of it, and wondering if the next day would bring them, but it never did; and presently the two of them always went back to London, and then she was Betty Wallingford again—only of course she was no more Betty Wallingford than she was a housemaid. She was nothing and no-one. Her mistress-mother, her mother-mistress, told her what to do; she and the man who sometimes came to see her, this Father Simon.

Of all the girls at school, two only now remained in her mind; indeed, she knew them a little still. She would have liked to be friends with Lester Grantham, who was now Lester Furnival, but it had never come about. At school Lester had never wanted to be bothered with her, though she had been in a vague way half-scornfully kind, and when she and Lady Wallingford met they had never got on very well. Lester had once or twice called with Evelyn Mercer, who was the other girl, but Betty did not like Evelyn. She might have borne Lester knowing about her being Bettina, but she would have been anguished by Evelyn's finding out, and Evelyn was the sort of person who did find things out. When Evelyn came to see her, she used to sit and talk to her; she had hunted her down at school sometimes just to talk to her. But it used to be horrible, and she would cry, and even now Evelyn would ask so many questions and tell so many horrid stories that Betty felt she could not bear it. Of course, she had to, because Evelyn sat, eying her and talking. So that presently she became the very image of Betty's fear, more even than Lady Wallingford; and one of her worse nightmares was of running away from Evelyn who was racing after her, calling "Bettina! Bettina!" And other acquaintances she had none.

During the war she had thought she would have to do a job and perhaps go away from home. She had registered, and she had been interviewed, by a nice oldish woman. But nothing else had happened. She had

23

been a little surprised, and she had even spoken of it to Lady Wallingford, who had only said: "You're not strong enough—mentally strong enough, I mean." So she supposed—and she was right—that Lady Wallingford had taken steps. After that, she had begun to worry over her mind; after that rather nice refugee had disappeared. During the little time she had known him, he had been rather comforting, but presently he had ceased to be about. And there was no-one again.

Until there had been Jonathan Drayton. She could not remember how they had first met, and they had certainly not met often. If her mother had not wished to have a painting of Father Simon, they would have met less often. But even Lady Wallingford was sometimes compelled to allow one obstinacy to get in the way of another. She had been startled—though not much more startled than Betty—when Jonathan began to talk of an engagement. Betty remembered how she had clung to him the first time he had kissed her, and what he had said of her, but she tried not to remember that, for she had always known it would be no good, and now Lady Wallingford had chosen to be offended at his painting, and it was all ended. Very soon they would be in the country again. Lady Wallingford was always saying that, now the war was over, they would go there permanently—"and then you shall settle down. I shall have to go up sometimes, but you need never leave it again." Betty was beginning to look on it as a refuge; once there, she would be Bettina altogether, and perhaps that would be peace.

But to-night it was no refuge. Jonathan was too near. He had sometimes talked to her about painting, and she had tried to understand, and even ask questions, though her mistress—no, her adopted mother—had said "Betty's rather backward" and repeated that she was mentally weak. But Jonathan had only said: "Thank God she's not cultured! and anyhow I'm not much more than adolescent myself," and gone on talking, and she had wanted to cry on his shoulder, as once or twice inexplicably she had. She never would again. She would be taken to hear Father Simon speak on Love. In a way that was a relief. While he talked she sat in a kind of trance and forgot everything. That was in Holborn; when he came to Highgate it was different and not so peaceful. She had to do something. He was always saying to her: "Do not trouble yourself; only do as I say." She would; in that and the maid's kitchen were her only hope.

She lay, waking and waiting—waiting for her mind to grow weaker, waiting for her memory of Jonathan to cease, waiting for an end. She was afraid of Lady Wallingford and desperately afraid of Evelyn. Evelyn would get everything about Jonathan out of her, and would tell people—no, she would not, for Evelyn was dead. In her sheer rush of gratitude Betty sat up in bed. It was almost her only individual movement for years. She drew a deep breath. Something of horror had stopped for ever. Evelyn, Evelyn was dead. Of course. Lester was dead too; she was a little sorry about Lester, but Lester had never wanted her. That had been Lester's husband this afternoon; he looked nice. At the time of the wedding she had been in Yorkshire; not that she would have been asked anyhow. Yorkshire—Oh well, Yorkshire; but Evelyn could never, never come to Yorkshire now. "Evelyn," she said to herself, clasping her knees, "Evelyn's *dead*." In her entire joy, she even forgot Jonathan—in her sudden sense of a freedom she had not known. She had at least no consciousness of impropriety; she was mentally strong enough for joy. She said it again, drawing breath, hugging herself, savouring it: "Evelyn's dead."

The door opened. Lady Wallingford came in. She switched on the light and saw Betty. Betty saw her, and before a word could be spoken or a glance exchanged, she thought: "People die." Lady Wallingford said: "Why are you sitting up like that?" and Betty answered, because it was so important: "Evelyn's dead."

For once Lady Wallingford was taken aback. She had never had much interest in Evelyn, though she was not as hostile to her as she had been to Lester, for she knew Betty was afraid of Evelyn. She did not altogether wish Betty to lose this, and she answered, almost immediately—but there had been a second's pause, a moment in which Betty all but triumphed: "Yes. But remember that that means she is still alive." She did not give this time to settle; she was well assured that the thought would return. She went on: "But we can't think of it now. Our Father needs you."

"Oh not *now*——" Betty exclaimed. "I'm so tired. I can't—after this afternoon—Mother, I *can't*." She spoke with more boldness than usual. The sense of freedom that Evelyn's death had given her was still strong, and an even larger sense that changes could happen which had risen in her mind when Lady Wallingford entered. People died. She looked at her mother almost as an equal; her mother would die. But she could not maintain her gaze. Lady Wallingford stared her down. As the girl's eyes fell, she said: "We are waiting. Dress and come down." She stayed for a moment, still staring; then she turned and went out.

Discouraged and miserably helpless, Betty got up and put on her clothes. She knew what would happen; it had happened before. She knew she went out, but where and with what result she did not know—only that afterwards she was again back in the house, and exhausted. Lady Wallingford always kept her in bed the next day. These occasions were known to the servants as "Miss Betty's turns". It was vaguely understood that Miss Betty was subject to something not quite nice. Something mental. Nor indeed were they far wrong, for the mind as well as the body suffered from those lonely excursions, and it was a question for her directors how long she would be able to bear them.

Her hands were trembling as she finished dressing. She had put on, and with difficulty fastened, a pair of outdoor shoes. If only, she thought, she did not have to leave the house! Or if she could know where she went and what she did! She might be braver then. It was this getting ready to go that frightened her, and the not knowing. Her tyrants never by any chance referred to her compulsory expeditions, except on the nights themselves. They would be waiting for her. She had forgotten Evelyn's death, and Lady Wallingford was perpetual. She looked at the clock; it was half-past one. There was no use in delay. She went down.

They were waiting, as she had known, in the drawing-room. Lady Wallingford was sitting by a table. Simon was walking softly up and down. When she came in he stopped and scanned her. Then he pointed to a chair. He said, in that husky voice she dreaded, though it was never unkind: "I want you to go out."

She was without initiative. She went to the chair and sat down. She said: "Yes, Father."

He said: "You shall be at peace soon. You could be at peace now if you did not fight. In a moment you will not fight; then you will be in peace. Presently you will always be at peace. Let yourself be in my will. I can send you; I can bring you back; only take the peace. Be in peace and you will be in joy. Why do you—no, you will not fight; you are not fighting; you are dying into peace; why should you not die in peace? Peace...."

The quiet husky soothing voice ran on, recapitulating the great words, bidding the sufficient maxims. She knew she would lose herself; now it did not seem so horrid; now she wondered she was not quicker to let go. She usually was. But to-night something interfered with the words. Her hands, quiet though they lay, were strangely warm, and the blood in them seemed to beat. Her body (though she did not then realize it) held a memory that her mind had forgotten. The strength of Jonathan's hands was still in her own, and rose up her arms, and stirred in her flesh. His voice, still subconditionally remembered in her ears, stirred in her corridors. She did not think of it but all her living body answered "Jonathan!" and on that cry rose against the incantation that all but appeased her. The word *love*, when the Clerk uttered it, was only a dim sound of distant wind, but it said "Jonathan!"; the word *peace* was great waters on a gentle shore, but it murmured "Jonathan!"; the word *joy* was an echo and no more, but it echoed: "Jonathan!" Even the afternoon, even the painting and all, had but made him more intense; as a man in sleep utters his love's name, so now, as she all but slept, her body sighed for its friend. She did not speak, but as she yielded to the spell, she moaned a little; she slept though with waking eyes, and she did not sleep peaceably. The Clerk knew it. He came near her; he spoke over her—he had a very great courage—those august words: "peace, joy, love". He used them for what he needed, and they meant to him—and to her—what he chose.

Lady Wallingford covered her eyes. She could not quite bear to see the nullification of life in the intellectual centre of life. She detested her daughter, and she wished to distress and pain her. But then she wished her, while she lived, to be still herself so that she should be distressed and pained. That other, who stood over the girl who was his daughter also, did not wish her to be herself, or even that only for a purpose. He wished her to be an instrument only; *peace*, *joy*, *love*, were but names for the passivity of the instrument. He was unique; yet he was no more than any man—only raised to a high power and loosed in himself.

Presently Lady Wallingford heard his voice near her. It said: "You didn't tell me she was so enamoured. It doesn't matter. I've found her in time." She moved her hand. He was standing by her, looking over to Betty where now she sat quietly in her chair, her eyes open, her body composed. He drew deep breaths; he said, so quietly that Lady Wallingford hardly heard, so strongly that the entranced girl rose at once to obey: "Go now and bring me the news."

She rose. Her eyes looked at him, simply, almost lingeringly. She gave him her attention, with a kind of delight. The last revolt had been abolished; a docile sweetness possessed her. Docility and sweetness were natural to her. In a quiet that might have been peace, in an attraction that might have been love, in a content that might have been joy, she turned from her director towards the door. Her exhaustion on the next day would come not only from what she was about to do, but from this surrender which would then have ceased. Yet every time her restoration was a little less; a day might come when this hypnotic quiescence would occupy her whole life. That day (the Clerk thought) would be soon. Then he would be able to send her for ever into the world she could now only visit.

Betty went out of the room. The Clerk followed her, and Lady Wallingford, drawn by a desire she half-dreaded, joined him and went with him. The house was warm and quiet. Sir Bartholomew was in Moscow; the servants were asleep in their rooms. Betty went to a lobby, took out a raincoat and a rough hat, and put them on. The two stood motionless, the tall man and the shorter woman, their arms hanging by their sides, their feet precisely together, their eyes fixed on the girl. They watched her go to the front door and open it wide. Beyond her lay the empty street, lit by the moon to a bluish pallor. The silence of it rushed in on them, a silence in which the quiet hall sounded as if, but a moment before, it had been noisy. Betty went out. The Clerk went quickly down the hall and almost closed the door, leaving it open but a chink. He stood by it, his head bent, intently listening. Lady Wallingford remained where she was, trembling a little. Hardly five minutes had passed when, in that perfect silence, deeper than any lull in any town, any stillness in any countryside, the faint-sound of slow dragging feet was heard. They were literally dragging, each was pulled along the path. The Clerk let go the door and stood back. It was pushed open a little farther, and through the crack Betty squeezed herself in. She was very pale, her eyes were almost shut, she drooped with the heaviness of her fatigue. She came in; she made a motion to push the door to; she stumbled forward and fell. The Clerk caught her; she lay against him. The Clerk looked over his shoulder at Lady Wallingford, who as at a sudden call ran forward. She bent down and picked up her daughter's feet. Between them the two creatures carried the girl upstairs; their monstrous shadows rising against the walls. They took her to her room and laid her on her bed. They undressed her and got her into the bed, all in silence and with the softest and quickest movements. Then they drew up chairs and sat down, one on each side. Lady Wallingford took up a notebook and a pen. The Clerk leaned his head close to Betty's and said something in her ear. He moved his head so that his ear was close to Betty's mouth, and in a voice hardly to be heard, with broken phrases and long intervals, she began to speak. He repeated, in a voice harder than was usual with him, what she said. Lady Wallingford wrote down the words. It was almost morning before the triple labour was done. The Clerk stood up frowning. Lady Wallingford looked at him. He shook his head slowly, and presently they both left the room, she to her own, he to the staircase and the hall.

Betty had gone out from the house into the street. She did not consciously remember what she had to do, and as she stood in the shadow of the porch she drew a deep breath or two. Something—if in the porch she had had a shadow, it would have been like her shadow, but it was not, and it was more solid—lay in the porch, against the door behind her. She did not notice it. She began to walk down the street, towards Highgate Hill and the City that lay below. She went lightly and gaily; these times were always happy and fortunate; she could not compare them with others, for she knew no others. All but these joyous hours were secluded from her. Ignorant of what she obeyed, but in a perfect volition of obedience, she went along. She did not know through what spectral streets she moved; she knew roads and turnings and recognized her way, but she did not name them. She was not thinking of them, for now she did not think. All that was, for the time, done. She only knew. But she did not know that the silence was any but an earthly silence, nor that the sky above her was the sky under which Lester and Evelyn walked. Nor did she think of any insolidity; if for a moment the fronts of the houses looked unearthly, she unconsciously attributed this to the effects of the moon. The world was as familiar as this world, and to her less terrifying.

It lay there, as it always does—itself offering no barriers, open to be trodden, ghostly to this world and to heaven, and in its upper reaches ghostly also to those in its lower reaches where (if at all) hell lies. It is ours and not ours, for men and women were never meant to dwell there long; though it is held by some that certain unaccountable disappearances have been into that world, and that a few (even living) may linger there awhile. But mostly those streets are only for the passing through of the newly dead. It is not for human bodies, though it has known a few—"Enoch, Elijah, and the Lady" though they not in London, but in the places where they died. It has certainly been thought, but the speculation is that of dreamers, that in the year of our great danger the grand attack of our enemies succeeded; that London and England perished; and that all we who then died entered it together and live there till we have wrought out our salvation—to enjoy (purgatorially) a freedom unpermitted on earth; and that our conquerors live on that earth, troubled and frenzy-driven by a mystical awareness of our presence. More justly, it is held by learned doctors that in times of much bloodshed that world draws closer (so to call a neighbourhood we cannot define) to this, that chance entry for the living is easier, and that any who wish to drive others there for their own purposes find the deathly work lighter. One day perhaps it will indeed break through; it will undo our solidity, which belongs to earth and heaven, and all of us who are then alive will find ourselves in it and alone till we win through it to our own place. It is full enough of passengers, but mostly alone, though those who died together may have each other's companionship there, as Lester and Evelyn had, and a few more fortunate friendships and intimate loves.

Betty Wallingford knew nothing of this. She walked in peace and gay, in her seeming body. She had been compelled in her body, and in her body she had left the house. That actual body lay now crouched in the porch of the house, unconscious, waiting her return. Lester's and Evelyn's flesh no longer waited them so; they had to find another way to the re-integration of the great identity of flesh and soul. But the days that had passed since their death had not held more for them than the few minutes since she had left the house had for her. In that state there might be ignorance, but even ignorance and fear meant only definite pause or definite action. The vagueness, the dreaming, the doubtful hanging-about are permitted only on the borders of intellectual life, and in this world they were rare. Neither angels nor insects know them, but only bewildered man. Far below Betty, as she came down the Hill, Lester and Evelyn walked. The City about them had not changed nor they. They were still troubled in their hearts by what did not at all trouble her.

She walked on. It was already morning; the day had rushed, in brightness and freshness, to meet her. It was a clear October morning—a little cold, with a few clouds, but agreeable to all her senses. She almost smelt it—a new pleasant smell mingling with the old London smell, but that itself (though heavier than the other) no longer unpleasant, if indeed it ever had been; the ground-bass of the whole absorbed music with which the lighter sun and sky mingled. Indeed the same effect struck her in sound, for she heard, as on similar journeys she had done, the distant noise of the waking City. It always seemed to her at first strange and then not strange. In general its citizens hardly notice it; they are a part of it, and their ears are deafened by it. But her hearing was now cleared and fresh, and she knew that it was happy and that she was happily going to it. She had to find it, or rather something in it, something which helped to compose it. All the sounds and times which went to make it were not equally important to her now. It was a question of time; she would come to the right time, for she had been directed to it, but there was a way to it, a part to be gone through first, a part of the City, not exactly disagreeable but strange. It was as if she were going through a part of her own past, though it was not always the same part, nor the same past. She knew that she only remembered certain parts of it. Someone had once told her that her mind wasn't very strong, "and indeed it isn't," she thought gaily, "but it's quite strong enough to do what it's got to do, and what it hasn't got to do it needn't worry about not doing." Who was it who had so joyously teased her so? to whom she had so joyously replied?

She began, as she came to the bottom of the Hill, to remember more clearly what did happen at these times. She had—they were hardly waking dreams, but she could not think of another word. Sometimes she seemed to be in a shadowy house, with the street faintly visible through the wall; sometimes she saw herself going by in a car with her mother. One way or another she was always in the dreams, and of some of them she was a little ashamed because she seemed to be making a frightful fuss. In ordinary dreams, as far as she knew, you did not criticize yourself. You were doing something or other and you were just doing it, but you rarely thought you might have done it very much better. Her shame however did not do away with her enjoyment; there was an agreeable exhilaration in her severe comments on herself. She began to try and recollect one or other of her dreams, but it was difficult, for she was now coming into the busy streets, and there was colour and sound and many people, and the sky was sparkling, and her heart swelled with mere delight. And in the midst of it all she was at King's Cross Station.

It was crowded but not unpleasantly. She knew at once what she had to do, or the first thing. She had to go and find that other self and say a kind encouraging word to it; she had to help herself. Cleverer people, no doubt, would help others, but she did not envy them, though she did admire. Helping herself was almost like helping another, and helping another was much like helping yourself. She made for the platform where the York train stood. The happy exhilaration of action was upon her. She remembered that you had to change at York for Palchester, and at Palchester for Laughton; and she remembered how that other she grew more and more distressed at each change and less and less capable of showing it. The reason, for the moment, evaded her, but it ought not to be so. "Be yourself, Betty," she said admonishingly, and saw herself on the platform outside a compartment. This, she knew at once, was her most recent journey. She and her mother had gone down in July, and this was July, and there was she and there was her mother. Her mother—she was in these dreams always surprised at her mother, for she definitely remembered her as domineering and powerful, but whenever she saw her in this world there seemed to be something lacking; she looked so blank and purposeless and even miserable. And there by her mother was the other Betty, quiet, wan, unhappy. The porters were calling out "Grantham, Doncaster, York"; the passengers were getting in. Betty came to the compartment. The dream was very strong. There was herself, her sister, her twin. She laughed at her; she said, gaily and yet impatiently: "Oh don't *worry*! Isn't it all a game? Why can't you play it?"

She did not know why she was so sure of the game, nor how she knew that it was her mother's game, and only a courtesy, if she could, to play it well. She added: "It won't hurt you." The other Betty said: "It does hurt me." She answered: "Well, if you can't stand a pinch—Oh darling, laugh!" The other Betty stood wretched and mute. Lady Wallingford said: "Get in, Betty. You travel first class as far as Laughton, you know." She added to a porter: "This part is for York?" The porter having just called out "Grantham, Doncaster, York", exercised a glorious self-restraint, and said: "Yes, lady." He spoke perhaps from habit, but here habit was full of all its past and all its patience, and its patience was the thunder of the passage of a god dominant, miraculous and yet recurrent. Golden-thighed Endurance, sun-shrouded Justice, were in him, and his face was the deep confluence of the City. He said again: "Yes, lady," and his voice was echoed in the recesses of the station, and thrown out beyond it. It was held in the air, and dropped, and some other phrase in turn caught up and held. There was no smallest point in all the place that was not redeemed into beauty and good—except Lady Wallingford's eyes and her young companion's white face. But the joyous face of that Betty who stood on the platform, whom her mother did not see, leaned towards her, and as the train began to move, cried out to her twin: "A game! only a game!" The girl in the train momentarily brightened and almost tried to smile.

Betty stood and watched it go. When it had disappeared—into a part, into a past, of this world—she turned. She paused, not quite knowing what she should do. Her exhilarated heart saddened a little; a touch of new gravity showed in her face. She felt as if she had delayed on an errand, yet she had been right to delay, for she had been directed by the City itself to this meeting. It had been given to her and enjoined on her but it had been somehow for her personal sake; now she must do her business for some other. She tried to remember what she had been bidden, but she could not. That did not matter; in this blessed place it would be shown to her. She walked slowly up the platform, and as she went the whole air and appearance of the station changed. With every step she took a vibration passed through the light; the people about her became shadowy; her own consciousness of them was withdrawn. She moved in something of a trance, unaware of the quickening of the process of time, or rather of her passage through time. The perfect composure of the City in which all the times of London existed took this wanderer into itself, and provided the means to fulfil her errand. When she had left her house, it had been late October; she had stood on the platform in the fullness of the preceding July; she walked now through the altering months, to every step a day, till when she came to the bookstall, some six months had gone by, and she stood by it on a dark morning in January, the January her mortal body in the porch of the house had not yet known, nor Simon the Clerk, nor any on earth. She had moved on into the thing happening, for here all things were happening at once. These were the precincts of felicity. The felicity of the City knew its own precincts, but as yet, while she was but a vagrant here, she could not know them as such. She was happy, yet as she came to the bookstall a vague contradiction of felicity rose in her heart and faded. It was right that she should do whatever it was she was about to do, yet she did not quite like it. She felt as if she were being a little vulgar, though she could not guess how. She was holding—how she could not guess; and the question hardly occurred to her—a few coins. Before her on the bookstall were the morning and weekly papers. Apologetically—she could not help feeling apologetic—she bought a number. She went into the waiting-room and sat down to read.

The reading had absolutely no meaning to her. Her eyes ran over, her memory took in, the printed lines. But for herself she neither understood nor remembered them. She was not doing it for herself but because she had been commanded. She read one paper, finished it, folded it, laid it down, took up another, and so through all. She read the future, but the future was not known to her; it was saved, by the redemption that worked in that place, for the master who had sent her there. Let him make his profit of it; her salvation was his peril. The activities and judgments of the world in that new January were recorded in her, but she, being magically commanded, was yet free. She lightly rose at last and left the papers lying. She went out of the waiting-room and of the station; she took her way again towards Highgate. By the time she had come into the street, she had moved again through receding time. It was again October, and a fresh wind was blowing.

Her mind now was a little subdued from her earlier joy. She caught herself looking forward to a tiresomeness, some kind of dull conversation. There were people waiting for her who would want things repeated or explained. "And I'm not," Betty protested, "very good at explaining. I've been trying to explain something to my mother for a long time, but I've never got it over." She spoke aloud, but not to anyone present; indeed there were few people present; the streets were emptier, and there was no-one by or in front of her. She spoke almost to the City itself, not in defence or excuse, but as a fact. She heard no answer, except that the air seemed to heighten, and the light in it to grow, as if it proposed to her something of encouragement and hope. If she had seen Jonathan's other picture she might have recognized the vibration of that light, though neither she nor anyone could have guessed why or how he had been permitted that understanding of a thing he had never known in itself. "And," she went on, "I shan't feel as good as this presently. I shall very likely have a headache too, which'll make it worse." The remark died into the air; she walked on, trying not to be peevish. She came—so quickly—to the bottom of the Hill, and as she saw it waiting to be climbed (so conscious did all the streets seem) she said, with the first touch of real distress: "It does seem a shame." It did—to leave this goodness for the stupid business before her; she knew it would be stupid, and she could feel the first symptoms of the headache. However, it could not be helped; someone had to do the job, and if it were she—— She became conscious that she was making something of a difficulty out of climbing the Hill, and quickened her steps. The dullness she expected would be but a game, and she would play it well. But as she mounted, the sense that she was near to leaving the City grew on her. She turned once or twice and looked back. It lay, lovely and light before her, but away to the East it was already a little shadowed, and the West was already rose and crimson as the sun sank. She would not, she knew, be here when it did sink; the night in this City was not for her. Another night waited her. It seemed to her that never when she had walked here before, had she felt it so hard to return. Then the sadness and the pain had taken her suddenly at the end. Now there was preparation; they approached, and she had become protestant, almost rebellious at their approach. Why leave? why leave? She was already on the edge of the shadow over the Hill's height, and all before her the sunset over the City—another sunset, another sun—glowed not as if the light were going but as if the night were coming, a holier beauty, a richer mystery. She closed her hand at her side, and it was warm as if she held another hand in hers, and that hand-holding surely belonged here. On the very junction of the two worlds—rather, in the very junction of them within her—the single goodness of the one precipitated itself into the other. She knew its name; she knew who it was who, in that, belonged to this. There someone was denying it; here it was native. She called aloud: "Jonathan!" On the edge of shadow, so near and so near the dark house that waited her, so near some power in which this bright self and joyous life would be again lost, she cried out on her lover. She stamped one small foot on the pavement. The demands of the other Betty were rising in her, but the energy of this was still with her. She just stopped herself saying: "I won't go!"; that would be silly, but she called, her very mildness mutinying, on the name of her only happiness, wishing to claim and clutch that happiness—she called again: "Jonathan! Jonathan!" Freely and fully her voice rang out, as never in all her young tormented life had her mortal mouth called. Immortal, she cried to immortality; and the immortal City let the word sound through it and gave it echo and greater meaning in the echo: "Jonathan! Jonathan!" Alone in the growing shadow, she looked down the Hill, and listened and waited. If he were there, perhaps she could be there; if not—— The night about her grew; she lingered still.

Far away, in London's mortal measurement, but brief time enough immortally, the two dead girls walked. It was not, to them, so very long since they had left the Park—a few days or even less. But Evelyn had reached what would have been on earth the point of exhaustion from tears; there was here no such exhaustion, but as if by a kind of reflexive action she stopped. She might begin again when she would have been capable of beginning again; at present she could not. She did not dare leave Lester, though she did not like Lester any the better for that. Lester still interfered with her chatter, and without her chatter this world was almost unbearable to her. She was afraid of losing that escape from its pressure, nor did she know how Lester could bear that pressure. And if Lester would not listen, there was no-one else to do so. Her fright required of her that relief, and she hated Lester for depriving her of it. Yet Lester still held her arm, and in default of better she dare not lose that pressure. And sometimes Lester did say something and encourage her to answer—only generally about silly uninteresting things.

Once, as they had been coming along Holborn, Lester had stopped and looked in one of those curious windows which were no windows. She had said hesitantly to her companion: "Evelyn, look, can you see any difference?" Evelyn had looked, but she had not seen anything particular. It seemed to be a shop with electric lamps and fires displayed—all vague and unreal enough. But Lester was looking at them seriously. She said: "That's the kind I've always meant to get. Do you see, the one in the back row?" Evelyn did not even want to look. She said in a high strained voice: "Don't be silly, Lester. What's the good?" It gave her some pleasure to retaliate; besides, she never had been interested in such convenient details. She would complain if things went wrong, but she would take no care to have them go right. Lester almost smiled; it was a sad little smile, but it was her first unpremeditated smile. She said: "No. But they do somehow look more real. And we both meant to get one. Richard was going to try and get me one for my birthday. Do be interested, Evelyn." Evelyn said sullenly: "You wouldn't be interested in what I was saying," and pulled away.

Lester with a small sigh had turned with her. That shop had for a moment seemed less like a façade and more like a shop. It had held the sort of thing that had once concerned her—not only for her own convenience, or to improve on her neighbours, but for a pleasure in its own neatness and effectiveness. As she turned away, at a corner, Evelyn felt her stop so suddenly that she herself gave a little squeal of fright. The grip on her arm relaxed, and then was so tightened that she squealed again in protest. But Lester had been rough and unkind. She had said: "Keep quiet——" and had choked and drawn a deep breath or two. Evelyn felt how unfair it was; first she was to talk, and then not to talk, and how could anyone know? She felt herself beginning to cry, and then they had gone on again in silence, up northward, till they had come out of all the parts of London she knew, and were in some long sordid street. There was still no-one else.

But suddenly there was another sound. High beyond and above them a voice called, piercing the air and shaking their hearts. Both girls abruptly stood still. It was a human voice, a girl's voice, crying high in the silence, with assurance and belief. Lester threw up her head; she did not recognize the voice but the note of it lifted her. It was a woman's call; and that was the way a woman should call in this City, the way she should call if she—if she too could dare. She thought of Richard as she had just now seen him in Holborn, and she opened her mouth to send his name also ringing over the streets, as this other name which she could not yet catch was ringing. She heard her voice, "as if hoarse with long disuse", say dully: "Richard!" The sound horrified her. Was this all she could do? She tried again. It was.

She made a third effort, and again she heard from her own mouth only the flat voice of the dead. She was possessed by it. Death, it seemed, was not over; it had only just begun. She was dying further. She could not call; presently she would not be able to speak; then not to see—neither the high stars nor the meaningless lights—yet still, though meaningless, faintly metropolitan. But she would find even this pale light too much, and presently would creep away from it towards one of those great open entrances that loomed here and there, for inside one of them she could hide from the light. Then she would go farther in, so as not to see even the entrance, in spite of the brick wall that stood before it; farther in, and a little way down the coiling stairs. If Richard came along the street then … no; perhaps she would wait at the entrance till he did, and then call him in this faint croak. She had pushed him away once, but now she would not push him away; she would call him and keep him; let him too find it—all the stairs, all the living dead. It was not the dead, as she had thought, it was the living who dwelled in those tunnels of earth—deep and O deep beyond any railways, in the tubes they themselves, thrusting and pushing, hollowed out for their shelter. Richard should no longer be pushed away; he should be there with her, prisoner with her, prisoner to her. If only he too would die, and come!

She saw all this in her mind for as long as it took that other voice to call once more. She saw it clearly—for an aeon; this was what she wanted; this was what she was. This was she, damned; yes, and she was damned; she, being that, was damned. There was no help, unless she could be something other, and there was no power in her to be anything other. As she stood, in a trance of horror at herself or at hell, or at both, being one, a word pierced her brain. The word was "Jonathan!" The far voice was calling: "Jonathan!" She knew the word; it was the name of Richard's friend. She had not herself much interest in Jonathan, but she had asked him to dinner because Richard liked him, she had studied his paintings with goodwill because Richard liked him. She recognized the name, and the name struck through her vision of the Pit. She was not yet so; no, she was not yet there; she was in the streets, and breathed still the open air, and knew the calls of love. Something, in or out of her mind, said to her: "Would it be unfair?" She answered, with the courage and good sense native to her, but with a new and holy shyness: "It would be perhaps extreme." "It would be your own extreme," the voice, if it were a voice, continued. She said: "Yes."

The unspoken dialogue ceased. The call from above had ceased. She seemed to have shut her eyes; she opened them. She saw Evelyn in front of her, running hard. She called, and even as she did so she realized that she could call Evelyn easily enough, and that that was not surprising—she called: "Evelyn!" The silent running figure looked back over its shoulder, and Evelyn's thin voice came to her clearly. It said: "That was Betty." It turned its head again and ran on.

Lester also began to run. The face that had looked back had startled her; it had been excited and pleased. She remembered Betty, and she remembered that Evelyn had not been very nice to Betty. They had once all three run in this way through the grounds of their school by the sea; indeed, as she ran, the bushes of those grounds showed through the houses and shops. Betty had run away, and Evelyn had run after Betty, and suddenly she herself had run after Evelyn. It had not been often she took the trouble, for Betty bored her, and anyhow Evelyn never did anything to Betty; even then she had been calling: "I only want to talk to you." But something in the talk made Betty cry, and for once Lester had interfered; and now, as then, they ran down the path; no, not down the path but up the street, towards Highgate, out to the bottom of the Hill. High above them a single figure watched them come.

Betty watched them; they were at first far away, and she did not know them. While she had gone out on her appointed way, she had been free from pain. But the terrible laws of that place gave her what she wanted when she insisted on it. Her distress, and now the nearness of her distress, might excuse a rebellion; it could not modify its result. She had stamped on the pavement, and (as in the old tales) the inhabitants of that place sprang at once into being. She had called on something she knew. But that something was more deeply engaged on its work in the world of the shadow behind her, and this world would not give her that. She saw at a distance the two running women, strange and remote as in a painting or a poem. She watched them curiously, and the time went by, as long to her as to Evelyn racing up the slope or to Lester outdistanced behind. Lester lost ground; she did not know clearly why she went, but Evelyn did; therefore the one ran faster and the other slower, for still in the outer circles of that world a cruel purpose could outspeed a vague pity. But the cruelty could not reach its end. Betty waited till, half-way up the Hill, the first running figure lifted its head slightly, so that she saw the face and knew it for Evelyn's. She took a step or two back, and the night of this world into which she had hesitated to advance took her as she retreated. Her nightmare possessed her; now it was happening. She screamed and turned and fled.

Evelyn called: "Betty! Betty! stop!" but to Betty's ears the name rang confused. It had been "Bettina!" in her dreams; it was "Bettina!" now. She ran. There was but a short street or two between her and the house; they were to her the natural streets, the sad unhappy streets of Highgate. She forgot her fear of the house in her fear of Evelyn. "Bettina! Bettina!" O lost, lost! but now nearer the house, and the cold quiet thing that waited her in the porch. "Bettina! Bettina!" No—she was there, and she and the shape by the door were no longer separate. A great exhaustion fell on her; her eyes closed; her body failed; she pushed weakly at the door and stumbled through. She fell; someone caught her; she knew nothing more.

Outside the house Evelyn stopped. For her that other world had not changed. It was as quiet and empty, as earthly and unearthly as ever. It was not quite dark; it never yet had been quite dark. The soft, intense, and holy darkness of that City was not known to her. She stood, gently panting, as a girl might who has wholeheartedly run from and been pursued by a welcome lover: so, and yet not so, for that swift and generous animality was not hers. The kind of rage that was in her was the eager stirring of the second death. She had wanted Betty, and now she did not know what she wanted. The house was before her, but she was afraid to try to enter it.

At that moment Lester caught her up. She said, with an imperious demand: "What are you doing, Evelyn? Can't you let her be?" and as she spoke she seemed to herself again to be saying something she had said before—away in those gardens by the sea, a great sea the sound of which, beyond her own voice, she could dimly hear as she had so often heard it in her bed at school. It was almost as if, behind her, the whole City moved. She half-lifted her hand to catch Evelyn by the shoulder, and that too she had once done; but she let it fall, for now the revolt in her flesh was too strong. Yet, as if she had been swung round by that once-impetuous hand, Evelyn turned. She said, as she had said before, in that foolish slurred voice whose protestations provoked disbelief: "What do you mean? I wasn't doing anything."

The answer shocked Lester back into fuller consciousness. They were no longer schoolgirls; they were—what were they? Women; dead women; living women; women on whose lips such words could have no meaning. The excuse of a child in a garden by the sea might have been accepted, if it had not been repeated here. But here it became dreadful. In the Park Lester could have half-smiled at it; she could not smile now. She spoke with a fuller and clearer voice than ever it had been in this world; she spoke as a woman, as Richard's wife, as something more than a vagrant, even if not yet a citizen; and she said: "Don't, my dear. It isn't worth it——" and as if by compulsion she added: "here."

Evelyn stopped, almost as if detaching herself from the other's hand, and took a step away. Lester looked up at the house. It seemed to her strange and awful. Betty had taken refuge in it, as once on a garden-seat among the bushes. Over it, close to it, a lone star hung. The other houses were shadowy and uncertain; this alone was solid and real. It stood out, and within its porch the entrance was as black as one of those other dark entrances which she feared. As she gazed, there came from the house a small human sound. It was someone crying. The half-suppressed unhappy sobs were the only noise that broke the silence. Evelyn's sobs and chattering teeth had broken it in the Park, but Evelyn was not crying now. It was Betty who was crying—among the bushes, in the house, without strength, without hope. Lester, with her own yearning in her bones, stirred restlessly, in an impatient refusal of her impatient impulse to go and tell her to stop. In those earlier days, she had not gone; she had hesitated a moment just so, and then turned away. Betty must really learn to stand up for herself. "Must she indeed?" Lester's own voice said to her. She exclaimed, with the fervent habit of her mortality: "Hell!"

The word ran from her in all directions, as if a dozen small animals had been released and gone racing away. They fled up and down the street, beating out the echo of the word with their quick pattering feet, but the larger went for the house in front of them and disappeared into the porch. She saw them, and was appalled; what new injury had she loosed? There was then no help. She too must go there. And Richard? She had thought that in this terrible London she had lost Richard, but now it seemed to her that this was the only place where she might meet Richard. She had seen him twice, and the second time with some undeclared renewal of love. What might not be granted a third time? voice? a word? Ghosts had spoken; ghost as he was to her in those first appearances, he too might speak. To go into the house might be to lose him. The quiet crying, still shockingly suppressed, continued. Lester hung irresolute.

Behind her, Evelyn's voice said: "Oh come *away*!" At the words Lester, for the first time in her life, saw a temptation precisely as it is when it has ceased to tempt—repugnant, implausible, mean. She said nothing. She went forward and up the steps. She went on into Lady Wallingford's house.

Chapter Five

THE HALL BY HOLBORN

Richard Furnival was as wakeful that night in his manner as Betty in hers. Once he had again reached his flat—it was taking him a long time to get used to saying "my flat" instead of "our flat"—and as the night drew on, he found himself chilled and troubled. He knew of a score of easy phrases to explain his vision; none convinced him. Nor had he any conviction of metaphysics into which, retaining its own nature, it might easily pass. He thought of tales of ghosts; he even tried to pronounce the word; but the word was silly. A ghost was a wraith, a shadow; his vision had been of an actual Lester. The rooms were cold and empty—as empty as any boarding-house rooms where the beloved has been and from which (never to return) she has gone. The afternoon with Jonathan had, when he left, renewed in him the tide of masculine friendship. But that tide had always swelled against the high cliff of another element, on which a burning beacon had once stood—and now suddenly had again stood. The sound of deep waves was in his ears, and even then his eyes had again been filled with the ancient fiery light. He had not, since he had first met Lester, lost at all the sense of great Leviathans, disputes and laughter, things native and natural to the male, but beyond them, and shining towards them had been that other less natural, and as it were more archangelic figure—remote however close, terrifying however sustaining, that which was his and not his, more intimate than all that was his, the shape of the woman and his wife. He had yet, for all his goodwill, so neglected her that he had been content to look at her so from his sea; he had never gone in and lived in that strange turret. He had admired, visited, used it. But not till this afternoon had he seen her as simply living. The noise of ocean faded; rhetoric ceased. This that he had seen had been in his actual house, and now it was not, and the house was cold and dark. He lit a fire to warm himself; he ate and drank; he went from room to room; he tried to read. But every book he opened thrust one message at him—from modern novels ("Aunt Rachel can't live much longer——") to old forgotten volumes ("The long habit of living indisposeth us for dying"; "But she is dead, she's dead…"). His teeth chattered; his body shook. He went to bed and dozed and woke and walked and again lay down, and so on. Till that night he had not known how very nearly he had loved her.

In the morning he made haste to leave. He was indeed on the point of doing so when Jonathan rang him up. Jonathan wanted to tell him about the Clerk's visit, and the Clerk's approval of the painting. Richard did his best to pay attention, and was a little arrested by the mere unexpectedness of the tale. He said, with a serious sympathy: "But that makes everything much simpler, doesn't it? He'll deal with Lady Wallingford, I suppose?"

"Yes," said Jonathan's voice, "yes. If I want him to. I don't believe I do want him to."

"But why not?" asked Richard.

"Because…. The fact is, I don't like *him*. I don't like the way he talks about Betty or the way he looks at paintings. You go and see him or hear him or whatever you can, and come on here and tell me. God knows I … well, never mind. I shall be here all day, unless Betty sends for me."

After this conversation, Richard was about to leave the flat, when he paused and went back. He would not seem to run away; if, by any chance, that presence of his wife should again appear, he would not be without all he could accumulate from her environs with which to greet her. Nor would he now seem to fly. He walked through the rooms. He submitted to memory, and in some poignant sense to a primitive remorse, for he was not yet spiritually old enough to repent. Then, quietly, he went out, and (unable quite to control his uselessly expectant eyes) walked through the streets till he reached Holborn.

It did not take him long to find the place of which he was in search. Behind Holborn, close to Great James Street, in a short street undamaged by the raids, were three buildings, one the largest, of a round shape, in the middle with a house on each side. They were not marked by any board, but as Richard came to the farther house, he saw that the door was open. A small exquisite carving of a hand, so delicate as to be almost a woman's or a child's hand, was fastened to the door-post, its fingers pointing into the house. Richard had never seen any carving that so nearly achieved the colour of flesh; he thought at the first glance that it was flesh, and that a real dismembered hand pointed him to the Clerk's lodging. He touched it cautiously with a finger as he went by and was a little ashamed of his relief when he found it was hard and artificial.

He walked on as far as the end of the street; then he walked back. It was a warm sunny morning for October, and as he paced it seemed to him that the air was full of the scent of flowers. The noise of the streets had died away; it was very quiet. He thought, as he paused before turning, how pleasant it was here. It was even pleasant in a way not to have anyone in his mind, or on his mind. People who were in your mind were so often on your mind, and that was a slight weariness. One would, of course, rather have it so than not. He had never grudged Lester anything, but here, where the air was so fresh and yet so full of a scent he just did not recognize, and London was as silent as the wood in Berkshire where he and Lester had been for a few days after their marriage, it was almost pleasant to be for a moment without Lester. His eyes averted themselves from where she was not lest she should unexpectedly be there. It was sufficient now to remember her in that wood—and even so, eclectically, for she had one day been rather difficult even in that wood, when she had wanted to go into the nearest town to get a particular magazine, in case by the time they did go on their return, it should be sold out, and he had not, for (as he had rightly and rationally pointed out) she could at a pinch wait for it till they got to London. But she had insisted, and because he always wished to consider her and be as unselfish as possible, they had gone. He was surprised, as he stood there, to remember how much he had considered Lester. A score of examples rushed vividly through his mind, and each of those he remembered was actual and true. He really had considered her; he had been, in that sense, a very good husband. He almost wondered if he had been too indulgent, too kind. No; if it were to do again, he would do it. Now she was gone, he was content to remember it. But also now she was gone, he could attend to himself. Luxuriating—more than he knew—in the thought, he turned. Luxury stole gently out within him, and in that warm air flowed about him; luxury, *luxuria*, the quiet distilled *luxuria* of his wishes and habits, the delicate sweet lechery of idleness, the tasting of unhallowed peace.

He remembered with equal distaste that he was on an errand, and felt sorry that Jonathan was not doing his own errand. Jonathan could, just as well as not; after all, it was Jonathan who wanted to marry Betty. However, as he had promised, as he was committed … it would be more of a nuisance to explain to Jonathan—and to himself, but he did not add that—than to go in. He contemplated the carved hand with admiration, almost with affection; it really was the most exquisite thing. There was nothing of Jonathan's shouting colours about it. Jonathan was so *violent*. Art, he thought, should be persuasive. This, however, was too much even for his present state of dreaming luxury. He came to, or almost came to, and found himself in the hall.

It was a rather larger hall than he had expected. On his left hand were the stairs; before him, the passage ran, with another ascending staircase farther on, to a kind of garden door. There was apparently another passage at the end turning off to the left. On his right was the door into the front room, which was open, and beyond it another door, which was shut. Richard hesitated, and began to approach the open door. As he did so, a short rather fat man came out of it, and said in a tone of much good humour: "Yes, sir?"

Richard said: "Oh good morning. Is this Father Simon's place?"

The short man answered: "That's right, sir. Can I do anything for you?"

"I just wanted to get some particulars for a friend," Richard said. "Is there anyone I could see?"

"Come in here, sir," said the other, retreating into the room. "I'm here to answer, as you may say, the first questions. My name's Plankin; I'm a kind of doorkeeper. Come in, sir, and sit down. They all come to me first, sir, and no-one knows better than I do what the Father's done. A tumour on the brain, sir; that's what he cured me of, a year ago. And many another poor creature since."

"Did he?" said Richard, a little sceptically. He was in the front room by now. He had vaguely expected something like an office, but it was hardly that; a waiting-room perhaps. There was a table with a telephone, a few chairs, and that was all. Richard was manoeuvred to a chair; the short man sat down on another by the table, put his hands on his knees, and looked benevolently at the visitor. Richard saw that, beside the telephone, there was also on the table a large-sized album and a pot of paste. He thought, but he knew one could not judge, that it looked as if Plankin had an easy job. But after a tumour on the brain——! He said: "I wanted to ask about Father Simon's work. Does he——"

The short man, sitting quite still, began to speak. He said: "Yes, sir, a tumour. He put his blessed hands on my head, and cured it. There isn't a man or woman in this house that he hasn't cured. I've never had a pain since, not of any kind. Nor they neither. We all carry his mark in our bodies, sir, and we're proud of it."

"Really?" said Richard; "yes; you must be. Does he run some kind of clinic then?"

"Oh no, sir," Plankin said. "He puts everything right straight away. He took the paralysis away from Elsie Bookin who does die typing, and old Mrs. Morris who's the head cook—he cured her cancer. He does it all. I keep an album here, sir, and I stick in it everything the papers say about him. But it's not like knowing him, as we do."

"No," said Richard, "I suppose not. Do you have many inquirers?"

"Not so very many, for the Father wants to be quiet here," said Plankin. "He sends most of them away after he's seen them, to wait. But they come; oh yes, they come. And some go away and some even come to the Relaxations."

"The Relaxations?" Richard asked.

"Oh well, sir," said Plankin, "you'll hear about them, if you stay. The Father gives us peace. He'll tell you about it." He nodded his head, swaying a little, and saying "Peace, peace."

"Can I see the Father then?" said Richard. Inside the room the warm air seemed again to be full of that attractive smell. He might have been in the very middle of the Berkshire wood, again, without Lester, but with an agreeable memory of Lester. The green distemper on the walls of the room was gently moving as if the walls were walls of leaves, and glints of sunlight among them; and the short man opposite him no more than a tree-stump. He could be content to sit here in the wood, where the dead did not matter and never returned—no more than if they had not been known, except for this extra exquisiteness of a happy dream. But presently some sort of surge went through the wood, and the tree-stump stood up and said: "Ah now that'll be one of the ladies. She'll tell you better than I can." Richard came to himself and heard a step in the hall. He rose to his feet, and as he did so Lady Wallingford appeared in the doorway.

She did not, when she saw him, seem pleased. She stood still and surveyed him. Except for the moment or two of introduction, he had not on the previous afternoon been face to face with her, and now he was struck by the force of her face. She looked at him, and she said coldly: "What do you want here?"

The challenge completely restored Richard. He said: "Good morning, Lady Wallingford. I came to ask a few questions about Father Simon. After yesterday, I was naturally interested."

Lady Wallingford said: "Are you sure this is a place for you?"

"Well," Richard answered, "I hope I'm not pig-headed, and I can quite believe that Jonathan may have been wrong." He remembered that morning's telephone conversation and added: "If his painting *was* what you thought it. I was wondering if I could meet—I don't want to intrude—meet Father Simon. He must be a very remarkable man. And if he had any public meetings—Knowledge is always useful."

"You run a certain risk," Lady Wallingford said. "But I've changed my mind a little about your friend's painting. Of course, there can be no nonsense about an engagement. I have quite other views for her. But if you really wish to learn——"

"Why not?" said Richard. "As for the engagement—that perhaps is hardly my business. I am only thinking of my own instruction." He began to feel that he was making progress. Jonathan was always apt to rush things. He took a step forward and went on engagingly: "I assure you——" He stopped. Another figure had appeared behind Lady Wallingford.

She seemed to know it was there, for without looking round she moved out of the doorway, so as to leave room for it to enter. Richard knew at once who it was. He recognized the shape of the face from Jonathan's painting, yet his first thought was that, in this case, Jonathan's painting was quite ridiculously wrong. There was no bewilderment or imbecility about the face that looked at him; rather there was a highness, almost an arrogance, in it which abashed him. He knew that on his right Plankin had dropped on his knees; he had seen Lady Wallingford move. That the movements did not surprise him was the measure of his sense of sovereignty. He resisted an impulse to retreat; he himself became bewildered; he felt with a shock that Simon was between him and the door. He knew the door was there, but he could not focus it properly. The door was not behind Simon; it was Simon: all the ways from this room and in this wood went through Simon. Lady Wallingford was only a stupid old witch in a wood, but this was the god in the wood. Between the tree-stump and the watching witch, he stood alone in the Berkshire wood; and Lester had gone away into the nearest town. He had not gone with her—because he had not gone with her. He had gone to please her, to consider her, which was not at all the same thing. So she had gone alone, and he was alone with the god in the wood, and the witch, and the tree-stump. The god was the witch's husband and father, his father, everyone's father; he loomed in front of him and over him. Yet he was also a way of escape from the wood and from himself. The high emaciated face was at once a wall and a gate in the wall, but the gate was a very old gate, and no-one had gone through it, except perhaps the witch, for many years——

Plankin stood up. Richard's head jerked. Simon was speaking. He said: "Mr. Furnival?" Richard answered: "Father Simon? How do you do?"

The Clerk came a pace into the room. He was wearing a black cassock, caught round the waist by a heavy gold chain. He did not offer his hand, but he said in a pleasant enough voice: "You've come to see us? That is kind." The faint huskiness of the voice reminded Richard of Lester's, which, clear enough at hand, always sounded slightly husky on the telephone. It had been, to him, one of her most agreeable characteristics. He had sometimes rung it up in order to hear that huskiness, carefully explaining the eroticism to himself, but undoubtedly enjoying it almost as happily as if he had not known it was eroticism. It had been in that voice that she had uttered the last thing he had ever heard her say—on the telephone, that too-fatal afternoon: "See you presently, darling." It leapt in his mind. He said: "Yes. Jonathan Drayton's painting made me interested. I hope it's permitted to call like this?"

A constriction passed across the Clerk's face. He answered: "It's free to everyone who cares. And any friend of Mr. Drayton's is especially welcome. He is a great man—only he must not paint foolish pictures of the City. London light is nothing like that. You must tell him so. What can we show you? We've no buildings, no relics, no curios. Only ourselves." He came farther into the room, and Richard saw that there were others behind him. There was a man who looked like a lorry driver, another like a clerk, another who might have been just down from the University. With them there were several women whom he did not immediately take in. These perhaps were those whom Simon had helped. Their eyes were all on the Clerk; no wonder, and again no wonder. Here, in this warm place, there was no illness, no pain, no distress. Simon would have seen to that. Perhaps no death, no ruined body, no horrible memory to mingle with amusing memories.

Simon said again: "Ourselves," and Richard, almost as if he pushed open the gate of the god, said suddenly: "I wish you'd known my wife," and the god answered in that husky voice, as if it came from deeper in the wood: "Is she dead?"

The harsh word did not break the calm. Richard said: "Yes." The god's voice continued: "Well, we shall see. Most things are possible. If I send for her, she may come." He lifted a hand. "Come, all of you," he said. "Come into the Relaxation. Come, Mr. Furnival."

As he used the commonplace phrase, he became again Simon the Clerk, a man to whom Richard was talking. He turned, and everyone turned with him and made way for him. He went into the hall, and in the general movement Richard found himself surrounded and carried along in the small crush. He went necessarily but also voluntarily. Simon's words rang in his ears: "May come ... may come.... If I send for her, she may come." Dead? may come? what was this hint of threat or promise? dead, and return? But she had come; he had seen her; not far from here he had seen her. The sudden recollection shocked him almost to a pause. Something touched his shoulder, lightly; fingers or antennae. He stepped forward again. They were going down the hall and turning into a narrow corridor, as if into a crack in the wall, insects passing into a crack; they were all passing through. They had come to another door, narrower than the passage, and here they went through one at a time, and the witch-woman who had been walking beside him stepped aside for him to pass through. It was Lady Wallingford, and she smiled friendlily at him, and now he smiled back and went on. Something just brushed his cheek as he did so; a cobweb in the wood or something else. He came into a clearing, an old wooden building, a hole; he did not precisely know which it was, but there were chairs in it, so it must be a room of some kind—rather like an old round church, but not a church. There was one tall armed chair. Simon was going across to it. Opposite to it was the only window the room possessed—a low round window, that seemed to be set in a very deep wall indeed, and yet it could not be, for he could see through it now, and into nothing but a kind of empty yard. He hesitated; he did not quite know where to go, but a light small hand, as if it were the carved hand he had seen on the doorpost of that house, crept into his arm, and guided him to a chair at one end of a rough half-circle, so that he could see at once the Clerk in his chair, and the tunnel-like window opposite. He sat down. It was Lady Wallingford who had led him. She withdrew her hand, and he almost thought that as she did so her fingers softly touched his cheek, light as cobweb or antennae. But she had gone right away now, to the other end of that half-moon of chairs, and was sitting down opposite him. Simon, he, Lady Wallingford, the window—four points in a circle; a circle— return and return; may come and may come. They were all sitting now, and Simon began to speak.

Richard looked at him. He knew the derivation of the word "Clerk", and that the original Greek meant "inheritance". The clerks were the inheritors; that was the old wise meaning—men who gathered their inheritance, as now, in that strange husky voice of his, the being on the throned seat was gathering his own. He was pronouncing great words in a foreign tongue; he seemed to exhort and explain, but then also he seemed to collect and receive. Was it a foreign tongue? it was almost English, but not quite English, and sometimes not at all English. Richard was rather good at languages, but this evaded him. It did not seem to evade the others; they were all sitting, listening and gazing. The voice itself indeed sounded more like a chorus of two or three than a single voice. They all died for a moment on a single English word; the word was *Love*.

The Clerk sat and spoke. His hands rested on the arms of his chair; his body was quite still; except that his head turned slightly as he surveyed the half-moon of his audience. The Jewish traits in his face were more marked. The language in which he spoke was ancient Hebrew, but he was pronouncing it in a way not common among men. He paused now and then to translate into English—or so it seemed, though only he knew if it was indeed so, and the English itself was strange and dull. A curious flatness was in his voice. He was practising and increasing this, denying accents and stresses to his speech. Wise readers of verse do their best to submit their voices to the verse, letting the words have their own proper value, and endeavour to leave to them their precise proportion and rhythm. The Clerk was going farther yet. He was removing meaning

35

itself from the words. They fought against him; man's vocabulary fought against him. Man's art is perhaps worth little in the end, but it is at least worth its own present communication. All the poems and paintings may, like faith and hope, at last dissolve; but while faith and hope—and desperation—live, they live; while human communication remains, they remain. It was this that the Clerk was removing; he turned, or sought to turn, words into mere vibrations. The secret School in which he had grown up had studied to extend their power over vocal sounds beyond the normal capacities of man. Generations had put themselves to the work. The healing arts done in that house had depended on this power; the healer had by sympathy of sound breathed restoring relationship into the sub-rational components of flesh.

But there were sounds that had a much greater spell, sounds that could control not only the living but the dead—say, those other living who in another world still retained a kinship and in some sense an identity with this. Great pronouncements had established creation in its order; the reversal of those pronouncements could reverse the order. The Jew sat in his chair and spoke. Through the lesser spells, those that held the spirits of those that already carried his pronunciation in their bodies, that held them fascinated and adoring, he was drawing to the greater. He would come presently to the greatest—to the reversal of the final Jewish word of power, to the reversed Tetragrammaton itself. The energy of that most secret house of God, according to the degree in which it was spoken, meant an all but absolute control; he thought, an absolute. He did not mean it for the creatures before him. To loose it on them would be to destroy them at once; he must precipitate it beyond. The time was very near, if his studies were true, at which a certain great exchange should be achieved. He would draw one from that world, but there must be no impropriety of numbers, either there or here; he would send one to that world. He would have thus a double magical link with infinity. He would begin to be worshipped there. That was why he had brought Richard in. Unknowingly, Richard's mind might hold precisely that still vital junction and communion with the dead which might offer a mode of passage. The Clerk did not doubt his own capacity, sooner or later, to do all by himself, but he would not neglect any convenience. He stirred, by interspersed murmurs, Richard's slumbering mind to a recollection of sensuous love, love which had known that extra physical union, that extra intention of marriage, which is still called marriage.

His eyes ceased to wander and remained fixed on the round window opposite. It looked on a yard, but it looked also on that yard in its infinite relations. There the entry of spirit might be. He drew nearer to the pronunciation; and that strange double echo in his voice, of which Richard had been partly aware, now ceased, and his voice was single. He knew very well that, at that moment, those other appearances of himself in Russia and China had fallen into trance. The deathly formula could only be pronounced by the actual human voice of the single being. There was in that round building one other who knew something of this most secret thing; she sat there, away on his right, and (with all her will) believed. She too knew that the moment was near, and that she too was engaged to it. But also she knew that her usefulness to him, save as one of these indistinguishable creatures who were his living spiritual food, was past.

In the early days of her knowledge of him, Sara Wallingford knew he had found her useful. It was different now. He did not need her, except for convenience of guarding their daughter; when he sent their daughter fully away, she would be—what would she be? A desertion greater than most human desertions would fall on her. The time was near. He had told her of it long since; she could not complain. The time was very near. When it came, and his triplicity was ended, she would be—what that painting had revealed; one of those adoring imbecilities. He had not troubled to deny it.

She remembered the awful beginning of the triplicity. It had been in that house in the North, and he had come to her, as he sometimes did, along garden ways at night. It had been the night after the conception of Betty, and she had known already that she had carried his child. It had not been she who desired it, nor (physically) he. But the child was to be to him an instrument she could not be. She hated it, before its conception, for that; and when she felt within her all the next day the first point of cold which grew and enlarged till after Betty's birth—"as cold as spring-water"—she hated it the more. And her hate did not grow less for what had happened on that second night.

She had known, as soon as she saw him, that he was bent on a magical operation. He did not now need, for the greater of his works, any of the lesser instruments—the wand, the sword, the lamps, the herbs, the robe. She had been in bed when he came. She was twenty-nine then, and she had known him for eight years. He did not need now to tell her to believe in him or to help him; she had been committed to that all those eight years. But in some sense the night of the conception had brought a change. Ever since then, though her subordination to him had grown, his need of her had grown less. On that night, however, she had not yet understood. She lay in her bed and watched him. He drew the curtains and put out the light. There were candles on the dressing-table, and her dressing-gown, with matches in its pocket, lay on a chair by the bed. She put out a hand to see that it was convenient.

36

He was standing between her bed and the great mirror. They had had that mirror put there for exactly such operations, and however dark the room there always seemed to be a faint grey light within the mirror, so that when she saw him in it, it was as if he himself and no mere image lived and moved there. He had put off his clothes, and he stood looking into the mirror, and suddenly the light in it disappeared, and she could see nothing. But she could hear a heavy breathing, almost a panting, and almost animal, had it not been so measured and at times changed in measure. It grew and deepened, and presently it became so low a moan that the sweat broke out on her forehead, and she bit her hand as she lay. But even that moan was not so much of pain as of compulsion. The temperature of the room grew hotter; a uterine warmth oppressed her. She sighed and threw the blankets back. And she prayed—to God? not to God; to him? certainly to him. She had given herself to his will to be the mother of the instrument of his dominion; she prayed to him now to be successful in this other act.

In the mirror a shape of grey light grew slowly visible; it was he, but it was he dimmed. There seemed to be two images of him in one, and they slid into and out of each other, so that she could not be certain which she saw. Both were faint, and there were no boundaries; the greyness itself faded into the darkness. The moaning had ceased; the room was full of a great tension; the heat grew; she lay sweating and willing what he willed. The light in the mirror went out. His voice cried aloud: "The candles!" She sprang from her bed and caught at her dressing-gown. She had it on in a moment and had hold of the matches; then she went very quickly, even in the dark, to the dressing-table, and was immediately striking a match and setting it to the candles. She did not quite take in, as she moved her hand from one to the other what she saw in the oval glass between, and as they caught she blew out the match and whirled swiftly round.

She almost fell at what she saw. Between her and the mirror, and all reflected in the mirror, were three men. One was nearer her; the other two, one on each side of him, were closer to the mirror. From the mirror three identical faces looked out, staring. She felt madly that that nearest form was *he*, her master, whose child she bore; but then the other—things? men? lovers? The sextuple horror, back and front, stood absolutely still. These others were no shadows or ghostly emanations; they had solidity and shape. She stared; her hand clutched at the table; she swayed, crumpled, and fell.

When she came to herself again he and she were alone. He had said a sentence or two to reassure her. It was (he said) indeed he who remained; the others were images and actual copies of him, magically multiplied, flesh out of flesh, and sent upon his business. The curtains were pulled back; the world was grey with dawn; and as she looked out over the moors she knew that somewhere there, through that dawn, those other beings went. The world was ready for them and they went to the world. He had left her then; and since that night there had been no physical intercourse between them. She—even she—could not have endured it. She believed that the he she knew was he, yet sometimes she wondered. At moments, during the next one-and-twenty years, while she worked for him and did his will, she wondered if it was the original whom she obeyed, or only one of those shapes sustained at a distance by the real man. She put the thought away. She read sometimes during those years of the appearance of a great religious philosopher in China, a great patriot preacher in Russia, and she guessed—not who; there was in them no *who*; but what they were. The war had for a while hidden them, but now that the war was over they had reappeared, proclaiming everywhere peace and love, and the enthusiasm for them broke all bounds, and became national and more than national; so that the whole world seemed to be at the disposal of that triplicity. A triple energy of clamour and adoration answered it. There were demands that these three teachers should meet, should draft a gospel and a policy, should fully rule the worship they provoked. It had been so with him in America, and would have been in England, had he not deliberately remained in seclusion. And she knew that in all the world only she, besides the Clerk who now sat before her in the throned seat, knew that these others were not true men at all, but derivations and automata, flesh of his flesh and bone of his bone, but without will and without soul.

She knew why he had kept himself in seclusion. He knew that, when he chose, that world was his for the taking. Rhetoric and hypnotic spells and healing powers would loose idolatry, but beyond all these was the secret and crafty appeal to every individual who came to him separately—the whisper, one way or another: "You are different; you are not under the law; you are particular." He played on both nerves; he moved crowds, but also he moved souls. The susurration of those whispers moved even many who would not otherwise easily have adored. She knew it bitterly, for it was so that she herself had been caught; and indeed she had been fortunate, for she had been useful, and she was the mother of his child. Would that ease abandonment? She knew it would not. Even when the deed was done for which Betty had been brought into the world, and their daughter dismissed into the spiritual places, she herself would be no nearer him. He was already almost spirit, except that he was not spirit. But soon he would have spirits for companions, and——

But before then, though he delayed his full public manifestation till that other work was done, it would have happened. When the communion with that other world was, through Betty, established, he would go

37

(she thought) into middle Europe, or perhaps farther—to Persia or India; and there those other shapes would come, each known to adoring multitudes, and there would be in secret a mystery of re-union, and then all would be in his hand.

She turned her eyes from him, she alone conscious of herself and him in all that group, and saw the rest losing their knowledge before him. They were beginning to sway gently to and fro; their faces were losing meaning; their arms and hands were rising slowly towards him. They were much like the insects in that painting, but their faces were more like his own; she knew when she looked at the painting that Jonathan had given him the face she had so often seen in this house, the blank helpless imbecile gaze. It was why she had been so angry. But *he* had not seen it. She looked at Richard, Jonathan's friend, and wondered if he too were beginning to sway and change.

In fact, if he were not, he was at least already in some danger of it. He had been thinking of love, and what love would mean if he had known someone who would love him perfectly. Lester was not always completely understanding. Something rhythmical in her did not always entirely correspond to him. He moved a little, as if expressing his own rhythm, forward-backward, backward-forward. His eyes opened a little wider, and as he did so they fell on the woman who sat opposite him. He saw her as he had seen her the previous afternoon, and suddenly he recollected Jonathan's paintings. He saw the insects, and he saw them here. He knew he was being caught in something; he made an effort to sit back, to sit still, to recover. The edge of things was before him; he thrust back. He thought of Lester, but not of her glory or her passion; he thought of her in a moment of irritation. He heard, in those precincts of infinity, the voice he had heard in other precincts, on Westminster Bridge. Vivid in his ears, she exclaimed to him: "Why have you kept me waiting?" His mind sprang alert; if she were waiting, what was he doing here?

He was again himself—"a poor thing but his own", or at least not in the sway of the creature on the throne. His native intelligence returned. He looked round; his eyes fell on the window. He heard the Clerk's voice, which was still speaking but now with such a small strange sound that Richard hardly knew it to be a voice at all. It was more like the echo of a voice thrown down a corridor, but not magnified, only diminished, as if it were passing out through the deep round window in the thick wall. But it was not so deep after all, though it was round; it was a window on a yard; an empty yard? no; for someone was in it, someone was looking in. A woman, but not Lester. He was profoundly relieved to find it was not Lester, yet he felt she was connected with Lester. She was coming in; she was coming through the wall. She was smiling, and as he saw the smile he recognized her. It was his wife's friend Evelyn, who had died with her. She was smiling at the Clerk, and as he looked back at the man on the throne he saw that constriction which was the Clerk's smile pass across his face. He heard, mingling with that echo of a human voice, another sound—a high piping sound, coming over distances, or falling as a bird's call from the sky, but this was no bird's call. Richard shut his eyes; still, through those shut eyes, he seemed to see the two smiling at each other. The exchanged smile, the mingled sound, was an outrage. He felt himself to be a witness of an unearthly meeting, of which the seeming friendliness was the most appalling thing. If he had known the word except as an oath, he would have felt that this was damnation. Yet there was only a smile—no pain, no outcry, no obscenity, except that something truly obscene was there. He saw, visibly before him, the breach of spiritual law. He saw a man sitting still and a woman standing just within the wall, a slight thing, and so full of vileness that he almost fainted.

He did not know how long it lasted; for presently they were all on their feet, and he too was able to stand up and then they were all going away.

Chapter Six

THE WISE WATER

It had been, earthly, about five that morning when Lester entered the house at Highgate. It had seemed only evening in the City she had left, for that other City was not bound either to correspondence or to sequence. Its inhabitants were where it chose they should be, as it engaged in its work of accommodating them to itself. They could not yet, or only occasionally, know contemporaneously. Lester still, in general, knew only one thing at a time, and knew them in a temporal order. There was indeed, nearer the centre of its life, another way of knowing, open to its full freemen and officers, but it was beyond these souls, and human language could not express what only sovereign and redeemed human nature could bear. Lester was finding out but slowly the capacities of her present existence, and even those she understood after her old manner. She was young in death, and the earth and its habits were, for this brief time, even more precious to her than they had been.

She paused, or so it seemed to her, inside the hall. It shook her with a new astonishment, and yet indeed it was but ordinary, to think that, so to enter, she had simply passed through the door. It was behind her, and she had not opened it. She had not the kind of mind that easily considered the nature of her own appearance to herself; on earth she had not, nor did she now. The sense of her passage encouraged her. She had no very clear idea that anyone would want to prevent her getting to Betty, but if she could go where she would she was strengthened in her purpose. She could, now, hear no sobs, though they were fresh in her ears. She saw the hall was dark, with a natural healthy darkness in which at first she felt some pleasure. She was free from the pale illumination of the dead. But presently it became clear to her that, dark though it might be, she could see in the dark. The whole hall, with its furniture, became distinct; shapes, though not colours, were visible to her. She felt again a sharp pang of longing for her own familiar things; it was indeed that pang that taught her that she could see, as a waking man finds himself in a strange room and knows by his immediate longing how strange it is. She did not wish to look at Lady Wallingford's properties. But she could not help it. She was there; it was dark; she could see in the dark. She stood and listened and heard no sound.

In fact, above her, Betty was not then crying. Her directors had left her, and she was lying exhausted—perhaps unconscious. Her mother had gone to her own room; there to copy out her notes of Betty's automatic speech. She had begun to do it years before, when the Clerk and she had begun their combined work, and now she could not bear to cease. She knew it was superfluous; he could keep the whole in his mind. At first he had sometimes forgotten a detail, but now never. He never even wished to read what she did; except as a kind of menial, he never used her. But she continued to work.

The Clerk had left Betty's room. He walked slowly to the head of the stairs. He was, for him, a little perplexed in his mind. For the first time now through several years, she had not, in her repetition of the world's rumours, mentioned his name. It was strange. It might be that some odd chance had kept him from the shouting columns of the daily records. It might be that she was growing too weak to report all. It might be that he himself—but that he could not visualize even to himself. Only he felt that the time for his precursor to be dispatched into the other world was very near. There she could see more clearly and universally; she could speak from her own knowledge and not from borrowed information and that information so limited. He had never been able yet to force her through more than a certain period—a few weeks only; if he attempted more she could only when she returned, moan "The rain! The rain!" Floods of water fell on her, it seemed, as if time itself changed to rain and drowned everything, or even swept everything away. When she was habituated to that world, it would be different. Then she would have no consciousness of return; then she could, slowly, grow into and through this rain, and learn what it hid. At present it seemed to threaten that in her which was still necessary to him. His face cleared; he came to the stairs and began to descend. The moon through the windows gave him light, though the hall was dark below. Half-way down he suddenly stopped. There was some living being below him.

He could not see in the dark as Lester could. No magic could give to him in himself the characteristics of the dead. Nothing but a direct shock of destruction, so sudden and immediate that even he could have no time to check it, could kill him, and he did not believe that that was at all possible. He had practised very steadily the restoration of himself against the quickest harm; his servants had, at his will, attempted his death and he had foiled them. But so doing, he had refused all possibilities in death. He would not go to it, as that other child of a Jewish girl had done. That other had refused safeguard and miracle; he had refused the achievement of security. He had gone into death—and the Clerk supposed it his failure—as the rest of mankind go—ignorant and in pain. The Clerk had set himself to decline pain and ignorance. So that now he had not any capacities but those he could himself gain.

He saw two eyes shining. He should have known what it was; he did not. He could not even see that it was a woman, or the ghost of a woman. He had not called it, and he did not expect it. But he did think that it was one of the lesser creatures of that other world. He had seen them sometimes in earlier rites, and once or twice something had followed Betty in, without her knowledge, as if drawn after her, and had lingered for a while in the hall. Such things had not come in human form, and he did not now expect human form. They came usually in the shapes of small monstrosities—things like rats or rabbits or monkeys or snakes, or even dwarfed vultures or large spiders and beetles. They were indeed none of these; they did not belong to animal nature. Had animal nature been capable of enduring the magical link, he would have used it for his purpose, but it was not. Once, long ago, he had tried it with a monkey, but the link had died with its own death; it had no rational soul, and if (after death) it lived at all, it was only its own happy past that lived; it could not grow into other communion. He supposed this to be a dim monstrosity of that ghostly kind. It awaited his will. It was useless to ask its name or kind; such beings were only confused and troubled by such questions and could not answer. They did not know what they were; they did sometimes—not always—know what they were about. He stood high above it, looking scornfully down, and he said: "Why are you here?"

Lester had seen him as he began to descend the stair. She had no idea who he was. Her first thought, as she looked up at that great cloaked figure, was that here at last was one of the native inhabitants of the new City, and that she had perhaps been encouraged into this house to meet him. Her second was that this was someone for whom she had been waiting. A childish memory of a picture or a tale of angels mingled with something later—an adolescent dream of a man of power, a genius, a conqueror, a master. Lester, like certain other women of high vitality and discontented heart, had occasionally felt that what she really needed was someone great enough to govern her—but to do that, she innocently felt, he (or she—there was no sex differentiation) would have to be very great. The vague dream had disappeared when she had fallen in love. Obedience to a fabulous ruler of shadows was one thing; obedience to Richard was quite another. He certainly rarely seemed to suggest it; when he did, she was rarely in agreement with him. Suddenly now the old adolescent dream recurred. She looked up at the high emaciated face, gazing down, and felt as if it were more than that of a man.

When however he spoke, she hardly heard the question. The voice which was husky to Jonathan was thick to her. She was not surprised; so perhaps these godlike beings spoke; or so perhaps she, uneducated in this sound, heard them. But she did just catch the words, and she answered, as meekly as she had ever thought she would: "I'm Lester. I've come to see Betty."

The Clerk heard below him what sounded like the single word "Betty". He did not hear more. He came down a step or two, peering. There was, he thought, a certain thickening of the darkness, a kind of moulded shape. He was sure now that something had followed Betty, but he was a little perplexed that it should—unless indeed it was something useless to him, being hungry and spiritually carnivorous. It was not in the shape of rat or monkey; it was roughly human, like a low tree rudely cut into human form. He lifted his hand and made over it a twisted magical sign, meant to reduce the intruder to the will that was expressed in it. He said: "Why?"

The sign, so loaded, was not without its effect, but its effect was consistent with Lester's nature and her present intention. It would have dissolved or subdued such momentary vitalities as, for instance, had sprung from her oath outside the house, but what had brought her into the house was a true purpose of goodwill; of help? she might have put it so: indeed she now began to answer so. She said: "To help——" and stopped. The word sounded pompous, not only before this god, but even to describe her intention. She almost felt herself blushing, as she thought of Betty and the times when she had not helped Betty. It was upon those vague and unexplored memories that the magical sign had power. The hall became to her suddenly full of shadows. Betty was on all sides of her, and so was she. She had no idea she had even seen Betty as many times as now she saw herself abandoning Betty. There were a mass of forms, moving, interpenetrating, and wherever her eyes saw a particular one it seemed to detach itself and harden and become actual. She saw herself ignoring Betty, snubbing Betty, despising Betty—in the gardens, in the dormitory, in the street, even in this hall. They were so vivid to her that she forgot the god on the stair; she was secluded from him in all this ghostly vehemence of her past, and the ghostliness of any apt to be truly more than ghost. She lost the images of herself; she saw only images of Betty—beginning to speak, putting out a timid hand, or only looking at her. She threw up her hand, in her old gesture, to keep them off. Her head span; she seemed swirled among them on a kind of infernal merry-go-round. If only any of them were the real Betty, the present Betty, the Betty she was coming to, the Betty she—fool!—had been coming to help. Where she had once refused to help, she was now left to need help. But that refusal had been laziness and indifference rather than deliberate malice—original rather than actual sin. It was permitted to her to recognize it with tears. The spiritual ecstasy ravaged her; she thought no more of help either given or taken; she was only in great need of it. She threw out her hand, in an effort to grasp, here or there, Betty's half-outstretched hand, but (actual as the figure seemed) hers never reached it; as the fingers almost touched, hers found emptiness, and there was Betty running away from her, down a garden-path, down a street, down the hall, infinitely down the hall. But the vague and impractical yet real sympathy she had once felt for Betty, the occasional interference she had bestowed, allowed her now a word of appeal. She cried out, pleading as she had never supposed she could or would plead: "Betty! please, Betty!"

As she spoke, she found herself alone. But she knew exactly where Betty was, and she knew she had no hope but there. Her dreams of a god had vanished among those too certain visions of a girl; she wholly forgot the appearance on the stairs in her desperate sense of Betty. She moved up the stairs, towards the help she needed, and in her movement she disappeared from the Clerk's own gaze. He was not aware that she passed him; to him it seemed that the roughly-moulded human form had dwindled and quivered and vanished, and the eyes had faded. It could not, he thought, this poor vagrant from the other world, this less than human or angelic monstrosity, bear the question which he had put to it, and it had fallen into nothingness below him. He was right enough in what, after his own manner, he had seen—the supernatural shaking of Lester's centre; but the processes of redemption were hidden from him. At the moment when she drew nearer to the true life of that City, he thought her to be dissolved. He went on calmly down the stairs, and opening the door passed into the earthly night.

But Lester, mounting, came to Betty's room, and opening no door passed on into it. This time indeed she knew she went through the door, but then the door, when she came to it, was no longer a serious barrier. It was still a door; it did not become thin or shadowy. But being a door, it was also in itself her quickest way. To open it would have been to go round by a longer path. She was growing capable of the movement proper to her state. She could not so have passed through the empty rooms or dim façades of her earlier experience; those shadowy images retained for her the properties of the world they imaged. But in this real world she could act according to her own reality. She went through the door. There, before her, stretched motionless in her bed, was Betty. Lester saw her clearly in the dark. She went on till she came to the foot of the bed; then she stood still.

She had never seen anyone look so exhausted and wan. The living girl's eyes were shut; she hardly drew breath; she too might have been dead, except that now and then she was shaken by a sudden convulsion. The dead Lester gazed at the seemingly dead Betty. Her heart sank; what help for her was here? what power in that shaken corpse to hold its own images at bay? If it were a corpse, then she and Betty were parted perhaps for ever. She might have left this reconciliation also too late, as she had left Richard. She had pushed Richard away; she had not gathered Betty in. She was to be left with her choice. She thought: "It isn't fair. I didn't know" and immediately regretted it. She had known—not perhaps clearly about Richard, for those unions and conflicts were of a particular kind, and the justice which must solve them was more intimate than she could yet understand, but she had clearly known about Betty. She had been very young then. But her refusal had been as definite and cold as the body at which she looked was definite and cold. Death for death, death to death, death in death.

The curtains at the windows were drawn back. The sun was rising; the room grew slowly bright with day. Lester stood there because she had nothing else to do. No impulse was upon her and no wish. She had nowhere to go. Evelyn was not in her mind. She knew she could do nothing unless she had help, and her only help lay useless before her. Presently she was aware of a step outside the room. There was a tap on the door; another. The door was gently opened, and a maid came in and paused. She looked at Betty; she looked round the room; she looked at Lester without seeing her. Lester looked back at her without interest; she was remote and irrelevant. It was not odd to be unseen; that, of course. Only Betty mattered, and Betty lay without sign. The maid went away. The morning light increased.

Suddenly Betty's eyes had opened. They were looking at Lester. A small voice, hardly audible even to Lester, inaudible to mortal ears, said: "Lester!" Lester said: "Yes," and saw that the other had not heard. The eyes widened; the voice said: "Lester!… but you're dead. Evelyn and you are dead." It added, dying on the sentence: "I'm so glad Evelyn's dead." The eyes closed. Exhaustion swallowed her.

Lester heard the relief in the dying words. She had forgotten Evelyn, but, fresh from that ghostly world where Evelyn and she had wandered, she retained some sense of companionship, and the relief—which was hostility—filled her with fear. She felt—though indirectly—the terror and the despair of those of the dead who, passing from this world, leave only that just relief behind. That which should go with them—the goodwill of those they have known—does not. There are those who have been unjustly persecuted or slain; perhaps a greater joy waits them. But for the ordinary man or woman to go with no viaticum but this relief is a very terrible thing. Almost, for a moment, Lester felt the whole City—ghostly or earthly or both in its proper unity—draw that gentle sigh. Disburdened, it rejoiced: at Evelyn's death? at hers? Was this to be all Betty and earth could give? a sigh of joy that she was gone? The form on the bed held all the keys. If she could speak so of one, that other waiting spirit felt no surety that she too might not be excluded, by failing voice and closing eyes, from the consciousness on which so much depended. It was awful to think how much did depend—how much power for everlasting decision lay there. Verdict, judgment, execution of judgment, hid behind those closed eyelids. Lester's impetuosity swelled in her. She wished to wake Betty, to bully her, to compel her to speak, to force help out of her. But she knew all such impetuosity was vain; and however, in her past, she had wrangled in private with Richard—and that was different; yes, it was different, for it was within the nearest image to love that she had known; it might be better or worse, but it was different; it was less permissible and more excusable—however that might be, she did not brawl in public. And she was in public now, in the full publicity of the spiritual City, though no inhabitants of the City except Betty were there. She had waited; she must wait. It was pain and grief to her sudden rage. She waited. The house, earthly, warm, lightened by the great luminary planet, was still to her a part of the City while Betty was there. Everything depended on Betty, and Betty on—on nothing that Lester yet knew.

The door of the room again opened. Lady Wallingford came in. She went to the bed and bent over Betty. She peered into her eyes, felt temples and wrists, and rearranged the bedclothes. Then she crossed to the window and drew one of the curtains a little, so that the sunlight no longer fell on her daughter's face. In so moving, she had passed round the foot of the bed. Lester began to step back; then she checked herself. She knew it did not matter; she was becoming different—how or why she did not know; but coincidence no longer meant contact. She had a faint sense, as she had done when she passed through the door, of something brushing against her. Her eyes blinked and were clear. Lady Wallingford went through the space which Lester seemed to herself to occupy, and so returned; it was all that could be said. The same space was diversely occupied, but the two presences were separate still. Lady Wallingford, exactly like a competent nurse, looked round the room and went out. Body and visionary body were again alone together. Outside the house a car was heard to start up and move off. Lady Wallingford was on her way to Holborn. Thither Richard was now walking along Millbank, while Jonathan in his room waited, with a fantastic but failing hope, for some word of Betty. And beyond them all, three continents murmured of their great leaders, and the two vegetable images of the Clerk swayed by his single will such crowds as he could sway, and he himself prepared for the operation which is called "the sending out", its other name being murder.

As the car's sound died away, Betty sat up. Bright in the shadow her eyes opened on Lester, tender and full of laughter. She pushed the bedclothes back, swung out her legs, and sat on the side of the bed. She said: "Hallo, Lester! What are you doing here?" The voice was full of a warm welcome; Lester heard it incredulously. Betty went on: "It's nice to see you anyway. How are you?"

Lester had waited for something, but hardly for this. She had not begun to expect it. But then she had never seen, face to face, the other Betty who had gone almost dancing through the City, nor guessed the pure freshness of joy natural to that place. She had heard only the high hill-call, and now (subdued as it might be to gay and friendly talk) she recognized the voice. She knew at once that a greater than she was here; it was no wonder she had been sent here for help. She looked at the girl sitting on the bed, whose voice was the only sound but Evelyn's that had pierced her nothing since she died, and she said, hoping that the other might also perhaps hear: "Not too frightfully well."

Betty had risen to her feet as Lester spoke. She showed signs of going across to the window, but on the other's words she paused. She said: "What's the matter? Can I do anything?"

Lester looked at her. There was no doubt that this was Betty—Betty gay, Betty joyous, Betty revitalized, but still Betty. This was no sorrowing impotence of misery, but an ardour of willingness to help. Yet to ask for help was not easy. The sense of fatal judgment was still present; the change in Betty had not altered that, and her glowing shape was vivid with it. The slightest movement of that hand, the slightest aversion of those eyes, would be still like any similar movement of those dead hands or that white face would have been, frightful with finality. To ask that this should be set aside, even to plead, was not natural to Lester. But her need was too great for her to delay. She said at once: "Yes; you can."

Betty smiled brilliantly at her. She answered: "Well, that's all right. Tell me about it."

Lester said, rather helplessly: "It's all those times … those times at school, and afterwards. I can't manage them without you."

Betty wrinkled her forehead. She said in some surprise: "Those times at school? But, Lester, I always liked you at school."

"Perhaps you did," said Lester. "But you may remember that I didn't behave as if I particularly liked you."

"Oh didn't you?" Betty answered. "I know you didn't particularly want me, but why should you? I was so much younger than you, and I expect I was something of a nuisance. As far as I can remember, you put up with me nobly. But I don't remember much about it. Need we? It's so lovely of you to come and see me now."

Lester realized that this was going to be worse than she had supposed. She had prepared herself to ask for forgiveness, but that, it seemed, was not enough. She must herself bring the truth to Betty's reluctant mind; nothing else than the truth would be any good. She would not be able entirely to escape from those swirling images of the past, if they were indeed images, and not the very past itself, by any other means than by Betty's dismissal of them. They were not here, in this room, but they were there, outside the door, and if she left the room she would be caught again among them. She did not understand how this different Betty had come to be, but the City in which she moved did not allow her to waste time in common earthly bewilderment. The voice was the voice she had wanted to imitate, the voice of the hill in the City. If the Betty of that moment and of this moment were the same, then perhaps Betty would understand, though there was in fact nothing to understand except her own perverse indolence. She said—it was the most bitter thing she had ever done; she seemed to taste on her tongue the hard and bitter substance of that moment; she said: "Try and remember."

Betty's eyes had been again wandering towards the sunlight at the window. She brought them back to look attentively at Lester, and she said quickly and affectionately: "Lester, you've been crying!"

Lester answered, in a voice from which, for all her growing vision and springing charity, she could not keep a rigidity of exasperation: "I know I've been crying, I——"

Betty interrupted: "But of course I'll remember," she said. "It was only that I didn't understand. What is it exactly you want me to remember?" She smiled as she spoke, and all the tenderness her mortal life had desired and lacked was visible in her. Lester felt an impulse to run away, to hide, even at least to shut her eyes. She held herself still; it had to be done. She said: "You might remember how I did behave to you, at school. And afterwards."

There was a long silence, and in it Lester's new life felt the first dim beginnings of exalted peace. She was not less troubled nor less in fear of what might come. She was, and must be now, the victim of her victim. But also she was now, in that world, with someone she knew, with someone friendly and royally disposed to good, with someone native to her and to that world, easy and happy. The air she breathed was fresh with joy; the room was loaded with it. She knew it as a sick woman knows the summer. She herself was not yet happy, but this kind of happiness was new to her; only, even while she waited, she recollected that once or twice she had known something like it with Richard—one night when they had parted under a street-lamp, one day when they had met at Waterloo. They belonged here, those times; yet those times were as true as those other sinful times that danced without. Her heart was tranquil. If she must go, she must go; perhaps this hovering flicker of known joy might be permitted to go with her. All that was noble in her lifted itself in that moment. The small young figure before her was her judge; but it was also the centre and source of the peace. She exclaimed, as if for Betty to know all was necessary to the fullness of the moment and to her own joy: "Oh remember! do remember!"

Betty stood attentive. The times of her happiness had been hitherto on the whole unclouded by her mortal life, except as she might sometimes vaguely remember an unpleasant dream. She set herself now to remember, since that, it seemed, was what was wanted, something she could lately have been contented to leave forgotten. It seemed to her also something of a waste on this glorious morning, with time happily before them, to spend it—however, she knew she wanted to remember. As soon as she knew that Lester wanted it, she too wanted it; so simple is love-in-paradise. She stood and thought. She was still smiling, and she continued to smile, though presently her smile became a little grave. She said: "Oh well, how could you know?"

Lester said: "I knew quite enough."

Betty went on smiling, but presently the smile vanished. She said, more seriously: "I do think Evelyn was rather unkind. But I suppose if she liked that sort of thing—anyhow we're not thinking of her. Well, now, that's done."

Lester exclaimed: "You've remembered?" and Betty, now actually breaking into a gay laugh, answered: "Darling, how serious you are! Yes, I've remembered."

"Everything?" Lester persisted; and Betty, looking her full in the eyes, so that suddenly Lester dropped her own, answered: "Everything." She added: "It was lovely of you to ask me. I think perhaps I never quite wanted to remember—Oh all sorts of things, until you asked me, and then I just did, and now I shan't mind whatever else there is. Oh Lester, how good you are to me!"

The tears came into Lester's eyes, but this time they did not fall. Betty's figure swam indistinctly before her, and then she blinked the tears away. They looked at each other, and Betty laughed, and Lester found herself beginning to laugh, but as she did so she exclaimed: "All the same——!" Betty put out her hand towards the other's lips, as if to hush her, but it did not reach them. Clear though they saw and heard each other, intimate as their hearts had become, and freely though they shared in that opening City a common good, still its proper definitions lay between them. The one was dead; the other not. The *Noli-me-tangere* of the City's own Lord Mayor was, in their small degree, imposed on them. Betty's hand dropped gently to her side. They half recognized the law and courteously yielded to it. Betty thought: "Of course, Lester was killed." She also thought, and she said aloud: "Oh but I was glad Evelyn was killed." Her voice was shocked; stricken, she looked at the other. She said: "How could I be?"

Lester had again forgotten Evelyn. She remembered. She became aware of Evelyn running, not now from her but towards her, towards them both. She herself now was at the other end of Evelyn's infinite haste; she shared with Betty the nature of the goal, and she felt at a distance Evelyn hurrying and almost there. She threw up her head, as she had thrown it up at the first call from the hill. She said—and now nothing deadened her speech; she said—in the voice that was to Richard her loveliest and lordliest: "I'll deal with Evelyn."

Betty answered, half-laughing and half-embarrassed: "I can't think why she scares me a little still. But I didn't mean to want her to be dead. Only she's all mixed up with *there*. I usen't to think of that much when I was here." There was no need to explain what she meant by "there" and "here". Their hearts, now in union, knew. "But lately I seem to have to sometimes. Now you've made me remember, I don't so much mind. Stay with me a little while, if you can; will you, Lester? I know you can't settle that; things happen. But while you *can*... I've a feeling that I've got to get through something disagreeable, and I don't want to make a fuss again."

"Of course I'll stay—if I may," said Lester. "But make a fuss—you!"

Betty sat down on the bed. She smiled again at Lester; then she began to talk, almost as if to herself, or as if she were telling a child a story to soothe it to sleep. She said: "I know I needn't—when I think of the lake; at least, I suppose it was a lake. If it was a river, it was very broad. I must have been very small indeed, because, you know, it always seems as if I'd only just floated up through the lake, which is nonsense. But sometimes I almost think I did, because deep down I can remember the fishes, though not so as to describe them, and none of them took any notice of me, except one with a kind of great horned head which was swimming round me and diving under me. It was quite clear there under the water, and I didn't even know I was there. I mean I wasn't thinking of myself. And then presently the fish dived again and went below me, and I felt him lifting me up with his back, and then the water plunged under me and lifted me, and I came out on the surface. And there I lay; it was sunny and bright, and I drifted in the sun—it was almost as if I was lying on the sunlight itself—and presently I saw the shore—a few steps in a low cliff, and a woman standing there. I didn't know who she was, but I know now, since you made me remember—Lester, I do owe you such a lot—it was a nurse I once had, but not for very long. She bent down and lifted me out of the water. I didn't want to leave it. But I liked her; it was almost as if she was my real mother, and she said: 'There, dearie, no-one can undo that; bless God for it.' And then I went to sleep, and that's the earliest thing I can remember, and after that only some things that belonged to it: some of the times I've been through London, and the Thames, and the white gulls. They were all in that part and in the other part too, the part I'm only just beginning to remember. And so were you, Lester, a little."

"I!" said Lester bitterly. It did not seem to her likely that she could have belonged to that world of light and beauty. Yet even as she spoke she irrelevantly thought of Richard's eyes at the corner in Holborn—and before that—before that—before she was dead; and she remembered how Richard had come to meet her once and again, and how her heart had swelled for the glory and vigour of his coming. But Betty was speaking again.

"I see now that you were, and now it seems all right. That was why I ran after you—Oh how tiresome I must have been! but it doesn't matter. I'm afraid I did make a fuss; I know I did over the headaches—there were some places where I knew I was going to have headaches—and over Evelyn. It really was rather silly of Evelyn. And then there was this house———"

She stopped and yawned. She threw herself back on the pillow and swung up her legs. She went on: "But I'm too sleepy now to remember all that I ought to about this house... And then there was Jonathan. Do you know Jonathan? he was very good to me. We might go and look at the Thames some time, you and I and Jonathan..." Her eyes closed; her hands felt vaguely about the bed. She said, in tones Lester could only just hear: "I'm so sorry. I just can't keep awake. Don't go. Jonathan will be coming.... Don't go unless you must. It's lovely having you here.... It was sweet of you to come ... Jonathan will ... dear Lester...." She made an uncertain movement to pull the bedclothes up over her; before the movement ended she was asleep.

Lester did not understand what she had been saying. In what strange way she had been known to Betty, more happily than ever she herself could have supposed, she did not know. Betty had been talking almost as if there had been two lives, each a kind of dream to the other. It would once have been easy to call the one life a fantasy, easy if this new, gay, and vivid Betty had not precisely belonged to the fantasy. She felt both lives within her too sharply now to call either so. There had been something like two lives in her own single life—the gracious passionate life of beauty and delight, and the hard angry life of bitterness and hate. It was the recollection of that cold folly which perhaps now made Betty seem to her—no; it was not. Betty was changing; she was dying back; she was becoming what she had been. Colour passed from her cheeks; the sweet innocence of sleep faded, and the pallor of exhaustion and the worn semblance of victimization spread. The hands twitched. She looked already, as men say, "near dead". Lester exclaimed: "Betty!" It had no effect. The change affected the room itself; the sunlight weakened; power everywhere departed. The girl who lay before Lester was the girl she had turned away from. The hands and head could no longer threaten judgment; they were too helpless. Yes, but also they had judged. What had been, in that other state, decided, remained fixed: once known, always known. She knew quite clearly that Betty had—forgiven her. The smile, the warmth, the loveliness, were forgiveness. It was strange not to mind, but she did not mind. If she did not mind Betty, perhaps she would not mind Richard. She smiled. Mind Richard? mind being forgiven—forgiven so—by that difficult obnoxious adorable creature? Let him come to her in turn and she would show him what forgiveness was. Till now she had not really understood it; occasionally in the past each of them had "forgiven" the other, but the victim had not much liked it. But now—by high permission, yes. And if Richard and Betty, then others; if this permission which now directed her life allowed, others. "Thus"—how did it go? "through all eternity I forgive you, you forgive me." Wine and bread, the poem had called it; wine and bread let it be. Meanwhile there was nothing to do but to wait till that happened which must happen. In some way she had now been left in charge of Betty. She must keep her charge. She must wait.

All this time, since first Lester had entered the house, the unhappy soul of Evelyn had also waited. At first it had almost followed Lester in, but it did not dare. Frightful as the empty appearance of the City was to it, to be enclosed in the house would be worse. She would be afraid of being shut up with Lester and Betty, certainly with Lester, almost with Betty. She hated the victim of her torment, but to be alone with her in that dark solid house—the thought ought to have been agreeable, but it was not at all agreeable. As for Lester, she hated Lester too. Lester had patronized her, but then Lester could. She had the power to be like that, and she was. She hated being alone in this place with Lester, though since she had run after Betty, even though she had missed her, she felt better. The street down which she had run after she had turned off from the hill, this street in which she now stood, had seemed more close, more helpful. The air held some sense of gain. This was more like the London she had known. The house should have been the climax; could she go in, she thought, it would be. Only she dared not go in. Lester was not to be trusted; Lester and Betty might be plotting.

After all, she was rather glad she had not caught up with Betty. Lester might have come up behind her, and then the two of them might have done things to her. Or they might have thought she would have run into the house, but she had not; she had been too clever for that—and for them. She walked a few steps away. It was no good standing too near; they would not come out—no, but if they should…. She could almost see them talking in the house, smiling at each other. She walked a little farther away, and turned her head over her shoulder as she went. On her face was the look which had shocked Lester when she had earlier seen that turned head. It was hate relieved from mortality, malice incapable of death. Within the house, Lester's own face had taken on a similar change; some element of alteration had disappeared. She herself did not, of course, know it; her attention had been taken up by the growing glory that was Betty. But even Betty's face had not that other lucidity. What had looked at Lester from Evelyn's eyes, what now showed in her own, was pure immortality. This was the seal of the City, its first gift to the dead who entered it. They had what they were, and they had it (as it seemed) for ever. With that in her eyes, Evelyn turned her head again and wandered slowly on.

She came on to the hill, and drifted down it, for having no choice of ways, and yet being oddly compelled to go on—if not into the house, then away from the house—she only retraced her steps, slowly going back, slowly going down. She was about a third of the way down when from far off the sound of the Name caught her. She could hardly there be said to have heard it; it was not so much a name or even a sound as an impulse. It had gone, that indrawing cry, where only it could go, for the eternal City into which it was inevitably loosed absorbed it into its proper place. It could not affect the solid houses of earth nor the millions of men and women toilfully attempting goodness; nor could it reach the paradisal places and their inhabitants. It sounded only through the void streets, the apparent façades, the shadowy rooms of the world of the newly dead. There it found its way. Other wanderers, as invisible to Evelyn as she to them, but of her kind, felt it—old men seeking lechery, young men seeking drunkenness, women making and believing malice, all harbourers in a lie. The debased Tetragrammaton drew them with its spiritual suction; the syllables passed out, and swirled, and drawing their captives returned to their speaker. Some went a little way and fell; some farther, and failed; of them all only she, at once the latest, the weakest, the nearest, the worst, was wholly caught. She did not recognise captivity; she thought herself free. She began to walk more quickly, to run, to run fast. As she ran, she began to hear the sound. It was not friendly; it was not likeable; but it was allied. She felt towards it as Lester had felt towards the cry on the hill. The souls in that place know their own proper sounds and hurry to them.

Something perhaps of fear entered her, to find herself running so fast. It was a steep road, and it seemed much longer than when she had run up it of her own volition. She ran, and she ran. She was running almost along the very cry itself, not touching the apparent pavement; it wailed louder below her. Her immortality was in her face; her spirituality in her feet; she was lifted and she ran.

She did not recognize the streets; she came at last round by King's Cross, on into the congeries of streets on the other side of the Euston Road, on towards Holborn. The cry grew quieter as she neared its source. What had been a wail in the more distant streets was a voice in the nearer. She still ran along it. At last, so running, she came through a small gate into a yard, and across it to a small low window. There she stopped and looked in. She saw a kind of hall, with people sitting on chairs, and away at the other end in a high chair, a man who was looking back at her. Or perhaps he was not actually looking back at her, but she knew he saw her. A dizziness of relief took her; here at last was someone else. She was so aware of him, and of his sidelong knowledge of her, that she hardly noticed she was moving forward and through the wall. A film of spiders' webs brushed against her; she broke through it. She had come back; at the very sight of him she had been able to return into the world of men. She had escaped from the horrible vague City, and here was he to welcome her.

He was smiling. She thought—as neither Jonathan nor Richard had done, that it was properly a smile, though again the smile was sidelong. He had reason, for when he saw her he knew that at last his writ ran in the spiritual City. He had known that it must be so, he being what he was. But that silence of Betty's about his future had almost troubled him. A deathly silence had seemed to hover round him, as if he had made an error in magic and could not recover himself. It was certainly time he sent out his messenger before him. But he knew now it was no error, for the silence had spoken. This was its first word—solitary, soon to be companioned. He would ride there presently upon their cries. He was overcoming that world.

The exchange of smiles—if that which had no thought of fair courtesy could be called exchange; at least some imitation of smiles—passed between them. Separately, each of them declined the nature of the City; which nevertheless held them. Each desired to breach the City; and either breach opened—directly and only— upon the other. Love to love, death to death, breach to breach; that was the ordering of the City, and its nature. It throve between Lester and Betty, between Richard and Jonathan, between Simon and Evelyn; that was its choice. How it throve was theirs. The noise of London, which was a part of it, rose at a distance outside the house—all its talk and traffic and turmoil. In the quiet of the hall the man said to the woman: "I shall want you soon." She said: "Take me out of it." And he: "Soon." He stood up; that was when Richard found himself going out of the hall.

Chapter Seven

THE MAGICAL SACRIFICE

An hour or so later Jonathan opened his door to Richard. He said: "I say, what's been happening? You look ghastly. Sit down; have a drink."

Richard was very white and unsteady. He dropped into a chair. Even the warm studio and Jonathan could not overcome the sense of that other thing which, ever since he had left the house in Holborn, had run cold in his blood. As Jonathan brought him the drink, he shuddered and looked rather wildly round. Jonathan said anxiously: "Here, drink this. Are you all right?"

Richard drank and sat for a little silent. Then he said: "I'd better tell you. Either I'm mad or.... But I'm not just wrong. I'm either right or I'm mad. It's no good telling me I was taken in by seeing a barmaid in a yard——"

"No; all right," said Jonathan. "I won't. I shouldn't be very likely to anyhow. Tell me what you like and I'll believe it. Why not?"

Richard began. He spoke slowly. He took care to be exact. He modified his description of his own sensations and emotions; he was as impartial as he could be. Once or twice he made an effort to be defensively witty; it was unsuccessful and he dropped it. As he came to the end, he grew even more careful. Jonathan sat on his table and watched him.

"I saw her come in. They looked towards each other and they smiled. And all I can tell you is that I know now what blasphemy is. It's not attractive and it isn't thrilling. It's just bloodcurdling—literally. It's something peculiarly different, and it's something which happens. It isn't talk; it happens. My eyes began to go dark with it, because I simply couldn't bear it. And then, before I went quite under, we were all standing up and going out—down that corridor. I don't know what would have happened if one of them had touched me then. We got into the hall, and there was a lot of shuffling and whispering, and then an ordinary voice or two, and then everyone had disappeared except the caretaker. I saw the front door and I went straight to it. I was just at it when he called me. I couldn't go back or turn round. I stood still—I don't know why; I suppose I was still in a nightmare. And outside I saw that filthy little hand pointing in behind me. He spoke over my shoulder in that damn husky voice of his, and he said——"

"Yes; all right," said Jonathan as Richard's voice went up a note or two. "Steady."

"Sorry!" said Richard, recovering. "He said: 'I won't keep you, Mr. Furnival. Come back presently. When you want me, I shall be ready. If you want your wife, I can bring her to you; if you don't want her, I can keep her away from you. Tell your friend I shall send for him soon. Good-bye.' So then I walked out."

He lifted his eyes and looked at Jonathan, who couldn't think of anything to say. Presently Richard went on, still more quietly: "And suppose he can?"

"Can what?" asked Jonathan gloomily.

"Can," said Richard carefully and explicitly, "do something to Lester. Leave off thinking of Betty for a moment; Betty's alive. Lester's dead, and suppose this man can do something to dead people? Don't forget I've seen one. I've seen that woman Mercer walk straight into his hall. I know she's dead; she looked dead. That's how I knew I saw her. No; not like a corpse. She was—fixed; as solid as you or me, but a deal more herself than either of us. If he made her come, can he make Lester come? If he can, I shall kill him."

Jonathan said, staring at the floor: "No, I wouldn't do that. If … if he *can* do anything of that kind, don't you see it mightn't make much difference if he *were* dead? I wouldn't kill him."

Richard got up. He said: "I see. No." He began to wander about the room. Presently he said: "I won't have him touch Lester." He added: "If I were to kill myself?"

Jonathan shook his head. "We don't know anything about it," he said. "You couldn't be sure of being with her. And anyhow it's a sin."

"Oh a sin!" said Richard peevishly, and was silent. His friend was on the point of saying: "Well, if souls exist, sins may," but he thought it would be tiresome, and desisted. Presently his eyes fell on the painting of those sub-human souls, and after staring at it he said abruptly: "Richard, I don't believe it. He may be able to hypnotize these creatures, but Lester wasn't much like them, was she? I don't believe he could control her unless she let him, and I shouldn't think she was much likely to let him. She wasn't, as I remember her, the kind of woman who likes being controlled, was she?"

Richard stopped. The faintest of smiles came to his lips. He said: "No. God help Father Simon if he tries to control Lester. Still"—and his face darkened again—"the plane was too much for her, and he might be."

They stood side by side and looked at the cloud of rising backs. Evelyn Mercer was one of them; would Lester be? was Betty meant to be? Their ladies called to them from separate prisons, demanding help and salvation. The corridor of iron rock opened—surely not for those sacred heads? surely those royal backs could never incline below the imbecile face. But what to do? Richard's habitual agnosticism had so entirely disappeared with the first sight of Evelyn that he had already forgotten it. Jonathan was beginning to think of seeking out a priest. But their tale was a wild thing, and he did not know what a priest could do. No priest could command Simon; nor exorcise Lester; nor enliven Betty. No; it was left to them.

He said: "Well, damn it, this isn't the only painting I've done. Let's look at the one Simon didn't like."

"I don't see what good that'll do," Richard said miserably, but he went round with his friend. He seemed to himself within himself to be standing alone among the insects, and he could not avoid the thought that perhaps now, somewhere, somehow, Lester was one of the insects—an irrational scuttling insect that would keep closer to him than any of the others would. That, if she were so, might still be left of their love, and that would be all. Their past would end in this, and this for ever. Only he knew she would not—unless Simon had utterly and wholly changed her very nature. She would, insect or woman or some dreadful insect-woman, keep away from him; and as he knew it, he knew he did not want her to. If she were that, he wanted her—in spite of the horror; if he could bear the horror!—to be by him still. Or perhaps he might come to some agreement with Father Simon—perhaps he instead of her—she would be very angry indeed if he did; he knew very well it would be a contest between them, if such a chance could be; pride clashing with pride, but also love with love. It would be unfair to do it without her knowledge, yet with her knowledge it could never be done. The thought flickered through his mind before he realized of what he was really thinking. When he did, he could hardly think of it; the terrible metapsychosis gnawed at him and would not be seen. He stared in front of him, and realized slowly that he was looking deeply into the light.

The massive radiance of that other painting flowed out towards him from the canvas; it had not surely, when he had seen it before, been as weighty as this? it had not so projected energy? He forgot Simon and the cluster of spiritual vermin; he forgot Lester, except that some changing detail of her hovered still in his mind—her hand, her forehead, her mouth, her eyes. The inscape of the painting became central. There, in the middle of this room, lay the City, ruined and renewed, submerged and gloriously re-emerging. It was not the sense of beauty but the sense of exploration that was greatest in him. He had but to take one step to be walking in that open space, with houses and streets around him. The very rubble in the foreground was organic and rising; not rising as the beetles were to some exterior compulsion but in proportion and to an interior plan. The whole subject—that is, the whole unity; shape and hue; rubble, houses, cathedral, sky, and hidden sun, all and the light that was all and held all—advanced on him. It moved forward as that other painting retired. The imbecile master and his companions were being swallowed up in distance, but this was swallowing up distance. There was distance in it, and yet it was all one. As a painting is.

He drew a deep breath. As he did so, a phrase from the previous day came back to him. He turned on Jonathan; he said, but his eyes were still on the canvas: "With plain observation and common understanding?"

"Yes," said Jonathan. "I'll swear it was. I don't wonder Simon didn't like it."

Richard could not bear the glow. It bore in upon him even more than it did on Jonathan—partly because it was not his painting, partly because he was already, despite himself, by his sight of Lester, some way initiated into that spiritual world. He walked to the window and stood looking out. The grey October weather held nothing of the painting's glory, yet his eyes were so bedazzled with the glory that for a moment, however unillumined the houses were, their very mass was a kind of illumination. They were illustrious with being. The sun in the painting had not risen, but it had been on the point of rising, and the expectation that unrisen sun had aroused in him was so great that the actual sun, or some other and greater sun, seemed to be about to burst through the cloud that filled the natural sky. The world he could see from the window gaily mocked him with a promise of being an image of the painting, or of being the original of which the painting was but a painting.

As he looked, he heard in the silence behind him a small tinkle. Something had fallen. Before his brain had properly registered the sound, he felt the floor beneath him quiver, and the tinkle was followed by a faint echo in different parts of the room. Things shook and touched and settled. The earth had felt the slightest tremor, and all its inhabitants felt it. It was for less than a moment, as if an infinitesimal alteration had taken place. Richard saw in the sky upon which his eyes were fixed a kind of eyelid-lifting, an opening and shutting of cloud. He caught no direct light, but the roofs and chimneys of the houses gleamed, whether from above or in themselves he could not tell. It passed and his heart lifted. He was suddenly certain of Lester— not for himself, but in herself; she lived newly in the light. She lived—that was all; and so, by God's mercy, he.

He thought the phrase, and though it was strange to him it was very familiar. But he did not, in that second, feel he had abandoned his agnosticism for what he knew to be Jonathan's belief. Rather his very agnosticism rose more sharply and healthily within him; he swung to a dance, and he actually did swing round, so that he saw Jonathan planted before his canvas and frowning at it, and on the floor a silver pencil which had rolled from the table. He walked across and picked it up, playing lightly with it, and as he began to speak Jonathan forestalled him. He said: "Richard, it *is* different."

"Different?" asked Richard. "How different?"

"I'm very good," Jonathan went on, but so simply that there was no egotism in the remark, "but I'm nothing like as good as this. I simply am not. I could never, never paint this."

Richard looked at the painting. But his amateur's eye could not observe with certainty the difference of which Jonathan seemed to be speaking. He thought he could have been easily persuaded that the shapes were more definite, that the mass of colour which had overwhelmed him before now organized itself more exactly, that the single unity was now also a multitudinous union—but he would not by himself have been certain. He said: "You're the master. How?"

Jonathan did not answer the question directly. He said, in a lower voice, almost as if he were shy of something in his own work: "I suppose, if things—if everything is like that, I suppose colours and paints might be. They must be what everything is, because everything is. Mightn't they become more themselves? mightn't they? It was what I wanted to do, because it was like that. And if the world is like that, then a painting of the world must be. But if it is…."

Richard went across to him. "If it is," he said, "we weren't done and can't be done. If it is, we aren't beetles and can't be beetles, however they grin at each other in their holes. By all possible plain observation and common understanding, we aren't. And as my own common understanding has told me on a number of occasions that Lester doesn't like being kept waiting, I'd better try not to keep her waiting."

"Is she waiting?" said Jonathan with a slow answering smile.

"I can't possibly tell you yet," said Richard. "But I shall try somehow to find out. Let's do something. Let's plainly observe. Let's go to Highgate and observe Betty. Let's persecute Lady Wallingford. Let's love Simon;

he likes love. Come on, man." He stepped back and waved his hand towards Highgate. "*Ecrasez l'infame.* Give them the point, gentlemen. And no heel-taps. Come. Have you ever seen Lester in a rage? 'Oh what a deal of scorn looks beautiful...' but I don't want it to get too beautiful."

He caught up his hat. Jonathan said: "I feel like a bit of my own painting. All right; come on. Let's get a taxi and go to Highgate and tell them where they stop. I don't quite know how."

"No," said Richard, "but the sky will or the earth or something. Simon control Lester? Simon couldn't control a real beetle. Nor could I, if it comes to that, but I don't pretend to. Come."

When they ran together out of the house, it was already something more than an hour since the Clerk had re-entered Betty's room. He knew that the crisis was on him; he had come to direct it. Up to now he had been content to send his daughter on her ghostly journeys as his messenger and in some sense his substitute. He had begotten her for this and for more than this; since she had grown out of early childhood he had trained her in this. Now the time of more had come, and the mystical rain which had defeated her should mock him no longer. The tale of the enchanters held a few masters—not many—who had done this. One of the earlier, another Simon, called the Magus, had slain a boy by magic and sent his soul into the spiritual places, there to be his servant. This Simon would make a stronger link, for he would send his child. But to establish that link properly, the physical body must be retained in its own proper shape, that in future all commands might be sent through it to its twin in the other air. The earlier Simon had kept the body of the boy in a casing of gold in his bedchamber, and (as it was said) angels and other powers of that air had visibly adored it, at the will of the magician laid upon them through the single living soul, and exposed all the future without the slow tricks that had otherwise to be used, and shown treasures and secrets of the past, until their lord became a pillar of the universe and about him the planetary heavens revolved. But in those days magicians had public honour; now for a little while a secret way was better. It was to be to-day no bloody sacrifice; only a compulsory dissolution of bonds between soul and body—a making for ever all but two of what must be at bottom for ever one; the last fact of known identity alone remaining. When that uncorrupting death was achieved, the body should be coffined for burial. After the burial it would be no less than natural that the distressed mother should go to her own house in the North to be quiet and recover; and no less than likely that she might take with her a not too great case—Betty was not large—of private effects. She could go, nowadays, by car. It would be easy, on the night before the funeral, to make from dust and air and impure water and a little pale fire a shape to be substituted for the true body. That should lay itself down in the coffin, clasping a corded brick or two to give it weight, for though magic could increase or decrease the weight of what already had weight, yet these magical bodies always lacked the mysterious burden of actual flesh. But it would serve for the short necessary time, and afterwards let earth go indeed to earth and dust to dust. The substitution made, and the true body laid in the chest, it could be conveyed away. It should lie in the lumber-room of the Northern cottage, and there serve him when he wished, until when he and his Types were united, and the world under him made one, he could house it becomingly to himself in his proper home.

The time had come. He could utterly pronounce the reversed Name—not that it was to him a Name, for his whole effort had been to deprive it of any real meaning, and he had necessarily succeeded in this for himself, so that it was to him no Name but vibrations only, which, directed as he chose, should fulfil what he chose. He had quite forgotten the original blasphemy of the reversal; the sin was lost, like so many common sins of common men, somewhere in his past. He did not now even think of there being any fact to which the Name was correspondent. He had, that very morning, aimed the vibrating and recessional power on the latest and the nearest of the dead—the wife of the man who had come foolishly inquiring. And though she had not come, yet her companion in death had come—one who was, it must have chanced, more responsive than she. He had his own intentions for her. But first a balance must be preserved; where one was drawn in one must go out. He had drawn back the other woman's soul to wait now outside the house; there she crouched till the act was finished. So prepared, he came into his daughter's room.

His mistress entered with him. In the eyes of the servants he was a foreign consulting doctor who had sometimes done Miss Betty good, and was a friend of the family. For the law, there was an ordinary practitioner who was well acquainted with her sad case and could do all that was necessary. Both of them would find now that for Betty they could do nothing. The pretence was to last just this hour; therefore his mistress came. Yet bringing the living woman it was unfortunate for him that he had not brought in with him the dead woman also whom he had left to her own ghostly place. So wise and mighty as he was, his wisdom had failed there. Had he done so, that poor subservient soul might have conveyed to him some hint of what else was in that room. He could see those he called; not, those he did not. He did not see the form that waited by the bed; he did not see Lester. He knew, of course, nothing of the exchange of redeeming love that had taken place between those two—no more than of that gallant Betty who had risen once from the lake of wise water. And if he had known anything, of what conceivable importance could the memories of two schoolgirls be to him? even though the memories of those girls should be the acts of souls? Because it would have been, and was, so unimportant, he did not see in the pale and exhausted girl in the bed any of the sudden runnels of roseal light which Lester now saw, as if the blood itself were changed and richly glowing through the weary flesh. Lester saw them—the blood hiding something within itself, which yet it did not quite succeed in hiding from any who, in whatever shy efforts of new life, had sought and been granted love. Lester might not have believed it, but then she did not have to try. She looked and saw; in that state what was, was certain. There was no need for belief.

The Clerk and she were very close. Lester did not recognize the identity of the shape she had seen on the stairs, and otherwise she did not know him. But as his great form came slowly into the room, she felt him to be of the same nature as that other shape. He now, and that he on the stairs, were inhabitants of this world in which she was. Their appearance, first in night and then in day, was overwhelming to her. The great cloak was a wrapping up of power in itself; the ascetic face a declaration of power. Those appearances, and that of the laughing Betty, belonged to the same world, but these were its guardians and masters. Lester felt unusually shy and awkward as she stood there; had he commanded then, she would have obeyed. She knew that she went unseen by men and women, but as his eyes passed over her she felt rather that she had been seen and neglected than that she had not been seen.

The giant, for so he seemed to her to be, paused by the bed. Lester waited on his will. So, behind him, did Lady Wallingford. Betty twitched a little, shifted restlessly, and finally turned on her back, so that she lay facing the gaze of her master and father. He said to her mother: "Lock the door." Lady Wallingford went back to the door, locked it, turned, and stood with her hand on the handle. The Clerk said to her again: "Draw the curtains." She obeyed; she returned. The room lay in comparative darkness, shut off and shut in. The Clerk said, in a gentle voice, almost as if he were waking a child: "Betty, Betty, it's time to go." But he was not trying to wake her.

Lester listened with attention. She believed that the giant was laying some proper duty on Betty, some business which she did not understand, but the inflexibility of the voice troubled her. The friendship which had sprung in the time of their talk made her wish to spare the present Betty this austere task. Besides she herself wished, as soon as was possible, to have a place in this world, to be directed, to have something to do. She made—she so rash, so real, so unseen—a sudden movement. She began: "Let me———" and stopped, for Betty's eyes had opened and in fear and distress were looking up at the Clerk, and her fingers were picking at the bedclothes, as the fingers of the dying do. Lester years before had seen her father die; she knew the sign. Betty said, in a voice only just heard through the immense stillness of the room: "No; no."

The Clerk thrust his head forward and downward. Its leanness, and the cloak round him, turned him for Lester to some great bird of the eagle kind, hovering, waiting, about to thrust. He said: "To go," and the words sprang from him as if a beak had stabbed, and the body of Betty seemed to yield under the blow. Only the fact that no blood gushed between her breasts convinced Lester that it was not so. But again and once again, as if the wounding beak drove home, the Clerk said: "To go ... to go." A faint sound came from the door; Lady Wallingford had drawn a sharp breath. Her eyes were bright; her hands were clenched; she was drawn upright as if she were treading something down; she said—the light word hung in the room like an echo: "Go."

Lester saw, though she was not directly looking. Her manner of awareness was altering. Touch was forbidden her; hers and Betty's hands had never met. Taste and smell she had no opportunity to exercise. But sight and hearing were enlarged. She could somehow see at once all that she had formerly been able to see only by turning her head; she could distinctly hear at once all sorts of sounds of which formerly one would deaden another. She was hardly aware of the change; it was so natural. She was less aware of herself except as a part of the world, and more aware of her friend. There was as yet no distrust of the grand shape opposite her, but the tiny vibration of that single syllable span within her. She saw Betty receding and she saw Betty struggling. She spoke with passion; and her voice, inaudible to those others, in the room, was audible enough to any of the myriad freemen of the City, to the alien but allied powers of heaven which traverse the City, to the past, present, and future of the City, to its eternity, and to That which everywhere holds and transfixes its eternity; audible to all these, clear among the innumerable mightier sounds of the creation, she exclaimed: "Betty!"

Her friend's eyes turned to her. They entreated silently, as years before they had entreated; they were dimming, but what consciousness they had still looked out—a girl's longing, a child's call, a baby's cry. A voice lower than Lady Wallingford's, so low that even the Clerk could not hear it, though he knew she had spoken, but perfectly audible to Lester and to any of that other company whose business it might be to hear, said: "Lester!" It was the same timid proffer of and appeal to friendship which Lester had once ignored. She answered at once: "All right, my dear. I'm here."

Betty's head lay towards her. The Clerk put out his hand to turn it again, so that his eyes might look into his daughter's eyes. Before it could touch her, the spiritual colloquy had gone on. Betty said: "I don't at all mind going, but I don't want him to send me." The voice was ever so slightly stronger; it had even a ripple of laughter in it, as if it were a little absurd to be so particular about a mere means. Lester said: "No, darling: why should he? Stay with me a little longer." Betty answered: "May I? Dear Lester!" and shut her eyes. The Clerk turned her head.

Lester had spoken on her spirit's instincts. But she did not at all know what she ought to do. She realized more than ever that she was parted from living men and women by a difference of existence, and realizing it she knew that the grand figure by the bed was not of her world but of that, and being of that, and being so feared, might be hostile, and might even be evil. She did not any longer squander power by trying to speak to him. She was not exactly content to wait, but she knew she must wait. She became conscious all at once of the delight of waiting—of the wide streets of London in which one could wait, of Westminster Bridge, of herself waiting for Richard on Westminster Bridge, as she had done—when? The day she was killed; the day before she was killed. Yes; on that previous day they had agreed to meet there, and he had been late, and she had been impatient; no wonder that, after death, she had been caught again to the scene of her impatience and played out again the sorry drama. Oh now she would wait, and he would come. She seemed, bodiless though in truth she was and knew it more and more, to feel her body tingling with expectation of him, with expected delight. She had once walked (he would have told her) in a kind of militant glory; she stood so now, unknowing. Her militancy was not now to be wasted on absurdities; as indeed it never need have been; there had been enough in herself to use it on. Her eyes, or what were once her eyes, were brighter than Lady Wallingford's; her head was up; her strong and flexible hands moved at her sides; her foot tapped once and ceased. The seeming body which the energy of her spirit flung out in that air was more royal and real than the entire body of Lady Wallingford. She gave her attention to the Clerk.

He was speaking, slowly, in a language she did not understand, and sternly, almost as if he were giving final instructions to a careless or lazy servant. He had laid his left hand on Betty's forehead, and Lester saw a kind of small pale light ooze out everywhere between his hand and Betty and flow over the forehead. Betty's eyes were open again, and they looked up, but now without sight, for Lester's own quickened sight saw that a film had been drawn over them. Betty was again receding. Lester said: "Betty, if you want me I'm here," and meant it with all her heart. The Clerk ceased to give instructions, paused, drew himself up, and began to intone.

All three women heard him, yet there was not a sound in the room. His lips moved, but they did not make the sound. The intonation was within him, and the intonation moved his lips; his mouth obeyed the formula. Presently, however, something syllabic did emerge. Lady Wallingford abruptly turned her back and leant her forehead against the door. The light on Betty's forehead expanded upward; in the dimness of the room it rose like a small pillar. Lester saw it. She was now incapable of any action except an unformulated putting of herself at Betty's disposal; she existed in that single act. It was then she became aware that the Clerk was speaking to her.

He did not think so. His intention and utterance were still limited to the woman on the bed. He was looking there and speaking there. He saw the almost dead face and the filmed eyes. But Lester saw a change. The eyes closed; the face relaxed. Betty slept, and slept almost happily. Lester felt the strange intoning call not to Betty but to her; it was she that was meant. Just as she realized it, she lost it. Her heart was so suddenly and violently racked that she thought she cried out. The intensity of the pain passed, but she was almost in a swoon from it, and all the sense of her physical body was in that swoon restored to her. She was not yet capable of the complex states of pain or delight which belong to the unbodied state, and indeed (though she must pass through those others) yet the final state was more like this world's in the renewal of the full identity of body and soul. She was unconscious for that time of the Clerk, of Betty, of the room, but she heard dimly sounds gathering at her feet; the intoning rose up her from below and touched her breasts and fell away. As she recovered, she looked down. She saw the bluish-green tinge of the death-light crawling round her ankles. She knew at once that that was what it was. She had not at all died till now; no, not when she tried to answer the voice from the hill and failed. Even that was but a preliminary to death, but this was dissolution. Better the vague unliving City than this, but she had come out of that City, and this was what lay outside; this lapping pool which, as it rose into her, mingled itself with her, so that she saw her limbs changing with it. She thought, in a paroxysm of longing, of the empty streets, and she made an effort to keep that longing present to her. She fought against dissolution.

But the backward-intoned Tetragrammaton continued to rise. It flowed up not equally, but in waves or sudden tongues. It reached up to her knees. The appearance of her clothes which had so long accompanied her had disappeared; looking down, she saw in that swimming bluish-green nothing but herself. She could see nothing but that, and she heard on all sides the intoning flow in on her.

Of one other thing she was conscious. She had been standing, and now she was no longer standing. She was leaning back on something, some frame which from her buttocks to her head supported her; indeed she could have believed, but she was not sure, that her arms, flung out on each side held on to a part of the frame, as along a beam of wood. In her fighting and sinking consciousness, she seemed to be almost lying along it, as she might be on a bed, only it was slanting. Between standing and lying, she held and was held. If it gave, as at any moment it might give, she would fall into the small steady chant which, heard in her ears and seen along her thighs, was undoing her. Then she would be undone. She pressed herself against that sole support. So those greater than she had come—saints, martyrs, confessors—but they joyously, knowing that this was the first movement of their re-edification in the City, and that thus in that earliest world fashioned of their earthly fantasies began the raising of the true houses and streets. Neither her mind nor her morals had prepared her for this discovery, nor did she in the least guess what was happening. But what of integrity she possessed clung to that other integrity; her back pressed to it. It sustained her. The pale dissolving nothingness was moving more slowly, but it was still moving. It had not quite reached her thighs. Below them she felt nothing; above she rested on that invisible frame. She could not guess whether that frame could resist the nothingness, or whether she on it. If it did not, she would be absorbed, living, into all that was not. She shut her eyes; say rather, she ceased to see.

At the moment when the anti-Tetragrammaton was approaching that in her which her fastidious pride had kept secluded from all but Richard, Betty suddenly turned on her bed. She did so with a quick heaving movement, and she spoke in her sleep. The Clerk had sunk on one knee, to bring his face and slow-moving lips nearer to hers. She had seemed to him already yielding to the spell, and at the unexpected energy of her turning, he started and threw back his head. He had been prepared, he thought, for any alteration in Betty, though he expected one particular alteration, but he was quite unprepared for this ordinary human outbreak of life. He threw back his head, as any close watcher might. But then, in his own mind, he was not supposed to be simply anyone. He missed, in the suddenness, the word which broke from the sleeping girl, as anyone might. But then he was certainly not simply anyone. The intoned vibrations, for less than a second, faltered; for a flicker of time the eyes of the master of magic were confused. He recovered at once, in poise and in speech and in sight. But what he saw there almost startled him again.

His books and divinations had told him, and the lesser necromantic spells he had before now practised on the dead had half-shown him, what he might expect to see. As he approached, after the graded repetitions, the greatest and most effective repetition—and the very centre of that complex single sound—he expected, visibly before him, the double shape; the all but dead body, the all but free soul. They would be lying in the same space, yet clearly distinct, and with the final repetitions of the reversed Name they would become still more distinct, but both at his disposal and subject to his will. He would divide without disuniting, one to go and one to stay, the spiritual link between them only just not broken, but therefore permanent. In his other necromancies on dead bodies he could only do it spasmodically, and only on those lately dead, and only for a little. But this was to be different. He had expected a double vision, and he had a double vision. He saw two shapes, Betty and another. But he had never seen the other before.

Had it been one of those odd creatures, such as that which he had almost seen in the hall, he would not have been taken by surprise, nor had it been any stranger inhabitant of the bodiless world. He knew that surprise does not become the magician, and is indeed apt to be fatal, for in that momentary loss of guard any attack upon the adept may succeed. His courage was very high; he would not have been startled at any tracery of low or high, at cherub or cacodemon. Or so he believed, and probably with truth. But he did not see cherub or cacodemon. He saw two sleeping girls—now one, and now the other, and each glancing through the other; and they were totally unlike. Not only so, but as he sought to distinguish them, to hold that bewildering conjunction steady to the analysis and disposal of his will, he saw also that it was the strange sleeper who lay wanly still with closed eyes, and Betty who slept more healthily than ever he had seen her sleep—fresh, peaceful, almost smiling. She had spoken, but he had not heard what she said. Only now, as he renewed, with all his will, the pronunciation of the reversed Name, he heard, in the very centre of the syllables, another single note.

Betty had indeed spoken a word, as a sleeper does, murmuring it. She had said, in a sleepy repetition of her last waking and loving thought: "Lester!" As the word left her lips, it was changed. It became—hardly the Name, but at least a tender mortal approximation to the Name. And when it had left her lips, it hung in the air, singing itself, prolonging and repeating itself. It was no louder than Betty's voice, and it had still some likeness to hers, as if it did not wish to lose too quickly the sense of the mortal voice by which it had come, and it retained still within it some likeness to the word "Lester!", as if it would not too quickly abandon the mortal meaning by which it had come. But presently it let both likenesses pass, and became itself only, and at that rather a single note than sequent syllables, which joyously struck itself out again and again, precisely in the exact middle of every magical repetition, perfect and full and soft and low, as if (almost provocatively) it held just an equal balance, and made that exact balance a spectacular delight for any whose celestial concerns permitted them to behold the easy dancing grapple. The air around it quivered, and the room and all within it were lightly shaken; and beyond the room and the house, in all directions, through all the world, the light vibration passed. It touched, at a distance, London itself, and in Jonathan's flat Richard saw the eye-flicker of light in the roofs and heard the tinkle of his friend's pencil as it fell.

Lester, lying with closed eyes, felt the change. She felt herself resting more quietly and more securely on her support; it might be said she trusted it more. Close beside her, she heard a quiet breathing, as if on some other bed near at hand a companion gently slumbered, friendly even in sleep. She did not see the tongue-thrusting Death lie still, or even here and there recoil, but she stretched out her legs, and felt them also to be resting on some support, and yawned as if she had just got into bed. She thought, in a drowsy happiness: "Well, that's saved her getting up," but she remembered no action of her own, only how once or twice, when she had been thirsty in the night, Richard had brought her a glass of water and saved her getting up; and in her drowsiness a kind of vista of innumerable someones doing such things for innumerable someones stretched before her, but it was not as if they were being kind, for it was not water that they were bringing but their own joy, or perhaps it was water and joy at once; and everything was altered, for no-one had to be unselfish any more, so free they all were now from the receding death-light of earth. She thought, all the same, "Darling, darling Richard!"—because the fact that he was bringing her his own joy to drink before she sank again to the sleep that was her present joy (but then waking had been that too) was a deed of such excelling merit on his part that all the choirs of heaven and birds of earth could never properly sing its praise; though there was a word in her mind which would do it rightly, could her sleepiness remember it—a not very long word, and very easy to say if someone would only tell her how. It was rather like a glass of water itself, for when all was said she did in her heart prefer water to wine, though it was blessed sometimes to drink wine with Richard especially one kind of wine whose name she could never remember, but Richard could; Richard knew everything better than she, except the things about which he knew nothing at all, for the word which was both water and wine—and yet not in the least mixed—had cleared her mind, and she could be gay with Richard now among all those things that either knew and the other not; and both of them could drink that word in a great peace. Now she came to think of it, the word was like a name, and the name was something like *Richard*, and something like *Betty* and even not unlike her own, though that was certainly very astonishing, and she knew she did not deserve it; still there it was—and anyhow it was not in the least like any of them, though it had in it also the name of the child Richard and she would one day have for they never meant to wait too long, and it would be born in a bed like this, on which she could now from head to foot luxuriously stretch herself; nor could she think why she had once supposed it to be hard and like wood, for it was marvellously spring-livened; spring of the world, spring of the heart; joy of spring-water, joy.

Oblivion took her. The task was done, and repose is in the rhythm of that world, and some kind of knowledge of sleep, since as a baby the Divine Hero closed his astonishing eyes, and his mother by him, and the princely Joseph, their young protector. Lester had taken the shock of the curse—no less willingly or truly that she had not known what she was doing. She had suffered instead of Betty, as Betty had once suffered through her; but the endurance had been short and the restoration soon, so quickly had the Name which is the City sprung to the rescue of its own. When recollection came to her again, she was standing by the side of the bed, but all the pale light had faded, and on the bed Betty lay asleep, flushed with her proper beauty and breathing in her proper content.

On the other side the Clerk still knelt. As soon as he heard that interrupting note, he had put out still more energy; he thought he had used it already, but for him there was always more, until his end should come indeed. He managed to complete the repetition into which the note broke, but the effort was very great. The sweat was on his forehead as he continued with the spell. He could just utter his own word as he willed, but he could not banish from it the other song. He put out his hand towards his mistress and beckoned, that she might lay her will with his. It was his folly. There is no rule more wise in magic than that which bids the adept, if the operation go awry, break it off at once. In the circles of hell there is no room for any error; the only maxim is to break off and begin again. When the Clerk saw before him the two shapes, he should have made an end. There had been an intrusion of an alien kind. He would not; say rather, he could not; he could not consent to leave it undominated. He was compelled therefore to summon his minion. The false slippery descent was opening, the descent so many of his sort have followed, according to which the lordly enchanters drop to lesser and lesser helps—from themselves to their disciples, to servants, to hired help, to potions and knives, to wax images and muttered murderous spells. Simon was not yet there, but he was going, and quickly.

Sara Wallingford was still leaning with her forehead against the door, and pressing it more closely. She knew, as far as she could, what the operation meant. But as the intoning had proceeded, her merely mortal hate got the better of her knowledge; she murmured: "Kill! kill!" She did not care what became of Betty, so long as Betty was dead. When, dimly, she heard the ringing opposition of the Name, she felt only a fear that Betty might live. And while with all her force she rejected that fear lest it should weaken the effort, she felt her master beckon. If indeed they had been, with whatever subordination, allies, there would have been between them an image of a truth, however debased, which might have helped. There was not. They had never exchanged that joyous smile of equality which marks all happy human or celestial government, the lack of which had frightened Richard in Simon's own smile; that which has existed because first the Omnipotence withdrew its omnipotence, and decreed that submission should be by living will, or perhaps because in the Omnipotence itself there is an equality which subordinates itself. The hierarchy of the abyss does not know anything of equality, nor of any lovely balance within itself, nor (if he indeed be) does the lord of that hierarchy ever look up, subordinate to his subordinates, and see above him and transcending him the glory of his household. So that never in all the myths, of Satan or Samael or Iblis or Ahriman, has there been any serious tale of that lord becoming flesh by human derivation; how could he be so supposed to submit, in bed or cradle? Simon himself, in the mystery of generation, had reserved something; he, like all his fellows, intended to dominate what he begot; therefore he and they always denied their purposes at the moment of achievement. "How shall Satan's kingdom stand, if it be divided against itself?" Messias asked, and the gloomy pedants to whom he spoke could not give the answer his shining eyes awaited: "Sir, it does not."

The man beckoned; the woman stood upright. She had no choice; she was his instrument only; she must go and be used. But (more than she guessed) she was also the instrument of her own past. As she took a step away, there came a tap on the door. It was very gentle, but to those two it was shattering in the silence—a blasting summons from the ordinary world. All three of them heard it. Lester heard it; to her it sounded precisely what it was, clear and distinct. To say she might have been alive again is too little; it was more happily itself, more sweetly promising, than if she had been alive. It was a pure and perfect enjoyment. She knew she could, if she chose, exert herself now to see who waited on the other side of the door, but she did not choose. It was not worth while; let the exquisite disclosure come in its own way. The Clerk's face convulsed; he made a gesture of prohibition. He was too late. Lady Wallingford's past was in her and ruled her; all the times when she had thought about the servants now compelled her. She was the servant of her servants. The glorious maxim (sealed for ever in the title of the Roman pontiff—*servus servorum Dei*) ruled her ingloriously. She was, for that second, oblivious of the Clerk. She put out her hand and switched on the light—there was no time to draw back the curtains; she unlocked and opened the door. She faced the parlour-maid.

The maid said: "If you please, my lady, there are two gentlemen downstairs who say they must see you. The gentleman who spoke said he didn't think you'd know his name but the other is Mr. Drayton. They say it's very urgent and to do with Miss Betty." She was young, pleasant, and inexperienced; her mildly surprised eyes surveyed the room, and rested on Betty. She broke out: "Oh she *is* looking better, isn't she, my lady?"

The news of Jonathan's arrival might, in her state of passion, have enraged Lady Wallingford; the impertinence of a servant outraged her past. It pulled her past and her together; unfortunately it pulled her together in the opposite direction from what was then going on. All the rebukes she had ever delivered rose in her; she did not see them, as Lester had seen her own actions, but her voice shook with them. She said: "You forget yourself, Nina." She went on: "Tell Mr. Drayton's friend I can't see them. Send them away and see I'm not interrupted again."

The maid shrank. Lady Wallingford stared angrily at her. As she did so, a curious sensation passed through her. She felt rooted and all but fixed, clamped in some invisible machine. A board was pressed against her spine; wooden arms shut down on her arms; her feet were iron-fixed. She could do nothing but stare. She heard her last dictatorial word: "see I'm not interrupted again". Was she not to be? The maid took a step back, saying hastily: "Yes, my lady." Lady Wallingford, immovable to herself, stared after her. She could not pursue.

She was not, however, then left to that doom. As the maid turned, she exclaimed: "Oh!" and stepped back, almost into her mistress. There was a sudden swiftness of feet; two forms loomed in the corridor. The maid slipped to the other side of the doorway and as Lady Wallingford broke—or was allowed to break—from the wooden beams which had appeared to close on her, Richard and Jonathan had passed her and come into the room.

54

Richard was speaking as he came. He said: "You must forgive this intrusion, Lady Wallingford. We know—Jonathan and I—that we're behaving very badly. But it's absolutely—I do mean *absolutely*—necessary for us to see Betty. If you believe in the Absolute. So we had to come." He added, across the room to Lester, without surprise, but with a rush of apology, and only he knew to whom he spoke: "Darling, have I kept you waiting? I'm so sorry."

Lester saw him. She felt, as he came, all her old self lifting in her; bodiless, she seemed to recall her body in the joy they exchanged. He saw her smile, and in the smile heaven was frank and she was shy. She said—and he only heard, and he rather knew than heard, but some sound of speech rang in the room, and the Clerk, now on his feet, looked round and up, wildly, as if to catch sight of the sound: she said: "I'll wait for you a million years." She felt a stir within her, as if life quickened; and she remembered with new joy that the deathly tide had never reached, even in appearance, to the physical house of life. If Richard or she went now, it would not much matter; their fulfilment was irrevocably promised them, in what manner soever they knew or were to know it.

Betty opened her eyes. She too saw Lester. She said: "Lester, you did stop! How sweet of you!" She looked round the room. Her eyes widened a little as she saw Richard; they passed unconcernedly over the Clerk and Lady Wallingford; they saw Jonathan. She cried out and sat up; she threw out her hands. He came to her and took them. He said, controlling the words: "You're looking better." He could not say more. Betty did not speak; she blushed a little and clung.

The Clerk looked down on her. The operation had failed; he did not doubt that he would yet succeed, but he must begin again. He did not permit himself any emotion towards whatever had interfered. It would waste his energy. These men were nothing. It had been in the other world that frustration had lain, and it should be seen to. Composing heart and features, he turned his head slowly towards Lady Wallingford. She took his will, and obeyed. She said: "We had better go downstairs. You can see, Mr. Drayton, that Betty is better: aren't you, Betty?"

"Much better," said Betty gaily. "Jonathan dear…" she paused; she went on: "I'll get up and dress. Go away for a few minutes, and I'll be down."

Jonathan said: "I'd much rather not leave you."

"Nonsense," said Betty. "I'm completely all right. Look, I'll be very quick. Mother, do you mind?"

It was the one thing that Lady Wallingford now minded more than anything else. But even hell cannot prevent that law of the loss of the one thing. She was full of rage—much of her own; something of the Clerk's which he had dismissed for her to bear. She was the vessel of such human passion as remained to him. She said: "If you will come down——?" The Clerk made a gesture with his hand as if to direct the two young men to pass in front of him, and his sudden constriction passed across his face. He looked particularly at Richard. But Richard was no longer the Richard of the house behind Holborn. He had tasted the new life in Jonathan's flat; he had drunk of it in his wife's eyes. As, while Jonathan spoke to Betty, he gazed at her, she began to withdraw, or rather it was not so much that she withdrew as that something—perhaps only the air of earth—came between them. But in that second of her immortal greeting, her passion and her promise, he had been freed from any merely accidental domination by the Clerk. She vanished; and, still at ease, he turned to meet Simon's look, and grinned back at him. He said: "You see, my dear Father, we had to make our own arrangements. But it was very kind of you to offer. No, no; after you. Lady Wallingford's waiting."

The unfortunate young maid had not known whether to go or stay. She had thought that Lady Wallingford might want the gentlemen shown out. She gathered, from the look Lady Wallingford gave her as she came though the door, that she had been wrong. The strange doctor followed; after him the two other visitors. Mr. Drayton paused to look back at Miss Betty; then he softly closed the door. The maid, even in her gloom, remembered that she had always said there was something between him and Miss Betty.

Chapter Eight

THE MAGICAL CREATION

All this while, Evelyn Mercer sat on the doorstep. It would once have seemed strange to her to think of herself sitting and hugging herself, as any old beggar-woman might, and she not old, though too much a beggar. She was acutely conscious of her beggary, ever since she had seen the man sitting in the chair. He had smiled and nodded at her, and she had expected and hoped he would speak. If he had only asked her a question, she could have told him everything—about her tiresome mother, and silly Betty, and cruel Lester. She did not expect him to talk, and all she wanted was for him to listen to her. She did not ask anything more; she was not the kind of girl that would. Lester was more like that, and even Betty.

In looking at him, she had become aware of her pain, which she had not been till then. It was not much more than a discomfort, a sense of pressure on her lungs. If she could talk, she would be able to appease it. He had sat nodding at her, as if he were telling her how right she was to come, and then he had stood up, and his nod as he did so had suddenly seemed to change. Instead of being a nod of welcome, it was now a nod of dismissal. She was to go; as she realized it, she yelped. She had not been able to help it. She had yelped rather like a lost cat, for she was frightened of being sent away, and the discomfort in her lungs had become immediately worse. But his head had still nodded dismissal. He was still smiling, and the smile had a kind of promise. Her own smile, which was the smile with which she had run after Betty, had become oddly fixed; she felt her face harden. As, still looking over his shoulder, in that mingling of promise and dismissal, he began to move away towards the door of the hall, she found that she herself was no longer in the hall but in the yard without. She had receded as he receded. She was up against the window, staring through it, but outside it, and sniffing at something in the air. It vaguely reminded her of fish, but it was not fish. She remained sniffing for some time, hoping that the man would come back. The smell had something to do with him, and he with the pain in her lungs. Presently she slipped away from the window-sill which she had been clutching; for the smell caused her to follow it. It was the kind of smell Betty had when Betty had to listen to her, though she had never understood that before. She began to run, out of the yard and along the street. Her head was stretched out; her eyes were bright, though they saw nothing except the pavement before them. She ran a long while, or not so long. When at last she stopped, it was outside a door—the door of the house from which she had hurried. Now she had hurried back.

As the semi-bestiality of her movement ceased, her muddled and obsessed brain managed to point that out to her. It even managed to suggest that to run for ever between those two points would be unsatisfactory. She had now made almost the same passage three times; and perhaps while she was in the streets that was all she could do. But how could she get out of the streets? She was not let go in there, and she did not dare go in here. She went right up to the door—the smell was strongest there; it was fish, surely—and stood by it listening. Betty was inside; for all she knew, *he* also might be inside. She even put her hand on the door. It sank through; she began to pull it back, and found it caught as if in a tangle of thorn. She felt a long sharp scratch before she got it loose. Tears came into her eyes. She was lonely and hurt. She looked at her hand through her tears, but it was a long time before she could see the scratch, almost as if neither scratch nor hand was there until she had found them. The hand itself was dim, because she had been crying; and dirty, because she had been leaning against the sill; and bleeding—at least, if she looked long enough it was bleeding. If the door was such a tangle of thorns, it was no use trying to go in. She went out of the porch and down the few steps. Her lungs were hurting her. She said aloud: "It isn't fair."

Lester had said the same thing, but as a rational judgment. This was not so much a rational judgment as a squeal. The squeal eased her lungs, and as she recognized this, she spoke again, saying: "Why won't anyone help me?" and found that her ease increased. She added: "I do think they might," and then the pain was no more than a slight discomfort. It seemed to her that the London air never had suited her, but she had never been able to agree with her mother where else they should live, so that somehow or other, because her mother had been inconsiderate, they had had to go on living in London. She was, at bottom, a little afraid that her mother too was in that dark house. Her mother didn't like fish; not that what she was waiting for was fish. It was the tall man who nodded his head.

She sat down on the bottom step, sideways, with her eyes on the door and her legs drawn up. She forgot about the scratch, except occasionally and resentfully because the door was a tangle of thorns. Whenever her lungs began to hurt her, she talked to herself aloud. Soon, though she did not realize it, she was keeping up a small continuous monologue. She did not talk of herself, but of others. The monologue was not (primarily) self-centred but mean. Men and women—all whom she had known—dwindled in it as she chattered. No-one was courteous; no-one was chaste; no-one was tender. The morning—for it was morning with her too—grew darker and the street more sordid as she went on.

In the middle of some sentence of attribution of foulness she stopped abruptly. The door had opened; there he was. He looked at her and she scrambled to her feet. He had come away from the conflict within the house, for purposes of his own. He had said to Lady Wallingford: "Keep her here." But he would not wait, for he knew that he had now a spy in the spiritual places, who could, when he could talk to her, tell him of Betty and what had interfered with the great operation. He had left her where she was, holding her by that sympathy between them, by her instinctive obedience to the reversed Name, which had made itself known to her in the curious smell. She had lingered in it, as he knew she would. Now, as she rose, he lifted a finger. He was still in his own world, and she in hers, but they were already visible to each other. He went so quickly that men did not see him, but behind him she was more truly invisible, as the actual streets of London were to her.

He came to the house behind Holborn, and he passed down the corridor into the secret hall. He went to his chair and sat down. Evelyn did not quite like to follow him there; she waited just inside the door. Her lungs were beginning to hurt her again, but she did not dare to speak without his permission. But she hoped he would soon be kind and not as cruel as Lester. The fish-smell was strong, and the hall dim. It might have been in the depth of waters; waters of which the pressure lay on her lungs, and the distance was dark round her. As she stood there, she felt both light and lightheaded, except for that increased pressure. She was floating there, and beyond her he sat like the master of all water-monsters, gazing away through the waters, and she must float and wait.

At the moment when the pain was becoming really troublesome, he turned his head. His eyes drew her; she ran forward and when she came to his seat, she sank on its steps as on the steps of the house. She had either to float or crouch; she could not easily stand. This did not astonish her; once she had been able to do something which now she could not do. The Clerk let her sit there; his eyes reverted to the distance. He said: "What do you know of that house?"

She began at once to chatter. After two sentences she found herself opening and shutting her mouth, but her voice had ceased. The pain was now really bad. She *must* speak, but she could only tell him what he wished to know. The tears again came into her eyes and ran down her face. That did not help. She choked and said—and immediately felt relief—"Betty was there, and Lester had gone to her."

The name of the obstacle, of that first interference, of the other girl on the bed, was Lester. The Clerk frowned; he had thought Betty was, through all the worlds, secluded from any companionship. He knew that there must always be some chance that a strange life, in those depths, should loom up, but he had supposed he had certainly cut his daughter off from any human friendship, and this sounded human. He had now to deal with it. He said: "Who is—Lester?"

Evelyn answered: "She was at school with Betty and me, and whatever she pretends now she didn't have any use for Betty then. She never liked her. She was killed—when I was." The last three words had to be spoken, but she shook all over as she spoke. When the Clerk said: "Was she a friend of yours?" she answered: "Yes, she was, though she was always hateful and superior. We used to go about together. She ought to be with me now."

The Clerk considered. He knew of the fierce hunger for flesh, for their physical habitations, which sometimes assails the newly dead, even the greatest. He knew how that other sorcerer of his race, the son of Joseph, had by sheer power once for awhile re-animated his body and held it again for some forty days, until at last on a mountainside it had dissolved into a bright cloud. What Jesus Bar-Joseph had not been able to resist, what he himself (if and when it was necessary) was prepared to do, he did not think it likely that this other creature, this Lester, would be able to resist. Especially if this other woman by him, her friend, drew her. He stretched out his hand over Evelyn's head, and she felt its weight where she crouched, though it was above her and did not touch her. He said: "What do you most want now?"

Evelyn answered: "To get back—or else to have someone to talk to. No-one will listen to me."

The constriction which was his smile showed on the Clerk's face, in sudden contempt for this wretched being, and for all those like her—how many millions!—who were willing to waste their powers so: talk of friends, talk of art, talk of religion, talk of love; all formulae and all facts dissolved in talk. No wonder they were hypnotically swayed by his deliberate talk. They swam and floated in vain talk, or sometimes they crouched in cruel talk. They fled and escaped from actuality. Unknowing, they spoke as he did, knowing; therefore they were his servants—until they dissolved and were lost. That might happen to this one. Let it, but before then perhaps she could be his auxiliary and draw that other shape from his daughter's bed.

It did not occur to him that he too was moving in the same direction. Sara Wallingford, Betty, Evelyn. Evelyn was a feebler instrument than Betty; even had there been no translucent Betty—and indeed for him there was none. But the helpless obedience of Betty was more exactly directed, more even of an accurate machine than this phantom in the worlds. There was indeed, even for her, a chance, could she have taken it. It lay precisely in her consenting not to talk, whether she succeeded or no. The time might be coming when she would have thrown that chance away, but for now she had it. She was looking up stealthily under his hand, that lay over her like a shadow on water; he was still gazing right away. But he said: "That might be done. I could give you a body—and as for talking, who would you most like to talk to?"

57

She knew that at once. In a voice stronger than she had hitherto been able to use in that world, she exclaimed: "Betty!"

He understood that. It seemed to him a poor and feeble wish, to be content to possess one other soul—to him who thought that numbers made a difference and even that quantity altered the very quality of an act, but he understood it. "The last infirmity of noble mind" can in fact make the mind so infirm that it becomes ignoble, as the divine Milton very well knew, or he would not have called it infirmity, nor caused Messias to reject it with such a high air; for paradise is regained not only by the refusal of sin but by the healing of infirmity. He looked down on her; she was touching her lips with her tongue. He said: "I could give you Betty."

She only looked up. He went on: "But first you must find her and this Lester. Then I will give her to you."

She said: "Always? Can I have her always?"

"Always," he said. As he spoke a hint of what he said was visible to them, a momentary sense of the infinite he named. The hall for each of them changed. It opened out for him; it closed in for her. He saw opening beyond it the leagues of the temporal world; he saw one of his Types exhorting crowds in a city of the Urals and another sitting in a chamber of Pekin and softly murmuring spells to learned men of China, and beyond them vague adoring shadows, the skies coalescing into shapes, and bowing themselves towards him. But for her the hall became a quite small room, which still seemed to grow smaller, where she and Betty sat, she talking and Betty trembling. Infinity of far and near lived together, for he had uttered one of the names of the City, and at once (in the way they wished) the City was there.

He dropped his hand nearer, and with a mortal it would have touched, but an infinity of division was between them (as between Betty and Lester), and it did not touch. He said: "You must get Lester away from her and bring her here. Then you shall have Betty. Go and look for them; look for them and tell me. Look and tell me; then you shall talk to Betty. Look and tell me. Go and find her; look and tell me...."

She was willing to yield to his command; she did yield. But she had not yet been dead long enough to know and use the capacities of spirit; she could not instantaneously pass through space, or be here and there at once. But that was what he wished, and his power was on her. She was to be at once with Betty and with him, to see and to speak. She was still aware of herself as having the semblance of a body, though it was dimmer now, and she still, as with the pain in her lungs or the words she heard or uttered, understood her spiritual knowledge in the sensations of the body. She was compelled now to understand, in that method, the coincidence of two places. She felt, by intolerable compulsion, her body and her head slowly twisted round. She opened her mouth to scream and a wind rushed into it and choked her. The pain in her lungs was terrible. In her agony she floated right up from the place where she sat; still sitting, she rose in the air. This apparent floating was the nearest she could get to the immaterial existence of spirit. She thought she heard herself scream, and yet she knew she did not; her torment was not to be so relieved. Presently she sank slowly down again on the steps of the pseudo-throne, but now rigid—contorted, and sealed in her contortion, staring. The Clerk had again lifted his eyes from her; inattentive to her pain, he waited only for tidings of that obstacle on whose removal he was set.

It was at this moment that Lester saw her. She had known that she had been withdrawn from Richard. The moment that had been given them was at once longer and more intense than the previous moments had been, and she was more content to let it go. Dimly there moved in her, since her reconciliation with Betty, a sense that love was a union of having and not-having, or else something different and beyond both. It was a kind of way of knowledge, and that knowledge perfect in its satisfaction. She was beginning to live differently. She saw Richard look where she had been, and saw him also content. The men went out of the room with Lady Wallingford. The room, but for the dead girl and the living girl, was empty. They spoke to each other freely now across the division. Betty said: "Darling, what happened?"

"Nothing," Lester answered. "At least, very little. I think he tried to push you somewhere, and then ... well, then he tried to push me."

"You're not hurt?" Betty asked, and Lester, with a rush of laughter, answered only: "*Here?*"

Betty did no more than smile; her gratitude possessed her. She stood and looked at her friend, and the charity between them doubled and redoubled, so that they became almost unbearable to each other, so shy and humble was each and each so mighty and glorious. Betty said: "I wouldn't have lost a moment, not a moment, of all that horrid time if it meant this."

Lester shook her head. She said, almost sadly: "But mightn't you have had this without the other? I wish you'd been happy then." She added: "I don't see why you couldn't have been. Need I have been so stupid? I don't mean only with you."

Betty said: "Perhaps we could go there some time and see." But Lester was not immediately listening; she was labouring with the unaccustomed difficulties of thought, especially of this kind of thought. Her face was youthfully sombre, so that it seemed to put on a kind of early majesty, as she went on: "Must we always wait centuries, and always know we waited, and needn't have waited, and that it all took so long and was so dreadful?"

Betty said: "I don't think I mind. I don't think, you know, we really did have to wait—in a way this was there all the time. I feel as if we might understand it was really all quite happy—if we lived it again."

Lester said, all but disdainfully: "Oh if we lived it *again*——"

Betty smiled. She said: "Lester, you look just like you used to sometimes"—and as Lester coloured a little and smiled back, she went on quickly: "There, that's what I mean. If we were living the other times *now*—like this—Oh I don't know. I'm not clever at this sort of thing. But the lake or whatever it was—and then Jonathan—and now you…. I feel as if all of you had been there even when you weren't, and now perhaps we might find out how you were even when you weren't. Oh well," she added, with a sudden shake of her fair head that seemed to loose sparkles of gold about all the room, "it doesn't much matter. But I'd like to see my nurse again. I wonder if I could."

"I should think," said Lester, "you could almost do anything you wanted." She thought, as she spoke, of the City through which she had come. Were the other houses in it—the houses that had seemed to her so empty then—as full of joy as this? but then perhaps also of the danger of that other death? If now she returned to them, would she see them so? if she went out of this house and—— She broke in on Betty who had now begun to dress with an exclamation: "Betty, I'd forgotten Evelyn."

Betty paused and blinked. She said, with a faint touch of reserve in her voice: "Oh Evelyn!"

Lester smiled again. "Yes," she said, "that may be all very well for you, my dear, and I shouldn't wonder if it was, but it's not at all the same thing for me. I made use of Evelyn."

Betty made a small face at herself and Lester in the mirror of her dressing-table. She said: "Think of the use she was trying to make of me!" and looked with a kind of celestial mischief over her shoulder at her friend.

"So I do," said Lester, "but it isn't the same thing at all, you must see. Betty, you do see! You're just being provoking."

"It's nice to provoke you a little," Betty murmured. "You're so much more *everything* than me that you oughtn't to mind. I might tempt you a little, on and off." Neither of them took the word seriously enough, nor needed to, to feel that this was what all temptations were—matter for dancing mockery and high exchange of laughter, things so impossible that they could be enjoyed as an added delight of love. But Betty swung round and went on seriously. "We *had* forgotten Evelyn. What shall we do?"

"I suppose I could go and look for her," Lester answered. "If she's still in those streets she'll be frightfully miserable…. She *will* be frightfully miserable. I must go." There rose in her the vague idea of giving Evelyn a drink, a cup of tea or a sherry or a glass of water—something of that material and liquid joy. And perhaps she ought to let Evelyn talk a little, and perhaps she herself ought to pay more serious attention to Evelyn's talk. Talk would not have checked the death-light, but if she could be a kind of frame for Evelyn, like the frame to which she had held or by which she had been held—perhaps Evelyn could rest there a little. Or perhaps—but Evelyn had first to be found. The finding of Betty had been like nothing she could ever have dreamed; might not the finding of Evelyn be too? There was a word, if she could only remember it for what she wanted—what she was thinking—now. Richard would know; she would ask Richard—after the million years. Compensation? no; recovery? no; salvation—something of all that sort of thing, for her and Betty and Evelyn, and all. She had better get on with it first and think about it afterwards.

They were silent—so to call it—while Betty finished dressing. Then Betty said: "Well now, shall I come with you?"

"Certainly not," said Lester. "You go down to your Jonathan. And if, by any chance, you should see Richard, give him my love." The commonplace phrase was weighted with meaning as it left her lips; in that air, it signified no mere message but an actual deed—a rich gift of another's love to another, a third party transaction in which all parties were blessed even now in the foretaste.

Betty said: "I wish you could come. Are you sure you wouldn't like *me* to? I shouldn't mind Evelyn a bit now, if she wanted to talk to me."

"No," said Lester, "I don't suppose you would. But I don't think it would be a terrifically good idea for Evelyn—yet, anyhow. No; you go on. And don't forget me, if you can help it."

Betty opened her eyes. She said, as Lester had said earlier, the sweet reminders interchanging joy: "Here?"

"No," Lester said. "I know, but it's all a little new still. And … *Oh!*"

The cry was startled out of her. Before Betty had begun dressing, she had pulled the curtains and put out the light. Lester had so turned that she was now facing the window, and there, within or without, looking at her, was Evelyn—an Evelyn whom Lester hardly recognized. She knew rather than saw that it was the girl she had once called her friend. The staring eyes that met hers communicated that, but in those eyes was the same death-light that had crept about her own feet. It was indeed so; the torment of twisted space was but the sign and result of a soul that was driven to obey because it had no energy within itself, nor any choice of obedience. Lester was by her at once; the speed of her movement depended now chiefly on her will. She disappeared in that second from Betty's sight. She threw out her hands and caught Evelyn's arms; the dead and living could not touch, but the dead could still seem to touch the dead. She cried out: "Oh Evelyn, my dear!"

Evelyn was mouthing something, but Lester could not hear what she was saying. That however was because Evelyn was not talking to her at all, but to the Clerk. She was saying: "I can see Lester; she's got hold of me. I can't see Betty."

The Clerk said: "Speak to her. Ask her what she's doing. Ask her to come away with you."

"Evelyn!" Lester exclaimed. "Evelyn! What's happening? Come with me." She spoke without any clear intention; she had no idea what she could do, but the sense of belonging to some great whole was upon her, and she trusted to its direction. It could save this tortured form as it had saved her.

Evelyn answered, as she had been told: "Lester, what have you been doing?" But these words, instead of gaining significance, had lost it; they emerged almost imbecilely.

"I?" said Lester, astonished. "I've been——" She stopped. She could not possibly explain, if indeed she knew. She went on "—putting things straight with Betty. But I was coming to you, indeed I was. Come and speak to Betty." She was aware, by her sharpened sight, that Betty was no longer in the room, and added: "She'll be back soon."

Evelyn, her eyes wandering round the room, said gasping: "I don't want to stop. Come with me."

Lester hesitated. She was willing to do anything she could, but she never had trusted Evelyn's judgment on earth, and she did not feel any more inclined to trust it now. Nor, especially since she had seen Evelyn's face turned on her at the bottom of the hill, and heard Evelyn's voice outside the house, did she altogether care to think into what holes and corners of the City Evelyn's taste might lead them. There was, she knew, in those streets someone who looked like a god and yet had loosed that death-light which had crept round her feet and now shone in Evelyn's eyes. She was not afraid, but she did not wish, unless she must, to be mixed up with obscenity. Her natural pride had lost itself, but a certain heavenly fastidiousness still characterized her. Even in paradise she preserved one note of goodness rather than another. Yet when she looked at that distressed face, her fastidiousness vanished. If she could be to Evelyn something of what Betty had been to her——? She said: "Do you want me?"

"Oh yes, yes!" the gasping voice said. "Only you. Do come."

Lester released her hold, but as she did so, two grasping hands went up and fastened on hers. They gave a feeble jerk, which Lester easily resisted, or indeed hardly had to resist. She had once disliked coming into this house; now, at the moment of new choice, she disliked leaving it. Her only friend in the new life was in it. But she could not refuse the courtesies of this London to her acquaintance in an earlier London. She gave a small sigh and relaxed her will. She moved.

Her relaxed will took her where Evelyn would, but at her own speed and in her own manner. She was aware of the space she covered but not of the time, for she took no more time than Evelyn did to turn herself back on the steps of the Clerk's chair. Not only space but time spread out around her as she went. She saw a glowing and glimmering City, of which the life was visible as a roseal wonder within. The streets of it were first the streets of to-day, full of the business of to-day—shops, transport, men and women, for she was now confirmed that not alone in the house she had left did that rich human life go on. It was truly there, even if (except through that house) she had no present concern with it. The dreadful silence she had known after death was no longer there; the faint sound of traffic, so common but oh so uncommon, came to her. It was London known again and anew. Then, gently opening, she saw among those streets other streets. She had seen them in pictures, but now she did not think of pictures, for these were certainly the streets themselves— another London, say—other Londons, into which her own London opened or with which it was intermingled. No thought of confusion crossed her mind; it was all very greatly ordered, and when down a long street she saw, beyond the affairs of to-day, the movement of sedan chairs and ancient dresses, and beyond them again, right in the distance and yet very close to her, the sun shining on armour, and sometimes a high battlemented gate, it was no phantasmagoria of a dream but precise actuality. She was (though she did not find the phrase) looking along time. Once or twice she thought she saw other streets, unrecognizable, with odd buildings and men and women in strange clothes. But these were rare glimpses and less clear, as if the future of that City only occasionally showed. Beyond all these streets, or sometimes for a moment seen in their midst, was forest and the gleam of marshland, and here and there a river, and once across one such river a rude bridge, and once again a village of huts and men in skins. As she came down towards what was to her day the centre of the City, there was indeed a moment when all houses and streets vanished, and the forests rose all round her, and she was going down a rough causeway among the trees, for this was the place of London before London had begun to be, or perhaps after its long and noble history had ceased to be, and the trees grew over it, and a few late tribes still trod what remained of the old roads. That great town in this spiritual exposition of its glory, did not omit any circumstance of its building in time and space—not even the very site upon which its blessed tale was sufficiently reared.

It was not for her yet to know the greater mystery. That waited her growth in grace, and the enlargement of her proper faculties in due time. Yet all she saw, and did not quite wonder at seeing, was but a small part of the whole. There around her lay not only London, but all cities—coincident yet each distinct; or else, in another mode, lying by each other as the districts of one city lie. She could, had the time and her occasions permitted, have gone to any she chose—any time and place that men had occupied or would occupy. There was no huge metropolis in which she would have been lost, and no single village which would itself have been lost in all that contemporaneous mass. In this City lay all—London and New York, Athens, and Chicago, Paris and Rome and Jerusalem; it was that to which they led in the lives of their citizens. When her time came, she would know what lay behind the high empty façades of her early experience of death; it was necessary that she should first have been compelled to linger among those façades, for till she had waited there and till she had known the first grace of a past redeemed into love, she could not bear even a passing glimpse of that civil vitality. For here citizenship meant relationship and knew it; its citizens lived new acts or lived the old at will. What on earth is only in the happiest moments of friendship or love was now normal. Lester's new friendship with Betty was but the merest flicker, but it was that flicker which now carried her soul.

The passage ended. Lester, exhilarated by the swiftness and the spectacle of the journey, stood in the yard, outside the hall. And Evelyn, on the steps of the chair, had been able to turn and felt the agonized rigour relax. The cramps of her spirit were eased. She stood up; she ran very fast, under the eyes of her master and under the shadow of his lifted hand, and came to Lester who, coming by an easier and longer way, became again aware of her, as she had not been on the way. Evelyn's face was still a little set, but the hard glaring misery was gone. Evelyn smiled at her; at least her face jerked; she, like the other inhabitants of that house, bore Simon's mark in her body. Lester looked away; it seemed to her more courteous not to meet what she privately regarded as an unspeakable grimace. But then Lester's standard for smiles had been, that day, considerably raised.

She said, looking round her at the yard and then through the window, and speaking more pleasantly than ever in this world she had spoken to Evelyn, but firmly: "What do you want me to do here? If," she added, still pleasantly, "you do want me to do anything."

Evelyn said: "*He* does. Come in." Her voice was stronger and more urgent; she tried again to pull Lester on. She had no power on the other; her pull was no more than a poor indication of what she wanted. Lester, having come so far, consented. She moved forward with Evelyn through the wall. She saw Simon and recognized him at once. He was no more a portent to her; the falling away of the death-light had taken from him something of his apparent majesty, and a kind of need and even peevishness showed in his face. He himself did not see her now—not even her eyes as he had done in the hall of the house. But Evelyn's manner told him that she was there. The link between them was Evelyn; on her depended the abolition of that obstacle.

But there was only one way of action. Had the Clerk himself been able to enter that other world of pattern and equipoise, of swift principles as of tender means, he might conceivably have been able to use better means. But he never had done, and there remained now the necessity of setting up a permanent earthly and magical link which he could control. He supposed, since he thought in those terms, that the coming of this Lester with Evelyn meant that Evelyn had some sort of hold on Lester, and not at all that Lester had merely come. He who babbled of love knew nothing of love. It was why he had never known anything of the Betty who had sprung from the lake, if lake it was, that lay in the midst of that great City, as if in the picture which Jonathan had painted the shadow of the cathedral had looked rather like water than mass, and yet (as always) light rather than water. It lay there, mysterious and hidden; only, as if from sources in that world as in this, the Thames and all rivers rose and flowed and fell to the sea, and the sea itself spread and on it vessels passed, and the traffic of continents carried news of mightier hidden continents; no ship laden in foreign ports or carrying merchandise to foreign ports but exhibited passage and the principle of passage, since passage was first decreed to the creation. Simon to turn that passage back upon itself? to turn back speech which was another form of that passage? let him first master the words of three girls, and drive them as he would.

He heard Evelyn say, as she came into the hall: "Here she is." He knew what had to be done and set himself to do it—to erect the material trap and magical link between himself and one dead girl that she might drag the other in. Let both be caught! The destroying anti-Tetragrammaton was not to be used for that, but there were lesser spells which deflected primeval currents. He stood upright; he set his deep fierce eyes on Evelyn; he began almost inaudibly to hum. The unseen motes in the air—and lesser points of matter than they—responded. After he had hummed awhile, he ceased and spat. The spittle lay on the floor at Evelyn's apparent feet, and was immediately covered by a film of almost invisible dust. The motes were drawn to it. Faint but real, a small cloud gathered against the floor.

He sighed. He drew in air, and bending towards the cloud which now stood up like a tiny pyramid he exhaled the air towards it. He reached his hands down towards the dust, and in the midst of his sighs he spat again. As his spittle fell on the dust, the pyramid thickened and became more solid. With a curious small whistling sound, as of air rushing through a narrow channel, the heap of dust enlarged and grew. There hung above it in that hall another sound as small as the whistling—the echo of a longing voice. It said: "Oh! Oh! a place for me?" and the Clerk's voice—was it a voice? to Lester, as now she heard the faint exchange it seemed no more than a mere lifting wave of the moon when the thinnest cloud obscures and reveals it— answered: "For you; for you." She herself was not permitted, or did not desire, then to speak; she was troubled faintly in her heart as that lifting wave came to her. Her own sins had not been of that kind; disordered in love, she had still always known that love was only love. She did not understand what was going on; only there was something disagreeable in that sign and countersign of agreement—"For me?" "For you." The Clerk stretched down his hands again, but now as if he sheltered the early flicker of a fire, and immediately the fire was there.

It came from his palms. It was not fire but an imitation of fire. The palms themselves gave no sign of it, and even through the seeming flames showed no reddening from the heat. The fire itself was pallid; it had no strength, but the flames darted down and hovered round the dust. They ran over it and clung to it, and as he encouraged them with mimetic movements of his hands, they sank deeper and were absorbed. As if their movement was communicated, the dust itself rose in sudden gushes and fell again, but each time the heap was larger than before. It was now about six inches high, and had grown more like a column than a pyramid. It was waving to and fro, as a single unbranched plant might, and the whistling came from it, as if a dying man were trying to breathe. The whistling was thin, but so was the plant, if it were a plant, which it was not, for it was still dust, even if organic dust. It was vaguely swaying and waving itself about, as if in search of something it had no means of finding, and the pallid fire played about it as it sought. Simon's heavy sighs exhaled above it and his hands shielded it, though (to Lester's apprehension) there was a great, almost an infinite, distance between those palms and it, as if she saw something of a different kind that was without relation to the place in which it stood. Suddenly for the third time the Clerk spat on it and this time it grew at once higher by almost another six inches, and its movement became more defined though no more successful. It was now certainly feeling out with its summit—with what would have been its head, but it had no head. The fire was absorbed into it, and disappeared; and as it did so the whole small column from being dust became a kind of sponge-like substance, an underwater growth. It began to try and keep a difficult balance, for it seemed to be slipping and sliding on the floor and by throwing itself one way and another just not falling. The thin whistling grew spasmodic, as if it had got some of its channels free, and was only here and there obstructed; and as the whistling ceased, so did the heavy breathing of the Clerk. He began to rise slowly from the position in which, like a witch-doctor, he had been half-crouching; but he did so in sudden jerks, and as he did so the spongy growth in sudden jerks followed him and grew.

With its first jerk there came another change. For the jerk was not only an upward movement, adding perhaps another three inches to its height, but also interior, as if the sponge shook itself and settled. It now stood more firmly, and with the next one or two similar movements it took on the appearance of a rudimentary human body. It was developing from its centre, for its feet and head were not visible, but only a something against its sides that might have been arms, and a division that might have been between its upper legs, and two faint swellings that might have been breasts. Soon, however, the arms did move outward, though they immediately fell, and below the centre the thing split into two stumps, on which, each in turn, it soundlessly stamped. It was now throwing its upper end violently about, as if to free itself from its own heaviness, but it failed and subsided into a continual tremor. With this tremor, its sponginess began in patches to disappear, and give place to some sort of smooth pale-yellowish substance, which presently had spread so far that it was the sponginess which grew on it in patches. Thus there stood now on the floor the rough form of a woman, a little under two feet high, and with the head gradually forming. The face, as far as it emerged, had no character; the whole thing was more like a living india-rubber doll than anything else, but then it did live. It was breathing and moving, and it had hair of a sort, though at present (as with such a doll) rather part of the formation of its head. It lifted its hands, as if to look at them, but its eyes were not yet formed, and it dropped them again; and then it seemed to listen, but though its ears were almost there, it could not hear—and indeed the only sound it could have heard was Simon's breathing, and that would only just have been audible even to a human ear.

Lester, as she watched, was a little surprised to find that the living doll was not more disgusting to her. It was faintly repellent, as an actual doll might be if it were peculiarly deformed or ugly. She disliked the spongy patches and the deadness of the apparent skin, but she could not feel strongly about it; not so strongly as Jonathan would have felt about a bad painting. She had a mild impulse to pick it up and put it right—pull and pat and order it, but she did not wish to touch it; and anyhow she did not know why it was there, nor why beside her she was aware that Evelyn was looking at it with such intensity, and even giving what seemed little squeals of pleasure as it grew. Indeed, Evelyn presently gave a quick forward movement, as if she were about to rush to the doll. She was checked by the Clerk's voice.

He said: "Wait. It's too cold." The fire was still pallid in the interior of his hands, and now he breathed on them as if to blow it into life, and it grew round each hand as if he had put on gloves of pale light, a light more like that of the false Tetragrammaton but not so deathly. With his hands thus encased, he took up the manikin between them and handled and dandled and warmed and seemed to encourage it, whispering to it, and once or twice holding it up above his head, as a father might his child, and as it turned its head, now grown, and looked over its shoulder, the girls saw that its eyes were open and bright, though meaningless. They saw also that it was longer and now nearly three feet in height, but it seemed to have no more weight, for still he cherished and caressed it, and held it out standing on one hand, as if it were no more than a shell. But that ended his play with it. He set it again on the floor, struck his hands together—as if to break the fire from them, and indeed the pale fire flew in sparks around him and about the hall, and his hands were clear of it. He looked at Evelyn, and said: "That is for you and your friend."

Evelyn's answer was heard both by him and Lester. She said: "*Both* of us?"

Simon answered: "You'll find the sharing of it better than most things. It's something for you to get into. It'll grow when you do, and you can go about in it. It will shelter you, and you will find presently you'll be able to talk to it, and it will understand better than anyone else, and answer you as you want. It won't need food or drink or sleep unless you choose. If I call you out of it sometimes, I'll always send you back, and if I call you it will be to get the woman you want."

Evelyn said: "Can't I have it for myself?" The Clerk slowly shook his head. He looked sideways at the motionless Lester. In what now seemed a dim air, Lester was not easily seen; unless the truth was that, even then, even in her attention, she was already farther away. Emboldened by that remoteness, Evelyn said, in what was meant to be a whisper and came out as a croak, almost as if the dwarf-woman (could she yet speak) might have spoken, in a sub-human voice: "*Must* she come?"

The Clerk said: "if you are to go, she must." But the hall grew colder as he spoke, so that Evelyn felt it and shivered and turned to Lester with a desperate and yet feeble ferocity. The dwarf-woman seemed to her now her only hope, a refuge from the emptiness and the threats, a shelter from enmity and cold, and if presently she could get Betty into it to be victimized, she would be, she thought, content. So she tried to catch at Lester's hand and succeeded, for Lester left it to her. She had, half-unconsciously, withdrawn herself from that short dialogue with a pure and grave disdain; whatever these others were talking of she refused to overhear. Had the hand that now clutched at her held any friendship or love, she would have felt it in her spirit and responded, or to any need. But this was rather greed than need, and yet its touch was now not even inconvenient to her. The beginnings of heaven are not so troubled. Only with the touch, she knew at once what Evelyn wanted, and she said gently: "I wouldn't go, Evelyn."

Evelyn said: "Oh I *must*. Do come, Lester. It can't hurt you."

Lester unexpectedly laughed. It was years since anyone had laughed in that hall, and now the sound, though low, was so rich and free, it so ran and filled the hall, that Evelyn gave a small scream, and the Clerk turned his head sharply this way and that, and even the dwarf-woman seemed to gaze more intently before her, with unseeing eyes. "No," Lester said, "I don't think it can. But it mayn't be too good for you."

Evelyn answered peevishly: "I wish you wouldn't laugh like that! And I want it. *Do* come. I've done enough things because you wanted them; you might just do this. Lester, *please*! I won't ask you for anything else. I swear I won't."

The echo of the laughter, which still seemed to sound, was cut off suddenly, as if in a sudden silence all there and all beyond heard her oath. The Clerk's constriction showed in his face, and Lester, though she did not altogether realize that the silly human phrase was now taken at its precise meaning, shuddered. If it had been but silliness, it might not have passed beyond the visionary façades of the City, but it was not. It was greed and clamorous demand, and it swept into the City's courts and high places and was sealed with its own desire. Lester said, almost as if, unknowing, she tried to forestall that sealing: "Come back with me. Come to Betty or your mother. Let's——" She saw the fixed immortality in Evelyn's eyes and ceased.

Evelyn pulled at her, and looked back at Simon, as if she were asking him to help. He did what he could. He knew he had no direct power on this alien spiritual thing until he could get into contact with it; and that, since he had been checked in the previous clash, he could only do now by a plausibility. He said, as if uttering some maxim of great wisdom: "Love is the fulfilling of the law." Lester heard him. At that moment, doubtful of her duty, the maxim was greater than the speaker. She was not particularly aware of loving Evelyn, but she acknowledged her duty. The inconvenience of plunging with Evelyn wherever Evelyn wished to plunge was a little tiresome—no more. She felt as Betty had done when Lester insisted on recalling the past—that it was a pity to waste so much time. The lifting lightness of her new life looked ruefully at the magical shape of the dwarf-woman; her fledgeling energy desired a freer scope. But there seemed to be no other way. She thought of Richard; she thought of Betty; she sighed a small sigh, but a sigh. She thought of Evelyn's tormented face, and the sigh ceased. She said suddenly, with one of those bursts of inspiration which are apt to possess noble and passionate hearts: "You'd be wiser to say that the fulfilling of the law is love." She had spoken, as it were, into the void, but then she went on to Evelyn: "Very well, if you want me to. But you'd be wiser—I'm sure you'd be wiser—to come away."

Evelyn did not answer. There was a pause of suspension in the whole hall. Then the dwarf-woman took a step forward. Under the Clerk's eyes, she began again to grow. She shook herself into shape as she did so, putting up her hands and settling her neck and head. There grew out of her smooth dead skin, into which the sponginess had now been wholly absorbed, fresh streaks and patches, ash-coloured, which spread and came together, and presently covered her, and grew loose, and wrapped itself round her like a dull dress. The dwarf pulled it into shape. There stood facing the Clerk, a short rather heavy-looking middle-aged woman, slightly deformed, with one shoulder a little higher than the other and one foot dragging a little, but undoubtedly, to all human eyes, a woman. Her eyes were brighter now, and she seemed both to see and hear.

The Clerk lifted a finger and she stood still. He bent his knee slowly, lowering himself till his face was on a level with hers. He was muttering something as he did so. He put his hands on her thighs, and from her thighs he passed them all over her. When he had finished, he leaned forward and very deliberately kissed her on the mouth. He sealed, so far as he could, a prison for those spirits, who had entered it by their own choice; and he judged he could do it well, for he knew the power that flesh—even impure and magical flesh—has on human souls, especially while they are still unused to that great schism in identity which is death. At first strangers in that other world, they may forget their bodies, but their bodies are their past and part of them and will not be forgotten. So that, sooner or later, these spiritual beings again strongly desire to be healed of their loss and whole. But this they cannot be until the whole of time is known to be redeemed, and when the hunger comes on them the blessed ones endure it smiling and easily, having such good manners that the time is no more to them than an unexpected delay before dinner at a friend's house.

He believed therefore that as, by proper magical means, a soul could within certain limits of time, be recalled to its body, so this false body might for a time ensnare and hold that other soul which was his enemy. He would have much preferred to operate necromantically on Lester's own proper body, and if Richard had remained under his influence he would have obtained through him some possession of hers which would have served for the first faint magical link with that body, and so set up a relation between them which might have brought her now corrupting flesh—or perhaps the scattered ashes of her cremated body— into this very hall. But Richard had failed him, and he had no time to take more subtle ways; the danger to his domination of Betty now arising from Jonathan and from Lester was too great. He knew that the government of this world would be driven by popular pressure to make some approach to him, and that in no very long period the fatal meeting with his Types would be forced on him—fatal because though at a distance they might be energized and driven by his will, yet when the three met they must dwindle and fade beside him. And first he must have sent his daughter into the spiritual world. He must be for ever before he could be now. So that altogether time was against him; the first condition of the universe was against him. He was hurried; he had to make haste. Therefore the magical trap; therefore its tossing, as he now proposed, into the ordinariness of earth.

He whispered into the ear of the dwarf-woman, still pressing his hands on it. He and it were now alone in the hall. It could not be said to hear him, but it received his breath. He was now separated from those two other children of earth, and they from him, unless he deliberately called them. He knew that their awareness must be now of and through the body they in some sense inhabited; not that they lived in it as in a place, but that they only knew through it. There was no limit to the number of spiritual beings who could know in that way through one body, for there was not between any of them and it any organic relation. The singleness of true incarnation must always be a mystery to the masters of magic; of that it may be said that the more

64

advanced the magic, the deeper the mystery, for the very nature of magic is opposed to it. Powerful as the lie may be, it is still a lie. Birth and death are alike unknown to it; there is only conjunction and division. But the lie has its own laws. Once even Lester had assented to that manner of knowledge, she must enter the City so. It remained to discover what she could do there.

In the front office of the house, the caretaker Plankin was standing by the door. He saw coming along from the side-passage a middle-aged woman. She was short and slightly deformed. Her eyes were fixed in front of her, and in spite of a dragging foot she was walking at a fair speed. She went by Plankin without noticing him and on into the street. He thought, as he watched her: "Ah, the Father hasn't healed her yet. But he will; he will. He'll put his mark in her body."

Chapter Nine

TELEPHONE CONVERSATIONS

Lady Wallingford sat in her drawing-room. Jonathan and Richard were with her, but she did not ask them to sit down. Jonathan leant on the back of a chair, watching the door. Richard paced up and down. Had Jonathan painted the scene, he might have shown a wilderness, with a small lump of that iron-grey rock in the centre, and near it a couched lion and a pacing leopard. It would have been a vision of principles, and so (even then) Jonathan, at least as the others appeared, took it in. He wondered, as he looked at Lady Wallingford, if she would ever move again; he wondered with what expectation Richard stepped and turned.

Yet it was the memory of something hardly more than an accident which chiefly held the woman rock-rigid in her chair. She knew what Simon proposed, though she did not know how he meant to fulfil his purpose. He had in mind a simpler and cruder thing than any magical dissolution. That had failed; there remained simple murder. She knew that that was what the night was to bring. But she was now only remotely aware of it, for though she no longer felt her body clamped in that frame which had shut on her in the bedroom, yet her anger was almost equally strong and imprisoned her from within. The maid's words: "Oh she *is* looking better, isn't she, my lady?" held her. She was furious that Betty should look better; she was almost more furious that the maid, even deferentially, should comment on it. The obnoxious fact was emphasized in the most obnoxious manner. It is the nature of things intensely felt as obnoxious so to emphasize themselves. She sat raging—immobile in her wilderness.

The maid herself was hovering in the hall. She did not like to stay, in case Lady Wallingford came out and saw her, or to go, in case Lady Wallingford rang for her, in which case the sooner she was there the better for her. She drifted uneasily about the foot of the stairs. Presently she heard above her a door shut. She looked up, Miss Betty was coming down the stairs.

Miss Betty was looking very much better. The maid lingered in admiration. Betty smiled gaily down at her, and the girl smiled shyly back. She ventured to say, with a sense of obscure justification: "You *are* better, aren't you, Miss Betty?"

"Much, thank you," said Betty, and added remorsefully: "I expect I've given you a lot of extra work, Nina."

"Oh *no*, Miss Betty," Nina said. "Besides, I'd have liked it. My grandmother used to be with Sir Bartholomew's mother, so in a way we're in the family. She was your nurse, Miss Betty."

Betty stopped on the third stair; then in a leap she was down them, and had caught hold of the girl's arm. Her face was alight; she exclaimed: "Your grandmother my nurse! Is she alive? where's she living? Do tell me, Nina."

Nina, surprised but pleased by this interest, said: "Why, she's living in London, over in Tooting. I go and see her most weeks."

Betty drew a deep breath. She said: "Isn't that marvellous? I want to see her. Can I? can I now?"

"She'd be very pleased if you did, Miss Betty," Nina said. "Only," she added more doubtfully, "I don't know if my lady would like it. I think there was some trouble between grandmother and my lady. She was sent away, I know, but Sir Bartholomew helped her. It's all a long time ago."

"Yes," said Betty—"when I was born and before you were. That'll be all right. Tell me the address; I'll explain to my mother."

"It's 59 Upper Clapham Lane," Nina answered. "It was once her own boarding-house, and then my brother and his wife took it over, only he's in Austria now. But my grandmother still lives there."

Betty said: "I shall go to-day. Thank you, Nina. I'll see you when I come back." She released the girl and went on into the drawing-room. She entered it, Jonathan thought, like water with the sun on it; the desert blossomed with the rose. The wild beasts in it were no less dangerous, but she was among them in the friendship and joy of a child. She slipped her hand in Jonathan's arm, and she said, smiling at them all: "Mother, I've just found out where my old nurse lives, and I'm going to see her. Isn't it marvellous? I've so often wanted to."

"You had better," said Lady Wallingford's dead voice, "have lunch here first."

"Oh need we?" Betty said. "Jonathan, won't you take me to lunch somewhere, and we could go on?"

"You were going to lunch with me anyhow," Jonathan said. "We can go anywhere you like afterwards."

"Do you mind, Mother?" Betty asked. "You see I really am absolutely all right."

As if the rock itself shifted, Lady Wallingford got to her feet. She would, under her paramour's instruction and for his sake, have put friendliness into her voice, had it been possible. It was not. She could neither command nor beguile. She said: "When will you be back?"

"Oh to dinner," said Betty. "May I bring Jonathan back?"

"No, thank you very much," Jonathan said hastily. "I couldn't to-night. Besides, you're dining with me, and after that we'll see. Let's go."

"All right," said Betty. "I'll ring you up, Mother, and tell you what we decide."

Jonathan looked at Richard. "What are you doing?" he asked.

Richard came lightly forward. He said to Lady Wallingford: "I've intruded quite long enough. It's been quite unforgivable, and I don't suppose you mean to forgive me, which would save us both trouble. Good-bye, and thank you so much. I'm glad that Betty is better, and that Sir Bartholomew will soon be back."

Betty exclaimed, and Lady Wallingford, still in that dead voice, said: "How do you know?"

"Oh the Foreign Office!" Richard said vaguely. "One can pick things up. Good-bye, Lady Wallingford, and thank you again. Come, children, or we shall get no lunch."

But, once outside the house, he disengaged himself. He sent off the two lovers and himself went on his way to his own flat. They, after the parting, went to lunch and the exchange of histories. Time was before them, and they had no need to hurry their understanding. After lunch they set out on their way to discover 59 Upper Clapham Lane. It was a largish respectable house, in reasonably good condition. Jonathan, as they looked at it, said: "*Is* everything brighter? or is it only being with you that makes me think so?—even than it was this morning?"

Betty pressed his arm. She said: "Everything's always as bright as it can be, and yet everything's getting brighter. Unless, of course, it's dark."

Jonathan shook his head. "Why," he said, "you should be able to see better than I—why you should have more plain observation and common understanding than I—well, never mind! Let's ring."

Presently they found themselves in Mrs. Plumstead's suite; she made it seem that by the way she welcomed them. She was a charming old lady, who was extremely touched and pleased by the unexpected appearance of Betty. She managed to treat it as at once an honour conferred and a matter of course, and made no allusion to the long separation. She did however with an awful aloofness once or twice allude to the parting between herself and Lady Wallingford, saying with an iciness equal to Lady Wallingford's: "I didn't suit my lady." Jonathan said, in answer: "You seem to have suited Betty very well, Mrs. Plumstead," and added ambiguously: "Without you she couldn't have been what she is."

Mrs. Plumstead, sitting upright, said: "No; my lady and me—we did not suit. But there's a thing that's been on my mind, my dear, all these years, and I think I ought to tell you. I'm free to say that I was younger then and apt to take things on myself, which I wouldn't do now, for I don't think it was quite proper. Her ladyship and I did not see eye to eye, but after all she was your mother, my dear, and no doubt meant you well. And if it was to be done again, perhaps I would not do it."

Jonathan thought that Mrs. Plumstead at that moment might have passed for Queen Elizabeth pronouncing upon the execution of Mary Queen of Scots. And then he forgot such literary fancies in the recollection of Betty's other life, and of the lake of which at lunch she had told him, and the high sky and the wise water and all the lordly dream, if it were a dream. Betty was leaning forward now, and gazing intently at the old lady. She said: "Yes, nurse?"

"Well, my dear," the old nurse went on, and ever so faintly blushed, "as I say, I was younger then, and in a way I was in charge of you, and I was a little too fond of my own way, and very obstinate in some things. And now I do not think it right. But you were such a dear little thing, and I did once mention it to my lady, but she was very putting-off, and only said: 'Pray, nurse, do not interfere'—her ladyship and I *never* suited—

and I ought to have left it at that, I do think now, but I was obstinate, and then you were such a dear little thing, and it did seem such a shame, and so——" the old nurse said, unaware of the intensity of the silence in the room—"well, I christened you myself."

Betty's voice, like the rush of some waterfall in a river, answered: "It was sweet of you, nurse."

"No; it wasn't right," Mrs. Plumstead said. "But there it is. For I thought then that harm it couldn't do you, and good it might—besides getting back on her ladyship: Oh I was a wicked woman—and one afternoon in the nursery I got the water and I prayed God to bless it, though I don't know now how I dared, and I marked you with it, and said the Holy Name, and I thought: 'Well, I can't get the poor dear godfathers and godmothers, but the Holy Ghost'll be her godfather, and I'll do what I can.' And so I would have done, only soon after her ladyship and I didn't suit. But that's what happened, and you ought to know now you're a grown woman and likely to be married and have babies of your own."

Betty said: "So it was you who lifted me out of the lake!"

Jonathan thought that Lady Wallingford's behaviour to her servants had been, on the whole, unfortunate. She had never credited the nurse she employed with such piety, decision, and courage (or obstinacy, if you preferred the word). And now as in some tales Merlin had by the same Rite issued from the womb in which he had been mysteriously conceived, so this child of magic had been after birth saved from magic by a mystery beyond magic. The natural affection of this woman and her granddaughter had in fact dispelled the shadows of giant schemes. And this then was what that strange Rite called baptism was—a state of being of which water was the material identity, a life rippling and translucent with joy.

Betty had stood up, and was kissing her nurse. She said: "Good-bye, nurse. We'll come again soon, Jon and I. And never be sorry; some day I'll tell you how fortunate it was." She added, quite naturally: "Bless me, now."

"God bless you, my dear," the old woman said. "And Mr. Drayton too, if I may take the liberty. And make you both very happy. And thank you for saying it was all right."

When they were outside the house, Betty said: "So that's how it was! But … Jon, you must tell me about it—what it's supposed to be."

Jonathan said grimly: "I don't know that you'll be much better off for my explaining. After all, it's you that are happening. I'm not sure that I'm not a little scared of you, darling."

"I'm not sure that I'm not a little scared myself," said Betty seriously. "Not badly, but a little. It's mixed up with discovering that you're really you—wonderful, darling, but rather terrifying. Let's go and look at your pictures, shall we? I've never yet looked at any of them properly, and yesterday I was shaking with fear of my mother. I don't mind her now at all."

"Anything," said Jonathan, "that pleases you pleases me. And God send that that shall be true until we die—and perhaps he will. Let's take a taxi. That's one great advantage of being engaged—one always has a perfectly good reason for taking taxis. All these things are added to one."

They spent some time in his room looking at various paintings, before Betty allowed herself to look at those two which still stood on their respective easels. She lingered for a long time before that of the City-in-light, and Jonathan saw her eyes fill with tears. He caught her hand and kissed it. She went close to him. She said: "I *am* a little scared, dearest. I'm not ready for it yet."

Jonathan said, holding her: "You're ready for much more than a painting … even if the colours have really become colours."

"It's terribly like a fact," Betty said. "I love it. I love you. But I'm *not* very intelligent, and I've got a lot to learn. Jon, you must help me."

Jonathan said only: "I'll paint you next. By the lake. Or no—I'll paint you, and all the lake living in you. It shall be quite fathomless, and these"—he kissed her hands again—"are its shores. Everything I've done is only prentice work—even these things. I don't much want to keep them any more."

"I'd just as soon you didn't keep the other one," Betty said. "Could you bear not to? I don't really mind, but it's rather horrid to have about—now."

"I could quite easily bear to get rid of it," Jonathan answered. "What shall we do with it? Give it to the nation? as from Mr. and Mrs. Jonathan Drayton on their wedding. Publicity, and all that."

"Ye-es," said Betty doubtfully. "I don't think I want the nation to have it. It seems rather rude to give the nation what we don't want."

"What *you* don't want," Jonathan corrected. "Myself, I think it's one of the better examples of my Early Middle Period. You must learn to think in terms of your husband's biography, darling. But if we're not to keep it and not to give it to the nation, what shall we do with it? Give it to Simon?"

Betty looked at him, a little startled: then, as they gazed, they each began to smile, and Jonathan went on: "Well, why not? He's the only one who's really liked it. Your mother certainly doesn't, and you don't, and I don't, and Richard doesn't. That's what we'll do. We'll take it down to Holborn and leave it for him. Betty, you won't go back to Highgate to-night?"

"Not if you don't want me to," said Betty. "Only I've got nothing with me, so I don't see how I can go to a hotel, even if we could find a room. And I don't at all mind going back."

"No, but I mind," Jonathan said, seriously. "To be honest, I don't think Simon's going to leave it at this. I'm not particularly bothered at the moment, because after what's happened I don't believe he's a chance. I think Almighty God has him in hand. But I'd like, as a personal concession, to have you under my eye. There's my aunt at Godalming. Or there's here. Or, of course, there's Richard's place. That's an idea, if he didn't mind; it's more fitted out for a woman."

Betty said: "It would be very nice of Lester." She did not know what Lester was now doing, but in that young and heavenly hero-worship which in heaven is always prejustified by fact and is one mode of the communion of saints, she was convinced that Lester was engaged on some great and good work. She was even willing in a modest candour to presume on Lester's goodwill. But instinctively she put forward her own. She said: "And anyhow, Jon, I was going to ask if we mightn't get Richard to come with us to dinner somewhere."

"I'd thought of that myself," said Jonathan. "We might; we most certainly might. I'd hardly met his wife, but she seemed a good sort—even before all that you told me."

"Oh she's a marvel," Betty exclaimed. "She's … she's like the light in that picture—and very nearly like you."

Jonathan looked at the City on the canvas. He said: "If I'm going to start serious work, and if we're giving Simon his picture, and if you feel like that about her—and if Richard would care for it, do you think we might offer him this? Unless you'd prefer to keep it?—as, of course, I should."

Betty opened her eyes. She said: "I think it's a marvellous idea. Jon, would you? I'd always wanted to give Lester something, but I never could, and if you'd give them this, it'd be perfect. If they'd take it."

"If they——!" said Jonathan. "My girl, do you happen to realize that this is, to date, my best work? Are you suggesting that any decent celestialness wouldn't be respectful?"

Betty, and all the air about her, laughed. She said demurely: "She mightn't know much about paintings, and she mightn't think them important—even yours."

"I'm not so sure that you do yourself," Jonathan said. But his lady protested anxiously: "Oh I do, Jon: well, in a way I do. Of course, I shall understand better presently."

Jonathan abruptly interrupted. "You're entirely right," he said. "But as and while I'm here, it's my job. We *will* ask Richard if he'd like it, and we'll ask him to dinner so as to ask him, and then we'll ask him if we can all sleep at his place—and on the way there we'll drop the other thing in on Simon. Come and help me telephone."

When he left the others Richard had returned to his flat. There he just managed to get to bed before he went to sleep. It was well into the afternoon before he woke, and woke more refreshed and serene than, as he lay there pleasantly aware of it, he could ever remember having felt in his life before, or at least not since he had been a very small child. This freshness and energy reminded him of that. He had no sense of nostalgia; he did not in the least wish to be small again and a child, but he could almost have believed he was now as happy as he remembered he had sometimes been then. An arch of happiness joined the then and the now, an arch he ought to have known all the time, under which or even in which he ought to have lived. It was somehow his fault that he had not, and yet it had never been there or but rarely. If this was life, he had somehow missed life, in spite of the fact that he had on the whole had a very pleasant and agreeable life. There was a great difference between what he had known and what he ought to have known. And yet he did not see how he could have known it.

When he got up, he found himself amused and touched by his own physical resilience. As he moved about the room, he misquoted to himself: "And I might almost say my body thought"; and then his mind turned to that other body which had meant so much to him, and he drifted aloud into other lines:

Whose   speech   Truth   knows   not   from   her   thought
Nor Love her body from her soul.

He had never before so clearly understood that sense of Lester as now when that second line must be rationally untrue. But his sleep had restored to him something he had once had and had lost—something deeper even than Lester, something that lay at the root of all magic, that the body was itself integral to spirit. He had in his time talked a good deal about anthropomorphism, and now he realized that anthropomorphism was but one dialect of divine truth. The high thing which was now in his mind, the body that had walked and lain by his, was itself celestial and divine. Body? it was no more merely body than soul was merely soul; it was only visible Lester.

68

His mind turned again to that house by Holborn. He thought of it, after his sleep, as a nightmare to which he need not return unless, for any reason, he chose. In the sleep from which he had come there could be no nightmares. They were possible only to his waking life, and sometimes from that cast back into the joy of sleep. He drew a deep breath. Simon was only an accident of a life that had not learned to live under that arch of happiness. It was astonishing how, this way, Simon dwindled. That last moment when something disagreeable had floated in at the window of the hall, some remote frigid exchange between imbeciles, was still repugnant to him. But now it was at a distance; it did not even distress him. What did distress him, as it crept back into his mind, was a memory of himself in the street outside the house, of his indulgent self. This unfortunately was no nightmare. He had, in that distant Berkshire wood, been just so; he had been kind to his wife. She (whatever her faults) had never been like that to him; she had never been dispassionately considerate. But he—he undoubtedly had. His new serenity all but vanished, and he all but threw his hairbrush at his face in the mirror, as he thought of it. But his new energy compelled him to refrain and to confront the face, which, as he looked at it, seemed to bear the impress of love behaving itself very unseemly. Her love had never borne that mark. Rash, violent, angry, as she might have been, egotistic in her nature as he, yet her love had been sealed always to another and not to herself. She was never the slave of the false *luxuria*. When she had served him—how often!—she had not done it from kindness or unselfishness; it had been because she wished what he wished and was his servant to what he desired. Kindness, patience, forbearance, were not enough; he had had them, but she had had love. He must find what she had—another kind of life. All these years, since he had been that eager child, he had grown the wrong way, in the wrong kind of life. Yet how to have done other? how to have learnt, as she had learnt, the language without which he could not, except for a conceded moment, speak to the imperial otherness of her glory? He must, it seemed, be born all over again.

A vague impression that he had heard some such phrase somewhere before passed through him. But it was lost, for as he dwelled on the strange notion of this necessary fact, it was swamped by the recollection of Simon. Not that he was now afraid of Simon's having any power over Lester. But if there was that newly visioned life, there was also—he had seen it—a creeping death that was abroad in the world. There was something that was not Lester, nor at all like her, issuing from that hideous little hall. Those who lay in that house, once sick, had been healed. Had they? He did not like to think of that healing. He would almost rather have remained unhealed; yes, but then he did not need healing. He thought uneasily of those who, themselves reasonably secure, urge the poor to prefer freedom rather than security. How could he have done it himself—have lived in pain? have perished miserably? Yet the cost of avoiding that was to be lost in the hypnotic mystery of the creeping death: an intolerable, an unforgivable choice! And perhaps, unless someone interfered, Simon would spread his miasma over the world: the nations swaying as he had seen men swaying. If even now——

The telephone interrupted him. Answering, he found at the other end a colleague of his at the Foreign Office, who began by asking whether Richard were (as he had said) coming back the next day. Richard said that he was. His colleague intimated that there was a particular reason, and (pressed to say more) asked whether Richard were not acquainted with the activities of a certain Simon the Clerk. Richard began to take an interest.

"Well—no and yes," he said. "I knew of him, and as it happens since this morning I may be said to know him. Why?"

"Since you've been away," his friend said, "it's become rather urgent to get into touch with him— unofficially, of course. It's more and more felt here that if the allied discussions could—could infiltrate through him and the other popular leaders there might be a better chance of ... of——"

"Of peace," said Richard.

"Well, yes," his colleague agreed. "They must, all three of them, be remarkable men to have such followings, and there don't seem, where they go, to be any minorities.... What did you say?"

"Nothing, nothing," said Richard. "No minorities?"

"No—or practically none. And it'll be in the best interests of the new World Plan that there should be no minorities. So that it's been hinted that if a kind of—well, not a conference exactly but a sort of meeting could be adumbrated.... Someone here thought you knew Simon."

"I do," said Richard. "And you want me to——"

"Well, since you know him," his colleague answered, "it'd be easy for you to ask him indefinitely, as it were. Could you manage it, d'you think? You can see the kind of thing we want. The fact is that there's a sort of pressure. Even the Russians are feeling it—and we hear a couple of Chinese armies have gone over complete to their own prophet. So the Government thinks it would rather deal with the three of them together than separately. If we could sound them——"

Richard was silent. This language was one he very well knew, but now it had a deeper sound than his colleague's voice could give it. The Foreign Office did not mean badly; it was no more full of "darkness and cruel habitations" than the rest of the world; and when Oxenstierna had complained of the little wisdom with which the world was governed, he had not clearly suggested how anyone was to get more. But if the official governments were beginning to yield to pressure, to take unofficial notice of these world leaders, then those healed bodies behind Holborn must be only a few of a very great number, and those swaying shoulders the heralds of great multitudes of devotion: devotion to what? to the man who had smiled at the dead woman, and claimed to hold Lester at disposal, and knelt in some obscure effort by Betty's bed, the man to whom the wicked little carved hand pointed. He himself might have been among the worshippers; he owed his salvation to his wife, for it was precisely the irreconcilability of his wife with Simon which had preserved him—and he most unworthy, given up to the social virtues, needing rebirth.

He did not know how great the multitudes were who followed those unreal Two; nor how unreal the Two were. He knew only the reports in the papers, and Simon. He seemed to feel again the light antennae-like touch on his cheek: he saw again the strange painting of the prophet preaching to insects: what insects? His colleague's voice went on: "Furnival, are you still there? You'd better know that Bodge"—Bodge was the Foreign Secretary—"is giving it his personal attention. He isn't here to-day, but he will be to-morrow. Couldn't you just sound this Father Simon by then?"

Bodge—the Cabinet room—the swaying shoulders and the lifted faces, the backs of the English ministers rising in the air, the corridor down which the nations could go, the window through which the dead had come. He said abruptly: "I don't know; I can't say. I'll be in to-morrow to report…. Yes; all right, I'll see…. Oh yes, I understand how urgent it is…. No; I don't promise anything. I'll come to-morrow. Unless," he added with a sudden absurd lightening of heart, "unless my wife interferes."

———————

The magical shape walked slowly along the Embankment. Hours had passed since it had emerged from the hidden place of its making into the streets of London; it had come out not by its own wish, for it could have no wish of its own, but under the compulsion of its lord in his last word, merely going, and anywhere. A poorly dressed, somewhat deformed woman went along the pavement. At first, following its maker's preoccupation, it had gone northward, towards the Highgate house. But as that preoccupation grew distant and was slowly lost, since he gave it no further guidance, it presently faltered and stood still, and then began to turn westward. It could not return, for that would be to disobey him; it could not go directly on, for that would be to stress his influence too far. It swung therefore in a wide arc, going always against the sun, and passing so down street after street and alley after alley. Sometimes, but not often, it faulted by taking a blind turning, and had to retrace its steps, but in general, as if it sniffed its way through the lower air, it was wonderfully accurate. But when, in its southward course, it came to the river, it hesitated and did not cross and abruptly turned off towards the east along its own side, and so on, until somewhere by Blackfriars it could see (could it indeed have seen anything at all) the still-lifted cross of St. Paul's. And there, a little way along Victoria Street, it ceased again and stood still.

It could not, for it was sensitive enough to some things, easily enter within the weight of those charged precincts. It avoided them precisely at the point where, had it been living woman, it might by sight or any other sense, have become conscious of them. So also those departed spirits who were now sealed to it were aware of its surroundings through what would have been its or their senses, had it or they lived. One of them had settled, almost happily, to such an existence. Evelyn (to give that spirit still the old name) was content merely to be again generally aware of earth; she did not care about the details. She was listening for its voice, even though at first that voice could only echo her own inaudible soliloquy. Perhaps afterwards it might even answer, and she and it would become an everlasting colloquy, but at the moment it did not. Those who passed it heard a kind of low croak coming from it, but not what it said. What it croaked to itself was a mass of comments and complaints: "But you would think, wouldn't you?" or "It's not as if I were asking much" or "I did think you'd understand" or "After all, fair is fair" or "She might" or "He needn't" or "They could at least" … and so on and on through all the sinful and silly imbecilities by which the miserable soul protects itself against fact. If this was Evelyn's pleasure, this was the pleasure she could have.

But Lester also, for the first time since her death, was aware of what we call the normal world. At first she was conscious of this body as a man is of his own; it was not hers, but it was in that way she knew the dragging foot, the dank palms, the purblind eyes. She knew the spasmodic croakings, as a man may hear his own exclamations. She disliked its neighbourhood, but there was no help for that, and by it alone she was aware of the material universe. So understood, that universe was agreeable to her. She knew and liked the feel of the pavement under the feet; she enjoyed through dim eyes the dull October day, and the heavy sky, and the people, and all the traffic. She seemed to be almost living again, for a little, and by no insistence of her own, in the world she had left.

At first she had not seemed, and had hardly desired, to control this body as it went on its way. She was passive to its haste. But as that haste dwindled, and as it began to circle round its centre, she felt a sense of power. She saw still, as from above, the false body swinging round, and it seemed improper that she herself should be so swung. The full sense of this came to her at almost the moment when that body hesitated by the river under the golden cross of the cathedral. As if from the height of the cross, Lester saw its circling path. There seemed—she almost thought it in human words—no sense in circling round and round Simon; he was no such attractive centre. Indeed, from the height at which she looked down he was no centre at all, except indeed that here and there in the streets she discerned a few forms engaged on precisely that wheeling worship. She knew them by their odd likeness to large beetles walking on their back legs. By an almost unconscious decision she checked the dwarf-woman just as it was about to move forward again. She said— and she just had to say, or at least to think: "No, no; the other way!" The shape tottered, twisted, and was reluctantly forced round. It began, jerkingly and slowly, but certainly, to retrace its steps along the Embankment. It went as if against a high wind, for it was going with the sun and against all the customs of Goetia. Had it been a living witch of that low kind, it would have resisted more strongly; being what it was, it did but find difficulty in going. But it went on, plodding, croaking, jerking, back towards Westminster.

Of Evelyn Lester was no longer immediately conscious. The magical form which united them also separated; through it they co-hered to each other but could not co-inhere. Lester had joined herself to this form for the sake of Evelyn, and Evelyn (so far as she could know) had been promptly removed. In fact, Evelyn no longer wanted her, for Evelyn was concerned only with her own refuge in this false shape, and with her own comfort in it. She did not much care whether it stayed or went, or how or where it went; she cared only that there should be, somewhere in the universe, a voice which, at first repeating, might presently come to respond to, her own. Lester was not unaware of the croaking voice, and justly attributed it to Evelyn, but she saw no reason to stop it. Sounds now came to her through a new kind of silence, a sweet stillness which they did not seem to break; of all the London noises none came so near to breaking it as that croak, but the silence, or perhaps she herself, withdrew a little, and the noise went about below it, as the dwarf-woman plodded below the clouds.

The clouds indeed were heavy in the sky. The river ran equally heavily with the weight of its mirk. A few boats rode on it; the Thames traffic, at this height of its course, had not renewed itself. Lester's attention turned to it, and the dwarf, folding her arms, paused conformably and leaned on the parapet. The Thames was dirty and messy. Twigs, bits of paper and wood, cords, old boxes drifted on it. Yet to the new-eyed Lester it was not a depressing sight. The dirtiness of the water was, at that particular point, what it should be, and therefore pleasant enough. The evacuations of the City had their place in the City; how else could the City be the City? Corruption (so to call it) was tolerable, even adequate and proper, even glorious. These things also were facts. They could not be forgotten or lost in fantasy; all that had been, was; all that was, was. A sodden mass of cardboard and paper drifted by, but the soddenness was itself a joy, for this was what happened, and all that happened, in this great material world, was good. The very heaviness of the heavy sky was a wonder, and the unutilitarian expectation of rain a delight.

The river flowed steadily on. Lester saw it, as if through the dwarf's eyes, and rejoiced. But she was aware that she was at the same time seeing some other movement, within or below it. She was looking down at it also. A single gull, flying wildly up beyond Blackfriars, swooped, wheeled, rose, and was off again down stream. London was great, but that gull's flight meant the sea. The sea was something other than London or than the Thames. Under the rush of the bird's flight—seen as once by another river other watchers had seen a dove's motion skirr and vanish—Lester, looking down, saw in the river the sub-surface currents and streams. Below the exquisitely coloured and moving and busy surface, the river by infinitesimal variations became lucid. On earth men see through lucidity to density, but to her it was as easy to see through density to lucidity. To her now all states of being were beginning to be of their own proper kind, each in itself and in its relationships, and not hampering the vision of others. So the Thames was still the Thames, but within it the infinite gradations of clarity deepened to something else. That other flow sustained and carried the layers of water above it; and as Lester saw it she felt a great desire to discover its source, and even that was mingled with the sudden human recollection that she and Richard had intended one day to set out to find for themselves the first springs of the Thames. So that even here she felt a high, new, strange, and almost bitter longing mingle still with the definite purposes of her past.

She looked—but now no longer from a height above the seagull, but only from her instrument's eyes on the Embankment—she looked up the river. But now she could not see past the great buildings of the Houses and the Abbey; and even those instituted masses seemed to her to float on that current of liquid beauty. As she looked at them the premonition of a pang took her; a sense of division, as if it was at that point that the lucid river flowed into the earthly river, so that beyond that point the way divided, and the source of the Thames was one thing and the springs of the sustaining tributary another. At that point or indeed at any; but always the same division at each. She was suddenly afraid. The strong current below the surface scared her. It flowed from under the bridge, cold and frightening, worse than death. The bridge above it where she and Richard had met this time and that was so frail. They had met above the surface Thames, but they had not guessed what truly flowed below—this which was different from and refused all earthly meetings, and all meetings coloured or overlooked by earth. Oh vain, all the meetings vain! "A million years?" not one moment; it had been the cry of a child. Her spiritual consciousness knew and shuddered. She could never exclaim so again; however long she waited, she only waited to be separated, to lose, in the end. The under-river sang as it flowed; all the streets of London were full of that sweet inflexible note—the single note she had heard in Betty's room, the bed on which she had safely lain. This was it—bed and note and river, the small cold piercing pain of immortal separation.

It passed. The time was not yet, though it was quite certain. The cruel clarity flowed by. She was left with a sense that she had better make the most of the present moment. She had thought she might be of use to Evelyn, but clearly she was not being; all she knew of Evelyn were these spasmodic croaks. What then? something she must do. Betty? Richard? Richard—with this body? She made herself aware of it. It would be revolting to him; it was almost revolting to her, even now, to think of going to her lover in this disguise. Yet if she could—? if they could speak? The shape was not so revolting, for what was it, after all? nothing. Before that great separation came, to take and give pardon and courage … if….

She was not clear how far she was responsible for what followed. Certainly she acted, but there was a pure precision about the process which surprised and delighted her, so that, had Betty or Richard been there, she could have laughed. She turned in herself again to the contemporary City, and the dwarf-woman, starting up, began again to walk. It came presently opposite Charing Cross Tube Station. There it stopped and turned and looked. Lester knew herself anxious to forewarn, to prepare, her husband; and she thought, not unnaturally, of the telephone. Matter to matter; might not this earthly shape use the things of earth? She did not dichotomize; mechanics were not separate from spirit, nor invention from imagination, nor that from passion. Only not even passion of spirit could create the necessary two pennies. She might be (she thought in a flash) immortally on her way to glory, but she had not got two pennies. She recollected the Good Samaritan who had, and with laughter in her heart she tossed a hand towards that sudden vivid image. She was not like Simon; she could not make two pennies. If she were to have them, someone would have to give them to her. She remembered, but not as a claim, that she too had given pennies in her time.

The dwarf in that pause had leaned again against the parapet. The ordinary traffic of London was going on, but as if Lester's pause had affected it, there came at the moment a lull and a silence. Through it there toddled slowly along an elderly gentleman, peering through his glasses at an evening paper. Lester, shyly and daringly, moved towards him. She meant to say: "I beg your pardon, but could you possibly spare me two pennies for the telephone?" But she had not yet control of that false voice, and the croak in which she spoke sounded more like "twopence as a loan". The elderly gentleman looked up, saw a poor shabby deformed creature staring glassily at him, heard the mumble, and hastily felt in his pocket. He said—and it was mercifully permitted him by the Omnipotence to be on this occasion entirely truthful: "It's all the change I've got." He raised his hat, in some faint tradition of "brave and ancient things", and toddled on. The magical body stood holding the pennies in its pseudo-hand, and Lester felt in her that something of a stir in glory which she had felt in seeing Richard's movements or Betty's smile. She was made free of adoration.

The dwarf, under her impulse, crossed the road and went into a telephone box. She put the two pennies in the slot and dialled a number. Lester was aware that there was no reply; Richard apparently was not at home. She felt a small pang at the thought of their empty flat; the desolation seemed to be approaching. It was most likely that he was at Jonathan's. She compelled her instrument to try again. A voice said: "Jonathan Drayton speaking." She caused her instrument to press the button. She said—and now her power was moving so easily in these conditions that something of her own voice dominated the croaking spasms and rang down the telephone: "Mr. Drayton, is Richard there?"

"Hold on," said Jonathan. "Richard!" For soon after Richard's conversation with the Foreign Office he had been rung up by Jonathan, and so warmly invited by both the lovers to join them that he had yielded and gone. Presently they were all to go and dine, but until then they had sat together talking and gradually, as far as possible, making clear to each other the mystery in which they moved. Betty showed an ever-quickened desire to get rid of the painting of the Clerk and his congregation; and both she and Jonathan had so pressed the other canvas on Richard that at last he had accepted it. He did so gratefully, for now, after all that he had seen, he found himself even more moved by it, so that at any moment he half-expected to find that he had missed the figure of Lester walking in the midst of it—if that swift and planetary carriage of hers could be called a walk—and even that he himself might find himself not without but within it and meeting her there. And the three of them in the room had begun, uncertainly and with difficulty—even Betty—to speak of the true nature of the streets there represented, when the telephone had rung.

At Jonathan's call Richard went across and took the receiver. He said: "Richard Furnival," and then, to his amazement, but not much to his amazement, he heard Lester's voice. It was interrupted by some kind of croak which he took to be a fault in the instrument, but he heard it say: "Richard!" and at the noble fascination of that familiar sound he answered, not as unsteadily as he feared: "Is it you, darling?" At the other end the dwarf leaned against the side of the box; nothing at either end, to any who saw, seemed in the least unusual. Along the wires the unearthly and earthly voice continued: "Listen, dearest. Presently someone is coming to see you; it's a short and rather unpleasant woman—at least, that's what it looks like. But I shall be with her, I hope—I do so hope. Will you be as sweet to me as you can, even if you don't like it?"

Richard said: "I've been all kinds of a fool, I know. But I'll do anything with you, if I possibly can. Jonathan and Betty are here."

"That's all right," the voice said. It added: "Once more. Before I go, before I give you up. Oh my sweet!"

The voice was so full of serene grief that Richard went cold. He said: "Nothing shall make me give you up. I've only just begun to find you."

"But you will, even if nothing makes you," the voice said. "It'll have to be like that. But I'll come first. Don't be too distressed about anything. And ask Jonathan to let me in: I'll speak to you inside. Good-bye. I do love you, Richard."

A kind of hubbub broke out on the telephone—another voice and the mechanic croaking—and then Lester's voice, dominating all: "Wait for us. Good-bye," and he heard the click of the receiver. He held his own a full minute before he slowly put it down. His two friends watched him coming back to them across the room. He said: "Something is coming here—a kind of woman. And Lester. I don't know anything more. She says she'll be with it."

"But—Lester…" Jonathan began.

"If that wasn't Lester," Richard said, "you're not looking at Betty now."

They both looked at her. She was standing by the window, and beyond her the October darkness was closing in. She said seriously: "Did she sound—disturbed?"

"Not about that," said Richard. He was silent; then he broke out: "Why isn't one taught how to *be* loved? Why isn't one taught anything?"

Betty said: "Don't worry, Richard; we can't be taught till we can learn. I wish Jonathan was going to get as good a wife as yours is. She wasn't like us; she hardly had to find out how to learn. Jon, take that thing off the easel, won't you? We'll get rid of it to-night. To-night."

She sounded almost impatient, but only because they had not already acted and the preaching horror was still in the room where they were and Lester was to come. Jonathan went and lifted the canvas. As he laid it face downwards on the table, he said: "Do you know what to-night is? All Hallows' Eve."

"A good night," said Richard, "for anything that has to be done."

"And a good night," Betty added, "for Lester to come to us here."

They fell into silence, and for the time that followed they remained mostly silent. Once Jonathan, muttering something about food, moved, and he and Betty spread a rough meal of bread and cheese and cold scraps and wine. There was not much, but there was enough, and they ate and drank standing, as Israel did while the angels of the Omnipotence were at their work in Egypt. The night was heavy without and the sound of rain. The sense of the crisis was sharp in them, and the expectation of that which came.

Presently the bell rang. They looked at each other. Richard said: "You go, Jonathan; she asked you to." Jonathan went to the street door and opened it. He saw in the night a short pale-faced woman and stood aside for her to come in. As it did so, he saw how blank its eyes were, how dead-dull its flesh. Yet he could have believed that, like a paralytic, it tried to recognize him and almost to smile. Neither of them spoke; it knew its way and went before him into the room where the others were.

They watched it come right in; they hardly watched but they heard Jonathan close the room-door. Then Betty said, in a low voice of welcome: "Lester!" She saw, as the others did not, the form of her friend beside this other thing; and yet what she saw, she saw less clearly than before. They were growing away from each other. Lester was bound to pass more wholly into that other world which cannot catch its true and perfect union with this until the resurrection of all the past; the occasional resurrection which then obtained for her

73

was rather purgatorial than paradisal, though sometimes the two were simply one. But Betty also was changing. That free, and (as it were) immaculate, self which had been by high disposition granted her was bound now to take on the conditions of its earthly place and natural heredity. The miracle that had preserved her was over, and she too must be subjected to the tribulations and temptations of common life. As she so drew apart her vision faded. One evening yet remained, and even now the other form and face were full of cloud.

But she saw her. Richard and Jonathan did not. They looked at that uncouth visitor, its blank struggling gaze, its lank hair, its dropped shoulder, its heavy hanging hands, its dragging foot, its dead flesh, its flopping dress, and could not speak. What had this to do with Lester? Lester herself, could she have felt regret, would in that moment have regretted that she had come. She did not. The Acts that were about to take place saw to that. They would, when the time came, see that she spoke what she had to speak, for she was already assenting to their will. It was why they had, since she had driven her present vehicle away from Charing Cross on the long walk to Jonathan's flat, quickened their purging. Up Villiers Street, along the Strand and Fleet Street, up Ludgate Hill, along the Old Bailey, they had worked on her. As the magical shape plodded on, its steps growing slower and heavier, through the rain and the dark, they troubled her with a sense of the physical body she had left. At first indeed, as the walk began, she had endured only a great wish that she had again the body as well as the soul of Lester, the body that Richard had loved and for which she had herself felt a small admiration. She wished, if she were to be thus materially before her husband, to give again the hand she had given, to speak to him with the mouth he had kissed. She had no physical desires except to be in his eyes her own physical self. But as she thought of it, she grew disturbed. Her faults, on the whole, had not been physical. Her body had carried no past of fornication or adultery, nor had she therefore mystically to free it from those avenging unions. She had not to disengage her flesh from those other bodies, or to re-engage her flesh so that its unions should be redeemed, approved, and holy. Nor had she been given to the other luxurious commitments of the flesh. She had not been particularly lazy or greedy; as bodies go, hers was reasonably pure. As bodies go—but even then? More and more disliking this body to which she was transitorily bound, she more and more came to consider her dealings with her own. All through that long walk, she re-lived them, and always she ended with this other false disrelish. She again and again began by being conscious of her looks, her energy, her swiftness; again and again she would (except for mere fastidiousness, which was of no account) have tempted others with it, though not to commit herself; again and again she melted to delicate pleasures and grew dependent on them, and as she did so, she woke to find herself in the end one with this other. It was this false deformed death of which she was proud, with which she tempted, in which she took her delight. Hers was this, or at least no more than this; unless, for again and again in the end the sudden impulse sprang—unless she could still let it be what it had been ordained to be, worthy in its whole physical glory of Betty, of Richard, of the City she felt about her, of all that was unfamiliar to her in the name of God. Her past went with her all that walk; and by the end of the walk her past had taught her this.

Yet, having so thought of herself in humility and serious repentance all the way, it was, when at last she came into Jonathan's room, of Richard that she thought. She was agonized for what she felt must be his horror if, seeming to be in this shape, she spoke. Betty's cry of welcome went unnoticed; she was here to speak, and now how could she—how could she—speak? He was staring at—her? no; but at this; and he was her husband; how could she treat her husband so? All the coldnesses and all the angers were but delirium and bitterness of love; she could have helped them perhaps, but now this she could not help, and this was worst of all. She had for a moment a terrible fear that this was they; even that this was she, and that he—Oh he by whom alone in that world she lived—would know that this was she. The silence became a fearful burden to them all. It was Betty who saved them. She broke into action; she dashed across the room; she caught Jonathan's and Richard's hands. She cried out: "Come over here!"

The relief of her action released them; uncertainly, they obeyed. She pulled them across to the window; she said: "Turn round, both of you; look out there." She nodded her golden head at the darkness, and to Jonathan it seemed as if a rain of gold drove through the night and vanished. They obeyed her still; one hand on the nearer shoulder of each she held them there. She turned her head over her shoulder; she exclaimed: "Lester, say something to us." Lester, in a rush of gratitude, did so. She said, it is true, no more than "Hullo!" but the voice was undoubtedly her voice, and (though no louder than on earth) it filled the room. Jonathan, hearing it, jumped a little. Richard did not; there was, in all the universe, no place in which that voice was not recognizable and good. He answered, with the immediate instinct of something that might yet be love: "Hullo, darling!"

74

Lester, dallying with peace and half-forgetful of the others, said: "Have I been very long? I'm so sorry." "Sorry" is a word that means many things; there is in general a friendliness about it, and now it meant all friendliness. "We took such a time." Her laugh sounded in their ears. "Have you been waiting?"

Betty took her hand off Richard's shoulder. In the intimacy of those two, her hand was a solecism. Lester's voice went on: "But I've been tiresome so often, darling. I've been beastly to you. I——"

He said: "You've never been tiresome," and she: "No; speak true now, my own. I——"

He said: "Very well; you have. And what in all the heavens and hells, and here too, does it matter? Do we keep accounts about each other? If it's the last word I speak I shall still say you were too good for me."

"And——?" she said, and her laughter was more than laughter; it was the speech of pure joy. "Go on, blessing—if it's our last word."

"And I'm too good for you," Richard said. "Let me turn round now. It's all right; I promise you it's all right."

"Do, darling," she said.

He turned, and the others with him. They saw the long room, and at the other end the painting of the City that dominated the room as if it and not the wall behind it were the true end of the room, as if the room precisely opened there on that space and those streets; and as if some unseen nature present there united both room and painting, the light in it was within the room also and vibrated there. The table with the remnants of the meal, the wine still in the glasses, the back of the other canvas lying on the table—all these were massive with the light. Between them and the table stood the dwarf-woman, but somehow it did not matter to any of them. The full and lovely voice said, almost as if a rich darkness spoke within the light: "It's nice to see you all again."

Betty said: "It's blessed to see you. But what *is* this, my dear?" She nodded at the dwarf.

Lester said: "It was made by—I don't, even know who he is, but by the man in your room."

Richard said: "He's called Simon, and sometimes the Clerk, and he thinks himself no end of a fellow. Has he hurt you?"

"Not a bit," said Lester. "I've been with it of my own choice. But now I've seen you, I know what to do—before I go away. It must be taken back to him."

So much was suddenly clear to her. She was here—and Richard and Betty, and Jonathan too, were here for this purpose. It was time the magical dwarf was driven back to Simon. It had come from him; it must go to him. The Acts of the City were in operation; she felt their direction. She only could compel this movement; she only return to the false maker the thing he had falsely made. It was full time.

Betty said: "We were going to take him that other thing—the painting Jon did of him. You haven't seen it; but that doesn't matter. It's very good, but it'd be much better if he had it altogether. So Jon's being a saint and giving it to him…. Lester, there's someone else with you!"

It was fortunate that the Acts of the City had allowed the three those minutes to become accustomed to the voice and to the shape. For now the shape took a quick step forward, and there broke from it a sudden confused noise. Neither Richard nor Jonathan at all recognized the human voice that was mixed with that croaking and cackling, but Betty recognized it. She had feared it too much and too often not to know. She did not step backwards, but she flinched, as if the noise had struck her. She exclaimed: "Evelyn!"

The noise ceased abruptly. Jonathan took a step forward, but Betty caught his arm. She said: "No, really, Jon; it's too silly. I'm not afraid; I know perfectly well I'm not afraid. I was only surprised. Lester, you needn't stop her. Were you talking to me, Evelyn?"

"No-one," said the dwarf with a slow effort and in a harsh imitation of Evelyn's voice, "cares about me. I don't expect much. I don't ask for much. I only want you, Betty. Lester's so cruel to me. She won't cry. I only want to see you cry." It tried to lift its hands, but they only waggled. The body drooped, and the head fell on one side. So askew, it continued to emit sounds mostly indistinguishable. Now and then a sentence stood out. It said at last, clearly and with a slight giggle: "Betty looked so funny when she cried. I want to see Betty cry."

Jonathan said under his breath: "God be merciful to us all!" Betty said: "Evelyn, if you want to talk, come and talk. I can't promise to cry, but I'll listen." Richard said: "Must we waste time?"

The dwarf's head jerked, and turned as far as it could from one to the other. It gave back a little. Before those three, as if the consciousness of their eyes oppressed it, it fell together a little more. It said, with a final great effort: "You hurt me when you look at me. I don't want you to look at me. I want to look at you. Betty, you used to be frightened of me. I want you to be frightened of me."

Jonathan said with a sudden decision. "We can't do anything. Let's do what we can do. If we're to do it, let's go now." He went to the table and took up the canvas.

Betty said: "Shall we, Lester?" and the other voice, again filling the room, answered: "We'd better. Evelyn can't manage this, and I've only one thing to do with it—to take it back. Let's go."

Richard went quickly past Jonathan to the table. He picked up his glass; he waved to the others and they came to him. He tried to speak and could not. But Betty did. She too took her glass; she held it up; she said: "Good luck, Lester!" and they all drank. Richard flung his glass to the floor. As it smashed, the dwarf with a little squeal turned round and began stumbling towards the door. The three friends went after it.

It was very late when they came into the street, but in the light of a near standard they saw a single taxi moving slowly along. The driver was a big man; he saw Jonathan's lifted hand, slowed, and leaning back opened the door. They stood round the dwarf while, slowly and in utter silence, it scrambled clumsily in. Before either of the young men could speak, Betty had followed it and sat down by it. They sat opposite. Jonathan could not quite remember giving the address, but he supposed he must have done, for the door was closed on them and the carriage moved off in the night. In spite of Betty's face opposite him a macabre horror fell on Jonathan; all he had ever read, in fiction or history, of fatal midnight drives recurred to him: discrowned kings fleeing, madmen carried off to Bedlam, or perhaps sane men by careful plottings certified as mad, gagged men borne to private assassinations, gangsters taken for rides by gangsters, and through all a ghastly element of another kind—arrest of heretics, seizure of martyrs, witches clutched or witches clutching—in all the cities of all the world midnight and dark coaches rolling and things unnameable for good or evil about to be done. Something still deeper—there was then, or had been, one plain simple act which could only be done in such a night. Unless this night were now about to give place to a more frightening day—a dawn on some town where such creatures lived as this opposite him or his own imagined insects and had their own occupation, grisly, unseen in this sun, but visible to sickness in another light so much like this but not this.

Beside him Richard leaned back free from such distress, for he had already known that distress. He had been used to think that nothing could shock him; he had been wrong. The universe is always capable of a worse trick then we suppose, but at least when we have known it we are no longer surprised by anything less. Jonathan's horrid nightmares, oppressive as they were to him, were less distressing than the pain of a mother listening to her child choking with bronchitis in the night. Richard's endurance now, like hers, was of present and direct facts. He had seen something which, in the full sense of the words, ought not to be, and never before had he felt the full sense of the words. This was what everything that ought not to be was—this quiet agreement that it should be. It was a breach in nature, and therefore in his own nature. His own self-indulgence was of this kind; his dispassionate consideration might be and might not—that depended on him. And now in this happier world he had thought to enter, a thing as extreme struck him. He could not disbelieve Lester when she spoke of going; he could not even doubt that it ought to be. But except for that "ought to be" the coldness in his heart was indistinguishable from the earlier chill. The new birth refused him. He was as yet ignorant of the fact that this was one method of its becoming actual. He despaired.

But Lester, when she had walked in the dead City, piercingly aware of her own rejection, had known that despair, and its inflexibility had entered her and grown in her. She no longer drove her one-time friend with her old impatience; her strength was now the other side of her willingness to wait "a million years" or to know she was not even to be allowed that. In their swift passage to the dark coach she had felt the rain on the false flesh; she had felt it as the premonition of that lucid flowing water of separation. A double charge was laid on her, to expel this thing from the streets of London, and then herself to go. The falsity must go to its place of origin to be destroyed; to go, so literally, dust to dust. The City must have what belonged to it in the mode in which it belonged. She thought no more of tubes and tunnels filled with horrors. Matter was purified and earth was free, or to become so. But instead of the tunnels flowed the inexorable river. She too must go.

She saw the taxi roll through the streets; she saw the four sitting in it. She knew that, if her new sight strengthened, she would see even more clearly the whole construction, not only of the vehicle, but of false mortality and true mortality. She almost did see Richard so, in his whole miraculous pattern, all the particles of him, of the strange creature who was in every particle both flesh and spirit, was something that was both, was (the only word that meant the thing he was) a man. She loved him the more passionately for the seeing. And then she saw Betty move. She saw her turn to that contorted thing in the corner which, under these vivid and suffering intelligences, was now beginning to lose even the semblance of a woman, and she saw her put her living hand on its dead paw. She heard Betty say: "Evelyn!" and then again: "Evelyn, let's talk!" and through a dim mumble she heard Evelyn say: "I don't want you now." She saw—and could not see farther—a fixed pallid mask of a face moulded in and looking out of the false flesh with a scared malice, and she too cried out: "Evelyn, don't leave us!" She even made an effort to dominate it, but that failed at once; the false flesh she could command but not now the thing within the flesh. Evelyn said: "I hate you." The dead paw—

now hardly five-fingered—made an effort to shake off Betty's hand, and when that tightened on it jerked and pulled in order to get away. As it succeeded, the taxi came to a stop.

Chapter Ten

THE ACTS OF THE CITY

On the vigil of the hallows, it was gloomily and steadily raining. Few people were out in the streets of London and the curtains at most windows were again drawn together. Even delight in the peace could hardly find satisfaction in keeping them wide on such a night. Unpropitiously, the feast approached.

The Clerk was sitting in his hall. He had remained secluded there since he had dismissed the false woman into the outer world, and with that (as he believed) the spirit that had interrupted his work. He was a little more troubled than he wished to admit to himself, and that for two reasons. He had been more pricked than he had allowed by Betty's silence about him when she repeated to him the tumultuous records of the world's future. There was, to his mind, but one explanation—that some new weakness had taken her, and when he had been defeated in his operation he had even been able to use that as an explanation. This other being—now imprisoned and banished from him—had affected her and silenced her. The future was not therefore as she had said. The alternative possibility—that the future was as she had said, and that he would so soon have utterly vanished from the world—was too dreadful for him. He encouraged his mind into illusion. Illusion, to the magician as to the saint, is a great danger. But the master in Goetia has always at the centre of his heart a single tiny everlasting illusion; it may be long before that point infects him wholly, but sooner or later it is bound to do so. It was infecting Simon now. It was hurrying him.

He was reluctant to do what he was being driven, by that scurry in his mind, to intend. He knew well that for the greater initiate to fall back on the methods of the lesser initiate was unwise. In sorcery as in sanctity there is no return. The master in any art who abandons the methods of his mastery and falls back on prentice habits runs a fearful risk. No lover, of any kind, not even the lover of himself, can safely turn from maturity to adolescence. His adolescence is in his maturity. The past may be recalled and redeemed in the present, but the present cannot be forsaken for the past. Lester was exposed to the true method; Evelyn was seeking the false. But the magician runs a greater risk even than Evelyn's, for if he begins to return, his works begin to return to him. All this Simon had learned many years before, but till now it had never been a temptation to him; now it was. He had begun to fall back on crude early methods of magic. He had already conceded to his need the making of the false body; now he was about to concede more. To recover Betty by spiritual means would mean much careful planning and working. He sat with his eyes fixed on that window through which he desired to see her spirit come, and he knew he must first suspend and separate her physical life. Her body, especially with this new knowledge, this love-relation to another, was her safeguard. He must at once, by easy and quick methods, overthrow her body. The great face that gazed towards the window was more like the face in Jonathan's painting than anyone, even Jonathan, had ever seen it before.

He turned his mind to his paramour. She was then sitting at her solitary dinner, in her house at Highgate, and presently she felt herself beginning to breathe heavily, and her left hand began to shake. She knew the signs, and she set herself to making her mind empty. Such communications demand a technique not dissimilar to that of prayer. First she thought of nothing but him; when she had nothing but his image in her mind, she set herself to exclude that too. Her coffee was before her; no-one would come till she rang. She sat—that woman only just past fifty, though since that very morning she had aged and looked full ten years older—gazing out over the coffee, a statue of quiet meditation; and the image of him faded from her mind, and she sank into an inner stillness. It was in that stillness, the stillness of the threshold of a ghostly temple, that she heard her own voice saying aloud: "Hair. Bring me her hair." She heard it clearly the first time she said it, but she heard herself repeat it several times before she acted; where once she would have moved at once. But she was stiff to-night and tired, and in great wanhope, and it was only slowly that at last she raised herself, pressing on the arms of her chair, and went clumsily upstairs to Betty's room. There, peering among the bristles of the brushes, she found two or three short golden hairs. She picked them carefully out, put them in an envelope, and going downstairs got out her car and drove down to Holborn. It was an hour afterwards that the maid found that, for the first time in her experience, her mistress had left the dining-room without ringing.

When she reached the house she found Plankin just about to lock the door. As she reached it, and he waited for her, she almost thought that the small carved hand showed through the darkness palely lit and in motion, waving her to go on. Plankin said: "Good evening, my lady. It's a nasty night." She nodded to him and he nodded back. He said: "It's good to belong to the Father and to be inside. We'll be in our beds soon, most of us. The Father's got good beds for those he takes care of," and as she went down the hall she heard him behind her still saying: "Good beds; good beds."

Round the corner, through the small door. The hall was dark. She switched on one light—the single light that was just over the door. It did not penetrate far—just enough to let her dimly see the Clerk sitting in the throned chair and something shining upon his knees. He was waiting for her. She went straight across to him, took the hairs out of the envelope, and gave them to him. He was sitting quite still and holding on his knees a little lump of what seemed paste. It was that which shone. He took the hairs from her and laid them on the paste; then he began to mould it. It was very small, not more than two inches long, and as he pressed and moulded it he made it less; presently it was not much more than an inch. Then, as if he needed more, he put his hand inside his cassock and took it out again full of a kind of soft amorphous stuff, also shining. He added that to what he already held and worked at it. There was in the hall now only the light over the door and the phosphorescent glow of the image.

When it was finished, it was a rough shape of a woman, nothing like so finished as that other larger shape he had made that morning. He stood up and put it on the seat of his chair. He said to the woman by him: "I will make the enclosure now. You shall hold it when we are ready," and she nodded. He took three paces to the front of the throne, and bending his great height he began to walk backward round it in a circle, drawing after him the point of his left thumb upon the floor. It left behind it a softly shining trail as if it were the streak of a snail's path. When he had finished the circle, he took a pace nearer the chair, and began another circle, and when that in turn was finished, he went in turn to the four points of the compass and joined the two circles by four straight lines. As he did so the air within the circles grew heavy and stifling, as if they formed a kind of round thick wall which shut out health and easy breath. He stood up and paused for a few moments as if to recover, then he lifted the fixed endoplasmic shape in his hands, turned, and took his seat again upon the now secluded throne. He nodded heavily at the woman, and she came and knelt in front of him with her face towards him. She seemed much older now than she had been when she entered the hall; it was the fallen face of a woman of ninety that stared at him, and was still ageing, and the hands she put out were older too, thin and faintly tremulous. He gave the image, built round those golden hairs, into them, and she held it at about the height of her shoulders, a little above his knees. The only sound now was that of the rain upon the roof.

The Clerk said: "Call her; call her often!" She obediently began; she could not make her voice anything but flat and lifeless, but she began automatically: "Betty!... Betty!... Betty!" and presently the repetition seemed to strengthen her. While she called, the Clerk put his hand again inside his cassock, but this time near his breast, and drew out what seemed a long needle. It too was bright, but with the brightness of actual steel; it was not like the doll, and it glinted in the efflorescence of the doll. There was about it almost a natural beauty, but the presence of that slip of loveliness accentuated the strange horror of the rest. The Clerk took it in his left hand. It had at its head a tiny gold knob, and on this he settled his forefinger, holding it about half-way down, between his thumb and his second and third fingers; the fourth came round to the ball of his thumb. He said: "Louder!" In that oppressive air, Sara Wallingford could not easily obey, but she made an effort, and her body unexpectedly responded. Her voice came out with a summons that was like a thin shriek: "Betty!... Betty!" And all the time she held up the doll to her master. The Clerk leant forward and raised the needle.

For almost a minute her voice shrieked alone, and then it was no longer alone. Other shrieks from the house beyond answered it and joined with it. The sudden multiplication of sound sang in her ears; she jerked and almost dropped the endoplasmic doll. She recovered herself immediately, but in that half-second's loss of control the Clerk had stabbed at the doll. The needle struck the tip of her middle right-hand finger, and as he pulled back his weapon a drop of blood stood out and oozed on to the fixed jelly. The Clerk looked at her; his eyes drew her yet more upright on her knees. Her finger continued to bleed; the shoulder of the doll showed crimson from the drops.

She went very white, and had stopped her high old woman's scream. It was he and not the secrets for which she had cared, and she did not know much of them, but something she could not help knowing, and what she knew made her afraid. His great face loomed over her and would not let her go. The face was the face of the Exile of Israel, of the old Israel and the new, and all Israel else was free to the Return. She saw, unknowing, as she looked up, the face of all exile, the face of the refusal of the Return, and it seemed to her as imbecile as it had been in the painting, though now indeed she had forgotten the painting. She tried to let go the doll, and failed. Her left hand could loosen it, but it remained fixed to her right, sealed to it by the blood. She held it in her left, and tried to pull her right free, but she could not. She felt indeed all the pain of the rending flesh, but the flesh was not rent. As her blood ran into the doll, so her heart's indifference passed into her flesh; her brain knew what ought to be, but her body refused her brain. The organic nature of her blood made her one with the doll, and more intimately much than the golden hairs could unite Betty to it. She realized the substitution that was taking place; she was likely to die in Betty's stead.

She knew she was about to die. She knew that the Clerk would not spare her and that even the thought of sparing would not occur to him. She had hated all things for his sake, and so did he, but now his hate was against her too. But she was allowed justice; she was allowed to hate even herself for his sake. After that instinctive effort to escape, she accepted that; she even gloried in it. Her heart flung itself up into that great alien sky of his face, and was absorbed in it. She had but one thing to ask, and that unvocally; that he should strike to kill before the doll had become even more she than Betty. She had a vague and terrible fear that the substitution might be so complete that Betty would not die. Let him stab before that happened! let him strike both of them into whatever waited! let her have but the chance to meet her daughter there, and see which of them could rule!

She was conscious of one other thing, though she did not properly know what it was. There passed through the face above her a series of vibrations, waves passing down it from forehead to chin. They reverberated in her as a kind of perpetual drumming, increasing as the face changed sea-like down from brow to point, and dying as the pause came, and again beginning as from beneath the hair the wave issued and swelled and sank and swelled, change after change of heavy cloud in that now to her almost shapeless sky. These waves, could she have realized it, came from the drumming rain—heavy, rapid, continuous; October closing in a deluge. The vigil of the saints was innumerably active in the City, and all London lay awake under it.

As if her prayer had moved the opaque cloud to yield to it, the slender steel flashed and struck again. She saw it; and, whether through his error or her shrinking, she felt the sudden sting in her forefinger—as if she were to be united to the image, member by member, blow by blow. But, for all the sudden pain and fear, it was not her mouth from which even now those screams were issuing; she after her first wound had become dumb. They came from two sources. The first was within the double barrier; it was held between her hands. In the head of the rough endoplasmic shape a hole opened, and out of the hole came screams much like her own had been. It was the most startling and the most dangerous. It had been the first sound of this which caused her to quiver and deflected Simon's aim, for it meant that a weakness and a peril were already within the circle. The wall had not yet been broken by any pressure from without—as the operation in Betty's bedroom had been. The magic here was mechanically shrilling under some turn within it; it was beginning to twist upon itself. The thing done was in active and antagonistic return.

But the noise was multiple; that scream was not solitary. Rising through the drumming of the rain—of which all this time the Clerk had never been entirely unaware, as it is said that those in deep prayer can hear and even consider sounds without distraction—came the screams from beyond the threshold, but now from only just beyond. Those who screamed were already at the door. The house had thrown them from its upper rooms, or rather that which had entered the house. All in the bedrooms and in the offices and the rest had been locked and silent and asleep when through the night and the rain that single taxi had rolled to the outer door. It stopped; the driver leaned back, put out his hand, and threw it open. Richard had been the first to descend; then Jonathan and Betty; lastly, the reluctant thing that had first got in. Jonathan gave some silver to the driver, and the vehicle disappeared into the darkness. They turned to the house; the carved hand glowed; and then, as they passed it, Betty put out a hand with a movement as if she brushed a twig away, and the thing went out suddenly. The dwarf, driven first of all the company, flinched as if it had itself been struck. It reached the door, and was halted, for though alone of all in London, it might of its nature have passed through that door yet the high and now dominating spirit who controlled it knew that neither her husband nor her friend's lover could. Jonathan began to use the knocker. Richard looked for a bell and could find none, until a thought struck him, and taking a step or two back he peered by the light of a sheltered match at the centre of the carved hand. He saw there a discoloured spot in the palm, something which might have been a bell, the nerve of the physical machinery of that house, whose brain (now secluding itself into imbecility) lay in the round hall within. They could not hear the sound of the bell, nor was Jonathan's hammering and occasional kicking at the door much more than a relief to his own feelings. The noise seemed deadened and only an echo of itself. Presently however a window went up above them, and a voice which Richard recognized as the doorkeeper's said: "What's all this? You can't see the Father now. It's too late."

"We've something for him," Jonathan called; "something of his own."

79

"You can't do anything for him, and you can't give him anything," the voice of Plankin said. "It's late; it's too late."

Another voice interrupted him. It came from the dwarf, but they knew it for Evelyn's and as it sounded the dwarf in a paroxysm of strength beat on the door with its hands. It cried: "Let me in! Let me in!"

Plankin, unseen above them, said: "I don't know, I'm sure. It isn't right to open the door after dark. The Father doesn't wish it. There's things in the dark that might frighten us."

Evelyn screamed: "Let me in! It's raining; you can't leave me in the rain." She added, more quietly and snivelling: "I shall catch a dreadful cold." The dwarf struck again at the door, and this time there broke out under the false hands a deep booming sound, as if the previous faint echo had now passed into a cavern of great depth. Jonathan had ceased to knock and Richard took his hand from the discoloured palm. This, at last, was the proper summons to that gatehouse; that which they had brought must itself demand entrance. At its call—dead woman and inorganic shape—the gatekeeper, if at all, would come down and open. They could not now hear Plankin for the noise, any more than they could see him for the night. They waited.

The door began to open—less than a crack; they could hardly have known it had not the dwarf, tearing and scrabbling, flung itself at the crack. Both its possessing spirits urged it there; there, with a yelp of delight, it pressed. The threshold shook; Betty and her friends felt it move, and the door, as if of its own accord, swung more widely back, revealing Plankin half-dressed, and carrying him with it. He stared at the intruder, as he staggered back. The dwarf sprang jerkily into the lit hall. Betty and the others followed, and as they did so the eyes of the gatekeeper changed. Dismay came into them; he gasped; he threw his hands to his head; he cried: "Oh! Oh!" Richard, as he saw and heard, remembered a phrase from their interview of that morning— "a tumour in the head". As he recollected it, and saw the dreadful consciousness of returning pain, he heard a clamour break out on the floor above. The dwarf had thrust past Plankin, and was scuttling away down the hall. As it pierced into the house the clamour grew—a hubbub of cries and thuds and shouts and hurrying feet and crashing doors. This was the Return, and this the operation of inflexible law.

They appeared; they came, stumbling and roaring, down the stairs—all those who carried the Clerk's mark in their bodies. First, an old woman, in a nightgown, eyes running tears and hand clutching her side where the cancer had begun again to gnaw, and she had been waked by it, with only one thought, and that all confused—to be healed, to get to her Comforter. A few steps behind came a young man partly dressed, coughing and spitting blood on to the stairs, and feeling vainly for the handkerchief he had in his first waking spasm forgotten. And after him a still younger man, who as he came was being twisted slowly back into deformity, his leg withering and drawing up, so that he was presently clinging to the banisters and hopping down sideways. Others followed, some with unseen ailments and some with open wounds, but all hurrying with one instinctive desire—to get to Simon, to find their Father, to be healed and at rest. Only one of all that household was not there—one, the paralytic, who had waked to find her flesh turning again a prison, she already half-immobile, and was now lying part in and part out of bed, anguished and alone in her room. The rest were down the stairs and in the hall and hurrying as best they could round the corner into that corridor in the wall to the hole that gave on the centre of all. In front of them, and quicker than any, went the dwarf, and as if in a miserable retinue they followed, Plankin the first. The hunt for the miracle-monger was up; they rushed to be again sealed his own, but there was something dangerous in the way they went.

Betty had paused in the open door till the scurry had gone by. Her hand was in Jonathan's, who still carried the canvas of the painting under his other arm. Richard was on Betty's other side. At last, she too began to move; she went quietly, and her face was very serious and calm. As they went down the hall, they saw that the walls there, and still more those of the narrow corridor when they entered it were running with drops and thin streams of water. Richard looked up. He saw that, here and there, the rain was beginning to come through the roof; he felt a few drops on his head, on his face, on his eyelids. But for the most part the rain was not yet upon the walls; it was the condensation of something in the air, some freshness of water that lay on them, but left the air dry and sterile for want of it. The walls absorbed it; under it they changed to a kind of slime.

When they came to the hall it was not so. There the roof was still sound, and the walls, as far as they could see, still dry. Before them the diseased throng were hurrying across the floor, and the three friends could not clearly see the dwarf beyond them or the two encircled figures beyond it. The woman, as all this crowd burst in, did not move, but the Clerk turned his eyes. Plankin was coming so fast that he outwent even the dwarf, who indeed seemed to pause and totter as it took there the first step, so that the others all broke out around it, and came first to the invisible barrier. That perhaps would not have held against any indifferent human being; it was not primarily meant for such protection—much less against divine scepticism or heavenly joy. Brutality might have trampled it. It was against them—the only thing about which the word can be properly used—illusion. But against these poor weak, demented and desirous things, it held sufficiently. They scattered about the outer circle, tottering and crawling round it, surrounding it, beating with their hands on an invisible wall, wailing and moaning, and one howling dog-like. The Clerk took no slightest notice; he was looking, and his eyes were very wary, at the other thing that now began to advance.

It walked more steadily now, as if it had found some centre of determination in itself. When Lester's influence had been on it, there had been in its movements an irrepressible jerkiness. But now that jerkiness had passed; it moved inflexibly, as if it neither could nor wished to stop. When it had almost reached the barrier, Betty pulled her hand from Jonathan's and ran after it. She caught up with it; in a swift and strong motion she caught its hand; she exclaimed: "Evelyn, do stop!"

The Clerk had been watching it come. Now he stood up. As he did so, he released from the intensity of his concentration the endoplasmic image in the hands of his paramour; it fell; and she, unable to let it go, fell forward also at that sudden unbalancing release. The Clerk had, at the same time, taken a step towards the barrier, so that she fell against the chair, and the doll, to which her hands were still fastened by her own blood, lay on the seat. She lay propped there, and she turned her head, so that she saw, at a little distance, not only the dwarf, of which she knew nothing, but handlinked with it her daughter, her rival and enemy. That Betty was wholly free from her. She saw her almost as Jonathan saw her, beautiful and good, very much Betty. That Betty was quite unlike the doll she helplessly held. The doll was all she had of Betty, and even the doll was becoming, as her blood soaked into it, less and less like Betty and more and more like herself. She was being, by an operation which her own will had in the beginning encouraged, slowly substituted for Betty. She lay, rigid and fixed, propped by the edge of the chair, and into the insatiable image through those two small pricks her blood continued to drain.

The Clerk made a quick savage motion, and the clamour of the diseased creatures ceased. He looked round the circle, collecting their pitiable eyes; then he raised his hand, pointing it at the dwarf, and he said: "Drag it away!"

Most of them ignored him. A few, of those least diseased, did look round at the dwarf, but they looked back at once. It was not disobedience but impotence that held them there. Someone—it was difficult to know who, in that throng—said feebly: "Make us well, Father!" The dwarf, dragging at Betty's hand, and pulling her after it, advanced another few steps. Now it was right up against the barrier, and had, with a definite and powerful thrust, got one foot just over the circle by some half an inch. There it seemed to halt, as if it could press no farther. Betty still clung to its hand; it was all she could do. She called out: "Lester, do help me! I can't hold her."

Indeed nothing—neither the Clerk's frown nor Betty's clasp—could now affect the mad determination of the lost spirit. Evelyn was over-ridden by the fear that even this refuge in which she somehow was might be snatched from her. She saw the barrier almost as a material wall; if she could get this body within it, she would be safe, or as safe as she could be. The attraction which that point exercised on the mere material image was strengthened by her own will; a false union held her and it. Since the house had been entered, there had been no need for Lester to drive the shape; it had been only too urgent to hurry on. Only Betty still clung to it. She flung out her other hand behind her, as if to Jonathan; and Jonathan sprang forward and caught it. As if aware of them for the first time, the Clerk lifted his eyes and saw the three friends.

Jonathan and Betty were too occupied to meet his eyes, but Richard did. And as he did, the sudden recollection of what this man had offered him rose bitterly in his heart. This fellow had offered to rule Lester for him, to give him back his wife or not as he might choose—he! He had been still lingering by the door, but now suddenly he too moved. If Lester was to go from him, she should go with all honours. He walked forward to join the others, and when he had reached them he took the canvas from under Jonathan's arm. He said: "Father Simon, my wife wishes us to return your property. Take it."

He lightly tossed the canvas towards the Clerk; it flew over the circles and struck Simon on the shoulder. The Clerk gave a sudden squeal. Richard went on, holding himself very upright and imperious: "If I had not been a fool in the past, you would not have been able to——"

"Darling, must you be quite so savage?" Lester's voice half-laughing interrupted. "Tell him what you ought to tell him—that will be enough."

Richard had forgotten his commission. Now he remembered. He said: "Yes … well … but I think it's too late. Lester is free of you, and Betty is free, and the world will soon be free. But just before it is—I was sent to offer you everything—all the kingdoms in it and their glory. You were to be asked to meet those others who are like you; you were, all three of you, to be… how do I know what? masters, for all I do know. But I think we've come in time. Let's see if your friends will."

A sudden silence fell. Richard listened—all of them, even the Clerk, all except Evelyn, listened—for that other voice. It did not then come. Lester was still clearly aware of what was happening. But she was also aware of a certain difference in her surroundings. She had seemed to enter the house with the others, even to come as far as the hall, but when the others had gone right in, when Richard had gone and had begun to speak, when she had broken in on him with that gay but serious protest, she had become aware that she was no longer related to that deformed image. It had itself released her, merely by entering the hall. For as it did so, and she for the first second with it, she had found herself once more in the rain. It was driving down over and past her on to—the Thames? some wide river, flowing, flowing on beneath her; and the pale ghastly light in the hall had changed. Within the rain a fresher light was opening. It shone on the rain and on the river; and the room with its companies was still there, but it stood on the river, which flowed through it, and in the rain, which fell through it. The light was like dawn, except that it had in it a tinge redder than dawn, and the same tinge was in the river and the rain, exquisite and blood-roseal, delicate and enriching. Only she felt again the awful sense of separation. It was like a sharp pain in a great joy. She gave herself to it; she could no other; she had consented long before—when she married Richard perhaps—or was consenting now—when she was leaving him. Her heart sank; without him, what was immortality or glory worth? and yet only without him could she even be that which she now was. All, all was ending; this, after so many preludes, was certainly death. This was the most exquisite and pure joy of death, in a bearing of bitterness too great to be borne. Above her the sky every moment grew more high and empty; the rain fell from a source far beyond all clouds. Below her the myriad drops, falling in slanting lines, struck the great river in innumerable little explosions, covering the whole surface. She saw each of them with an admirable exactitude—each at the same time as she saw all, and the flowing river and the empty sky, and herself no longer bodily understood, but a point, a point reflected from many drops and pierced by many drops, a spark of the light floating in the air. But she was not very conscious of herself as herself; she no longer thought of herself as bearing or enjoying; the bitterness, the joy and the inscape of those great waters were all she knew, and among them the round hall, with those mortal figures within it, and its window open, as she now saw it, on the waters. Even Richard's figure there had lost its immediate urgency; something once necessary and still infinitely precious, which had belonged to it, now lay deep, beyond all fathoming deep, in the current below, and could be found again only within the current or within the flashing rain. Of any future union, if any were to be, she could not begin even to think; had she, the sense of separation would have been incomplete, and the deadly keenness of the rain unenjoyed.

The rain did not seem to her to be driving into the round hall; if it did, it was there invisible to her. The window was open, and she became aware that towards the window, from a great distance, two forms were moving. They came walking upon the waters, great-headed, great-cloaked forms, forms like Simon, two Simons far beyond the hall, coming towards the hall and Simon. She thought at first there were more—a whole procession of Simons, but it was not so; there were but the two. They were going directly towards the window, one behind the other, and as she saw them she had a sudden sense that never, never, would she have asked either of them to bring her a drink of water in the night. She would have been terrified of what they brought; there would have been something in the glass—as if the Richard of past days had put secret poison in the drink; and much worse than that, for human malice was but human malice, and comprehensible and pardonable enough to any human; but this would have been a cool and immaterial—and the worse for being immaterial—antipathy to—to? to all, a drink the taste of which would have been a separation without joy. They came on, as it were below her—not that she had at all a place to see them from—and as they passed or seemed to pass, she had a moment's terror that it was not they but she. The great-headed, great-cloaked, steadily walking forms were wholly unlike her, but yet they were she—double, immense, concealed, walking through the unfelt rain on the unyielding water, antipathetic, relegated to antipathy; as if in the shadowy City of her early death she had gone another way, and through the deep tunnels and tribes had come out on this water, and (grown in them to this size and covered in them with this wrapping to hide herself) were walking on to some quiet and awful consummation. This had been the other way, the way she had just not gone. Behind them, as they went, the faint roseal glow in the waters and the rain gathered thicker and followed, and deepened as it followed. The colour of it—rose or blood or fire—struck up the descending lines of rain and was lost somewhere in that empty upper sky above her; but below it was by now almost a wall which moved after those forms; and absorbed and changed the antipathy they diffused; and all behind them the freshness of the waters and the light was free and lovely.

On earth—that is, among those earthly—the turn of the night had come. The morning of the feast imperceptibly began, though none of them knew it—none? the Clerk knew. As a man feels the peculiar chill that comes, especially in early spring or late autumn, with the rising sun, so he, long before any sun had risen, felt a new coldness in the hall. The air within the charmed circle was heavy, but as the Acts of the City took charge and the nearness of all the hallows grew everywhere within the outer air, it became dank and even more oppressive with a graveyard chill. More than humanity was holy and more than humanity was strange. The round hall itself, and its spare furnishings, and the air in it were of earth, and nothing could alter that nature. The blessedness of earth was in them and now began to spread out of them. There too were the hallows, and their life began to awake, though the City itself seemed not yet awake. Invisible motions stirred, and crept or stepped or flew, as if a whole creation existed there unseen. The Acts of the City were at hand. Simon's eyes were still on the dwarf, which by now had pressed still farther into the barrier, as if it was working its way through some thick moulded stuff which could not quite halt it. It was delayed also by its paw, being still caught in Betty's; for all its spasmodic tugging it could not quite free itself from that young passionate clasp. But it had dragged Betty herself very near the barrier. Her other hand was in Jonathan's, and his arm was round her. As her foot touched the outer circle, she looked round at him and said: "Don't hold me now, Jon. I must go with her."

Jonathan said: "You'll do nothing of the sort. What's the good? Let her go where she wants. It's I who need you, more than ever she can."

Betty answered breathlessly: "No, really, Jon. I *must* go; after all, we did know each other. And you're different; you can manage. Besides, I shouldn't be the least good to you if—— Let me go, darling. I can't leave her to die again. I was glad she was dead the first time, so I must be with her now."

Jonathan tried to resist, but all his energy, and all the energy of his art, was in vain. He set his feet; they slipped. He dragged at Betty's slim form; it advanced. He said: "Don't; it's hell. What shall I do?"

Betty, faintly, panted: "Hell? it won't hurt me; of course it won't. I *must* go; darling, let me."

Their voices, quiet enough, were dreadfully loud in the hall where there was no other sound, except always of the rain. Jonathan called: "Richard, come and help me!"

Richard said—and if there was an impurity in his answer, it was hardly avoidable; a deadly touch was in his heart and more than Jonathan he knew that certain departures must be; if he spoke with the least possible impatience, it was but mortal—Richard said: "I shouldn't worry. You won't have her if you keep her; when she wants to go she ought to go."

His eyes were still on the Clerk, and the Clerk's on Betty. At this moment, suppose as he might that he still had his whole ancient purpose in mind, it was a dream and an illusion. The sight of his daughter and slave, whole, well, and free, distracted him. He forgot the theory of magic, the principle of the physical and spiritual categories of identity, the philosophy and metaphysic of Goetia. Spells had failed and images had failed. He was more a common man than ever before, and he forgot all but the immediate act. That remained: killing remained. He saw the body of Betty, and the hand that held the needle crept slowly up his side. Inch by inch she drew nearer; inch by inch he raised the weapon. He fixed his eyes on her throat.

They were all now in a world of simple act. The time for thought, dispute, preparation was done. They were in the City. They were potent to act or impotent to act, but that was the only difference between any of them. The eyes of the woman who lay, incapable of act, against the abandoned chair, were also on Betty and greedy with the same murderous desire. The diseased creatures, also incapable, who lay around the circle, trembled and moaned a little with their helpless longing for the act of healing. She and they alike yearned towards act, and could not reach it. The dwarf-form was still in motion, and its motions as it forced its way on were both its own and Evelyn's—it magically drawn to its origin, she spiritually driving to her refuge. Betty felt that invisible soft mass press against her everywhere—against head and breasts, hands and thighs and legs. She gasped out to Jonathan: "Let go—you must. I may; not you. Only one of us, and I knew her." She wrenched her own hand free from his and struck it backward against him, as Lester had struck at Richard, one gesture whether accurst or blest. In the fierceness of her knowledgeable love, she struck so hard—all heaven in the blow—that he loosed his arm from her and fell back a pace. Richard caught and steadied him. At that moment, as Betty entered the circle, the rain broke in.

It came with a furious rush, as if it had beaten the roof down under it. But in fact the roof had not fallen. The rain drove through it, and down over all of them, torrential, but torrential most over the centre of the circle as if the centre of a storm was settled there. Under the deluge the doll on the chair at once melted; it ran over the woman's hands and wholly disappeared, except for a thin film of liquid putrescence which covered them, pullulating as if with unspermed life. She saw it, and under it her hands still bloody; she shook them wildly and tried to tear at them, but the thin pulsing jelly was everywhere over them, and her fingers could not get through it. For the first time in her life she began to sob, with a hideous harsh sound; and as her obstinacy melted like the doll under the rain she scrambled to her feet and made for Simon, the tears on her aged cheeks, clutching at him, with those useless and helpless hands. He did not notice her; it was his misfortune.

As if the barrier itself had also disappeared under the rain, the dwarf-figure began suddenly to move loosely. It slipped and almost fell over; then it righted itself and tottered on. But at the same time it began to lose even the rough shape it had. The rain poured down on it; its head ran thickly into its shoulders; then it had no head nor shoulders, but still it staggered forward. The paw that Betty held became damp mud in her grasp and oozed through her fingers; its legs, such as they were, bent and came together, and then it had no legs, and was only a lump which was madly bumping on, and then at the edge of the second circle it lost power altogether and toppled down, dropping just within that circle, and falling in great splashes of mud over Simon's feet. He had, so far, the adoration he desired.

Betty had stood still where she had lost hold. Simon looked once at the splashes; then, as quick as the holy rain itself, he flung himself forward and struck with his steel at his daughter's throat. The weapon touched her, swerved, scratched, and was gone. The two young men had moved, but something had been before them. The bloody and filthy hands of the old woman, blind with her tears, had caught Simon's upper arm as he launched himself, and the thrust was deflected. The hand that held the steel was pulled away, and, opening as it fell, dropped the weapon. Betty put out her hand and lightly caught it. She glanced at it curiously, and as she stepped back to Jonathan gave it to him with a smile. The Clerk furiously and with a strange cry flung himself round after his mistress, and as they swung in a clutching frenzy and she falling backward before him, he saw across and beyond her the window of the hall, and there he saw and knew his end.

There stood in the window two shapes which he at once recognized. They were exactly alike; their huge all-but-skeleton heads were thrust a little forward; their cloaks of darkness were wrapped round them; their blank eyes were turned to him. They had, in the beginning, been exactly like him, but his human flesh, even his, carried a little the sense of its own experiences, and theirs only indirectly and at one remove. They had therefore the effect now of slightly sinister caricatures of him—as the doll, though more horribly, of Betty and the dwarf of any woman. It was the nature of that world to produce not so much evil art as bad art, and even Jonathan's painting was more truthful to its reality than any reproduction of its own. But each reproduction had its own proper quality. The heavenly rain drove on these shapes without visible effect; they were, however perversely, of human flesh, and indeed, in so far as they were anything, were Simon himself. The grace drove against them from behind, as if it were driving them back to him; or perhaps it had been their coming which stirred and shook the unseen clouds, and left a void the living waters rushed in to fill. The roseal glow behind them in the waters was now very deep and filled the window with what was becoming not so much a glow as a fume of colour. An opaque cloud gathered. It had been so when that other Jew ascended; such a cloud had risen from the opening of the new dimensions into which he physically passed, and the eyes of the disciples had not pierced it. But that Jew had gone up into the law and according to the law. Now the law was filling the breach in the law. The blood of all victims and the fire of all avengers was in it—from Abel to those of London and Berlin—yet it was merely itself. It was an act, and as an act it followed, of its own volition, wave-like, high-arching. The shapes began to advance, and it also. The Clerk stood rigid, at his feet the body of his mistress; across the floor those other Clerks came on.

He made, within himself, one last effort. But these were too much he; all the years, in the most secret corner of his heart, he had sustained them so. His thoughts had shaped their brains, his words their voices. He had spoken in himself and in them. What he now said to them, he must say to himself. He began to bid them stop, but as he did so he found himself stiffen into an even more fixed rigidity. He tried to look them down, but he could no more catch any meaning in their eyes than he could see his own. He moved his hand to trace against them in the air a significant and compelling figure of magic, and he felt the earth shake under him and the burden of the air weigh on him to crush him as he did so. To unmake them he must unmake himself. There was only one other possibility; he might attempt, here, with no preparation, to unite them again with himself, and make them again he. He must act, and the act might be successful. He consented.

He crossed the barrier; he went forward. They too, each head slightly turning towards him, continued to advance, in the steady measure of his own steps as his of theirs. He began to murmur spells, of which the beating rhythm mingles with those which sustain flesh, but he felt again a creeping in his own flesh, and desisted. In the seclusion of the circles, protected by them, he might have found and practised a distinction. Here, in the confusion of the rain, he could not. It beat on him, and he could not think; it drove against him, and he could not see. He went on against it, but the growing roseal light confused him still more. It bewildered him, and he lost sight of the shapes until suddenly they loomed out of it very close to him. He unexpectedly thought "This is death", and knew himself weaken at the thought.

He managed to pronounce a word of command. They stopped, but then also he too stopped. He obeyed himself. He knew he needed time—time and shelter from the rain and the rose-light, and the rose-smell; which was not only a rose-smell but a smell of blood and of burning, of all those great crimson things. He smelt crimson between him and them, and saw it too, for that rich colour had ceased to over-arch them, and was sweeping down and round them, gathering and thickening, as if from light it were becoming liquidity, and yet he could not feel it. It grew and shut them in, all three, two not able to speak, and one not daring to speak. Only through it there went out from all three a blast of antipathy. He hated them, and since they held his hate they hated him. The hate seemed to swell in a nightmare bubble within the rose which was forming round them, cloud in cloud, overlying like petals. Simon made a quick half-spring as if to overleap it, and so did they; but he failed and fell back, and so did they. The smell of the rose was changing to the smell of his last act, to the smell of blood. He looked down; he saw below him the depth of the rose. A sudden fresh blast of rain fell on him and drove him deeper, and so those others. It flashed past him in an infinity of drops, as of points falling—at first crystal, then of all colours, from those almost too dark to be seen through to those almost too bright to be seen. They fell continuously between him and those other faces, in which he could now see those waves passing which his devotee had seen in his own face. The bright showers of the hallows flashed, and beyond him he could see only his multiplied self; and all he could do against them was only done to himself.

The rose began to withdraw. He felt himself carried with it, and slipping more deeply into it. The smell of blood was in his nostrils; the touch of burning on his flesh; this was what the crimson must be to him. He stared, as he sank and as that in which he was held moved in its own fashion, at the rain of swift-darting points between him and himself. The City, so, was visible to him. "If I go down into hell, thou art there"; but if I go down into thee——? If even yet he could attend to those points, he would escape hell; he would never have been in hell. If he could not, he had his changing and unchanging faces to study. He stared at them, imbecile; imbecile, they stared back—farther and farther, deeper and deeper, through the rose and the burning and the blood.

At the moment when the Clerk met the other Clerks, when the rose-light began to thicken and swim and gather round them, the three friends also felt that final blast of rain, falling on and even through them. Jonathan and Richard shrank under it, as under a burst of ordinary rain. Betty, still fresh from the lake of power, the wise waters of creation, lifted her face to it and felt it nourishing her. It was she who saw, as the driving torrent dwindled and passed, a fume of crimson rising, as if the rain had so fallen on the shaping rose that it sent up a cloud as of the smell of rose-gardens after rain. The smell lingered, but the cloud sank. As if she looked down a great distance she saw a small pool crimson in the light, and that too vanishing, till it was no more than the level of dark wine in a wine cup, and within it, before it vanished, she saw the whole City through which she had so often passed, vivid and real in that glowing richness. But she lost that sight as she realized that the City opened all ways about her and the hall in which she stood, in which also the daylight now visibly expanded. She heard the early noises of London outside the hall. She sighed with delight, and turned to the morning joy; smiling, she turned to her lover. He looked back at her, he still young and already a master in a certain knowledge of that City. Yet it was not he—it was Richard over whom the Acts of the City more closely hovered, and he whose face, like Lester's once in Betty's own room, was touched with the sombre majesty of penitence and grief and a young death.

But there were others in the hall. The diseased, except for an occasional sob, were silent now, the clear light showing them more pitiable. The body of Sara Wallingford lay where she had fallen; she had not moved. It was neither she nor the sick whom Betty and her friends first saw. Before them, in what had once been the circle, were the two dead and living girls. They seemed to be in their earthly shapes, their earthly clothes. Betty took a step or two towards them, and there, in an overpowering ordinariness, they stood, as any three young women might, deciding occupation, exchanging chat. It was Evelyn who spoke. Her eyes darting from Betty to Lester and back, she said: "Don't you interfere with me. I won't let you. I won't. Don't try."

Lester said: "Look, Evelyn, we've often gone out together; let's do it again. Come with me to-day and we'll think what there is to do."

Betty made a motion to speak, but Lester smiled at her and she ceased. The voices and the words might have been of any moment in the past. Lester went on: "Come, you might as well. I'm sorry if I've been … stupid. It was wrong. If I ever made use of you, come and make use of me. I only want you to. I do. I do. Let's go and see what we can find!"

Evelyn said: "I suppose you think that's kind. You think it's clever to be kind, don't you? I always hated being with you, and I daresay sooner or later I can find someone else there, thank you."

"Yes," said Lester, "I'm afraid you may."

The words, to all but Evelyn, brought a sinister thought of that other strange world. But Evelyn was past noting even that. When her shelters had melted round her, she had not known in her despair what she would do; and now she only knew that she would not let herself be caught. Lester and Betty were trying to catch her, to keep her, to pain her; they had always hated her. But she would beat them. She made a rush; she ran between them; she dodged the hands that were not flung out; she cried: "Let me go" to those who had not held her. She ran to the window; the yard outside was very lonely and spectral. She almost hesitated. But she looked back over her shoulder and saw Lester move. She cried out: "You thought you'd got me, didn't you?"

They saw the immortal fixity of her constricted face, gleeful in her supposed triumph, lunatic in her escape, as it had had once a subdued lunatic glee in its cruel indulgences; and then she broke through the window again and was gone into that other City, there to wait and wander and mutter till she found what companions she could.

Betty looked at Lester, and they were silent. Then Lester said: "We might have found the waters together, she and I. Well, I must go. Good-bye, my dear. Thank you for being sweet."

Betty exclaimed: "But what about——" Out of sheer courtesy to those who might hear her, she checked herself, but her eyes were on the unhappy throng, and she made a small gesture with her hand. She did not know who they were nor how they came to be in that house, but she saw what they were suffering. Lester shook her head. She said: "They are for you, my dear. You can do it; you've done harder things. It'll take something out of you, of course, but you can. Good-bye." She looked across at Richard. She said: "Dearest, I did love you. Forgive me. And thank you—Oh Richard, *thank you*! Good-bye, my blessing!" She stood, quiet and very real, before them; almost she shone on them; then the brightness quivered in the air, a gleam of brighter light than day, and in a flash traversed all the hall; the approach of all the hallows possessed her, and she too, into the separations and unions which are indeed its approach, and into the end to which it is itself an approach, was wholly gone. The tremor of brightness received her.

Betty was the first to move. She looked at those who remained in the hall, besides her own friends. She was, since Lester had spoken, clear what was to be done. But she felt a little as she had done on Highgate Hill, though now even more at peace. A troublesomeness was approaching, the result of the act to which she was, by her friend's word, committed. The act was to be hardly hers, yet without her it could not be. But now that other companion for whom on the hill she had sighed and called was with her; the extra grace involved an extra labour; without the labour, of what value the grace? She said impulsively: "Jon, I will try not to be tiresome."

He did not answer directly, but he put his arm about her shoulders, and said: "What about your mother?"

They went to her. They knelt and looked and touched and spoke. She showed no sign, lying there living but inert. It would be long before she came to herself, and then she would not come to herself. When presently she woke and tried to move, she would wake without knowledge, without memory, lost to all capacity and to all care. She would not know who she was or where she was or who those were that were about her or what they did—not even what they did for her, for the things that were done—the dressing, the feeding, the taking into the air—would be things to which she could attach no words. She had given herself away, and her self would be no longer there, or rather (as if it were a new-born child) would have to be cared for and trained afresh. But since in that gift she had desired the good of another and not her own, since she had indeed willed to give her self, the City secluded her passion, and took her gift to its own divine self. She had, almost in a literal physical sense, to be born again; at least she had to grow again, and over the growth her daughter was to preside. That tenderness was to meet her needs, and (if she could ever speak) to answer her stumbling words. She was now almost in that state to which her master had willed to reduce their child; the substitution was one of the Acts of the City. Her spiritual knowledge lay unconscious, as it were in the depth of the separating and uniting waters; her body under the common sun. Resurrection must be from the very beginning, and meanwhile Betty was to do for her mother, while she lived, all that love could do.

But it would be certainly, for a long while, a thinner and wanner Betty who would do so. For now, when it was clear that she could do nothing there for her mother, she and Jonathan rose from their knees. She said: "Well…" and she kissed him. Then she saw Richard. They looked at each other; she smiled and put out her hand, and he came slowly across. She went to meet him, and gave him also her mild lips. He said: "Thank you for the picture." She pressed his hand and then she had turned again and gone across to the nearest of those sick and sorry creatures who were lying or crouching there. Her immortality was strong in her as she came to him; it happened to be Plankin. She took his hands in hers; the joy of the City in her, she kissed him on the mouth; she looked into his eyes. She said, after a minute: "You'll be well." He looked, at first, bewildered; then, slowly, relieved; then, suddenly, joyous. He half-scrambled to his feet from where, his head on his knees, he had been sitting, and uttered some sort of incoherent cry. Betty said clearly: "That'll be all right," released herself, and went on. She passed, so, round the whole circle, holding, touching, healing—simply and naturally, and with all the gaiety that she could. But though her voice did not falter nor her hands lose their strength, yet as she went on she herself changed. She grew paler; she had to pause to recover as time after time she rose and left renewed wholeness behind. Jonathan had followed her all the while, and presently, as she came near the end, she was leaning on his arm for the necessary step or two between one and another. As the high heavenly power in her was poured into those tormented beings, so the power, and still more quickly the joy of the power, passed from her. She who had risen from the waters was still that she, and could not be lost unless she betrayed herself, but these energies were for a purpose, and were to be spent on that purpose. Have and not-have; not-have and have—sometimes one the first and sometimes the other; but by both she and Lester and all came to the City, though the union of both and the life of the union, the life of that final terrible and triumphant *Have!* was yet far beyond them, and even to envisage it would be to refuse the way to it. Her miraculous life passed into those others, and she herself, without any apparent gain to herself from her voice and smile and gesture and free love, was left wholly to her old. At the end she wavered and nearly fell. Jonathan held her, and they turned and came, but she hardly, back towards Richard, who took her other arm, and so she paused, white and worn, supported by her lover and her friend. She murmured, with a last flashing smile: "That's done!"

All those whom she had healed were on their feet—moving, chattering, tidying themselves. They did not seem to know what exactly had happened; at least they showed no awareness of Betty and did not even look at her. Someone said: "I knew the Father would help us," and someone else: "It might have been a dream," and someone else: "Goodness! what a fright!" And then a whole noise of voices broke out and a little laughter, and Betty looked pleadingly at Jonathan, and the three began to move slowly towards the door. The morning of the feast was bright in the hall. As they came near the door, and Betty's white frailty was only just holding up and holding level, Plankin suddenly ran up to them. He said: "Excuse *me*, miss and gentlemen, but there's one more upstairs—Elsie Bookin who does the typing. She used to have the paralysis, and if she thinks she's got it again I daresay she couldn't get down with the rest of us. But she may feel bad, and if so be as you were going upstairs, I'm sure she'd be thankful."

Jonathan began to say something. Betty pressed his arm. She looked at Plankin, and the faintest of wry smiles turned her lips. With a final effort she pulled herself up. She said: "Oh well…. Yes. Jon, do you mind…?"

Descent into Hell

Chapter I

THE MAGUS ZOROASTER

*

"It undoubtedly needs," Peter Stanhope said, "a final pulling together, but there's hardly time for that before July, and if you're willing to take it as it is, why——" He made a gesture of presentation and dropped his eyes, thus missing the hasty reciprocal gesture of gratitude with which Mrs. Parry immediately replied on behalf of the dramatic culture of Battle Hill. Behind and beyond her the culture, some thirty faces, unessentially exhibited to each other by the May sunlight, settled to attention—naturally, efficiently, critically, solemnly, reverently. The grounds of the Manor House expanded beyond them; the universal sky sustained the whole. Peter Stanhope began to read his play.

Battle Hill was one of the new estates which had been laid out after the war. It lay about thirty miles north of London and took its title from the more ancient name of the broad rise of ground which it covered. It had a quiet ostentation of comfort and culture. The poor, who had created it, had been as far as possible excluded, nor (except as hired servants) were they permitted to experience the bitterness of others' stairs. The civil wars which existed there, however bitter, were conducted with all bourgeois propriety. Politics, religion, art, science, grouped themselves, and courteously competed for numbers and reputation. This summer, however, had seen a spectacular triumph of drama, for it had become known that Peter Stanhope had consented to allow the restless talent of the Hill to produce his latest play.

He was undoubtedly the most famous inhabitant. He was a cadet of that family which had owned the Manor House, and he had bought it back from more recent occupiers, and himself settled in it before the war. He had been able to do this because he was something more than a cadet of good family, being also a poet in the direct English line, and so much after the style of his greatest predecessor that he made money out of poetry. His name was admired by his contemporaries and respected by the young. He had even imposed modern plays in verse on the London theatre, and two of them tragedies at that, with a farce or two, and histories for variation and pleasure. He was the kind of figure who might be more profitable to his neighbourhood dead than alive; dead, he would have given it a shrine; alive, he deprecated worshippers. The young men at the estate office made a refined publicity out of his privacy; the name of Peter Stanhope would be whispered without comment. He endured the growing invasion with a great deal of good humour, and was content to see the hill of his birth become a suburb of the City, as in another sense it would always be. There was, in that latest poetry, no contention between the presences of life and of death; so little indeed that there had been a contention in the *Sunday Times* whether Stanhope were a pessimist or an optimist. He himself said, in reply to an interviewer's question, that he was an optimist and hated it.

Stanhope, though the most glorious, was not the only notorious figure of the Hill. There was Mr. Lawrence Wentworth, who was the most distinguished living authority on military history (perhaps excepting Mr. Aston Moffatt). Mr. Wentworth was not in the garden on that afternoon. Mrs. Catherine Parry was; it was she who would produce the play, as in many places and at many times she had produced others. She sat near Stanhope now, almost as tall as he, and with more active though not brighter eyes. They were part of that presence which was so necessary to her profession. Capacity which, in her nature, had reached the extreme of active life, seemed in him to have entered the contemplative, so much had his art become a thing of his soul. Where, in their own separate private affairs, he interfered so little as almost to seem inefficient, she was so efficient as almost to seem interfering.

In the curve of women and men beyond her, other figures, less generally famous, sat or lay as the depth of their chairs induced them. There were rising young men, and a few risen and retired old. There were ambitious young women and sullen young women and loquacious young women. They were all attentive, though, as a whole, a little disappointed. They had understood that Mr. Stanhope had been writing a comedy, and had hoped for a modern comedy. When he had been approached, however, he had been easy but firm. He had been playing with a pastoral; if they would like a pastoral, it was very much at their service. Hopes and hints of modern comedies were unrealized: it was the pastoral or nothing. They had to be content. He consented to read it to them; he would not do more. He declined to make suggestions for the cast; he declined to produce. He would like, for his own enjoyment, to come to some of the rehearsals, but he made it clear that he had otherwise no wish to interfere. Nothing—given the necessity of a pastoral—could be better; the production would have all the advantage of his delayed death without losing any advantage of his prolonged life. As this became clear, the company grew reconciled. They gazed and listened, while from the long lean figure, outstretched in its deck-chair, there issued the complex intonation of great verse. Never negligible, Stanhope was often neglected; he was everyone's second thought, but no one's first. The convenience of all had determined this afternoon that he should be the first, and his neat mass of grey hair, his vivid glance, that rose sometimes from the manuscript, and floated down the rows, and sank again, his occasional friendly gesture that seemed about to deprecate, but always stopped short, received the concentration of his visitors, and of Mrs. Parry, the chief of his visitors.

It became clear to Mrs. Parry, as the afternoon and the voice went on, that the poet had been quite right when he had said that the play needed pulling together. "It's all higgledy-piggledy," she said to herself, using a word which a friend had once applied to a production of the *Tempest*, and in fact to the *Tempest* itself. Mrs. Parry thought that this pastoral was, in some ways, rather like the *Tempest*. Mr. Stanhope, of course, was not as good as Shakespeare, because Shakespeare was the greatest English poet, so that Stanhope wasn't. But there was a something. To begin with, it had no title beyond *A Pastoral*. That was unsatisfactory. Then the plot was incredibly loose. It was of no particular time and no particular place, and to any cultured listener it seemed to have little bits of everything and everybody put in at odd moments. The verse was undoubtedly Stanhope's own, of his latest, most heightened, and most epigrammatic style, but now and then all kinds of reminiscences moved in it. Once, during the second act, the word *pastiche* floated through Mrs. Parry's mind, but went away again on her questioning whether a *pastiche* would be worth the trouble of production. There was a Grand Duke in it, who had a beautiful daughter, and this daughter either escaped from the palace or was abducted—anyhow, she came into the power of a number of brigands; and then there was a woodcutter's son who frequently burned leaves, and he and the princess fell in love, and there were two farmers who were at odds, and the Grand Duke turned up in disguise, first in a village and then in the forest, through which also wandered an escaped bear, who spoke the most complex verse of all, excepting the Chorus. The Chorus had no kind of other name; at first Mrs. Parry thought they might be villagers, then, since they were generally present in the forest, she thought they might be trees, or perhaps (with a vague reminiscence of *Comus*) spirits. Stanhope had not been very helpful; he had alluded to them as an experiment. By the end of the reading, it was clear to Mrs. Parry that it was very necessary to decide what exactly this Chorus was to be.

She had discouraged discussion of the play during the intervals between the four acts, and as soon as it was over tea was served. If, however, the poet hoped to get away from discussion by means of tea he was mistaken. There was a little hesitation over the correct word; fantastic was dangerous, and poetic both unpopular and supererogatory, though both served for variations on idyllic, which was Mrs. Parry's choice and won by lengths. As she took her second cup of tea, however, she began to close. She said: "Yes, idyllic, Mr. Stanhope, and so significant!"

"It's very good of you," Stanhope murmured. "But you see I was right about revision—the plot must seem very loose."

Mrs. Parry waved the plot up into benevolence. "But there are a few points," she went on. "The Chorus now. I don't think I follow the Chorus."

"The Chorus *could* be omitted," Stanhope said. "It's not absolutely necessary to a presentation."

Before Mrs. Parry could answer, a young woman named Adela Hunt, sitting close by, leant forward. She was the leader of the younger artistic party, who were not altogether happy about Mrs. Parry. Adela had some thoughts of taking up production herself as her life-work, and it would have been a great advantage to have started straight away with Peter Stanhope. But her following was not yet strong enough to deal with Mrs. Parry's reputation. She was determined, however, if possible, to achieve a kind of collaboration by means of correction. "O, we oughtn't to omit anything, ought we?" she protested. "A work of art can't spare anything that's a part of it."

"My dear," Mrs. Parry said, "you must consider your audience. What will the audience make of the Chorus?"

"It's for them to make what they can of it," Adela answered. "We can only give them a symbol. Art's always symbolic, isn't it?"

Mrs. Parry pursed her lips. "I wouldn't say symbolic exactly," she said slowly. "It has a significance, of course, and you've got to convey that significance to the audience. We want to present it—to interpret."

As she paused, distracted by the presentation by the poet of two kinds of sandwiches, Adela broke in again.

"But, Mrs. Parry, how can one interpret a symbol? One can only *mass* it. It's all of a piece, and it's the total effect that creates the symbolical force."

"Significant, not symbolical," said Mrs. Parry firmly. "You mustn't play down to your audience, but you mustn't play away from them either. You must"—she gesticulated—"intertwine … harmonize. So you must make it easy for them to get into harmony. That's what's wrong with a deal of modern art; it refuses—it doesn't establish equilibrium with its audience or what not. In a pastoral play you must have equilibrium."

"But the equilibrium's in the *play*," Adela urged again, "a balance of masses. Surely that's what drama is— a symbolical contrast of masses."

"Well," Mrs. Parry answered with infuriating tolerance, "I suppose you might call it that. But it's more effective to think of it as significant equilibrium—especially for a pastoral. However, don't let's be abstract. The question is, what's to be done about the Chorus? Had we better keep it in or leave it out? Which would you prefer, Mr. Stanhope?"

"I should prefer it in, if you ask me," Stanhope said politely. "But not to inconvenience the production."

"It seems to be in the forest so often," Mrs. Parry mused, dismissing cake. "There's the distant song in the first act, when the princess goes away from the palace, and the choric dialogue when…. It isn't Dryads, is it?"

A friend of Adela's, a massive and superb young man of twenty-five, offered a remark. "Dryads would rather wreck the eighteenth century, wouldn't they?"

"Watteau," said a young lady near Adela. "You could have them period."

Mrs. Parry looked at her approvingly. "Exactly, my dear," she said. "A very charming fantasy it might be; we must take care it isn't precious—only period. But, Mr. Stanhope, you haven't told us—are they Dryads?"

"Actually," Stanhope answered, "as I told you, it's more an experiment than anything else. The main thing is—was—that they are non-human."

"Spirits?" said the Watteau young lady with a trill of pleasure.

"If you like," said Stanhope, "only not spiritual. Alive, but with a different life—even from the princess."

"Irony?" Adela exclaimed. "It's a kind of comment, isn't it, Mr. Stanhope, on futility? The forest and everything, and the princess and her lover—so transitory."

Stanhope shook his head. There was a story, invented by himself, that *The Times* had once sent a representative to ask for explanations about a new play, and that Stanhope, in his efforts to explain it, had found after four hours that he had only succeeded in reading it completely through aloud: "Which," he maintained, "*was*the only way of explaining it."

"No," he said now, "not irony. I think perhaps you'd better cut them out."

There was a moment's pause. "But we can't do that, Mr. Stanhope," said a voice; "they're important to the poetry, aren't they?" It was the voice of another young woman, sitting behind Adela. Her name was Pauline Anstruther, and, compared with Adela, she was generally silent. Now, after her quick question, she added hastily, "I mean—they come in when the princess and the wood-cutter come together, don't they?" Stanhope looked at her, and she felt as if his eyes had opened suddenly. He said, more slowly:

"In a way, but they needn't. We could just make it chance."

"I don't think that would be nearly as satisfactory," Mrs. Parry said. "I begin to see my way—the trees perhaps—leaves—to have the leaves of the wood all so helpful to the young people—so charming!"

"It's a terribly sweet idea," said the Watteau young lady. "And so true too!"

Pauline, who was sitting next her, said in an undertone: "True?"

"Don't you think so?" Watteau, whose actual name was Myrtle Fox, asked. "It's what I always feel—about trees and flowers and leaves and so on—they're so *friendly*. Perhaps you don't notice it so much; I'm rather mystic about nature. Like Wordsworth. I should love to spend *days* out with nothing but the trees and the leaves and the wind. Only somehow one never seems to have time. But I do believe they're all breathing in with us, and it's such a comfort—here, where there are so many trees. Of course, we've only to sink into ourselves to find peace—and trees and clouds and so on all help us. One never need be unhappy. Nature's so terribly good. Don't you think so, Mr. Stanhope?"

Stanhope was standing by, silent, while Mrs. Parry communed with her soul and with one or two of her neighbours on the possibilities of dressing the Chorus. He turned his head and answered, "That Nature is terribly good? Yes, Miss Fox. You do mean 'terribly'?"

"Why, certainly," Miss Fox said. "Terribly—dreadfully—very."

"Yes," Stanhope said again. "Very. Only—you must forgive me; it comes from doing so much writing, but when I say 'terribly' I think I mean 'full of terror'. A dreadful goodness."

"I don't see how goodness can be dreadful," Miss Fox said, with a shade of resentment in her voice. "If things are good they're not terrifying, are they?"

"It was you who said 'terribly'," Stanhope reminded her with a smile, "I only agreed."

"And if things are terrifying," Pauline put in, her eyes half-closed and her head turned away as if she asked a casual question rather of the world than of him, "can they be good?"

He looked down on her. "Yes, surely," he said, with more energy. "Are our tremors to measure the Omnipotence?"

"We'll have them in shades of green then," Mrs. Parry broke in, "light to dark, with rich gold sashes and embroidery running all over like twigs, and each one carrying a conventionalized bough—different lengths, I think. Dark gold stockings."

"To suggest the trunks?" asked Adela's friend Hugh Prescott.

"Quite," Mrs. Parry said, and then hesitated. "I'm not sure—perhaps we'd better keep the leaf significances. When they're still—of course they could stand with their legs twined…."

"What, with one another's?" Adela asked, in a conscious amazement.

"My dear child, don't be absurd," Mrs. Parry said. "Each pair of legs just crossed, so"—she interlaced her own.

"I could never stand still like that," Miss Fox said, with great conviction.

"You'd have your arms stretched out to people's shoulders on each side," Mrs. Parry said dubiously, "and a little gentle swaying wouldn't be inappropriate. But perhaps we'd better not risk it. Better have green stockings—we can manage some lovely groupings. Could we call them 'Chorus of Leaf-Spirits', Mr. Stanhope?"

"Sweet!" said Miss Fox. Adela, leaning back to Hugh Prescott, said in a very low voice, "I told you, Hugh, she'll ruin the whole thing. She's got no idea of mass. She ought to block it violently and leave it without a name. I wouldn't even have 'Chorus'. I hope he won't give way, but he's rather weak."

However, Stanhope was, in the politest language, declining to have anything of the sort. "Call it the Chorus," he said, "or if you like I'll try and find a name for the leader, and the rest can just dance and sing. But I'm afraid 'Leaf-Spirits' would be misleading."

"What about 'Chorus of Nature-Powers'?" asked Miss Fox, but Stanhope only said, smiling, "You will try and make the trees friendly," which no one quite understood, and shook his head again.

Prescott asked: "Incidentally, I suppose they will be women?"

Mrs. Parry had said, "O, of course, Mr. Prescott," before the question reached her brain. When it did, she added, "At least … I naturally took it for granted…. They are feminine, aren't they?"

Still hankering after mass, Adela said, "It sounds to me more like undifferentiated sex force," and ignored Hugh's murmur, "There isn't much fun in that."

"I don't know that they were meant to be either male or female," Stanhope said. "I told you they were more of an experiment in a different kind of existence. But whether men or women are most like that is another matter." He shed an apologetic smile on Mrs. Parry.

"If they're going to be leaves," Miss Fox asked, "couldn't they all *wear* huge leaves, so that no one would know if they were wearing knee-breeches or skirts?"

There was a pause while everyone took this in, then Mrs. Parry said, very firmly, "I don't think that would answer," while Hugh Prescott said to Adela, "Chorus of Fig-leaves!"

"Why not follow the old pantomime or the present musical comedy," Stanhope asked, "and dress your feminine chorus in exquisite masculine costume? That's what Shakespeare did with his heroines, as often as he could, and made a diagram of something more sharp and wonderful than either. I don't think you'll do better. Masculine voices—except boys—would hardly do, nor feminine appearances."

Mrs. Parry sighed, and everyone contemplated the problem again. Adela Hunt and Hugh Prescott discussed modernity between themselves. Pauline, lying back, like Stanhope, in her chair, was thinking of Stanhope's phrases, "a different life", "a terrible good", and wondering if they were related, if this Chorus over which they were spending so much trouble were indeed an effort to shape in verse a good so alien as to be terrifying. She had never considered good as a thing of terror, and certainly she had not supposed a certain thing of terror in her own secret life as any possible good. Nor now; yet there had been an inhumanity in the great and moving lines of the Chorus. She thought, with an anger generous in its origin but proud and narrow in its conclusion, that not many of the audience really cared for poetry or for Stanhope's poetry—perhaps none but she. He was a great poet, one of a very few, but what would he do if one evening he met himself coming up the drive? *Doppelgänger*, the learned called it, which was no comfort. Another poet had thought of it; she had had to learn the lines at school, as an extra task because of undone work:

> *Magus Zoroaster, my dead ch*
> *is own image walking in the g*

She had never done the imposition, for she had had nightmares that night, after reading the lines, and had to go sick for days. But she had always hated Shelley since for making it so lovely, when it wasn't loveliness but black panic. Shelley never seemed to suggest that the good might be terrible. What would Peter Stanhope *do*? what could he? if he met himself?

They were going: people were getting up and moving off. Everyone was being agreeably grateful to Stanhope for his lawn, his tea, and his poetry. In her fear of solitude she attached herself to Adela and Hugh and Myrtle Fox, who were all saying good-bye at once. As he shook hands he said casually: "You don't think they are?" and she did not immediately understand the reference to the measurement of Omnipotence by mortal tremors. Her mind was on Myrtle, who lived near her. She hated the pang of gratitude she felt, and hated it more because she despised Miss Fox. But at least she wouldn't be alone, and the thing she hated most only came, or had so far only come, when she was alone. She stuck close to Myrtle, listening to Adela as they went.

"Pure waste," Adela was saying. "Of course, Stanhope's dreadfully traditional"—how continually, Pauline thought, people misused words like dreadful; if they knew what dread was!—"but he's got a kind of weight, only he dissipates it. He undermines his mass. Don't you think so, Pauline?"

"I don't know," Pauline said shortly, and then added with private and lying malice: "I'm no judge of literature."

"Perhaps not," Adela said, "though I think it's more a question of general sensitiveness. Hugh, did you notice how the Parry talked of significance? Why, no one with a really *adult* mind could possibly—— O, good-bye, Pauline; I may see you to-morrow." Her voice passed away, accompanied by Hugh's temporary and lazy silence, and Pauline was left to Myrtle's monologues on the comforting friendliness of sunsets.

Even that had to stop when they reached the Foxes' hole. Myrtle, in a spasm of friendship for Messias, frequently called it that. As they parted upon the easy joke, Pauline felt the rest of the sentence pierce her. She took it to her with a sincerity of pain which almost excused the annexation—"the Son of Man hath not where to lay his head." It was the cry of her loneliness and fear, and it meant nothing to her mind but the empty streets and that fear itself. She went on.

Not to think; to think of something else. If she could. It was so hopeless. She was trying not to look ahead for fear she saw it, and also to look ahead for fear she was yielding to fear. She walked down the road quickly and firmly, remembering the many thousand times it had not come. But the visitation was increasing—growing nearer and clearer and more frequent. In her first twenty-four years she had seen it nine times; at first she had tried to speak of it. She had been told, when she was small, not to be silly and not to be naughty. Once, when she was adolescent, she had actually told her mother. Her mother was understanding in most things, and knew it. But at this the understanding had disappeared. Her eyes had become as sharp as when her husband, by breaking his arm, had spoiled a holiday in Spain which she—"for all their sakes"—had planned. She had refused to speak any more to Pauline that day, and neither of them had ever quite forgiven the other. But in those days the *comings*—as she still called them—had been rare; since her parents had died and she had been sent to live with and look after her grandmother in Battle Hill they had been more frequent, as if the Hill was fortunate and favourable to apparitions beyond men; a haunt of alien life. There had been nine in two years, as many as in all the years before. She could not speak of it to her grandmother, who was too old, nor to anyone else, since she had never discovered any closeness of friendship. But what would happen when the thing that was she came up to her, and spoke or touched? So far it had always turned aside, down some turning, or even apparently into some house; she might have been deceived were it not for the chill in her blood. But if some day it did not....

A maid came out of a house a little farther down a road, and crossed the pavement to a pillar-box. Pauline, in the first glance, felt the sickness at her heart. Relieved, she reacted into the admission that she was only twenty-three houses away from her home. She knew every one of them; she had not avoided so much measurement of danger. It had never appeared to her indoors; not even on the Hill, which seemed to be so convenient for it. Sometimes she longed always to stay indoors; it could not be done, nor would she do it. She drove herself out, but the front door was still a goal and a protection. She always seemed to herself to crouch and cling before she left it, coveting the peace which everyone but she had ... twenty-one, twenty.... She would *not* run; she would*not* keep her eyes on the pavement. She would walk steadily forward, head up and eyes before her ... seventeen, sixteen.... She would think of something, of Peter Stanhope's play—"a terrible good". The whole world was for her a canvas printed with unreal figures, a curtain apt to roll up at any moment on one real figure. But this afternoon, under the stress of the verse, and then under the shock of Stanhope's energetic speech, she had fractionally wondered: a play—was there a play? a play even that was known by some? and then not without peace ... ten, nine ... the Magus Zoroaster; perhaps Zoroaster had not been frightened. Perhaps if any of the great—if Cæsar had met his own shape in Rome, or even Shelley … was there any tale of any who had?… six, five, four….

Her heart sprang; there, a good way off—thanks to a merciful God—it was, materialized from nowhere in a moment. She knew it at once, however far, her own young figure, her own walk, her own dress and hat—had not her first sight of it been attracted so? changing, growing…. It was coming up at her pace—*doppelgänger, doppelgänger*: her control began to give … two … she didn't run, lest it should, nor did it. She reached her gate, slipped through, went up the path. If it should be running very fast up the road behind her now? She was biting back the scream and fumbling for her key. Quiet, quiet! "A terrible good." She got the key into the keyhole; she would not look back; would it click the gate or not? The door opened; and she was in, and the door banged behind her. She all but leant against it, only the *doppelgänger* might be leaning similarly on the other side. She went forward, her hand at her throat, up the stairs to her room, desiring (and with every atom of energy left denying that her desire could be vain) that there should be left to her still this one refuge in which she might find shelter.

Chapter II

VIA MORTIS

*

Mrs. Parry and her immediate circle, among whom Adela Hunt was determinedly present, had come, during Pauline's private meditations, to several minor decisions, one of which was to ask Lawrence Wentworth to help with the costumes, especially the costumes of the Grand Ducal Court and Guard. Adela had said immediately that she would call on Mr. Wentworth at once, and Mrs. Parry, with a brief discontent, had agreed. While, therefore, Pauline was escaping from her ghostly twin, Adela and Hugh went pleasantly along other roads of the Hill to Wentworth's house.

It stood not very far from the Manor House, a little lower than that but still near to the rounded summit of the rise of ground which had given the place half its name. Lawrence Wentworth's tenancy was peculiarly suitable to the other half, for his intellectual concern was with the history of battle, and battles had continually broken over the Hill. Their reality had not been quite so neat as the diagrams into which he abstracted and geometricized them. The black lines and squares had swayed and shifted and been broken; the crimson curves, which had lain bloody under the moon, had been a mass of continuous tiny movement, a mass noisy with moans and screams. The Hill's chronicle of anguish had been due, in temporalities, to its strategic situation in regard to London, but a dreamer might have had nightmares of a magnetic attraction habitually there deflecting the life of man into death. It had epitomized the tale of the world. Prehistoric legends, repeated in early chronicles, told of massacres by revolting Britons and roaming Saxons, mornings and evenings of hardly-human sport. Later, when permanent civilization arose, a medieval fortalice had been built, and a score of civil feuds and pretended loyalties had worn themselves out around it under kings who, though they were called Stephen or John, were as remote as Shalmanezer or Jeroboam. The Roses had twined there, their roots living on the blood shed by their thorns; the castle had gone up one night in fire, as did Rome, and the Manor House that followed had been raised in the midst of another order. A new kind of human civility entered; as consequence or cause of which, this Hill of skulls seemed to become either weary or fastidious. In the village that had stood at the bottom of the rise a peasant farmer, moved by some wandering gospeller, had, under Mary Tudor, grown obstinately metaphysical, and fire had been lit between houses and manor that he might depart through it in a roaring anguish of joy. Forty years later, under Elizabeth, the whispering informers had watched an outlaw, a Jesuit priest, take refuge in the manor, but when he was seized the Death of the Hill had sent him to its Type in London for more prolonged ceremonies of castration, as if it, like the men of the Renascence, seemed to involve its brutal origin in complications of religion and art. The manor had been forfeited to the Crown, but granted again to another branch of the family, so that, through all human changes, the race of owners had still owned. This endured, when afterwards it was sold to richer men, and even when Peter Stanhope had bought it back the house of his

93

poetry remained faintly touched by the dreadful ease that was given to it by the labour and starvation of the poor.

The whole rise of ground therefore lay like a cape, a rounded headland of earth, thrust into an ocean of death. Men, the lords of that small earth, dominated it. The folklore of skies and seasons belonged to it. But if the past still lives in its own present beside our present, then the momentary later inhabitants were surrounded by a greater universe. From other periods of its time other creatures could crawl out of death, and invisibly contemplate the houses and people of the rise. The amphibia of the past dwelt about, and sometimes crawled out on, the slope of this world, awaiting the hour when they should either retire to their own mists or more fully invade the place of the living.

There had been, while the workmen had been creating the houses of the new estate, an incident which renewed the habit of the Hill, as if that magnetism of death was quick to touch first the more unfortunate of mortals. The national margin of unemployment had been reduced by the new engagement of labourers, and from the work's point of view reduced, in one instance, unwisely. A certain unskilled assistant had been carelessly taken on; he was hungry, he was ill, he was clumsy and slow. His name no one troubled to know. He shambled among the rest, their humorous butt. He was used to that; all his life he had been the butt of the world, generally of an unkind world. He had been repeatedly flung into the gutter by the turn of a hand in New York or Paris, and had been always trying to scramble out of it again. He had lost his early habit of complaining, and it only added to his passive wretchedness that his wife kept hers. She made what money she could by charing, at the market price, with Christmas Day, St. Stephen, and such feasts deducted, and since she usually kept her jobs, she could reasonably enjoy her one luxury of nagging her husband because he lost his. His life seemed to him an endless gutter down which ran an endless voice. The clerk of the works and his foreman agreed that he was no good.

An accidental inspection by one of the directors decided his discharge. They were not unkind; they paid him, and gave him an extra shilling to get a bus some way back towards London. The clerk added another shilling and the foreman sixpence. They told him to go; he was, on the whole, a nuisance. He went; that night he returned.

He went, towards the buses a mile off, tramping blindly away through the lanes, coughing and sick. He saw before him the straight gutter, driven direct to London across the lanes and fields. At its long end was a miserable room that had a perpetual shrill voice.

He longed to avoid them, and as if the Hill bade him a placable farewell there came to him as he left it behind him a quiet thought. He could simply reject the room and its voice; he could simply stop walking down the gutter. A fancy of it had grown in him once or twice before. Then it had been a fancy of some difficult act; now the act had suddenly become simple.

Automatically eating a piece of bread that one of the men had given him, he sat down by the roadside, looking round him to find the easiest way to what had suddenly become a resolve. Soft and pitiless the country stretched away round him, unwilling that he should die. He considered. There were brooks; he knew it was impossible for him to hold himself down in them while he drowned. There were motors, cars, or buses; apart from his unwillingness to get other people into trouble, he feared lest he should be merely hurt or maimed. He wanted to get himself completely out of trouble. There were the half-finished buildings away behind him. A magical and ghostly finger touched his mind; in one of those buildings he remembered to have seen a rope. In a dim way, as he sat gnawing his bread, he felt that this was the last trouble he would give to his fellows. Their care this time would be as hasty and negligent as ever, but it would be final. If the rope were not there, he would find some other way, but he hoped for the best. He even believed in that best.

He got up, sometime in the early evening, and began to plod back. It was not far and he was not old. In covering the short distance he covered age also, toiling doubly through space and time. The Republic, of which he knew nothing, had betrayed him; all the nourishment that comes from friendship and common pain was as much forbidden to him as the poor nourishment of his body. The Republic had decided that it was better one man, or many men, should perish, than the people in the dangerous chance of helping those many. It had, as always, denied supernatural justice. He went on, in that public but unspectacular abandonment, and the sun went down on him.

Under the moon he came on the Hill to a place which might have been an overthrown rather than an arising city. The chaos of that revolution which the Republic naturally refuses had rolled over it, or some greater disaster, the Vesuvian terror of Pompeii, or an invisible lava of celestial anger, as that which smote Thebes, or the self-adoring Cities of the Plain. Unfinished walls, unfilled pits, roofless houses, gaping holes where doors and windows were to be or had been spread before him. His body was shaking, but he went on. Here and there a ladder stretched upward; here and there a brazier burned. An occasional footstep sounded. The cold moon lit up the skeletons of houses, and red fires flickered rarely among them. He paused for a moment at the edge of the town, but not in doubt, only to listen if a watchman were near. From mere physical stress he whimpered a little now and then, but he did not change his purpose, nor did the universe invite him to change. It accepted the choice; no more preventing him than it prevents a child playing with fire or a fool destroying his love. It has not our kindness or our decency; if it is good, its goodness is of another kind than ours. It allowed him, moving from shadow to shadow, cautious and rash, to approach the house where he remembered to have seen the rope. All the afternoon the rope had been visible to his eyes. He knew exactly where it was; and there indeed it was. He slunk in and touched it, shivering and senseless but for the simple sense of life. The air of that infected place suffered his inhalations and filled his lungs as he dragged the rope, gently and softly, towards the nearest ladder beyond.

The ladder frightened him, lest it should be too much boarded, or else, bone-white in the moon, should, while he climbed, expose his yet living body to those universals who would have him live. But it was open for him, and he crouched within the lower shell of a room, holding the rope, peering, listening, waiting for he did not guess what until it came. He thought once he heard hurrying feet at a distance, but they were going from him, and presently all was again quiet. The moonlight gently faded; the white rungs grew shadowy; a cloud passed over the sky, and all was obscured. The heavens were kind, and the moon did not, like the sun, wait for a divine sacrifice in order to be darkened. A man served it as well. He rose, and slipped to the foot of his ladder. He went softly up, as the Jesuit priest had gone up his those centuries earlier, paying for a loftier cause by a longer catastrophe. He went up as if he mounted on the bones of his body built so carefully for this; he clambered through his skeleton to the place of his skull, and receded, as if almost in a corporeal ingression, to the place of propinquent death. He went up his skeleton, past the skeleton frames of the ground floor, of the first floor. At the second the poles of the scaffold stretched upward into the sky. The roof was not on, nor his life built up. He dragged himself dizzily on to the topmost landing, pulling the rope after him, and there his crouching mind stayed. The cloud passed from the moon; another was floating up. His flesh, in which only his spirit now lived, was aware of the light. He still hoped for his best; he lay still.

Presently he peered over. The world allowed him to be capable and efficient at last; no one had seen him. The long gutter of his process was now coiled up into the rope he held; the room with its voice was away in and looked on him from the silent moon. He breathed, and a cloud floated over it again. There was nothing more to happen; everything had already happened except for one trifle which would be over soon. He tiptoed to the scaffold pole on his right hand, uncoiling the rope as he went; he pulled and gently shook it. It was slender, but it seemed strong. He took one end of the rope, began to fasten it to the end of the pole, and suddenly hesitated. It was a long rope; suppose it were too long, so that when he jumped he fell to the ground and was not dead but broken. Then all those people, who, more fortunate than he, had governed him and shoved him into his gutter, would come to him again—he could hear a footstep or two of theirs upon the ground now, and lay still while they sounded and ceased—they would come to him and mind him and turn him out again, down a miry path under a perpetual talking moon that knew no wane. This was his one chance, for ever and ever, of avoiding them. He knew he must not miss it.

He measured out the rope to twice the length of his outstretched arms, and when the ruined city was once more silent he peered over, letting that measured section run through his hands. The end dangled much more than his height from the ground, and at that he twisted and knotted the next yard or two around the pole, straining against it, tugging it, making certain it could not ease loose. The moon emerged as he finished, and in a panic he dragged up the loose end, and shrank back from the edge, well back, so that no watcher should see him from the road. There, lying flat on his empty belly, he began his penultimate activity. He knotted, as best he could, the end of the rope about his neck, with a great and clumsy, but effective, slip knot. He tried it again and again, more fearful than ever lest its failure, because of his own, should betray him back into a life which his frenzy felt as already ghostly. He felt that he could not bear that last betrayal, for he would never have courage to repeat this mighty act of decision. The dreadful universe perhaps would spare him that, if he were careful now. He was very careful.

As, exhausted by the necessary labour, he lay flat on that stage of the spectral ascent, amid the poles and unroofed walls, he did not consider any future but unfortunate accident or fortunate death. He was almost shut up in his moment, and his hope was only that the next moment might completely close him in. No dichotomy of flesh and spirit distressed or delighted him, nor did he know anything of the denial of that dichotomy by the creed of Christendom. The unity of that creed has proclaimed, against experience, against intelligence, that for the achievement of man's unity the body of his knowledge is to be raised; no other fairer stuff, no alien matter, but this—to be impregnated with holiness and transmuted by lovely passion perhaps, but still this. Scars and prints may disseminate splendour, but the body is to be the same, the very body of the very soul that are both names of the single man. This man was not even terrified by that future, for he did not think of it. He desired only the end of the gutter and of the voice; to go no farther, to hear no more, to be done. Presently he remembered that time was passing; he must be quick or they would catch him, on his platform or as he fell, and if he fell into the safety of their hands he would fall into his old utter insecurity. All he knew of the comfort of the world meant only more pain. He got awkwardly to his feet; he must be quick.

He was not very quick. Something that was he dragged at him, and as he crawled to the edge dragged more frantically at something still in him. He had supposed he had wanted to die, and only at the last even he discovered that he wanted also not to die. Unreasonably and implacably, he wanted not to die. But also he wanted not to live, and the two rejections blurred his brain and shook his body. He half struggled to his feet in his agony; he twisted round and hung half over, his back to the abyss; he clutched at the rope, meaning to hold it and release it as he fell, to such an extreme of indecision pretending decision did his distress drive him, and then as the circling movement of his body ended, twining the rope once more round his neck, he swayed and yelped, and knew that he was lost, and fell.

He fell, and as he fell he thought for a moment he saw below him a stir as of an infinite crowd, or perhaps, so sudden and universal was it, the swift rush of a million insects towards shelter, away from the shock that was he. The movement, in the crowd, in the insects, in the earth itself, passed outward towards the unfinished houses, the gaps and holes in half-built walls, and escaped. When at last he knew in his dazed mind that he was standing securely on the ground, he knew also, under the pale light which feebly shone over the unfashioned town, that he was still alone.

He stood for a moment in extreme fear that something would break out upon him from its hiding-place, but nothing moved, and as his fear subsided he was at leisure to begin to wonder what he had to do there. He recognized the place; it was the scene of his last job, the job from which he had been dismissed, the place to which, for a reason, he had returned. The reason? He looked round; all was quite still. There were no footsteps; there were no braziers, such as he had half expected, for he had thought a watch was set at night. There was no moon in the sky, perhaps it was not night. Indeed it was too light for night; perhaps it was dawn, but there was not yet a sun. As he thought of dawn and another day, he remembered why he was there. He had come there to die, and the rope was on the platform above. He did not quite understand why he was standing at the foot of the ladder, for he seemed to remember that he had mounted it, up to his head, unless he had jumped down to frighten something that had vanished, but it did not matter. What mattered was that dawn was here, and his time was short. Unless he acted, his chance and he would be lost. He went again, very quickly and anxiously, up the ladder. At the top he got on to the platform and hurried to find the rope. He had had it ready; he must not waste it. He looked round for it. The rope was not there.

At first he did not believe. This was certainly the place, though in the dawn which was less bright than the moon, and he knew he had hated the moon because it watched him, the corners of that stage between earth and sky were now in darkness. But he went and peered into them and felt. Uselessly. He knelt down, staring round, unaware of any sickness or exhaustion, only of anxiety. He almost lay down, screwing up his eyes, dragging himself round. It was all useless. The rope was not there.

By now, as he raised his head and looked out, the silence was beginning to trouble him, and the pallid dawn. It was good that the light should not grow, but also it was terrifying. There had not been much time, or had there? He could not attend to it; the absence of the rope preoccupied him. Could someone, out of the world that was filled with his rich enemies, have come, while he was down at the foot, doing something he could not remember, and run up the ladder quietly, and stolen back his rope as he himself had stolen it? Perhaps the men who had sent him off that day, or even his wife, out of the room, stretching a lean hand and snatching it, as she had snatched things before—but then she would have snarled or shrilled at him; she always did. He forgot his caution. He rose to his feet, and ran round and round seeking for it. He failed again; the rope was not there.

By the ladder he stood still, holding on to it, utterly defeated at last, in a despair that even he had never felt before. There had always been present to him, unrecognized but secure, man's last hope, the possibility of death. It may be refused, but the refusal, even the unrecognized refusal, admits hope. Without the knowledge of his capacity of death, however much he fear it, man is desolate. This had gone; he had no chance whatever. The rope was gone; he could not die. He did not yet know that it was because he was already dead.

The dead man stood there, a vast dead silence about him and within him. He turned his head this way and that. He no longer minded whether anyone came, and no one did come. He looked back over his shoulder at his platform and its dark corners. Some things were yet concealed. There was shadow; his eyes looked at it for a long while, some days or weeks, without interest or intelligence. Presently there was a stir in it, that presently ceased. He had been looking at it all that time, over his shoulder, still standing there and holding his ladder; his body, or what seemed to him to be his body, his whole consciousness of distances and shapes that seemed not to be he, slowly conforming itself to its intelligence of this other world. The silence of the dead was about him, the light of the dead was over him. He did not like the corners of darkness or the stir in the corners, and presently as he stood there he began to feel that he could get away from them. He knew now that he would not find the rope, that he would not take again the means he had once taken to escape from pain and fear, but in that utter quiet his despair began to discover itself to be more like contentment. He slid on to the ladder, vaguely determined to get as far as he could from the platform of transition. He went soundlessly down, and as he came to ground and loosed his hold he sighed; he took a step or two away and sighed again, and now for pure relief. He felt, through all his new world, the absence of men, the mere absence therefore of evil. The world which was to be represented, there, by the grand culture of Battle Hill, could offer him, after his whole life, no better thing than that it should keep away. Justice, so far, rescued him; what more there was had not yet begun to work. He wandered away over the Hill.

Chapter III

QUEST OF HELL

*

It was in the house of the suicide that Lawrence Wentworth now sat. The dead man's corpse, discovered hanging in the morning, had been hugger-mugger interred, the body that then existed being then buried. With such bodies of past time the estate had no concern except to be silent about them, which it very successfully was. Wentworth, when he took the house, heard nothing of the most unfortunate incident, nor had any idea of what had happened in the space which now, properly closed and ceilinged, he had taken for his bedroom, any more than he saw through the window of his study the dead man occasionally return to the foot of the ladder which, in his world, still reached from earth to scaffolding. Neither of them was aware of the other.

Wentworth had at least one advantage over many other military historians; he had known war. He had served with some distinction, partly from luck, and partly from his brain, which organized well. He had held a minor position on an army staff, and he had been alert at moving masses of men about, and fitting them in, and removing them again. He could not win battles, but he could devise occupation for armies. He could always, when necessary, find somewhere for them to go and something for them to do, and he could deal with any objections to their going or doing that were raised. His mind reduced the world to diagrams, and he saw to it that the diagrams fitted. And as some such capacity is half of all ordinary leadership in war, he really had an insight into the technical side of the great military campaigns of the past. He could see what Cæsar or Napoleon had done, and why, and how; it was not to be expected that he could have seen it, as they did, before it happened. He had never had a friend or a lover; he had never, in any possible sense of the word, been "in love".

Yet, or perhaps therefore, his life had been pleasant to him, partly by the Fortune which confirms or ruins the care of generals, partly through his own instinctive tactical care. Only of late, especially since he had come to the Hill, the pleasantness had seemed to waver. He was not much over fifty, but his body was beginning to feel that its future was shortening, and that it had perhaps been too cautious in the past. His large opaque eyes, set widely in a squarish face, were acquiring a new restlessness. Also he had begun to dream. Something moved more sharply in his sleep, as the apparition of Pauline's terror moved more surely in the streets; the invisible life of the Hill quickening its pressure upon mental awareness.

It was a little dream, of no significance, as Mrs. Parry would have said; it was only a particular development of a common dream-thing, the state of something going on. He had no reason for disliking it except that it recurred. It was not complex; it was remarkably simple—simple and remarkable. He was climbing down a rope; he did nothing but climb down a rope. It was a white rope, so white that it shone of its own clarity in the pitch-black darkness where it and he existed, and it stretched up high above him, infinitely high, so that as he looked he could not see where or to what it was fastened. But that it was fastened both above and below was clear, for it was taut in his hands and between his legs, twisted expertly round it. He was not sliding down it; he was descending by the aid of knots which, though he could feel them against his hands and legs, he could never actually see in the rope as it emerged from his hands past his eyes. The descent was perplexing, for he never felt himself move and yet he knew he was continually farther down,

down towards the bottom of the rope, the point and the place where it was secured beneath him. Once or twice he looked down and saw only the twined white strands stretching away in the black abyss. He felt no fear; he climbed, if he climbed, securely, and all the infinite black void did not terrify him; he would not fall. Nor did he fear the end—not *fear*; no monstrosity awaited him. On the other hand, he did, waking, remember to have felt the very slightest distaste, as if for a dentist. He remembered that he wanted to remain on the rope, but though he saw neither top nor bottom he was sure, in the dream, that that was impossible. A million yards or years of rope stretched above him; there might be a million years or yards below him. Or a hundred, or a score, or indeed but two or three. He climbed down, or else the rope climbed up, and about them was everlasting silence and the black night in which he and the rope only were visible, and only visible to himself.

It was mildly disagreeable; the more, and perhaps, if he had thought about it, only, because dreams, though negligible on waking, are so entirely ineluctable in sleep. Sleep had, all his life, been a pleasant thing to Wentworth; he had made of it an art. He had used himself to a composure that had readily accommodated itself to him. He made it a rule to think of pleasant things as he stretched himself in bed: his acquaintances sometimes, or the reviews—most of the reviews—of his last book, or his financial security, or his intentions about his immediate future work, or the permanent alterations he hoped he had caused in universal thought concerning Cæsar's employment of Balearic slingers during the campaigns in Gaul. Also, deliciously, his fancies would widen and change, and Cæsar would be drawing out cheques to pay his London Library subscriptions, or the Balearic slingers would be listening to him as he told them how they used to use their slings, and the next thing he would know would be either his housekeeper tapping at the door, or the light of morning, or, sometimes, the dream.

For this assault in sleep there were at least two personal reasons in his waking life, besides the nature of the Hill or the haunter of his house; one of them very much in the forefront of his mind, the other secret and not much admitted. The first was Aston Moffatt; the second was Adela Hunt. Aston Moffatt was another military historian, perhaps the only other worth mentioning, and Wentworth and he were engaged in a long and complicated controversy on the problem of the least of those skirmishes of the Roses which had been fought upon the Hill. The question itself was unimportant; it would never seriously matter to anyone but the controversialists whether Edward Plantagenet's cavalry had come across the river with the dawn or over the meadows by the church at about noon. But a phrase, a doubt, a contradiction, had involved the two in argument. Aston Moffatt, who was by now almost seventy, derived a great deal of intellectual joy from expounding his point of view. He was a pure scholar, a holy and beautiful soul who would have sacrificed reputation, income, and life, if necessary, for the discovery of one fact about the horse-boys of Edward Plantagenet. He had determined his nature. Wentworth was younger and at a more critical point, at that moment when a man's real concern begins to separate itself from his pretended, and almost to become independent of himself. He raged secretly as he wrote his letters and drew up his evidence; he identified scholarship with himself, and asserted himself under the disguise of a defence of scholarship. He refused to admit that the exact detail of Edward's march was not, in fact, worth to him the cost of a single cigar.

As for Adela, he was very well aware of Adela, as he was aware of cigars, but he did not yet know what he would give up for her, or rather for the manner of life which included her. As Aston Moffatt was bound either to lessen or heighten Wentworth's awareness of his own reputation, so Adela was bound either to increase or abolish his awareness of his age. He knew time was beginning to hurry; he could at moments almost hear it scamper. He did not very well know what he wanted to do about it.

He was sitting now in his study, his large body leaning forward over the table, and his hands had paused in measuring the plan that lay in front of him. He was finding the answer to Aston Moffatt's last published letter difficult, yet he was determined that Moffatt could not be right. He was beginning to twist the intention of the sentences in his authorities, preferring strange meanings and awkward constructions, adjusting evidence, manipulating words. In defence of his conclusion he was willing to cheat in the evidence—a habit more usual to religious writers than to historical. But he was still innocent enough to be irritated; he felt, as it were, a roughness in the rope of his dream, and he was intensely awake to any other slights from any quarter. He looked sharply to see if there were more Moffatts in the world. At that inconvenient moment on that evening Adela arrived, with Hugh. It was long since he had seen her in the company of one young man: alone, or with one woman, or with several young men and women, but not, as it happened, so. He stood up when they were announced, and as they came in, Adela's short red-and-cream thickness overshadowed by Hugh's rather flagrant masculinity, he felt something jerk in him, as if a knot had been first tied and then suddenly pulled loose. He had written but that morning in an article on the return of Edward IV, "the treachery of the Earl destroyed the balance". Remote, five hundred years away, he felt it in the room; a destruction of balance. Then they were sitting down and Adela was talking.

She explained, prettily, why they had come. Hugh, watching, decided that she must not behave quite so prettily. Hugh had no jerks or quavers. He had decided some time since that Adela should marry him when he was ready, and was giving himself the pleasurable trouble of making this clear to her. There was a touch too much gusto in her manner towards Wentworth. She had been, as he had, and some others of the young, in the habit of spending an evening, once a fortnight or so, at Wentworth's house, talking about military history and the principles of art and the nature of the gods. During the summer these informal gatherings were less frequent, because of tennis and motor-rides and the nature of men and women. Hugh meant that for Adela they should stop altogether. He observed an intimacy; he chose that it should not continue, partly because he wished Adela to belong to him and partly because the mere action of breaking it would show how far Adela was prepared to go with him. His mind made arrangements.

Adela explained. Wentworth said: "Very well, I'll do anything I can. What is it you want?" He felt ungracious; he blamed Aston Moffatt.

"O, the costumes," Adela answered. "The Guard especially. The Grand Duke has a guard, you see, though there didn't seem to be much point in it. But it has a fight with the robbers, and if you'd see that it fought reasonably well…." She did not trouble to enlarge on her own view that the fight ought to be quite unrealistic; she knew that Mr. Wentworth did not much care for non-realistic art, and till recently she had preferred her mild satisfaction with her invasion of Wentworth's consciousness to any bigotry of artistic interpretation.

Hugh said: "It'd be frightfully good of you to give me a hand with my Guard, Mr. Wentworth." He infused the "Mister" with an air of courteous deference to age, and as he ended the sentence he stretched and bent an arm in the lazy good humour of youth. Neither of the others analysed stress and motion, yet their blood was stirred, Adela faintly flushing with a new gratification, Wentworth faintly flushing with a new anger. He said, "Are you to be the Grand Duke then, Prescott?"

"So Mrs. Parry seems to suggest," Hugh answered, and added, as if a thought had struck him, "unless—Adela, d'you think Mr. Wentworth would take the part himself? Isn't that an idea?"

Before Adela could answer Wentworth said: "Nonsense; I've never acted in my life."

"I'm quite sure," Hugh said, leaning comfortably forward with his elbows on his knees and his strong hands interlocked, "that you'd be a better father for the princess than I should. I think there's no doubt Adela'll have to be the princess."

"O, I don't see that," said Adela, "though it's true Mrs. Parry … but there are lots of others. But, Mr. Wentworth, would you? You'd give it a kind of …", she thought of "age" and substituted "force". "I was saying to Hugh as we came along that all it needs is force."

"I certainly wouldn't take it away from Prescott," Wentworth said. "He's much better at these games than I could be." He had tried to give to the words a genial and mature tolerance, but he heard them as merely hostile; so did the others.

"Ah, but then," Hugh answered, "you know such a lot about battles and history—battles long ago. You'd certainly be more suitable for Adela's father—sir."

Wentworth said: "I'll keep myself for the Guard. What period did you say?"

"They seem to think 1700," Adela said. "I know Mrs. Parry said something about eighteenth-century uniforms. She's going to write to you."

Hugh stood up. "So we oughtn't to keep you," he added. "Adela and I are going back to talk to her now. Come on, duchess—or whatever it is they call you."

Adela obeyed. Wentworth noted, with an interior irritation, that she really did. She moved to rise with something more than consent. It was what he had never had—consent, yes, but not this obedience. Hugh had given her his hand to pull her up, and in that strained air the movement was a proclamation. He added, as she stood by his side: "Do change your mind, sir, and show us all how to be a *Grand Siècle* father. I'll ask Mrs. Parry to put it to you."

"You certainly won't," Wentworth said. "I've no time to be a father."

"Odd way of putting it," Hugh said when they were outside. "I don't know why your Mr. Wentworth should be so peeved at the idea. Personally, I rather like it."

Adela was silent. She was well aware of the defiance—nor even a defiance, the rumour of a struggle long ago—that Hugh had brought into the conversation. Wentworth had been relegated, for those few sentences, to his place in the shadowy past of Battle Hill. The notice he had taken of her had been a dim flattery; now it was more dim and less flattering. She had been increasingly aware, since she had met Hugh, of her militant blood; of contemporary raid and real contest, as of some battle "where they charge on heaps the enemy flying". But she did not quite wish to lose Lawrence Wentworth; he had given her books, he had friends in London, he could perhaps be useful. She desired a career. She could be sensationally deferential on

Thursday, if, as she expected, she went to him on Thursday. There had been, at the last gathering, ten days before, an agreement on next Thursday. She had just accomplished this decision when Hugh said: "By the way, I wanted to ask you something. What about next Thursday?"

"Next Thursday?" she said, startled.

"Couldn't you come out somewhere in the evening?"

"But …" Adela paused, and Hugh went on: "I thought we might have dinner in town, and go to a show if you liked."

"I'd love it," Adela said. "But it needn't be Thursday?"

"I'm afraid it must," Hugh answered. "There's tennis at the Foxes' on Monday, and Tuesday and Wednesday I shall be late at work, and Friday we're to read the play, and the Parry's almost certain to want us on the Saturday too."

Adela said again: "I'd love it, but I was going to Mr. Wentworth's on Thursday. I mean, we've been going rather steadily, and last time I practically promised."

"I know you did," said Hugh. "So did I, but we can't help it."

"Couldn't we go another week?" Adela asked.

"With this play about?" Hugh said sardonically. "My dear, we're going to be clutched by rehearsals every evening. Of course, we can leave it if you'd rather, but you said you'd like to see that thing *The Second Pylon*—it's your style—and as it's only on till Saturday … well, as a matter of fact, I got a couple of tickets for Thursday on the chance. I knew it'd be our only night."

"Hugh!" Adela exclaimed. "But I want frightfully to see it; they say it's got the most marvellous example of this Surrealist plastic cohesion. O, Hugh, how splendid of you! The only thing is…."

"Pauline'll be going to Wentworth's, won't she?" Hugh said. "And probably others. He can talk to them."

They were both aware that this would be by no means the same thing. They were equally both aware that it was what was about to happen; and that by Thursday evening it would have happened. Adela found that her hesitation about the future had already become a regret for the past: the thing had been done. A willing Calvinist, she said: "I hope he won't think it rude. He's been very nice."

"Naturally," Hugh answered. "But now it's up to you to be nice. Grand Dukes ought to be gratified, oughtn't they?"

"You asked him to be the Grand Duke," Adela pointed out.

"I asked him to be your father," Hugh said. "I don't think I had any notion of his being a Grand Duke."

He looked at her, laughing. "Write him a note on Wednesday," he said, "and I'll ring him up on Thursday evening from London, and ask him to make my excuses to you and Pauline and the rest."

"Hugh!" Adela exclaimed, "you couldn't!" Then, dimpling and gurgling, she added: "He's been very kind to me. I should hate him to feel hurt."

"So should I," Hugh said gravely. "Very well; that's settled."

Unfortunately for this delicate workmanship, the two or three other young creatures who had shared, with Adela, Hugh, and Pauline, the coffee and culture of Wentworth's house, were also deflected from it on that Thursday by tennis or the play; unfortunately, because the incidents of the Saturday had left him more acutely conscious at once of his need for Adela and of his need for flattery. He did not fully admit either; he rather defended himself mentally against Hugh's offensiveness than surrendered to his knowledge of his desire. Even so he refused to admit that he was engaged in a battle. He demanded at once security and victory, a habit not common to those great masters whose campaigns he studied. He remembered the past— the few intimate talks with Adela, the lingering hands, the exchanged eyes. Rather like Pompey, he refused to take measures against the threat on the other side the Rubicon; he faintly admitted that there was a Rubicon, but certainly not that there might be a Cæsar. He assumed that the Rome which had, he thought, admired him so much and so long, was still his, and he desired it to make his ownership clear. He was prepared to overlook that Saturday as not being Adela's fault as soon as the Thursday should bring him Adela's accustomed propinquity; perhaps, for compensation's sake and for promise of a veiled conclusion, a little more than propinquity. It was the more shattering for him that her note only reached him by the late post an hour or so before his guests usually arrived.

She had had, she said, to go to town that day to see about the stuff for her costume; things would be rushed, and she hadn't liked to make difficulties. She was dreadfully distressed; she might well be, he thought, with a greater flush of anger than he knew. He glanced at another note of excuse almost with indifference. But he was still ruffled when Pauline arrived, and it was with a certain abruptness that he told her he expected no one else but Prescott.

When, ten minutes later, the telephone bell rang, and he heard Prescott's voice offering his own regrets and explaining that absolutely unavoidable work kept him at the office: would Mr. Wentworth be so good as to apologize to Adela?—he was not sure if he were glad or sorry. It saved him from Prescott, but it left him tiresomely alone with Pauline. Pauline had a recurrent tendency to lose the finer points of military strategy in an unnecessary discussion of the sufferings of the rank and file; neither of them knew that it was the comfort of his house and his chairs—not to reckon her companionship with men in grief—which incited her. He did not think he wanted to have to talk to Pauline, but he was pleased to think he need not carry Hugh's message to Adela. He could not, of course, know that Adela was then squeezed into the same telephone box as Hugh. She had objected at first, but Hugh had pleasantly overpersuaded her, and it was true she did want to know exactly what he said—so as to know. And it was attractive to hear him telephone apologies to her when she was close at his side, to listen to the cool formality with which he dispatched ambassadorial messages to phantom ears, so that her actual ears received the chill while her actual eyes sparkled and kindled at his as he stood with the receiver at his ear. He said—as Wentworth only realized when he had put down his own receiver—"and would you be kind enough to make my apologies to Adela?" She mouthed "and the others" at him, but he shook his head ever so little, and when, as he put back the receiver, she said, "But you ought to have sent your message to Pauline at least," he answered, "Wentworth'll see to that; I wasn't going to mix you up." She said, "But supposing he doesn't, it'll look so rude," expecting him to answer that he didn't care. Instead of which, as they emerged from the call-box, he said, "Wentworth'll see to it; he won't like not to." She sat down to dinner infinitely more his accomplice than she had been when she had met him first that evening.

In effect he was right. Wentworth had received a slight shock when the single name reached his ears, but it was only on his way back to the study that he realized that he was being invited to assist Prescott's approach towards Adela. He must, of course, enlarge the apology, especially since Adela anyhow wasn't there, as he hadn't troubled to explain. Prescott could find that out for himself. Since he didn't know—a throb of new suspicion held him rigid outside his study door. It was incredible, because Prescott wouldn't have sent the message, or any message, if he and Adela had been together. But they were both away, and that (his startled nerves reported to his brain) meant that they were together. His brain properly reminded him that it meant nothing of the sort. But of that saving intelligence his now vibrating nervous system took no notice whatever. It had never had a chance to disseminate anarchy before, and now it took its chance. Fifty years of security dissolved before one minute of invasion; Cæsar was over the Rubicon and Pompey was flying from Rome. Wentworth strode back into the study and looked at Pauline much as Pompey might have looked at a peculiarly unattractive senator.

He said: "Prescott can't come either. He sends you his apologies," and with an extreme impatience waited to hear whether she had any comment to make upon this, which might show what and how much, if anything, she knew. She only said, "I'm sorry. Is he working late?"

It was exactly what Wentworth wanted to know. He went back to his usual seat at the corner of his large table, and put down his cigar. He said, "So he says. It's unfortunate, isn't it, just the evening Adela couldn't come?" He then found himself pausing, and added, "But we can go on talking, can't we? Though I'm afraid it will be duller for you."

He hoped she would deny this at once; on the other hand he didn't want her to stop. He wanted her to want to stop, but to be compelled to go by some necessary event; so that her longing and disappointment could partly compensate him for Adela's apparently volitional absence, but without forcing him to talk. He wished her grandmother could be taken worse suddenly. But she made no sign of going, nor did she offer him any vivid tribute. She sat for a minute with her eyes on the floor, then she looked at him and said: "There was something I thought of asking you."

"Yes?" Wentworth said. After all, Prescott probably was at his office, and Adela probably—wherever she had to be.

Pauline had not formally intended to speak. But Lawrence Wentworth was the only person she knew who might be aware of … what these things were and what they demanded. And since they were thus left together, she consented to come so far as to ask. She disdained herself a little, but she went on, her disdain almost audible in her voice: "Did you ever come across"—she found she had to pause to draw equable breath; it was difficult even to hint—"did you ever read of any tale of people meeting themselves?"

Momentarily distracted, Wentworth said: "Meeting themselves? What, in dreams?"

"Not dreams," Pauline said, "meeting themselves … in the street … or anywhere." She wished now she hadn't begun, for to speak seemed to invite its presence, as if it were likely to hover outside, if not inside, the house; and she would have to go home by herself to-night the whole way…. Or, since she had betrayed its privacy, supposing it followed up her betrayal and came now….

"There's a picture of Rossetti's," Wentworth said; "were you thinking of that?"

101

"Not a picture," Pauline said; "I mean, have you ever read of its happening? Shelley says it happened to Zoroaster."

"Indeed," Wentworth said. "I don't remember that. Of course I've heard of it as a superstition. Where have you come across it? Has anyone you know been seeing themselves?"

His mind was drifting back to Adela; the question rang hard. Pauline felt the obstruction, and stayed. She said, "I knew a girl who thought she did. But don't let me bother you."

"You aren't bothering me," Wentworth said by force of habit. "On the contrary. I never remember to have come across anything of the sort, though I've a notion it was supposed to foretell death. But then almost any unusual incident is supposed to foretell death by the savage—or let's say the uncivilized—mind. Death, you see, is inevitably the most unusual incident, and so—by correspondence—the lesser is related to the greater. Anthropology is very instructive in that way. The uneducated mind is generally known by its haste to see likeness where no likeness exists. It evaluates its emotions in terms of fortuitous circumstance. It objectifies its concerns through its imagination. Probably your friend was a very self-centred individual."

Pauline said coldly, "I don't know that she was," while Wentworth wondered if Adela and Prescott had finished the supper they were not, of course, having together. Their absence was a fortuitous circumstance. He evaluated his emotions in its terms, and (like any barbarian chief) objectified his concerns by his imagination. She could find out the difference between Prescott and himself. But he didn't mind; he didn't mind. He curvetted on that particular horse for a while, and while curvetting he took no notice of Pauline's remark until the silence startled his steed into nearly throwing him. Still just remaining seated, he said, "O, she isn't, isn't she?" and thought how lank, compared to Adela, Pauline was—lank and blank. She had no capacity. Exactly what capacity she lacked he did not carefully consider, assuming it to be intellectual: the look, not the eyes; the gesture, not the hand. It was Adela's mental alertness which he knew he would have grudged Prescott, if he could grudge anybody anything. This conversation about people seeing themselves was the dullest he had ever known; he looked covertly at the clock on the mantelpiece; at the same moment Pauline, also covertly, looked at her wrist-watch. She had been a fool to say anything; the only result was to expose her more consciously to that other approach. She had better get home, somehow, before she did anything sillier. She said, "Thank you," and couldn't think of anything else. She got up therefore, and said the only thing left.

"My grandmother's not been so well to-day. Would you forgive me if I deserted you too? We're treating you shockingly, aren't we?"

Wentworth got up alertly. "Not a bit," he said. "I'm sorry. I'm sorry you feel you ought to go." It occurred to him that, later on, he might walk down toward the station. If he met them together, he would at least be justified. They might have met at Marylebone, of course, even if he did meet them; and if he didn't, they might be coming by a later train. He might wait for the next. Perhaps it would be wiser not to go—he couldn't, in his position, hang about for ever and ever. People chattered. But he would decide about that when this superfluous being had been dismissed. He went with her to the door, was genial and bright, said good night, snarled at the time she took getting to the gate, and at last was free to make up his mind.

He could not do it. He was driven by his hunger as the dead man who had come to that unbuilt house had been driven by his, and for some time he wandered about his rooms as that other shape had gone through the streets, seeking peace and finding none. At last he found himself in his bedroom, looking out of the window, as the dead man had stood there looking over the ruins of history, from the place of his skull. Wentworth stood there now for some seconds, exercising a no more conscious but a still more deliberate choice. He also yielded—to the chaos within rather than the chaos without. The dead man had had reason to suppose that to throw himself down would mean freedom from tyranny, but Wentworth was not so much of a fool as to think that to thrust himself into the way of possible discovery would mean any such freedom. A remnant of intelligence cried to him that this was the road of mania, and self-indulgence leading to mania. Self-preservation itself urged him to remain; lucidity urged him, if not love. He stood and looked and listened, as the dead man had looked and listened. He heard faint hurrying footsteps somewhere on the Hill; the moon was covered by a cloud. The shadow provoked him; in it they might be, now, passing the end of his road. He must act before it was too late. He would not go to spy; he would go for a walk. He went out of the room, down the soft swift stairs of his mind, into the streets of his mind, to find the phantoms of his mind. He desired hell.

He strode out on his evening walk. He walked down the length of his road; if that led towards the station it could not be helped, nor if at a point it joined the road which Adela would take from the station. He was a man, and he had a right to his walk. He was not a child, neither the child that had lost its toy and cried for it, nor the child that had lost its toy and would not let itself care, nor the child that had lost its toy and tried to

102

recover it by pretending it never did care. It may be a movement towards becoming like little children to admit that we are generally nothing else. But he was; he was a man, he was going for his walk.

At the junction of roads, as at a junction of his mind, he stopped and waited—to enjoy the night air. His enjoyment strained intently and viciously to hear the sounds of the night, or such as were not of too remote and piercing a quality to reach him. The wind among the hills was fresh. He heard at a distance a train come in, and the whistle of its departure. One or two travellers went by; one, a woman, hurrying, said something to him as she passed—good night or good morning; it sounded, in his strained joy, like both. He became aware that he was visible in the moon; he moved back into shadow. If he saw them coming he could walk away or walk on without seeming to be in ambush. He was not in ambush; he was out for a walk.

An hour and more went by. He walked back, and returned. His physical nature, which sometimes by its mere exhaustion postpones our more complete damnation, did not save him. He was not overtired by his vigil, nor in that extreme weariness was the vision of a hopeless honour renewed. He paced and repaced, cannibal of his heart. Midnight passed; the great tower clock struck one. He heard the last train come in. A little up the road, concealed in the shadow, he waited. He heard the light patter of quick feet; he saw, again, a woman go hurrying by. He thought for a moment she was Adela, and then knew she was not. Other feet came, slower and double. The moon was bright; he stood at the edge of his own skull's platform; desire to hate and desire not to hate struggled in him. In the moonlight, visible, audible, arm in arm, talking and laughing, they came. He saw them pass; his eyes grew blind. Presently he turned and went home. That night when at last he slept he dreamed, more clearly than ever before, of his steady descent of the moon-bright rope.

Chapter IV

VISION OF DEATH

*

Pauline's parents had both died a few years before, and she had been put in Battle Hill to live with her grandmother for two reasons. The first was that she had no money. The second was that her uncle refused "to leave his mother to strangers". Since Pauline's mother had never liked her husband's parents, the girl had practically never seen the old lady. But the blood relationship, in her uncle's mind, connoted intimacy, and he found an occupation for an orphan and a companion for a widow at one stroke of mercy. Pauline was furious at the decisive kindness which regulated her life, but she had not, at the time when it interfered, found a job, and she had been so involved with the getting to Battle Hill that she discovered herself left there, at last, with her grandmother, a nurse, and a maid. Even so, it was the latent fear in her life that paralysed initiative; she could respond but she could not act. Since they had been on the Hill and the visitations had grown more frequent, she felt that deep paralysis increasing, and she kept her hold on social things almost desperately tight. Her alternative was to stop in altogether, to bury herself in the house, and even so to endure, day by day, the fear that her twin might resolve out of the air somewhere in the hall or the corridor outside her own room. She hated to go out, but she hated still more to stop in, and her intelligence told her that the alternative might save her nothing in the end. Rigid and high-headed she fled, with a subdued fury of pace, from house to gathering, and back from gathering to house, and waited for her grandmother to die.

Her grandmother, ignoring the possible needs of the young, went on living, keeping her room in the morning, coming down to lunch, and after a light early dinner retiring again to her room. She made no great demands on her granddaughter, towards whom indeed she showed a delicate social courtesy; and Pauline in turn, though in a harsher manner, maintained towards her a steady deference and patience. The girl was in fact so patient with the old lady that she had not yet noticed that she was never given an opportunity to be patient. She endured her own nature and supposed it to be the burden of another's.

On an afternoon in early June they were both in the garden at the back of the house; the walls that shut it in made it a part of the girl's security. Pauline was learning her part, turning the typescript on her knees, and shaping the words with silent lips. The trouble about some of them was that they were so simple as to be almost bathos. Her fibres told her that they were not bathos, until she tried to say them, and then, it was no

103

good denying, they sounded flat. She put the stress here and there; she tried slowness and speed. She invoked her conscious love to vocalize her natural passion, and the lines made the effort ridiculous. She grew hot as she heard herself say them, even though she did not say them aloud. Her unheard melody was less sweet than her memory of Stanhope's heard, but she did not then think of him reading, only of the lines he had read. They were simple with him; with her they were pretentious and therefore defiled.

She looked up at Mrs. Anstruther, who was sitting with her eyes closed, and her hands in her lap. Small, thin, wrinkled, she was almost an ideal phenomenon of old age. Some caller, a day or two before, had murmured to Pauline on leaving: "She's very fragile, isn't she?" Pauline, gazing, thought that fragile was precisely not the word. Quiet, gentle, but hardly passive and certainly not fragile. Even now, on that still afternoon, the shut eyes left the face with a sense of preoccupation—translucent rock. She was absent, not with the senility of a spirit wandering in feeble memories, but with the attention of a worker engrossed. Perhaps Stanhope looked so when he wrote verse. Pauline felt that she had never seen her grandmother before and did not quite know what to make of her now. A light sound came from the garden beyond. Mrs. Anstruther opened her eyes and met Pauline's. She smiled. "My dear," she said, "I've been meaning to ask you something for the last day or two." Pauline thought it might be the hot afternoon that gave the voice that effect of distance; it was clear, but small and from afar. The words, the tone, were affectionate with an impersonal love. Pauline thought: "She might be talking to Phœbe"—Phœbe being the maid—and at the same time realized that Mrs. Anstruther did so talk to Phœbe, and to everyone. Her good will diffused itself in all directions. Her granddaughter lay in its way, with all things beside, and it mingled with the warm sun in a general benediction.

Pauline said: "Yes, grandmother?"

"If by any chance I should die during the next few weeks," Mrs. Anstruther said, "you won't let it interfere with your taking part in the play, will you? It would be so unnecessary."

Pauline began to speak, and hesitated. She had been on the point of beginning formally: "O, but——" when she felt, under the lucid gaze, compelled to intelligence. She said slowly: "Well, I suppose I should have...."

"Quite unnecessary," Mrs. Anstruther went on, "and obviously inconvenient, especially if it were in the last few days. Or the last. I hoped you wouldn't think of it, but it was better to make sure."

"It'll look very odd," said Pauline, and found herself smiling back. "And what will the rest of them think?"

"One of them will be disappointed; the rest will be shocked but relieved," Mrs. Anstruther murmured. "You've no proper understudy?"

"None of us have," Pauline said. "One of the others in the Chorus would have to take my part ... if I were ill, I mean."

"Do any of them speak verse better than you?" Mrs. Anstruther asked, with a mild truthfulness of inquiry.

Pauline considered the Chorus. "No," she said at last, sincerely. "I don't think ... I'm sure they don't. Nor Adela," she added with a slight animosity against the princess. Her grandmother accepted the judgment. "Then it would be better for you to be there," she said. "So you'll promise me? It will very nearly be a relief."

"I'll promise certainly," Pauline said. "But you don't feel worse, do you, my dear? I thought you'd been stronger lately—since the summer came in."

"'I have a journey, sir, shortly to go'," Mrs. Anstruther quoted. "And a quieter starting-place than our ancestor."

"Our ancestor?" Pauline said, surprised. "O, but I remember. He was martyred, wasn't he?"

Mrs. Anstruther quoted again: "'Then the said Struther being come to the stake, cried out very loudly: *To him that hath shall be given,* and one of the friars that went with him struck at him and said: *Naughty heretic, and what of him that hath not?* and he shouted with a great laughter, pointing at the friar, and calling out: *He shall lose all that he hath,* and again *The Lord hath sent away the rich with empty bellies.* Then they stripped him, and when he was in his shirt he looked up and said: *The ends of the world be upon me*; and so they set him at the stake and put the fire to the wood, and as the fire got hold of him he gave a loud cry and said: *I have seen the salvation of my God,* and so many times till he died. Which was held for a testimony that the Lord had done great things for him there in the midst of the fire, and under the Lady Elizabeth the place was called Struther's Salvation for many years.'"

Mrs. Anstruther stopped. "And perhaps the Lord did," she said, "though I would not quite take Foxe's word for it."

Pauline shuddered. "It was a terrible thing," she said. "How he could shout for joy like that!"

"Salvation," Mrs. Anstruther said mildly, "is quite often a terrible thing—a frightening good."

"A ..." said Pauline, and paused. "Mr. Stanhope said something like that," she ended.

"Peter Stanhope is a great poet," her grandmother answered. "But I don't think many of you can possibly understand his play. You may; I can't tell."

"Mrs. Parry understands it, all but the Chorus," Pauline said. "And Adela and Myrtle Fox understand even that."

Mrs. Anstruther's look changed. She had been contemplating the fact of Stanhope's poetry with a gaze of awe; there entered into that awe a delicate and extreme delight. She said: "My dear, I used to know Caroline Parry very well. No one has destroyed more plays by successful production. I sometimes wonder—it's wrong—whether she has done the same thing with her life. It's wrong; she is a good creature, and she has behaved very well in all her unrehearsed effects. But I feel she relies too much on elocution and not enough on poetry."

Pauline meditated on this. "I don't think I quite understand," she said. "How the elocution?"

"You're a little inclined to it yourself, my dear," Mrs. Anstruther answered. "Your elocution is very just and very effective, but a certain breath of the verse is lacking. No one could have been kinder to me than you have. We've done very well together—I as the patient and you as the keeper. That's what I mean by elocution."

She turned on her granddaughter eyes full of delight and affection. Pauline could only sit and stare. Then slowly a blush crept up her face, and she looked hastily away.

"Ah, don't be distressed," the old woman said. "My dear, you've been perfect. You're in trouble over something, and yet you've always been kind. I wish I could have helped you."

"I'm not in any trouble," Pauline said with a slight harshness, "except now. Have I been stupid, grandmother?"

"That," Mrs. Anstruther said, "was perhaps a little less than intelligent. Why do you refuse to lean?"

"I don't," Pauline said bitterly, "but there's no——" She was on the point of saying "no help in leaning"; she recovered herself, and changed it to "no need to lean".

"O, my dear child," Mrs. Anstruther murmured gently, "that's almost like the speech days at my school. Ask Peter Stanhope to tell you how to read verse."

Confused between metaphor, implication, and rebuke, and the voice that disseminated sweetness through all, Pauline was about to protest again when Phœbe came out into the garden. She came up to her mistress, and said: "Mrs. Lily Sammile has called, madam, and wants to know if you are well enough to see her."

"Certainly," Mrs. Anstruther said. "Ask Mrs. Sammile to come out here." And as Phœbe disappeared: "Do you know her, Pauline?"

Pauline, standing up and folding her typescript with a precision that was almost respect, said: "Hardly *know*. She meets one continually, and she's at things. She calls. I never met anyone who'd called on her, now I come to think of it. I don't even know where she lives."

"There are all sorts of places to live on this hill," Mrs. Anstruther said, and Pauline heard in the voice an undertone of ambiguity. For a moment her fear took her; she looked hastily round. There was no sign of her twin. "All sorts of places to live."

"Many habitations," she answered with forced lightness, and went to meet the visitor who appeared from the house.

Mrs. Sammile was younger than Mrs. Anstruther, and much quicker in movement. She was much more restless. Her feet pattered on the path, her eyes glanced everywhere; she suggested by her whole bearing that time was in a hurry, and there was very little time for—something. Perhaps the contrast of Mrs. Anstruther's repose heightened this excitement. She was shorter than Pauline, and her eyes looked up at the girl almost anxiously. She said: "I've only just looked in. But it was so *long* since I'd seen you."

"We met yesterday, if you remember," Pauline answered, smiling. "But it was good of you to come."

"I don't, I hope, intrude?" Mrs. Sammile went on, as she shook hands with the old woman. Mrs. Anstruther murmured something vague, and Pauline said it more definitely: "Of course not, Mrs. Sammile, we're delighted."

"Such glorious weather—but trying, isn't it?" the visitor prattled nervously on, rather like a chicken fluttering round the glass walls of a snake's cage. "I always think any weather's trying, heat or cold. And it always seems to be one or other, doesn't it?"

"So pleasant," said Mrs. Anstruther politely. "Like sex, one can't imagine anything not one or the other. Or, of course, a combination."

"If," Pauline added, valiant but aware of failure, "if we could make our own weather…."

Lily Sammile slewed round a little towards her. "If we *could*!" she said. "I thought yesterday that you were looking a little tired, my dear."

"Was I?" Pauline answered. "Perhaps I was," and added agonizingly, "It's the spring, I expect."

The other looked at her, turning still a little more away from Mrs. Anstruther, and seeming to become a little quieter as she did so. She said: "I do think the world's rather trying, don't you?"

"I do," Pauline said with a heartfelt throb of assent, and more earnestly than she knew. "Very trying." It certainly was hot. She felt that three in the garden were too many, and wondered if her grandmother, in case she was feeling tired, ought to be offered an opportunity of going indoors. If June were so sultry, what would July be? The time was still; no sound came. A lifting palpitation took her; she shuddered. Her grave: who walked on, or was it from, her grave? The thing she had so often seen? into which—she knew now—she feared to be drawn, to be lost or not to be lost, to be always herself as the enfeebled element in something else. Never yet within walls, but the heat crept round her, a preliminary invasion; the heat came over or through walls, and after the heat its centre.

The violent sensation receded. She came to herself to find herself staring rudely at Mrs. Sammile's face. It was a face that had been beautiful, rounded and precious with delight, sustained just sufficiently by its bones to avoid, as for instance Adela Hunt's hardly avoided, the reproach of plumpness; and was still full in places, by the ears and round the jaw; only the cheeks were a little macabre in their withdrawal, and the eyes in their hint of hollows about them. Pauline, stirred by the sad recollection of her other self, thought that Mrs. Sammile looked more like death than her grandmother, more like a living death, than which, on this hill where her own ancestor and so many others had died, what could be more likely?

Mrs. Sammile was saying softly: "Perhaps she's asleep; I don't want to wake her. You look so tired. If I could be any use...."

Pauline thought, as she looked back, that she had been unjust to Mrs. Sammile's eyes. They were not restless, as she had thought. They were soothing; they appealed and comforted at once. She said: "I've had bad dreams."

Mrs. Sammile said: "I've had them too, sometimes," and Pauline almost felt that even her dream, to call it that, was less trouble than those other undescribed nightmares. But before she could speak the visitor went on: "But there are cures, you know."

She had spoken, perhaps, a little more loudly, for Mrs. Anstruther's voice answered equably: "There is, of course, sleep. Or waking. Is there anything else?"

Mrs. Sammile looked round, and her answer held the earlier suggestion of hostility. She said, defensively: "Pleasanter dreams. On a hill like this, one ought to have a choice. There are so many."

Pauline said: "Can you change dreams, Mrs. Sammile?"

"O, everyone can," the other answered. She leant towards Pauline and went on: "There are all sorts of ways of changing dreams." She put a hand on the girl's. "All tales of the brain. Why not tell yourself a comforting tale?"

"Because I could never make up a satisfying end," Pauline said, "and the tale wouldn't stop—no tale that I could think of. There was always something more that had got to happen and I could never feel—not in my best tale—that I was quite certainly telling it."

"You must let me tell you tales instead," Lily Sammile answered. "Come and see me."

"I'd like to, but I don't think I know where you live, Mrs. Sammile," Pauline said, and paused on the implied question.

Mrs. Sammile said: "O, we shall meet. And if we can't find a tale we'll do as well. Cross my hand with silver, and I'll not only tell you a good fortune, I'll make you one. Like the Bible—wine and milk without money, or for so little it hardly counts."

Pauline looked at Mrs. Anstruther. "Mrs. Sammile is offering us all we want without any trouble," she said. "Shall we take it and be grateful?"

"Exquisite rhetoric," her grandmother allusively answered, but faintly, and Pauline went on to the visitor: "And would one always enjoy oneself then?"

"Why not?" Mrs. Sammile said. "Everything lovely in you for a perpetual companion, so that you'd never be frightened or disappointed or ashamed any more. There are tales that can give you yourself completely and the world could never treat you so badly then that you wouldn't neglect it. One can get everything by listening or looking in the right way: there are all sorts of turns."

Phœbe reappeared by Mrs. Anstruther's chair. "Miss Fox and Mr. Stanhope, madam," she said, and retired with a message.

Pauline said, as she stood up, "It'd be too wonderful," and then, "Aren't you rather tired, grandmother? Wouldn't you rather go upstairs and let me see them indoors?"

"My dear," Mrs. Anstruther said, "as long as Peter Stanhope comes to see me, I shall receive him. At least, until Mrs. Sammile gives us the effect of Shakespeare without Shakespeare. Give me your arm."

She stood up, and leaning on the girl took a step or two forward, as Myrtle Fox, followed by Stanhope, came into the garden, and hurried across to her.

"Dear Mrs. Anstruther, how nice to see you again," Myrtle said. "It seems such a long time, but you know how rushed one is! But I felt I must come to-day. Do you know Mr. Stanhope? We met in the street and came along together."

Mrs. Anstruther allowed herself to be embraced and kissed without any further welcome than a smile; then she held out her hand.

"This is a great honour, Mr. Stanhope," she said. "I'm very glad to welcome you here."

He bowed over her hand. "It's very kind of you, Mrs. Anstruther."

"I've owed you a great deal for a long while now," she said, "and I can do no more than acknowledge it. But I'm grateful that I can do that. Do you know Mrs. Sammile?"

Stanhope bowed again; Myrtle let out a new gush of greeting, and they all sat down.

"I really came," Stanhope said after a little interchange, "to ask Miss Anstruther if she had any preference in names."

"Me?" said Pauline. "What sort of names?"

"As the leader of the Chorus," Stanhope explained. "I promised Mrs. Parry I'd try and individualize so far—for the sake of the audience—as to give her a name. Myself, I don't think it'll much help the audience, but as I promised—I wondered about something French, as it's to be eighteenth century, La Lointaine or something like that. But Mrs. Parry was afraid that'd make it more difficult. No one would understand (she thought) why leaves—if they are leaves—should be *lointaine*...."

He was interrupted by Myrtle, who, leaning eagerly forward, said: "O, Mr. Stanhope, that reminds me. I was thinking about it myself the other day, and I thought how beautiful and friendly it would be to give all the Chorus tree-names. It would look so attractive on the programmes, Elm, Ash, Oak—the three sweet trees—Hawthorn, Weeping Willow, Beech, Birch, Chestnut. D'you see? That would make it all quite clear. And then Pauline could be the Oak. I mean, the Oak would have to be the leader of the English trees, wouldn't he—or she?"

"Do let Mr. Stanhope tell us, Myrtle," Mrs. Anstruther said; and "You'd turn them into a cosy corner of trees, Myrtle," Pauline interjected.

"But that's what we want," Myrtle pursued her dream, "we want to realize that Nature can be consoling, like life. And Art—even Mr. Stanhope's play. I think all art is so consoling, don't you, Mrs. Sammile?"

Mrs. Anstruther had opened her mouth to interrupt Myrtle, but now she shut it again, and waited for her guest to reply, who said in a moment, with a slight touch of tartness, "I'm sure Mr. Stanhope won't agree. He'll tell you nightmares are significant."

"O, but we agreed that wasn't the right word," Myrtle exclaimed. "Or was it! Pauline, was it significant or symbolical that we agreed everything was?"

"I want to know my name," Pauline said, and Stanhope, smiling, answered, "I was thinking of something like Periel. Quite insignificant."

"It sounds rather odd," said Myrtle. "What about the others?"

"The others," Stanhope answered firmly, "will not be named."

"O!" Myrtle looked disappointed. "I thought we might have had a song or speech or something with all the names in it. It would sound beautiful. And Art ought to be beautiful, don't you think? Beautiful words in beautiful voices. I do think elocution is so important."

Pauline said, "Grandmother doesn't care for elocution."

"O, Mrs. Anstru——" Myrtle was beginning, when Mrs. Anstruther cut her short.

"What does one need to say poetry, Mr. Stanhope?" she asked.

Stanhope laughed. "What but the four virtues, clarity, speed, humility, courage? Don't you agree?"

The old lady looked at Mrs. Sammile. "Do *you*?" she asked.

Lily Sammile shrugged. "O if you're turning poems into labours," she said. "But we don't all want to speak poetry, and enjoyment's a simple thing for the rest of us."

"We do all want to speak it," Stanhope protested. "Or else verse and plays and all art are more of dreams than they need be. They must always be a little so, perhaps."

Mrs. Sammile shrugged again. "You make such a business of enjoying yourself," she said with almost a sneer. "Now if I've a nightmare I change it as soon as I can." She looked at Pauline.

"I've never had nightmares since I Couéd them away," Myrtle Fox broke in. "I say every night: 'Sleep is good, and sleep is here. Sleep is good.' And I never dream. I say the same thing every morning, only I say Life then instead of Sleep. 'Life is good and Life is here. Life is good'."

Stanhope flashed a glance at Pauline. "Terribly good, perhaps," he suggested.

"Terribly good, certainly," Myrtle assented happily.

Mrs. Sammile stood up. "I must go," she said. "But I don't see why you don't enjoy yourselves."

"Because, sooner or later, there isn't anything to enjoy in oneself," Stanhope murmured, as she departed.

Pauline took her to the gate, and said good-bye.

"Do let's meet," Mrs. Sammile said. "I'm always about, and I think I could be useful. You've got to get back now, but sometime you needn't get back...." She trotted off, and as she went the hard patter of her heels was the only sound that broke, to Pauline's ears, the heavy silence of the Hill.

The girl lingered a little before returning. A sense of what Miss Fox called "significance" hung in her mind; she felt, indeterminately, that something had happened, or, perhaps, was beginning to happen. The afternoon had been one of a hundred—the garden, a little talk, visitors, tea—yet all that usualness had been tinged with difference. She wondered if it were merely the play, and her concern with it, that had heightened her senses into what was, no doubt, illusion. Her hands lay on the top bar of the gate, and idly she moved her fingers, separating and closing them one by one for each recollected point. Her promise to her grandmother—death was not to interrupt verse; the memory of her ancestor—death swallowed up in victory—Struther's Salvation, Anstruther's salvation; elocution, rhetoric, poetry, Peter Stanhope, Lily Sammile, the slight jar of their half-philosophical dispute; her own silly phrase—"to make your own weather"; tales of the brain, tales to be told, tales that gave you yourself in quiet, tales or the speaking of verse, tales or rhetoric or poetry; "clarity, speed, courage, humility". Or did they only prevent desirable enjoyment, as Lily Sammile had hinted? One would have to be terribly good to achieve them. And terribly careful about the tales. She looked down the street, and for an instant felt that if she saw It coming—clarity, speed, courage, humility—she might wait. She belonged to the Chorus of a great experiment; a thing not herself.

The   Magus   Zoroaster,   my   dead   child,
Met his own image walking in the garden.

If those four great virtues were needed, as Peter Stanhope had proposed, even to say the verse, might Shelley have possessed them before he discovered the verse? If she were wrong in hating them? if they had been offered her as a classification, a hastening, a strengthening? if she had to discover them as Shelley had done, and beyond them....

She must go back. She pulled herself from the gate. Mrs. Sammile had just reached the corner. She looked back; she waved. The gesture beckoned. Pauline waved back, reluctantly. Before she told herself tales, it was needful to know what there was in verse. She must hear more.

She was not offered more. The visitors were on the point of departure, and Mrs. Anstruther was certainly tired. She roused herself to beg Stanhope to come again, if he would, but no more passed, except indeed that as Pauline herself said good-bye, Stanhope delayed a moment behind Miss Fox to add: "The substantive, of course, governs the adjective; not the other way round."

"The substantive?" Pauline asked blankly.

"Good. It contains terror, not terror good. I'm keeping you. Good-bye, Periel," and he was gone.

Later in the day, lying unsleeping but contented in her bed, Mrs. Anstruther also reviewed the afternoon. She was glad to have seen Peter Stanhope; she was not particularly glad to have seen Lily Sammile, but she freely acknowledged, in the words of a too often despised poet, that since God suffered her to be, she too was God's minister, and laboured for some good by Margaret Anstruther not understood. She did not understand clearly what Mrs. Sammile conceived herself to be offering. It sounded so much like Myrtle Fox: "tell yourself tales".

She looked out of the window. There would be few more evenings during which she could watch the departure of day, and the promise of rarity gave a greater happiness to the experience. So did the knowledge of familiarity. Rarity was one form of delight and frequency another. A thing could even be beautiful because it did not happen, or rather the not-happening could be beautiful. So long always as joy was not rashly pinned to the happening; so long as you accepted what joys the universe offered and did not seek to compel the universe to offer you joys of your own definition. She would die soon; she expected, with hope and happiness, the discovery of the joy of death.

It was partly because Stanhope's later plays had in them something of this purification and simplicity that she loved them. She knew that, since they were poetry, they must mean more than her individual being knew, but at least they meant that. He discovered it in his style, in words and the manner of the words he used. Whether his personal life could move to the sound of his own lucid exaltation of verse she did not know. It was not her business; perhaps even it was not primarily his. His affair had been the powerful exploration of power after his own manner; all minds that recognized power saluted him. Power was in that strange chorus over which the experts of Battle Hill culture disputed, and it lay beyond them. There was little human approach in it, though it possessed human experience; like the *Dirge* in *Cymbeline* or the songs of Ariel in the *Tempest* it possessed only the pure perfection of fact, rising in rhythms of sound that seemed inhuman because they were free from desire or fear or distress. She herself did not yet dare to repeat the Chorus; it was beyond her courage. Those who had less knowledge or more courage might do so. She dared only to recollect it; to say it would need more courage than was required for death. When she was dead, she might be able to say Stanhope's poetry properly. Even if there were no other joy, that would be a reason for dying well.

Here, more than in most places, it should be easy. Here there had, through the centuries, been a compression and culmination of death as if the currents of mortality had been drawn hither from long distances to some whirlpool of invisible depth. The distances might be very long indeed; from all places of predestined sepulchre, scattered through the earth. In those places the movement of human life had closed— of human life or human death, of the death in life which was an element in life, and of those places the Hill on which she lived was one. An energy reposed in it, strong to affect all its people; an energy of separation and an energy of knowledge. If, as she believed, the spirit of a man at death saw truly what he was and had been, so that whether he desired it or not a lucid power of intelligence manifested all himself to him—then that energy of knowledge was especially urgent upon men and women here, though through all the world it must press upon the world. She felt, as if by a communication of a woe not hers, how the neighbourhood of the dead troubled the living; how the living were narrowed by the return of the dead. Therefore in savage regions the houses of sepulchre were forbidden, were taboo, for the wisdom of the barbarians set division between the dead and the living, and the living were preserved. The wisdom of other religions in civilized lands had set sacramental ceremonies about the dying, and dispatched the dead to their doom with prayers and rites which were not meant for the benefit of the dead alone. Rather, they secured the living against ghostly oppression; they made easy the way of the ghosts into their own world and hurried them upon their way. They were sped on with unction and requiem, with intercessions and masses; and the sword of exorcism waved at the portal of their exodus against the return of any whom those salutations of departure did not ease. But where superstition and religion failed, where cemeteries were no longer forbidden and no longer feared; where the convenient processes of cremation encouraged a pretence of swift passage, where easy sentimentality set up a pretence of friendship between the living and the dead—might not that new propinquity turn to a fearful friendship in the end? It was commonly accepted that the dead were anxious to help the living, but what if the dead were only anxious for the living to help them? or what if the infection of their experience communicated itself across the too shallow grave? Men were beginning to know, they were being compelled to know; at last the living world was shaken by the millions of spirits who endured that further permanent revelation. Hysteria of self-knowledge, monotony of self-analysis, introspection spreading like disease, what was all this but the infection communicated over the unpurified borders of death? The spirits of the living world were never meant to be so neighbourly with the spirits of that other. "Grant to them eternal rest, O Lord. And let light eternal shine upon them." Let them rest in their own places of light; far, far from us be their discipline and their endeavour. The phrases of the prayers of intercession throb with something other than charity for the departed; there is a fear for the living. Grant them, grant them rest; compel them to their rest. Enlighten them, perpetually enlighten them. And let us still enjoy our refuge from their intolerable knowledge.

As if in a last communion with the natural terrors of man, Margaret Anstruther endured a recurrent shock of fear. She recalled herself. To tolerate such knowledge with a joyous welcome was meant, as the holy Doctors had taught her, to be the best privilege of man, and so remained. The best maxim towards that knowledge was yet not the *Know thyself* of the Greek so much as the *Know Love* of the Christian, though both in the end were one. It was not possible for man to know himself and the world, except first after some mode of knowledge, some art of discovery. The most perfect, since the most intimate and intelligent, art was pure love. The approach by love was the approach to fact; to love anything but fact was not love. Love was even more mathematical than poetry; it was the pure mathematics of the spirit. It was applied also and active; it was the means as it was the end. The end lived everlastingly in the means; the means eternally in the end.

The girl and the old woman who lay, both awake, in that house under the midnight sky, were at different stages of that way. To the young mind of Pauline, by some twist of grace in the operation of space and time, the Greek maxim had taken on a horrible actuality; the older vision saw, while yet living, almost into a world beyond the places of the dead. Pauline knew nothing yet of the value of those night vigils, nor of the fulfilment of the desire of truth. But Margaret had, through a long life, practised the distinction, not only between experience and experience, but in each experience itself between dream and fact. It is not enough to say that some experiences are drugs to the spirit; every experience, except the final, has a quality which has to be cast out by its other quality of perfection, expelled by healthy digestion into the sewers where the divine scavengers labour. By a natural law Margaret's spirit exercised freely its supernatural functions and with increasing clearness looked out on to the growing company of the Hill.

Lights in the houses opposite had long since been put out. The whole rise of ground, lying like a headland, or indeed itself like some huge grave in which so many others had been dug, was silent in the darkness, but for one sound; the sound of footsteps. Margaret knew it very well; she had heard it on many nights. Sometimes in the day as well, when the peace was deepest within her and without, she could hear that faint monotonous patter of feet reverberating from its surface. Its distance was not merely in space, though it seemed that also, but in some other dimension. Who it was that so walked for ever over the Hill she did not know, though in her heart she did not believe it to be good. The harsh phrase would have been alien to her. She heard those feet not as sinister or dangerous, but only—patter, patter—as the haste of a search for or a flight from repose—perhaps both. Ingress and regress, desire and repulsion, contended there. The contention was the only equilibrium of that haunter of the Hill, and was pain. Patter, patter. It sounded at a distance, like the hurrying feet of the woman on her own garden path that afternoon. She had heard, in old tales of magic, of the guardian of the threshold. She wondered if the real secret of the terrible guardian were that he was simply lost on the threshold. His enmity to man and heaven was only his yearning to enter one without loss. It did not matter, nor was it her affair. Her way did not cross that other's; only it was true she never sank into those circles of other sensation and vision but what, far off, she heard—patter, patter—the noise of the endless passage.

There moved within her the infinite business of the Hill into which so much death had poured. First there came the creation of new images instead of those of every day. Her active mind still insisted on them; she allowed its due. The Hill presented itself before her with all its buildings and populace; she saw them, small and vivid, hurrying. She would even sometimes recognize one or other, for the briefest second. She had seen, in that re-creation by night of the Hill by day, Pauline going into a shop and Peter Stanhope talking in the street, and others. She remembered now, idly, that she had never seen the woman who had called on her that day, though she had seen Myrtle Fox running, running hard, down a long street. Distinct though the vision was, it was but momentary. It was the equivalent of her worldly affairs, and it lasted little longer; in a second it had gone.

It had enlarged rather. It reduplicated itself on each side, and its inhabitants faded from it as it did so, seeming themselves to pass into other hills. Presently there was no living form or building on that original Hill, and it was no longer possible to tell which had been the original, for a great range swept right across the sky, and all those heights were only the upper slopes of mountains, whose lower sides fell away beneath her vision. The earth itself seemed to lie in each of those mountains, and on each there was at first a populous region towards the summit, but the summit itself rose individual and solitary. Mountains or modes of consciousness, peaks or perceptions, they stood; on the slopes of each the world was carried; and the final height of each was a separate consummation of the whole. It was, as the apprehended movement upon each of them died away, in the time before the dawn that they rose there, nor had the sun risen, though they were not in darkness. Either a light emanated from themselves or some greater sun drew towards them from its own depth.

Then—it was not to say that they faded, but rather that she lost them, becoming herself one of them and ignorant of the rest. It was very silent; only small sounds came up to her as if someone was climbing below. The noises were so faint that in the air of earth they would have been lost. Had she been woman she would not have known them; now that she was not woman alone but mountain, the mountain knew that it was not from its own nature alone that the tiny disturbances came. There was movement within it certainly; rush of streams, fall of rocks, roar of winds through its chasms, but these things were not sound to it as was that alien human step. Through all another single note sounded once; a bell. Minutely she knew that the public clock of the Hill had struck one. It was a remote translation of a thing, for the dawn began.

It came from above, and as the light grew the mountain that was she became aware again of its fellows, spread out around no longer in a long range but in a great mass. They stretched away on all sides. At the increase of the sun there grew also an increase of fugitive sound; and she became aware of a few wandering shapes on the heights about her. Some climbed on; others, instead of welcoming the light as lost mountaineers should do, turned to escape it. They hurried into such caves or crevasses as they could find. Here and there, on a great open space, one lay fallen, twisting and dragging himself along. They seemed all, even those who climbed, grotesque obtrusions into that place of rock and ice and thin air and growing sun, a world different from theirs, hers and not hers. A divided consciousness lived in her, more intensely than ever before.

In the time of her novitiate it had seemed to her sometimes that, though her brains and emotions acted this way or that, yet all that activity went on along the sides of a slowly increasing mass of existence made from herself and all others with whom she had to do, and that strong and separate happiness—for she felt it as happiness, though she herself might be sad; her sadness did but move on it as the mountaineer on the side of a mountain—that happiness was the life which she was utterly to become. Now she knew that only the smallest fragility of her being clung somewhere to the great height that was she and others and all the world under her separate kind, as she herself was part of all the other peaks; and though the last fragility was still a little terrified of the dawn which was breaking everywhere, she knew that when the dawn reached the corner where she lay it would, after one last throb of piercing change under its power, light but the mountain side, and all her other mighty knowledge would after its own manner rejoice in it. She had not much strength in these days—that she which was Margaret Anstruther and lay in her bed on Battle Hill—but such as she had it was her business to use. She set herself to crawl out of that darkened corner towards the light. She turned from all the corner held—her home, her memories, Stanhope's plays, Pauline; with an effort she began her last journey. It might take hours, or days, or even years, but it was certain; as she moved, crawling slowly over the rock, she saw the light sweeping on to meet her. The moment of death was accepted and accomplished in her first outward movement; there remained only to die.

On her way and in her bed, she dozed a little, and in that light sleep—dream within dream or vision within vision—she seemed to be walking again in the streets of Battle Hill, as if, having renounced it, it was restored to her. It was still night there; the lamps were lit in the streets; the rustle of the many trees was substituted for the silence of the mountains. But the great mountains were there, and the light of them, and their inhabitants; though the inhabitants did not know the soil on which they lived. In a foretaste of the acute senses of death she walked among them, but they did not see her. Outside her own house she saw Pauline come out and look bitterly this way and the other, and start to walk down the road, and presently as if from the mountain side another Pauline had grown visible and came to meet the first, her head high and bright as the summit, her eyes bright with the supernatural dawn, her movements as free and yet disposed as the winds that swept the chasms. She came on, her feet which at first made no noise, beginning to sound on the pavement as she took on more and more of mortal appearance, and the first Pauline saw her and turned and fled, and the second pursued her, and far away, down the dark streets and round the dark mountain, they vanished from sight. And then again, and now she was not by her own house but in another street towards the top of the hill, she saw a man walking hurriedly on, a man strange to her, but after him followed a crowd of others, young men and children, and all of them with his face. They pursued him, as the vision of Pauline had pursued the vision of Pauline, but this time with angry or plaintive cries, and he hurried on seeking something, for his restless eyes turned every way and sometimes he peered at the gutter and sometimes he looked up at the dark window, till presently he turned in at one of the gates, and about the gate his company seemed to linger and watch and whisper. Presently she saw him at a window, looking down; and there were at that window two forms who did not seem to see each other, but the second she knew, for he had been at her house once not so long ago, and it was Lawrence Wentworth. He too was looking down, and after a little he was coming out of the gate, and after him also came a figure, but this time a woman, a young woman, who pursued him in his turn, and for whom also he lay in wait.

But the other man too had now come out into the street, only it was no more the street of a town but a ruined stretch of scaffolding or bone or rock, all heights and edges and bare skeleton shapes. He was walking there on the mountain though he did not know it, any more than he noticed the light. He walked and looked up and round, and her eyes met his, and he made a sudden movement of wonder and, she thought, of joy. But as they looked, the dream, which was becoming more and more a dream, shifted again, and she heard quick and loud the patter-patter of those footsteps with which, as if they marked a region through or round which she passed, such experiences always began and ended. She was on the Hill, and all the houses were about her, and they stood all on graves and bones, and swayed upon their foundations. A great stench went up from them, and a cry, and the feet came quicker, and down the street ran Lily Sammile, waving and calling, and checked and stood. She looked at a gate; Pauline was standing there. The two neared each other, the gate still between them, and began to talk. "No more hurt, no more pain, no more but dreams", a voice said. Margaret Anstruther put out a hand; it touched a projection in the rock on which she was lying in her journey towards corporeal death. She clung to it, and pulled herself forward towards Pauline. The nurse in the room heard her and turned. Mrs. Anstruther said: "I should like to see Pauline; will you ask her——" and at that she woke, and it was striking one.

RETURN TO EDEN

*

Margaret Anstruther had seen, in her vision, a single house, with two forms leaning from the same window. Time there had disappeared, and the dead man had been contemporaneous with the living. As if simultaneity approached the Hill, the experiences of its inhabitants had there become co-eval; propinquity no longer depended upon sequence.

The chance that brought Lawrence Wentworth into such close spiritual contact with the dead was the mere manner of his ill luck. His was not worse than any other's, though the hastening of time to its end made it more strange. It grew in him, like all judgment, through his negligence. A thing of which he had consistently refused to be aware, if action is the test of awareness, drew close to him: that is, the nature of the Republic. The outcast of the Republic had climbed a forlorn ladder to his own death. His death entered into the Republic, and into the lives of its other members. Wentworth had never acknowledged the unity. He had never acknowledged the victims of oppression nor the presence of victimization. It may be that such victimization is inevitable, and that the Republic after its kind must be as false to its own good as the lives of most of its children are to theirs. But Wentworth had neither admitted nor rejected this necessity, nor even questioned and been hurt by it; he had merely ignored it. He had refused the agony of the *res publica*, and of temporal justice. Another justice sharpened the senses of his *res privata*. He was doubly open to its approach—in his scholarship, where the ignoring of others began to limit, colour, and falsify his work, and in his awareness of supernatural neighbours, if any should be near. One was.

The dead man had stood in what was now Wentworth's bedroom, and listened in fear lest he should hear the footsteps of his kind. That past existed still in its own place, since all the past is in the web of life nothing else than a part of which we are not sensationally conscious. It was drawing closer now to the present; it approached the senses of the present. But between them still there went—patter, patter—the hurrying footsteps which Margaret Anstruther had heard in the first circle of the Hill. The dead man had hardly heard them; his passion had carried him through that circle into death. But on the hither side were the footsteps, and the echo and memory of the footsteps, of this world. It was these for which Wentworth listened. He had come back into his own room after he had heard those steady and mocking footsteps of Hugh and Adela, and the voices and subdued laughter accompanying them. He had himself wandered up and down, and come to a rest at last at the finished window where, with no wall before him, the dead man had peered. He also peered. He listened, and his fancy created for him the unheard melody of the footsteps. His body renewed and absorbed the fatal knowledge of his desire. He listened, in the false faith of desire. It could not be that he would not hear, out of those double footsteps, one true pair separating themselves, coming up the street, approaching the gate; that he would not see a true form coming up the drive, approaching the door. It must happen; his body told him it must happen. He must have what he wanted, because … but still those feet did not come. The dead man stood by him, arm to arm, foot by foot, and listened, the rope in his hand, and that night neither of them heard anything at all.

The evening and the morning were the first day, or a few hours, or a few months, or both at once. Others followed. The business of the Hill progressed; the play went forward. Pauline fled, and Margaret died, or lived in process of death. Hugh went up and down to the City. Adela went about the Hill. Wentworth, now possessed by his consciousness of her, and demanding her presence and consent as its only fulfilment, went about his own affairs. "Blessed is he whosoever shall not be offended in Me"; the maxim applies to many stones of stumbling, and especially to all those of which the nature is the demand for a presence instead of the assent to an absence; the imposition of the self upon complacency. Wentworth made his spiritual voice hoarse in issuing orders to complacency, and stubbed his toes more angrily every day against the unmovable stone.

Once or twice he met Adela—once at Mrs. Parry's, where they had no chance to speak. They smiled at each other—an odd smile; the faintest hint of greed, springing from the invisible nature of greed, was in it on both sides. Their greeds smiled. Again he ran into her one evening at the post office—with Hugh, and Hugh's smile charged theirs with hostility. It ordered and subdued Adela's; it blocked and repulsed Wentworth's. It forced on him the fact that he was not only unsuccessful, but old; he contended against both youth and a rival. He said: "How's the play going?"

"We're all learning our parts," Adela said. "There doesn't seem to be time for *anything* but the play. Shall we ever get another evening with you, Mr. Wentworth?"

He said: "I was sorry you could neither of you come." That, he thought, would show that he hadn't been taken in.

"Yes," said Hugh; the word hung ambiguously. Wentworth, angered by it, went on rashly: "Did you have a pleasant time?"

He might have meant the question for either or both. Adela said: "O well, you know; it was rather a rush. Choosing colours and all that."

"But fortunately we ran into each other later," Hugh added, "and we almost ran at each other—didn't we, Adela?—so we fed in a hurry and dashed to a theatre. It might have been much worse."

Wentworth heard the steps in his brain. He saw Hugh take Adela's arm; he saw her look up at him; he saw an exchanged memory. The steps went on through him; double steps. He wanted to get away to give himself up to them: life and death, satisfaction of hate and satisfaction of lust, contending, and the single approach of the contention's result—patter, patter, steps on the Hill. He knew they were laughing at him. He made normal noises, and abnormally fled. He went home.

In his study he automatically turned over his papers, aware but incapable of the organic life of the mind they represented. He found himself staring at his drawings of costumes for the play, and had an impulse to tear them, to refuse to have anything to do with the grotesque mummery, himself to reject the picture of the rejection of himself. But he did not trust his own capacity to manage a more remote force than Adela—Mrs. Parry. Mrs. Parry meant nothing to him; she could never become to him the nervous irritation, the obsession, which both Aston Moffatt and Adela now were. His intelligence warned him that she was, nevertheless, one of the natural forces which, like time and space, he could not overcome. She wanted the designs, and she would have them. He could refuse, but not reject, Adela; he could reject, but he certainly could not refuse, Mrs. Parry. Irritated at his knowledge of his own false strength, he flung down the rescued designs. Under them were his first drafts; he tore them instead.

The evening wore into night. He could not bring himself to go to bed. He walked about the room; he worked a little and walked, and walked a little and worked. He thought of going to bed, but then he thought also of his dream, and the smooth strange rope. He had never so much revolted against it as now; he had never, waking, been so strongly aware of it as now. It might have been coiled in some corner of the room, were it not that he knew he was on it, in the dream. Physically and emotionally weary, he still walked, and a somnambulism of scratched images closed on him. His body twitched jerkily; the back of his eyes ached as if he stared interiorly from the rope into a backward abysm. He stood irritably still.

His eyes stared interiorly; exteriorly they glanced down and saw the morning paper, which, by an accident, he had not opened. His hands took it up, and turned the pages. In the middle he saw a headline: "Birthday Honours", and a smaller headline: "Knighthood for Historian". His heart deserted him: his puppet-eyes stared. They found the item by the name in black type for their convenience: "Aston Moffatt".

There was presented to him at once and clearly an opportunity for joy—casual, accidental joy, but joy. If he could not manage joy, at least he might have managed the intention of joy, or (if that also were too much) an effort towards the intention of joy. The infinity of grace could have been contented and invoked by a mere mental refusal of anything but such an effort. He knew his duty—he was no fool—he knew that the fantastic recognition would please and amuse the innocent soul of Sir Aston, not so much for himself as in some unselfish way for the honour of history. Such honours meant nothing, but they were part of the absurd dance of the world, and to be enjoyed as such. Wentworth knew he could share that pleasure. He could enjoy; at least he could refuse not to enjoy. He could refuse and reject damnation.

With a perfectly clear, if instantaneous, knowledge of what he did, he rejected joy instead. He instantaneously preferred anger, and at once it came; he invoked envy, and it obliged him. He crushed the paper in a rage, then he tore it open, and looked again and again—there it still was. He knew that his rival had not only succeeded, but succeeded at his own expense; what chance was there of another historical knighthood for years? Till that moment he had never thought of such a thing. The possibility had been created and withdrawn simultaneously, leaving the present fact to mock him. The other possibility—of joy in that present fact—receded as fast. He had determined, then and for ever, for ever, for ever, that he would hate the fact, and therefore facts.

He walked, unknowing, to the window, and stared out. He loomed behind the glass, a heavy bulk of monstrous greed. His hate so swelled that he felt it choking his throat, and by a swift act transferred it: he felt his rival choking and staggering, he hoped and willed it. He stared passionately into death, and saw before him a body twisting at the end of a rope. Sir Aston Moffatt ... Sir Aston Moffatt.... He stared at the faint ghost of the dead man's death, in that half-haunted house, and did not see it. The dead man walked on his own Hill, but that Hill was not to be Wentworth's. Wentworth preferred another death; he was offered it.

As he stood there, imagining death, close to the world of the first death, refusing all joy of facts, and having for long refused all unselfish agony of facts, he heard at last the footsteps for which he had listened. It was the one thing which could abolish his anger; it did. He forgot, in his excitement, all about Aston Moffatt; he lost sight, exteriorly and interiorly, of the dangling figure. He stood breathless, listening. Patter—patter; they were coming up the road. Patter—patter; they stopped at the gate. He heard the faint clang. The footsteps, softer now, came in. He stared intently down the drive. A little way up it stood a woman's figure. The thing he had known must happen had happened. She had come.

He pushed the window up—careful, even so, not to seem to go fast, not to seem to want her. He leaned out and spoke softly. He said: "Is that you?" The answer startled him, for it was Adela's voice and yet something more than Adela's, fuller, richer, more satisfying. It said "I'm here." He could only just hear the words, but that was right, for it was after midnight, and she was beckoning with her hand. The single pair of feet drawn from the double, the hand waving to him. He motioned to her to come, but she did not stir, and at last, driven by his necessity, he climbed through the window—it was easy enough, even for him—and went down to meet her. As he came nearer he was puzzled again, as he had been by the voice. It was Adela, yet it was not. It was her height, and had her movement. The likeness appeased him, yet he did not understand the faint unlikeness. For a moment he thought it was someone else, a woman of the Hill, some one he had seen, whose name he did not remember. He was up to her now, and he knew it could not be Adela, for even Adela had never been so like Adela as this. That truth which is the vision of romantic love, in which the beloved becomes supremely her own adorable and eternal self, the glory and splendour of her own existence, and her own existence no longer felt or thought as hers but of and from another, that was aped for him then. The thing could not astonish him, nor could it be adored. It perplexed. He hesitated.

The woman said: "You've been so long."

He answered roughly: "Who are you? You're not Adela."

The voice said: "Adela!" and Wentworth understood that Adela was not enough, that Adela must be something different even from Adela if she were to be satisfactory to him, something closer to his own mind and farther from hers. She had been in relation with Hugh, and his Adela could never be in relation with Hugh. He had never understood that simplicity before. It was so clear now. He looked at the woman opposite and felt a stirring of freedom in him.

He said: "You waved?" and she: "Or didn't you wave to me?"

He said, under her eyes: "I didn't think you'd be any use to me."

She laughed: the laugh was a little like Adela's, only better. Fuller; more amused. Adela hardly ever laughed as if she were really amused; she had always a small condescension. He said: "How could I know?"

"You don't think about yourself enough," she said; the words were tender and grateful to him, and he knew they were true. He had never thought enough about himself. He had wanted to be kind. He had wanted to be kind to Adela; it was Adela's obstinate folly which now outraged him. He had wanted to give himself to Adela out of kindness. He was greatly relieved by this woman's words, almost as much as if he had given himself. He went on giving. He said: "If I thought more of myself?"

"You wouldn't have much difficulty in finding it," she answered. "Let's walk."

He didn't understand the first phrase, but he turned and went by her side, silent while he heard the words. Much difficulty in finding what? in finding it? the it that could be found if he thought of himself more; that was what he had said or she had said, whichever had said that the thing was to be found, as if Adela had said it, Adela in her real self, by no means the self that went with Hugh; no, but the true, the true Adela who was apart and his; for that was the difficulty all the while, that she was truly his, and wouldn't be, but if he thought more of her truly being, and not of her being untruly away, on whatever way, for the way that went away was not the way she truly went, but if they did away with the way she went away, then Hugh could be untrue and she true, then he would know themselves, two, true and two, on the way he was going, and the peace in himself, and the scent of her in him, and the her, meant for him, in him; that was the she he knew, and he must think the more of himself. A faint mist grew round them as they walked, and he was under the broad boughs of trees, the trees of the Hill, going up the Hill, up to the Adela he kept in himself, where the cunning woman who walked by his side was taking him, and talking in taking. He had been slow, slow, very slow not to see that this was true, that to get away from Hugh's Adela was to find somewhere and somehow the true Adela, the Adela that was his, since what he wanted was always and everywhere his; he had always known that, yet that had been his hardship, for he must know it was so, and yet it hadn't seemed so. But here in the mists under the trees, with this woman, it was all clear. The mist made everything clear.

She said: "In here." He went in; a wooden door swung before and behind him.

It was quite dark. He stood. A hand slipped into his hand, and pressed it gently. It drew him forward, and a little to one side. He said aloud: "Where are we?" but there was no answer, only he thought he heard the sound of water running, gently, a lulling and a lapping. It was not worth while, against that sound, asking again where he was. The darkness was quiet; his heart ceased to burn, though he could hear its beating, in time with the lapping and lulling waters. He had never heard his heart beating so loudly; almost as if he were inside his own body, listening to it there. It would be louder then, he thought, unless his senses were lulled and dulled. Likely enough that if he were inside his own body his senses would be lulled, though how he got there or how he would get out.… If he wanted to get out. Why? Why fly from that shelter, the surest shelter of all, though he could not be quite there yet because of the hand that guided him, round and round in some twisting path. He knew that there were hundreds of yards, or was it millions, of tubes or pipes or paths or ropes or something, coiled, many coils, in his body; he would not want to catch his foot in them or be twisted up in them—that was why the hand was leading him. He pressed it, for acknowledgment; it replied. They were going downhill now, it seemed, he and his guide, though he thought he could smell Adela, or if not Adela, something like Adela, some growth like Adela, and the image of a growth spread in his brain to trees and their great heavy boughs; it was not a lapping but a rustling; he had come out of himself into a wood, unless he was himself and a wood at the same time. Could he be a wood? and yet walk in it? He looked at that question for a long time while he walked, and presently found he was not thinking of that but of something else; he was slipping his fingers along a wrist, and up an arm—only a little way, for he still wished to be led on the way, though everything was so quiet he could hardly think there was any need. He liked going on, away, away, away, from something behind, or indeed outside, outside the wood, outside the body, outside the door. The door wouldn't open for anyone; it was his door, and though he hadn't fastened it, it wouldn't open, because it knew his wish, and his wish was to leave the two who had worried him outside the door. It was fun to think they were playing games on him when he wasn't there; running round under his windows, and he was quite away, and they would never know, even if he saw them again, where and how and why he had been. It was good for him to be here, and great fun; one day he would laugh, but laughter would be tiring here, under trees and leaves, leaves—leaves and eaves—eaves and eves; a word with two meanings, and again a word with two meanings, eves and Eves. Many Eves to many Adams; one Eve to one Adam; one Eve to each, one Eve to all. Eve….

They stopped. In the faint green light, light of a forest, faint mist in a forest, a river-mist creeping among the trees, moon in the mist, he could just see the shape of the woman beside him. He might be back again in Eden, and she be Eve, the only man with all that belonged to the only man. Others, those whose names he need not then remember, because they were the waking animals of the world—others were inconsiderable to the grand life that walked now in this glade. They hardly belonged to it at all; they belonged outside, they were outside, outside the sealed garden, no less sealed for being so huge, through a secret gate of which he had entered, getting back to himself. He was inside and at peace. He said aloud: "I won't go back."

His companion answered: "You needn't go back *really*—or you can take it with you if you do. Wouldn't you like to?"

It took a while for this to reach him. He said, at last: "This? all this, d'you mean?" He was a little disturbed by the idea that he might have to go back among the shapes that ran about, harsh and menacing, outside the glade or the garden or the forest, outside the mist. They betrayed and attacked him. One had made fun of him and exposed him to her paramour. That was outside; inside, he knew the truth, and the truth was that she was quite subordinate to him. He breathed on her hand, and it was turned into stone, so that she couldn't carry it, but it sank to the ground, slowly, in that misty air, and she was held there, crying and sobbing, by the weight of her petrified hand. He would go away for a year or two, and perhaps when he came back he would decide to set her free by blowing on the stone hand. The whole air of this place was his breath; if he took a very deep breath, there would be no air left, outside himself. He could stand in a vacuum, and nothing outside himself could breathe at all, until he chose to breathe again; which perhaps he wouldn't do, so that he could infinitely prevent anything at all from existing merely by infinitely holding his breath. He held his breath for a century or so, and all the beasts and shapes of the wilderness, a tall young satyr and a plump young nymph among them, who were dancing to the music of their own chuckles, fell slowly down and died. The woman now beside him didn't die, but that was because she could live without air, of which he was glad, for he wanted her to go on living, and if she had needed air she would have died. He would have destroyed her without meaning to.

She was saying, eagerly: "Yes, yes, yes: better than Eve, dearer than Eve, closer than Eve. It's good for man to be alone. Come along, come along: farther in, farther in: down under, down under."

Down under what? down under where? down under the air that was or wasn't? but he was there under the air, on the point of breathing out everything that would be just right. Why had he been so long content to have things wrong? it all came out of that silly name of Eve, which had prevented him realizing that he was what counted. Eve had never told him he had made her, and so he wouldn't make her again, she should be left all a twisted rag of skin in the vacuum, and he would have a world in which no one went to the City, because there was no City unless he—but no, he wouldn't have a City. Adela....

He found he had been holding his breath; he released it. He found he was lying down, and that the woman was not there. He had exhaled, with a deep permission to Adela to exist. Now he was sleeping after that decision and act. He was awake in his sleep, and the moon was pouring itself over him. He wasn't on a rope now. The moon was pouring down, quite out of the sky; presently there wouldn't be any moon, only a hole in the sky: down, down! He felt hands moving over him, the moonlight changing to hands as it reached him, moon-hands, cool and thrilling. The hands were delighting in him; these were what he would take back to his own world, if he went. The moon would always be his, though all the moonlight had poured down now, and there was a hole, a dark hole, because the moon had emptied itself of its glory, and was not there any more; he was at first in the smallest degree troubled, for if odd things could disappear like this, could he be certain that his own Adela would live? yes, because he was a god, and sometime he would make another moon. He forgot it now; he was quite given up to the hands that caressed him. He sank into oblivion; he died to things other than himself; he woke to himself.

He lay quiet; beyond heart and lungs he had come, in the depth of the Hill, to the bottom of the body. He saw before him, in the disappearing moonlight, a place of cisterns and broad tanks, on the watery surface of which the moon still shone and from which a faint mist still arose. Between them, covering acres of ground, an enormous shape lay, something like a man's; it lay on its face, its shoulders and buttocks rose in mounds, and the head beyond; he could not see the legs lower than the thighs, for that was where he himself lay, and they could not be seen, for they were his own. He and the Adam sprang from one source; high over him he felt his heart beat and his lungs draw breath. His machinery operated, far away. He had decided that. He lay and waited for the complete creation that was his own.

The Adam slept; the mist rose from the ground. The son of Adam waited. He felt, coming over that vast form, that Hill of the dead and of the living, but to him only the mass of matter from which his perfect satisfaction was to approach, a road, a road up which a shape, no longer vast, was now coming; a shape he distrusted before he discerned it. It was coming slowly, over the mass of the Adam, a man, a poor ragged sick man. The dead man, walking in his own quiet world, knew nothing of the eyes to which his death-day walk was shown, nor of the anger with which he was seen. Wentworth saw him, and grew demented; was he to miss and be mocked again? what shape was this, and there? He sprang forward and up, to drive it away, to curse it lest it interpolated its horrid need between himself and his perfection. He would not have it: no canvassers, no hawkers, no tramps. He shouted angrily, making gestures; it offended him; it belonged to the City, and he would not have a City—no City, no circulars, no beggars. No; no; no. No people but his, no loves but his.

It still came on, slowly, ploddingly, wearily, but it came; on down the road that was the Adam in the bottom of Eden, determinedly plodding as on the evening when it had trudged towards its death, inexorably advancing as the glory of truth that broke out of the very air itself upon the agonized Florentine in the Paradise of Eden: "ben sem, ben sem, Beatrice"; the other, the thing seen, the thing known in every fibre to be not the self, woman or beggar, the thing in the streets of the City. No, no; no canvassers, no beggars, no lovers; and away, away from the City into the wood and the mist, by the path that runs between past and present, between present and present, that slides through each moment of all experience, twisting and twining, plunging from the City and earth and Eve and all otherness, into the green mist that rises among the trees; by the path up which she was coming, the she of his longing, the she that was he, and all he in the she—patter-patter, the she that went hurrying about the Hill and the world, of whom it was said that they whom she overtook were found drained and strangled in the morning, and a single hair tight about the neck, so faint, so sure, so deathly, the clinging and twisting path of the strangling hair. She whose origin is with man's, kindred to him as he to his beasts, alien from him as he from his beasts; to whom a name was given in a myth, Lilith for a name and Eden for a myth, and she a stirring more certain than name or myth, who in one of her shapes went hurrying about the refuge of that Hill of skulls, and pattered and chattered on the Hill, hurrying, hurrying, for fear of time growing together, and squeezing her out, out of the interstices of time where she lived, locust in the rock; time growing together into one, and squeezing her out, squeezing her down, out of the pressure of the universal present, down into depth, down into the opposite of that end, down into the ever and ever of the void.

He was running down the path, the path that coiled round the edge of Eden, and the mist swooped to meet him. He had got right away from the road which was the shape of the Adam outstretched in the sleep precedent to the creation of fact, the separation of Eve, the making of things other than the self. He ran away into the comforting mist, partly because he liked it better, partly because there was nowhere else. He ran from sight; he found sensation. Arms met and embraced, a mouth kissed him, a sigh of content was loosed to him and from him. He was held, consoled, nourished, satisfied. Adela; he; sleep.

The door swung after him. He was standing on Battle Hill, not far from his house, but higher, towards the cemetery, towards the height. There, waiting for him, was a girl. She exactly resembled Adela. She came towards him softly, reached her hand to him, smiled at him, put up her mouth to him. It was night on the Hill. They turned together and went down it; after the single footsteps the double sounded again, his own and the magical creature's drawn from his own recesses: she in him, he in him. He was complacent; they went home.

Chapter VI

THE DOCTRINE OF SUBSTITUTED LOVE

*

Pauline sat back in her chair, and her arms lay along its arms. A rehearsal was taking place in the grounds of the Manor House, and she had ended her part in the first act. She was free to watch the other performers, and to consider the play once more. By now they had all got more or less accustomed to that speaking of verse aloud which our uneducated mouths and ears find so difficult, being less instructed than the more universal Elizabethan must have been. Pauline remembered again, with a queer sense of inferiority, that no Elizabethan audience, gods or groundlings, can have felt any shock of surprise or awkwardness at a play opening with a high rhodomontade of sound. No modern audience would put up with going to the first night of a new play to hear the curtain sweep up on such an absurd and superb invocation as:

g be the heavens with black; yield, day, ı

ts, importing change ...

and so on. On the other hand, they accepted plays beginning with the most ordinary prose. Even rhodomontade demands a peculiar capacity, and to lose its bravery perhaps hampers some other bravery of the spirit; to lose even one felicity is to be robbed of more than we have a right to spare. Certainly Stanhope had spared them any overwhelming magniloquence; his verse was subdued almost to conversation, though as she listened and read and studied and spoke it, she became aware that the rhythm of these conversations was a great deal more speedy and vital than any she could ever remember taking part in. All Mrs. Parry's efforts to introduce a stateliness of manner into the Grand Ducal court, and a humorous but slow—O so slow—realism into the village, and an enigmatic meandering meditativeness into the Chorus could not sufficiently delay the celerity of the lines. Once or twice Stanhope, having been consulted, had hinted that he would rather have the meaning lost than too firmly explained, and that speed was an element, but after a great deal of enthusiastic agreement they had all gone on as before. She herself had been pleasantly ticked off by Mrs. Parry that very afternoon for hurrying, and as Stanhope hadn't interfered she had done her best to be adequately slow. It was some recompense to sit now and listen to Adela and Mrs. Parry arguing with, or at least explaining to, each other. Adela, true to her principles of massing and blocking, arranged whole groups of words in chunks, irrespective of line and meaning, but according to her own views of the emotional quality to be stressed. She had just unexpectedly broken one line with a terrific symbolical pause.

"I am," she said to her Woodcutter, and pausing as if she had invoked the Name itself and waited for its Day of Judgment to appear, added in one breath, "only the perception in a flash of love."

Pauline encouraged in herself a twinge of wonder whether there were anything Adela Hunt were less only; then she felt ashamed of having tried to modify the line into her own judgment, especially into a quite unnecessary kind of judgment. She knew little enough of Adela, and the result was that she lost the sound of the woodcutter's answer—"A peremptory phenomenon of love". She thought, a little gloomily, that malice could create a fair number of peremptory phenomena for itself, not perhaps of love, but easily enjoyable, like

Myrtle Fox's trees. Malice was a much cosier thing than love. She was rather glad they were not doing the last act to-day; that act in which Periel—male or female, no matter!—spirit, only not spiritual—she—began and led the Chorus; and where everyone came in, on the most inadequate excuses, the Princess and her lover and the Grand Duke and the farmers and the banditti and the bear; and through the woods went a high medley of wandering beauty and rejoicing love and courtly intelligence and rural laughter and bloody clamour and growling animalism, in mounting complexities of verse, and over all, gathering, opposing, tossing over it, the naughting cry of the all-surrounding and overarching trees.

It troubled her now, as it had not done when she first read it, as it did not the others. She wondered whether it would have troubled her if, since the day of his first call, she had not sometimes heard her grandmother and Peter Stanhope talking in the garden. It was two or three weeks ago, since he had first called, and she could not remember that they had said anything memorable since except a few *dicta* about poetry—but everything they said was full and simple and unafraid. She herself had rather avoided him; she was not yet altogether prepared in so many words to accept the terror of good. It had occurred to her to imagine those two—the old woman and the poet—watching the last act, themselves its only audience, as if it were presented by the imagined persons themselves, and by no planned actors. But what would happen when the act came to an end she could not think, unless those two went up into the forest and away into the sounds that they had heard, into the medley of which the only unity was the life of the great poetry that made it, and was sufficient unity. Under the influence of one of those garden conversations she had looked up in her old school Shelley the lines that had haunted her, and seen the next line to them. It ran:

That apparition, sole of men, he saw;

and it referred, of course, to Zoroaster. But she couldn't, watching the play, refrain from applying it to Stanhope. This apparition, sole of men—so far as she had then discovered—he had seen; and she went back to wonder again if in those three lines Shelley, instead of frightening her, was not nourishing her. Supposing—supposing—that in this last act Peter Stanhope had seen and imagined something more awful even than a vision of himself; supposing he had contemplated the nature of the world in which such visions could be, and that the entwined loveliness of his verse was a mirror of its being. She looked at the hale and hearty young man who was acting the bear, and she wondered whether perhaps her real bear, if she had courage to meet it, would be as friendly as he. If only the woodcutter's son had not learned the language of the leaves while they burned in the fire! There was no doubt about that speech: the very smell and noise of the fire was in it, and the conviction of the alien song that broke out within the red flames. So perhaps the phoenix cried while it burned.

Someone sat down in the next chair. She looked; it was Stanhope. Mrs. Parry and Adela concluded their discussion; Adela seemed to be modifying her chunks of words—sharpening ends and pushing them nearer till they almost met. Presumably Mrs. Parry was relying on later rehearsals to get them quite in touch, and even, if she were fortunate, to tie them together. The rehearsal began again. Stanhope said: "You were, of course, quite right."

She turned her head towards him, gravely. "You meant it like that then?" she asked.

"Certainly I meant it like that," he said, "more like that, anyhow. Do you suppose I want each line I made to march so many paces to the right, with a meditation between each? But even if I could interfere it'd only get more mixed than ever. Better keep it all of a piece."

"But you don't mind," she asked, "if I'm a little quicker than some of them?"

"I should love to hear it," he answered. "Only I think it's probably our business—yours and mine—to make our own feelings agreeable to the company, as it were. This isn't a play; it's a pleasant entertainment. Let's all be pleasantly entertaining together."

"But the poetry?" she said.

He looked at her, laughing. "And even that shall be Mrs. Parry's," he said. "For this kind of thing is not worth the fretfulness of dispute; let's save all that till we are among the doctors, who aren't fretful."

She said suddenly, "Would you read it to me again one day? is it too absurd to ask you?"

"Of course I'll read it," he said. "Why not? If you'd like it. And now in exchange tell me what's bothering you."

Taken aback, she stared at him, and stammered on her answer. "But—but——" she began.

He looked at the performers. "Miss Hunt is determined to turn me into the solid geometry of the emotions," he said. "But—but—tell me why you always look so about you and what you are looking for."

"Do I?" she asked hesitatingly. He turned a serious gaze on her and her own eyes turned away before it. He said, "There's nothing worth quite so much vigilance or anxiety. Watchfulness, but not anxiety, not fear. You let it in to yourself when you fear it so; and whatever it is, it's less than your life."

"You talk as if life were good," she said.

"It's either good or evil," he answered, "and you can't decide that by counting incidents on your fingers. The decision is of another kind. But don't let's be abstract. Will you tell me what it is bothers you?"

She said, "It sounds too silly."

Stanhope paused, and in the silence there came to them Mrs. Parry's voice carefully enunciating a grand ducal speech to Hugh Prescott. The measured syllables fell in globed detachment at their feet, and Stanhope waved a hand outwards.

"Well," he said, "if you think it sounds sillier than that. God is good; if I hadn't been here they might have done the *Tempest*. Consider—'Yea—all which—it inher-it—shall dis-solve. And—like this—insub-stantial pag-eant fa-ded.' O certainly God is good. So what about telling me?"

"I have a trick," she said steadily, "of meeting an exact likeness of myself in the street." And as if she hated herself for saying it, she turned sharply on him. "There!" she exclaimed. "Now you know. You know exactly. And what will you say?"

Her eyes burned at him; he received their fury undisturbed, saying, "You mean exactly that?" and she nodded. "Well," he went on mildly, "it's not unknown. Goethe met himself once—on the road to Weimar, I think. But he didn't make it a habit. How long has this been happening?"

"All my life," she answered. "At intervals—long intervals, I know. Months and years sometimes, only it's quicker now. O, it's insane—no one could believe it, and yet it's there."

"It's your absolute likeness?" he asked.

"It's me," she repeated. "It comes from a long way off, and it comes up towards me, and I'm terrified—terrified—one day it'll come on and meet me. It hasn't so far; it's turned away or disappeared. But it won't always; it'll come right up to me—and then I shall go mad or die."

"Why?" he asked quickly, and she answered at once, "Because I'm afraid. Dreadfully afraid."

"But," he said, "that I don't quite understand. You have friends; haven't you asked one of them to carry your fear?"

"Carry my fear!" she said, sitting rigid in her chair, so that her arms, which had lain so lightly, pressed now into the basket-work and her long firm hands gripped it as if they strangled her own heart. "How can anyone else carry my fear? Can anyone else see it and have to meet it?"

Still, in that public place, leaning back easily as if they talked of casual things, he said, "You're mixing up two things. Think a moment, and you'll see. The meeting it—that's one thing, and we can leave it till you're rid of the other. It's the fear we're talking about. Has no one ever relieved you of that? Haven't you ever asked them to?"

She said: "You haven't understood, of course…. I was a fool…. Let's forget it. Isn't Mrs. Parry efficient?"

"Extremely," he answered. "And God redeem her. But nicely. Will you tell me whether you've any notion of what I'm talking about? And if not, will you let me do it for you?"

She attended reluctantly, as if to attend were an unhappy duty she owed him, as she had owed others to others and tried to fulfil them. She said politely, "Do it for me?"

"It can be done, you know," he went on. "It's surprisingly simple. And if there's no one else you care to ask, why not use me? I'm here at your disposal, and we could so easily settle it that way. Then you needn't fear it, at least, and then again for the meeting—that might be a very different business if you weren't distressed."

"But how can I not be afraid?" she asked, "It's hellish nonsense to talk like that. I suppose that's rude, but——"

"It's no more nonsense than your own story," he said. "That isn't; very well, this isn't. We all know what fear and trouble are. Very well—when you leave here you'll think to yourself that I've taken this particular trouble over instead of you. You'd do as much for me if I needed it, or for any one. And I will give myself to it. I'll think of what comes to you, and imagine it, and know it, and be afraid of it. And then, you see, you won't."

She looked at him as if she were beginning to understand that at any rate he thought he was talking about a reality, and as she did so something of her feeling for him returned. It was, after all, Peter Stanhope who was talking to her like this. Peter Stanhope was a great poet. Were great poets liars? No. But they might be mistaken. Yes; so might she. She said, very doubtfully: "But I don't understand. It isn't *your*—you haven't seen it. How can you——"

He indicated the rehearsal before them. "Come," he said, "if you like *that*, will you tell me that I must see in order to know? That's not pride, and if it were it wouldn't matter. Listen—when you go from here, when you're alone, when you think you'll be afraid, let me put myself in your place, and be afraid instead of you." He sat up and leaned towards her. "It's so easy," he went on, "easy for both of us. It needs only the act. For what can be simpler than for you to think to yourself that since I am there to be troubled instead of you, therefore you needn't be troubled? And what can be easier than for me to carry a little while a burden that isn't mine?"

She said, still perplexed at a strange language: "But how can I cease to be troubled? Will it leave off coming because I pretend it wants you? Is it your resemblance that hurries up the street?"

"It is not," he said, "and you shall not pretend at all. The thing itself you may one day meet—never mind that now, but you'll be free from all distress because that you can pass on to me. Haven't you heard it said that we ought to bear one another's burdens?"

"But that means——" she began, and stopped.

"I know," Stanhope said. "It means listening sympathetically, and thinking unselfishly, and being anxious about, and so on. Well, I don't say a word against all that; no doubt it helps. But I think when Christ or St. Paul, or whoever said *bear*, or whatever he Aramaically said instead of *bear*, he meant something much more like carrying a parcel instead of someone else. To bear a burden is precisely to carry it instead of. If you're still carrying yours, I'm not carrying it for you—however sympathetic I may be. And anyhow there's no need to introduce Christ, unless you wish. It's a fact of experience. If you give a weight to me, you can't be carrying it yourself; all I'm asking you to do is to notice that blazing truth. It doesn't sound very difficult."

"And if I could," she said. "If I could do—whatever it is you mean, would I? Would I push my burden on to anybody else?"

"Not if you insist on making a universe for yourself," he answered. "If you want to disobey and refuse the laws that are common to us all, if you want to live in pride and division and anger, you can. But if you will be part of the rest of us, and live and laugh and be ashamed with us, then you must be content to be helped. You must give your burden up to someone else, and you must carry someone else's burden. I haven't made the universe and it isn't my fault. But I'm sure that this is a law of the universe, and not to give up your parcel is as much to rebel as not to carry another's. You'll find it quite easy if you let yourself do it."

"And what of my self-respect?" she said.

He laughed at her with a tender mockery. "O, if we are of that kind!" he exclaimed. "If you want to respect yourself, if to respect yourself you must go clean against the nature of things, if you must refuse the Omnipotence in order to respect yourself, though why you should want so extremely to respect yourself is more than I can guess, why, go on and respect. Must I apologize for suggesting anything else?"

He mocked her and was silent; for a while she stared back, still irresolute. He held her; presently he held her at command. A long silence had gone by before he spoke again.

"When you are alone," he said, "remember that I am afraid instead of you, and that I have taken over every kind of worry. Think merely that; say to yourself—'he is being worried', and go on. Remember it is mine. If you do not see it, well; if you do, you will not be afraid. And since you are not afraid...."

She stood up. "I can't imagine not being afraid," she said.

"But you will not be," he answered, also rising, certainty in his voice, "because you will leave all that to me. Will you please me by remembering that absolutely?"

"I am to remember," she said, and almost broke into a little trembling laugh, "that you are being worried and terrified instead of me?"

"That I have taken it all over," he said, "so there is nothing left for you."

"And if I see it after all?" she asked.

"But not 'after all'," he said. "The fact remains—but see how different a fact, if it can't be dreaded! As of course it can't—by you. Go now, if you choose, and keep it in your mind till—shall I see you to-morrow? Or ring me up to-night, say about nine, and tell me you are being obedient to the whole fixed nature of things."

"I'll ring up," she said. "But I ... it sounds so silly."

"It is silly sooth," he answered, "and dallies with the innocence of love. Real sooth, real innocence, real love. Go with God." They shook hands, and slowly, looking back once, just before she reached the lane, she went out of his sight.

Stanhope, turning his eyes from her parting figure, looked at the rehearsal and then settled himself more comfortably in his chair. A certain superficial attention, alert and effective in its degree, lay at the disposal of anyone who might need it, exactly as his body was prepared to draw in its long outstretched legs if anyone wanted to pass. Meanwhile he disposed the rest of his attention according to his promise. He recollected Pauline; he visualized her going along a road, any road; he visualized another Pauline coming to meet her. And as he did so his mind contemplated not the first but the second Pauline; he took trouble to apprehend the vision, he summoned through all his sensations an approaching fear. Deliberately he opened himself to that fear, laying aside for awhile every thought of why he was doing it, forgetting every principle and law, absorbing only the strangeness and the terror of that separate spiritual identity. His more active mind reflected it in an imagination of himself going into his house and seeing himself, but he dismissed that, for he desired to subdue himself not to his own natural sensations, but to hers first, and then to let hers, if so it should happen, be drawn back into his own. But it was necessary first intensely to receive all her spirit's conflict. He sat on, imagining to himself the long walk with its sinister possibility, the ogreish world lying around, the air with its treachery to all sane appearance. His own eyes began to seek and strain and shrink, his own feet, quiet though actually they were, began to weaken with the necessity of advance upon the road down which the girl was passing. The body of his flesh received her alien terror, his mind carried the burden of her world. The burden was inevitably lighter for him than for her, for the rage of a personal resentment was lacking. He endured her sensitiveness, but not her sin; the substitution there, if indeed there is a substitution, is hidden in the central mystery of Christendom which Christendom itself has never understood, nor can.

Since he could not take, nor would have admitted, her hate and rejection, her passion was received into the lucidity of his own spirit. The experience itself, sharply as his body took it, was less sharp for him; not that he willed it so, but because his senses received their communication from within not from without, and there is in all holy imagination from goodwill a quality of greatness which purifies and stablizes experience. His goodwill went to its utmost, and utmost goodwill can go very far. It went to all but actual vision, and it excluded his intellectual judgment of that vision. Had he been asked, at that moment, for his judgment, he would have answered that he believed sincerely that Pauline believed sincerely that she saw, but whether the sight was actual or not he could not tell. He would have admitted that it might be but a fantastic obsession of her brain. That made no difference to his action. If a man seems to himself to endure the horrors of shipwreck, though he walks on dry land and breathes clear air, the business of his friend is more likely to be to accept those horrors as he feels them, carrying the burden, than to explain that the burden cannot, as a matter of fact, exist. Given all reasonable talk as well, wherever there is intelligence enough for exchange and substitution to exist, there is place enough for action. Only when the desire of an obsession has carried its subject beyond the interchanges of love can the power of substituted love itself cease. It would have been small use for any adept, however much greater than Peter Stanhope, to have offered his service to Wentworth, where he sat in his own room with the secret creature of substantial illusion at his feet caressing his hand; for from that haunting, even while it was but an unmaterialized anguish within his blood, Wentworth had had no desire, more than the desire of maddened pride, to be exquisitely free.

So devoted to the action of his spirit, Stanhope sat on among the sounds of laughter and gaiety and half-serious wrangles that rose around him. It was not a long while that he was left to sit alone; perhaps Pauline had not more than partly advanced on her return when someone came across to interrupt and consult him. He gave a full attention, for that other concern is not measured by time but by will. To give freedom to both, he would return to his task when opportunity next offered; afterwards, when they had all gone away, and he was alone. But that was rather for the sake of his own integrity of spirit than that more was needed. The act of substitution was fully made; and if it had been necessarily delayed for years (could that have been), but not by his fault, still its result would have preceded it. In the place of the Omnipotence there is neither before nor after; there is only act.

Pauline went out through the open door of the house, for the Manor was now almost a public building of happiness, and began to make her way towards her home. Just as she left, one of the other girls, who was only then arriving for her part, had delayed her with a question, a minute matter about a borrowed pattern for a dress, and possible alterations. Pauline also had given her attention, and now, walking down the road, went on thinking of it—and whether Mary Frobisher would really be well advised to move the left seam an eighth of an inch back, considering Mary Frobisher's figure. It was another thing for her, and the hang of the frock had been as satisfactory as could be hoped. But Mary—she stopped to smell the pinks in a garden she was passing. Pinks were not very showy flowers, but they had a fragrance. It was perhaps a pity they had so few in their own garden; she had once or twice thought of asking her grandmother to order the gardener to get some more, since the gardener certainly wouldn't otherwise do it. But Mrs. Anstruther was always so content with immediate existence that it seemed a shame to bother her about proximate existence. Pauline wondered if she, when she was ninety-seven, would be as little disturbed by the proximate existence of death as her grandmother seemed to be. Or would she be sorry to be compelled to abandon the pleasant wonder of this world, which, when all allowances were made, was a lovely place, and had——

She nearly came to a full stop; then, with slackened steps, she went on, blinking at the sunlight. She realized she had been walking along quite gaily. It was very curious. She looked down the road. Nothing was in sight—except a postman. She wondered whether anything would come into sight. But why was she so careless about it? Her mind leapt back to Stanhope's promise, and she knew that, whatever the explanation might be, she had been less bothered for the past ten minutes than ever before in any solitude of twenty years. But supposing the thing came? Well, then it came, but till it came why suppose it? If Peter Stanhope was taking trouble, as he was, because he said he would, there was no conceivable reason for her to get into trouble. She had promised to leave it to him; very well, she would. Let him—with all high blessing and gratitude—get on with it. She had promised, she had only to keep her promise.

So she put it to herself, but within herself she knew that, except just to ratify her promise, even that act of her mind was superfluous. It was an act purely of extra delight, an occasion of obedience. She wouldn't worry; no, because she couldn't worry. That was the mere truth—she couldn't worry. She was, then and there, whatever happened later, entirely free. She was, then and there, incapable of distress. The world was beautiful about her, and she walked in it, enjoying. He had been quite right; he had simply picked up her parcel. God knew how he had done it, but he had. A thing had, everywhere and all at once, happened. A violent convulsion of the laws of the universe took place in her mind; if this was one of the laws, the universe might be better or worse, but it was certainly quite different from anything she had ever supposed it to be. It was a place whose very fundamentals she had suddenly discovered to be changed. She hadn't any clear idea of what Stanhope was doing, and that didn't matter, except that she ought, as soon as possible, to find out and try to understand. That was merely her duty, and might—the thought crossed her mind and was gone—be her very great happiness. Meanwhile, she would go on walking. And if she came to her self, well she came to her self. No doubt Peter Stanhope would be doing something about it. A kitten on a wall caught her eye; it put its head down; she stretched her arm and stood on tiptoe to stroke it, and so doing for a while she forgot Stanhope and the universe and Pauline.

The rehearsal had long been over, and the Manor left again to its owner. Stanhope had returned to his own proper activity of work, when, exactly as the clock in his study chimed nine, the telephone bell rang.

He took up the receiver.

"Peter Stanhope speaking," he said.

"Pauline," said a voice. "You told me to ring you up."

"I was waiting for you," he answered. "Well?"

"Well … there was a kitten and pinks and a pattern for a frock and a postman who said the rain was holding off," said the voice, and paused.

"Cautious man," said Stanhope, and waited.

"Well … that was all," the voice explained.

"Really all?" Stanhope asked.

"Really all," the voice answered. "I just went home. It *is* real, I suppose?"

"Entirely," said Stanhope. "Aren't you sure of it?"

"Yes, O, yes," said the voice. "It … I … I wanted to thank you. I don't know what you did——"

"But I've told you," he murmured, and was cut short.

"——but I did want to thank you. Only—what happens now? I mean—do I——" It stopped.

"I should think you did," said Stanhope, gravely. "Don't you? It seems a perfectly good idea."

"Ah, but do you mean that?" she protested. "It looks so like taking advantage."

"You'll be as involved morally as you are verbally, if you talk like that," he said. "Taking advantage! O my dear girl! Don't be so silly! You've got your own job to do."

"What's that?" she asked.

"Being ready to meet it," he answered. "It'll be quite simple, no doubt, and even delightful. But if I were you I'd keep my faculties quiet for that. If meeting is a pleasure, as we so often tell people, you may as well enjoy the pleasure."

"I hadn't really thought of it being that," said the voice.

"But now?" he asked.

"Yes … I … I suppose it might," she said.

"Do you see any reason whatever why it shouldn't? Since we're agreed you won't have any opportunity to be afraid," he added.

"It's funny," she said, after another pause, "but do you know I feel as if I'd never really looked at it till now. At least, perhaps the first time, when I was quite small, but I was always shut up when I talked about it, and then sometimes I saw it when … when I didn't like it…."

"I don't quite follow," Stanhope said. "When you didn't like it?"

He couldn't see the blush that held Pauline as she sat by the telephone table, but he heard the voice become smaller and softer as she said, "When I wasn't being very good. There wasn't much money in the house, and once there was a shilling my mother lost, and then there were sweets. It was just after I'd bought the sweets that I saw it coming once. It was horrid to see it just then, but it was beastly of me, I know."

"Well, that's as may be," Stanhope said. "The limits of theft are a high casuistical problem. Read Pascal and the Jesuits—especially the Jesuits, who were more ordinary and more sensible. The triumph of the bourgeois."

"But I knew it was wrong," Pauline exclaimed.

"Still your knowledge may have been wrong," Stanhope demurred. "However, don't let's argue that. I see what you mean. Self-respect and all that. Well, it won't do you any harm to feel it knows you. Much the best thing, in fact."

"Y—yes," Pauline said. "Yes—I do think so really. And I'm not to worry?"

"You are most emphatically to remember that I'll do the worrying," Stanhope said. "Ring me up at any time—day or night; only if no one answers at night remember that, as Miss Fox so rightly told us, sleep is good, and sleep will undoubtedly be here. But sleep isn't separation in the Omnipotence. Go in peace, and wish me the same, for friendship's sake."

"O how can I?" she said, startled. "How can I wish peace to you? You are peace."

"M'm," Stanhope said. "But the more if you will have it so. Try."

"Good night then," she answered slowly. "Good night. Thank you. Go … in peace."

Her voice had faltered so that she could hardly speak the words, and when she rose from her seat she was on fire from head to foot. Guilt or shame, servile fear or holy fear, adoration or desperation of obedience, it burned through her to a point of physical pain. The blood rode in her face and she panted a little in the heat. She could not have answered, had anyone spoken to her; her tongue seemed to have said its last words on earth. Never, never, her heart sang, let her speak again, never let the silence that followed her daring, her presumptuous invocation, be broken. It had been compelled, she had been commanded; a God had been with her—not Peter Stanhope, but whatever answered him from her depth.

She looked at her watch; it was not yet time for her evening visit to her grandmother. She looked round; a book lay on the table. It was the volume of Foxe with the account of her ancestor's martyrdom; Mrs. Anstruther had been reading it again. She walked to it, and with one hand, the knuckles of the other pressed against her slowly cooling cheek, turned the pages to find the place. Something from it was vaguely coming to her mind. "They set him to the stake and put the fire to the wood, and as the fire got hold of him he gave a great cry and said, *I have seen the salvation of my God*…. The Lord had done great things for him there in the midst of the fire." The Lord, she thought, made a habit of doing things in the midst of a fire; he had just brought her to say "Go in peace" in another. She glowed again to think of it. But it was the first phrase she had looked for; "I have seen the salvation". It had never occurred to her, any time she had read or remembered the martyrdom, that Struther was anything but a demented fanatic; a faint distaste that she should come of his blood had touched her. It now occurred to her that Struther might have been talking flat realism. She put the book down, and looked out of the window. It was—all of a sudden—remarkably easy to look out of the window. She might even walk down to the gate and look at the street. The parcel was completely in some one else's care, and all she had to do was to leave it. She hoped it was not troublesome to Peter Stanhope, but it wouldn't be. He and whatever he meant by the Omnipotence would manage it quite well between them. Perhaps, later on, she could give the Omnipotence a hand with some other burden; everyone carrying everyone else's, like the Scilly Islanders taking in each other's washing. Well, and at that, if it were tiresome and horrible to wash your own clothes and easy and happy to wash someone else's, the Scilly Islanders might be intelligent enough. "Change here for Scilly," she said aloud as she came to the gate.

"My dear!" said a voice beside her.

Pauline jumped. It was a fairly high wall, and she had been preoccupied; still, she ought to have seen the woman who was standing outside, alone against the wall on her left. For a moment something jarred, but she recovered. She said, "Oh, good evening, Mrs. Sammile. I didn't see you."

The other peered at her. "How's your grandmother?" she asked.

"Rather weaker, I'm afraid," Pauline said. "It's kind of you to ask."

"And how are you?" Lily Sammile went on. "I've been——" but Pauline unintentionally cut through the sentence.

"Very well indeed," she murmured, with a deep breath of pleasure. "Isn't it a lovely night?"

The other woman strained a little forward, as if, even in the June evening, she could not see her clearly. She said, "I haven't seen you about lately: you haven't wanted to see me. I thought perhaps you might."

Pauline looked back smiling. How, in this quietness of spirit, could she have thought she wanted anything changed? But the old lady had wanted to help, and though now she did not need the help, the goodwill remained. She said, leaning over the gate: "Oh, I'm much better now."

"That's good," the other woman said. "But take care of yourself. Think of yourself; be careful of yourself. I could make you perfectly safe and perfectly happy at the same time. You really haven't any idea of how happy you could be."

Her voice was infinitely softer than Pauline could remember it. In the full light of day, the other woman had seemed to her slightly hard, her voice a light third hammer to her feet. She pattered everywhere, upstairs, downstairs, in my lady's chamber, in any chamber; but now her figure was dim and her feet still, and her voice soft. As soft as the dust the evening wind was blowing down the street. Dust of the dead, dust of the Struther who had died in flame. Had he been happy? happy? happy? Pauline was not sure whether she or her companion had spoken the word again, but it hung in the air, floating through it above, and the dust was stirred below, and a little dizziness took her and passed. Lazily she swung the gate.

She said, as if to draw down the floating mist: "Happy? I … I happy?"

The other murmured: "Happy, rich. Insatiate, yet satisfied. How delicious everything would be! I could tell you tales that would shut everything but yourself out. Wouldn't you like to be happy? If there's anything that worries you, I can shut it away from you. Think what you might be missing."

Pauline said: "I don't understand."

The other went on: "My dear, it's so simple. If you will come with me, I can fill you, fill your body with any sense you choose. I can make you feel whatever you'd choose to be. I can give you certainty of joy for every moment of life. Secretly, secretly; no other soul—no other living soul."

Pauline tingled as she listened. Shut up within herself—shut up till that very day with fear and duty for only companions—with silence and forbearance as only possibilities—she felt a vague thrill of promised delight. Against it her release that day began already to seem provisional and weak. She had found calm, certainly; only ten minutes earlier that calm had seemed to her more than she could ever have hoped. She loved it still; she owed to it this interval of indulgent communion with something other than calm. The communion threatened the calm with a more entrancing sensation of bliss; she felt almost that she had too rashly abandoned her tribulation for a substitute that was but a cold gift, when warm splendour had been waiting to enrapture her. In the very strength of her new-found security she leaned from it, as from the house itself; as within a tower of peace, with deliberate purpose she swung the gate more wide. Inconceivably she all but regretted the fear that would have been an excuse, even a just reason, for accepting a promise of more excitement of satisfaction than peace and freedom could give or could excuse. Peace had given her new judgment, and judgment began to lament her peace. If she opened the gate, if the far vision of her returning vision gave her speed and strength to leap from it to this more thrilling refuge! And while her heart beat more quickly and her mind laboured at once to know and not to know its desires, a voice slid into her ear, teasing her, speeding her blood, provoking her purpose. It spoke of sights and sounds, touches and thrills, and of entire oblivion of harm; nothing was to be that she did not will, and everything that she willed, to the utmost fulness of her heart, should be. She would be enough for herself. She could dream for ever, and her dreams should for ever be made real. "Come soon," it said, "come now. I'll wait for you here. In a few minutes you'll be free, and then you'll come; you shall be back soon. Give me your hand and I'll give you a foretaste now." A hand came into hers, a pulse against her wrist beat with significance of breathless abandonment to delirious joy. She delayed in a tremulous and pleasurable longing.

"But how," she murmured, "how can all this happen? how do I know what I want? I've never thought … I don't know anyone … and to be alone.…"

"Give me your hand," the other said, "then come and dream, till you discover, so soon, the ripeness of your dreams." She paused, and added, "You'll never have to do anything for others any more."

It was the last touch, and false, false because of the habit of her past and because of Stanhope's promise. The fountain of beauty had sprung upward in a last thrust; it broke against the arched roof of his world, and the shock stung her into coldness. Never have to do anything—and she had been promising herself that she would carry someone's parcel as hers had been carried, that she would be what he said she could. Like it or not, it had been an oath; rash or wise it stood.

"An oath, an oath, I have an oath in heaven." She had been reading more verse of late, since she had had to speak Stanhope's, and the holy words engulfed her in the sound which was so much more than she. "An oath, an oath.… Shall I lay perjury upon my soul?" The wind, rising as if to a storm, screamed "perjury" through the sky that held the Hill and all; false, false! she perjured in that last false gleam. She was come; "false, fleeting, perjured Clarence! Seize on him, Furies".… The word, Antæan, sprang hundred-voiced around her, and held her by every gripping voice. Perjury, on her soul and in her blood, if now she slipped to buy sweets with money that was not hers; never, till it was hers in all love and princely good, by gift and gift and gift beyond excelling gift, in no secrecy of greed but all glory of public exchange, law of the universe and herself a child of the universe. Never till he—not Pascal nor the Jesuits nor the old chattering pattering woman but he; not moonlight or mist or clouding dust but he; not any power in earth or heaven but he or the peace she had been made bold to bid him—till they bade her take with all her heart what nothing could then forbid. An oath, an oath, an oath in heaven, and heaven known in the bright oath itself, where two loves struck together, and the serene light of substitution shone, beyond her understanding but not beyond her deed. She flung the gate shut, and snatched her hands away, and as it clanged she was standing upright, her body a guard flung out on the frontier of her soul. The other woman was at the gate—of garden or world or soul—leaning to but not over it, speaking hurriedly, wildly, and the voice rising on the wind and torn and flung on the wind: "Everything, anything; anything, everything; kindness to me … help to me … nothing to do for others, nothing to do with others … everything, everything…."

The door behind her was opened; the maid's voice said doubtfully: "Miss Pauline?"

Pauline, rigid at her post, said, turning her head a little: "You wanted me?"

Phœbe murmured: "Your grandmother's asking for you, Miss Pauline, if you could come."

Pauline said, "I'm coming." She looked over the gate; she added in a voice hard with an unreasoning hostility: "Good night." She ran in.

Chapter VII

JUNCTION OF TRAVELLERS

*

The dead man walked in his dead town. It was still, quiet and deserted; he too was quiet in it. He had now, for long, no need to worry. Nagging voice and niggling hunger were gone. It was heaven enough; he sought nothing else. Dead or alive, or neither dead nor alive, he was free from the sick fear which the Republic had imposed on him. The stigmata of his oppression burned and ached no more. His tired feet had lightness; his worn form energy. He did not know or care if he were in the body or out of the body. For the first time he needed nothing, and nothing distressed him. He walked, sat, stretched himself out. He did not sleep, for he did not need sleep. Sometimes he wondered a little that he was never hungry or thirsty. It was an odd place he was in, but he did not grow tired of it any more than of walking through it. So much the better if he were not hungry or thirsty or tired. As for luxuries, he could not have missed them, for he had never had them, nor, then and there, was it permitted him to feel any want.

The faint light persisted. Time had no measurement except by the slow growth of his interior quiet, and to him none. All the capacities of satisfaction in one ordinary life, which have their fulfilment in many ways, in him there were concentrated on that quiet. Monotony could not exist where all duration was a slow encouragement of rest. Presently he even found himself looking up into the sky for the moon. The moon in his mind was, since his death, connected with the world he had known, with his single room and his wife, his enemies and tyrants. He felt, now, safe from it; he seriously expected its appearance, knowing that he was free. If the big pale ball had floated up, a balloon in which everything harmful was borne away, busy but not with him, he would have been mildly pleased. He knew that that balloon was for ever cut off from him. Moon, balloon, it could not drop anyone among these shells of houses. If it did, whoever it dropped would be caught in the shells. He had been a good-tempered little victim, but there were one or two in the past whom he could placidly have borne to see scrabbling and thrusting at the scaffolding and cage. He did not exactly resent, in that quiet, anything they had done—a foreman, a mate, a brother, a wife, but perhaps, as the unmeasured time did pass, he felt a little more strongly that he would enjoy his freedom more if he saw them defeated. In the past they had taken everything from him. It would not be unpleasant now to see them raging with a wish to get at him, and, in that air, defeated.

He sat opposite his ladder, after a long, long while, and let the fancy grow. It was then that he first noticed a change. The light was growing stronger. It was, again, a long while between the first faintest hint of it and any notice he took, and again between his first faint wonder and his belief, and again between belief and certainty. At the end of all those long periods, there was not much perceptible difference in the sky. Centuries passed before that difference grew more marked, but that too came. He had sat watching it, dimly, peacefully. He rose then, not quickly but more quickly than he had been used to move. He stirred with a hardly discernible unease.

It seemed as if the light were spreading steadily down, from somewhere away in the height. He did not positively see that any patch of sky was whiter than the rest, but he was looking for such a patch. The increase must have a centre of expansion. It must come from somewhere. No moon, no sun, no cause of illumination. Only sometimes a kind of wave of movement passed down the sky, and then it was lighter. He did not like it.

If he had asked himself why, he could not have easily answered. It did not disturb his quiet. He was as lonely and peaceful as before. No sound was in his City, foot or voice. But vaguely the light distracted him from his dim pleasure of imagining, imagining disappointment. His imagination could hardly, by ordinary standards, be said to be good or bad. It was a pleasure in others' anger, and bad; but the anger was that of tyrannical malice, and the imagined disappointment of it was good. Some such austere knowledge the Divine John saw in heaven, where disappointed hell is spread and smokes before the Lamb. But the Lamb and the angels do not imagine hell to satisfy their lust, nor do he nor the angels determine it, but only those in hell; if it is, it is a fact, and, therefore, a fact of joy. In that peace which had been heaven to the vagrant, he had begun to indulge a fancy of his own; he went beyond the fact to colour the fact.

Light grew. He began to walk. He had done so, often enough, through that great period of re-creation, for pure pleasure of change. Now he had, for the first time, a purpose unacknowledged. He wished to escape the light. It was desirable that he should still be left alone. He did not trust the light to let him alone. It was desirable that he should be free to make pictures for himself and to tell himself tales. He did not trust the light to let him do it. He moved gently; there was no need, here, to run. The need that was not concealed from him, his first inclination to run. He had run often enough for others' pleasure, but this was the first time he had been tempted to run for his own. The light still gently spread. As gently he went away from it, down the hill. His choice was in this direction; it was brightest, by a little, at the top.

As, through a still unmeasured period, he went drifting, changes came on the hill. He did not at first notice them. Long as he had wandered, he had not marked detail of building there. But, unnoticed, details had altered. It was now a town half-built, not ruined. When he had climbed that skeleton shape of a house, or of himself, he had done so in the midst of a devastation. As he went away from it towards the bottom the devastation became incomplete erection. Houses were unfinished, roads unmade, yet they were houses and roads. Roofs were on, scaffolding gone. The change was irregular, more as if some plants had outgrown others than as if order had been established by man. He went soundlessly down the slope of the thickening vegetation, and as on the bare height the light was fullest, so here instead of light, shadows grew thicker. Between them the pallid light of his experience grew stronger by contrast. He would not look at the new light; there was increased for him by opposition the presence of the old.

He had gone some way, and some time, unnoticing, inclined to linger upon his tales and dreams, when he was startled into knowledge. He had turned his back upon light and had not remarked erection. He saw suddenly, at a distance in front of him, a flash. He stopped and stared. It was no longer a flash but a gleam. He was looking at, far off, the reflection of light upon glass—of what he would, in lost days, have called the sun upon a window.

A thrust of fear took him; he could not, for a moment, go on. He stood blinking; after a while, he turned his head. There was behind him a long space of shadows and pale light, but beyond that, away beyond the house where he had died, there was a broad stretch of high ground, bare and rocky, rising higher than he had ever thought, and all bright with, he supposed, the sun. A rich, golden splendour, beyond all, at the height of all, played flashing upon some other glittering surface; it was not glass there, but ice. He stared back as he had stared forward. He could not dare return to *that*, also he was unwilling to go on down towards the gleaming window below. That meant the world; he could not, after so much peace, return to the world. Why could he not sit and imagine a moon and thwarted creatures dropped from the moon into a world that mocked them? It was not much to ask.

It was too much; he could not have it. False as the Republic had been to him, making his life dreadful, he had not deserved, or he could not have, an infinity of recompense. He could not have this in utter exchange for that. Exchange had been given; temporal justice, for what it is worth, done. Now incidents were no more counted, on this side or the other. He must take the whole—with every swiftness of the Mercy, but the whole he must have.

He saw that the exhibition of light was moving towards him. It had reached the house where he had died. He noticed, even in his alarm, that the buildings now ended there. In his earlier wanderings he had gone among the ruins both above and below it, but now the bare rock rose above—or ice, as he had first thought. It went up, in blocks and irregularities of surface, until, some distance beyond, it opened on one broad sweep, smooth and glittering, rounding towards the top of the Hill; upon it, by some trick of sight, the sunlight seemed active. It was not changed, but it ran. It hastened in sudden charges of intensity, now across, now down. The unchanging rock beneath the unchanging sun responded to that counter-marching, evoked into apparent reordination. It was perhaps this which terrified him, for there the earth was earth still and yet alive. In the strict sense of the words it was living stone.

He stood for some minutes staring, and entranced. But at some sudden charge downwards from the height towards the house, and him beyond it, he broke. He gave a little cry, and ran. He ran down towards the bottom of the Hill, among the houses, towards that house where the glass was. As he ran he saw, for the first time since he had entered that world, other forms, inhabitants of a state for which there were no doubt many names, scientific, psychological, theological. He did not know the names; he knew the fact.

The return of time upon itself, which is in the nature of death, had caught him. Margaret Anstruther had, in a vision within a dream, decided upon death, not merely in her own world but in that other. Her most interior heart had decided, and the choice was so profound that her past experiences and her present capacities could only obey. She had no work of union with herself to achieve; that was done. But this man had died from and in the body only. Because he had had it all but forced on him, he had had opportunity to recover. His recovery had brought to him a chance of love. Because he had never chosen love, he did not choose it then. Because he had never had an opportunity to choose love, nor effectively heard the intolerable gospel proclaimed, he was to be offered it again, and now as salvation. But first the faint hints of damnation were permitted to appear.

He was running down a street. It was a street that closed in on him. He did not notice, in his haste, that it was a street much like those in which most of his life had been spent. He saw, in front of him, at a great distance, two living forms, a man and a girl; at which he ran with increased speed. Since he had begun to go down the Hill he had lost his content in being alone; he smelt solitude as if it were the odour of bare rock, and he hated it. He heard, more vividly with every step, no sound. He could not hear those forms walking, but he saw them; it was enough; he ran. He was catching them up, running very fast through his old life to do it. When he was within a hundred yards the girl looked over her shoulder. He checked in midpace, his foot heavily thudding down, and he almost falling. He saw, with sharp clarity, the face of the girl who had been his wife. Her mouth was opening and shutting on words, though the words were silent. It had always been opening and shutting. At once, without looking round, the figure arm in arm with hers released itself, stopped, and as if moving by the direction of that busily talking mouth, took a step or two backwards. Then it paused, and with a weary care began slowly to turn itself round. The dead man saw the movement. It became terribly important that he should escape before the youth he had been caught him and dragged him in, to make a third with them, and to listen again to that hated and loathed voice—always perhaps; the prisoner of those two arms, the result and victim of his early desire. He ran hastily back again up the street.

Presently he glanced behind him, and could not see them. He trotted a little farther, looked round again, saw the street still empty—the street that was recovering the appearance of a street upon the Hill—and dropped to a walk. Only he could not go on right to the end, though he had come thence, for he could see across it a beam of faint but growing sun, as the ocean beams at the end of a road. He did not think of the image, for he had not seen the sea, since his childhood; and that time would not be remembered until he reached it. An instinct, none the less, warned him; so he did not make his way to where, ready for him, in that twisting maze of streets and times, a gutter child played on his only seaside holiday, and cried because a bigger boy had bullied him. Sea or sun—sun to him—it was the light he wished to avoid. He hesitated, and took a side turning, where under the eaves some darkness was left.

The image was growing more complex and more crowded, for, as if the descending light, the spreading harshness of rock and ice,[1] crowded them into the streets grew shorter, more involved, themselves more populous with figures. Once it was a sneering foreman, who drove his face-hidden shape towards him; once—how he got there he did not know—it was someone's back on a ladder carrying a rope, going up no doubt, but perhaps coming down to throw the rope round him before he slipped away. Once he turned from a figure leaning against a lamp-post, quite still, with a stealthy suspense, as if it might dodge round the lamp-post, pretending that the post hid what it could not hide, and making to play a game that was not a kind game. And each time he slipped away or turned away, it was more like running away, and continually he would see, here and there in the distance, the beam of light on icy rock and sniff the bitter smell of the place of no return.

So presently he was running very quickly, with a sense that they were now after him. They had begun to be bolder, they were leaning out of windows, stumbling out of streets, lurching, shambling, toiling after him. He had read somewhere of a man being trampled to death, and he thought of that now; only he could not envisage death, any more than Pauline the end of luxurious dream. He could only think of trampling. He ran faster then, for he did not see how he would ever be able to get up, those apparitions of his terror would be too many and too strong. For the first time in that world he began to feel exhausted; and now the streets were slipping by, and the feet were coming up, and in a central daze in that dance of time and truth all round him, he felt himself stopping. He dimly consented; he stood still.

As he did so, there came about him also a cessation. The street was still; the feet silent. He drew a breath. He saw in front of him a house, and at a window, a window with glass where no light gleamed, he saw a face, the face of an old woman, whom never in all his life had he seen before. He saw her as a ghost in the shadow, within the glass, but the glass was only a kind of faint veil—of ceremony or of habit, though he did not think of it so. He felt it did not matter, for he and the other were looking directly at each other. He wanted to speak; he could not find words to utter or control. He broke into a cry, a little wail, such as many legends have recorded and many jokes mocked. He said: "Ah! ah!" and did not think it could be heard.

The old face looked at him, and he was trembling violently, shaking to see the apparition of this world's living, as they shake to see the phantasms of the dead. He knew he was not afraid, as they are often afraid; this was almost the first face he had seen, in the body or out of the body, of which he was not afraid. Fear, which separates man from man, and drives some to be hostile, and some tyrannical, and some even to be friendly, and so with spirits of that state of deathly time, there abandoned him. Fear, which never but in love deserts mortal man, deserted him there. Only he could not do or say any more. He stared, hungrily, hopefully. He waited, selfishly certain she would go, sweetly sure she would stay. She said, as he waited: "My dear, how tired you look!"

To Margaret herself the images were becoming confused. She did not, for a good part of the time, know of any, being engaged merely, beyond her own consciousness, in passing through that experience which in her dream had meant crawling over the stretch of open rock. Some hint of memory of it recurred to her at moments. She had on this evening known nothing but a faint sense of slow dragging in her limbs, an uneasiness in her body as if it lay rough, a labouring in her breath as if she toiled. Then she had felt herself lying on rock, holding a spike of rock, and instinctively knew she had to do something, and clasped the spike with energy—it had to do with Pauline; and a bell—the great bell of the dead, or the bell of the living on the Hill, or her own little bell, or all at once—had rung; and as it did so, she saw a strange face looking at her from a crevice of darkness below. Then she knew it; it was the face of the strange man in her dream. She was aware that Pauline was coming over the rock through a door of great stones like Stonehenge, but Pauline was behind, and across in front of a gleam of mountain light that pierced her room was the shadow of the weary and frightened face. She said with a fresh spring of pure love, as if to Pauline or Phœbe or anyone: "My dear, how tired you look!"

He tried to answer, to thank her, to tell her more, to learn salvation from her. His life, in and out of the body, had forgotten the time when a woman's voice had last sounded with friendship in his ears. He wanted to explain. This face was neither light nor darkness but more tolerable and deeper than either, as he felt it, for it had lived towards him in love. He made efforts to speak, and seemed to himself to do no more than cry out again, wordlessly and wailingly. The sound he made communicated his fear, and she answered him from her withdrawn experience of death, as from his less withdrawn spirit of poetry Stanhope had answered Pauline—nothing could be worth such distress. Or nothing, at least, but one thing—the coming out of it into tender joy. She said: "But wait: wait for it."

Pauline had come in from the garden, and as she ran through the hall she was furiously angry with herself. She did not very well know what the woman in the street had offered, beyond indefinable sweet and thrilling excitements. But she felt, her foot on the first stair, that she had regretted, that she had grudged and been aggrieved with, the new change in her life. She had almost, if by God's mercy not quite, wished that Peter Stanhope had not interfered. No range of invective—and she had a pretty, if secret, range—sufficed her for herself. She struck her hand against the wall as she ran, and wished that it was her head, or that someone—Stanhope for preference, but it didn't much matter; anyone would do—would pick her up and throw her violently over the banisters to the floor below, knocking the breath out of her body, and leaving her bruised and gasping, looking like the fool she was. She put all herself into despising herself, and her scorn rode triumphant through her: a good thing under direction, but dangerous to the lonely soul. So ambiguously repentant, she came into her grandmother's room, and saw suddenly that the justice of the universe had taken her earlier word and abandoned her.

It was not so, but at the window there was a face; and she had, in the first shock, supposed it was hers. The obsession of her visitation returned, through the double gate of her repining and her rage. It was coming, it was come, it was here. Her wild spirit sickened in her; and as she felt its power dissolve, she sprang to the other power the knowledge of which, at least, her anger had preserved. Ashamed of betrayal, unashamed of repentance and dependence, she sprang. She knew with all her soul's consent that Peter Stanhope had taken over her fear; was, now, one with it; and it was not, for he was in power over it. Among the leaves of his eternal forest he set it, and turned it also to everlasting verse. Evading or not evading, repining or not repining, raging or not raging, she was Periel; she was the least of the things he had created new; *ecce, omnia nova facio.* She was a line of his verse, and beyond that—for the thought of him took that high romantic self-annihilation and annihilated it in turn—she was herself in all freedom and courage. She was herself, for the meeting with herself. She stepped forward—lightly, almost with laughter. It was not yet she.

As she gazed, she heard her grandmother speak. The room, for those three spirits, had become a place on the unseen mountain: they inhabited a steep. The rock was in them, and they in it. In Margaret Anstruther it lived; it began to put out its energy of intellectual love. At least to the dead man it was felt as love, as love that loved him, as he longingly and unknowingly desired. This holy and happy thing was all that could be meant by God: it was love and power. Tender to the least of its creatures, it submitted itself to his need, but it is itself always that it submits, and as he received it from those eyes and the sound of that voice he knew that another thing awaited him—his wife, or the light, or some renewal of his earlier death. Universal, it demanded universality. The peace communicated there was of a different kind from the earlier revival of rest. And the woman said: "It's done already; you've only got to look for it."

As Pauline had moved forward, the face at the window disappeared from her sight. She drew breath; it had been an accident of light; there had been no face. She turned to look at her grandmother, and saw her lying very still, her eyes on the window as if she could still see something there. Quiet as she lay, she was in action. Her look, her voice, showed it: her voice, for she spoke, but very low, and Pauline could not hear the words. She caught the sound; lightly she threw herself on her knees by the bed—and half fulfilled her earlier passionate desire for subordination. For the first time in her young distracted life her energy leapt to a natural freedom of love. She ran swiftly down the way her master had laid open; she said, in words almost identical with his: "Let me do something, let me carry it. Darling, do let me help." Margaret gave her hand a small gentle pressure, but kept her eyes beyond her still.

The silence in that place became positive with their energies, and its own. The three spirits were locked together, in the capacity of Margaret's living stone. The room about them, as if the stillness expressed its nature in another mode, grew sharply and suddenly cold. Pauline's mind took it as the occasional sharp alteration of a summer evening; she moved to go and turn on the electric fire, for fear her grandmother should feel the chill, and that natural act, in her new good will, was no less than any high offer of goodness and grace. But Margaret knew the other natural atmosphere of the icy mountain, where earthly air was thin in the life of solitude and peak. It was the sharp promise of fruition—her prerogative was to enter that transforming chill. The dead man also felt it, and tried to speak, to be grateful, to adore, to say he would wait for it and for the light. He only moaned a little, a moan not quite of pain, but of intention and the first faint wellings of recognized obedience and love. All his past efforts of good temper and kindness were in it; they had seemed to be lost; and they lived.

But that moan was not only his. As if the sound released something greater than itself, another moan answered it. The silence groaned. They heard it. The supernatural mountain on which they stood shook, and there went through Battle Hill itself the slightest vibration from that other quaking, so that all over it china tinkled, and papers moved, and an occasional ill-balanced ornament fell. Pauline stood still and straight. Margaret shut her eyes and sank more deeply into her pillow. The dead man felt it and was drawn back away from that window into his own world of being, where also something suffered and was free. The groan was at once dereliction of power and creation of power. In it, far off, beyond vision in the depths of all the worlds, a god, unamenable to death, awhile endured and died.

---

1. It is evident that something is amiss with the syntax of this passage; the following is a suggested alternative sequence: (...) *for, as if the descending light crowded them into the spreading harshness of rock and ice, the streets grew shorter* (...)

———————

DRESS REHEARSAL

*

Among the many individualized forms, dead or living, upon the Hill, there was one neither dead nor living. It was the creature which had lingered outside the illusion of Eden for the man who had consented to its company. It had neither intellect nor imagination; it could not criticize or create, for the life of its substance was only the magical apparition of its father's desires. It is said in the old tales that the devil longs to become incarnate that he may challenge the Divine Word in his own chosen house of flesh and that he therefore once desired and overshadowed a maid. But even at the moment of conception a mystical baptism fell on the child, and the devil was cast out of his progeny at the moment of entrance. He who was born of that purified intercourse with angelic sacrilege was Merlin, who, wisest of magicians, prophesied and prefigured the Grail-quest, and built a chapel to serve the Table till Logres came to an end, and the Merciful Child Galahad discovered the union in a Mass of the Holy Ghost which was sung by Messias among a great company of angels. Since that frustrating transubstantiation the devil has never come near to dominion over a mortal woman. His incubi and succubi, which tempt and torment the piety of anchorites, are phantasms, evoked from and clouded and thickened with the dust of the earth or the sweat of the body or the shed seed of man or the water of ocean, so as to bewilder and deceive longing eyes and eager hands.

The shape of Lawrence Wentworth's desire had emerged from the power of his body. He had assented to that making, and again, outside the garden of satisfied dreams, he had assented to the company of the shape which could not be except by his will and was imperceptibly to possess his will. Image without incarnation, it was the delight of his incarnation, for it was without any of the things that troubled him in the incarnation of the beloved. He could exercise upon it all arts but one; he could not ever discover by it or practise towards it the freedom of love. A man cannot love himself; he can only idolize it, and over the idol delightfully tyrannize—without purpose. The great gift which this simple idolatry of self gives is lack of further purpose; it is, the saints tell us, a somewhat similar thing that exists in those wholly possessed by their End; it is, human experience shows, the most exquisite delight in the interchanges of romantic love. But in all loves but one there are counterpointing times of purposes; in this only there are none.

They had gone down the hill together, the man and that creature of illusion which had grown like the flowers of Eastern magic between the covering and uncovering of a seed. The feminine offspring of his masculinity clung to him, pressing her shoulder against him, turning eyes of adoration on him, stroking his fingers with her own. The seeming trance prolonged itself in her in proportion as it passed from his own senses; he could plunge again into its content whenever the creature looked at or spoke to him. Their betrothal had been celebrated thus before they began to walk down the hill, and in that betrothal a fraction of his intelligence had slept never to wake. During the slow walk his child dallied with his senses and had an exquisite perception of his needs. Adela walked by him and cajoled him—in the prettiest way—to love her. He was approached, appeased, flattered, entreated. There flowed into him from the creature by his side the sensation of his absolute power to satisfy her. It was what he had vehemently and in secret desired—to have his own way under the pretext of giving her hers. This was the seed which grew in his spirit and from which in turn his spirit grew—the core of the fruit and also the fruit of the core. The vagrant of matter murmured to him; it surrounded him with devotion, as very well it could, seeing what the only reality of its devotion was. He did not need to say much, nor himself to initiate approach. It took all that activity upon itself; and the sweet reproaches which its mouth offered him for having misunderstood and neglected and hurt it were balm to his mind. He had hurt her—then he had not been hurt or she did not know it. He was wanted—then he need not trouble to want or to know he wanted. He was entreated by physical endearments—in languorous joy he consented to gratify the awful ambiguity of his desire.

At his own gate they had paused. There, for a little, he almost recovered himself; his habitual caution leapt into action. He thought for himself: "Suppose anyone saw us?" and looked anxiously up at the windows. They were dark; his servants were asleep in their own rooms at the back of the house. He glanced up and down the road; no one was about. But his caution, having struck one note, passed to another; he looked down at the creature who stood opposite him. It was Adela in every point, every member and article: its hair, its round ears, its full face, its plump hands, its square nails, its pink palms, its gestures, its glances. Only that appealing softness was new, and by that same appealing softness he knew clearly for an instant that it was not Adela who had returned by his side.

He stared at it and a shudder seized him; he took a half-step away, and the first chance of escape was offered. He wondered, desperately, perhaps in a little hope, if it would say good-night and go away. His hand was on the latch of the gate, yet he hesitated to do anything so certain as to go sharply through. He looked up and down the street; perhaps someone would come. He had never before wanted to see Hugh Prescott; now he did. If Hugh would come and slip his arm through Adela's and take her away! But Hugh could not save him unless he wanted the thing that was Hugh's, and not this other thing. The thought of Hugh had done all it could when it reminded him of the difference between the real and the unreal Adela. He must face jealousy, deprival, loss, if he would be saved. He fled from that offer, and with a sudden snarl clutched his companion by the arm. It leaned closer to him, and otherwise circumstance lay still. It yearned to him as if it feared to be disappointed, which indeed at the bottom of his heart he infinitely did. It put one hand upon his heart. It said, in a breathless whisper: "You won't send me away?" Adela and his refusal to know Adela in relation to Hugh rose in him; sensuality and jealousy twined. He swung open the gate. It said: "Be kind to me, be whatever you want, but don't send me away." He had never been able to dream of a voice so full of passion, and passion for him. The hand that smoothed his heart was the hand that had lain in Hugh's, yet it was not; he crushed it in his own, relieved from agony and released to a pretended vengeance. His mind became giddy. He caught the whole form tighter, lest indeed Hugh should come striding out of the night, tall as a house, and stretch out a huge animal hand, and pull her from his arm. He moved to the threshold; as if it swooned against him it drooped there with all its weight upon his heart and side. He muttered thickly: "Come on, come on," but it seemed past movement. Its voice still murmured incoherent passion, but its limbs were without strength to take the step. He said: "Must I carry you?" and the head fell back, and the voice in a trance of abandonment answered: "Carry me, carry me." He gathered it to his arms and lifted it; it lay there, no more than an easy weight.

As he moved, his mind spoke, or more than his mind. The whole air of the Hill said in his ear, with a crisp intelligence: "You fool, that's not Adela; you couldn't carry Adela. What do you think you'll get out of anything that isn't Adela?" He recognized well enough that the real Adela might have given him considerable trouble to lift, but his whole damnation was that he would not choose the trouble to lift the real Adela. This thing was light in his arms, though solid to his heart, and his brain was dazed by its whispers. He came over the threshold, and when they had entered the garden it found its feet again, and went along with him to the complacency of his dream.

Since that night it had come to him often, as on that night it had been all he could desire. It had been an ape of love's vitality, and a parody also of its morality. It possessed a semblance of initiative, and it had appeased, as is all lovers' duty, the fantasies of his heart; it had fawned on him and provoked him. He had no need of the devices against fertility which, wisely or unwisely, the terrible dilemmas of men drive them to use, for he consummated a marriage whose infertility was assured. This, which it made clear to him for his satisfaction, a little troubled him, for it reminded him, until he managed to forget, of its true nature. He was outraging his intelligence with this invited deceit, and he did not wish to know it. But it passed, for he was given good measure after his kind. There was no lack of invention and pleasure, for the other forming of sterile growth from sterile root was far off, lying in the necessity of the stir of distant leaves on the side of the mountain where he had no thought to come.

The days went by, and still he was consoled. In the mornings it had gone; in the early summer dawns it wakened him to whisper farewells, and his heavy drugged sleep only understood that here also it was fulfilling his need. He had not at first very clearly understood why or where it was going, but he did not then care, for it promised him, leaning naked over him, that it would always return. Whether it were then Adela or a being like Adela he was too full of slumber to care; it was going; he need not trouble; for whenever he needed her, it would return. If it were Adela, she ought to get away; if it were not Adela, it ought still to go away, because there would be the morning and the world.… So much his drowsiness let through to him; and it went, showing him itself, in a faithful copy of his half-realized wishes, to the end. For contenting him with its caution, it gathered up the articles of its apparent dress, and presently all clothed it stole across the room, and by the door it turned, and with one gesture promised him itself again. In the dawn, at once by that gesture clothed and unclothed, it had shone before him, a pale light burning against the morning, the last flickering fire of the corpse-candles of the insubstantial; then it had passed, and left him to sleep. So when later they brought him his early tea, he was alone; but that day while he drank, he found the thought of the Adela of past days a little disagreeable—no longer troublesome or joyous but merely disagreeable. He would have to meet her, no doubt, one day; meanwhile he was entirely at peace, and he did not want to think of anything at all. He lay and drank, and was still.

As the days went by, he found that his child kept her promise. He could not conceive a way of coming that, sooner or later, she did not take, nor a manner of love that, sooner or later, she did not fulfil. Since it was more and more Adela, he was instinctively careful never to conceive a meeting which conflicted with the possibilities of the actual Adela; he asked of his nightly bedfellow nothing but secret advents or accidental encounters. But these gradually he multiplied; and always it answered. By chance, in the street, at first by late night, but afterwards earlier. For once this Adela said to him, in a casual phrase, to which only his own veiled knowledge gave a double meaning: "They won't remember if they see me." So he dared to walk with it sometimes for variation, but then they went always through the lower darker streets of the Hill, and at first they met no one whom he knew, and presently no one at all. But Adela Hunt wondered sometimes why she never seemed to run against Lawrence Wentworth by chance in the streets of Battle Hill.

Yet, in the order of the single universe known to myriads of minds, the time and place that belongs to each of those myriads has relation to others; and though the measurement of their experiences may differ, there is something common to them all in the end. Sometimes where time varies place is stable; or where places intermingle time is secure, and sometimes the equilibrium of both, which is maintained in so many living minds, swings into the place of the dead. Sometimes the dead know it, and sometimes the living; a single clock ticks or a single door opens in two worlds at once. The chamber of that dark fundamental incest had had the dead man for its earliest inhabitant, though his ways and Wentworth's had been far apart—as far as incest from murder, or as self-worship from self-loathing, and either in essence false to all that is. But the self-worship of the one was the potential source of cruelty, as the self-loathing of the other was the actual effect of cruelty; between them lay all the irresolute vacillations of mankind, nourishing the one and producing the other. All who had lived, or did or could live, upon Battle Hill, leaned to one or the other, save only those whom holy love had freed by its revelation of something ever alien from and conjoined with the self.

In Wentworth's old dream he had climbed down a rope securely and not unpleasantly, much as the world of our culture sways on the rope from the end of which the outcasts of civilization swing in a strangled life. Since the phantom of Adela had come to him the dream had disappeared. He slept deeply. If he woke she would be there by his side, petting or crooning to him; until one night he thought how pleasant it would be to wake and look on her asleep, and the next time he woke, there indeed she was, disposed to his wish. But he found it troubled him; as he looked at her in the silence he began to wonder, and to think of the other Adela sleeping in her own house. For a little he tried to find pleasure in considering how in effect he possessed her without her knowledge or will, but the effort was too much for his already enfeebled mind. He found himself disliking the life of the actual Adela; he could be so happy with the substance by him if only the other were dead. But to know that she did not know … and that perhaps one day Hugh…. He had forgotten Hugh in these last weeks, and in a hasty retreat to oblivion he woke the creature from its apparent slumber, and in its yearnings and embraces lost actuality again and lost himself. He whispered to her then that she must never sleep when he woke, so drawing another veil between himself and the truth.

It was some nights afterwards that the dream returned. For the first time it troubled him. He was climbing in the darkness down that shining rope of silver, even more peacefully than ever he had climbed before. He was descending, he now vaguely imagined, towards a companion who waited for him far below, where the rope was fastened to the side of a cave in an unseen wall. The companion had waited, was waiting, would wait; it would never grow tired either of him or of waiting for him; that was why it was there, with its soft bare arms, and its sweet eyes closed in the dream of his approach. As he descended, in that warm expectation, a terrible sound broke on him. The abyss groaned. From above and below, from all sides, the rending grief of a hardly tolerable suffering caught him; he clung horribly to his rope, and the rope shook in the sound. The void became vocal with agony; the hollow above and the hollow below came together in that groan of the very air, and it echoed from unseen walls, and re-echoed, and slowly died. Only once it came. It was succeeded by the ancient silence. He listened breathlessly, but it did not recur. It had turned the dream into a nightmare for him; he shook on his rope, and struggled in his body, and so he awoke, and there by his side, waking also, was the companion he sought. He clutched it and hid himself against it; he hid his ears between its breasts and its hands, lest the night should groan again. In his haste to hide himself, as if like others he bade the mountains fall on him and the hills cover him, and in the darkness of the room, he did not see the inhuman countenance. It had grown haggard and old; its fulness fell away; its eyes were blurred. The meaning which he had given it had departed; an imbecile face stared blankly over him. The movements its body made were sufficient to cover his distress, but they had been jerky and inorganic, as if an automaton repeated its mechanical motions, and as if the mechanism were running down. For less than the time it took him to find refuge with her the creature that lay there was millions of years older than the dying woman by whom Pauline watched, while the pain of a god passed outwards from the mountain depths, as from those where Prometheus hung, or downwards from the cross that stood upon a hill that also was of skulls. It united itself with all spiritual anguish that received and took part with it; it fell away from the closed ears in the beds of Gomorrah. The dead man looked at Margaret, Pauline thought of Stanhope and was at peace as it ceased. The renewed phantasm of peace received again the desire that sprang in the heart of its father and lover, and throve and grew beautiful on it. Her terrible and infinite senility receded; Lawrence Wentworth's strong deceit forbade her to pass on to death and recalled her to apparent life. The suicide in the body had lost the vision of his destruction; the suicide in the soul had not yet reached his own. The thing became lovely with Adela's youth, and its lover slept.

In the morning, however, alone as usual, Wentworth was less at peace than had been his wont since the thing had come to him. In those earlier hours the night and his nightly companion were always indistinct. He preferred that indistinctness; he preferred, in the bright July mornings, to think of his work—the books he was reading, the book he was writing. He remembered that he had still a letter to write against Aston Moffatt, and had already begun it. But though he thought about his next unwritten sentence he could not ever manage to write it down. He would often go to his study in his dressing gown to get his papers, refusing to remember why they were not, as in the old days they used to be, lying by his bedside, or remembering only that it was because of the pleasant fantasies of his brain. So long as he could, in those early hours, pretend that it was only a mental fantasy he felt happier; he did not, just for those hours, quite like to admit that it was physical, because its actuality would have seemed in some way more immoral than a mental indulgence. His mind was certainly losing power. Afterwards as the day grew on, and the strength of his masculinity returned and swelled in him, he came to repose on his knowledge of its actual presence. But that morning he was troubled; he felt obscurely that something was attacking his peace. He moved restlessly; he got up and walked about; he tried to find refuge in this or the other thought; he failed. He would not go out that day; he sat about the house. And as the day went on he became aware that he feared to go out lest he should meet Adela Hunt, the real Adela Hunt on some real errand. He could not bear that; he could not bear her. What right had she to make his beloved a false image of her? It was after a solitary lunch and a fretful hour of work that he allowed himself at last to long for the succubus by day, and by day, knocking at his door—and he guessed who knocked and hurried himself to open it—it came. It sat in his room, and talked to him, with his own borrowed intelligence. It spoke of Cæsar and Napoleon, of generals and campaigns—traditions it could not know, history it could not recall, humanity it could not share. And still, though he was less unhappy, he was unhappy, for all that day, till the sun began to go down, he was haunted by a memory of another Adela. Even when his hand was on her bare arm, or hers caressing his, he was dimly troubled. He wanted to pull the curtains, to lock the doors, to bar out what was in his brain by barring his house, to be with what was irreconcilably not the world. He wanted either to shut himself wholly away from the world in a sepulchre of desire and satiety and renewed desire; or to destroy, if not the world, at least one form that walked in the world.

His trouble was increased by the likelihood of the intrusion of the world of the other Adela. He had, weeks since, sent to Mrs. Parry drawings and descriptions for the Grand Ducal uniforms. She had rung him up once or twice about them, and she was beginning to insist on his going round to her house to approve the result. He did not want to go to her house. He would be expected to be at the play, the performance of which was approaching, and he did not want to be at the play. Adela would be acting, and he didn't want to see her in her eighteenth-century costume, or any more at all. He would have to speak to her and he did not want to speak to her. He wanted to be alone with his fantasies. It was all the busy world, with Adela as its chief, that still hampered him. He could, of course, shut himself away, but if he were to enjoy the phantasm of Adela as he wanted to, his servants must see her and bring her tea and accept her as a visitor, and then what would they think if they heard of the actual Adela being seen somewhere else at the same time? Or if, by chance, the actual Adela should call?

It knew, with that accuracy with which it always prevented his desires, that he was disturbed about something it could not, until night came, cure. It spent on him a lingering gaze of love, and said: "I must go." It caught and kissed his hand in a hungry fire, and it looked up at him fervently and said: "To-night? Dear Lawrence, to-night?" He said "To-night," and desired to add the name. But he had never yet been able to do so—as if the name were indeed something actual, sacramental of reality. He said "To-night," and pressed it and kissed it and took it to the door, which he shut quickly, as he always did, for he had an uneasy wonder whether it ever went anywhere, once it had parted from him, and he did not wish to see it fade before his eyes into the air which, this summer, was growing so intolerably bright.

The unusual brightness had been generally noticed. It was not a heat-wave; the weather was too gay and airy for that. It was an increase in luminous power; forms stood out more sharply, voices were heard more clearly. There seemed to be a heightening of capacity, within and without. The rehearsals of the play increased in effect, a kind of swiftness moved in the air; all things hastened. People said: "What a beautiful summer!" and went on saying it. One afternoon Pauline heard Stanhope, who had replied to that phrase a score of times, vary the reply by saying with some surprise: "O, the summer, do you think?" But his interlocutor had already been wafted away.

It was two days since the promise of substituted love, and it was their first meeting. She took advantage of her precursor's remark to say, as she shook hands, and their glances exchanged affection: "What then, if it isn't the summer?"

He shrugged delicately. "Only, does it seem like the summer?" he asked.

"Not very," she said. "But what do you think?"

"The air within the air, perhaps," he answered, half-serious. "The thing that increases everything that is, and decreases everything that isn't."

Pauline said, not upon any impulse of conventional chatter, "And which am I?"

"O *is*," he said, "*is*, decidedly. Unfortunately, perhaps, in many ways, but final. You haven't had any meetings yet?"

She began to answer and was cut short by new arrivals. It was the day of the dress rehearsal, and even the sophisticated practitioners of Battle Hill felt a new excitement.

Climax was at hand. The young and more innocent actors triumphed in a delight modified by fear of their incapacity; the more experienced feared the incapacity of others. Adela Hunt, for instance, was anxious that Periel and the Chorus should be her adequate background, and that her dramatic lover should adore her urgently. He, a nice boy and shy, was too conscious of the Chorus individually to rise quite to the height of them in a mass. His voice still faltered with the smallest vibration of awareness upon the invocation of the fire. Mrs. Parry had pointed out to him that he must be used to burning leaves, and he had agreed; still, at the height of the verse, he trembled a little with the stress. The Bear, on the other hand, was distracted between his own wish to be ursine and Mrs. Parry's to be period. His two great moments, however, were in action rather than speech. One was a heavy pursuit of the Princess; at the other he and Periel intertwined in a dance among all the personages, drawing them into a complexity of union. He was not a pantomime bear; no assistant completed quadrupedicity; he walked bowed but upright, a bear's head, high furred boots, furred coat and gauntlets, making up the design which signified or symbolized the growling mass of animal life. Nor, though he and the spirit of the spirits danced together, did they ever meet or speak; between them always moved the mortal figures and harmonized their incommunicable utterances.

It was the reputation of Peter Stanhope which had so largely increased the excitement of this year's drama. Public attention was given to it; articles appeared in New York and paragraphs in Paris. Seats had to be reserved for a few—a very few—very distinguished visitors; many others could be and had to be refused. The Press would be there. A palpitation of publicity went through the cast; the world seemed to flow towards Battle Hill. There was no denying that it was an event, almost a moment in the history of the imagination; recognized as such by, at least, a not inconsiderable minority of those who cared for such things, and a quite inconsiderable minority of those who did not, but who read everything in their papers. Even the cast were provided with tickets; and the rehearsal itself was guarded by a policeman. A popular member of the Chorus also stood by the gate and scrutinized all arrivals, as if the bear and the spirit purged creation by power and knowledge.

The pressure of this outer world had modulated and unified the producer, the performers, and every one else concerned with the play. Harmony became so necessary that it was actually achieved, fate and free-will coinciding. Stanhope became so desirable that he was compelled to promise to say a few words at the end. A deference towards him exhibited itself. Adela rebuked Pauline for speaking lightly of the great man.

"I didn't know that you admired him so much yourself," Pauline said.

Adela, with an unfailing grasp of the real values of the world, said: "Even if I didn't, he is respected by some very fine judges. But I've come to see there is more in him than I'd thought. He's got a number of curiously modern streaks under his romanticism."

When Adela mentioned romanticism Pauline, and most other people, changed the conversation. Otherwise it was a prelude to a long and complete denunciation of all romantics as the enemies of true art. True art had been recently defined, by a distinguished critic, as "the factual oblique", and of the factual oblique romanticism, it seemed, was incapable, being neither clear enough to be factual or clever enough to be oblique. The factual oblique, incidentally, had not yet revealed to Adela the oblique fact that she never mentioned romanticism when she was with Hugh; any conversation in which it seemed likely to appear was deflected before it arrived. Pauline, not having been able to deflect, merely altered.

"There's Mr. Wentworth," she said. "I do hope he approves of the Guard."

"He ought to have looked at them before," Adela said severely. "He's been terribly slack. I suppose you haven't seen him lately?"

"No, not with grandmother and the play and everything," Pauline answered. "Have you?"

Adela shook her head. Wentworth was moving slowly across the lawn towards them. His eyes were on the ground; he walked heavily, and it was as if by accident that he at last drew level with them. Pauline said: "Good afternoon, Mr. Wentworth."

He looked up at her, and blinked. It was true the air was very clear and the sun very bright, yet Pauline was astonished by the momentary difficulty he seemed to find in focusing her. When he had got her right, he slowly smiled, and said: "Ah! Good afternoon, Miss Anstruther."

Adela Hunt abruptly said: "Mr. Wentworth!" He jumped. Slightly but definitely he jerked, and only then looked round. He looked, and there was perplexity in his eyes. He stared at the surprised Adela; he seemed taken aback at seeing her, and almost to resent it. A disagreeable shock showed in his face, and was gone, as he answered: "Oh, yes; Miss Hunt," a statement, not a greeting: a piece of information offered to the inquiring mind. Adela could not help noticing it, and was almost too astonished to smile. She couldn't believe the look had been acted, yet he couldn't really be surprised. She wondered if he were indeed secretly angry, if it were a poor mad insult of an outraged mind, and decided it couldn't be.

She said briskly: "I hope you've approved of the uniforms." He took a step back. He said, in real distress: "Oh, hush, hush, not so loud," and in turn he blinked at her, as if, when he had taken in her words, they surprised him more. Little though she could know it, they did. He had supposed, in the night and the morning, that he had hated the Adela of the world; he had had her in his imagination as an enemy and a threat. He had overrated her. She was, in fact, nothing like what he had, and now he had met her he had hardly recognized her. There had been a girl talking to—to—the name had again escaped him—to the other girl, whose shape had reminded him of his nightly mistress; she had turned her head, and it had been his mistress, and then again it was not. It could not be, for this one was remote and a little hostile; it was not, for this one was nothing like as delightful, as warm, as close-bewildering. She spoke, and it was strange, for he expected love; he did not want that voice except in love, and now it—at first—said strange things. With relief he realized it was not *his* voice—so he called it, admirably exact; this was not the voice of *his* mistress, and his mistress was most particularly he. This distressed him; it was loud, harsh, uncouth. It was like the rest of the tiresome world into which he had been compelled to enter—violent, smashing, bewildering by its harsh clamour, and far from the soft sweetness of his unheard melody. It was not without reason that Keats imagined the lover of unheard melody in reverie on stone images; the real Greek dancers would have pleased him less. But though Wentworth was shocked by the clumsy tread and the loud voice, they relieved him also. He had hated once; but then he had not wanted to hate—it disturbed him too much; and now he knew he did not. He need not resent the grossness of the world; enough if, by flight, he rejected it. He had his own living medicament for all trouble, and distaste and oblivion for everything else—most of all for this noisome parody of his peace.

Adela said, modulating her voice: "Have you got a headache? what a shame! it's good of you to turn out, but we do want to be sure everything's all right. I mean, if we must have uniforms. Personally …"

Wentworth said, in a voice of exhaustion: "Oh, please!" In this stridency, as it seemed to him, there was a suggestion of another disastrous noise—the nightmare of a groan, tearing up the abyss, setting the rope swinging. The dull, heavy, plain thing opposite him became identified to his pained sense with that dreadful break-up of his dream, and now he could not hide. He could not say to the hills of those comforting breasts: "Cover me". The sound sang to his excruciated body, as the sight oppressed it. The two imprisoned and split him: they held him and searched his entrails. They *wanted* something of him. He refused to want anything but what he wanted.

While Adela stared, half offended by his curious moan, he withdrew himself into his recesses, and refused to be wanted. Like the dead man on his flight down the hill, he declined communion. But he, to whom more room and beauty in life had been given, chances of clarity and devotion, was not now made frightening to himself. He had not known fear, nor did he find fear, nor was fear the instrument of salvation. He had what he had. There were presented to him the uniforms of the Grand Ducal Guard.

A voice as loud but less devastating than Adela's, for it recalled no unheard melodies, said behind him: "Mr. Wentworth! at last! we're all ready for you. Pauline, the Guard are over by the beeches: take Mr. Wentworth across. I'll be there in a minute." Mrs. Parry, having said this, did not trouble to watch them do it. She went on.

Pauline smiled at Wentworth's dazed and Adela's irritated face. She said: "I suppose we'd better. Would you, Mr. Wentworth?"

He turned to her with relief. The sound of her voice was quieter than the rest. He had never before thought so, but now certainly it was. He said, "Yes, yes; let's get away."

Pauline saw Adela as they turned from her, a Gorgon of incredulity. Her heart laughed, and they went. As they passed over the grass, she said: "I do hope you haven't a headache? They're so trying."

He answered, a little relieved to be away from the dull shouting oppression of Adela: "People are so noisy. Of course ... anything I can do ... but I can't stop long."

"I shouldn't think it would take more than a few minutes," Pauline said. "You'll only have to say yes or no—practically. And," she added, looking round at the whole chaos of glory, and instinctively discerning Stanhope in the distance, "as it's too late for anything else, you might be so very kind as to enjoy us for what we are, and say yes."

Hugh Prescott, grand-ducally splendid and dramatically middle-aged, ran after them. He said, as he caught them up: "Hallo, Mr. Wentworth! I hope my Guard'll be correct."

Wentworth had been soothed by Pauline's voice. It had to his mind, after Adela's, something of that quality he desired. It mingled with him; it attracted him; it carried him almost to that moment he knew so well, when, as the desire that expressed his need awoke and grew in him, there came a point of abandonment to his desire. He did not exactly will, but he refused to avoid. Why, indeed, he had once asked himself, swiftly, almost thoughtlessly, should he avoid? He asked himself no more; he sighed, and as it were, nestled back into himself, and then it would somehow be there—coming from behind, or speaking in his ear, or perhaps not even that, but a breath mingling with his, almost dividing from his to mingle with it, so that there were two where there had been one, and then the breath seemed to wander away into his palm where his hand lay half-closed, and became a hand in his own hand, and then a slow arm grew against his, and so, a tender coil against him or a swift energy of hunger, as his mood was, it was there, and when the form was felt, it could at last be seen, and he sank into its deep inviting eyes. As he listened to Pauline he suddenly knew all this, as he had never known it before; he almost saw it happen as a thing presented. Her voice created, but it separated. It brought him almost to his moment, and coiled away, with him in its toils. It directed him to the Guard; it said, with an intensity that Pauline had never uttered, but he in his crisis heard: "Take us as we are, and say yes; say yes or no ... we are ... we are ... say yes ...", and another voice, "Is the Grand Duke's Guard correct?" They became, as he paused before the displayed magnificence, a chorus swinging and singing: "We are ... we are ... we are.... Is the Guard correct?... Say, say, O say ... is the Guard, is the Guard correct?"

It was not. In one flash he saw it. In spite of his diagrams and descriptions, they had got the shoulder-knots all wrong. The eighteenth century had never known that sort of thing. He looked at them, for the first moment almost with the pure satisfaction of the specialist. He almost, somewhere in him, joined in that insane jangle: "No, no, no; the Guard is wrong—O, wrong. Say ... I say...." He looked, and he swung, as if on his rope, as if at a point of decision—to go on or to climb up. He walked slowly along the line, round the back, negligent of remarks and questions, outwardly gazing, inwardly swinging. After that first glance, he saw nothing else clearly. "Say yes or no...." The shoulder-knots could be altered easily enough, all twelve, in an hour or so's work. Or pass them—"take us as we are ... say yes." They could be defended, then and there, with half a dozen reasons; they were no more of a jumble than Stanhope's verse. But he was something of a purist; he did not like them. His housekeeper, for that matter, could alter them that evening under his direction, and save the costume-makers any further trouble. "Is the Guard, is the Grand Duke's Guard, correct?"

A voice penetrated him. Hugh was saying: "One must have one's subordinates exact, mustn't one?" There was the slightest stress on "subordinates"—or was there? Wentworth looked askance at him; he was strolling superb by his side. Pauline said: "We could alter some things, of course." His silence had made her anxious. He stood away, and surveyed the backs of the Guard. He could, if he chose, satisfy and complete everything. He could have the coats left at his house after the rehearsal; he could do what the honour of his scholarship commanded; he could have them returned. It meant only his being busy with them that one evening, and concerning himself with something different from his closed garden. He smelt the garden.

Mrs. Parry's voice said: "Is the Guard correct?" He said: "Yes." It was over; he could go.

He had decided. The jingle was in his ears no more. Everything was quite quiet. The very colours were still. Then from a distance movement began again. His future was secure, both proximate and ultimate. But his present was decided for him; he was not allowed to go. The devil, for that afternoon, promptly swindled him. He had cheated; he was at once cheated. Mrs. Parry expected him to stop for the rehearsal and oversee the movement of the Guard wherever, in its odd progress about the play, it marched on or marched off. She made it clear. He chattered a protest, to which she paid no attention. She took him to a chair, saw him in it, and went off. He had no energy to oppose her. No one had. Over all that field of actors and spectators—over Stanhope and Pauline, over Adela and Hugh, over poetry and possession and sacred possession the capacity of one really capable woman imposed itself. The moment was hers, and in view of her determination the moment became itself. As efficient in her kind as Margaret Anstruther in hers, Catherine Parry mastered creation, and told it what to do. She had taken on her job, and the determination to fulfil her job controlled the utterance of the poetry of Stanhope and delayed the operation of the drugs of Lilith. Wentworth struggled and was defeated, Adela writhed but obeyed, Peter Stanhope laughed and enjoyed and assented. It was not perhaps the least achievement of his art that it had given to his personal spirit the willingness to fulfil the moment as the moment, so that, reserving his own apprehension of all that his own particular business meant to him, he willingly subordinated it to the business of others at their proper time. He seconded Mrs. Parry as far as and in every way that he could. He ran errands, he took messages, he rehearsed odd speeches, he fastened hooks and held weapons. But he only seconded her. The efficiency was hers; and the Kingdom of God which fulfilled itself in the remote recesses of his spacious verse fulfilled itself also in her effective supremacy. She stood in the middle of the field and looked around her. The few spectators were seated; the actors were gathering. Stanhope stood by her side. The Prologue, with his trumpet, ran hastily across the stage to the trees which formed the background. Mrs. Parry said: "I think we're ready?" Stanhope agreed. They retired to their chairs, and Mrs. Parry nodded vigorously to the Prologue. The rehearsal began.

Wentworth, sitting near to Stanhope, secluded himself from it as much as possible, reaching backward and forward with closed eyes into his own secrecies. At the extreme other end of activity, Pauline, waiting with the Chorus for the Woodcutter's Son's speech, upon which, as he fed the flames, the first omnipotent song was to break, also gave herself up to delight. If the heavens had opened, it was not for her to deny them, or even too closely to question or examine them. She carried, in her degree, Peter Stanhope and his fortunes—not for audience or other publicity but for the achievement of the verse and the play itself. It was all very well for Stanhope to say it was an entertainment and not a play, and to be charmingly and happily altruistic about her, and since he preferred her to fall in with Mrs. Parry's instructions she did it, for everyone's sake including her own. But he was used, anyhow in his imagination, to greater things; this was the greatest she had known or perhaps was ever likely to know. If the apparition she had so long dreaded came across the field she would look at it with joy. If it would sit down till the rehearsal was over…. She smiled to herself at the fantasy and laughed to think that she could smile. The Woodcutter's Son from beside her went forward, carrying his burden of twigs. His voice rose in the sublime speculations of fire and glory which the poet's reckless generosity had given him. He spoke and paused, and Pauline and all the Chorus, moving so that their own verdure showed among the trees, broke into an answering song.

She was not aware, as the rehearsal proceeded, of any other sensation than delight. But so clear and simple was that delight, and so exquisitely shared by all the performers in their separate ways, that as between the acts they talked and laughed together, and every one in the field, with the exception of Lawrence Wentworth, joined in that universal joy—so single and fundamental did it become that once, while again she waited, it seemed to her as if the very words "dress rehearsal" took on another meaning. She saw the ceremonial dress of the actors, but it did not seem to her stranger than Mrs. Parry's frock or Stanhope's light suit. All things, at all times and everywhere, rehearsed; some great art was in practice and the only business anyone had was to see that his part was perfect. And this particular rehearsal mirrored the rest—only that this was already perfected from within, and that other was not yet. The lumbering Bear danced; the Grand Duke uttered his gnomic wisdom; the Princess and the Woodcutter's Son entered into the lucid beauty of first love; the farmers counted their pence; and the bandits fell apart within.

It was in the pause before the last act that the dark thought came to her. She had walked a little away from the others to rest her soul, and, turning, looked back. Around the place where lately the fire had burned, the Prologue and some of the Guard were talking. She saw him lift his trumpet; she saw them move, and the uniforms shone in the amazing brightness of the sun, and suddenly there came to her mind another picture; the woodcut in the old edition of the *Book of Martyrs*. There too was a trumpet, and guards, and a fire, and a man in it. Here, the tale said, and she had not remembered it till now, here where this stage, perhaps where this fire lay, they had done him to death by fire.

She had had the last act in mind as she turned, the act in which physical sensation, which is the play of love, and pardon, which is the speed of love, and action, which is the fact of love, and almighty love itself, all danced together; and now a shadow lay across it, the shadow of death and cruelty, the living death. The sun was still bright, colours vivid, laughter gay, and the shadow was the centre of them all. The shadow was a hollow, filled with another, quite different, fact. She felt the pang of the last hopelessness. If the living who walked in the gutters of mind or spirit, if the present misery of the world, were healed, or could be forgotten, still there sprang out of the hollow the knowledge of the dead whose unrecompensed lives had gone before that joy. The past accused her, made terrible by the certain history of her house. His blood was in her and made demands on hers. He had gone willingly to death, chosen it, insisted on it; his judges had been willing enough to spare him if he would commit himself to a phrase or two. But still in the end they had inflicted death, and agony in death; and the world that had inflicted and enjoyed and nourished itself on agony was too like the world in which she moved, too like Hugh and Adela and Catherine Parry and the rest. She had been lost in a high marvel, but if that joy were seriously to live it must somehow be reconciled with the agony that had been; unless hollow and shell were one, there was only hollow and shell.

She walked back, and as she did so Stanhope saw her and came across.

"Well," he said, "it all seems going very well."

She said, with a coldness in her voice that rose from the creeping hollow of the darkness. "You think so?… did you know an ancestor of mine was burnt alive just here?"

He turned to walk by her. "I did," he said. "I'd read it, of course—after all, it's my house—and your grandmother spoke of it."

She said: "Well?" and then repentantly, "I'm sorry but … we're all so happy. The play, the fire—*our* fire, it's all so wonderful. And yet we can do *that*. How can we be happy, unless we forget? and how can we forget? how can we dare forget?"

He said: "Forget nothing. Unless everything's justifiable, nothing is. But don't you forget, perhaps, something else?"

She looked at him with question. He went on: "Mightn't his burden be carried too?"

She stopped; she said staring: "But he's dead!"

"And so?" Stanhope asked mildly, and waited.

She said: "You mean … you can't mean…?" As her voice hung baffled, there arose gigantic before her the edge of a world of such incredible dimensions that she was breathless at the faint hint. Her mouth opened; her eyes stared. Her head was spinning. She said: "But…."

Stanhope took her arm to propel her gently forward; then, letting it go, he said: "A good deal of our conversation consists of saying *but* to each other. However, who shall fail to follow when … and so forth. 'But—' Periel?"

"But he's dead," she repeated. It was not what she meant to say.

"So you remarked," Stanhope said gently. "And I asked you what that had to do with it. Or words to that effect. You might as well say he had red hair, as for all I know he may have had. Yes, yes, Mrs. Parry."

He raised his voice and waved back. "We shall be delaying the rehearsal," he said. "Come along—all things in their order."

She asked, inadvertently, as she quickened her steps to keep pace with him: "Do you tell me to try and carry *his* fear?"

"Well," he answered, "you can't make contract; so far, it's true, death or red hair or what not interferes. But you might, in the Omnipotence, offer him your—anything you've got. Only I should intend to have it first."

"Intend to have it?" she asked breathlessly.

"Intend to have joy to offer," he said. "Be happy—take all the happiness, if it's there, that you may not offer the Lord what costs nothing. You must have a small private income to try and help support even a Marian martyr. Heavens, they *are* waiting. To your tent, O Periel." As she ran he exclaimed after her. "Perhaps that's the difference between Israel and Judah! they went to their own tents and left David to his. Hence the Dispersion … and the Disappearance."

"What disappearance, Mr. Stanhope?" Mrs. Parry asked.

He had come level with her while he was still speaking, and he made a small gesture. "Nothing, Mrs. Parry. Of the saviour of his own life. How well this act opens, doesn't it?"

As Pauline, escaping Mrs. Parry's eye, ran across the stage, and threaded her way between the persons to her position, her mind was more breathless than she. She felt again, as in a low but immense arc rising above the horizon of her world, or perhaps of the earth itself, the hint of a new organization of all things: a shape, of incredible difficulty in the finding, of incredible simplicity found, an infinitely alien arrangement of infinitely familiar things. The bottom had dropped out of her universe, yet her astonished spirit floated and did not fall. She was a little sick with running, running into this other world. She halted, turned, addressed herself. She turned to the play where martyrdom had been—to the martyrdom. "I have seen the salvation of my God." The salvation throbbed in the air above her; it thrilled in the mortal light. "'Unto him that hath shall be given' … 'what of him that hath not?'" A voice, neither of the martyr nor his executioner, answered, singing, with a terrible clarity of assured fact—fact, the only thing that can be loved: "from him that hath not shall be taken away even that which he seemeth to have". A trumpet was crying, crying for the execution of the justice of the Queen's Majesty on a convicted and impenitent heretic. His blood was in her veins; dazed with her own will, she struggled to pay the dues of her inheritance. The sudden crowd of adorned figures thronged before her. He was not there; he was dead centuries since. If centuries meant anything; perhaps they didn't—perhaps everything was all at once, and interchanged devotion; perhaps even now he burned, and she and her friends danced, and her grandmother died and lived, and Peter Stanhope wrote his verse, and all the past of the Hill was one with its present. It lived; it intermingled; not among these living alone did the doctrine of substituted love bear rule. Her intention rose, and was clear, and withdrew, as the stage opened for her advance. About her the familiar and transfigured personages moved; this was the condition and this the air of supernatural life. *Ecce, omnia nova facio.* The incantation and adoration of the true substance of experience sounded. She fulfilled her part in a grave joy, aspiring to become part of that substance. All drew to its close; the dress rehearsal ended. Remained only the performance of the play.

Chapter IX

THE TRYST OF THE WORLDS

*

As if the world of that other life to which this in which Margaret Anstruther lay was but spectral, and it to this, renewed itself with all its force in the groan he heard, as if that groan had been but its own energy of freeing itself, the dead man found when it ceased that he was standing alone among the houses. He remembered the vanished apparitions clearly enough, two images of beauty. He had seen an old woman and a young, though the younger form had been faint with distance. The colour which she hinted was obscured; in the older there was no colour but softness of light. Now he was in the street. His back was to the house. He was looking along the road, and he saw, beyond it, at the point where the light of the sun, whatever sun, lay halted, the house and the ladder he knew. He saw the light beyond it, softer than before, as it were of one kind with that of the woman with whom he had spoken. The house itself was dark; the ladder was white with a bony pallor against it, but it held no sun. There it stood, waiting for him to go back.

There had been an opening up within him. He had run in his life after other men, and in his second life away from other selves. His unapt mind had been little use to him. It had been trying to please others or himself, naturally and for long properly. He was relieved of this necessity. There was only one way to go, and the only question if he should go. He could move, or not. He knew this, yet, like Pauline when she kept her promise to Stanhope, he knew that he had already chosen, had come into obedience, and was no longer free. He began to walk. He had not realized that the choice was there until the choice had been made. Wentworth, turning from the Grand Ducal Guard, did not realize it even then; as Macbeth did not know he had accepted his deed when he accepted the means, and conceded his sin to his conviction of success.

In effect, the dead man's choice, like all choices of the kind, had been less than it seemed. He could go, or he could wait till he was driven. In the hastening or delaying of the end lies all distinction in the knowledge of the end when at last it comes. At rare moments speed is determined; all else is something else. He went, and with more energy than he had ever known. The lost power of his missed youth awoke in him, and of his defrauded manhood. It was needed. He had not taken a dozen steps before the memory of his latest experience became as faint as the old woman's voice had been. He did not again feel his old fear, but he was intensely aware of ignorance. There were now no shapes. He was alone, and the pallid ladder of the dark house stood before him. The light beyond was soft, but promised nothing. As he went soundlessly he had no thought but that it was better to do at once what must be done, and that he had seen, if only in a fading apparition, the tender eyes of love.

He passed the finished houses; he came among those which, by the past or future, had been unbuilt. As he reached them he heard a faint sound. He had come again into the peculiar territory of the dead. He heard behind him a small rustle, as if of dead leaves or snakes creeping out from dry sticks. He did not think of snakes or leaves, nor of the dead leaves of a great forest, the still-existent nothingness of life. Those who had known the green trees were tangled and torn in the dry. The tragedies of Peter Stanhope carried the image of that pain-piercing nothing. The dead man, like Pauline, had lived with thorns and hard wood, and at last they had destroyed him as pitilessly as the Marian martyr. He did not therefore conceive them now as anything but a mere sound. It went with him along the road, and when he had come fully out at the end into the space where the ladder of bone led again to a darkness of the grave, it had become louder. He heard it on all sides. He stopped and turned.

The shapes were standing in a great crowd watching him. Mostly they had his form and face, and they stood, in the infinite division of past moments, but higgledy-piggledy, sombrely staring. He saw in front, parodying earthly crowds, the children—different ages, different sizes, all looking with his small pointed hungry face. In the massed multitude behind there were, at points, different faces, faces of any few creatures who for one reason or another had mattered to his mind. He saw his wife in several places; he saw the face of a youth who had been the nearest he had known to a friend; he saw those he had disliked. But, at most, these others were few.

The crowd did not move, except that sometimes other single forms slipped out of the ruined houses, swelling it as crowds are swelled in London streets. It was useless, had he desired it, to attempt to return. He turned away from them again, but this time not merely from them but towards something, towards the ladder. He laid a hand on it. The long hard dry rustle came again, as the whole crowd fell forward, bones shifting and slipping as some moving vitality slid through them. They closed towards him, their thronged circles twisting round the house and him as if they were the snake. His mortal mind would have given way, could it have apprehended such a strait between shadowy bone and shining bone; his immortal, nourished by belief in the mother of his soul, remained clear. His seeming body remained capable. He exercised his choice, and began to go up the ladder. At once, with a horrid outbreak of shifting leaves and snapping sticks and rustling bodies, they were about its foot, looking up. The living death crowded round the ladder of bone, which it could not ascend. White faces of unvitalized, unsubstantial, yet real, existence, looked up at him mounting. Nothingness stared and panted, with false breath, terrible to those who live of choice in its phantasmal world. But for him, who rose above them to that stage set in the sky, the expanded point and culminating area of his last critical act, the place of skull and consciousness, of life and death and life, for him there entered through the grasp he had on the ladder shafts an energy. He looked neither down nor up; he went on. A wind had risen about him, as if here the movement of the leaves, if leaves, shook the air, and not the air the leaves. It was as if a last invisible tentacle were sent up by the nothingness to draw him back into the smooth undulations below, that its sterility might bury him in a living sepulchre; the identities of the grave moving in a blind instinct to overtake and seize him. Now and then some of them even began to mount a few rungs, but they could get and keep no hold. They fell again to their own level.

He did not see this, for his eyes were above. In the same sense of nothing but action he climbed the last rungs, and stood on the stage from which he had been flung. But he had hardly stepped on to it before it changed. He had come back from his own manner of time to the point in the general world of time from which he had fled, and he found it altered. The point of his return was not determined by himself, but by his salvation, by a direction not yet formulated, by the economy of means of the Omnipotence, by the moment of the death of Margaret Anstruther. Therefore he came into the built house, and the room where Wentworth slept. The open stage closed round him as he came upon it. The walls rose; there was a ceiling above. He knew he stood in a room, though the details were vague. It was ghostly to him, like that other in which, a short time before, he had stood. There the old woman had been a vivid centre to him. Here he was not, at first, aware of a centre. In this other world he had not been astonished at the manner in which things happened, but now he was a little uncomfortable. He thought at first it was because he could have had no business in such a room during his earlier life. So perhaps it was, but if so, another cause had aroused the old uneasiness—the faint hint of a slither of dry leaves, such as he had heard behind him along the road, but now within the room. It displeased and diseased him; he must remove himself. It was almost his first quiet decision ever; he was on the point to enter into actions of peace. The courtesy that rules the world of spirits took him, and as the creature that lay in the room had not entered except under Wentworth's compulsion, so this other made haste to withdraw from its intrusion. Also he was aware that, having re-entered this place and point of time, this station of an inhabited world, by the ladder of bone from the other side, he must go now farther on the way. He had the City in his mind; he had his wife in mind. He could not tell by what means or in what shape he would find her, or if he would find her. But she was his chief point of knowledge, and to that he directed himself. Of the necessity of getting a living he did not think. Living, whether he liked it or not, was provided; he knew that he did like. He went carefully across the dim room and through the door; down the stairs, and reached the front door. It opened of itself before him, so he thought, and he peered out into the road. A great blackness was there; it changed as he peered. As if it fled from him, it retreated. He heard the wind again, but now blowing up the street. A shaft of light smote along with it. Before wind and light and himself he saw the night turn, but it was not the mere night; it was alive, it was made of moving and twisting shapes hurrying away of their own will. Light did not drive them; they revealed the light as they went. They rose and rushed; as they disappeared he saw the long drive before him, and at its end, in the street proper, the figure of a girl.

In a different darkness, mortally illumined, Pauline, not far away, had that previous evening been sitting by her grandmother's bed. It was, to her, the night after the rehearsal. She had come home to find Margaret awake, alert, inquiring, and after she had spoken of the details of the afternoon, she had not been able, nor wished, to keep from speaking of the other thing that filled and threatened her mind. Her grandmother's attention still seemed to her acute, even if remote. Indeed, all mortal things were now remote to Margaret unless they were vividly consistent with the slope over which she moved. She felt, at intervals, someone being lifted and fed, someone hearing and speaking intelligible words. Only sometimes did definiteness from that other casual state enter her; then she and it were sharply present. For the rest she only saw vague images of a great good, and they faded, and at rarer intervals in the other single consciousness of slow—but slow!—movement over a surface, an intense sweetness pierced her. She moaned then, for it was pain; she moaned happily, for it was only the last inevitable sloth of her body that made its pain, resisting, beyond her will, the translucent energy. She always assented. She assented now to what Pauline was saying, sitting by her bed, her fingers interlocked and pressed against her knee, her body leaning forward, her breath drawn with a kind of slow difficulty against the beating passion of her heart's presagements. She was saying: "But how could one give backwards?"

Margaret could not, at that point of experience, explain metaphysics. She said: "If it's like that, my dear?"

Pauline said: "But if he took it? I thought—there—I might: but now, I daren't."

She saw Margaret's smile flash at her across rocks. It went and the voice said: "You think it's yours?"

Pauline answered, abruptly checking abruptness: "I don't…. Do I?"

"You think one of the two's yours—joy or misery," Margaret said, "or both. Why, if you don't, should you mind?"

Pauline for a minute struggled with this in silence: then, evading it, she returned to time. "But four hundred years," she exclaimed.

"Child," her grandmother said, "I can touch Adam with my hand; you aren't as far off."

"But how could he take it before I'd given it?" Pauline cried, and Margaret said: "Why do you talk of *before*? If you give, you give to It, and what does It care about *before*?"

Pauline got up and walked to the window. It was drawing towards night, yet so translucent was the pale green sky that night and day seemed alike unthinkable. She heard in the distance a single pair of hurrying feet; patter, patter. She said, in a muffled voice: "Even the edge frightens me."

"Peter Stanhope," Margaret said, "must have been frightened many times."

"O—poetry!" Pauline exclaimed bitterly. "That's different; you know it is, grandmother."

"In seeing?" Margaret asked. "And as for being, you must find out for yourself. He can carry your parcels, but not you."

"Couldn't he?" Pauline said. "Not that I want him to."

"Perhaps," Margaret answered. "But I think only when you don't need it, and your parcels when you do."

Her voice grew faint as she spoke, and Pauline came quickly back to the bed.

"I'm tiring you," she said hastily. "I'm sorry: look, I'll go now. I didn't mean to talk so much."

Margaret glanced at her, and said in a whisper: "But I'd so much rather die talking." All talk of the divine thing was pleasant to her, even if this beating of wings in the net, wings so dear and so close, was exhausting in the thin air. Pauline, looking down for a second after her good-night, thought that a change had taken place. The eyes had closed, though the girl was by no means sure that they were not as alert now as they had been when they were open and watching.

Yet a proportion between the old woman and external things had been withdrawn; another system of relations might have been established, but if so it was unapprehensible by others. But the change in customary relations was definitely apprehensible. She looked small, and yet small was hardly the word; she was different. The body had been affected by a change of direction in the spirit, and only when the spirit was removed would it regain for a little while its measurable place amongst measurable things. It could be served and aided; but the ceremonies of service were now made to something strange that existed among them. The strangeness communicated itself, by a kind of opposition, to the very bed in which that body was stretched; it became a mound of earth lifted up to bear the visiting victim. The woman who was their companion had half-changed into a visitor from another place, a visitor who knew nothing of the world to which she was still half-native. The unknown and the known mingled, as if those two great parents of humanity allowed their mingled powers to be evident to whoever watched. The mound, in the soft light of the room, presented itself to Pauline as if its low height was the crown and peak of a life; the long journey had ended on this cavity in the rounded summit of a hill. She considered it gravely so before she turned and, leaving the nurse in charge, went to her own room.

She was not asleep when later in the night she was called. Her grandmother, the nurse said, needed her. Pauline pulled a dressing-gown on her and went across. Mrs. Anstruther was sitting in the bed, propped by pillows; her eyes looking away out of the room. As if she dared not turn her gaze away, she said, as Pauline came up: "Is that you, darling?"

"Me," the girl answered. "Did you want me?"

"Will you do something for me?" Mrs. Anstruther said. "Something rather odd?"

"Why, of course," the girl said. "Anything. What is it?"

"Would you be so very charming as to go out and see if anyone wants you?" Mrs. Anstruther said, quite distinctly. "Up by Mr. Wentworth's."

"She's wandering," the nurse whispered. Pauline, used to Mrs. Anstruther's extremely unwandering habits, hesitated to agree. But it was certainly rather odd. She said, with a tenderness a little fractured by doubt, "Wants *me*, darling? Now?"

"Of course, *now*," her grandmother answered. "That's the point. I think perhaps he ought to get back to the City." She looked round with a little sigh. "Will you?"

Pauline had been about to make the usual unfelicitous efforts of the healthy to persuade the sick that they are being rightly served. But she could not do it. No principle and no wisdom directed her, nor any conscious thought of love. She merely could not do it. She said: "By Mr. Wentworth's? Very well, darling." She could have helped, but did not, adding: "I don't think it's very likely."

"No," said Margaret, and Pauline was gripped by a complete sense of folly. "'I don't think it's … No.'" She said: "I don't know a thing. I'll go." And turned. The nurse said, as she moved to the door: "Sweet of you to be so nice. Come back in ten minutes or so. She won't realize the time."

"I'm going," Pauline said, distantly and distinctly, "as far as Mr. Wentworth's. I shall be as quick as I can." She saw a protest at the nurse's mouth, and added: "At once."

She dressed quickly. Even so, in spite of her brave words to the nurse, her doubts were quicker. In spite of her intention, she reasoned against her promise. Three words dogmatized definition at her: "Her mind's wandering; her mind's wandering." Why, obeying that wandering mind, should she herself wander on the Hill? Why, in a lonely street, under the pale shining sky, should she risk the last dreadful meeting? The high clock struck one; time drew to the night's nadir. Why go? why go? Sit here, she said, almost aloud, and say "Peace". Is it peace, Jehu? cry peace where there is no peace; *faciunt solitudinem et pacem vocant*. She would make a solitude round the dying woman and call it peace; the dying woman would die and never know, or dying know and call it well; the dying woman that would not die but see, or die and see; and dead, see and know—know the solitude that her granddaughter had called peace. Up and up, the wind was rising, and the shuffle of leaves under the moon, and nothing was there for her to find, but to find nothing now was to be saved from finding nothing in the place where whatever she now did was hid and kept and saved. The edge of the other world was running up along the sky, the world where everyone carried themselves but everyone carried someone else's grief: Alice in Wonderland, sweet Alice, Alice sit by the fire, the fire burned: who sat by the fire that burned a man in another's blood on the grass of a poet's house, where things were given backward, and rules were against rights and rights against rules, and a ghost in the fire was a ghost in the street, and the thing that had been was the thing that was to be and it was coming, was coming; what was coming? what but herself? she was coming, she was coming, up the street and the wind; herself—a terrible good, terror and error, but the terror was error, and the error was in the terror, and now all were in him, for he had taken them into himself, and he was coming, down all the roads of Battle Hill, closing them in him, making them straight: make straight the highways before our God, and they were not for God took them, in the world that was running through this, its wheel turning within this world's air, rolling out of the air. No peace but peace, no joy but joy, no love but love. Behold, I come quickly. Amen, even so, come….

She caught up a hat and flung herself at the door, her blood burning within her, as the house burned around. The air was fiery to her sense; she breathed a mingled life, as if the flames of poetry and martyrdom rose together in the air within the air, and touched the outer atmosphere with their interior force. She ran down the stairs, but already her excitement, being more excitement than strength, flagged and was pain. Action was not yet so united with reaction as to become passion. The doubt she must have of what was to come took its old habitual form. Her past pretended to rule her, *de facto* sovereign, and her past was fear. It was midnight, the Hill was empty, she was alone. It could only be that her ghostly image lay, now, in wait for her to emerge into its desolate kingdom. She grit her teeth. The thing must be done. She had promised her grandmother; more important still, she had promised the nurse. She might have confided to the first what she would never concede to the second. It was that then she saw the telephone.

At first, as she paused a minute in the hall, to settle herself—to settle her determination that that woman who had talked of wandering minds should not find her foolish expectation fulfilled—at first she did not think of Stanhope; then inevitably, with her grief stirring in her, she did. To think of him was to think, at once, of speaking to him. The telephone. She thought: "One o'clock and he's asleep; don't be a fool." She thought: "'Any hour of the day or night'." She thought: "I oughtn't to disturb him," and then with the clarity of that world of perpetual exchange: "I ought to disturb him." It was her moral duty to wake him up, if he was asleep and she could. She smiled, standing in the hall where the new light of the summer sky dimly shone. Reversal had reached its extreme; she who had made a duty of her arrogance had found a duty in her need. Her need retreated beneath the shock. At precisely the moment when she could have done without him she went to ask for him; the glad and flagrant mockery of the Omnipotence lay peaceful in her heart as she dialled his number, her finger slowing a little on the last figure, as if the very motion were a delight too sweet to lose by haste. The receiver at her ear, as if she leant to it, she waited. Presently she heard his voice.

She said, again grave: "Are you awake enough to hear me?"

"Complete with attention," he answered. "Whatever it is, how very, very right of you! That's abstract, not personal. Concede the occasion."

"The occasion," she said, "is that I'm going out up the Hill because my grandmother's asked me to, and I was a little afraid just now … I'm not."

"O blessed, blessed," Stanhope murmured, but whether he thought of her or the Omnipotence she did not know. He added, to her: "Go in peace. Would you like me to come?"

"No, of course not," she answered, and lingering still a minute said: "I thought I wanted to ring you up, but when I did I didn't. Forgive me."

"If it gives you any pleasure," he said, "but you might have needed forgiveness in fact if you hadn't. God's, not mine. Pardon, Periel, like love, is only ours for fun: essentially we don't and can't. But you want to go….. You'll remember?"

"For ever," she said, "and ever and ever. Thank you." She put the receiver firmly down, opened the door, and went out into the street. The pure night received her. Darkness was thick round the houses, but the streets lay clear. She was aware, immediately, of some unusualness, and presently she knew what it was. She was used to shadows lying across the pavements, but now it was not so. On either side of the street they gathered and blocked and hid the buildings, climbing up them, creepers of night, almost in visible movement. Between those masses the roads lay like the gullies of a mountain down which an army might come—broad and empty, prepared for an army, passes already closed by scouts and outposts, and watched by the dazzling flashes which now and then and here and there lit the sky, as if silver machines of air above the world moved in escort of expected power. Apart from those momentary dazzling flashes light was diffused through the sky. She could see no moon, only once or twice in her walk, at some corner, between the cliffs of darkness, far away on the horizon, she half-thought she saw a star—Hesper or Phosphor, the planet that is both the end and the beginning, Venus, omega and alpha, transliteration of speech. Once, far behind her, she thought she heard hurrying footsteps, but as she went on she lost them. She went quickly, for she had left behind her an approaching point to which she desired to return, the point of hastening death. She went peacefully, but while, days before, it had been Stanhope's intervention that had changed her mood, now she had come, by the last submissive laughter of her telephone call, into the ways of the world he had no more than opened. She went with a double watchfulness, for herself and for that other being whom her grandmother had sent her to meet, but her watchfulness did not check her speed, nor either disturb the peace. She turned, soon enough, into the street where Lawrence Wentworth's house stood, not far from the top of the Hill in one direction, from the Manor House in another, and, beyond all buildings, from the silent crematorium in a third. The street, as she came into it, looked longer than she had remembered. It had something of the effect by which small suburban byways, far inland, seem to dip towards the sea, though here it was no sea but a mere distance of road which received it. She slackened her pace, and, flicking one hand with her gloves, walked towards the house.

She reached it at last, and paused. There was at first no sign of any living creature. She looked up at it; the shadows were thick on it, seeming to expand and contract. The small occasional wind of the night, intermittently rising, caught them and flung them against it; they were beaten and bruised, if shadows could take the bruise, against its walls; they hid windows and doors; there was only a rough shape of the house discernible below them. She thought, in a faint fancy, too indistinct to be a distress, of herself flung in that steady recurrence against a bleak wall, and somehow it seemed sad that she should not be bruised. A gratitude for material things came over her; she twisted her gloves in her fingers and even struck her knuckles gently together, that the sharp feel of them might assure her of firm flesh and plotted bone. As if that slight tap had been at a door, to announce a visitor, she saw a man standing outside the shadow, close by the house.

She could not, in the moon, see very clearly what he was. She thought, by something in his form, that she had seen him before; then, that she had not. She thought of her grandmother's errand, and that perhaps here was its end. She waited, in the road, while he came down the drive, and then she saw him clearly. He was small and rather bent; obviously a working man and at that an unsuccessful working man, for his clothes were miserably old, and his boots gaped. Yet he had presence; he advanced on her with a quiet freedom, and when he came near she saw that he was smiling. He put up his hand to his tattered cap; the motion had in it the nature of an act—it had conclusion, it began and ended. He said, almost with a conscious deference such as she could have imagined herself feeling for Stanhope had she known nothing of him but his name: "Good evening, miss. Could you tell me the way to London?"

There was the faintest sound of the city's metal in his voice: dimly she knew the screech of London gate. She said: "Why, yes, but—you don't mean to walk?"

He answered: "Yes, miss, if you'll be so kind as to tell me the right road."

"But it's thirty miles," she cried, "and … hadn't you better…." She stopped, embarrassed by the difficulties of earth. He did not look inferior enough to be offered money; money being the one thing that could not be offered to people of one's own class, or to anybody one respected. All the things that could be bought by money, but not money. Yet unless she offered this man money he did not, from his clothes, look as if he would get to London unless he walked.

He said: "I'd as soon walk, miss. It isn't more than a step."

"It seems to be considerably more," she said, and thought of her grandmother's errand. "Must you go now or could you wait till the morning? I could offer you a bed to-night." It seemed to her that this must be the reason why she was here.

He said: "I'd as soon not, though thank you for offering. I'd rather start now, if you'll tell me the way."

She hesitated before this self-possession; the idea that he needed money still held her, and now she could not see any way to avoid offering it. She looked in his serene quiet eyes, and said, with a gesture of her hand, "If it's a question of the fare?"

He shook his head, still smiling, "It's only a matter of starting right," he answered, and Pauline felt absurdly disappointed, as if some one had refused a cup of coffee or of cold water that she had wanted to bring. She was also a little surprised to find how easy it was to offer money when you tried—or indeed to take it: celestially easy. She answered his smile: "Well, if you won't…." she said, "Look then, this is the best way."

They walked a few steps together, the girl and the dead man, till, at a corner a little beyond Wentworth's house, she stopped.

"Down there," she said, pointing, "is the London road, you can just see where it crosses this. Are you sure you won't stay to-night and go in the morning—fare and all?" So she might have asked any of her friends, whether it had been a fare or a book or love or something of no more and no less importance.

"Quite, miss," he said, lifting his hand to his cap again in an archangelic salute to the Mother of God. "It doesn't matter perhaps, but I think I ought to get on. They may be waiting for me."

"I see," she said, and added with a conscious laughter, "One never knows, does one?"

"O I wouldn't say *never*, miss," he answered. "Thank you again. Good-night, miss."

"Good-night," she said, and with a last touch of the cap he was gone down the road, walking very quickly, lightly, and steadily. He went softly; she was not sure that she could hear his tread, though she knew she had not been listening for it. She watched him for a minute; then she turned her head and looked up the cross-road on the other side of the street. That way ran up towards the Manor House; she thought of her telephone call and wondered if Stanhope were asleep or awake. She looked back at the departing figure, and said after it aloud, in an act of remembered goodwill: "Go in peace!"

The words were hardly formed when it seemed to her that he stopped. The figure surely stood still; it was swaying; it was coming back—not coming back, only standing still, gesticulating. Its arms went up toward heaven in entreaty; then they fell and it bent and clutched its head with its hands. An agony had fallen on it. She saw and began to run. As she did so, she thought that her ears caught for an instant a faint sound from behind her, as of a trumpet, the echo of the trumpet of that day's rehearsal done or of the next day's performance not yet begun, or of a siren that called for the raising or lowering of a bridge.

So faintly shrill was the sound, coming to her between the cliffs of a pass from a camp on the other side the height, that her senses answered as sharply. The sound was transmitted into her and transmuted into sight or the fear of sight. "The Magus … my dead child … his own image." She was running fast; the stranger had gone an infinite distance in that time; she was running as she had run from her own room, and now she knew she had been right when she stopped, and it was a trap. Everything—she was running, for she could not stop—had been a part of the trap; even the shelter she had sometimes found had been meant only to catch her more surely in the end. Ah, the Magus Zoroaster had set it for her, all that time since, and her grandmother was part of its infinitely complicated steel mechanism, which now shut her in, and was going off—had gone off and was still going off, for ever and ever going off, in the faint shrill sound that came from behind her where Stanhope sat working it, for Zoroaster or Shelley were busy in front, and in front was the spring of the death and the delirium, and she had been tricked to run in that ingenious plot of their invention, and now she could no more stop than she could cease to hear the shrill whirr of the wheel that would start the spring, and when it cracked at last there would be her twin shape in the road. It was for this that the inhuman torturer who was Stanhope had pretended to save her, and the old creature who was her grandmother and talked of God had driven her out into the wild night, and the man who would not take her offer had fetched her to the point and the instant. Earth and sky were the climax of her damnation; their rods pressed her in. She ran; the trumpet sounded; the shape before her lifted his head again and dropped his hands and stood still.

She was coming near to him, and the only fact of peace to which her outraged mind could cling was that so far it was still he and not the other. Every second that he so remained was a relief. His back might open any moment and her own form leap hastily down from its ambush now among his veins and canals or from his interior back-throbbing heart. It did not; it became more definitely a man's back, as she neared it, but she saw it shaking and jerking. It was a great back, clothed in some kind of cloth doublet, with breeches below, and a heavy head of thick hair above; and the arms suddenly went up again, and a voice sounded. It said, in a shout of torment: "Lord God! Lord God!"

She stopped running a dozen yards off and stood still. It was not her decision; she was brought to a stand. The cry freed her from fear and delirium, as if it took over its own from her. She stood still, suddenly alert. The trap, if there had been a trap, had opened, and she had come out beyond it. But there was another trap, and this man was in it. He cried again: "Lord God!"

The trumpet had ceased blowing. She said in a voice breathless only from haste: "Can I help you?"

The man in front became rigid: he said: "Lord God, I cannot bear the fear of the fire."

She said: "What fire?" and still with his back to her he answered: "The fire they will burn me in to-day unless I say what they choose. Lord God, take away the fear if it be thy will. Lord God, be merciful to a sinner. Lord God, make me believe."

She was here. She had been taught what to do. She had her offer to make now and it would not be refused. She herself was offered, in a most certain fact, through four centuries, her place at the table of exchange. The moment of goodwill in which she had directed to the City the man who had but lately died had opened to her the City itself, the place of the present and all the past. He was afraid, this martyr of her house, and she knew what to do. There was no doubt about it at all. She knew that the horror of the fire had overcome him. He was in the trap in which she had been but now; the universe had caught him. His teacher, his texts, his gospel had been its bars, and his judges and executioners were springing it; and the Lord God himself was, in that desperate hour, nothing but the spring that would press him into the torment. Once the Lord had been something else; perhaps still…. He was praying passionately: "Make me believe; make me believe." The choice was first in her; Omnipotence waited her decision.

She knew what she must do. But she felt, as she stood, that she could no more do it than he. She could never bear that fear. The knowledge of being burnt alive, of the flames, of the faces, of the prolongation of pain. She knew what she must do. She opened her mouth and could not speak. In front of her, alone in his foul Marian prison, unaware of the secret means the Lord he worshipped was working swiftly for his peace, believing and unbelieving, her ancestor stood centuries off in his spiritual desolation and preluding agony of sweat. He could not see beyond the years the child of his house who strove with herself behind and before him. The morning was coming; his heart was drained. Another spasm shook him; even now he might recant. Pauline could not see the prison, but she saw him. She tried to choose and to speak.

Behind her, her own voice said: "Give it to me, John Struther." He heard it, in his cell and chains, as the first dawn of the day of his martyrdom broke beyond the prison. It spoke and sprang in his drained heart; and drove the riotous blood again through his veins: "Give it to me, give it to me, John Struther." He stretched out his arms again: he called: "Lord, Lord!" It was a devotion and an adoration; it accepted and thanked. Pauline heard it, trembling, for she knew what stood behind her and spoke. It said again: "Give". He fell on his knees, and in a great roar of triumph he called out: "I have seen the salvation of my God."

Pauline sighed deeply with her joy. This then, after so long, was their meeting and their reconciliation: their perfect reconciliation, for this other had done what she had desired, and yet not the other, but she, for it was she who had all her life carried a fear which was not her fear but another's, until in the end it had become for her in turn not hers but another's. Her heart was warm, as if the very fire her ancestor had feared was a comfort to her now. The voice behind her sang, repeating the voice in front, "I have seen the salvation of my God."

Pauline turned. She thought afterwards that she had had no choice then, but it was not so. It was a movement as swift, as instinctive, as that with which one hand flies to balance the other, but it was deliberate. She whirled on the thing she had so long avoided, and the glorious creature looked past her at the shouting martyr beyond. She was giddy with the still violence of this last evening; she shut her eyes and swayed, but she was sustained by the air about her and did not fall. She opened her eyes again; there—as a thousand times in her looking-glass—there! The ruffled brown hair, the long nose, the firm compressed mouth, the tall body, the long arms, her dress, her gesture. It wore no supernatural splendour of aureole, but its rich nature burned and glowed before her, bright as if mortal flesh had indeed become what all lovers know it to be. Its colour bewildered by its beauty; its voice was Pauline's, as she had wished it to be for pronouncing the imagination of the grand art. But no verse, not Stanhope's, not Shakespeare's, not Dante's, could rival the original, and this was the original, and the verse was but the best translation of a certain manner of its life. The glory of poetry could not outshine the clear glory of the certain fact, and not any poetry could hold as many meanings as the fact. One element co-ordinated original and translation; that element was joy. Joy had filled her that afternoon, and it was in the power of such joy that she had been brought to this closest propinquity to herself. It had been her incapacity for joy, nothing else, that had till now turned the vision of herself aside; her incapacity for joy had admitted fear, and fear had imposed separation. She knew now that all acts of love are the measure of capacity for joy; its measure and its preparation, whether the joy comes or delays.

Her manifested joy whirled on her with her own habitual movement. She sprang back from that immortality; no fear but a moment's truce of wonder and bodily tremor. She looked in her own eyes and laboured to speak; a shout was in her. She wished to assent to the choice her beatitude had made. The shout sank within her and rose without; she had assented, then or that afternoon or before this life began. She had offered her joy to her betrayed ancestor; she heard now, though she saw nothing but those brilliant and lucid eyes, the noise of his victorious going. The unseen crowd poured and roared past her. Her debt was paid, and now only she might know why and when she had incurred it. The sacrifice had been accepted. His voice was shouting in her ears, as Foxe said he had shouted, *To him that hath shall be given*. He had had; she had been given to him. She had lived without joy that he might die in joy, but when she lived she had not known and when she offered she had not guessed that the sacrificial victim had died before the sacrificial act was accomplished; that now the act was for resurrection in death. Receding voices called still; they poured onwards to the martyrdom. The confusion that was round him was her own confusion of hostile horror at the fact of glory: her world's order contending with distraction—what distraction!

One called: *What of him that hath not*? but who could be that had not? so universal, in itself and through its means, was the sublime honour of substituted love; what wretch so poor that all time and place would not yield a vicar for his distress, beyond time and place the pure vicariate of salvation? She heard the question, in that union of the centuries, with her mortal ears, as she heard excited voices round her, and the noise of feet, and the rattle at a distance of chains. She saw nothing, except the streets of the Hill and herself standing on the Hill. She felt no grief or fear; that was still to come or else it had been, according to choice of chronology. Her other self, or the image in which she saw both those choices in one vision, still stood opposite her, nor was its glory dimmed though and as her own intensity absorbed it.

After the shouted question she did not hear a reply, other sounds covered it. The scuffling, the rattling, the harsh alien voices went on; then the voice she had heard calling on the Lord cried: *The ends of the earth be upon me*. The roads had been doubled and twisted so that she could meet him there; as wherever exchange was needed. She knew it now from the abundant grace of the Hill or the hour: but exchange might be made between many mortal hearts and none know what work was done in the moment's divine kingdom. There was a pause, ominous down all the years; a suspense of silence. Then suddenly she smelt burning wood; the fire was lit, he in it. She heard the voice once more: *I have seen the salvation of my God*.

He stood in the fire; he saw around him the uniforms—O uniforms of the Grand Duke's Guard—the mounted gentlemen, the couple of friars, the executioners—O the woodcutter's son singing in the grand art!—the crowd, men and women of his village. The heat scorched and blinded and choked him. He looked up through the smoke and flame that closed upon him, and saw, after his manner, as she after hers, what might be monstrous shapes of cherubim and seraphim exchanging powers, and among them the face of his daughter's æviternity. She only among all his children and descendants had run by a sacrifice of heart to ease and carry his agony. He blessed her, thinking her some angel, and in his blessing her æviternity was released to her, and down his blessing beatitude ran to greet her, a terrible good. The ends of the world were on them. He dead and she living were made one with peace. Her way was haunted no more.

She heard the cry, and the sky over her was red with the glow of fire, its smell in her nostrils. It did not last. Her beatitude leant forward to her, as if to embrace. The rich presence enveloped her; out of a broken and contrite heart she sighed with joy. On the inhaled breath her splendour glowed again; on the exhaled it passed. She stood alone, at peace. Dawn was in the air; *ecce omnia nova facio*.

Soon after, as she came back to the house, she saw Stanhope approaching. She waited, outside her gate. He came up, saying with a smile: "Awake, lute and harp"—he made a gesture of apology—"I myself will awake right early." She put out her hand.

"I owe you this," she said. "I owe you this for ever."

He looked at her. "It's done then?" he asked, and she: "It's done. I can't tell you now, but it's done."

He was silent, studying her, then he answered slowly: "Arise, shine; your light is come; the glory of the Lord is risen upon you." His voice quickened: "And you'll do it well, taking prettily and giving prettily, but the Lord's glory, Periel, will manage to keep up with you, and I shall try."

"Oh, you!" she said, pressing and releasing his hand: "but you've got such a start!"

He shook his head. "No," he said, "our handicaps are all different, and the race is equal. The Pharisees can even catch up the woman with the mites. Those who do not insist on Gomorrah." She said: "Gomorrah?" and the chill of the word struck even through her contemplation. She remembered the unanswered question of her vision:*What of them that have not?* As if the answer had been reserved for these lower circles, he gave it. He said: "The Lord's glory fell on the cities of the plain, on Sodom and another. We know all about Sodom nowadays, but perhaps we know the other even better. Men can be in love with men, and women with women, and still be in love and make sounds and speeches, but don't you know how quiet the streets of Gomorrah are? haven't you seen the pools that everlastingly reflect the faces of those who walk with their own phantasms, but the phantasms aren't reflected, and can't be. The lovers of Gomorrah are quite contented, Periel; they don't have to put up with our difficulties. They aren't bothered by alteration, at least till the rain of the fire of the Glory at the end, for they lose the capacity for change, except for the fear of hell. They're monogamous enough! and they've no children—no cherubim breaking into being or babies as tiresome as ours; there's no birth there, and only the second death. There's no distinction between lover and beloved; they beget themselves on their adoration of themselves, and they live and feed and starve on themselves, and by themselves too, for creation, as my predecessor said, is the mercy of God, and they won't have the facts of creation. No, we don't talk much of Gomorrah, and perhaps it's as well and perhaps not."

"But where?" she cried.

"Where but here? When all's said and done there's only Zion or Gomorrah," he answered. "But don't think of that now; go and sleep if you can, or you'll be nervous this afternoon."

"Never," she said. "Not *nervous*."

"Well, that's as it may be," he said. "Still, sleep. The Sabbath and all that, even for the cattle. Be a lamb, and sleep."

She nodded, went obediently through the gate, and paused, saying: "I shall see you presently?"

"Making my concluding appearance," he said. "Unless the Lord decides to take his own call. The author has seemed to be out of the house rather often, but he may have been brought in at last. Till when, Periel, and with God."

Chapter X

THE SOUND OF THE TRUMPET

*

Mrs. Parry, rising that morning to control the grand occasion, and excluding from her mind as often as possible the image of a photograph in the papers of herself and Peter Stanhope side by side, "author and producer", found a note from Lawrence Wentworth waiting on her breakfast table. It was short and frigid. It said only that he had caught a feverish chill and would not be at the performance. Even so, it had given him some trouble to write, for it had demanded contact, and only a desire that he should not be, by some maddening necessary inquiry, disturbed in his solitude, had compelled him to write it. He had sent it round very early, and then had returned to sit in his study, with curtains drawn, to help him in his sickness.

"Very odd weather to catch a feverish chill," Mrs. Parry thought, looking through her window at the dancing sunlight. "And he might have returned his ticket, and he might have sent good wishes." Good wishes were precisely what Wentworth was incapable of sending anywhere, but Mrs. Parry could not know that. It was difficult to imagine what either Zion or Gomorrah would make of Mrs. Parry, but of the two it was certainly Zion which would have to deal with her, since mere efficiency, like mere being, is in itself admirable, and must be coloured with definite evil before it can be lost. She made a note to tell the Seating

Committee there was a seat to spare. If there were no other absentee, if none of the cast were knocked down by a car, blown up by a geyser, or otherwise incapacitated, she would think herself fortunate. She had had a private word with Pauline the day before, after the rehearsal. Rumours of Mrs. Anstruther's condition had reached her, and she wanted, in effect, to know what Periel was going to do about it. She had always been a little worried about it, but one couldn't refuse parts to suitable people because of elderly grandmothers. Periel, however, had been entirely sensible; with the full consent, almost (Mrs. Parry understood) under the direction of the grandmother. She would, under God, be there. Mrs. Parry had not too much belief in God's punctuality, but she was more or less satisfied, and left it at that. If misadventure must come, the person best spared to it would be Peter Stanhope himself. Mrs. Parry would willingly have immolated him on any altar, had she had one, to ensure the presence of the rest, and the success of the afternoon; it was why he admired her. She desired a public success, but more ardently she desired success—the achievement. She would have preferred to give a perfect performance to empty seats rather than, to full, it should fail from perfection.

She was given her desire. Even the picture was supplied. Stanhope, approached by photographers, saw to that. He caused her to be collected from her affairs at a distance; he posed by her side; he directed a light conversation at her; and there they both were: "Mr. Stanhope chatting with the producer (Mrs. Catherine Parry)." She took advantage of the moment to remind him that he had promised to say something at the end of the play, "an informal epilogue". He assured her that he was ready—"quite informal. The formal, perhaps, would need another speaker. An archangel, or something."

"It's angelic of *you*, Mr. Stanhope," she said, touched to a new courtesy by his, but he only smiled and shook his head.

The photographs—of them, of the chief personages, of the Chorus—had been taken in a secluded part of the grounds before the performance. Stanhope lingered, watching, until they were done; then he joined Pauline.

"How good Mrs. Parry is!" he said sincerely. "Look how quiet and well-arranged we all are! a first performance is apt to be much more distracted, but it's as much as our lives are worth to be upset now."

She said thoughtfully: "She is good, but I don't think it's altogether her: it's the stillness. Don't you feel it, Peter?"

"It doesn't weigh on us," he answered, smiling, "but—yes."

She said: "I wondered. My grandmother died this morning—five minutes after I got back. I wondered if I was—imagining—the stillness from that."

"No," he said thoughtfully, "but that may be in it. It's as if there were silence in heaven—a fortunate silence. I almost wish it were the *Tempest* and not me. What a hope!

> *I'll deliv*
> *promise you calm seas, auspicio*
>
> *til so expeditious, that shall catch*
> *oyal fleet far off."*

His voice became incantation; his hand stretched upward in the air, as if he invoked the motion of the influences, and the hand was magical to her sight. The words sprang over her; auspicious gales, sail so expeditious, and she away to the royal fleet far off, delivered, all delivered, all on its way. She answered: "No; I'm glad it's you. You can have your *Tempest*, but I'd rather this."

He said, with a mild protest: "Yet he wrote your part for you too; can you guess where?"

"I've been educated," she answered, brilliant in her pause before they parted. "Twice educated, Peter. Shall I try?

> *rily, merrily, shall I live now*
> *· the blossom that hangs on the b*

Bless me to it."

"Under the Mercy," he said, and watched her out of sight before he went to find a way to his own seat.

The theatre was almost full; late-comers were hurrying in. The gate was on the point of being closed—two minutes, as the notices had stated, before the beginning of the play—when the last came. It was Mrs.

Sammile. She hurried through, and as she came she saw Stanhope. As he bowed, she said breathlessly: "So nice, isn't it? Have you got everything you want?"

"Or that we don't——" Stanhope began, but she chattered on: "But it's a good thing not to have, isn't it? Perfection would be so dull, wouldn't it? It's better to think of it than to have it, isn't it? I mean, who was it said it's better to be always walking than to get there?"

"No, thank you very much," he said, laughing outright. "I'd rather have perfection than think of it, though I don't see why we shouldn't do both. But we mustn't stop; you've only a minute and a half. Where's your ticket? This way." He took her round to her seat—at the end of a row, towards the front—and as he showed it to her he said, gravely: "You won't mind getting there for once, will you? Rather than travelling hopefully about this place the whole afternoon."

She threw a look at him, as he ran from her to his own seat, which perplexed him, it seemed so full of bitterness and despair. It was almost as if she actually didn't want to sit down. He thought, as he sank into his chair, "But if one hated to arrive? if one only lived by not arriving? if one preferred avoiding to knowing? if unheard melodies were only sweet because they weren't there at all? false, false ..." and dismissed his thought, for the Prologue stood out before the trees, and the moment of silence before the trumpet sounded was already upon them.

It sounded, annunciatory of a new thing. It called its world together, and prepared union. It directed all attention forward, as, his blasts done, the Prologue, actors ready behind and audience expectant before, advanced slowly across the grass. But to one mind at least it did even more. At the dress rehearsal it had announced speech to Pauline, as to the rest; now it proclaimed the stillness. It sprang up out of the stillness. She also was aware of a new thing—of speech in relation to the silence in which it lived.

The pause in which the Prologue silently advanced exhibited itself to her as the fundamental thing. The words she had so long admired did not lose their force or beauty, but they were the mere feel of the texture. The harmony of motion and speech, now about to begin, held and was composed by the pauses: foot to foot, line to line, here a little and there a little. She knew she had always spoken poetry against the silence of this world; now she knew it had to be spoken against—that perhaps, but also something greater, some silence of its own. She recognized the awful space of separating stillness which all mighty art creates about itself, or, uncreating, makes clear to mortal apprehension. Such art, out of "the mind's abyss", makes tolerable, at the first word or note or instructed glance, the preluding presence of the abyss. It creates in an instant its own past. Then its significance mingles with other significances; the stillness gives up kindred meanings, each in its own orb, till by the subtlest graduations they press into altogether other significances, and these again into others, and so into one contemporaneous nature, as in that gathering unity of time from which Lilith feverishly fled. But that nature is to us a darkness, a stillness, only felt by the reverberations of the single speech. About the song of the Woodcutter's Son was the stillness of the forest. That living stillness had gathered the girl into her communion with the dead; it had passed into her own spirit when the vision of herself had closed with herself; it had surrounded her when she looked on the dead face of Margaret; and now again it rose at the sound of the trumpet—that which is before the trumpet and shall be after, which is between all sentences and all words, which is between and in all speech and all breath, which is itself the essential nature of all, for all come from it and return to it.

She moved; she issued into the measured time of the play; she came out of heaven and returned to heaven, speaking the nature of heaven. In her very duty the doctrine of exchange held true, hierarchical and republican. She owed the words to Stanhope; he owed the utterance to her and the rest. He was over her in the sacred order, and yet in the sacred equality they ran level. So salvation lay everywhere in interchange: since, by an act only possible in the whole, Stanhope had substituted himself for her, and the moan of a God had carried the moan of the dead. She acted, and her acting was reality, for the stillness had taken it over. The sun was blazing, as if it would pierce all bodies there, as if another sun radiated from another sky exploring energies of brilliance. But the air was fresh.

She was astonished in the interval to hear Myrtle Fox complaining of the heat. "It's quite intolerable," Miss Fox said, "and these *filthy* trees. Why doesn't Mr. Stanhope have them cut down? I do think one's spirit needs *air*, don't you? I should die in a jungle, and this feels like a jungle."

"I should have thought," Pauline said, but not with malice, "that you'd have found jungles cosy."

"There's such a thing as being too cosy," Adela put in. "Pauline, I want to speak to you a minute."

Pauline allowed herself to be withdrawn. Adela went on: "You're very friendly with Mr. Stanhope, aren't you?"

"Yes," Pauline said, a little to her own surprise. She had rather meant to say: "O not very" or "Aren't you?", or the longer and more idiotic "Well I don't know that you'd call it friendly". But it struck her that both they and every other living creature, from the Four-by-the-Throne to the unseen insects in the air, would call it friendly. She therefore said, "Yes," and waited.

"O!" said Adela, also a little taken aback. She recovered and went on: "I've been thinking about this play. We've done so much with it—I and Mrs. Parry and the rest...." She paused.

"Myrtle," Pauline said, "remarked yesterday that she felt deeply that it was so much *ours*."

"O," said Adela again. The heat was heavy on her too and she was pinker than strictly the Princess should have been. The conversation hung as heavy as the heat. A determination that had hovered in her mind had got itself formulated when she saw the deference exhibited towards him by the outer world that afternoon, and now with a tardy selfishness she pursued it. She said: "I wonder if you'd ask him something."

"Certainly—if I can decently," Pauline answered, wondering, as she heard herself use the word, where exactly the limits of decency, if any, in the new world lay. Peter, she thought, would probably find room for several million universes within those limits.

"It's like this," Adela said. "I've always thought this a very remarkable play." Pauline's heavenly nature said to her other, without irritation but with some relevance, "The hell you have!" "And," Adela went on, "as we've all been in it here, I thought it'd be jolly if we could keep it ours—I mean, if he'd let us." She realized that she hated asking favours of Pauline, whom she had patronized; she disliked subordinating herself. The heat was prickly in her skin, but she persevered. "It's not for myself so much," she said, "as for the general principle...."

"O, Adela, be quick!" Pauline broke in. "What do you *want*?"

Adela was not altogether unpractised in the gymnastics of Gomorrah. Her spirit had come near to the suburbs, and a time might follow when the full freedom of the further City of the Plain would be silently presented to her by the Prince of the City and Lilith his daughter and wife. She believed—with an effort, but she believed—she was speaking the truth when she said: "I don't want anything, but I think it would be only right of Mr. Stanhope to let us have a hand in his London production."

"Us?" Pauline asked.

"Me then," Adela answered. "He owes us something, doesn't he? and," she hurried on, "if I could get hold of a theatre—a little one—O, I think I could raise the money...."

"I should think you could," Pauline said, "for a play by Mr. Stanhope."

"Anyhow, I thought you might sound him—or at least back me up," Adela went on. "You do see there's nothing personal about it?" She stopped, and Pauline allowed the living stillness to rise again.

Nothing personal in this desire to clothe immortality with a career? Nothing unnatural perhaps; nothing improper perhaps; but nothing personal? Nothing less general than the dark pause and the trees and the measured movements of verse? nothing less free than interchange of love? She said: "Adela, tell me it's for yourself, only yourself, and I'll do it if I can."

Adela, extremely offended, and losing her balance, said: "It isn't. We shall be as good for him as he will be for us."

"A kind of mutual-profit system?" Pauline suggested. "You'd better get back; they'll be ready. I'll do whatever you want—to-morrow."

"But——" Adela began; however, Pauline had gone; where Adela did not quite see. It was the heat of the afternoon that so disjoined movement, she thought. She could not quite follow the passage of people now—at least, off the stage. They appeared and disappeared by her, as if the air opened, and someone were seen in the midst of it, and then the air closed up, and opened again, and there was someone else. She was getting fanciful. Fortunately there was only one more act, and on the stage it was all right; there people were where she expected them. Or, if not, you could find fault; that refuge remained. She hurried to the place, and found herself glad to be there. Lingering near was the Grand Duke. He contemplated her as she came up.

"You look a little done," he said, gravely and affectionately.

"It's the heat," said Adela automatically.

"It's not so frightfully hot," Hugh answered. "Quite a good afternoon. A little thunder about somewhere, perhaps."

The thunder, if it was thunder, was echoing distantly in Adela's ears; she looked at Hugh's equanimity with dislike. He had something of Mrs. Parry in him, and she resented it. She said: "I wish you were more sensitive, Hugh."

"So long as I'm sensitive to *you*", Hugh said, "it ought to be enough. You're tired, darling."

"Hugh, you'd tell me I was tired on the Day of Judgment," Adela exclaimed. "I keep on saying it's the heat."

"Very well," Hugh assented; "it's the heat making you tired."

"I'm not tired at all," Adela said in a burst of exasperated rage, "I'm hot and I'm sick of this play, and I've got a headache. It's very annoying to be so continually misunderstood. After all, the play does depend upon me a good deal, and all I have to do, and when I ask for a little sympathy...."

Hugh took her arm. "Shut up," he said.

She stared back. "Hugh——" she began, but he interrupted her.

"Shut up," he said again. "You're getting above yourself, my girl; you and your sympathy. I'll talk to you when this is over. You're the best actor in the place, and your figure's absolutely thrilling in that dress, and there's a lot more to tell you like that, and I'll tell you presently. But it's time to begin now, and go and do as I tell you."

Adela found herself pushed away. There had been between them an amount of half-pretended mastery and compulsion, but she was conscious of a new sound in Hugh's voice. It struck so near her that she forgot about Pauline and the heat and Stanhope, for she knew that she would have to make up her mind about it, whether to reject or allow that authoritative assumption. Serious commands were a new thing in their experience. Her immediate instinct was to evade: the phrase which sprang to her mind was: "I shall have to manage him—I can manage him." If she were going to marry Hugh—and she supposed she was—she would either have to acquiesce or pretend to acquiesce. She saw quite clearly what she would do; she would assent, but she would see to it that chance never assented. She knew that she would not revolt; she would never admit that there was any power against which Adela Hunt could possibly be in a state of revolt. She had never admitted it of Mrs. Parry. It was always the other people who were in revolt against her. Athanasian in spirit, she knew she was right and the world wrong. Unathanasian in method, she intended to manage the world ... Stanhope, Mrs. Parry, Hugh. She would neither revolt nor obey nor compromise; she would deceive. Her admission to the citizenship of Gomorrah depended on the moment at which, of those four only possible alternatives for the human soul, she refused to know which she had chosen. "Tell me it's for yourself, only yourself...." No, no, it's not for myself; it's for the good of others, her good, his good, everybody's good: is it my fault if they don't see it? manage them, manage them, manage her, manage him, and them. O, the Princess managing the Woodcutter's Son, and the Chorus, the chorus of leaves, this way, that way; minds twiddling them the right way; treachery better than truth, for treachery was the only truth, there was no truth to be treacherous to—and the last act beginning, and she in it, and the heat crackling in the ground, in her head, in the air. On then, on to the stage, and Pauline was to ask Stanhope to-morrow.

Pauline watched her as she went, but she saw the Princess and not Adela. Now the process of the theatre was wholly reversed, for stillness cast up the verse and the verse flung out the actors, and though she knew sequence still, and took part in it, it was not sequence that mattered, more than as a definition of the edge of the circle, and that relation which was the exhibition of the eternal. Relation in the story, in the plot, was only an accident of need: there had been a time when it mattered, but now it mattered no longer, or for a while no longer. Presently, perhaps, it would define itself again as a need of daily life; she would be older than her master, or younger, or contemporaneous; now they were both no more than mutual perceptions in a flash of love. She had had relation with her ancestor and with that other man more lately dead and with her grandmother—all the presently disincarnate presences which lived burningly in the stillness, through which the fire burned, and the stillness was the fire. She danced out of it, a flame flung up, a leaf catching to a flame. They were rushing towards the end of the play, an end, an end rushing towards the earth and the earth rushing to meet it. The words were no longer separated from the living stillness, they were themselves the life of the stillness, and though they sounded in it they no more broke it than the infinite particles of creation break the eternal contemplation of God in God. The stillness turned upon itself; the justice of the stillness drew all the flames and leaves, the dead and living, the actors and spectators, into its power—percipient and impercipient, that was the only choice, and that was for their joy alone. She sank deeper into it. The dance of herself and all the others ceased, they drew aside, gathered up—O on how many rehearsals, and now gathered! "Behold, I come quickly! Amen, even so...." They were in the groups of the last royal declamations, and swept aside, and the mighty stage was clear. Suddenly again, from somewhere in that great abyss of clarity, a trumpet sounded, and then a great uproar, and then a single voice. It was the beginning of the end; the judgment of mortality was there. She was standing aside, and she heard the voice and knew it; from the edge of eternity the poets were speaking to the world, and two modes of experience were mingled in that sole utterance. She knew the voice, and heard it; all else was still. Peter Stanhope, as he had promised, was saying a few words at the close of the play.

There was but one small contretemps. As, after moving on to the stage and turning to face the audience, Stanhope began to speak, Mrs. Sammile slid down in, and finally completely off, her chair, and lay in a heap. She had been very bright all the afternoon; in fact, she had been something of a nuisance to her immediate neighbours by the whispered comments of admiration she had offered upon the display of sound and colour before her. As the crash of applause broke out she had been observed to make an effort to join in it. But her hands had seemed to tremble and fail. Stanhope was to speak before the last calls, and the applause crashed louder when he appeared. It was in the midst of that enthusiasm that Mrs. Sammile fainted.

Chapter XI

THE OPENING OF GRAVES

*

Whatever mystery had, to Pauline's exalted senses, taken its place in the world on that afternoon, it seemed to make no difference to the world. Things proceeded. Her uncle had arrived from London during the performance, and had had to have his niece's absence explained to him, first by the maid and later by the niece. After the explanation Pauline remembered without surprise in her shame that she used to dislike her uncle.

Margaret Anstruther was buried on the next day but one, to the sound of that apostolic trumpet which calls on all its hearers to rise from the dead, and proclaims the creation on earth of celestial bodies, "sown in corruption, raised in incorruption; sown in dishonour, raised in glory; sown in weakness, raised in power". "Be steadfast, unmovable ... your labour is not in vain in the Lord." Pauline heard with a new attention; these were no longer promises, but facts. She dared not use the awful phrases for herself; only, shyly, she hoped that perhaps, used by some other heavenly knowledge, they might not be altogether inapplicable to herself. The epigram of experience which is in all dogma hinted itself within her. But more than these passages another stranger imagination struck her heart: "Why are they then baptized for the dead?" There, rooted in the heart of the Church at its freshest, was the same strong thrust of interchange. Bear for others; be baptized for others; and, rising as her new vision of the world had done once and again, an even more fiery mystery of exchange rolled through her horizons, turning and glancing on her like the eyed and winged wheels of the prophet. The central mystery of Christendom, the terrible fundamental substitution on which so much learning had been spent and about which so much blood had been shed, shewed not as a miraculous exception, but as the root of a universal rule ... "behold, I shew you a mystery", as supernatural as that Sacrifice, as natural as carrying a bag. She flexed her fingers by her side as if she thought of picking one up.

The funeral over, her uncle hastened action. The moment for which they had all been waiting had arrived; his mother was dead. So now they could clear things up. The house could be sold, and most of the furniture. Pauline could have a room in a London hostel, which he would find her, and a job in a London office, which he had already found her. They discussed her capacities; he hinted that it was a pity she hadn't made more of the last few years. She might have learned German while sitting with Margaret, and Spanish instead of taking part in plays. She would have to be brisker and livelier. Pauline, suppressing a tendency to point out that for years he had wished her to be not brisk or lively, but obedient and loving, said she would remember. She added that she would have a little money, enough to buy her bread. Her uncle said that a woman couldn't live on bread, and anyhow a job was a good thing; he didn't wish his niece to waste her time and energy. Pauline, thinking that Stanhope had said the same thing differently, agreed. Her uncle, having put everything he could into somebody's hands, left her to live for a few days in the house with the maid, and rushed back to London with his wife, whose conversation had been confined to assuring Pauline that she would get over it presently.

Pauline might have believed this if she had been clear what it was that she was expected to get over. Of one thing it was true; she no longer expected to see the haunting figure of her childhood's acquaintance and youthful fear. She remembered it now as one remembers a dream, a vivid dream of separation and search. She had been, it seemed, looking for a long while for someone, or perhaps some place, that was necessary to her. She had been looking for someone who was astray, and at the same time she had been sought. In the dream she had played hide-and-seek with herself in a maze made up of the roads of Battle Hill, and the roads were filled with many figures who hated—neither her nor any other definite person, but hated. They could not find anything they could spend their hate on, for they slipped and slithered and slid from and through each other, since it was their hate which separated them. It was no half-self-mocking hate, nor even an immoral but half-justified hate, certainly not the terrible, enjoyable, and angry hate of ordinary men and women. It was the hate of those men and women who had lost humanity in their extreme love of themselves amongst humanity. They had been found in their streets by the icy air of those mountain peaks of which she had once heard her grandmother speak, and their spirits had frozen in them. Among them she also had gone about, and the only thing that had distinguished her from them was her fear lest they should notice her. And while she hurried she had changed, in her bygone dream, and she was searching for some poor shadow of herself that fled into the houses to escape her. The dream had been long, for the houses had opened up, as that shadow entered, into long corridors and high empty rooms, and there was one dreadful room which was all mirrors, or what was worse than mirrors, for the reflections in those mirrors were living, though they hid for a while and had no being till the shadow at last came speeding into the room, but then they were seen, and came floating out of their flickering cells, and danced the shadow into some unintelligible dissolution among them. It was from that end that she sought to save the miserable fugitive. When in her memory she reached that point, when the shadow was fleeing deeper into Gomorrah, and she fled after it on feet that were so much swifter than its own and yet in those infinite halls and corridors could never overtake it while it fled—when the moment of approach down the last long corridor to the last utter manifestation of illusion drew near, she heard far off a trumpet, and she could remember nothing more but that she woke. She remembered that she woke swiftly, as if a voice called her, but however hard she tried she could not well recollect whose voice it was; perhaps that also was part of the dream, or perhaps it was the nurse's voice that had called her on the morning her grandmother had died. Perhaps; perhaps not. Under all the ceremonies of the days, under the companionship of her people, under her solitude, under her gradual preparations for departure and her practice of studies which were to make her more efficient in whatever job her uncle and the operation of the Immortals should find her, under sun and moon alike, she waited. She waited, and remembered only as a dream the division between herself and the glorious image by which the other was to be utterly ensouled.

It was observable, however, on the Hill, how many of the inhabitants were unwell. Mrs. Sammile had fainted, and had not been seen about since. Someone had offered to take her home in a car, but she had declined, declaring that she was all right, and had disappeared. Myrtle Fox, though she had got through the performance, had gone home crying, and had been in bed ever since. She could not sleep; a doctor had been called in, but he did not help her. She took this and that, and nothing did good. She would doze a little, and wake crying and sobbing. "It's all this excitement," her mother said severely, and opinion began to blame the play for Myrtle's illness. Lawrence Wentworth remained shut in his house; even his servants hardly saw him, and the curtains of his study were generally drawn. "It isn't human," his parlour-maid said to next door's parlour-maid. Some of the actors and some of the audience were also affected by what was generally called the local influenza epidemic. The excitement of the play or the brightness of the summer or the cold winds that even under such a sun swept the Hill, or some infection more subtle than these, struck the inhabitants down.

Neither Adela nor Hugh were among them. Hugh, like Mrs. Parry, went on efficiently dealing with the moment. Adela suffered, from the heat, from the thunder, from suppressed anxiety, but she did not go to bed. Pauline, even had she been free from her family, could not have carried out her promise, for immediately after the performance Stanhope disappeared for a few days; it was understood he had gone away for a change. Pauline could do no more than assure Adela that, as soon as he returned, she would look for an opportunity. "But I can't," she said, "do more than that. I can't butt in on him with a club, Adela. If it's for all of us, why not do it yourself? If it was for you personally, of course you might feel awkward, but as it isn't...." Adela said it certainly wasn't, and went off peevishly.

As a result the management of Hugh had to be postponed. He had not, in fact, made that formal proposal which was necessary if Adela was to feel, as she wished, that she had a right and a duty to manage him. In order not to thwart him, Adela controlled herself more than was her habit when they were together. Obedience and revolt being both out of the question, she compromised temporarily that she might manage permanently. It was in such a compromise that they had been walking one evening on the Hill two or three days after Margaret Anstruther's burial. By accident, on their return, they took a road which led past the gates of the cemetery, and as they came by Hugh said idly: "I suppose Pauline'll be going now her grandmother's dead."

Adela had not thought of this. She said immediately: "O, I shouldn't wonder if she stopped—moved to a smaller house or something. She *can't* go yet."

Hugh said: "You didn't go to the funeral, darling?"

"Of course not," Adela answered. "I hate being morbid." As if to prove it she lingered to look through the gates. "There are so *many* of them," she added.

"Yes," Hugh said, with what faintly struck Adela as unnecessary obtuseness, "you can't get round death with any kind of adjective, can you?"

"I don't want to get round anything with adjectives," Adela almost snarled. "Thank God we've got away from any pretence. It's so unimportant when one doesn't pretend. When one's dead, one's dead, and that's all there is to it."

Hugh said, "Yes, but what's all there is to it? I'm that old-fashioned thing, an agnostic; I don't know. I like to be clear on what I know and what I don't know, and I don't like day-dreams, either nice or nasty, or neither."

"O, nor do I," said Adela. "But you must sometimes think how nice it would be if something particular happened. I call that common sense."

"Within limits," Hugh said, putting his arm over her shoulders. "I sometimes let myself think, for a certain time, or a definite distance—say, from here to your house—how pleasant something would be—having fifty thousand pounds a year, say. But when I come to your house, or wherever it is, I stop."

"Do you?" said Adela, more impressed than she admitted to herself.

"Always," said Hugh. "And then—O, concentrate on making another fifty. Day-dreaming without limits is silly."

Adela shook her head. "I suppose I imagine rather intensely," she said. "I seem to see things *obliquely*, if you know what I mean. They're alongside the actual thing, a sort of tangent. I think really that's what all art is—tangential."

The word had hardly left her lips when a voice, tangential to her ear, said: "Do let me persuade you, Miss Hunt."

Adela, with a jump, looked round, and saw Lily Sammile. There was, at that part of the cemetery wall, a lean-to erection of boards, a kind of narrow shelter, almost a man's height, and having a rough swinging door at the nearer end. It had been there before anyone could remember, and it stayed there because no one could remember to have it taken away. It was very old and very weather-stained. It was almost a tool-shed, but then the necessary tools were, more conveniently, kept elsewhere. Everyone supposed that someone else used it. At the door of this shed, close to the cemetery railing, stood the woman who had spoken. She was leaning forward, towards Adela, and holding on to a bar of the gate. Now she put a hand on Adela's bare arm. It was gritty to the skin, which felt as if a handful of rough dust was pressed down, and pricked and rubbed it. The voice was rough too; it mumbled through a mouthful of dust. Adela pulled her arm away; she could not answer; she thrust closer to Hugh.

The woman said, after a pause during which they stared at her, and saw her dishevelled, hatless, hair of grey ashes, and cheeks almost as grey: "Come and get away. Dust—that's what you want; dust."

Hugh said easily: "Not a bit, Mrs. Sammile. We both want a great deal more."

The woman answered: "You may, but she doesn't. She's a——"

They could not catch the word, her voice so muffled it. Adela took two steps back, and said in a little squeak: "Hugh!"

Hugh slipped his arm round her. He said firmly, though less easily than before: "Well, we must be getting on. Come along, darling."

Lily Sammile began to cry. The tears ran down her face and left streaks in the greyness, as if they crept through and over grime. She said miserably: "You'll wish you had; O, you'll wish you had." She was standing with her back to the gate, leaning against it, and as she ceased to speak she became rigid suddenly, as if she listened. Her eyes widened; her nose came out over an indrawn lip; her cheeks hollowed in her effort. There was no need for the effort. They could hear the sound that held her; a faint rustle, a dry patter. It came from beyond her, and she twisted her head round—only her head—and looked. So, distracted by the movement, did the other two. They saw movement in the graves.

Most were quiet enough; their inhabitants had passed beyond any recall or return, and what influence they had on the Hill was by infection rather than by motion. But the estate was still new, and the neat ranks of sepulchres did not reach far into the enclosure. They lay along the middle path mostly; the farthest away was the mound that covered Margaret Anstruther. That too was quiet: its spirit could not conceive return. It was between the earlier graves and hers that the disclosure began, as if the enclosed space was turning itself over. The earth heaved; they felt, where they stood, no quiver. It was local, but they saw—there, and again there—the mounds swell and sway and fall in a cascade of mould, flung over the green grass. Three or four in all, dark slits in the ground, and beyond each a wide layer of dust. It did not stop there. The earth was heaving out of the dark openings; it came in bursts and rushes—in a spasmodic momentum, soon exhausted, always renewed. It hung sometimes in the air, little clouds that threatened to fall back, and never did, for they drifted slowly to one side, and sank again on what had earlier dropped. Gravitation was reversed; the slowness and

154

uncertainty of the movement exposed the earth's own initiation of it. The law of material things turned; somewhere in that walled receptacle of the dead activity was twisted upon itself. The backward movement of things capable of backward movement had begun. The earth continued to rise in fountains, flung up from below; and always at their height, their little height above the ground, the tops of those fountains swayed, and hurled themselves sideways, and dropped, and the rest fell back into the hidden depth of the openings, until it flung itself up once more. The gentle low patter of rough earth on gravel paths floated over the gates to the ears of the three who were still standing there.

There was a more deathly silence without the gates than within. The old woman, with twisted head, her body almost a pattern of faintly covered bones against the iron bars, was rigid; so were Adela and Hugh. They stood staring; incredulous, they gazed at the exhibited fact. So incredible was it that they did not think of the dead; ghosts and resurrections would have been easier to their minds, if more horrible, than this obvious insanity, insanity obvious in its definite existence. They were held; then, to instinctive terror, the frantic cause presented itself. Adela screamed, and as the dead man's moan had been answered in the mountain her scream was caught and prolonged in the other woman's wailing shriek. The shriek was not human; it was the wind rushing up a great hollow funnel in a mountain, and issuing in a wild shrill yell. It tore itself out of the muffled mouth, and swept over the Hill, a rising portent of coming storm. Myrtle Fox heard it in her long night of wakefulness, and her body sickened. Pauline heard it, and felt more intensely the peace that held her. Stanhope heard it, and prayed. Before the sound had died, Lily Sammile had jerked from the gate, and thrown herself at the dark shed, and disappeared within, and the swinging door fell to behind her.

As she sprang, Adela sprang also. She screamed again and ran. She ran wildly up the road, so fast that Hugh, who followed, was outdistanced. He called after her. He shouted: "Adela, it's nothing. The earth was loose and the wind was blowing. Stop." She did not stop. He kept up the pursuit down a street or two, but his own action offended him. Much though the vision had for the moment affected him, he was, as soon as he began to move, more immediately affected and angered by his situation. There might be explanations enough of what he thought he had seen—he spared a curse for Lily Sammile—but more certain than what he thought he had seen was what he knew Adela was doing. She was, faster than he, running and screaming over Battle Hill. He was angry; suppose some one met her! He raised in his own mind no reasonable pretext for abandoning her, nor did he disguise his intention from himself, but after a corner or two he simply stopped running. "Perfectly ridiculous!" he said angrily. "The earth was loose, and the wind was blowing." He was free as Pauline herself from Lilith, but without joy. There was, between the group to which his soul belonged and hers, no difference, except only that of love and joy, things which now were never to be separated in her any more.

Adela ran. She had soon no breath for screaming. She ran. She did not know where she was going. She ran. She heard a voice calling behind her: "The earth's loose and the wind's blowing", and she ran more wildly. Her flesh felt the touch of a gritty hand; a voice kept calling after her and round her: "The earth's loose; the wind's blowing." She ran wildly and absurdly, her full mouth open, her plump arms spasmodically working, tears of terror in her eyes. She desired above all things immediate safety—in some place and with some one she knew. Hugh had disappeared. She ran over the Hill, and through a twisted blur of tears and fear recognized by a mere instinct Lawrence Wentworth's house. She rushed through the gate; here lived some one who could restore her to her own valuation of herself. Hugh's shouted orders had been based on no assent of hers to authority; however much she had played at sensual and sentimental imitations of obedience, she hated the thing itself in any and every mode. She wanted something to condone and console her fear. There was a light in the study; she made for it; reached the window, and hammered on the glass, hammered again and again, till Wentworth at last heard and reluctantly drew himself from the stupor of his preoccupation, came slowly across the room and drew back the curtain.

They confronted each other through the glass. Wentworth took a minute or two to recognize whose was the working and mottled face that confronted him, and when he recognized it, he made a motion to pull the curtain again and to go away. But as she saw the movement she struck so violently at the glass that even in his obsession he was terrified of others hearing, and slowly and almost painfully he pushed the window up and stood staring at her. She put her hands on the sill and leant inwards.

She said: "Lawrence, Lawrence, something's about!"

He still stood there, looking at her now with a heavy distaste, but he said nothing, and when she tried to catch his hand he moved it away. She looked up at him, and a deeper fear struck at her—that here was no refuge for her. Gomorrah closed itself against her; she stood in the outer wind of the plain. It was cold and frightful; she beat, literally, on the wall. She sobbed, "Lawrence, help me."

He said, "I don't know you," and she fell back, astounded. She cried out: "Lawrence, it's me, it's me, Adela. You know *me*; of course you do. Here I am—I've come to you. There's something dreadful happening and I've come to you."

He said dully: "I don't want to know you. Go away; you're disturbing me." And he moved to shut the window down.

At this she leant right forward and stared up at his eyes, for her fear desired very strongly to find that he was only defending himself against her. But his eyes did not change; they gazed dully back, so dully and so long that she was driven to turn her own away. And as she did so, sending a wild glance around the room, so urgently had she sought to find out his real desire and so strong was his rejection of her, and so fast were all things drawing to their end, that she saw, away beyond the light of the reading-lamp, a vague figure. It was in the shadows, but, as if to meet her, it thrust its head forward, and so again fulfilled its master's wish. For to Adela there appeared, stretched forward in the light, her own face, infinitely perfected in sensual grace and infinitely emptied of all meaning, even of evil meaning. Blank and dead in a spiritual death it stared vacantly at her, but undoubtedly it was she. She stood, staring back, sick and giddy at the horror, and she heard Wentworth say: "Go away; I don't want to help you; I don't know you. Go away."

He closed the window; he began to draw the curtains; the creature disappeared from her sight. And by the wall of Gomorrah she fainted and fell.

He saw her fall, and in his bemused mind he felt her as a danger to his peace. He stood looking down at her, until, slowly turning a stiff head, he saw the reflection of his doubt in the eyes of his mistress, the gleam of anxiety which reflected his own because it was concerned with himself. Reluctantly therefore he went out and half-lifted, half-dragged the girl to the gate, and got her through it, and then got her a little way down the road, and so left her lying. He mistily wondered, with a flat realism, if she would awake while he laboured, but the stupor of her horror was too deep. She lay there prone and still, and he returned.

But, as if in that effort he had slid farther down the rope of his dream, when he returned he was changed. He sat down and his creature crept up to him and took and nuzzled his hand. As she did so he became aware for the first time that he did not altogether want her. She was not less preferable than she had been for long to the real Adela, but she was less preferable now than his unimaged dream. He wanted to want her; he did not want her to go; but he could not—not as he had done. Even she was a betrayal, she was a thing outside. It was very good, as it always was, observant of his slightest wish. It sat by him, blinking at the fire. This year, in his room curtained from the sun, it was cold; he had had a fire kept up for the last few days, in spite of his servants' astonishment. He could not, as he sat, think what he wanted, unless indeed to want her, for he feared somehow to let her go: when he did he would be at the bottom of his rope. He had been given rope enough, but there was a bottom, and a dark hole, and him in the hole. He saw this dimly and was unwilling to slide lower, yet not to slide was to stop out where other things and other images were, and he was unwilling to be there also. He looked round several times, thinking that he would see something else. He thought of a girl's body lying in the road, but he could not get off his rope for that, not even if he wished, and most certainly he did not wish. Something else: something connected with his work, with the Grand Duke's Guard. What Grand Duke? The unbegotten Adela by his side said, in a low voice which stammered now as it had not before, as if it were as much losing control as was his own mind: "W-what Grand D-Duke, darling? w-what w-work?" The Grand Duke's Guard—a white square—a printed card—yes, a notice: a meaning and a message, a meeting. He remembered now. It was the annual dinner of a small historical society to which he and a few others belonged. He remembered that he had been looking forward to it; he remembered that he would enjoy going, though he could not remember for a few minutes who else came to it. He did not trouble to say anything, however; he was too tired—some drag, some pulling and thrusting had exhausted him more than he knew; he had to roll a body in the uniform of the Grand Duke's Guard, or to protect himself from hitting against its dark mass as he swung on his rope; but that was over now, and he could forget, and presently the two of them stirred and went—mumblingly and habitually—to bed.

It could not be supposed, when Adela was found soon after by a young constable on his beat, that Mr. Wentworth had had anything to do with her. The constable found her name from letters in her handbag, and presently he and others roused her people and she was got to her own temporary place, her own room. She remained unconscious till the morning; then she woke. Her temperature and her pulse were at first normal, and at first she could not recall the night. But presently it returned to her. She felt herself running again from the opening graves to the sight of the meaningless face; Hugh was running after her. Hugh was running out of the graves and driving her on to meet the face. She too, like Myrtle Fox, screamed and vomited.

Her mother rang up Hugh. There was an acrimonious conversation. Mrs. Hunt said that she had trusted Adela to Hugh's care. Hugh said that Adela had insisted on being alone, which, considering the rate at which she had run away, he felt was approximately true. Mrs. Hunt said that Adela was actually at death's door.

Hugh said she would probably be wise enough not to ring the bell. Mrs. Hunt said that she herself insisted on seeing him; Adela was in no state to see anybody. Hugh said he would give himself the pleasure of leaving some flowers sometime. He knew he was behaving brutally, and that he was in fact more angry and less detached than he made his voice sound. He had left her to run, but had presently gone round and had at last reached her home in time to observe the confusion that attended her being brought home. He would have spoken, but he hated Mrs. Hunt, and he hated scenes, especially scenes at two in the morning, when his always equable passion for Adela was at ebb. So he had gone home, and indulged irritation. Nevertheless he intended to be efficient to the situation; the flowers should be taken and Adela seen that evening. He had no intention of leaving any duty unfulfilled—any duty of exterior act. He did not quite admit that there was any other kind, except in so far as outer efficiency dictated the interior.

Pursued by Hugh in her nightmares, Adela had no sense of ease or peace in his image. She ran in that recurrent flight from him through an arch that was Wentworth towards the waiting face, and as she was carried towards it, it vanished, and she was beginning again. As she ran she repeated lines and bits of lines of her part in the play; the part she was continually trying and continually failing to learn, the part that repeated to her a muddle of words about perception and love which she could never get in the right order. Sometimes Mrs. Parry was running beside her and sometimes Mrs. Sammile; at least, it had Mrs. Sammile's head though the body was Peter Stanhope's, and it said as it ran: "What you want is perception in a flash of love; what you love is a flash in a want of perception; what you flash is the want in a love of perception; what you want is what you want …" and so always. Others of her acquaintance were sometimes about her in the dream of chaos which had but one element of identity, and that was the race she ran and the conditions of the race. She came again under the arch that was Wentworth, and this time there was a change, for she found Pauline running beside her. Pauline's hand was in hers; she clutched it, and the speed of her running dwindled, as if a steadiness entered it. She said in a squeak: "Pauline!"

Pauline, leaning over the bed, and feeling her hand so fiercely held—she had called as soon as she heard Adela was ill—said: "Yes, my dear?"

Her voice gave its full value to the last word: it rang in the air of the dream, a billow of comprehensible sound.

Adela stopped running. She said: "Will you help me?"

"Of course," Pauline said, thinking rather ruefully of asking Stanhope. "What do you want me to do?"

Adela said breathlessly: "I want to stop. I want to know my part."

"But you did know your part," Pauline answered. "You knew it beautifully, and you did it beau … you did it."

Adela said: "No, no; I've got to find it, and she can give it to me."

"She?" Pauline asked.

"Lily, she … Sammile, whatever she's called," Adela cried. "In the shed by the cemetery."

Pauline frowned. She remembered Lily Sammile very well. She remembered her as something more than an old woman by a gate, or if, then a very old woman indeed by a very great gate, where many go in who choose themselves, the gate of Gomorrah in the Plain, illusion and the end of illusion; the opposite of holy fact, and the contradiction of sacred love. She said, very quickly: "Let me run for you, Adela; you can keep quiet. I can run faster than you," she added truthfully. "I've got longer legs. Let me run instead of you. Don't worry about Mrs.——" she could not say the name; no name was enough for the spirit that lay in Gomorrah, in the shed by the cemetery, till the graves were opened—above or below, but opened.

Adela said, "No, no; no one can do anything. She can make my head better. She can give me something. You can't do anything; you didn't see it in the house."

Pauline said: "But let's try at least. Look, let me go and learn your part." She was not quite sure, as she said it, whether this came under the head of permissible interchanges. She had meant it but for the part in the play, but this new fashion of identities was too strong for her; the words were a definition of a substitution beyond her. Adela's past, Adela's identity, was Adela's own. A god rather than she, unless she were inhabited by a god, must carry Adela herself; the god to whom baptism for the dead was made, the lord of substitution, the origin and centre of substitution, and in the sides of the mountain of the power of substitution the hermitages of happy souls restored out of substitution. A fanfare of recovered identities surrounded her; the single trumpet shrilled into diversities of music.

Adela said: "In the shed by the cemetery. I shall know my part there. Go and ask her."

Her hand shook Pauline's in her agitation, and the movement was a repulsion. Pauline, flung off upon her errand, was by the same energy repelled from her errand. Her own body shook; she was tossed away from the grand gate of Gomorrah where aged Lilith incunabulates souls. She sprang up, driven by necessity, and Adela, opening her eyes which all this while had been shut, met hers. They gazed for a moment, and then

157

Adela screamed. "Go away," she cried; "you won't, and if you do it'll be worse. You're a devil; you want me not to know. Go away; go away."

"Adela, darling," Pauline said, oblivious of repulsion in a distressed tenderness, "it's Pauline. Don't be unhappy; I'll do all I can."

"You won't, you won't," Adela screamed. "You'll spoil everything. You're torturing me; you're tearing my bones out of me; you're scraping my bones. I hate you, I hate you; go away."

Pauline heard Mrs. Hunt running up the stairs, drawn by that shriek of denial. She exclaimed, torn herself by so much pain: "I'll go, I promise. If you want——"

"No," Adela screamed, throwing her arm over her eyes, "you'll hurt us all. You don't care about us; you don't love any of us. You'll help Hugh to shut me up in the graves with it; he's got something in his room … it isn't me … it isn't …"

Her mother was by her, murmuring and soothing; her single look told Pauline to go, and she went. She let herself out of the house, and walked up the street, trying to settle her mind. It ought to be possible to determine what to do. Was it good for Adela, but who was to decide what was good for Adela? She—or Adela? Or someone else? Peter? but she wouldn't ask Peter, only what would he say if she did? "The Omnipotence"? Coming on the word, she considered it, and it worked upward to her freeing. She would do what Adela wanted, for it was Adela's need, and she had no reason against; she would do it in the Omnipotence, in the wood where leaves sang. Whoever was found there was subject to it, to the law of exchanged good. The Hill rose before her in the sunshine, and on its farther side the place from which her twin, now deeply one with her, had come. The mountains of impersonality have yet their hidden sides, and she was climbing towards them, in the point which was one with the universe. She knew herself going towards a thing that must be done. The growth of earth into heaven and heaven into earth approached in time a point it had already occupied in space. She could see no one else in the streets; she went lonely, and repeated to herself as she went those lines in which Peter's style individualized felicity. Up, and still up … where the brigands hid in a shelter and cave of the wood, and shared but did not exchange. Oh, happy and happy to have attributions of property for convenience of grace; thrice-happy that convenience of grace could dispose of property: *tam antiqua, tam nova, vita nova, nova creatura*, a new creature, no more in any sense but new, not opposed to the old, but in union with the old; new without any trick of under-meaning, new always, and now new. Up, and up, and presently down again a little; she was looking out towards the City where she was to be. She saw, away over open ground, the smoke of a train, it was carrying to the City some of those who lived or had lived upon the Hill and were leaving it or flying from it. Was the rest of the world shaken with entranced joy? Perhaps that was not discoverable, for speech of such things came only when it was permitted, and to one the world was new and to one not, to one redeemed and to one not. Yet beyond such differences there lay some act, and this was so whether or not, known or not. Perhaps to Peter to-morrow—no, to-night, for she herself must leave the Hill to-morrow, and never before had parting held such joy. Parting was a fact; all facts are joyous; therefore parting was joyous. With that unnecessary syllogism delicately exhibiting itself as a knowledge of truth, she found herself at the shed by the hill.

There it was. She had seen it a hundred times. The rough door as usual was swung to. She looked at it. This then was where Lily Sammile lived? "I could live in a nutshell and count myself king of infinite space, were it not that I have bad dreams." Was the counting of oneself king of space when one lived in a nutshell one of the bad dreams? Unheard melodies—the rigid figures on the Grecian vase? To enjoy nutshell as nutshell, vase as vase! She rapped at the door; there came no other sound. She rapped again; as if the wood thinned before her, she heard a quick breathing from within. She did not knock again; she laid a hand on the door and gently pressed.

It swung. She peered in. It was dark inside and very long and narrow and deep. Its floor slid away, hundreds of yards downward. There was no end to that floor. A little distance within the shed the woman was sitting on the earth, where the floor began to slope. She was not alone; the occupiers of the broken-up graves were with her. They were massed, mostly, about the doorway; in the narrow space there was room for infinities. They were standing there, looking at their nurse, and they were hungry. The faces—those that were still faces—were bleak with a dreadful starvation. The hunger of years was in them, and also a bewildered surprise, as if they had not known they were starved till now. The nourishment of the food of all their lives had disappeared at once, and a great void was in their minds and a great sickness. They knew the void and the sickness. The nourishment drawn from full lives had carried Margaret Anstruther and her peers over the bare mountain, and they had passed, but when the sun of the mountain struck on the people of infinite illusion it struck on all their past lives and they lived at last in the starvation they had sought. Religion or art, civic sense or sensual desire, or whatever had drugged the spirit with its own deceit, had been drawn from them; they stared famished at the dry breasts of the ancient witch. They had been freed from the grave, and had come, in their own faint presences, back to the Hill they knew, but they could not come farther on to the Hill, in the final summer of mortality, than to this mere outbuilding. Their enchantress sat there, the last illusion still with her, the illusion of love itself; she could not believe her breasts were dry. She desired infinitely to seem to give suck; she would be kind and good, she who did not depend, on whom others had depended. They stood there, but she would not see them; she who was the wife of Adam before Eve, and for salvation from whom Eve was devised after the mist had covered the land of Eden. She would not see, and she would not go to the door because of that unacknowledged crowd, but she sat there, cut off from the earth she had in her genius so long universally inhabited, gazing, waiting, longing for some of the living to enter, to ask her for oblivion and the shapes with which she enchanted oblivion. No one came; oblivion had failed. Her dead had returned to her; her living were left without her. The door swung.

Pauline saw her sitting, an old woman crouched on the ground. As the girl gazed the old woman stirred and tried to speak; there issued from her lips a meaningless gabble, such gabble as Dante, inspired, attributes to the guardian of all the circles of hell. The angelic energy which had been united with Pauline's mortality radiated from her; nature, and more than nature, abhors a vacuum. Her mind and senses could not yet receive comprehensibly the motions of the spirit, but that adoring centre dominated her, and flashes of its great capacity passed through her, revealing, if but in flashes, the single world of existence. Otherwise, the senses of her redeemed body were hardly capable yet of fruition; they had to grow and strengthen till, in their perfection, they should give to her and the universe added delight. They now failed from their beatitude, and lived neither with intuitive angelic knowledge nor immediate angelic passage, but with the slower movement of the ancient, and now dissolving, earth.

Lilith, checked in her monotonous gabble by the radiant vision who let in the sun's new light, stared at it with old and blinking eyes. She saw the shape of the woman; and did not know beatitude, however young. She supposed this also to be in need of something other than the Omnipotence. She said, separating with difficulty words hardly distinguishable from gabble: "I can help you."

"That's kind of you," Pauline answered, "but I haven't come to you for myself."

"I can help anyone," the old woman said, carefully enunciating the lie.

Pauline answered again: "Adela Hunt wants you." She could and would say no more and no less. She recommended the words to the Omnipotence (which, she thought, it was quite certain that Adela Hunt did want, in one or both senses of the word).

The other said, in a little shriek of alarm, such as an old woman pretending youth might have used for girlish fun, "I won't go out, you know. She must come here."

"She can't do that," Pauline said, "because she's ill."

"I can cure everyone," the other answered, "anyone and everyone. You."

"Thank you very much, but I don't want anything," Pauline said.

The figure on the earth said: "You must. Everyone wants something. Tell me what you want."

Pauline answered: "But I don't. You can't think how I don't. How could I want anything but what is?"

The other made in the gloom a motion as if to crawl forward. Illusion, more lasting than in any of her victims, was in her. At the moment of destruction she still pressed nostrums upon the angelic visitor who confronted her. She broke again into gabble, in which Pauline could dimly make out promises, of health, of money, of life, or their appearances, of good looks and good luck, or a belief in them, of peace and content, or a substitute for them. She could almost have desired to find it in her to pretend to be in need, to take pity, and herself to help the thing that offered help, to indulge by her own goodwill the spiritual necromancy of Gomorrah. It was not possible. The absolute and entire sufficiency of existence rose in her. She could no more herself deny than herself abandon it. She could ask for nothing but what was—life in the instant mode of living. She said: "O don't, don't."

The woman seemed to have drawn nearer, through that wriggling upon the ground; an arm poked out, and a hand clutched, too far off to catch. A voice rose: "Anything, everything; everything, anything; anything, everything: every——"

"But I don't *want* anything," Pauline cried out; and as she heard her own vain emphasis, added with a little despairing laugh: "How can I tell you? I only want everything to be as it is—for myself, I mean."

"Change," said the shape. "I don't change."

Pauline cried out: "And if it changes, it shall change as it must, and I shall want it as it is then." She laughed again at the useless attempt to explain.

At the sound of that laugh Lilith stopped, in movement and speech, and all the creatures that stood within vision turned their heads. The sterile silence of the hidden cave exposed itself, and the single laughter of the girl ran over it, and after the laughter the silence itself awoke. As if the very air emanated power, the stillness became warm; a haze of infinite specks of gold filled the darkness, as if the laughter had for a moment made its joy, and more than its joy, visible. The sombre air of the chill city of the plain was pierced by the joy of the sons of God which exists even there. Lilith shrieked and flung up her arms; and a sudden thin wail followed the shriek, the wail of all those dead who cannot endure joy. The advent of that pure content struck at the foundations of the Hill, and the wail went up from all the mortal who writhed in sickness and all the immortal who are sick for ever.

There was a noise of cracking and breaking wood. A cloud of dust rose. Pauline threw her head back, involuntarily shutting her eyes. The dust was in her nostrils; she sneezed. As she recovered and opened her eyes, she saw that the old shed had collapsed before her. It lay, a mass of broken and discoloured wood, upon the ground. The thrust she had given to the door had been too much for it, and it had fallen.

Chapter XII

BEYOND GOMORRAH

*

"Then this," Stanhope said, "is a last visit?"

"Yes," Pauline said. "I'm going up to London to-morrow morning."

"You'll like the work," Stanhope went on. "Odd—to know that when you don't know what it is. You do know that?"

"Under the Mercy," she said. "I'm to see my uncle's man to-morrow at twelve, and if he approves me I shall start work at once. So then, my uncle says, I can stay with them for a few days till I've found rooms or a room."

"You'll send me the address?" he asked.

She answered: "Of course. You'll stop here still?"

He nodded, and for the minute there was silence. Then she added: "Most people seem to be trying to move."

"Most," he said, "but some won't and some can't and some needn't. You must, of course. But I think I might as well stop. There are flowers, and fruit, and books, and if anyone wants me, conversation, and so on—till the plague stops."

She asked, looking at him: "Do you know how long it will last?"

He shrugged a little: "If it's what my grandmother would have called it," he said, "one of the vials of the Apocalypse—why, perhaps a thousand years, those of the millennium before the Judgment. On the other hand, since that kind of thousand years is asserted to be a day, perhaps till to-morrow morning. We're like the Elizabethan drama, living in at least two time-schemes."

She said: "It is that?"

"'As a thief in the night'," he answered. "Could you have a better description? Something is stealing from us our dreams and deceptions and everything but actuality."

"Will they die?" she asked.

"I don't think anyone will die," he said, "unless—and God redeem us all!—into the second death. But I think the plague will spread. The dead were very thick here; perhaps that was why it began here."

"And Adela?" she asked, "and Myrtle?"

"Why, that is for them," he answered.

But she opened on him a smile of serenity, saying: "And for you."

"I will talk Nature to Miss Fox," he said, "and Art to Miss Hunt. If they wish. But I think Prescott may be better for Miss Hunt; he's an almost brutal realist, and I shall remain a little Augustan, even in heaven."

"And I?" she asked, "I?"

"*Incipit vita nova*," he answered. "You—by the way, what train are you catching to-morrow? I'll come and see you off."

"Half-past ten," she said, and he nodded and went on:

"You'll find your job and do it and keep it—in the City of our God, even in the City of the Great King, and … and how do I, any more than you, know what the details of Salem will be like?"

She stood up, luxuriously stretching. "No," she said, "perhaps not. I suppose poets are superfluous in Salem?"

"I have wondered myself," he admitted. "But you needn't realize it so quickly. If the redeemed sing, presumably someone must write the songs. Well—I'll see you at the station to-morrow?"

"Yes, please," she said, as they moved to the door, and then silently down the drive under a night blazing with stars. At the gate she gave him her hand. "It seems so funny to be talking about trains in the easier circles of …" As she hesitated he laughed at her.

"Are you afraid to name it?" he asked, and with a blush she said hastily:

"… heaven. O good night."

"Till to-morrow and good night," he said. "Go with God."

She took two steps, paused and looked back. "Thank you for heaven," she said. "Good night."

The next morning they were on the platform together, chatting of her prospects and capacities, when as they turned in their walk Pauline said: "Peter, look—there's Mr. Wentworth. Is he coming to London too? He looks ill, doesn't he?"

"Very ill," Stanhope said gravely. "Shall we speak?" They moved down the platform, and as Wentworth turned his head in her direction Pauline smiled and waved. He looked at her vaguely, waggled a hand, and ceased. They came to him.

"Good morning, Mr. Wentworth," Pauline said. "Are you going to London too?"

He looked away from them with an action as deliberate as if he had looked at them. He said in a low mumble: "Must excuse me … bad chill … bones feel it … can't remember bones … faces … bones of faces, I mean."

Stanhope said: "Wentworth! *Wentworth!* … stop here."

The voice seemed to penetrate Wentworth's mind. His eyes crawled back along the platform, up to Stanhope's face; there they rested on the mouth as if they could not get farther than the place of the voice, they could not connect voice and eyes. He said: "Can't stop … must get to …" There, exhausted, he stopped.

Pauline heard their train coming. She said: "May I travel with you, Mr. Wentworth?"

At that he came awake; he looked at her, and then again away. He said in a tone of alarm: "No, no. Told you Guard was right. Travelling with a lady. Good-bye, good-bye," and hastily and clumsily made off up the platform as the train drew in. He scrambled into a distant compartment. Pauline sprang into her own, and turning looked at Stanhope.

"O Peter!" she said, "what's wrong?"

He had been gazing after Wentworth; he turned back to her. "I think he has seen the Gorgon's head that was hidden from Dante in Dis," he said. "Well…. Pray for him, and for me, and for all. You will write?"

She stretched her hand from the window. "Will I write?" she said. "Good-bye. But, Peter, ought I to do anything?"

"You can't do anything unless he chooses," he answered. "If he doesn't choose…. Pray. Good-bye. Go in peace."

His eyes challenged her on the word; this time she did not pause. "Go in peace," she said, "and thank you still." The train began to move; he waved to her till she was out of sight, and then went out of the station to walk in the streets and sit by the beds of Battle Hill.

Wentworth sat in his corner. He felt he had forgotten something, and slowly and laboriously he went over in his mind all that he ought to possess. He found it difficult to remember why he had left his house at all. His servants had refused to stay; they had all gone that morning; so he had had to go. He couldn't take the trouble to get others; he hadn't enough energy. He would come to London, to an hotel; there he would be quiet, and not see any ghosts. A horrible screaming ghost had looked in through his window, a ghost that had fallen down in a fit, and he had had to go out and drag it away so that other ghosts could find it. He had been afraid of them since, and of those two just now who had made mouths at him, calling him by a strange word. He was going somewhere too. He was going to a supper. He had his evening things with him in his bag. It would be necessary to dress for the supper, the supper of scholars, of historical scholars, and he was an historical scholar. He remembered what he was, if not who he was. It was true he had said the Grand Duke's Guard was correct though it wasn't, but he was an historical scholar, and he was going to his own kind of people, to Aston Moffatt.

As the name came to him, Wentworth sat up in his corner and became almost his own man again. He hated Aston Moffatt. Hate still lived in him a little, and hate might almost have saved him, though nothing else could, had he hated with a scholar's hate. He did not; his hate and his grudge were personal and obscene. In its excitement nevertheless he remembered what he had left behind—his watch. He had over-wound it weeks ago, on some day when he had seen a bad play, and had put it by to have it mended. But it was too much trouble, and now he had left it in his drawer, and couldn't tell the time. There would be clocks in London, clocks all round him, all going very quickly, because time went very quickly. It went quickly because it was unending, and it was always trying to get to its own end. There was only one point in it with which he had any concern—the time of the last supper. It would be the last supper; he would not go and meet Aston Moffatt again. But he would go to-night because he had accepted and had his clothes, and to show he was not afraid of Moffatt. That was the only time he wanted to know, the time of his last supper. Afterwards, everything would look after itself. He slept in his corner, his last sleep.

The train stopped at Marylebone, and he woke. He muddled on, with the help of a porter, to the Railway Hotel. He had thought of that in the train; it would save bother. He usually went to some other, but he couldn't remember which. The ordinary habits of his body carried him on, and the automatic habit of his mind, including his historic automatic. History was his hobby, his habit; it had never been more. Its austerity was as far from him now as the Eucharists offered in the Church of St. Mary la Bonne, or the duties of the dead, or the ceremonies of substituted love. He automatically booked a room, ate some lunch, and then lay down. This time he did not sleep; the noise of London kept him awake; besides he was alone. The creature that had been with him so long was with him no more. It had gone upstairs with him for the last time two nights before, and had his former faculties lived he would have seen how different it was. After the passage of the dead man it had never quite regained its own illusive apparition; senility and youth had mingled in its face, and in their mingling found a third degree of corruption. At the hour of the falling in of the shed of Lilith it had thinned to a shape of twilight. Meaning and apparent power had gone out of it. It was a thing the dead man might have met under his own pallid sky, and less even than that. In the ghostly night that fell on the ruins of Gomorrah it had tottered round its father and paramour, who did not yet know through what destruction they went. His eyes were dimmed. Those who look, in Stanhope's Dantean phrase, on the head of the Gorgon in Dis, do not know, until Virgil has left them, on what they gaze. In the night she was withdrawn; the substance of illusion in her faded, and alongside his heavy sleep she changed and changed, through all degrees of imbecile decay, till at last she was quite dispelled.

He was alone. He lay awake, and waking became aware of his ancient dream. Now he was near the end of his journey. He saw below him the rope drawn nearer and nearer to the wall, if it were a wall. He looked up; above him the rope seemed to end in the moon, which shone so fully in the dark, millions of miles away. Down all those miles he had slowly climbed. It was almost over now; he was always a little lower, and when he stood up he did not lose the dream. Through his bathing and dressing and going down and finding a taxi he was still on his rope. He felt once for his watch, and remembered he had not got it, and looked up at the shining silver orb above, and found that that was his watch. It was also a great public clock at which he was staring; but he could not make it out—moon or watch or clock. The time was up there; but he could not see it. He thought: "I shall be just in time." He was, and only just; as close to its end as to the end of the rope.

He got into his taxi. It went off along the High Street, and then was held up behind a policeman's arm. He was looking out of the window, when he thought a creaking voice said in his ear, as if a very old woman was in the seat beside him: "Madame Tussaud's". He did not look round, because no one was ever there, but he stared at the great building which seemed to glow out of the darkness of the side of the abyss, and there rose in him the figure of what it contained. He had never been there, though in a humorous moment he had once thought of taking Adela, but he knew what was in it—wax images. He saw them—exquisitely done, motionless, speechless, thoughtless; and he saw them being shifted. Hanging on his rope, he looked out through the square of light in the darkness and saw them all—Cæsar, Gustavus, Cromwell, Napoleon, Foch, and saw himself carrying them from one corner to another, and putting them down and picking them up and bringing them somewhere else and putting them down. There were diagrams, squares and rectangles, on the floor, to show where they should go; and as he ran across the hall with a heavy waxen thing on his shoulder he knew it was very important to put it down in the right diagram. So he did, but just as he went away the diagram under the figure changed and no longer fitted, and he had to go back and lift the thing up and take it off to another place where the real diagram was. This was always happening with each of them and all of them, so that six or seven or more of him had to be about, carrying the images, and hurrying past and after each other on their perpetual task. He could never get the details correct; there was always a little thing wrong, a thing as tiny as the shoulder-knots on the uniforms of the Grand Duke's Guard. Then the rope vibrated as the taxi started again, and he was caught away; the last vestige of the history of men vanished for ever.

Vibration after vibration—he was very near the bottom of his rope. He himself was moving now; he was hurrying. The darkness rushed by. He stopped. His hand, in habitual action, had gone to his pocket for silver, but his brain did not follow it. His feet stepped, in habitual action, off the rope, on to the flat ground. Before him there was a tall oblong opening in the dark, faintly lit. He had something in his hand—he turned, holding it out; there was a silver gleam as it left his hand, and he saw the whole million-mile-long rope vanishing upward and away from him with incredible rapidity towards the silver moon which ought to have been in his waistcoat pocket, because it was the watch he had overwound. Seeing that dazzling flight of the rope upwards into the very centre of the shining circle, he thought again: "I'm just in time." He was standing on the bottom of the abyss; there remained but a short distance in any method of mortal reckoning for him to take before he came to a more secret pit where there is no measurement because there is no floor. He turned towards the opening and began his last journey.

He went a little way, and came into a wider place, where presently there were hands taking off a coat he discovered himself to be wearing. He was looking at himself; for an instant he had not recognized his own face, but he did now, over a wide shining oval thing that reminded him of the moon. He was wearing the moon in front of him. But he was in black otherwise; he had put on a neat fantastic dress of darkness. The moon, the darkness, and he—only no rope, because that had gone away, and no watch, because he had done something or other to it, and it had gone away too. He tried to think what a watch was and how it told him the time. There were marks on it which meant something to do with time, but he didn't know what. Voices came to him out of the air and drove him along another corridor into another open space. And there suddenly before him was Sir Aston Moffatt.

The shock almost restored him. If he had ever hated Sir Aston because of a passion for austere truth, he might even then have laid hold on the thing that was abroad in the world and been saved. If he had been hopelessly wrong in his facts and yet believed them so, and believed they were important in themselves, he might have felt a touch of the fire in which the Marian martyr had gone to his glory, and still been saved. In the world of the suicides, physical or spiritual, he might have heard another voice than his and seen another face. He looked at Sir Aston and thought, not "He was wrong in his facts", but "I've been cheated". It was his last consecutive thought.

Sir Aston was decidedly deaf and extremely talkative, and had a sincere admiration for his rival. He came straight across to Wentworth, and began to talk. The world, which Wentworth had continuously and persistently denied in favour of himself, now poured itself over him, and as if in a deluge from heaven drove him into the depths. Very marvellous is the glorious condescension of the Omnipotence; the myth of the fire which was rained over the plain now incarnated itself in Sir Aston Moffatt. Softly and gently, perpetually and universally, the chatty sentences descended on the doomed man, each sentence a little prick of fire, because, as he stood there, he realized with a sickness at heart that a voice was talking and he did not know what it was saying. He heard two sounds continually repeated: "Went-worth, Went-worth". He knew that those two noises meant something, but he could not remember what. If all the faces that were about him would go away he might remember, but they did not go. They gathered round him, and carried him forward in the midst of them, through a doorway. As he went through it he saw in front of him tables, and with a last flash of memory knew that he had come there to eat and drink. There was his chair, at the bottom left corner, where he had always sat, his seat in the Republic. He went to it with an eager trot. It was waiting for him as it had always waited, for ever and ever; all his life and from the creation of the world he had sat there, he would sit there at the end, looking towards the—he could not think what was the right name for the tall man at the other end, who had been talking to him just now. He looked at him and tried to smile, but could not, for the tall man's eyes were blank of any meaning, and gazed at him emptily. The Republic deserted him. His smile ceased. He was at last by his chair; he would always sit there, always, always. He sat down.

As he did so, he knew he was lost. He could not understand anything about him. He could just remember that there had been one moment when a sudden bright flash had parted from him, fleeing swiftly across the sky into its source, and he wanted that moment back; he wanted desperately to hold on to the rope. The rope was not there. He had believed that there would be for him a companion at the bottom of the rope who would satisfy him for ever, and now he was there at the bottom, and there was nothing but noises and visions which meant nothing. The rope was not there. There were faces, which ceased to be faces, and became blobs of whitish red and yellow, working and twisting in a horrible way that yet did not surprise him, because nothing could surprise him. They moved and leaned and bowed; and between them were other things that were motionless now but might at any moment begin to move and crawl. Away over them was a huge round white blotch, with black markings on it, and two long black lines going round and round, one very fast and one very slow. This was time, too fast for his brain, too slow for his heart. If he only had hold of the rope still, he could perhaps climb out of this meaningless horror; at least, he could find some meaning and relation in it all. He felt that the great blotch had somehow slid up and obscured the shining silver radiance into which a flash out of him had gone, and if he could get the rope he could climb past, or, with great shuddering, even through the horrible blotch, away out of this depth where anything might be anything, and was anything, for he did not know what it was. The rope was not there.

163

He shrank into himself, trying to shut his eyes and lose sight of this fearful opposite of the world he had known. Quite easily he succeeded. But he could not close his ears, for he did not know how to manage the more complex co-ordination of shoulders and arms and hands. So there entered into him still a small, steady, meaningless flow of sound, which stung and tormented him with the same lost knowledge of meaning; small burning flames flickered down on his soul. His eyes opened again in mere despair. A little hopeless voice came from his throat. He said, and rather gasped than spoke: "Ah! ah!" Then everything at which he was looking rushed together and became a point, very far off, and he also was a point opposite it; and both points were rushing together, because in this place they drew towards each other from the more awful repulsion of the void. But fast as they went they never reached one another, for out of the point that was not he there expanded an anarchy of unintelligible shapes and hid it, and he knew it had gone out, expiring in the emptiness before it reached him. The shapes turned themselves into alternate panels of black and white. He had forgotten the name of them, but somewhere at some time he had thought he knew similar forms and they had had names. These had no names, and whether they were or were not anything, and whether that anything was desirable or hateful he did not know. He had now no consciousness of himself as such, for the magical mirrors of Gomorrah had been broken, and the city itself had been blasted, and he was out beyond it in the blankness of a living oblivion, tormented by oblivion. The shapes stretched out beyond him, all half turned away, all rigid and silent. He was sitting at the end, looking up an avenue of nothingness, and the little flames licked his soul, but they did not now come from without, for they were the power, and the only power, his dead past had on him; the life, and the only life, of his soul. There was, at the end of the grand avenue, a bobbing shape of black and white that hovered there and closed it. As he saw it there came on him a suspense; he waited for something to happen. The silence lasted; nothing happened. In that pause expectancy faded. Presently then the shape went out and he was drawn, steadily, everlastingly, inward and down through the bottomless circles of the void.

The Greater Trumps

CHAPTER I

THE LEGACY

'… perfect Babel,' Mr. Coningsby said peevishly, threw himself into a chair, and took up the evening paper. 'But Babel never was perfect, was it?' Nancy said to her brother in a low voice, yet not so low that her father could not hear if he chose. He did not choose, because at the moment he could not think of a sufficiently short sentence; a minute afterwards it occurred to him that he might have said, 'Then it's perfect now.' But it didn't matter; Nancy would only have been rude again, and her brother too. Children were. He looked at his sister, who was reading on the other side of the fire. She looked comfortable and interested, so he naturally decided to disturb her.

'And what have you been doing to-day, Sybil?' he asked, with an insincere goodwill, and as she looked up he thought angrily, 'Her skin's getting clearer every day.'

'Why, nothing very much,' Sybil Coningsby said. 'I did some shopping, and I made a cake, and went for a walk and changed the library books. And since tea I've been reading.'

'Nice day,' Mr. Coningsby answered, between a question and a sneer, wishing it hadn't been, though he was aware that if it hadn't been … but then it was certain to have been. Sybil always seemed to have nice days. He looked at his paper again. 'I see the Government are putting a fresh duty on dried fruits,' he snorted.

Sybil tried to say something, and failed. She was getting stupid, she thought, or (more probably) lazy. There ought to be something to say about the Government putting a duty on dried fruits. Nancy spoke instead.

'You're slow, auntie,' she said. 'The correct answer is: "I suppose that means that the price will go up!" The reply to that is, "Everything goes up under this accursed Government!"'

'Will you please let me do my own talking, Nancy?' her father snapped at her.

'Then I wish you'd talk something livelier than the Dead March in *Saul*,' Nancy said.

'You're out of date again, Nancy,' jeered her brother. 'Nobody plays that old thing nowadays.'

'Go to hell!' said Nancy.

Mr. Coningsby immediately stood up. 'Nancy, you shall not use such language in this house,' he called out.

'O, very well,' Nancy said, walked to the window, opened it, put her head out, and said to the world, but (it annoyed her to feel) in a more subdued voice, 'Go to hell.' She pulled in her head and shut the window. 'There, father,' she said, 'that wasn't in the house.'

Sybil Coningsby said equably, 'Nancy, you're in a bad temper.'

'And suppose I am?' Nancy answered. 'Who began it?'

'Don't answer your aunt back,' said Mr. Coningsby, still loudly. 'She at least is a lady.'

'She's more,' said Nancy. 'She's a saint. And I'm a worm and the child of….'

She abandoned the sentence too late. Her father picked up his paper, walked to the door, turned his head, uttered, 'If I am wanted, Sybil, I shall be in my study,' and went out. Ralph grinned at Nancy; their aunt looked at them both with a wise irony.

'What energy!' she murmured, and Nancy looked back at her, half in anger, half in admiration.

'Doesn't father *ever* annoy you, auntie?' she asked.

'No, my dear,' Miss Coningsby said.

'Don't we ever annoy you?' Nancy asked again.

'No, my dear,' Miss Coningsby said.

'Doesn't anyone ever annoy you, aunt?' Ralph took up the chant.

'Hardly at all,' Miss Coningsby said. 'What extraordinary ideas you children have! Why should anyone annoy me?'

'Well, we annoy father all right,' Nancy remarked, 'and I never mean to when I begin. But Ralph and I weren't making all that noise—and anyhow Babel wasn't perfect.'

Sybil Coningsby picked up her book again. 'My dear Nancy, you never do begin; you just happen along,' she said, and dropped her eyes so resolutely to her page that Nancy hesitated to ask her what she meant.

The room was settling back into the quiet which had filled it before Mr. Coningsby's arrival, when the bell of the front door rang. Nancy sprang to her feet and ran into the hall. 'Right, Agnes,' she sang: 'I'll see to it.'

165

'That'll be Henry,' Ralph said as she disappeared. 'Wasn't he coming to dinner?'

'Yes,' his aunt murmured without looking up. One of the things about Sybil Coningsby that occasionally annoyed other people—Ralph among them—was her capacity for saying, quite simply, 'Yes' or 'No,' and stopping there, rather as if at times she were literally following Christ's maxim about conversation. She would talk socially, if necessary, and sociably, if the chance arose, but she seemed to be able to manage without saying a lot of usual things. There was thus, to her acquaintances, a kind of blank about her; the world for a moment seemed with a shock to disappear and they were left in a distasteful void.

'Your aunt,' Mr. Coningsby had once said, 'has no small-talk. It's a pity.' Ralph had agreed: Nancy had not, and there had been one of those continual small rows which at once annoyed and appeased their father. Annoyed him—for they hurt his dignity; appeased him—for they at least gave him a dignity to be hurt. He was somebody then for a few minutes; he was not merely a curiously festering consciousness. It was true he was also a legal officer of standing a Warden in Lunacy. But his emotions worried him with a question which his intellect refused to define—what, what exactly was the satisfaction of being a Warden in Lunacy? Fifty-eight; fifty-nine. But Sybil was older; she was over sixty. Perhaps in a few years this gnawing would pass. She was contented: no doubt time would put him also at peace.

He was not thinking of this while he sat in the room they called his study, looking at the evening paper and waiting for dinner. He was thinking how shameful Nancy's behaviour had been. She lacked respect, she lacked modesty, she almost lacked decency. All that he had done … no doubt her engagement to—her understanding with—whatever it was she had along with this young Henry Lee fellow—had hardened her. There had been a rather vague confidence, a ring had appeared, so had Henry quite often. But to what the engagement was tending or of what the understanding was capable—that Mr. Coningsby could not or had not been allowed to grasp. He sat thinking of it, consoling himself with the reflection that one day she'd be sorry. She wasn't … she was … confused; all confused … confusion confounded … yes…. Suddenly Nancy was in the room—'Look here, old thing'—no, he wasn't asleep; she was saying it. He hated to be discovered asleep just before dinner; perhaps she hadn't noticed—'and all that. Come and talk to Henry a minute before we eat.'

If her father had been quite clear how far the apology had gone, he would have known whether he might reasonably accept it. But he wasn't, and he didn't want to argue because of not having been asleep. So he made a noise in his throat and got up, adding with a princely magnanimity, 'But don't be rude to your aunt: I won't tolerate*that*.'

Nancy, glowing with her past brief conversation with Henry, and looking forward to the immediate future with zest, subdued an inclination to point out that it was she who had called Sybil a saint, and they both returned to the drawing-room.

Although Mr. Coningsby had known his daughter's *fiancé*—if indeed he were that—for some months now, he still felt a slight shock at seeing him. For to him Henry Lee, in spite of being a barrister—a young, a briefless barrister, but a barrister—was so obviously a gipsy that his profession seemed as if it must be assumed for a sinister purpose. He was fairly tall and dark-haired and dark-skinned, and his eyes were bright and darting; and his soft collar looked almost like a handkerchief coiled round his throat, only straighter, and his long fingers, with their quick secret movements—'Hen-roosts,' Mr. Coningsby thought, as he had thought before. A nice thing for Nancy to be tramping the roads—and Nancy was a gipsy name. That was her mother's fault. Names had for him a horrid attraction, largely owing to his own, which was Lothair. That disastrous name had to do with his father's godmother, a rich old lady with a passionate admiration for Lord Beaconsfield. To please that admiration her godson's first child had been named Sybil; the second Lothair. It might have been Tancred or Alroy; it might even have been Endymion. Mr. Coningsby himself allowed that Endymion Coningsby would have been worse. The other titles would no doubt have been allocated in turn, but for two facts; first, that the godmother abandoned politics for religion and spent large sums of money on Anglican sisterhoods; second, that there were no more children. But the younger was at once there, and there too soon to benefit by the conversion which would have saved others. Lothair—always, through a document-signing, bank-corresponding, cheque-drawing, letter-writing, form-filling, addressed, directoried, and important life, always Lothair Coningsby. If only he could have been called Henry Lee!

He thought so once more as they settled to dinner. He thought so through the soup. Something had always been unfair to him, luck or fate or something. Some people were like that, beaten through no fault of their own, wounded before the battle began; not everybody would have done so well as he had. But how it dogged him—that ghastly luck! Even in the last month Duncannon (and everyone knew that Duncannon was well off) had left him … no honest, useful, sincere legacy, but a collection of playing-cards, with a request that it should be preserved intact by his old friend, the legatee, Lothair Coningsby, and a further request that at the said legatee's death the collection should be presented to the British Museum. About that the legatee refused to think; some of the packs were, he believed, rather valuable. But for a couple of years or so, or anyhow for a year, nothing could be done: too many people knew of it. There had even been a paragraph in one of the papers. He couldn't sell them—Mr. Coningsby flinched as the word struck him for the first time—not yet awhile anyhow.

'Father,' Nancy said, 'will you show us Mr. Duncannon's playing-cards after dinner?' Mr. Coningsby just checked a vicious sneer. 'Henry,' Nancy went on, 'saw about them in the papers.' Mr. Coningsby saw a gipsy reading torn scraps of newspapers under a hedge. 'And he knows something about cards. What a lot you *do* know, Henry!' Yes, in a fair, cheating yokels out of their pennies by tricks or fortune-telling: which card is the pea under? Something like that, anyhow. Bah!

'My dear,' he said, 'it's rather a painful business. Duncannon was my dear friend.'

'Still, father, if you would…. He'd have loved people to be interested.'

Mr. Coningsby, looking up suddenly, caught a swift, tender smile on Sybil's face, and wondered what she was grinning at. Nancy had hit on the one undeniable fact about the late Mr. Duncannon, and he couldn't think of any way of getting round it. But why should Sybil be amused?

'I'd be very grateful if you would, sir,' the young man said. 'I do find them interesting—it's in my blood, I suppose,' he added, laughing at Nancy.

'And can you tell fortunes? Can you tell mine?' she answered joyously.

'Some by cards and some by hands,' he said, 'and some by the stars.'

'O, I can tell some by hands,' she answered. 'I've told father's and auntie's. Only I can't understand father's line of life—it seems to stop at about forty, yet here he is still alive.' Mr. Coningsby, feeling more like a death's head than a living Warden in Lunacy, looked down again.

'And Miss Coningsby's?' Henry asked, bowing towards her.

'O, auntie's goes on for ever, as far as I can see,' Nancy answered, 'right round under the finger.'

Henry for a moment looked at Sybil a little oddly, but he said nothing, and the chatter about palmistry was lost in Ralph's dominating the conversation with an announcement that those things, like Spiritualism, were all great rubbish. 'How can you tell from the palm of my hand whether I'm going to be ill at fifty or have a fortune left me at sixty or go to Zanzibar at seventy?'

'Hands are strange things,' Henry said. 'Nobody knows very much about them yet.'

'Eh?' said Ralph, surprised.

'Auntie's got the loveliest hands I ever saw,' Nancy said, sending a side-glance at Henry, and meeting the quick astonishment of his eyebrows. This being what he was meant to show—because she did think she had good hands, the rest of her being tolerable but unnoticeable, hair, face, figure, and everything—she allowed her own hand for a moment to touch his, and added, 'Look at them.'

They all looked, even Sybil herself, who said softly, 'They are rather nice, aren't they?'

Her brother thought privately that this remark was in execrable taste; one didn't praise one's own belongings, still less oneself. What would people think if he said his face was 'rather nice'?

'They're dears,' said Nancy.

'Jolly good,' said Ralph.

'They're extremely beautiful,' said Henry.

'There's a very striking hand in the British Museum,' Mr. Coningsby said, feeling the time had come for him to break silence, 'belonging to an Egyptian king or something. Just a giant head and then in front of it a great arm with the fist closed—so.' He illustrated.

'I know it, sir,' Henry said, 'the hand of the image of Rameses: it is a hand of power.'

'The hand of power! I thought that was something to do with murderers; no, of course, that was glory,' Nancy said, adding immediately, 'And now, father, do let's look at the cards while we have coffee.'

Mr. Coningsby, seeing no easy way out, gloomily assented. 'Where did you have them put, Sybil?' he asked as the whole party rose.

'In the chest in your study,' she answered. 'The catalogue's with them.'

'Catalogue?' Ralph said. 'He did it in style, didn't he? Fancy me making a catalogue of my old tennis racquets.'

'These cards,' Mr. Coningsby said with considerable restraint, 'were not worn-out toys. They are a very valuable and curious collection of remarkable cards, gathered together with considerable difficulty and in some sense, I believe, priceless.'

Nancy pinched Henry's arm as they followed their father from the dining-room. 'The dear!' she said. 'I've heard him say the same thing himself, before they belonged to him.'

Ralph was whistling. 'O, but I say now, priceless?' he said. 'That'd be pretty valuable, wouldn't it?'

167

'I don't know exactly what the value would be to collectors, but considerable,' Mr. Coningsby said as he opened the large wooden chest, and then, thinking of the British Museum, added in a more sullen voice, 'Considerable.'

Sybil took from the chest a fat writing-book. 'Well, shall I read the descriptions?' she asked. 'If someone will call out the numbers.' For each pack was contained in a special little leather cover, with a place on it for a white slip containing a number.

'Right ho!' Ralph said. 'I'll call out the numbers. Are they in order? It doesn't look like it. Number ninety-four.'

'I think I will read, Sybil,' Mr. Coningsby said. 'I've heard Duncannon talk of them often and it's more suitable. Perhaps you'd pick them up and call the numbers out. And then the young people can look at them.'

'Give me that chair, then, if you will, Henry,' Sybil assented. Her brother sat down on the other side of a small table, and 'the young people' thronged round it.

'Number——,' Sybil began and paused. 'Ralph, if you wouldn't mind going on the same side as Nancy and Henry, I could see too.'

Ralph obeyed, unaware that this movement, while removing an obstacle from his aunt's gaze, also removed his own from the two lovers. Sybil, having achieved the maximum of general satisfaction with the minimum of effort, said again, 'Number——'

'I didn't think you'd be very interested, aunt,' Ralph, with a belated sense of apology, threw in.

Sybil smiled at him and said again, 'Number——'

'I have never known your aunt *not* be interested in anything, my boy,' Mr. Coningsby said severely, looking up, but more at Sybil than at Ralph, as if he were inclined to add, 'and how the devil she does it I can't think!'

'Darling,' said Nancy, 'aunt's a perfect miracle, but can't we leave her for now and get on with the cards?'

'We are on the point of "getting on" with them, as you call it, Nancy,' her father answered. 'I wish you'd remember this is something of an ordeal to me, and treat it more seriously.'

Nancy's hand, under the table, squeezed its impatience into Henry's and relieved her tongue. When the momentary silence had achieved seriousness but had not reached self-consciousness, Sybil's voice collected and, as it were, concluded it with the words, 'Number ninety-four.'

'Ninety-four,' Mr. Coningsby read out, '"French; *circa* 1789. Supposed to have been designed by David. A special Revolutionary symbolism. In this pack the Knaves are painted as a peasant, a beggar, an *aubergiste*, and a *sansculotte* respectively; the Queens (Marie Antoinette) have each a red line round the neck, as if guillotined; the Kings are reversed; over the ace is the red cap of liberty. Round the edge of each card is the legend, *La République, une, libre, indivisible*."'

'Number nine,' Sybil said, and put down another pack.

'Nine,' read Mr. Coningsby. '"Spanish pack, eighteenth century. The Court cards are ecclesiastical—cardinals, bishops, and priests. It is unlikely that this pack was ever used for playing; probably it was painted as an act of devotion or thanksgiving. See Appendix for possible portraits."'

'Number three hundred and forty-one,' Sybil said.

'"Most rare,"' Mr. Coningsby read. '"Very early pack of Tarot cards. I have not been able to trace the origin of these; they have some resemblances to a fifteenth-century pack now in the Louvre, but would seem to be even earlier. The material of which they are made is unusual—? papyrus. The four suits are, as usual, sceptres, swords, cups, and coins; the Greater Trumps are in the following order (numbered at the foot in Roman): (i) The Juggler, (ii) The Empress, (iii) The High Priestess, or Woman Pope——"'

'The what?' Nancy exclaimed. 'What! Pope Joan? Sorry, father, I didn't mean to interrupt.'

'"(iv) The Pope—or Hierophant, (v) The Emperor—or Ruler, (vi) The Chariot, (vii) The Lovers, (viii) The Hermit, (ix) Temperance, (x) Fortitude, (xi) Justice, (xii) The Wheel of Fortune, (xiii) The Hanged Man."'

'Jolly game of bridge we could have with these,' Ralph remarked. 'I lead the Hanged Man.'

There was a tremendous pause. 'Ralph, if you can only make fun——' Mr. Coningsby began, and stopped.

'Do go on,' Sybil Coningsby's voice implored. 'I should have had to say something silly if Ralph hadn't. It's so exciting.'

Mr. Coningsby gave a suppressed grunt, fortunately missed Nancy's low-breathed comment on it—'The Hanged Man!'—and proceeded.

'"(xiv) Death, (xv) The Devil, (xvi) The Falling Tower, (xvii) The Star, (xviii) The Moon, (xix) The Sun, (xx) The Last Judgement——"'

Mr. Coningsby paused to shift his eyeglasses; in a perfect silence the others waited.

'"(xxi) The Universe, (o) The Fool."'

'Nought usually comes at the beginning,' Ralph said.

'Not necessarily,' said Sybil. 'It might come anywhere. Nought isn't a number at all. It's the opposite of number.'

Nancy looked up from the cards. 'Got you, aunt,' she said. 'What about ten? Nought's a number there—it's part of ten.'

'Quite right, Nancy,' Mr. Coningsby said with something like pleasure. 'I think the child has you, Sybil.'

'Well, if you say that any mathematical arrangement of one and nought really makes ten——' Sybil smiled. 'Can it possibly be more than a way of representing ten?'

'It doesn't matter, anyhow,' Nancy hastily said. 'Aren't they fascinating? But why are they? And what do they all mean? Henry, why are you looking at them like that?'

Henry indeed was examining the first card, the Juggler, with close attention, as if investigating the smallest details. It was a man in a white tunic, but the face, tilted back, was foreshortened, and darkened by the brim of some black cap that he wore: a cap so black that something of night itself seemed to have been used in the painting. The heavy shadow and the short pointed beard hid the face from the observer. On the breast of the tunic were three embroidered circles—the first made of swords and staffs and cups and coins, balanced one on the other from the coin at the bottom to the apex of two pointing swords at the top; and within this was a circle, so far as Nancy could see, made up of rounded representations of twenty of the superior cards each in its own round; and within that was a circle containing one figure, but that was so small she couldn't make out what it was. The man was apparently supposed to be juggling; one hand was up in the air, one was low and open towards the ground, and between them, in an arch, as if tossed and caught and tossed again, were innumerable shining balls. In the top left-hand corner of the card was a complex device of curiously interwoven lines.

Henry put it down slowly as Nancy spoke and turned his eyes to her. But hers, as they looked to plunge into that other depth—ocean pouring into ocean and itself receiving ocean—found themselves thwarted. Instead of oceans they saw pools, abandoned by a tide already beyond sight: she blenched as a bather might do in the cold wind across an empty shore. 'Henry!' she exclaimed.

It was, surely, no such great thing, only a momentary preoccupation. But he was already glancing again at the cards; he had already picked up another, and was scrutinizing the figure of the hierophantic woman. It had been drawn sitting on an ancient throne between two heavy pillars; a cloud of smoke rolled high above the priestly head-dress and solemn veil that she wore, and under her feet were rivers pouring out in falling cataracts. One hand was stretched out as if directing the flow of those waters; the other lay on a heavy open volume, with great clasps undone, that rested on her knees. This card also was stamped in the top left-hand corner with an involved figure of intermingled lines.

'Well!' said Nancy, as she stared at it.

'But, look here,' Ralph asked, 'does one play with them, or what?' He peered over Henry's shoulder. 'Old Maid, I suppose; and Beggar my Neighbour with the first.'

'They're very wonderfully done, aren't they?' Sybil Coningsby asked, and herself delicately picked up one of what her brother had called the Greater Trumps. It was the nineteenth card—that named the Sun—and was perfectly simple: the sun shone full in a clear sky, and two children—a boy and a girl—played happily below. Sybil smiled again as she contemplated them. 'Aren't they the loveliest things?' she breathed, and indeed they were—so vivid, so intense, so rapturous under that beneficent light, of which some sort of reflection passed into Sybil's own face while she brooded. Or so it seemed to Henry, who had put down his card when Ralph spoke and over Nancy's bent head was now watching her aunt. Sybil looked up and saw him. 'Aren't they perfect, Henry?' she asked.

'They are very, very fine,' Lee said, and yet seemed a little puzzled, as if he had expected something, but not quite that.

'But what—are—they—all—about?' Ralph asked. 'What's the idea of it?'

'Duncannon used to tell me,' Mr. Coningsby said; he had put down his catalogue now, and was standing by the table with the others; his high, bald forehead gleaming a little in the light, his thin, dissatisfied face bent towards the pack, 'that the Tarot cards were an invention of the fourteenth century, though supposed by some to be Egyptian.' He stopped, as if everything were explained.

'Stupendous bit of work—inventing them,' Ralph said gravely. 'But why did anyone bother? What I mean—it seems rather … rather needless, doesn't it?'

'We have a tale about them,' Henry Lee began, with a cautious ease, and Mr. Coningsby said, 'We?'

Ever so slightly the young man flushed. 'I mean the gipsies,' he answered lightly, and added to Nancy, 'That's your fault, darling, for always pretending that I'm a real gipsy with a caravan, a tin kettle, and a grandmother with a black pipe.'

'Wouldn't she love these cards?' Nancy said enthusiastically. 'Henry, darling, do have a grandmother, so that she can tell us stories about Tarots, and perhaps even tell fortunes with—what did you call them, father?—the Greater Trumps.'

'Well,' said Ralph, abandoning the whole subject, 'shall we look at some more?'

'At least, I've a grandfather——' Henry said to Nancy; but 'O, a grandfather!' she mocked him. 'But he lives in a house with electric light, doesn't he? Not in a caravan under the moon. Still, can he tell us what this is?' She picked up the last card, that numbered nought, and exhibited it. It might have needed some explanation, for it was obscure enough. It was painted with the figure of a young man, clothed in an outlandish dress of four striped colours—black and grey and silver and red; his legs and feet and arms and hands were bare, and he had over one shoulder a staff, carved into serpentine curves, that carried a round bag, not unlike the balls with which the Juggler played. The bag rested against his shoulder, so that as he stood there he supported as well as bore it. Before him a dragonfly, or some such airy creature, danced; by his side a larger thing, a lynx or young tiger, stretched itself up to him—whether in affection or attack could not be guessed, so poised between both the beast stood. The man's eyes were very bright; he was smiling, and the smile was so intense and rapt that those looking at it felt a quick motion of contempt—no sane man could be as happy as that. He was painted as if pausing in his stride, and there was no scenic background; he and his were seen against a flatness of dull gold.

'No,' said Henry, 'that's the difficulty—at least, it's the unknown factor.'

'The unknown factor in what?' Mr. Coningsby asked.

'In——' Henry paused a second, then he added, 'in telling fortunes by the Tarots. There are different systems, you know, but none of them is quite convincing in what it does with the Fool. They all treat it as if it were to be added to the Greater Trumps—making twenty-two.'

'So there are twenty-two,' Mr. Coningsby said. 'I've just read them out.'

'No, sir,' Henry answered, almost reluctantly, 'not exactly. Strictly there are the twenty-one and the nought. As Miss Coningsby said. And you see the nought—well, it's nought—nothing—unaccountable.'

'Well, shall we look at some more?' Ralph asked.

'Can you tell fortunes by them?' Nancy said eagerly, but Henry shook his head.

'Not properly,' he answered; 'at least, I'd rather not try. It can be done; my grandfather might know. They are very curious cards, and this is a very curious pack.'

'Why are they curious cards?' Nancy went on questioning.

Henry, still staring at them, answered, 'It's said that the shuffling of the cards is the earth, and the pattering of the cards is the rain, and the beating of the cards is the wind, and the pointing of the cards is the fire. That's of the four suits. But the Greater Trumps, it's said, are the meaning of all process and the measure of the everlasting dance.'

'Some folk-lore survival, I suppose?' Mr. Coningsby said, wishing that his daughter hadn't herself got mixed up with a fellow very much like a folk-lore survival.

'Certainly it may be that, sir,' the young man answered, 'from the tales my people used to tell round their fires while they were vagabonds.'

'It sounds frightfully thrilling,' Nancy said. 'What *is* the everlasting dance, Henry darling?'

He put his arm round her as Mr. Coningsby turned back to his chair. 'Don't you know?' he whispered. 'Look at the seventh card.'

She obeyed; and on it, under the stamped monogram, she saw the two lovers, each aureoled, each with hands stretched out; each clad in some wild beast's skin, dancing side by side down a long road, that ran from a far-off point right down to the foreground. Her hand closed on Henry's and she smiled at him. 'Just that?' she said.

'That's at least the first movement,' he answered; 'unless you go with the hermit.'

'Sybil, I'm waiting,' Mr. Coningsby said, and Sybil hastily picked up another pack, while Ralph very willingly collected and put away the Tarots.

But the interest had flagged. Henry and Nancy were preoccupied, Mr. Coningsby and his son were beginning to be bored, and in a few minutes Sybil said pleasantly, 'Don't you all think we've looked at about enough for to-night?'

'She really does know when to stop,' Mr. Coningsby thought to himself, but he only said cheerfully, 'Just as you like, just as you like. What do you say, Henry?'

'Eh?... O, just as you like,' Henry agreed with a start.

'I vote we push them back then,' Ralph said, even more cheerfully than his father. 'Jolly good collection. But those what-you-may-call-them are the star lot.'

Hours later, by the door, the sight of a single star low in the heavens brought one of the 'what-you-may-call-thems' back to Nancy's mind. 'O, and darling,' she said, 'will you teach me how to tell fortunes by those other cards—you know, the special ones?'

'The Tarots?' Henry asked her, with a touch of irony in his voice.

'If that's what you call them,' she said. 'I can do a bit by the ordinary ones.'

'Have you got the sleight of hand for it?' he asked. 'You have to feel how the cards are going, and let yourself do what they mean.'

Nancy looked at her hands, and flexed them. 'I don't see why not, unless you have to do it very quickly. Do try me, Henry sweet.'

He took both her hands in one of his. 'We'll try, darling,' he answered; 'we'll try what you can do with the Greater Trumps. If it's the pack I think it is. Tell me, do you think your father would ever sell them to me?'

'Why? Do you want them?' she asked in surprise. 'Henry, I believe you're a real gipsy after all! Will you disguise yourself and go to the races? O, let's, and I'll be the gipsy maiden—"Kind sir, kind sir,"' she trilled, 'and everyone'll cross my palm with pound notes because I'm so beautiful, and perhaps the King will kiss me before all the Court ladies. Would you like that? He might give me a diamond ring too, and you could show it to the judges when they came to tea. No, don't tell me they won't, because when you're a judge they will, and you'll all talk about your cases till I shall only have the diamond ring to think about and how the King of England once gave it to Nancy the little gipsy girl, before she became Lady Lee, and tried to soften her husband's hard heart for the poor prisoners the ruffians in the police brought to him. So when you see me dreaming you'll know what I'm dreaming of, and you must never, never interrupt.'

'I don't really have much chance, do I?' Henry asked.

'O, cruel!' she said, 'to mock your Nancy so! Will you call me a chatterbox before all the world? or shall I always talk to you on my fingers—like that?'—they gleamed before him, shaping the letters—'and tell you on them what shop I've been to each day, as if I were dumb and you were deaf?'

He caught a hand in one of his, and lightly struck the fingers of his other over its palm. 'Don't flaunt your beauties,' he said, 'or when I'm a judge you'll be before me charged with having a proud heart, and I'll send you to spoil your hands doing laundry-work in a prison.'

'Then I'll trap the governor's son, and escape,' she said, 'and make a ballad of a wicked judge, and how first he beat and then shut up his own true sweetheart. Darling, you must be getting on. I'll see you to-morrow, won't I? O, good night. Do go home and sleep well. Good night. Don't let anything happen to you, will you?'

'I'll stop it at once,' he said. 'If anything starts to happen, I'll be very angry with it.'

'Do,' she said, 'for I don't want anything to happen ever any more. O, good night—why aren't you gone? It doesn't take you long to get home, does it? You'll be asleep by midnight.'

But when she herself fell asleep Henry was driving his car out of London southward, and it was long past midnight before he stopped it at a lonely house among the Downs.

———————————————

CHAPTER II

THE HERMIT

An old man was sitting alone in a small room. He was at a table facing the door; behind him was another door. The walls were bare of pictures: the table was a large one, and it was almost completely covered with a set of Tarot cards. The old man was moving them very carefully from place to place, making little notes on a sheet of paper, and sometimes consulting an old manuscript book that lay by him. He was so absorbed that he did not hear the step outside, and it was not till the door opened that he looked up with a sudden exclamation. Henry Lee came lightly into the room.

'Why, Henry!' the old man said. Henry looked at the table, let his eyes run over the whole arrangement of the cards, and smiled.

'Still no nearer, grandfather?' he asked.

'Nearer? No, no, not nearer yet,' his grandfather answered. 'Not quite, yet awhile. But I shall do it.' He sighed a little. 'I keep the account very carefully,' he said, 'and some day I shall do it. I spend all my time on it.'

Henry nodded towards the other door. 'And—*they*?' he asked, lowering his voice a trifle.

'Yes,' the old man said. 'I watch them too. But, you know—it's too difficult. But I must do it at last. You're not … you're not coming back to help me, are you?'

'Why, I may even do that,' Henry said, taking off his motoring-coat.

Aaron Lee got to his feet. He was certainly very old—nearly a century, one might think, looking at the small wizened figure, dark-skinned and bald; but his movements, though slow, were not uncertain: his hands were steady as he leaned on the table, and if his voice shook a little, it was with excitement and not from senility.

'What do you mean, Henry?' he asked. 'Have you found out anything? What have you heard? Have you—have you the secret?'

Henry sat down on the edge of the table, and idly fingered one of the cards. 'Don't believe me too much,' he said. 'I don't believe myself. I don't know about the secret—no, I think we still have to find that out. But I think'—he dropped the card and looked burningly at his grandfather—'I think I have found the originals.'

Aaron gave a short gasp. 'It's not possible,' he began, and fell into a fit of trembling so great that he dropped again into his chair. When to a degree it had passed, he said once more, 'It's not possible.'

'You think not?' the younger man asked.

'Tell me,' Aaron exclaimed, leaning forward, 'what are they? Why do you believe—how can you—that——' His voice stopped, so anxious was he, but after a moment's pause he added—'Tell me; tell me.'

'It is so unlikely,' Henry began, 'and yet with *them* there is nothing either likely or unlikely, is there? One cannot tell how they will move to-morrow. Tell me first, grandfather, do you still watch my future every day?'

'Every day by the cards,' Aaron said.

'And did yesterday promise nothing for to-day?' the young man asked.

'Nothing that I thought important,' Aaron answered. 'Something was to come to you, some piece of good luck; the ace of cups lay on the Wheel of Fortune—but I thought it had to do with your law. I put it by to ask you about when you came.'

'You are old, grandfather,' Henry said. 'Are the cups only deniers for you to think so?'

'But what *could* I think?' Aaron protested. 'It was a day's chance—I couldn't…. But what is it? What have you found?'

'I have told you I am betrothed,' Henry went on, using the solemn word as if deliberately, 'and her father has had left him—by a friend of his who is dead—a collection of playing-cards…. O, the usual thing, except for a set of the symbols. He showed them to us and I tell you, grandfather, I think it is the very one original set. I've come here to-night to see.'

'Have you got them?' the old one asked eagerly, but Henry shook his head.

'Time enough,' he said. 'Listen, among *them* is not the Chariot an Egyptian car, devised with two sphinxes, driven by a Greek, and having on it paintings of cities and islands?'

'It is just that,' the other said.

'And Death—is not Death a naked peasant, with a knife in his hand, with his sandals slung at his side?'

'It is so,' the other said again.

'Certainly then they are the same,' Henry concluded. 'But let us look at *them*, for that's why I have come.'

The old man got up, and took from an inner pocket of his coat a key. He walked slowly to the inner door, and Henry followed him. He put the key in the lock, turned it, and opened the door. Within the room they were on the point of entering, and directly before them, there hung from ceiling to floor thick black curtains, and for a moment, as he laid his hand on one of these, the old man hesitated. Then he half pulled it aside, half lifted it, and went through, holding it so that his grandson might enter after him.

The place into which they came was smaller than the outer room. It was hung all round with a heavy black stuff, and it was filled with a curious pale light, which certainly did not come through any window or other opening. The colour of that pale light was uncertain; it seemed to change softly from one hue to another—now it was red, as if it were the reflection of a very distant fire; now it was green, as if diffused through invisible waters that covered them; now it was darker and half obscured by vapour; now those vapours were dispelled and the clear pallor of early dawn exhibited itself within the room. To this changing phenomenon of light the two men paid no attention; they were gazing at a table which stood in the centre.

It was a table made of some strange kind of wood: so much could be seen from the single central support which opened at the bottom into four foot-pieces, and each of these again into some twelve or fourteen claws, upon the whole fifty-six of which the table rested. But the top was hidden, for it was covered by a plate of what looked like gold, marked very intricately with a pattern, or perhaps with two patterns, one of squares, and one of circles, so that the eyes, as with a chess-board, saw now one and now the other as predominant. Upon that plate of gold were a number of little figures, each about three inches high, also of gold, it seemed, very wonderfully wrought; so that the likeness to the chess-board was even more pronounced, for to any hasty spectator (could such a one ever have penetrated there) the figures might have seemed like those in a game; only there were many of them, and they were all in movement. Gently and continuously they went, immingling, unresting—as if to some complicated measure, and as if of their own volition. There must have been nearly a hundred of them, and from the golden plate upon which they went came a slight sound of music—more like an echo than a sound—sometimes quickening, sometimes slowing, to which the golden figures kept a duteous rhythm, or perhaps the faint sound itself was but their harmonized movement upon their field.

Henry took a few steps forward, slowly and softly, almost as if he were afraid that those small images would overhear him, and softly and slowly Aaron followed. They paused at a little distance from the table, and stood gazing at the figures, the young man in a careful comparison of them with his memory of the newly found cards. He saw among them those who bore the coins, and those who held swords or staffs or cups; and among those he searched for the shapes of the Greater Trumps, and one by one his eyes found them, but each separately, so that as he fastened his attention on one the rest faded around it to a golden blur. But there they were, in exact presentation—the Juggler who danced continuously round the edge of the circle, tossing little balls up and catching them again; the Emperor and Empress; the masculine and feminine hierophants; the old anchorite treading his measure and the hand-clasped lovers wheeling in theirs; a Sphinx-drawn chariot moving in a dancing guard of the four lesser orders; an image closing the mouth of a lion, and another bearing a cup closed by its hand, and another with scales but with unbandaged eyes—which had been numbered in the paintings under the titles of strength and temperance and justice; the wheel of fortune turning between two blinded shapes who bore it; two other shapes who bore between them a pole or cross on which hung by his foot the image of a man; the swift ubiquitous form of a sickle-armed Death; a horned mystery bestriding two chained victims; a tower that rose and fell into pieces, and then was re-arisen in some new place; and the woman who wore a crown of stars, and the twin beasts who had each of them on their heads a crescent moon, and the twin children on whose brows were two rayed suns in glory—the star, the moon, the sun; the heavenly form of judgement who danced with a skeleton half freed from its grave-clothes, and held a trumpet to its lips; and the single figure who leapt in a rapture and was named the world. One by one Henry recognized them and named them to himself, and all the while the tangled measure went swiftly on. After a few minutes he looked round: 'They're certainly the same; in every detail they're the same. Some of the attributed meanings aren't here, of course, but that's all.'

'Even to that?' Aaron asked in a low voice, and pointed to the Fool in the middle of the field.

It was still: it alone in the middle of all that curious dance did not move, though it stood as if poised for running; the lynx or other great cat by its side was motionless also. They paused—the man and the beast—as if struck into inactivity in the very midst of activity. And all about them, sliding, stepping, leaping, rolling, the complex dance went on.

'That certainly,' Henry said, turning slowly away.

The old man took a step to meet him. 'But then,' he whispered, so that his faint voice blended with the faint music, 'but then we can find out—at any moment—what the dance says? We can tell what the future will be—from what the present is?'

Henry spread out his hands towards the table, as if he were laying something down. 'That could be done, I suppose,' he answered. 'But if the Fool does not move, how will it affect divination? Don't your books tell you anything?'

'There are no writings which tell us anything at all of the Fool,' Aaron said.

They stood still for what might have been two or three minutes, watching that unresting movement, hearing that unceasing sound, themselves changed from moment to moment in that altering light; then Aaron said, 'Come away now. I don't like to watch too long, unless I am working at the order of the dance.'

Henry stood for a moment longer. 'I wonder if you can know the dance without being among the dancers,' he said.

'But we are,' the old man answered hurriedly; 'we are—everything is.'

'O, as everything is,' Henry uttered scornfully, 'as stones or winds or ships. But stones and winds and ships don't *know*. And to know——' He fell silent, and stood meditating till the other pulled at his arm; then, a little reluctantly, he turned to withdraw, and between the curtains and through the doorway they came into the outer room. Aaron locked the door and went back to his seat at the table, whence he looked inquiringly at his grandson.

'What will you do now about the cards?' he asked.

Henry came back from his secret thoughts with an abrupt movement of his body, and smiled, though his eyes remained brilliant and sombre. 'I don't know,' he admitted. 'Remember, I've only just seen them.'

'This owner, this father—will he sell them?' Aaron asked.

Henry played a tune on the table. 'If he doesn't,' he answered slowly, 'I don't know quite how…. He is supposed, at his death—or before, perhaps—to give them to the British Museum. All of them.'

'What?' Aaron cried out in something like terror. 'But that's imbecile. Surely he'd sell—if we offered him enough.'

Henry shook his head. 'I don't know,' he said. 'He's a man who's got pretty well everything he wants and finds it entirely useless to him. He doesn't need money at all badly. He can think of nothing that will give him pleasure, and because of that he doesn't like other people to have too much pleasure. No, he isn't cruel; he's even kind in his own way. But he holds on to his own as a child does to a broken toy—because one day it might want it or because it doesn't like to see another child playing with what was once its own.'

'But money?' Aaron urged.

'I tell you he doesn't want money,' Henry said.

'Wouldn't he give it to his daughter?' Aaron asked more hopefully. 'Are you going to marry her?'

'He can't easily give her one pack out of the whole collection, and the rest to the Museum,' Henry answered. 'Yes—I shall marry her. I think perhaps—but that doesn't matter. But if he gives her the whole lot he will be bothered by his friend's wish; and if he gives her one pack he will be bothered by the explanations; and if he leaves it all to the Museum he will be bothered by losing it.'

'But how will he lose it—if he keeps it while he's alive?' the old man asked.

'I think he's already unhappy, even while he's alive, at the idea of losing at his death so much that he could never enjoy,' Henry said. 'He is for ever waiting for satisfaction.'

Aaron Lee leaned forward. 'But it's necessary that he should sell it or give it—or lose it somehow,' he said anxiously.

'It would be very difficult for him to lose it,' the other answered. 'And how do you know what virtue might pass from the cards?'

'Only violence … that's unwise,' Aaron answered. 'But to take them … to take them for this purpose … I don't see the wrong.'

'Mr. Lothair Coningsby would see the wrong,' Henry said drily. 'And I doubt if I could persuade Nancy.'

'What's she to do with it?' his grandfather asked contemptuously.

Henry smiled again, a bright but almost threatening flash of amusement. 'I wonder,' he said. 'But, whatever I wonder, be certain, grandfather, that I'm determined not to go against her till….'

He stopped for so long that Aaron said, 'Till—till when?'

'Till I've seen whether the image of the Lovers has another use,' Henry finished. 'To know—to see from within—to be aware of the dance. Well, we shall see.' His eyes fixed on the inner door, he added slowly, 'Nancy—Nancy—Nancy.'

Aaron said: 'But you must do something soon. We can't run any risk. An accident——'

'Or a spasm of gloom,' Henry added, 'and the cards would be in the Museum. Yes, you're right; we can't wait. By the way, do you ever see anything of Joanna?'

'I haven't seen her for months,' the old man answered, with a slight shudder. 'She came here in the summer—I told you.'

'I know you did,' Henry said. 'Is she still as mad as ever? Is she still crying out on the names of the old dead gods?'

The other moved uneasily. 'Don't let's talk of it. I am afraid of Joanna.'

'Afraid of her?' Henry said scornfully. 'Why, what can she do to harm us?'

'Joanna's mad, with a terrifying madness,' Aaron said. 'If she knows that the Tarots might be brought back to their originals and the working of the mystery be complete——'

'What could an old woman and an idiot boy do?' Henry asked.

'Call them an insane prophetess and a young obedient Samson,' Aaron answered. 'I dream of her sometimes as if she belonged to *them*. If she thought the body of her child was found and formed and vivified … and if she knew of the cards, she might…. A mad hierophant … a hieratic hate….'

'Mightn't she be appeased if she thought her child was found?' Henry asked.

'If she thought that we kept it from her?' the old man said. 'Ask your own blood, Henry, what your desire would do. Your spirit is more like hers than mine. When she and I were young together, I set myself to discover the prophetic meaning of the dance, but she imagined herself a partner in it, and she studied the old tales and myths of Egypt—thirty years she studied them, and her child was to be a Mighty One born within the measure. It was born, and the same day it died——'

Henry interrupted him sharply. 'You've never told me this,' he said. 'Did Joanna mean knowingly to create life within the dance? Why did the child die? Who was the father?'

'Because its heart was too great, perhaps, or its body too feeble: how should I know?' his grandfather answered. 'She married a man who was reckoned knowledgeable, but he led an evil life and he was a plaything compared to Joanna. She longed to adore him, and she could only mock at him and herself. Yet she was fierce for him after the flesh, and she made him her child's father and hated him for his feebleness. She would strike and taunt him while the child was in her womb—for love and anger and hate and scorn and fear. The child was a seven-months child, and it died. The father ran away from her the day before it was born, and the same night was killed in a street accident when he was drunk. But Joanna, when she heard that the child was dead, screamed once and her face changed, and the Tarot cards that she sought (as we have all done), and the myth of gods that she studied, and the child that should have been a lord of power and was instead a five-hours-old body of death—these tangled themselves in her brain for ever; and for fifty years she has sought the thing that she calls Osiris because it dies and Horus because it lives and at night little sweet names which only Stephen hears. And it has one and twenty faces, which are the faces of them within and of the Tarots, and when she finds the limbs that have been torn apart by her enemy, who is her husband and is Set and is we who seek the cards also, she thinks she will again become the Queen of Heaven, and the twice twenty-one gods shall adore her with incense and chanting. No doubt she is mad, Henry, but I had rather deal with your other mad creature than with her.'

Henry meditated for some time, walking about the room in silence; then he said, 'Well, there's no reason why she should hear of it, unless she snuffs the news up out of the air.'

'She may even do that,' Aaron said. 'Her life is not as ours, and the air and the lords of the sceptres are one.'

'In any case, I don't see what she can do to interfere with us,' Henry answered. 'She had her chance and lost it. I will see that I don't lose mine. As for Coningsby——' He walked up and down the room for a few minutes in silence; then he said, 'I've a good mind to try and get them here for Christmas. It's a month off—that ought to give me time. You could manage, I suppose?'

'What good would that be?' his grandfather asked.

Henry sat down again. 'Why, it's clear,' he said, 'that we shall have to let them know something—Nancy and her father anyhow. If he's got to give us the cards he's got to have a reason for doing it, and so far as I can see——'

'You're not going to show him *them*?' Aaron exclaimed, glancing over his shoulder at the door of the inner room.

'Why not?' Henry asked lightly. 'What does it matter? There're all sorts of explanations. Besides, I want to show Nancy, and she'll be able to work on him better if he's seen them.'

'But he'll tell people!' Aaron protested.

'What can he tell them?' Henry asked. 'And, if he does, who's to believe him? Besides—after we've got the cards … well, we don't know what we can do, do we? I'm sure that's the best. See, I'll ask Nancy—and she'll bring her aunt, I suppose——'

'Her aunt?' Aaron interrupted sharply. 'How many are you going to bring? Who is this aunt?'

'Her aunt,' Henry said, 'is just the opposite to her father. As serene and undisturbed as … as *they* are. Nothing puts her out; nothing disturbs her. Yet she isn't a fool. She'll be quite harmless, however: it won't matter whether she sees or not. She'll be interested, but not concerned. Well, Nancy and her aunt and her father. I'll try and dodge the brother; he's simply a bore. There'll be the three of them, and me; say, for—Christmas Day's on a Saturday, isn't it?—say, from Thursday to Tuesday, or a day or two longer. Well?'

'But will he come?' Aaron asked doubtfully.

'I think he may,' Henry said. 'Oh, of course he won't want to, but, as he won't want to do anything else in particular, it may be possible to work it. Only you'd better keep Joanna out of the way.'

'I don't know in the least where she is,' the old man said irritably.

'Can't you find out by the cards?' Henry smiled. 'Or must you wait for the Tarots?' On the word his face changed, and he came near to the table. 'We will certainly have them,' he said in a low, firm voice. 'Who knows? perhaps we can find out what the Fool means, and why it doesn't dance.'

Aaron caught his sleeve. 'Henry,' he breathed, 'if—if there should be an accident—if there should—who would get the cards?'

'Don't be a fool,' Henry said roughly. 'Haven't you always told me that violence breaks the knowledge of the cards?'

'They told me so,' the old man answered reluctantly, 'but I don't see … anyhow, we needn't both….'

'Wait,' his grandson answered, and turned to pick up his coat. 'I must get back.' He stretched himself, and laughed a little. 'Nancy told me to have a good night,' he said, 'and here I am spending it talking to you.'

175

'Don't talk too much to these people of yours,' Aaron grumbled, 'Nancy or any of them.'

His grandson pulled on his coat. 'Nancy and I will talk to one another,' he said, 'and perhaps what we say shall be stranger talk than ever lovers had before. Good night. I will tell you what I can do about it all in London.'

CHAPTER III

THE SHUFFLING OF THE CARDS

The Coningsbys usually went to Eastbourne for Christmas. The habit had been begun because Mr. Coningsby had discovered that he preferred hotel life for those few days to having his own house treated as an hotel. Groups of young people would arrive at any hour of day or night, and Nancy or Ralph, if in, would leap up and rush to welcome them, or, if not in, would arrive soon after, inquiring for friends who had already disappeared. Mr. Coningsby disapproved strongly, but for once found himself helpless, so sudden was the rush; he therefore preferred to be generous and give everyone a thorough change. It was never quite clear whether he regarded this as on his sister's account chiefly or on his children's. She was supposed to need it, but they were supposed to enjoy it, and so after the first year they all went back each Christmas to the same hotel, and Mr. Coningsby put up with playing bridge and occasionally observing the revels and discussing civilization with other gentlemen of similar good nature.

It annoyed him slightly at times that Sybil never seemed quite grateful enough for the mere change—as change. Even the profound content in which she normally seemed to have her being—'sluggish, sluggish,' Mr. Coningsby said to himself when he thought of it, and walked a little more briskly—even that repose must surely be all the pleasanter for a change. There were always some nice women about for her to talk to. Of course, she was pleased to go—but not sufficiently pleased to gratify Mr. Coningsby: he was maddened by that continuous equable delight. She enjoyed everything—and he, he enjoyed nothing.

But this year things were different—had got, or anyhow were going, to be different. It had begun with Ralph, who, rather confusedly, had intimated that he was going to have a still more thorough change by going off altogether with some friend of his whose people lived somewhere near Lewes. Mr. Coningsby had not said much, or did not seem to himself to have done so, but he had made it clear that he disliked such secession from the family life. To summer holidays spent with friends he had (he hoped) never objected, but Christmas was different. Christmas was, in fact, the time when Mr. Coningsby most nearly realized the passage of time and the approach of age and death. For Christmas every year had been marked by small but definite changes, through his own childhood, his youth, his marriage, his children's infancy and childhood, and now there were only two possibilities of change—the coming of a third generation or the stopping of Christmas. Each year that Mr. Coningsby succeeded in keeping Nancy and Ralph by him for Christmas postponed either unwelcome change, and enabled him to enter the New Year with the pretence that it was merely the Old Year beginning over again. But this year his friend's death had already shaken him, and if he and Sybil and Nancy—an engaged Nancy—were to be without Ralph, the threat of an inevitable solitude would loom very near. There would be a gap, and he had nothing with which to fill the gap or to meet what might come through it; nothing except the fact that he was a Warden in Lunacy, and had all the privileges of a Warden—such as going in to dinner before the elder sons of younger sons of peers. He did not know where, years before, he had picked up that bit of absurd knowledge, in what odd table of precedence, but he knew it was so, and had even mentioned it once to Sybil. But all the elder sons of younger sons of peers whose spectres he could crowd into that gap did not seem to fill it. There was an emptiness brought to mind, and only brought to mind, for it was always there, though he forgot it. He filled it with his office, his occupation, his family, his house, his friends, his politics, his food, his sleep, but sometimes the emptiness was too big to be filled thus, and sometimes it rolled up on him, along the street when he left the home in the morning, blowing in at evening through the open window or creeping up outside when it was shut, or even sometimes looking ridiculously at him in the unmeaning headlines of his morning paper. 'Prime Minister', he would read, 'Announces Fresh Oil Legislation'—and the words would be for one second all separate and meaningless—'Prime Minister'—what was a Prime Minister? Blur, blot, nothingness, and then again the breakfast-table and *The Times* and Sybil.

Ralph's announced defection therefore induced him unconsciously to desire to make a change for himself, and induced him again to meet more equably than he otherwise might have done Nancy's tentative hints about the possibility of the rest of them going to Henry's grandfather. It didn't strike him as being a very attractive suggestion for himself, but it offered him every chance of having Nancy and Henry as well as Ralph to blame for his probable discomfort or boredom or gloom, and therefore of lessening a concentration on Ralph, Ralph's desertion, change, age—and the other thing. Sybil, when he consulted her, was happy to find him already half-reconciled to the proposal.

'I'm afraid it'll be very dull for you,' he said.

'O, I don't think so,' she answered. 'It'll have to be very dull indeed if it is.'

'And of course we don't know what the grandfather's like,' he added.

'He's presumably human,' Sybil said, 'so he'll be interesting somehow.'

'Really, Sybil,' Mr. Coningsby answered, almost crossly, 'you do say the most ridiculous things. As if everybody was interesting.'

'Well, I think everybody is,' Sybil protested, 'and things apart from their bodies we don't know, do we? And considering what funny, lovely things bodies are, I'm not especially anxious to leave off knowing them.'

Her brother kept the conversation straight. 'I gather that he's old but quite active still, not bedridden or anything.'

'Then we shan't be expected to sit with him,' Sybil said happily, 'and, as Nancy and Henry certainly wouldn't want to, you and I will be much freer.'

'If I thought I was expected to sit with a senile old man——' Mr. Coningsby said in alarm, 'but Henry implied that he'd got all his faculties. Have you heard anything?'

'Good heavens, no!' said Sybil, and, being in what her brother called one of her perverse moods, added, 'I love that phrase.'

'What phrase?' Mr. Coningsby asked, having missed anything particular.

'Good heavens,' Sybil repeated, separating the words. 'It says everything almost, doesn't it? I don't like to say "Good God" too often; people so often misunderstand.'

'Sometimes you talk exactly in Nancy's irresponsible way, Sybil,' her brother complained. 'I don't see any sense in it. Why should one want to say "Good God"?'

'Well, there isn't really much else to say, is there?' Sybil asked, and added hastily, 'No, my dear, I'm sorry, I was only....' She hesitated for a word.

'I know you were,' Mr. Coningsby said, as if she had found it, 'but I don't think jokes of that kind are in the best of taste. It's possible to be humorous without being profane.'

'I beg your pardon, Lothair,' Sybil said meekly. She tried her best not to call her brother 'Lothair,' because that was one of the things which seemed to him to be profane without being humorous. But it was pain and grief to her; there wasn't all that time to enjoy everything in life as it should be enjoyed, and the two of them could have enjoyed that ridiculous name so much better together. However, since she loved him, she tried not to force the good God's richness of wonder too much on his attention, and so she went on hastily, 'Nancy's looking forward to it so much.'

'At her age,' Mr. Coningsby remarked, 'one naturally looks forward.'

'And at ours,' Sybil said, 'when there isn't the time there isn't the necessity: the present's so entirely satisfactory.'

Mr. Coningsby just stopped himself saying, 'Good God,' with quite a different intonation. He waited a minute or two and said, 'You know Henry's offered to take us down in his car?'

'Nice of him,' Sybil answered, and allowed herself to become involved in a discussion of what her brother would or would not take: at the end of which he suddenly said, 'O, and by the way, you might look through those packs of cards and put in a few of the most interesting—and the catalogue—especially the set we were looking at the other evening. Nancy asked me; it seems there are some others down there, and Henry and she want to compare them. A regular gipsy taste! But if it amuses them.... He's promised to show her some tricks.'

'Then I hope,' Miss Coningsby said, 'that Nancy won't try to show them to us before she's practised them. Not that I mind being surprised in an unintentional way, but it'd show a state of greater sanctity on her part.'

'Sanctity!' Mr. Coningsby uttered derisively. 'Nancy's not very near sanctity.'

'My dear, she's in love,' his sister exclaimed.

'And what's that got to do with sanctity?' Mr. Coningsby asked triumphantly, and enjoyed the silence to which Sybil sometimes found herself driven. Anyone who didn't realize the necessary connexion between love and sanctity left her incapable of explanation.

'Tricks' was hardly the word which Nancy would have used that same evening, though it was one which Henry himself had used to her a week or so before. It wanted still some ten days to Christmas, and in the fortnight that had elapsed since the examination of the late Mr. Duncannon's legacy the subject of the cards had cropped up several times between the two young people. Nancy had the natural, alert interest of youth, as Sybil had the—perhaps supernatural—vivid interest of age, and Henry's occasional rather mysterious remarks had provoked it still more. She had, in fact, examined the cards by herself, and re-read the entry in the catalogue, and looked up 'Tarot' in the encyclopædia without being much more advanced. As she sat now coiled in front of the dining-room fire, playing gently with her lover's fingers, at once stirred and soothed by the contact, she suddenly twisted round to face him in the deep chair to her right.

'But, Henry, dearest, what is it you mean?' she said. 'You keep on talking of these cards as if they were important.'

'So they are,' Henry answered. 'Exactly how important depends on you, perhaps.'

Nancy sat up on her heels. 'Henry,' she said, 'are you teasing me or are you not? If you are, you're not human at all; you're a black-maned devil from Hell, and I've got engaged to you by the worst mistake that ever happened. And if you're not, then show some pity, and leave off talking like a doctor about some bit of my inside that I don't understand. How and why and when and where and what have I got to do with the cards? If you don't tell me, I shall go straight down to father and say you've insulted me.'

'Then you don't know what you'd miss,' Henry said.

Nancy threw out her arms. 'O wretched me!' she cried dramatically. 'Henry, if I pretend I don't want to know, are you sure you'll play up? You won't take a mean advantage, will you?'

'If you really don't want to know,' he told her, 'I certainly won't tell you. That's the whole point. Do you *really*want to know?'

'Have I bared my heart to have it mistrusted?' she said. 'Must I pine away in an hour or so to persuade you? Or will it do if I sob myself to sleep on the spot? As I used *not* to say when we did *Julius Cæsar* at school, if you don't tell me, "Portia is Brutus' harlot, not his wife." What a nasty little cad and cat Portia was—to squeeze it out of him like that! But I swear I'll give myself a wound "here in the thigh" unless you *do* tell me, and bleed to death all over your beautiful trousers.'

He took her hand in his so strongly that her eyes changed to immediate gravity.

'If you want to know,' he said, 'I will tell you what I can here; and the rest—there. If you can bear it.'

'Do as you will,' she answered seriously. 'If it's no joke, then try me and let me go if I fail. At that,' she added with a sudden smile, 'I think I won't fail.'

'Then bring the Tarot cards now, if you can,' he said. 'But quietly. I don't want the others to know.'

'They're out—father and Ralph,' she answered. 'I will go and get them,' and on the word was away from the room.

For the few minutes that elapsed before she returned he stood looking absently before him, so that he did not at once hear her entrance, and her eyes took him in, his frown, his concentrated gaze, the hand that made slight unpurposed movements by his side. As she looked, she herself unconsciously disposed herself to meet him, and she came across the room to him with something in her of preparation, as if, clear and splendid, she came to her bridal; nor did they smile as they met, though it was the first time in their mutual acquaintance that so natural a sweetness had been lacking. He took the cards from her, and then, laying his hand on her shoulder, lightly compelled her towards the large table in the middle of the room. Then he drew the cards from their case, which he threw carelessly from him to the floor, and began to separate them into five piles.

'Look,' he said, 'these are the twenty-two cards—the twenty-one and the one which is nothing—that we looked at the other night. Those are the Greater Trumps, and there's nothing to tell you about them now; they must wait till another time. But these others are the four suits, and you will see what we did not carefully look at then—they're not the usual designs, not clubs and spades and hearts and diamonds, but staffs or sceptres, and swords and cups and coins—or deniers: those last are shaped sometimes as pentacles, but this is the better marking. And see—there are fourteen and not thirteen in each suit, for besides the Knave and Queen and King there is in these the Knight: so that here, for instance, are the Knave—or Esquire—of sceptres, and the Knight, Queen, and King of sceptres; and so with the swords, the cups, and the deniers. Look, here they are.'

She bent above them, watching, and after a moment he went on.

'Now these cards are the root and origin of all cards, and no one knows from where they came, for the tale is that they were first heard of among the gipsies in Spain in the thirteenth century. Some say they are older, and some even talk of Egypt, but that matters very little. It isn't the time behind them, but the process in them, that's important. There are many packs of Tarot cards, but the one original pack, which is this, has a secret behind it that I will show you on Christmas Eve. Because of that secret this pack, and this only, is a pack of great might.'

He paused again, and still she made no movement. He glanced at her hands resting on the edge of the table, and resumed.

'All things are held together by correspondence, image with image, movement with movement: without that there could be no relation and therefore no truth. It is our business—especially yours and mine—to take up the power of relation. Do you know what I mean?'

As she suddenly looked up at him, she almost smiled.

'Darling,' she murmured, 'how couldn't I know *that*? I didn't need the cards to tell me. Ah, but go on: show me what it means in them.'

For another second he paused, arrested: it was as if she had immediately before her something which he sought far off. A little less certainly he again went on, his voice recovering itself almost immediately.

'There is in these suits a great relation to the four compacted elements of the created earth, and you shall find the truth of this now, if you choose, and if the tales told among my people and the things that were written down among them are true. This pack has been hidden from us for more than two centuries, and for all that time no one, I think, can have tried it till to-night. The latest tale we know of is that once, under Elizabeth, a strange ancestor of mine, who had fled to England from the authority of the King of Spain, raised the winds which blew the Armada northward past Scotland.'

Nancy wrinkled her forehead as he paused. 'Do you mean,' she began, 'do you mean that he … I'm sorry, darling, I don't seem to understand. How could he raise the winds?'

'"The beating of the cards is the wind",' he answered, 'but don't try and believe it now. Think of it as a fable, but think that on some point of the sea-shore one of those wild fugitives stood by night and shook these cards—these'—he laid his hand on the heap of the suit of staffs or sceptres—'and beat the air with them till he drove it into tumult and sent the great blasts over the seas to drive the ships of King Philip to wreck and destruction. See that in your mind; can you?'

'I can,' she said. 'It's a mad picture, but I can.'

He stooped to pick up the case, and restored to it the swords, the staffs, and the cups, and the Greater Trumps, all in silence; then he laid it by, and took up the suit of deniers, or coins, or pentacles.

'Now,' he said, smiling at her, 'shall we see what your hands and mine can do?'

'Tell me,' she answered.

He gave the fourteen cards to her, and, standing close by her, he made her hold them in both hands and laid his own over hers. 'Now listen,' he said in her ear, speaking slowly and commandingly; 'you will think of earth, garden-mould, the stuff of the fields, and the dry dust of the roads: the earth your flowers grow in, the earth to which our bodies are given, the earth which in one shape or another makes the land as parted from the waters. Will you do as I say?'

Very serious, she looked up at him. 'Yes, Henry,' she said, and her voice lingered a little on the second word, as if she gave herself so the more completely to his intention. He said again: 'Earth, earth of growing and decaying things—fill your mind with the image of it. And let your hands be ready to shuffle the cards. Hold them securely but lightly, and if they seem to move let them have their way. Help them; help them to slide and shuffle. I put my hands over yours; are you afraid?'

She answered quite simply, 'Need I be?'

'Never at all,' he said, 'neither now nor hereafter. Don't be afraid; these things can be known, and it's good for us to know them. Now—begin.'

She bent her mind to its task, a little vaguely at first, but soon more definitely. She filled it with the thought of the garden, the earth that made it up, dry dust sometimes, sometimes rich loam—the worms that crawled in it and the roots of the flowers thrusting down—no, not worms and roots—earth, deep thick earth. Great tree-roots going deep into it—along the roots her mind penetrated into it, along the dividing, narrowing, dwindling roots, all the crannies and corners filled with earth, rushing up into her shoulder-pits, her elbows sticking out, little bumps on those protracted roots. Mould clinging together, falling apart; a spade splitting it, almost as if thrust into her thoughts, a spadeful of mould. Digging—holes, pits, mines, tunnels, graves—no, those things were not *earth*. Graves—the bodies in them being made one with the earth about them, so that at last there was no difference. Earth to earth—she herself earth; body, shoulders, limbs, earth in her arms, in her hands.

There were springs, deep springs, cisterns and wells and rivers of water down in the earth, water floating in rocky channels or oozing through the earth itself; the earth covering, hampering, stifling them, they bursting upwards through it. No, not water—*earth*. Her feet clung to it, were feeling it, were strangely drawing it up into themselves, and more and more and higher and higher that sensation of unity with the stuff of her own

179

foundation crept. There were rocks, but she was not a rock—not yet; something living, like an impatient rush of water, was bubbling up within her, but she felt it as an intrusion into the natural part of her being. Her lips were rough against each other; her face must be stained and black. She almost put up her wrist to brush the earth from her cheek—not her hand, for that also was dirty; her fingers felt the grit. They were, both hands, breaking and rubbing a lump of earth between them; they were full and heaped with earth that was slipping over them and sliding between the fingers, and she was trying to hold it in—not to let it escape.

'Gently, gently,' a voice murmured in her ear. The sound brought her back with a start, and dispelled the sensation that held her; she saw again the cards in her hands, and saw now that her hands, with Henry's lying over them, were shuffling the cards, each moment more quickly. She was trying to keep up with the movement, she wasn't initiating it—and that feeling of earth escaping was in fact only this compulsion which the cards were exercising. They were sliding out and sliding back—now she saw the four of deniers on top, and now the ace, and now the Esquire, and now the King, a hatted figure, with a four-forked beard, holding the coin—or whatever it was—in a gloved hand. It shone up at her, and a card from below slipped out, and her fingers thrust it back, and it covered the King—the nine of deniers. A slight sound reached her—a curious continuous sound, yet hardly a sound at all, a faint rustle. The cards *were* gritty, or her hands were; or was it the persistent rubbing of her palms against the edges of the cards? What was that rustling noise? It wasn't her mere fancy, nor was it mere fancy that some substance was slipping between her fingers. Below her hands and the cards she saw the table, and some vague unusualness in it attracted her. It was black— well, of course, but a dull heavy black, and down to it from her hands a kind of cloud was floating. It was from there that the first sound came; it was something falling—it was earth, a curtain, a rain of earth falling, falling, covering the part of the table immediately below, making little sliding sounds—earth, real black earth.

'Steady,' said the voice in her ear. She had a violent impulse to throw the cards away from her—if she could, if she could rend her hands from them, but of course she couldn't: they, earthy as they were, belonged to this other earth, the earth that was slipping everywhere over and between her fingers, that was already covering the six of deniers as it slid over the two. But there were other hands; hers weren't alone; she pressed them back into her lover's, and said, keeping her voice as steady as she could: 'Couldn't we stop?'

Breath deeply drawn answered her: then Henry's voice. 'Yes,' it said. 'Steady, steady. Think with me, think of the cards—cards—drawings—just drawings—line and colour. Press them back, harder: use your hands now—harder.'

It was as if a brief struggle took place between her hands and that which they held: as if the thing refused to be governed and dominated. But it yielded; if there had been any struggle, it ceased. Her strong hands pressed back the cards, pushed them level; her thumb flicked them. Henry's hands left hers and took the suit. She let hers drop, took a step away, and looked at the table. There lay on it a little heap of what seemed like garden mould.

Faintness caught her; she swayed. Henry's arm round her took her to a chair. She gasped out, 'I'm all right. Stop a minute,' and held on to the arm. 'It's nothing,' she said to herself, 'it's quite simple. It's only that I'm not used to it—whatever it is.' That it was any kind of trick did not even enter her mind; Henry and that sort of trick could not exist together. Earth on the dining-room table. Aunt Sybil would wonder why it was there. She deliberately opened her eyes again, and her mouth opened in spite of her. It was still there.

'All right?' Henry's voice said.

Nancy made a great effort. 'Yes,' she said. 'Henry, what's happened? I mean——'

'You're frightened!' he said accusingly.

'I'm not frightened,' she said.

'If you are, I can't tell you anything,' he said. 'I can't share with you unless you want me to. This is only the beginning: you'd better understand that at once.'

'Yes, darling,' she said. 'Don't be cross with me. It's a little sudden, isn't it? Is it … is it real?'

He picked up some of the earth and scattered it again.

'Quite,' he said. 'You could grow evergreens in it.'

'Then,' said Nancy, with a slightly hysterical note in her voice, 'I think you'd better ring for Agnes to clear it up.'

'Touch it,' he said, 'feel it, be sure it's real.'

'I wouldn't touch it for anything,' she exclaimed. 'Do ring, Henry. I want to see Agnes taking it away in a dustpan. That'll prove it's real.'

Agnes indeed removed it in a dustpan, without any other emotion than a slight surprise and a slight perplexity. It was clear that she couldn't think what Miss Nancy and her young man had been about; but it was also clear that she supposed whatever they had been about had resulted in a small heap of earth on the dining-room table, which she efficiently removed, and then herself disappeared. Nancy lay back in her chair, and there was a complete silence for a long time.

At last she stirred and looked at Henry. 'Tell me now,' she said.

He leaned against the mantelpiece, looking down on her. 'I've told you,' he answered. 'I told you at first; at least, I hinted at it. There is correspondence everywhere; but some correspondences are clearer than others. Between these cards'—he pointed to the leather case in which he had replaced the denier suit—'and the activities of things there is a very close relation....'

She broke in. 'Yes, darling; don't explain it, just tell me,' she said. 'What you said about the wind, and this, and everything.'

'Earth, water, air, and fire,' he said. 'Deniers, cups, sceptres, swords. When the hands of a man deal in a certain way with the cards, the living thing comes to exist.'

She looked down at the hands that lay in her lap. 'Hands,' she said. 'Can they do it?'

'They can do anything,' he said. 'They have power.'

'But why the cards…?' she asked.

He smiled at her, and suddenly she threw out her arms to him and he leant and caught her in his own. The movement gathered her, but it was she who was raised from her chair, not he who was brought down to that other level, and even while he murmured to her his voice was charged with an exultant energy, and when upon her moving he loosed her at last there was in his action something of one who lays down a precious instrument till it shall be required. Or, since he kept his eyes on her, something of one who watches a complex and delicate piece of machinery to see if everything runs smoothly, and the experiment for which it is meant may be safely dared.

Nancy patted her hair and sat down again. 'Next time,' she said, 'I shall be more prepared.'

'There is to be a next time?' he asked, testing a screw in the machinery.

Her eyes were seriously upon him. 'If you choose,' she said, 'and you will, won't you? If you want me to help, I will. But next time perhaps you'd better tell me more about it first. Why *does* it happen?'

'I don't know why,' he said, 'but how is clear enough. These cards are in touch with a thing I'll show you at Christmas, and they're in touch with … well, there aren't any words for it—with the Dance.'

'The Dance?' she asked.

'The Dance that is … everything,' he answered. 'You'll see. Earth, air, fire, water—and the Greater Trumps. There's a way to all knowledge and prophecy, when the cards and they are brought together. But, O Nancy, Nancy, if you'll see what I see and want what I want, there's a way—if it can be found, there's a way.' He caught her hands in his. 'Hands,' he cried, 'hands among *them* and all that they mean. Feel it; give it to me; take it.'

She burned back to his ardour. 'What will you do?' she asked, panting.

He held her hands more tightly. 'Who knows?' he answered, rising on the wings of his own terrific dream. 'Create.'

———————————————

CHAPTER IV

THE CHARIOT

On the Wednesday before Christmas, Henry had arranged to take the Coningsbys to his grandfather's house. Mr. Coningsby had decided to give them a week of his Christmas vacation from the preoccupations of a Warden in Lunacy, and Henry was very willing that the chances of those critical days should have so long a period in which to be tested. The strange experiment which he and Nancy had tried had left him in a high state of exaltation; he felt his delight in her as a means to his imagined end. Of its effect upon Nancy herself he found it difficult to judge: she did not refer to it again, and was generally rather more silent with him than was her wont. But his own preoccupations were intense, and it may be it was rather his preoccupation than her own which shrouded and a little constrained her. To the outer world, however, she carried herself much as usual, and only Sybil Coningsby noted that her gaiety was at times rather a concealment than a manifestation. But then among that group only Sybil was aware of how many natural capacities are found to be but concealments, how many phenomena disappear before the fact remains. It was long since in her own life the search had begun; with eyes that necessarily veiled their passion she saw in her niece the opening of some other abyss in that first abyss which was love. Mr. Coningsby had spoken more truly than he thought when he accused Sybil of an irresponsibility not unlike Nancy's; their natures answered each other across the years. But between them lay the experience of responsibility, that burden which is only given in order to be relinquished, that task put into the hands of man in order that his own choice may render it back to its creator, that yoke which, once wholly lifted and put on, is immediately no longer to be worn. Sybil had lifted and relinquished it; from the freedom of a love more single than Nancy's she smiled at the young initiate who from afar in her untrained innocence beheld the conclusion of all initiations.

She stood now on the steps of the house and smiled at Henry, who was beside her. Nancy was in the hall; Mr. Coningsby was telephoning some last-minute instructions in lunacy to the custodians of lunacy who were for a while to occupy the seat of the warden. Ralph had gone off that morning. It was late afternoon; the weather was cold and fine.

Sybil said: 'Have I thanked you for taking us down, Henry?'

He answered, his voice vibrating with great expectation, 'It's a delight, Aunt Sybil: mayn't I call you that too?'

She inclined her head to the courtesy, and her eyes danced at him as she said, 'For Nancy's sake or mine?'

'For all our sakes,' he answered. 'But you're very difficult to know, aren't you? You never seem to move.'

'Simeon Stylites?' she asked. 'Do I crouch on a tall pillar in the sky? What an inhuman picture!'

'I think you are a little inhuman,' he said. 'You're everything that's nice, of course, but you're terrifying as well.'

'Alas, poor aunt!' she said. 'But nowadays I thought maiden aunts were nothing uncommon?'

'A maiden aunt——' he began and stopped abruptly. Then he went on with a note of wonder in his voice, 'That's it, you know; that's exactly it. You're strange, you're maiden, you're a mystery of self-possession.'

She broke into a laugh, almost as delightful, even to him, as Nancy's. 'Henry, *mon vieux*,' she said, 'what do you know about old women?'

'Enough to know you're not one,' he said. 'Aunt Sybil—Sibyl—your very name means you. You're the marvel of virginity that rides in the Zodiac.'

'That,' she said, 'is a most marvellous compliment. If I wasn't in furs I'd curtsey. You'll make me wish myself Nancy's age—for one evening.'

'I think it's long,' he said, 'since you have wished yourself anything but what you are.'

She was prevented from answering by Mr. Coningsby, who hurried Nancy out before him on to the steps and shut the door. They all went down to the car, and a policeman on the pavement saluted Mr. Coningsby as he passed.

'Good evening, good evening, constable,' he said. 'Here.' Something passed. 'A merry Christmas.'

'Gracious,' Nancy said in Henry's ear, 'father's almost jovial.'

'That,' Henry answered, 'is because he doesn't regard the police as human. He'd never be harsh to a dog or a poor man. It's those of his own kind that trouble and fret him.'

'Well, darling,' she said, 'I've never heard you speak of standing a policeman a drink.' She slipped her hand into his. 'O, I'm so thrilled,' she went on, 'what with you and Christmas and … and all. Is that policeman part of it, do you think? Is he in the sceptres or the swords? Or is he one of your mysterious Trumps?'

'What about the Emperor?' Henry threw at her, as Mr. Coningsby, who had stopped to speak to the constable, probably about the safety of the house, came to the car. Sybil was already in her seat. Nancy slipped into hers, as Mr. Coningsby got in next to Sybil: Henry closed the door, sprang in, and started the car.

There was silence at first. To each of them the movement of the car meant something different and particular; to the two men it was movement *to* something, to the two women it was much more like movement *in* something. Mr. Coningsby felt it as a rush towards an immediate future to which he had been compelled and in which he gloomily expected defeat. Henry's desire swept on to a future in which he expected trial and victory. But to Nancy and Sybil separately the future could not be imagined except as a blessed variation on what they knew; there was nowhere to go but to that in which they each existed, and the time they took to go was only the measure of delight changing into delight. In that enclosed space a quadruple movement of consciousness existed, and became, through the unnoticeable, infinitesimal movements of their bodies, involved and, to an extent, harmonized. Each set up against each of the others a peculiar strain; each was drawn back and controlled by the rest. Knowledge danced with knowledge, sometimes to trouble, sometimes to appease, the corporeal instruments of the days of their flesh.

A policeman's hand held them up. Henry gestured towards it. 'Behold the Emperor,' he said to Nancy.

'You're making fun of me, my dear,' she half protested.

'Never less,' he said seriously. 'Look at him.'

She looked, and, whether the hours she had given to brooding over the Tarots during the last few days, partly to certify her courage to herself, had imposed their forms on her memory, or whether something in the policeman's shape and cloak under the lights of the dark street suggested it, or whether indeed something common to Emperor and Khalif, cadi and magistrate, prætor and alcalde, lictor and constable, shone before her in those lights—whichever was true, it was certainly true that for a moment she saw in that heavy official barring their way the Emperor of the Trumps, helmed, in a white cloak, stretching out one sceptred arm, as if Charlemagne, or one like him, stretched out his controlling sword over the tribes of Europe pouring from the forests and bade them pause or march as he would. The great roads ran below him, to Rome, to Paris, to Aix, to Byzantium, and the nations established themselves in cities upon them. The noise of all the pausing street came to her as the roar of many peoples; the white cloak held them by a gesture; order and law were there. It moved, it fell aside, the torrent of obedient movement rolled on, and they with it. They flashed past the helmed face, and she found that she had dropped her eyes lest she should see it.

With the avoidance of that face she seemed to have plunged herself deeper into the dream, as if by avoiding it she had assented to it and had acknowledged its being and power. They were not stopped again, but yet, as the car ran smoothly on, she seemed to see that white-clothed arm again and again, now in the darkness beyond the headlights, now pointing forward just outside the window. The streets were busy with Christmas shoppers, but the car shut them out and her in, and, though they were there, it was running steadily away from them—as if down a sloping road while they were all on the high level banks on either hand. They never actually did go down that road, but—as in nightmare—they were always on the very point of plunging. Nancy held desperately to her recollection of a car and a policeman and Henry; she was really beginning to pull herself together when suddenly—somewhere on the outskirts of London—the car slowed for a moment outside the gate of a large building. Over the gate was a light, and under the light was a nurse holding a big key. A gate—a light—a nurse; yet one lobe of her brain showed her again a semblance of one of the Tarot cards—ceremonial robes; imperial head-dress, cloak falling like folded wings, proud, austere face lifted towards where in the arch of the gate, so that the light just caught it, was a heraldic carving of some flying creature. Someone, somewhere—perhaps her father behind her—grunted a little, and the grunt seemed to her as if it were wrung from a being in profound pain. And then the car quickened again, and they were flying into the darkness, and away in the roads behind them was that sovereign figure and the sound of a suffering world coming up to it out of the night.

She would have liked to speak to Henry, but she couldn't. She and he were in the same car, side by side, only she wasn't at all clear that there was anyone else in the car at all, or that it was a car, that it was anything but herself mysteriously defined to her own knowledge. She was in a trance; the car, though moving, was still—poised, rushing and motionless at once, at the entrance to a huge, deep, and dark defile, from which on either side the mighty figures rose, themselves at once swift and still, and fled past her and yet were for ever there. Indefinable, they defined; they made and held steady the path that was stretched for her. It was a cloud; it was the moon; it was vapour and illusion—or it was the white cloak of the Emperor and the clear cold face of the Empress, as she had seen them when she pored over the Greater Trumps. But the darkness of the low defile awaited her; deeper and deeper, motionless and rushing on, they—she and her companions— were sinking into it. She dared not speak to Henry; he was there, but he was guiding the car; if he were distracted for a moment they might all crash into utter ruin. She let herself take one side-glance at him, a supplication in her heart, but never a finger stirring; and, even as she saw his face, she remembered to have seen it elsewhere. There was a painting—somewhere—of a chariot, driven by some semi-Greek figure scourging on two sphinxes who drew that car, and the face in the painting was Henry's. Henry's, and yet there was a difference … there was some other likeness: was it (most fantastic of all dreams!) her aunt? The faces, the figures, all rushed together suddenly; something that was neither nurse nor policeman, Empress nor Emperor, Sybil nor Henry, sphinx nor charioteer, grew out of and possessed them all. It was this to which they were rushing, some form that was immediately to be revealed, some face that would grow out of….

The car slowed, wheeled as if sweeping round a curve in the road, and suddenly—despite herself—she screamed. For there, with light full on it, thrown up in all its terrible detail, gaunt, bare, and cold, was a man, or the image of a man, hanging by his hands, his body thrust out from the pole that held it, his head dropping to one side, and on it a dreadful tangled head-dress. It hung there right before her, and she only knew that it was the wrong way up—the head should have been below; it was always so in the cards, the Hanged Man upside down. But here the Hanged Man was, livid and outstretched before her, his head decked but above. She screamed and woke. At least, everyone supposed she woke. Henry was solicitous and her father was irritable, and, after all, it was only a village war memorial with a rather badly done crucifix.

They took her away from it and Henry comforted her, and she settled down again, apologizing with the most utter shame. A bad dream, of course.

'Darling, of course it was,' Henry murmured.

'Of course it was,' her father snapped.

'Of course it is,' Sybil Coningsby said. 'One wakes, Nancy.'

So then they went on again, and, except for one other unusual incident—but that was certainly not a dream—reached their destination undisturbed. The incident indeed occurred not far away.

The car had slid through a village—the nearest village to his grandfather's, Henry told them, and at that a couple of miles away. It had issued thence past the church and rectory on to an upland road, and climbed steadily across the Downs. Mr. Coningsby looked out at the winter darkness and shuddered, thinking of London, Eastbourne, and the next five or six days. Henry had just looked over his shoulder to say 'Not far now,' much as one of Dante's demons might have spoken to a soul he was conducting to its particular circle in Hell. He looked back, swore, and jammed on the brakes. The car protested, slid, and came to a standstill. Six feet in front of it an old woman squatted on the ground, right in the middle of the road. Two feet behind her stood a tall, rough-looking young fellow, as if waiting.

'Good God!' said Mr. Coningsby.

The old woman was apparently speaking, but, shut in the car, they could not hear. Henry opened the door and jumped out. Mr. Coningsby opened his window; Nancy and Sybil instinctively did the same.

'Welcome home, Henry!' the old creature said, in a high shrill voice. Henry took a couple of steps forward—the unknown man moved level with the squatting hag. In the lights of the car she was seen to be very old, shrivelled, and brown. She was wrapped head and body in a stained shawl that had once been red; one foot, which was thrust out from under a ragged skirt, wore a man's heavy boot. She pushed a hand out from beneath the shawl and waggled the skinny fingers at Henry as if in grotesque greeting.

'What are you doing here?' he asked fiercely.

'He, he!' the grotesque being tittered at him. 'I've come to see Aaron, Henry. I'm very tired. Won't you take me up in your grand coach? Me and Stephen. Good little Stephen—he takes care of his grandmother—his gran——' She went off into an indescribable fit of chuckling and choking. Henry looked at Stephen. 'Get her out of the way,' he said.

The man looked stupidly back. 'She does what she likes,' he said, and turned his eyes again on the old woman.

'Two nice ladies and one nice gentleman,' she babbled. 'Kind lady'—she peered at Nancy, who was leaning from the window—'kind lady, have your fortune told? He'—she jerked a thumb at Henry—'thinks he knows fortunes, but is he a goddess? Good luck to you, kind lady, to meet a goddess on the roads. Great good luck for you and your children to have a goddess tell you your doom.'

Henry said something in a low voice that the others couldn't hear. Sybil opened her door and got out of the car. Mr. Coningsby said sharply, 'Sybil, come back,' but she only threw him a smile and remained standing in the road. Most reluctantly he also got out. The hag put her head on one side and looked at them.

'Is the young miss afraid of the goddess?' she said. 'Or will she help me look? Blessings on whoever finds him.'

'Out of my way, Joanna,' Henry said, with anger in his voice.

'Henry dear,' Sybil said, 'is she going our way?'

He made a fierce gesture, but did not reply.

'Do you know her, Henry?' Mr. Coningsby said sharply.

'Father!' Nancy breathed, and touched his arm. 'Don't be cross with us; Henry couldn't help it.'

'Us,' Mr. Coningsby thought. 'You … us … O!'

'Do you want to come to the house?' Henry asked.

'What house?' she shrilled. 'Fields, rivers, sea—that's his house. Cover for you, beds for you, warmth for you, but my little one's cold!'

Henry looked over at his friends and made a sign to them that all would be well in a moment. The hag thrust her head on one side and looked up at him.

'If you know——' she cried, more wildly than before. 'Curses on you, Henry Lee, if you know and don't tell me. I'm an old fool, aren't I, and you're a clever man and a lawyer, but you've gone to live in houses and forgotten the great ones who live in the gipsy tents. And if you find so much as a shred of skin and don't tell me, so much as the place where a drop of blood has soaked into the ground and don't tell me, you shall be destroyed with the enemy when I and my son take joy in each other again. I'll curse you with my tongue and hands, I'll lay the spell on you, I'll——'

'Be quiet,' he said harshly. 'Who are _you_ to talk, Joanna, the old gipsy-woman?'

184

'Gipsy I was,' she said, 'and I'm something more now. Ha, little frightened ones! Ha, Henry Lee the accursed! Stephen! Stephen!'

'Aye, grandmother,' the man said.

'Say the answers, say the answers. Who am I?'

The man answered in a voice entirely devoid of meaning, 'A goddess are you.'

'What's the name of the goddess?' she shrilled.

'Isis the Wanderer,' he said mechanically.

'What does Isis the Wanderer seek?'

'The flesh and the bones and the heart of the dead,' he answered, and licked his lips.

'Where are the flesh and the bones and the heart of the dead?' she shrilled again.

'Here, there, everywhere,' he said.

'Good Stephen, good Stephen,' she muttered, appeased; and then suddenly scrambled to her feet. Henry jumped forward to interpose himself between her and the other women, and found himself in turn blocked by Stephen. They were on the point of closing with each other when Sybil's voice checked them.

'And where does the Divine Isis search?' she asked in a perfectly clear voice of urgent inquiry.

The old woman turned her eyes from Nancy to Sybil, and a look of delight came into her face. She took a step or two towards the other.

'Who are you,' she said, 'to speak as if you knew a goddess? Where have we seen each other?'

Sybil also moved a step forward. 'Perhaps in the rice-fields,' she said, 'or in the towns. I don't remember. Have you found anything that you look for?'

The old creature came nearer yet, and put out her hand as if to feel for Sybil's. In turn Miss Coningsby stretched out her own, and with those curiously linked hands they stood. Behind, on the one side, the two young men waited in an alert and mutually hostile watch; on the other, Mr. Coningsby, in a fever of angry hate, stood by Nancy at the car door; the Downs and the darkness stretched about them all.

'Aren't you a stranger and a Christian rat?' the hag said. 'How do you know the goddess when you meet her in Egypt?'

'Out of Egypt have I called my son,' Sybil said. 'Could you search for the god and not belong to his house?'

'Worship me then, worship me!' the insane thing cried out. 'Worship the Divine Isis!'

'Ah, but I've sworn only to worship the god,' Sybil answered gently. 'Let Isis forgive me, and let us look for the unity together.'

'They've parted him and torn him asunder,' the creature wailed. 'He was so pretty, so pretty, when he played with me once.'

'He will be so lovely when he is found,' Sybil comforted her. 'We'll certainly find him. Won't you come with me and look?'

The other threw up her head and snuffed the air. 'It's coming,' she said. 'I've smelt it for days and days. They're bringing him together—the winds and waters are bringing him. Go your way, stranger, and call me if you find him. I must be alone. Alone I am and alone I go. I'm the goddess.' She peered at Sybil. 'But I will bless you,' she said. 'Kneel down and I'll bless you.'

Mr. Coningsby made a sound more like a real Warden in Lunacy than ever in his life before as the tall furred figure of his sister obeyed. But Nancy's hand lay urgently on his shoulder, even had he meant to interfere. Sybil kneeled in the road, and the woman threw up her arms in the air over her, breaking into a torrent of incomprehensible, outlandish speech, which at the end changed again to English—' This is the blessing of Isis: go in peace. Stephen! Stephen!' He was by her in a moment. 'We'll go, Stephen—not with them, not to-night. Not to-night. I shall smell him, I shall know him, my baby, my Osiris. He was killed and he is coming. Horus, Horus, the coming of God!' She caught the young man by the arm, and hastily they turned and fled into the darkness. Sybil, unaided, rose to her feet. There was a silence, then she said charmingly, 'Henry, don't you think we might go on now?… It doesn't look as if we could be of any use.'

He came to hold the door for her. 'You've certainly done it,' he said. 'How did you know what to say to her?'

'I thought she talked very sensibly,' Sybil said, getting into the car. 'In her own way, of course. And I wish she'd come with us—that is, if … would it be very rude to say I gathered she had something to do with your family?'

'She's my grandfather's sister,' he answered. 'She's mad, of course; she—but I'll tell you some other time. Stephen was a brat she picked up somewhere; he's nothing to do with us, but she's taught him to call her "grandmother," because of a child that should have been.'

'Conversation of two aunts,' said Sybil, settling herself. 'I've known many wilder minds.'

'What were you at, Sybil?' Mr. Coningsby at last burst out. 'Of all the scandalous exhibitions! Really, Henry, I think we'd better go back to London. That my sister should be subjected to this kind of thing! Why didn't you interfere?'

'My dear, it would mean an awful bother—going back to London,' Sybil said. 'Everything's settled up there. I'm a little cold, Henry, so do you think we could go fairly fast? We can talk about it all when we get in.'

'Kneeling in the road!' Mr. Coningsby went on. 'O, very well—if you will go. Perhaps we shall smell things too. Is your grandfather anything like his sister, Henry? If so, we shall have a most agreeable Christmas. He might like me to kneel to him at intervals, just to make things really comfortable.'

Sybil laid a hand on his knee. 'Leave it to me to complain,' she said. 'All right, Henry; we all know you hated it much more than the rest of us.' Nancy's hand came over the seat and felt for hers; she took it. 'Child, you're frozen,' she said. 'Let's all get indoors. Even a Christian rat—all right, Henry—likes a little bacon-rind by the fire. Lothair dear, I was going to ask you when we stopped—what star exactly is that one over there?'

'Star!' said Mr. Coningsby, and choked. He was still choking over his troubles when they stopped before the house, hardly visible in the darkness. He was, however, a trifle soothed by the servant who was at the door and efficiently extricated them, and by the courtesies which the elder Mr. Lee, who was waiting just within the hall, immediately offered them. He found it impossible not, within the first two minutes, to allude to the unfortunate encounter; 'the sooner', he said to himself, 'this—really rather pleasant—old gentleman understands what his sister's doing on the roads the better.'

The response was all he could have wished. Aaron, tutored at intervals during the last month by his grandson in Mr. Coningsby's character and habits, was highly shocked and distressed at his guests' inconvenience. Excuses he proffered; explanations he reasonably deferred. They were cold; they were tired; they were, possibly, hungry. Their rooms were ready, and in half an hour, say, supper…. 'We won't call it dinner,' Aaron chatted on to Mr. Coningsby while accompanying him upstairs; Sybil and Nancy had been given into the care of maids. 'We won't call it dinner to-night. You'll forgive our deficiencies here—in your own London circle you'll be used to much more adequate surroundings.'

'It's a very fine house,' said Mr. Coningsby, stopping on what was certainly a very fine staircase.

'Seventeen-seventeen,' Aaron told him. 'It was built by a Jacobite peer who only just escaped attainder after the Fifteen and was compelled to leave London. It's a curious story; I'll tell it you some time. He was a student and a poet, besides being a Jacobite, and he lived here for the rest of his life in solitude.'

'A romantic story,' Mr. Coningsby said, feeling some sympathy with the Jacobite peer.

'Here's the room I've ventured to give you,' Aaron said. 'You can't see much from the windows to-night, but on a clear day you can sometimes just catch a glimpse of the sea. I hope you've everything. In half a hour, then, shall we say?'

He pattered away, a small, old, rather bent, but self-possessed figure, and Mr. Coningsby shut his door. 'Very different from his sister,' he thought. 'Curious how brothers and sisters *do* differ.' His mind went to Sybil. 'In a way,' he went on to himself, 'Sybil's rather irresponsible. She positively encouraged that dreadful old woman. There's a streak of wildness in her; fortunately it's never had a chance to get out. Perhaps if that other had had different surroundings … but if this is her brother's house, why's she wandering about the country? And, anyhow, that settles the question of giving Henry those cards. I shall tell Nancy so if she hints at it again. Fancy giving poor dear Duncannon's parting gift—the things he left me on his very death-bed—to a fellow with a mad gipsy for an aunt! Isis,' he thought, in deep disgust, 'the Divine Isis. Good God!'

CHAPTER V

THE IMAGE THAT DID NOT MOVE

Much to her own surprise when she found it out in the morning, Nancy slept extremely well: rather to his own disgust, so did her father. No one ever thought of asking Sybil—or, at least, no one ever listened to the answer; it was one of the things which wasn't related to her. She never said anything about it, nor, as a consequence, did anybody else; it being a certain rule in this world that what is not made of vivid personal importance will cease to be of social interest. The shoemaker's conversation therefore rightly returns to leather. Nancy woke and stretched, and, as her senses returned, considered healthily, voluptuously, and beautifully the immediate prospect of a week of Henry, interspersed with as much of other people as would make him more rare if not more precious. It occurred to her suddenly that he might already be downstairs, and that she might as well in that case be downstairs herself. But as she jumped out of bed—with the swinging movement—she swung into a sudden change of consciousness. Here they were—at his grandfather's, and here then all his obscure hints and promises were to be explained. He wanted something; he wanted something of her, and she was not at all clear that she wasn't rather frightened, or anyhow a little nervous, when she tried to think of it. She took a deep breath. Henry had something to show her, and the earth had grown in her hands; however often she washed them she never quite seemed to get away from the feel of it. Being a semi-educated and semi-cultured girl, she dutifully thought of *Macbeth*—'the perfumes of Arabia', 'this little hand'. For the first time in her life, however, she now felt as if Shakespeare had been talking about something more real than she had supposed; as if the words echoed out of her own deep being, and again echoed back into it—'cannot cleanse this little hand'. She rubbed her hands together half-unconsciously, and then more consciously, until suddenly the remembrance of Lady Macbeth as she had once seen her on the stage came to her, and she hurriedly desisted. Lady Macbeth had turned—a tall, ghostly figure caught in a lonely perdition—at the bottom corner of the stage, where the Witches … what was it they had sung?

weird sisters, hand

·s of the sea and lan·

'Posters of the sea and land,'—was that what she had been yesterday in the car—in her sleep, in her dreams? Or that mad old woman? The weird sisters—the old woman and Aunt Sybil—hand in hand, posters of the sea and land? Posters—going about the world—from point to point in a supernatural speed? Another line leapt at her—'Peace! the charm's wound up'. Wound up—ready for the unwinding; and Henry ready too. Her expectation terrified her: this day which was coming but not yet quite come was infinite with portents. Her heart filled and laboured with its love; she pressed a hand against it to ease the bursting pain. 'O Henry,' she murmured aloud, 'Henry!' What did one do about it? What was the making of earth beside this? This, whatever it was—this joy, this agony—was not out of key with her dreams, with the weird women; it too posted by the sea and land; the universe fell away below the glory of its passion.

She rose, unable any longer to sit still, drawing deep breaths of love, and walked to the window. The morning as it grew was clear and cold; unseen, miles away, lay the sea. Along the sea-shore, between earth and water, was the woman of the roads now hobbling? Or were the royal shapes of the Emperor and the Empress riding out in the dark heavens above the ocean? Her heart laboured with power still, and as that power flooded her she felt the hands that rested on the window-frame receive it; she leaned her head on the window and seemed to expect mysteries. This was the greatest mystery; this was the sea and land about which she herself was now a fortunate and happy poster.

It was too early; Henry wouldn't be about yet. But she couldn't go back to bed; love and morning and profound intention called to her. Her aunt was in the next room; she decided to go there, and went.

Her aunt, providentially, was awake, contemplating nothing with a remote accuracy. Nancy looked at her.

'I suppose you do sleep?' she said. 'Do you know, I've never found you asleep?'

'How fortunate!' Sybil said. 'For after all I suppose you've generally wanted something—if only conversation?'

Nancy, wrapping herself in her aunt's dressing-gown as well as her own, sat down, and looked again, this time more attentively.

'Aunt Sybil,' she said, 'are you by any chance being offensive?'

'Could I and would I?' Sybil asked.

'Your eyes are perpetually dancing,' Nancy said. 'But is it true—do I only come to you when I want something?'

'Why,' said Sybil, 'if you're asking seriously, my dear, then by and large the answer is yes.' She was about to add that she herself was quite content, but she saw something brooding in Nancy's face, and ceased.

'I don't mean to be a pig,' Nancy said. Sybil accepted that as a soliloquy and said nothing. Nancy added, 'I'm not all that selfish, am I?'

'I don't think you're particularly selfish,' her aunt said, 'only you don't love anyone.'

Nancy looked up, more bewildered than angry. 'Don't love?' she said. 'I love you and father and Ralph very much indeed.'

'And Henry?' Sybil asked.

'Well—Henry,' Nancy said, blushing a little, 'is different.'

'Alas!' Sybil murmured, but the lament was touched with laughter.

'What do you mean—"alas"?' Nancy asked. 'Aunt Sybil, do you *want* me to feel about everybody as I do about Henry?'

'A little adjustment here and there,' Sybil said, 'a retinting perhaps, but otherwise—why, yes! Don't you think so?'

'Even, I suppose,' Nancy said, 'to Henry's great-aunt or whatever she was?' But the words died from a soft sarcasm to a softer doubt: the very framing of the question, as so often happens, was itself an answer. 'Her body thought'; interrogation purged emotion, and the purified emotion replied to the interrogation. To love....

'But I can't,' she exclaimed, 'turn all *this*'—she laid her hand on her heart—'towards everybody. It can't be done; it only lives for—him.'

'Nor even that,' Sybil said. 'It lives for and in itself. You can only give it back to itself.'

Nancy brooded. After a while, 'I still don't see how I can love Joanna with it,' she said.

'If you give it back to itself,' Sybil said, 'wholly and utterly, it will do all that for you. You've no idea what a lot it can do. I think you might find it worth trying.'

'Do you?' Nancy said soberly; then she sighed, and said with a change of tone, 'Of course I simply adore this kind of talk before breakfast. You ought to have been a missionary, Aunt Sybil, and held early services for cannibals on a South Sea Island.'

'The breakfast,' Sybil said gravely, 'would have a jolly time listening to the bell before the service—if I had a bell.'

'O, you'd have a bell,' Nancy said, 'and a collection of cowrie-shells or bananas, and open-air services on the beach in the evening. And Henry and I would lean over the side of our honeymoon liner and hear your voice coming to us over the sea in the evening, and have—what is it they have at those times?—*heimweh*, and be all googly. And father would say, "Really, Sybil!" without being googly. Well, thank you for your kind interest in a Daughter of the Poor.' She kissed her aunt. 'I do, you know,' she said, and was gone.

The day passed till dinner without anything particularly striking having taken place. They looked over the house; they lunched; they walked. *The Times* arrived, sent up from the village, about midday, and Mr. Coningsby settled down to it. Henry and Nancy appeared and disappeared; Sybil walked and rested and talked and didn't talk, and contemplated the universe in a serene delight. But after dinner and coffee there came a pause in the conversation, and Aaron Lee spoke.

'My grandson thinks,' he said to his visitors, 'that you'd be interested to see a curiosity which we have here.'

'I'm sure anything——' answered Mr. Coningsby, who was feeling rather inclined to be agreeable.

Nancy said to Henry in a low voice, 'Is it whatever you meant?' and he nodded.

The old man rose. 'If I may trouble you, then, to come with me,' he said, leading the way from the room, and Mr. Coningsby sauntered after his sister without the smallest idea that the attack on his possession of the Tarot cards was about to begin. They came into Aaron's room; they crossed it and stood about the inner locked door. Aaron inserted the key; then, before turning it, he looked round and said, 'Henry thinks that your ownership of a particular pack of our gipsy cards may make you peculiarly interested in … in what you'll see. The pack's rather rare, I believe, and this'—he unlocked the door—'is, I may say, very much rarer.'

Henry, from the back, watched him a little anxiously. Aaron had not been at all eager to disclose the secret dancing images to these strangers; it was only the absolute necessity of showing Mr. Coningsby an overpoweringly good reason for giving away the cards that had at last convinced him. A day's actual acquaintance with Mr. Coningsby had done more towards conviction than all Henry's arguments—that, and the knowledge that the Tarot cards were at last in the house, so close to the images to which, for mortal minds, they were the necessary key. Yet, under the surface of a polite and cultured host which he had presented, there stirred a longing and a hostility; he hated this means, yet it was the only means to what he desired. In the conflict his hand trembled and fumbled with the door-handle, and Henry in his own agitation loosed Nancy's arm. She felt his trouble and misunderstood it. 'Darling,' she murmured, 'you don't mind us seeing, do you? If you do, let's go away.'

'You *must* see,' he answered, low and rapidly, 'you especially. And the others too—it's why they're here.'

She took his 'here' to mean at that door, and his agitation to be the promise of the mystery he had spoken of, and delighted to share it with him. 'You'll tell me everything,' she whispered. 'I'll do whatever you want.' Her eyes glowed at him as he looked at her. He met them, but his preoccupation was heavy upon him. 'Your father,' he whispered back, 'get your father to give me the cards.'

The door was open. Aaron said, 'You'll excuse me if I go first; there's a curtain.' He stepped forward, passed between the hangings, stepped aside, and raised them, so that, one by one, the others also came into the light of the inner chamber—Mr. Coningsby first, then Sybil, then the two young ones. Aaron let the curtain fall, and joined them where they stood, he and Henry closing them in on either side.

The light had been tinged with red when they entered; but it changed, so swiftly that only Aaron noticed it, to a lovely green, and then—more slowly—to an exquisite golden beauty. Aaron's eyes went to Henry's, but the young man was looking at the moving images; then they passed to the visitors—to Nancy, who also was raptly gazing at the spectacle; to Mr. Coningsby, who was surveying it with a benevolent generosity, as if he might have shown his host something similar in his own house, but hadn't thought it worth while; to Sybil, who was half-smiling in pure pleasure at the sight.

'These,' Aaron said, 'are a very ancient secret among the folk from whom Henry and I come, and they have never been shown to anyone outside our own people till now. But since we are to be so closely joined'—he smiled paternally at Nancy—'the reason against revealing them hardly exists.'

He had to pause for a moment, either because of his inner excitement or because (as, for a moment, he half-suspected) some sense stronger than usual of the unresting marvel before them attacked him and almost beat him down. He mastered himself, but his age dragged at him, and his voice trembled as he went carefully on, limiting himself to what Henry and he had agreed should be said.

'You see those little figures? By some trick of the making they seem to hold—what we call—the secret of perpetual motion. You see—how they are dancing—they do it continually. They are—we believe—in some way magnetized—by the movements of the earth—and they—they vibrate to it.'

He could say no more. He signed to Henry to go on, but Mr. Coningsby unintentionally interrupted.

'Very curious,' he said, 'very interesting indeed.' He looked all round the room. 'I suppose the light comes from behind the curtains somehow?'

'The light comes from the figures,' Henry said.

'Does it indeed?' Mr. Coningsby said, as if he was perfectly ready to believe anything reasonable, and even to refrain from blaming his host for offering him something perfectly unreasonable. 'From the figures? Well, well.' He settled his eyeglasses and leaned forward. 'Are they moving in any order?' he asked 'or do they just'—he waggled his hand—'jump?'

'They certainly move in order,' Henry answered, 'all but one: the one in the centre. You may recognize them; the figures are those which are painted on the Tarot cards you showed us.'

'O, really?' Mr. Coningsby said, a small suspicion rising in him. 'Just the same kind, are they? Well, well. But the cards aren't moving the whole time. At least,' he added, half in real amusement, half in superior sarcasm, 'I hadn't noticed it.'

'No,' Henry agreed. 'But, if you'll excuse me, sir, the point is rather that the cards explain—or anyhow may be supposed to explain—the movements of these figures. We think probably that that's what all fortune-telling by cards comes from, but the origin's been forgotten, which is why it's the decadent and futile thing it is.'

Nothing occurred to Mr. Coningsby in answer to this; he didn't understand it but he didn't want to be bothered with an explanation. He strolled forward till he stood by the table. 'May one pick them up?' he asked. 'It's difficult to examine the workmanship properly while they're all bustling round.'

'I don't think I should touch them, sir,' Henry said, checking his grandfather's movement with a fierce glance. 'The balance that keeps them dancing must be very delicate.'

'O, just as you like,' Mr. Coningsby said. 'Why doesn't the one in the middle dance?'

'We imagine that its weight and position must make it a kind of counterpoise,' Henry answered. 'Just as the card of the Fool—which you'll see is the same figure—is numbered nought.'

'Has he a tiger by him for any particular reason?' Mr. Coningsby inquired. 'Fools and tigers seem a funny conjunction.'

'Nobody knows about the Fool,' Aaron burst in. 'Unless the cards explain it.'

Mr. Coningsby was about to speak again when Sybil forestalled him.

'I can't see this central figure,' she said. 'Where is it exactly, Mr. Lee?'

Aaron, Henry, and her brother all pointed to it, and all with very different accents said, 'There.' Sybil stepped slightly forward, then to one side; she moved her head to different angles, and then said apologetically, 'You'll all think me frightfully silly, but I can't see any figure in the middle.'

'Really, Sybil!' her brother said. 'There!'

'But, my dear, it isn't there,' she said. 'At least, so far as I can possibly see. I'm sorry to be so stupid, Mr. Lee, because it's all quite the loveliest thing I ever saw in the whole of my life. It's perfectly wonderful and beautiful. And I just want, if I can, to see where you say this particular figure is.'

Henry leant forward suddenly. Nancy put her left hand up to where his lay on her shoulder. 'Darling,' she said, 'please! You're hurting me.' He took no notice; he did not apparently hear her. He was looking with intense eagerness from Sybil to the golden images and back. 'Miss Coningsby,' he said, reverting unconsciously to his earlier habit of address, 'can you see the Fool and his tiger at all?'

She surveyed the table carefully. 'Yes,' she said at last, 'there—no, there—no—it's moving so quickly I can hardly see it—there—ah, it's gone again. Surely that's it, dancing with the rest; it seems as if it were always arranging itself in some place which was empty for it.'

Nancy took hold of Henry's wrist and pulled it; tears of pain were in her eyes, but she smiled at him. 'Darling, must you squeeze my shoulder quite so hard?' she said.

Blankly he looked at her; automatically he let go, and though in a moment she put her own hand into the crook of his arm he did not seem to notice it. His whole attention was given to Sybil. 'You can see it moving?' he uttered.

On the other side, Aaron was trembling, and putting his fingers to his mouth as if to control it and them. Sybil, gazing at the table, did not see him. 'But it seems so,' she said. 'Or am I just distracted?'

Henry made a great effort. He turned to Nancy. 'Can you see it?' he asked.

'It looks to me to be in the centre,' she said, 'and it doesn't seem to be moving—not exactly moving.'

'What do you mean—not exactly moving?' Henry asked, almost harshly.

'It isn't moving at all,' said Mr. Coningsby. 'It's capitally made, though; the tiger's quite lifelike. So's the Fool,' he added handsomely.

'I suppose I meant not moving,' Nancy said. 'In a way I feel as if I expected it to. But it isn't.'

'Why should you expect it to?' Henry asked.

'I can't think,' Nancy admitted. 'Perhaps it was Aunt Sybil saying it *was* that made me think it ought to be.'

'Well,' Sybil said, 'there we are! If you all agree that it's not moving, I expect it isn't. Perhaps my eyes have got St. Vitus's dance or something. But it certainly seems to me to be dancing everywhere.'

There was a short and profound silence, broken at last by Nancy. 'What did you mean about fortune-telling?' she said, addressing ostensibly Mr. Lee, but in fact Henry.

Both of them came jerkily back to consciousness of her. But the old man was past speech; he could only look at his grandson. For a moment Henry didn't seem to know what to say. But Nancy's eager and devoted eyes were full on him, and something natural in him responded. 'Why, yes,' he said, 'it's here that fortunes can be told. If your father will let us use his pack of cards?' He looked inquiringly across.

Mr. Coningsby's earlier suspicion poked up again, but he hesitated to refuse. 'O, if you choose,' he said. 'I'm afraid you'll find nothing in it, but do as you like. Get them, Nancy; they're in my bag.'

'Right,' said Nancy. 'No, darling,' as Henry made a movement to accompany her. 'I won't be a minute: you stay here.' There had been a slight effect of separation between them, and she was innocently anxious to let so brief a physical separation abolish the mental; he, reluctant to leave Aaron to deal with Mr. Coningsby's conversation, assented.

'Don't be long,' he said, and she, under her breath, 'Could I?' and was gone. As she ran she puzzled a little over her aunt's difficulty in seeing the motionless image, and over the curious vibration that it seemed to her to possess. So these were what Henry had meant; he would tell her more about them presently, perhaps, because he certainly hadn't yet told her all he meant to. But what part then in the mystery did the central figure play, and why was its mobility or immobility of such concern to him? Though—of course it wasn't usual for four people to see a thing quite still while another saw it dancing. Supposing anyone saw her now, could they think of her as quite still, running at this speed? Sometimes one had funny feelings about stillness and motion—there had been her own sensation in the car yesterday, but that had only been a feeling, not a looking, so to speak. No one ever saw a motionless car tearing along the roads.

She found the Tarot pack and ran back again, thinking this time how agreeable it was to run and do things for Henry. She wished she found it equally agreeable to run for her father. But then her father—it was her father's fault, wasn't it? Was it? Wasn't it? If she could feel as happy—if she *could* feel. Could she? Could she, not only do, but feel happy to do? Couldn't she? Could she? More breathless within than without, she came again to the room of the golden dance.

She was aware, as through the dark screen of the curtain she entered the soft spheral light and heard, as they had all heard, that faint sound of music, of something changed in three of those who waited for her. Henry and her father were standing near each other, as if they had been talking. But also they were facing each other, and it was not a friendly opposition. Mr. Coningsby was frowning, and Henry was looking at him with a dominating hostility. She guessed immediately what had been happening—Henry had himself raised the possibility of his buying or being given or otherwise procuring the cards. And her father, with that persistent obstinacy which made even his reasonable decisions unreasonable, had refused. He was so often in a right which his immediate personal grievance turned into a wrong; his manners changed what was not even an injury into something worse than an insult. To be so conscious of himself was—Nancy felt though she did

190

not define it—an insult to everyone else; he tried to defy the human race with a plaintive antagonism—even the elder sons of the younger sons of peers might (he seemed to suggest) outrage his decencies by treading too closely on his heels. So offended, so outraged, he glanced at Henry now.

She came to them before either had time to speak. Aaron Lee and Sybil had been listening to the finished colloquy, and both of them willingly accepted her coming.

'Here we are,' she said. 'Henry, how frightfully exciting!' It wasn't, she thought at the same moment, not in the least. Not exciting; that was wholly the wrong word for this rounded chamber, and the moving figures, and the strange pack in her hand by which the wonder of earth had happened, and the two opposed faces, and Aaron Lee's anxious eyes, and the immortal tenderness of Sybil's. No—not exciting, but it would serve. It would ease the moment. 'Who'll try first?' she went on, holding out the Tarots. 'Father? Aunt? Or will you, Mr. Lee?'

Aaron waved them on. 'No, no,' he said hurriedly. 'Pray one of you—they're yours. Do try—one of you.'

'Not for me, thank you. I've no wish to be amused so——' Her father hesitated for an adverb, and Sybil also with a gesture put them by.

'O, aunt, do!' Nancy said, feeling that if her aunt was in it things would be safer.

'Really, Nancy. I'd rather not—if you don't mind,' Sybil said, apologetic, but determined. 'It's—it's so much like making someone tell you a secret.'

'What someone?' Henry said, anger still in his voice.

'I don't mean someone exactly,' Sybil said, 'but things … the universe, so to speak. If it's gone to all this trouble to keep the next minute quiet, it seems rude to force its confidence. Do forgive me.' She did not, Nancy noticed, add, as she sometimes did, that it was probably silly of her.

Nancy frowned at the cards. 'Don't you think we ought to?' she asked.

'Of course, if you can,' Sybil answered. 'It's just—do excuse me—that I can't.'

'You sound,' Henry said, recovering a more normal voice, 'on remarkably intimate terms with the universe. Mayn't it cheat you? Supposing it had something unpleasant waiting for you?'

'But,' said Sybil, 'as somebody says in Dickens, "It hasn't, you know, so we won't suppose it." Traddles, of course. I'm forgetting Dickens; I must read him again. Well, Nancy, it's between you and Henry.'

Nancy looked at her lover. He smiled at her at first with that slight pre-occupation behind his eyes which always seemed to be there, she thought a little ruefully, since the coming of the Tarots. But in a moment this passed, and they changed, though whether she or that other thing were now the cause of their full, deep concentration, she could not tell. He laid his hand on hers that held the Tarots.

'And what does it matter which?' he said. 'But I'd rather we tried yours, if you don't mind.'

'Can't we try them together?' she asked, 'and say good night to separation?'

'Let's believe we've said it,' he answered, 'but you shall try them for us both and let me read the fates. Do you believe that it's true?'

'Is it true?' she asked.

'As the earth in your hands,' he answered, and Mr. Coningsby's hostility only just conquered his curiosity, so as to prevent him asking what on earth Henry meant. 'It's between those'—he pointed to the ever-moving images—'and your hands that the power flows, and on the power the cards move. See.'

He turned her, and Aaron Lee, who stood between her and the table, moved hastily back. Then, taking the cards from their case, he made her hold them in her hands, as she had held the suit of deniers on that other evening, and the memory of it came back on her with sudden force. But this time, having settled her hands, he did not enclose them in his own; instead, he stepped away from her and waved away Sybil also, who was close on her left side, so that she stood alone, facing the golden table, her hands extended towards it, holding within them the whole pack of cards, opened a little fanwise so that from left to right the edges made a steeply sloping ascent.

'Move forward, slowly,' he said, 'till I tell you to stop. Go on.'

The earth that had lain in her hands … and now she was to go forward a step, or stop. It was not beyond her power to withdraw; she might pause and laugh and apologize to them all—and to Henry privately and beyond all—and lay aside the things she held. It was not beyond her power to refuse to enter the light that seemed now to grow to a golden sheen, a veil and mist of gold between her and the table; she could step back, she could refuse to advance, to know, to be. In the large content of the love that filled her she had no strong desire to find her future—if the cards indeed could tell her of it—though she could not feel, as Sybil did, that the universe itself was love. But, pausing on the verge of the future, she could find no reason noble enough for retreat—retreat would be cowardice or … no, nothing but cowardice. She was Henry's will; she was her own will to accomplish that will; having no moral command against her, she must needs go on.

She took a step forward, and her heart beat fast and high as she seemed to move into the clouded golden mist that received her, and fantastically enlarged and changed the appearance of her hands and the cards within them. She took another step, and the Tarots quivered in her hold, and through the mist she saw but dimly the stately movement of the everlasting measure trodden out before her, but the images were themselves enlarged and heightened, and she was not very sure of what nature they were. But nothing could daunt the daring in which she went; she took a third step, and Henry's voice cried to her suddenly, 'Stop there and wait for the cards.'

She half-turned her head towards him at the words, but he was too far behind for her to see him. Only, still looking through that floating and distorting veil of light, she did see a figure, and knew it for Aaron's: yet it was more like one of the Tarots—it was the Knight of Sceptres. The old man's walking-stick was the raised sceptre; the old face was young again, and yet the same. The skull-cap was a heavy medieval head-dress—but as the figure loomed it moved also, and the mist swirled and hid it. The cards shook in her hands; she looked back at them, and suddenly one of them floated right out into the air and slowly sank towards the floor; another issued, and then another, and so they followed in a gentle persistent rain. She did not try to retain them; could she have tried she knew she could not succeed. The figures before her appeared and disappeared, and as each one showed, so in spiral convolution some card of those she still held slipped out and wheeled round and round and fell from her sight into the ever-swirling mist.

They were huge things now, as if the great leaves of some aboriginal tree, the sacred bodhi-tree under which our Lord Gautama achieved Nirvana or that Northern dream of Igdrasil or the olives of Gethsemane, were drifting downward from the cluster round which her hands were clasped. The likenesses were not in her mind, but the sense of destiny was, and the vision of leaves falling slowly, slowly, carried gently upon a circling wind that touched her also in its passage, and blew the golden cloud before it. She grew faint in gazing; the grotesque hands that stretched out were surely not those of Nancy Coningsby, but of a giant form she did not know. With an effort she wrested her eyes from the sight, and looked before her, only more certainly to see the dancers. And these now were magnified to twenty times their first height; they were manikins, dwarfs, grotesques, yet living. More definitely visible than any before, a sudden mingled group grew out of the mist before her. Three forms were there—with their left arms high-arched, and finger-tips touching, wheeling round a common centre; she knew them as she gazed—the Queen of Chalices, holding her cup against her heart; and the naked figure of the peasant Death, his sickle in his right hand; and a more ominous form still, Set of the Egyptians, with the donkey head, and the captives chained to him, the power of infinite malice. Round and round, ever more swiftly, they whirled, and each as it passed seemed to stretch out towards her the symbol of itself that it carried; and the music that had been all this while in her ears rose to the shrieking of a great wind, and the wind about her grew strong and cold. Higher still went the shrieking; more bitterly against her the fierce wind beat. The cold struck and nipped her; she was alone and her hands were empty, and the bleak wind died; only she saw the last fragments of the golden mist blown and driven upon it. But as it passed, and as she gaspingly realized that her lover and friends were near her, she seemed yet for a moment to be the centre of that last measure: the three dancers whirled round her, their left hands touching over her head, separating and enclosing her. Some knowledge struck to her heart; and her heart ached in answer, a dull pain unlike her glorious agony when it almost broke with the burden of love. It existed and it ceased.

Henry's voice said from behind her: 'Happy fortune, darling. Let's look at the cards.'

She felt for the moment that she would rather he looked at her. There she was, feeling rather pitiable, and there were all the cards lying at her feet in a long twining line, and there was her father looking a trifle annoyed, and there was Henry kneeling by the cards, and there was Aaron Lee bending over him, and then between her and the table at which she didn't want to look came the form of her aunt. So she looked at her instead, which seemed much more satisfactory, and went so far as to slip an arm into Sybil's, though she said nothing. They both waited for Henry, and both with a certain lack of immediate interest. But this Henry, immersed in the cards, did not notice.

'You're likely to travel a long distance,' he said, 'apparently in the near future, and you'll come under a great influence of control, and you'll find your worst enemy in your own heart. You may run serious risks of illness or accident, but it looks as if you might be successful in whatever you undertake. And a man shall owe you everything, and a woman shall govern you, and you shall die very rich.'

'I'm so glad,' Nancy said in a small voice. She was feeling very tired, but she felt she ought to show a little interest.

'Henry,' she went on, 'why is the card marked nought lying right away from the others?'

'I don't know,' he said, 'but I told you that no one can reckon the Fool. Unless you can?' he added quickly, to Sybil.

'No,' said Sybil. 'I can see it right away from the others too.' She waited a minute, but, as Henry showed no signs of moving, she added in a deliberately amiable voice: 'Aren't you rather tired, Nancy? Henry dear, it's been the most thrilling evening, and the way you read fortunes is superb. I'm so glad Nancy's to be successful. But would you think it very rude if she and I went to bed now? I know it's early, but the air of your Downs....'

'I beg your pardon?' Henry said. 'I'm afraid I wasn't listening.'

Sybil, even more politely, said it all again. Henry sprang to his feet and came over to them. 'My darling, how careless of me,' he said to Nancy, while his eyes searched and sought in hers, 'of course you must be fagged out. We'll all go back now—unless,' he added politely to Mr. Coningsby, 'you'd like to try anything further with'—there was the slightest pause—'your cards.'

'No, thank you,' Mr. Coningsby said frigidly. 'I may as well take them down myself'; and he looked at them where they lay on the floor.

'I'll come back and collect them as soon as I've seen Nancy along,' Henry answered. 'They'll be safe enough till then.'

'I think I would as soon take them now,' Mr. Coningsby said. 'Things have a way of getting mislaid sometimes.'

'Nothing was ever mislaid in this room,' Henry answered scornfully.

'But the passages and other rooms might be less fortunate,' Mr. Coningsby sneered. 'Nancy can wait a minute, I'm sure.'

'Nancy,' she said, 'will pick them up while you're talking about it,' and moved to do it. But Henry forestalled her, though his dark skin flushed slightly, as he rose with the pack, restored it to its case, and ostentatiously presented it to Mr. Coningsby, who clasped it firmly, threw a negligent look at the dancing figures, and walked to the opening in the curtains. Henry drew Nancy from her aunt into his own care, and followed him; as they passed through she said idly: 'Why do you have curtains?'

He leaned to her ear. 'I will show you now, if you like,' he said; 'the sooner the better. Are you really too tired? or will you see what larger futures the cards show us?'

She looked back at the room. 'Darling, will to-morrow do?' she said. 'I do feel rather done.'

'Rest, then,' he answered; 'there's always sound sleep in this house. To-morrow, I'll show you something else—if,' he added, speaking still more softly, 'if you can borrow the cards. Nancy, what good can they possibly be to your father?'

She smiled faintly. 'Did you quarrel with him about them?' she said, but as she saw him frown added swiftly, 'None.'

'Yet he *will* hold on to them,' Henry said. 'Don't you think they belong to—those behind us?'

'I suppose so,' Nancy said uncertainly. 'I feel as if we all belonged to them, whatever they are. Your golden images have got into my bones, darling, and my heart's dancing to them instead of to you. Aren't you sorry?'

'We'll dance to them together,' he said. 'The images and the cards, and the hands and the feet—we'll bring them all together yet.'

'That's what your aunt said,' she answered, 'something coming together. What did she mean by Horus?'

'My aunt's as mad as your father,' he answered, 'and Horus has been a dream for more than two thousand years.'

CHAPTER VI

THE KNOWLEDGE OF THE FOOL

It was some time later, their visitors having all retired, after more or less affectionate partings, that Henry came to his grandfather in the outer room. The old man was waiting eagerly; as the door shut behind his grandson he broke out, 'Did you hear? Did she mean it?'

Henry came across and sat down. 'She must have meant it,' he said; 'there's no conceivable way by which she could have known what we need. Besides, unless she was playing with us—but she wouldn't, she's not that kind. So if she saw——' He got up again and walked in extreme excitement about the room. 'It can't be—but why not? If we've found the last secret of the images! If time's at last brought sight along with the cards!'

Aaron put his hand to his heart. 'But why should she be able to see? Here have all our families studied this for centuries, and none of them—and not you nor I—has ever seen the Fool move. There's only a tale to tell us that it does move. Why should this woman be able to see it?'

'Why should she pretend if she doesn't?' Henry retorted. 'Besides, I tell you she's a woman of great power. She possesses herself entirely; I've never seen anything dismay or distract her. She's like the Woman on the cards, but she doesn't know it—hierophantic, maid and matron at once.'

'But what do you mean?' Aaron urged. 'She knew nothing of the cards or the images. She didn't know why they danced or how. She's merely commonplace—a fool, and the sister of a fool.'

'None of us has ever known what the Fool of the Tarots is,' the other said. 'You say yourself that no one has ever seen it move. But this woman couldn't see it in the place where we all look for it. She saw it completing the measures, fulfilling the dance.'

'She doesn't know the dance,' Aaron said.

'She doesn't know what she does or doesn't know,' Henry answered. 'Either she was lying, I tell you, or by some impossible chance she can see what we can't see: and if she can, then the most ancient tale of the whole human race is true, and the Fool does move.'

'But then she'll know the thing that's always been missing,' Aaron almost sobbed. 'And she's going away next week!'

'It's why she could manage Joanna as she did,' Henry went on unheeding. 'She's got some sort of a calm, some equanimity in her heart. She—the only eyes that can read the future exactly, and she doesn't want to know the future. Everything's complete for her in the moment. It's beautiful, it's terrific—and what do we do about it?' He stopped dead in his walk and stared at Aaron.

'She's going away next week,' the old man repeated.

Henry flung himself back into a chair. 'Let us see,' he said. 'The Tarots are brought back to the images; there is a woman who can read the movements rightly; and let us add one more thing, for what it's worth—that I and Nancy are at the beginning of great experiments. On the other hand, the Tarots may be snatched from us by the idiot who pretends to own them; and the woman may leave us and go God knows where; and Nancy may fail. But, fail or not, that's a separate thing, and my own business. The other is a general concern, and yours. When the Tarots have been brought back to the dancers, and we can read the meaning of the dance, are you willing to let them go?'

'But let us see then,' Aaron said, 'what we can do to keep them.'

Henry looked over at him and brooded. 'If we once let them out of this house we may not see them again—they will be hidden in the Museum while we and our children die and rot: locked in a glass case, with a ticket under them, for hogs' faces of ignorance to stare at or namby-pamby professors to preach about.' He leapt to his feet. 'When I think of it,' he said, 'I grow as mad as Joanna, with her wails about a dismembered god. Shall we let the paintings and the images be torn apart once more?'

Aaron, crouching over the table, looked up sneeringly. 'Go and pray to Horus, as Joanna does,' he said, 'or run about the fields and think yourself Isis the Divine Mother. Bah! why do you jump and tramp? I'm an old man now, desire is going out of me, but if I'd your heat I'd do more with it than waste it cursing and shouting. Sit down; let us talk. There are four days before they go.'

Henry stamped. 'You can't be sure of four hours,' he said. 'Any moment that fool may take offence and be off. Get over to-morrow safely, and he can't go on Christmas Day, but after that how can we keep him against his will?'

'By leaving him to use his will,' Aaron said.

Henry came slowly back to the table. 'What do you mean?' he asked. 'You won't run the risk of violence, will you? How can we? We don't know what the result on the Tarots may be; there are warnings against it. Besides—it would be hard to see how to do it without—— O no, it's impossible.'

Aaron said, 'He has the Tarots—can't he be given to the Tarots? Is wind nothing? Is water nothing? Let us give him wind and water, and let us see if the obstinacy that can keep the cards will bring him safely through the elements of the cards. Don't shed blood, don't be violent; let's loose the Tarots upon him.'

Henry leaned forward and looked at the ground for a long time. 'I've thought of something of the sort,' he said at last. 'But there's Nancy.'

Aaron sneered again. 'Spare the father for the child's sake, hey?' he said. 'You fool, what other way is there? If you steal the cards from him, if you could, can you show them to her or use them with her? D'you think she won't be bothered and troubled, and will that be good for your experiment? She'll always be worried over her honesty.'

'I might show her that our use and knowledge is a high matter,' Henry said uncertainly, 'and teach her....'

'All in time, all in time,' the old man exclaimed, 'and any day he may give the Tarots to the Museum. Besides, there's the woman.'

'The woman!' Henry said. 'That's as great a difficulty. Can you persuade her to come and live with you and be the hierophant of the images of the cabalistic dance?'

'If,' said Aaron slowly, stretching out a hand and laying it on the young man's arm, 'if her brother was— gone, and if her niece was married to you, would it be so unlikely that she should live with her niece? If her niece studied the images, and loved to talk of them, and asked this woman for help, would it be so unlikely that she would say what she can see?' He ceased, and there was a pause.

At last—'I know,' Henry said. 'I saw it—vaguely—even to-night I saw it. But it may be dangerous.'

'Death is one of the Greater Trumps,' Aaron said. 'If I had the strength, I would do it alone; as it is, I can't. I haven't the energy or will to control the cards. I can only study and read them. You must do the working, and however I can help you I will.'

'The Greater Trumps——' Henry said doubtfully. 'I can't yet use—that's the point with Nancy—I want to see whether she and I can live—and she mustn't know——'

'There are wind and water, as I told you before,' the old man answered. I don't think your Mr. Coningsby will manage to save himself even from the twos and threes and fours of the sceptres and cups. He has no will. I am more afraid of Joanna.'

'Joanna!' Henry said. 'I never heard that she saw the movement of the Fool.'

Aaron shrugged. 'She looked to find that out when she had succeeded in carrying out her desire,' he said.

'She was right,' Henry said.

'And has Sybil Coningsby carried out her desire?' Aaron asked. 'What was it, then?'

'I can't tell you,' Henry said, 'but she found it and she stands within it, possessing it perfectly. Only she doesn't know what she's done. But she doesn't matter at the moment, nor Joanna. Only Nancy and ... and that man.'

'Shall there then be only Nancy?' Aaron asked softly.

Henry looked back at him steadily. 'Yes,' he answered, 'unless he can overcome the beating of the cards.'

'Be clear upon one thing,' Aaron said. 'I will have no part in this which you are wanting to achieve with *them*. I do not want even to know it. If all things go well, it will be enough for me to have restored the knowledge of the dance, and perhaps to have traced something of the law of its movement. But supposing Nancy—later—discovers somehow, in the growth of her wisdom, what you've done? Have you considered that?'

'I will believe,' Henry said, 'that if indeed it's the growth of her wisdom that discovers it, her wisdom will justify me. She'll know that one man must not keep in being the division of unity; she'll acknowledge that his spirit denied something greater than itself and perished inevitably. His spirit? His mere habitual peevish greed.'

'You will take that risk?' Aaron said.

'It is no risk,' Henry answered; 'if it were, then the whole intention is already doomed.'

Aaron nodded, and got to his feet. 'Yet ten minutes ago you weren't so certain,' he said.

'I hadn't then determined,' Henry answered. 'It's only when one has quite determined that one understands.'

'When will you do it?' Aaron asked. 'Do you want me to help you? You should consider that if what you do succeeds, then the girl may be too distressed to go your way for a while.'

'If it may be,' Henry said slowly, 'I will wait over to-morrow, for to-morrow I mean to show her the fortunes of nations. But we must not wait too long—and you're right in what you say: she will need time, so that I won't try to carry her with me till later. And if after Christmas her father should determine to go ... it would be done more conveniently here. Let's see how things fall out, but if possible let it be done on Christmas Day. He always walks in the afternoon—he told me weeks ago that he hasn't missed a sharp walk on Christmas afternoon for thirty-four years.'

'Let it be so, then,' his grandfather answered. 'I will talk to the women, and do you rouse the winds. If by any chance it fails, it can be tried again. At a pinch you could do it with the fire in the car when you return.'

Henry made a face. 'And what about Nancy and her aunt?' he asked.

Aaron nodded. 'I forgot,' he said. 'Well, there will be always means.'

CHAPTER VII

THE DANCE IN THE WORLD

The sense of strain that had come into being on the Thursday night existed still on the morning of Christmas Eve. Henry and Mr. Coningsby were markedly the centres of conflicting emotions, and Mr. Coningsby was disposed to make his daughter into the battle-field since she seemed to hesitate to support him with a complete alliance. He alluded, as the two of them talked after a slightly uncomfortable breakfast, to the unusual sight which had been exposed to them the night before.

'I must say,' he remarked, 'that I thought it showed poorer taste than I had hoped for in Henry, to try that trick of the moving dolls on us.'

'But why do you call it a trick, father?' Nancy objected. 'They *were* moving: and that was all Henry said.'

'It was not by any means all,' Mr. Coningsby answered. 'To be quite candid, Nancy, he disappointed me very much; he practically tried to swindle me out of that pack of cards by making an excuse that the dolls were very much like them. Am I to give up everything that belongs to me because anyone has got something like it?'

Nancy thought over this sentence without at once replying.

Put like that, it did sound unreasonable. But how else could it be put, to convince her father? Could she say, 'Father, I've created earth, and seen policemen and nurses become emperors and empresses, and moved in a golden cloud where I had glimpses of a dance that went all through my blood?' Could she? Could she tell him that her mind still occasionally remembered, as if it were a supernatural riddle, the shock of seeing the crucifix with its head above its feet, and the contrast with the Hanged Man of the cards? She said at last, 'I don't think Henry meant it quite like that. I'd like you to be fair to him.'

'I hope I'm always fair,' said Mr. Coningsby, meaning that he couldn't imagine Eternal Justice disagreeing with him, 'but I must say I'm disappointed in Henry.'

Nancy looked at the fire. Dolls? She would have been annoyed, only she was too bothered. Her father must be there, if she could only get at him. But, so far as that went, he might as well be shut away from her in the gleaming golden mist. He might as well be a grey automaton—he was much more like a moving doll than the images of the hidden room, than Henry, than Sybil and Joanna hand in hand, than the white-cloaked governor of the roads, than Henry, than the witches of Macbeth's encounter, than the staring crucifix, than the earth between her hands, than Henry…. She looked at him dubiously. She had meant to ask him if she and Henry might have the Tarot pack again that evening, because Henry wanted to tell her something more, and she wanted to know. But he wouldn't, he certainly wouldn't. Might she borrow them for an hour without asking him? It wouldn't hurt them or him. They were on his dressing-table; she had seen them there, and wondered why he hadn't locked them away. But she knew—it was because he hadn't really expected them to be taken; he had only wanted to be nasty to Henry. Suppose she asked him and he refused—it would be too silly! But was she to lose all this wonder, which so terrified and exalted her, because he wanted to annoy Henry? O, in heaven's name what would a girl who was trying to love *do*?

Love (presumably) at that moment encouraged Mr. Coningsby, meditating on his own fair-mindedness and his generous goodwill, to say, 'I'd always be willing for him to borrow them, if I could be sure of getting them back. But——'

Nancy lifted eyes more affectionate than she knew. 'If I promised I'd give them back, father, whenever you liked?'

Mr. Coningsby, a little taken aback, said evasively, 'It isn't you I'm doubtful about. You're my daughter, and you know there's such a thing as decency.'

It would be only decent, Nancy thought, for her not to take the cards for use without his consent; but it would also be only decent for him to lend them. She said, 'You'd trust me with them?'

'Of course, of course, if the necessity arose,' Mr. Coningsby said, a trifle embarrassed, and feeling glad that the necessity couldn't arise. Nancy, relieved from her chief embarrassment, decided that the necessity *had* arisen. She felt that it would be silly to compel her father to a clearer statement. She said, as clearly as possible, 'I'll take care of them,' but Sybil came into the room at that moment and the remark was lost. Nancy, a little bewildered by the sudden appearance in her life of a real moral problem, and hoping sincerely that she had tried to solve it sincerely, slid away and went to look for Henry.

It was with Henry, and holding the Tarots, that she entered the room that evening and passed the curtains; together they stood before the golden images. Nancy felt the difference; what had on the previous night been a visit of curiosity, of interest, was now a more important thing. It was a deliberate repetition, an act of intention, however small; but it was also something more. By her return, and her return with Henry, she was inviting a union between the mystery of her love and the mystery of the dance. As she stood, again gazing at it, she felt suddenly a premonition of that union, or of the heart of it. It must be in herself that the union must be, in a discovery of some new state perhaps as unlike her love and her vision as they were unlike the ignorant Nancy of the previous year—there was no other place nor other means, whatever outward change took place. All that she did could but more deeply reveal her to herself; if only the revelation could be as good and lovely as … as Henry found her. Could she believe in herself so? Dared she trust that such a beauty was indeed the final answer, or could be made so?

But before she could search out her own thoughts he spoke to her.

'You saw last night how fortunes can be told,' he said. 'The cards that you held are the visible channel between the dance and you. You hold them in your hands and——'

'Tell me first,' she said, 'now we're here alone, tell me more of this dance. It's more than fortune-telling, isn't it? Why do the cards make earth? Why do you call some of them the Greater Trumps? Is it only a name? Tell me; you must tell me now.'

He drew a deep breath, began to speak, and then, checking, made a despairing movement with his hands. 'O, how shall I explain,' he cried out, 'what we can only be taught to imagine? what only a few among my own people can imagine? I've brought you here, I've wanted you here, and now it's too much for me. There aren't any words—you'll think me as mad as that wretched woman on the roads.'

'How do you know I think her mad?' Nancy said. 'Did Aunt Sybil seem to? You must try and tell me, Henry—if you think it's important. If you don't,' she added gravely, lifting serious eyes to his, 'I should be sorry, because it would all be only a conjurer's trick.'

He stood away from her a step or two, and then, looking not at her but at the table, he began again to speak. 'Imagine, then, if you can,' he said, 'imagine that everything which exists takes part in the movement of a great dance—everything, the electrons, all growing and decaying things, all that seems alive and all that doesn't seem alive, men and beasts, trees and stones, everything that changes, and there is nothing anywhere that does not change. That change—that's what we know of the immortal dance; the law in the nature of things—that's the measure of the dance, why one thing changes swiftly and another slowly, why there is seeming accident and incalculable alteration, why men hate and love and grow hungry, and cities that have stood for centuries fall in a week, why the smallest wheel and the mightiest world revolve, why blood flows and the heart beats and the brain moves, why your body is poised on your ankles and the Himalaya are rooted in the earth—quick or slow, measurable or immeasurable, there is nothing at all anywhere but the dance. Imagine it—imagine it, see it all at once and in one!'

She did not speak, and after a minute's silence he broke out again.

'This is all that there is to learn; our happiest science guesses at the steps of a little of it. It's always perfect because it can't be anything else. It knows nothing of joy or grief; it's movement, quick as light, slow as the crumbling of a stone tomb in the jungle. If you cry, it's because the measure will have it so; if you laugh, it's because some gayer step demands it, not because you will. If you ache, the dance strains you; if you are healthy, the dance carries you. Medicine is the dance: law, religion, music, and poetry—all these are ways of telling ourselves the smallest motion that we've known for an instant before it utterly disappears in the unrepeatable process of *that*. O Nancy, see it, see it—that's the most we can do, to see something of it for the poor second before we die!'

The very dance itself seemed to have paused in her, so motionless her light form held itself, so rapt in its breathless suspension as the words sounded through her, and before her eyes the small shapes of glory turned and intertwined.

'But once,' he went on, '—some say in Egypt long before the Pharaoh heard of Yussuf Ben-Yakoob, and some in Europe while the dreaming rabbis whispered in the walled ghetto over fables of unspeakable words, and some in the hidden covens of doctrine which the Church called witchcraft—once a dancer talked of the dance, not with words, but with images; once a mind knew it to the seventy-eighth degree of discovery, and not only knew it, but knew how it knew it, so beautifully in one secret corner the dance doubled and redoubled on itself. And then the measure, turning here and there, perpetually harmonious, wrought out these forms of gold in correspondence with something at least of itself, becoming its own record, change answering to change. We can't guess who, we can't tell how, but they were carried in the vans of the gipsies about Europe till they were brought here, and here they still are.'

She moved a hand and he paused; as if willing to speak from herself, she said—the voice and the words desiring a superfluous but compensating confirmation, as of step answering to step: 'To look at these then is to have the movement made visible? this is what is going on … now, immediately now? Isn't there anything anywhere that isn't happening there?'

He pointed to the table. 'This is the present,' he said, 'and this is the only present, and even that is changed before it can be known.'

'Yet you said,' she answered, 'that this unknown man knew how it was to be known. How was that? and why, dearest, are the figures—the images, I mean—made as they are?'

'It would need another seer to explain,' he said, 'and that seer would have to pass behind the symbols and see them from within. Do you understand, Nancy? Do you understand that sometimes where one can hardly go, two may? Think of that; and think what might be seen and done within the dance if so much can be seen without. All we know is that the images are the twenty-one and the nought, and the four fours and the four tens. Doubtless these numbers themselves are of high necessity for proper knowledge, but their secret too is so far hidden within the dance.'

'Yet you must have considered the shapes, darling?' she asked.

'The shapes, perhaps, are for two things,' he answered more slowly, 'for resemblance and for communication. On the one hand they must mean some step, some conjunction, some—what we call a fact—that is often repeated in the infinite combinations; on the other, it must be something that we know and can read. This, I think, is what was meant, but even the secondary meaning has been lost—or was lost while the cards were separated from the golden images, as if a child were taken from its mother into some other land and never learned her language, that language which should have been the proper inheritance of its tongue.'

He stopped short, as if the thought troubled him, and the girl, with the same memory in her mind, said, 'Did the woman on the road mean that when she talked to us?'

'I don't care what she meant,' he said almost harshly. 'Neither she nor anyone but ourselves concerns us now. No one but ourselves has a proper right to talk of the cards or the images.'

He glanced at her as he spoke, but, smiling very slightly, she let the utterance die, and said only: 'Tell me more of the cards.'

'The cards were made with the images,' he answered; 'the mark in the corner of each of them is the seal of the bottom of each golden shape; seventy-eight figures and as many seals on as many cards. The papyrus paintings are exactly the same as the figures; they are the paintings of the figures. This, as I told you a month ago, when we first saw them, is the only perfect set, correspondence to correspondence, and therefore the only set by which the sublime dance can be read. The movement changes incessantly, but in every fractional second it is so, and when these cards are brought to it they dispose themselves in that order, modified only by the nature of the hands between which they are held, and by the order into which they fall we read the fortune of whoever holds them.'

'But the suits, you said, are the elements?' she asked.

He nodded. 'But that is in the exterior world; they are the increasing strength of the four elements, and in the body of a man there are corresponding natures. This is the old doctrine of humours which your schoolmistress taught you, no doubt, that you might understand Ben Jonson or what not.'

'And the others?' she said; 'the Greater Trumps?'

He came near to her and spoke more low, almost as if he did not want the golden dancers to know that he was talking of them. 'They,' he said, 'are the truths—the facts—call them what you will—principles of thought, actualities of corporate existence, Death and Love and certain Virtues and Meditation and the Benign Sun of Wisdom, and so on. You must see them—there aren't any words to tell you.'

'The Devil—if it is a devil?' she said.

'It is the unreasonable hate and malice which moves in us,' he answered.

'The Juggler—if it is a juggler?' she asked.

'It is the beginning of all things—a show, a dexterity of balance, a flight, and a falling. It's the only way he—whoever he was—could form the beginning and the continuation of the dance itself.'

'Is it God then?' Nancy asked, herself yet more hushed.

Henry moved impatiently. 'What do we know?' he answered. 'This isn't a question of words. God or gods or no gods, these things are, and they're meant and manifested thus. Call it God if you like, but it's better to call it the Juggler and mean neither God nor no God.'

'And the Fool who doesn't move?' she said after a pause.

'All I can tell you of that,' he said grimly, 'is that it is the Fool who doesn't move. There are tales and writings of everything but the Fool; he comes into none of the doctrines or the fortunes. I've never yet seen what he can be.'

'Yet Aunt Sybil saw him move,' she said.

'You shall ask her about it some time,' he answered, 'but not yet. Now I have told you as much as I can tell of these things; the sense of them is for your imagination to grasp. And when you have come to understand it so, then we may see whether by the help of the Tarots we may find our way into the place beyond the mists. But meanwhile I will show you something more. Wait for me a minute.'

He paused, considering; then he went to a different part of the curtains and disappeared through what she supposed was another opening in them. She heard a sound, as if he were opening a window, then he came back to her.

'If you look up at this room from without,' he said, 'you will see it has four windows in it. I have opened the eastern one. Now see.'

He went to the part of the table nearest to the window he had opened, and, feeling beneath it, drew out a curved ledge, running some third of the way round the table. It was some three feet wide, and it reached, when it was fully extended, almost to the curtains; it also was of gold, and there were faint markings on it, though Nancy could not see very well what they were—some sort of map of the world, she thought. Henry turned a support of wood to hold it rigid and began to lay the Tarot cards upon it. He spread the Greater Trumps along the table edge in the order of their numbering. But he began, not with the first, but with the second card, which was that of the Empress, and so on till he came to the pictures which were called xx The Last Judgement—where a Hand thrust out of cloud touched a great sarcophagus and broke it, so that the skeleton within could arise, and xxi The World—where a single singing form, as of a woman, rose in a ray of light towards a clear heaven of blue, leaving moon and sun and stars beneath her feet. The first, however, which showed a Juggler casting little balls into the air, he laid almost in the middle, resting it upon the twelfth card, which was the Wheel of Fortune, and supporting it against the edge of the table itself behind, over which it projected; under the Wheel of Fortune he hid the Fool. Having done this carefully, he went on very quickly with the rest of his task. He took the four suits and laid them also on the ledge from left to right, the deniers, the cups, the sceptres, the swords. Of each suit he laid first, against and slightly overlapping the Greater Trumps, the four Court cards—the King, the Queen, the Knight, the Esquire; in front of, and again overlapping these, the ten, the nine, the eight, and the seven; then, similarly arranged, the six, the five, and the four; then the three and the two; and in front of all, pointing outwards, the ace of each suit, so that the whole company of the Tarots lay with their base curved against the table of the dance, and pointing with a quadruple apex towards the curtains behind which was the open window.

As soon as this was done he stepped back to Nancy, thrust an arm round her, and said: 'Look at the curtains.' She obeyed, but not continuously; her eyes turned back often to the cards on the ledge, and it was while she gazed at them that she became aware how, in the movement of the dance, the Juggler among the images had approached the corresponding card. He seemed to her to run swiftly, while still he kept the score or so balls spinning over him in the air, and as he went he struck against the card and it slid from its place. Its fall disturbed the Wheel of Fortune on which it stood, and immediately the whole of the cards were in movement, sliding over and under each other—she gazed, enchanted, till Henry whispered in her ear, 'The curtain!'

She looked, and at first instead of a curtain she saw only the golden mist in which she had found herself on the previous night. But it was already gathering itself up, dissipated, lost in an increasing depth of night. At first she thought the curtains had disappeared and she was looking out through the open window, but it was hardly that, for there was no frame or shape. The dark hangings of the room here lost themselves in darkness. She had not passed through the mist, but she was looking beyond it, and as within it her own fortune had been revealed so now some greater thing came into conjunction with the images, and the cards moved under the union of the double influence. For within the darkness a far vision was forming. She saw a gleam of green close before her; she heard for an instant what seemed the noise of waves on the shore. Then against that line of greenish-blue a shore actually grew; she saw the waves against it. As she gazed, it dwindled, growing less as what was beyond it was shaped in the darkness. Small and far, as if modelled with incredible minute exactitude, there emerged the image of a land with cities and rivers, railways and roads. The shape defined itself and was familiar; she was looking at a presentation of Holland and Belgium and Northern France, and—for, even as she understood, the limits expanded and what she saw seemed to grow smaller yet, as wider stretches came into view—there were the Alps, there was Italy; that dome of infinitesimal accuracy, above like infinitesimal detail, was St. Peter's—and beyond were more seas and islands and the sweep of great plains. Before her breath had thrice sighed itself out she saw India and Asia, with its central lakes, and Everest, its small peak dazzling white against the dark, and, as she breathed again, Tibet expanded into China, and the horizon of that mysterious night fled yet farther away and closed at length upon the extreme harbours of Japan. The whole distance lay before her, and she knew certainly within her that she was seeing

199

no reproduction or evoked memory, but the vast continents themselves, with all that they held. She looked on the actual thing; earth was stretched before her, and the myriad inhabitants of that great part of earth.

Fast in Henry's arm, as if leaning forward from a height, she strained to see; and something of man's activities she did indeed discern. There were moving specks on certain roads—especially away in Northern China; and, since there chiefly she could trace movement, without deliberate intention concentrated on it. It grew larger before her, and the rest of the vision faded and diminished. She unconsciously desired to see, and she saw men—companies of men—armies—all in movement—details she could not hold her gaze steadily enough to observe, but there was no doubt that they were armies, and moving. There was a town—they were about it—it was burning. Her concentration could not but relax, and again all this receded, and again before her the whole of Europe and of Asia lay. But now the seas and continents were no longer still; they were shaken as if with earthquake; they were dissolving, taking fresh shapes, rising into, changing into, the golden images that danced upon their golden ground. Only here they danced in night upon no ground. They started from the vanishing empires and nations; cities leapt together, and Death came running instead; from among the Alps the Imperial cloak swept snow into itself; rivers poured into the seas and the seas into nothing, and cups received them and bearers of cups, and a swift procession of lifted chalices wound among the gathering shapes. From Tibet, from Rome, some consummation came together, and the hierophant, the Pope of the Tarots, took ritual steps towards that other joined beauty of the two lovers for which her grateful heart always searched. All earth had been gathered up: this was the truth of earth. The dance went on in the void; only even there she saw in the centre the motionless Fool, and about him in a circle the Juggler ran, for ever tossing his balls.

She felt, being strangely, and yet not strangely, conscious of his close neighbourhood, Henry draw himself together as if to move. She felt him move—and between those two sensations she saw, or she thought she saw, a complete movement in the dance. Right up to the hitherward edge of the darkness the two lovers came; they wheeled back; her eyes followed them, and saw suddenly all the rest of the dancers gathering in on either side, so that the two went on between those lines towards where the Fool stood still as though he waited them. After them other opposing forms wheeled inward also, the Emperor with the Empress, the mitred hierophant with the woman who equalled him; and the first twain trod on the top of the Wheel of Fortune and passed over; before them rose the figure of the Hanged Man, and they disjoined to pass on either side and went each under his cross, and Death and the Devil ran at them, and they running also came to a tower that continually fell into ruin and was continually re-edified; they passed into it, and when they issued again they were running far from each other, but then the golden light broke from each and met and mingled, and over them stars and the moon and the sun were shining; yet a tomb lay in their path, and the Fool— surely the motionless Fool!—stretched out his hand and touched it, and from within rose a skeleton; and it joined the lovers in their flying speed, and was with each, and the Fool was moving, was coming; but then she lost sight of lovers and skeleton, and of all the figures there were none left but the Juggler who appeared suddenly right under her eyes and went speedily up a single path which had late been multitudinous, and ran to meet the Fool. They came together; they embraced; the tossing balls fell over them in a shower of gold— and the golden mist covered everything, and swirled before her eyes; and then it also faded, and the hangings of the room were before her, and she felt Henry move.

CHAPTER VIII

CHRISTMAS DAY IN THE COUNTRY

It had been settled at dinner on Christmas Eve that the three Coningsbys would go to the village church on Christmas Day. Mr. Coningsby theoretically went to church every Sunday, which was why he always filled up Census forms with the statement 'Church of England.' Of the particular religious idea which the Church of England maintains he had never made any special investigation, but he had retained the double habit of going to church on Christmas morning and for a walk on Christmas afternoon. In his present state of irritation with the Lees he would rather have walked to church than not have gone, especially as Aaron pleaded his age and Henry professional papers as reasons for not going. But Aaron had put the car and chauffeur at his disposal for the purpose, so that he was not reduced to any such unseemly effort. Mr. Coningsby held strongly that going to church, if and when he did go, ought to be as much a part of normal life as possible, and ought not to demand any peculiar demonstration of energy on the part of the church-goer.

Sybil, he understood, had the same view; she agreed that religion and love should be a part of normal life. With a woman's natural exaggeration, she had once said that they were normal life, that they were indeed life. He wasn't very clear whether she usually went to church or not; if she did, she said nothing much about it, and was always back in time for meals. He put her down as 'Church of England' too; she never raised any objection. Nancy went under the same heading, though she certainly didn't go to church. But her father felt that she would when she got older; or that, anyhow, if she didn't she would feel it was right to do so. Circumstances very often prevented one doing what one wished: if one was tired or bothered, it was no good going to church in an improper state of mind.

Nancy's actual state of mind on the Christmas morning was too confused for her to know much about it. She was going with her father partly because she always had done, but even more because she badly needed a short refuge of time and place from these shattering new experiences. She felt that an hour or so somewhere where—just for once—even Henry couldn't get at her was a highly desirable thing. Her mind hadn't functioned very clearly during the rest of the time they had spent in the inner room; or else her memory of it wasn't functioning clearly now. Henry had explained something about the possibility of reading the fortunes of the world in the same manner as those of individuals could be read, but she had been incapable of listening; indeed, she had beaten a rather scandalous retreat, and (for all his earlier promises of sound sleep) had lain awake for a long time, seeing only that last wild rush together of the Fool and the Juggler, that falling torrent of balls breaking into a curtain of golden spray, which thickened into cloud before her. One last glance at the table had shown her upon it the figure of the Fool still poised motionless, so she hadn't seen what Aunt Sybil had seen. But she had seen the Fool move in that other vision. She wanted to talk to her aunt about it, but her morning sleep had only just brought her down for breakfast, and there had been no opportunity afterwards before church. She managed to keep Sybil between herself and her father as they filed into a pew, and sat down between her and a pillar with a sense of protection. Nothing unusual was likely to happen for the next hour or two, unless it was the vicar's new setting of the Athanasian Creed. Aaron Lee had remarked that the man was a musical enthusiast, doing the best he could with the voices at his disposal, assisted by a few friends whom he had down at Christmas. This Christmas, it seemed, he was attempting a little music which he himself had composed. Nancy was quite willing that he should—nothing seemed more remote from excitement or mystery than the chant of the Athanasian Creed. During the drive down her father had commented disapprovingly on the Church's use of that creed. Sybil had asked why he disliked it. Mr. Coningsby had asked if she thought it Christian; and Sybil said she didn't see anything very un-Christian about it—not if you remembered the hypothesis of Christianity.

'And what,' Mr. Coningsby said, as if this riddle were entirely unanswerable, 'what do you call the hypothesis of Christianity?'

'The Deity of Love and the Incarnation of Love?' Sybil suggested, adding, 'Of course, whether you agree with it is another thing.'

'Certainly I agree with Christianity,' Mr. Coningsby said. 'Perhaps I shouldn't put it quite like that. It's a difficult thing to define. But I don't see how the damnatory clauses——'

However, there they reached the church. Nancy thought, as she looked at the old small stone building, that if Henry was right about the dance, then this member of it must be sitting out some part of the time on some starry stair. Nothing less mobile had ever been imagined. But her intelligence reminded her, even as she entered, that the apparent quiescence, the solidity, the attributed peace of the arched doorway was one aspect of what, in another aspect, was a violent and riotous conflict of … whatever the latest scientific word was. Strain and stress were everywhere; the very arch held itself together by extreme force; the latest name for matter was Force, wasn't it? Electrical nuclei or something of that sort. If this antique beauty was all made of electrical nuclei, there might be—there must be—a dance going on somewhere in which even that running figure with the balls flying over it in curves would be outpaced. She herself outpaced Sybil by a step and entered the pew first.

And she then, as she knelt decorously down, was part of the dance; she was the flying feet passing and repassing; she was the conjunction of the images whose movement the cards symbolized and from which they formed the prophecy of her future. 'A man shall owe you everything'—everything? Did she really want Henry to owe her *everything*, or did she—against her own quick personal desire—desire rather that there should be something in him to which she owed everything? 'And a woman shall govern you'—that was the most distasteful of all; she had no use at all for women governing her; anyhow, she would like to see the woman who would do it. 'And you shall die very rich'—by this time she had got up from her knees, and had sat down again—well, that was very fortunate. If it meant what it said—'You shall die very rich'—but the forms of Death and the Devil and the Queen of Chalices had danced round her, and the words shook with threat, with promise, with obscure terror. But what could even that do to harm her while Henry and she together dared it? While that went on, it was true in its highest and most perfect meaning; if that went on, she would die very rich.

A door opened; the congregation stirred; a voice from the vestry said: 'Hymn 61. "Christians, awake," Hymn 61.' Everyone awoke, found the place, and stood up. The choir started at once on the hymn and the procession. Nancy docilely sent her voice along with them.

> *istians, awake, salute the happy*
> *'on the Saviour of the world was*
> *) u——*

Her voice ceased; the words stared up at her. The choir and the congregation finished the line—

> *adore the mystery of love.*

'The mystery of love.' But what else was in her heart? The Christmas associations of the verse had fallen away; there was the direct detached cry, bidding her do precisely and only what she was burning to do. 'Rise to adore the mystery of love.' What on earth were they doing, singing about the mystery of love in church? They couldn't possibly be meaning it. Or were they meaning it and had she misunderstood the whole thing?

The church was no longer a defence; it was itself an attack. From another side the waves of some impetuous and greater life swept in upon her. She turned her head abruptly towards Sybil, who felt the movement and looked back, her own voice pausing on 'the praises of redeeming love.' Nancy, her finger pointing to the first of those great verses, whispered a question, 'Is it true?' Sybil looked at the line, looked back at Nancy, and answered in a voice both aspirant and triumphant, 'Try it, darling.' The tall figure, the wise mature face, the dark ineffable eyes, challenged, exhorted, and encouraged. Nancy throbbed to the voice that broke into the next couplet—'God's highest glory was their anthem still.'

She looked back at the hymn and hastily read it—it was really a very commonplace hymn, a very poor copy of verses. Only that one commanding rhythm still surged through her surrendered soul—'Rise to adore the mystery of love.' But now everyone else was shutting up hymn-books and turning to prayer-books; she took one more glance at the words, and did the same.

The two lovers had run straight on—not straight on; they had been divided. Separately they had run up the second part of the way, separately each had danced with the skeleton. She could see them now, but more clearly even than them she remembered the Juggler—'neither God nor not God,' Henry had said—running to meet the unknown Fool. 'Amen,' they were singing all round her; this wasn't getting very far from the dance. It hadn't occurred to her that there was so much singing, so much exchanging of voices, so much summoning and crying out in an ordinary church service. Sybil's voice rose again—'As it was in the beginning, is now——' ' What was in the beginning and was now? Glory, glory.

Nancy sat down for the Proper Psalms, though she was aware her father had looked at her disapprovingly behind Sybil's back. It couldn't be helped; her legs wouldn't hold her up in the midst of these dim floods of power and adoration that answered so greatly to the power and adoration which abode in her heart, among these songs and flights of dancing words which wheeled in her mind and seemed themselves to become part of the light of the glorious originals of the Tarots.

She was still rather overwhelmed when they came to the Athanasian Creed, and it may have been because of her own general chaos that even that despised formulary took part in the general break-up which seemed to be proceeding within her. All the first part went on in its usual way; she knew nothing about musical setting of creeds, so she couldn't tell what to think of this one. The men and the boys of the choir exchanged metaphysical confidences; they dared each other, in a kind of rapture—which, she supposed, was the setting—to deny the Trinity or the Unity; they pointed out, almost mischievously, that though they were compelled to say one thing, yet they were forbidden to say something else exactly like it; they went into particulars about an entirely impossible relationship, and concluded with an explanation that something wasn't true which the wildest dream of any man but the compiler of the creed could hardly have begun to imagine. All this Nancy half-ignored.

But the second part—and it was of course the setting—for one verse held her. It was of course the setting, the chance that sent one boy's voice sounding exquisitely through the church. But the words which conveyed that beauty sounded to her full of sudden significance. The mingled voices of men and boys were proclaiming the nature of Christ—'God and man is one Christ'; then the boys fell silent, and the men went on, 'One, not by conversion of the Godhead into flesh, but by taking of the manhood into God.' On the assertion they ceased, and the boys rushed joyously in, 'One altogether, not'—they looked at the idea and tossed it airily away—'*not* by confusion of substance, but by unity'—they rose, they danced, they triumphed—'by unity, by unity'—they were silent, all but one, and that one fresh perfection proclaimed the full consummation, each syllable rounded, prolonged, exact—'by unity of person.'

It caught the young listening creature; the enigmatic phrase quivered with beautiful significance. Sybil at her side somehow answered to it; she herself perhaps—she herself in love. Something beyond understanding but not beyond achievement showed itself, and then the choir were plunging through the swift record of the Christhood on earth, and once more the attribution of eternal glory rose and fell—'is now,' 'is now—and ever shall be.' Then they were all kneeling down and the vicar was praying in ritual utterance of imperial titles for 'our sovereign lord King George.'

For the rest of the service Nancy moved and rose and sat and knelt according to the ritual, without being very conscious of what was going on. She felt two modes of being alternating within her—now the swift rush of her journey in the car, of her own passion, of the images seen in the night, of the voices roaring upward in the ceremonies of Christmas; now again the pause, the silence and full restraint of the Emperor, of Sybil, of her own expectation, of that single voice declaring unity, of the Fool amid the dance of the night. She flew with the one; she was suspended with the other; and, with downcast eyes and parted lips, she sought to control her youth till one should disappear or till both should come together. Everything was different from what it had so lately seemed; even the two who sat beside her. Her respect for her aunt had become something much more like awe; 'Try it, darling,' was a summons to her from one who was a sibyl indeed. Her father was different too. He seemed no more the absurd, slightly despicable, affected and pompous and irritating elderly man whom she had known; all that was unimportant. He walked alone, a genie from some other world, demanding of her something which she had not troubled to give. If she would not find out what that was, it was no good blaming him for the failure of their proper relation. She, she only, was to blame; the sin lay in her heart whenever that heart set itself against any other. He might be funny sometimes, but she herself was very funny sometimes. Aunt Sybil had told her she didn't love anyone; and she had been slightly shocked at the suggestion. The colour swept into her cheeks as she thought of it, sitting still during the sermon. But everything would be different now. She would purify herself before she dared offer herself to Henry for the great work he contemplated.

At lunch it appeared that his ordinary work, however, was going to occupy him for the afternoon as well as the morning. He apologized to her for this in a rather troubled way, and she mocked him gently.

'Father's going,' she said, 'and you'll be shut up. It'll be perfect heaven to look at the furniture or read a murder story—only your grandfather doesn't seem to have many murder stories, does he, darling? All his literature seems so very serious, and quite a lot of it's in foreign languages. But there's yesterday's paper, if I'm driven to it.'

'I must do it,' Henry said, rather incoherently. 'There's no other way.'

'Where there's a will there's a way,' she said. 'You haven't got the will, Henry. You don't think the world's well lost for me.'

'I've a will for what's useful,' he said, so seriously that she was startled.

'I know you have, dearest,' she said. 'I'm not annoying you, am I? You sounded as if you were going to do something frightfully important, that I hadn't a notion of.'

He found no answer to that, but wandered off and stood looking out of the window into the frosty clearness of the day. He dared not embrace her lest she should feel his heart beating more intensely than ever it had beaten for his love; nor speak lest his voice should alarm her sensitive attention to wonder what he purposed. It was one thing to see what had to be done, and if it had not been for Nancy he could have done it easily enough, he thought. But to sit at lunch with her and 'the murdered man.' If she ever knew, would she understand? She must, she must! If she didn't, then he had told his grandfather rightly that all his intention was already doomed. But if she did, if she could see clearly that her father's life was little compared to the restoration of the Tarots, so that in future there might be a way into the mystical dance, and from within their eyes might see it, from within they—more successful than Joanna—might govern the lesser elements, and perhaps send an heir to all their knowledge out into the world. If they perished, they perished in an immense effort, and no lesser creature, though it were Nancy's father or his own—though it were Nancy herself, should she shrink—must be allowed to stand in the way. She would understand when she knew; but till she had learned more he dared not tell her. It would be, he told himself, cruel to her; the decision for both of them must be his.

The sombre determination brooded over the meal. As if a grey cloud had overcast the day and the room, those sitting at the table were dimmed and oppressed by the purpose which two of them cherished. Aaron's eyes fixed themselves, spasmodically and anxiously, on the women whom his business was to amuse; Henry once or twice, in a sudden sharp decision, looked up at Mr. Coningsby, who went on conversing about

Christmas lunches he had known, about lunches in general, the ideal lunch, the discovery of cooking, fire, gas-fires, air, space, modern science, science in the Press, the present state of newspapers, and other things. Sybil assisted him, more talkative than usual, because the other three were more silent. Nancy felt unexpectedly tired and chilly, though the room was warm enough. A natural reaction of discouragement took her, a natural—yet to her unnatural—disappointment with Henry. Her eyes went to him at intervals, ready to be placated and delighted, but no answering eyes met hers. She saw him, once, staring at his own hands, and she looked at them too, without joy, as if they were two strange instruments working at a little-understood experiment. The dark skin, the long fingers, the narrow wrists—the hands that had struck and caressed hers, to which she had given her free kisses, which she had pressed and stroked and teased—they were so strange that they made her union with them strange; they were inhuman, and their inhumanity crept deeper into the chill of her being. Her glance swept the table; five pairs of hands were moving there, all alien and incomprehensible. Prehensile … monkeys swaying in the trees: not monkeys … something more than monkeys. She felt Sybil looking at her, and refused to look back. Her father's voice maddened her; he was still talking—stupid, insane talk. He a Warden in Lunacy! He was a lunatic himself, the worse for being uncertifiable. O, why didn't he die?

A fork and spoon tinkled. Mr. Coningsby was saying that forks came in with Queen Elizabeth. She said, quite unexpectedly, 'In Swift's time people used to say "Queen Elizabeth's dead" instead of "Queen Anne's dead."'

Henry's hand jerked on the cloth, like some reptile just crawled up from below the table. She went on perversely, 'Did you know that, Henry?'

He answered abruptly, 'No,' and so sharp was the syllable that it left all five of them in silence, a silence in which either Elizabeth or Anne might have passed from a world she knew to a world she could not imagine. Sybil broke it by saying, 'It was the change of dynasty that made their ends so important, I suppose? No one ever said "George II is dead," did they?'

'Aren't we being rather morbid?' Aaron asked, in a kind of high croak, almost as if the reptile Nancy had imagined had begun to speak. Cold … cold … and cold things making discordant noises. O, this wouldn't do: she was being silly. She made an effort and reminded herself that this was Mr. Lee speaking—and it was a gloomy conversation: not so much gloomy as horrid. Everyone was unnatural—at least, Henry was unnatural, and her father was overwhelmingly natural, and Mr. Lee…. He was saying something else. She bent her attention to it.

'There are some manuscripts,' he was saying, 'you might like to look at this afternoon. Some poems, part of a diary, a few letters.'

'I should like to very much,' Sybil said. 'What sort of a man does he seem to have been?'

'I'm afraid I've not read them carefully enough to know,' Aaron replied. 'He was, of course, disappointed; the cause had been ruined, and his career with it.'

Sybil smiled. 'He believed that?' she asked. 'But how foolish of him!'

Henry said, 'Is it foolish to give oneself to a purpose and die if it perishes?'

'Disproportioned, don't you think?' Sybil suggested. 'One might die rather than forsake a cause, but if the cause forsakes you——? They're pathetic creatures, your lonely romantics. They can't bear to be mistaken.'

Nancy shivered again. Even Sybil's lovely voice couldn't help giving the word 'mistaken' rather a heavy and fatal sound. 'Mistaken'—utterly mistaken. To mistake everything life had concentrated in, to be *wrong*, just*wrong*…. O, at last the meal was ending. She got up and followed her aunt and Aaron to the drawing-room, loathing herself and everybody else, and especially the manuscript relics of the unfortunate peer.

Henry saw Mr. Coningsby off. 'Which way shall you go?' he asked.

'I shall walk as far as the village and back,' his guest said. 'If I see the vicar I shall congratulate him on the service this morning—bright, short, and appropriate. A very neat little sermon too. Quiet and convincing.'

'What was it about?' Henry said, against his will trying to delay the other. He looked at him curiously: 'bright, short, and appropriate' were hardly the words for the thing that was gathering round him who had spoken. The reared tower of his life was already shaking; and it was Henry whose hand pushed it.

'O, behaving kindly—and justly,' Mr. Coningsby said. 'Very suitable to the villagers who go. Well, I mustn't delay. I'll be off.'

'Take care you take the left path at the division as you come back,' Henry said.

'Quite, quite; the left,' Mr. Coningsby said, and disappeared. Henry went his own way—not to the drawing-room, where Nancy, with all her heart but much against her temper, expected him to look in for a few minutes. He didn't. She cursed herself, and went on staring at the peer's extremely eighteenth-century diary, taking no part in the chat of the other two. Sybil began reading a poem aloud.

CLARINDA: ON RECEIVING A LETTER

cruel Clarinda, must this Paper show
thy Fortune that I now may know?
h still the Town retain thee, perjured
ot some Thought of me the Town inv
forgotten when I did depart,
ou oblivious of a Faithful Heart?
ir to thee is but a grateful Pain,
y pretended by the Amorous Swain;
, in me Despair is all my Sense
teful as impoverished Joy's Pretence–

'Impoverished Joy's pretence'—Nancy knew that was what she was feeling, and knew how hateful it was. At the same time she realized that she was feeling tired—O, so absolutely tired. She must get away and lie down and rest: she'd be better then by tea-time. And perhaps Henry would be free, and impoverished Joy need no longer pretend. When the poem was finished, she said, rather ungrateful to the wretched peer, 'He wasn't a very good poet, was he? I suppose Clarinda had thrown him over. Mr. Lee, would you think me a perfect pig if I went and lay down and went to sleep? I'm only just keeping my eyes a little way open.'

'My dear girl, of course,' Aaron said. 'Anything you like. I'm so sorry. You're not overtired, are you?'

'No, O no,' Nancy protested. 'It's just … it's just … that I'm unutterably sleepy. I can't think what's come over me.'

As he went to open the door, she smiled at her aunt. Sybil said in a low voice, 'Being in love is a tiring business—I mean getting into love. Sleep well, darling.'

She slept at least without dreams, unless that sudden vision of her father falling from a high precipice from which she woke and sprang up was a dream. It was his scream that had wakened her; was it—or was it that howling wind? There was something driving against the windows; for a moment she thought it was a great white face staring in, then she knew it for snow—heavy, terrific snow. Bewildered, she blinked at it. The day had changed completely: it was dark, and yet, from the unlit room, white with snow. The wind or the scream sounded again, as, still half-asleep, she clung to the bed and gazed. Her father—he must be in by now. It was close on five. Her father—faces looking for him—her father crying out. She ran uncertainly to the door, and, driven by an unknown fear, went hurrying to the hall. There was Sybil and Aaron—Sybil with her coat on, Aaron protesting, offering…. Nancy came up to them.

'Hallo,' she said. 'I say, aunt, you're not going out, are you?'

Sybil said something that was lost in the noise of the blizzard; Nancy looked round. 'Where's father?' she asked.

'Out,' Sybil said. 'I was just going to meet him.'

'Hasn't he come back?' Nancy said. 'But, I say, he'll never find his way….' If only she hadn't dreamed of his being thrown over a precipice. There was no precipice here. But he'd screamed.

'But it's absurd,' Aaron said. 'Henry'll go. I'll call him. I've let the chauffeur go home. But Henry'll go.'

Sleep was leaving Nancy, but dream and fear and cold took her. Her father ought to have been back long ago—and where *was* Henry? He couldn't be working all this time, in this tumult. He and her father were missing—and her aunt was going out—and she?

'I'll go,' she said. 'You can't go, aunt. I'll go.'

'You,' Sybil said, 'can go and look for Henry. We can't leave Mr. Lee to do everything. I've no doubt your father's all right, but he may be glad of an arm. Even mine. Help Mr. Lee to shut the door.'

If her father had taken the wrong road—if hands were guiding him the wrong way—if he were being thrust——

Sybil opened the door: the wind struck at their throats and half-stifled them; the snow drove at their faces. Over her shoulder Sybil said, 'It is rather thick.'

'O, don't go,' Nancy said. 'You'll be flung over the edge too. I'll go—I hated him—I'll go. What can you *do?*'

'You go and find Henry,' Sybil said, leaning forward against the wind. 'I can adore the mystery of love.' The tall figure was poised for a moment against the raging turmoil beyond and around, then it took a couple of steps forward and was lost to sight. Aaron struggled to close the door, desperately alarmed; it had been no part of his intention that Sybil also should be exposed to the powers that were abroad. But he hadn't been able to stop her. Nancy, in a torment of anger at herself, flung forward to help him; that done, she turned and fled to find Henry. Where was Henry? Some terror beat in her: Henry and her father—a scream in the storm. She ran into Henry's room; he wasn't there. She rushed out again—to other rooms; she raced through the house, and couldn't find him. Was he in the room of the images? If so, the old man must open it for her. But

Aaron had vanished too, and the wind was howling even louder round the house. She burst in on the maids in the kitchen thrilling at the storm—'Mr. Lee; where's Mr. Lee?' Before they could answer with more than the beginning of stammered ignorance she was off again. Well, if he wasn't here she would go without him. She *must* go. She rushed into her own room, and as she pulled on her coat she gazed out of the window on the wild chance of seeing her father's returning figure, though (could she have thought) she would have remembered that her room looked out over the terrace at the side of the house. But it was then that she saw Henry.

He was standing at one end of the terrace facing slantingly out so as to command from a distance the road that led to the village, and to be himself unseen except from one or two higher windows. He was standing there; she could only just see his figure through the dark snow-swept day, but it was he—certainly it was he. What he was doing there she couldn't think; he couldn't be watching for her father—that would be silly. He must have a reason, but, whatever the reason, it must wait; his business now was to come with her. She flew out of the room, downstairs, along a corridor that led to a small door giving on to the other end of the terrace, just beside the drawing-room which occupied the bottom corner of the house; not more than thirty yards from Henry she'd be then. She opened it and desperately fought her way out.

The next thing she knew was that the wind had flung her back against the wall of the house and was holding and stifling her there. Bludgeons of it struck her; snow and wind together choked her. She turned her head to face the wall, drew a sobbing breath or two, and cried out 'Henry' once. Once, for she could hardly hear herself, and with her remaining intelligence she kept her breath for other things. Surely Henry couldn't be out in this; the wind beat and bruised her again, thrusting her against the wall. For a moment she forgot everything, and reached out to find the doorway and drag herself into shelter, but even as her hand touched the edge she tore it away. No, Henry wasn't indoors and he was out here; and her business was to get to him. She began to edge along the wall. He had been standing at the extreme end of the terrace; so if she worked along the wall, and then (if necessary) crawled out on her hands and knees, she ought to find him. Unless he had gone….

She ventured to look over her shoulder. The wind, even in its violence, was rhythmical; it rose to its screaming height and ceased a little, and then began to rise again. In a pause she looked and could see only the falling snow. She looked back just in time to avoid a blast that seemed almost to smash at her as if it were a great club, and went on struggling along the wall. Aunt Sybil was out in this, and her father, and Henry. In God's name, why Henry? Her father by accident, and Sybil by—by love. Love—O, to get away from this, and anyone who liked could have love! 'No, no,' she gasped. 'No, darling; I'm sorry.' She looked round once more and saw—not Henry, but another shape. In the snow, leaping up through the air, preluding the new blast of wind that blinded and strangled her, there swept a wild figure waving in each hand a staff of some kind, and another like it followed. She saw the swinging clubs, she heard shrieking—the wind shrieking—and almost lost her footing as the renewed strength of it came against her. For some minutes she clung to the wall; mad memories that the crisis of the last half-hour had driven from her mind returned. Death with the sickle—earth from the deniers—the gipsy who drove the Armada—and the powers of the wind screamed again as if once more they saw the dismasted and broken ships swept before them through the raging seas. Henry—where was Henry? What was Henry doing out at the end of the terrace? Before the thought had formed in her mind she herself screamed—one protesting shriek: 'Henry, my darling, don't, don't!' And as she did so she began to struggle on again towards an end which she did not dare imagine. Whatever it was, she must be there; Sybil had told her to find Henry—but Sybil must be dead by now; nothing could live in this storm, any more than the Spanish vessels flung on the Scottish rocks. Sybil must be dead—well, then, it all lay on her; she was left to do the bidding of a greater than herself. And if Sybil wasn't dead—Sybil who had seen the Fool moving, who had said 'Try it, darling.' 'Try it'—and she was crawling along the house-wall! Though Death ran at her, though the Hanged Man faced her, though the Tower fell upon her, though a skeleton rose in her path—'Rise to adore the mystery of love.' She pulled herself upright and passionately flung round to face the wind and snow.

Something, away, among them, was moving: something was sweeping up and down. She forced herself a step out from the wall: there was the end, there was where Love meant her to be, there then was where she was except for the slight inconvenience of getting there. Another step; another—she was, by the mere overwhelming force of the storm, driven down, she stumbled and fell on to one knee; there she looked up to those moving shapes and knew them for hands. Regularly, monotonously, they swept down and out, holding something; they were huge, gigantic—as her own had seemed in the golden mist. As her own in the golden mist, so these in the white surges of the snow, and the snow swept out from them. On one knee she fought to get nearer—to face another terror, she dimly felt, but of a different kind. This, if that other were true, this could be stopped. The great hands swept down again, and colossal snowflakes drove towards her on a renewed blast that drove her down literally to hands and knees. But she crawled and dragged herself on; she was almost there; she was under them—those awful moving origins of storm. She kneeled upright, she struck up at them and missed, they had swept right outward and as they more lightly turned she flung at them with her own hands outstretched. She caught and held them, but as they struggled with hers in that first surprise, and dragged themselves away and up, bringing her to her feet with them, something that they held slipped and was gone. She clutched and clung to them, holding them in, pressing them back, and as she did so and was drawn inward with them she fell forward and knew suddenly that she lay on Henry's breast.

Lost in the concentration and movement of the spell, he did not know she was near him till his hands were seized and, pulling them frantically away, he dragged her grey-coated form up with them out of the storm. It was against his heart before he knew it; he had one spasm of terror lest something unknown had turned on him, lest an elemental being, a bearer of staffs, had crept near to embrace its master. He cried out, then, recovering, checked, and then again broke into a shout of rage. 'You fool,' he cried, 'you fool! You've knocked the cards away!' In his hand he held but a few; peering at them in the dusk, he discerned but the four princely chiefs; the rest, as she clutched them, had slipped or blown off, and were now tossing in the wind which rose from them, seething with power, vagabond and uncontrolled. Even with her weight against him he took a step or two forward, but her arms clung round his shoulders and he could not shake himself free. The catastrophe—the double catastrophe, for the magical instruments were lost, and the wild whirlwind was free—struck at his heart; he stood, still, stricken. She half-raised her head. 'Henry, please don't,' she murmured.

'You've stopped it,' he said. There could be no secrets now; by another way than either had intended they had been brought into knowledge of each other, and might speak clearly.

'Stop it now,' she urged. 'Darling, don't do it. Not this way.'

'I can't stop it,' he said. 'I haven't got them. You've—— Get in, get in: we mustn't be here. Anything may happen.'

In that great rending of both their spirits they could not clamour. The Tower that each had raised—the Babel of their desired heavens—had fallen in the tumult of their conflicting wills and languages, and a terrible quiet was within their hearts. They were joined in an unformulated union of despair. He accepted the arm about his shoulder; he put his own arm round her. 'Back,' he said, 'to the wall; to the door. Come.'

The storm was still soaring upward and outward from around them, so that their way was at first easier. But before they reached their refuge it had spread more wildly; battle raged in the air, and the heavens, once disturbed only at a distance where the invoked disturbance struck them, were now themselves in full action. Natural and supernatural riot ruled everywhere. Once Nancy was torn from him, and only as if by chance their clutching hands re-gripped, frenzied with the single desire and power of preservation. Twice they were beaten down amid the already heaping snow, and had to drag themselves along till an accidental and local lull in their enemy let them scramble to their feet. They were dashed against the wall; they were held motionless by the madness of the elements. At last they came, almost broken, to the harbour of the open doorway. They stumbled through the drift that was forming in it, and the need for new labour presented itself. But other human aid was near. Henry, half-blind, staggered towards the kitchen, called the maids, and ordered one of them to help him to clear the doorway and fasten the door, while the other took charge of Nancy. With his last effort he saw the lock turned, the bolt driven home; then he dropped to the floor of the passage, unconscious at once of his purpose, his thwarting, and his accomplishment.

————————————

CHAPTER IX

SYBIL

Sybil Coningsby stepped out into the storm and tried to see before her. It was becoming very difficult, and the force of the wind for the moment staggered and even distressed her. She yielded to it a little both in body and mind; she knew well that to the oppositions of the world she could in herself offer no certain opposition. As her body swayed and let itself move aside under the blast, she surrendered herself to the only certain thing that her life had discovered: she adored in this movement also the extreme benevolence of Love. She sank before the wind, but not in impotence; rather as the devotee sinks before the outer manifestations of the

God that he may be made more wholly one with that which manifests. Delaying as if both she and it might enjoy the exquisite promise of its arrival, it nevertheless promised, and, as always, came. She recovered her balance, swaying easily to each moment's need, and the serene content which it bestowed filled again and satisfied her.

It satisfied, but for no more than the briefest second did she allow herself to remain aware of that. Time to be aware, and to be grateful for that awareness, she enjoyed; literally enjoyed, for both knowledge and thankfulness grew one, and joy was their union, but that union darted out towards a new subject and centre. Darted out and turned in; its occupation was Lothair Coningsby, and Lothair was already within it. It did not choose a new resting-place, but rather ordered its own content, by no greater a movement than the shifting of the accent from one syllable back to the other. So slight a variation as gives the word to any speaker a new meaning gave to this pure satisfaction a new concern. She was intensely aware of her brother; she drew up the knowledge of him from within her, and gave it back within her. In wave after wave the ocean of peace changed its 'multitudinous laughter' from one myriad grouping to another. And all, being so, was so.

Such a state, in which the objects of her concern no longer struck upon her thoughts from without, recalled by an accident, a likeness, or a dutiful attention, but existed rather as they did in their own world—a state in which they were brought into being as by the same energy which had produced their actual natures—had not easily been reached. That sovereign estate, the inalienable heritage of man, had been in her, as in all, falsely mortgaged to the intruding control of her own greedy desires. Even when the true law was discovered, when she knew that she had the right and the power to possess all things, on the one condition that she was herself possessed, even then her freedom to yield herself had been won by many conflicts. Days of pain and nights of prayer had passed while her lonely soul escaped; innocent joys as well as guilty hopes had been starved. There had been a time when the natural laughter that attended on her natural intelligence had been hushed, when her brother had remarked that 'Sybil seemed very mopy.' She had been shocked when she heard this by a sense of her disloyalty, since she believed enjoyment to be a debt which every man owes to his fellows, partly for its own sake, partly lest he at all diminish their own precarious hold on it. She attempted dutifully to enjoy and failed, but while she attempted it the true gift was delivered into her hands.

When the word Love had come to mean for her the supreme greatness of man she could hardly remember: one incident and another had forced it on her mind—the moment when her mother, not long before death, had said to her, 'Love, Sybil, if you dare; if you daren't, admit it'; the solemn use of the name in the great poets, especially her youthful reading of Dante; a fanatic in a train who had given her a tract: *Love God or go to Hell*. It was only after a number of years that she had come to the conclusion that the title was right, except perhaps for *go to*—since the truth would have been more accurately rendered by *be in Hell*. She was doubtful also about *God*; *Love* would have been sufficient by itself but it was necessary at first to concentrate on something which could be distinguished from all its mortal vessels, and the more one lived with that the more one found that it possessed in fact all the attributes of Deity. She had tried to enjoy, and she remembered vividly the moment when, walking down Kingsway, it had struck her that there was no need for her to try or to enjoy: she had only to be still, and let that recognized Deity itself enjoy, as its omnipotent nature was. She still forgot occasionally; her mortality still leapt rarely into action, and confused her and clouded the sublime operation of—of It. But rarely and more rarely those moments came; more and more securely the working of that Fate which was Love possessed her. For it was fatal in its nature; rich and austere at once, giving death and life in the same moment, restoring beyond belief all the things it took away—except the individual will.

Its power rose in her now and filled her with the thought of her brother. As she came from the drive into the road she looked as alertly as she could before her in case he staggered into sight. Whether she was going to find him or not she couldn't tell, but it was apparently her business to look for him, or she wouldn't have felt so strongly the conviction that, of all those in the house, she alone was to go out and search. That she should be walking so lightly through the storm didn't strike her as odd, because it wasn't really she who was walking, it was Love, and naturally Love would be safe in his own storm. It was, certainly, a magnificent storm; she adored the power that was displayed in it. Lothair, she thought, wouldn't be adoring it much at the moment: something in her longed passionately to open his eyes, so that the two of them could walk in it happily together. And Nancy, and Henry—O, and Aaron Lee, and Ralph, and everyone they all knew, until the vision of humanity rejoicing in this tumultuous beauty seemed to show itself to her, and the delight of creation answered the delight of the Creator, joy triumphing in joy.

It was the division in the road where Lothair might go wrong: to take the right-hand path would lead him away over the Downs. If she got there without meeting him, should she go on or herself turn up the other road? She had long ago discovered that Love expected you to do the best you could to solve such questions before leaving It to decide. The intellect had to be finely ready before It deigned to use it. So she tried to think, and kicked something in the road.

It wasn't her brother at any rate, she thought, yet it had felt as if it were soft and alive. She bent down, put her hand out, and, grasping something just at her feet, gathered it up—to discover that it was a rather large kitten. Where it came from she couldn't think—probably from the Lees' house. She warmed and caressed and petted it, till the half-frozen brute began to pay some attention, then she undid a button of her coat and thrust in her hand and wrist, extended upon which the kitten lay contentedly purring. Sybil went on, smiling to think that perhaps Lothair had passed her and was already safe; the Power that governed her would be quite capable of dragging her out of the house to save a kitten from cold. She adored It again: perhaps the kitten belonged to some child in the village, and she was taking a four-mile walk in a snowstorm to make a child and a kitten happy. Lothair, she thought, would be honestly puzzled by that, and (she thought more regretfully) while he was honestly puzzled he probably wouldn't be encouraged to take the four-mile walk. So everyone would be satisfied.

The storm lifted, and she found herself at the parting of the roads, and there, by the hedge, on the extreme wrong side, was a crouching figure. The snow was beginning to pile round it; the wind and flakes seemed to be rushing at it and centring on it. Sybil, holding the kitten firmly, went quickly across the road. For a moment, as she ran, she thought she saw another form, growing out of the driving snow—a tall figure that ran down on the white stairs of the flakes, and as it touched earth circled round the overwhelmed man. Before it a gleam of pale gold, as of its own reflection, since no break in the storm allowed the sinking sun to lighten the world, danced in the air, on the ground, on hands that were stretched out towards the victim. They seemed to touch him, as in the Sistine Chapel the Hand of God for ever touches the waking Adam, and vanished as she reached it. Only, for a moment again, she saw that gleam of flying gold pass away into the air, lost within the whiteness and the gloom. Then she was by him; she leaned down; she touched a shoulder, and held and shook it gently. She herself knelt in the snow to see the better—it was Lothair. His hat was gone; his glasses were gone; his coat was half-off him, flying loose; the buttons, she found, as she tried, with one hand, to pull it round him, were all off. He was blue and dangling.

'What a thing it is to be a Warden in Lunacy,' Sybil thought, 'and how much like a baby the dear looks! and how he'd hate to think so! Lothair! Lothair, darling! Lothair!'

He took no notice, save that he seemed to relax and sink even lower. 'O dear,' Sybil sighed, 'and I can't put the kitten down!' She pulled at the coat till she got it more or less properly over him; then she stood up, put her left arm round him beneath the shoulders, and made an enormous effort to pull him up also. It was impossible; he was too heavily irresponsible. She stilled herself—either Love would lift him or Love would in some other way sufficiently and entirely resolve the crisis that held them. The practised reference possessed her, and then, kneeling by him, she went on shaking him and calling to him: 'Lothair! Lothair! Lothair!'

He opened dull eyes on her. "S that you, Sybil?' he said. 'Are they go'?'

'Are who gone?' she said. 'Do take me home, Lothair. It's such a terrific storm.'

"ur quite all righ',' he muttered. 'Jus' res' a min' an' I'll get alon'. Are they go'?'

She shook him again. 'I've never been out in such weather. Lothair, you always look after me. Do, please, please, take me back!'

She put a poignant wail into her voice that disturbed him. He made his first movement. 'I'll look a'ter you,' he said. 'I'll take … back in min'. Didn' know you were here.'

'I came to you to meet you,' she said, distraught and appealing. 'And I'm out in it too.'

He gently shook his head, as he had often done over her folly. 'Silly o' you,' he said. 'Ver' silly. Stop indoors. Did they hit you?'

She clutched his shoulder with a strength that brought him back to clearer consciousness. 'Ow!' he said, 'Sybil, be careful. We must get on. You shouldn't have come out.' But even as he began to struggle slowly to his feet he looked round, still only half-restored. 'Funny,' he went on. 'Sure I saw them. Running by me, beating me. Each side. Great men with clubs.'

She thought of the figure she had seemed to see, but she answered, 'I've not seen them, my dear. O, Lothair, help me up.' Her arm was in his as she spoke, and, so twined, they both struggled awkwardly to their feet. The kitten, alarmed at the earthquake, stuck its claws into Sybil's wrist. She rubbed it with her little finger to pacify it, and it slowly removed them. Once on his feet, Mr. Coningsby began to take charge. 'Keep your arm in mine, and don't be frightened. It was a good thing you saw me—you'd have been quite lost. I'd stopped for a minute—get my breath. Had you better hold on—both hands?'

'One's enough, I think,' Sybil said. 'We'd both better keep our coats round us, and we shall have to hold them.'

She didn't feel like producing the kitten, and also she was engaged in secretly getting him on to the right road: she didn't think Love meant them to stand in the snow arguing which was the way to go. And if Lothair thought it was the left....

He vacillated, but not between the roads. The screaming and howling of the blizzard grew louder, and as they moved away from the hedge, both huddled against the wind, for his crouching dragged her upright body down, he paused. 'I wonder,' he gasped, 'if ... hadn't better ... shelter there ... a bit.'

'O, take me back,' said Sybil. 'I've got you.' The ambiguity of those words pleased her immensely, and she said them over again, more slowly, separating them, enjoying the exquisite irony of the universe, which made them even more subtle than at first she had seen. For certainly *she* hadn't got him; something other than she was, as she had known it would, carrying and encouraging them both.

'Yes,' Mr. Coningsby panted. 'You're quite all right.'

'Good God,' said Sybil she thought she might allow herself that, in the circumstances—'yes. Only don't leave me.'

'I won't——' he began, but had to abandon it, and merely gasp, 'No.'

They went on, struggling back along the way she had come so easily. Most of the time he hung on her arm, leaned on her, or even stumbled and fell against her. But he murmured protective assurances at intervals, and Sybil, her arm pulled and wrenched, her breath knocked from her at every stumble, couldn't help thinking how really charming and affectionate he was. Because he certainly thought he was helping her on, and he never grew irritable through all that task of salvation, or not beyond panting once or twice, 'Can't think ... why you ... came out. Horrible day'; and once, 'Good thing you ... found me.'

'It was,' she answered. 'I'm very grateful.' He was really moved, even in his present state, by the thought of her danger; he was very good. 'My dear,' she said, pressing his arm.

Slowly, under that imperious command of death, they drove their way onward; each, with more or less strength and intensity, devoted to the other's preservation. Away on the terrace, Nancy clung to the terrible moving hands, and the magical invocation of wind and snow broke from the hands of the practitioner and rode free: storm to the tenth degree of power was loosed without control.

Fortunately, when, unknown to them, that mischief chanced, they were already near the drive; fortunately for them also, the wider dissemination of the origins of storm weakened it a little directly round them. But as they turned in for the last effort to reach the house, Mr. Coningsby almost halted; only Sybil's determination kept him moving; as a mere human being, she felt that if the kitten stuck its claws in her once more she should forget that she loved it. It had done so whenever her brother fell against her, and whenever he dragged her over to him. 'Need you hold on *quite* so firmly, darling?' she silently asked it. 'You're quite safe, you know. Sparrows falling to the ground, and so on. I suppose you're like us; you've made your mind up *not* to fall to the ground, whether your heavenly Father knows it or not. O, Lothair dear, you nearly had me over. Kitten, don't please. That is, if either of you could possibly manage without.'

Mr. Coningsby almost halted. Right in front of them—in the blind tumult they had almost collided—were other figures; three of them, it seemed. Sybil peered forward.

'I ... told ... you so....' her brother managed to articulate; 'men ... with clubs.'

One figure seemed to have a kind of club; indeed, as it struggled on, Sybil saw that it had, but it was rather a staff on which it leant than a club. But the other two hadn't. They were all going more slowly than the two behind them, who had, indeed, everything considered, come along with remarkable speed. Or, *everything* considered, perhaps not so remarkable.

'They're making for the house, I expect,' Sybil said. 'Though how they can see their way ...' Unobtrusively she guided her brother to one side. 'We'd better catch them up,' she added.

Mr. Coningsby nodded. He was drifting again towards unconsciousness. 'Then all of us have good res',' he said; Sybil could only just hear him. 'Nice quiet time.'

There was, even Sybil admitted, something attractive in the idea of a nice quiet time. She peered again at the other travellers as they drew level, and saw that the middle one of the three was a woman, a small woman hanging on the arms of the others, but talking. Sybil could just catch the sound of a voice: then the man nearest her turned his face towards her, and she recognized it.

'Ralph!' she cried.

'Hallo, aunt!' Ralph gasped. 'Hell of a day ... what ... you doing ... out in it?'

'Walking,' Sybil said vaguely, but he couldn't hear her, and the conversation ended. He made some inquiring gesture in front of him; she nodded. All five of them beat on together. But the sound from the woman went on, and even pierced the storm and reached Sybil's ears; it was a kind of chanting. The shrill voice mingled with the wind and was the only thing that was not silenced by it. Its scream answered the wind's scream; though it was blown away, it was not lost, but carried as if on the music of a mad unison. The storm sang with its companion, reinforced her, made way for her. A word or two came to Sybil.

'… coming … coming … the whole one shall awake….'

Ralph turned his head with difficulty and made a face at her. Discreetly turned from her brother, she grimaced back. She wondered—could it be the old gipsy Henry had called Joanna? That might explain why these others held so straight a course for the house. But with what wild song was she challenging or hailing the blizzard? and what energy of insane vision so filled her as to give her voice and spirit this strength, though her body hung on the arms of her supporters? Certainly it was not for Sybil Coningsby to deny the dismemberment through earth of the ever-triumphant Osiris, nor the victory that the immortal freshness of Love continually won over his enemies. If it was Love that the old woman was praising now, the shrill voice didn't quite sound like it. But it might be; with the sweet irony of Perfection, one could never tell. It was never what you expected, but always and always incredibly more.

Something dim loomed in front of them; they were there—they were right up against the front door, Lothair and the kitten and Ralph and these others and she herself: not for salvation from death, but for the mere manifestation of its power, she adored the Mystery of Love. She pressed the bell steadily; Ralph hammered on the door; the other man—Stephen, if it was Stephen—beat on it with his stick. Her brother fell against the door-post. The old woman turned her head—Sybil and she gazed at one another, their eyes recognizing mysteries of remote initiations.

'Perfectly hellish weather!' Ralph said.

They heard someone within. The door was opened by Aaron himself, and the blizzard and they entered together. Sybil helped her brother in; then she gave Ralph a quick hand with the door. It closed gradually and was made fast. Her back against it, Sybil turned gently, removing the kitten from her numb arm, and saw Lothair sinking on to a seat; Stephen leaning against the opposite wall; and Joanna, all dripping with melting snow, facing a snarling Aaron.

'I've come,' she cried, 'I've come. Don't hide him, Aaron. I've come to see him wake.'

CHAPTER X

NANCY

It was still hardly six o'clock. Mr. Coningsby had been put to bed, after Nancy had flown to welcome him and her aunt—to rather more than welcome her aunt, perhaps, for Sybil felt in the clinging embrace something she could have believed to be a clutching despair. She looked at the girl intently as they drew apart. Nancy's face was colourless, her eyes very tired: the new light which had for weeks shone from her was eclipsed, and her movements were heavy and troubled. 'Where's Henry?' Sybil casually asked. 'O, shut away somewhere,' Nancy said, and shut herself away even more secretly.

Ralph was introduced and taken to have hot drinks and a hot bath. It appeared that he had determined to rush across in his car from the house where he was staying, to hurl Christmas greetings at his people on Christmas Day, and then to tear back. He was slightly ashamed of the intention, more especially as in the first excited feeling of safety he had told Sybil that he had thought it would please his father.

'That was very nice of you, Ralph,' she said warmly.

'O, I don't know,' he answered vaguely. 'I mean—he was looking a bit aged the other day, I thought, and if a man's getting on … well, I mean he *likes* people to think about him a bit, I suppose. I mean, it wouldn't matter two grey Grimalkins to me whether anyone came to see me on Christmas Day or not; there's always plenty of people about anyhow. But he doesn't seem to get up to more than about forty per h. at the best, does he?'

'And what's yours normally?' Sybil said gravely.

'O, I don't know; say, a lusty sixty,' Ralph meditated. 'But I'm rather a quiet one really, Aunt Sybil. I mean——'

Here he was interrupted, and only given time hastily to explain how the storm had caught and held the car; how he had at last got out and gone a little way to see if there was another road or anything; how he had lost his way back, and then encountered the other two wanderers, with whom he had gone along—partly because

211

they had seemed to be aiming somewhere, partly to give Joanna an arm. 'And I must say,' he added quietly and hastily to Sybil, 'the set of carols that she sung all the time curdled anything in me that the snow didn't. O, she was a lively little Robin Redbreast.'

Sybil thought, as she herself was carried off—quite unnecessarily, she assured them—that there was something not wholly inapplicable in the phrase. The two women were apparently the least exhausted of all the five. Joanna was sitting on one of the hall chairs; her old red cloak pulled round her, and snow melting and pouring from her on every side. Aaron obviously wasn't a bit pleased, but nothing could be done. He couldn't push Joanna and Stephen out into the blizzard, and no one naturally would help him, and they wouldn't go. 'But I wonder,' Sybil thought, 'why they dislike each other so. Is it just family, or is it something special?'

She would not go to bed, certainly not, but hot drinks—yes; and a hot bath—yes; and a complete change—yes. Drinks and baths and changes were exquisite delights in themselves; part of an existence in which one beauty was always providing a reason and a place for an entirely opposite beauty. As society for solitude, and walking for sitting down, and one dress for another, and emotions for intellect, and snowstorms for hot drinks, and in general movement for repose, repose for movement, and even one movement for another, so highly complex was the admirable order of the created universe. It was all rather like Henry's charming little figures in their perpetual dance; perhaps they were a symbol of it; perhaps that was what was meant by Aaron's uncertain phrase about being magnetized by the earth. They were the most beautiful things, with that varying light irradiating and striking outward from each, and a kind of gold aureole hanging in the air, which had expanded and heightened while Nancy's fortune was being tried. As she saw them again in her mind she saw at the same time the faint golden gleam that had possessed the air around her brother. She knew where the golden light came from among the images; it came from the figure of the Fool who moved so much the most swiftly, who seemed to be everywhere at once, whose irradiation shone therefore so universally upward that it maintained the circle of gold high over all, under which the many other rays of colour mingled and were dominated now by one, now by another. It had been, this afternoon, as if some figure—say, the Fool himself—had come speeding down from his own splendid abode of colour to her brother's side. She contemplated the idea; so, one might imagine, only no imagination could compass it, so did the beautiful perfection which was in and beyond all things make haste to sustain its creatures in their need; immediacy to immediacy. She moved her foot lazily through the water of the bath, and half-pretended, half-believed, that little sparkles of gold rose and floated off as she did so: then she abandoned the fancy hastily. 'I'm getting mythical,' she said aloud; 'this is the way superstitions and the *tantum mali* arise. Only,' she added, in a charming apology, 'I knew I was doing it, and I *have* left off. People,' she went on thinking, 'have killed one another on questions like that—did you or did you not see a golden sparkle? Well, the answer is, No, I didn't, but I saw the ripples in the water, and the top of my toe, and even though it may annoy Lothair, it is a very well-shaped toe. How sweet of Love to have a toe like that!'

She wondered as she dressed where Henry was; she'd rather expected to find him also in the hall. Nancy's 'shut away somewhere' had been obscure—not merely in the meaning but in the tone. It hadn't been bitter; it hadn't been plaintive; it had been much more like an echo of despair. Despair? Had Henry refused to come out or something? had he a complex about snow? did it make him go what Ralph—if she had the phrase right—called 'ga-ga'? If so, Nancy's winters—except for the luck of the English climate, to which Lothair (judging from his continual protests about it) had a profound objection—Nancy's winters might be rather trying. Henry might have to hibernate. She imagined Nancy teaching her children: 'Mother, what animals hibernate?' 'Bears, tortoises, hedgehogs, and your father.' Squirrels, snakes? did snakes and squirrels hibernate? It couldn't be that; he wouldn't have become a barrister if the Long Vacation was merely a prelude to a sound sleep. So awkward if he could only have summer clients. 'Nobody could have much affiance in a barrister who could only take summer clients.'

She re-ordered her thoughts; this was mere dithering. But dithering was rather nice; occasionally she and Nancy had dithered together. Nancy. What was wrong with the child? She had sat down to put on her shoes, and—one off and one on—she turned to her habitual resource. She emptied her mind of all thoughts and pictures; she held it empty till the sudden change in it gave her the consciousness of the spreading out of the stronger will within; then she allowed that now unimportant daily mind to bear the image and memory of Nancy into its presence. She did not, in the ordinary sense, 'pray for' Nancy; she did not presume to suggest to Omniscience what it would be a thoroughly good thing if It did; she merely held her own thought of Nancy stable in the midst of Omniscience. She hoped Nancy wouldn't mind, if she knew. If, she thought, as, the prayer over, she put on her other shoe—if she had believed in a Devil, it would have been awkward to know whether or not it would be permissible to offer the Devil to Love in that way. Because the Devil might dislike it very much, and then…. However, she didn't believe in the Devil, and Nancy, up to lunch anyhow, had believed in a—if not the—mystery of Love. She determined to go and see if Nancy by any chance would like her to listen. Besides, there was Lothair—who in a strange home would certainly want her to be somewhere about. Also there was Joanna—Sybil rather looked forward to a conversation with Joanna, who seemed to her to have, on the whole, a just view of the world, if rather prejudiced against the enemies of Horus.

On the point of going downstairs, she checked herself. It was possible that Nancy, relieved from anxiety about her father, was not downstairs, but in her own room next door. Sybil considered this, and decided, if she were, that there would be no harm in venturing a visit; it could easily be ended. She went and knocked. A high, shaking voice said, 'Come in.'

Nancy was lying on the bed; she barely looked round as her aunt entered, and, on the point of speaking, gave up the effort.

She looked worse than she had done downstairs; a more complete collapse showed in her. Sybil, from the door, beheld a dying creature, one in whom the power of Life was on the point of evacuating its last defences. But she looked also a creature betrayed, one in whom the power of Life had changed to Death while she was still aware. The storm that had attacked the bodies of others might have crushed her soul; a wan recognition of the earth lingered in her eyes before she fell into entire ruin. Sybil came swiftly across the room.

'What's the matter, darling?' she said.

Nancy made a small movement with one hand, but didn't answer. Sybil sat down on the bed, and very lightly took the hand in her own. They remained so for some minutes in silence; then, in a voice hardly breaking it, Sybil said:

'All beauty returns. Wait a little.'

Nancy trembled, as if the storm shook her from within; she said 'No' in a moan and was silent. But the moan was at least life; the denial was at least consciousness; and Sybil ventured then so far as to put an arm round the girl's shoulders. There she rested silent again, bending all the power that she had to find what remote relic of power still existed somewhere in that strange overthrow. Time went past, but after a long while Nancy's fingers had closed ever so little more tightly on Sybil's hand; her shoulder pressed ever so little more willingly against the encircling arm. The blizzard without struck again and again at the window, and suddenly for the first time Nancy shuddered when she heard it. In a horrible stifled voice she said, 'You don't know what that is.'

Sybil tightened her grasp and gathered Nancy more closely into eternity. As if the remorseless will of that peace broke her into utterance, Nancy said, still in the same horrible voice, 'It's Henry killing father.'

The executive part of Sybil's mind had been so disciplined that it was not allowed to be startled. She said, and though her voice was low it was full of profounder wisdom than the words seemed to carry: 'He came back with me.'

'If he didn't,' Nancy answered, 'if he'd died out there, if I'd died, the storm would have stopped. It won't stop, now. It'll go on for ever. It's Henry killing father, and he can't leave off. I've stopped him.'

Her brother's fancy of 'great men with clubs' came into Sybil's mind for a perplexing moment. She dismissed it gently, not to break the deeper labour on which she was engaged. She answered with all the tenderness of her certainty: 'You couldn't do anything at all unless you were let, could you? And if you were let stop it, then stopping it was the most perfect thing that could happen. Only *you* mustn't stop now.'

The storm shook and rattled at the windows. Nancy jerked violently and cried out: 'Nothing can stop it. He's lost them; he can't.'

'What is it that's lost?' Sybil asked commandingly, and the girl answered in almost a shriek, 'The Tarots, the magical leaves.' She went on in a high torment: 'He had them; he beat them up and down; he made the storm to kill father, and I knocked them away, and they're gone, and nothing can stop the wind and the snow for ever. It'll find father and it'll drown the whole world. Hear it dancing! hear it singing! that's the dance Henry keeps in his little room.'

'I know the dance,' Sybil said instantly. 'Nancy, do you hear? I know the dance, and the figures that make the dance. The crown's gold over them, and there's a movement that Henry's not known yet. Do you suppose that storm can ever touch the Fool?'

Why she used the words she didn't know, but something in them answered the girl in the same terms in which she had cried out. Her face changed; there came into it a dim memory of life. She said, arrested in the midst of terror and death, 'The Fool——'

'I saw the gold in the snow,' Sybil said,' and your father was in it and safe. Do you think the Tarots can ever escape while the Fool is here to hold them?'

'They say he doesn't move,' Nancy breathed.

'But I saw him move,' Sybil answered, eternal peace in her voice, 'and there's no figure anywhere in heaven or earth that can slip from that partner. They are all his for ever.'

'The snow?' Nancy said.

'And you and I and Henry and your father,' Sybil answered. 'It is only the right steps we have to mind.' She was not very clear what language she was using; as from the apostles on Pentecost, the single gospel flowed from her in accents she had not practised and syllables she had never learned. She added, deeply significant: 'Your father came back with me; mayn't Henry be waiting for you?'

As a proselyte in the streets of Jerusalem, drawn from the parts of Libya about Cyrene, hearing a new message in a familiar tongue, Nancy looked up for the first time.

'Why?' she said.

'Do you think the mystery of Love is only between those who like one another?' Sybil said. 'Darling, you're part of the mystery, and you'll be sent to do mysterious things. Tell me—no, never mind the storm; it's nothing; it's under the feet of the Fool—tell me what's happened.'

Uncertainly at first, and in no sort of order, Nancy began to pour out her story of all that she had known of the Tarots. She broke off, she went back to the beginning and leapt to the end, she confused her own experiences with what Henry had told her, and that again with what she believed Henry to desire, and all of it with her outraged will to love. It was confusion, but in the confusion, as if in a distant unity of person, went the motionless and yet moving figure of the Fool, and about his feet as he went flowed the innocent and ardent desire of the girl who told it to do all that she could—for Henry perhaps, but, even more than for Henry, for the unfathomable mystery of which she had known something and had half-hoped, half-despaired to know more.

Sybil herself, being prepared for anything at any moment, as those who have surrendered themselves must naturally be, all amazement being concentrated in a single adoring amazement at the mere fact of Love, and leaving no startled surprise for the changes and new beauties that attend It—Sybil herself listened gravely and intelligently to the tale. She saw, not in her own mind so much as in Nancy's, the whole earth, under the stress of what had been heard and seen, taking on a strange aspect. She saw—but this more in her own mind—the remote figure of the Juggler, standing in the void before creation was, and flinging up the glowing balls which came into being as they left his hands, and became planets and stars, and they remained some of them poised in the air, but others fell almost at once and dropped down below and soared again, until the creating form was lost behind the flight and the maze of the worlds. She saw, as the girl's excited voice rushed on, the four great figures between whom the earth itself hovered—the double manifestation of a single fact, the body and soul of human existence, the Emperor and the Empress, and diagonally opposite them, the hierophants male and *fe*male, the quadruple security of knowledge and process upon earth. The rushing chariot of the world came from among them, and it again parted, and on one side went the Hermit, the soul in its delighted solitude of contemplation, and on the other the Lovers, the soul in its delighted society of terrestrial love.

'And earth came out of them,' Nancy said breathlessly. Earth and air and fire and water—the lesser elements pouring down from below the Greater Trumps, but these also in the dance, and in each of those four cataracts she saw the figure of the Fool, leaping and dancing in joy. 'So I thought it was the Hanged Man, and I screamed.' Nancy had dashed to another part of the tale, and Sybil remembered the crucifixions of her past, and by each of them, where she herself hung and screamed and writhed, she saw the golden halo and the hands of the Fool holding and easing her, and heard his voice murmuring peace. 'And what shall we do? what shall we do?' the young creature babbled at last, and, half-risen, clutched hard at Sybil and broke into a storm of tears. But as she wept and agonized Sybil's hands held and eased her and Sybil's voice murmured peace.

How far her vivid intelligence at the moment believed the tale was another matter. Whether the pieces of painted papyrus and the ever-moving images, the story of newly created earth and the swift storm, Henry's desire and her brother's firmness, the sight of her own eyes and the vision of the rest, Nancy's tragic despair and Joanna's wild expectation—whether all these corresponded to some revelation of ultimate things she could not then tell, nor did she much mind. The thing that immediately concerned her was Nancy's own heart. There was the division; there, justified or not, were bewilderment and fear. If it were delusion that possessed her, still it was clear that that delusion was too deep and far-reaching to be torn up by a few easy words of bright encouragement. If it were not delusion, if the strange and half-mystical signs and names of the Greater Trumps had meaning and life, then no doubt in the due time of beneficence her own concern with them would be revealed. She held Nancy more closely.

'Dearest,' she said, 'your father's safe. Do you understand that?'

'Yes,' Nancy sobbed.

'Tell me then—there, darling, quietly; all is well, all is most well—tell me, where's Henry?'

'In his own room, I suppose,' Nancy said brokenly. 'I—I ran away from him—when I knew.'

'Did he want you to—run away?' Sybil asked slowly.

'I don't know—no,' Nancy said. 'But I couldn't stop. He'd been doing that awful thing—and I was terrified and ran away—and I love him. I can't live if I don't find him—and now I never shall.'

'But, darling, that's not loving *him*,' Sybil gently protested. 'That's only preferring to live, isn't it?'

'I don't care what it is,' Nancy sobbed again. 'If I could do anything, I would, but I can't. Don't you understand—he tried to *kill* father? There's just Death between them, and I'm in the middle of it.'

'Then,' Sybil said, 'there's something that isn't death, at least. And you might be more important than Death, mightn't you? In fact, you might be life perhaps.'

'I don't know what you mean,' Nancy said, wresting herself free suddenly. 'O, go away, Aunt Sybil. I'm going mad. Do go away.'

Sybil sat back on the bed. 'Stand still and listen,' she said. 'Nancy, you said it yourself, there's death and there's you. Are you going to be part of death against Henry and against your father? or are you going to be the life between them? You'll be power one way or another, don't doubt that; you've got to be. You've got to live in them or let them die in you. Make up your mind quickly, for the time's almost gone.'

'I can't do anything,' Nancy cried out.

Sybil stood up and went over to her. 'Your father came back with me,' she said. 'Go and see if Henry still has any idea of going anywhere with you. Go and see what he wants, and if you can give it to him do. I'll see to your father and you see to Henry. Do let's get on to important things.'

'*Give* it to him!' Nancy exclaimed. 'But….'

'Dearest,' Sybil said, 'he may not want *now* what he wanted two hours ago. People change their minds, you know. Yes, honestly. Go and live, go and love. Get farther, get farther—now, with Henry if you can. If not—listen, Nancy—if *not*, and if you loved him, then go and agonize to adore the truth of Love. Now.' She gave the girl a little gentle shake, and moved away to the door, where she stopped, looked over her shoulder, said, 'I should be as quick as I could, darling,' and went.

Nancy stared after her. 'Go to Henry'? 'go and live'? 'go and love'? To be life or death between her lover and her father? Her hands to her cheeks, she stood, brooding over the dark riddle, seeing dimly some sort of meaning in it. Something had kept her father alive; something held her father and herself—if that something were waiting for her to move? to go to Henry? She couldn't think what she could do there, or of what, divided and united at once by a terrible truth, they could possibly even speak. Life wasn't all speaking. Love was being something, in some way. Was she now to be driven to be *that*, in the way that—who knows what?—chose? Slowly she began to move. Henry probably wouldn't want her, but…. She went gradually and uncertainly towards his room.

He was sitting, as she had been lying, in darkness. When she had knocked and got no answer, she had taken the risk of annoying him and had gone in, switching on the light. She saw him sitting by his table and switched it off again. Then she went delicately across the room, kneeled by him, touched him lightly, and said, 'Henry!'

He did not answer. In a little she said again, 'Darling,' and as still he made no sound she said no more, only went on kneeling by his chair. After many minutes he said, 'Go. Go away.'

'I will,' she answered sincerely, 'if you want me to, if I can't help. Can I help?'

'How can you help?' he said. 'There's nothing for any of us but to wait for death. We shall all be with your father soon.'

'He's back, quite safe,' she said. 'Aunt Sybil met him and brought him back.'

'It was a pity; the storm will have to find him out again,' he answered. 'Go and be with him till that happens.'

'Must it happen?' she asked, and he laughed.

'Unless you have a trick to lure back the chalices and the staffs,' he said. 'If you can, you can put them in their order and seal up the storm. But since they are rushing and dancing about the sky I can't tell how you'll do it. Perhaps if you talked to those that are left——'

'Mightn't we?' she asked, but he did not understand her.

'Try it,' he mocked her again. 'Here are the four princes; take them and talk to them. Perhaps, since you struck all the rest loose, these will tell you where they are. O, to be so near, so near——!'

'I should have done it all the same if I'd known,' she said, 'but I didn't know—not that I should do that. I only wanted to hold your hands still.'

'They'll be still enough soon,' he mocked, 'and so will yours'; and suddenly his hand felt for and caught hers. 'They're beautiful hands,' he said; 'though they've ruined the world, they're beautiful hands. Do you

215

know, Nancy, that you've done what thousands of priests and scientists have talked about? This is the end of the world. You've killed it—you and your beautiful hands. They've sent the snow and the wind over the whole world, and it'll die. The dance is ending: the Juggler's finished with one ball.'

'Love them a little then,' she said, 'if you're sure. If you're quite sure.'

'Can you bring back the staffs?' he asked, 'from the one to the ten? Shall I open the window for you to call or catch them? Maybe one's on the window-sill now.'

'Can't the images help?' she asked. 'I don't know, but you should. Isn't there any way in which they could command the Tarots?'

She felt him stiffen in the darkness. 'Who told you that?' he said. 'I can't tell. I don't know anything of what can be done from within. If….'

'If——' she answered, and paused. 'I will do anything with you that I can. What would you like me to do?'

His figure turned and leaned towards her. 'You?' he said. 'But you hated what I was doing, you wanted to save your father—of course you did; I'm not blaming you—but how can you help me now?'

She broke unexpectedly into a laugh, the sound of which surprised some solemn part of her nature but seemed to bring freedom at once into herself and into the dark room, so that she felt relieved of her lingering fear. 'O, Henry darling,' she said, 'must those dancers of yours concentrate on my father? Haven't they any way of doing things without bothering the poor dear? Don't you think they might manage to save the world and yet leave him alone? Henry sweetest, how serious you are about it all!'

'You can laugh,' he said uncertainly, not as a question nor yet in anger, but as if he were feeling after some strange fact. 'You can laugh … but I tell you it is the end of the world.'

She scrambled to her feet. 'I begin to agree with Aunt Sybil,' she said; 'it isn't quite decent to break into the poor thing's secrets when it's gone to such trouble to keep them quiet. But since you and I together drove things wrong, shall you and I together see—only see, darling—if we can put them straight?'

'You're afraid of the Tarots,' he said; 'you always have been.'

'Never again,' she said, 'or yes—perhaps again. I'll be afraid again, I'll fall again, I'll hate and be angry again. But just for a moment there's something that runs and laughs and all your Tarots are flying along with it, and why shouldn't it catch them for us if we ask it very nicely? Only we won't hurt anyone, will we, if we can help it? Nothing's important enough for that.'

He got to his feet heavily. 'There's no way anywhere without hurting someone,' he said.

'Darling, how gloomy you are,' she said. 'Is this what comes of making blizzards and trying to kill your own Nancy's own father? Perhaps there's a way everywhere without hurting anyone—unless,' she added, with a touch of sadness clouding the full gaiety that had seized her, 'unless they insist on being hurt. But let's suppose they won't, and let's pretend they don't, and let's be glad that my father's safe, and let's see if the golden dancers can call back the staffs and the cups. I think perhaps we owe the world that.' She kissed him lightly. 'It was sweet of you to pick out a nice soothing way of doing what you wanted,' she said. 'Some magicians would have put him in a barn and set it on fire, or forced him into a river and let him drown. You've a nice nature, Henry, only a little perverted here and there. All great geniuses are like it, they say. I think you must be a genius, darling; you take your job so solemnly. Like Milton and Michael Angelo and Moses. Do you know, I don't believe there's a joke in all the Five Books of Moses. I can't see very well, Henry, but I think you're frowning. And I'm talking. And talking and frowning won't do anything, will they? O, hark at it! Come along, my genius, or we shan't save the world before your own pet blizzard has spoilt it.'

'There's no other way,' he said, 'but I warn you that you don't know what may happen. Perhaps even this isn't a way.'

'Well, perhaps it isn't,' she answered. 'But they are dancing, aren't they, dearest? And perhaps, if we mean to love——'

'Do you love me still then?' he asked.

'I never loved you more and yet I never loved you less,' she told him. 'O, don't let's stop to ask riddles. And, anyhow, I wasn't thinking of you, so there! Come, darling, or your aunt will be doing something curious. Yours is a remarkable family, Henry; you get all het up over your hobbies. And so you shall if you like, bless you! only not just now.'

'Joanna——' he exclaimed, unconsciously following her as she drew him towards the door. 'Is she here?'

'She is,' Nancy said, 'but we won't worry about her now. Take me to them, darling, for the dance is in my ears and the light's in my eyes, and this is why I was born, and there was glory in the beginning and is now and ever shall be, and let's run, let's run, for the world's going quickly and we must be in front of it to-night.'

—————————

CHAPTER XI

JOANNA

In the hall below, the kitten stretched itself and yawned. Sybil had put it down when she was once well inside and asked one of the maids to look after it. But there had been no time yet; Mr. Coningsby, Ralph, Sybil herself, had to be seen to. And now there were still Joanna and Stephen. Aaron Lee, looking at his sister with something very much like watchful hatred, said: 'Now you're here, Joanna, you'd better get into bed. And so,' he added, jerking his head at Stephen, 'had he.'

'Yes, Aaron,' said Joanna docilely, with a little giggle. 'It's a bad night to be out in, isn't it?'

Aaron glanced round him; the three, except for the kitten, were alone in the hall.

'Why have you come?' he asked.

'To see you, dear,' the old woman said. 'So's Stephen. He's very fond of you, Stephen is. Aren't you, Stephen?'

'Yes, grandmother,' Stephen answered obediently.

'He's very big, isn't he?' Joanna ran on. 'Much bigger than you, dear Aaron.' She hopped off her chair and began to prowl round the hall, sniffing. Presently she came to the kitten and stood staring at it. The kitten rubbed itself against her leg, felt the wet, and sprang aside. The old woman, bending, scratched its head, and began muttering to it in words which the others couldn't hear.

The kitten jumped up, fell down, twisted over itself, dashed off, and dashed back. Joanna gesticulated at it, and it crouched watching her.

'You'd better get to bed, Joanna,' Aaron exclaimed to her. 'Get those things off and get between the blankets. You'll be ill if you don't.'

'You fool, Aaron,' Joanna said. 'Illness can't touch me any more than death. I shall never be ill. I shall be transformed when the body that's lost is made whole.' She turned her face towards him. 'And where'll you be then, Aaron? Screeching among the tormentors.'

'You're mad,' Aaron answered. 'You're a mad old woman hobbling about in a dream.'

She left the kitten and almost ran back to him. 'Dream, hey?' she snarled. 'Little dream, Aaron Lee, for you that help to hide my baby.'

'Your baby's dead,' Aaron snarled back, as the two small old creatures faced each other fiercely and despitefully. 'Don't you know that by now?'

She caught at his coat, and at the movement of her arm the water that still ran from her was flung wide-spattering around. 'My baby never dies,' she cried, 'and you know it. That's why you hate me.' Her whole manner changed. 'But you're right, dear Aaron,' she mumbled, 'yes, you're right. Give me your bed to sleep in and your plate to eat from and I'll give you a plate and a bed one day in a finer house than this. Give me a kiss first, Aaron, and I'll never set Stephen on to you to twist the news of the grave where you've hidden him out of your throat. Kiss me, Aaron.'

She was up against him, and he stepped sharply back to face her. His foot came down on the tail of the kitten, which was smelling at his shoes. It yelped; Aaron tottered and lost his footing, staggering a pace or two away. He turned fiercely on the kitten, which had dashed wildly across the hall.

'Put it out,' he cried, 'put it back in the snow. Who brought it in? Stephen, catch it and put it out.'

The young man, who all this while had been leaning dully against the wall, the snow melting from him, his eyes following Joanna wherever she went, moved uncertainly. Joanna made no sign, and he, with movements that seemed clumsy but were exact, first attracted the kitten and then caught it up in his great hands.

'What shall I do with it, grandmother?' he said.

'Put it out,' Aaron called to him.

'Ah, no, don't put it back in the snow,' Joanna said. 'Ah, it's a cunning little cat; it's very small, but everything's small at first. It'll grow; it'll grow. Let it sleep in my blankets, Aaron; the cats know where the blood fell, and they sit in a circle round the hidden place watching for God. Have you ever found their eyes looking at you, Aaron, when you were shuffling the cards? little green eyes looking up at you? little claws that scratched? Give it to me, and it'll sleep till the right time comes.'

'No cat'll come to you in those drenched clothes,' Aaron said, with a curious flat effort at common sense. But, unhearing, she beckoned to Stephen, and, when he came, took the kitten from him. It wriggled a little in her hands and mewed once, but it did not make any serious effort to escape. She held it near her face, peering and muttering at it, and it stared back at her. The colloquy of their eyes lasted some dozen seconds; then

Joanna said: 'Show me where I'm to rest, Aaron.' A maid returned at the moment. Aaron conferred with her and then said abruptly to Joanna, 'Go along with Amabel; she'll show you.' Then to Stephen, 'And you—come with me. You can rub yourself down and have some food.'

'Ah, let Stephen sleep in the same room with me,' Joanna cried, 'for we're used to it and we're uneasy apart. Haystack or lych-gate or king's house or quarry, it's all one to us so long as there's Stephen to watch while I'm dreaming and me to wake while Stephen sleeps. Only he can't see my dreams, and though I see his they're only water and wind and fire, and it's in earth that the other's hidden till Horus comes.'

With the word a quietness fell on her; she brought the kitten against her cheek and crooned to it, as she followed the bothered and dubious Amabel away.

Stephen presumably 'had some food,' but he was not at the late and bewildered dinner to which, soon after, Aaron sat down with Sybil and Ralph. Aaron muttered something about Henry's probably being busy, and seemed to take it for granted that Nancy, after her experience of the storm, was also in bed. Sybil, when she grasped this, thought that Nancy might have been annoyed to have it thought so, but then even Sybil had not quite grasped the true history of the afternoon. She knew that Nancy believed that Henry had loosed the storm on Mr. Coningsby, by means of the magical operation of the power-infused Tarots. But she was not aware of the short meeting of Henry and Aaron, when the younger man had recovered consciousness to find his grandfather, summoned by an agitated maid, bending over him. In a few sentences, as he came to himself, he told Aaron what had happened. Aaron stepped back, appalled.

'But then,' he faltered, 'we can't stop the winds,' and his face paled. 'We shall all be killed.'

'Yes,' Henry said. 'That's the end of all our dreams.'

As he spoke he had gone away to his own room, to sit in darkness brooding over his hope and his defeat, waiting for the crash that must come when the force of the released elements broke in on the house, and had sat so till Nancy came to him. But Aaron had refused, in his own mind, to believe it; it couldn't be so. Something might happen, some wild chance might save them. He had never cared much for Henry's intrusion into the place of the powers, and Henry might easily be wrong. The manuscripts told them this and that, but the manuscripts might be wrong. In the belief that they were true, Henry and he had plotted to destroy his guest—but the storm might be a coincidence; Coningsby might be safe; in an ordinary storm he would be; it wasn't as if, all put together, it was a long distance or a great danger, *unless*—unless the snow and wind had been aimed at him. If they were not, if it was chance, if indeed the Tarots and the images had no power in themselves and were but passive reflections of more universal things, if the mystery of both was but a mystery of knowledge and prophecy and not of creation and direction—why then—the stranger would come back safely, and, if he did, why then they would all be safe. That some of the paintings should be lost was indeed a catastrophe; no one now could justly divine the movement of the images and their meaning. The telling of fortunes would be for ever but a childish game, and never the science of wisdom. But he would be alive. The long study in which he had spent his years might partly fail. But he would be alive. On the very verge of destruction, he cried out against destruction; he demanded a sign, and the sign was given him. Lothair Coningsby came stumbling into the hall, and when Aaron saw him he drew great breaths of relief. The storm was but natural; it would cease.

In this recovered quiet of mind he was able to deal with immediate practical questions; he was even able to confront Joanna with his old jealousy and hatred. Since, many years before, the images had come into his possession, since his father and he had—O, away in his boyhood!—taken them (with what awful and breathless care! what almost eye-shutting reverence!) from the great round old silver case—only some six inches high, but marvellously huge in diameter—in which for centuries, so his father had told him, this hidden secret of the gipsies had been borne about the world, covered by wrappings and disguises, carried in waggons and carts, unknown even to most of their own wandering bands, who went straying on and did not know that one band of all those restless companies possessed the mystery which long since some wise adept of philosophical truths had made in the lands of the east or the secret houses of Europe: Egyptian or Jew or Christian heretic—Paulician, Bogophil, or Nestorian—or perhaps still farther off in the desert-circled empire of Abyssinia, for there were hints of all in the strange medley of the sign-bearing images, and the symbols wore no accepted or traditional aspect; their familiarity was foreign, they had been before the building of churches and sects, aboriginal, infinite: but, from wherever they came, he who had made them, and the papyrus paintings with them, up to seventy-eight degrees of knowledge, had cased and hidden them, and sent them out on everlasting wanderings without as they kept among themselves the everlasting dance within. But at that making and hiding the Tarot cards had lain in due mysterious order on and about the golden base of the Tarot images, each subtly vibrating to the movements of its mightier golden original, as that in turn moved in correspondence to the movement of that full and separate centre of the created dance which it microcosmically symbolized. There was to be a time, the legends said, when one should arise who should understand the mystery of the cards and the images, and by due subjection in victory and victory in subjection should come to a secret beyond all, which secret—it had always been supposed by those few who had looked on the shapes, and few they had been even over the centuries—had itself to do with the rigid figure of the Fool. But the dark fate that falls on all mystical presentations, perhaps because they are not presentations only, had fallen on this; the doom which struck Osiris in the secular memory of Egypt, and hushed the holy, sweet, and terrible Tetragrammaton in the ritual of Judah, and wounded the Keeper of the Grail in the Castle of the Grail, and by the hand of the blind Hoder pierced the loveliest of all the Northern gods, and after all those still everywhere smote and divided and wounded and overthrew and destroyed; by the sin of man and yet by more and other than the sin of man, for the myth of gods and rebellious angels had been invoked—by reason, no doubt, to explain, but by something deeper than reason to frame the sense of a dreadful necessity in things: the need that was and yet must not be allowed to be, the inevitability that must be denied, the fate that must be rejected, so only and only by such contradictions of mortal thought did the nature of the universe make itself felt by man. Prophesied itself within itself by the Tower that fell continually or by the fearful shape of Set who was the worker of iniquity ruling over his blinded victims, prophesied thus within itself, the doom came to pass on the mystery of the images, none knew when, for some said as long since as the son of the first maker, who fell from his father's wisdom, and others but in the very generation that preceded the speaker's. But, whenever the sin was done, it chanced upon a night that one opened the silver case, sealed with zodiacal signs, and, daring the illustrious beauty that shone forth, thrust in his hands and tore out the translucent painted leaves, thinking that by them alone he might tell the fortunes of men and grow rich by his fellows' yearning to know what was to be, or wantonly please an idle woman in the low chambers of Kieff or Paris. The images he dared not touch, and the golden base that carried them he could not. So he fled, completing the sacrilege, and died wretchedly, the tale said, but rather because it was thought proper that the sinner should suffer than because anything certain was known. Thus the leaves of the presentation were carried one way, and the golden shapes another, and the people of the secret waited in hope and despair, as Israel languishes till the Return, and the Keeper till the coming of the Haut Prince, and Osiris the slain till Horus overcome his foes, and Balder in the place of shades till after Ragnarok, and all mankind till the confusions of substance be abolished and the unity of person be proclaimed. But, even when the paintings had been found by chance and fate and high direction in the house of Lothair Coningsby, yet the wills of the finders had been set on their own purposes, on experiment of human creation or knowledge of human futurity, and again the mystical severance had manifested in action the exile of the will from its end.

To that last conclusion, as his thoughts recalled the myth, Aaron, sitting at the dinner-table, did not permit himself to reach. In his father's time it had been determined, by a few among the wanderers, that the far-borne images should be carried no farther, since it was yearly becoming more difficult to evade the curiosity and power of the magistrates; enough money, from some rich and many poor, had been gathered, a solitary house had been found, and the treasure had been given into the charge of the oldest of the Lees. The room had been prepared and the silver chest carried in, and, that the influence of the dance might more quickly draw to itself its lesser instruments, the images had been set upon the new-shaped table. But upon their father's death the knowledge of the charge had been, as it were, separated between Aaron and Joanna, and both again misunderstood the requirements of devotion, Joanna in hot dreams of her child, Aaron in cold study of the continuous maze. Her madness drove her wide, his folly kept him still; and when she came to him he forbade her even a sight of the sacred thing. So through years their anger grew between them, and now she lay in his home.

He hated and feared her, yet he did not well know what in her he feared and hated. He did not much think she would dare to touch the images, and, anyhow, without Henry's aid or his own she could not find them through the outer and inner chambers. It was perhaps no more than the intensity of her desire, and the mad energy which for her turned the names of Egypt to living and invocable deities, and within that her own identification of herself with the Divine Mother and Seeker. It was strange and absurd, but it was also rather terrifying—she was so much one with her dream that at times her dream invaded like the mists of the Nile his own knowledge of her as Joanna. But she was here, and nothing could be done. Perhaps Miss Coningsby, who seemed from Henry's account to have been remarkably successful with her on the road, would be able to quieten her if she fell into one of her fits. Sybil, while she ate and drank, and maintained the conversation as well as could be, considering the spoiled dinner, their preoccupied minds, and the increasing hurricane without, contemplated at the same time the house and its occupants. She saw it, against the background of a dark sky filled with tumultuous snow, part of it yet its opposite, its radiance of enclosed beauty against a devastation of wilder beauty, and in the house she saw the lovely forms of humanity each alive with some high virtue, each to its degree manifesting the glory of universal salvation. Her brother, industrious, as generous as he knew how to be, hungry for peace, assured, therefore, of finding peace; Henry and Nancy—Henry, she thought, had been a little mistaken if he imagined that violence of that kind would bring him to the kingdom; stillness rather, attention, discipline—but Henry and Nancy—she ardently hoped they were together and moving into peace; Ralph with his young freshness and innocence; Aaron with his patient study and courtesy—even if the courtesy had hidden some other intention, as, if Nancy were right, it probably had, still courtesy in itself was good and to be enjoyed: yes, certainly good was not to be denied in itself because motives were a little mixed. Her own motives were frequently mixed; the difference between delighting in ... well, in the outrageous folly of mankind (including her own) and provoking it grew sometimes a little blurred. She was uneasily conscious that she sometimes lured her butcher in London into showing off his pomposity, his masterful attitude towards his employees, because it seemed to her so wonderful that he should be able to behave so. 'My fault,' Sybil sighed to herself, and offered herself once more as a means whereby Love could more completely love the butcher. Not, of course, that Love didn't completely love the butcher already, but through her perhaps ... however, that argument was for the theologians. Anyhow, with that sin in her mind it was not for her to rebuke Aaron or Nancy. Before perfect Love there wasn't much to choose between them. At the same time, without excusing herself, it was up to the butcher to see that he wasn't drawn, if he didn't want to be, even as subtly as she knew she did it; and in the same way it was up to her to see that the charm of Aaron's manners didn't any further involve her brother in disagreeable experiences. The courtesy was one thing; the purpose of the courtesy was another thing; there need be no confusion of substance. She smiled back at Aaron. 'And where,' she asked, 'is my kitten?'

'In my sister's room, as a matter of fact,' Aaron answered. 'If you want it——'

She signed a negative. 'Why, no,' she said, 'of course not. Did I tell you that I found it in the snow? I thought it must belong to the house.'

Aaron shook his head. 'Not here,' he answered. 'We never have any animals here, especially not cats.'

'Really?' Sybil said. 'Don't you like them, Mr. Lee? Or doesn't the air suit them? Or do they all refuse to live in the country and want to get to London, to the theatres and the tubes? Are the animals also forsaking the countryside?'

He smiled, saying, 'It isn't a social law, Miss Coningsby, but it's a rather curious fact. They—the cats we've had from time to time, for one reason or another—they spend all their time round my study door, miaowing to get into the room of the images.'

Ralph looked up; this was the first he had heard of a room with images.

'Dogs too,' Aaron went on, 'they do the same thing. In fact, we've had a mighty business sometimes, getting them away—when we've had one. It'd snarl and bite and go almost mad with rage before it'd be taken back to its kennel. And there was a parrot Henry had when he was a boy—a cousin of mine gave it to him, a magnificent bird—Henry left the door of its cage unfastened by accident one night, and we found it the next morning dead. It had gone on dashing itself against the door of the room till it killed itself.'

There was a moment's silence; then Ralph said: 'Parrots are jolly useful things. I know a man—he's at Scotland Yard, as a matter of fact, and he has to see all sorts of cranks and people who think other people are conspiring or fancy they're on the track of dope-gangs ... of course not the very silliest kind, but those that there just might be something in—well, he got so fed up that he had a parrot in his room, put it away in the window opposite his table so that it was at the back of anyone else, and he taught it, whenever he stroked his nose several times, to say "And what about—last—Tuesday—week?" It had an awfully sinister kind of croak in its voice, if you know what I mean, and he swore that about half his people just cleared out of the room without stopping to ask what it meant, and even most of those that didn't were a bit nervy most of the rest of the time. He got a shock once though, because there was a fellow who'd lost a lot of money racing on the Tuesday week, and when he was reminded of it suddenly like that, he just leapt up and cursed for about twenty minutes straight off before getting down to his business again.'

'That,' said Sybil with conviction, 'was an admirable idea. Simple, harmless, and apparently effective. What happened to the parrot, Ralph?'

'O, well, it got all out of hand and a bit above itself,' Ralph answered. 'It kept on all the time asking "What about last Tuesday week?" till my friend got sick of it. Especially after some fellow tried to do him in one Tuesday with a hammer. So he had to get rid of it. But he always thought it'd be a brainy notion for solicitors and business men and vicars and anybody who had a lot of callers.'

'Beautiful!' Sybil said. 'The means perfectly adapted to the end—and no fuss. Would you jump, Mr. Lee, if someone asked you what you were doing last Tuesday week?'

'Alas, I am always leading the same life,' Aaron said. 'There hasn't been a day for years—until this Christmas—that I've had cause to remember more than any other. No, I shouldn't jump.'

'And you, Ralph?' Sybil asked.

'Well—no,' Ralph said, 'I should have just to think for a minute…. I mean, in Scotland Yard and all. But—no, not after a second.'

'How innocent the old are,' Sybil said, smiling to Aaron. 'I shouldn't jump either.'

'No, but then you never *do* jump, do you, Aunt Sybil?' Ralph protested. 'When that girl we had smashed a whole trayful of china in the hall, you just said, "O poor dear, how worried she'll be!" and dipped out there like a homing-pigeon.'

'Well, so she was worried,' Sybil answered. 'Frightfully worried. But about your animals, Mr. Lee. What's the explanation, do you think?'

Aaron shrugged delicately and moved his hands. 'Who knows?' he answered. 'It sounds fantastic to say the images draw them, but what other cause can there be? Some mesmeric power … in the balance, in the magnetic sympathies.'

'Magnetic sympathy over cats?' Sybil said, a little dubiously. 'Cats never struck me like that. But you won't let my kitten bang itself against the door, will you? Or not till we've tried to amuse it in other ways first.'

'I'll see to its safety myself,' Aaron said. 'I shall be looking in on Joanna, and I'll either bring it away or warn her to keep it safe. She'll treat it carefully enough, with her unfortunate delusions about Egypt. Isn't Ra the Sun God shown in a cat's form?'

'I haven't an idea,' Sybil answered, smiling. 'Perhaps the kitten is Ra, and I carried the Sun God home this afternoon. It doesn't, if one might say so, seem exactly the Sun God's best day.'

They listened to the blizzard for a minute or two; then Sybil looked at her watch. 'I think, if you'll pardon me, Mr. Lee,' she said, 'I'll just run and look in on my brother. He might be glad of a word.' The three of them rose together.

'Present my regrets again,' Aaron bowed. 'It was an entirely unexpected accident and a most regrettable result.'

Sybil curtsied back. 'Thank you so much,' she murmured. 'Lothair will—or will not—think so. But I can't altogether think so myself, if (you don't mind me being frank?), if Henry *did* arrange for the storm.'

He stepped back, startled. 'The storm,' he cried more loudly, 'the storm's only winter snow.'

'But is all winter snow the same storm?' she asked. 'That is, if I've got it right. But isn't it divinely lovely? Do excuse me; I must just see Lothair.' She turned and went.

'Aunt Sybil,' Ralph said in the pause after her departure, 'would find a torture-chamber divinely lovely, so long as she was the one on the rack. Or a broken-down Ford. Or draughts. Or an anaconda.'

———

CHAPTER XII

THE FALLING TOWER

In Aaron's workroom the noise of the blizzard was very high. The two who crossed the room heard it, and heard it roaring still higher as Henry unlocked the inner door. But when they had entered that other room, just as they passed through the curtains, there was a change. The high screech of the wind altered by an infinitely small but complete variation. Nancy heard it no longing screaming, but singing. Her hand in Henry's, she paused between the hangings.

'Do you hear? my dear, do you hear?' she exclaimed. Holding the hangings for her, and listening, he looked back. 'I hear,' he said. 'It's catching us up, Nancy.'

'No, but that's gone,' she protested. 'It sounds different here. Hark!'

As he dropped the curtain, the habitual faint music of the room greeted them. It seemed to the girl that the roar of the wind was removed to an infinite distance, where it mingled with other sounds, and was received into the feet of the dancers, and by them beaten into fresh sound. She stood; she looked; she said to Henry: 'Have you the Tarots, darling?'

He held them out, the suit of sceptres, the suit of deniers, the princely cards of cups and staves.

'I wonder,' she said, 'if we shall be able to find our way in by them alone.'

He looked at her fully for the first time since on the terrace their eyes had beheld each other in the snow.

'I can't tell; this has never happened before,' he said. 'What I tried to do has failed; perhaps it was better that it failed. I did what seemed wise——'

'I know you did,' she said. 'Dearest Henry, I know you did. I do understand that, though I understand so little. There's nothing between us at all. You did—and I did—and now here we are. But you've always talked as if there was a way to—what do you call them?—the Greater Trumps, and as if the Greater ruled the Lesser.'

'Certainly they do,' he answered, 'and therefore the suits are less than the Trumps. But it may be a very dangerous thing to thrust among them as we are, so—half-prepared.'

'Still, we can't wait, can we?' she said. 'And if time would let us, my heart won't—it's beating too hard. Kiss me, Henry, and, in case we are divided, remember that I always wanted to love. And now for the cards. Look, will you hold them or shall I? and what's the best thing to do?'

'Do as you did the other night,' he said, 'and I will put my hands round yours, and hold the eight high cards that are left to us; and then let's move towards the table as you did, but this time we will not stop till we are compelled. And God help us now—if there be a God—for I do not know what we can do or say if we come knowingly into the measure of the dance.'

'All is well; all is most well,' she murmured, and they put themselves in the order he had proposed, but he more fearfully than she. Then, the Tarots pointed towards the dancers, they took the first slow step forward together.

As they did so, the golden mist flowed out again to meet them, and flowed round them as it had compassed her but two nights before. This time, so intent was her will upon its work, she did not look up to him at all, and it was he who was startled by the apparent distortion of her face below his, by the huge enlargement of their hands, by the gigantic leaves that shook and quivered in their clasp, trembling till the very colours upon them seemed to live and move, and the painted figures floated as if of their own volition from the mortal grasp that held them. He did not dare pause, nor could he feel a trace of faltering in the girl who stepped forward, foot by foot, so close to him; only there passed through his mind a despairing ironic consciousness that not thus, certainly not thus, had he purposed to attempt the entrance into the secret dance. He had meant to go victoriously, governing the four elemental powers, governing the twin but obedient heart and mind that should beat and work in time with his, lover and friend but servant also and instrument. By her devotion to his will he had hoped to discover the secret of domination, and of more—of the house of life where conquerors, heroes, and messiahs were sent out to bear among men the signs of their great parentage. And now he was drawn after her. It had been she who had pointed the way, the thought of which had been driven from his mind by the catastrophe that had overwhelmed it. It was she who went first, not by his will but by her own—nor could he then guess how much, to Nancy's own heart, her purpose and courage seemed to derive from him. His power was useless till she drew it forth; it worked through her, but it was from him that it still obscurely rose. Though she ruled instead of him in the place of the mist, it was he who had given her that sovereignty, and it seemed to her then that, though all dominions of heaven and earth denied it, she would acknowledge that profound suzerainty while her being had any knowledge of itself at all.

She pressed on. The great leaves shook and parted and drifted upon the wind, which, as before, seemed to stir in the golden cloud. As one by one they were carried off they took on the appearance of living forms; the transparency which was illumined with the crimson and azure tints of the Queen of Chalices floated before her, farther and farther away, and was indeed a crowned and robed woman bearing the crimson cup; the black and purple of the Esquire of Deniers showed for a moment before it was swallowed up in the cloud as a negro youth in an outlandish garment holding aloft a shining bronze coin, and all surrounded by a halo of light which had once been the papyrus where had been figured the now-living shape. Her hands below her were lucent and fiery in the mist; the golden cloud above those pale shapes, infused with crimson fire of blood, dazzled and dazed her; they were more splendid and terrific even than the visions that rose from them and fled upon the wind. Around them, closing them in, supporting them, were other mighty hands—his. Of his presence otherwise she was by now unaware; she might, but for those other hands, have been alone. But those four hands that by mischance had loosed the winds and the waters on earth were stretched out to recover the power they had inadvertently cast away. The power within her, the offspring of her transmuted love, longed in itself, beating down her own consciousness, for some discovery beyond where mightier power should answer it. She pressed on.

It was at the fourth step that Henry lost her. Still aware of the irony of their movement, still aware of himself as against her, and of both of them as against the mystery of paintings and images, he lost himself for less than a moment in a regret that things should have turned to this result. This was not what he had meant to be; his mind added that this was not what should have been, and almost before his reproach had grown from his pulse into his thought she was gone. His hands were empty; the cloud swirled about him, but he had now no companion. He took a single solitary step; then he ceased to move. He hesitated in the mist; the wind struck him as if it had swept the girl away and was minded to fling him into ruin. He pressed back and fought against it, but not for his own sake then so much as for hers. It pressed him, not in sudden blasts, but with a steady force, so that he could, by leaning against it, just maintain himself. As if he were still on the terrace fighting the storm, he set himself against this oppression, as if indeed all that had chanced since had never been, but for one unrealized change. On the terrace his danger and hers had been known to him with equal urgency. But in fact, since then much had happened. His own schemes had been scattered; her love for him, her love for something greater than him, had shone in his darkness; her laughter had stirred it, her voice had called him from it. Following her, he had come so far; he filled his mind now with desire for her salvation. Let himself go, let the world perish, so only that she walked safely among the perils of this supernatural world. He had mocked at her fear, and now fear for her was in his heart. The mist was in his throat and nostrils; he was choking in it. His eyes were blind, his head swam, in that terrible golden cloud. But, more than that, he knew chiefly that her hands were gone, and that she also was alone.

It was then that the hands took him. At first he did not realize, he did not even notice, what was happening. Filled with a sense of Nancy's possible danger, himself choking and groping in that intolerable shining cloud, and fighting all the time to keep securely upright in the persistent wind, he hardly felt the light clasp that took hold of one ankle. But as he began to move his foot he found it fixed, and fixed by what felt like a hand. He looked hastily down; nothing could be seen through the floating gold. He tried to pull his foot up from the ground; he could not do it. On the point of bending to free his ankle, he hesitated; the mist was so thick down there. He jerked it sharply; the grasp of whatever held it grew tighter, and something slid round the other ankle and held fast. Certainly they were hands; he felt the fingers and thumbs. On the realization he stood still; against these adversaries it was no use battling like a frightened child. Perhaps if something hostile indeed lived in this world he could overcome it—so long as his will held. But what was his will to do?

His feet were being drawn together. He set his will against it, but compulsion moved them. He swept an arm round him, and as it came to his rear his wrist also was seized, and the arm was drawn against his back and held there. The grasp was not harsh, it was even gentle, but it was absolute. It, or another like it, caught his other wrist and drew that also back. The wind ceased; it might have been blowing merely to delay him until the imprisonment was complete.

For what seemed hours nothing more happened, only he was held. His strong and angry imagination strove in vain to find some method of release, and miserably failed. There came to him out of the mist, which had receded a little from him, the sound of music, now increasing, now diminishing, as if something went past him and again returned. He could, once or twice, have believed that he heard voices calling, but they also died away. A faint light shone at intervals; the mist shook as if trembling with a quick passage. But more than these hints of existences he could not catch. He stood there, seeing nothing else. His heart began to faint; this perhaps was the end. Motionless in the place of the Tarots, as motionless as the Fool that stood in the centre—he himself, indeed, a fool of the Tarots. And Nancy—was she also held—her young delight, her immortal courage, her desire for love, in this unchanging golden mist? 'If we are divided, remember that I always wanted to love.' There was nothing here to love but himself—if indeed he wanted to love.

The hours grew into days, into years. Imperceptibly the grasp had tightened; that round his ankles had drawn them together, and that also round his wrists. He was still incapable of movement, but his incapacity was more closely constrained; he was forced more tightly into the mere straight shape of his enclosed body, for the mist closed again round him and moulded itself to his form. He was defined as himself, a bas-relief of him was shaped on that cloud, now almost plastic in its consistency; he could breathe and that was all. His thoughts began to fail within him; he was aware only of his senses, and they were now limited to the sight and feel of the mist. If it had not been for the slight tingling everywhere which the golden vagueness seemed to cause as it pressed on him, and the strong grasp upon his limbs, he would not have been conscious of anything at all—there would have been nothing of which to be conscious. He could no longer even strive to free himself, for the very idea of freedom was passing from him. There was no freedom for there was no knowledge; he was separated from all that he had been, except that dimly, within or without, in that æonian solitude, there occasionally loomed something of a memory of one or other of the Greater Trumps of the Tarots. Somewhere, very vaguely, he would think that he saw in front of him, fashioned of the mist, yet thrown up against the mist, the hierophantic Woman or the Lovers, or the great Tower which reached almost out of sight, so loftily it grew up and then always—just as his dimmed eyes strained to see the rising walls— tottered and swayed and began in a horrible silence to fall apart, but never quite apart. It was raised by hands which, from within the rising walls, came climbing over, building themselves into a tower, thrusting those below them into place, fists hammering them down, so that the whole Tower was made up of layers of hands. But as it grew upward they changed; masonry below, thinner levels of masonry above, and, still above, masonry changing into hands, a few levels of moving hands, and (topmost of all) the busy working fists and fingers. And then a sudden spark of sunlight would fall on it from above and the fists would fall back out of sight, and the hands would disjoin, swiftly but reluctantly, holding on to each other till the ruin tore them apart, and the apparent masonry, as it was rent by some invisible force, would again change back into clutching and separating hands. They clung together fantastically; they shivered and writhed to avoid some principle of destruction that lurked within them, and as he felt that ugly living twist and evasion they would altogether fade back into the mist from which they grew. The years went by, and every now and then, once in every four or five, the Tower was again shown, and each time it was a little closer than before.

The years grew into centuries. He was no longer looking at anything; sight also had departed. Very slowly the Tower had moved right up against him; he could see it no more, for he was one with it. A quiver began at the bottom of his spine, spreading through his loins, and then it ceased, and he felt rigidity within him—up, up, till he was petrified from loins to head, himself a tower of stone. Even so, he meant to do something, to lift a great marble arm and reach up and pick the stars from heaven and tangle them into a crown—a hard sharp golden crown—for a head such as Nimrod's, perhaps his own. He was setting up a gigantic image of himself for heaven and earth to adore. He was strong and great enough to do what no man had done before, and to stand on the top of some high place which would be stable among the circling lights of the celestial world. And then always, just as he felt his will becoming fixed and strong enough to raise his arm and break the clasp of those cold hands, just as he dreamed of the premonitory prick of the starry spikes upon his head, something within him began to fall. He trembled with giddiness; he would have swayed but could not. There ran a downward rippling through his flesh; his lower jaw dropped; his knees shook; his loins quivered; he was dragged at from within in every direction; he was on the edge of being torn into destruction. Then again slowly he was steadied, and again his long petrifaction proceeded, and so through cycle after cycle of years the making and breaking of his will went on, and slowly after many repetitions his heart failed within him and he assented to the impossibility of success. The stars were beyond his reach; Babel was for ever doomed to fall—at the last minute, when the plains of heaven lay but a few yards beyond its rising structure, confusion invaded it, and spread, and the incoherent workers fled, and the elements of the world roared out each upon its own passage, and came together again in wars and tumults, conflicts and catastrophes. But now, each time that he felt the dreadful ruin go falling through him, he heard also one voice rising among that strange and shattering chorus and saying: 'Remember I wanted to love.' Out of each overthrow it sounded, and at every overthrow more clearly. This alone of all his past was urgent; this alone had meaning in the void to which his purpose crashed.

It came more quickly; it was repeated again and again; it grew shorter, words dropping away from it. The centuries ended; a quicker rush of years began; vehemently the call reached him, and as he strove to answer it with some single willingness of intention, the hands of the supernatural powers released their hold. He moved and stumbled; times rushed round him; something brushed against his legs; the mist swirled and broke, and as he stepped uncertainly forward he found himself looking into the face of Joanna, and then the golden cloud again swept between them, and parted once more the two most passionate seekers of the Tarots.

CHAPTER XIII

THE CHAPTER OF THE GOING
FORTH BY NIGHT

Mr. Coningsby had been lying in bed for some time, but he was not asleep. He was restless; his mind was restless. It was all very well, this going to bed, this being put to bed in case he got a bad cold, but—but—he had a continual vision of Sybil before his eyes. Sybil, he had rather dimly gathered, wasn't in bed, and wasn't in the least proposing to go: and if she was up, why was he where he was? Of course, it showed a very nice spirit, no more than he would have expected of the old man, who didn't seem to know anything about Henry's indescribable fatuous insolence in hoping, in rather more than hoping, even expecting, or something like it, that he should be given a set of cards which were part of the only memory he himself possessed of an old and dear friend, a friendship the value of which a young pigeon-stealer like Henry couldn't possibly know; gipsies never made friends, or only of their own kind, vagrants and beggars, the kind of person Nancy had never met—though certainly the grandfather seemed different: probably the mother—the daughter—had run away, only the name was identical, so it must have been the father, but then the family would be the same—however, Aaron Lee was a very different kind of creature, and had behaved very properly. Still, though in the first shock of getting back he had allowed himself to be looked after and waited on and almost cosseted—still, the fact remained that after an hour or so of solitude he didn't like the idea. He wasn't so old that he couldn't be out in a snowstorm and laugh at it. He did a kind of mocking laugh at the blizzard swirling about the curtained windows, to which the blizzard responded by making such a frantic attack on the house that Mr. Coningsby unintentionally abandoned his laughter and looked uneasily at the curtains. If the infernal thing broke the glass and burst in, a nice sight he'd look, dancing round the room and trying to get dressed in a hurry. He had a momentary glimpse of himself feeling for a stud on a snowy dressing-table and trying to fix a tie which continually, 'torn but flying,' streamed away upon the wind. Really, there was a lot to be said for getting up. Besides, Sybil was up, and Sybil wasn't a girl any longer, and, though he'd been out in the storm longer than she had, yet he was a man and he had been rather underlining his own active habits, in an only half-unconscious comparison of himself with the rest. Aaron, Sybil—he supposed Nancy and Henry were up too—while he was tucked up with a hot-water bottle. A hot-water bottle! That was all that the young thought their parents wanted. 'And when,' thought Mr. Coningsby, led on by the metaphor, 'when they get into hot water, with their jumpings and their jazzings, and their nigger-minstrels and their night-clubs, who do they go to to get them out? To the old fellow tucked up with the bottle.' Nothing less likely than any appeal in a crisis by Nancy or Ralph to their father could well have been imagined, but that actual division was hidden from him in his view of the sentimental. They were all up—dining probably. No one so far had brought him any dinner: however, perhaps they weren't dining yet. 'I'm a fair-minded man,' Mr. Coningsby thought; 'I dare say dinner's a bit late. So much the better. I shall get up. If my sister can be about, so can I.'

The feeling under the last sentence was, in fact, not so simple as it seemed—and he knew it. There floated in his mind, though he avoided it, a horrible wonder whether in effect he had really saved Sybil quite as much as he thought. Lothair Coningsby was in many things fantastic, but he was not merely stupid. He never insisted on seeing facts wrongly, though he did a busy best to persuade the facts to arrange themselves according to his personal preference. But sometimes a fact refused—Nancy's arrangement with Henry, Ralph's determined departure for Christmas—and then there was nothing to do but to condole with himself over it or to look at it and send it away. The afternoon's experience had been a fact of such a kind. He had meant to be saving Sybil, he had thought he was saving her, he had been very anxious about her, but now, in his warm comfort of repose, he couldn't help seeing that she had been very active about it all; her voice had been very fresh, and she had … she certainly had … been gently singing to herself while they waited for the door to open. He himself had not been singing, but then he didn't generally sing; he believed in opening his mouth at the proper times, and outside a shut door in a howling snowstorm wasn't one of them. She'd come out to meet him—yes, of course; but which of them—O, good heavens, *which* of them—had really been thankful for the other's presence? Perhaps it didn't matter; perhaps they'd both been thankful? Reciprocal help. Sybil rather believed in reciprocity, so that was all right. So did he, only, in the way the world went, he always seemed having to be more reciprocal than anybody else. But this afternoon?

This was becoming intolerable. The wind banged at the window again and startled him into decision. He would get up. It was Christmas Day—by heaven, so it was! He had never spent Christmas evening in bed. He always took a good-natured part in any fun that there was. Fun perhaps was too much to expect in this house, but there'd be talk, no doubt, and perhaps—Aaron had hinted as much—a rather unusual wine; perhaps a little music or what not. Anyhow, what not or no what not, he wasn't going to lie here like an abandoned log while the other logs were … well, were downstairs. Sybil should see that if she had helped him, it was only momentary: and if he'd helped her, then it was silly for her to be up and him not. And then, if the storm did burst his window, he'd be able to move to another room more easily. So any way and every way it was better to get up. Especially as everyone seemed to have forgotten him: his host, Henry, Nancy, Sybil—everyone. Well, he would go down: he wouldn't complain, but if anyone expressed surprise he might just say a word—'O, well, lying by oneself——'; 'Unless one's really ill, one likes to see something of people——'; perhaps, even better, 'I thought I'd rather be among you,' with just the faintest stress on the 'among you'—not enough for them to treat him as an invalid, but just enough to cause a flicker of regret in Sybil's and perhaps Aaron's heart; he didn't much expect to cause even a flicker in Nancy's, and he rather hoped that Henry would be a little annoyed.

While he was dressing, he went on trying over various words to say. Every now and then the English language appeared to Mr. Coningsby almost incapable of expressing his more delicate shades of emotion. But then life—getting other people to understand exactly what you meant and wanted and thought and felt—was a very complex business, and, as he never wanted to push himself on others, he was usually satisfied if he could lightly indicate what he was feeling. One mustn't be selfish—especially on Christmas Day. He abandoned a plaintive, 'I thought perhaps you wouldn't *mind* me coming down,' in favour of a jocund, 'Ha, ha! Well, you see, I didn't need much putting right. Ah, Sybil, you … your … you don't….' Rather peevishly he gave that up. He simply could not think of anything at all jocund to say to Sybil. He finished dressing and went to the door. His hand on it, he switched off the light, opened it, and stepped out. His room was near the top of the staircase, next to Aaron's bedroom. The corridor into which he came ran to his right and left, at each end turning into a short concluding corridor. In the extreme corner to his right was the door of Aaron's study, within which lay that curious inner room, exposed to the wind on almost all sides, where were the absurd little marionettes. He had been rather pleased when he used the word to Henry, and it recurred to him as he stared towards it. For, much to his surprise, he saw a small procession going stealthily along the corridor. It had only just passed his door when he opened it, quietly, as it happened, and had not heard him. Indeed, the tall young masculine back at which he found himself gazing was what had startled him. It wasn't Henry's; it wasn't anybody's that he knew. It was wearing a chauffeur's outdoor coat, but as its arms stuck inches out beyond the sleeves and its neck rose high and thick over the collar it probably wasn't the chauffeur. Besides the chauffeur wouldn't be wandering about like that in his master's house. Mr. Coningsby's eyes passed it as he wondered, and lit on someone whom he vividly remembered. There, her eyes on the ground, a blanket clutched round her—'extraordinary dress!' the astonished and already indignant visitor thought—was the old madwoman they had encountered on their journey down. O, it was she undoubtedly: the tangled white hair brought that other evening back in full recognition, and the bent form, and the clutching hand holding the blanket round its neck. She was following something; her head was thrust forward and downwards. Mr. Coningsby instinctively leaned sideways and craned to see what it was, and saw, a yard or so in front of her, a kitten. He stared blankly, as the curious train went on—first the kitten, going gently, pausing now and then with a sudden kittenish crouch, then getting up and going on again, its head turning from side to side; and after it the old woman, with that amazing blanket; and after her the young man in the coat three sizes and more too small for him. Mr. Coningsby's flesh crept at the mere sight of them. Why a kitten? why should even a mad old hag go so softly and carefully after a kitten? Perhaps it was her kitten and she was trying to catch it; she wasn't hurrying it or hurrying after it; if it stopped, she stopped; when it went on, she went on. And so with the third member of the procession, who copied her in all things—moving or staying as she did. It was uncanny; it was rather horrible. His hand still on the door-handle, Mr. Coningsby for a few moments stood gaping after them.

Aaron presumably knew about it—but did he? This wretched woman had seemed to dislike Aaron; supposing he didn't know! It didn't seem very likely he'd let her meander round the house in a blanket after a kitten, nor a young ruffian covered only by a coat that didn't fit him—not anyhow with Nancy and Sybil about. Sybil, it was true, had seemed to get on with them remarkably well, but even so…. Suppose Nancy had met them … what on earth would a—for all her faults—ordinary nice young girl do? Suppose the old devil dropped the blanket by accident—or purposely? Mr. Coningsby revolted at the idea—revolted against the whole mad fact. He let go of the handle and said in a surprisingly firm voice, 'Hallo, there!'

No one took the smallest notice of him. By now he couldn't see the kitten, but the procession was nearing the end of the corridor. At least he ought to see where they went. It was possible that they'd been having baths or something, like himself—no, not like himself. The notion that he and the old woman had shared a bath, that they could have anything at all in common—even the very idea of a bath—was extraordinarily offensive. Besides, the kitten? The kitten might, from the way it was going, have been a maid showing a visitor to her room, but of course it wasn't. Unless it was a new kind of marionette. If any kitten started to show him to his room—— Well, he was going after them, he was going to make quite certain that they didn't run into Nancy. It'd be enough to give her a shock. And he wasn't going to have Sybil kneeling down as if she were in church; she'd been to church once to-day already. Blessing, indeed! Mr. Coningsby went down the corridor after the others with a firm determination to allow no sort of blessing whatever within any reasonable distance of him while he was alive and sane. Except, of course, in a church.

They were outside the door of Aaron's study; he heard the kitten mewing at it. Joanna—if that was her name—opened it. Mr. Coningsby called out again, quite loudly this time, 'Hallo, you there!' But the 'you there' took no notice; they were going in. Mr. Coningsby broke into a run and then checked—after all, his host *might* have given Joanna the use of the room. He considered the possibility and rejected it; Aaron had apparently had a quite different view of Joanna. No, there was some hanky-panky about.

An awful thought for a moment occurred to him that she might be merely going to let the kitten out into the garden or somewhere; people did let kittens out into gardens, and a nice fool he'd look if that were so. But surely on a night like this—and anyhow not on the first floor—and not into a study. He became shocked at himself; he was almost vulgar. Very much more angry, he reached the study door.

The others, including the kitten, were inside. As Mr. Coningsby came into the room he heard the mewing again, plaintive and insistent; he saw the little beast on its hind legs against the inner door—not that it was so little; it struck him that it was within an inch or so of being a proper cat, and the noise it was making was much louder than feline infancy produces. Joanna was almost beside it, but she had had to go round Aaron's great table while the cat had dashed below it. And a little behind her, just turning the table-corner, was Stephen. Mr. Coningsby remembered that behind that other door were the images of gold. Those were what she was after, of course—gipsies—golden statues—theft. He said loudly, 'Now then, now then, what are you doing there?'

She stopped, for this time she heard him, and looked over at him. Her eyes blinked at him from the tanned wrinkled old face under the matted hair, over the blanket fastened together (he now saw) by a strap round her. She said, 'Keep away; you're too late.'

'I fancy you'll find I'm just in time,' Mr. Coningsby answered, and walked into the room, going round the table on the opposite side to Stephen. 'Does Mr. Lee know you're here?'

She chuckled unpleasantly, then nodded at him. 'He'll know,' she said, 'he'll soon know. Wait till I bring him out.'

'Out?' Mr. Coningsby said. 'What do you mean—out?'

She pointed to the door, and her voice sank to a whisper as she said, 'What he has *there*.'

'What he has there,' Mr. Coningsby said, 'is his business. I thought that was what you were after, and it's a good thing for you I happened to be about. I suppose you were going to rob him? Well, you won't this time. Now you get away, and take your damned kitten with you—if it is yours.'

She clutched the handle of the door and began to speak, but Mr. Coningsby, in the full tide of satisfaction, swept on.

'Leave go of that door. Come on; we'll go downstairs together. A nice piece of work, upon my word! You ought to know better, at your age.'

The cat yowled at the door. Joanna glowered, and then said, 'You—*you'll* stop me finding my baby?'

'Your what?' Mr. Coningsby exclaimed. 'O, don't be silly; there's no baby there. There's only a set of marionettes—pretty things, but nothing like a baby. And don't try and put me off with that kind of talk. Get you away.'

'Ah! ah!' the old creature cried out with extraordinary force, 'you're one of them, you're one of the sons of Set.'

The cat yowled louder than ever. For a moment Mr. Coningsby felt strangely alone, as the sound went through the room, and he heard and saw the claws tearing at the door. He thought of that continuous movement behind it; he saw the straining beast and the snarling woman; he saw the dull face of the idiot behind her; he heard the noise of the storm without—and he wished very much that someone else was by his side. There was something wrong about the images, the house, the very wind; cat and storm howled together, and the old woman suddenly shrieked, 'He's over you, he's over you. Get away before he strikes. All his enemies are close to death. The cats are up; the god's coming.'

'Nothing is over me,' Mr. Coningsby said in a voice that became high and shrill in spite of himself. 'Let that door alone.'

'It isn't you that'll stop it,' she screeched back, 'nor a million like you. They'll take you and cut you in a thousand pieces, they'll embalm you alive in the pyramids of hell, they'll drown you among the crocodiles that are tearing your father, they'll flay you with the burning knives of Anubis, and your heart shall be eaten in the place of justice.' She turned towards the door and turned the handle. Mr. Coningsby was on her in a moment, pressing it shut, and incidentally kicking the cat away. As he jumped he almost wished that he'd left her alone; it was all horrible, and he loathed the old voice screaming curses at him. It was of course absolute nonsense, but some minute atom of his mind dragged on the words 'embalmed alive.' Embalmed alive—he of all people!

'No, you don't!' he said. 'Leave that door alone. Ah! ow!'

The cat had leapt back at him and was madly clawing at his legs. Mr. Coningsby kicked at it and missed. It hung on to his trousers, then it fell off and flung itself at his ankles. It was in a state of raging lunacy, almost as wild as Joanna, who dropped the blanket so that it fell back from her shoulders, and herself clutched at him with clawing fingers. Mr. Coningsby avoided her, kicked again at the cat, and desperately held on to the door. But he was suddenly torn from it. Joanna, as she clawed at his throat, had shrieked out a call to her companion, and Stephen, leaping past her, caught Coningsby round the waist, and with a great heave wrenched him away from the door and held him high in the air. Head and feet downwards, he hung, jerking, kicking, choking out anathemas.

'What shall I do with him, grandmother?' Stephen said. 'Shall I throw him out into the storm?'

227

The old woman turned her eyes to the window, but, alert in hatred, saw that it was too small; to push a struggling full-sized body through it would not easily be done even by Stephen. 'Throw him there,' she said, pointing across the room, and at once Stephen obeyed. Mr. Coningsby was sent hurtling through the air into the extreme corner of the room, where he hit the walls first and then crashed to the floor. By mere chance his head escaped; he fell bruised, shocked, and dazed, but still in some sort of consciousness. For one fratricidal second fear and pride warred in his heart, and pride won. He lay for some minutes where he had been flung, till rage so bubbled in him that he began painfully to wriggle over, obstinately determined to see what those creatures were doing. He could not see, for the inner door was open and they had disappeared. They were busy then—he had been right—about the golden images; robbery—robbery with violence. A long, long, long sentence for Stephen, and Joanna—Mr. Coningsby's professional knowledge supplied him with a clear view of Joanna's future. But that couldn't happen if they got away, and unless he did something they might get away. He was too confused by his fall to think of the extreme unlikelihood of Joanna's going out into the storm clothed only in a blanket, and carrying in a fold of it a collection of little golden figures; had he thought of it he would have believed Joanna capable of it, and perhaps he would have been right. For when she stood on the threshold of that inner room and peered into the cloud that filled it, when she beheld the rich mystery that enveloped the symbols of our origins, she had cried out once upon the name of the god, and from that moment she lost touch with the actualities of this world. She pressed on: Stephen, behind her, made violent movements and noises as if to hold her back, but over her shoulder she turned on him a face of such destructive malignity that he shrank back, and crouched defensively down by the door, only whispering from there, 'Don't go, don't go.'

All this was hidden from Mr. Coningsby, who, with a growing determination to stop it, was getting, slowly and gruntingly, to his feet. 'Fortunate,' he thought as he did so, 'fortunate I brought my other glasses with me! Losing one pair in the storm—shouldn't have seen anything of this—didn't someone say Ralph had called? Get hold of Ralph—not always thoughtful—couldn't stand seeing his father thrown about the room, like a … like a *quoit*. Just as well he didn't see—soon settle this nonsense. Ugh! What's that?'

As he came finally to his feet, and adjusted the extra pair of glasses, the gold chain of which had kept them attached if not in position, he saw the first wraiths of mist faintly exuding from the inner room. 'What the devil is it?' he thought, staring. "Tisn't snow; 'tisn't smoke … or is it? Has that infernal old woman set the place on fire?' He went forward a little, keeping the big table between himself and the other door, just in case Joanna and Stephen dashed out at him again, and then he saw the whole doorway filling with it. He had an impression that there were a great many people before his eyes, a crowd of them, just there in the doorway, but that could hardly be so, unless of course other wanderers had taken refuge in this house from the storm, but then they wouldn't be here, they'd be in the kitchen or somewhere. It wasn't people; it was mist or smoke or something. He remembered suddenly that such a faint vapour had seemed to enwrap Nancy and the table when she had her fortune told, but he hadn't taken much notice, because he had then been, as ostentatiously as possible, looking another way. If the old woman was asking about *her* fortune, Mr. Coningsby felt he could tell her exactly what it would be, only she wasn't there to be told. Nothing was there but the cloud and … again … an indefinable sensation of lots of people, all moving and turning.

'It's those damned figures,' Mr. Coningsby thought. 'I expect they shake everything, all that gyrating nonsense. Good God, it's getting thicker.' He turned, ran through the outer door, and shouted as loudly as he could, 'Fire! Fire!'

As he opened his mouth for the third shout, he stopped on the 'F——' For there came from below a sudden crash, a crash that was answered from different parts of the house by a noise of smashing and splintering, and then the wind was howling louder and nearer than before. 'Great Christ!' Mr. Coningsby cried out, in mere ingenuity of perplexed anxiety, 'what the devil's that?' He had guessed even as he spoke; the doors and windows were giving way before the blizzard. 'The snow's getting in and the fire's getting out,' he thought, distractedly staring back over his shoulder. 'O, my Father in heaven, what a Christmas!'

Downstairs, Aaron and Ralph were still gating at one another in the dining-room when the crash came. At the noise of it they both exclaimed, but Ralph was the first in the hall. He saw there how the front door had given way under the tireless assaults of the storm, which, as if imbued with a conscious knowledge of its aim, had been driving like a battering-ram at the house since the return of Sybil and her brother. It might have been pursuing and hunting him down; the loosened leaves of invocation might have been infused— beyond any intention—with Henry's purpose, and the vague shapes whom Lothair Coningsby had thought he saw in the snow-swept roads might have been hammering with a more terrible intensity at the door which had closed behind him. At last those crashing buffets had torn lock and bolt from the doorpost; the door was flung back, and the invading masses of snow and wind swept in. The floor of the hall was covered before anyone could speak; the wind—if it were not rather the dance of searching shapes—swept into every corner.

A picture or two on the walls were torn off and flung down lest they concealed the fugitive; tables were tossed about; an umbrella-stand was kicked to the extreme end of the hall. A howl of disappointment went up, and the snow drove over the first few stairs, as if the pursuit was determined never to stop until its prey had been discovered.

Ralph gaped for a moment, then plunged for the door. 'Come on!' he yelled. 'Call everyone! Come and shut it.' He pulled it a little forward and was thrown back again along with it. 'Come on!' he cried stentorianly to Aaron. 'No time to waste! Call the others!'

But Aaron was stupefied. The comfortable reassurances in which he had clothed himself were torn away by the same giant hands that were wrecking his house. This was no unexpected winter storm, but supernaturally contrived death, and, whatever scope it had, this place was its centre. If it were to sweep, eschatological and ultimate, over the world, that destruction was but an accident. The elementals, summoned from their symbols, were still half-obedient to the will that had called them. His brain called to him to give him their desire, to take the stranger and throw him out beyond the threshold, that he might there be beaten and stunned and crushed and stifled and buried, a sacrifice now not to magical knowledge but to the very hope of life. And again his brain answered and told him that he could not, that the storm itself had brought to the stranger a friend and to himself two enemies. There was no one in the house but Henry who would do his bidding, and even if Henry could be found in the darkness where he had hidden himself, what could he and Henry do against Coningsby and his son? A more sinister thought leapt in his mind—what if Henry himself could be made the offering? might not these raging powers be satisfied with the body of the sorcerer who had invoked them? might not Coningsby and his son and he himself manage to make that offering? At least then Aaron Lee would be alive, and now nothing in the whole universe mattered but the safety of Aaron Lee. He looked wildly round, and then Ralph left the door and ran back to him, seizing his arm, and crying, 'Call someone! We've got to shut the door and barricade it—then the windows! Hallo, everybody! *Hallo!* Come here! you're wanted! *Come—here—everyone!*'

The servants—which meant two maids and the cook—had come already, bursting into the hall from their own quarters, and screaming that the back doors were broken down. One of the maids was hysterical with the continued roar of the blizzard, and was screaming and howling continuously. The other, almost equally alarmed, was quieter, and it was on her that Ralph fixed.

'Hallo!' he said, 'come along! Look here, we've got to try and get the door held. We'll get a good big table and barge it to with that behind it, and someone else can get some rope or something. The dining-room table's best, don't you think? It's the biggest thing I've seen.' He had her by the arm and was rushing her to the dining-room. 'O lor', won't anything keep that gramophoning misery behind us quiet? No, don't go back, for God's sake. Here—now smash everything off it—that's right! O, don't stop to pick them up, girl!—what's your name? what? Amabel?—all right, Amabel, just pitch them off, so! Now this way—that's it! careful! careful! blast that leg!—sideways, I think—so; yes, so—gently; don't get flustered. Hark at the polish!' as the table-top screeched against the doorpost. They tottered out with it.

'Can I help, Ralph?' his aunt's voice said behind him. Sybil had been half-upstairs when the door had given way, and she had come quickly back to the hall, but her arrival had been unnoticed in the feminine rush that had preceded it.

'Hallo!' said Ralph breathlessly, as they fought to get the table long side on to the storm; it was only the accident of a recess that had enabled them to get it out of the dining-room at all, and at the moment it was being driven steadily towards the stairs, with Ralph and Amabel holding on to it at each end, like the two victims who were dragged prisoners to the power of Set in the Tarot paintings. Sybil caught Amabel's end, and her extra weight brought the other round; Ralph was suddenly spun round in a quarter of a circle, and then they were all pushing towards the door. Ralph, over his shoulder, yelled at Aaron, the cook, and the hysterical maid, 'Cord! Miles of cord!'

'Wouldn't it be easier to close the door first, Ralph?' Sybil said, looking back at him.

'Be *better*,' Ralph said, 'but easier? You try it.'

Sybil looked at Amabel. 'Can you hold it?' she said. 'I think if we shut the wind out first....' She let go of the table, went down the hall, took hold of the door, and pushed it gradually shut. 'There,' she said, 'that's what I meant. Don't you think that's simpler, Ralph?'

'Much,' said Ralph, a little astonished either at his aunt's suggestion or at her expert dealing with the door, he wasn't sure which: but he assumed there must have been a momentary lull. He and Amabel rushed the heavy table up, and were just setting it with its broad top against the door as Ralph said, 'Now we've only got to fix——' when another voice joined in. From high above them—'Fire!' called Mr. Coningsby. 'Fire!'

The hall broke into chaos. Amabel, startled, let go her end of the table, which crashed to the ground only an inch from Sybil's foot. The hysterical maid broke into a noise like a whole zoological garden at once. The cook, who had been going steadily, and rather heavily, towards the stairs, stopped, turned to Aaron, and said, 'Mr. Lee, sir, did you hear that?' Aaron ran to the stairs, and, checking at the bottom, cried out some incoherent question. Ralph said, in a penetrating shout: 'What? What?' then in a much quieter voice he added, 'Well, if it's fire, it's not much use barricading the door, is it? Look here, let's wedge it with that chair just for a moment till——'

'Fire!' Mr. Coningsby called out again.

'Go and see, Ralph,' Sybil said. 'It may be a mistake.'

'Probably is,' Ralph answered. 'Right ho, but let's just push that chair in here. Amabel bright-eyes, give it over here, will you? and then go and smother that fog-horn. There, so; another shove, aunt; so!'

Somehow the table and the heavy hall chair were wedged across the door. Ralph, letting go, looked at his barricade doubtfully. 'It won't hold for more than a second,' he said, 'but—I'll pop up and see what's biting him now. If there's really anything, I'll tell you.'

He shot off, and, overtaking Aaron half up the stairs, arrived with him on the landing where his father was restlessly awaiting them.

'It's that old woman,' Mr. Coningsby broke out at once to Aaron. 'She's got into your private room, where the marionettes are, and there's a lot of smoke coming out. I don't suppose she's done much damage yet, but you'd better stop her. Come on, Ralph my boy, we may need you; there's a nasty violent ruffian with her, and I'm not strong enough to tackle him alone.'

As they ran down the corridor, Ralph heard another splintering crash from one of the rooms. 'Window!' he thought. 'This is looking nasty! Lord send it isn't a fire! Eh?'

The last syllable was a bewildered question. They had reached the door of Aaron's room, and there the strange apparition billowed—the golden mist swirled and surged before them. Its movement was not rapid, but it had already completely hidden from their sight the opposite wall, with its inner door, and was rolling gently over the large writing-table. It was exquisitely beautiful, and, though Ralph's first thought was that it certainly wasn't smoke, he couldn't think what it really was. He gaped at it; then he heard Aaron at his side give a piteous little squeal of despair. His father at the same time said, 'I can't think why she doesn't come *out*. It's such a funny colour.'

'Well,' Ralph said, 'no good staring at it, is it? Look here, this is more important than the door; we'd better have a line of people to the—damn it, father, it can't be *smoke*!'

Mr. Coningsby only said, 'Then what is it?'

'Well, if she's inside,' Ralph exclaimed, 'I'm going in too. Look here, Mr. Lee….'

But Aaron was past speech or attention. He was staring in a paralysed horror, giving little moans, and occasionally putting up his hands as if to ward off the approaching cloud. From within and from without the dangers surrounded him, and Henry was nowhere about, and he was alone. Within that cloud was Joanna—Joanna alone with the golden images of the dance, Joanna who thought he had kept them from her, who knew herself for the Mother of a mystical vengeance, who went calling day and night on her Divine Son to restore the unity of the god. What was happening? what was coming on him? what threat and fulfilment of threat was at hand?

Ralph thought, 'The poor old chap's thoroughly upset; no wonder—it's a hectic day,' and went forward, turning to go round the table.

'Take care, my boy,' Mr. Coningsby said. 'I'll come with you—I don't think it can be fire. Only then—— What's the matter?'

Ralph, with an expression of increasing amazement, was moving his arms and legs about in front of the mist, rather as if he were posturing for a dance in front of a mirror. He said in a puzzled tone, 'I can't get through. It's too thick.'

'Don't be absurd,' his father said. 'It's quite obviously not *thick*. It's hardly more than a thin veil—of sorts.' He added the last two words because, as the rolling wonder approached them, it seemed here and there to open into vast depths of itself. Abysses and mountainous heights revealed themselves—masses of clouds were sweeping up. 'Veil' perhaps was hardly the word.

Ralph was being driven back before it; he tried to force his hand through it, and he seemed to be feeling a thick treacle—only it wasn't sticky. It wasn't unpleasant; only it was unpierceable. He gave way a step or two more. 'Damned if I understand it,' he said.

Mr. Coningsby put up his own hand rather gingerly. He stretched it out—farther; it seemed to touch the mist, but he felt nothing. Farther; he couldn't see his hand or his wrist, still he felt something. Farther, something that felt exactly like another hand took hold of his lightly. He exclaimed, jerked his hand away, and sprang back. 'What was that?' he said sharply.

Aaron was watching with growing horror the steady approach of the mist. But it was not merely the approach that troubled him; it was the change in it. The cloud was taking on form—he could not at first distinguish what the form was, and then at one point he suddenly realized he was looking at a moving hand, blocked out of the golden mist, working at something. It was the size of an ordinary man's hand, and then, while he looked, he missed it somehow, as a stain on a wall will be one minute a cat's head and the next but an irregular mark. But as he lifted his eyes he saw another—more like a slender woman's hand—from the wrist grasping upward at … at yet another hand that reached downward to it; and then those joining fingers had twisted together and became yet a third that moved up and down as if hammering, and as it moved was covered and hidden by the back of a fourth. His gaze swept the gathering cloud; everywhere it was made up of hands, whose shape was formed by it, and yet it was not the mist that formed them, for they were the mist. Everywhere those restless hands billowed forward; of all sizes, in all manner of movement, clasping, holding, striking, fighting, smoothing, climbing, thrusting out, drawing back, joining and disjoining, heaving upward, dragging down, appearing and disappearing, a curtain of activity falling over other activity, hands, and everywhere hands. Here and there the golden shimmer dulled into tints of ordinary flesh, then that was lost again, and the aureate splendour everywhere shone. The hands were working in the stuff, yet the stuff which they wrought was also hands, so that their purpose was foiled and thwarted and the workers became a part of that which was worked upon. Over and below and about the table the swelling and sinking curtain of mystery swept—if it were not rather through it, for it did not seem to divide or separate the movement, and the cloud seemed to break from it on the side nearest Aaron, just as it filled all the air around. The room was hidden behind it, nearer and nearer to the door it came, and the three were driven back before it.

Or, rather, Ralph and his father were. Aaron had not moved from the doorway, and now, as he understood the composition of that mist, he cried out in terror. 'It's alive!' he shrieked, 'it's alive! it's the living cloud! Run, run!' and himself turned and went pattering as fast as he could towards the stairs, sending out an agonized call to Henry as he fled. The cloud of the beginning of things was upon him; in a desperate effort to escape he rushed down the staircase towards the hall. But his limbs were failing him; he went down half a dozen steps and clung to the balustrade, pale, trembling, and overwhelmed.

Mr. Coningsby looked after him, looked back at the mist, which had now almost filled the room, retreated a little farther, and said to Ralph, with more doubt than usual in his voice, 'Living cloud? D'you see anything living about it?'

'Damn sight too solid,' Ralph said, 'at least it's not quite that either—it's more like … mortar or thick custard or something. Where does it come from?'

On the point of answering, Mr. Coningsby was again distracted. There was a noise of scampering from within the mist, and out of it suddenly dashed the kitten, or cat, or whatever it was, which tore between them and half-way down the corridor, where it stopped abruptly, looked all round it, mewed wildly, tore back, and hurled itself into the cloud. Before either Mr. Coningsby or Ralph could utter a word, it shot out again more frenziedly than before, and this time rushed to the head of the stairs, where it broke into a fit of mad miauling, ran, jumped, or fell half down them past the step where Aaron clung, and in full sight of the front door crouched for the spring.

Sybil had been doing her best to soothe the hysterical maid, not without some result. Her back being to the stairs, she did not at first see what was happening there, though she heard—as everyone in the house did— the cries of Aaron and the yowling of the cat. She gave the maid a last word of tender encouragement, a last pat of heartening sympathy, and swung round. As she did so, the cat and Aaron both moved. The cat took one terrific leap from the stairs right across the hall, landed on Ralph's barricade, dropped on to the floor, slithered, snarled, and began scratching at the table. Aaron at the same time took another step or two down, slipped, lost his footing, and crashed down. Sybil ran to him. 'O, my dear,' she cried, but he answered her frantically, 'My feet won't take me away. They won't let me escape.'

'Are you hurt?' she asked, and would have helped him up, but he shook his head, moaning, 'My ankle, my ankle.' She kneeled to look at it, soothing him a little, even then, by the mere presence of unterrified and dominating serenity. Equanimity in her was not a compromise but a union, and the elements of that union, which existed separately in others, in her recognized themselves, and something other than themselves, which satisfied them. That round which her brother, exasperated and comforted at once, was always prowling; that to which Nancy had instinctively turned for instruction; that which Henry had seen towering afar over his own urgencies and desires—that made itself felt by Aaron now. In the same moment, by chance a silence fell in the house; the wind sank without, and all things seemed about to be ordered in calm. It was but for a moment. There was, for that second, peace; then again the cat howled by the door, and, as if in answer to the summons, the blizzard struck at it again, and the feeble barriers gave. The chair and table were tossed aside, the door was flung back, the snow poured again into the house, this time with double strength.

231

It swept through the hall; it drove up the stairs; in its vanguard the cat also raced back. And from above, itself rushing forward with increased speed, the cloud of the mysteries drove down to meet it. The two powers intermingled—golden mist with wind and snow; the flakes were aureoled, the mist was whitened. Confusion filled the house; the mortal lives that moved in it were separated each from the rest, and each, blinded and stumbling, ran for what shelter, of whatever kind, it thought it could find. Voices sounded in cries of terror and despair and anger; and the yowling of the cat and the yelling of the storm overbore them; and another sound, the music of the room of the images—but now grown high and loud and passionate—dominated and united all. Dancing feet went by; golden hands were stretched out and withdrawn. The invasion of the Tarots was fulfilled.

Only Sybil, contemplating Aaron's swelling ankle, said, 'I think, Mr. Lee, if you *could* manage to hobble up just these few stairs to a room somewhere, perhaps we could deal with it better.'

CHAPTER XIV

THE MOON OF THE TAROTS

Nancy found herself alone. The mist round her was thinning; she could see a clear darkness beyond. She had known one pang when she felt Henry's hands slip from round hers; then she had concentrated her will more entirely on doing whatever might be done to save whatever had to be saved from the storm, which now she no longer heard. But the fantastic mission on which she was apparently moving did not weigh upon her; her heart kept its lightness. There had come into her life with the mystery of the Tarots a new sense of delighted amazement; the Tarots themselves were not more marvellous than the ordinary people she had so long unintelligently known. By the slightest vibration of the light in which she saw the world she saw it all differently; holy and beautiful, if sometimes perplexing and bewildering, went the figures of her knowledge. They were all 'posters of the sea and land,' and she too, in a dance that was happy if it was frightening. Nothing was certain, but everything was safe—that was part of the mystery of Love. She was upon a mission, but whether she succeeded or not didn't matter. Nothing mattered beyond the full moment in which she could live to her utmost in the power and according to the laws of the dance. The dance of the Tarots, the dance of her blood, the dance of her mind, and whatever other measure it was in which Sybil Coningsby trod so high and disposed a movement. Hers couldn't be that *yet*, couldn't ever perhaps, but she could understand and answer it. Her father, Henry, Ralph, they were all stepping their parts, and she also—now, now, as the last shreds of the golden mist faded, and, throbbing and glad, she came into the dark stillness which awaited her.

On the edge of it she paused. The room of the images had been vaguely in her expectation, but if that indeed were where she stood then she could see nothing of it. Complete and cool night was about her. She glanced down; her hands were empty of the cards, but lifted as if she were still holding them, and she was aware that her palms were gently throbbing and tingling. It was something like neuralgia—only it wasn't in the least like neuralgia. But if there could be a happy neuralgia, if some nerve could send to her brain the news of power and joy continually vibrant, then that was how her hands felt. It might so easily have been disagreeable, but it was not disagreeable; it was exquisite. Part of its very exquisiteness, indeed, was the knowledge that if this delight had been overstressed or uncontrolled then it would have been disagreeable. But the energy that thrilled there was exactly right; its tingling messages announced to her a state of easy health as the throbbing messages of diseased mankind proclaim so often a state of suffering. Joy itself was sensuous; she received its communication through the earth of which she was made.

She kept her hands very still, wondering at them. They had been so busy, with one thing and another, in the world, continually shaping something. What many objects had rested against those palms—chair-backs, cups, tennis-rackets, the hands of her friends, birds, books, bag-handles, umbrellas, clothes, bed-clothes, door-handles, ropes, straps, knives and forks, bowls, pictures, shoes, cushions—O, everything! and always she had had some purpose, her hands had been doing something, making something, that had never been before—not just so. They were always advancing on the void of the future, shaping her future. In Henry's—exchanging beauty and truth; in her father's—exchanging … the warm blood took her cheeks as she thought ashamedly of him. In Sybil's—not long since, receiving strength, imparting the tidings of her own feebleness. Full of the earth of the Tarots; holding on to Henry's to stay the winds and waters of the Tarots. She stretched them out to either side of her; what could she do now to redeem the misfortune that threatened? what in this moment were her hands meant to shape by the mystical power which was hidden in them? She remembered the old woman's hands waving above Sybil's head; she remembered the priest's hand that very morning raised for the ritual blessing; she remembered hands that she had seen in painting, the *Praying Hands* of Dürer, the hands of Christ on the cross or holding off St. Mary in some drawing of the garden tryst, the hands of the Divine Mother lifting the Child, the small hand of the Child Himself raised in benediction; she remembered the stretched hand of the Emperor directing the tumults of the world; the hands of the Juggler who tossed the balls, the hand of the Fool as he summoned the last danger from its tomb, the lifted hands of the Juggler and of the Fool as they came together, before the rain of gold had hidden them that evening from her sight.

It was no doubt a thing to wonder at, the significant power of man's hands. She thought of the unknown philosopher who had wrought the Tarot images; his hands had been filled with spiritual knowledge; they perhaps had guided his mind as much as his mind his hands. What would the fortune-telling palmistry with which she had played have discovered in those passive and active palms? the centres of wisdom and energy, which had communicated elemental strength to the images and the paintings, so that other hands could release at their will earth and air and water and fire to go about the world? Release and direct. She stretched out her arms, instinctively passionate to control the storm which she believed, outside her present sense, to be raging over earth; and, as the back of her hands shone lucidly before her in the dark, she felt against them from beyond the first cold touches of the snow.

At the touch she became rigidly attentive. It was time then; something was about to happen. The darkness round her was changing. She could see below her again a gleam of gold; at first she thought it was the base upon which the images had danced, but it was not that, it was not clear and definite enough. It was rather the golden mist, but it was shaken now by an intrusion of white flakes. The confusion was at first far below her, but presently it was rushing upward, and as it came nearer and became larger she realized that she was indeed still standing in the secret room, in the darkness that had once been curtains; below her expanded the wide open spaces of the Downs. They too were covered with snow, but the tumult was less, and unmingled with that other strange glow: they lay, a winter vision, such as she had seen before in fields or towns. She saw them, white and silent, and then there swept up from the turmoil in the house a giant figure, a dimly defined form waving a huge club from which the snow poured in a continuous torrent. It rose, rushing towards her, and she thrust out her hands towards it, and it struck its club against them—they felt the blow, the blast of an icy wind, and were numbed, but life tingled in them again at once, and the ghostly shape was turned from his course, and sent plunging back into the turmoil from which it came. Others rushed up after it; the invoked elementals were seeking a larger scope. From raging about and in the house they were bursting abroad over the Downs, over the world where men kept Christmas, one way or another, and did not know that everlasting destruction was near. Between that threat and its fulfilment stood the girl's slender figure, and the warm hands of humanity in hers met the invasion and turned it. They moved gently over the storm; they moved as if in dancing ritual they answered the dancing monstrosities that opposed them. It was not a struggle but a harmony, yet a harmony that might at any moment have become a chaos. The column of whirling shapes arose and struck, and were beaten abroad under the influence of those extended palms, and fell in other whirling columns; and so the whole of the magical storm was sent pouring back into the place of its origin; and out on the Downs, over villages and roads, over the counties and cities of England, over rivers and mountains, there fell but the natural flakes of a snowy Christmas.

The carols of Christmas, wherever they were sung that night, were sung in ignorance of the salvation which endured among them, or in ignorance at least of the temporal salvation which the maiden-mother of Love preserved. But the snow ceased to fall as the night drew on, and before midnight the moon rode in a clear sky. Yet another moon shone over the house on the Downs, like that which was among the one and twenty illuminations of the Greater Trumps. For there, high between two towers, the moon shines, clear and perfect, and the towers are no longer Babels ever rising and falling, but complete in their degree. Below them again, on either side of a long and lonely road, two handless beasts—two dogs, or perhaps a wolf and a dog—sit howling, as if something which desired attainment but had not entered into the means of attainment cried out unprofitably to the gentle light disseminated from above; and again below, in the painting of mysterious depths, some other creature moves in the sea, in a coat of shell, clawed and armed, shut up in itself, but even itself crawling darkly towards a land which it does not comprehend. The sun is not yet risen, and if the Fool moves there he comes invisibly, or perhaps in widespread union with the light of the moon which is the reflection of the sun. But if the Tarots hold, as has been dreamed, the message which all things in all places and times have also been dreamed to hold, then perhaps there was meaning in the order as in the paintings; the tale of the cards being completed when the mystery of the sun has opened in the place of the moon, and after that the trumpets cry in the design which is called the Judgement, and the tombs are broken, and then in the last mystery of all the single figure of what is called the world goes joyously dancing in a state beyond moon and sun, and the number of the Trumps is done. Save only for that which has no number and is called the Fool, because mankind finds it folly till it is known. It is sovereign or it is nothing, and if it is nothing then man was born dead.

She stood above the world, and her outstretched and down-turned palms felt the shocks, and she laughed aloud to see the confusion of clubs striking upward and failing to break past the small shields that were defending the world from them. She laughed to feel the blows as once she had laughed and mocked at Henry when his fingers struck her palm; danger itself was turned into some delight of love. As if her laughter were a spiritual sword, the last great rush of spectral giants fell back from it: the two-edged weapon of laughter sprang from her mouth, as some such conquering power springs from the mouth of the mystical hero of the Apocalypse. The laughter and the protection that are beyond the world entered her to preserve the world, and, still laughing for mere joy of contact and conflict, she moved forward. The ghostly elementals broke and fled in chaos; a grey swirl of snow received them, and then the golden mist was around her again and she was sinking and moving forward through it. It swirled and shook and condensed; darkness sprang through it. She stood by the golden base, empty of images, in the room where the dark hangings enclosed her; and then she saw across the table, confronting her, the wild face of Joanna, and her clutching hands, and her mouth gnashing itself together upon incoherent words.

Nancy's hands dropped to her side; the joy that possessed her quietened; she became still. All then was not yet done. The storm had been turned back, but she did not know if it was quenched, and this mad personification of storm raged at her a few feet off. Joanna had come to the inner room, when the mist already drawn from its hiding-place among or in the dancing figures by the operation of the lovers had filled the whole chamber; she had entered through the breach which they had made in the constraining power that localized the images, or, to put it another way, she had been received into the vapour which they had loosed from the expanding dance. As Henry had seen her for a moment, so she had seen him; she entering, he returning. His mortal purpose had been overthrown, and his mind had accepted that and submitted. But hers, thwarted long since, had overthrown the mind itself in its collapse. Babel had overwhelmed her being; she walked among the imagined Tarots seeking for the love which she held to be her right, her possession, her living subject. Wild, yet not more wild than most men, she sought to nourish the god in her own way, and that way was by the dream of Horus and vengeance and torments. Full of that hope, tenderness mingled with cruelty, devotion with pride, government with tyranny, maternity with lust, she raged among the symbols of the everlasting dance, and madly believed that, by virtue of her godhead, she ruled it and was more than a part of it. Henry and she had seen each other, then she had rushed on. She rushed into the centre of the room, where now the mist blew in widening circles round the empty base, and saw the void. There, where all restoration should have lain was nothing; there, where the slain god should have lived, the very traces of his blood had vanished; for she had passed the fallen Tarot paintings in her haste, and they lay behind her, hidden and neglected, upon the floor. But she saw Nancy, and at Nancy she now gazed and gibbered. The silence for some seconds was yet unbroken; the old woman mouthed across the empty pedestal, but no sound came from her. Nancy, unafraid but aware of her ignorance before this questing anger, after the pause said, half-faltering: 'You're … still looking?'

The old woman's face lit up with a ghastly certainty. She nodded vehemently. 'Ah,' she said, 'still looking, kind lady. Kind lady, to hide him there!'

Nancy moved her hands a little. 'Indeed,' she said, 'I haven't hidden him. Tell me what you want and I'll help look.'

Joanna went off into a fit of ironical chuckling. 'O, yes, you'll help,' she said. 'O, you'll help! You've helped all this long time, haven't you? But it was you who ran about the tent and peeped underneath to see if the child was there! Peeping here and peeping there! and wriggling through at last to take him away!'

'What have I taken?' Nancy said, knowing the madness, half-convinced by it, and half-placating it. 'What could I take from you? I'll give it back, if you'll tell me, or I'll look for it everywhere with you.'

Joanna, up against the table of the Tarots, leaned across it suddenly and caught Nancy's hand in her own. The girl felt the old fingers clutch her and squeeze into her with a numbing strength, so that the free activity in which she had moved during her conflict with visions was now imprisoned and passive. She resisted the impulse to struggle and let her hand lie still.

'I'll look for it,' Joanna said. 'I know where you keep him. The blood in the blood and the body in the body. I'll let him out of you.' She wrenched the girl nearer, and sprawled over the table, leaning her head towards Nancy's breast. 'I hear him,' she breathed. 'It's he that's beating in you. I'll let him out.'

234

Nancy shook suddenly. The laughter that had been in her had died away; a fantastic wonder possessed her whether she might now be paying for her mastery of the storm. Better perhaps to have died with Henry in the snow than … but this was nonsense: she wasn't going to die. She was going to live and find Henry, and show him the palms that had taken the snow, and make him kiss them for reward, and lay hers against his, his that had begun and sent the clubbed elementals right into hers, and all ways adore the mystery of Love. The mystery of Love couldn't be that she should die here … with only the old woman near. Aunt Sybil would come, or Mr. Lee, or her father…. Meanwhile, she must try and love this old woman.

She was jerked forward again. Joanna scrambled upright and dragged Nancy in turn across the table; then, holding her tight-stretched, she bent her head down towards her, and gabbled swiftly: 'The hand you took him with, the hand of power, the hand of magic—there, there, that's where we let him out. The middle of the hand—didn't you know? that's where the god goes in and out.' She twisted the girl's hand upward and scratched at the palm with the nails of her other hand. 'I shall see him,' she ran on, 'in the first drop of blood, the blood that the cats smell out; that's why the cat brought me here, the cat that lives in the storm, the tiger that runs by the Fool. It'll come'—her nails tore at the hand—'and he'll come out of it. My own, my little one, my sweet chuck! come, come along, come.'

The pain struck Nancy as being quite sufficient; it suggested to her that she might scream—scream out—call out. There wouldn't, she thought, be much harm in calling out. But also she must love this old woman—wish her well—understand her—see her goodness. But the old woman was one and she was one—and she couldn't see any clear reason why the old woman should spoil hands that Henry had said were beautiful. She made a final effort to break away, and didn't succeed: almost upside down as she felt she was, that was hardly surprising. So she called in as steady a voice as possible: 'Aunt! Henry! Father! Aunt! Aunt Sybil!'

Her voice ceased abruptly. Instead of any of these appearing out of the golden mist that hid the doorway from her, there was a sudden soft thud, and on the table close up to her stretched arm appeared a cat. Nancy in the few minutes she had spent with Sybil in the hall had heard and seen nothing of the cat, and had had no opportunity since. And she had never heard or seen one in the house. But there it crouched, mewing, turning its head from her to Joanna and back again, unsheathing and sheathing its claws, moving its restless tail. Nancy's first thought as she saw it was, 'It's got no hands,' and this seemed to her so horrible that she nearly lost control. It had no hands, it had no spiritual instruments of intention, only paws that patted or scratched, soft padded cushions or tearing iron nails—all four, all four, and no hands. The cat put one paw suddenly on her arm, and she almost shrieked at that soft dab. It tried to lift its paw, but its claws were entangled in the light stuff of the afternoon frock she had on, and were caught. After a moment's struggle it ripped them out, and Nancy seemed to hear the sound of the light stuff tearing—absurd, of course, but if it should tear it right away, and her arm lay bare like her wrist and hand, and the cat and Joanna both tore and scratched … Love…. She must love Joanna. Joanna wanted something, and, though she was afraid Joanna wouldn't find it, she herself must try and love.

Never since the child had died had Joanna been nearer than then to finding the power of whom she told herself fantastic tales, than when the girl's struggling will fixed itself again on that centre. In the place of the images the god offered himself to his seekers, through the effort of his creature. In the depth of Nancy's eyes as she turned them on Joanna, in the sound of her voice as she spoke, he allowed his mystery to expand, as she said, 'Indeed, it isn't here. I'd help you if I could. It'll do it if we let it.'

The old woman did not meet her eyes; she was looking at the cat. 'The cat that lives in the storm,' she said. 'Go, my dear; go and show me. You brought me here—show me; show me. She's got it in her, hasn't she? go and get it out.'

The cat stared at her; then it turned its eyes to Nancy's face, and, keeping them fixed there, seemed to swivel its body slowly round. Nancy had an awful thought, 'It's going to spring! it's got no hands and it's going to spring! It'll tear me because it's got no hands!' In the last of the Tarot cards, in the unnumbered illumination, she had seen something like that—a beast rearing against the Fool: in the midst of the images, rigid in the centre of the base, she had seen it, a beast rearing against the Fool. It had not then seemed to be attacking exactly; rather it had seemed as if poised in the very act of a secret measure trodden with its controlling partner among the more general measure trodden by all the shapes. The Fool and the tiger, the combined and single mystery—but it was going to spring. She brought up her other hand from where it had held the edge of the table, to help her keep her footing against Joanna's strong pull; and she slipped a little more forward as she did so, bringing her face too near to that crouched energy that was gathering itself … too near, too near. Her hand came up, clutched, missed, for the cat slithered aside snarling, and then, as her hand came down on the golden table, crouched again, and was unexpectedly caught by its neck. A high, peevish voice said, 'Good God! what is all this? Let go at once, you wretched creature! Do you hear me? Let my daughter alone. *Damn you, woman, let my daughter alone!*'

CHAPTER XV

THE WANDERERS IN THE
BEGINNING

The descent of the golden mist separated the inhabitants of the house from the sight of each other, with the single exception of Sybil and Aaron. The servants, caught in the hall, clung together, not daring to move yet frightened to remain where they were. They felt in the closeness of hands and bodies the only suggestion of safety, as, long since, our scarcely human ancestors crowded together against night and the perils of the night. The cook gasped continuously; her hysterical companion was reduced to a shaking misery of moans; even the silent Amabel quivered spasmodically as she clutched the arms of her unseen colleagues. Between them the mist rolled and stayed.

In the corridor above, ignoring social divisions, reducing humanity to an equality of bewildered atoms, it had swept between Ralph and his father. Ralph, frankly defeated by this inexplicable amazement, fell back against the wall in a similar stupor to the cook's. A world upon which he had all his life relied had simply ceased to exist. Mists on mountains, fogs in towns, he had heard of; sea-fogs and river-mists. But here was neither sea nor river, neither mountain nor town. Existence as he knew it had just gone out. In a minute or two he would pull himself together and do something. But this stuff, as he leaned against the wall, was damned unpleasant: the wall gave to his back, and he came hastily upright, feeling gingerly for it. He couldn't feel it; he couldn't feel any difference between anything.

He brought his hand towards his thigh, trying to touch himself, and couldn't: where he ought to be was nothing but this thick consistency. He closed his hand upon itself, and what felt like fingers pressed more deeply into the same shifting and resisting matter. He could feel himself all right, so long as he didn't definitely try to find himself. But when he did, he wasn't there. That was silly: he was there. He put up both hands to his head—at least to where his head ought to have been, and still, if his head was there, he couldn't get it. This porridge-like substance oozed between his fingers and clung to them—porridge or thin mud. He had had a tooth out once, and afterwards felt as if the tooth was still there. Suppose his whole body had been pulled out, and he were only feeling as if it were there. But the rest of the world? That was gone too. Suppose everything had just been pulled out—leaving only the place where it had been, and himself feeling the place, seeming sometimes full and sometimes empty? For a moment he visualized a hole in the air, out of which the round world had been neatly and painlessly extracted, but his mind, unused to metaphysical visions, refused to pursue this thought, and restored him to the simple view that he was feeling very funny, probably a bit overtired with all this snow. Nevertheless, he couldn't forget that never in his life, fresh, tired, or overtired, had he searched for himself and not found himself. His hold on sanity depended on the fact that the fingers of either hand did sometimes rub together as he moved them, though the two hands never quite met each other. If they only could, he would be getting back to normal; something would have joined. There would have been a kind of shape, a point of new beginning, a definite fixture, in this horrible mess, where at present were only two wandering feelers, antennæ moving about in a muddy mass. He wondered abruptly what his father was feeling like, but no sound—yes, but there was a sound, four sounds. Four separate notes of music, in an ascending scale, came to him, faint and monotonously repeated—la, la, la, la; la, la, la, la; la, la, la, la. Well, sooner or later perhaps this incredible nightmare would *stop*.

Mr. Coningsby had found himself cut off from Ralph with as much sudden expedition as Ralph had experienced. But, unlike his son, he did not feel the cloud that so surrounded and deprived him as being thickly material. It was an offence, certainly, but an offence of shocked bewilderment. It removed his world from him as it had removed Ralph's and, like Ralph and the servants, he instinctively put out his hand to find companionship. He found—not companionship certainly, but what he had found before, another hand that laid hold of his, a strong, gentle, cold, strange hand. He pulled his own hastily back, and the other let it go. It had rather invited than constrained him, and it did not attempt to control. He rubbed his fingers together distastefully, and pretended that it might have been Joanna's hand or Stephen's. Anything else—it couldn't be anything else. It might be Henry's or Aaron's—it might even have been Ralph's. Only he was, in spite of himself, certain that it hadn't been Ralph's or Aaron's or Henry's, and, in spite of himself, he didn't believe it to be Stephen's or Joanna's; it had been too cold and strong for any mortal hand. It was then—it wasn't; certainly it wasn't. Or if it was, then the only thing to be done was to keep out of the way of these released marionettes. 'Robots!' Mr. Coningsby indignantly thought, though how the Robots had got from their table to the corridor he didn't attempt to explain. He would get right out of the house—but the storm was outside. It cut him off from his home, from London, from trains and taxis; it shut him in and he must stay in. And within was the mist. There was, Mr. Coningsby realized, absolutely nowhere in the universe he could get to. He was *there*, and *there* he was going to stop.

Blundering along what he supposed to be the corridor, he exclaimed aloud, 'Lunacy!' At the word all sorts of dim memories of his work awoke, only he seemed to be on the wrong side of them. He had never heard of a lunatic whose delusion was that a whirling snowstorm shut him up in a golden cloud, where cold hands touched his. Some lunatics were violent and had to be held down by others' hands. What if he, struggling in this horror, became violent, and those hands held him? suppose his mind was, by their judgements, mad? Lunacy—lunacy—what was lunacy? what was the mad mind wrestling with contemptuous and powerful enemies? what was he doing at the moment? If he should be caught and carried away for ever into the depths and distances which opened now and then before him—the mist falling away on either side and making a league-long valley of itself, or heaving up and leaving a great abyss round which it swirled and then covered it again. Borne into it … taking precedence, O, for ever and ever taking desolate and lunatic precedence of the elder sons of younger sons of peers. They would always be behind him; they could never catch him up. As if bound upon a great wheel, spinning round, with lives bound to it—no wonder he was giddy; the mist or the wheel had made him so. That was why he saw the depths—as the wheel turned; it didn't go quickly, but it was always revolving, and he had been on it for so long, so many years, and now he was old and sinking deeper and deeper down. But the elder sons would never catch him up; they were tied to it too.

His head was aching with the dizziness of the revolutions all the same; wheels within wheels—he had heard that phrase before. The mists were revolving round him or he in them: which—what—was it? Wheels within wheels—there had been some phrase of glory, angels or something, wheels full of eyes, cycles in cycles all vigilant and intelligent, revolving. These weren't eyes; these were hands. Perhaps hands were eyes; if the eye of the body was dark, if the hand had no power—a vague wheel of innumerable hands all intertwined and clasped and turning, turning faster and faster, turning out of mud and into the mist, hands falling from it, helplessly clutching.…

It was at this moment that Mr. Coningsby, blindly edging along the corridor, his own hands feeling nervously along the wall, touched a door-handle he turned it, went in, found himself in his own room, still miraculously and mercifully free from mist, and slammed the door behind him. It was at the same moment that a voice within him said in tones of startled concern, 'Nancy? Sybil?' If they were out there, as of course they were—he had seen Sybil in the hall when he was calling 'Fire!' down the stairs. But Sybil—he knew it and admitted it at last—didn't matter. In any unusual variation of normal things—snowstorms or shipwrecks or burning houses—he could have regarded himself as Sybil's superior. But this was entire subversion of normal things, a new world, a world of lunacy, and he was not superior to her there. Confronted with any utterly new experience, he was her inferior, for he existed only in his relationships, and she—she existed in herself. There was certainly no point in his looking for Sybil.

All this he understood in a swift revelation; but he understood also that Nancy was different. Nancy was not merely his daughter—she was much more likely to find him useful than Sybil was. And he didn't trust Henry to look after her; he had always thought that Henry was more concerned with himself than with Nancy. Poised three steps within the room, Mr. Coningsby turned round and looked unhappily at the closed door. Must he really go back into that mist on the chance of being useful to her? It seemed he must. 'Blast!' Mr. Coningsby said aloud, in a rare explosion of disgust. Sybil, Ralph, Henry—any of these might be looking after her; yes, but he didn't *know* they were. Besides, there was Joanna. His altruism excited into action by this opportune dislike (as so often happens: even love often owing more to hate than perfection of love could altogether approve), he went back to the door, and observed disagreeably that the golden cloud was beginning to ooze through it. He was past surprise by now; he didn't even try to see that it was coming through the keyhole or anywhere except straight through the wood. There it was, growing thicker. In that case it was just as well that he'd already determined to leave the room, since things would soon be as bad within as without. Very well; only this time he must keep his head; he wouldn't be any use to Nancy if he lost it. No nonsense about wheels or hands that were eyes or distances. This was a house; it had a fog in it; he was Lothair Coningsby, and he was going to find his daughter in case she was frightened by an ugly old woman. Very well. He opened the door.

Actually, when he had gone a little distance down the corridor, he thought the mist wasn't too bad. He even ventured to open his mouth, and say in a curiously subdued voice, 'Nancy!' He didn't quite admit that he didn't want any—anybody—anybody with inhuman hands to hear him, but he knew it would be very inconvenient if they did. But nothing at all happened, blessedly. So he took a few more steps and said 'Nancy' again. This time another form stepped against his own—very nearly crashed into him—and a voice said, 'She hasn't come back then?'

Mr. Coningsby, recovering from a spasmodic fear that the new appearance might be one of the presences of the cloud, peering closer, saw that it was Henry, and his fear spoke angrily: 'What d'ye mean—come back? Why aren't you with her?'

'Because I can't get there,' Henry said. 'God only knows where she is, and if He does He knows why I'm not there.'

'Don't stand there talking about God,' Mr. Coningsby snapped, 'Tell me what devil's trick you've played on her.'

'When I tried to kill you,' Henry began in a low, monotonous voice, as if he had often said it over to himself, 'because I thought you stood in the way of the entrance into the——'

'When you what?' Mr. Coningsby cried out, 'tried to kill *me*? Are you mad? When did you try to kill me?' The nightmare was getting worse; he couldn't really be standing in this accursed welter of golden cloud talking to his daughter's lover of his own plotted murder. Had there been any trying to kill him? or had he been killed? and was this mist the ghostly consequence of death? He checked in time to hear Henry say:

'When I brought the storm out of the Tarots. I poured the waters on you out of their vessels and I beat the winds against you with the staffs because you wouldn't give up the cards. But she went away to stop it.'

'Stop it!' Mr. Coningsby said, clutching at the first words he really understood. 'I should think she would stop it! What under heaven are you talking about?' He peered closely at Henry's face, and was struck silent by what he saw in eyes of which the brightness had been dulled. Pallid and fixed, the face looked back at him; mild and awful, the voice answered him, 'I meant to use her, and now I can't find her. She's gone beyond me, and I can't catch her up. You may.'

'I certainly will,' Mr. Coningsby said. 'I—I—— Where *is* she?'

'She's gone into the dance,' Henry said, 'and I don't know whether even she can hold her past there. I was a fool once and dreamed, and I tried to kill you because you were in the way of my dreams.'

'You were a fool all right,' Mr. Coningsby said, 'and if this utterly detestable nonsense you're talking means anything, you were a great deal worse than a fool. Pull yourself....'

Henry looked at him, and he stopped. No man with a face of that colour and of that agony would be talking nonsense—not if he knew it. If the storm had been—but storms *weren't*! Nor, of course, was mist. Nancy was trying to stop the storm—he'd got that much—and she'd gone into the dance. That, whatever else it meant, meant those damned silly marionettes in their infernal black magic of a room—where Joanna had been going. He had known all the time that Joanna would be in it somehow.

He pushed past Henry, rather thankful even in his angry distraction to feel Henry's undoubted body as he shoved it away, and said, 'I'll deal with you after. If you can't find her, I will.'

Unexpectedly docile, Henry said: 'You may. That may be the judgement. Do it; do it, if only you can.'

Mr. Coningsby had gone on several paces when he, without quite knowing why, looked back over his shoulder. It was a silly thing to do, he knew, with this God-forsaken mist all round him, and when he had done it he knew it all the more. For looking back was like seeing things reversed; he was looking back in two ways at once. He saw Henry, but he saw him upside down—a horrible idea. Nevertheless, there it was: Henry was, in the ridiculous reflections of the mist, hanging in the void, his head downwards; his hands out of sight behind him somewhere, his leg—one leg—drawn up across the other—it was the other he was hanging by. For a full minute Mr. Coningsby stood gaping over his shoulder at that vision seen in one of the opening hollows of the cloud, then a driving gold as of storm swept across it, and he could see no more. He turned his head again, but now he stood still. He was feeling sick and ill; he was feeling very old; he wished Sybil were with him. But she wasn't, and however sick and ill and old he was, still Nancy was somewhere about, in danger of being frightened, if nothing worse, by that loathsome hag of a Joanna. He went on, and for the first time since his childhood prayed, prayed that he mightn't look round again, prayed that Nancy at least when he found her might be whole and sane, prayed that if Sybil was any good, Sybil might pretty soon turn up, prayed that he might keep his mind steady and do for the best whatever he had to do. The mist opened in front of him in one of its sweeping unfoldings, and he was aware of figures moving in it, tall figures emerging and disappearing, and it covered them again, and again those cold fingers closed round his own. Mr. Coningsby said, in a voice that shook despite his efforts, 'Who are you?' The fingers warmed suddenly to his, and became a grasp; a voice in answer to his exclaimed, 'Hallo, father!' and he realized that it was Ralph's, though he would have sworn that the touch hadn't been Ralph's when it first caught him. But he must have been mistaken. He said in enormous relief: 'Hallo, my boy! glad to find you.'

'I'm damned glad,' Ralph answered, and his head appeared close to his father's. 'You're solid, anyhow.'

'Whereabouts are we?' Mr. Coningsby asked.

'Where we were, I suppose,' Ralph said. 'By that doorway into the study or whatever it was. I've not done much moving since, I can tell you. Funny business this.'

'It's a wicked and dangerous business,' Mr. Coningsby cried out. 'I'm looking for Nancy. That fiend's left her alone, after trying to kill me.'

'What fiend?' Ralph asked, even more bewildered. 'Who's been trying to kill you?'

'That devil's bastard Henry,' Mr. Coningsby said, unwontedly moved as he came to speak of it. 'He said so. He said he raised the storm so as to kill me.'

'Henry!' Ralph exclaimed. 'Raised a storm. But I mean—O, come, a storm!'

'He said so,' Mr. Coningsby repeated. 'And he's left Nancy in that room there with that gibbering hag of an aunt of his. Come on with me; we've got to get her out.'

'I see,' said Ralph. 'Yes; O, well, let's. I don't mind anything so long as it's firm. But raised a storm, you know! He must be a bit touched. I always thought he was a trifle gibbery himself.'

'O, everyone's mad in this damned house,' Mr. Coningsby said. 'I suppose we're going right?'

'Well, I can't see much,' Ralph answered, 'but perhaps we are. I mean—if we're not we shall find out. What's that?'

They had both bumped into something. Mr. Coningsby, his language becoming less restrained every time he spoke, cursed and felt for it. But it was Ralph's less maddened brain which found the explanation. 'It's the table,' he said suddenly. 'The big table we saw from the doorway.'

'Then we'd better get round it,' Mr. Coningsby said. 'The room where those gargoyles are is on the other side. I wish I could smash every one of them into fragments and cram them down his gulping throat.'

Hand still in hand, they groped round the table, and, when they judged they were almost opposite the inner door, struck out towards it. After two or three cautious steps, 'It's getting thinner,' Mr. Coningsby said.

Ralph was more doubtful, but, dutifully encouraging, he had just answered, 'Perhaps you're right,' when he was startled by his father nearly falling. Mr. Coningsby's raised foot had come down on something that jerked and heaved under it. He cried out, staggered, recovered himself, and came to a halt as the thing rose in their pathway. It was in the shape of a man; it was a man; it was the fellow that had been with the witch; it was Stephen. He must have been lying across the threshold of the inner room. He looked at them with dull hostility.

'Get back,' he said. 'You can't come here. She's there.'

'She is, is she?' Mr. Coningsby said. 'Here, Ralph, move him.'

Ralph started to obey. He put a hand on Stephen and began to say, 'Look here, you must let us by,' when Stephen leapt at him, and the two were locked in a wild struggle. Mr. Coningsby just avoided their first collision, and slipped past them as they swayed. Both of them, clutching and wrestling, went, under the impulse of Stephen's rush, back into the outer room; all the emotions of fear and anger that had been restrained in their separate solitudes now broke into activity through the means of that hostile embrace. In the mysterious liquefaction of everything which had distressed Ralph, in the outbreak of the mysteries of the vagrant goddess which had terrified Stephen, each of them found something recognizable, natural, and human, and attacked it. The beings who possessed the cloud were veiled by it from both of them; like primeval men of undeveloped capacities, they strove with whatever was near. So had dim tribe battled with tribe—and earlier yet, before tribes were, before the beasts that grew into tribes, when the stuff that is the origin of all of us had brought forth only half-conscious shapes, such struggles had gone on. The nature of the battles of all the world was in them; to pass or not to pass—neither knowing clearly why, except that great command intensely swayed their spirits—was the centre of their conflicting wills. The gateway was taboo, for the goddess had entered; mystical age, nourishing wisdom, had gone into the sanctuary and must be inviolate. The gateway must be forced, for kinship was in danger; mystical womanhood, unprotected helplessness, was abandoned within and must be saved. Religion had commanded, and the household: the unknowing champions of either domination panted and fought in the outer courts of the mystery. The mist rolled into and over them; it possessed and maddened them. Life strove with life, and life poured itself into them to maintain the struggle. In such unseeing obedience, at that very moment, in the wider world, armies poured to battle, for causes as obscurely known. They battered and struck; they had no hope but destruction and no place but war. Ignorant of all but simple laws, they closed and broke and struck and closed again, and the strength of earth fought in them for mastery.

But of that manifestation of primitive violence Mr. Coningsby saw nothing: he had glimpsed the inner doorway and went hurriedly through it. Within, all was clear: clear so that he could know, unknowing, another mystery of mankind. For there, in the room with the dark hangings, through or in which had appeared to the initiate the vision of the painted world, he saw the solemn intention of sacrifice, the attempted immolation of the victim to the god. Fate had fallen on deity, and only by bursting the doors of human life could deity be relieved. Humanity, caught up into dooms and agonies greater even than its own, was madly attempting to relieve them, and itself with them. Over the golden altar of blood the body of the girl lay stretched; on one side the hierophant clutched her wrist and tore at the mystery of the hand, which means so much in its gentle and terrible power; and on the altar itself, as if some god had descended to aid and quicken the sacrifice, the cat lay crouched in a beautiful and horrible suspense before its spring. As far as the struggling bodies without from the holy striving of joyous imaginations, so far within was the grotesque group from the sacred and necessary offering which (the testimony of the myths declares) releases, after some spiritual manner, the energies of the gods. But it was not wholly alien; and that which is common to all was the purpose of death.

Mr. Coningsby, as he broke into the charmed circle, saw the priestess, the cat, and the body of the sacrifice. It was on the last that his attention was concentrated, and he cried out in a voice rather of objection than of protest, but that was the result of fifty years of objection to life rather than of protest against it. He ran forward, grabbed the cat, lifted it, and flung it with violence at the doorway, much as Stephen had flung him away not long before. Joanna screeched at him, and he swore back at her. Dominant for the first time in his life, moved for the first time by those two great virtues, strength and justice, he commanded her, and for a moment she flinched. She was distracted from the hand she held by the hand that gripped her shoulder— before its owner had time to realize how offensive to his normal habits such a grip was. Nancy at the same moment twisted her wrist and jerked her own scratched hand away, standing once more upright on the other side of the table. Mr. Coningsby ran round the table to her. She put her arm round him and realized suddenly how much she owed to him—owed because she was a blundering servant of Love to this other blundering servant of Love, owed from her struggling goodwill to his struggling goodwill: and how full of goodwill his labouring spirit was. He was a companion upon the Way, and how difficult she had made the Way to him! She hugged his arm, not so much in gratitude for this single service as in remorse for her impatient past.

'O, thank you, darling,' she said. 'You did come just at the right time.'

'Are you all right?' Mr. Coningsby said. 'Are you all right? Has she hurt you? What was she doing?'

'She was looking for something,' Nancy said, 'and she thought I'd got it. But I haven't. If I only knew exactly what it was! Perhaps Aunt Sybil could find out if we could get them together. Ask her to come downstairs, won't you, father?'

'I'll ask her to come downstairs,' Mr. Coningsby said. 'I'll ask her to come down into the cellars, and I'll ask her if she minds the doors being locked on her, and if she'd very much mind if we tied her up for the dancing, raving monstrosity of ugly hell that she is. Looking for something!'

At any rate, Nancy thought, that would give them a chance of finding Sybil on the way, and perhaps something more satisfactory than cellars would open. She couldn't feel, for all her smarting hand, that locking Joanna in a cellar would do any real good. Nothing but giving Joanna what she wanted or getting Joanna to change her wants would be any real good. She pressed her hand to her heart; it was smarting dreadfully; the blood stood along the scratches. She didn't want to show it in case her father became more annoyed with Joanna, but the sooner she could find Henry or (if needs must) bathe it herself the better. She began gently to edge Mr. Coningsby round the table. She said, 'Let's go with her at least. I'm sure Aunt Sybil could help. She knows what the lost thing is.'

Mr. Coningsby felt a shock of truth. Sybil did seem to know—Sybil had quietened this old hag—the lost thing—he took an automatic step or two forward. Joanna had already retreated a little, and was darting angry eyes round the room. She went back yet farther, and, as Nancy also moved, the golden cloud which hung behind the old woman rolled back, disclosing on the ground at her feet the paintings of the Tarots which had fallen from the hands of the lovers that evening. They lay there, throbbing and vibrating. With a scream of rage and delight she dropped to her knees and scraped them together in her hands.

'What——' Mr. Coningsby began, surprised, and ended in a different voice. 'Are those my cards? What under heaven are my cards doing there?' He rushed round the table, and Nancy ran with him.

But they were too late. Joanna was on her feet again, had turned, was running off into the mist, clutching the paintings. The other two ran also, and, as if their movement was itself a wind, the mist rolled back from before them, driven to either side and about their feet and floating over their heads. But, as Joanna ran, her hands fingered the cards, and she cried out in ecstasy.

They broke into the outer room, and at the sound of that shrill rapturous voice the two combatants ceased to struggle. She was upon them, and both of them, startled at the coming of such a hierophant in such exaltation, released the other and fell back. But Stephen sent a word to her, and she answered: 'I'm finding him, I'm finding him. I'll burn them first and then he'll come. He'll come in the fire: the fire is for Horus, Horus in the fire.'

She was by him and out of the room, and still she worked the magic in her hands, and by now, so swift and effective was her insanity, she had separated the suit of the swords from the rest, and was setting them in some strange order. She made of them a mass of little pointed triangles, three living symbols to each triangle, and the King of the Swords, whose weapon quivered and glowed as if in flame, she thrust on top of them all, and laid her own hand over it, warming it into life. And as she came into the longer corridor, already the sparks went about her, and she was calling, 'Little one, little one! I'm coming. They shan't hurt you any more. I'll drive them away—your mother'll save you. I can hear you—I'm coming.'

Behind her those who pressed were parted. At the door of the outer room Mr. Coningsby's strength went from him. He staggered, and would have fallen had not Nancy held him, and Ralph, by whom they paused, sprang to her help. Nancy gave her brother one swift, delightful smile and exclaimed to him, 'Look after him, there's a dear. I must go.'

'Right ho!' Ralph said, and took his father's arm as Nancy released it. Stephen uncertainly looked at them, then he left them and followed Nancy. She came into the longer corridor and saw before her Henry leaning on the balustrade at the top of the stairs. Joanna, checking as she went, had lifted the swords that were beginning to shoot from between her hands in little flames, and was thrusting them continually forward towards him in sharp spasms of motion. And about them the cloud gathered into shapes and forms, and through all the translucent house Nancy was aware of golden figures unceasingly intertwining in the steps of the fatal dance.

CHAPTER XVI

'SUN, STAND THOU STILL
UPON GIBEON'

Sybil, with a great deal of difficulty, although it did not occur to her to call it that, had managed to get Aaron downstairs and into the drawing-room. She had wanted him to be helped to his bedroom, but this he had altogether refused. He wouldn't go up those stairs; he wouldn't go back into the thicker mist; he would go down; he would get away if he could. She wasn't to leave him—everyone else had left him—and they would be on him.

'They?' Sybil asked as she helped him cautiously along. 'Splendid, Mr. Lee. You *could* get upstairs almost as well, you know. Easier, in fact. No, all right—if you'd rather. They?'

'They,' Aaron babbled. 'They're all round us, they always are, but we shall see them. I daren't see them. I daren't. I can't see anything: it's too bright.'

'It *is* very bright,' Sybil said. 'If it wasn't so late, I should think the sun was shining. But I never heard of the sun shining at ten o'clock on Christmas night. Gently; that's perfect.'

'The sun!' Aaron said. 'The sun's gone out for ever; we're all blind. Lame and blind, so that we can't escape them.'

Sybil smiled at him. 'Well, then,' she said, 'I wouldn't worry about escaping. Leave that to Nancy and Henry, unless they're sensible enough not to worry either. I wasn't at their age. I tried to insist on escaping; fortunately, I didn't. That's the bottom.'

'How can you tell?' Aaron exclaimed. 'Can you see? can you see through the mist and the snow?'

'Fairly well,' Sybil said. 'I wonder if Amabel—Amabel, could you give Mr. Lee your arm on the other side?'

The words reached Amabel where she was clasped with her companions. They reached her out of the bright cloud; she raised her head, felt it against her eyes, and promptly shut them again. Sybil looking across the hall at them—the hall that in this curiously golden-tinted snow looked more lovely, though more ruinous, than she had thought any mortal thing could look—considered a moment, and then in a firmer voice called again, 'Amabel!' Snowstorms were all very well, but it was silly to get into a state of crouching hysterics over a snowstorm; Amabel's immediate job was to be of use. Normally one wouldn't order other people's servants about, and she said to Aaron between two calls: 'Will you forgive me, Mr. Lee? Perhaps if you called her...?'

Aaron, however, it was clear, had no notion of doing anything of the sort; the words didn't seem to mean anything to him. Sybil called for the third time, with an imperious certainty: 'Amabel! will you come here?'

Amabel heard the voice and looked up again. In the awful vagueness of the hall, tumultuous with cloud and storm, she saw figures moving. A mingled sense of her duty and of wild adventure filled her. She released the cook and the other maid; she said faintly but definitely, 'I'm coming.'

'Well, come, then,' Sybil said, still slightly imperious. 'My dear girl, do hurry. I know it's very unusual, but we may as well be useful.'

Amabel dashed through the mist, terrified but exultant. It swirled round her; it carried her along; she was swept, deliriously panting, to the side of the strange lady who walked in the cloud as others did by day, and laughed at the storm as others did at spring, and closed doors that the whole power of the world dashed open, and carried an old man safely through chaos to——

'Where to, madam?' she asked, an attentive executant once more.

Serenely Miss Coningsby smiled at her—a smile that Amabel felt to be even brighter than the golden glow about them: so much brighter that for a moment the glow was only the reflection of the smile.

'How dear of you!' Miss Coningsby said. 'So—yes. I thought the drawing-room. You and my nephew made rather a mess of the dining-room, didn't you?'

Amabel smiled back, a thing she didn't much believe in doing as a rule, having been for some months with a lady who held that if you smiled at your servants they would do everything for you, and also held that you had a right to see that they did. The company proceeded slowly to the drawing-room, and Aaron was made as comfortable as possible on a divan. Sybil, kneeling by him, bared his ankle and looked at it.

'It doesn't,' she said, 'seem very bad.' She laid her hand over it; thinking how charming Aaron Lee's courtesy had been, very willing to be courteous in her turn. He looked up at her and met her eyes, and his anxious babblings stopped.

Her hand closed round the ankle; her mind went inwards into the consciousness of the Power which contained them both; she loved it and adored it: with her own thought of Aaron in his immediate need, his fear, his pain, she adored. Her own ankle ached and throbbed in sympathy, not the sympathy of an easy proffer of mild regret, but that of a life habituated to such intercession. She interceded; she in him and he in her, they grew acquainted; the republican element of all created things welled up in them both. Their eyes exchanged news. She throbbed for an instant not with pain but with fear as his own fear passed through her being. It did but pass through; it was dispelled within her, dying away in the unnourishing atmosphere of her soul, and with the fear went the pain. Her hand had fastened on him; she smiled at him, and then with the passing of that smile before her recovered serenity her hand was released. She sank back on to her heels, and said, her voice full of a deep delight: 'O, no, not very bad.'

Of what exactly she spoke she hardly knew, but he answered her in the greater sense. 'Let them come then,' he said. 'I was a fool ever to think I knew.'

'Why, no,' she said. 'Only perhaps you sprained your ankle—hurrying.'

Negligent of his supposed hurt, he put his feet to the floor and stood up; then, as if from the weight he put on them, he flinched. 'But the cloud! the living cloud!' he cried. 'And Joanna's there!'

She came, in a complex movement of harmony, to her feet. 'Yes,' she said thoughtfully, 'Joanna might perhaps be a little carried away. Ought we to go and see if we can find her?'

'Must we find her?' he said irresolutely. 'Let her fight them if she wants to. Must we go back into the mist?'

'What is this mist you see?' Sybil asked. 'Why do you call it a living cloud?'

'It's the cloud from which the images were first made,' he said, almost whispering. 'It hides in everything; it's the golden hands that shape us and our lives. It's death to see them; no one can bear it.'

'Are our hands so different?' Sybil said.

'So many degrees less,' he answered, 'in life and power. There have been those whose palms were touched, when they were born, by figures leaning over the cradles: some by one and some by another.' His words came faster, as if he would keep her where she stood, keep her by his talk in forgetfulness of the dangers without. 'Napoleon … Cæsar. There was one who came to Olympias on the night when Alexander was conceived, and to the mother of Samson. Great priests—the hierophant touched their hands when they were tiny. Death sometimes—Joanna's child—and the innocents of Bethlehem. And others that we can't see, others beyond the seventy-eight degrees.'

'Yet all this time,' Sybil said, 'Joanna cries for her child.'

He caught her arm. 'Leave her alone,' he cried. 'Perhaps she'll turn the magic against the princes, then she'll die, she'll be blasted. Keep your hands from her.'

'Why, she blessed me once with hers,' Sybil answered. 'And I can't see this mist of yours, though I agree there's a new loveliness in things. Let's go.'

'If you enter the cloud, you'll never come out,' he cried again. 'The hands'll drag you down, the hands of the beginning.'

'Let's go and see,' she said. 'There are the others, and there's always a way through all mists.' She looked at Amabel, who was listening in puzzled and fearful silence. 'Thank you, my dear,' she said. 'Shall we go back now?'

She moved forward and out into the hall. Aaron, half-willing, half-unwilling, followed her, hobbling either from his hurt or his fear, if indeed the two were separate. Amabel, in the mere growing certainty that to be near Miss Coningsby was to be as near safety as possible, followed; but she took care to follow her master. Somehow she didn't think Miss Coningsby, if she should look round, would like to see her pushing on out of her place. So, biting her lips a trifle nervously, and as nervously settling her sleeves at her wrists, she controlled her impulse to thrust right up against the strange lady and contented herself with keeping her eyes fixed on the tall assured figure which passed through the drawing-room door and came out among....

Among the powers and princes of the dance. For Amabel, as she in turn came into the hall, had the most bewildering vision of a multitude of invaders. She couldn't at once grasp it, but as she gazed and panted she saw that the whole house had changed. The walls, the stairs, the doors, the ceiling, were all alive. They were formed—all that she could see of them through snow and mist—of innumerable shapes, continuously shifting, sliding over and between each other. They were in masses of colour—black mostly, she seemed to see, but with ripples of grey and silver and fiery-red passing over them. Dark pillars of earth stood in the walls, and through them burning swords pierced, and huge old cups of pouring waters were emptied, and grey clubs were beaten. She screamed once despairingly, and Miss Coningsby looked round over her shoulder. But the very movement, though in a way reassuring, was immediately more terrifying; for it seemed to divide even that solitary figure of comfort, and there were two shapes before her: one was the strange lady and one was a man, in a great white cloak and a golden helmet with a crown round it. As if treading a dance together, the two went forward—and the king or emperor or whatever he was also looked back over his shoulder. Amabel was near fainting, but as she met the awful eyes that shone at her she was gathered together and strengthened. She had her duty to do, she reminded herself; if the storm stopped, they'd want the hall tidied up. She must be there in case the hall wanted tidying up. She forgot, in that necessity, the eyes that called to her, and the lord of secular labour vanished from her sight, for she was herself part of the hierarchy that is he. She stood still, concentrated on that thought: 'If the storm stops, they'll want the hall tidied up—tidied up—tidied.' She wished spasmodically that those sudden shining figures wouldn't come between her and Miss Coningsby, and determined, early in the New Year, to have her eyes seen to. Meanwhile, if the storm stopped....

High above them, at the top of the stairs, Nancy looked down. She saw below her Sybil standing in the middle of the hall: she saw the storm in its elemental shapes of wind and water dancing about her. The sight kept her gaze momentarily even from Joanna in front of her, and in that moment she saw Sybil imperiously put out her left hand.

She remembered that movement: once, not so long ago, her father had come home tired and with a bad chill, and she and Ralph had been making rather a row dancing to the gramophone or something—she remembered the exact gesture with which Sybil had flung a hand out towards them while going on some errand. She hadn't needed to speak; the hand had somehow tossed them into subjection. Ralph and she had rather awkwardly broken off and begun chatting—quite quietly chatting—instead. Nancy smiled as the memory touched her in the recognition of the gesture, and smiled again to see the flagging of the white whirlwind. Sybil stood there, one hand flung out, looking up, and Nancy's eyes went back to the two in front of her, to Henry and Joanna facing each other now.

They went back to meet Henry's. He was looking past Joanna and the burning threat which was leaping and darting from the agile, hateful hands; he was looking, as he had never looked before, at the girl who had come again from among the mystery of the images. She looked back at him and laughed, and beckoned him by throwing out her hands towards him; and in simultaneous movement both she and Henry took a few running steps and came together on Joanna's left.

'You're safe,' he said abruptly, holding her.

'And you, darling?' she breathed anxiously.

'I?' he said. 'O, yes, I'm safe'; and then, as if realizing the new danger, 'But run, run quickly; she's got the magic in her hands and she may do anything. Get away, dearest and best; leave me to deal with her.'

'You do it so well, don't you, sweetheart?' she mocked. 'O darling, you never ought to be let deal with anyone but me.'

The throbbing voice caught him away from the danger near them. He said: 'And you then?'

'Ah! me,' she said, 'that was given to you alone: that's your only gift. Do you want more?'

'Haven't you that also—you who have all the rest?' he said.

She answered, smiling, 'If you give it me. But don't give it me too soon. Love isn't all that easy—even with you. Darling, your aunt's very angry: let's talk to her together.'

Obedient to her initiative, he turned with her. Between them and the top of the stairs the half-naked creature stood, sparks flying off from those spasmodically thrusting hands and little flames breaking from them. The paintings between those hands were thrusting of their own volition as nights before they had slid and rubbed in Nancy's. But the old woman was not facing them; she did not seem even to have noticed Henry's movement. She glared round her, unseeing, or rather seeing everywhere hostility; she cried out accusing and cursing the whole world of things that had caught away her victim, who was also the casket of the hidden god, and had left her but this solitary weapon of magical fire. At the top of that height, between the lovers on one side and Sybil below her on the other, she broke into a paroxysm of despair and desire, supplicating and reassuring the lost child, denouncing the enemies that held him apart. Between the young lovers hand in hand on one side, and on the other the solitary figure of Sybil, whose hand was still stretched out over shapes that might, as Nancy saw them, have been blown heaps of snow or might have been such forms as had come rioting up from the centre of the storm but were now still and crouching—between those reconciled minds the distracted voice of Joanna pealed on. Nancy had meant to speak, to try to soothe or satisfy, but she dared not. If she did, if she asked and was answered, it would not be an answer that she could comprehend. Witches at the stake, with the fire already about them, might have been shrieking so, with as little chance that the stricken hearers would know the names they adjured. But it was not of witches that Nancy thought, for all the screams and the flames; she heard a more human cry. She heard the wail that rang through the curses, and it was a wail that went up from the depths of the world. Her hand clasped Henry's passionately, for the sound of that universal distress terrified her young soul. On the edge of a descent an antique misery was poised, and from the descent, from the house, from the earth, misery beyond telling lamented and complained—to men who could not aid, to gods who made no sign, for it was the gods themselves that had been lost. 'Ah! ah! ah!'—something final was gone, something beyond description precious: 'ah! ah! ah!'—the little child was dead. They were weeping for it everywhere, as they had been always. She who stood there screamed and stabbed for torment of hate and loss, and from marshes and cities all desire that had not learnt its own futility rose and swelled in hers. The litany of anguish poured out as if it were the sound of the earth itself rushing through space, and comfortless for ever the spinning globe swept on, turning upon itself, crying to itself; and space was the echo of its lament, and time was the measure of its sobs. But more than mere awe of such unavailing grief and desire awoke in Nancy then: cold at her heart, a personal fear touched her and stayed. It was a fear of that actual moment, but futurity lived in it. One hand was in Henry's, but the other was torn by Joanna's nails. Joanna stood in the way; beyond her the way led on to Sybil. She could see Sybil—ever so far off, in that descent upon which the great stairs opened. But Joanna stood in her, overarching the way, pouring out her voice like the way itself. She wanted to go to Sybil, and that voice was in the way—O folly of cowardice! that voice was the way. Why didn't Sybil move? why didn't Sybil come? Around her, before her, glimmering in the red glow that was uncertainly breaking from those ever-busy hands, she saw the mighty golden shapes looming. They were looming out of the cloud which was at once their background and yet they. It was difficult to see, but she caught the form of the designs she had studied—the one and twenty revelations of the Greater Trumps. The red glow leapt and faded; but the crown of the Emperor, but the front of the sphinx-drawn Chariot, but the stretched sickle of the image of Death, but the sandals of the two children playing together under an unshaped sun, themselves shedding the light by which they played, but the girdle of the woman who danced alone—all these and other fragmentary visions struck on her straining eyes. The glow faded; her dazzled eyes refused to see more distinction in those walls of mist. But as she shut them she heard Sybil call, and then she heard a sudden rush close by her. She opened her eyes hastily, in time to see—of all mad things—the cat that had crouched on the altar dash down the stairs towards Sybil. That wild and alien thing which Sybil had found in the magical storm, which had followed Joanna to her room and led her thence to the room of the images, which had almost made a way for the snow to break into the house, which had dashed from snow to mist and from mist to snow as if it were the living secret of uncontrolled power, which had instinctively assisted at the attempted sacrifice to uncontrolled desire, itself unshaping since lacking the instruments of shape, now rushed to the foot of the stairs, and absurdly checked itself, and then with high feline grace stepped across the hall to Sybil's feet.

Sybil dropped her hand towards it and dropped it a soft word; it jumped delicately towards her hand and played round her foot, and jumped again. As it rushed, as it stayed, Joanna's cry also ceased. The power of it was withdrawn; all power, all utterance, was withdrawn. The unexpected silence was more awful than even the wailing, for it was not a silence of relief but of impotence. The cry of the world was choked; the ball, tossed from the Juggler's hand, revolved in unspoken anguish. The madwoman reeled once, as if she had been struck on the mouth; then, recovering, turned darting eyes to Sybil in the hall below. Through the silence Sybil called to her: 'The child's found, Joanna; the child's alive and lovely. All's well; the child's found.' Joanna tried to speak and could not. She shuffled towards the stair; she turned her pointing hands, bearing their fiery weapon, as if she herself carried the sword of the crowned chieftain of fire, downward towards that other confronting form. Sybil took a step forward, the cat leaping up against her, and called again: 'He's here. Come and adore.'

In a forced and horrible croak, as if speech broke through against commandment and against control, Joanna said: 'It's you all the time. I shall see him when you're dead. When you're dead and the world's destroyed, I'll see my desire.'

Amabel, crouching by the drawing-room door, saw the strange lady, her left hand rising and falling in a dance with the leaping cat, stretch out the right as if in invitation. The open palm, the curved fingers, the arching thumb, took on a reflection of the cloud that hung over all things: it seemed to Amabel that Miss Coningsby held out a golden hand towards the staircase down which Joanna was beginning to creep. The hand which had helped Lothair and comforted Nancy and healed Aaron, which had picked up the kitten and closed the door and controlled the storm, was stretched to gather in this last reverted madness of man. It lay there, very still, the centre of all things, the power and the glory, the palm glowing with a ruddy passion veiled by the aureate flesh—the hand of all martyrs, enduring; of all lovers, welcoming; of all rulers, summoning. And, as if indeed it summoned, the cloud of gold rushed down towards it, but it moved in shapes and figures, the hands of all the symbols stretched towards the hand that, being human, was so much more than symbol. Nancy and Henry from above beheld them, hands imperial and sacerdotal, single and joined, the working hands that built the Tower, the helpless hands that formed the Wheel, white hands stretching from the snow, fiery hands thrusting from between Joanna's that burned downwards and vanished, all activities rushing towards that repose through which activity beat in the blood that infused it. So the hand of the Juggler had been stretched to cast and catch the tossed balls of existence; so the hand of the Fool had at last fulfilled the everlasting promise and yielded its secrets to the expected hour. The cloud swirled once around that open palm, as the intermingling shapes trod out a last circling measure, hiding all other forms, so that the hand itself was all that could be seen as the rapturous powers wheeled inwards to it. For an infinitesimal fraction of time the immortal dance stood still to receive the recollection of that ever-moving and never-broken repose of sovereign being. Then suddenly they were gone, and the cloud was gone, and everywhere, breaking from Sybil's erect figure, shone a golden light, as of the fullness of the sun in his glory, expanding in a rich fruition. Over the snow spread and heaped around, over Aaron and the others by him, over the stairs and the landing and those who were on it, and so over and through the whole house, the light shone, exquisite and full of promise, radiant and full of perfection. The chaos of the hall was a marvel of new shape and colour; the faces of those who stood around were illumined from within. It was Christmas night, but the sunlight shed itself about the whole house, and in the sunlight, between Sybil and Joanna, seriously engrossed, two small strange children played. The mystery which that ancient seer had worked in the Greater Trumps had fulfilled itself, at that time and in that place, to so high a point of knowledge. Sybil stood there, and from her the sun of the Tarots ruled, and the holy children of the sun, the company of the blessed, were seen at least by some of the eyes that watched. For Amabel saw them and was ignorantly at peace; and Aaron saw them and was ashamed; and Nancy and Henry saw them, and Nancy laughed for mere joy of seeing, and when he heard it Henry felt his heart labour as it had never done before with the summons and the power; and Sybil saw them and adored, and saw beyond them, running down the stairs between herself and Nancy as if he were their union, and poised behind Joanna as if he supported and protected her, the vivid figure of the Fool. He had come from all sides at once, yet he was but one. All-reconciling and perfect, he was there, running down the stairs as he had run down the storm. And as he passed, receiving and bestowing light, Nancy, on an impulse, turned and kissed Henry—before the light should vanish, so that she might have done it, might have done it if in days to come she should ever find herself a part of that dreadful cry which had gone up from the world. But even in the kiss she felt her smarting hand throbbing an answer, an answer and an oath that years should see valiantly kept. When she looked back, the figure of the Fool was gone; she heard Joanna cry out in a natural voice, and she saw the children cease from their play and look up, and then Joanna ran down the rest of the stairs, and, as she reached the bottom, cried out once more as if in pain, and stumbled and fell.

The cry shook the golden light; it vanished. Amabel, gazing, saw Miss Coningsby in the hall and the old woman lying in a heap at the foot of the stairs, and before she had time to move she saw the other visitors come flying down them. They came very swiftly, but as if they also came in order; the lovers first, still hand in hand, and after them Mr. Coningsby, still anxiously watching Nancy, and thinking as fast as he could that he must keep in touch with her, whatever happened. And after him again came Ralph and Stephen, distracted

245

from their mutual hostility, but with all their strength ready and vigilant. The three great orders of grace and intellect and corporeal strength, in those immature servants of their separate degrees, gathered round the place where Sybil kneeled by Joanna, and the search within and the search without were joined.

Mr. Coningsby peered over Henry's shoulder. 'Has she collapsed?' he said hopefully.

Nancy had kneeled down also, and Sybil's hands and hers were busy with easing and helping. Amabel, released at last from what she felt must have been a deliciously thrilling nightmare, ran of her own accord to get some water. Aaron came over to the rest. Joanna opened her eyes, and they fell on Nancy. She looked, uncertainly and then eagerly, at the grave young face bending over her, then a great gladness shone in her own. She put out a trembling hand, and Nancy clasped it. She murmured something, and Nancy in similar indistinguishable words answered. Sybil stood up, and Mr. Coningsby edged round to her.

'What's she doing?' he asked, not quite knowing why he was speaking in a whisper. 'Is she apologizing or what?'

Sybil did not immediately answer. She looked at him with a smile; then with the same smile she looked round the hall, and her eyes lingered on a little heap that lay where she had been standing just before, a little heap of golden dust, strewn with charred and flimsy scraps, so light that already one or two were floating away in the mere stir of the air. The presentation of the dance was for ever done. She looked at them tenderly; then she turned back to her brother, and said, 'She has found her child.'

'Has she?' Mr. Coningsby said. 'Where?' And he also looked round the hall, as if he suspected that Joanna's child was likely to be a fresh nuisance.

'She thinks Nancy is her child,' Sybil said.

Mr. Coningsby stared, tried to grasp it, moved a little, was gently pushed out of the way by Amabel with an 'Excuse me, sir,' glowered after her, and said: 'Nancy?'

'She thinks so,' Sybil answered.

'But … but, I mean … what about the age?' her brother protested. 'She can't think a girl of twenty—forty, perhaps, if she thought she'd grown up, or four if she hadn't. But not twenty.'

'She's looking at something immortal,' Sybil said. 'Age….' She delicately shrugged it away.

Mr. Coningsby stared at her, and then realized that he was a little frightened of her, though he couldn't think why. 'But,' he began again, and suddenly remembered a single simple fact, 'but I thought her child was a *boy*. I'm sure someone told me it was a boy. She doesn't think Nancy's a boy, does she? Don't you mean Henry?'

'No,' Sybil said, 'I mean Nancy. I don't think it much matters about girl or boy. She thought her child was Messias.'

'O!' Mr. Coningsby said. 'And is Nancy Messias?'

'Near enough,' Sybil answered. 'There'll be pain and heart-burning yet, but, for the moment, near enough.'

THE END

Many Dimensions

CHAPTER I
THE STONE

'Do you mean,' Sir Giles said, 'that the thing never gets smaller?'

'Never,' the Prince answered. 'So much of its virtue has entered into its outward form that whatever may happen to it there is no change. From the beginning it was as it is now.'

'Then by God, sir,' Reginald Montague exclaimed, 'you've got the transport of the world in your hands.'

Neither of the two men made any answer. The Persian, sitting back in his chair, and Sir Giles, sitting forward on the edge of his, were both gazing at the thing which lay on the table. It was a circlet of old, tarnished, and twisted gold, in the centre of which was set a cubical stone measuring about half an inch every way, and having apparently engraved on it certain Hebrew letters. Sir Giles picked it up, rather cautiously, and concentrated his gaze on them. The motion awoke a doubt in Montague's mind.

'But supposing you chipped one of the letters off?' he asked. 'Aren't they awfully important? Wouldn't that destroy the—the effect?'

'They are the letters of the Tetragrammaton,' the Persian said drily, 'if you call that important. But they are not engraved on the Stone; they are in the centre—they are, in fact, the Stone.'

'O!' Mr. Montague said vaguely, and looked at his uncle Sir Giles, who said nothing at all. This, after a few minutes, seemed to compel Montague to a fresh attempt.

'You see, sir?' he said, leaning forward almost excitedly. 'If what the Prince says is true, and we've proved that it is, a child could use it.'

'You are not, I suppose,' the Persian asked, 'proposing to limit it to children? A child could use it, but in adult hands it may be more dangerous.'

'Dangerous be damned,' Montague said more excitedly than before, 'It's a marvellous chance—it's … it's a miracle. The thing's as simple as pie. Circlets like this with the smallest fraction of the Stone in each. We could ask what we liked for them—thousands of pounds each, if we like. No trains, no tubes, no aeroplanes. Just the thing on your forehead, a minute's concentration, and whoosh!'

The Prince made a sudden violent movement, and then again a silence fell.

It was late at night. The three were sitting in Sir Giles Tumulty's house at Ealing—Sir Giles himself, the traveller and archaeologist; Reginald Montague, his nephew and a stockbroker; and the Prince Ali Mirza Khan, First Secretary to the Persian Ambassador at the court of St. James. At the gate of the house stood the Prince's car; Montague was playing with a fountain-pen; all the useful tricks of modern civilization were at hand. And on the table, as Sir Giles put it slowly down, lay all that was left of the Crown of Suleiman ben Daood, King in Jerusalem.

Sir Giles looked across at the Prince. 'Can you move other people with it, or is it like season-tickets?'

'I do not know,' the Persian said gravely. 'Since the time of Suleiman (may the Peace be upon him!) no one has sought to make profit from it.'

'Ha!' said Mr. Montague, surprised. 'O come now, Prince!'

'Or if they have,' the Prince went on, 'they and their names and all that they did have utterly perished from the earth.'

'Ha!' said Mr. Montague again, a little blankly. 'O well, we can see. But you take my advice and get out of Rails. Look here, uncle, we want to keep this thing quiet.'

'Eh?' Sir Giles said. 'Quiet? No, I don't particularly want to keep it quiet. I want to talk to Palliser about it—after me he knows more about these things than anyone. And I want to see Van Eilendorf—and perhaps Cobham, though his nonsense about the double pillars at Baghdad was the kind of tripe that nobody but a broken-down Houndsditch sewer-rat would talk.'

The Prince stood up. 'I have shown you and told you these things,' he said, 'because you knew too much already, and that you may see how very precious is the Holy Thing which you have there. I ask you again to restore it to the guardians from whom you stole it. I warn you that if you do not——'

'I didn't steal it,' Sir Giles broke in. 'I bought it. Go and ask the fellow who sold it to me.'

'Whether you stole by bribery or by force is no matter,' the Prince went on. 'You very well know that he who betrayed it to you broke the trust of generations. I do not know what pleasure you find in it or for what you mean to use it, unless indeed you will make it a talisman for travel. But however that may be, I warn you that it is dangerous to all men and especially dangerous to such unbelievers as you. There are dangers within the Stone, and other dangers from those who were sworn to guard the Stone. I offer you again as much money as you can desire if you will return it.'

'O well, as to money,' Reginald Montague said, 'of course my uncle will have a royalty—a considerable royalty—on all sales and that'll be a nice little bit in a few months. Yours isn't a rich Government anyhow, is it? How many millions do you owe us?'

The Prince took no notice. He was staring fiercely and eagerly at Sir Giles, who put out his hand again and picked up the circlet.

'No,' he said, 'no, I shan't part with it. I want to experiment a bit. The bastard asylum attendant who sold it to me——'

The Prince interrupted in a shaking voice. 'Take care of your words,' he said. 'Outcast and accursed as that man now is, he comes of a great and royal family. He shall writhe in hell for ever, but even there you shall not be worthy to see his torment.'

'—said there was hardly anything it wouldn't do,' Sir Giles finished. 'No, I shan't ask Cobham. Palliser and I will try it first. It was all perfectly legal, Prince, and all the Governments in the world can't make it anything else.'

'I do not think Governments will recover it,' the Prince said. 'But death is not a monopoly of Governments. If I had not sworn to my uncle——'

'O it was your uncle, was it?' Sir Giles asked. 'I wondered what it was that made you coo so gently. I rather expected you to be more active about it to-night.'

'You try me very hard,' the Prince uttered. 'But I know the Stone will destroy you at last.'

'Quite, quite,' Sir Giles said, standing up. 'Well, thank you for coming. If I could have pleased you, of course.... But I want to know all about it first.'

The Prince looked at the letters in the Stone. 'I think you will know a great deal then,' he said, salaamed deeply to it, and without bowing to the men turned and left the house.

Sir Giles went after him to the front door, though they exchanged no more words, and, having watched him drive away returned to find his nephew making hasty notes.

'I don't see why we need a company,' he said. 'Just you and I, eh?'

'Why you?' Sir Giles asked. 'What makes you think you're going to have anything to do with it?'

'Why, you told me,' Montague exclaimed. 'You offered me a hand in the game if I'd be about to-night when the Prince came in case he turned nasty.'

'So I did,' his uncle answered. 'Yes—well, on conditions. If there is any money in it, I shall want some of it. Not as much as you do, but some. It's always useful, and I had to pay pretty high to get the Stone. And I don't want a fuss made about it—not yet.'

'That's all right,' Montague said. 'I was thinking it might be just as well to have Uncle Christopher in with us.'

'Whatever for?' Sir Giles asked.

'Well ... if there's any legal trouble, you know,' Montague said vaguely. 'I mean—if it came to the Courts we might be glad—of course, I don't know if they could—but anyhow he'd probably notice it if I began to live on a million—and some of these swine will do anything if their pockets are touched—all sorts of tricks they have—but a Chief Justice *is* a Chief Justice—that is, if you didn't mind——'

'I don't mind,' Sir Giles said. 'Arglay's got a flat-footed kind of intellect; that's why he's Chief Justice, I expect. But for what it's worth, and if they did try any international law business. But they can't; there was nothing to prevent that fellow selling it to me if he chose, nor me buying. I'll get Palliser here as soon as I can.'

'I wonder how many we ought to make,' Montague said. 'Shall we say a dozen to start with? It can't cost much to make a dozen bits of gold—need it be gold? Better, better. Better keep it in the same stuff—and it looks more for the money. The money—why, we can ask a million for each—for what'll only cost a guinea or two....' He stopped, appalled by the stupendous vision, then he went on anxiously, 'The Prince did say a bit any size would do, didn't he? and that this fellow'—he pointed a finger at the Stone—'would keep the same size? It means a patent, of course; so if anybody else ever did get hold of the original they couldn't use it. Millions ... millions....'

'Blast your filthy gasbag of a mouth!' Sir Giles said. 'You've made me forget to ask one thing. Does it work in time as well as space? We must try, we must try.' He sat down, picked up the Crown, and sat frowning at the Divine Letters.

'I don't see what you mean,' Reginald said, arrested in his note-taking. 'Time? Go back, do you mean?' He considered, then, 'I shouldn't think anyone would want to go back,' he said.

'Forward then,' Sir Giles answered. 'Wouldn't you like to go forward to the time when you've got your millions?'

Reginald gaped at him. 'But … I shouldn't have them,' he began slowly, 'unless … eh? O if I'm going to … then I should be able to jump to when … but … I don't see how I could get at them unless I knew what account they were in. I shouldn't be that me, should I … or should I?'

As his brain gave way, Sir Giles grinned. 'No,' he said almost cheerfully, 'you'd have the money but with your present mind. At least I suppose so. We don't know how it affects consciousness. It might be an easy way to suicide—ten minutes after death.'

Reginald looked apprehensively at the Crown. 'I suppose it wouldn't go wrong?' he ventured.

'That we don't know,' Sir Giles answered cheerfully. 'I daresay your first millionaire will hit the wrong spot, and be trampled underfoot by wild elephants in Africa. However, no one will know for a good while.'

Reginald went back to his notes.

Meanwhile the Prince Ali drove through the London streets till he reached the Embassy, steering the car almost mechanically while he surveyed in his mind the position in which he found himself. He foresaw some difficulty in persuading his chief, who concealed under a sedate rationalism an almost intense scepticism, of the disastrous chance which, it appeared to the Prince, had befallen the august Relic. Yet not to attempt to enlist on the side of the Faith such prestige and power as lay in the Embassy would be to abandon it to the ungodly uses of Western financiers. Ali himself had been trained through his childhood in the Koran and the traditions, and, though the shifting policies of Persia had flung him for awhile into the army and afterwards into the diplomatic service his mind moved with most ease in the romantic regions of myth. Suleiman ben Daood, he knew, was a historic figure—the ruler of a small nation which, in the momentary decrease of its two neighbours, Egypt and Assyria, had attained an unstable pre-eminence. But Suleiman was also one of the four great world-shakers before the Prophet, a commander of the Faithful, peculiarly favoured by Allah. He had been a Jew, but the Jews in those days were the only witnesses to the Unity. 'There is no God but God,' he murmured to himself, and cast a hostile glance at a crucifix which stood as a war memorial in the grounds of a church near the Embassy. '"Say: for those who believe not is the torment of hell: an evil journey shall it be."' With which quotation he delivered the car to a servant and went in to find the Ambassador, whom he discovered half-asleep over the latest volume of Memoirs. He bowed and waited in silence.

'My dear Ali,' the Ambassador said, rousing himself. 'Did you have a good evening?'

'No,' the young man answered coldly.

'I didn't expect you would,' his chief said. 'You orthodox young water-drinkers can hardly expect to enjoy a dinner. Was it, so to speak, a dinner?'

'I was concerned, sir,' the Prince said, 'with the Crown of Suleiman, on whom be the Peace.'

'Really,' the Ambassador asked. 'You really saw it? And is it authentic?'

'It is without doubt the Crown and the Stone,' Ali answered. The Ambassador stared, but Ali went on. 'And it is in the hands of the infidel. I have seen one of these dogs——'

His chief frowned a little. 'I have asked you,' he said, '—even when we are alone—to speak of these people without such phrases.'

'I beg your Excellency's pardon,' the Prince said. 'I have seen one of them use it—by the Permission—and return unharmed. It is undoubtedly the Crown.'

'The crown of a Jew?' the Ambassador murmured. 'My friend, I do not say I disbelieve you, but—have you told your uncle?'

'I reported first to you, sir,' the Prince answered. 'If you wish my uncle——' He paused.

'O by all means, by all means,' the Ambassador said, getting up. 'Ask him to come here.' He stood stroking his beard while a servant was dispatched on the errand, and until a very old man, with white hair, bent and wrinkled, came into the room.

'The Peace be upon you, Hajji Ibrahim,' he said in Persian, while the Prince kissed his uncle's hand. 'Do me the honour to be seated. I desire you to know that your nephew is convinced of the authenticity of that which Sir Giles Tumulty holds.' He eyed the old man for a moment. 'But I do not clearly know,' he ended, 'what you now wish me to do.'

Hajji Ibrahim looked at his nephew. 'And what will this Sir Giles Tumulty do with the sacred Crown?' he asked.

'He himself,' the Prince said carefully, 'will examine it and experiment with it, may the dogs of the street devour him! But there was also present a young man, his relation, who desires to make other crowns from it and sell them for money. For he sees that by the least of the graces of the divine Stone those who wear it may pass at once from place to place, and there are many who would buy such power at a great price.' The formal phrases with which he controlled his rage broke suddenly and he closed in colloquial excitement, 'He will form a company and put it on the market.'

The old man nodded. 'And even though Iblis destroy him——' he began.

'I implore you, my uncle,' the young Prince broke in, 'to urge upon his Excellency the horrible sacrilege involved. It is a very dreadful thing for us that by the fault of our house this thing should come into the possession of the infidels. It is not to be borne that they should put it to these uses; it is against the interests of our country and the sanctity of our Faith.'

The Ambassador, his head on one side, was staring at his shoes. 'It might perhaps be held that the Christians derive as much from Judah as we,' he said.

'It will not so be held in Tehran and in Delhi and in Cairo and in Beyrout and in Mecca,' the Prince answered. 'I will raise the East against them before this thing shall be done.'

'I direct your attention,' the Ambassador said stiffly,' to the fact that it is for me only to talk of what shall or shall not be done, under the sanction of Reza Shah who governs Persia to-day.'

'Sir,' the Prince said, 'in this case it is a crown greater than the diadem of Reza Shah that is at stake.'

'With submission,' the old man broke in, 'will not your Excellency make representations to the English Government? This is not a matter which any Government can consider without alarm.'

'That is no doubt so,' the Ambassador allowed. 'But, Hajji Ibrahim, if I go to the English Government and say that one of their nationals, by bribing a member of your house, has come into the possession of a very sacred relic they will not be in the mind to take it from him; and if I add that this gives men power to jump about like grasshoppers they will ask me for proof.' He paused. 'And if you could give them proof, or if this Sir Giles would let them have it, do you think they would restore it to us?'

'Will you at least try, sir?' Ali asked.

'Why, no,' the Ambassador answered. 'No, I do not think I will even try. It is but the word of Hajji Ibrahim here. Had he not known of the treachery of his kinsmen and come to England by the same boat as Giles Tumulty we should have known very little of what had happened, and that vaguely. But as it is, we were warned of what you call the sacrilege, and now you have talked to him, and you are convinced. But what shall I say to the Foreign Minister? No; I do not think I will try.'

'You do not believe it,' the Hajji said. 'You do not believe that this is the Crown of Suleiman or that Allah put a mystery into it when His Permission bestowed it on the King?'

The Ambassador considered. 'I have known you a long while,' he said thoughtfully, 'and I will tell you what I believe. I know that your family, which has always been known for a very holy house, has held for centuries certain relics, and has preserved them in great secrecy and remoteness. I know that among them tradition has said that there is the Crown of the King, and that, but a few weeks since, one of the keepers was bribed to part with this Crown—if such it be—to an Englishman. I believe that many curious powers exist in such things, lasting for a longer or shorter time. And—because I believe Ali—I believe that it has seemed to him that a man has been here and there in a moment. But how, or whether indeed, this has been I do not know, and I do not desire to argue upon it with the English ministers.' He shook his head. 'I risked too much even when I permitted you semi-officially to try and buy it back from Sir Giles.'

'But he would not sell it,' the Prince cried.

'A very natural feeling,' the Ambassador said, and added rather incautiously, 'If I had it myself I don't suppose I should sell it.'

'Then,' the Prince insisted, 'if your Excellency will do nothing, it is for me to act. There is a sin upon my house till I recover the Crown.'

'And what will you do, my friend?' the Ambassador asked.

'I shall cause all my relatives and my acquaintances in Persia to know of it, and I will take such an oath that they will certainly believe,' the Prince answered. 'I will send the news of it through all the palaces and bazaars. I will cause this sacrilege to be known in every mosque, and the cry against the English shall go from Adrianople to Hong Kong. I will see if I can do a little in all the places of Islam.'

'You will make the English Government curious, I believe,' the Ambassador said, 'and you may kill a few soldiers. But I do not think you will recover the Crown. Also you will do these things against my will.'

Hajji Ibrahim said suddenly, 'By the Permission it was taken; by the Permission it will return. When the Unity deigned to bestow the Stone upon the King it was not that he might go swiftly from place to place. I think it shall return to the Keepers only when one shall use it for the journey that is without space, and I do not think that shall be you, my nephew, nor any of us. Let spies be set upon the infidels and let us know what they do. But do not let us wake the bazaars. I do not think that will help you at all.'

'And the English Government?' the Ambassador asked.

'A soft word in the ear of a friend,' the Hajji said. 'Be very friendly with them—and that your Excellency may well do, for you are almost as one of them. But speak only of a relic and not of the virtues of the relic; seek peace and ensue it, as their scriptures say. The English will not have war for the sake of Giles Tumulty, unless their pride is touched.' He rose to his feet. 'The Peace be upon you,' he said and went to the door.

CHAPTER II
THE PUPIL OF ORGANIC LAW

'You ought to know by now,' Lord Arglay said into the telephone, 'that I can't possibly put any money into your companies…. Cæsar's wife…. No, I am…. O never mind…. Yes…. Certainly…. As much as you like…. Lunch then.' He put the receiver back. 'It's an extraordinary thing,' he went on to Chloe Burnett, as she lifted her hands again to the typewriter, 'that Reginald won't realize how careful I have to be of what my money is in. It's a wonder I have any private income at all. As it is, whenever I give a decision in a financial case I expect to be left comparatively penniless in a month or two.'

'Does Mr. Montague want you to invest?' Miss Burnett asked.

'He wants me to give him five hundred, so far as I can understand,' Lord Arglay said, 'to put in the best thing that ever was. What is the best thing that ever was?'

Miss Burnett looked at her typewriter and offered no opinion.

'I suppose that I ought to think the Twelve Tables were,' the Chief Justice went on, 'officially—or the Code Napoléon—but they're rather specialist. And anyhow when you say "that ever was," do you mean that it's stopped being? Or can it still be?… Miss Burnett,' he added after a pause, 'I was asking you a question.'

'I don't know, Lord Arglay,' Chloe said patiently. 'I never can answer that sort of question. I suppose it depends on what you mean by "was." But oughtn't we to get on with the rest of the chapter before lunch?'

Lord Arglay sighed and looked at his notes. 'I suppose so, but I'd much rather talk. *Was* there ever a best thing that ever was? Never mind; you're right as usual. Where were we? The judgement of Lord Mansfield——' He began dictating.

There was, in fact, time for an hour's work before Mr. Montague arrived for lunch. Chloe Burnett had been engaged six months before by Lord Arglay as general intellectual factotum when he had determined to begin work on his *Survey of Organic Law*. When the Chief Justice was at the Courts she spent her time reducing to typed order whatever material Lord Arglay left ready for her the night before. But during the vacation, since he had remained in town, it had become a habit for them to lunch together, and neither Chloe's intention of withdrawing or Mr. Montague's obvious uneasiness caused Lord Arglay to break it.

'Of course you'll lunch here,' he said to Chloe, and to Mr. Montague's private explanations that the matter in hand was very secret, 'That's all right; two can spoil a secret but three make a conspiracy, which is much safer.'

'And now,' he said to his nephew after they were settled, 'what is it? What do you want me to put my money in this time? I shan't, of course, but what's it all about?'

'Well, it's a kind of *transport*,' Reginald said. 'It came to me through Uncle Giles, who wanted me to help him in an experiment.'

'Was it a dangerous experiment?' Lord Arglay asked.

'O I don't think *dangerous*,' Montague answered. 'Unusual perhaps, but not dangerous. When he came back from Baghdad this time he brought with him a funny kind of a thing, something … well, something like a crown and something … something…'

'Something not,' said Lord Arglay. 'Quite. Well?'

'Made of gold,' Reginald went on, 'with a stone—*that* size … in the middle. Well, so he asked me over to help him experiment, and there was a man from the Persian Embassy there too, who said it was what Sir Giles thought it was—at least, he'd bought it as being—but that doesn't matter. Well now, this thing—I know you won't believe it—it sounds so silly; only you know I did it. Not Sir Giles—he said he wanted to observe, but I did. The Persian fellow was rather upset about it, at least not upset, but a bit high in the air, you know. Rather frosty. But I'm bound to say he met us quite fairly, said he was perfectly willing to admit that we had it, and to make it clear to us what it was; only he must have it back. But that would have been too silly.'

As Mr. Montague paused for a moment Lord Arglay looked at Chloe. 'It's a fact I've continually observed in the witness box,' he said abstractedly, 'that nine people out of ten, off their own subject, are incapable of lucidity, whereas on their own subject they can be as direct as a straight line before Einstein. I had a fellow once who couldn't put three words together sanely; we were all hopeless, till counsel got him on his own business—which happened to be statistics of the development of industry in the Central American Republics; and then for about five minutes I understood exactly what had been happening there for the last seventy years. Curious. You and I are either silent or lucid. Yes, Reginald? Never mind me, I've often been meaning to tell Miss Burnett that, and it just came into my mind. Yes?'

'O he was lucid enough,' Reginald said. 'Well it seems this thing was supposed to be the crown of King Suleiman, but of course as to that I can't say. But I can tell you this.' He pointed a fork at the Chief Justice. 'I put that thing on my head—' Chloe gave a small gasp—'and I willed myself to be back in my rooms in Rowland Street, and there I was.' He stopped. Lord Arglay and Chloe were both staring at him. 'There I was,' he repeated. 'And then I willed myself back at Ealing, and *there* I was.'

Chloe went on staring. Lord Arglay frowned a little. 'What do you mean?' he said, with a sound of the Chief Justice in his voice.

'I mean that I just was,' Reginald said victoriously. 'I don't know how I got there. I felt a little dizzy at the time, and I had a headache of sorts afterwards. But without any kind of doubt I was one minute in Ealing and the next in Rowland Street, one minute in Rowland Street and the next in Ealing.'

The two listeners looked at each other, and were silent for two or three minutes. Reginald leaned back and waited for more.

Lord Arglay said at last, 'I won't ask you if you were drunk, Reginald, because I don't think you'd tell me this extraordinary story if you were drunk then unless you were drunk now, which you seem not to be. I wonder what exactly it was that Giles did. Sir Giles Tumulty, Miss Burnett, is one of the most cantankerously crooked birds I have ever known. He is, unfortunately, my remote brother-in-law; his brother was Reginald's mother's second husband—you know the kind of riddle-me-ree relationship. He's obscurely connected with diabolism in two continents; he has written a classic work on the ritual of Priapus; he is the first authority in the world on certain subjects, and the first authority in hell on one or two more. Yet he never seems to do anything himself; he's always in the background as an interested observer. I wonder what exactly it was that he did and still more I wonder why he did it.'

'But he didn't do anything,' Reginald said indignantly. 'He just sat and watched.'

'Of two explanations,' Lord Arglay said, 'other things being equal, one should prefer that most consonant with normal human experience. That Giles should play some sort of trick on you is consonant with human experience; that you should fly through the air in ten minutes is not—at least it doesn't seem so to me. What do you think, Miss Burnett?'

'I don't seem to believe it somehow,' Chloe said. 'Did you say it was the Crown of Suleiman, Mr. Montague? I thought he went on a carpet.'

Lord Arglay stopped a cigarette halfway to his lips. 'Eh?' he said. 'What a treasure you are as a secretary, Miss Burnett! So he did, I seem to remember. You're sure it wasn't a carpet, Reginald?'

'Of course I'm sure,' Reginald said irritably. 'Should I mistake a carpet for a crown? And I never knew that Suleiman had either particularly.'

Lord Arglay, pursuing his own thoughts, shook his head. 'It would be like Giles to have the details right, you know,' he said. 'If there was a king who travelled so, that would be the king Giles would bring out for whatever his wishes might be. Look here, Reginald, what did he want you to do?'

'Nothing,' Reginald answered. 'But the point is this.' Confirming the Chief Justice's previous dictum he became suddenly lucid. 'The Persian man told us that small fractions taken from the Stone—it's the Stone in the Crown that does it—have the same power. Now, if that's so, we can have circlets made—with a chip in each, and just think what any man with money would give to have a thing like that. Think of a fellow in Throgmorton Street being able to be in Wall Street in two seconds! Think of Foreign Secretaries! Think of the Secret Service! Think of war! Every Government will need them. *And we have the monopoly.* It means a colossal fortune—colossal. O uncle, you *must* come in. I want a thousand: I can get six hundred or so quietly—not a word must leak out or I could do more, of course. Give me five hundred and I'll get you fifty thousand times five hundred back.'

Lord Arglay disregarded this appeal. 'Did you say the other man belonged to the Persian Embassy?' he asked. 'What did he want anyway?'

'He wanted it back,' Reginald said. 'Some sort of religious idea, I fancy. But really Sir Giles only needed him in order to make sure it was authentic.'

'If Giles thought it *was* authentic,' Lord Arglay said, 'I'd bet any money he wanted to tantalize him with it. If there was an *it*, which of course I don't believe.'

'But I saw it, I touched it, I used it,' Reginald cried out lyrically. 'I tell you, I did it.'

'I know you do,' the Chief Justice answered. 'And though I shan't give you the money I'm bound to say I feel extremely curious.' He got up slowly. 'I think,' he said, 'the telephone. Excuse me a few minutes. I want to try and catch Giles if he's in.'

When he had gone out of the room a sudden consciousness of their respective positions fell on the other two. Reginald Montague became acutely aware that he had been revealing an immense and incredible secret to a girl in his uncle's employment. Chloe became angrily conscious that she could not interrogate this young man as she would have done her own friends. This annoyed her the more because, compared with Lord Arglay's learning and amused observation, she knew him to be trivial and greedy. But she, though certain of a greater affection for the Chief Justice than he had, was a servant and he a relation. She thought of the phrase again—'the Crown of Suleiman.' The crown of Suleiman and Reginald Montague!

'Sounds awfully funny, doesn't it, Miss Burnett?' Mr. Montague asked, coming carefully down to her level.

'Lord Arglay seemed to think Sir Giles was having a joke with you,' she answered coldly. 'A kind of mesmerism, perhaps.'

'O that's just my uncle's way,' Reginald said sharply. 'He likes to pull my leg a bit.'

'So Lord Arglay seemed to think,' Chloe said.

'No, I mean Lord Arglay,' Reginald said more irritably than before.

'You mean Lord Arglay really believes it all?' Chloe said, surprised. 'O do you think so, Mr. Montague?'

'Lord Arglay and I understand one another,' Reginald threw over carelessly.

'One another?' Chloe said. 'Both of you? But how splendid! He's such an able man, isn't he? It must be wonderful to understand him so well.' She frowned thoughtfully. 'Of course I don't know what to think.'

'Ah well, that doesn't so much matter, does it? I mean——' He hesitated.

'O I know it isn't my money that comes in,' Chloe hastened to say. 'I do realize that, Mr. Montague.'

'It isn't a question of money—not first of all,' Reginald protested. 'It's a matter of general interest.'

Chloe said nothing, chiefly because she was a little ashamed of herself, but the result was almost worse than if she had made another effort. The commenting silence extended itself for some minutes and was broken at last by Lord Arglay's return.

'Well,' he said, 'I've been talking to Giles. I'm bound to say he swears it's quite right, and sticks to you in every particular, Reginald. However, he's asked us to go over to-night and see. Miss Burnett, can you come?'

'O but, Lord Arglay, ought I to…' Chloe said doubtfully; and 'I don't suppose Miss Burnett would find it very interesting,' Reginald hastily threw in.

'Civilized man,' Lord Arglay said, 'is known by the capacity of his intellect to produce convincing reasons for his emotions. *Convincing*, Reginald. Say anything you like, except to suggest that anyone wouldn't be interested in this new interstellar traffic of yours. Besides, I need my secretary. I shall be out this afternoon and I officially request her to spend her time looking up all the references to Suleiman the son of David that she can find. We will all dine here at seven and then go to Ealing. That suit you, Miss Burnett? You, Reginald? Right.'

Reginald got up to go. 'Well, you won't finally decide against coming in until to-night, will you, uncle?' he said. 'Good-bye, Miss Burnett. Don't let my uncle persuade you to come if you don't want to.'

'I won't,' Chloe said politely, 'as I shan't be able to have a financial interest. Good-bye, Mr. Montague.'

When Reginald had gone—'And why the scratch, Miss Burnett?' Lord Arglay asked. 'Quite right, of course, but why to-day especially? Generally you just let Reginald fleet by. Why this unwonted sharpness?'

'I beg your pardon,' Chloe said. 'I don't quite know. It was impertinent of me. I didn't mean to be rude to you.'

'Not in the least impertinent,' the Chief Justice answered. 'Quite remarkably relevant. But why to-day?'

'I think it was his talk of the Crown of Suleiman,' Chloe said reluctantly. 'Somehow…'

Arglay shook his head. 'I wouldn't pin much to that. My belief is still that Giles has been hocussing that young man. But I'm curious to know why; and anyhow it wouldn't do me any harm to know as much as you about the son of David. I can't think of another fact about him at present. So you dig out what you can and then clear off and be back by seven.'

'Are you going out, Lord Arglay?' Chloe asked.

'Certainly not,' the Chief Justice said. 'I am going to lie in my deepest armchair and read *When Anarchy came to London*, which has an encouraging picture of the Law Courts being burnt on the cover. Till seven, then.'

The dinner was largely occupied, much to Reginald's boredom, by Chloe's account of what she had discovered about King Suleiman and Lord Arglay's comments on it. It seemed she had been right in her remembrance that the Majesty of the King made its journeys accompanied by the Djinn, the doctors of the law, and the viziers, upon a carpet which accommodated its size to the King's needs. But there were also tales of the Crown and the Stone in the Crown, and (more general) of the Ring by virtue of which the King understood all languages of men and beasts and Djinn and governed all created things, save only the great Archangels themselves who exist in immediate cognition of the Holy One. 'For,' said Chloe thrilling, 'he was one of the four mighty ones—who were Nimrod and Sheddad the Son of Ad, and Suleiman and Alexander; the first two being infidels and the second two True Believers.'

'Alexander?' Arglay said in surprise. 'How jolly! Perhaps Giles will produce the helmet of the divine Alexander too. We shall have a regular archaeological evening, I expect. Well, come along, *Malbrouck s'en va t'en guerre…*.' He carried them off to the car.

Sir Giles received the party with an almost Christ-like, 'What went ye out for to see?' air, but he made no demur about producing the Crown for their examination. The Chief Justice, after examining it, showed it to Chloe.

'And the markings?' he asked her.

Chloe said nervously, 'O you know them, Lord Arglay.'

'I know they are Hebrew,' the Chief Justice said, 'and I know that Sir Giles is sneering at me in his heart. But I haven't an idea what they are.'

'I suppose you've never had a Hebrew Rabbi before you?' Sir Giles said. 'That's how you judges become educated men, isn't it? The letters——'

'I asked Miss Burnett, Giles,' Lord Arglay interrupted, and Sir Giles with a shrug waited.

'They are the four letters of the Tetragrammaton, the Divine Name,' Chloe said still more nervously. 'Yod, He, Vau, He. I found it out this afternoon,' she said suddenly to Sir Giles, 'in an encyclopedia.'

'Some of us write encyclopedias,' Arglay said, '—that's you, Giles; some of us read them—that's you, Miss Burnett; some of us own them—that's me; and some of us despise them—that's you, Reginald.'

'Encyclopedias are like slums,' Giles said, 'the rotten homes of diseased minds. But even Hoxton has to pretend to live, it thinks, and of course it doesn't know it stinks.'

Arglay was looking at the letters. 'The Divine Name,' he said musingly. 'Yod, He, Vau, He. Umph. Well…. We were going to experiment, weren't we?' he added, almost as if recovering himself. 'Who begins? Reginald, suppose you show us.'

'Certainly,' Montague said. 'Now look here, uncle, let's really show you. Tell me something I can bring you from your study.'

'Bring me the pages of manuscript on the small table by the window,' Arglay answered at once. 'The top one is marked *Chapter IV*.'

Montague nodded and taking the Crown put it on his head; he settled it comfortably, then taking a step or two backwards sat down in the nearest convenient chair. Lord Arglay watched him attentively, occasionally darting his eyes sideways towards Sir Giles, who—as if bored with the repetition of a concluded experiment—had turned to the papers on which he had previously been working. Chloe suddenly caught Arglay's arm; he put up his other hand and pressed hers. At once they found themselves looking at an empty chair. Chloe cried out; Arglay took a step towards the chair. Sir Giles, looking round, said casually; 'I shouldn't get in the way; he may be back at any moment, and you might get a nasty knock.'

'Well, I'm damned,' Lord Arglay said. 'It's all——' he began, looking at Chloe, but, impressed by the vivid excitement that possessed her, ceased in the middle of the reassuring phrase he had begun. They waited in silence.

It was only about two or three minutes before, suddenly, they saw Reginald Montague again in front of them. He sat still for another minute or two, then he stepped forward and gave the Chief Justice several pages of manuscript. 'Well, uncle?' he asked triumphantly.

Arglay took the papers and looked at them. They were those on which he had been making notes that afternoon, and he had, he knew, left them on his table. He turned them over in silence. Chloe released his arm suddenly and sat down. Sir Giles strolled back to them. 'Interesting exhibit, what?' he said.

The Chief Justice's mind admitted the apparent fact. It was impossible, but it had happened. In less than five minutes these papers had been brought from Lancaster Gate to Ealing. He loosed the little sigh which always preceded his giving judgement and nodded. 'I don't know whether it's the Crown of Suleiman, Giles,' he said, 'or some fantasia of your own. But it certainly seems to work.'

'What about trying it, uncle?' Reginald said invitingly, removing the gold circlet from his head and holding it out. 'It's quite simple. You just put it on and wish firmly to go—wherever you choose.'

'Wishing firmly is a very difficult thing,' Lord Arglay said. 'But if you can I suppose I can.' He took the Crown and looked at Chloe. 'Where shall I go, Miss Burnett?' he asked.

'Somewhere quiet,' Sir Giles interjected. 'If you choose the House of Commons or London Bridge or anything like that you'll cause a sensation. Try your—' he paused a moment, 'dining-room,' he added.

'I'd rather go somewhere I didn't know,' Arglay said.

'Go to my sitting-room, Lord Arglay,' Chloe put in swiftly. 'I don't suppose you even remember what the address is. On—let me think—on the table is last week's *New Statesman*.'

'There isn't likely to be any other fellow there?' Sir Giles asked. 'No? All right, Arglay. Better sit down; it's apt to jar you, they say. Now—will yourself there.'

Lord Arglay took the Crown in both hands and set it on his head. Chloe involuntarily compared the motion with Montague's. Reginald had put it on with one hand as if he were settling a cap; against his thin form the Chief Justice's assured maturity stood like a dark magnificence. He set on the Crown as if he were accepting a challenge, and sat down as if the Chief Justice of England were coming to some high trial, either of another or of himself. Chloe, used to seeing and hearing him when his mind played easily with his surroundings, used to the light courtesy with which he had always treated her, had rarely seen in him that rich plenitude of power which seemed to make his office right and natural to him. Once or twice, when, in dictating his book, he had framed slowly some difficult and significant paragraph, she had caught a hint of it, but her attention then had been on her work and his words rather than his person. She held her breath as she looked, and her eyes met his. They were fixed on her with a kind of abstract intimacy; she felt at once more individual to him than ever before and yet as if the individuality which he discerned was something of which she herself was not yet conscious. And while she looked back into them, thrilling to that remote concentration, she found she was looking only at the chair, and was brought back at once from that separate interaction to the remembrance of their business. She started with the shock, and both the men in the room looked at her.

'Don't be frightened,' Sir Giles said, with an effort controlling his phrases, and 'It's all right, you know,' Montague added coldly.

'I'm not frightened, thank you,' Chloe said, hating them both with a sudden intensity, but she knew she lied. She *was* frightened; she was frightened of them. The Crown of Suleiman, the strange happenings, Lord Arglay's movements—these were what had stirred her emotions and shaken her, and those shaken emotions were loosed within her in a sudden horror, yet of what she did not know. It seemed as if there were two combinations; one had vanished, and the other she loathed, but to that she was suddenly abandoned. It was ridiculous, it was insane. 'What on earth are you afraid of?' she asked herself, 'do you think either of them is going to assault you?' And beyond and despite herself, and as if thinking of some assault she could not visualize or imagine she answered, 'Yes, I do.'

Lord Arglay, as he sat down wearing the Crown, had directed his eyes and mind towards Chloe. For the first few moments half a score of ordinary irrelevant thoughts leapt in his mind.

She was efficient, she was rather good-looking, she was, under the detached patience with which she took his dictation, avid of ideas and facts, she was desirous—but of what Lord Arglay doubted if she knew and was quite certain he did not. He put the irrelevancies aside, by mere habitual practice, held his mind empty and prepared, as if to receive some important answer which could then be directed to its proper place in the particular order to which it belonged, allowed the image of Chloe Burnett and the thought of her home to enter, and shut his mind down on them. The Crown pressed on his forehead; he involuntarily united the physical consciousness and the mental; either received the other. His interior purpose suddenly lost hold; a dizziness caught him, through which he was aware only of a dominating attraction—his being yearned to some power above, around, within him. The dizziness increased and then was gone; his head ached; the Stone pressed heavily on it, then more lightly. He found himself opening his eyes.

He opened them on a strange room, and realized that he was standing by the door. It was a not too well furnished room—not, obviously, his own kind. There were two comfortable armchairs; there was a book-case; a table; another chair; pictures; a little reproduction of the Victory of Samothrace, a poor Buddha, a vase or two. On the table a box of cigarettes and a matchbox; some sort of needlework; a book; the *New Statesman*. Lord Arglay drew a deep breath. So it worked. He walked to the table, then he went over to the window and looked out. It was the ordinary suburban street, a few ordinary people—three men, a woman, four children. He felt the curtains—they seemed actual. He felt himself with the same result. He went back to the table and picked up the *New Statesman*, then he sat down in one of the comfortable chairs as if to consider. But as he leant back against the cushions he remembered that the experiment was only half done; he could consider afterwards. The immediate thing was to return with the paper; if that were done, all was done that could be at the moment. 'I wish there were someone here to speak to,' he thought. 'I wonder—I suppose they would see me.' He thought of going down into the street and asking his way to some imaginary road, but the difficulty in passing anyone outside Chloe Burnett's room occurred to him and he desisted. Return, then. He gripped the *New Statesman* tightly, and began to think of Sir Giles at Ealing. But the notion of introducing Sir Giles offended him; so, almost as much, did the thought of Reginald Montague, and he was content at last to make an image, as near as possible, of the room from which he had come, with the thought of his secretary attached to it. 'My dear child,' Lord Arglay said unconsciously, and shut his eyes.

When, after a similar play of feeling to that which he had experienced before, he opened them to see Reginald Montague in front of him there flashed across his mind the idea that the Crown had somehow muddled things. But it was gone as he came to himself and recognized that he had indeed returned. He looked at his watch; the whole episode had taken exactly five minutes. He sat for a minute, then he got up, walked across to Chloe and gave her the paper. 'Yours, I think, Miss Burnett? I'm sorry to give you the trouble of carrying it back,' he said, and wondered whether he had only imagined the look of relief in her eyes. 'Well,' he went on to the other two, 'it seems you're quite right. I don't know what happens or how, but if this sort of thing can go on indefinitely, space doesn't exist—for purposes of travel.'

'You see it?' Reginald cried out.

'Certainly I see it,' Lord Arglay answered. 'It's a little startling at first and I want to know several more things, but they can wait. At the moment I have enough to brood on. But we're forgetting our duty. Miss Burnett, wouldn't you like to try the ... to put on the Crown of Suleiman?'

'No,' said Chloe. 'No, thank you, Lord Arglay. Thank you all very much, but I think I had better go.'

'Go—at once?' Arglay asked, 'But give me a few more minutes and we'll all go back together.'

'I shouldn't press Miss Burnett to stop if she wants to go,' Sir Giles said. 'The station is about the fourth turning on the right.'

'Thank you, Sir Giles,' Chloe answered him. 'Thank you for showing me the—the Crown. Good night, Mr. Montague. Good night, Lord Arglay.'

'All right, Giles,' Arglay stopped a movement Tumulty had not made. 'I'll see Miss Burnett out.' As the room door closed behind them he took her arm. 'Why the rush?' he asked gently.

'I don't ... I don't really know,' Chloe said. 'I'm being rather silly but I felt I couldn't stop there just now. It is rather upsetting, isn't it? And ... O I don't know. I'm sorry to seem a fool.'

'You are not in the least like a fool,' the Chief Justice said equably. 'And you will tell me to-morrow what the matter is. Are you sure you are all right now?'

'Quite all right,' Chloe said as he opened the door for her. 'Yes, really, Lord Arglay.' She added with a sudden rush of temper, 'I don't like Sir Giles.'

'I couldn't,' Arglay smiled at her, 'have much use for a secretary who *did* like Sir Giles. Or Reginald either, for that matter. A vulture and a crow—but that's between ourselves. Well, if you will go, good-night.'

'Good-night,' Chloe said, took a step forward, and looked back suddenly. 'You aren't going to try it again yourself?'

'Not I,' Lord Arglay said. 'I'm going to talk to them a little and then go. No more aerial flights to-day. Till to-morrow then.' He watched her out of the gate and well along the street before he returned to the others.

He discovered then that Reginald had not been wasting his time.

Anxious to lay hands as soon as possible on some of the colossal fortune that seemed to be waiting, the young man had extracted permission from Sir Giles to make an effort to remove a small chip from the Stone, and had been away to bring a chisel and hammer from the tool-box. Arglay looked at Tumulty.

'You're sure it won't damage it?' he asked.

'They all say it won't,' Sir Giles answered. 'The fellow I had it from and Ali Khan who was here the other night and the manuscripts and all. The manuscripts are rather hush-hush about it—all damnably veiled and hinting. "The division is accomplished yet the Stone is unchanged, and the virtues are neither here nor there but allwhere"—that kind of thing. They rather suggest that people who get the bits had better look out, but that's Reginald's business—and his covey of company-promoters. He'd better have a clause in the agreement about not being responsible for any damage to life or limb, but it's not my affair. *I* don't care what happens to them.'

'Who is this Ali Khan?' Arglay asked, watching Reginald arrange the Stone conveniently.

'A fellow from the Persian Embassy,' Sir Giles told him. 'He was on to me almost as soon as I reached England, wanting to buy it back. So I had him out here to talk to him about it, but he couldn't tell me anything I didn't know or guess already.'

Reginald struck the chisel with the hammer, and almost fell forward on to the table. For, unexpectedly, since the Stone had been hard enough to the touch, it yielded instantaneously to the blow, and, as Reginald straightened himself with an oath, they saw, lying on the table by the side of the Crown, a second Stone apparently the same in all respects as the first.

'Good God!' Lord Arglay exclaimed, while Reginald gazed open-mouthed at the result of his work and Sir Giles broke into a cackle of high laughter. But they all gathered round the table to stare.

Except that one Stone was in the Crown and the other not they could not find any difference. There was the same milky colour, flaked here and there with gold, the same jet-black markings which might be letters and might be only accidental colouring, the same size, the same apparent hardness.

'"The division is accomplished yet the Stone is unchanged,"' Lord Arglay quoted at last, looking at his brother-in-law. 'It is, too. This is all very curious.'

Tumulty had thrust Reginald aside and was peering at the two Stones. After a minute, 'Try it again, Reginald,' he said—'the new one, not the old. Come round here, Arglay.' He caught the Chief Justice by the arm and brought him round the table. 'There,' he said, 'now watch.' He himself, while Lord Arglay leant forward over the table, moved a step or two off and squatted down on his heels, so that his eyes were on a level with the Stone. 'Now slowly, Reginald, slowly.'

Montague adjusted it, set the chisel on it, raised the hammer and struck, but this time with less force. The watchers saw the chisel move down through the Stone which seemed to divide easily before it and fall asunder on both sides. Sir Giles scrambled to his feet and he and Lord Arglay leaned breathlessly forward. There on the table, exactly alike, lay two Stones, each a faithful replica of its original in the Crown.

Montague put the chisel and hammer down and stepped back. 'I say,' he said, 'I don't like this. Stones don't grow out of one another in this way. It's … it's uncanny.'

'Stones don't carry you five miles through the air and back usually,' Arglay said drily. 'I think you're straining at a gnat. Still…' The perfect ease with which the Stone had recreated itself, a ghastly feeling of its capacity to go on producing copies of itself to infinity, the insane simplicity, the grotesque finality, of the result, weighed on his mind, and he fell silent.

Sir Giles, alert and eager, picked them up. 'Just a moment,' he said, 'let me weigh them.'

He went to a corner of the room where a small balance stood in a glass case, and put one of the Stones on the scales. For a minute he stared at it, then he looked over his shoulder at the Chief Justice.

'I say, Arglay,' he cried, 'it doesn't weigh anything.'

'Doesn't weigh——' Lord Arglay went across to him. The Stone lay in the middle of the scale, which remained perfectly poised, balanced against its fellow, apparently unweighted by what it bore.

'But——' Arglay said, 'but——But it *does* weigh…. I mean I can feel its pressure if I hold it. Very light, but definite.'

'Well, there you are,' Giles said. 'Look at it.' With the tweezers he picked up a gramme weight and dropped it on the other scale, which immediately sank gently under it.

'There,' he said, 'the balances are all right. It just doesn't weigh.' He took up the Stone and they returned to the table, where all three stood staring at the marvel, until Sir Giles grew impatient.

'We look like Hottentots staring at an aeroplane,' he said. 'Reginald, you baboon-headed cockatoo, show a little gratitude. Here instead of a mere chip you can give every one of your degenerate Jew millionaires a stone as big as the first one, and you stand gaping like a cow with the foot-and-mouth disease.'

Reginald made an effort at recovery. 'Yes,' he answered rather quaveringly, 'yes, of course I see that. It made me feel funny somehow. But—yes, of course. It'll save any difficulty about chipping the original, and they'll look much better—much. Can I leave them here to-night?'

'Why, you're scared out of what wits you've got,' Sir Giles said. 'What about you, Arglay? Will you have one?'

'No,' Lord Arglay said soberly. 'I think not; not to-night. I feel rather as if I'd been scared out of what wits I'd got, and was just getting over it. If I were you, Reginald, I should think a great many times before I started that transport scheme of yours.'

'Eh?' said Reginald. 'But surely Sir Giles is right? This'll make it even easier.'

'Just as you like,' Lord Arglay said. 'I think I will go now, Tumulty. I should like to come and see it again soon, if I may.'

Sir Giles nodded casually, and as casually bade his visitors good-night.

On the way back to town Lord Arglay said very little, and ignored Reginald's occasional outbreaks of mingled hope and nervousness. He found himself wishing Chloe Burnett had not gone; he would have liked to have his own silence buttressed by another instead of harassed by a futile and spasmodic volubility. His mind gazed blankly at the riddle of the three Stones in an awe which he usually kept for Organic Law. There must be some conclusion, he felt, but he couldn't think—not yet. '—pay even more,' he heard at his side and drove faster. 'Is there no intelligent creature about?' he thought. 'I wish that girl hadn't—no, perhaps it's as well. Damn it, I'm muddled.'

He reached his house almost at the same time that Chloe by a slower and longer method came to her own, full of similar half-conscious anxieties and alarms. She found, opened, and read a couple of letters that awaited her, and realized when she had finished that she knew nothing of their contents, and did not particularly want to know. She put down the *New Statesman* in its place on the table, took off her things, and looked vaguely round the room. It was here then that Lord Arglay had been during that unbelievable and terrifying disappearance; to this the Crown of Suleiman had transported him. The Crown of Suleiman … the Lord Chief Justice…. Chloe Burnett. It might have happened but she didn't believe it; at least, except that she couldn't disbelieve in that sharp spasm of fear. She moved towards a chair and noticed, with a slight annoyance, that she had forgotten to shake the cushions up when she left the house that evening. Or had another visitor——? Chloe dropped into the chair where Lord Arglay had sat and burst into tears.

CHAPTER III
THE TALE OF THE END OF DESIRE

When Miss Burnett arrived at the Chief Justice's house the next morning she found him reading his correspondence in a perfectly normal way. He looked up to welcome her and considered her carefully. 'No worse?' he said. 'Good night? Well, you missed something even more eerie.'

'O Lord Arglay! Nothing happened?'

'Something happened all right,' Arglay answered, and his face grew grave. 'Up to last night,' he went on, 'I thought Giles was monkeying about with something, and playing tricks on Reginald for some infernal reason of his own. But I don't know now; I really don't. He didn't seem to expect what did happen.'

'But, Lord Arglay! What did?'

The Chief Justice told her. Chloe sat gazing at him. 'It multiplies itself?' she breathed. 'But it must be something—magical, then. Something unnatural.'

Arglay shook his head. 'I wouldn't say that,' he answered. 'Atoms do it, or electrons, or something. But I admit to having a nasty jar when I saw the three things all exactly alike. Somehow the sight of Reginald producing stones of Suleiman ben Daood at the rate of two a minute with a chisel—it didn't seem decent.'

'That,' Chloe said with conviction, 'is what I felt; that's why I ran away. Lord Arglay, could...' she hesitated, 'could those letters be real?'

'If they are, if the Stone is,' the Chief Justice said, 'it looks as if it were real in another manner—more or less real than we are. No, that's absurd, of course. There can't be degrees in Reality. But we know that we can pass through space by its means—we both know that—and I have seen what was one become two, and then three, and lose nothing in the process. And now this morning...' He gave her a letter and she read—

'*Foreign Office,*
'10 *May.*

'MY DEAR CHIEF JUSTICE,

'I wonder if you could spare me a few minutes to-day, and if so whether you would mind ringing up and making an appointment. Nothing to do with you directly, but the fact is we have been approached—very tentatively—on a little matter relating to your brother-in-law Sir Giles Tumulty. And as, on the few occasions when I've met him, he always seemed to me rather a difficult man to deal with, I thought my way might be smoother if I could have a chat with you first. Pray forgive me for troubling you.

'Yours very truly,
'J. BRUCE CUMBERLAND.'

Miss Burnett looked up. 'You think it's the same thing?'

'I shouldn't wonder,' Lord Arglay answered. 'Of course it may not be. Giles always seems to be conducting several lines of research at once, some perfectly harmless and one or two perfectly loathsome. But the F.O. has had trouble with him once or twice before—obscure troubles no one seemed to know the rights of, except Giles who (it is said) was the proximate cause of one Secretary's resignation. I don't wonder Bruce Cumberland hesitates to tackle him.'

'Who is Mr. Cumberland?' Chloe asked.

'One of the smaller great guns there,' Arglay told her. 'A Permanent Official in many impermanent offices. But I've rung up already and made an appointment for twelve. I want——'

There was a tap at the door and a maid came in. 'Sir Giles Tumulty would like to see you, my lord,' she said.

'Sir Giles——? O bring him in, bring him in,' Arglay said and met the visitor at the door. 'Hallo, Tumulty, what brings you here so early?' he asked.

Sir Giles came briskly in, threw Chloe a glance, and sat down. 'Three things,' he said. 'My house was burgled last night, I'm going to Birmingham to-day, and I want to warn you, or rather other people through you.'

'Burgled?' Arglay said. 'Casually or deliberately? And by whom, or don't you know?'

'Of course I know,' Sir Giles said. 'It's the Embassy people; I shouldn't be a bit surprised to find Ali Khan did it himself. I'm only surprised they didn't try to tackle me. They did it pretty well on the whole, felt under my pillow while I was trying not to snigger, and went all over the study, got what safe there is open, and made very little noise. I dare say I shouldn't have heard them if I hadn't been awake.'

'Did they get what they wanted?' Arglay asked.

'Get it?' Sir Giles almost shrieked. 'Do you suppose, Arglay, that any set of half-caste earthworms would find anything I wanted to hide? No, they didn't. Suleiman and I are going off to see Palliser at Birmingham to-day. But I thought I'd leave one of those little fellows with you and one with Reginald. I've dropped his in on him and here's yours.' He pulled one of the Stones from his pocket and threw it on to the table. 'And now for the warning. You're mixed up with all this Whitehall crowd of simians, Arglay, and for all I know the Persians may be trying to pull the strings they dance to. Well, if you hear anything about it, tell them to be careful. For if they try to get the Crown out of me they'll get more than they want. Tell them if they give me any trouble I'll make enough Stones to build a wall round London. I'll sell them at two a penny to the children in the streets. I'll set up a Woolworth's to show nothing but Stones. The whole population of this blasted sink you call London shall be playing hop-scotch with them. I'll give them relics enough, and you tell them so. I've written to Ali Khan warning him and referring him to you for confirmation.' He started to go, and stopped. 'O and if they try and get me knocked on the head *that* won't help. For I'll leave it in proper keeping and I'll have a mausoleum of relics built over me. So they know.'

With which Sir Giles flung out of the room, but he was back again before Lord Arglay could say more than 'Cheery creature!'

'My own advice to both of you,' he said, 'is to say nothing at all whatever leprous hooligan from the Foreign Office or the Embassy you may be pestered with. You play your office, Arglay, and Miss Burnett can play her sex. Justice and innocence, that's your line, though I don't suppose either of you's either.'

He was gone again, this time for good, and they heard the front door close.

'Giles always reminds me of the old riddle,' Lord Arglay said in a moment. 'Would you rather be more abominable than you sound or sound more abominable than you are? The answer is I would rather be neither but I am both. And now what do we do?' He looked at his watch. 'I go to the Foreign Office,' he said, and considered. 'I think, Miss Burnett, if anyone comes from the Persian Embassy you had better see them. Don't know anything; just be obliging. I've asked you to take any message that comes, to interview any callers—that sort of thing. Lord Arglay was particularly anxious—you know. I'm not sure that I oughtn't to cut adrift altogether, but there's Bruce Cumberland, and, as a matter of fact, I'm horribly curious. Well, I'll go. I'll tell them to show anyone from the Embassy in to you. Good-bye, and good luck. I shall be back to lunch.'

'They may want you to lunch at the Foreign Office,' Chloe suggested.

'Then I shan't,' Lord Arglay said firmly. 'We must talk the whole thing over. O and this?' He picked up the Stone. 'I think this shall go in my private safe upstairs. Good-bye. You might sort out the notes for the next chapter of *Organic Law*.'

Chloe did her best, but even the thesis of law as a growing and developing habit of the human mind, with its corollary of the distinction between organic consciousness expressed in law and inorganic rules imposed from without, failed to hold her. It might be true that the whole body of criminal law was, by its nature, inorganic, which was the point the Chief Justice had reached, though whether in agreement or opposition she had no idea, but she could not keep her mind away from what seemed an organism of unexpected power. 'It must be alive,' she found herself saying, and went on to ask herself, 'But then does it know? Does it know what it does and what we do to it? Who ever heard of a living stone?' She went on, nevertheless, thinking along that road. 'Does it know what Mr. Montague is doing with it? What else can it do? and can it do anything to us?'

The maid came in. 'A gentleman from the Embassy is downstairs, Miss Burnett,' she said. 'Lord Arglay told me to show him up. Will that be all right?'

'Certainly,' Chloe said nervously, 'yes, please bring him in.'

In a minute the maid announced 'Mr. Ibrahim,' and vanished. A little old gentleman, in Western dress but for his green turban, walked placidly into the room.

'Do sit down,' Chloe said, mastering her agitation. 'Probably the maid told you that Lord Arglay was so sorry he had had to go out, but he hoped you would be good enough to leave any message with me. If possible.'

Hajji Ibrahim bowed and sat down. 'You know, I think, what I have come about?' he said.

'I'm sorry, but Lord Arglay didn't tell me—only that it might be rather important,' Chloe answered.

The Hajji smiled slightly. 'I believe that Lord Arglay did not tell you,' he said, 'but I think you must have seen something last night when you went with him to Sir Giles Tumulty's house.'

'If you know that,' Chloe answered, disagreeably surprised, 'you will know that I left before Lord Arglay and wasn't with him there—not for long.'

'Long enough,' the Hajji nodded. 'Do not let us dispute on that, Miss Burnett—it was Miss Burnett your servant said?—or we shall waste our time and our spirit. You know what it is we are seeking, though you may not know all that it means. It is the End of Desire.'

'The end of desire?' Chloe repeated.

'It is called the White Stone and the Stone of Suleiman ben Daood (on whom be the Peace!),' the Hajji went on, 'and it has other names also. But that is its best name, as that is its best work. Now that it is at large in the world it may bring much sorrow. I think Lord Arglay would be wise to do what he can to bring it back. No,' he added as he saw Chloe about to make another effort at denial, 'you are acting in good faith but it is quite useless. I can see that you know the thing if not the work.'

'If you have any definite message,' Chloe said, 'I shall be most careful to give it to Lord Arglay.'

'I think you have a premonition of the message,' Hajji Ibrahim answered. 'Tell me, have you not seen certain of the marvels of the Stone and are you not afraid in your heart? Else why should you be so shaken at speaking with me?'

'I am not shaken,' Chloe said indignantly.

The other smiled. 'Child,' he said, 'you have done what you can to be loyal, but you cannot control your eyes, and there is fear at the back of them now. Do not fear us who serve the Stone but fear those who attempt to rule it.'

'What is this Stone?' Chloe asked, hoping rather vainly that the intensity of her feeling would sound like a mere business interest.

'I will tell you what is said of it,' the Hajji said, 'and you shall tell Lord Arglay when he returns. It is said that in the Crown of Suleiman ben Daood there was a strange and wonderful Stone, and it is said also that this Stone had belonged of old to the giants, to Nimrod the hunter and his children, and by its virtue Nimrod sought to build Babel which was to reach to heaven. And something of this kind is certainly possible to those who have the Stone. Before Nimrod, our father Adam (the Peace be upon him!) had it, and this only he brought with him out of Paradise when he fled before the swords of the great ones—Michael and Gabriel and Raphael (blessed be they!) And there are those who say that before then it was in the Crown of Iblis the Accursed when he fell from heaven, and that his fall was not assured until that Stone dropped from his head. For yet again it is told that, when the Merciful One made the worlds, first of all He created that Stone and gave it to the Divine One whom the Jews call Shekinah, and as she gazed upon it the universes arose and had being. But afterwards it passed from Iblis to Adam, and from Adam to Nimrod, and from Nimrod to Suleiman, and after Suleiman it came into the sceptre of Octavianus who was called Cæsar and Augustus and was lord of Rome. But from Rome it came with Constantine to New Rome, and thence eastward—only in hiding—till our lord Muhammed (blessed be he!) arose to proclaim the Unity. And after he was received into the Mercy it belonged to seven Khalifs, and was taken into Spain when the Faith entered there, and some say that in his wars Charlemagne the Emperor found it and set it under the hilt of his sword, which was called Joyeuse because of it, and from that the Franks made a war-shout and cried *Montjoy St. Denis*. And because of its virtue and his will the Emperor made himself lord of the world. After him the world became very evil, and the Stone made for itself a place of repose and remained therein until to-day. This is the tale of the Stone of Suleiman, but its meaning is in the mind of him who hears it.'

Chloe Burnett said abruptly, 'And they use it for——'

The Persian smiled. 'They use it as they will,' he said. 'But there are those who know it by its name which I have told you.'

'But can the end of desire be an evil?' Chloe said.

'If the End is reached too violently it may mean chaos and madness,' Ibrahim told her. 'Even in lesser things it is not everyone who can bear to be carried hither and thither, in time or place or thought, and so in the greater it is necessary to grow accustomed to the Repose of the End. I think if you were to set it on your head now and offer your soul to it, the strength of your nature would be overthrown and not transformed by its own strength, and you would be destroyed. There is measure and degree in all things, even upon the Way.'

'The Way?' Chloe asked.

'The Way to the Stone, which is in the Stone,' the old man said. 'Yet you have a hint of the holy letters on your forehead, and Allah shall bring you to the Resignation. For you are of Islam at heart.'

'I—of Islam?' Chloe cried. 'Do you mean a Muhammedan?'

'There is no God but God and Muhammed is the Prophet of God,' the old man intoned gravely. 'Yet the Resignation is within. Say what you will of this to your master, but bid him if he is a wise judge assist us in the restoration of the Stone.'

'But if Sir Giles bought it——' Chloe began.

'He that sold it and he that bought it alike sinned,' the Hajji answered. 'Tell your lord that at any time I will come to him to speak of it if he will. For I do not wish my nephew to let war loose on the world.'

'War?' Chloe exclaimed.

'It is the least of the plagues, perhaps,' Ibrahim said. 'But tell your master and bid him think what he will do.'

Gravely he took his leave, with a murmured benediction, and left Chloe in a state of entire upheaval to await Lord Arglay's return.

When he came she saw that he was himself perplexed and troubled. But with the exception of asking whether she had had a visitor he said nothing, either of information or inquiry, until after lunch. When they were back in his study he gave her cigarettes and sat down opposite her. 'And now,' he said; 'let's talk. No—stop—let us have … what Giles left with us here too.' He went for the Stone and set it, rather seriously, on the table by them. 'Now for your visitor,' he said.

Chloe went over the conversation as far as she could. When she had finished——

'You didn't tell him about the division of the Stone?' Lord Arglay asked.

'I didn't tell him anything at all,' Chloe said. 'I didn't have the chance. He did all the talking.'

'Well, that was the idea, after all. I did exactly the same, only less tactfully,' Arglay assured her. 'Bruce Cumberland was in the extreme jumps, all nicely hidden of course, but there without a doubt. He was so sorry—not at all—yes, but he was, only I was the only respectable person in touch with Sir Giles. And they wanted, they very much wanted—well, in short they wanted to know what Sir Giles had been up to. Yesterday, it appears, at some conference on the finances of Baluchistan or the reform of the gendarmerie in the suburbs of Erzerum, the Persian Ambassador whispered in Birlesmere's ear—he's the Foreign Secretary, you know. There was a matter of a relic, feloniously abstracted, under cover of a payment which was really a bribe, by one of our nationals. The Ambassador himself had no use for it, nor, he thought, had Riza Khan—but the populace, the fanatical Muhammedan populace … his lordship the Secretary would understand. Well, Birlesmere's used to these unofficial hints, only it seems for the last month things *have* been a bit more restive than usual all over the Near East, in expanding circles. So he began to sit up. Could his Excellency tell him at all…? His Excellency, *most* unofficially, had heard rumours of Suleiman, and a crown, and even—without any sort of accusation—of Sir Giles Tumulty. He didn't press, he didn't even ask, for anything; he only remarked that rumours were about. Pure friendship. Of course if his Britannic Majesty's Government could reassure him, just in case the Imams (or whatever) went to Riza Khan. There was even a young fellow at the Embassy inclined to make trouble; he would be exchanged certainly—Moscow perhaps. Still…. Birlesmere was pushed; he had to go off to Sandringham last night, so he switched Cumberland on to it. Who did me the honour to remember that I was Sir Giles's brother-in-law, and begged me to sound him. Had I heard? Could I think? Would I investigate—delicately? I promised I would, told him nothing, and came away. So there we are.'

They sat and looked at each other. Then Lord Arglay said, 'I can only think of one thing to be done at once, and that's to stop Reginald. He won't want to run risks with the Government, at least I shouldn't think so, though he's thinking in millions. But he *must* keep quiet anyhow till I can see Giles again. City five seven three eight,' he added into the telephone.

'You'll see Sir Giles when he comes back?' Chloe asked.

'I shall see *everybody*,' Lord Arglay said. 'Giles and the Ambassador and your Hajji and Cumberland again and so on. If I'm in the centre of it I'm going to enjoy it. Is that Mr. Montague's? Is Mr. Montague in?... Lord Arglay.... That you, Reginald?... Look here, I've just been in touch with the Foreign Office and I'm rather anxious about you. It's most important you should do and say nothing, absolutely *nothing*, about the Stone at present. You've got one, haven't you? Sir Giles left one with you?... Yes—well you mustn't even *look* at it yet. I'll tell you ... what?'

Chloe watched anxiously. In a minute, 'O my dear God in heaven!' Lord Arglay said. 'No ... O yes, keep it quiet *now*.... Who is Angus M. Sheldrake?... yes, *who*? Who? *I* don't know his name.... Oh. Can we get at him?... No, I don't think you'd better; perhaps I will.... Good-bye.'

He looked round. 'Reginald has sold a Stone to a fellow who has made a fortune in gallipots and other pottery ware and is called Angus M. Sheldrake. He is an American and may have left London by now.'

'But,' Chloe cried, 'do you mean he's sold his one Stone already?'

'No,' Lord Arglay said. 'He has divided it and sold the new one.'

'But he was going to have it set!' Chloe said.

'But he had a chance of meeting Angus M. Sheldrake, who is the richest man that ever motored across Idaho, and as Angus was leaving London Reginald scrapped the setting, took an hour to convince him, and did it. While Bruce Cumberland was talking to me about the necessity of caution. Caution! With Reginald being creative. Do you know I entirely forgot he could do that? Ring up the Savoy and see if the unmentionable Sheldrake is still there.'

Chloe leapt to the telephone. After a few minutes—'He's left London till Monday,' she said.

'And to-day's Friday,' Lord Arglay said. 'I wish I had Reginald in the dock on an embezzlement charge. Well—I don't want to see the Ambassador till I've seen Giles; not after this morning. You know I'm terrified in case he*does* start multiplying—either he or Reginald. But I can't bring him back quicker; if I try he'll just stop away. I really don't see what else we can do—till Monday. I can talk to Reginald of course, and I will.'

'Do you believe in it?' Chloe asked.

'In the Stone?' Arglay said. 'I suppose I do—in a sense. I don't know what your friend means by calling it the end of desire.'

'What do you think he meant by saying that the way to the Stone was in the Stone?' Chloe asked again. 'And what is the way?'

'I do not know what he meant,' Arglay answered, 'though certainly the way to any end is in that end itself. For as you cannot know any study but by learning it, or gain any virtue but by practising it, so you cannot be anything but by becoming it. And that sounds obvious enough, doesn't it? And yet,' he went on as if to himself, 'by becoming one thing a man ceases to be that which he was, and no one but he can tell how tragic that change may be. What do you want to be, Chloe?'

The use of her name was natural enough to pass outwardly unheeded, if not unnoticed by some small function of her mind which made a sudden movement of affection towards him.

'I do not know,' she said.

'Nor I,' he said, 'for myself any more than for you. I am what I am, but it is not enough.'

'You—the Chief Justice,' she said.

'I am the Chief Justice,' he answered, 'but the way is in the end, and how far have I become justice? Still'—he recovered lightness and pointed to the typescript of *Organic Law*—'still we do what we can. Well—— Look here now, you can't do anything till Monday. If there are any developments I will let you know.'

'Are you sure I can't do anything?' she said doubtfully.

'Neither of us can,' Arglay answered. 'You may as well clear off now. Would you like to use the Stone to go home by?'

'No, thank you,' she said. 'I think I'm afraid of the Stone.'

'Don't think of it more than you can help between now and Monday,' Arglay advised her. 'Go to the theatre to-night if you can. If anything happens messenger boys in a procession such as preceded the queen of Sheba when*she* came to Suleiman shall be poured out to tell you all.'

'I *was* going to the theatre,' she said, 'but I thought of postponing it.'

'Nonsense,' said the Chief Justice. 'Come on Monday and we'll tackle Sir Giles and the Ambassador and Angus M. Sheldrake and Reginald and the Hajji and Bruce Cumberland—and if there are any more we will deal with them also. Run along.'

By midnight however Chloe almost wished she had not followed Lord Arglay's advice. For she was conscious that the evening had not been a success, and that the young man who accompanied her was conscious of it too. This annoyed her, for in matters of pleasure she had a high sense of duty, and not to cause gaiety appeared to her as a failure in morals. Besides, Frank Lindsay was working very hard—for some examination in surveying and estate agency—working in an office all day and then at home in the evening, and he ought to be made as happy as possible. But all her efforts and permissions and responses had been vain; she had said good night to her companion with an irritable sense of futility which she just prevented herself expressing. He had, as a matter of fact, been vainly contending all the evening, without knowing it, against two preoccupations in Chloe's mind—the Stone and Lord Arglay. Not only did the Stone lie there, a palpitating centre of wonder and terror, but against the striving endeavour of Frank Lindsay's rather pathetic culture moved the assured placidity of Lord Arglay's. It did not make Frank less delightful in the exchanges discoverable by him and her together, but it threw into high relief the insufficiency of those exchanges as more than an occupation and a means of oblivion; it managed to spoil them while providing no substitute and no answer for the desires that thrilled her.

It seemed to her that all things did just so much and no more. As, lying awake that night, she reviewed her activities and preoccupations, there appeared nothing that consumed more than a little part of her being, or brought her, by physical excitement or mental concentration, more than forgetfulness. Nothing justified her existence. The immortal sadness of youth possessed her, and a sorrow of which youth is not always conscious, the lucid knowledge of her unsatisfied desires. There was nothing, she thought, that could be trusted; the dearest delight might betray, the gayest friendship open upon a treachery and a martyrdom. Of her friends, of her young male friends especially, pleasant as they were, there was not one, she thought, who held that friendship important for her sake rather than for his own enjoyment. Even that again was but her own selfishness; what right had she to the devotion of any other? And was there any devotion beyond the sudden overwhelming madness of sex? And in that hot airless tunnel of emotion what pleasure was there and what joy? Laughter died there, and lucidity, and the clear intelligence she loved, and there was nothing of the peace for which she hungered.

Her thought went off at a tangent to Reginald Montague's preoccupation with the Stone. If there could be an end to desire, was it thus that it should be used? Was it only that men might hurry the more and hurl themselves about as if the speed of Chloe Burnett or Reginald Montague were of moment to the universe? She hated Montague, she hated Sir Giles, she hated Frank Lindsay—poor dear!—she hated—no, she did not hate Lord Arglay, but she hated the old man who had come to her and talked of kings and prophets and heroes till she was dizzy with happiness and dread. Most of all she hated herself. The dark mystery of being that possessed her held no promise of light, but she turned to it and sank into it, content so to avoid the world.

CHAPTER IV
VISION IN THE STONE

Lord Arglay spent some part of the same evening in trying to define the process of his thought on organic law and a still larger part in contemplation of the Stone in his possession. The phrase that had most struck him in Chloe's account of her conversation with Hajji Ibrahim was not, as with her, 'the Way to the Stone which is in the Stone,' but the more definite 'movement in time and place and thought.' The same question that had struck Sir Giles inevitably occurred to him; if in place, then why not in time? He wondered whether Sir Giles and Palliser, whoever Palliser might be, were making experiments with it that very evening at Birmingham. The difficulty, he thought, was absurdly simple, and consisted merely in the fact of the Stone itself. Supposing you willed to return a year, and to be again in those exact conditions, interior and exterior, in which you had been a year ago—why then, either you would have the Stone with you or you would not. If you had, you were not the same: if you had not, then how did you return, short of living through the intervening period all over again? Lord Arglay shuddered at the possibility. It would be delightful, he thought, to know again the thrill which had gone through him when he had heard of his appointment to the office he held. But to have to go again through all those years of painful appeals, difficult judgements, distressing decisions, which so often meant unhappiness to the innocent—no. Besides—supposing you did. When you reached again this moment you would again return by virtue of the Stone—and so for ever. An infinite series of repetitions of those same few years, a being compelled to grow no older, a consciousness forbidden to expand or to die. So far as Lord Arglay could see five minutes' return would be fatal; if, now, he willed himself back at the beginning of his meditations necessity would keep him thinking precisely those thoughts through an everlasting sequence. For if you willed yourself back you willed yourself precisely to be without the Stone; otherwise you were not back in the past as the past had truly been. And Lord Arglay had a suspicion that the Stone would be purely logical.

Yes, he thought, but what, in that sense, were the rules of its pure logic? How could you exist in that past *again* except by virtue of the Stone? if that were not there you yourself could not be there. The thing was a contradiction in terms; you could not be in the past without the Stone yet with the Stone you could not be in the past. Then the Stone could not act in time. But Chloe's visitor had said it could. And a Stone that could create itself out of itself and could deal as it had dealt with space ought to be able to deal in some way or other with time. For time was the same thing as space, or rather duration was a method of extension—that was elementary. 'Extension,' he thought, 'I extend myself into—into what? Nothingness; the past is not; it doesn't exist.' He shook his head; so simple a solution had never appealed to him. Every infinitesimal fraction of a second the whole universe peeled off, so to speak, and passed out of consciousness, except for the extremely blurred pictures of memory, whatever memory might be. Out of existence? that was his difficulty; was it out of existence? He remembered having read somewhere once a fantastic theory that whenever a man made a choice, a real choice—whenever he definitely did one of two things he also did at the same moment the other and brought an entire new universe into being that he might do so. For otherwise an infinite number of potentialities would exist for ever unfulfilled—which, the writer had said, though Lord Arglay had forgotten his reasons, was absurd. It had occasionally consoled him, or at least had appeared to him as a not disagreeable hope, when the Court had rejected an appeal from a sentence of death, to think that at the same time, in a new universe parting from this one as the Stone before him had parted from its original, they had allowed it. In which case a number of Christopher Arglays must exist; the thought almost reduced him to idiocy. But in the same way the past might, even materially, exist; only man was not aware of it, time being, whatever else it was, a necessity of his consciousness. 'But because I can only be sequentially conscious,' he argued, 'must I hold that what is not communicated to consciousness does not exist? I think in a line—but there is the potentiality of the plane.' This perhaps was what great art was—a momentary apprehension of the plane at a point in the line. The Demeter of Cnidos, the Praying Hands of Dürer, the *Ode to a Nightingale*, the Ninth Symphony—the sense of vastness in those small things was the vastness of all that had been felt in the present. Would one dare wish to *be* the Demeter? to be—what? Stone? yes, presumably stone. But stone of an intense significance—to others; but to itself? Agnosticism checked him; no one knew. No one knew whether the Demeter had consciousness, or if so of what kind. Lord Arglay abandoned art and returned to the question of time.

Frankly he was not going to risk perpetual recurrence. He had no intention—his mind chilled suddenly within him as he thought of Giles Tumulty. Would that insane scientist mind risking recurrence—for someone else? If he could find someone who didn't see the catch, he would risk it quite happily, the Chief Justice thought, and stood up in agitation. Some wretched laboratory assistant, some curator, some charwoman even, anyone who would put that bit of gold on their heads and try to will themselves back ten minutes. If his own thought was right … Giles would watch the fellow thinking, doing, being, the same thing for ever. But no—that would involve Sir Giles being there to give him, whoever it might be, the Stone. Only a past Giles though, not the present. The Giles whom the victim knew—there needn't be a real Giles at all. But then the victim would just disappear—he wouldn't be there at all. Well, Giles, he knew, would sacrifice anyone in creation just to prove that. And would look, with a grin of pleasure, at the placards announcing a sensational disappearance. In the horror of approaching a conception of real hell Lord Arglay for the first time since his childhood found himself almost believing in God from sheer fright.

He walked about the room. He had meant to try and think out the future but this agony was too much for him. Who was the Palliser Giles was working with? He flung himself at such works of reference as he possessed—a *Whitaker*, a *Who's Who*—and found him. Abel Timothy Palliser, Professor of Relative Psychology at the University of Birmingham, born 1872, educated—and so on, unmarried. Career—and so on. Author of *Studies in Hypnotic Consciousness*; *The Mind as a Function of Approach*; *The Discontinuous Integer*. The titles, in his present state, seemed to Lord Arglay merely sinister. He had a moment's vision of two men playing with victim after victim. Well, they wouldn't succeed with him—they didn't know of Sheldrake—they might trick Reginald, and though Reginald was a besotted idiot, still even Reginald—'Ass,' Lord Arglay said, 'they're in Birmingham,' and immediately went on, 'How do I know they're in Birmingham? They may have taken a late train—but they needn't take a train! Fool that I am, this thrice infernal Stone will do it for them! O damn the day when that accursed Giles——'

In the middle of the imprecation he stopped and made himself sit down. A small voice within him said 'Something must be done about this.' After all, he might be wrong; the Stone might act, in time, in ways he could not foresee. Or Chloe might have got Hajji Ibrahim's words wrong. His first impulse was to go to Sir

Giles and stop whatever devilry might be taking place. But, short of violence, it would be difficult to stop Tumulty doing whatever he wanted. An alternative was to find out, if he could, exactly what the powers of the Stone were, and the only person who could tell him that, so far as he could see, was Hajji Ibrahim. At the moment, Lord Arglay realized, he himself was the passive centre of the whole affair; the Government, the Embassy, Sir Giles, Reginald, all their activities were communicated to him. It might be possible to lay Sir Giles out; on the other hand, Giles was an awkward enemy and might lay him out, and then the confusion would, he thought more or less impartially, be worse. It looked like the Embassy first, and in something under five minutes he was speaking to Hajji Ibrahim on the telephone.

'I am Lord Arglay,' he said. 'I wonder, Hajji, if you could spare me ten minutes.'

'I will come at once,' the answer reached him. 'You are willing to help us, yes?'

'I am willing to talk to you,' the Chief Justice answered. 'You will be round here immediately? Good.'

It took him, however, when the Hajji arrived, more than ten minutes to reach tactfully the two questions he was anxious to have answered. What *was* the Stone? and what could it do?

'What is it in itself, I mean?' he urged. 'Yes, Miss Burnett told me its history—but what is it? Is it a new element?'

'I think it is the First Matter,' the Hajji told him, 'from which all things are made—spirits and material things.'

'Spirits?' Arglay said. 'But this is matter;' he pressed a finger on the Stone.

'Matter to matter,' Ibrahim answered, 'but perhaps mind to mind, and soul to soul. That is why it will do anything you ask it—with all your heart. But you must will truly and sincerely.'

'In the matter of time,' Arglay, after a moment's meditation, went on, 'can it transfer a man from one point to another?'

'Assuredly,' the Hajji said. 'But you must remember that the Keepers of the Stone have not for centuries of generations laid hands on it, far less used it for such things. It has been kept in profound seclusion, and now that it is loose I fear greatly for the world. I think this Giles Tumulty has little reverence and few scruples.'

'So do I,' Lord Arglay said grimly. 'He has told you that he will multiply it?'

'He has threatened us with the most awful and obscene sacrilege,' the Hajji answered, trying to keep his voice calm. 'He has sworn that he will divide the Indivisible for his own ends.'

'But *time*——' Arglay, returning to his point, laid the problem before the Persian but he got no satisfaction.

'I tell you since the Shah Ismail laid hands on it five hundred years ago no one has desecrated it so,' Ibrahim insisted. 'For he perished miserably with all his house. How should I know in what manner the Holy Thing permits itself to be used? Give me the Stone which you have and let us seek the other.'

'Others,' Lord Arglay said. 'The affair's gone farther than you think, Hajji. And it won't be an easy thing to get it back from Giles without worse trouble.'

'Cannot your Government seize it?' the other asked, but Arglay shook his head.

'To be perfectly frank,' he answered, 'I doubt if the Government would go to extremes unless they realized something of its value. And then—I hope for the best—but it's no use blinking the possibility—then, if they knew its value, they mightn't very much want to give it back.'

'Ali Khan will raise all the deserts and bazaars against them,' Ibrahim said—'Egypt and Arabia, Africa and Syria and Iraq and Iran and India and beyond.'

'I dare say,' Arglay answered gloomily. 'But Ali Khan won't have the Stone. And if it comes to raising the Government can do a little. Besides, what do you suppose the other Powers would be doing—if the whole of Islam was at war? No, Hajji, I wouldn't trust the Government so far as to tell them what it can do.'

'I know,' the Hajji answered. 'I did but seek for your thought. I have told Ali Khan we shall never recover it by war.'

'What is worrying *me*,' the Chief Justice went on, 'is what devil's tricks Giles may be playing all this while and what I ought to be doing to stop them.'

'Ask it if you will,' Ibrahim said.

'Eh?' Lord Arglay stared.

'Ask it to illuminate your mind and show you what your brother is doing at this moment. The manuscripts tell us that it moves in the world of thought as in the world of action. Only take care that you are not snared in his thought so that your mind cannot return to itself.'

'If it can do all this,' Arglay said, 'cannot it reunite itself and return of its own virtue, if you will it so?'

'No,' the Hajji answered, 'for it will do nothing for itself of itself, neither divide nor reunite. One Stone has no power upon its Type unless they are under the will of a single mind. Unless indeed——' He paused.

'Unless——?' Lord Arglay asked.

'Unless anyone should will that it and he should be with the Transcendence,' Ibrahim said in a very low voice. 'But I do not know who would dare that; and if he presumed and failed he would be destroyed and the Stone he held would be left in the world where he failed. For the Stone is he, and will go where he goes and no farther. But if he came to the End … I do not know; these are very terrible things.'

'And can none of the house of the Keepers,' the Chief Justice asked, 'dare to will this thing to save the Stone from its enemies?'

'I have asked that,' Ibrahim answered, 'but we know too little and too much. We know we are not worthy, and we do not know what is its will. Ali Khan desires to redeem the Stone for the sake of his Faith and I for the honour of my house, and my brothers in Persia for their glory or their peace, but we dare not bring these things into the Transcendence.'

Lord Arglay was silent again. His mind told him the Persian's meaning but his being did not respond to it. Long since he had left these questions aside, unless—as in rare moments he sometimes fantastically hoped— the nature of law was also the nature of God. But if so it was not in the Transcendence but in the order of created things. In a minute or two he brought the talk back to the immediate necessities.

'Do you tell me,' he said, 'that I can know what Giles is doing or purposing?'

'The Traditions say so,' Ibrahim answered. 'But it is a perilous thing to undertake; for you must sink into the life of thought and you may not easily return.'

'I am a worm and no man,' Lord Arglay said, 'but if Giles can catch *me* in his mental perversities——'

'Take care,' the Hajji interrupted him. 'I think it is not your strength that shall save you.'

The Chief Justice suppressed his words but he was conscious that a very strong sense of pride was on tip-toe within him, anxious to defy Giles and all his works. He waited till it had sunk down a little, and said: 'What shall I do then? For if any wretched charwoman is being trapped to-night…' It was ridiculous, he thought at the same moment, how his mind kept running on charwomen. But he had a vision of some thin, rather harassed, grey-haired female being persuaded to take the Stone and being caught in an everlasting cleaning of some stone corridor. All wrong metaphysically, no doubt, he protested—but possible—no, not possible: no more than sudden passage from place to place or a Stone that divided itself and was yet unchanged.

Ibrahim answered, 'You need but take it into your hand and will.'

'And you?' Arglay said. 'Will you do it with me?'

The Hajji hesitated. 'It is almost sacrilege,' he murmured, 'yet it is with a right desire. I dare not use my will, but I may sit by you while you use your own. So much is perhaps not against my oath…. Under the Protection.' He stretched out his hand. 'Take the Stone and let it lay in your palm, and I will put my hand over it, and set your desire to know what Giles Tumulty does and purposes.'

'And for the return?' Arglay asked.

'That is with Allah,' Ibrahim said. 'Will you dare it now?'

For all answer the Chief Justice pulled an armchair near and parallel to his visitor's; then he sat down in it and laid his arm on the arm of the chair. On his palm the Stone rested. Ibrahim laid his own hand lightly over it and so they remained.

Arglay, as he leaned back, formed in his mind, out of the impulse of distaste which grew in it, the image of Giles Tumulty. He suppressed, as quickly as he could, the criticisms of his brother-in-law which he was tempted to make to himself; he compelled them to define the central idea more exactly. Then he released upon that image the anxiety which had possessed him; he made a demand of it and sent it out to compel an answer. The antipathy he always felt grew stronger but it was controlled and directed by his intention; Giles's mind should lie open to his, he was determined. He felt, but without attending to it, Ibrahim's hand quiver upon his, as he was still vaguely aware of the chair on which he was sitting. Slowly those details of sensation vanished, and instead he became aware that he was holding, or seemed to be holding, a living thing, a moving, pulsating something which he hated. It was approaching him; he drove his detestation forward to meet it. The sensation of enclosing it in his hand disappeared; physical connection ceased, and he seemed to know as a mental experience alone. Only that experience now existed; he was repelled, yet since nothing but repulsion was to be felt it was that which passionately concerned his whole being. He allowed that repulsion to enter him, but as his spirit seemed to retire before it, so at the same time it overcame and dominated it. There ensued a moment's balance between those contending forces; they swung equal and then the effort ceased. His mind was aware of an ordered arrangement, as if in the outer world it had been considering the plan of a great city; he concentrated his attention even more strongly, and found himself conscious of an overpowering desire.

But it was a consciousness purely intellectual; the normal confusion of the mind by the emotions was absent. He was not concerned to excuse, justify, or condemn the desire he felt existing; rather he observed it merely. Nor indeed was he at first clear what he was considering, until there shaped itself against the darkness a face, a large, youthful, eager face which was gazing at him with a docile attention. It had red hair, a rather squab nose, a high colour, a weak mouth slightly open, brown and expectant eyes. His mind remarked that it was a face hitherto unseen; it reported at the same time a hatred of the face, combined with a desire to see it hurt and damaged—yet not in mere uselessness but in the process of extracting some personal profit out of its existence and its pain. The face removed itself to a little distance and developed into the whole figure of a young man, a lower middle-class young man, who was speaking. A small, very distant voice floated into his mind. 'Yes,' it was saying, 'yes, sir; and then?' He heard another strange voice—an older, sharper voice—say, 'That's the whole thing; you understand?' and the rest of his being underwent a sudden spasm of delight.

'Christ Almighty,' Lord Arglay thought suddenly, 'this is happening,' and with the momentary distraction the form flickered and seemed to fade. But he made a desperate effort to hold it, and at once a strength flowed out from him. The young man's figure no longer appeared alone; it was in a room, a long room, with windows, instruments, books, and there was another figure by it. A tall, lean, oldish man, with a sharp anxious face, was standing there, playing with something in his hand. It was one of the Stones—no, it was the Crown itself, and with the sight his mind realized what and where it was. It was looking out, his mind, through Giles Tumulty's eyes; it was Giles Tumulty's desire that it knew; it was Giles Tumulty's experiment that was beginning—and Christopher Arglay's mind that watched it.

But that mind was so detached that it seemed incapable of staying or hastening the intention that flowed around it; as often as it turned inwards to realize its own separate existence the appearances which it beheld mingled and faded. It was suspended and observant.

Yet, as if on the outskirts of its own nature, it presently found itself observing other thoughts. Much the same argument that Arglay had already gone over flashed through it; scattered phrases—'if he just disappears'—'time and place'—'I wonder what Arglay would say to this'—struck it and passed. The figure of the young man put out its hand and received something from the tall man. Lord Arglay's mind made an effort forward. 'Stop, you fool,' it knew itself thinking, and heard Giles's voice say, close and loud, 'Calm now, quite calm. Just make as near an image of what you were doing as you can.'

The alien mind that received those words shuddered with the horror. But the mental habits of so many years befriended it then; it realized, as it felt the pang, that it could do nothing then and there. It must act in its own medium; on the crowd of diabolic curiosities that surged around it, it could produce no effect. 'I am here,' Lord Arglay's mind said to itself, 'by my will and the virtue of the Stone. I can do nothing here—nothing. I must return by virtue of the Stone.' It sought to shut out the vision in front of it; it sought to concentrate on itself and to will to know again the vehicle that was natural to it. And even as it did so Lord Arglay heard a voice saying to him: 'Have you seen? have you seen?'

He was lying back in his own chair. Beside him Hajji Ibrahim was looking anxiously at him. The Stone? yes, the Stone still lay quietly enough on his palm. Lord Arglay stared at it as if his eyes would never shift. Then very slowly he got to his feet and laid it carefully on the table. As he did so Ibrahim repeated: 'Have you seen?'

'Yes,' Lord Arglay said, again slowly. 'Yes, I have seen. And if what I have seen is true, and if it is as I fear it may be, I will choke Giles Tumulty's life out of him myself. Have *you* seen?'

'I think I slept and dreamed. And in my dream——' the Hajji said, and described the room and the two forms. But he went on—'Also I saw a little brownish man standing by a table, and his eyes were all alight with curiosity and desire. Also I saw,' and he began to tremble, 'that they had again divided the Stone; for they did not give the Crown to the youth, but only a Stone. I think they are very evil men.'

'I believe you care more about the division of the Stone than about the harm they may do with it,' Arglay dispassionately said.

'Certainly I do,' the Hajji answered, 'for the one is an offence against the Holy One, but the other only against man. He who divides the Unity is a greater sinner than he who makes a mock of his brother.'

'You may be right,' Lord Arglay said, 'but of the Unity I know nothing, and of man I know something.' He stamped suddenly with sheer rage. 'Why did I return?' he cried out.

'You did wisely,' the Hajji said, 'for you had not gone to fight his will but to observe it. You will not find it easy, I know now, to break Giles Tumulty's will, and you could not have done it in that way. Consider that, if what you fear has happened, this young man's mind will not perhaps suffer so much, for in the very nature of things he will not know that he is living but that one period of past time over and over again, until the day when the End of Desire shall come indeed; nay, for all we know, he may be saved from many evils so.'

'He may be saved from what you will,' Lord Arglay said, and his face set as he spoke, 'but no human being shall be turned into an automaton at the will of Giles Tumulty while I am living and sane.'

There was a short silence, then Arglay went on. 'But you are so far right that we do not know what arrangements Giles has made, nor what the end of this experiment of his may be. And till we know where the Types of the Stone all are—if that is what you call them—we must move slowly. To-morrow I will go to the Foreign Office again, and after that we will talk with one another further.'

The Hajji stood up. 'The Peace be upon you,' he said.

'It will be a peace that passeth all understanding then,' the Chief Justice answered, and took him to the door.

CHAPTER V
THE LOSS OF A TYPE

Nor was Lord Arglay any nearer to an apprehension of that mystical Peace when he discovered on the next morning, that everybody had taken advantage of the week-end to vanish from London. Mr. Bruce Cumberland was expected back on Monday; so was Mr. Reginald Montague; so was Mr. Angus M. Sheldrake. As for Sir Giles he might be back any moment, but so far as he was expected at all it was on Monday. The Persian Ambassador even (not that he was wanted) had gone to Sandringham,—so *The Times* said—where presumably he and Lord Birlesmere were being diplomatic. London—to the Chief Justice's irritation—consisted of himself, the Hajji, and Chloe, neither of whom seemed at the moment to be much good to him. He thought of confronting Sir Giles, wherever he might be, but he was unwilling to give his brother-in-law that advantage of circumstances which he would then undeniably possess, and at last he resigned himself to spending a day of enmity deferred which, if it did not make his heart sick, made it at least extremely and unusually sullen.

He would not have been any happier if he had known what was happening, on that same Saturday morning, at a country house some fifty miles out of London, the property of Mr. Sheldrake and his occasional retreat from high finance and the complications of industry when he was in England. The Chief Justice had done him some wrong in limiting him to gallipots; actually there were few branches of production and distribution in which he had not, somehow or other, a share. These had mostly come to him from his father, as Rivington Court had come to him from his mother, and Sheldrake's own additions had consisted of several large motor factories and the establishment of an Atlantic Airways Company to the first, and an entirely unnecessary though quite beautiful wing to the second. Neither it nor the Atlantic Airways would probably have come into existence but for Cecilia Sheldrake, who, having been forestalled in her desire to be the first woman to fly the Atlantic, had determined that at least most of the others who did so should do it by her permission. Her husband had founded the company, as he had built the wing, in order that she might have everything she wanted to play with, and when he had bought the Stone from Reginald Montague he had done it with a similar intention in his mind.

In actual fact it had taken a longer time to persuade Sheldrake to buy than Reginald had admitted to his uncle. But the surprising chances of that Friday—the coming of Sir Giles with the Stone, the meeting with Sheldrake at an unexpected conference on the same morning, the discovery that the richest man of Idaho, of the States, of the world (report varied) was a young fellow not quite so old as he himself was—all these had convinced Reginald that what, at a pinch, he would have been driven to call Providence was on his side, and had given him an increased audacity. He had caught Sheldrake by mentioning, almost in one breath, transport, the Lord Chief Justice, and a rare stone, thus attacking at once through the American's sense of business, security, and romance. Certainly there had been a few minutes' danger when the Stone was discovered to be no jewel, as jewels are ordinarily known; indeed, Reginald had been driven to a rather hasty demonstration, which, in its turn, startled Sheldrake so greatly as seriously to endanger the negotiations. Two ideas, however, occurred to the financier, though he spoke of neither to Reginald; one was motor-cars and airways, the other was his wife. To protect the one and delight the other made it the aim of his morning to procure the Stone, and the eventual seventy-three thousand guineas at which it changed hands was a lesser matter. Neither of them were ever quite clear how that particular sum was reached; though Reginald flattered himself that the guineas made it a far more reputable transaction than if it had been merely pounds. He had pressed on Sheldrake the advisability of secrecy, but he had been compelled to admit that a few other Stones of the kind were in existence—not more than half a dozen. The American had displayed some curiosity as to their owners, but here the mere facts enabled Montague to be firm. He admitted that Sir Giles Tumulty had one; he thought the Chief Justice had; and he himself—well, of course, he had kept one, that was reasonable. But he said nothing of his intention to spend the afternoon creating a few more Stones nor of the names of buyers which were already floating in his mind. On his side Sheldrake said nothing of his intention to communicate the mystery at least to his wife, nor of his anxiety to procure, if he anyhow could, the other existing examples of it. Equally satisfied, equally unsatisfied, they parted, and while Reginald went first to his office and then to Brighton, Sheldrake went straight by car to Rivington Court.

He waited however till the next day, and till he had, rather nervously, at a very early hour the next morning, tried a few more minor experiments, before he spoke of the new treasure. The experiments were tried cautiously, in a small wood near the house, and were limited to the crossing of a brook, the passage of a field, and so on, concluding with the grand finale of a return to his own room, where he contentedly locked the Stone away and went to breakfast. It was some time later, not very long before lunch, while Lord Arglay raged in London, that he took his wife across the terraces and lawns to a hidden summer-house and revealed the secret to her.

Cecilia took it with surprising calm—took, indeed, both the secret and the Stone with a similar calm. She was delighted, she was thrilled, but with an obscure and egoistical acceptance of things she was not wildly surprised. If such treasures existed, they did so, both she and her husband felt, chiefly for Cecilia Sheldrake. Her life had refused her only one thing—to be the first woman to fly the Atlantic, and Cecilia, like everyone else, felt that life owed her every sort of gratification in return for that disappointment. Not that anything could really make up for it, but other tributes might help her to forget. Even miracles were reasonable since they happened for her, and Angus, in the depths of his nature, though his brain moved more slowly, felt that a world whose chief miracles were the existence of Cecilia and her existence as his wife might easily throw in a few more to make things pleasant for her. She did indeed open her eyes a little at the price, but that also seemed reasonable since it was for her, and she was more ready to risk extended experiments than her husband had been. Indeed it was she who made what must up to then have been the longest journey yet taken by those high means—at least for some centuries—in going direct to her bedroom in London and returning with a dress she had left behind and had changed her mind about on the way down the day before. When she had safely returned——

'Darling, how sweet of you!' she cried to Angus. 'I never had anything like it before.'

'I don't suppose many people have, or will have,' Angus said, with justice. 'Not many will have the chance.'

'But will *anybody*?' Cecilia said, a little shocked. 'Are there more of them?'

'Only about half a dozen, I gathered,' Angus told her. 'And I don't know who's going to buy them.'

Cecilia looked depressed. 'Where did they come from?' she asked in a moment.

'Sir Giles Tumulty brought them from the East, Montague said,' Angus answered. 'He's a traveller and explorer.'

His wife looked at him meditatively. 'You don't think he'd sell them *all*?' she asked. 'O Angus, if somebody else got hold of them.'

'Well, Sir Giles has,' Sheldrake pointed out.

'O him!' Cecilia said. 'I mean somebody else like us.' She sat up suddenly. 'Angus! What about Airways?'

'I know,' Angus said, 'I thought the same thing. It might be awkward. Of course, it's not so bad because you'd want to be pretty sure of anyone before you lent them the Stone.'

Cecilia shook her head. 'We mayn't know everything,' she said. 'They may have cheated you. This Mr. Montague didn't *say* it was the only one?'

'Sweetheart, he said it *wasn't*,' Angus pointed out.

'Then he *has* cheated you,' Cecilia said impatiently. 'O Angus, we *must* put it right. After all, the Airways ought to have control, oughtn't they?'

'It may be a little awkward,' Angus answered. 'I think one of them is with the Lord Chief Justice.'

Cecilia opened her eyes. 'But I thought judges weren't supposed to have financial interests,' she exclaimed. 'Isn't it corruption?… Angus, they can't *make* them, can they?'

'What!' said her husband, startled. 'Make them? O no—at least I suppose not. They came from the East.'

'Yes, but do they *make* them in the East, or dig them up, or magnetize them, or something?' Cecilia persisted. 'Angus dear, you must see what I mean. If there was a mine now, how dreadful it would be.'

'Darling, I think you're getting unnecessarily alarmed,' Sheldrake protested. 'There can't be a mine—not possibly—not of stones that do this.'

'Why not?' Cecilia asked.

'Well, could there? It isn't reasonable,' her husband urged. 'Stones like this *must* be rare.' But he looked uneasily at it as he spoke.

'Anyhow—it's near lunchtime—anyhow I think you ought to do something. Get it forbidden by law or something.'

'But then what about us?' Sheldrake asked.

Cecilia took his arm. 'Darling,' she said, 'you're awfully slow. There could always be a special license to the Airways.'

'It'd be very difficult to explain to the Home Secretary without telling him everything, and I don't know that I want to tell him everything,' Angus murmured. 'Besides, if one license is granted others could be, and suppose you got a Labour Government in again?'

Cecilia almost stamped. 'I suppose you could buy a monopoly or a charter or something of that sort for twenty-one years or so?' she asked plaintively. 'Darling Angus, we do want to stop it going further, don't we?'

'O rather, yes,' Angus agreed. 'It's the explaining that will be difficult.'

'It won't be any more difficult for you than for me to explain to Elise how this frock came down here,' his wife said. 'Dearest, it's a lovely present and I do thank you *enormously*. But if you could just prevent anyone else having one, it would be too perfectly sweet! You will try, won't you?'

'O I'll try,' Angus answered, kissing her. 'But it'll take some doing. There'd have to be an Act, I'm afraid—and if the Lord Chief Justice was nasty——'

'He wouldn't have anything to do with politics though, would he?' Cecilia asked. 'And as a matter of fact he might, if you put it to him nicely, be willing to sell.'

They returned to the house to lunch.

About the same time a less elaborate lunch was being served in the inn of the village close by to Chloe Burnett and Frank Lindsay. Chloe had been half-unwilling to leave London, for fear the Chief Justice should want her, but a sense of duty, a necessity to recompense Frank for the unsatisfactory result of the Friday evening, had compelled her to accept his suggestion; though, for some undefined reason, she had caused him to take Lancaster Gate on the way. Lord Arglay's house had offered no more information than she expected, but the sight of it enabled her more freely to devote all her energies to making the day's amusement a success. She had received with interest and encouragement Frank's serious efforts towards culture, although a part of her mind remotely insisted on comparing his careful answers with Lord Arglay's casual completeness. Sir Giles's epigram on encyclopedias—'the slums of the mind'—recurred to her, and she went so far to meet it as to admit that Frank's information was rather like a block of model dwellings compared with the tumultuous carelessness of a country house. The contrast had been suddenly provoked by Frank's short lecture in answer to her question—'O by the way, what is a Sufi?'

'It is a Muhammedan sect,' he had answered. 'Muhammed, you know, who was a fanatical monotheist, wrote the Koran, or rather claimed that the Koran had been delivered to him by Gabriel.' He had gone on, with what seemed a good many references to Muhammed. Chloe's intelligence reminded her that by the phrase 'Muhammed was a Fanatical monotheist' he meant what Lord Arglay—or was it the Hajji?—had meant by saying 'Our lord the Prophet arose to proclaim the Unity,' but she found the one phrase unusually trying after the other. As penance and compensation she allowed her hand, which lay lightly in Frank's, to give it a small squeeze of thanks, and diverted his attention by saying, 'O what a jolly house!'

The lecture had taken place soon after lunch while they were wandering in the lanes round the village. There was in fact very little of the house to be seen—it was too far off and hidden by trees, but perhaps sufficient to justify Chloe in saying, 'Let's go through that gate and get a bit nearer.'

'You'll be trespassing,' Frank said, looking at the obviously private road on the other side.

Chloe laid her hand on the latch and gazed along the empty road. 'Frank, in two minutes,' she said, 'there will rush round that corner a herd of maddened cows—look, there they are. I shall take refuge behind this gate, and I pull you in too.' She did, and shut it after them. 'Being here, don't you think we might just go as far as that bend and see if we can see the house better?'

'Certainly,' Frank said obligingly. 'As a matter of fact, according to English law, trespassers——'

'O don't talk about the law,' Chloe said very hastily. 'I don't want anyone but Lord—the Chief Justice to talk to me about that.'

'Poor dear, you must get enough of it. I forgot you live with it perpetually,' Lindsay answered. 'You must be jolly glad to get away from it a bit.'

Chloe, with a certain throb of conscience, attended to the house, of which a great deal more became visible as they reached the bend. The private road ran on towards it, but both the trespassers lingered.

'It is rather jolly, isn't it?' Frank said, and stopped dead. Chloe gave a cry of fear. For before the words had been well spoken or heard the air in front of them seemed suddenly to quiver, a quick brightness shone within it, and they found standing in front of them, where no one had been, whither no one had come, a well-dressed young lady. She seemed to be equally startled, and her gurgling cry caught up Chloe's shriek. There was a minute's silence while they gazed, then——

'The Stone,' Chloe cried out. 'You've got the Stone.'

Rather shaken still, the stranger looked at her, but hostilely.

'What do you mean? what stone?' she asked.

'You must have it,' Chloe said breathlessly. 'I know—I've seen. It was exactly that; the wind, the light, the—you. You *have* got the Stone.'

Her words sounded almost accusingly. Mrs. Sheldrake unconsciously clenched her hand a little more tightly round what was, surely, her property, and said: 'I suppose you know you're trespassing?'

Frank re-acted to the commonplace remark, feeling that he must have been day-dreaming a few moments. The new arrival had, of course, walked up the road.

'We're so sorry,' he said. 'As a matter of fact we came in to shelter——' He paused in a confused realization that he had been on the point of repeating Chloe's preposterous tale about the cows.

'To shelter!' the lady said.

'Well, no, not to shelter,' Frank stammered, feeling suddenly angry with Chloe, who was still staring, almost combatively. 'I'm so sorry—I mean—we just came a step or two in to look at the house. From here, I mean. We weren't going nearer. I do apologize, I—I——'

Cecilia looked at Chloe. 'What did you mean by the Stone?' she asked again.

'I mean the Stone,' Chloe said with a clear vigour. 'Is there another then, or have you bought one?'

Cecilia came a step nearer. 'What do you mean about the Stone?' she asked, and made a mistake which in a less startled moment she would not have made. 'You had better tell me,' she added.

Chloe flushed a little. 'I shall certainly not——' she began, and stopped as a confused dream of Lord Arglay, Charlemagne, Gabriel, the Tetragrammaton, and the End of Desire swept across her. 'I beg your pardon,' she went on. 'It was only that I was so surprised.'

'Is this Mr. Montague?' Cecilia asked, abruptly shifting her attack to Frank, who was too taken aback to do more than begin a hasty denial before Chloe interrupted him.

'No,' she said, 'he has nothing to do with it. Are you Mrs. Sheldrake?'

'I am Mrs. Sheldrake,' the other said, 'but what do you know?'

Chloe hesitated. 'I know that you have one of the Stones,' she said, 'but it ought not to have been bought or sold. It wasn't Mr. Montague's and it can't be yours.'

'Don't be absurd,' Cecilia said sharply. 'How many of these Stones are there then?'

'I don't know,' Chloe answered truthfully. 'There was only one at first, but that can't be yours for that was in the Crown.'

'The Crown? what Crown?' Cecilia asked again, feeling that this was intolerable. There were, it seemed, goodness knows how many of these Stones—and now there was more talk of a Crown—as if seventy-three thousand guineas oughtn't to have bought the whole thing. She was half-inclined to throw the Stone in the girl's face—only that would be silly; as a mere precaution she ought to keep it.

Chloe said anxiously, 'You ought to see Lord Arglay; the Chief Justice, I mean. He could tell you better than I can. He's Mr. Montague's uncle and he warned him not to sell it.'

'Is it Lord Arglay's property then?' Cecilia answered.

'I don't know whose property it is,' Chloe admitted rather helplessly. 'But you ought to be very careful what you do with it.'

'I should like very much to see Lord Arglay,' Mrs. Sheldrake said, 'if he could make things any clearer.' She lifted the hand that held the Stone. 'Can we reach him by this?'

'Certainly not,' Chloe said, with a return of firmness. 'We can't use the Stone of Suleiman for that.'

'My good girl,' Cecilia said contemptuously, 'that's what it's for.'

'It isn't,' Chloe cried out, 'and if you use it for that you've got no business with it. Any more than Mr. Montague. It's for getting somewhere.'

'Well,' said Mrs. Sheldrake, 'I want to get to Lord Arglay. Will you tell me how and where I can find him? Or must I do it myself?'

'O don't,' Chloe said. 'He's in London, I think.' She gave the address. 'But he won't be pleased if you use the Stone.'

'I shall go,' Mrs. Sheldrake announced, 'by car. And now don't you think you'd better get out of these grounds?'

Mr. Lindsay, who had been anxious to do so for the last five minutes, flung her a vicious glance and started. Chloe, who wanted to say a good deal without saying anything, gave her intelligence the victory and accompanied him. But over at the gate she seized his hand and forced him to run with her. 'Quick,' she said, 'quick. We must get back to London.'

'London?' Frank protested. 'Why on earth——? Why, it's not three yet. Surely——'

'O we *must*,' Chloe exclaimed. 'I must see Lord Arglay. I must find out if I've done right. I must see what he says to her.'

'But surely he can manage her *without* you,' Frank said. 'It can't be so absolutely vital to you to be there. If she's got something that doesn't belong to her, I shouldn't think she really does want to see him——I should think it was all bluff. If,' he added, 'you'd tell me what it's all about I should know better what we ought to do.'

What they ought to do was not Chloe's concern; what she was going to do she knew perfectly well. She was going straight back to Lancaster Gate; so straight that the idea of telephoning occurred to her only to be dismissed. Nor had she any intention of explaining to Frank; she had been agreeable to him all day, it was now his turn to start being agreeable. She kept up a steady speed towards the inn.

'I can't explain now,' she said after a moment or two. 'If I possibly can I'll tell you some other time. The Foreign Office comes into it,' she added, as an exciting suggestion. 'But don't talk now—run.'

It appeared to Frank the most curious day in the country with a girl friend that he had ever spent. Short of Bolsheviks—in whom he was reluctant to believe, being a typical Liberal in politics, though he professed a cynical independence—he couldn't imagine why the Foreign Office should come in. But he was genuinely anxious to please Chloe, and though he offered one or two more disjointed protests he headed the car for London as soon as possible, once they had reached the inn; warning Chloe, however, that this little two-seater was unlikely to be able to arrive before whatever kind of magnificent car the Sheldrakes owned.

'O but we *must*,' she said. 'Try, Frank, try. I *must* be there when she gets there. I must know what's happening.'

'But what is this blessed Stone?' Frank asked.

'Darling, don't worry now,' Chloe urged him. 'Just see to getting on. Lancaster Gate, you know. As quick as ever.'

'I might be a taximan,' Frank let out. 'All right.'

They fled through various lanes and emerged on a more important side road which would take them on to the main road for London. As soon as they did so however Frank began to slow down. A short distance in front of them, halfway up the steep bank, was another car, and out of it Mrs. Sheldrake was scrambling.

'O don't stop,' Chloe cried, but Cecilia had recognized them and run into the middle of the road.

'Stop,' she said, and Frank was compelled to obey. She came up and addressed Chloe.

'A most annoying thing has happened,' she said, 'and perhaps you'll help us. The Stone's somewhere over there.' She pointed to the bank and the hedge. 'I was looking at it in the car and Angus—Mr. Sheldrake—had to swerve suddenly and it flew out of my hand, and now he can't find it.'

'What!' Chloe exclaimed.

'It must be there,' Cecilia went on sharply. 'I was just holding it up to the sun, to get the colour in the light, and the car jerked, and it had gone. But it's only just over there, it must be, and I thought you wouldn't mind helping us look.'

Chloe was out of the car in a moment. 'You've lost it,' she said. 'O Mrs. Sheldrake!'

'It can't possibly be *lost*,' Cecilia assured, rather annoyed. 'And please—I'm afraid I don't know your name—remember that it's my property.'

'We can settle that after,' Chloe said, beginning to mount the bank. 'We can't possibly leave it lying about for someone to pick up. We can ask Lord Arglay whom it ought to belong to.'

'This,' Frank put in before Mrs. Sheldrake could speak, 'is Miss Burnett. She is the Chief Justice's secretary,' he added as impressively as possible, as Chloe caught the hedge at the top of the bank, pulled herself up, and wriggled and pushed through. 'My name is Lindsay.'

Cecilia eyed the bank. 'Well, Angus?' she called.

A rather strained voice answered her from above—'No, no luck. O—er—are you helping? Somewhere about here, we thought.'

'Will you help me too, Mr. Lindsay?' Cecilia asked. 'So tiresome, all this business. But one can't afford to throw away seventy thousand guineas.' Some reason, after all, had to be given to this young man who was obviously in a state of mere bewilderment, and perhaps the price——

So far she was right. He gaped at her. 'A stone,' he said. 'But what kind of a stone then?'

'O about *so* large,' Cecilia told him. 'A kind of cream colour, with gold flakings, and funny black marks. *Will* you? It would be so good of you. Miss Burnett's too kind. All four of us ought to find it, oughtn't we? Thank you.'

272

He began to help her to climb. Why Chloe, who had been so intent on rushing to London—but of course if the stone was really worth seventy thousand—seventy thousand, it would be rather fascinating even to see a stone worth that.

But half an hour's search, though they all tramped round, parted the thick grass, bent and grovelled and peered, brought them no nearer success. Cecilia, Angus felt, could hardly have chosen a worse place to look at the Stone; nor could Angus, his wife felt in turn, have chosen a worse place to swerve. For besides the bank and hedge by the road, at this particular point two fields were divided by another thorny hedge, at the base of which the grass on each side grew long. There were nettles and thistles and much larger stones on which the men seemed to be continually kneeling, and they all had a feeling that any one of the others might be trampling it into the ground at any moment. And Cecilia distrusted Chloe and Frank, and Chloe distrusted Cecilia and Angus, and Frank was wondering what the whole business meant, and Angus was wondering who the strangers were, and as they searched this wonder, suspicion, and irritation grew every moment more violent. But the End of Desire remained hidden.

At last, as they met in their circumambulations, Frank murmured to Chloe, 'Is this really our business? Is it your Stone or theirs?'

'It isn't mine,' Chloe said, trying not to sound irritable but conscious she was looking hot and dirty and anxious, 'but it isn't really theirs. They bought it all right, but they oughtn't to have it.'

'Are you tired out, Mr. Lindsay?' Cecilia called impatiently. 'It *must* be somewhere here.'

'Yes, Mrs. Sheldrake,' Frank rebelled suddenly, 'but Miss Burnett wanted to get to London, and really we seem to be going over the same ground again and again.'

'Please don't stop then,' Cecilia said. 'I'm sorry to have kept you.'

'O nonsense,' Chloe broke in. 'Of course we must stop. We *must* find it. We can't let a thing like that be about loose. If *someone's* got it at least we shall know where it is, if not whose.'

'There's no question of that,' Cecilia threw at her, 'since we paid for it. As it is, I think your friend Mr. Montague has cheated us.'

'He is *not*——' Chloe began and then remembered she was looking for the End of Desire. With a muddled prayer to the Stone—since, being a modern normally emotional girl she was, quite naturally, an idolater— she stopped and, to her own astonishment, experienced a sudden flicker of amused peace, accompanied by a clearer intellectual survey.

'But we are getting confused, I think,' she said.

At this moment Angus, having stung himself again, swore violently and got up, kneeling on something sharp as he did so. Moved by this exactly as by unexpected opposition at a board meeting he began to decide things at once. 'We can't go on like this,' he said. 'After all, so long as things are left undisturbed here we're damn well certain to find it if I have every blade of grass pulled up separately. The point is—do you want to go to London now, Cecilia, or back to the Court?'

His wife looked at Chloe, who knew the Chief Justice. Let her talk to him while she sat ignorant? Never. If they couldn't find this stone they could anyhow get on the track of the others.

'London,' she said. 'But you had better stop here, Angus, and perhaps Mr. Lindsay will go back to the Court and send someone to you.'

Chloe felt clear that this would do what she wanted with Frank without her interfering. She went on moving the grass with her foot and looking at the ground, as did everyone else except Frank who glanced back towards the road and said coldly, 'I'm afraid that's impossible. Miss Burnett wants to go to London too.'

There was a short silence. Then Angus, still murmuring curses, said abruptly to his wife, 'Then you'd better take the car and get on to London with Miss Burnett. And I'll stop here, and then perhaps Mr. Lindsay won't mind going back to the Court.'

'I shall very much mind,' Lindsay answered. 'I am going to take Miss Burnett to London at once—myself. I daresay someone will pass pretty soon who'll take a message for you.'

Chloe's hand on his arm distracted him. 'Frank dear,' she said, '*Would* you go? I know it sounds beastly, but if you would....'

Frank stared at her. 'Do you want me to?' he asked stupidly.

'I don't—I don't—want you to,' Chloe in confusion murmured. 'But I think it would be—O sporting—of you. It's not a bit nice, but I think we ought.'

'I think it's perfectly insane,' Frank answered in a low voice. 'Do you want them to have their own way altogether?'

'Not altogether,' Chloe protested, also speaking softly, 'but it seems as if we ought,' she ended again lamely.

Frank, in a very bad temper, gave way. 'O anything you like, of course,' he said coldly. 'I go back to this Court then, and after that I can come to London by myself, I suppose?'

'I know it's beastly, Frank,' Chloe answered appealingly. 'I'd go myself or I'd come with you—I'd love to come with you—but I must get to Lord Arglay as soon as Mrs. Sheldrake.' She was not quite clear why, since she realized even then that two sentences of Cecilia's conversation would let the Chief Justice know everything. But she could not yet face that abolition of her own secret desires which the abandonment of any attempt to witness their meeting would involve. Besides, Frank would be bound to want to know—still, it was hard on him and it was quite natural he should turn away and say to Sheldrake very politely, 'Miss Burnett thinks your suggestion a very good one, and so do I. Will Mrs. Sheldrake take her on to London then?'

Cecilia with a cold grudge assented. But Chloe said suddenly to Angus—'O but, Mr. Sheldrake, if you *do* find it, you'll tell us, won't you? That would be only fair.' Angus agreed. 'If I find it I'll let you know at once,' he said. 'At Lord Arglay's?'

'Please,' Chloe said gratefully, and tried to catch Frank's eye. She failed, and went sadly to the bank. She was always doing the selfish thing, she felt. But after all Lord Arglay might—might very easily—want several things done at once when he knew the situation. She wished she wanted to be with Frank a little more strongly. Duty with a strong inclination looked so dreadfully selfish besides duty with a mild inclination. She sat down gloomily in the Sheldrakes' car and it moved off.

The two men looked at each other. 'I don't understand what all this is about,' Frank said, 'or whose this precious stone is. But I have your word that if you find it while I'm gone, or at all for that matter, you'll let us know.'

'I don't mind telling you what *I* know,' Angus answered. 'I bought, from a fellow named Montague, who seems to be a nephew of this Lord Arglay your friend's so keen on, a rather valuable stone for my wife. She understood that it was—well, practically, unique—and now there seems to be some question on our side of misrepresentation, and on yours—theirs, I mean,—of other rights in the property. I daresay it can all be settled by a few minutes' chat between me and Lord Arglay or whoever knows, but till then, since I've parted with my money, I consider I've a right to hold the stone. But I'm anxious to be quite fair and I'll certainly let you or Miss Burnett know if it's found. I shall have a very careful search made, and if it's necessary I shall buy both these fields.'

'I see,' Frank said, a little impressed by this method of dealing with difficulties. 'And you want me to go and let your people know where you are.'

'If you will,' Angus assented. 'It's very good of you, but you'll agree that Miss Burnett seemed almost as keen as my wife.'

'O yes' Frank answered gloomily. 'What's the best way to your place from here?'

Sheldrake told him and he departed, car and all. Angus, allowing about an hour before he was relieved, lit a cigarette and sat down under the hedge to wait. He was too tired to do any more searching; indeed, when the cigarette was finished, he found himself disinclined to move in order to reach another, but, stretching himself out, lay half-asleep and half-brooding.

He was only partly conscious of feet that sounded on the other side of the hedge, though a certain subconscious knowledge told him that someone was coming along a footpath that ran alongside the hedge, a couple of feet away. As they came nearer however he moved so as to be just in time to see a tall figure take a short stride up to the hedge, reach up and pick something from the top of the intertwining twigs. A sudden fear assailed him. The stranger was back on the footpath before Angus could scramble to his feet, and was beginning to move away by the time he reached the hedge.

'Hi!' Angus cried out, seriously alarmed. 'Hi, you!'

The stranger paused and looked back. He was a tall, rather dark young man, of about thirty, carrying sketching materials, and he looked at Angus with a certain hard surprise.

'Hi!' said Angus again. 'Is that mine?'

The young man looked at him, took a step or two farther on, and said over his shoulder, 'Is what yours?'

Angus ran a few feet along his side of the hedge and said, 'What you've just picked up. If it's a funny looking stone, it's mine.'

'Is it really?' the stranger said. 'And why did you put it there?'

'Never mind about all that,' Sheldrake said impatiently. 'Just hand it over, will you?'

The young man began to walk slowly on, and Angus, tripping over roots and stones every other second, kept pace with him, cursing aloud.

'I ask you,' the stranger said to the sky, 'what would *you* think? I pick a—something—from a hedge and am vociferously told that it belongs to *him*'—he threw a disagreeable glance at Sheldrake. 'And you, I suppose,' he said bitterly, 'were looking for it?'

'I had been,' Angus said, almost falling once more. 'I had only just sat down.'

'Well, if you will take a rest in the middle of pitch and toss—' the young man flung over. 'If it's yours how did it get to the top of the hedge?'

'My wife threw it there from a car,' Sheldrake answered incoherently as they reached the bank of the high road.

'And then went away, car and all,' the stranger said looking at the empty road. 'Family happiness. Is marriage a success?'

'Don't be a damned idiot,' Angus snapped. 'Give me that stone at once.'

The stranger pondered. 'I half-believe you,' he said, 'but only half. And anyhow I may tell you I dislike nothing so much as to be called Hi. I don't mind calling myself I, though of course—yes, I know what you're going to say—there's no proof of it. It's a convenience elevated into a philosophy—yes, I agree. But even so I don't like strangers using what is, so to speak, my own pet name for myself. And still more do I dislike their aspirating it. An aspirate so generously bestowed is almost snobbish. I don't say—'

'Will you give me that stone?' Sheldrake shouted.

'If you had asked me politely,' the young man went on gravely, 'I probably should—more out of surprise than conviction. Holy awe and so on. But as it is—no. However, if it's yours, you shall have it. My name is Oliver Doncaster, and I am staying for a few weeks at Mrs. Pentridge's in the village over there. I am now going there to tea. *After* tea'—he looked at his watch—'a quarter to five say, about six, if you will call and convince me you shall have your stone. What is your name—besides Hi, which is, I suppose, generic?'

Angus tried to pull himself together; he felt such a fool wrangling through a hedge. Besides he was not finally certain that this fellow had the stone. 'I beg your pardon if I was rude,' he said, 'but it was all so sudden….'

'Very sudden,' Doncaster agreed politely.

' … and I was so anxious to stop you, that I just called out…. If you would let me see what it was you took out of the hedge….'

'It was,' the other allowed, 'a stone. It just happened to catch my eye. After six I shall be delighted to let it catch yours. Never mind about your name if you'd rather keep it dark. In about an hour or so then? So pleased to have—well, this is hardly a meeting, is it?—heard from you. Good-bye, good-bye.' He waved his hand gracefully and went off along the footpath which here turned to the left and took him to a gate half-way along the field. By the time Angus had got to the bottom of the bank he had come into the road, passed across it, and disappeared down a side lane.

At tea he examined his find. It seemed dull enough indoors, though the colour was pure and the markings curious, but it lacked something of the golden light with which it had seemed to shine in the afternoon sun. A little disappointed he went up to his bedroom and paused on the way at another door.

'Hallo,' he said, 'may I come in?'

In the bed in this room lay Mrs. Pentridge's mother, Mrs. Ferguson, who had been paralyzed from the waist downward for the last year. Opinion in the house was silently divided whether it would have been better for her to be taken altogether or not. Mr. Pentridge thought it would be a merciful release for her. Mrs. Pentridge thought it was a merciful blessing that she had been so far spared. Mrs. Ferguson disguised her own opinion, if she had one, and concentrated her energies on making the most of what visitors and what talk she could still have. Doncaster had fallen into what he felt to be a ridiculous habit of showing her his day's work after tea, and was even, half-seriously, trying to teach her his own prejudices about art; not that he allowed himself to call them that. Mrs. Pentridge, who was also in the room, examining pillow-cases, welcomed him as warmly as her mother.

'Did you get a nice view, Mr. Doncaster?' she asked.

He sat down smiling. 'A very pretty bit of work,' he said. 'No, Mrs. Ferguson, I don't mean mine—I mean the thing I was trying to do. But I had to alter one branch. I couldn't somehow find out exactly what spot nature meant me to stand at. Now look there——' He held out the sketch and Mrs. Ferguson stared at it while he expatiated. Mrs. Pentridge went on with her pillow-cases. When at last he rose—'O by the way,' he said, 'I'm expecting a man in a few minutes to talk about something I found. Look, did you ever see a stone like that?' He passed it over to Mrs. Ferguson. 'Look at the colour, isn't it exquisite?'

'What is it?' the old lady asked.

'Lord knows,' said Oliver. 'I should like it to be chrysoprase, but I don't suppose it is. The Urim and Thummim perhaps.'

'That was what the high priest had on his breast-plate,' Mrs. Ferguson said, looking at the Bible that lay by her bedside. 'I remember that well enough.'

'I'm sure you do,' Oliver said smiling.

'I was little enough when I heard about them,' Mrs. Ferguson went on. 'At the Sunday school it was. I remember it because I learned them the Sunday before I went to the treat for the first time. Urim and Thummim, that was it. I remember Susie Bright pretending to look for them all the way home in the ditch. O I do wish I could run now as well as I could then.'

Mr. Sheldrake's knock at the door below passed unnoticed. For Mrs. Pentridge had dropped her pillow-cases, and with staring eyes was watching her mother struggling up in bed. She sat up, she gasped and gazed, her hands drooped and waved in front of her. She began to shift round; oblivious of Oliver's presence she felt for the side of the bed and began to slip her feet over it. 'Mother,' shrieked Mrs. Pentridge and flew to one side as Oliver leapt to the other. Mrs. Ferguson, panting with surprise and exertion, came slowly to her feet, and holding on to her two supporters, took a step or two forward.

'I'm all right,' she gasped, released Oliver, took another step, 'quite all right,' and let go of her daughter. 'I think,' she added, 'I must be feeling a bit better to-day.'

There was a stupendous silence. Mr. Sheldrake knocked again at the front door.

CHAPTER VI
THE PROBLEM OF TIME

Sir Giles lay back in a chair and grinned at Professor Palliser. 'Well,' he said, 'we've spent twenty-four hours on it and here's the result.' He read from a paper.

'1. It is of no known substance.
2. It answers to no re-agents.
3. It can be multiplied by division without diminution of the original.
4. It can move and cause movement from point to point, without leaving any consciousness of passage through intervening space.
5. It can cause disappearance—possibly in time.'
'Certainly in time,' Palliser said, but Sir Giles shook his head.
'Only possibly,' he answered, 'we don't know that your bright young pathological specimen has gone back in time; we only know he isn't here and the Stone is. I thought you told a very good story this morning to that mother of his.'

'I don't like it,' Palliser answered seriously. 'It's all very disturbing. I suppose the police will be coming here soon.'

'I should think certainly,' Sir Giles agreed. 'But I heard him say good night. And there's no reason why you should murder him—I suppose there isn't?—and no way for you to do it. So I can't see that you're likely to be troubled seriously. And anyhow they haven't got a body nor any trace of one. Let's get on with the inquiry.'

'I expect you're right,' the Professor said. 'What do you think we ought to do next?'

Sir Giles leaned forward. 'If this assistant of yours has moved in time,' he said, 'if he has gone back, wherever he's gone to, I suppose he might have gone forward instead?'

'I suppose so,' Palliser assented slowly.

'Then that seems to be the next thing,' Sir Giles said. 'But that I think we shall have to do ourselves. We can't run any risk of giving too much away. And, I don't see any chance of being permanently lost there because the future must be the present some time.'

'All the same, I shouldn't go too far at first,' Palliser suggested. 'A quarter of an hour, say.'

Sir Giles took a Stone from the table, and was about to speak when Palliser suddenly went on. 'Look here, Tumulty, if it worked that way, it wouldn't be a certainty, would it? Supposing I project myself an hour forward and find I'm sitting in this room—and then suppose I return to the present and go to my bedroom and have myself locked in for two hours, say, how can I be doing what I saw myself doing? And the shorter the time the more chance of proving it wrong. In six days anything might happen, but in six minutes…'

Sir Giles brooded. 'You probably wouldn't remember,' he pointed out. 'But I like the idea of your defying the future, Palliser. Try it and see.' Palliser's tall lean form quivered with excitement. 'It would snap the chain,' he said. 'We should know we weren't the mere mechanisms of Fate. We should be free.'

'I sometimes think,' Sir Giles answered reflectively, 'that I'm the only real scientist in this whole crawling hotbed of vermin called England. There isn't one of all of you that doesn't cuddle some fantastic desire in his heart, and snivel over every chance of letting it out for an hour's toddle. Do be intelligent, Palliser. How can any damned happening break the chain of happenings? Why do you want to be free? What good could you do if you were free?'

'If a man can defeat the result of all the past,' the Professor said, 'if he can know what is to be and cause that it shall not be——'

'O you're drunk,' said Sir Giles frankly. 'You're drunk with your own romantic gin-and-bitters. If you're going to be sitting here in an hour's time you're going to be, even if this bit of prehistoric slime has to bump you on your crazy noddle and shove you into a chair all on its own. But try it, try it and see.'

'Well, you try it too,' Palliser said sullenly. 'I'm going to keep you under my eye, Tumulty. None of your kidnapping games for me.'

'You romantics are always so suspicious,' Sir Giles said. 'But for once I don't mind. Let's try it together. Where's the Crown?'

Palliser took it out of the old safe in which it had rested all night, and sat down beside Tumulty. 'How long do we make it?' he asked. 'Half an hour?'

'Good enough,' Sir Giles answered. 'You locked the door? Right. Now—where's the clock? Half-past eleven. Wait. Let me write it on a bit of paper—so, and put that on the table. What's the formula?'

'To be as we shall be at twelve o'clock, I suppose,' Palliser said, and the two—Palliser wearing the Crown, Sir Giles clutching the Stone—framed the wish in their minds.

' … though I don't suppose I can tell you anything new,' Palliser ended, looking at the police inspector.

Sir Giles looked round over his shoulder—he was standing by the window—but he was only half-attending. Had or had not the experiment succeeded? He couldn't remember a thing out of the ordinary. He had sat with Palliser for what seemed a long time—but which the clock had shown to be only ten minutes, and had been vaguely conscious of a rather sick feeling somewhere. And then they had looked at one another and Palliser had abruptly said, 'Well?' He had stirred and stood up, looked at the slip of paper with '11.30' written on it, looked at the clock which marked twenty to twelve, looked back at Palliser, and said with some irritation, 'God blast the whole damned thing to hell, I don't know.'

'What do you mean?' or something like it, Palliser had asked. The picture was becoming fainter, but roughly he could still fill it in. Every minute made all that had happened in that half hour more of a memory; but had it happened at all or was it memory to begin with? And was what was happening now actually happening or was it merely foresight?

Sir Giles in a burst of anger and something remarkably like alarm, realized that he didn't know.

He remembered the knocking, the caretaker, the entrance of the inspector to whom Palliser was talking—very well the Professor was doing, Sir Giles thought, only he probably hadn't realized the difficulty; he wouldn't, not with that kind of cancer-eaten sponge he called an intellect. 'But I *remember*,' Tumulty thought impatiently. 'How the hell could I remember if it hadn't happened? There'd be nothing to remember.' He plunged deeper. 'But at twelve I should remember. Then if it's come off—I remember what hasn't happened. I'm in a delusion. I'm mad. Nonsense. I'm in the twelve state of consciousness. But the twelve state couldn't be unless the eleven to twelve state had been. Am I here or am I sitting in that blasted chair of Palliser's knowing it from outside time?'

He had a feeling that there was another corollary just round the corner of his mind and strained to find it. But it avoided him for the moment. He looked over his shoulder to find that the inspector was going, and as soon as the departure was achieved rushed across the room to Palliser. 'Now,' he said, 'what *has* happened? O never mind about your fly-blown policeman. *What has happened?*'

'Nothing has happened,' Palliser said staring. 'It evidently doesn't work in the future.'

'You seem jolly sure about it,' Sir Giles said. 'How do you *know*? You wanted to be as you would be at twelve, didn't you? Well, how do you know you're not? You seem to remember, I know; so do I.'

'Well then,' Palliser argued—'Yes, I see what you mean. This is merely knowledge—premature knowledge? Umph. Well, let's return to eleven-thirty.' He took a step towards the safe, but Sir Giles caught him by the wrist. 'Don't do that, you fool,' he said. 'Why the hell didn't I see it before? If you once go back, you'll bind yourself to go on doing the same thing—you *must*.'

Palliser sat down abruptly and the two looked at each other. 'But you said the present would be bound to become the future,' he objected.

'I know I did,' Sir Giles almost howled at him. 'But don't you see, you fool, that the action of return must be made at the starting-point? That's why your oyster-stomached helot vanished; that's the trick that's caught you now. I won't be caught; there must be a way out and I'll find it.'

'Look here, Tumulty,' Palliser said, 'let's keep calm and think it out. What do you mean by the action of return being made at the starting-point?'

'O God,' Sir Giles moaned, 'to be fastened to a man who doesn't know how to ask his mother for milk! I mean that you must condition your experiment from without and not from within; you must define your movement before you make it or your definition will be controlled by it. You can say *I will go and return in such and such a manner*, but if you only say *I will go* your return is ruled by sequence. Can't you think, Palliser?'

'Then we *are* in the future?' Palliser said, 'and we can't go back to live that half-hour? Well, does it very much matter?'

'If we are,' Sir Giles said, 'we—O it's no good trying to explain to you.' He began to walk about and then went back to the chair in which he had been sitting originally and stared at it. 'Now am I there?' he asked grimly, 'or am I here?'

There was a silence of some minutes. Then Palliser said again, 'I still can't see why you're so excited. That half-hour wasn't of any importance, surely?'

Sir Giles, having reached his limit of exasperation, became unexpectedly gentle. He went back to Palliser and said almost sweetly, 'Well, don't worry over it, don't hurt your brain, but just try and follow. If this is a forecast in consciousness, that consciousness is, so to speak, housed somewhere. And it's housed in your body. And where's your body? And how do you get your mind-time and your body-time to agree?'

'My body is here,' Palliser said, patting it.

'O no,' Sir Giles said, still sweetly. 'At least perhaps it is and perhaps it isn't. Perhaps all this is occupying a millionth part of a second and we're still sitting there.'

'But Pondon disappeared?' Palliser objected, 'into his past, I suppose? Mayn't we have disappeared into our future?'

'I hope we have,' Sir Giles assented. 'But we seem to remember—or to know—what happened, don't we? We seem to know that we talked and the police came and so on? Did it happen or has it got to happen or hasn't it happened and will it never happen? If we will to return we seem to me—but of course I'm a little child crooning on your knee—to be in a constant succession of the same period. And if we don't?'

'Well, we go on,' the Professor said.

'Till we become conscious of death?' Sir Giles asked. 'And then what happens? Till these apparent bodies die and corrupt and our minds return to our real bodies and live it again—is that the truth? Years and years and years and all in less than a second and all to be repeated—do you like it, Palliser?'

'But Pondon disappeared,' the Professor said again.

'You keep on repeating that,' Sir Giles told him. 'Don't you see, you cow, that the conditions may be different? Whatever the past is, it has been in everyone's knowledge; whatever the future is it hasn't.'

'What do you propose to do about it, anyhow?' the Professor asked.

Sir Giles considered. 'I propose to think over it for a few days,' he said, 'and see if I can think of any formula to find out, first where that assistant of yours is and secondly where we are. Also to see if Whitehall is doing anything, because I'm not going to be taken by surprise by *them*, not under present conditions. So I shall go back to London this afternoon.'

All the way to Euston—he didn't want to use the Stone again at the moment—Tumulty brooded over the problem that confronted him. He devised several formulæ for getting into touch with the unfortunate Mr. Pondon; the most obvious experiment—that of willing him back—had been tried by himself and the Professor on the previous evening without success. It seemed that the Stone could not be used to control others; its action was effective only over the action of whoever held it. Sir Giles regretted this rather keenly; the possibility of disarranging other people's lives had appeared to him a desirable means of experiment, since he was on the whole reluctant to conduct experiments on himself. That state of being which lies between mysticism, madness, and romanticism, had always been his chosen field, but it was a field in which few suitable subjects grew. He found it impossible not to desire to be able to dispose of objectionable people by removing them to some past state of being, and he almost sent a telegram to Palliser urging him to acquaint Mrs. Pondon and the police with the facts of the case and to inquire whether the police 'in the execution of their duty' would be bound to follow the vanished assistant to the day before yesterday. Pondon had certainly gone of his own free will, even if his superior had refrained from explaining the possibilities clearly enough. However, Pondon could wait a few days. That morning, Sir Giles had noticed in their short interview, he had cut himself while shaving; it afforded Tumulty a certain pleasure to think of that small cut being repeated again and again until he himself had time, inclination, and knowledge to interfere. But the other problem worried him more considerably. That missing half hour haunted him; had he lived through it or had he not, and if he had not could even the Stone release him from the necessity of doing so?

He began to wonder if the Stone could help him, but he didn't see how, unless it could present thoughts to his mind—or to other people's. If there was someone he could trust to tell him what could be learnt from such a trial of the Stone? He thought of Lord Arglay, a trained and detached, and not unsympathetic, mind. Palliser was no good because Palliser was mixed up with it. And you couldn't go to everyone asking them to help you look for half an hour you had mislaid. Also Arglay would know if Whitehall were moving—not that he minded very much if it were.

At Euston he took a taxi to the Chief Justice's.

Lord Arglay's Saturday afternoon therefore broke suddenly into activity. Some time after tea, while he was playing with the idea of bringing *Organic Law* into the Stone's sphere of activity, though he felt certain the Hajji would disapprove of any such use, he was startled by the announcement that Mrs. Sheldrake had called. 'Miss Burnett is with her, sir,' the maid added.

'Now what on earth,' Lord Arglay said as he went to the drawing-room, 'is Chloe doing with Mrs. Sheldrake? How did she get hold of her, I wonder? and has she brought her here to be instructed or to be frightened?'

It soon appeared however that if anyone were frightened it was Chloe herself. Mrs. Sheldrake took the conversation into her own hands, with a brief explanation of her connection with the Stone and a light reference to the fact that it had been, for the moment, mislaid. She wanted to know, since Miss Burnett had mentioned Lord Arglay several times, whether he claimed any rights in the Stone.

'Not in that particular Type,' Lord Arglay said.

'Type, Lord Arglay?' Cecilia asked. 'How do you mean—Type?'

'The position is a little obscure,' the Chief Justice said, considering rapidly Mrs. Sheldrake's appearance and manner, Mr. Sheldrake's riches and position (which he had looked up), and the desirability of subduing them both without antagonism. 'I say Type because the Stones which exist—and there are several—are apparently derivations from one Original, though (and perhaps therefore) possessed of the same powers. But how far they are to be regarded as being identical with it, for proprietary reasons, I cannot at the moment say. Nor in whom the title to the property inheres. I may add that certain foreign representatives are deeply interested, and the Government is observing matters. I think that in the present situation your husband should preserve the utmost secrecy and caution. His title appears to me uncertain, both so far as the acquisition of his Type is concerned and in the relation of that Type to the Original.'

He delivered this with occasional pauses for meditation and with a slight pomposity which he put on at necessary moments. Mrs. Sheldrake, a little impressed, nevertheless appeared to receive it with frigidity.

'But Lord Arglay,' she said, 'we can't be expected to sit quiet while other people use our property in order to ruin our companies. I am thinking of the effect it may have on Atlantic Airways. What is this original you are talking about?'

'It is the centre of the derivations,' Lord Arglay said at random, but ridiculously enough the phrase in Chloe's mind suddenly connected itself with 'the End of Desire.' The chance and romantic words came to her like a gospel, none the less emotionally powerful that at the moment she didn't understand it. What were the derivations? She had a vague feeling that the sentence suggested Lord Arglay himself as the centre though she knew he would have been the first to mock at the ascription. But there was certainly something in them that referred, if not to him, then to something connected with him. He was walking on some firm pavement, where she wanted to be walking too.

She came back to hear Mrs. Sheldrake end a sentence—'opinion on it.'

'Madam,' Lord Arglay said, 'it must be clear to you that I can give no opinion until a case is before the Court. I am not a solicitor or a barrister. I am the Chief Justice.'

'But we must know what to *do*,' Mrs. Sheldrake said. 'Don't you even know where the original, whatever it is, came from?'

Lord Arglay suppressed a desire to offer her a précis of the Hajji's history of the Stone of Suleiman, and leaned forward.

'Mrs. Sheldrake,' he said, 'by the folly of my nephew you have come into actual—if not legal—possession of a Type of a Stone which is said to be regarded by millions as a very holy relic, and the ownership of which may have the most important repercussions. I beg you to act with great care. I venture to suggest that you should at least consider the propriety of giving it into my care until more is known and decided. It is, I know, an audacious proposal, but the seeming audacity is due to the anxiety with which I regard the situation. I am not speaking casually. I do not think it likely, but in certain remote yet not impossible circumstances I can believe that even your life and your husband's might be in danger. Consult with him and believe me that this warning is meant very, very seriously.'

'That,' he thought, 'ought to worry her.' She was staring at the ground now, and he threw a side glance at Chloe, whose face reinforced his words.

Cecilia felt baffled. She saw nothing to do at the moment but to talk to Angus and take other ways of finding out the mystery. As she began to shape a phrase of dubious farewell the door was thrown open and Sir Giles Tumulty came in. He nodded to Arglay and stared at the visitors.

'Busy, Arglay?' he asked. 'I want to talk to you.'

'I want to talk to *you*,' the Chief Justice said, with something in his voice that made Chloe look up suddenly and even distracted Cecilia, to whom he turned. 'I can do no more for you now, Mrs. Sheldrake,' he ended.

'It's very unsatisfactory,' she complained. 'I almost think I had better go to the Ambassador. You see, we don't come under your jurisdiction, if that's what you call it. We belong to the States.'

'Quite,' Lord Arglay said, waiting for her to go.

'After all someone must know to whom the Stone belongs, and who can or can't sell it,' Cecilia went on.

'Hallo,' Sir Giles said, 'have you got one too? Is this yours, Arglay, or is it Reginald's? I hope you didn't overcharge for it.'

Cecilia almost leaped at him. 'O,' she said, 'I'm afraid I don't know your name, but can you tell me anything about this Stone? It's all so very mysterious. We—my husband and I—bought it from a Mr. Montague, and now we are told it's very doubtful whether he had the right to sell it.'

'Of course he had the right,' Sir Giles said. 'I gave him one yesterday morning.'

'Was it yours then to begin with?' Cecilia asked.

'Certainly,' Sir Giles said. 'Does anyone deny it?'

'Yes,' Lord Arglay said, 'and you know they do.'

'O a set of religious maniacs,' Sir Giles tossed them aside. 'Do you, Arglay?'

The Chief Justice paused for a half second, then his training won.

'No,' he said, 'I don't deny it for I don't know. But I want to talk to you about it, Tumulty, after this lady has gone.' He felt it was rude but he couldn't help it. A more urgent matter than Mrs. Sheldrake's trouble was obsessing him. That she had actually lost the Stone he had not understood; her references to that part of the adventure had been so general as to leave the impression that her husband was finding it just as she set off with Chloe.

Now she retaliated by turning her back full on him and saying to Tumulty: 'I should like to talk with you, Sir Giles. Could you spare me half an hour at Grosvenor Square?'

Sir Giles's first impulse was to tell her to go to hell. But he felt that Lord Arglay had changed in something; his previous good temper had gone. Tumulty had been through too many dangerous experiences in remote parts of the world not to recognize hostility when he met it, and he knew that Arglay was hostile now. Why he couldn't imagine but that was the fact. If Arglay was going to turn nasty it might be as well to be in with this woman, whoever she was. If she had bought the Stone there must be money and therefore power and probably position, and perhaps a counterweight to the Chief Justice's enmity. Not that it mattered very much; he wasn't going to spend any time shooting at Arglay with any possible kind of inconvenient elephant rifle. But obviously these two weren't on the best of terms, and Sir Giles's generally diffused contempt suddenly crystallized in a definite hatred of this large man looming in front of him. He accepted a card, refused to make a definite promise; he wasn't going to be rung up as if he were her chauffeur—but said something about ringing up, and with a malicious benevolence got rid of her. She departed, her mind stabilized by his brusque assurance that she had an entire right to her Stone. Chloe half rose; Lord Arglay waved her back. Sir Giles flung himself into a chair. 'Now,' he said, 'what's *your* trouble, Arglay—that is, if it's fit for your … secretary … to hear.' It was the minutest pause before 'secretary'; both his hearers remarked it, and neither of them took any notice of it.

'I want to know,' Arglay said, 'what you've been doing at Birmingham.'

Genuinely surprised, Sir Giles stared at him. 'But that's exactly what I want to tell you,' he said. 'I want you to find out, one way or another, what *has* happened.'

'I promise you I will do that,' Arglay answered. 'But you shall tell me first what you have done.'

'Don't talk to me like that,' Sir Giles snapped back. 'You're not in your bestial Law Courts now. Palliser and I made an experiment this morning, and I'm not at all clear——'

'I want to know,' Arglay interrupted, 'about your experiment last night.'

More and more astonished, Sir Giles sat up. 'Last night?' he said, 'what do you know about last night? Not that there's anything particular to know. You're not interested in Palliser's kindergarten school, are you?'

'Who was the man you gave the Stone to?' the Chief Justice insisted, 'and what happened to him?'

'Now how do you know all that?' Sir Giles said meditatively. 'God strike you dead, Arglay, have you been spying on me with that blasted bit of dried dung? You have, have you? So it does do something with knowledge. Good, that's what I wanted to know. Now listen. This morning Palliser and I——'

'What happened to the man last night?' Lord Arglay said again.

'O how the hell do I know?' Sir Giles said fretfully. 'That's part of the whole thing. You can have him—I don't want him. He's probably messing round last week—no, we said twelve hours so he won't be. As a matter of fact I thought he might come back in another twelve but we were there—at least, Palliser was—by nine this morning and he hadn't. But you can go and look for him. Only I want you to tell me first whether I'm here or not.' He succeeded in outlining his problem.

In spite of himself Lord Arglay was held by it.

'But so far as I'm concerned, it's certainly you—the normal corporeal sequential you I'm talking to,' he said. 'I've not missed half an hour.'

'I know *that*,' Sir Giles moaned. 'I know that what's happening now is happening to you. But I don't know whether I'm knowing it all first of all. It's this damned silly business of only actually experiencing the smallest minimum of time and all the rest being memory that does me in. I know it was memory at twelve o'clock but if I'd lived through it all it would still be memory. O for God's sake, Arglay, don't be as big a fool as Palliser. I suppose you've got *some* brains; after all they made you Chief Justice. And if you can see what happened in Birmingham last night you can see what happened there this morning. You needn't be afraid; we can define the whole thing first of all, so you're bound to come back all right.'

'I will do nothing at all,' Lord Arglay said, 'until I have done what I can for your——' he paused on the word 'victim' which sounded theatrical. 'And even then,' he said, slurring it, 'I do not know what I can do, for I do not think this Stone was meant to be used to save such men as you from the consequences of their actions.'

'What *do* you think it was meant for?' Sir Giles said. 'And not so much of this infant school Scripture lesson. I'd see your inside torn out, Arglay, before I asked you to save me. I want to know what *does* happen and if you won't tell me the nearest warder in the Zoological Gardens will do as well.'

'Then you can go and ask him,' Lord Arglay said, recovering something of his good temper, partly because he began to discern that, somehow or other, the unfortunate assistant might be given a chance of return, and partly because he did not dislike seeing Sir Giles really thwarted. 'I'm not going to do a thing without very great care. And you'd better take care what you do because, if you're right, you'll have to do it all again.'

'O my lord God Almighty,' Sir Giles said, 'can't you see that, *if* I'm right, I can't choose till next time? You are a louse-brained catalept, Arglay.' His interest in pure thought vanished and his personal concern returned. 'So you're not going to do anything, aren't you?' he said.

'Not for a day or two,' Lord Arglay said. 'It'll do you all the good in the world, Giles, to be a little uncertain of yourself. Well, you can't object to that way of putting it, surely; you are exactly a little uncertain of yourself, aren't you?'

Sir Giles said nothing. He sat for a minute or two gazing at the Chief Justice, then he got up, and with a conversational, 'Well, well, well,' walked straight out of the room. Lord Arglay looked at Chloe.

'I refrain from saying "Curiouser and curiouser,"' he said, 'but I can't think of anything else to say. The efficient Giles has been caught. How just a compensation! The Stone is a very marvellous thing.' His voice, even on the words, changed into gravity. 'And now,' he went on, 'suppose you tell me what did happen this afternoon.'

When she had done so—'Then for all we know one of them is lying about the English country-side?' the Chief Justice said. 'Pleasant hearing for our friend the Hajji. And now for my experiments.' He went over his experiences of the previous evening.

'So,' he ended, 'we know it moves in time and space and thought. And in what else?'

'But what else is there?' Chloe said.

'The Hajji talked of the Transcendence,' Lord Arglay answered. 'But who knows what he meant or if what he meant is so?'

Chloe said, almost with pain, 'But what do *you* think he meant?'

'Child,' Lord Arglay said, 'I am an old man and I have known nothing all my life farther or greater than the work I have taken to do. I have never seen a base for any temple nor found an excuse to believe in the myths that are told there. I will not say *believe* or *do not believe*. But there is one thing only of which I have wondered at times, and yet it seemed foolish to think of it. It will happen sometimes when one has worked hard and done all that one can for the purpose before one—it has happened then that I have stood up and been content with the world of things and with what has been done there through me. And this may be pride, or it may be the full stress of the whole being and delight in labour—there are a hundred explanations. But I have wondered whether that profound repose was not communicated from some far source and whether the life that is in it was altogether governed by time. And I am sure that state never comes while I am concerned with myself, and I have thought to-day that in some strange way that state was itself the Stone. But if so then assuredly none of these men shall find its secret.'

'Is that the end of desire?' Chloe said.

'I have no desire left at all,' Lord Arglay said, 'but I think that other is the better ending of desire. And though I cannot tell how you should seek for it, I think it waits for everyone who will have it. Also I think that perhaps the Stone chooses more than we know; and yet that is a fantasy, is it not?'

'*Was* there a stone in the Crown of Suleiman?' she said, 'and was Suleiman the wisest of men?'

'So they say,' Lord Arglay answered. 'And will you seek for wisdom in the Stone?'

'What is wisdom?' Chloe said.

'And that, child,' Lord Arglay answered again, 'though I am an interpreter of all the laws of England, I do not know.'

CHAPTER VII
THE MIRACLES AT RICH

Half-way down the stairs Mrs. Pentridge and Oliver Doncaster began to realize that someone was knocking, loudly and continuously, at the door. But the spectacle of Mrs. Ferguson in front of them, progressing, in the dressing gown which she had put on, from stair to stair with an alertness which her age, to say nothing of her paralysis, would have seemed to forbid, so occupied and distracted them that it was with reluctance that Mrs. Pentridge at last rushed to open, and with delight that she said, hastily returning, 'It's for you, sir.'

'Eh?' said Oliver, 'me? O nonsense! O damn!' He remembered the lunatic who wanted the stone, and strode across. 'Hallo,' he said, 'O it *is* you! Well, yes; yes, I'm sorry, but we're in a bit of a confusion just now owing to a paralyzed old lady suddenly skipping like the high hills. Could you wait a few minutes or go and have a drink or something?'

'No, I couldn't,' Sheldrake said. 'You've made me come all this way and given me all this trouble, and now you talk to me about an old woman. An old woman won't stop you giving me my stone.'

'By the way, what did I do with it?' Doncaster asked vaguely. 'I know I had it a few minutes ago. Now what—I remember, I was showing it to Mrs. Ferguson when she began to curvet. I wonder if she dropped it somewhere.'

Sheldrake swore under his breath, then ceased as an incredible idea came into his mind. 'Who's Mrs. Ferguson?' he asked.

'Mrs. Ferguson is my landlady's mother,' Doncaster said. 'Who having been in bed to my knowledge since just before I came last year is now jazzing like a two-year-old. Peep round the door. Well, you don't suppose I'm going to interrupt her by asking for my—I mean your—at least I mean you said your—pebble, do you? Bless her, she's like a child at a Sunday school treat.'

Sheldrake became more and more uneasy. If this infernal old woman—if the Stone could cure—if it got about——'Look here,' he said quite untruly to Oliver, 'I've got to get on to London and I want to take my property with me. A joke's a joke, but——'

'And a jubilee's a jubilee,' Oliver said. 'Still, I see your point. Well, wait a minute——Good heavens, she's going out.'

Mrs. Ferguson indeed was coming straight to the door. When she reached it Oliver pulled Sheldrake aside. 'Still feeling better, Mrs. Ferguson?' he asked.

'Much better, thank you, sir,' the old lady said. 'But I feel as if I could do with a little fresh air, and if it looked a nice evening I was thinking I'd just pop along and see my sister Annie. I haven't seen much of her this year owing to her asthma and my not being able to get out. Mary, my dear,' she added to Mrs. Pentridge, 'I think I'll dress.'

'O mother,' said Mrs. Pentridge, 'do you think you ought to go out? Suppose you were taken bad again?'

Mrs. Ferguson smiled serenely. 'I shan't be taken bad,' she said, 'I never felt better in all my life. And I owe it all to you, Mr. Doncaster,' she added.

'Me?' said the surprised Oliver.

'I felt the strength just pouring into me from that stone you gave me, sir,' Mrs. Ferguson assured him. 'I've got it tight. You don't want it back this minute, do you, sir?'

'Certainly not, Mrs. Ferguson,' Doncaster said promptly. 'Keep it an hour or two and see how you feel.'

'O nonsense,' Sheldrake broke in,—'look here, Mrs.——'

'Shut up,' said Oliver. 'That's all right, Mrs. Ferguson. Carry on.'

'I won't shut up,' Sheldrake shouted. 'What the hell do you think you're doing, throwing other people's property about?'

'How do I know it's your property?' Oliver shouted back. 'I pick a bit of stone out of a hedge and you pop up out of a sound sleep and say your wife threw it there and will I give it back? Who are you, anyhow?'

'My name is Sheldrake, Angus M. Sheldrake,' the other answered. 'I'm the chairman of Atlantic Airways and half a dozen other things. I gave seventy thousand pounds for that stone and I want it back at once.'

'Then you won't get it back at once,' Oliver retorted, 'not if you were the chairman of the Atlantic, Pacific, Indian, Arctic, and Antarctic air, sea, and land ways, and the Tube railways too. Not if you offered me another seventy thousand—at least, you might then. I don't know, so don't tempt me. Or rather do, so that I can say, "Keep your dross." Start with fifty thousand, and go up by fives.'

'By God,' Sheldrake said, 'I'll have you all in prison for this.'

'Don't be a fool,' Oliver answered crossly. 'Go and wake up Job Ricketts and tell him to arrest old Mrs. Ferguson for stealing your stone. I should like to see you explaining.'

The quarrel raged in this manner until Mrs. Ferguson, cloak and bonnet on, came to the door to start. 'Is it the gentleman's stone, sir?' she asked anxiously.

'He doesn't know, I don't know,' Oliver told her. 'Get you along, Mrs. Ferguson, but don't let it go out of your possession. I call everybody to witness,' he said loudly, addressing Mrs. Ferguson, Mrs. Pentridge, Sheldrake, the chauffeur, and the villagers who were beginning to collect, 'that Mrs. Ruth Ferguson retains the property in question—namely, a stone—on my instructions until I am satisfied of the bona-fides of the claimant, one Angus M. Sheldrake on his own confession. There,' he added to Sheldrake.

'What the devil do you suppose is the good of that?' Sheldrake said furiously.

'I don't really know,' Oliver said comfortably, 'but it creates a right impression, don't you think?'

'But do you expect me to prove the whole bally thing to any fool who stops me in the street or any pickpocket who sneaks it?' Sheldrake raged.

'To be accurate, it was you who stopped me and wanted to pick my pocket—in effect,' Oliver said. 'And we might as well spend the next two or three hours proving your bona-fides as not, don't you think?'

'I'm not going to let that woman out of my sight,' Sheldrake said. 'Where she goes I go.'

'Her people shall be thy people and her gods thy gods,' Oliver murmured. 'Sudden conversion of a millionaire. The call of the old home. Way down on the Swanee River. O Dixie, my Dixie, our fearful trip is done.'

'O go to the devil,' Sheldrake said, leaping back to his car. 'Barnes, follow that damned old woman in the black bonnet.'

'Yes, sir,' the chauffeur said obediently, and the procession started—Mrs. Ferguson and Mrs. Pentridge in front, Oliver strolling a few paces behind, the car rolling along in the road, parallel to him, and an increasing crowd of villagers, dissolving, reforming, chattering and exclaiming as the astonishing news spread. Rather owing to this tumultuous concourse than to any weakness on Mrs. Ferguson's part it took them an hour to reach the mile-distant town of Rich-by-the-Mere, commonly called Rich, where Mrs. Ferguson's asthmatic sister lived. By the time they reached her street the crowd was a mob, the car was doing the best it could among the excited groups, and Oliver had been pushed forward on to Mrs. Ferguson's heels. The old lady knocked at the door, which was opened in a minute, and there followed immediately a loud scream.

'Ruth!' cried a voice.

'All right, Annie,' Mrs. Ferguson was heard to protest and the excitement in the crowd grew louder.

Sheldrake felt almost off his head with anger, despair, and doubt. He had realized during the slow crawl that to go to the police would be to broadcast the rumours of the Stone, but what was to happen he could not guess. That he would recover it he had no real doubt, but he wanted to recover it quietly and get out of England with it at the earliest possible moment. He peered out of the car to see Oliver, his back against the door of the house, giving a dramatic description of Mrs. Ferguson's recovery to as many of the crowd as could hear him; he saw, remotely, the helmets of one or two policemen approaching slowly; he saw windows and doors open all round and new conversations leaping up every moment; he even discerned one or two members of the crowd scribbling in small notebooks, and dropped back with an oath. But he sat up again in a moment and managed to attract Oliver's attention, who slid through the crowd to the car.

'Look here,' he said, 'this is past a joke. I apologize if I was rude. I can prove anything you want me to. But as a matter of fact the stone does belong to me, and I must rely on you to get it back. You believe me, don't you?'

'I do really,' Oliver said. 'You were a bit uppish, you know, but I don't understand what's happened. Of course, it's all nonsense about the stone healing her, but as things have turned out we shall have to go gently. We can't have the poor old thing pushed back into bed because we take it away brutally. Leave it to me and I'll get it back for you to-night. Where do you live?'

Angus told him. Oliver grimaced. 'A bit of a way,' he said, 'but I suppose it was my fault. Well, I'll try and collect it gently to-night or to-morrow morning.'

'Excuse me, sir,' a voice beside him said, 'but can you tell me whether it's true that an old lady has been cured of cancer by a piece of magnetic iron? Does it belong to you or to this other gentleman? And is it true that she   '

Oliver and Sheldrake stared at each other. Suddenly Oliver looked round. Out of the window of the house Mrs. Pentridge was leaning.

'O Mr. Doncaster,' she called, 'do please come. Auntie's asthma's gone. It went in the middle of a cough. O do come.'

The noise broke out deafeningly. Mr. Sheldrake flung himself down in the car, and the small reporter fought his way beside Oliver to the door.

The next morning they all read it. Chloe at Highgate in a paper purchased when she saw the placards, Lord Arglay at Lancaster Gate in the *Observer*, Sir Giles at Ealing in his housekeeper's *Sunday Pictorial*, Professor Palliser at Birmingham in the *Sunday Times*, Reginald at Brighton (though this was purely by accident, in a paper he picked up in the smoking-room of his hotel). It was even stated long afterwards, in a volume of memoirs, that at Sandringham the Majesty of England, augustly chatting with Lord Birlesmere (the Minister in attendance), the Persian Ambassador, and the author of the memoirs, had graciously deigned to remark that it was a very extraordinary affair. In the papers, Lourdes, the King's Evil, the Early Christians, Mrs. Eddy, Mesmer, and other famous healers were introduced and, almost, invoked. For the scenes in Rich all night had been such 'as to baffle description.' Once it had been understood that this impossible thing was happening, that health was being restored, and that so simply, so immediately, the house was almost rushed before the police could guard it. The two old ladies—Mrs. Ferguson and her sister—with Mrs. Pentridge were rushed up the stairs by Oliver, who, with one policeman by him, stationed himself near the top, exhorting, arguing, fighting. The crowd in the street was, with usual and immediate sympathy, continually dividing to let cripples through or the blind and the deaf. Many came rushing to borrow the Stone for the sick who could not come. Sheldrake's car, opposite the front-door, was turned into a kind of Grand Stand. By midnight the whole place was in a tumult. The loss of the Stone itself became an imminent danger. Sheldrake was continually telling the police that it belonged to him; the police were concerned with more difficult matters. But the reporters had it. 'The Stone,' they all declared, 'was said to belong to Mr. Angus M. Sheldrake, the well-known …' and so on. It was known all over England on that Sunday morning that Mr. Angus M. Sheldrake owned—whether at the moment he actually possessed was a little doubtful—a miraculous Stone which healed all illnesses at a mere wish.

'Well, really,' Lord Arglay said to himself, 'Reginald seems to have done it this time.'

Reginald was much of the same opinion. But neither he nor anyone else of those concerned had any idea what to do next. The Persian Ambassador took advantage of the afternoon quiet at Sandringham to point out to Lord Birlesmere that if this were true, and if it were due to the relic of which he had spoken, and if the news were telegraphed abroad the most serious consequences might ensue. Lord Birlesmere took note of his Excellency's communication, and, later on, got through to Rivington Court on the telephone. He had met Sheldrake two or three times and Angus came to speak. But when he understood that the Foreign Secretary was hinting at a personal interview he gave a little laugh.

'My dear Lord Birlesmere,' he said, 'I couldn't if I would. Not without a couple of thousand soldiers and machine guns. They're all round the place, camping in the grounds, knocking at the doors. Every town in the district has discharged its halt and maimed here, and they all want me to heal them.'

'And do you?' Lord Birlesmere asked, fascinated by the idea.

'What?' said Mr. Sheldrake.

'But aren't,' Lord Birlesmere went on, changing the subject, 'aren't the County Authorities doing anything?'

'They've drafted all the police that they have to spare,' Sheldrake told him, 'and they're communicating with London. But it doesn't look as if that would help me till to-morrow.'

'I'll talk to the Home Office people,' Birlesmere said. 'You won't mind promising not to leave England or get rid of the Stone till I've seen you?'

Sheldrake hesitated. His chief wish was to get out of England with the Stone; on the other hand his chances of doing so in the face of an antagonistic Foreign Office were small, and he was conscious that there were certain crises in which the Foreign Office would offer no strings for him to pull—the ends would all discreetly disappear. He did not completely understand why the Foreign Office was interfering at all; the Stone hardly seemed to be their pigeon. He had gathered from Cecilia when she returned the night before, or rather when he had himself returned that morning, that the Government was mixed up with it; and of course the Stone was said to have come from abroad. Still——

'Well,' he said, 'if you'll get me out of this at once I don't mind promising to see you before I leave.'

'But can't you really get away?' Lord Birlesmere asked.

It seemed to him inconceivable that any crowd could really prison a man in his own country house, but that was because he had never seen it happen. The concourse round Mr. Sheldrake's front-door, between that and the garage, trying to look in, and even to get in, at the windows, continually flowing in through the gates, occupying the lawns, the terraces, and the gardens, consisted of more people than Lord Birlesmere had seen in all his life. They were quiet while they were not interfered with, in an uncertain quiet. They doubted whether it was much good their coming. They might, before evening, disperse from sheer discouragement and hunger; but the one or two attempts made by an insufficient band of police to shift them had merely produced irritation and, once or twice, something like serious trouble.

Lord Birlesmere, discovering all this by gentle questioning, at last, with some sort of qualified promise, put the receiver back and stared at it. Soldiers were all very well, but the Government was shaky enough, and what would the Opposition papers say if he used the Army to hold back a crowd of suffering English men and women from their chance of healing, and to ensure the escape of an American millionaire with the source of healing in his possession? The Opposition would know, as well as Mr. Sheldrake, as well as Lord Birlesmere himself, that the idea of the Stone doing anything was rubbish. He wished the Prime Minister was in London, but he wasn't; he was in Aberdeen. The best thing was obviously to get Sheldrake quietly to London—perhaps later the crowd would disperse a bit—and then there was this Sir Giles Tumulty the Persian Ambassador had mentioned—an interview there. What on earth had Bruce Cumberland been doing, if anything? The thought of the Ambassador suggested to Lord Birlesmere that it might be just as well if he did not learn too much from the Persian; he didn't want to be put too clearly in possession of the views of a friendly Government. Sheldrake had certainly better be removed quietly. He took such measures as suggested themselves.

On the same Sunday evening the Hajji came round to Lord Arglay's house. The Chief Justice threw down the latest edition of a special evening paper and greeted him with a certain pretended cynicism. 'This, I suppose,' he said, 'is the evil you prophesied for the world—all this healing, I mean?'

'There is not a great deal of healing so far; there is a great deal of desire for healing,' Ibrahim answered. 'That may be an evil.'

'If Sheldrake gets off to America with it, there'll be an evil all right,' Lord Arglay said. 'I wouldn't be a bit surprised if they passed a special act to prevent him.'

'Can your Parliament do such things?' the Hajji asked.

'O rather,' Lord Arglay said. 'Prevention of Removal of Art Treasures, I should think. It'll take Sheldrake as long as we like to prove the Stone isn't an Art Treasure. Or they may claim that the sale is invalid because it never was Reginald's; only then you'd want a real claimant. And who could that be? Not me, obviously; not Giles—he wouldn't; not the Ambassador—they'd have to give it back to him.'

'You think they would not?' said the Hajji.

'I am absolutely and perfectly sure they would not,' Lord Arglay said. 'And really, Hajji, I don't know that I blame them. After all, it's not the kind of thing that any one man or family or country even ought to keep. I'm not at all sure it ought to be in existence at all, but after what I've seen I can't think how to destroy it. If you dropped it into the Atlantic I should be afraid of it floating to the Esquimaux or some such people. And it can't be left loose. Look at what happens when it is.'

'What then.' the Hajji said, 'do you think should be done with it?'

'I can't think,' Lord Arglay said. 'Unless the League of Nations? With a special international guard? No? I was afraid you wouldn't agree.'

'You are mocking at it and me,' the Hajji said.

'No, I'm not,' the Chief Justice assured him. 'I'm a little de-normally-mented about it. But I take it very seriously. When the English take anything very seriously they always become a trifle delirious. People tell you that we aren't logical, but it isn't true. Only our logic is a logic of poetry. We are the Tom o' Bedlam of the nations, the sceptics of the world, and we have no hope at all, or none to speak of—that is why we are always so good at adopting new ideas. Look at the way Reginald adopted the Stone.'

The Hajji went on looking at him gravely. 'And what are you going to do now?' he said.

'I'm in several minds,' Lord Arglay said. 'And one is to take the Stone and will myself wherever what you call its Types are and collect them all one by one, whether their present possessors agree or not, and then will myself inside Vesuvius with them all. And one is to go and look for this Pondon fellow. And another is to go and knock Giles on the head. That's three—and the fourth? The fourth is to take the Stone and will it to do what it will with me.'

'And that is the most dangerous of all,' the Hajji said.

'After all,' Arglay argued, 'if Miss Burnett seems to think she can get wisdom from it, why shouldn't I?'

'Does she?' the Hajji asked.

'No, of course she doesn't,' Lord Arglay said irritably. 'It was I who asked her that. Hajji, I'm just rambling. But what in God's name can we *do*?'

The Hajji brooded. 'I think that it only knows,' he said. 'But I dare not use it at all, because it is so great and terrible, and I do not think you believe in it enough for it to reveal its will. What of this friend of yours?'

'Who?' Lord Arglay said blankly.

'This Miss Burnett,' Ibrahim answered. 'Does she believe?'

Lord Arglay stared at him. 'What if she does? What can she believe *in*?' he said. 'Are you proposing to play some such trick on her as Giles did on Pondon? Because if so, Hajji, I may as well tell you I shall stop it. Besides, why do you think she'd find out?'

'If—no, it is impossible,' the Hajji said. 'But I dreamed that I saw the Name of Allah written on her forehead as it is written on the Stone. And it is certain that the way to the Stone is in the Stone.'

'Then,' Lord Arglay said, not unreasonably, 'why don't you take it?'

'Those of my house,' the Hajji answered reluctantly, 'who were of the Keepers have sworn always to guard and never to use the Relics they keep. Neither this nor a yet more sacred thing.'

'What else is there then?' Arglay asked.

'There is that which is in the Innermost,' the Hajji answered, 'that which controls all things. And I fear lest by the knowledge of the Stone any shall come to find this other thing. For it is said that even Asmodeus when he wore it sat on the throne of Suleiman ben Daood in Jerusalem, and if your Giles Tumulty——'

'I expect even Asmodeus was a gentleman compared with Giles,' Lord Arglay said. 'But seriously, Hajji, do you mean that there is something else behind? And if so what is it?'

'I must not tell you,' Ibrahim said.

'Quite,' Lord Arglay answered, half as a gibe, half as a submission. 'It's all very useful, isn't it? Well, Hajji, will you help me to find this Pondon man? Is there any particular formula?'

'I think you had need be careful,' Ibrahim answered. 'For if you will to return to the worlds that were you will not have the Stone with you.'

'Giles's idea seemed to be,' Lord Arglay said, 'that one could will to return to the past for ten minutes or so.'

'I do not see how you can bring this man back from the past without the Stone, and if you return to the past you will not have the Stone,' the Hajji said doubtfully. 'Besides, though you can return to your own past, I do not know whether you can return to his.'

'But why can't I go to him *now*,' Lord Arglay said, 'wherever he is *now*? Damn it, man, he must be somewhere*now*.'

'If you are right, he is nowhere at all *now*,' the Hajji said. 'He has not yet reached *now*. He is in yesterday.'

'O Lord!' the Chief Justice said. 'But he must be somewhere in space.'

'O in space he is no doubt here or there or anywhere,' Ibrahim answered. 'For yesterday's space is exactly where to-day's space is.'

'And to-morrow's also?' Lord Arglay said.

'I think that is true,' the Hajji told him. 'But to-morrow's exists only in a greater knowledge than ours and it can only be experienced in that diviner knowledge. Therefore to experience the future, though not perhaps to foresee the future, it is necessary to enter the soul of the world with the inward being.'

'Then Giles did not miss that half-hour?' Lord Arglay said, and explained the situation. The Hajji shook his head. 'I think,' he answered, 'that he has known, in an infinitely small fraction of time, all his future until he enters the End of Desire.'

'He has foreknown that which he is now experiencing?' Lord Arglay asked.

'I think so,' Ibrahim answered. 'But though he knew it I do not think it is now within his memory, nor will be until he reaches the end. For to remember the future he must have foreknown his memory of that future, and yet that he could not do without first foreknowing it without memory. So I think he is spared that evil. Exalted for ever be the Mercy of the Compassionate!'

CHAPTER VIII
THE CONFERENCE

The room at the Foreign Office was large enough not to be crowded. Lord Birlesmere sat in a chair dexterously arranged at the corner of a table, thus allowing him to control without compelling him to preside. Next to him sat Lord Arglay with Chloe by his side; opposite was Mr. Sheldrake in a state of very bitter irritation. Reginald Montague was in an equal state of nervousness next to Chloe. Mr. Doncaster was next to Sheldrake, and a little apart were Professor Palliser and Sir Giles Tumulty. At the bottom of the table were Mr. Bruce Cumberland and a high police official. The Persian Embassy was not represented. It was about 11 o'clock on Monday.

Lord Birlesmere leant a little forward. 'Gentlemen,' he began, 'you know, I think, why we have troubled you and why you have consented to come here. The very surprising demonstrations at Rich during the week-end are a matter which do not concern this particular Office, but—as most of you at any rate know—those demonstrations are said to be connected with a substance, reputedly a relic, in the existence and preservation of which a foreign Power has declared itself to be interested. I need not detain you now to explain to what extent that Power's representatives have taken official action. But I may say, in passing, that I myself have reason to believe that certain agitations and disturbances in the Near East during the last two months have the same cause....'

'What cause?' Mr. Sheldrake interrupted irritably.

'A concern,' Lord Birlesmere flowed on, 'with the existence and disposal of this hypothetical relic. I am anxious to discover, on behalf of the Government, of what nature this is, whether it is one or many, to whom it now belongs, and in whose possession it now is, and how far the claims of any foreign Power can be justified. I need not say that I and any other representatives of the authorities here will treat every communication made as confidential, or that if any of you wish to make a private statement we shall be pleased to give you immediate opportunities.'

Nobody leapt at the opportunity. Lord Birlesmere said across the table: 'I believe, Mr. Sheldrake, you claim that this supposed relic belongs to you?'

'I know nothing whatever about relics,' Sheldrake answered. 'I know that only last Friday I bought from Mr. Montague a kind of stone which he assured me could produce certain remarkable results. I tested his claims and they seemed justified; and as a result of these tests I gave him my cheque for seventy-three thousand guineas.'

'Did you understand,' Lord Birlesmere asked, 'that this was the only stone of its kind in existence?'

'No,' Sheldrake admitted rather reluctantly, 'I understood there were three or four.'

'And by a series of events this Stone came into the hands of Mr. Doncaster and thence to the police, performing apparently some remarkable cures on its way—yes,' Lord Birlesmere said, 'we needn't go into that now. Except, Mr. Doncaster, that you think these cures may really have been produced by the Stone? Or anyhow,' he added, seeing that Oliver was prepared to discuss this for a long time, 'you see nothing against that hypothesis?'

'Well, nothing except——' Oliver began.

'Practically nothing at the moment,' Lord Birlesmere substituted. 'Quite. Well now, Mr. Montague, would you mind telling us where *you* got the Stone?'

'My uncle gave it me,' Reginald said very quickly. 'Sir Giles.' He met Sir Giles's eyes and shivered a little.

Lord Birlesmere, having reached the desired point by a more gentle method than by mere attack, looked at Sir Giles with an engaging smile. 'I wonder whether you would mind telling us exactly what you know about the Stone, Sir Giles,' he said.

'I don't *mind* telling you,' Sir Giles said, 'but I'm damned if I see why I should. Why on earth should I tell this private detective agency everything about my personal affairs, because an auriferous Yankee loses his purse?'

Lord Arglay observed round the table a slight perplexity, except where Mr. Sheldrake jerked upright and Reginald stared downwards. In an undertone to Chloe he said: 'I don't really know why he should, do you?' But Chloe was looking, rather inimically for her, at Sir Giles.

Lord Birlesmere glanced at Bruce Cumberland, who said: 'Merely as a friendly act, Sir Giles, you might be willing to assist the inquiry.'

'But in the first place,' Sir Giles answered, 'I don't see any friends here—except perhaps the Professor, and secondly, I don't know what I've got to do with the inquiry. Whoever's been curing the village idiots of England it isn't me. I've got something else to do than to cure old women of paralytic delirium.'

'The properties of the Stone…' Mr. Cumberland began again.

'The properties of the Stone,' Sir Giles interrupted, 'are for scientists to determine—not politicians, policemen, and prostitutes.'

Mr. Sheldrake jerked again, and kept his eyes away from Chloe with an effort. So did everyone else, except Lord Arglay who smiled at her and then looked at Lord Birlesmere. The Foreign Secretary, caught between ignoring the word and thus appearing to allow it and protesting and thus permitting the whole conversation to wander off on to a useless path, said in a perfectly audible voice to Mr. Sheldrake: 'Sir Giles, like other great men, is a little eccentric in his phrases sometimes,' but Sir Giles refused to be excused.

'Well, I suppose the Foreign Secretary *is* a politician,' he said, 'and a Scotland Yard Commissioner *is* a policeman. Eh? Very well then——!'

Bruce Cumberland leaned across towards the Chief Justice. 'Perhaps,' he said in a hoarse whisper, 'Miss Burnett would like to withdraw. I mean, you see….'

Chloe's hand touched Lord Arglay's arm. 'Don't make me go,' she breathed to him.

'Ah,' Lord Birlesmere said, delighted at the suggestion, 'now if in the unusual circumstances Miss Burnett would oblige me personally by rendering the inquiry easier…. We want,' he went on rather vaguely, 'to have no restraints imposed, though if the matter were less urgent…'

'My dear Birlesmere,' Arglay said patiently, 'neither Miss Burnett nor I have the least objection to Sir Giles using any language he finds congenial. We haven't even a police-court acquittal against us, and any apology seems to me to be chiefly due to the English language which is being wildly misused. Pray consider our feelings unruffled.'

'Very good of you,' Lord Birlesmere, rather perplexed, murmured, and returned to Sir Giles who was feeling in a waistcoat pocket and snarling at the Chief Justice. 'The point is, Sir Giles,' he said, 'that it is necessary for the Government to know, first, what justification there is for foreign claims to the Stone; secondly, what properties the Stone possesses; and thirdly, how many there are in existence.'

'The answers,' Tumulty said, 'are that no foreign claim to the Stone has any validity, that Professor Palliser and I are at work on an investigation of its qualities, and that I cannot tell you how many stones exist for a reason I can show you.' He felt in his pocket again.

'The qualities,' Lord Birlesmere said, 'are said to include rapid transit through space and singular curative powers.'

'Transit through *time* and space,' Sir Giles corrected him. 'Two hundred miles or two hundred hours.' He pushed his chair a little away from the table and set another—his own—Stone on his knee. 'Don't crowd me, gentlemen,' he went on, 'or I shall have to remove myself at once. This is not the Stone Mr. Sheldrake flung away.'

'Like the poor Indian,' Oliver Doncaster put in, being a little tired of having no chance to say anything, but no one took any notice except the Chief Justice who, glancing at Sheldrake, altered Shakespeare into Pope by murmuring 'whose untutored mind.'

'If the Government,' Sir Giles went on, 'wish to conduct an inquiry into the nature of the Stone I shall be happy to assist them by supplying examples.' He covered the Stone on his knee with both hands and apparently in some intense effort shut his eyes for a minute or two. The inquiry looked perplexed and doubtful, and it was Chloe who suddenly broke the silence by jumping to her feet and running round the table. Sir Giles, hearing the movement, opened his eyes just as Palliser thrust his chair back in Chloe's path, and leapt up in his turn, throwing as he did so about a dozen Stones, all exactly similar, on to the table. Everybody jumped up in confusion, as Chloe, still silent, caught Palliser's chair with a vicious jerk that unbalanced and overthrew the Professor, and sprang towards Tumulty. Sir Giles, the Stone clasped in one hand and his open knife still in the other, met her with a snarl. 'Go to hell,' he said, and slashed out with the knife as she caught at his wrist.

'Miss Burnett! Miss Burnett!' half the table cried. 'Miss Burnett! Sir Giles!' Lord Birlesmere exclaimed. Mr. Sheldrake, his mouth open in dismay, caught up two or three of the Stones and looked at them. Lord Arglay, leaning over the table, struck Doncaster's shoulder sharply: 'Get that knife away from him,' he said, and himself ran round after Chloe. Palliser, scrambling to his feet, thrust himself in Doncaster's way. 'Lord Birlesmere,' he called. 'I protest! I demand that you shall stop this attack.'

'Get out, you——' Sir Giles yelled at Chloe. The knife had shut on her fingers and blood was on her hand. But her other had already caught Tumulty's wrist and was struggling with his for the Stone. Lord Arglay's arrival did not seem materially to help her; it was Tumulty, who, as everyone rushed to do something to end the scuffle, let go of the Stone, slipped to one side, reached the table, and caught up one or two of the Types which, to the Chief Justice's hasty glance, seemed to cover it. There were by now half a dozen bodies between Chloe and Sir Giles, who however had only distanced a foe to meet a fidget. Sheldrake clutched at him. 'What are you doing?' he shrieked. 'What are you doing with my stone?'

'Lord Birlesmere,' Sir Giles said, 'unless you stop that hell-cat of Arglay's I'll ruin everything. I'll go off and flood the country with Stones. I can and I will.'

Lord Birlesmere said passionately, 'Miss Burnett, please be quiet. You'd better go; you'd really better go.'

The Chief Justice gave Chloe a handkerchief. 'You attend to Tumulty, Birlesmere,' he said. 'The real proceedings are only just beginning. All mankind has been searching for this Stone, and now the English Government has got it.'

Lord Birlesmere came back to the table and stood by Sir Giles. 'What does it *mean*?' he said.

'I will tell you now,' Tumulty answered. 'Anyone who has this Stone can heal himself of all illnesses, and can move at once through space and time, and can multiply it by dividing it as much as he wishes. There will be no need of doctors or nurses or railways or tubes or trams or taxis or airships or any transport—except for heavy luggage, and I'm not sure about that—*if* I scatter this Stone through the country. How do you like the idea? Look,' he said, 'I'll show you. Will to be somewhere—in Westminster Abbey.' He thrust one of the Types into the Foreign Secretary's hand, who took it, looked at it, looked at Sir Giles, hesitated, then seemed to concentrate—and suddenly neither he nor Tumulty were there.

As the others jumped and gaped Arglay said to Chloe, 'You can't do any more. They have it here. Go back home and wait for me.'

'I suppose I was a fool,' Chloe said in a low tone. 'But I did so hate to see him sitting there, and *know* what he was doing. And if I'd screamed at them no one would have done anything.'

Arglay nodded. 'It is clear,' he began, 'that here—no, never mind. I'll tell you presently. Wait.' He stepped to the table and picked up one of the Types. Mr. Bruce Cumberland began to say something. Lord Arglay looked at him and went back to Chloe. 'Take this,' he said. 'No, take it. Thrice is he armed, of course, but I would rather you could come to me.'

'I don't like to touch it,' Chloe looked at it in a kind of awe.

'To the pure all things are pure, even purity,' Lord Arglay said. 'Take it, child. And keep it near you, for I do not think we know what may happen, but I think the Stone is on your side.'

'What do you mean?' Chloe asked. 'On our side?'

'I haven't an idea,' Lord Arglay answered. 'But I think so. Now go. Go to Lancaster Gate and wait for me. Go before the Foreign Secretary and that Gadarene swine return.' He took her to the door, and as he returned was met by Mr. Bruce Cumberland.

'Has Miss Burnett gone?' the secretary said. 'I don't know whether Lord Birlesmere might not want her not to go before——'

'My dear Mr. Cumberland,' the Chief Justice said, 'your certainties are as mixed as your negatives. Hasn't Lord Birlesmere been asking her to go in every kind of voice? And now I've urged her to, just to please him. And you're still not happy. How difficult you diplomats are!'

'But she took one of the Stones,' Bruce Cumberland protested.

'Well,' Lord Arglay said, sitting down leisurely, 'I can easily make you another—ten, twenty more. At least, I can't, because I don't want to annoy Suleiman ben Daood—on whom be the Peace! as my friend the Hajji would say. If it belongs to him. But you can make them for yourself. What a time Giles is, showing Birlesmere the tombs in Westminster Abbey!'

Bruce Cumberland gave up the argument and they waited in silence for the return of the others. When this took place Sir Giles, with a glance round the room and a triumphant grin at Arglay, flung himself into a chair. Lord Birlesmere stood leaning on the table for some time. Then he said: 'I think, gentlemen, there is nothing more that can profitably be done now. I am very much obliged to all of you.' He paused, bowed, added something in a low voice to Mr. Sheldrake, and sat down. The American did the same thing. Lord Arglay watched thoughtfully till the others had withdrawn, and Lord Birlesmere was looking at him restlessly. He considered for a moment the three opposite him, and said quietly. 'No, Birlesmere; you're like Salisbury, you're backing the wrong horse. And if Mr. Sheldrake wants to get his seventy thousand pounds restored I think that he's riding the wrong way. As for you, Tumulty, I don't think you know where you're riding.' He got up and strolled slowly to the door.

The important conference now began. That Sir Giles was a member of it was due largely to the importance he seemed to have as the origin and scientific investigator of the Stone rather than to any actual need of him. But his impatience prevented a good deal of time being lost in an international wrangle, since neither Birlesmere nor Sheldrake wished more Types to exist than could be helped, while Tumulty was entirely reckless. All that he wanted was opportunity to investigate the qualities of the Stone, without exposing himself to any serious risk of unexpected results; and this he saw a chance of obtaining by an understanding with the Government. But to both of the others the monopoly of the Stone was rapidly becoming a matter of the first importance, and under pressure from Sir Giles something very like the first draft of a new Anglo-American treaty was reached in half an hour or so. Sheldrake had vague personal and semi-official relations with the President, and promised to bring the whole thing privately to his notice. With instruments of this nature at their disposal, and a judicious use of them, he and the Foreign Secretary saw infinite possibilities of developing power. Only one thing stood in their way, and it was this hindrance they were anxious for Sir Giles to remove. At present the successful use of the Stone depended entirely on the individual will. But for purposes of national control, it was necessary that the controllers should be able to move masses of men without the masses having a choice. It was clear that no army which had been supplied with Types of the Stone could be relied on. Mutiny might be dangerous but transit of this sort would be safe and easy. For the first time in history the weakest thing was on a level, was indeed better off, than the strongest. Besides, as Sir Giles with a certain glee pointed out, in war nothing but mortal wounds would be any use; others could be healed at once, and wars would become interminable. It was Lord Birlesmere who asked whether, if the Stone could heal so easily, it could also repair wastage; that is, prove a substitute for food. 'But then,' he added, startled, 'it would practically confer immortality. The world would in time become over-crowded; you would be adding without taking away.'

'You might,' Sir Giles said, 'use it as the perfect contraceptive.'

Mr. Sheldrake looked down his nose. The conversation seemed to him to be becoming obscene.

'Under control,' Lord Birlesmere said thoughtfully, 'always, always under control. We *must* find out what it can do; you must, Sir Giles.'

'I ask nothing better,' Sir Giles said. 'But you Puritans have always made such a fuss about vivisection, let alone human vivisection.'

'No one,' Lord Birlesmere exclaimed, 'is suggesting vivisection. There is a difference between harmless experiments and vivisection.'

'I can have living bodies?' Sir Giles asked.

'Well, there are prisons—and workhouses—and hospitals—and barracks,' Birlesmere answered slowly. 'Judiciously, of course. I mean, a careful investigation of the possibilities.' He was distracted by Mr. Sheldrake's clamour for a licensed monopoly of the Stone for use in transit.

It took longer to satisfy the American than the scientist. Lord Birlesmere was perfectly willing to give up bodies to experiment, so far as he could, but he was very reluctant to interfere with the right of any citizen into whose possession the Stone might come, to use it as he chose. Yet nothing else, it was clear, would be of any use.

The possession of the Stone would have to be made illegal. And therefore the Types would have to be recovered. Of such Types, besides those on the table, there were at least four—Professor Palliser had one ('I'll answer for him,' Sir Giles said), Reginald Montague ('and you can deal with him,' he added, 'frightening him will do it'), Lord Arglay, and Miss Burnett.

They looked at each other. It might be rather a difficult thing to persuade the Chief Justice to give up anything he had a right to possess and an interest in keeping.

'What about a secret Order in Council?' Sheldrake soared to new heights of romanticism.

'I don't know the legal aspect,' Birlesmere muttered. 'And he probably would. The English law is a difficult study, my dear Mr. Sheldrake, and Lord Arglay would probably know a good deal about it. I might consult the Law Officers—but even then—and Miss Burnett too. Being his secretary makes it so awkward....'

There was a prolonged silence. Then Sir Giles said suddenly: 'What about this foreign Power of yours?'

'What about it?' Birlesmere asked in surprise.

'Persia, wasn't it?' Sir Giles said. 'I had some carpet-weaver of theirs to dinner to find out about the Stone. And if they burgled me—and I'm almost sure they did—what about a neat little burglary at Lancaster Gate? And at—where does that girl live?'

Birlesmere shook his head. 'It means them getting the Stone,' he objected, 'and I'd much rather Arglay had it. Well, I'll think about it. Perhaps a friendly appeal——'

Sir Giles made a peculiar noise and rather reluctantly abandoned the subject. He disliked any Types being in Arglay's and Chloe's possession, but his dislike was not strong enough to urge him to extreme action. But as, a little later, a temporary agreement having been arrived at, he left the Foreign Office, it occurred to him that if the Stone had shown his own action to the Chief Justice, it could be used also to discover what was in Arglay's mind, and to suggest other modes of action. With this idea possessing him he rejoined Palliser, who was staying at Ealing.

290

CHAPTER IX
THE ACTION OF LORD ARGLAY

Lord Arglay, insisting on writing some business letters after lunch, insisted also that Chloe should wait his convenience and rest until he was ready for her. It was consequently not until after tea that he lit one of his very occasional cigars, and standing in front of the fireplace said: 'And now, Miss Burnett, what do you make of it?'

'I feel an awful ass,' Chloe told him, 'going for Sir Giles like that. But I couldn't think of anything sane to do—I was so angry.'

'The wrath of the Lamb,' Arglay said. 'But I didn't mean about yourself; you saved the Lord Chief Justice throwing an inkstand at Giles, which would have been more scandalous, but perhaps more effective, if I had hit him. It might even have killed him. I really meant—about the situation. Suppress, if you can, your righteous supernatural anger with him, and tell me why you hate him so.'

'I *don't* hate him,' Chloe said. 'I only want to stop him doing anything at all with the Stone. He oughtn't to have it.'

'So far as we know, he bought it,' Lord Arglay pointed out.

'But it isn't *his*,' Chloe pleaded, 'not really.'

'Mrs. Sheldrake used much the same argument to convince me that *all* the Types ought to be her husband's,' Arglay answered. 'Only she said, they *are* his, really. Try and be masculine and rational. *Why* isn't it his?'

Chloe made an obviously intense effort. 'I think I hate the way he looks at it,' she said. 'He doesn't care about *it*, only about the way it works. He doesn't care about Suleiman—or Charlemagne—or…. He only wants to see what it will do.'

'And being an incurable romantic,' Arglay said, 'you hate him being merely utilitarian. Well, I don't suppose anyone else, for a thousand years or so, has barked their knuckles for the sake of Suleiman the King. I should think you were the first of the English to do it. Still—it's hardly reason enough for your disliking Giles quite so much.'

Chloe went on looking for reasons. 'He doesn't *care* about it a bit,' she protested. 'He throws it about as if it were of no importance at all. And he doesn't care how much he cuts it up.'

'And why do we care?' Lord Arglay asked.

Chloe smiled. 'I don't know,' she said, 'I don't know a bit, but I do. Don't you know?'

The Chief Justice frowned at his cigar. 'I will offer you two alternatives,' he said. 'First, we are both disgracefully sentimental. We wallow in tradition. And when a traditional thing appears to produce unusual results we can't help being affected. Giles is stronger-minded. Suleiman and our lord the Prophet leave him unmoved. *J'y suis, j'y reste*, and so on. I hate being less efficient than Giles, but I fear it, I promise you I fear it.' He shook his head despairingly.

'And the other alternative?' Chloe said.

'The other? O the other is that we're right in being affected,' Lord Arglay answered, 'that amid all this mess of myths and tangle of traditions and … and … febrifuge of fables, there is something extreme and terrible. And if so, Giles had better be careful.'

'Which do you believe?' Chloe asked.

'My dear girl, I haven't a notion,' the Chief Justice told her. 'I don't see a little bit how we can decide. It's a question—let's be perfectly frank—of which we want to believe.'

'Which do you then?' Chloe persisted.

'I don't want to believe either. I hate being foolish and I dislike being pious,' Arglay said. 'Do you choose first. How will you know and receive the Stone?'

'He said it was the End of Desire,' Chloe murmured.

'And shall that be romance or truth for you?' Arglay asked. 'Make up your mind and tell me, child; what will you have the Stone to be?'

'I would have it to be the End of Desire indeed,' Chloe said. 'I would have it to be something very strong and—satisfying. I am afraid of it but I—don't laugh—I love it.'

Lord Arglay looked at her thoughtfully. Then, 'Do you believe in God?' he asked.

'I suppose so,' Chloe said, 'I think I do when I look at the Stone. But otherwise—I don't know.'

'Well,' said Lord Arglay, 'I will make you a fair proposal—I will if you will. It's all perfectly ridiculous, but since I saw those people this morning I feel I must be with them or against them. So I suppose I'm against them. Not, mind you, on the evidence. But I refuse to let you believe in God all by yourself.'

Chloe looked up at him, her eyes shining. 'But dare I believe that the Stone is of God?' she said. 'And what do I mean by God—except…' she half added and stopped.

'Except——?' Arglay asked, but she silently refused to go on and he said: 'If you will believe this way, then I also will believe. And we will set ourselves against the world, the flesh, and the devil, and not sit in the seat of Giles Tumulty. But I would have you be careful there for I think he hates you.'

'But what can he do?' Chloe asked in astonishment.

'If I have seen his mind, as I believe I did,' Lord Arglay said, 'he may also see yours. Unless the Stone has varying powers. I would have you consider very closely in what way you may work with the Stone for God. Also I would have you keep it on you day and night that you may escape by it if need be.'

'But what need can there be?' Chloe asked.

'Child,' Lord Arglay answered, 'it is clear that these men cannot stop where they are. They must either abandon the Stone to chance and itself or they must seek to possess it. Now I do not think it is well that they should wholly possess it, and I think that you and I should keep our Types while we can. I do not know whether the Types can be united, but if I were Birlesmere I would strive for that, and the united Stone would give sole power. If this is what he does they may attempt anything within or without the Law. Fortunately,' he added pensively, 'the interpretation of the law so often depends on the Courts. To-morrow I will talk to the Hajji.'

'But what will you do with it in the end?' Chloe asked.

'Why, that we shall see,' Lord Arglay said. 'For the Law is greater than the Courts, and in the end the Courts shall submit to the Law. But meanwhile you shall consider how you will follow this God that we have decided to believe in, who, it seems, may give wisdom through the Stone. And then we will free Giles's prisoner in the past.' He paused and considered Chloe with an anxious protectiveness. 'But if you need me,' he said, 'come to me at any hour of the day or night.'

Chloe met his eyes gravely. 'I will remember,' she said, 'and—and I do believe in God.'

'In spite of the fact that Giles Tumulty exists, so do I,' Lord Arglay said, 'though in a man of past fifty it's either an imbecility or a heroism.'

'And what for a girl of twenty-five?' Chloe asked.

'O in her it's either a duty or a generosity,' Lord Arglay said, 'but for a secretary it's a safeguard. One must have something to explain or counter-balance one's employer!…'

At Ealing Sir Giles got up in a rage. 'Why the hell can't I find out?' he asked, throwing one of the Types on the table.

The question seemed reasonable enough. For in their preliminary investigations that afternoon both he and the Professor had found out all they wanted. Having worked out what seemed a moderately safe formula they had experimented first on such minds as Sir Giles's housekeeper, the Professor's old aunt, Lord Birlesmere, and others. After something of the same experiences which Lord Arglay had undergone, the results had been satisfactory enough. Sir Giles, rather to his annoyance, had been conscious of a strongly marked, if muddled, desire that some malignant old beast should go to China, mingled with an anxiety whether a girl called Lizzie should be getting into trouble. The process was similar in each case. There opened before the eyes of the holder of the Stone the scene then before the eyes of the subject of the investigation, there arose within his mind the occupation of the subject's mind, but in words rather than in ill-defined vision. The presence of the Stone in the hand remained throughout as a kind of anchor, so that the connexion with the actual world was never entirely lost, and could at will be wholly re-established.

But when Sir Giles, rather pleased at being able apparently to get his own back on the Chief Justice, attempted the most important experiment, he found the result negligible. He framed the formula; he called up the consciousness of Arglay; he intensified his will. There appeared gradually before him the familiar study as seen from in front of the fire-place; Chloe was sitting in front of him. Sir Giles was aware of thinking that Arglay had an admirable taste in women, that though of course this girl was not really intelligent she could probably take the Chief Justice in. This consciousness went on repeating itself again and again. He tried to empty his mind, but it was no good. The image of Chloe occupied it, with a sort of detached irritation, until he recalled himself in a fit of anger.

'You try, Palliser,' he said shortly. 'Arglay can't be so demented on that girl that he can think of nothing else. But I'm damned if he seems to, unless the Stone's gone wrong.'

The Professor tried, with a little more success. 'The Chief Justice,' he said, 'seems to be thinking of protecting God.'

'Of what?' Sir Giles shrieked.

'That was the impression I got,' Palliser said. 'A strong wish to protect and a sense that protection was valueless, and the idea—the word God recurring. All aimed at the girl.'

'I know Arglay's a legal hurdy-gurdy,' Sir Giles said, 'but even he wouldn't play that tune. But why can't I get any result?'

'You don't think,' Palliser asked rather nervously, 'that it's because you'd already decided what he was thinking?'

'Don't be a damned fool,' said Sir Giles. 'I hadn't decided. I know his feeling about the girl, of course. She's a presentable bitch and there's only one thing an unmarried senility like Arglay *could* be thinking. You don't mean to tell me he's merely altruistic? But he can't be thinking of lechery the whole time. He must be talking to her about something—even God.'

The Professor continued persistent. 'You don't think you're imposing your view on him?' he said. 'After all, these others—your housekeeper and the rest—we didn't know or care what they were thinking about. But Arglay and this girl—you do or you say you do.'

'Well, you don't seem to be much nearer,' Sir Giles snapped. 'What's this blithering imbecility about protecting God?'

'I may not have got it quite right,' Palliser admitted. 'But I certainly had the idea of protection, and of God. It may have been the girl he wanted to protect.'

'A damn good word, protection,' Tumulty sneered, and for a minute or two seethed up and down the room. Then he broke out: 'Do you mean to tell me Arglay can read my mind and I can't read his?'

'You know best,' Palliser answered. 'You know how far he knew what you were doing, and how far you know what he was.'

'He knew something about that Boy Scout of yours,' Sir Giles said, 'so he must have *seen* something. By the way, I suppose he—what was his filthy name? Pondon?—is going on his merry-go-round just the same? I'd like to have a look at him. I suppose we can?'

'Only take care you don't get caught up in the past too,' Palliser said. 'But I should think you could see him if you wanted to. As I understand it, all the past still exists and it's merely a matter of choosing your point of view.'

'I don't see,' Sir Giles said thoughtfully, 'I really don't see how he's ever going to get back. Birlesmere's quite right—what we want is to control the damned thing. If I could do that I'd—I'd make Arglay an infant in arms and his girl an … an embryo again. Friday—Saturday—Sunday—Monday. It'll very soon be four days to the minute since your fellow willed. I suppose he just goes on willing when he reaches the top point?'

'The Stone being there too?' Palliser asked.

'I suppose so,' Sir Giles meditatively answered. 'If the past is continually scaled off the present, the Stone is scaled off too. And he goes on willing and dropping it. Let's have a look at him, Palliser!' Palliser hesitated a little. 'We want to be careful only to look,' he said. 'Don't forget that half-hour.'

Sir Giles looked black. 'I don't,' he said harshly. 'But we can't do anything about that now. And we only want to see the past from the present. Come along, Palliser, let's try it. I desire—I will—to see—what was his name? Hezekiah? O, Elijah—I will without passing into the past to see Elijah Pondon—something like that, eh? What was the exact time—a quarter to seven, wasn't it? It's almost that now.'

'Suppose,' Lord Arglay said to Chloe, 'two persons, each holding the Stone or its Type, wished opposite things at once, what would happen then?'

'Nothing probably,' Chloe said.

'I wonder.' Lord Arglay looked at the Type before them. 'Nothing—or would the stronger will…? The point is this—you know the wretched fellow Giles trapped? Well, he willed of course; they must have persuaded him so far. But he must have willed merely in obedience, in anxiety to please, in a kind of good-feeling—you see——? And at the moment he held a Type.' He paused.

'Yes?' Chloe asked.

'It's all very difficult,' Lord Arglay sighed. 'But if the Stone is—what the Hajji says—indivisible and that sort of thing, mustn't all the Types be, so to speak, *one*? It sounds raving lunacy—but otherwise I don't see … And if they are, and if a fellow had one of the Types for a moment, could we enlarge that moment by some other Type so that he saw—and did or didn't do what he did before? Do you see?'

'Not very well,' Chloe said frankly. 'Wouldn't you be altering the past?'

'Not really,' Lord Arglay went on arguing. 'If the Types are one then at his moment of holding *his* this fellow in Birmingham held this one, and there his present touches our present.'

'But then—you mean that Time is in the Stone, not the Stone in Time?' Chloe asked.

'Eh?' said Lord Arglay, 'do I? I believe I do. Lucid mind! But keep your lucidity on the practical aspect. Eschew the higher metaphysics for a moment, and tell me—don't you think we might offer him other ways *at* that moment?'

'Why are we to be so anxious to help this poor man?' Chloe asked. 'You do dislike Sir Giles almost as much as I do, don't you, Lord Arglay?'

'I dislike tyranny, treachery, and cruelty,' the Chief Justice said. 'And I think that this fellow has been betrayed and tyrannized over. Whether it's cruelty depends on what his past was like. Besides, it's got to be a kind of symbol for me—an omen. I can't believe the Stone likes it.'

'I don't suppose it does,' Chloe said seriously.

A little startled, Lord Arglay looked at her. 'My dear child,' he said, 'do you really think——?' But as she looked up at him it was so clear that she did think exactly that, and that it seemed quite natural to her, that he abandoned his protest. 'We are,' he thought to himself, 'becoming anthropomorphic a little rapidly. We shall be asking the Stone what it would like for breakfast next.' He played privately with the fancy of the Stone absorbing sausages and coffee, and then decided to postpone any protest for the moment. 'After all, I don't know any more than she does,' he meditated, 'perhaps it *would* like sausages and coffee. Shall I end with a tribal deity? Well then, God help us all, it shall be at least *our* deity and not Giles's and Sheldrake's and Birlesmere's. Much nicer for everyone, I should think. Now that we know we create gods, do not let us hesitate in the work.' He blinked inwardly at the phrase and proceeded. 'But I have promised to believe in God, and here is a temptation to infidelity already, since I know that any god in whom I can believe will be consonant with my mind. So if I believe it must be in a god consonant with me. This would seem to limit God very considerably.'

'Do I really think what?' Chloe asked.

For a moment he did not answer. He considered her as she sat before him, leaning a little forward, gravity closed over fire, waiting for his answer, and 'Yet it is very certain,' Lord Arglay thought, 'that things beyond my conscious invention exist and are to be believed. Also that if I choose to attribute such an admirable creation to God I am thereby enlarging my own ideas of him, which by themselves would never have reached it. So that in some sense I do believe outside myself.'

'Nothing, nothing,' he said to Chloe. 'Return we to our sheep, our ewe lamb. If his will worked merely in courtesy, might it not be swept by a stronger will?' He began to walk up and down the room. 'You know, Chloe, I've a good mind to try it.'

'Do be careful,' Chloe said, with considerable restraint.

'I shall be extremely careful,' Lord Arglay told her. 'But don't forget we are rather relying on the Stone to assist us. I admit that it's purely logical and won't go against our wills, but perhaps it might even elucidate the will. Anyhow,' he added suddenly, 'I'm going to try. But what the devil do I say to it?'

He took up a pencil and a sheet of paper and sat down, remaining for some minutes engrossed. When he had at last, in deep concentration, made several marks on the paper he threw it to Chloe. 'There,' he said.

It looked almost like a magical diagram. There was a rectangle in the centre, with two or three small sketches within it which might have been meant for human figures. Above it was written '6.45 or thereabouts, and next to it 'Pondon'. Underneath 'I will that in the unity of the Stone I may know that moment and show this present moment to him who is in the past, and that I may return therefrom.'

'The last phrase,' Lord Arglay said, 'sounds singularly unlike a courageous English gentleman. But I shall do no good at all by being stuck in last Friday. Otherwise it's almost as good as the Hajji.'

'I think the Hajji would have added one thing,' Chloe answered, and blushing a little wrote at the end 'Under the Protection'; then she said hastily, 'What is the drawing meant to be?'

'That is the room where Giles's experiment took place,' Lord Arglay explained. 'The squizzle on the right is Pondon, the Greek decoration on the left is Palliser, and the thousand-legged Hindu god underneath is Giles himself. It's to help the mind. With the greatest respect to the informing spirit of the Stone I don't want to leave more to it than I can help.' He looked at his watch. 'Six-thirty-three,' he said. 'Ought one to give the Stone a little rope?'

'You think the exact time necessary?' Chloe asked.

'Not logically, no,' Arglay said. 'It's merely to help my own mind again. Strictly one could reach six-forty-five on Friday from anytime now. But the nearer we are the sharper the crisis seems to me to be. Silly, but true.'

294

'And what do I do?' Chloe asked.

Arglay looked at her a little wryly. 'I think you'd better just sit still,' he said. 'You might pray a little if you feel sufficiently accustomed to believing in God.' He picked up the Stone and settled himself in his armchair. But before he could begin to concentrate Chloe had moved her own chair to face him, and leaning forward, laid her right hand over his that held the Stone. With her left she picked up the diagram.

'Let me try too,' she said. 'I'd rather not be left here alone.'

'Be warned,' Lord Arglay answered. 'You may find yourself merely taking down the history of Organic Law. Or even continually knocking Palliser's chair away from him and getting your fingers cut infinitely often.'

'Let me try,' she urged again. 'Or do you think I might spoil it?'

'No,' Arglay said. 'I think you may save it. For I am sure you are the only one of all of us who is heartily devoted to the Stone. Well, come along then. Are you comfortable?'

Chloe nodded. 'Under the Protection,' she said softly and suddenly, and Lord Arglay, smiling a little but not at all in scorn, gravely assented: 'Under the Protection.' And silence fell on the room.

Chloe was later on very indistinct in her own mind on what had actually happened or seemed to happen. She was even shy of explaining it to Lord Arglay, though she did manage to give him a general idea, encouraged by the fact that he seemed to accept it as a perfectly normal incident. For after some few minutes while she gallantly strove to keep her mind fixed on the diagram at which she was gazing, and the unfortunate Mr. Pondon, and Lord Arglay's almost unintelligibly fixed passion for restoring him, and such difficult and remote things, it seemed to her as if an inner voice very like Arglay's said firmly: 'My dear child, don't blether. You know perfectly well you don't care about this at all. Do let us be accurate. Now.'

She made, or so she thought, a general vague protest that she was anxious to do what he wanted, but Arglay, or the Stone, or whatever it was that was dominating her, swept this aside; she forgot it in the sudden rush of her consciousness to its next point of rest. And this point seemed to be the memory of Mr. Frank Lindsay. She found herself remembering with a double poignancy at once how satisfactory and how unsatisfactory he was. The poor dear did and was everything he could be; he held her hand pleasantly, he kissed well, he displayed becoming zeal, and if his talk was a little dull … yes, but his talk was not dull but alien. Talk, they all—and two or three other young men arose in Chloe's mind—they all failed to be memorable in talk. There came to her almost a cloud of phrases and sentences in different voices—preceding, accompanying, following, incidents that had certainly not been talk. They had been extremely delightful—incidents and companions alike—she was an ungrateful creature. But her palm rested on something that was warmer and closer and steadier than any kiss on that palm had been, and the ends of her fingers touched a hand that was warm and intimate and serene. And again the voice that was Arglay's or the Stone's said within her: 'Go on, child.' In a sudden reaction it seemed to her that she hated that intimate but austere government. She hung suspended between it and Frank Lindsay. Times upon times seemed to pass as she waited, without the power of choice between this and that, hating to lose and fearing to gain either because of the loss of the other that such gain must bring. She must, she thought vaguely, be getting very old, too old to be loved or desired, too old to desire. Her memories were spectral now; her companions and peers very faint and circling round her in an unnoticing procession. And besides them what else had there been in her life? There came to her a phrase—the *Survey of Organic Law.*—*Organic Law* had never meant very much to her, and this increasing loneliness and age was law, organic law. But again there pierced through that loneliness the double strength upon which her hand rested. The words grew sacramental; they had not existed by themselves but as the communication—little enough understood—of a stored and illuminated mind. Who was it, long before, had used those words? And suddenly at a great distance she saw the figure of Lord Arglay as he stood in Sir Giles's room holding the Stone—the Justice of England, direct in the line of the makers and expositors of law. Other names arose, Suleiman and Charlemagne and Augustus, the Khalifs and Caesars of the world, of a world in which a kiss was for a moment but their work for a longer time, and though they grew old their work was final, each in its degree, and endured. Between those figures and her young lovers, now, in her increasing age, she could not stop to choose; immediately and infinitesimally her mind shifted and she forgot her throbbing past. It avenged itself at once; the names grew cold and the figures vague as she dwelled in them. She seemed to meet the eyes of the ghostly Arglay, and he smiled and shook his head. No longer strong but very faint the same voice said to her: 'Go on, child.' But where and how was she to go? A cold darkness was about her and within her, and at the end of that darkness the high vision of instruction and fair companionship was fading also in the night. Despairingly she called to it; despairingly with all her soul she answered: 'I will go on, I will, but tell me how.' The phantom did not linger gently to mock or comfort her; it was gone, and around her was an absolute desolation which she supposed must be death. All the pain of heart-ache she had ever known, all negligences, desertions, and betrayals, were gathered here, and were shutting themselves up with her alone. Beyond any memory of a hurt and lonely youth, beyond any imagination of an unwanted and miserable age, this pain fed on itself and abolished time. She lay stupefied in anguish.

From somewhere a voice spoke to her, an outer voice, increasing in clearness; she heard it through the night. 'Child,' Lord Arglay was saying with a restrained anxiety, and then, still carefully, 'Chloe! Chloe, child!' She made a small effort towards him, and suddenly the pain passed from her and the outer world began to appear. But in the less than second in which that change took place she saw, away beyond her, glowing between the darkness and the returning day, the mild radiance of the Stone. Away where the apparition of Lord Arglay had seemed to be, it shone, white interspersed with gold, dilating and lucid from within. Only in the general alteration of her knowledge she was aware of that perfection, and catching up her breath at the vision she loosed it again in the study and found the Chief Justice watching her.

Lord Arglay's own experience had been much more definable. He shaped in his mind the image of the room in which he had seen the three men, formulated as clearly as he could his desire to offer Pondon a way of return and made an effort towards submitting the whole thing to whatever Power reposed in the Stone. He took all possible care to avoid any desire towards an active imposition of his will, since it appeared to him that such a desire involved not only danger to himself, but probable failure in his attempt. Less moved, in spite of his protestations, by the mere romanticism of the thing than Chloe, unaffected by titles and traditions and half-ceremonial fables, he yet arrived at something of the same attitude by a process of rationalism. He did not know how far the Stone was capable of action—perhaps not at all; but until he did know a great deal more about its potentialities than he did at the moment, he refused to do more than make an attempt to provide Pondon with a way of return. How far, and in what manner, such a return would present itself to the consciousness of Sir Giles's victim, he could not tell; the endeavour was bound to be experimental only. But he did not primarily wish to move himself to the building at Birmingham; he wanted to bring that complex of minds and place and time again into the presence of the Stone. He resolved his thoughts into lucidity and sat waiting.

For what seemed a long while nothing happened. Concentrated on his thought he remained unconscious of the look of strain that gradually occupied Chloe's face; at first he was vaguely conscious of her, then he lost her altogether. For though there was at first no change either in his surroundings or in his thought yet change there was. Something was pressing against his eyes from within; he felt unnaturally detached, floating, as it were, in his chair. A slight nausea attacked him and passed; his brain was swimming in a sudden faintness. The room about him was the same and yet not the same. The table at his right hand seemed to be multiplied; a number of identical tables appeared beyond it in a long line stretching out to a vague infinity, and all around him the furniture multiplied itself so. Walls that were and yet were not transparent sometimes obscured it and sometimes dissolved and vanished. He saw himself in different positions, now here, now there, and seemed to recognize them. Whenever his mind paused on any one of these eidola of himself it seemed to be fixed, and all the rest to fade, and then his mind would relax and again the phantasmagoria would close in, shifting, vanishing, reappearing. He became astonishingly aware of himself sitting there, much more acutely so than in any normal action; a hand was still on his, but it was not Chloe's or was it Chloe's? No, it was another hand, masculine, more aged; it was … it was the Hajji's. Lord Arglay began to think: 'But this is Friday then,'—with an effort abolished the thought, and went on keeping the problem in his mind clear. The myriad images of himself that vacillated about him were vastly disconcerting—and there were other people too, his servant, the Hajji, Chloe. He was doing or saying something with each of them. It was like a dream, yet it was not like a dream for distinct memory hovered round him, and he found that only by a strong inhibition could he prevent himself submitting to it and being conscious only of some precise moment. The apprehensions began to deepen downwards and outwards but not by the mere inclusion of neighbouring space. An entirely new plane of things thrust itself in and across various of the appearances; in an acute angle almost like a wedge a different room thrust itself down over a picture of himself talking to the Hajji, but within this wedge itself were infinite appearances, swelling like a huge balloon with a painted cover and loosing fresh balloons and new thrusting wedges in all directions. In one group of superimposed layers he was aware of Giles doing a thousand things, and then suddenly, as if in a streak of white light driving right across the whole mirage he was aware of Giles watching. In a new resolution he turned from Giles to Pondon, but he couldn't see Pondon, or not at all clearly; it seemed to him certainly that Pondon now and again was walking about, was walking towards him, down a floor that ran level with his eyes, straight towards the bridge of his nose. The physical discomfort of the sensation was almost unbearable, but Lord Arglay held on. Pondon now like a tiny speck was right up against him, and then the discomfort vanished. A hand—not Chloe's, not the Hajji's, was closing round the Stone in his own hand. Lord Arglay made another act of submission to the Stone; all times were here and equal—if the captive of the past could understand.

The Stone seemed to melt, and almost before he had realized it to reharden; the intruding hand was gone. There was a faint crash somewhere, a sensation of rushing violence. Lord Arglay found himself on his feet and gasping for breath while before him Chloe lay pallid and silent and with shut eyes in her chair.

He stood still for a few seconds till he was breathing more normally and had become more conscious of his surroundings; then, feeling slightly uncertain of his balance, he sat down again. He became aware that his hand and Chloe's were now closely interlocked; in the hollow between the two he felt the Stone. He looked more carefully at his secretary; he put out his other hand and felt the table near him; then he sighed a little. 'And I wonder,' he said to himself, 'if anything has happened. Heavens, how tired I am! And what on earth is happening to this child? She looks as if she were going through it too. Dare one do anything?... I wonder why Giles shot across like that. *He* didn't seem to do anything. I wonder—I wonder about it all. Where is Pondon? Where is Giles? Where am I? And above all where is my admirable secretary?'

Very gently he disengaged their hands, but not entirely, restoring them to the position they were in at the beginning of the experiment. He looked at his watch; it marked six forty-seven. 'I wonder,' Lord Arglay said, still staring at it, 'if Pondon caught the connexion. It's all very difficult.... I seem,' he added, 'to remember saying that before. Well ...' He leant forward a little and said, softly, but clearly, 'Chloe ... Chloe ... Chloe, child!'

———————————

CHAPTER X
THE APPEAL OF THE MAYOR OF RICH

Oliver Doncaster, having been suddenly thrown over both by Mr. Sheldrake and Lord Birlesmere, and finding himself in London with nobody wanting him, determined to return to his holiday village. As he walked to the station he found himself considerably irritated by the treatment he had received. He had been asked by the police to be good enough to attend this conference, and now he was flung into the street with the other less important people. No one had explained anything to him. He didn't even know who half the people he had seen were. He had heard Lord Arglay's name and recognized it; he had a vague recollection of having once read an extremely outspoken book by Sir Giles on the religious aspect of the marriage customs of a tribe of cannibals in Polynesia. But who Palliser was or the girl who had landed Palliser on the floor he had no idea, nor why she had done it. Why had she rushed round and flown at Sir Giles's throat? 'I almost wish,' he thought, 'she'd flown at mine. Or Sheldrake's. I should have liked to help her wring Sheldrake's neck. I wonder if she hurt herself much. Anyhow it won't matter if she's got one of the Stones. Why the devil didn't I take one? Why does no one tell me what it's all about? Why did Sir Giles cut the Stone to bits? And why did that girl want to stop him?' As far as Rich he entertained himself with such questions.

Rich itself, when he arrived there, seemed to be similarly, but rather more angrily, engaged. There were groups in the streets and at the doors; there were dialogues and conversations proceeding everywhere. There were policemen—a number of policemen—moving as unnoticeably as possible through the slightly uncivil population. In fact it was, Doncaster thought, as much like the morning after the night before on a generous scale as need be. It occurred to him that he would go round and see Mrs. Ferguson's sister on his way; it would be interesting to know whether she remained in her recovered health—if he could reach her, of course, because as he wandered towards her street the groups seemed, in spite of the continually pacing police, to be larger and more numerous. The street itself however was passable, though not much more, and he had just turned into it, when he was startled into a pause by a high shrill voice some distance off which called over the street, 'Where's the Stone? Take me to the Stone.'

Oliver looked at the people near him. One man shook his head placidly and said, 'Ah there he is again.' But the rest were listening, he thought, almost sullenly, and one or two muttered something, and another gave a short laugh. Conversations ceased; a policeman, wandering by, caught Oliver's eye, and seemed to meet it dubiously as if he were not quite certain what to do.

'Where's the Stone?' the voice shrilled again. 'I want to see. Won't some kind friend take a poor old blind man to the Stone?'

'What is it?' Oliver said to his nearest neighbour, the man who had laughed.

'That's old Sam Mutton,' the man said in a surly scorn. 'Stone-blind and half-dotty. He's heard of this Stone and he's made his grand-daughter take him about the town all day to look for it.' He lifted his own voice suddenly and called back, 'No use, Sam, the police have got it. It's not for you and me to get well with it.'

The cry went over the silent street like a threat. But in answer the old man's voice came back, 'I can't see. I want to see. Take me to the Stone.' Each sentence ended in what was nearly a prolonged shriek, and as Oliver took a pace or two forward he saw the speaker in front of him. It was a very old man, bald and wizened, approaching slowly, leaning on the one side on a stick, on the other on the arm of a girl of about twenty, who, as they moved, seemed to be trying to persuade him to return. She was whispering hurriedly to him; her other hand lay on his arm. Even at a little distance Oliver noticed how pale she was and how the hand trembled. But the old man shook it off and began again calling out in that dreadful agonized voice, 'I want to se-ee; take me to the Sto-one.'

On the moment the girl gave way. She collapsed on the ground, her arm slipping from the old man's grasp so that he nearly fell, and broke into a violent fit of hysterics. Two or three women ran to her, but above her rending sobs and laughter her grandfather's voice went up in a more intense refrain. 'Where's the Stone? I can't see. Nancy, I can't see, take me to the Stone.' The policeman had come back and was saying something to Oliver's neighbour who listened sullenly. '—get him home,' Oliver heard, and heard the answer, 'You get him home—if you can.' The policeman—he looked young and unhappy enough—went up to the old man, saying something in a voice that tried to be comfortable and cheering. But old Sam, if that were his name, turned and clutched at him, and broke out in a shrill senile wail of passion that appalled Oliver, 'I'm dying, I'm dying. I want to see before I die. I'm dying. I want to see. O kind, kind friends, will no one bring me to the Stone?'

'The police have got the Stone,' Oliver's neighbour called. 'Who cares if you want to see? The police have got the Stone.'

'God blast the police,' said someone the other side of Oliver, and a young working man, of about his own age, thrust himself violently forward opposite the constable. 'You, damn you, you've killed my wife. My wife's dead, she died this morning, and the baby's dead—and they'd have lived if I'd got the Stone.' He made sudden gestures and the policeman, letting go of the old man, stepped back. Oliver saw two or three more helmets moving forward in support, and a voice behind him said sharply, 'Now then, now then, what's all this?'

He looked round. A group of men were pushing past him. One was a short fierce-looking man, with an aggressive moustache; beside him was an older and larger man, with a grave set face. Behind these two were a police-inspector and two or three constables.

'What's all this?' said the little man angrily. 'Constable, why aren't you keeping the street clear? Don't you know your orders? Who's this man? Why are you letting him make all this noise? What's he got to do with it? Don't you know we can hear him all over the town? Gross incapacity. You'll hear more of this.'

The young constable opened his mouth to speak and shut it again. The tall man laid his hand on his companion's arm. 'One man can't do everything, Chief Constable,' he said in a low voice. 'And Sam's a difficult person to deal with. I think we'd better leave it to the inspector here to deal with things quietly.'

'Quietly?' the Chief Constable snapped. 'Quietly! Look here, Mr. Mayor, you've been at me all day to do things quietly, and I've given in here and given in there, and this is the end of it.' He looked over his shoulder, 'Clear the street at once, inspector,' he said. 'And tell that old dodderer that if he makes another sound I'll have him in prison for brawling.'

The Mayor said firmly, 'You can't arrest him; he's a well-known character here, and everyone's sorry for him and his grand-daughter. Besides, it's natural enough that he should be crying out like this.'

'I don't care whether it's natural or not,' the Chief Constable answered. 'He's not going to do it here. Now, inspector, I'm waiting.'

The inspector signed to his men, who began to make separate and gentle movements forward. But after a step or two the advance flickered and ceased. The general murmur, 'Now then, now then, you can't hang about here,' died in and into the silence with which it was received. The crowd remained sullenly fixed.

'Inspector!' the Chief Constable said impatiently.

The inspector looked at Oliver who was close to him, recognized his kind, and said in a low almost plaintive voice. 'Now, sir, if you'd start some of them would get away.'

'And why the devil,' Oliver asked very loudly, 'should we get away?'

There was a stiffening in the crowd near him, a quick murmur, almost the beginning of a cheer. The Mayor and the Chief Constable both looked at Oliver.

'Say that again, my man,' the latter said, 'and I'll have you in prison for resisting the police.'

298

'The Lord Chief Justice,' Oliver said, more loudly still, 'is entirely opposed to the action of the Government.' He had hardly meant to say that, but as soon as it was said he thought hastily that in the morning's conference the Chief Justice *hadn't* seemed to be exactly one with the Government. But he realized in a minute that his sentence, meaning one thing, had meant to his hearers quite another. A more definite noise broke out around him. 'This,' he thought, 'is almost a roar.'

The Chief Constable began to say something, but the Mayor checked him with a lifted hand. 'Do I understand you, sir,' he asked, 'to say that the Chief Justice considers the action of the Government illegal? Do you speak from your own certain knowledge?'

Oliver thought of saying, 'Well, I don't know about *illegal*,' but the phrase was so deplorably weak that he abandoned it. Besides, in that large room at the Foreign Office—Lord Birlesmere, Sir Giles, Chloe's bleeding fingers—'The Chief Justice's secretary,' he said clearly, 'was seriously injured this morning in—protesting against—the action of—certain associates of the Government, and the Chief Justice takes the most serious view of the situation.'

This might be a little compressed, he felt; Lord Arglay's actual words had seemed a trifle less official. And seriously injured? Still…

The inspector stood still, looking worried, and glanced gloomily at the Chief Constable, who was making half-audible noises. The Mayor considered Doncaster evenly. Somebody behind shouted, 'The Government's broken the law,' and Oliver felt a little cold as he heard this final reduction of his own sentences to a supposed fact. In the following silence, 'I want the Stone' the old man wailed again.

'We all want the Stone,' another voice called, and another, 'Who cares what they say? We want the Stone.' Cheers and shouts answered. A man stumbled heavily against the inspector, who was thrown back upon the Chief Constable.

The incident might have become a mêlée if the Mayor had not intervened. He held up both arms, crying in a great voice, 'Silence, silence! Silence for the Mayor,' and went to a horse-trough near by motioning to Oliver to follow him; by whose assistance he mounted on the edge of the trough. Holding to an electric light standard he began to address the crowd.

'Good people,' he said in a stentorian voice, 'you all know me. I will ask you to return to your homes and leave me to discover the truth about this matter. I am the Mayor of Rich, and if the people of Rich have been injured it is my business to remedy it and help them. If, as appears, the Stone of which we have heard is able to heal illness, and if the Government are using it, as swiftly as may be, for that purpose, it is the duty of all good citizens to accept what delay the common good of all demands. But it is equally their right to be assured that the Government is doing its utmost in the matter, day and night, so that not a single moment may be lost in freeing as many as may be from pain and suffering. I shall make it my concern to discover this at once. I know the hindrances which must, and I fear those which may, follow on what has happened. I will myself go to London.' He paused a moment, then he went on. 'Some of you may know that my son is dying of cancer. If it is a matter of ensuring swiftness and order he and I will be the last in all the country to claim assistance. But I tell you this that you may be very sure that he shall not suffer an hour longer than need be because of the doubts or fears or stupidities of the servants of the people. Return to your homes and to-morrow at this time you shall know all that I know.' He paused again and ended with a loud cry, 'God save the King.'

'God save the King!' yelled Oliver in a thrill of delight, and assisted the Mayor to descend. Who turned on him at once and went on talking before the Chief Constable could interrupt. 'I shall want you,' he said. 'I want all the information you can give me, and I may need your personal help. Are you free? But it doesn't matter whether you are or not. I demand your presence in the name of the King and by the authority of my office. We will go to the Town Hall first. Barker,' he went on, to a man behind him, 'see that the car is kept all ready in front of the Town Hall. Inspector, I rely on you to see that the promise I have made is published everywhere, and I warn you that the bench will examine very carefully any case of reported brawling brought before them in this connexion. Chief Constable, I am obliged for your assistance, but I think the situation is well in hand, and the chief magistrate can dispense with any outside help. Come along, young man—what is your name?'

What account exactly Oliver gave the Mayor he was never very clear. But, whatever it was, it was bound to confirm in the other's mind the importance of the Stone and the need for urging immediate action on the Government. Once in the Town Hall, Oliver found himself in a maze of action. There was a small, stout, and facetious alderman who was apparently being left in charge as deputy mayor; there was an auburn and agitated Town Clerk; there were the girl typists who are spread all over England; there were commissionaires and chauffeurs and telephones and councillors and a male clerk—Oliver had had no idea so many people could accumulate in the seat of authority of a small country town. He was rather curious to learn what the

Mayor's own name was, and at last by dint of studying the notices on the wall discovered that it was Clerishaw—Eustace Clerishaw. He had hardly fixed on this when its owner was on him again.

'I shall want you to come with me,' the Mayor said. 'I am going to London at once.'

'But what good shall I be?' Oliver asked, as he was hurried to the door, but without any real regret at finding himself thus caught up again in the operations of the Stone.

'I may,' the Mayor went on, 'want to see Lord Arglay, but I shall go to the Home Office first.'

'If you get as much satisfaction as we did at the Foreign Office,' Oliver answered, 'you'll be there for months. What do you think they'll do?'

The Mayor, taking no notice, pushed him out of the Town Hall and followed him. There was a large crowd at the entrance, and a cheer went up when they appeared. As they hurried down to the car which stood in readiness a policeman sprang to open it and Oliver recognized the young constable he had seen before. They scrambled in; the policeman banged the door, and put his head in

'Good luck, sir,' he said. 'Good luck and give them hell.'

'Heavens above,' thought Oliver as he sat down, 'the Pretorian Guard's beginning to mutiny.'

For the rest of the journey he was undergoing a close interrogation, and by the time they reached London the Mayor seemed more or less satisfied. He sat back and stretched his legs.

'The Deputy Mayor, with the help of my clerk and so on,' he said, 'is getting into touch with all the Mayors in the affected district. During Sunday crowds from at least five other centres came out to Rich, and returned, I fear, with very little satisfaction. I have been asked questions by all the Mayors, but until I found you I had very little information to go on.'

'I shouldn't think you'd got much now,' Oliver said.

The Mayor looked at his notes. 'As I understand,' he went on, slowly, 'the matter is at present in the hands of the Foreign Office, and some kind of strain exists between that Department and the Lord Chief Justice. I heard from Mr. Sheldrake—whom I saw for a few minutes yesterday—that Lord Arglay was in some way connected with the whole thing—indeed, Mrs. Sheldrake seemed to think he was responsible for the trouble. But I have always been very much impressed by such of Lord Arglay's judgements as I have been able to read and follow, and I was greatly struck by an article of his I once read on the Nature of Law. A little abstract, perhaps, but very interesting; he defined law provisionally as "the formal expression of increasing communal self-knowledge" and had an excursus comparing the variations in law with the variations in poetic diction from age to age, the aim being to discover the best plastic medium for expression in action. Very interesting.'

'He didn't look a bit like that this morning,' Oliver said. 'He just surveyed everything, though he moved quickly enough when that foul Tumulty creature was slashing round with a knife—at least, he told me to move.'

'I think the best plan,' the Mayor said unheeding, 'would be for you to go straight to him. He may not, in his position, be able to do anything, but he said in that article that law should be an exposition of, not an imposition on, the people—so he may be more or less in sympathy. Yes, you go there—I had the address looked up—while I go to the Home Secretary's; it's no use trying Whitehall—I'd better go to his private house first. If I can get no satisfaction....'

'Do you expect to?' Oliver asked.

The Mayor was silent for a few minutes, then he said quite quietly, 'No, I don't. I expect there'll be trouble before we get our way. That's why I want to know about the Chief Justice. If he's on our side it will help us amazingly.'

Oliver tried to imagine the large placid form who had sat comfortably opposite him at the conference leading the crowd from Rich-by-the-Mere to attack London. But though that picture faded too quickly, he realized as he thought that the assistance of the Chief Justice would give the riot an emblem of authority which would transform it into a rebellion. Only he couldn't see Lord Arglay doing it, and he was no nearer to seeing it when the Mayor turned him out of the car at Lancaster Gate and went off, leaving him staring at the front door which concealed the Justice of England. The Justice of England, he reflected, might be out; nothing in the present state of things was more probable. A little more cheerfully he rang the bell, and his hopes were defeated. The maid would see if Lord Arglay was at home. Mr. Doncaster? Would he take a seat?

'Doncaster?' Lord Arglay said, looking at Chloe. 'Doncaster? Ought I to.... I do, vaguely.'

'I think he was there this morning,' Chloe said, 'Just a minute.' She looked among her papers. 'Yes, he was. I made a list of their names in case they should be useful.'

'I sometimes think,' Arglay said, glancing down the slip of paper she gave him, 'that the law of cause and effect isn't really understood. Since whatever you do is bound to be justified, justification is produced. This

Mr. Doncaster comes merely as a result of your having written down his name. Shall we ask him what he thinks—poor deluded wretch!—made him call here?'

They had, at the moment of Oliver's arrival, been arguing whether it was safe for Chloe to go home alone. She had wished to go as usual; the Chief Justice had offered his car, his servants ('though none of them,' he put in, 'would be useful'), and himself to take her. Alternatively, was there no friend she could telephone to, who could call at the house and look after her. 'If you won't stop here, that is.'

But this, considering that the servants knew nothing of the crisis, and considering also matters of dress and convenience, Chloe declined to do. She was more uncertain about summoning Mr. Lindsay. Frank *had* been rather badly treated—and he was almost certain to be in, working—and he would love to be called on. Ought she to give him the pleasure? 'But we should have to tell him,' she said aloud, half-unconsciously.

'The papers,' Lord Arglay said, 'have already done a good deal of that. And a friend of yours——' with a gesture he opened the secret to her friend's entrance.

Duty could sometimes be pleasure, Chloe thought looking at him, and certainly pleasure sometimes looked remarkably like duty. Still … after all, Frank *had* had a difficult Saturday. And nothing at all of a Sunday, since she had refused to stir out for fear she might be wanted. After a brief explanation therefore she got through to Frank, offered a tepid request, and came back feeling unexpectedly gloomy. It was then that Oliver had arrived.

'Yes, O yes,' Chloe said, 'I should ask him. I'll go and wait for Mr. Lindsay in the hall.' That, she felt, described her existence—she would always be waiting for someone in the hall. While the great people talked in studies and drawing-rooms. She rather hoped Frank wouldn't come, then she could get off by herself before the Chief Justice had finished with this Mr. Doncaster. What was the shortest time she could decently wait?

'Show Mr. Doncaster in,' Lord Arglay said to the maid. 'And when a Mr. Lindsay whom I'm expecting comes, show *him* in. If,' he went on to Chloe, 'this fellow has anything really secret I'll take him away, while you tell your friend as much as you choose of the story. If you can remember it, which is more than I shall be able to do soon. I do wish I knew what, if anything, had happened at Birmingham. If that fellow Pondon has come back what a difficulty he'll have explaining to the police! Mr. Doncaster? Why yes, I remember you this morning now—Miss Burnett, if you remember Miss Burnett, remembered you before. Do sit down.'

'Thank you very much, Lord Arglay,' Oliver said, obeying.

'An extraordinary business, isn't it?' the Chief Justice went on. 'How goes your end?—whichever *is* your end. For I'm ashamed to say I am not quite clear what party you are of, so to speak. Mr. Sheldrake's, wasn't it?'

Oliver crossed his legs. 'I represent,' he said gravely, 'the people. I am the autos of their autocratic mouth. I am the sovereign will. I am….' The solemn tone of his mock proclamation faded, and he ended, lamely and seriously, 'the people.'

Lord Arglay observed the change of tone and looked at him carefully. 'And how do the people come in?' he asked.

Oliver, as best he could, explained. As he began he felt a fool, but his eyes lit on the strip of black silk across Chloe's hand—she had declined to attempt to heal it by the Stone—and he derived therefrom a certain strength. After all, this girl had knocked the Professor over and attacked Sir Giles; she had thrust herself across the will of that unpleasant little beast. And Sir Giles had been left with Sheldrake at the Foreign Office when the rest of them were turned out. And the people were clamouring for life and health from that Mystery which the police, on behalf of the American, had pouched.

'I don't quite see,' Lord Arglay said when he had done, 'on what grounds you asserted so strongly that I disapproved of the Government.'

'Well, sir,' Oliver said, 'I thought you approved of Miss Burnett.'

'I always approve of Miss Burnett,' Arglay answered. 'It would be temperamentally impossible to me to have a secretary of whom I disapproved. But approving of Miss Burnett has not, from the beginning, been necessarily equivalent to disapproving of the Government.'

'But in this case, sir…?' Oliver suggested.

The Chief Justice shook his head. 'No, no,' he said. 'In the first place I don't know what they are doing; in the second, I neither approve nor disapprove of governments, but of men, and that only according to the order and decision of the laws. I am a chair, Mr. Doncaster, not a horse—not even Rosinante.'

'But if Don Quixote came before the chair?' Oliver asked.

'I should think he is very likely to, if he goes on as he is at present,' Arglay said drily. 'But even then—Don Quixote or Don Juan or the Cid Ruy Diaz the Campeador—it is all one. I have not eyes to see nor mouth to speak but as the laws shall direct me.'

'But if it is a case beyond any law?' Oliver said.

'There is no case beyond law,' the Chief Justice answered. 'We may mistake in the ruling, we may be deceived by outward things and cunning talk, but there is no dispute between men which cannot be resolved in equity. And in its nature equity is from those between whom it exists: it is passion acting in lucidity.'

'Mr. Lindsay,' the maid said, opening the door. Chloe stood up swiftly and went forward to meet him, and as she did so it seemed to Oliver as if Arglay's last phrase took on a sudden human meaning. A vivid presence passed him, and he found himself gravely reconstructing the meaning of those words. On a sudden impulse he turned to Lord Arglay. 'Is that what you would call Miss Burnett's action this morning?' he asked.

For a moment the Chief Justice frowned; it appeared to him unnecessary that this Mr. Doncaster should remark on anything Chloe had chosen to do. But the neatness of the phrase placated him; he looked at Oliver with cautious but appreciative eyes. 'I will admit, at least,' he said, 'that, entirely as a private man, I regard Giles Tumulty as something very nearly without the law.' He stepped forward to meet Frank.

The half-hour which followed was not one on which Chloe looked back, for some time, without growing hot. It was largely, she felt, Mr. Doncaster's fault for arriving so late; it was largely Frank's for arriving so soon. He had been dragged from his surveyor's studies to take her home, and she didn't want to go—not until she knew whether this Mayor was coming. But if she didn't go at once she must explain, and how could she explain in front of Mr. Doncaster? And why did Frank look so *dull*? And why, in an effort to be conversational, must he ask her at once if she had hurt her hand? And why was the Chief Justice displaying a remote intention of leaving her to talk to Frank while he went back to Mr. Doncaster? She managed to introduce them, in order (by the exercise of a certain dexterity which she was uneasily conscious Lord Arglay patiently humoured), to move the conversation—it was no more lightly done—on to the common subject of Mr. Sheldrake. But it continually showed signs of breaking into two halves, and at the end of about a quarter of an hour she began wretchedly to make the first preparations for departure. She put one or two papers together, she opened her handbag, and saw within it the white silk handkerchief in which her Type of the Stone had been wrapped. Under cover of a monologue of Lord Arglay's she pushed aside the soft opaqueness and gazed at the Mystery. Nothing, she thought, had ever looked more feebly useless, more dull and dead, than that bit of white stone. The flakings were not gold, they were yellow; they were obviously merely accidental and it was only a perverse fancy that could see in the black smudges the tracing of the Divine Name. She put her hand down sharply to cover it again, and found that her fingers were unwilling to move. Dared she so, in action, deny the Stone? Thought was multitudinous but action single. A pushing aside or a ritual veiling?—one it must be. Nobody could see or know what she did, yet she felt as if an expectancy lay around, as if something waited, docile but immortal, the consequences of her choice. 'Cowardly fool!' Chloe said to herself and, so protesting against her own action, drew Lord Arglay's handkerchief ceremonially over the Stone.

In spite of her delay she had reluctantly gone, attended by Mr. Lindsay, before the Mayor of Rich arrived at Lancaster Gate. He was shown in at once and Oliver, hastily presenting him to the Chief Justice, said urgently: 'Well, what happened?'

The Mayor answered slowly: 'I have had to remind the Home Secretary that the office of Mayor is filled, not by the decision of the Government, but by the choice of the people.'

'Have you indeed?' Oliver said.

'I had some difficulty in getting to see him,' the Mayor went on, 'and when I did he was bent on assuring me that the matter was being dealt with. I pressed him to tell me more. I pointed out that I was responsible for order in the town, and that the effect of maintaining secrecy would be highly damaging. We had a long discussion and in the end I was compelled to point out to him that, if no satisfactory statement were made, I should be driven to place the resources of the mayoralty at the disposal of any constitutional agitation that might arise. I was very careful to say "constitutional." It was then that he threatened me with removal and I reminded him that the Mayors came by vote of the Town Council who are chosen by the people.'

CHAPTER XI

THE FIRST REFUSAL OF CHLOE BURNETT

Chloe's chief regret, when she and Frank got out of her bus at Highgate, was that there was a quarter of an hour's walk before them. She made a half-hearted effort—half-hearted on his account as much as hers—to persuade him to return at once, but when this failed she resigned herself to his inevitable desire to discuss the whole matter. Saturday afternoon's experience, the Sunday papers, things said that evening, had made it impossible to keep from him the secret of the Stone. But, accustomed to him as she was, she seemed to hear in his voice a hint of anxiety which at first she attributed to his concern for her.

'It shows you things in your mind?' he said as they turned a corner.

'Apparently,' Chloe assented. 'At least, it showed Lord Arglay Sir Giles's mind.'

He was silent for a minute or two. Then: 'Tells you things?' he went on, following his own thoughts.

Chloe considered. 'Tells you?' she asked at last.

'Things you mightn't know—or might have forgotten,' he answered. 'It would make things clear to you, wouldn't it? If it shows you thoughts.'

'I suppose it might,' Chloe said, rather vague about what he meant and a little irritated at her vagueness. There was another short silence.

'And it can be separated?' Frank said.

'No,' said Chloe firmly, 'it can't. Or only by people like Sir Giles.'

The pause after this began to annoy her; the conversation was going in spasms like hiccups. 'Let's talk of something else,' she said. 'It's only a month to the exam., isn't it? I do hope you'll get through.'

'I suppose,' he answered lightly, 'you wouldn't like to lend me the Stone?'

'To——' Chloe stared. 'The Stone? Whatever for?'

'Well,' said Frank, 'if it shows you things—I mean, if it helps the mind, the memory or whatever … well, don't you see—if one could remember at the right time——' He made a second's pause and went on 'That's where an examination's so unfair; one can't remember everything just at the minute and just forgetting one single fact or formula that one knows perfectly well throws the whole thing out. It isn't even a case of wanting to be sure one would remember, because one *would* remember if one didn't forget—I mean, if one wasn't afraid of forgetting. It isn't, in that way, as if there was any unfairness. I wouldn't dream of taking an unfair advantage; it wouldn't really be doing more than taking an aspirin if one had a headache on the day. Lots of the fellows have mnemonics—it'd only be feeling that one had a pretty good system. It isn't as if——'

'Frank, do *stop*,' Chloe said. 'What is it you want?'

'I've just told you,' Frank said. 'Would you lend me the Stone just till after my exam.?'

'No, I wouldn't,' Chloe answered. 'I'm sorry, Frank, but I really can't.'

'Well—if you don't want to part with yours—I quite understand—would you … make one for me?' Frank asked. 'You know how important it is for me to get through, darling. I don't know what'll happen if I muff it.'

'I suppose you'll go in again,' Chloe said, anger growing within her. It was only, she warned herself, that Frank didn't—and, not knowing all about it, couldn't—understand. But nobody—nobody—did understand, she least of all.

'Well—perhaps,' Frank said, defeated by this realism. 'But it'd be much more convenient to get through at once. It might mean a great deal more than a year later on—it gives one a better chance.' Chloe made a small effort. 'Dear Frank,' she said, 'I hate to seem a pig, but I couldn't … I couldn't do that—not with the Stone.'

'But it wouldn't be unfair,' Frank urged. 'Anyone who can manage any way of remembering things does—short of writing them down. It's only just to safeguard the mind against a sort of stage-fright; just a sort of … of … cooling-mixture.'

'O God,' Chloe said suddenly, 'is there no end?'

Frank looked at her in a hurt surprise. 'I shouldn't think I was asking very much,' he said, 'not if you really want me to pass. You might know that I wouldn't ask you to do anything unfair. It doesn't put me in a better position; it only prevents me being in a worse. They'd all do as much if they could.'

'I don't care if they would or not. I don't care whether it's right or fair or whatever you call it or not,' Chloe answered. 'Frank, do try and see it. It's just that we can't use the Stone like that.'

'But why not?' Frank asked in mere bewilderment. 'If it can do all those things? Your Lord Arglay's been using it, hasn't he?'

'Not for himself,' Chloe answered.

'But I'm not asking you to use it for yourself. It's really an unselfish thing you'd be doing in lending it to me, or giving me one,' Frank urged. 'I did think you'd like me to pass—but I suppose you don't care about that either.'

'Don't be beastly, Frank,' Chloe said.

'It doesn't look much like it, anyhow,' the misguided Frank went on. 'You don't seem to mind other people being helped—and I don't understand *why* you won't. You've always been out to make the best of your chances, and you won't do the same for me. You'd use it quick enough to save yourself being sacked, I expect.'

'I wouldn't,' Chloe said sharply. 'I wouldn't use it to buy myself food if I was starving.'

'O don't talk rubbish,' Frank said and fell into sullenness.

They walked on silently. He had dropped her arm or she had dropped his; anyhow, they were disjoined. Her hands were empty but for the handbag, and in that ridiculous bag the absurd Cause. It seemed from its seclusion to taunt her. 'Throw me away,' it seemed to be saying, 'throw me into the gutter. Am I worth all this trouble?' It wouldn't, she thought, with a touch of sanity, please Frank any better if she did—not Frank. He wouldn't appreciate the gesture. Besides, it wasn't her business to throw it away. 'I am yours,' the Stone gibed at her, 'your own—throw me away. You're in danger of throwing him away.' From somewhere her memory brought up a text—'My lovers and friends hast thou set afar from me; and hid my acquaintance out of my sight.' She didn't want him to go like this.

'Darling,' she breathed tentatively, 'don't be cross. I'd do anything I could.'

'That,' said Frank coldly, 'isn't true, Chloe. It's a quite simple thing and you won't do it. Very well; it's your Stone. But it's no good saying you'd do it if you could. You can and you won't.'

'Do it,' something said to her, 'do it. Why ever not? Are you setting up to know what's right? Do it, and be a real friend to him.' Friendship—after all, ought she to do for her friend what she wouldn't do for herself? Ought she to break her heart and do it? Was it only her own wish she was safeguarding?

From her own point of view it was by the mercy of the Stone that Frank said again at this moment, with a touch of superior and angry rationalism—'Yes, you can and you won't.'

'Very well then,' Chloe said, stopping dead. 'I can and I won't. And now go away. Go away or I shall hate you. Go.'

'I prefer to see you right home,' Frank said formally.

'I don't want you to,' Chloe said. 'I can't bear it. O Frank, do go.'

'I don't want to be nasty,' he said irresolutely, 'but I can't see why you won't. I've explained to you that it wouldn't be unfair.'

'I know, I know,' Chloe said. 'Good-night. I'll write to-morrow.'

'O well, good-night,' Frank answered, and found himself looking after her in a temper of which he had never imagined she could be the cause. 'So ridiculous,' he thought; 'women never can reason clearly, but I did think she was more intelligent. It isn't very much to ask her to do for anyone she professes to like. But it's always the same; everybody wants to have their own way.'

Still meditating on the insufficiency of human virtue he turned back towards the terminus at the bottom of Highgate Hill. Anxious, however, as he might be, to see Chloe's point of view, it eluded him with persistent ingenuity. As a friend, as something—well, different from a friend—she ought to have wanted to help him. Not that he found it easy to accept the Stone, but his incredulity was a good deal intimidated by the sudden arrival of Mrs. Sheldrake on the Saturday, the columns of the Sunday papers, the rather mysterious position of Lord Arglay, and Chloe's own great concern with it. He thought rather vaguely of radium, vita-glass, magnetism, and psycho-analysis, the possibility of some quickening power exercised on the brain, or some revitalization of the nervous functions. The last phrase appeared plausible enough to cover all instances of recovery to health and what—so far as he could see—was a sort of mind-reading. As for movement in space … perhaps it was hardly so satisfactory there. Nervous functions would have to be thoroughly vitalized in order——

A fresh voice interrupted him. He looked up to see another friend—but this time a young man.

'Hullo, Carnegie,' he said gloomily.

Albert Carnegie looked at him with an irritating cheerfulness.

'What's the gloom about?' he asked. 'Why the misery?'

'I'm not miserable,' Lindsay said perversely. 'Why should I be miserable?'

'Sorry,' Carnegie answered. 'I thought you were looking a bit under the weather.'

'It's this damned examination, I expect,' Lindsay said. 'I've been sticking to it close enough, these last days.'

Carnegie turned. 'I'll walk back with you,' he said. 'How's Miss Burnett?'

'Well enough, I suppose,' Miss Burnett's friend answered. 'But she's got mixed up with all the business about this Stone in the papers, and she's a bit on edge about it.'

'What, the Stone that makes people well?' Carnegie asked.

'Makes anyone do anything,' Lindsay told him, 'so far as I can understand. Makes people fly or jump or see into each other's minds, so they say.'

'Fly!' the other exclaimed.

'Well, if you don't call getting from one place to another in practically no time flying, I don't know what you do call it,' Lindsay said. 'And I saw something like it happen myself, so I can't say it's all tripe.'

'Do you mean you saw someone move through the air by using this Stone?' Carnegie asked.

'I saw a woman suddenly appear where she hadn't been—and Chloe says she's seen it done, seen Lord Arglay disappear and reappear and have been somewhere in between. It all sounds nonsensical enough, but what with what I saw and Chloe and the papers together I don't know what to think.'

Carnegie walked on for some distance in silence, his mind occupied with a side of the question which had so far only occurred to Mr. Sheldrake and Reginald Montague and to them in a limited sense. But Carnegie's occupation happened to be in the headquarters of the National Transport Union, and while Lindsay was talking there came to him the idea that if—only if, because of course there couldn't—but *if* there were anything to it, then it was the sort of it that the General Secretary of the Union would think was most distinctly his own business. Any violent disturbance of transport would be, and this would be a very violent disturbance. At least if there were more than one, or perhaps a few Stones. It was against nature that there should be more.

'I suppose there are only one or two Stones in existence, so far as we know?' he said in a few minutes, as casually as possible.

'It doesn't seem to matter,' Lindsay answered, still brooding over his grievance. He broke into a short explanation of his desires and was gratified by the concentration with which Carnegie listened. 'So that,' he ended, 'I really don't think it's too much to suggest. It gives her no trouble and no one could call it unfair.'

'And every single one of these things has the same power?' Carnegie asked.

'I know it's all ridiculous, but that's their story,' Lindsay agreed. 'So one would think that Chloe…'

'And who have got them now?' Carnegie interrupted.

'Well, Chloe has, and this Sheldrake man, and Arglay I suppose … I wish Chloe wasn't with Arglay; I think he's none too good an influence. These lawyers are such hidebound pedants very often, and Chloe's rather open to suggestion. I don't mean that she's weak exactly, but she's rather over-anxious to please, and doesn't take her own line sometimes as strongly as she ought to. Now she might have seen that in a thing like this she ought to exercise her own judgement and not be dominated by legal forms.'

'Yes,' said Carnegie, whom Chloe only interested at the moment as one of the holders of the Stone. 'Anyhow there must be a good few knocking about at the present moment, and more to be made at any time?'

They had come out into the main road opposite a large *Evening News* placard which announced 'Interview with Mrs. Ferguson.' Another close by stated 'Where the Stone came from,' and a *Star* placard 'The Stone—Government Action. Official.' The *Evening Standard's* 'The Situation at Rich' was comparatively out of date. Carnegie looked at them. It might be, it certainly was, a hoax somehow or other, but even as a hoax he thought the General Secretary would like to know. The only question was—now or in the morning? At the Tube entrance he left Lindsay who went on his way meditating over Chloe's perversity.

If he had been able to press his request again at that moment he might have gained it. For Chloe was lying in bed, miserable enough, and, with her habitual disposition (as Mr. Lindsay had very nearly understood) to wonder if she had behaved unkindly to others, was almost regretting her firmness. It seemed now so small a thing that Frank had wanted, and she might have been merely selfishly one-ideaed—and her own ideaed—in refusing him. After all, Lord Arglay had made use of the Stone. Yes, but that *had* been for someone else's good. And had not she been asked only to help another's good? it wasn't her examination. And would not Lord Arglay have had her use it for her own good? had not he bidden her use it, if need were, if there were danger? Yes, danger, but Frank's desire to pass an examination could hardly be called danger. (Besides even in danger—could she?) She couldn't see Lord Arglay using it to make himself Chief Justice, though he might to ensure a right judgement and proper sentence. But had she any right to inflict on Frank her own interpretation of what the Chief Justice's will might be? Frank had no particular use for the Chief Justice. It would be, she thought, convenient if they could ask of Suleiman ben Daood himself what the proper use of the Stone was, though even Suleiman, as far as she remembered the legends she had studied a few days before, had fallen sometimes from wisdom. Asmodeus had sat on his throne, and Pharaoh's daughter had deceived him, and he had built altars to strange gods. She remembered Lord Arglay's bargain of that evening; was she really supposed to be believing in God? And if so, who? or what? Suleiman's? Presumably. Or

Octavius Caesar's or Charlemagne's or Haroun-al-Raschid's—supposing they all had one? Or the Stone's own God?

Half-unconsciously her hand felt for it where it lay under her pillow in its silken veil, and as she touched it sleep or some other healing power flowed through her. Asleep or awake, at once or after a long time—it seemed both in the dream that possessed her—she seemed to see before her a great depth of space that changed itself while she looked into it and became a hall with carved pillars and a vast crowd surging through it. Far off she heard a roaring that grew louder and by its own noise divided and ordered the crowd so that the many small scurrying figures were heaped in masses on either side. She felt herself somewhere among them, but not in any one place; she was carried through them, seeing all round her brown faces and long dark beards and bright turbans and cloaks, the roaring still in her ears. And then the crowd opened before her and she saw suddenly the great centre of the whole, but first in masses and only afterwards its own central height. For to right and left as she gazed there expanded huge gatherings of seated men: on the one side men in the same cloaks and head-dresses she had already seen, with little rolls or boxes fastened to their foreheads and wrists, and some of them held antique parchment in their hands. Their faces were Jewish, and mostly very old and lined with much thought, only here and there she saw one and another young and ardent and again one and another still older than most but astonishingly full and clear and happy. Over against them, but with a broad aisle between them were another company, in many different garbs and all unknown to her; or almost all, for among the turbans and helmets and diadems she saw suddenly a Chinese mandarin sitting gravely watchful, and another whose bearded face came to her as if she had looked on it in a gallery of high statuary among divine heads of Aphrodite and Apollo, of Theseus and Heracles and Aesclepius. But most of the rest were strange and terrible, only not so terrible as those on whom her eyes next rested. For beyond these, and again in two opposing companies, she saw figures that seemed larger or lesser than mortal man, and other figures who were of other natures and kept in them only a faint image of humanity. There a seeming fountain twisted its ascending and descending waters into such a simulacrum, and there again was one having many heads, and one again whose writhing arms encircled him round and round and sometimes leapt forth and were again retrieved till it seemed as if the ancient Kraken itself had become human. Over and among them flew many birds and by their flights her glance was drawn upward till she saw that the whole roof of that place was formed of birds, vibrating and rising and falling with persistent but unequal motion, with colours gleaming and iridescent or dull and heavy. In front there hung immovable one huge monster of a bird like the father and lord of all that are of the eagle and vulture tribe, with his eyes filmed and his head and dreadful beak a little on one side as though he listened to all he could not see. And as she shuddered and looked down she saw below him a number of huge lions' heads, and the red jaws opened in a terrific roar as the beasts seemed, some to crouch before the spring, some to be high-ramping in a wild fury. In this last astonishment all former wonder was swallowed up—and that she felt surprise and awe she knew even then, and knew also that she did not truly dream, but even while the beasts raged and roared there passed between them a note of music and a voice sang 'Praise to the Eternal One; glory and honour and adoration be to the Lord God of Israel; blessed be He!' and immediately the noise of the beasts sounded in one answering roar and was still, and they also. Then Chloe saw them stand fixed, on the steps of a throne, six on the one side, six on the other; and the throne itself was above and behind them, carved as it were out of sapphire, very deep and clear; and on the throne a king sat, with a crown on his head. In the crown was the Stone, and it shone with a soft whiteness, and in it, amid the gold, in a deep blackness the letters of the Name were moving and glowing. Below the throne Chloe saw the companies assembled, the companies of the doctors of the Law and of the ambassadors from many lands, and the awful Djinn and Angels, diabolic or divine, who waited on the word of Suleiman ben Daood, king in Jerusalem. Then she looked again at the king, and saw that his right hand lay closed upon his vestmented knees, but while she looked he lifted it slowly up, the whole assemblage bowing themselves to the ground, and opened it. But what was in or on it Chloe did not see, for there leapt upon her from it a blinding light, and at once her whole being felt a sudden devastating pain and then a sense of satisfaction entire and exquisite, as if desires beyond her knowledge had been evoked and contented at once, a perfect apprehension, a longing and a fulfilment. So intense was the stress that she shrieked aloud; immediately it was gone, and she found herself standing upright by the side of the bed, trembling, open-mouthed, holding agonizedly to its framework.

She sank onto it and remained exhausted. Only it seemed in a little that the noise of the lions was still in her ears and a voice with it. Gradually she found the voice was saying: 'Miss Burnett! Miss Burnett! Are you all right, Miss Burnett?' and knew it for the landlady's.

'Yes, Mrs. Webb, yes, all right, thank you,' Chloe stammered. 'It was just—it was—it was something in my sleep. I'm so sor—I mean, I was—please, it's quite, quite all right.'

'Are you sure?' Mrs. Webb said, still doubtfully. 'I thought you were being killed.'

'Thank you so *very* much,' Chloe said again, and then in a sudden rush of heroic virtue got to her feet, struggled across the room, unlocked the door, and spoke comfortingly to the anxious Mrs. Webb till the old lady at last went away. Chloe shut the door, with a desolating sense that she had forgotten everything, went back to bed, and as she stretched herself down into it went off immediately into a profound sleep.

So profound and effective was it that she was rather more than half an hour late the next morning in arriving at Lancaster Gate, where she found Lord Arglay in a high state of excitement. 'Don't apologize,' he said, 'but I thought you were never coming. Nothing wrong? No, all right, that's merely my rubbing it in. Look at this and all will be forgiven.' He held out to her the morning paper, directing her eyes to a remote paragraph. 'Strange Incident at Birmingham,' she read. 'Missing Man Burgles Laboratory.'

'The laboratory assistant Elijah Pondon who was supposed to have lost his memory at Birmingham was discovered this morning in curious circumstances. When the senior demonstrator visited the laboratory late last night during Professor Palliser's absence in London, whose assistant the missing man was, he found Pondon already there. His entrance is at present inexplicable as he had no key, and the laboratory had not been in use during yesterday. Efforts to obtain a statement have not so far succeeded, as he appears to be in a dazed condition. It is supposed he must have some means of entry known only to himself.'

'"Means of entry known only to himself,"' Lord Arglay said. '"Dazed condition!" I should think he probably*was* in a dazed condition. But we've done it, child. We've given him a means of entry known … and so forth.'

'We?' Chloe said.

'We,' Lord Arglay said firmly. 'By virtue of the Stone, if you like, but after all it was we who determined and tried—determined, dared, and done. Heavens, how pleased I am!' His mood changed and he began to walk up and down the room. 'I wonder what Pondon makes of it,' he said. 'Does he know anything? does he guess anything? What did he see, feel, or do? or didn't he do, feel, or see anything? Has he just linked up with Friday night? or does his memory…' His voice died as he meditated.

Chloe fingered the paper. 'Do you think we ought to know?' she asked.

'I don't know about "ought,"' Lord Arglay answered, 'but I should very much like to know. Why?'

'I was wondering,' Chloe said. 'I could go to Birmingham if you liked and talk to him a little.'

'Things are getting so frightfully complicated,' the Chief Justice sighed. 'There's the Government and Sheldrake and Giles and the Persians and the Mayor—all busy about it.' Chloe mentally added Frank Lindsay to the list, and might (had she known in what confidences Mr. Lindsay's irritation had resulted) have added also the Secretary of the National Transport Union. But she said nothing.

'I don't really like letting you out of my sight,' Arglay went on. 'Yet it *might* be useful to know what this Pondon knows—if anything,' he added dubiously. 'Is there anyone who could go with you? What about your friend Mr. Lindsay?'

'No, O no,' Chloe said, stopped, and went on. 'But what do you think could possibly happen, Lord Arglay? They haven't any reason to do anything to *me*.'

'I told you last night,' the Chief Justice answered, 'that they're bound to want to get all the Types into their possession—Sheldrake and the Government anyhow, and I suppose the Persians, only they don't stand a chance. And now there'll be the Mayor too; I don't believe he realizes yet that I have one.'

'You didn't tell him?' Chloe asked.

'No,' Arglay answered. 'I'm becoming very shy of telling anyone anything about the Stone. But he's bound to hear, and then he'll be at me to go down to Rich on a mission of healing. Well, I won't.'

This possibility was a new idea to Chloe and for a few moments she gazed at Lord Arglay in silence.

'You won't?' she asked at last, consideringly.

'I withdraw "won't,"' he answered, 'because I don't really know from moment to moment what I shall be doing. I may. I may find myself sitting in the market place or the Old Moot Hall or whatever they have there, handing the Stone to one after another, and watching the sick take up their beds and walk. Or at least get off them. O don't, don't let's go into that now. Would you like to go to Birmingham?'

'I think I should rather,' Chloe said. 'I should like to see the man you saved. And whether he feels anything about it.'

Lord Arglay went to the telephone. With his hand on the receiver he paused. 'Do you remember Mr. Doncaster?' he asked.

'Yes, of course,' Chloe said. 'Why?'

'Did you like Mr. Doncaster?' Lord Arglay went on.

'He seemed quite nice and intelligent, I thought,' Chloe answered. 'I didn't trouble about him much.'

'Would you mind him coming to Birmingham with you?' Arglay said.

'It seems quite unnecessary,' Chloe objected. 'But no—not if you would like him to. It's nice of you to worry—' she added suddenly.

The Chief Justice, engaged in ringing up the hotel where the Mayor and Oliver had found a night's shelter, waved a hand, and then, while waiting for Oliver to be found, said: 'After all, when this is over—I suppose it will be, some time—there is *Organic Law*. If you like. Not that you really care for Organic Law, do you, child?'

She answered his smile with another, flushing a little, then she said: 'I do see something of it, I think. But it seems so far away from…'

'People,' Lord Arglay said. 'And yet so is the Stone. Or it looks like it. On our last night's hypothesis—Is that Mr. Doncaster? This is Lord Arglay. Mr. Doncaster, are you doing anything urgent to-day, either for yourself or for Don Quixote?… I was wondering whether you could and would take Miss Burnett to Birmingham…. O the same story…. Yes, she'll tell you all about it in the train…. Do. Good-bye.—So that's settled.'

'I don't know what use he's going to be,' Chloe said.

'O—lunch,' said Lord Arglay, 'and tickets … have you any money, by the way? I'll get you some … and to keep an eye on your back in case a Persian attacks you with a yataghan or what not.'

'And what use am I going to be?' Chloe asked.

'You will be of one chief use,' Arglay answered. 'You will discover all that is possible of the nature of the Stone.' He put his arm over her shoulders and she reached up her hand and took his. 'It may be,' he went on, 'that before these things are ended we shall have great need of knowing … and perhaps of trusting … the Stone.'

CHAPTER XII
NATIONAL TRANSPORT

The General Secretary of the National Transport Union listened to his subordinate the next morning with considerable incredulity. It was, in fact, only the caution necessary to his official position that prevented him being openly contemptuous, and even that caution was strained.

'Do you expect me to believe that a man can fly through walls and ceilings?' he asked.

'No, sir,' Carnegie said deferentially. 'I don't expect you to believe anything—I don't know that I do. But I thought you'd like to know what was being said.'

'But who's saying it—except some friend of yours?' the General Secretary asked. 'I mean—it's not evidence, is it?'

'My friend mentioned Lord Arglay, sir,' Carnegie ventured. 'That's really what made me decide to tell you.'

'What!' the General Secretary said, 'I'd forgotten that bit. D'you mean the Chief Justice?'

'Yes, sir. This girl is his secretary.'

Mr. Theophilus Merridew got up and went across to the fireplace, at which he stood staring.

'It's obviously got twisted round somehow,' he said at last irritably. 'But what on earth could get twisted into such a fantastic tale? I think I'd better see your friend, Carnegie.'

'Yes, sir,' Carnegie said. 'You won't forget that he may not really have meant to tell me so much?'

'I shouldn't think he did,' the General Secretary answered. 'If I hadn't always found you a very reliable fellow—and if it wasn't for Lord Arglay—I met him once on a Commission and he seemed a very level-headed sort of man. But this…. No, I won't. The whole thing's too ridiculous…. But what the devil can it be they've got hold of? Tell me all about it again.'

Carnegie did so, stressing his own unbelief and his anxiety merely to bring it to his chief's notice as part of his official duty, however wild the rumour might be, in anything that had to do with transport.

'Can't we get hold of a bit of this precious Stone?' Merridew asked at the end. 'Who's got it?'

'Well, sir, the girl's got a bit—because Lindsay wanted it, and I understood Lord Arglay had, and of course the Government because of this affair at Rich. I don't know who else. O! Sheldrake.'

'What!' said Merridew. 'What, the Atlantic Airways man? Why didn't you say so before? I know Sheldrake well enough—I'll go and see *him*. Whatever bit of truth there is behind this he'll have got hold of. And if the bit of truth is anything we ought to know about—he won't want an upset any more than we do.'

'I thought he was on the other side, sir,' Carnegie said smiling.

'Profits mean employment, employment means profits,' said Mr. Merridew. 'Didn't we agree on that at the last Conciliation Conference? Very well then. I'll see if I can get him at once.'

It happened therefore a little later that morning that Sheldrake was asked if he could see Mr. Merridew, who for one reason or another was a fairly frequent caller and was admitted.

'I've come on a funny business,' he said cheerfully, sitting down. 'I want to know anything you can tell me about this Stone of yours.'

'Eh?' said Sheldrake, really surprised, for he could imagine no reason why Merridew should take an interest in a medicinal stone. And there had been nothing else in the papers. 'The Stone? Why do you want to know about the Stone?'

The General Secretary, equally in fear of ridicule and negligence, went carefully.

'I want to know what truth there is in this rumour that Lord Arglay's putting about,' he said, 'that it's going to do something queer to transport.'

'Transport?' Sheldrake asked with a pretence of renewed surprise. 'Does Lord Arglay say that?'

'No, no,' Mr. Merridew said. 'You don't catch me committing myself to that, not with a lawyer. I don't mind letting his name drop in, so to speak, between you and me, but actually perhaps I'd better say—what truth there is in this rumour that's got about? I needn't tell you that, whatever it is, we don't want transport reduced any more than you do.'

Sheldrake thought for a minute or two. On the one hand he wasn't anxious to bring anyone into the secret; on the other, to have the Union at his back would bring extra pressure to bear on the Government, of whose intentions he still remained doubtful. It had been desirable that he should recover his own Stone, but it was absolutely necessary that he should stop any ideas—still more any copies—of it from getting about. That would be, if not ruin, at least very considerable inconvenience. And it would mean very considerable inconvenience to Mr. Merridew's clients also, of that he was sure. Weighing all this in his mind, and throwing into the balance Mr. Merridew's own reputed and experienced discretion, he decided to speak. He gave, without names, a summary of how it had reached him, of the concern felt in high quarters, of its powers medicinal and expeditory. And finally he drew from his inner waistcoat pocket the absurd Thing itself, and, very carefully holding it, displayed it to Mr. Merridew, who sat staring at it.

'Well,' he said at last, 'that's not going to damage transport, is it? It looks like nothing on earth. What's it supposed to *do*? What … what is it?' he ended helplessly.

Sheldrake shook his head. 'Tumulty says something about it being an original.'

'Original enough,' Mr. Merridew murmured, still staring.

'And Lord Arglay told my wife it was the centre of the derivations,' Sheldrake added.

'Centre of what derivations?' Merridew asked, more bewildered than ever. 'Look here, Sheldrake, can't you show me what it'll do? What *happens* when you … use it, if that's the word?'

Sheldrake being not unwilling to convince him, Mr. Merridew emerged from the next few minutes in a startled and very anxious condition. It seemed clear indeed that transport was going to be in a serious state of collapse if the Stone was multiplied. On the other hand he very naturally and very badly wanted it. 'But what's this girl doing with it?' he asked. 'Carnegie told me that his friend said she was Arglay's secretary and she had one.'

'I know, I know,' Sheldrake said. 'Arglay and she have them, and I wish they hadn't. But I can't get Birlesmere to do anything drastic; this Chief Justice is too important to be … just dealt with, so he says. I don't suppose he'll do anything with it, but I wish to God we had them all under lock and key. It's not safe while they're about in the world.'

Merridew got up meditatively. 'Well, anyhow,' he said, 'we run together in this. You'll let me know of any developments?'

'I will,' Sheldrake answered. 'And keep it quiet. You won't want your conferences to get nervy. Tell me if you manage to get hold of Arglay's.'

'I don't know about Arglay's,' Merridew said, 'but I wonder whether…. All right. Good-bye for now.'

He returned to his office still in profound meditation and when he had reached it sent for Carnegie.

'This friend of yours,' he began, 'the fellow who told you about the Stone—I've seen Sheldrake, and I'm bound to say it seems a serious business—you keep your mouth shut, Carnegie, and stand by me, and I'll look after you … understand? Very well. As I was saying, this friend of yours—who is he?'

Carnegie explained Frank Lindsay.

'Well off?' asked Mr. Merridew. 'No, of course not. And he was a bit up in the air over it, was he? Is he a … sensible fellow? the kind that can see where his own interests lie?'

'I think so, sir,' Carnegie said. 'He always seemed to me a pretty level-headed chap. Reads a good deal, but I suppose he has to do that.'

'Yes … umph … well,' said the other. 'Get him round here, will you, Carnegie? Ask him to look in here at lunch time; ask him to lunch—no, better not; that would look too eager. Ask him to look in and see me. You needn't let him know what you've told me. Just that I was speaking of the Stone and you mentioned you knew someone who knew this Miss Burnett who is the Chief Justice's secretary. See?'

Carnegie saw at any rate sufficiently well to lure Frank round to the offices of the Union, and there introduced him to Mr. Merridew, who was extremely interested and affable.

'Ah, Mr. Lindsay, how kind of you! Do sit down. Don't go, Carnegie, don't go. It's a shame to trouble you about this, Mr. Lindsay, but if you can help us I needn't say how grateful I should be. Of course I quite understand that this is all confidential. Now I'm in a state of great anxiety, very great anxiety indeed, and when Carnegie let out that he knew you and that you were in touch with the Lord Chief Justice and so on, I thought a little chat couldn't at any rate do any harm. It's all about this Stone of yours.'

'Not of mine, I'm afraid,' Frank said. His first feeling on waking that morning had been that he had been rather hard on Chloe, but as he dressed and became more clearly aware that the examination was one morning nearer this had given way to the feeling that Chloe had been very hard on him. In which opinion he still remained. 'I've not even seen it properly.'

'It's Miss Burnett who has it?' Mr. Merridew asked half-casually.

'It is,' said Frank. 'And of course Lord Arglay.'

'Ah, yes, Lord Arglay,' Merridew assented. 'Lord Arglay—have you ever met him?'

'Once,' Frank said.

'Lord Arglay is a delightful man in himself, I believe,' Merridew went on, 'but I'm not sure that he isn't in some ways a little narrow-minded. A lawyer is almost bound to be perhaps. However, that's neither here nor there. My own trouble is quite simple. I'm responsible, as far as any man is, for all the members of this Union getting shelter and food from their jobs. Now, I've not seen this Stone, and I can hardly believe what's said, but it's said—it is *said*—that it means there's some new method of movement. I suppose it's a kind of scientific invention.'

'I really don't know,' Frank said, as Mr. Merridew paused. 'I only know what Miss Burnett told me. O and Mrs. Sheldrake seemed very anxious about it.'

'Ah, the ladies, the ladies!' the General Secretary smiled. 'A little credulous, perhaps—yes? But I do feel that, if there should be anything in it, I ought to know *what*. And as between a lady, a lawyer, and, if I may say so, a man of the world like yourself, I naturally preferred to get into touch with you. After all—I don't know what your political views may be, but after all someone ought to think of these millions of hardworking men whose livelihood is in danger.'

'But I don't see quite what *I* can do,' Frank said. 'Miss Burnett wouldn't lend me the Stone.'

'She wouldn't, you think,' Merridew asked, casually looking down at his papers, 'sell it?'

'Eh? sell it?' Frank exclaimed. 'No, I don't—I'm almost sure she wouldn't. Besides Mrs. Sheldrake said something about seventy thousand pounds.'

'Ah, well, a poor Trades Union could hardly go to that—but then I'd be quite willing only to borrow it,' Merridew said. 'If for instance you by any chance had one of them—I'd willingly pay a good sum for the privilege of borrowing it for a little while. Say——' he estimated Frank for a moment and ended—'a few hundreds even. It's of such *dire* importance to my people.'

Frank considered, and the more he considered the more certain he became that to offer Chloe, if she were still in her last night's mood, a few hundreds would be the same as offering her a few millions or a few pence. In these silly tempers it would mean nothing to her.

'I can ask her, of course,' he said reluctantly.

'If she should lend it to you for any reason——' Mr. Merridew thoughtfully said. 'If, I mean, you had any need of it and—as she naturally would—she passed it on to you, perhaps you'd bear me in mind.'

'I don't think she's likely to do that,' Frank said.

'Or even if you could borrow it sometime—I don't mean exactly without her knowing, though if she didn't happen to want it…. I understand Lord Arglay has one, and I suppose if Miss Burnett works there she could always use his—if you happened across it some time…. I don't know whether Miss Burnett is one of those young ladies who always leave their umbrellas or their handbags or something behind them——'

'No,' Frank said, 'she isn't.'

'Well, if she did'—Merridew went on—'or, as I say, if you borrowed it for any purpose of your own—well, if you had it in any way, and would show it me, I should be very glad to pay a fee. Better spend a few hundreds first than a few millions on unemployment pay, you know, is the way I look at it. Prevention is better than cure.'

'I see,' Frank answered.

He was not at all clear what he did see, moving in his mind, what kind of action half-presented itself and then withdrew, but to borrow the Stone for his examination, just for the day or two, couldn't do any harm. And if this fellow was willing to pay … Chloe should have it, of course; she'd only about thirty pounds at her back. Or at least they might split it—she was always very good about paying if things were rather tight, and she'd probably rather … only then she'd have to know. And if as a matter of fact she hadn't known, if there *were* any way of borrowing it, if…

'I see,' he said again, and there was a silence. Suddenly he stood up. 'Well, I must be going,' he said. 'Yes, I see, Mr. Merridew. Well, if anything should happen——'

'Any time, day or night,' the General Secretary said. 'Carnegie will give you my address. And of course any expenses—taxis or anything—good-bye.'

He watched Frank out and when Carnegie returned—'I wish there was a quicker way,' he said. 'I shall go to the Home Office after lunch, but I don't suppose they'll let one out of their hands. I wouldn't if I was them. It's up to you to keep on top of your friend, Carnegie. If he wants it himself for this examination of his we may just have tipped the balance. Though he mayn't be able to do it even so. Well, we must see. And now try and make an appointment for me with the Home Office this afternoon.'

The Home Secretary was a charming politician whose methods differed from Lord Birlesmere's in that while the Foreign Secretary preferred at least to appear to direct the storm, Mr. Garterr Browne allowed it to blow itself out, after which he pointed out to it exactly what damage it had done. He got up to shake hands with Mr. Merridew and directed his attention to another visitor who was standing by the table.

'May I introduce you to Mr. Clerishaw, the Mayor of Rich-by-the-Mere?' he said. 'Mr. Merridew, the General Secretary of the National Transport Union. Do sit down, both of you. I fancy this business may be a trifle long. Don't be alarmed, Mr. Merridew—I know what you want, at least I can guess. My difficulty is … but perhaps Mr. Clerishaw had better explain. A man always puts his own case best.'

There were those who asserted that this phrase, which was a favourite with Mr. Garterr Browne, had been responsible for more quarrels in his party and crises in the Cabinet than any other formula for twenty years. After hearing it, a man was always convinced that he did, and was consequently more reluctant to abandon his case than before. The Mayor needed no convincing, but neither was he anxious to waste energy.

'I have already stated my case to you, sir, as a member of the Government,' he said. 'I cannot see that anything is to be gained by repeating it.'

'I think, Mr. Mayor,' the Home Secretary said, 'that you will find it is more necessary to convince Mr. Merridew than to persuade me.'

'How so?' the Mayor asked.

'Because Mr. Merridew is one of my difficulties, I fancy,' the Minister answered. 'Mr. Secretary, tell me how much publicity do you desire for the tale of this absurd Stone?'

'What!' Merridew exclaimed—'publicity? I don't want any publicity at all—that's the point. I want to know whether the Government are taking steps to control all of these precious Stones that are in existence … I mean, if there's anything in them. Or to have immediate assurances that there is nothing.'

'Yes, but Mr. Clerishaw wants a great deal of publicity,' Mr. Garterr Browne smiled. 'O a very great deal. He objects to any kind of secrecy.'

Mr. Merridew settled himself firmly in his chair. 'And why?' he asked, very much as a General Secretary should.

The Mayor turned on him. 'Great God, sir,' he said almost fiercely, 'do you want to condemn thousands of men and women to suffering?'

'I don't,' Merridew said, 'and because I don't I want the Stone withdrawn from … from circulation.'

'Don't you know,' the Mayor cried out, 'that there are those well and happy to-day who have been in pain and grief for years—all by the healing powers of this Stone?'

'O you mean the people at Rich?' Merridew exclaimed. He had entirely forgotten, in his concern with transport, the virtues of the Stone which had caused so much disturbance in Rich during the week-end. But his phrase sounded as if he relegated the people at Rich to sickness or health indifferently, and the Mayor took a step forward.

'I speak for the people at Rich,' he said, 'for I am the Mayor of Rich. By what right do you speak and for whom?'

'I speak,' Merridew answered, sincerely if somewhat habitually moved, 'for the sons of Martha.' He had found Mr. Kipling's poem of the greatest use in emotional speeches from the platform; that and some of Mr.

Masefield's verses were his favourite perorations. But the Mayor, not having read much modern verse, was merely astonished.

'For what?' he asked.

'"For the sailor, the stoker of steamers, the man with the clout,"' murmured the Home Secretary, who had heard Mr. Merridew before. 'For the workers—some of them anyhow.'

'And what have the workers to lose because of the Stone?' the Mayor asked. 'Are not they also the people?'

'Of course they're the people,' the General Secretary exclaimed, 'they *are* the people. And are they to lose their livelihood because of a few cures?'

'Perhaps,' the Home Secretary put in, 'you haven't realized, Mr. Mayor, that this very interesting Stone has other qualities, so I am told, besides the curative. In short....'

He gave a brief explanation of those qualities. The Mayor listened frowning.

'But I confess,' Mr. Garterr Browne ended, 'I didn't know that these facts—these apparent facts—would have reached Mr. Merridew so soon. However, as it is——' He got courteously off the storm, and signed to it to go ahead.

'That,' Merridew said, 'is my case. If it's some scientific invention, as I suppose it is, it ought to be State property, and its introduction into the economic life of the country must only be brought about very, very gradually.'

'While the poor die in misery,' the Mayor commented.

'Damn it, sir,' Mr. Merridew exclaimed, 'I am speaking for the poor.'

'For the sick and dying?' the Mayor asked. 'For the blind and the paralytic and the agonized? Do as you will about economics—but the body is more than raiment.'

'Not without raiment—not for long,' Mr. Garterr Browne said. 'But go on with the discussion. What were you about to say, Mr. Secretary?'

'I protest against the way my words are twisted,' Merridew cried. 'I've no possible objection to the medicinal use of the Stone.'

'Nor I to its economic suppression,' the Mayor answered and they both looked at Mr. Garterr Browne.

'Beautiful,' the Minister breathed. 'When democracy lies down with democracy.... And how, gentlemen, do you propose to use the Stone all over the country while at the same time keeping it under close guard?'

'The doctors——' Merridew began.

'Hardly,' the Minister said. 'For it must be in the hands and at the will of those who are to be healed. And I don't myself see what is to prevent the ... the healee from going off by its means, once he is cured. We shan't be able to keep it quiet. And then there will be Stones everywhere. I'm not objecting. I'm only saying that we must use it either fully or not at all.'

'Then in the name of God, use it!' the Mayor cried out.

'And ruin hundreds and thousands of homes!' Merridew followed him. 'Suppress it, I say.'

Mr. Garterr Browne waved both hands at the storm. 'You see?' he asked it courteously, and after a few moments' silence added, 'If the Government heal the sick they starve the healthy. If, on the other hand, they protect the healthy they doom the sick.'

Both his visitors felt a sudden touch of horror. The dilemma came at them so suddenly, and on so vast a scale, that they mentally recoiled from it. Neither of them was thinking at the moment of any others than those on whose behalf he imagined himself speaking. But to each of them the placid voice of the Home Secretary called up a vision of another hemisphere of danger and distress; and over that danger and that distress floated, ironically effective, the Stone. Of the two the Mayor suffered the more, for he had the keener sight, and at the same time the remembrance of his own son struck at his heart. He saw the silent railways and the idle workers at the same time that he heard the moans of the dying man and knew them for the moans of one among thousands. He turned sharply on the Minister.

'Is there no way of administering relief,' he asked, 'by the most careful vigilance?'

'There is no way to protect the Stone if we are to use the Stone,' Mr. Garterr Browne said. 'And now, gentlemen?'

'I cannot believe it,' the Mayor cried out. 'Is the mind of man incapable of dealing with this problem? Or is the Stone sent to mock us?'

'Well ... mock?' the Minister asked, 'mock?... But I think probably its value has been much exaggerated. We have, of course——'

'But I have seen these things happen,' the Mayor said.

'No doubt, no doubt. As I was saying,' the Minister went on, 'we have, of course, our own scientists at work on it. Analyzing, you know.'

'Who are your scientists?' the Mayor asked.

'Sir Giles Tumulty primarily,' the other answered. He had never heard of Sir Giles till the previous evening, but his manner implied that the name ought to settle the Mayor. 'And no doubt he—they—will find some means to isolate the curative while—shall we say inhibiting?—the non-curative elements. But you must give us time.'

'And am I to go back to Rich and tell the people to die?' the Mayor asked.

'You talk as if your townsfolk were all the people,' Merridew muttered. 'Aren't there any others to watch for the people than you? What of the Unions? Are my members to starve that your townsfolk may be more cheerful?'

'It seems,' the Mayor said heavily, 'that this Stone is a very subtle thing.'

Mr. Garterr Browne felt that his own mind was at least as good as the Stone if it came to subtlety. It had been a difficult situation, and now everything was coming right. He looked almost gratefully at Mr. Merridew, but received no answering glance. The General Secretary was beginning to feel anxious about the future.

'At least,' the Mayor said suddenly, 'you will have the whole matter laid before Parliament, so that we may know what resolution is come to, and for what reason.'

'I very certainly will not,' Mr. Garterr Browne said, startled at this new threat of tempest. 'Why, Parliament isn't even sitting. I shall let the Cabinet know. Can't you trust us to do our best?'

Neither of his visitors seemed anxious to do so. Both of them were thinking of the crowds, of voices crying out questions, of the demand of the common people for security and food and content. In the faint noise of the traffic of London that came to them in the room there seemed to be something which must either be laid hold of or itself lay hold. Merridew saw before him the massed ranks of his Conference. There was here a thing which allowed, it seemed, of no arrangement; here was no question of percentages and scales and wage-modifications over long periods—things that could be explained and defended. If it got out, if the Stone were used publicly, the whole of his Unions would be raging round him, and all the allied trades. Yet if the Stone were refused, he seemed to see in the upright and dangerous figure of the Mayor a threat of other action, of the outbreak of the sick and the friends of the sick. He foresaw division and angry strife, and suddenly looking at the Home Secretary he cried out in answer to the plaintive appeal—'But this is civil war!'

The Mayor looked over at him. 'I do not think you are wrong, Mr. Secretary,' he said. 'We are coming perhaps to evil days.'

'But really, gentlemen,' the Minister began, and then changing his intention addressed himself to the Mayor. 'Do you not see,' he said, 'that more will suffer if the Stone is used than if it is kept secret? I am sure we all sympathize with those who are in need of one sort or another, but you cannot build up a house by pulling it down, nor do good to some by doing harm to many. Besides, so little has really been discovered about this … discovery that it's too soon to take a gloomy view. You, I am sure, Mr. Mayor, will explain this to the people of Rich.'

'And if the people of Rich lynch me in the street I shall think it natural,' the Mayor answered.

There was a knock at the door and a secretary entered. 'Lord Birlesmere is very anxious to see you, sir,' he said. 'He telephoned from the Foreign Office just now to know if he could come across.'

'Of course, of course,' Mr. Garterr Browne answered, and then, as the secretary went out, turned to his visitors. 'Well,' he said, 'I must break off the discussion. But please don't let there be any misunderstanding. The Government will take steps to find out what the truth really is. As I said before, there is always likely to be exaggeration. And then I will let you know its decision. Pray, gentlemen, exercise all your restraining influence, and do not let there be any talk of civil war. This is a civilized community. Your interests—the interests of those you represent—townsfolk or unionists—will be safe in our hands. I shall be writing to you both in a few days. No, Mr. Mayor, I can't discuss it further at present. Important things are bound to take time.'

As the two were ushered out Mr. Garterr Browne shook his head thoughtfully at the still ominous storm. 'What is quite certain,' he said, 'is that no one must be allowed to believe in this Stone any more. It simply must not be allowed.'

'Wandsworth?' Professor Palliser said, staring at Sir Giles. 'Why did you go there?'

'Can't you guess?' Sir Giles asked. 'Then I suppose you won't guess what happened. Well, I don't mind telling you, Palliser, that for once neither did I. Nor the Governor, who is a beefy lump of idiocy. He got quite upset when he saw it.'

'Saw what?' Palliser asked. 'What have you been doing?'

'I'll tell you,' Sir Giles answered. 'I ought to have foreseen perhaps—but one doesn't know what the logic of the damned thing is. Well, I went to Wandsworth. You know what they have at Wandsworth?'

'Not specially,' Palliser said. 'A common, isn't there? And a prison?'

'And a Hottentot missionary college, and a seminary for barmaids,' Sir Giles added. 'What do they have at Wandsworth Prison early in the mornings?'

'Parades?' Palliser, all at sea, ventured. 'Breakfast? Chapel?'

'Try all three,' Sir Giles answered. 'Executions, Palliser. That's what I went for. There aren't so many that I could afford to miss one, especially just after Birlesmere had given me a practically free hand. So I got a letter out of him and the Home Office scullion and down I went. After all, I argued, if this infernal Stone is a kind of rendezvous of the past and the future and every sort of place I didn't see why it shouldn't push a man over an interruption, like death. There is only one kind of death which is fixed and that's executions. Even at hospitals you can't be certain to an hour or two, and anyhow very often there people don't die intelligently; they lose themselves and drift. But the fellow who's going to be executed knows about it all right. The ape-creature who called himself the Governor wouldn't let on to me whether he usually drugged the victim, but I saw to it he didn't drug this one. I wanted all the intelligence I could find—not that there was much anyhow; he was an undersized slug who'd poisoned a woman because she'd run away with him without having any money, so far as I could understand. Not that it mattered. I got there before he'd had his breakfast, and had a little talk, asked him if he'd like to live and so on. The warder had been cleared out of the cell, so it was all right. I don't know what the wretched creature thought I was offering him, but he screamed with gratitude—quite a fascinating ten minutes, all twisting and slobbering. In fact, I began to think I shouldn't get the idea into the maggot-hole he had for a brain, but I did, and made him have a good breakfast too. Then the chaplain came in and talked about life in heaven, but my murderer was all for life on earth, and I was worth a dozen mongrel-faced chaplains to him. So he was pinioned so that he could hold one of the Stones—you ought to have seen the Governor looking like a Sunday school superintendent in a night club or something worse—and I told him to put everything he knew into choosing to live. And off we went—he and the hangman and the chaplain and the Governor and I and everyone. The funniest thing you ever saw, Palliser—if you ever did see anything funny. And there was the trap and everything. Well, do you know it was only then it occurred to me that I ought to be underneath—in the pit thing he drops into. It delayed matters a bit, but at last they grasped what I wanted: anyone except a malformed baby of two months would have understood me sooner than that Governor: and round and down I went. And down he came.'

Sir Giles paused. 'And now,' he resumed, 'what do you think happened?'

'How do I know?' Palliser exclaimed. 'He was dead?'

'No,' Sir Giles said thoughtfully, 'No, I shouldn't say he was dead.'

'He was alive!' Palliser cried. 'Does it really do away with death?'

'Well, yes, I suppose in a way he was alive,' Sir Giles said. 'He was quite conscious and so on—one could see that. The only thing was that his neck was broken.'

Palliser gaped at him. In a moment Sir Giles resumed. 'There he was. Neck broken, everything as it should be, the body dead so to speak. But *he* wasn't. I can see now that it was my fault in a way. I was thinking in terms of continuation of life, so I put him on to that idea, and of course he swilled it down with his coffee. But we both forgot to arrange the conditions, so that the ordinary physical process wasn't interfered with. Yet on the other hand his consciousness just stopped there, *in* his body or wherever it lives. A damn funny result, Palliser. If you could have seen his eyes while he hung there kicking——'

Palliser interrupted. 'But what did you do?' he asked.

Sir Giles shrugged. 'O well, they cut him down, and stuck him in a bed somewhere privately, and the chaplain postponed any more of the resurrection and the life and the Governor went off to get more instructions. And I hung about a bit—in fact, I've been there all day on and off; but there doesn't seem to be any change. There he lies, all broken up, and just his eyes awake. No use at all to me or anyone, damn and blast him for a verminous puppy-dog!'

Palliser moved uneasily. 'I'm beginning to be afraid of it,' he said. 'I wish we knew what it was.'

'It's the First Matter,' Sir Giles said. 'I told you that was what I thought it was, and I'm more sure than ever now. It's that which becomes everything else.'

'But how does it work?' Palliser asked. 'How does all this movement happen? How does it carry anyone about in space?'

'It doesn't,' Sir Giles answered immediately. 'Can't you see that it doesn't move people about like an aeroplane display? Once you are in contact and you choose and desire and will, you go into it and come out again where you have desired because everything is in it, anyhow. Do try and see further than a wax doll on a Christmas tree can.'

'So that if you were set in contact you might, even if you only partly knew...?' Palliser began slowly and stopped.

'I expect so,' Sir Giles said sweetly, 'if your hearse of a mind could only get to the cemetery a bit quicker. What might you?'

'I was thinking of Pondon,' Palliser went on. 'That might explain how it was that he's ... returned?'

'He's what?' Sir Giles said sharply. 'What d'you mean, Palliser? He hadn't a Stone, had he?'

'Your brother-in-law must have done it,' Palliser answered, feeling some pleasure at the connexion. 'You know you thought you saw him when we were trying to get at Pondon the other night and failed. There seems to have been a paragraph in the paper, but I missed that. But when I got to Birmingham yesterday morning, he was there. He'd been found in the laboratory when my demonstrator went in at about ten o'clock. He was a bit bewildered then, I gathered, so I went round to see him. And who do you think I found there?'

'Arglay!' Sir Giles exclaimed. 'By God, I'll tear Arglay into bits.'

'Not Arglay,' Palliser went on, 'but that girl who was with him—his secretary. She'd told him some tale and got on his right side, for there he was talking away to her, and telling her how he couldn't make out what had happened. I was rather sorry I'd turned up at first, though he was quite all right with me—asked me if the vibrations were all right. You remember we told him some tale about testing etheric vibrations—on the lines of my *Discontinuous Integer*?'

'He was damn near being a discontinuous integer himself,' Sir Giles said snappily. 'And what had Arglay's woman to say about it?'

'I don't like it,' Palliser answered. 'O she didn't *say* much, just cooed at him now and then. But from what he said, while he was doing his job as usual, he found his hand holding this Stone—and he knew he'd been holding it, so (as far as I could understand) he took a tighter grip and said to himself, "This is where I ought to be." And then he remembers pitching right over, and there the demonstrator found him. But that girl and Arglay have had something to do with it, and if they're going to interfere continually——'

Sir Giles put up a hand as if for silence, and sat meditating for several minutes. Then he drew a deep breath and got up. 'I'm going to try something,' he said. 'I've had enough of this young Hecate mixing herself up with my affairs because that bestial leprachaun who employs her tells her to. I'll give Miss Chloe Burnett something else to do with her mind, and perhaps with mine. If she can use the Stone so can other people. Where is it? Go away now, Palliser, and let me try.'

It was perhaps the greatest mistake which Giles Tumulty had ever made to allow what had been in general a cold, if rather horrible, sincerity of investigation into remote states of mind to become violently shaken by a personal hatred of his brother-in-law. He and Arglay had always mutually despised each other, but until now they had never been in conflict. The chances of the last few days however had turned them from contemptuous acquaintances into definite enemies. Indeed at that moment, though no one of those connected with the progress of the Stone and its Types had realized it, the Chief Justice and his secretary were becoming the only single-minded adherents it possessed. Lord Arglay certainly could not be thought to feel any passionate devotion to it; but he strongly disliked all that he saw and felt of the greed by which it was surrounded. The Persian Government, the English Government, the American millionaire and his wife—these he knew; and there were others he did not know—Merridew and Frank Lindsay; even, in some sense, though a holier, the Mayor of Rich and the Hajji Ibrahim. All for good or evil desired to recover the Stone, and use it, and most of them desired greatly to possess all its Types as well. Doncaster and Mrs. Pentridge hardly knew enough or were hardly in sufficient contact with the movements it had caused to make any demand. But Lord Arglay, at once in contact and detached, at once faithless and believing, beheld all these things in the light of that fastidious and ironical goodwill which, outside mystical experience, is the finest and noblest capacity man has developed in and against the universe. And now this itself was touched by a warmer consciousness, for as far as might be within his protection and certainly within his willing friendship, there was growing the intense secret of Chloe's devotion to the Mystery. As if a Joseph with more agnostic irony than tradition usually allows him sheltered and sustained a Mary of a more tempestuous past than the Virgin-Mother is believed to have either endured or enjoyed, so Lord Arglay considered, as far as it was clear to him, his friend's progress towards the End of Desire. To that shelter and sustenance she had eagerly returned from her absence on the Birmingham errand, and she and her companion were now telling him and the Hajji, who had been summoned, of the occurrences of that errand.

Of one thing however Chloe did not speak. She might have gradually revealed it to Lord Arglay, but she certainly was not going to mention it before the Hajji, and as in a way Mr. Doncaster was it or the occasion of it she could not before him. Chloe had usually found a fairly long train journey—especially in the first class compartment Lord Arglay had naturally assumed she would take—in the company of an intelligent and personable young man who rather obviously admired her, a very pleasant, and even exciting, method of spending the time. There was so happy a mixture of the known and the unknown; there was all the possibility of advance and yet all the surety of withdrawal—there was in short such admirable country for campaigning that she could not very clearly understand why she had to-day looked at it without any thought of a campaign. She had thrown out a squadron or so to check Mr. Doncaster's early moves, and had with small expenditure of effort immobilized him. The journeys were ended and there was no regret. She must, Chloe thought when she became conscious of this, be terribly excited. But she was not excited. She only wanted to serve the Stone—and Lord Arglay—as much as Lord Arglay—and the Stone—wanted. There was a slight doubt in her mind which of them, if it came to a crisis, was the more important, but it hadn't come to a crisis and very likely never would. Once or twice her experience in the operation which she and the Chief Justice had directed occurred to her; with the suggestion of a possibility that there indeed a choice beyond her knowledge had been made and a first separation from mortality dutifully and sadly undergone. It would have seemed to her silly and pretentious to put it like that, but when she said to herself: 'I don't think perhaps I shall care about it so much,' it might have meant much the same thing, at least to any of the Types of the Stone or to the wisdom of Suleiman ben Daood, king in Jerusalem.

'We went to the University first,' Doncaster was saying, 'but he wasn't there, and they didn't or wouldn't know anything, so we went to his house.'

'How did you find it?' the Chief Justice put in.

'Telephone Directory,' Doncaster said. 'That was my idea—I thought in his position he'd almost *have* to be on, and he was. But it was Miss Burnett got us into the house—the usual kind of house; just the thing you'd expect of him. He lived with his mother, and I thought we could swear we were journalists; but before I could say anything——' He paused and looked at Chloe.

'And what did Miss Burnett swear you were?' Lord Arglay asked.

'I said we were his friends,' Chloe answered, with a simplicity and a certainty in her voice which—Arglay thought—would have opened any doors. Some new completeness seemed to be growing in her. He permitted himself to test it with another question.

'And did you also think it was the kind of house you would expect of him?' he asked, throwing a side glance of humorous apology at Doncaster.

Chloe frowned a little. 'I don't think I know,' she said. 'I mean, I didn't expect anything. It was—it was a house, and he and his mother lived in it. I don't see what more one could say.'

'It didn't,' Arglay asked again, 'seem to you of any particular kind?'

'It was a very nice house,' Chloe said, 'but—no, I didn't notice anything else.'

'It had an aspidistra in the window,' Doncaster put in.

'It certainly had,' Chloe agreed, 'and a very good aspidistra too. I admired it.'

Lord Arglay signed to Doncaster to go on—after a slightly perplexed glance at Chloe, he obeyed.

'So Miss Burnett said, "We are his friends," and his mother let us in and took us to the aspidistra, and presently he came in. So we—at least Miss Burnett—told him she knew all about it....'

'Did you?' Arglay interrupted.

'Well, in a way,' Chloe answered. 'It seemed as if he thought he had seen me before; he looked at me so hesitatingly at first. And I said I knew something of what had happened, and was anxious to know if we could do anything more to help him. So we ... we stammered a little at one another, and then he broke out. He said he didn't know what had happened. He remembered Professor Palliser talking to him about etheric vibrations, and asking him to test them by wishing—he said wishing—to be at an earlier point of time, and then he wondered if he had been.'

'He was very muddled about it all,' Doncaster added. 'And about what happened afterwards: he was doing his job in his usual manner and suddenly he felt as if he were holding on to a post and something was saying to him, "This is the Way." He couldn't get nearer than that. And he saw a kind of photograph in the air.'

'A what?' Lord Arglay exclaimed.

'He didn't say a photograph,' Chloe cried out. 'He said a picture.'

'He said, to be exact, "a picture just like a photograph,"' Doncaster insisted, 'of the same room. And it got bigger. But go on, Miss Burnett.'

'I think he saw them in the Unity,' Chloe said. 'He said he felt as if he were standing between them, and he didn't know which he ought to be in, but it was frightfully important for him to choose rightly. And he wondered which the Professor and his friends wanted. But then he thought he saw …' she hesitated … 'me in one of them, and moved to ask whether I wanted to see the Professor!'

'And then crashed,' Doncaster ended. 'And knew nothing more. It was at that point that the Professor arrived. He looked a trifle embarrassed when the mother brought him in and he saw Miss Burnett— embarrassed first and then rather annoyed. So there was general conversation for awhile, and I chatted to the Professor—at least, I asked him what he thought of it all, while Miss Burnett and Pondon talked. And then we came away.'

'I like the notion that he thought you wanted Palliser,' Lord Arglay said contentedly. 'The Stone seems to have a subtle irony of its own. But why *you*? Very much pleasanter for him, of course; but I had an idea, from what you said, that I was doing most of the work. Why didn't he see me?'

'It may be,' the Hajji said, 'that it was by your work that this man beheld her. For all that you showed him was the Stone, and it may be that Miss Burnett's work was in the Stone, and that he beheld her there. It was, in its degree, redemption which you offered him, and if she was toiling also at redemption—the Way to the Stone is in the Stone.'

'And yet his desire was to do what Palliser wished,' Arglay demurred.

'His desire was to fulfil good as he knew it,' the Hajji said. 'Therefore he was capable of receiving within those conditions the End of Desire, which is eternally good.'

'All times are within it and all places, it seems,' Arglay said. 'Are not therefore its own Types within itself?'

'I think that is true,' the Hajji answered. 'Certainly therefore this Thing contains its own Unity; it is for us to find the path by which that Unity may be manifested.'

'It seems to me,' Doncaster began….

For some time Chloe had been conscious of a restlessness which she had been trying in vain to subdue. She was tired or something, she supposed, but things looked different somehow. What a lot of bother everyone was making! after all, there were other things in the world. And all this talk about redemption and the End of Desire. The end of desire was to get what you wanted. The Hajji was rather a silly little old man, she thought, with his Compassionates and his Muhammeds and his Peace be upon him and his under the Protection— what protection and from what? A little intelligent watchfulness was all the protection she needed, and she could supply that herself. As for Lord Arglay—Lord Arglay, it occurred to her, was unmarried, and if not rich—he could hardly be that—still he must have…. And no-one but Reginald Montague to leave it to! Old men sometimes … after all he wasn't repulsive. If he married Chloe Burnett, Chloe Burnett would have a more comfortable life. And if he didn't marry still he was the kind of man who would probably treat his mistress very fairly. Suppose he had one already? That must be seen to. Chloe Burnett might not be exactly beautiful, but she had (so she had been told) a genius for making the most of herself and her art. There wouldn't be many mistresses who could outdo her if it really came to a tussle.

The Hajji stopped speaking, Lord Arglay stirred, and Chloe woke to sudden anxiety. What on earth had she been thinking? Thoughts had passed through her mind in their usual way, but not—surely not!—usual thoughts. Had she really been guessing how much money Lord Arglay had, and whether she could get it? Had she really been planning to use the hands clasped beneath her chin to trap him? Now if it had been this young Doncaster man … his hair would be rather pleasant to pull rather hard, he had thick hair; and well-made wrists, better than Frank's. Not that there would be any need to give up Frank, or anyhow not entirely. Chloe Burnett could deal with them as Sir Giles dealt with Arglay and the Hajji or the fellow at Birmingham, a silly fellow as she remembered him. Useful no doubt in a way, and amusing to think of him lost in the past. But very, very dull and only meant to be made use of by other people much more intelligent—Sir Giles for instance.

'Bloody fool!' Chloe said aloud.

As Oliver Doncaster had just begun 'It seems to me——' her words caused, even in that company, a moment's attention. Oliver stopped speaking with a shock and found himself faced with the unbelievable. The Hajji turned on her a look of sudden alarm. Lord Arglay, taking her in with a side glance, said casually—'Not you, Mr. Doncaster; I think probably Palliser. But in any case we have for the moment done what we can. Would it be too much to ask you to call in the morning?'

Oliver had had earlier some general expectation of seeing Chloe home. But he wasn't as clear as the Chief Justice that the words hadn't been meant for him, and of course if that was what she thought the sooner he got away the better. Dare he risk shaking hands? He offered her his as charmingly as possible. 'Very well, Lord Arglay,' he said. 'Good-night, Miss Burnett. Thank you for letting me come to Birmingham.'

Chloe gave him her hand and looked at him. Oliver who had been all day conscious of being held at an emotional distance discovered, with the second shock in two minutes, that he was being deliberately invited to be—understanding. Her fingers caressed for a moment the back of his hand; her mouth shaped itself for the kiss the circumstances forbade; her eyes mourned rebukingly over his departure. 'Good-night, Mr. Doncaster,' said a voice full of suggestions of intimacies that, so far as he could remember, hadn't happened, 'We may meet—again—in the morning then?'

'She can't have meant him,' the Chief Justice thought to himself. 'But it certainly sounded as if she did. "Bloody fool"—it's the way these modern young creatures talk. Yes, but not here, not—with other people about—to me. I shouldn't have thought she'd have done that. Still—she did. No,' he thought suddenly. 'I don't believe it. She never talked like that—except for amusement or from bitterness. And never *so*. She is civilized; she is in obedience to the Law.'

He had been taking Oliver to the door while he was thinking and once that was closed he hastened back to the study. Chloe was standing by the fireplace, looking round the room. Lord Arglay had seen her standing just there often enough, but in her eyes now there was a difference. They surveyed, they considered, they calculated; so much he saw before she brought them back to meet his with a smile. But even that had something unnatural about it, a determination of quite another kind from that which had on other occasions once or twice appeared in the depths of her look, a hardness alien to the secretary the Chief Justice knew. For a moment, as their glances met, this gave place to a sudden bewilderment, but before he could say a word she had turned aside and was looking towards the window. Lord Arglay looked round for the Hajji, who had apparently withdrawn into some corner, and found him at last by his elbow. In that room they were far enough from Chloe not to be heard if they spoke softly, and in a such a tone the Hajji said: 'Something has frightened you?'

'No,' Arglay answered, 'not frightened. I was a little startled, but I expect it's all right. No doubt Miss Burnett is a little overtired.'

'I do not know Miss Burnett,' the Hajji said, 'except that I saw the Name upon her forehead. But I have watched her eyes, and I think you are right to be anxious.'

'Why?' Arglay said abruptly.

'Her eyes and her mouth have changed,' the Hajji answered. 'They are curious and greedy—and even malicious. And if, as I think, she is not by nature greedy or malicious….'

He paused, but Arglay only said, 'Well?'

'Then,' the Hajji concluded, 'something or someone is making her so.'

In case Chloe should catch his eyes again Lord Arglay looked at the Hajji and said, 'It seems a damn silly thing to try to do. What good would it be?'

'It might be a good deal of good,' the Hajji said, 'if indeed they desire to obtain the Types which you have. But even if not, have you never known men act from hate and anger alone?'

'And is this also, if it is so,' Lord Arglay said, ironically, 'part of the miracle of the Stone?'

'I warned you that there might be much evil,' the Hajji answered, and fell silent.

Lord Arglay glanced again at Chloe. 'You think they may be playing tricks on her?' he asked, but more as if in courteous conversation than in inquiry, and the other did not trouble to answer. At last, 'Well,' he went on, 'if this is so I will do what can be done.'

'Will you try and find her in the Stone?' the Hajji asked.

'No,' Arglay answered, 'no, I do not think I will take up the Stone. Between her and me I will not have any even of these things.'

'You love her?' the Hajji said, half in statement, half in interrogation.

'Why, I do not very well know what love may be,' Lord Arglay said, 'but so far as is possible to men I think that there is Justice between her and me, and if that Justice cannot help us now I do not think that any miracles will.'

'This is a very rare thing,' the Hajji said doubtfully.

'My secretary,' Lord Arglay said, half-lightly, half-seriously, 'is a very rare young lady.' His voice became entirely serious, as he added, 'And if it is Giles, I will perhaps kill him to-morrow. But now I will see what is at work here.'

'Cannot I help you?' the other asked.

'No,' Arglay said. 'I will do this alone. Good-night.'

He shook hands and opened the door. The Hajji, without going nearer, bowed to Chloe and walked out. Lord Arglay shut the door and strolled across the room.

'I thought he was never going,' Chloe said.

The remark was so perfectly normal that for a moment the Chief Justice felt almost idiotically defeated. But something reminded him that Chloe had never been the kind of secretary who remarked in that way on her employer's visitors. She would have thought it presumptuous and rude, and the affection that had grown between them had never made her more careless of her behaviour as a subordinate or as a friend. In both capacities the remark was inadmissible, and Lord Arglay knew it as he took the last three steps that brought him level with her. He smiled at her and for a moment considered.

'Do you feel very tired?' he asked.

'Well, it was a hell of a journey,' Chloe said, 'but no—not if you want me, I mean.'

'Too tired,' Lord Arglay said, 'to do a little *Organic Law*?'

Chloe looked at him blankly for a moment. 'O!' she exclaimed, and before she could add any more the Chief Justice went on easily, 'I want you to consider it in connexion with our last night's resolution. I want you to *think*.' His voice on the last word became suddenly authoritative.

Chloe laid a hand on his arm. 'I am *rather* tired,' she said, 'but of course if you must have it done——' The hand slid down his arm to his hand and lingered there. Lord Arglay took it and held it. 'Yes, *think*,' he said. 'Think, very carefully, yourself.'

Chloe pouted. 'What about?' she said. 'Isn't there anything better to do? It's you that ought to think, not me.'

'Good God!' Lord Arglay said, really annoyed, 'don't talk such rubbish, child.'

A quick tremor shook Chloe, she released his hand, and slid round to face him. 'Am I a child?' she said, and suddenly anger contended with cunning in her eyes. She paused uncertainly, as if something within her, unaccustomed to the instrument it was using, was fumbling with it; she half put out her hand again and withdrew it; she leaned forward but whether in desire or hate Arglay could not tell. He kept his eyes on her now, saying nothing for a moment that the remembrance of the Chloe Burnett he knew might gather more mightily within him. For the change that had come upon her was provoked by no natural alteration of mood, and for a moment he wondered whether indeed he had been wise in this extremity to refuse the mysterious capacities of the Stone. If he could use it to rescue Pondon might he not with a thousand times more reason use it here? Might it not be a wise and proper thing to do? But however wise or proper it might be he knew he could not; to do so would be already to confess defeat—there was something else on which he relied and it was the mere fact that they two were what they were and had been what they had been.

He said, with a certain slowness, 'Child, I would have you think of what we chose to do.'

'I do not want to think of anything that is past,' she answered sullenly, and to that he said in a growing passion of authority, 'But I will have you do this, and therefore you shall do it now. I will have you do it.'

She moved her head from side to side as if to avoid the charge he laid upon her; then, abandoning a direct refusal, she said in almost a whisper, 'But first let us think of other things.'

'Child,' he answered, 'the things of which you would think are neither here nor there, nor do you think of them. You think and you shall think of all that we have done together, and of how we determined to believe in God.'

'I will believe in you instead,' Chloe said and took a small step forward in the small distance that separated them.

The sentence was so unexpected, she was herself so close, that Arglay for a moment hesitated. It was not so much desire for her that filled him as a willingness to accept himself on those terms, to take this offered substitution. To play deity to an attractive young girl—there was, for a moment he felt, a certain point to the idea. But even as the point pricked him ever so slightly he smiled to think of it, and the consciousness of the prick passed from him. His own belief in God was still small, but his feeling for Organic Law was very strong, and his dislike of any human being pretending to be above that Law was stronger still. The temptation rose and was lost in its absurdity. And yet.... She looked up with an inviting smile. He took her suddenly by one shoulder with his hand.

'You will not believe in me,' he answered, 'as more than a servant of that which you serve. Answer me—what is that?'

'It is nothing with which you have anything to do,' she said, 'unless you will do also what I will.'

He smiled at her in a sudden serenity. 'Now I know that I shall have my way,' he said, either to her or to that which was within her, and added to her alone, 'since it is impossible that we should be so separated for ever.'

'You!' she said harshly, 'Will you govern me with your bit of filthy pebble?'

'I have no need of the Stone,' he answered, still smiling at her, 'for all that is in the Stone, except the accidents of time, is here between us and perhaps more than is in the Stone. And in that you will answer me. Tell me, child, what it is you serve.'

319

She wrenched her shoulder away from him. 'Keep your beastly hands away,' she cried. 'I am my own to keep and command.'

'And if that shall be true to-morrow,' Lord Arglay said, 'it is not true now.' His voice took on a sternness and he looked on her with a high disdain. 'Answer,' he said; 'will you make me wait? Answer—what is it that you serve?'

She moved back a step or two, and suddenly he put out his hand, caught her wrist, and pulled her back close to him; then, his eyes on hers, he said: 'Child, you know me and I know you among the deceptions. What is it, what is it that you serve?'

She gave a stifled cry, and slipped forward so that he caught her—'I know,' she said, 'I know. Hold me; I know.'

When at last he moved she stood up and did something to her hair; then she looked at him with a faint smile. 'I do know,' she said.

'Then I think it is more than I do,' Lord Arglay said. 'But that is very possible.'

'Have I been saying anything—very silly?' she asked, picking up her handbag and looking for her powder-puff.

The Chief Justice considered her. 'How do you feel?' he asked. 'Well enough to talk a little about it?'

'Quite,' Chloe answered, sitting down, and adding after a moment's pause, 'Have I been a nuisance?'

'Don't you remember?' Lord Arglay asked. 'Suppose you tell me first—whatever seemed to happen.'

'I don't know that anything exactly happened,' Chloe said. 'I just began to think about … began to think in a different way.'

'In *quite* a different way?' Arglay interrupted. 'I mean, in a way you had never thought before?'

The colour flamed in Chloe's cheeks. But she met his eyes and answered, 'Partly. I don't think I ever*calculated* before—not so much anyhow. Or not at the same time that I felt …' she struggled bravely on and ended … 'desirous.'

The Chief Justice considered again. He had seen the farewell she had taken of Doncaster; he had observed, when he had returned to the study, the valuation to which she was bringing its furniture; he had remarked the cold intention in her eyes when the two of them were talking; and he decided that in this case desire and calculation were two different things. But by what means, if by any outside herself, had they been loosed?

'It came on you suddenly?' he asked.

'It came,' she answered, 'as if I thought I was walking down one road and found I was walking down another. It didn't even come; it was there. I lived into the midst of it.'

'And it?' Arglay said, 'it seemed like some other self of yours? Did you know yourself in it?'

'In a way,' she answered, 'all the things that I have sometimes hated most in myself. But not altogether. Never—no, in all my life, I never wanted so utterly to grab without giving anything at all, never before.' In her agitation she stood up. 'I'm not like that,' she said, 'O indeed I'm not.'

'No,' Lord Arglay said, 'but I think I could guess who is, and whose mind was thrust upon yours then. But even he, even in the Stone, could only affect you through your own habits and emotions. So that both he and you troubled and hid your heart.' He paused for a moment and went on. 'Child, in those past times that you speak of, how have you governed yourself?'

'By this and that,' Chloe said. 'By trying to think clearly and by trying to be as nice as I could to people.'

'It is very well said,' Lord Arglay answered. 'I do not think Giles or anyone else will easily overcome that guard of yours.'

'I will take care of that,' Chloe said in quite a different voice. 'I shan't be caught twice.'

'Well,' Lord Arglay answered comfortably, looking round the room, 'I mayn't be what Reginald's unfortunate American would call rich, but I should think I am quite the most well-to-do person you know. So if you are going to make an attempt on anyone it will probably be on me again. Which won't matter, will it?'

'No,' said Chloe, 'though it seems funny that it shouldn't. And in a way it does.'

'O la la! in a way——' Lord Arglay said. 'But only in a way conformable to the Stone. Now it *is* funny, if you like, how determined I was not to use the Stone. One might have thought I didn't care *what* happened to you. I might have been the Hajji; indeed I was worse than the Hajji, for he at least thought about using it.'

'Why—if I may—why didn't you?' Chloe asked shyly, but her eyes were glad as she looked at him.

'I couldn't see that it was going to be of the slightest use,' he answered. 'It just wasn't there. Or else—since we have decided to believe in it—it was there anyhow, and to have it materially wouldn't have helped.'

'Is there then something greater than the Stone?' she asked. 'I dreamed last night that the King lifted up his hand and there was a great light.'

'Also the Hajji spoke of a greater secret,' he answered. 'I do not think Giles quite knows what he is doing.'

'Do you think it is dangerous to him?' Chloe said.

'Anything that one uses is apt to become one's master,' Arglay answered. 'And if the Stone should become Giles's master—what would he find it to be?'

Chloe looked at her fingers. 'Do you think,' she said doubtfully, 'we ought to try and … warn him or … help him … or anything?'

'Help him—help Giles?' Lord Arglay exclaimed. 'My dear child, don't be absurd! After he … O you're tired out; I shall take you home. Unless—I ask you again—unless you'll stop here?'

'Not to-night, please,' she said. 'I shall be quite safe now. If he tries it again, I shall just *think*.'

'Do,' Lord Arglay approved. 'My present problem in *Organic Law* is this—Good heavens, you want to know! O come along, you're merely making altruism into a habit.'

CHAPTER XIV
THE SECOND REFUSAL OF CHLOE BURNETT

Lord Arglay asserted later that whenever Chloe declared that she would be quite safe something perilous was certain to be approaching. But since he knew that she was in possession of one of the Types and therefore had at her disposal a means of escape from any crisis and a place of refuge in his own house it did not seem to him that she was likely to be in any unavoidable danger. For alternatively if any one of those who were bound to regard them as enemies should seize on the Type she had, then his object would be achieved. The Stone possessed, there would be no point in harming Chloe; it would indeed be a stupid and risky thing to do, arousing that very attention which it was important to avoid. It appeared therefore to the Chief Justice that though she might be inconvenienced she could not be seriously endangered.

This argument, though sound within its limits, suffered from the same trouble that invalidates all human argument and makes all human conclusion erroneous, namely, that no reasoning can ever start from the possession of all the facts. The two facts which Lord Arglay's reasoning left out of account were, first, the inclusion of the Prince Ali among the pursuers of the Stone, and second Chloe's increasing determination not to use her Type for her own safety. It was this omission which proved his conclusion wrong and did actually put her in peril.

For whatever the Persian Ambassador might diplomatically desire, and whatever the Hajji Ibrahim might religiously assert, Ali had no intention at all of relinquishing his efforts—if necessary, his militant efforts— to recover all the Types if possible, and if not at least one; by the possession of which he hoped to procure the rest. His first objective had been Sir Giles. But Sir Giles had made it clear that any attempt to recover the Type in his possession would mean a multiplication of Stones which from Ali's point of view would be not only sacrilegious but extremely troublesome. He had not for some days been at all clear where the rest of the Types were. Reginald Montague had apparently had one, but then—he gathered from the papers—so had Sheldrake; were they one or two? Ali could not, in his position, afford to make a number of violent and unsuccessful efforts to recover it or them; the Ambassador's modernity and the Hajji's piety might agree in removing him to Moscow or having him recalled to Tehran before he achieved what he wanted, should either of them suspect what was happening. He had not dared so far to make any effort to excite the temper of the East. But he had, with the greatest caution, sounded the minds of one of his friends in the Embassy; he intended to gather about himself a small group of similar spirits in order that when a convenient time came he might, if necessary, strike in several directions at once.

Nothing however was further from his mind than that he should be rung up by Sir Giles Tumulty. It was not the first telephonic conversation which had proceeded between the Embassy and the English that morning; the Hajji and Lord Arglay had been talking earlier. The Chief Justice had briefly explained that all was well with Miss Burnett, and had added that he was still in two minds about going off to Ealing and quite simply killing Sir Giles.

'What good do you think that would be … in the End?' the Hajji said.

'I haven't an idea what good it would be in the End,' Lord Arglay assured him, 'but it seems as if it might be a considerable good here and now. After all, we can't be expected to put everything off because of the End or we should just be putting off the End itself. At least it seems so to me, but I'm no metaphysician.'

'What would Miss Burnett desire?' the Hajji asked.

'That's my only difficulty,' Lord Arglay explained. 'I don't think she'd like it—and yet I don't know. Everybody else would be pleased. I might be hanged but I should be almost certain to have a memorial statue somewhere, probably by Epstein. I like Epstein too. Well, I suppose I shan't.'

He might however have been almost inclined to turn the only half-fantastic idea into an act if he had overheard Sir Giles a quarter of an hour later. The whole history of Tumulty's dealings with the Stone had roused in him a state of increasing irritation with Lord Arglay and his secretary. There had been the spying on him, as he chose to call it, at Birmingham; Arglay's refusal to investigate the half-hour's break; the affray at the Conference; his own impotence to understand Arglay's mind; the rescue of Pondon. And now…. He was not very clear what had interfered with his domination of Chloe. He had, after the usual preliminary attention and concentration, become aware of looking through Chloe's eyes much as Arglay had looked through his own. He had been aware of a feeling for the Chief Justice which, since it certainly wasn't his own, must be Chloe's. He had attempted to turn that emotion into his own desire to use Arglay and then throw him aside. But he had not reached to the extremer places of Chloe's own manner of experience; it had been but her conscious thought that he could dominate, working inwards from without. He had so far conquered that his intention had imposed itself on her as her own, although with the changed appearance which, in their turn, her physical and mental desires had wrought in it. But at the time when Lord Arglay had called upon his friend with the authority to which she was accustomed and which she loved, Giles's will had been swept aside. A darkness fell upon him; he became aware of the Stone in his hands, it seemed to move in them and itself to thrust him back. He dropped it suddenly as if just in time to avoid its growth against him, and took, as he became again conscious of his outer surroundings, a few angry steps about the room. 'I don't know if this is a damned nightmare,' he grunted, 'but it felt as if I was going to be swallowed by the bloody thing. I wonder if I'm letting the idea of getting back at Arglay and his whore run away with me. One does, sometimes; and that's just death to observation. I wish there was someone else who could tackle them. And by God,' he exclaimed, 'there is. I suggested it to Birlesmere myself—there's the Persian.'

As he thought about it he decided that this, in default of a better, was the momentary solution. The Prince Ali was probably still anxious to recover the Stone, and if he happened to kill Chloe or Arglay in the process so much the better. Anyhow, even to lose their Types would certainly annoy them, and if at the worst Ali or his friends failed or suffered there was no particular harm done to Sir Giles himself. 'Ali and this screaming peahen can fight it out together,' he said, and looked up the number of the Persian Embassy.

The Prince was considerably surprised when he was first told that Sir Giles Tumulty wanted to speak to him, but he condescended to answer.

Sir Giles was obscenely abrupt. On condition that he was left alone he would give the Persian a chance of recovering something, if Ali thought it worth while. Was he to be left alone? The Prince, as abruptly, agreed. Then at Lancaster Gate and wherever the secretary hibernated, were Types of the Stone, if they were wanted.

'But why,' the Prince said curiously, 'do you tell me this?'

'What in hell's name does that matter to you?' Sir Giles asked. 'I gave him one when I thought you were after me, just to make you and your company of date-eaters think a bit. But he annoys me, and I'd rather you had it.'

The Prince thought, but did not say, that the Foreign Office would hardly have agreed. Sir Giles had thought of it but he was far too angry with his brother-in-law to care about all the Foreign Offices in Europe.

'Well, there you are,' he said. 'I suppose you can hire somebody to do the job.'

'That I will see to,' the Prince said. 'If this is true I cannot thank you, but I will at least ignore you.'

'You'll do what?' Sir Giles almost yelled, but recovered himself and slammed down the receiver. 'And I hope they assault the girl and assassinate Arglay,' he thought to himself as he prepared to go out again to Wandsworth.

The exact measures which the Prince took were, not unnaturally, never explained. But by the time that Chloe, after an uneventful day, returned home, they had been carried out. His friend had left London for Brighton and Reginald Montague. He himself was waiting for night.

Chloe and the Chief Justice had—quite seriously—discussed the possibility of attempting to recover all the Types and of escaping with them from England. But neither of them, especially as they grew less and less inclined to use it—or, as Chloe had said—to dictate to it, had been quite prepared to take such extreme measures. Lord Arglay viewed with a certain hesitation the annexation of Sheldrake's Type, for which after all he had paid and from which he was presumably entitled to get such satisfaction as he legally could. The Mayor of Rich had called to ask the Chief Justice to draw up a public statement and petition on behalf of all the sick, and on the first draft of this Lord Arglay, with a wry smile, had spent some time. Rich, he gathered from the papers, was still in a state of simmering discontent. Oliver Doncaster had called, very uncertain of his behaviour in Chloe's company, and rather defeated at finding that everything seemed normal. No one alluded to her remark of the previous night, and the Chief Justice being in the room all the time there was no opportunity for him to make the running on the strength of her own behaviour. As, rather gloomily, he departed, Lord Arglay looked at Chloe. 'Of course he doesn't appreciate Giles,' he said.

'But what must he think of *me*?' Chloe asked despairingly.

'I can't begin to imagine,' Lord Arglay said. 'Nor as a matter of fact can he. You can, but you needn't at the moment. For I am utterly convinced that Austin—Austin!—never said '*Attribuat igitur rex legi, quod lex attribuit ei, videlicet dominationem et potestatem. Non est enim rex ubi dominatur voluntas et non lex.*' Don't you know the sound of Bracton's voice, when you hear it? "Therefore let the king attribute to the law that which the law attributes to him, namely, domination and power. For where the will rules and not the law is no king." You haven't checked your references, child, and, as a result, you've got this whole page of quotations wrong.'

Chloe bit her lips, crossed out the attribution, and plunged back into legal histories.

This unfortunate lapse, the more maddening that it had been a page she had written out some weeks earlier, and before the Stone had preoccupied her mind, was annoying her when she returned that night. For she had rather prided herself on her secretarial efficiency, and Lord Arglay's quite pleasant, but quite firm, criticism of it distressed almost as much as it pleased her. Almost, because she thought as she took off her hat how much worse it would have been if he had pretended that, because of their friendship, it didn't matter. 'It was,' he had said, 'no doubt the prophetic soul of your wide world dreaming on things to come. But don't let it be dreaming too much about the law-makers who are gone, will you? Or let us be quite clear when it is.' Chloe kicked herself again and made some coffee.

The incident however sent her to bed even more certain of the edge of incapacity and void upon which she dwelt than she normally was. What with Frank Lindsay being angry with her for one thing (and even now she wasn't clear that she had been right), and Lord Arglay being critical of her for another (and she was quite clear that she had been hopelessly careless), she seemed to herself a sufficiently ineffectual creature. It was true she couldn't much care whether Frank was angry or not, and didn't in a sense mind whether Lord Arglay was displeased or not; if the one didn't understand, well, she couldn't help it, and of the other she would always be secure no matter how unhappy he might, very properly and rightly, make her. Still, if this was the result of her emotional and intellectual life—merely to annoy everybody! She looked at herself in the glass and wondered as on several other occasions during the last few days what the Hajji had meant by saying that the Name was upon her forehead. The Name of the God in which she and Lord Arglay had decided to believe? What did you do if you had decided to believe in God? So far as her early training served her, she thought you gave up your will to His. *Non est enim rex ubi dominatur voluntas*—for where the will rules there is no king. But Bracton—damn her stupidity!—had been talking of feudal law, and yet…. She wandered slowly back and lifted from her handbag the Type of the Stone that she carried, to lay it under her pillow for the night. 'The End of Desire' … 'the Stone which is between you and me.' You gave up your will, did you? Your will by itself produced pretty poor results, it seemed. *Attribuat igitur*—let the king attribute to the law … But how to find the law? 'The Way to the Stone which is in the Stone.' The Stone, Lord Arglay, God—the End of Desire. Was this then what her absurd childish prayers meant? 'Our Father which art in heaven,' she thought, 'Hallowed be Thy name, Thy kingdom come, Thy will be done on earth as it is in heaven'—and what did that mean? Of course if it all did mean something it was quite easy to believe she hadn't yet understood, but in that case she wanted, she wanted very much, to understand; and very much indeed, with her body and mind and everything else, she desired the End of Desire. Still thinking about it, still trying over to herself the first few phrases of that august ritual of intercession she got into bed, laid the Type of the Stone under her pillow, and settled herself to sleep.

Or to think. But bed, as Chloe had on other occasions discovered, is not really a good place in which to try and do both, even sequentially. When she decided that she had thought enough and ought to go to sleep, for fear the next day should find her making a muddle of more quotations, she found it was too late. Bits of her previous thoughts half imaged themselves to her, and disappeared before she could do more than recognize them. She thought of getting up and reading, but she couldn't think of any book in her rooms which she wanted to read—not even Mr. Ford Madox Ford's novels or the life of Sir Edward Marshall-Hall (which, a fortnight before, had seemed to her to unite law and interest—Chloe had never quite freed herself from the idea that she ought to read in her leisure something that had a bearing on her work). And anyhow——

She lay very still suddenly. Something, surely something, had sounded. Only the door-handle. But it had, ever so faintly, clicked. Doors did make noises in the night—but door-handles? She felt hastily round to see if she could remember a door-handle clicking. Was there somebody—had somebody come for the Stone? She thrust both hands under her pillow in a panic, and her fingers closed about it. The moonlight came half across the room, alongside her bed; surely no one at least could reach its—and her—head, and the Stone, unseen. She began to strain her eyes towards the foot; then she shut them, in case there was anyone, and that she might be thought asleep; then she partly opened them that she might see what was happening. There was a faint movement somewhere, as if of a breath being loosed, then another silence. Chloe's right hand grasped the Stone; her left held the bed-clothes tightly. What, what, if there was anyone there, was she to do? O for Lord Arglay now!

She remembered suddenly, still desperately watching, what he had said, 'Come to me'—yes, but how was she to come? O why wouldn't he come to her? 'Come to me.' But how—but of course the Stone. She only had to make use of the Stone and all would be safe. In the thrill of assured safety she all but made a face at the unknown, if there were an unknown. And there was; for one second on the edge of the dark an edge of a finger showed. Something was moving towards her in the night. Well, that was all right; they could go on moving. She had only to will and——She had only to will … to use the Stone. In a horror of anguish she understood the choice that was presented to her.

Her thoughts went through her head like Niagara. Lord Arglay had told her but even Lord Arglay didn't feel like that about the Stone and she had said to Frank she wouldn't use it if she were starving and what was the man doing and what would he do if she screamed and even if she did perhaps Mrs. Webb wouldn't come down this time and what could she do if she did? O it wasn't fair, it wasn't fair! How could she use the Stone? yet how could she bear not to if whoever it was came nearer? He was probably trying to see if her hands were empty; well, they weren't. He won't know if I've got it in my hand or not, she thought. Could she sit up, switch on the light, and with the Stone in her hand dare him to move? No—it was too risky; he'd think of something she wasn't prepared for and perhaps snatch it from her. Then she would use it; after all she was using it to save it. She was doing for it what it could not do for itself. She was protecting it. Not being a reader of religious history Chloe was ignorant what things have been done in the strength of that plea, or with what passionate anxiety men have struggled to protect the subordination of Omnipotence. But in her despair she rejected what churches and kings and prelates have not rejected; she refused to be deceived, she refused to attempt to be helpful to the God, and being in an agony she prayed more earnestly. The God purged her as she writhed; lucidity entered into her; she turned upon her face, and with both hands beneath her pillow holding the Stone, she lay still, saying only silently in her panting breath: 'Thy will, … do … do if Thou wilt; or'—she imagined the touch of the marauder on the calf of her leg and quivering in every nerve added—'or … not.'

In the darkness the Prince Ali almost made a movement of delight. He had got into the house, by the aid of certain hangers-on of the hangers-on of the Embassy; secret service, from which even a minor Embassy is not entirely exempt, sets up connexions which are useful at times, and judicious inquiries that afternoon by a gentleman in search of lodgings had let him know which Chloe's room was. The actual seizure of the Stone he had not dared to entrust to anyone else, but he had been disturbed to find Chloe still awake. He had reckoned on sleep, darkness, and chloroform, but he had not dared cross the moonlight while she lay awake, for he had some idea of how swiftly the Stone would work and he had no wish to be confronted with an empty bed. Now that she had turned on to her face, however, his opportunity was at hand. He felt very carefully for the chloroformed pad, and at that moment a cloud began gradually to obscure the moonlight. The Prince hesitated and determined to wait for that fuller darkness; while he waited he took out his electric torch with his left hand, and rehearsed his movements. A few quiet steps to the top of the bed, the torchlight on her head, the pad over her mouth. He was practically certain that the Stone would be under her pillow—or perhaps in a bag round her neck; at any rate once she was unconscious he would be able to search at leisure, with the room light on. It would, he felt, have been more satisfactory to his outraged creed to destroy the woman who had done dishonour to the sacred thing even by possessing it, and to avenge upon her the insult offered to his God. But this relief he could hardly allow himself; Allah himself must punish. The moonlight had disappeared; the room lay in darkness, he stepped forward, his finger on the switch of the torch.

When Chloe had heaved herself round with that last movement her heart had been beating wildly, and her breath coming in quick pants. Now as she lay she felt both of them beginning to move more quietly and more largely; she drew long and deep breaths and her heart composed itself to a corresponding rhythm. She still saw before her mental vision the edge of a finger against a darkness, or rather not now the edge but the finger itself, and at its back an indeterminate shape as if it were thrust a little forward from the whole hand; and she realized that it was not the same finger which she had seen a few moments earlier. Between these two palenesses therefore she lay, the one remembered, the other beheld, yet both present, and, almost as if in the uncertainty before sleep, she was vaguely conscious that the two came together and formed one stream of pale but increasing light. From somewhere beyond her, where her hands clasped the Stone, that narrow line of light emerged; she lay within it and it passed through and about her without hindrance. The more clear it grew to her knowledge, the more clearly within she enunciated the formula she had shaped with such pain and at last unconsciously abandoned the formula itself for the meaning that lay within it.

'Do, or do not,' she silently uttered, and fell even mentally into stillness in order that unhindered that action might or might not take place. The light grew suddenly around her; some encumbrance for a moment touched her mouth and would have interrupted her appeal, had it been vocal; a vibration went through her, as if a note of music had been struck along her whole frame, and far off she heard as it were a single trumpet at the gate of the house of Suleiman with a prolonged blast saluting the dawn.

The police-constable on his beat outside had come slowly down the road, and from a few yards off saw a dark heap at the door of Mrs. Webb's house. He broke into a run, bent over it for a minute, then straightened himself, and blew his whistle. It was the body of a man that lay there; they found afterwards that it was burnt as if by lightning and broken as if cast from an immense distance. The constable's whistle sounded again as if with a prolonged blast saluting the dawn.

CHAPTER XV
THE POSSESSIVENESS OF MR. FRANK LINDSAY

Neither Mrs. Webb nor Miss Burnett were of much use to the police in that morning investigation. Neither of them recognized the body, and though it had lain huddled against the front door of the house, there was nothing to show that, alive or dead, it had ever been inside the door. Besides which, burning and breaking, as that body was burnt and broken, are not injuries which the two women seemed very capable of inflicting, and the inspector in charge leaned to the idea that it had been brought from a distance and dropped at this spot. The usual inquiries were set on foot, with a casual jest or two about the possibility of the Rich Stone being responsible. But Miss Burnett was not prevented from departing to her employment, though some care was taken to see that she actually went to Lord Arglay's as she had professed to intend; since with these modern girls, as someone remarked, you never knew. The police had cause to be glad that they had not interfered, since in quite a short time the Home Office was intimating to them that the whole incident had better be kept as quiet as possible, and the stop-press paragraph which, by the chance of a belated journalist, had appeared in one morning paper had better be left without any sequel.

The Chief Justice had listened in silence to Chloe's account of the night.

'And that blast of sound went on,' she ended, 'and it seemed to be a long time before I understood it was just a police whistle, and all that light was just the moon. And then I knew that whatever it was had gone away; so I got up and looked out of the window. And there they were.'

'The police?'

'The police. They saw me and I asked a question or two, and they asked more—of Mrs. Webb too. But they couldn't do anything to us. I don't even know whether … what they had was what I saw.'

'It may not have been,' Arglay said, 'But I think it is likely. Did you see the … the result?'

'Yes,' Chloe said, her face white but rather with awe than horror or fear, 'it was as if it had been struck by lightning.'

'It wasn't Giles?'

'It was someone I have never seen before,' Chloe answered. 'A dark man, a foreigner I think. Not a negro but someone Eastern.'

'As a Persian, for instance?' Lord Arglay asked. 'Though how they knew of you I don't understand. Well, we can ask the Hajji if he knows anything—I don't think he'd be in it. He seems to have too low an opinion of violence and too high an opinion of you.'

Chloe looked at her feet and said nothing, and in a moment the Chief Justice went on. 'Yes, we will talk to him, and also I will speak to Bruce Cumberland. He won't want the thing broadcast, if it is the Persians, and it may save you some trouble. At any rate, you will sleep here now.'

'Yes,' Chloe said simply, 'I will. Shall I send a note to Mrs. Webb explaining?'

'Do,' Arglay said, 'while I telephone.'

Mr. Bruce Cumberland, when he heard the news, took the steps he was expected to take. The police were warned to be careful in their inquiries, and to turn those inquiries to discovering whether any member of the

Persian Embassy was missing. But before Lord Arglay had finished talking to the Hajji a caller arrived at Lancaster Gate.

Mr. Frank Lindsay had seen the newspaper paragraph, and alone among its readers had known the street for Chloe's. He did not seriously connect her with 'the dead body of a man found early that morning,' but there flashed through his mind the notion that here was an opportunity for an anxious inquiry. Within that opportunity another possibility lay curled, vivid with a delectable poison. Sometimes with, sometimes without, his own consent, Merridew's proposal had demanded consideration, each time more urgently, each time more plausibly. But however reasonable it had begun to seem, since after all it would do Chloe no harm and himself a great deal of good, he could not discover how to carry it out without a depressing sacrifice of his own proper pride. She had refused his suggestion almost—no, quite—rudely; she had dismissed him; she had promised to write and had not written. Even for the sake of his examination and (what of course did not weigh with him) the fee Merridew had spoken of—for a fee, nothing more, was what it was—even for these things Lindsay could not see how to make any movement towards a reconciliation. But every day made the need of that reconciliation more urgent, if it was to be in time to be any use, if (he said to himself) they were to be on their old terms again, and hardly knew that by the phrase he meant very new terms indeed. It was not that Chloe would bear any malice, but that swift willingness of hers to hurry all occasion of mischief into oblivion at times rather annoyed him; it seemed a little undignified, and was one of the things in which he suspected the influence of Lord Arglay encouraged her in lessening herself. Of course, it was different when he was concerned, though even then it was difficult for him to be gracious when she so speedily abolished the opportunity for grace. She ran where he walked, and he thought walking the more handsome movement. But now—with a dead body in the street—yes, a real concern was permissible. And if that concern repaid its possessor in other ways—but he was not thinking of that, he was thinking of a dead body. He was perfectly correct, but a more accurate vision would have told him that he was thinking also of a dying soul, and that his own.

She would be at Lancaster Gate, and to Lancaster Gate, rather nervously, he went. The telephone seemed inadequate to his anxiety; an actual meeting, a clasping hand, a reassuring embrace, if possible, if the Chief Justice was out of the way, seemed to be demanded. From every point of view he hoped that Lord Arglay would be out of the way.

Lord Arglay, seeing the maid speak to Chloe and seeing also Chloe's glance at himself, cut short his conversation with the Hajji, and, hearing that Mr. Lindsay had called, took immediate steps to be out of the way. 'You can call me for a minute when he's going,' he said, 'if you think it would look more courteous. But do as you like about that. The Hajji won't be here just yet.'

'But I don't know that I want you to go,' Chloe said uncertainly. 'No, I'm sorry, I didn't mean to put it like that. I didn't mean to talk as if I had a right....'

'I feel,' Lord Arglay said, 'that God—it's curious how easily one accepts the idea; atavism, I suppose—would rather I went; at least, the God in your friend. There is courtesy everywhere, and this, so to speak, is that. Besides, now I know you're safe, I should like him to.'

Chloe did her amiable best to reassure Mr. Lindsay, but she felt all the time that she couldn't much mind whether he were reassured or not. Unless indeed he had undergone a conversion of which she would not look for the signs for fear they should not be there. She said nothing about the invasion of the night and at first took great care not to mention the Stone. Yet since it was so much in her thoughts she did find herself wishing that he, so young, so ignorant, so well-intentioned, as he seemed to her, could feel as she felt about it, or could at least see what she felt, and when after about a quarter of an hour she felt that he might as well go, she said hesitatingly: 'You do understand, Frank, about the other night, don't you?'

Frank, whose inner thoughts had also been occupied with the Stone, said brightly: 'O of course, of course. Don't worry; that's quite all right. I see what you meant,' and wondered, for the fifteenth time, whether she had brought it with her or left it at Highgate. It wasn't on any of the tables, but her handbag lay by the typewriter; could it be——

'Would you like just to speak to Lord Arglay?' Chloe said.

That meant that she was expecting him to go, he thought very swiftly; if he said yes would she leave the room? or would she send a maid? It was growing urgent, this need of the Stone, though, of course, he could perhaps take her home. But where did she keep it? Suppose she had it round her neck in a bag? Girls did; and then——Even his mind refused to contemplate what measures, and in them what treachery, might be necessary: after all, they had been friends. 'Yes' then, and pray heaven she went to tell Lord Arglay herself.

'Perhaps it would be better,' he said.

She kissed him—persevering upon the Way—pressed his hand, went to the door, threw him a last smile, and disappeared. And he, swiftly and quietly, his eyes on the closed door, moved to her work-table, opened the bag, felt the Stone, withdrew it, stared at it, slipped it into his trouser pocket, where he thought among his keys and money it would be least noticeable, re-fastened the bag, and almost ran to the window. And even then there were two or three minutes given him for repentance, before Chloe opened the door for the Chief Justice, and stepped softly aside, as a secretary should, that her employer might enter. This careful subordination had always pleased Lord Arglay, and after the occurrences of the last few days gave him an increasing joy, as if it were part of the habitual ritual that surrounded his office, but much more delightful, more dear, and in some way more important than the rest.

Lord Arglay shook hands. Mr. Lindsay, a trifle awkwardly, apologized for disturbing Miss Burnett at her work. Lord Arglay said that any friend of Miss Burnett's was free at all times to disturb her in her work, which owing to her sense of form was rapidly becoming a great deal more her work than it was his. Mr. Lindsay said that the paragraph in the paper had alarmed him; he had been afraid there might have been some disturbance in the street, or even that some attack…. Lord Arglay said that he had feared the same thing and had been very anxious until Miss Burnett arrived. Mr. Lindsay was greatly indebted to Lord Arglay. Lord Arglay hoped that Mr. Lindsay would believe that their common friendship with Miss Burnett put his own house at Mr. Lindsay's disposal at such—or any—times. The maid announced Mr. Ibrahim. Mr. Lindsay was again obliged and must go. Lord Arglay regretted, understood, and parted. The maid showed Mr. Lindsay out.

With his departure the three in the study seemed to enter into a common concern. The Hajji, as the sound of the front door closing was heard, said quite simply: 'It was Ali.'

'That is your nephew?' Lord Arglay said.

'He was my nephew,' the Hajji answered, 'but more than death has separated us. For he also has wished to lay violent hands upon the Stone.'

Lord Arglay said, as he motioned to them to be seated, 'Hajji, the whole world seems to agree with him there.'

'It is the worse for all of us,' the Hajji answered sadly.

'You are sure of this?' Arglay asked, as he too sat down.

'As sure as I can be without seeing him,' Ibrahim said. 'He is not at the Embassy this morning, none knows where he has gone, and I know what he unwisely desired.'

'I am very sorry for your house,' Lord Arglay said, 'for this is becoming a very terrible thing. But because of others will you tell us what you think happened last night? Why did this man die?'

The Hajji looked at Chloe. 'Tell me,' he said, 'what you did when you knew that someone was in your room.'

Chloe tried to express it. 'I didn't think I ought to use the Stone for myself,' she said, 'and I didn't think I knew what it willed for itself, so I—I did nothing except hope that it would—deal with things.'

'Of itself?' the Hajji asked softly.

'I suppose so,' Chloe admitted. 'I didn't know what I ought to do.'

The Hajji nodded slowly, and looked at Lord Arglay. 'It should be clear to you what has come about,' he said. 'A thing has happened which has not been possible for a thousand years.'

'I can quite believe that,' Lord Arglay said. 'A thousand years seem to be considerably less than a day in this case. But I am not at all clear what this thing is.'

'This Holy Thing has been kept in seclusion,' Ibrahim answered, 'through many centuries, and in all that time none of its keepers have approached or touched it. And since Giles Tumulty stole it men have grasped at it in their own wisdom. But this woman has put her will at its disposal, and between it and her the union may be achieved by which the other Hiddenness is made manifest.'

'What is the other Hiddenness?' Lord Arglay asked.

The Hajji hesitated, then he turned his eyes back to Chloe and seemed to ask a question of her. What answer he saw on the forehead at which he gazed she could not guess, but he spoke then in a low and careful voice.

'In the Crown of Suleiman the Wise—the Peace be upon him!—' he said, 'there was a Stone, and this Stone was that which is the First Matter of Creation, holy and terrible. But on the hand of the King there was a Ring and in the Ring another secret, more holy and terrible than the Stone. For within the Ring there was a point of that Light which is the Spirit of Creation, the Adornment of the Unity, the Knowledge of the Loveliness, the Divine Image in the mirror of the worlds, just and true. This was the Justice and the Wisdom of Suleiman, by which all souls were made manifest to him and all causes rightly determined. Also when within the Holy of Holies in the Temple that the King made he laid his crown upon the Ark and between the wings of the Cherubim, and held his hand over it, the Light of the Ring shone upon the Stone and all things had peace. But when the King erred, building altars to strange gods, he dared no longer let the Light fall upon the Stone; also he put aside the Ring and it is told that Asmodeus sat upon his throne seven years. But I think that perhaps the King himself had not all that time parted from his throne, how closely soever Asmodeus dwelt within his soul. And of the hiding place of the Ring I do not know, nor any of my house; if it is on earth it is very secret. But the Light of it is in the Stone and all the Types of the Stone—and the Power of it is in the soul and body of any who have sought the union with the Stone, so that whoever touches them in anger or hatred or evil desire is subjected to the Light and Power of the Adornment of the Unity. And this I think my nephew did, and this is the cause of his blasting and hurling out.'

He looked straight at Chloe. 'But woe, woe, woe to you,' he said, 'if from this time forth for ever you forget that you gave your will to the Will of That which is behind the Stone.'

Chloe started to her feet with a cry. 'It isn't true,' she broke out, 'it isn't true! What have I done to bring all this on me? I can't bear it; it isn't, it mustn't be true.'

Lord Arglay's voice answered her. 'All is well,' he said, 'all is well, child. You shall do nothing that you cannot do and bear nothing that you cannot bear. I will see to that.' He held out his hand towards her, and, shaken and terrified, she caught it. 'Sit down,' he went on, smiling at her, 'and we will know what all this is.'

'What are you,' the Hajji asked, more astonished than indignant, 'to promise to govern the Stone?'

'Why, in some sense,' Lord Arglay said, smiling again, 'I am at the moment, as you say, the Light that is in the Stone. Not that I ever meant or wanted to be.'

'I do not understand you,' the Hajji exclaimed in bewilderment. 'You act as if you believed in the Stone, yet you talk like an infidel. Are you for or against this Sanctity?'

'That it may decide for itself,' Lord Arglay said. 'I am no light to my own mind, I promise you. But if what you say is true, and the Stone is a thing of goodness, and has saved this child last night, then we may agree yet.'

The Hajji shook his head. 'I do not understand,' he said almost pitifully. 'Why will you always mock?'

'I do not mock,' Arglay answered, 'or if I do I would have you consider whether this may not be part of your Mystery. But we will not now talk of the place of mockery among the gifts of the King Suleiman, although if he never smiled at himself the Court of the King must have been a very sombre place. I have known other Courts which were so, but they were, often, without any kind of light. Let us talk quietly of this.'

He drew from his pocket a small jewel case and laid it on the table, then he released his hand from Chloe's and touched her shoulder as she sat. 'Is everything well?' he said.

She looked at him, in a returning serenity. 'Everything,' she said, 'I was afraid.'

'Do not be afraid,' he said. 'Consider that we, if anything at all can be, are in the knowledge of the illuminated Stone.'

He opened the case, and his Type lay before them, but in it there was a change. The Stone was glowing with a stronger colour than before; its size was no greater but its depth seemed, as in some great jewel, to be infinitely increased, and in that depth the markings which had seemed like letters arose in a new and richer darkness. It expanded within; and the eyes of those who gazed were drawn down the shapes of the Tetragrammaton into its midst where the intervolutions of cream and gold mingled themselves in what was more like cloud than Stone. The Hajji looked and covered his eyes with his hand, pronouncing in a low voice the formula of the Unity. Lord Arglay looked and there came upon his face a half-smile of such affectionate irony as that with which he had glanced at Chloe—'this thing,' he seemed to say, 'cannot be and yet it is.' Chloe looked, and unconsciously put out her hand toward the Stone, not as if to take hold, but naturally as if it were on the point of clasping that of some sufficient lover. It moved forward and then sank and rested on the table close to the Stone, and Lord Arglay, including it also in his gaze, wondered suddenly at the kinship between the two. For the hand and the Stone were to his eyes both softly translucent; though the shapes were different, the matter of both was the same, and if the one was to be raised the other was capable of raising it. He permitted for a moment the fancy that that hand was but pausing before it lifted up, not the Stone, but the whole round world, playing with it as a ball upon its palm. He remembered the Hand thrust out from a cloud in many an early painting to image the Power behind creation, and the hand that lay open before him seemed meant to receive that creation as it came into being. He saw—even while, rightly wise in his own proper generation among these things, he refused to believe too easily—that the Stone no longer rested on the table but that it threw out of itself colour shaped into the table: the walls and furniture were in themselves reflections of that Centre in which they secretly existed; they were separations, forms, and clouded visibilities of its elements, and he also and other mortals who moved among them. The Stone quivered with its own intense and hidden life, and through the unknown hand that appeared close beside it there passed an answering quiver. Arglay saw it and held his breath for what might ensue. But nothing more ensued, or nothing that could be apprehended by his critical mind. The hand which had been for a moment a mystery of the same nature as the Stone resolved itself again into the hand of Chloe Burnett. The Stone, parted to his vision again from the world, lay on the table where he had set it. He looked up suddenly and as Chloe also moved their eyes met.

'And still,' he said, 'even so, you *did* muddle up those quotations.'

She smiled across at him. 'Am I not forgiven?' she asked.

'No,' Lord Arglay said thoughtfully, 'no, I do not think you are *forgiven*.' He considered the Stone again. 'Lay your Type here,' he went on, 'and let us see if they agree.'

She went across the room to her typewriting table, picked up and opened her bag, looked into it, felt in it, looked again, and turned to him with an exclamation. 'It isn't here,' she cried.

The Hajji looked round with a start of attention; Lord Arglay went swiftly over to her. 'Was it there?' he asked.

'Certainly it was,' Chloe cried. 'I looked at it this morning just before Frank came in.'

Arglay turned back towards the table where the Type lay. 'Can the two already have become one?' he said. 'Are all the Types of the Stone restored?'

Ibrahim joined them, asking, 'What is the matter?'

'I had a Stone here,' Chloe said, agitation growing in her—'not an hour ago it was here, and now it is gone.'

The Hajji gazed, and shook his head. 'I do not think they are yet all one,' he said, 'for no soul has yet made itself a way for the Stone to be what it will in itself. I think it is more likely that you have been robbed of it.'

Lord Arglay frowned, but before he could speak Chloe broke out in an exclamation of horror. 'O no,' she cried, 'no,' and looked at him with troubled eyes.

'Who has been here since you saw it?' the Hajji asked, and the girl, still staring at Arglay, answered, 'It couldn't be,' but more in fear than doubt.

'Why, all of us are capable of all misfortunes at all times,' the Chief Justice answered. 'Are you very certain that it was here?'

'I am quite certain,' Chloe answered, 'for I … I adored it while you were telephoning.'

'And are you certain,' Arglay said to Ibrahim, 'that the Types of the Stone are not yet made one?'

'I am not certain,' he answered, 'who can be certain of the movement of Justice? But I think that a further devotion is needed.'

Lord Arglay turned back to Chloe. 'Well,' he said, 'there is no need for us to decide, for there is nothing that we could do. If it has been taken, let us desire that goodwill may go with it, and that I will very gladly do.'

'But I must go after him,' Chloe said, 'I must make him give it back. It is my fault—perhaps I ought to have given it to him. Only … O what have I done?'

'Nothing but what was wise,' Arglay said. 'Let us forget it. You and I are here, and also a Type of the Stone. Let it rest at that, and we are where we were before.'

'Not quite,' the Hajji said, 'for as there is but one End, so there is now but one Stone with you, and it may be one path for the Stone. It may be that the path and the Stone and the End are shown you that they may be one.'

Lord Arglay had turned to go to the Type that remained when he was interrupted by the entrance of the maid with a telegram. He took it from her, opened and read it, and gave a low exclamation. Then, 'There is no immediate answer,' he said, and as the maid went out he went back to the other two.

'They have dealt with Reginald,' he said. 'Your friends again, I expect, Hajji.'

Chloe said, 'What has happened to Mr. Montague?'

'They have killed him,' Arglay answered, and for once negligent of an absurdity read the telegram aloud.

'From the Hotel Montespan, Brighton. Gentleman seriously injured by burglars and afterwards died here registered as Reginald Montague Rowland Street West gave your name as that of relation burglar unfortunately escaped but no apparent trace of theft would like to confer Gregson manager.'

After a moment's silence Arglay said, 'I am sorry for Reginald. He was a fool but he wasn't malevolent…. And now there is only us—and the others.'

'Shall you go to Brighton?' the Hajji asked.

'Certainly I shall go,' Lord Arglay said, 'for if by chance it was not a thing done to gain the Stone then any that he had may still be there. I do not think that I shall find one, but I will take no risks. Besides, as things are, I would not have even Reginald's death quite unnoticed, whatever catastrophe awaits us.'

'And this Type that you have?' Ibrahim asked, pointing to it.

'That I will leave here,' Lord Arglay said, 'and Miss Burnett shall guard it for the few hours that I shall be gone. They will not attack the house of the Chief Justice in full daylight, and if any come to take it in the name of the Law then Miss Burnett shall do what she chooses. And you, Hajji?'

'If this is true,' Ibrahim answered, 'I will not go back to those who are already shedding blood.'

'Then you also shall be here,' Lord Arglay said, 'And you two shall talk together and see if there is anything to be done. For so far,' he added in an unwonted outbreak of anger, 'I have done nothing at all. Nothing. I have been only a useless loquacity.'

'It isn't true,' Chloe said.

'Well—if you can think of anything, except trying to bring a laboratory assistant out of yesterday …' the Chief Justice answered, still bitterly.

'You may have been more than you know,' the Hajji put in.

'O I may …' Lord Arglay said. 'They also serve who only sit about and chat. But after believing in God——'

'Ah but you do!' Chloe cried, 'and is that doing nothing?'

Lord Arglay looked at her. 'It is giving a new name to old things,' he said. 'Or perhaps an old name to new things. Don't worry, child. I will go to Brighton, and do you consider the doctrine that is within the Stone.'

CHAPTER XVI
THE DISCOVERY OF SIR GILES TUMULTY

The same afternoon, while Lord Arglay was hearing at Brighton of the extraordinary events (so the manager called them) of the previous night—how someone, so far untraced, must have got into Mr. Montague's room, and how Mr. Montague's mutilated body had been discovered there in the morning; while he himself was finding that there was no trace of any Type of the Stone among Reginald's belongings—while this separation of a single Type from the rest was proceeding, Lord Birlesmere and Mr. Garterr Browne sat in a room at the Home Office and talked. Lord Birlesmere was agitated; Mr. Garterr Browne was calm and bright.

'Tumulty tells me nothing,' the Foreign Secretary was saying. 'I tried to get hold of him yesterday, but I couldn't. That fellow Palliser who was with him would only say that he hoped in time to find some way of control.'

'It might be awfully useful if he did,' Mr. Garterr Browne said, 'I see that. But it's going to take time, and I don't think at present either of us can afford the time.'

'That's quite true. I don't know what's happened,' Birlesmere answered, 'but there was an unpleasant note in the Persian man's voice. I've just seen him, and they're more sure of themselves. He even began to hint at Geneva and perhaps something more.'

'Well,' Mr. Garterr Browne went on, 'I think I may say that, as soon as I heard of it, I saw what would have to be done. One thing, anyhow, I don't know about Persia, but I think it'll quiet things here.'

'And what's that?' Birlesmere asked.

Mr. Garterr Browne smiled slyly. 'Ask yourself,' he said, 'why people—this Mayor, for instance—are making such a fuss about the Stone. Why, because they think it *does* things.'

'So it does,' Lord Birlesmere said.

'Never mind whether it does or not,' Garterr Browne said sharply. 'The point is that they believe it does. Very well. What do we want to do then? Stop them believing it. How do we do that? Tell them, and show them, that it doesn't.'

'But it does,' Lord Birlesmere said again.

'The first thing I said to myself,' Mr. Garterr Browne went on, 'when I realized it, was—people must simply not be allowed to believe in it. The second thing was—thank God it's stone.'

Lord Birlesmere sat and stared. Mr. Garterr Browne sat and smiled, then he resumed.

'How can one stop them believing in it? As I've just said—tell them it doesn't work; show them it doesn't work. And if it does, show them something that doesn't.'

'Good God!' Lord Birlesmere exclaimed.

'Stone,' the other said, still smiling, 'isn't rare. Marked stone isn't rare. Of course, to a shade the markings…. I don't say that the tints are exactly…. But near enough. I got hold of a man, and I went over his place, and I found bits. I've known him rather well for years—he was a contractor for the new Government buildings—and I found a bit of what I wanted.'

He pulled out a drawer and extracted something from it which he threw across to Lord Birlesmere. It was a fragment of square stone, having a black streak or two in it. But it was a poor imitation of the Stone of Suleiman, and so Lord Birlesmere, having considered it, felt compelled to say.

'No one would take it for the same thing,' he said.

'No one who hasn't got the original is likely to be able to compare,' Garterr Browne said. 'And who's got it? Sheldrake—well, he must keep his for the present; the Persians—well, if they know we'll keep it quiet they won't want to make a fuss; Tumulty and Palliser—well, they must be careful in their experiments, but they're not likely to act in public; you—that's all right; Arglay—that is a little awkward, but he's a sensible fellow and we'll talk to him. I fancy Merridew's trying to get a bit but I don't think he has yet—and anyhow he'll want it kept quiet; he was here saying so.'

'But, good God,' Lord Birlesmere said, 'people won't believe that these cures and so on didn't happen.'

'We shan't ask them to,' Garterr Browne explained. 'They may *have* happened; they don't happen now. Something has changed—the Stone has been exposed to the air or something. Rays … rays might have been exhausted. Tumulty and I'll manage a convincing statement. Just keep it firmly in your mind that people must not be allowed to believe in it.'

'But then why worry about having this thing?' Birlesmere asked. 'You can tell them all that anyhow.'

Mr. Garterr Browne almost winked. 'You wait,' he said. 'That Mayor's coming round here again, and it'll sound more convincing if I produce this. Besides—I'm not certain, but I *may* decide to get a few scientific opinions on the virtue and age of the thing, a few doctors or something.'

'They certainly won't believe that *that* did anything,' Lord Birlesmere said.

'Nor very likely did the other,' Garterr Browne answered. 'Think of the number of people who *don't* believe in it now, and those who don't want to. All we need for public opinion is a focus.' He got up in great glee and pointed to the bit of stone. 'This is the focus.' He made gestures with both hands. 'We concentrate,' he said, 'by a semi-official statement. Now how many people, in face of that, and their neighbours, are going on believing in an obviously absurd Stone? Ask yourself, Birlesmere, would you?'

'If I'd *seen* it …' Lord Birlesmere began.

'Pooh! coincidence,' said the other. 'Pure coincidence.'

'And suppose one of the original Stones gets about somehow?' Birlesmere asked. 'How will the Government look then? It's a damned risky business, Browne, and I don't half like it.'

'Nor you mayn't,' Mr. Garterr Browne, a little huffed, answered. 'But you don't like simplicity. Look here—this *is* the Stone, don't you see? It is; it just is. And it doesn't do anything at all. Of course, we shall try and get hold of all the others. Tumulty ought to do that.'

'Tumulty won't do anything but what he wants,' Birlesmere said. 'And I don't like the way the Persians are talking. Suppose it *does* come up at Geneva?'

'Well, give them this,' the Home Secretary suggested. 'Who's to know? They only want it for a temple or something, I suppose, so this would be just as good. It isn't as if it was a matter of practical importance. And would even they know the difference? Why, I can hardly believe there is any.'

'O I think there is,' Birlesmere protested. 'The marking looks different.'

'O the marking, the marking,' said Mr. Garterr Browne impatiently. 'God's truth, man, what does the marking matter? Here am I faced with a riot or a strike and you with a war, and there you sit bleating about the marking. If you get to rock-bottom, if you come down to actual facts, it is that or this. Which will you have?'

'O this of course,' Lord Birlesmere said.

'Do you agree to my telling this Mayor, when he comes in a few minutes, that this is it?' the other pressed again.

'Yes, O yes,' Birlesmere assented. 'Only you must back me up too with the Persian.'

'United we stand, divided we fall,' Mr. Garterr Browne almost sang. 'It's quite simple, Birlesmere, so long as you keep firmly in mind that people *must not* be allowed to believe in it. In fact, of course, they don't believe in it; nobody could. So we're only making their real minds clear to them.'

'But——' the Foreign Secretary began.

'I know, I know,' the other interrupted. 'You used it, didn't you? You and Tumulty. Yes, but, my dear fellow, are you sure you did? Looking back now, are you sure it wasn't a kind of illusion? You may know it wasn't because you have the Stone, but will those who haven't it know?'

The telephone rang and he bent to it. 'O bring him in,' he said. 'Now here is the Mayor; now you see.'

The Mayor came in heavily. His meeting with Merridew had shaken his determination far more than he had known at the time, for since then he had become gradually aware of how strong, within his public feeling and his desire for the good of the common folk, had been the hope to save that son who lay cancer-stricken at home, and also of what a strong case Merridew might present for the suppression of the Stone. He had supposed good to be single, and it was divided; to be clear, and it was very clouded; to be inevitable, and it was remotely receding. With dull eyes, and a heart almost broken by public and private pain, he faced the Home Secretary.

'I have come to know if you have any news for me,' he said.

Mr. Garterr Browne shook a sympathetic head. 'I am afraid,' he said, 'that what I have is, in a sense, worse even than you might fear. In fact, we have discovered that the matter has settled itself.' He paused and the Mayor stared at him; then he resumed. 'Yes, settled itself. You see,' he picked up the stone that lay on the table, 'you see apparently this thing changes; at least, I mean a change comes in it. It doesn't *retain* its powers. Lord Birlesmere here will bear me out that we have been very much startled and shocked to find that after a while the qualities of the Stone, the special qualities both of transport and medicine, disappear. It becomes apparently just an ordinary piece of … mineral. We are, as I told you, having it investigated, but our advisers report to the worst effect, and I am bound to say that what Lord Birlesmere and I myself have been able to see has confirmed us in accepting that report. It may be that the air has a … a modifying effect or that some inherent virtue becomes exhausted—like radium, I mean like radium doesn't, if you follow me. It may be that some central ray-diffusing nucleus disperses itself gradually. I couldn't say. But as a result—well, there we are. Nothing happens. I chanced,' Mr. Garterr Browne went on suddenly, apparently resolving to do the whole business well, while he was about it—'I happened to have neuralgia early this morning rather badly, and so of course I thought…. But there it is, my neuralgia didn't stop. I'm very sorry to have to tell you this, for I know what you must be feeling, what indeed I'm feeling myself. But there it is. Truth will out.'

With this sudden peroration Mr. Garterr Browne put the stone back on his table and looked at the Mayor. The Mayor, without invitation, sat down suddenly. He stared at the stone which, up to now, he had not seen.

'This is it?' he asked.

'This is it,' Mr. Garterr Browne said regretfully, while Lord Birlesmere inhaled audibly and thought of that earlier moment when Lord Arglay's secretary had made a scene in a Government office on behalf of the Stone of Suleiman. How much quieter things were, he considered, round Browne's stone! If only it could be kept up, and after all there was no reason why it shouldn't be. No one could tell, except by the general growth of peace and quiet, which stone had really better exist. Strong measures perhaps, but difficult times required strong measures.

The Mayor said slowly: 'Do your scientific men, your doctors, assure you that this is quite useless?'

'Alas, yes,' Mr. Garterr Browne said reluctantly.

'And what of the other Stones?' the Mayor asked. 'Have they also become useless?'

'Well, so far as we can test them,' the Home Secretary answered, with an air of complete frankness. 'There are one or two we haven't got, of course. There's Sir Giles Tumulty's; he's working on it, so no doubt we shall hear.'

There was a short silence. Then the Mayor said, 'It is certain that this Stone can do nothing?'

'It is perfectly certain,' Mr. Garterr Browne answered, tasting the words as if he were enjoying the savour of the truth that they contained, 'that this stone can do nothing.'

The Mayor stretched out his hand, picked up the stone, looked at it, turned it over in his hand, and then sat for a moment holding it. At this last moment of his hopes, when he realized that, in consequence of this new discovery of the mysterious nature of the stone, he was about to return to Rich disappointed and crushed and compelled to crush and disappoint—at this moment it was impossible for him not to make one last personal effort. It was useless, of course, but if any virtue remained, if, defeated in the State, he could still succeed in the household by some last lingering potency, if he could help his son——He shaped the wish to himself and put all his agony and desire into it, clutching tightly the useless bit of matter meanwhile, and the two Ministers watched him with rather obvious patience. At last he stirred, put it down, and stood up.

'It seems I can do no more,' he said. 'I will go back to Rich and tell them that there is no hope.'

'A great pity,' Lord Birlesmere said, speaking for the first time; and 'A very great pity,' said Mr. Garterr Browne, adding, both to create a good impression and with an eye to any extremely improbable future eventualities, 'Of course, if any fresh change should occur, if (for example) it should be in any way *cyclic*, I pledge you my word to let you know. But I haven't much hope. A most remarkable phenomenon—that it should have reasonably aroused such hope.'

'A very common phenomenon—that the dying should hope for life,' said the Mayor, and with one abrupt farewell went out.

'And now,' Garterr Browne said, leaning across his table towards Birlesmere, '*now* for Tumulty.'

The Foreign Secretary in turn leant a little forward, so that to observant eyes, perhaps to Lord Arglay's, the two might have seemed, as they bowed towards each other across the office table and the mock stone, like two figures of cherubim bowing over another Ark than that which was in the Temple of Suleiman, and over the false treasures of an illusory world. The light of the Shekinah was hidden, but there was something of a light in Mr. Garterr Browne's eyes as he said, 'Birlesmere, now we've got rid of him, now he's been worked, is there any reason why *we* shouldn't have it'—he dropped his voice a little—'and stick to it? You and I and Sheldrake if we must, and Tumulty to experiment? It may be able to do very great things. Life—for all we know; and gold—for all we know; and control.'

Lord Birlesmere paled a little, but he also had felt during the last few days a small and strange desire moving in his heart, and he did not dispute with his colleague. He only said, 'Can it be done?'

'Let us talk to Tumulty,' Mr. Garterr Browne answered and took up the telephone.

It was, however, much later in the evening before Sir Giles could be got hold of. He had that day been again to Wandsworth considering the detestable bed where the living and broken victim of his experiment lay, sustained against all likelihood in a dreadful mortality by the rigorous operation of the Stone. He had then proceeded to a hospital where he proposed to institute a series of experiments to see how far health could be restored or abolished, and to note the effect of the Stone upon bodies in a state of disease, and he had made arrangements to visit a madhouse on the next day, where among the merely imbecile he hoped to be able to measure the degree of personal will necessary for any working. He was consequently both tired and snappy when the Home Secretary began talking, and shut down on the conversation in a few minutes.

'It's always the same damnable chit-chat,' he muttered, as he went up to his bedroom and flung his Type on a table by the bed. 'Always this infernal control. I'd control *them* fast enough if I could. If I could get past whatever sailor's knot the thing tied itself into the other day when I wanted to try it on that bitch of Arglay's. Can't that hog-headed paroquet of a Secretary have Arglay and her jailed for something or other? I can't get rid of a notion that she's peering over the blasted thing at me. Am I losing my nerve and beginning to see things?' He had sat down, half-undressed, on the side of the bed, and in a sudden outbreak of rage he picked up the Stone again. 'Damn you,' it was Chloe whom he half-unconsciously apostrophized, 'are you tucked away in it as if it was Arglay's bed? I only wish I could get at you.'

As he spoke the Stone seemed to open in his hand. He found himself looking into it, down coils of moving and alternated splendour and darkness. Startled, he dropped it on the table, or would have done, but that, as he loosed it, instead of falling, it hung in the air, dilating and deepening. It was no more a mere Stone, it moved before him as a living thing, riven in all its parts by a subdued but increasing light. He sprang up and took a step or two away, nor did it pursue, but he somehow found himself no farther off. He backed, cursing, to the extreme other side of the room, but there once more he found himself close to what had by now become a nucleus of movement which passed outward from it into the very walls and furniture. They, so far as the mind which was now striving to steady itself, could discern, were themselves shifting and curving. He put out his hand to the bed and found himself holding the cord of one of the pictures; he stepped aside, and one foot was on the pillows of the bed and one crashing through the glass of the wardrobe. 'The damn thing'll get me down if I'm not careful,' he thought, and made a great effort to hold himself firm, and see in its natural shape the room he knew so well. But, whether within or without, the awful change went on; it was as if the room itself, and he with it, were being sucked into the convolutions of the Stone. Its darkness and its light were no more merely before him but expanding upwards and downwards till they rose to his head and descended to his feet; he felt himself drawn against all his efforts into some unnaturally curved posture—he knew of pain somewhere but could not keep his mind on it. For before him in arch after arch, as if veil after veil were torn swiftly aside, that which was the Stone was opening its heart to him. His eyes could not properly see, nor his brain understand, what those swift revelations held; he thought once or twice he saw himself, he was sure he caught sight of Lord Arglay moving in some abstracted meditation upon some serious concern. And then suddenly he saw her; he saw her lying in bed asleep, far off but very clear, and felt himself beginning to be entirely drawn down the long spiral passages through which he gazed. He set, in one last gigantic effort, his whole will against this movement, and for a moment seemed to stay it. So clear was the vision that he saw Chloe stir and turn a little in her sleep. In a suddenly renewed rage he felt himself cry out at her, 'O go to hell,' and as the words, from within or without, reached his mind, Chloe stirred again and woke. He saw her wake; his eyes met hers; he saw them but saw in them no recognition—not of horror or anger or fear; nor indeed of pity or mercy or distress. She looked at him through the distances, and as if unconsciously put a hand beneath her pillow. And as she did so the vision passed and he saw her no more.

For now, and now that sense of pain in his limbs grew stronger, he saw That which had lain beneath her pillow; within the Stone he saw the Stone. Not in the sense of which the Hajji had spoken or Lord Arglay had talked to Chloe, but for him more agonizingly the way to the Stone lay indeed within the Stone. Its greatness was all about him, yet its smallness lay, glowing gold, at the remote centre. There was something or someone behind and partly above it, and below in a fiery circle of guardianship he saw figures that seemed each to wear it in ring or crown, in swordhilt or sceptre, and then the Stone in the centre changed and was the Stone no more.

For whatever brooded over it had moved, and at the movement the light leaped out at him, and suddenly Giles Tumulty began to scream. For at once the light and with it the pain passed through him, dividing nerve from nerve, sinew from sinew, bone from bone. Everywhere the sharp torment caught him, and still, struggling and twisting, he was dragged down the curving spirals nearer to the illumination into which he was already plunged. And he remembered—now suddenly he remembered how he had seen in a vision what was to be. He had willed to be in the future, and since that could not be, for the future as yet had lain only in the Mind to which it equally with the past was present, the Stone had revealed the future to him. He remembered; he knew what was to happen, for the merciful oblivion was withdrawn; he saw himself gathered, a living soul, into the centre of the Stone. That which he had been to men, that by which he had chosen to deal with others, by that he was to be dealt with in his turn. The wheeling and looming forms of giant powers amid whom he was drawn turned on him their terrible and curious eyes; under the gaze of everlasting dominations he was exposed in a final and utter helplessness. He was conscious also of a myriad other Giles Tumultys, of childhood and boyhood and youth and age, all that he had ever been, and all of them were screaming as that relentless and dividing light plunged into them and held them. He was doing, it seemed, innumerable things at once, all the things that he had ever done, and yet the whole time he was not doing, he was slipping, slipping down, and under and over him the Glory shone, and sometimes it withdrew a little and then pierced him again with new agony. And now he was whirling round and round, having no hold above or footing below, but being lost in an infinite depth. Above him the light was full of eyes, curious and pitiless, watching him as he had often watched others, and a subtle murmur, as of some distant words of comment or of subdued laughter came to him. From the spirals of time and place he felt himself falling, and still he fell and fell.

When they found him, but a few moments after that raucous scream had terrified the household, he was lying on the floor amid the shattered furniture twisted in every limb, and pierced and burnt all over as if by innumerable needle-points of fire.

CHAPTER XVII
THE JUDGEMENT OF LORD ARGLAY

Twenty-four hours after his theft, Frank Lindsay had begun to realize that the emotions which accompany possession are sometimes as hard to deal with as the difficulties which precede possession. Before he had had the Stone in his pocket he had seen quite clearly what he would do; he would divide it, keep one part, and pass the other on to Mr. Merridew in return for a fee. That two identical Stones would result from the division he had not understood, only that each part of a divided Stone possessed the virtues of the whole. But he found that such a proceeding was by no means easy. His irritation with Chloe had prepared the way for his desire of success in his examination, winged by the promised fee, to pass into action; but when action was for the moment over, he found the second step more difficult than the first. He had been squeezed by circumstances and a narrow chance into the first act, but time opened before him for the second, and he could not move. He continually found himself staring at the Stone; he continually fingered his pocket-knife, and even took it out and opened it. But he could not put the edge to its work.

For one thing the Stone itself surprised him. He had not understood from Chloe—and for a good reason, since at that time she had not made herself a path for the Will of the Stone, and the Light within it had not expanded in proportion—that it was so strange, so active, and even so terrible an object. He was—he had to admit—frightened of touching it; he felt as if it would bleed at a cut and pour out its life before him. He hesitated even to touch it; it looked sometimes as if it would burn him if he lifted it. On the other hand, he could not bring himself to part entirely in his mind from Chloe by passing it on to Mr. Merridew in its completeness. He thought of ringing Carnegie up and refrained; vaguely it seemed to him that Chloe might, she *might*, be willing to lend him one of them if he didn't. After all, she might take another view of his needs even now, even if she found out; but he realized that if she found out that it had passed to Merridew, his own days would be short in her land. And at that he began to realize that he was very near finding Chloe indispensable to him, or (as he called it) loving her. He didn't want her to leave him, and while he had the

Stone (he thought hopefully, in the manner of lovers of the sort) he could bribe, or lure, or bully her into nearness. The idea had occurred to him in the night, and he took it with him to the offices where he worked, and his own small room.

The only difficulty in the way of re-establishing relations with Chloe while retaining the Stone was the explanation of how he had got it. He hardly saw himself saying to her, 'I have stolen this from you, and I want to use it. But if you are very nice to me I will not give it to anyone else, though I might make a hundred or two by doing so. I will, that is, buy you with a hundred pounds and the preservation in my own hands of your property.' The nearest he got to saying that even to himself was to recollect that she had occasionally, in times of financial stress, jested, half-mockingly, half-grimly, on the amount for which she would sell herself. But he realized that anyone who offered five pounds, or indeed five pence, would stand a better chance than he himself coming with such a bargain. Besides, of course, he didn't want her to sell herself; he wanted her to love him—in exchange for his loss of a hundred pounds and his promise only to use the Stone for his own purposes.

It was at that moment she arrived, following up an office-boy, who just had time to say, 'Miss Burnett to see you,' before he was dazzled out of the way by her smile as she passed. The smile vanished as she shut the door behind her; she turned on the wretched, goggling, and gasping Frank a face which he had never seen before. Chloe laughing, Chloe irritable, Chloe impatient, Chloe affectionate, Chloe attentive, Chloe provocative, these and many another he had known—but this, this was hardly Chloe. It was not that she looked angry or harsh; there was rather in her face a largeness of comprehension, a softness of generosity and lovely haste to meet any approach, which bewildered him.

'Dear Frank,' she said, tenderly, 'how silly of you!'

Frank went on goggling. She added simply, 'I couldn't come yesterday because Lord Arglay was away till very late, and I didn't like to leave it while he had told me to stop. Not that it mattered. So I had to come here.' She smiled at him. 'Darling,' she added, 'you were rather rash, weren't you? and a little rude?'

Frank's mind tried vainly to understand. He was being accused—it must in the circumstances surely be an accusation? what could she do except ask, or appeal, or accuse? Only this didn't sound like any of the three; it was more like sympathy. But if he were being accused, it was of a breach of manners and not of morals, which put him at a disadvantage, since the second can be defended on the grounds of some better, or at least different, morality, but the first is a matter of taste and defence is only communicable by emotion. Of her emotions at the moment he was altogether ignorant.

'Rude?' he said, 'rude? What do you mean—rude?'

'Well …' Chloe sketched a gesture. 'You might have asked me again first if you needed it so much.'

Whether this subtlety was from the Stone or from her own feminine mind was hidden at the place where the Stone and her mind were finding their union. The only answer of which Frank was capable was criticism in turn.

'I did ask you,' he said, 'and you wouldn't…. But anyhow, I don't know…'

He could not finish. Her swift and luminous eyes prevented him, passing in front of him with what shone in them, as they turned his excuses and denials aside, like a new and overwhelming mastery and knowledge. She came lightly to him and paused.

'Will you give it back to me?' she said simply and stretched out her hand.

In the stress of the moment he almost did. They had, they had been friends, great friends. They had had good times together; she had mocked and teased and helped and liked him; their hands and their mouths, their voices and their glances, were familiar. All but the sovereign union had been theirs, and if, for Chloe, that sovereign union had by now been made with other worlds, and if its image and instrument in this world lay between her and her other friend and master, yet of these things Frank was ignorant. And since assuredly that full and sovereign union permits no exclusion of any beauty, since the august virtue of its nature is to receive into itself all which partakes of its own divine benignity, since there—and there alone—is neither one nor many, neither lesser nor greater, but all is perfect and free, since even in its reflections upon earth the marvellous liberty of the children of God is to be experienced by all who devoutly and passionately desire, then even at that single moment Frank Lindsay might have entered into its sweetness and strength could he have met her as she came, and answered her in such a voice as that in which she asked. But such a voice can carry no selfish complaint, no wrangling excuse; it is a sound which, native to heaven, can on earth be vocal and audible only between spirits already disposed to heaven. So disposed, for all of clumsiness or roughness or anger or haste or folly that needed still to be cleared and enlightened, she stood and faced him. So indisposed, for all of industry and care and thought and study, he stood and looked away.

'Give what back?' he mumbled.

She sighed a little, and a faint shadow came upon her. She dropped her hand and said gravely, 'Will you give me back the Stone that you have taken?'

Between denial and excuse he hesitated; then, abandoning both, he began, 'Chloe, I don't think you quite understand——'

'Need I understand more?' she asked.

'It's like this——' he began again, and again she checked him.

'There is no need,' she said, and then more swiftly, 'Frank, dear Frank, will you do this?'

He made another effort, letting go the pretence of ignorance. 'Are *you* asking me to?' he said. 'I mean, do *you* want it?'

'No,' she said, and ceased.

'But if you don't want it, then why…. I mean, mightn't it as well be here—or even——' He was a little disappointed by her negative, and yet uncertain of the wisdom of introducing Merridew.

'It does not matter much where it is, I think,' she said, and again affection broke into her voice as she said, 'I'm not asking for it; I'm asking you.'

'You're asking me for it,' he said intelligently.

'No,' she answered again. 'I am asking you to restore it, if you will, before——'

'Before?' he asked, really startled. Surely Arglay, surely she, couldn't be thinking of the police! Curiously enough, he had never thought of the police until now. But she wouldn't, she couldn't, not with him! And Arglay couldn't be such a cad.

'Before'—for the first time she faltered—'I don't know; perhaps before it is restored. But that doesn't matter; only I can't wait. Lord Arglay is expecting me; he let me come because he knew I wanted to, but I can't wait. Frank, if you have liked what we have had, you and I, will you give me back the Stone?'

'It isn't that I wouldn't—soon,' Frank answered.

'Will you now?' she asked.

'I think we ought to talk it over a little,' he said defensively. 'I think you ought to try and get my point of view. I think I——'

She moved away and walked, a little sadly, to the door. There she paused and looked back. 'Thank you for everything you have done for me,' she said. 'They were good times. Good-bye, darling.'

He began to stammer some further explanation, but she was gone, and he stood alone with an emptiness and an uncertain fear invading his heart. In his haste, when she had entered, he had flung his morning paper over the Stone, which had been lying on the table, and now he moved that away, and again looked at the thing which he had denied her. He thought uncertainly of the examination, and unpleasantly of Mr. Merridew; of course, if she really wanted—It was a long while before, still disturbed, but still following the way he had begun to tread, he rang up Carnegie at the Union offices. Nor even then had he ventured to divide the Stone; he would talk to them first.

Carnegie, a cheque in his pocket, and the General Secretary's urgent instructions in his mind, arrived as quickly as possible, and as quickly as possible cut short Frank's talk, and procured the exhibition of the Stone. He agreed to every condition Frank made about having it returned—or a part of it—for the examination, passed over the cheque, picked up a spare envelope, slipped the Stone into it, put it down for a moment on the table again, and slapped Frank on the shoulder.

'Good man!' he said. 'Merridew will be frightfully bucked, and you may find he can be useful to you yet. He will if he can after this. Well, I must get back at once. On the twenty-third you want it then?'

He grinned cheerfully at Frank, moved to pick up the packet, and looked vaguely at the table. 'Where——' he began, picked up an empty envelope, the only one in sight, and said with some sharpness, 'Where the devil is it?'

They both looked, they separated and sorted papers, they searched table and floor, they looked inside the envelope a dozen times, and still the Stone was undiscoverable.

'What's the idea?' Carnegie asked. 'Is this a joke?'

'Don't talk rubbish,' Frank answered sharply. 'Did you put it in your pocket?'

It seemed not, though the cheque had remained in Frank's. Carnegie searched, threatened, expostulated; Frank, maddened by an implied accusation of a theft of money, snapped, and later raged. They searched and quarrelled; they hunted and denounced. And for all their effort and anger and perplexity, the Stone of the King was not to be found.

But while Frank had, after her departure, still been standing, dimly puzzled and unhappy, Chloe had been on her way back to Lancaster Gate, back to the Hajji and Lord Arglay and the Unity in the Stone. All the previous afternoon she had watched it, or—to the best of her power—prayed, or meditated, or talked or listened to that foreign doctor of the mysteries. The realization of the theft of her Type had caused that which remained to seem very precious to her; the thought of the attempt in her room and of the death of Reginald Montague had brought the sense of necessary action very close, but she did not yet see what that action was to be. The Hajji had talked as if but one stage had been reached; she had made an opportunity, he implied, for the Stone, and the Indwelling of the Stone, to operate in the external world, but there it could at best only heal and destroy and its place was not there. He would not formulate for her what more remained, and she reposed now on the hope, the more than hope, that Lord Arglay and the Stone would direct her. Her unhappiness about Frank lay rather round than in her; she saw it as a sadness rather than felt it as a sorrow, for within she was withdrawn to an intention of obedience and a purpose not yet unveiled.

She got out at the Tube station, smiled at the newspaper man, picked up an agitated old lady's umbrella, threw a glance over the Park, and came after a short walk to the house. When she opened the study door she was at first unobserved, for Lord Arglay was standing with his back to the door listening to the Mayor of Rich. At least, she supposed it must be the Mayor, from what he was saying, and from Oliver Doncaster's presence a few paces distant. The Hajji was sitting close by. The Stone, infinitely precious, glowed upon the table. On another smaller table were her typewriter, her notebooks, one pile of ordered manuscript which was the first few chapters of *Organic Law*, and another pile of papers which were the notes and schemes and drafts and quotations and references for the remainder. She closed the door softly behind her and for a minute or so stood and gazed.

Her gaze took in, it seemed, the symbols and instruments of her life, but they were real things and she felt with increasing happiness that what was there had, however hidden, run through her life. The muddled, distressed, amusing thing that her life had been resolved itself into four things in that room—the manuscript, and Oliver Doncaster, and Lord Arglay, and the Stone. Whatever was coming, it was good, and she was fortunate, that her work had entered into the Chief Justice's attempt to formulate once more by the intellect the actions of men; she was fortunate to have had even so small a part in the august labour. Whatever was coming, it was good that all her transitory loves should touch with so pleasant a glance as Oliver Doncaster's her renewed entrance. She remembered how she had thought of his hair, and with a secret smile she assented—not in desire but in a happy amusement. 'The dear!' she thought, caught his eyes, saw the admiration in them, preened herself on it for a moment's joy, and looked on. Of the Hajji and the Mayor she felt little; they knew and did things, but they answered to no need or capacity within her except as teachers or clients. And of Lord Arglay and of the Stone she could not think, only she hoped that, whatever happened, neither of them would be lost to her for ever.

She took off her hat and coat, went and put them on her chair, and came softly back. The Mayor saw her and stopped. Lord Arglay questioned her with his eyes; she shook her head. He nodded, and considered; then he said:

'It seems then, as the Hajji said yesterday, that there remains but this Type. And three of us are agreed that there is but one End. But the Hajji declares that there is but one Path also.'

'And what is that?' Chloe asked.

'It is through the Restoration of the Stone,' the Hajji said, but before he could add anything Lord Arglay went on, 'Only the Mayor here believes that there is another Path, for having heard'—his little finger indicated Oliver—'that we preserve the Stone he has come here to ask me to use it for all sorts of good things.'

'But I thought,' Chloe said, 'that the Government———'

Lord Arglay allowed himself to smile. 'The Government,' he said, 'have found that the Stone has unfortunately exhausted its powers.'

'What!' Chloe exclaimed.

The Hajji got up. 'It is the most horrible blasphemy,' he said.

'Why, that may be so,' Lord Arglay said, 'though I can very well believe that the stone they have produced is an exact presentation of the feeling between Birlesmere and Garterr Browne. So that even in such a blasphemy the Justice of things is maintained.'

'But exhausted———?' Chloe asked, staring at the marvel which from its place directed the movements of her heart.

'O la la!' Lord Arglay answered, 'let us forget their tricks.' He too looked at the Stone, and added, almost as if speaking to it, 'But what can you expect, with such an Executive?' Then he went on, 'So the Mayor has come to us, and he would have us do what we may with the Stone to cure all the broken and diseased men in his city.'

He paused, but Chloe only waited for him to proceed as (he thought) she had so often done while he dictated the sentences of *Organic Law*. He went on.

'And here therefore we are,' he said, 'wondering what path to follow. For the Mayor and the Hajji disagree, and Mr. Doncaster and I have no clear idea, and though doubtless the Stone knows very well it does not give us much help. What do you think?'

She shook her head, and as she did so the Mayor broke once more into his plea for those whom he sought to serve. But after a while he stopped.

Lord Arglay said, 'All this is true and dreadful enough. But even yet I am not clear what should be done.'

'If you are afraid to act——' the Mayor cried out.

'No,' Lord Arglay said, 'I do not think I am afraid.'

'Then divide the Stone,' the Mayor exclaimed, 'and let me have a part, and do what you will with the other.'

The Hajji made a movement, but Lord Arglay checked him with a hand, and said, 'No, that I will not do; for I am still the Chief Justice—though I cannot think I shall be so for very long—and it is not in my judgement to commit any violence upon the Stone.'

'Then for God's sake say what you will do,' the Mayor cried out in pain, 'and put an end to it all.'

Lord Arglay stood for a minute in silence, then he began to speak, slowly and as if he gave judgement from his seat in the Court.

'I think there are few among my predecessors,' he said, 'who have had such a matter to decide, and that not by the laws of England or Persia or any mortal code. But God forbid that when even such a matter is set before us we should not speak what we may. For if this is a matter of claimants then even those very terrible opposites shall abide the judgement of the Court to which chance, or it may be something more than chance, has brought them, as it was said in one of the myths of our race that a god was content to submit to the word of the Roman law. But it is not in our habit to wash our hands of these things, whatever god or people come before us. Also this is a question, it seems, between God and the people. It is a very dreadful thing to refuse health to the sick—but it is more tragic still to loose upon earth that which does not belong to the earth, or if it does only upon its own conditions and after its own mode. Therefore I would not compel the Stone to act or ask any grace from it that it did not naturally give. And it is clear to us at least since last night that this thing belongs only to itself. So that I say that it is necessary first that it may be offered again to itself, but whether or how that may be done I do not yet know. For of all of us here one has sworn an oath and will keep it, and one claims the Stone for his purposes, and two are unlearned in its way. And therefore there is but one Path for the Stone, and since she has made herself that we will determine the matter so.'

He looked at Chloe, and his voice changed. 'Are you to be the Path for the Stone?' he said.

'That is as you will have me,' Chloe answered.

'Are you to be?' he asked, with a tender irony. 'Will you sit on the throne of Suleiman, and of all those who have possessed the Stone, kings and law-givers, Nimrod and Augustus and Muhammed and Charlemagne, will you only restore it to its place?'

Chloe flushed, and looked at him in distress. 'Am I being silly?' she asked. 'I do not compare, I was only asking what you wanted me to do.'

'Be at peace,' he answered, 'for no man has yet measured his own work, and it may be you shall do more than all these. They laboured in their office, and you shall work in yours. But why will you have me tell you what to do?'

'Because you said that the Stone was between us,' she answered, 'and if that is so how otherwise can I move in the Stone?'

'And if I tell you to do it?' he asked.

'Then I will do what I may,' Chloe said.

'And if I tell you not to do it?' he asked again.

'Then I will wait till you will have it done,' she said, 'for without you I cannot go even by myself.'

He looked at her in silence for a while, and as they stood there came through the open window the shouting of the newspaper boys. 'More Rioting at Rich,' they called, 'Official Statement.' 'The Stone a Hoax.' 'Rumours of War in the East.' 'Rumours of War … rumours of war.'

Lord Arglay listened and looked. Then, 'Well,' he said, 'whether I believe I do not know and what I believe I most certainly do not know. But it is either that or this. And since this is in your mind I also will be with your mind and I will take upon me what you desire. So, if there is indeed a path for the Stone, in the name of God let us offer it that path, and let whatever Will moves justly in these things fulfil itself through us if that is its desire.' He lifted up the Stone, kept it for a moment raised upon his hand in the full view of all of them, and held it a little out towards Chloe. 'Go on, child,' he said.

With the words there came to her the memory of her other experience in that room, when in dream or vision she had heard some such voice command her and struggled desperately to obey. There was no struggle or desperation in her movement or consciousness now as, so summoned, she went forward and paused in front of him, holding out her joined hands below his. He lowered his own gently till it lay in the cup of hers, and said in a voice shaken beyond his wont, 'Do you know what you must do?'

She looked at him with a docile content. 'I have nothing at all to do,' she said, and the Hajji cried suddenly aloud, 'Blessed for ever be the Resignation of the elect.'

'Under the Protection,' Lord Arglay said, with the smile he had for her, and, as she answered, in a voice that only he could hear, 'Under the Protection,' he leaned his hand very gently so that, as if almost of its own motion, the Stone rolled over into hers. She received it, moving a step or two backward till she stood a little apart from them. The Hajji broke into the Protestation of the Unity—'There is no God but God and Muhammed is the Prophet of God.'

The Mayor had turned half aside and had sat down, but he looked back now at the figures before him. Oliver Doncaster gazed with the ardent worship of young love at Chloe, but he also was in the rear. Upright, attentive, providential, Lord Arglay maintained his place, and stood nearest to her of all who watched.

She turned her eyes from his at last, downwards upon the Stone. It lay there, growing every moment more dark and more bright within itself; it seemed larger than it had been, but they could not properly judge because of the movement within it. Chloe looked at it, and suddenly there came into her mind the memory of Frank Lindsay. 'Poor darling,' she felt with a renewed rush of pity and affection, 'he didn't, he couldn't, understand.' In her own understanding she offered his failure and his mischief to That which she held, and with him also (moved by a large impulse which she endured without initiating, but with which she gladly united herself) all those who for any purpose of good or evil had laid their hands or fixed their desires upon the Stone. Vague in image, but intense in appeal, her heart gathered all—from herself to Giles Tumulty—in a sudden presentation of them to the Mystery with which they had trafficked.

Opposite her the eyes of Christopher Arglay had been watching it also. But as, in the passion of her intercession, she raised her hands and bent her head as if to carry the Stone into her breast and brood above it there, his gaze slid along those arms to her form, and took in not only that but the open window and the sky beyond.

He looked out, and in the sky itself there was a change. There was movement between him and the heavens; the chimneys and clouds and sky took on the appearance of the Stone. He was looking into it, and the world was there, continents and cities, seas and their ships. The Stone was not these, yet these were the Stone—only there was movement within and beyond them, and from a point infinitely far a continual vibration mingled itself with the myriad actions of men. And then, in the foreground of that vastidity, he saw rising the Types of the Stone, here and again there appearing and through all those mingled colours rushing swiftly together. Loosed from their cells and solitudes upon earth, living suddenly in conjoining motion, closing within themselves the separation which men had worked on them, those images grew into each other and were again made one. For a moment he saw the Unity of the Stone at a great distance within the Stone which was the world, and then the farther Mystery was lost in the nearer. Colour and darkness were a great background for her where she stood; they concentrated themselves upon her; through her they poured into the Stone upon her hands, and behind her again appeared but the sky and the houses of a London street.

The Hajji's voice called: 'Blessed be the Merciful, the Compassionate! blessed!' and he got to his knees, immediately afterwards prostrating himself towards the window, the East, and Mecca. Moved by the action and by some memory of churches and childhood, Oliver also knelt down; so that of all those in the room only the figure of Lord Arglay remained still upright and vigilant before her as the great change went on.

The strength of the appeal within her faded; it had achieved itself and she was hastened to what remained in her will. She became conscious of the movement of her hands and her head, and stayed them, for they seemed to suggest, however slightly, a removal and possession of the Stone. Her hands went a little from her, the Stone exposed upon them; they lifted a little also, and her head was raised and thrown back. But still her eyes were upon it, and her will abolished itself before its own. Where before she had prayed 'Do or do not,' now she did not even pray. Her thought and her feeling passed out of her knowledge; she was the Path and there was process within her, and that was enough.

It was not given to her—or to most of the others—to see the operation by which that Mystery returned to its place. For the Hajji's eyes were hidden, and the Mayor still brooded over the needs of men and was but half-attentive, and Oliver Doncaster's look was for Chloe rather than the Stone. Only the justice of Lord Arglay, in the justice of the Stone which lay between himself and the woman he watched, beheld the manifestation of that exalted Return. He had seen the Types come together and pass through her form, colouring but never confusing it, till they had entered entirely into the Type upon her hands. But scarcely had the last vestige of entwined light and dark grown into the One which remained, scarcely had he seen her in herself standing again obedient and passive, than he saw suddenly that the great process was reversing itself. As all had flowed in, so now all began to flow out, out from the Stone, out into the hands that held it, out along the arms and into the body and shape of which they were part. Through the clothes that veiled it he saw that body receiving the likeness of the Stone. Translucency entered it, and through and in the limbs the darkness which was the Tetragrammaton moved and hid and revealed. He saw the Mystery upon her hands melting into them; it was flowing away, gently but very surely; it lessened in size and intensity as he watched. And as there it grew less, so more and more exquisitely and finally it took its place within her— what the Stone had been she now was. Along that path, offered it by one soul alone, it passed on its predestined way—one single soul and yet one not solitary. For even as she was changed into its nature her eyes shone on her mortal master with an unchanged love and in the Glory that revealed itself there was nothing alien to their habitual and reciprocal joy. The Stone that had been before them was one with the Stone in which they had been; from either side its virtue proclaimed itself in her. At last the awful change was done. She stood before him; her hands, still outstretched, were empty, but within her and about her light as of a lovely and clearer day grew and expanded. No violent outbreak or dazzling splendour was there; a perfection of existence flowed from her and passed outward so that he seemed both to stand in it and to look on it with his natural eyes. With such eyes he saw also, black upon her forehead, as if the night corresponding to that new day dwelled there for a while apart, the letters of the Tetragrammaton. She stood, so withdrawn, as the Stone sank slowly through her whole presented nature to its place in the order of the universe, and that mysterious visibility of the First Matter of creation returned to the invisibility from which it had been summoned to dwell in the crown of Suleiman the King. As in the height of his glory the Vicegerent of the Merciful One had sat, terrific and compulsive over spirits and men, and the Stone had manifested above him, so now from the hands stretched to grasp it and the minds plotting to use it, from armies and conspiracies, greed and rapine, it withdrew through a secluded heart. She stood, and the light faded and the darkness vanished; she stood, one moment clothed in the beauty of the End of Desire, and then swiftly abandoned. She was before him, the hands stretched not to hold but to clasp, the eyes wide with an infinite departure; she exclaimed and swayed where she stood, and Lord Arglay, leaping to her as she fell, caught a senseless body in his arms.

CHAPTER XVIII

THE PROCESS OF ORGANIC LAW

Cecilia Sheldrake was always, everybody said, extraordinarily kind to her husband, which may have been why he committed suicide some ten years after the vanishing of the Stone. No one quite believed, and very few people understood, what her hints to her intimate, and indeed her less intimate, friends exactly meant; that she and he had possessed some marvellous thing by which anyone could go anywhere, and that, having nearly lost it once in a motor-car, he had shortly afterwards entirely lost it in her drawing-room. She never reproached him, or not after the first year or two, and even then never with the virulence of the first week. They had, people gathered, been looking together at whatever it was—nobody remembered and nobody cared to remember, and then he had mislaid it. At least, for the first year or two he had mislaid it, and after then nobody ever understood quite what he had done with it—sat on it or swallowed it or sold or secreted it, according as it seemed to the hearer most like an egg, a bon-bon, a curiosity, or a jewel. But somehow he had got rid of it, and Cecilia's life was ruined. As, very justly, it actually was—first, by the discontent which she perpetually nursed, and secondly, by the drastic financial rearrangements which followed on her husband's suicide.

Mr. Garterr Browne, being unmarried, and having definitely himself preserved the Type which he had had, found himself in the difficult position of having nobody but himself to blame. His position therefore was so far worse than Mrs. Sheldrake's, and it was for a few months made worse still by his having at odd times to deal with the doctors and scientists whom he had summoned to report on his own substitute for the Stone. Fresh reports kept arriving for quite a long time from scientific men of whom he had never heard, but who (with an indecently unselfish ardour) kept on taking an interest in the remarkable cures at Rich and their relation to the wretched fragment which Mr. Garterr Browne had handed on to his earlier advisers and they had passed to their friends who were interested. Exactly how it was that he and Lord Birlesmere could never afterwards be persuaded to take the same view on any question, not even the Prime Minister, whose Government was twice wrecked, ever properly understood.

Between those two politicians, between Sheldrake and his wife, between Carnegie and Frank Lindsay, there lay continually suspicion, anger, and hatred. Negligent of them and their desires, the Mystery had left them to their desires, and with those companions they lived. For it was not in the nature of the Stone to be forgotten, and even in her village Mrs. Ferguson entertained her friends with the tale of her recovery rather from an unappreciated love of it than because she was as talkative as she seemed.

The Persian Embassy fell silent; Professor Palliser fell silent. Only one event caused a common flicker of satisfaction to rise in the hearts of the professor, the millionaire, the thwarted General Secretary (who never understood what the trouble had been about), and the politicians. That event was the sudden resignation of his office by Lord Arglay.

For in the house at Lancaster Gate Chloe Burnett lay, uncomprehending and semi-paralysed, for a long nine months of silence. On the same day when at Wandsworth the unhappy wreckage of a man passed into death, and his bed lay empty, the wreckage of his saviour was carried to a bed in the Chief Justice's house. Her mouth was silent, her eyes were blank, and that whole side of her which was not for ever still shook every now and then with uncontrollable tremors. The doctors stated that it was a seizure, a verdict on which only once did Lord Arglay permit himself to say that, whatever it was, it was precisely not that. All the rest of the time he maintained a silence—his secretary had been taken ill while at work, and since apparently she had no relations and no friends with a better claim, and since he felt that it was probably his fault for overworking her, and since the house was large, it was better that she should remain. This was the general interpretation which Lord Arglay allowed to arise. 'For if,' he said to the Hajji before the latter returned to Persia, 'if we profess that this is the End of Desire, fewer people than ever will want to experience it.'

'Her spirit is in the Resignation,' the Hajji said.

'Quite,' Lord Arglay answered. 'So, you may have seen by this morning's paper, is mine. As entirely, but in another sphere.'

'Did you not hold,' the Hajji asked, 'that your office was also of the Stone?'

'I have believed it,' Lord Arglay answered, 'but for one thing I will not now make that office a personal quarrel between these men and myself, though I think that otherwise even the Government would find it difficult to turn me out. But the Law is greater than the servants of the Law, and shall I make the Law a privy garden for my own pride? Also since this child has come to such an end I will have none but myself, so far as is possible, be her servant for the rest of her time.'

'I do not understand your mind,' Ibrahim said. 'Have you known and seen these things and yet you do not believe in the Stone?'

'Who said I did not believe?' Lord Arglay asked. 'I believe that certain things have emerged from illusion, and one of them I have resigned for its sake and the other I will watch for hers.'

'You are a strange man,' the Hajji said. 'Farewell then, for I suppose you will never be in Persia.'

'Do not despise us too much,' Lord Arglay said. 'It is our habit here to mock at what we love and contemn what we desire, and that habit has given us poets and lawgivers and saints. Good-bye, Hajji.'

'The Mercy of the Compassionate be with you,' the Hajji said.

'And even in that, for a reason, I will believe,' Lord Arglay answered, and so they parted.

To Frank Lindsay Arglay sent a short note, saying nothing of the Stone but only that Miss Burnett had suffered from—he paused and with a wry smile wrote—a seizure, that she remained at Lancaster Gate, and that he would at all times be very happy to see Mr. Lindsay there. Frank however did not come. For a number of days he intended to answer the note, but he could think of nothing to say that seemed adequate. If Chloe wanted to see him, he argued, she would send a special message; it was not his business to intrude. So safeguarding himself from that intrusion he safeguarded himself also from any, and all that he might have known of the conclusion of the Mystery was hidden from him. He passed however a not unsuccessful life in his profession, and the only intruder he found himself unable to cope with was death.

But every few days through months Oliver Doncaster called and saw Chloe and talked a little with Lord Arglay, and it was to him only that Arglay on a certain day sent a note which read:

'MY DEAR DONCASTER,

'Chloe died yesterday evening. The cremation will be on Thursday. If you could call here about eleven we might go together.

'Yours,
'ARGLAY.'

There had been no change and no warning of that conclusion. Whatever process had been working in her body, since the day when her inner being had been caught with the Stone into the Unity, closed quietly and suddenly. The purgation of her flesh accomplished itself, and it was by apparent chance that Arglay was with her when it ceased. He had paused by the bedside before going to his own room next to hers for the night. As he looked he saw one of those recurrent tremors shake her, but this time it was not confined to one side but swept over the whole body. From head to foot a vibration passed through her; she sighed deeply, and murmured something indistinguishable. So, on the moment, she died.

Arglay saw it and knew it for the end. He made no immediate move until he touched with his fingers the place where the epiphany of the Tetragrammaton had appeared. 'Earth to earth,' he said, 'but perhaps also justice to justice and the Stone to the Stone.' His hand covered her forehead. 'Under the Protection,' he murmured. 'Good-bye, child,' and so, his work at an end, left her.

In the car, as they returned from the crematorium, Oliver Doncaster said to him, almost bitterly, 'Was it a wise thing to tell her to do it?'

'Why, who can tell?' Lord Arglay answered. 'But she sought for wisdom, and what otherwise should such spirits as hers do upon earth?'

'She might have had love and happiness,' the young man said, 'and others too. There was always a light about her.'

'Why, so it seemed,' Lord Arglay said, and after a moment's pause, looking out of the window of the car, he went on. 'But who can tell how that light came to be? It is but a few weeks since I gave sentence upon a man before me who had murdered through some sudden jealousy the girl he was to marry. And when, as is the ritual, I asked him if he had anything to say, he cried out that though I might hang him justly, for he confessed his crime, yet that there was a Justice against which he had sinned which was greater than I and had already purged him. And though I have never made it my habit to do as some of my brethren do, offering their own moral opinions and the ethical and social rules of their own world, and condemning the guilty by such verbiage as well as by the law, I answered him that this also might be possible and that such a Justice might already be fulfilled in him. But if indeed there be any such sovereign Justice, may not this child have found a greater thing than either you or I could give her? Could she do more, while she was upon the stepping stones, than smile at the water that ran by her?'

'Must the water always run by?' Oliver said.

'It is its nature, as it was hers to pass over it,' Lord Arglay answered. 'And it may be that she has come into the light that was about her and the God in whom we determined to believe.'

At Lancaster Gate he bade Doncaster farewell, came again into his study, and stood still to look round it. His charge was at an end, and for all he could tell there were still before him years of life. Something must be done, and instinctively he looked at the MS. of the *Survey of Organic Law* which had lain so long neglected, then he walked over and picked it up. The typewritten sheets bore in places his own alterations and in places hers. There were sheets of annotations she had typed and sheets of references in her writing. Lord Arglay looked at them, and for a moment it seemed to him an offensive thing that another handwriting should be mixed with theirs. Yet after a moment he smiled: to accept such a ruling would indeed be to go against the whole nature of the Stone and the work they had done together. For here was this lesser work, and if it were worth doing—as it might be—and if without someone to supply necessary detail it would probably not be done—was not this also as much in the nature of organic law as the operation of the Stone?...

'Besides,' Lord Arglay said aloud, 'in a year's time, child, I should be finding an excuse. I think I will not find an excuse. The way to the Stone is in the Stone, and I will choose to do this thing rather than to leave it undone or to be driven back to it by the weariness of time.'

He walked across to the telephone, looked at it distastefully, and turned the pages of the directory.

With his hand on the receiver, 'Also,' he said, although the King wrote Ecclesiastes, yet the Courts gave judgement in Jerusalem. This, I suppose, is Ecclesiastes.... Paddington 814.... Is that the Lancaster Typewriting Agency?'

The Place of the Lion

CHAPTER I

THE LIONESS

From the top of the bank, behind a sparse hedge of thorn, the lioness stared at the Hertfordshire road. She moved her head from side to side, then suddenly she became rigid as if she had scented prey or enemy; she crouched lower, her body trembling, her tail swishing, but she made no sound.

Almost a mile away Quentin Sabot jumped from the gate on which he had been sitting and looked at his wrist-watch.

'I don't see much sign of this bus of yours,' he said, glancing along the road.

Anthony Durrant looked in the same direction. 'Shall we wander along and meet it?'

'Or go on and let it catch us up?' Quentin suggested. 'After all, that's our direction.'

'The chief use of the material world,' Anthony said, still sitting on the gate, 'is that one can, just occasionally, say that with truth. Yes, let's.' He got down leisurely and yawned. 'I feel I could talk better on top of a bus than on my feet just now,' he went on. 'How many miles have we done, should you think?'

'Twenty-three?' Quentin hazarded.

'Thereabouts,' the other nodded, and stretched himself lazily. 'Well, if we're going on, let's,' and as they began to stroll slowly along, 'Mightn't it be a good thing if everyone had to draw a map of his own mind— say, once every five years? With the chief towns marked, and the arterial roads he was constructing from one idea to another, and all the lovely and abandoned by-lanes that he never went down, because the farms they led to were all empty?'

'And arrows showing the directions he wanted to go?' Quentin asked idly.

'They'd be all over the place,' Anthony sighed. 'Like that light which I see bobbing about in front of me now.'

'I see several,' Quentin broke in. 'What are they—lanterns?'

'They look like them—three—five,' Anthony said. 'They're moving about, so it can't be the road up or anything.'

'They may be hanging the lanterns on poles,' Quentin protested.

'But', Anthony answered, as they drew nearer to the shifting lanterns, 'they are not. Mortality, as usual, carries its own star.'

He broke off as a man from the group in front beckoned to them with something like a shout. 'This is very unusual,' he added. 'Have I at last found someone who needs me?'

'They all seem very excited,' Quentin said, and had no time for more. There were some dozen men in the group the two had reached, and Quentin and Anthony stared at it in amazement. For all the men were armed—four or five with rifles, two with pitchforks; others who carried the lanterns had heavy sticks. One of the men with rifles spoke sharply. 'Didn't you hear the warning that's been sent out?'

'I'm afraid we didn't,' Anthony told him. 'Ought we?'

'We've sent a man to all the crossroads this half hour or more,' the other said. 'Where have you come from that you didn't meet him?'

'Well, for half an hour we've been sitting on a gate waiting for a bus,' Anthony explained, and was surprised to hear two or three of the men break into a short laugh, while another added sardonically, 'And so you might wait.' He was about to ask further when the first speaker said sharply, 'The fact is there's a lioness loose somewhere round here, and we're after it.'

'The devil there is!' Quentin exclaimed, while Anthony, more polite, said, 'I see—yes. That does seem a case for warning people. But we've been resting down there and I suppose your man made straight for the cross-roads and missed us.' He waited to hear more.

'It got away from a damned wild beast show over there,' the other said, nodding across the darkening fields, 'close by Smetham. We're putting a cordon of men and lights round all the part as quickly as we can and warning the people in the houses. Everything on the roads has been turned away—that's why you missed your bus.'

'It seems quite a good reason,' Anthony answered. 'Was it a large lioness? Or a fierce one?'

'Fierce be damned,' said another man, who possibly belonged to the show. 'It was as tame as a white mouse, only some fool startled it.'

'I'll make it a darn sight tamer if I get a shot at it,' the first man said. 'Look here, you gentlemen had better get straight ahead as fast as you can. We're going to meet some others and then beat across the fields to that wood—that's where it'll be.'

'Can't we help you?' Anthony asked, looking round him. 'It seems such a pity to miss the nearest thing to a lion hunt we're ever likely to find.'

But the other had made up his mind. 'You'll be more use at the other end,' he said. 'That's where we want the numbers. About a mile up that way there's the main road, and the more we've got there the better. It isn't likely to be on any road—not even this one—unless it just dashes across, so you'll be pretty safe, safer along here than you will be across the fields with us. Unless you're used to country by night.'

'No,' Anthony admitted, 'not beyond an occasional evening like this.' He looked at Quentin, who looked back with an expression of combined anxiety and amusement, murmuring, 'I suppose we go on then—as far as the main road.'

'Yoicks—and so on,' Anthony assented. 'Goodnight then, unless we see you at the end. Good luck to your hunting.'

'It ought to be forbidden,' a man who had hitherto been silent said angrily. 'What about the sheep?'

'O keep quiet,' the first man snapped back, and during the half-suppressed wrangle the two friends parted from the group, and stepped out, with more speed and more excitement than before, down the road in front of them.

'What enormous fun!' Anthony said, in an unintentionally subdued voice. 'What do we do if we see it?'

'Bolt,' Quentin answered firmly. 'I don't want to be any more thrilled than I am now. Unless it's going in the other direction.'

'What a day!' Anthony said. 'As a matter of fact, I expect it'd be just as likely to bolt as we should.'

'It might think we were its owners,' Quentin pointed out, 'and come trotting or lolloping or whatever they do up to us. Do you save me by luring it after you, or do I save you?'

'O you save me, thank you,' Anthony said. 'These hedges are infernally low, aren't they? What I feel I should like to be in is an express train on a high viaduct.'

'I hope you still think that ideas are more dangerous than material things,' Quentin said. 'That was what you were arguing at lunch.'

Anthony pondered while glancing from side to side before he answered. 'Yes, I do. All material danger is limited, whereas interior danger is unlimited. It's more dangerous for you to hate than to kill, isn't it?'

'To me or to the other fellow?' Quentin asked.

'To—I suppose one would have to say—to the world in general,' Anthony suggested. 'But I simply can't keep it up now. I think it's splendid of you, Quentin, but the lioness, though a less, is a more pressing danger even than your intellectual errors. Hallo, here's a gate. I suppose this is one of the houses they were talking about.'

They stopped before it; Quentin glanced back along the road they had come, and suddenly caught Anthony by the arm, exclaiming, 'There! There!'

But his friend had already seen. A long low body had slithered down the right hand bank some couple of hundred yards away, had paused for a moment turning its head and switching its tail, and had then begun to come leaping in their direction. It might have been mere friendliness or even ignorance—the two young men did not wait to see; they were through the gate and up the short garden path in a moment. In the dark shelter of the porch they paused. Anthony's hand touched the knocker and stayed.

'Better not make a row perhaps,' he said. 'Besides, all the windows were dark, did you notice? If there's no one at home, hadn't we better keep quiet?'

There was no reply unless Quentin's renewed clasp of his arm could be taken for one. The straight path to the gate by which they had entered divided a broad lawn; on each side of it the grass stretched away and was lost in the shade of a row of trees which shut it off from the neighbouring fields. The moon was not high, and any movement under the trees was invisible. But the moonlight lay faintly on the lawn, the gate, and the road beyond, and it was at the road that the two young men gazed. For there, halting upon her way, was the lioness. She had paused as if she heard or felt some attraction; her head was turned towards the garden, and she was lifting her front paws restlessly. Suddenly, while they watched, she swung round facing it, threw up her head, and sent out a long howl. Anthony felt feverishly at the door behind him but he found no latch or handle—this was something more than the ordinary cottage and was consequently more hostile to strangers. The lioness threw up her head again, began to howl, and suddenly ceased, at the same instant that another figure appeared on the lawn. From their right side came a man's form, pacing as if in a slow abstraction. His

344

hands were clasped behind him; his heavy bearded face showed no motion; his eyes were directed in front of him, looking away towards the other side of the lawn. He moved slowly and paused between each step, but steps and pauses were co-ordinated in a rhythm of which, even at that moment of strain, the two young men were intensely aware. Indeed, as Anthony watched, his own breathing became quieter and deeper; his tightened body relaxed, and his eyes left turning excitedly towards the beast crouching in the road. In Quentin no such effect was observable, but even he remained in an attitude of attention devoted rather to the man than the beast. So the strange pattern remained until, always very slowly, the stranger came to the path down the garden, and made one of his pauses in its midst, directly between the human and the animal spectators. Anthony thought to himself, 'I ought to warn him,' but somehow he could not; it would have seemed bad manners to break in on the concentrated silence of that figure. Quentin dared not; looking past the man, he saw the lioness and thought in hasty excuse, 'If I make no noise at all she may keep quiet.'

At that moment a shout not very far away broke the silence, and at once the garden was disturbed by violent movement. The lioness as if startled made one leap over the gate, and her flying form seemed to collide with the man just as he also began to take another rhythmical step. Forms and shadows twisted and mingled for two or three seconds in the middle of the garden: a tearing human cry began and ceased as if choked into silence, a snarl broke out and died swiftly into a similar stillness, and as if in answer to both sounds there came the roar of a lion—not very loud, but as if subdued by distance rather than by mildness. With that roar the shadows settled, the garden became clear. Anthony and Quentin saw before them the form of a man lying on the ground, and standing over him the shape of a full grown and tremendous lion, its head flung back, its mouth open, its body quivering. It ceased to roar, and gathered itself back into itself. It was a lion such as the young men had never seen in any zoo or menagerie; it was gigantic and seemed to their dazed senses to be growing larger every moment. Of their presence it appeared unconscious; awful and solitary it stood, and did not at first so much as turn its head. Then, majestically, it moved; it took up the slow forward pacing in the direction which the man had been following; it passed onward, and while they still stared it entered into the dark shadow of the trees and was hidden from sight. The man's form still lay prostrate, of the lioness there was no sign.

Minutes seemed to pass; at last Anthony looked round at Quentin. 'We'd better have a look at him, hadn't we?' he whispered.

'What in God's name has happened?' Quentin said. 'Did you see … where's the … Anthony, what's happened?'

'We'd better have a look at him,' Anthony said again, but this time as a statement, not an enquiry. He moved very cautiously nevertheless, and looked in every direction before he ventured from the shelter of the doorway. Over his shoulder he said, 'But there *was* a lioness? What did you think you saw?'

'I saw a lion,' Quentin stammered. 'No, I didn't; I saw…. O my God, Anthony, let's get out of it. Let's take the risk and run.'

'We can't leave him like this,' Anthony said. 'You keep a watch while I run out and look, or drag him in here if I can. Shout if you see anything.'

He dashed out to the fallen man, dropped on a knee by him, still glancing quickly round, bent over the body, peered at it, caught it, and rising tried to move it. But in a moment he desisted and ran back to his friend.

'I can't move him,' he pouted. 'Will the door open? No. But there must be a back way. We must get him inside; you'll have to give me a hand. But I'd better find the way in first. I can't make it out; there's no wound and no bruise so far as I can see: it's the most extraordinary thing. You watch here; but don't go doing anything except shout—if you can. I won't be a second.'

He slipped away before Quentin could answer—but nothing, no shout, no roar, no snarl, no human or bestial footfall, broke the silence until he returned. 'I've found the door,' he began, but Quentin interrupted; 'Did you see anything?'

'Damn all,' said Anthony. 'Not a sight or a sound. No shining eyes, no—— Quentin, *did* you see a lion?'

'Yes,' Quentin said nervously.

'So did I,' Anthony agreed. 'And did you see where the lioness went to?'

'No,' Quentin said, still shooting glances over the garden.

'Are there two escaped animals then?' Anthony asked. 'Well, anyhow, the thing is to get this fellow into the house. I'll take his head and you his—— O my God, what's that?'

His cry, however, was answered reassuringly. For the sound that had startled him was this time only the call of a human voice not far off, and it was answered by another still nearer. It seemed the searchers for the lioness were drawing closer. Lights, many lights, were moving across the field opposite; calls were heard on the road. Anthony turned hastily to Quentin, but before he could speak, a man had stopped at the gate and exclaimed. Anthony ran down the garden, and met him as, others gathering behind him, he came through the gate.

'Hallo, what's up here?' he said. 'What—— O is it you, sir?'

He was the man with whom the friends had talked before. He went straight to the prostrate man, bent over him, felt his heart and touched him here and there; then he looked up in perplexity.

'Fainted, has he?' he said. 'I thought it might—just possibly—have been this damned beast. But it can't have been; he'd have been mauled if it had touched him—and I don't suppose it would. Do you know what happened?'

'Not very well,' Anthony said. 'We *did* see the lioness, as it happened, in the road—and we more or less sprinted up here—and then this man, whoever he is——'

'O I know who he is,' the other said. 'He lives here; his name's Berringer. D'you suppose he saw the creature? But we'd better move him, hadn't we? Get him inside, I mean?'

'We were just going to,' Anthony said. 'This door's shut, but I've got the back one open.'

'Right ho!' the other answered. 'I'd better slip in and warn his housekeeper, if she's about. One or two of us will give you gentlemen a hand.' He waved to the small group by the gate, and they came in, to have explained what was needed. Then their leader went quickly round the house while Anthony, Quentin, and the rest began to lift the unconscious Mr. Berringer.

It was more difficult to do so than they had expected. To begin with they seemed unable to get the proper purchase. His body was not so much heavy as immovable—and yet not rigid. It yielded to them gently, but however they tried to slip their arms underneath they could not at first manage to lift it. Quentin and Anthony had a similar difficulty with the legs; and indeed Anthony was so startled at the resistance where he had expected a light passivity that he almost fell forward. At last, however, their combined efforts did raise him. Once lifted, he could be carried easily enough along the front of the house, but when they tried to turn the corner they found an unplaceable difficulty in doing so. It wasn't weight; it wasn't wind; it wasn't darkness; it was just that when they had all moved they seemed to be where they were before. Anthony, being in front, realised that something had gone wrong, and without being clear whether he were speaking to the body or the bearers, to himself or his friend, said sharply and commandingly: 'O come *on*!' The general effort that succeeded took them round, and so at last they reached the back door, where the leader and a disturbed old woman whom Anthony assumed to be the housekeeper were waiting.

'Upstairs,' she said, 'to his own bedroom. Look, I'll show you. Dear, dear. O do be careful'—and so on till at last Berringer was laid on his bed, and, still under the directions of the housekeeper, undressed and got into it.

'I've telephoned to a doctor,' the leader said to Anthony, who had withdrawn from the undressing process. 'It's very curious; his breathing's normal; his heart seems all right. Shock, I suppose. If he saw that damned thing——You couldn't see what happened?'

'Not very well,' said Anthony. 'We saw him fall, and—and—— It was a lioness that got away, wasn't it? Not a lion?'

The other looked at him suspiciously. 'Of course it wasn't a lion,' he said. 'There's been no lion in these parts that I ever heard of, and only one lioness, and there won't be that much longer. Damned slinking brute! What d'ye mean—lion?'

'No,' said Anthony, 'quite. Of course, if there wasn't a lion—I mean—— O well, I mean there wasn't if there wasn't, was there?'

The face of the other darkened. 'I daresay it all seems very funny to you gentlemen,' he said. 'A great joke, no doubt. But if that's what you think's a joke——'

'No, no,' Anthony said hastily. 'I wasn't joking. Only——' He gave it up; it would have sounded too silly. After all, if they were looking for a lioness and found a lion … well, if they were looking for the lioness*properly*, it presumably wouldn't make much difference. Besides, anyhow, it couldn't have been a lion. Not unless there were two menageries and two—— 'O God, what a day!' Anthony sighed; and turned to Quentin.

'The highroad, I think,' he said. 'And any kind of bus anywhere, don't you? We're simply in the way here. But, damn it!' he added to himself, 'it *was* a lion.'

———————————

CHAPTER II

THE EIDOLA AND THE ANGELI

Damaris Tighe had had a bad night. The thunder had kept her awake, and she particularly needed sleep just now, in order to be quite fresh every day to cope with her thesis about *Pythagorean Influences on Abelard*. There were moments when she almost wished she had not picked anyone quite so remote as Abelard; only all the later schoolmen had been done to death by other writers, whereas Abelard seemed—so far as theses on Pythagorean Influences went—to have been left to her to do to death. But this tracing of thought between the two humanistic thinkers was a business for which she needed a particularly clear head. She had so far a list of eighteen close identifications, twenty-three cases of probable traditional views, and eighty-five less distinct relationships. And then there had been that letter to the *Journal of Classical Studies* challenging a word in a new translation of Aristotle. She had been a little nervous about sending it. After all, she was more concerned about her doctorate of philosophy, for which the thesis was meant, than for the accuracy of the translation of Aristotle, and it would be very annoying if she made enemies—not, of course, the translator— but … well, anyone. And on top of all that, had come that crash of thunder, every now and then echoing all through the black sky. No lightning, no rain, only—at long intervals, just whenever she was going off to sleep at last—thunder, and again thunder. She had been unable to work all the morning. It looked, now, as if her afternoon would be equally wasted.

'We hear,' Mrs. Rockbotham said, 'that he's quite comatose.'

'Dear me,' Damaris said coldly. 'More tea?'

'Thank you, thank you, dear,' Miss Wilmot breathed. 'Of course you didn't really know him *well*, did you?'

'I hardly know him at all,' Damaris answered.

'Such a wonderful man,' Miss Wilmot went on. 'I've told you, haven't I, how—well, it was really Elise who brought me into touch—but there, the instrument doesn't matter—I mean,' she added looking hastily over at Mrs. Rockbotham, 'not in a human sense. Or really not in a heavenly. All service ranks the same with God.'

'The question is,' Mrs. Rockbotham said severely, 'what is to be done to-night.'

'To-night?' Damaris asked.

'To-night is our monthly group,' Mrs. Rockbotham explained. 'Mr. Berringer generally gives us an address of instruction. And with him like this——'

'It doesn't look as if he would, does it?' Damaris said, moving the sugar-tongs irritably.

'No,' Miss Wilmot moaned, 'no … no. But we can't just let it drop, it'd be too weak. I see that—Elise was telling me. Elise is *so* good at telling me. So if you would——'

'If I would what?' Damaris exclaimed, startled and surprised. What, what could she possibly have to do with these absurd creatures and their fantastic religion? She knew, from the vague gossip of the town, from which she was not altogether detached, that Mr. Berringer, who lived in that solitary house on the London Road, and took no more part in the town's activities than she did herself, was the leader of a sort of study circle or something of that kind; indeed, she remembered now that these same two ladies who had broken in on her quiet afternoon with Abelard had told her of it. But she never attended to their chatter with more than a twentieth of her mind, no more than she gave to her father's wearisome accounts of his entomological rambles. Religions and butterflies were necessary hobbies, no doubt, for some people who knew nothing about scholarship, but they would not be of the smallest use to Damaris Tighe, and therefore, as far as possible, Damaris Tighe very naturally left them out of her life. Occasionally her father's enthusiasm broke through her defences and compelled attention; it always seemed extraordinary to Damaris that he could not in her politeness realise her boredom. And now….

Mrs. Rockbotham interrupted Miss Wilmot's lengthier explanation. 'You see,' she said, 'we meet once a month at Mr. Berringer's, and he gives us an Instruction—very instructive it always is—about thought-forms or something similar. But I suppose he won't be able to this time, and none of us would like—I mean, it might seem pushing for any of us to take his place. But you, as an outsider…. And your studies are more or less about methods of thought, I understand?'

She paused, and Damaris supposed they were.

'I thought, if you would read us something, just to keep us in touch with—well, the *history* of it, at least, if nothing else,' Mrs. Rockbotham ambiguously concluded, 'we should all be greatly obliged.'

'But,' Damaris said, 'if Mr. Berringer is … incapacitated, why not suspend the meeting?'

'No, I don't want to do that,' Mrs. Rockbotham answered. 'It would be very awkward, anyhow, to let everybody know before nine to-night—some of them live miles out——'

'You could telegraph,' Damaris put in.

'And in the second place,' Mrs. Rockbotham went on steadily, 'I don't think Mr. Berringer would like us to treat it as if it all depended on him. He always insists that it's an individual effort. So we must, in the circumstances, get someone else.'

'But where will you hold the meeting?' Damaris asked. She didn't want to offend Mrs. Rockbotham who, though only a doctor's wife, had influential relations, among whom was the owner of that literary weekly of which her cousin Anthony Durrant was a sub-editor or something of the sort. Damaris had had an occasional article, done for the public of course, printed there already, and she was anxious to keep the gate open. Indeed it occurred to her at once that if she could only find among her various MSS. a suitable paper, she might use it both for that evening and for *The Two Camps*, which was the name of the weekly. It had originally been meant to be symbolical of the paper's effort to maintain tradition in art, politics and philosophy while allowing the expression of revolt; though Anthony insisted that it signified the division in the contributors between those who liked it living and intelligent and those who preferred it dying and scholarly, represented by himself and Damaris. He had told her that in a moment's exasperation, because she had insisted on talking of the paper instead of themselves. Anthony was always wanting to talk of themselves, which meant whether she loved him, and in what way, and how much, whereas Damaris, who disliked discussing other people's personal affairs, preferred to talk of scholarship or abstract principles such as whether and how soon *The Two Camps* would publish her essay on *Platonic Tradition at the Court of Charlemagne*. Anthony had gone off in rather a bad temper finally, saying that she had no more notion of Plato than of Charlemagne, and that her real subject was *Damaristic Tradition at the Court of Damaris*; upon which he swore he would write a long highbrow article and publish it—Damaris being, for that purpose, a forgotten queen of Trebizond overthrown by the Saracen invasion. 'Nobody'll know any better,' he had said, 'and what you need very badly indeed is a thoroughly good Saracen invasion within the next fortnight.'

Mrs. Rockbotham was explaining that she had been talking to Mr. Berringer's housekeeper on the telephone. The usual small arrangements had, of course, been made for the meeting, and the housekeeper, though a little reluctant, was under pressure compliant. Mr. Berringer was still lying quite quiet—unconscious, Dr. Rockbotham had said. Mrs. Rockbotham and Miss Wilmot however both thought it more likely that the unconsciousness was of the nature of trance, Mr. Berringer's soul or something having gone off into the spiritual world or somewhere, probably where time didn't exist, and not realizing the inconvenient length of the period that was elapsing before its return.

'And suppose,' the over-suppressed Miss Wilmot broke out, 'suppose he came back *while we were there*! What he might tell us! He'd even be able to tell you something, Elise, wouldn't he?'

The whole thing sounded extremely disagreeable to Damaris. The more she thought about it, the sillier it looked. But was it worth while, if Mrs. Rockbotham chose to be silly, refusing her request, and running the risk of a hostile word dropped in that influential relative's ear?

'But what sort of thing do you want?' she asked slowly.

Mrs. Rockbotham considered. 'If you could tell us something about thought-forms, now,' she said. 'That's what we're trying to shape—I can't go into it all—but perhaps a few remarks about … well, now, Plato? Mr. Berringer told us that Plato wrote a good deal about ideas, and didn't you tell me you had several studies in Plato almost done?'

Damaris thought of the Charlemagne paper, but rejected it as being too historical for this purpose. She thought of a few other titles, and suddenly—

'If it would be any good to you,' she said, 'I have some notes on the relation of Platonic and mediaeval thought—a little specialist, I'm afraid, but it would be the best I could do. If it's really any use——'

Mrs. Rockbotham sat up with a delighted smile. 'How good of you, Miss Tighe,' she exclaimed. 'I knew you'd help us! It will be exactly right, I'm sure. I'll call for you in the car at half-past eight. And thank you so much.'

She stood up and paused. 'By the way,' she asked, 'what's your paper called?'

'*The Eidola and the Angeli*,' Damaris answered. 'It's just a comparison, you know; largely between the sub-Platonic philosophers on the one side and the commentators on Dionysius the Areopagite on the other, suggesting that they have a common pattern in mind. But some of the quotations are rather quaint and might attract your friends.'

'I'm perfectly certain it will be delightful,' Mrs. Rockbotham assured her. '*The—the Eidola*. What were they? But you'll tell us that, won't you? It's really too kind of you, Miss Tighe, and I only hope one day I shall be able to do something to show my appreciation. Good-bye till half-past eight.'

Damaris, with the firm intention that Mrs. Rockbotham should have her hope fulfilled by assisting, if necessary, to print the paper in question, said good-bye, and herself took her visitors to the car. Then she went back to her study and set to work to find the lecture. When she did, it appeared even more technical than she had supposed. The main thesis of a correspondence between the development of the formative Ideas of Hellenic philosophy and the hierarchic angelicals of Christian mythology was clearly stated. But most of the quotations were in their original Greek or Latin, and Damaris was compelled to sit down and translate them at once, for fear of later hesitation about an adequate word, into bearable English. She took the opportunity to modify it here and there, in case she hurt Mrs. Rockbotham's feelings, changing for example, 'superstitious slavery' into 'credulous piety' and 'emotional opportunism' into 'fervent zeal'. Not that Mrs. Rockbotham was likely to be worried by any insult to the schoolmen or Dionysius the Areopagite—she added a couple of sentences explaining 'Areopagite'—but Damaris had only the remotest notion what these ladies supposed themselves to be doing, and even in pure scholarship it was never worth while taking risks unless you were pretty sure. The highly intellectualized readers of *The Two Camps* were almost certain to be free from any prejudice in favour of either the *eidola* or the *angeli*, but with Mr. Berringer's disciples one couldn't tell. She altered 'priestly oppression' into 'official influence' almost automatically, however, recalling that Anthony had told her that a certain number of clergymen took in the periodical, and after a couple of hours' work felt fairly ready. It would, at worst, give her a chance of reading her paper, which she liked doing; things sounded different when they were read aloud. At best—well, at best, one never knew; someone useful might be there. Damaris put the MS. ready and went down to dinner.

At dinner her father began talking. They sat opposite each other in the small dining-room into which two bookcases holding works on Proclus, Iamblichus, St. Anselm, and the Moorish culture in Spain had lately crept. The maid supplied them with food, and Damaris—to a less nourishing effect, but with a similar efficiency—supplied her father with conversation. He was more than usually thrilled to-day; never had he seen so many butterflies, and yet they had all escaped him.

'There was a great one on the oak at the top of the hill,' he said, 'and it vanished—really vanished—just as I moved. I can't think what sort it was—I couldn't recognize it; brown and gold it seemed. A lovely, lovely thing!'

He sighed and went on eating. Damaris frowned.

'Really, father,' she said, 'if it was as beautiful as all that I don't see how you can bear to go on eating mutton and potatoes so ordinarily.'

Her father opened his eyes at her. 'But what else can I do?' he said. 'It *was* a lovely thing; it was glinting and glowing there. This is very good mutton,' he added placidly. 'I'm glad I didn't miss this too—not without catching the other.'

Damaris looked at him. He was short and rather plump, and he was enjoying the mutton. Beauty! She didn't know that she hated him, and certainly she didn't know that she only hated him because he was her father. Nor did she realize that it was only when she was talking to him that the divine Plato's remarks on beauty were used by her as if they meant anything more than entries in a card-index. She had of course heard of 'defence mechanisms', but not as if they were anything she could have or need or use. Nor had love and Heloise ever appeared to her as more than a side-incident of Abelard's real career. In which her judgment may have been perfectly right, but her sensations were wildly and entirely wrong.

'Plato says——' she began.

'O Plato!' answered Mr. Tighe, taking, as if rhythmically, more vegetables.

'—that,' Damaris went on, ignoring the answer, 'one should rise from the phenomenal to the abstract beauty, and thence to the absolute.'

Mr. Tighe said he had no doubt that Plato was a very great man and could do it. 'But personally,' he added, 'I find that mutton helps butterflies and butterflies mutton. That's why I like lunching out in the open. It was a marvel, that one on the oak. I don't see what it can have been. Brown and gold,' he added thoughtfully. 'It's very curious. I've looked up all my books, and I can't find anything like it. It's a pity,' he added irrelevantly, 'that you don't like butterflies.'

Meaning to be patient, Damaris said, 'But, you know, I can't take up everything.'

'I thought that was what you just said Plato told you to do,' her father answered. 'Isn't the Absolute something like everything?'

Damaris ignored this; her father on Plato was too silly. People needed a long intellectual training to understand Plato and the Good. He would probably think that the Good was the same thing as God—like a less educated monk of the Dark Ages. Personification (which was one of her side subjects) was a snare to the unadept mind. In a rare mood of benignity, due to her hopes for her paper, she began to talk about the improvement in the maid's cooking. If time had to be wasted, it had better be wasted on neutral instead of irritating subjects, and she competently wasted it until it was time to get ready for the meeting.

As she stepped into Mrs. Rockbotham's car, she heard the thunder again—far away. She made conversation out of it.

'There's the thunder,' she said. 'Did it keep you awake last night?'

'It did rather,' Mrs. Rockbotham said, pressing the self-starter. 'I kept on expecting to see the lightning, but there wasn't a single flash.'

'And not a drop of rain,' Damaris agreed. 'Curious. It must be summer thunder, if there is such a thing! But I do hate lying awake at night.'

'Naturally—with all your brain-work,' the other said. 'Don't you find it very tiring?'

'O well, of course, it gets rather tedious sometimes,' Damaris agreed. 'But it's interesting too—comparing different ways of saying things and noting the resemblances.'

'Like Shakespeare, I suppose?' Mrs. Rockbotham asked, and for a moment took Damaris by surprise. 'Shakespeare?'

'Haven't they found out where he got all his lines from?' her friend said. 'I remember reading an article in *Two Camps* a few weeks ago which showed that when he wrote, "Egypt, you are dying," he was borrowing from somebody else who said, "England is dying, because sheep are eating men." Marlowe or Sir Thomas More.'

'Really?' Damaris asked, with a light laugh. 'Of course, Shakespeare's not my subject. But what did he mean by sheep eating men?'

'It was something to do with agriculture,' Mrs. Rockbotham answered. 'He didn't mean it literally.'

'O of course not,' Damaris agreed. 'But the lamb's become so symbolical, hasn't it?'

'Hasn't it?' Mrs. Rockbotham assented, and with such prolonged intellectual conversation they reached *The Joinings*, as Mr. Berringer's house was called, with some vague and forgotten reference to the cross-roads near by. The thunder crashed again, as they got out, much nearer this time, and the two ladies hurried into the house.

While Mrs. Rockbotham talked to the uncertain and uneasy housekeeper, Damaris looked at the assembled group. There were not very many members, and she did not much care for the look of any of them. Miss Wilmot was there, of course; most of the rest were different improvisations either upon her rather agitated futility or Mrs. Rockbotham's masterful efficiency. Among the sixteen or seventeen women were four men— three of whom Damaris recognized, one as a Town Councillor and director of some engineering works, one as the assistant in the central bookshop of the town, the third as the nephew of one of the managing ladies, a Mrs. Jacquelin. Mrs. Jacquelin was almost county, the sister of a local Vicar lately dead; she called herself Mrs. Roche Jacquelin on the strength of a vague connexion with the Vendean family.

'However does this Mr. Berringer interest them all at once?' Damaris thought. 'What a curious collection! And I don't suppose they any of them know anything.' A warm consciousness of her own acquaintance with Abelard and Pythagoras stirred in her mind, as she smiled at the Town Councillor and sat down. He came over to her.

'Well, Miss Tighe,' he said briskly, 'so I hear you are to be good enough to talk to us to-night. Very unfortunate, this collapse of Mr. Berringer's, isn't it?'

'Very indeed,' Damaris answered. 'But I'm afraid I shan't be very interesting, Mr. Foster. You see I know so little of what Mr. Berringer and you are doing.'

He looked at her a little sharply. 'Probably you're not very interested,' he said. 'But we don't really do anything, except listen. Mr. Berringer is a very remarkable man, and he generally gives us a short address on the world of principles, as one might call it.'

'Principles?' Damaris asked.

'Ideas, energies, realities, whatever you like to call them,' Mr. Foster answered. 'The underlying things.'

'Of course,' Damaris said, 'I know the Platonic Ideas well enough, but do you mean Mr. Berringer explains Plato?'

'Not so much Plato——' but there Mr. Foster was interrupted by Mrs. Rockbotham, who came up to Damaris.

'Are you ready, Miss Tighe?' she asked. 'Yes? Then I will say something first, just to have things in order, and then I will ask you to speak. After that there may be a few questions, or a little discussion, or what not, and then we shall break up. Will you sit here? I think we may as well begin.' She tapped on the table before her, and as the room grew silent proceeded to address it.

'Friends,' she began, 'you have all heard that our leader, Mr. Berringer—may I not say our teacher?—has passed into a state of unconsciousness. My husband, who is attending him, tells me that he is inclined to diagnose some sort of brain trouble. But perhaps we, who have profited by our teacher's lessons, may think that he is engaged upon some experiment in connexion with some of his work. We all remember how often in this very room he has urged us to work and meditate until we became accustomed to what he called ideas, the thought-forms which are moulded by us, although of course they exist in a world of (as he has so often told us) their own. Many of us can no longer walk in the simple paths of childhood's faith—perhaps I should say alas! But we have found in this new doctrine a great suggestiveness, and each in our own way have done our best to carry it out. It seemed therefore a pity to omit our monthly meeting merely because our leader is in—shall I say?—another state. We can always learn, and therefore I have asked Miss Damaris Tighe, who besides being a dear friend of mine and also known to some of you, is a deep student of philosophy, to speak to us to-night on a subject of mutual interest. Miss Tighe's subject is——' She looked at Damaris, who murmured '*The Eidola and the Angeli*'—'the idler and the angels'—We shall all listen to her with great interest.'

Damaris stood up. Her attention for the moment was centred on the fact that she was Mrs. Rockbotham's dear friend. She felt that this was a promising situation, even if it involved her wasting an evening among people who would certainly never know an *eidolon* if they met it. She moved to the table, laid down her handbag, and unfolded her manuscript. As she did so she sniffed slightly; there had seemed to come from somewhere—just for the moment—an extremely unpleasant smell. She sniffed again; no, it was gone. Far away the thunder was still sounding. Mrs. Rockbotham had composed herself to listen; the remainder of the members desisted from their gentle and polite applause.

'Ladies and gentlemen,' Damaris began, 'as I have already said to Mrs. Rockbotham and to Mr. Foster, I fear I have only a very inadequate substitute to-night for—for what you are used to. But the cobbler, we know'—she was reading now from her manuscript—'must stick to his last, and since you have done me the honour to ask me to address you it may not be without interest for me to offer you a few remarks on a piece of research I have recently been attempting to carry out. Mr. Foster'—she looked up—'in the course of a very interesting conversation which I had with him just now'—she bowed to Mr. Foster who bowed back—'alluded to your study of a world of principles. Now of course that has always been a very favourite subject of human study—philosophical study, if I may call it that—although no doubt some ages have been more sympathetic to it than others. Ages noted for freedom of thought, such as Athens, have been better equipped for it than less-educated times such as the early mediaeval. We perhaps in our age, with our increased certainty and science and learning, can appreciate all these views with sympathy if not with agreement. I, for instance'—she smiled brightly at her audience—'no longer say "Four angels round my bed", nor am I prepared to call Plato *der grosse Pfaffe*, the great priest, as was once done.'

She sniffed again; the smell had certainly recurred. In a corner Miss Wilmot moved restlessly, and then sat still. Everything was very quiet; the smell slowly faded. Damaris resumed——

'But it was that phrase which suggested to me the research with which my paper deals. You will all know that in the Middle Ages there were supposed to be various classes of angels, who were given different names—to be exact' ('and what is research if it is not exact?' she asked Mrs. Rockbotham, who nodded), 'in descending order, seraphim, cherubim, thrones, dominations, virtues, princes, powers, archangels, angels. Now these hierarchized celsitudes are but the last traces in a less philosophical age of the ideas which Plato taught his disciples existed in the spiritual world. We may not believe in them as actually existent—either ideas or angels, but here we have what I may call two selected patterns of thought. Let us examine the likenesses between them; though first I should like to say a word on what the path was by which the imaginations of the Greek seer became the white-robed beings invoked by the credulous piety of Christian Europe, and familiar to us in many paintings.

'Alexandria——'

As if the word had touched her poignantly Miss Wilmot shrieked and sprang to her feet. 'Look, look,' she screamed, 'On the floor!'

Damaris stared at the floor, and saw nothing unusual. But she had no long time to look. Miss Wilmot was crouching back in her corner, still shrieking. All the room was in disorder. Mrs. Rockbotham was on her feet and alternately saying fiercely—'Miss Wilmot! Dora! be quiet!' and asking generally, 'Will someone take her out?'

'The snake!' Dora Wilmot shrieked. 'The crowned snake!'

So highly convinced and convincing did the words sound that there was a general stir of something remarkably like terror. Damaris herself was startled. Mr. Foster was standing close to her, and she saw him look searchingly round the room, as she had felt herself doing. Their eyes met, and she said smiling, 'Do you see anything like a crowned snake, Mr. Foster?'

'No, Miss Tighe,' Mr. Foster said. 'But I can't perhaps see what she sees. Dora Wilmot may be a fool, but she's a sincere fool.'

'Can't you get her away, Mr. Foster?' Mrs. Rockbotham asked. 'Perhaps you and I together—shall we try?'

'By all means,' Foster answered. 'By all means let us try.'

The two of them crossed to the corner where Miss Wilmot, now risen from crouching and standing upright and flat against the wall, had with that change of position left off screaming and was now gently moaning. Her eyes were looking past Damaris to where at that end of the room there was an empty space before the French windows.

Mrs. Rockbotham took her friend's arm. 'Dora, what do you mean by it?' she said firmly. 'You'd better go home.'

'O Elise,' Dora Wilmot said, without moving her eyes, 'can't you see? look, look, there it goes!' Her voice dropped to a whisper, and again she uttered in a tone of terror and awe: 'the snake! the crowned snake!'

Mr. Foster took her other hand. 'What is it doing?' he asked in a low voice. 'We can't all see clearly. Tell me, quietly, what is it doing?'

'It is gliding about, slowly,' Miss Wilmot said. 'It's looking round. Look, how it's moving its head! It's so *huge*!'

In the silence that had fallen on the room Damaris heard the colloquy. She was very angry. If these hysterical nincompoops were to be allowed to interrupt her careful analysis of Platonic and mediaeval learning, she wished she had never taken all that trouble about her paper. 'Crowned snake indeed,' she thought. 'The shrieking imbecile! Are they never going to get her away?'

'Yes, O yes!' Miss Wilmot moaned, 'I daren't stop. I—no, no, I daren't stop!'

'Come then,' Mr. Foster said. 'This way; the door's just here by you. But you're not afraid of it, are you?'

'Yes … no … yes, I am, I am,' Dora moaned again. 'It's too—O let's get away.'

Mrs. Rockbotham released the arm she held. Mr. Foster, one hand still holding Miss Wilmot's, felt with his other for the door-handle. Damaris was watching them, as were all the rest—without her indignation—when suddenly everyone sprang into movement. There was a rush for the door; screams, not Miss Wilmot's, sounded. Damaris herself, startled and galvanized, moved hastily forward, colliding with a heavy mass in flight which turned out to be Mrs. Roche Jacquelin. For from behind her, away towards those open windows, soft but distinct, there had come, or seemed to come, the sound of a gentle and prolonged hiss. Terror caught them all; following Mr. Foster and his charge, they squeezed and thrust themselves through the door. Only Damaris, after that first instinctive movement, restrained herself; only Mrs. Rockbotham, a little conscious of dignity still, allowed herself to be last. After the panic those two went, drawn by it but resisting its infection. The room lay empty and still in the electric light, unless indeed there passed across it then a dim form, which, heavy, long, and coiling, issued slowly through the open window into a silent world where for that moment nothing but the remote thunder was heard.

CHAPTER III

THE COMING OF THE BUTTERFLIES

Anthony shook his head reproachfully at Damaris over the coffee cups.

'You know,' he said, 'if I were a sub-editor on anything but a distinguished literary paper, I should say you were playing with me—playing fast and loose.'

'Don't be absurd, Anthony,' Damaris answered.

'I come and I go,' Anthony went on, 'and you will and you won't. And——'

'But I've told you what I will,' Damaris said. 'I'm not sure whether you and I could make a success of marriage. And anyhow I won't think about anything of the kind till I've got my degree. Of course, if you think more of yourself than of me——'

'Well, naturally I do,' Anthony interrupted. 'Who doesn't? Am I a saint, or an Alexandrian gnostic? Don't let's ask rhetorical questions, darling.'

'I'm not doing anything of the kind,' Damaris said, coldly. 'But you must be willing to wait a little while. I'm not sure of myself.'

'It's all you are sure of—besides Abelard,' Anthony said. 'And with you, that covers everything else.'

'I think you're rather unkind,' Damaris answered. 'We both like each other——'

'Dearest, I don't like you a bit,' Anthony interrupted again. 'I think you're a very detestable, selfish pig and prig. But I'm often wildly in love with you, and so I see you're not. But I'm sure your only chance of salvation is to marry me.'

'Really, Anthony!' Damaris got up from the table. 'Chance of salvation, indeed! And from what, I should like to know?'

'Nobody else,' Anthony went on, 'sees you as you are. Nobody else will give you such a difficult and unpleasant time as I do. You'll never be comfortable, but you may be glorious. You'd better think over it.'

Damaris said nothing. Anthony, it was clear, was in one of his difficult fits; and if it hadn't been for *The Two Camps*——. There was a short silence, then he too stood up.

'Well,' he said, 'you've not been eaten by the lion, and I've been mauled by the lioness. I think I will now go and look for the other lioness.'

Damaris half-turned and smiled at him over her shoulder. 'Do I maul you?' she asked. 'Am I a pig and a prig—just because I like my work?'

Anthony gazed at her solemnly. 'You are the Sherbet of Allah, and the gold cup he drinks it out of,' he said slowly. 'You are the Night of Repose and the Day of Illumination. You are, incidentally, a night with a good deal of rain and a day with a nasty cold wind. But that may be merely Allah's little game.'

'I hate being bad friends with you,' Damaris said, with perfect truth, and gave him her hand.

'But I', said Anthony, as he kissed it, 'hate being good friends. Besides, I don't think you could be.'

'What, a bad friend?'

'No, a good one,' Anthony said, almost sadly. 'It's all right, I suppose; it isn't your fault—or at least it wasn't. You were made like it by the Invisibles that created you.'

'Why are you always so rude to me, Anthony?' she asked, as wistfully as she thought desirable, but keeping rather on the side of intellectual curiosity than of hurt tenderness.

'I shall be ruder to the other lioness,' he said. 'It's only a way of saying, "Hear thou my protestation"—and making quite sure you do.'

'But what do you mean—look for the lioness?' Damaris asked. 'You're not anxious to find it, are you?'

Anthony smiled at her. 'Well, you want to work,' he said, 'and I could do with a walk. And so, one way and another——' He drew her a little closer to him, but as she moved they both suddenly paused. There struck momentarily into their nostrils—what Damaris recognized and Anthony didn't—a waft of the horrible stench that had assailed her on the previous night in the house where Mr. Berringer lay insensible. It was gone in a second or two, but to each of them it was obvious that the other had smelt it.

'My God!' Anthony said involuntarily, as Damaris shuddered and threw back her head. 'What's the matter with your drains?'

'Nothing,' Damaris said sharply. 'But what—did you smell something?'

'*Smell*,' Anthony exclaimed. 'It was like a corpse walking. Or a beast out of a jungle. What on earth is it?' He sniffed experimentally. 'No, it's gone. It *must* be your drains.'

'It isn't our drains,' Damaris said crossly. 'I smelt it at that house last night, only not nearly so strongly; but how it got here——! It can't be the frock—I wasn't wearing it. How horrible!'

They were standing staring at one another, and she shook herself abruptly, then, recovering her normal remoteness, 'I shall go and have a bath,' she said. It occurred to her that the smell might be, in some way, clinging to her hair, but she wasn't going to admit to Anthony that anything about her could be even remotely undesirable, so she ended—'It makes one feel to need it.'

'It does,' Anthony said. 'I suppose the lioness——'

'In a town—unseen? My dear Anthony!'

He looked out of the window at the street and the houses opposite. People were going by; a car stopped; a policeman came into sight. 'Why, no,' he said, 'I suppose not. Well—it's funny. Anyhow, I'm off now. Goodbye, and do think about salvation.'

'Goodbye,' she said. 'Thank you for coming, and if I ever seem to need it I will. But I've read a good deal about salvation, you know, in all those tiresome texts of one sort and another.'

'Yes,' Anthony answered, as they came into the hall. 'Reading isn't perhaps—the texts are not quite the ritual. Send for me if you want me at any time. I love you. Goodbye.'

He came into the street, frowning, though at what he hardly knew. It was usually at Damaris. He was on these visits provoked by her ignorance of his intelligence; he was provoked even more deeply by her ignorance of his authority over himself. Walking slowly away, he had often asked himself whether—in that momentary opportunity of choice which recurrently presented itself to his mind—he ought not so to exercise it as to turn his preoccupation from her. Only he did not see what good would be done, assuming that he could and did. She thought herself so intellectual and scholarly and capable—and so she was. But she was also an absurd, tender, uncertain little thing, with childish faults of greediness and conceit, and Anthony felt strongly that no one except himself was likely to recognize the childishness. They all took her at her own valuation, and some liked her and some disliked her. But to him she so often seemed like a child with its face against the window-pane, looking for the rain to stop so that the desired satisfaction might arrive. Her learning, her articles, her doctorate—and the picnic would be ended and she would be fortunate if she were not, like most people, tired and cross and unhappy before the end of the day. Perhaps then he could be really of use—good. And if he chose to do it, it was his business. So on the whole he thought that Authority—which meant his decision—was on the side of going on. Only then Authority must control his own mental and physical irritations a little better. Self-reverence was absurd, self-knowledge was hopeless; self-control—perhaps a little more....

He switched his thoughts on to another track. For the past forty hours Quentin and he had discussed, whenever they had been together in the rooms they shared in Notting Hill, little but the mysterious business of Tuesday night. They had gone over every incident without result. Lionesses didn't change into lions; nor did lions appear on small country lawns. But then what had happened? Had they been under some sort of hypnotism? Who was this very odd Mr. Berringer, in whose garden lions leapt out of nothing and who (he had gathered from Damaris) went off into reputed trances? Quentin had been almost terrified ever since, poor fellow! He seemed to think one or other of the beasts was on his track. And now this tale of a woman's hysterics and a crowned snake; and this horrible smell that had penetrated into the Tighes' dining room. Of course, that a woman should be upset—of course, that the drains should go wrong—— But it was the other thing that held his concern. He had felt, it seemed to him now, a curious fascination as he gazed at that immense and royal beast—not terror at all; he had for an instant been almost inclined to go out and meet it. But what about the lioness? Well—there was no getting away from it—the lioness had just vanished, whatever people with guns might say. Vanished.

Revolving alternately the possibility of a lioness being changed into a lion, and of Damaris being converted to humility and love, he walked on along the road into which he and Quentin had turned two days earlier, until he had passed the cross-roads and drawn near to the house of the meeting. Why he was going here he wasn't a bit clear, unless—which seemed silly—it were on the chance of seeing the lion again. His mind recalled it as it had stood there: majestic, awful, complete, gazing directly in front of it, with august eyes. And huge—huger than any lion Anthony had ever seen or dreamt of. The lions he had seen had been a kind of unsatisfactory yellow, but this in spite of the moonlight had been more like gold, with a terrific and ruddy mane covering its neck and shoulders. A mythical, an archetypal lion.

By the gate, when he reached the house, were two men; a car stood by. One of the men was Mr. Tighe, complete with the paraphernalia of active entomology; the other was a stranger who, as Anthony came up, got into his car and drove off. Mr. Tighe exclaimed with pleasure as he recognized Anthony, and shook hands.

'And what brings you down this way?' he asked happily.

'O—things!' Anthony answered. He suspected that Mr. Tighe would take this to mean Damaris, but he didn't mind that. Mr. Tighe and he had, though they never spoke of it, a common experience. Damaris treated her father's hobby and her lover's heart with equal firmness, and made her profit out of both of them. 'Lionesses don't keep you from your butterflies?'

'They seem to think it's gone farther away. I don't suppose it would hurt me,' Mr. Tighe said. 'And even if it did—when I think of the number of butterflies I've caught—I should feel it was only fair. Tit for tat, you know. The brutes—if you can call a butterfly a brute—getting a little of their own back. They deserve to.'

'In England perhaps,' Anthony allowed, 'but do you think altogether?' He liked to talk to Mr. Tighe, and was content for a few minutes to lean on the gate and chat. 'Haven't the animals had it a good deal their own way on the earth?'

The other shook his head. 'Think of the great monsters,' he said. 'The mammoth and the plesiosaurus and the sabre-toothed tiger. Think of what butterflies must have been once, what they are now in the jungles. But they will pass with the jungles. Man must conquer, but I should feel a sympathy with the last campaign of the brutes.'

'I see—yes,' Anthony said. 'I hadn't thought of it like that. Do you think the animals will die out?'

'Perhaps,' Tighe said. 'When we don't want them for transport—or for food—what will be left to them but the zoos? The birds and the moths, I suppose, will be the last to go. When all the trees are cut down.'

'But,' objected Anthony, 'all the trees won't be cut down. What about forestry and irrigation and so on?'

'O' Mr. Tighe said, 'there may be tame forests, with artificially induced butterflies. That will be only a larger kind of zoo. The real thing will have passed.'

'And even if they do,' Anthony asked, 'will man have lost anything very desirable? What after all has a lioness to show us that we cannot know without her? Isn't all real strength to be found within us?'

'It may be,' Mr. Tighe answered. 'It may be that man will have other enemies and other joys—better perhaps. But the older ones were very lovely.'

They ceased speaking, and remained leaning on the gate in silence. Anthony's eyes, passing over the garden, remained fixed where, two nights before, he had thought he saw the form of a lion. It seemed to him now, as he gazed, that a change had taken place. The smooth grass of the lawn was far less green than it had been, and the flowers in the beds by the house walls, on either side of the door, were either dying or already withered. Certainly he had not been in a state to notice much, but there had been left with him a general impression of growth and colour. Neither growth nor colour were now there: all seemed parched. Of course, it was hot, but still….

There was a sudden upward sweep of green and orange through the air in front of him: he blinked and moved. As he recovered himself he saw, with startled amazement, that in the centre of the garden, almost directly above the place where he had seen the lion, there floated a butterfly. But—a butterfly! It was a terrific, a colossal butterfly, it looked as if it were two feet or more across from wing-tip to wing-tip. It was tinted and coloured with every conceivable brightness; green and orange predominating. It was moving upward in spiral flutterings, upward to a certain point, from which it seemed directly to fall close to the ground, then again it began its upward sweep, and again hovered and fell. Of the two men it seemed to be unaware; lovely and self-sufficient it went on with its complex manœuvres in the air. Anthony, after a few astonished minutes, took his eyes from it, and looked about him, first with a general gaze at all his surroundings, then more particularly at Mr. Tighe. The little man was pressed against the gate, his mouth slightly open, his eyes full of plenary adoration, his whole being concentrated on the perfect symbol of his daily concern. Anthony saw that it was no good speaking to him. He looked back at the marvel in time to see, from somewhere above his own head, another brilliancy—but much smaller—flash through the air, almost as if some ordinary butterfly had hurled itself towards its more gigantic image. And another followed it, and another, and as Anthony, now thoroughly roused, sprang up and aside, to see the better, he beheld the air full of them. Those of which he had caught sight were but the scattered first comers of a streaming host. Away across the fields they came, here in thick masses, there in thinner lines, white and yellow, green and red, purple and blue and dusky black. They were sweeping round, in great curving flights; mass following after mass, he saw them driving forward from far away, but not directly, taking wide distances in their sweep, now on one side, now on another, but always and all of them speeding forward towards the gate and the garden beyond. Even as a sudden new rush of aerial loveliness reached that border he turned his head, and saw a cloud of them hanging high above the butterfly of the garden, which rushed up towards them, and then, carrying a whirl of lesser iridescent fragilities with it, precipitated itself down its steep descent; and as it swept, and hovered, and again mounted, silent and unresting, it was alone. Alone it went soaring up, alone to meet another congregation of its hastening visitors, and then again multitudinously fell, and hovered; and again alone went upward to the tryst.

Bewildered and distracted, Anthony caught his companion's arm. Mr. Tighe was by now almost hanging to the gate, his hands clutching frenziedly the topmost bar, his jaws working. Noises were coming from his mouth; the sweat stood in the creases of his face. He gobbled at the soft-glowing vision; he uttered little cries and pressed himself against the bars; his knees were wedged between them, and his feet drawn from the ground in the intensity of his apprehension. And over him faster and thicker the great incursion passed, and the air over the garden was filled with butterflies, streaming, rising, sinking, hovering, towards their centre, and faster now than Anthony's eyes could see the single host of all that visitation rose and fell, only whenever he saw it towards the ground, it turned upwards in a solitary magnificence and whenever, having risen, it dropped again, it went encircled by innumerable tiny bodies and wings.

Credulous, breathless, he gazed, until after times unreckoned had passed, there seemed to be a stay. Lesser grew the clouds above; smaller the flights that joined them. Now there were but a score and now but twelve or ten—now only three tardy dancers waited above for the flight of their vision; and as again it rose, but one—coming faster than all the rest, reaching its strange assignation as it were at the last permitted moment, joining its summoning lord as it rose for the last time, and falling with it; and then the great butterfly of the garden floated idly in the empty air, and the whole army of others had altogether vanished from sight, and from knowledge. It also after a short while rose, curvetting, passed upward towards the roof of the house, settled there for a moment, a glowing splendour upon the red tiles, swept beyond it, and disappeared.

Anthony moved and blinked, took a step or two away, looked round him, blinked again, and turned back to Mr. Tighe. He was about to speak, but, seeing the other man's face, he paused abruptly. The tears were running down it; as his hands released the bars Anthony saw that he was trembling all over; he stumbled and could not get his footing upon the road. Anthony caught and steadied him.

'O glory, glory,' Mr. Tighe said. 'O glory everlasting!'

Anthony said nothing; he couldn't begin to think of anything to say. Mr. Tighe, apparently collecting himself, went an unconscious pace or two on, and stopped.

'O that I should see it!' he said again. 'O glory be to it!' He wiped away his tears with his knuckles, and looked back at the garden. 'O the blessed sight!' he went on. 'And I saw it. O what have I done to deserve it?'

'What … what do you think….' Anthony desisted, his companion was so obviously not listening. Mr. Tighe in a little run went back to the gate, and bobbed half across it, making inarticulate murmurs. These gradually ceased, and, pulling himself upright, he remained for a few minutes gazing devoutly at the garden. Then with a deep sigh he turned to face Anthony.

'Well,' he said normally, 'I suppose I ought to be getting back. Which way are you going?'

'I think I'll come back with you,' Anthony answered. 'I don't feel capable of walking on as I meant to. Besides,' he added diffidently, 'I should be very much obliged to you if you could explain this.'

Mr. Tighe picked up his net, which was lying on the road, patted himself here and there, gave a final beatific glance at the garden, put his cap straight, and began to walk on. 'Well, as to explaining,' he said doubtfully, 'I couldn't tell you anything you don't know.'

'It seems to me someone ought to be able to tell me quite a lot I don't know,' Anthony murmured, but Mr. Tighe only answered, 'I always knew they were real, but to think I should see them.'

'See them?' Anthony ventured.

'See the kingdom and the power and the glory,' Mr. Tighe answered. 'O what a day this has been!' He looked round at the tall young man pacing by his side. 'You know, I did believe it.'

'I am quite sure you did,' Anthony answered gravely. 'I wish you'd believe as well, Mr. Tighe, that I only want to understand, if I can, what it seems to you happened over there. Because I can't think that I really saw a lot of butterflies vanishing entirely. But that was what it looked like.'

'Did it now?' Mr. Tighe said. 'Well, but the thing is—— You see, it proved they were real, and I always believed that. Damaris doesn't.'

'No,' Anthony agreed, with a doubtful smile, 'Damaris probably doesn't—whatever you mean by real. But she will.'

'Will she?' Mr. Tighe replied, with an unexpected scepticism. 'Well perhaps … one of these days.'

'If there is any reality,' Anthony said vigorously, 'then Damaris shall jolly well know it, if I have anything to do with her. Wouldn't she like to hear me say so, bless her for a self-absorbed little table-maker. But about this reality of yours——'

Mr. Tighe seemed to make an effort or two at phrases, but presently he gave it up. 'It's no good,' he said apologetically, 'if you didn't see it, it's no good.'

'I saw clouds and clouds of butterflies, or I thought I did, all just disappearing,' Anthony repeated. 'And that monstrous one in the middle.'

'Ah, don't call it that,' the older man protested. 'That … O that!'

He abandoned speech in a subdued rapture; and in a despair at making anything of anything Anthony followed his example. Something very queer seemed to be going on at that house in the country road. The lion—and the butterflies—and the tale Damaris had, with apparent laughter and real indignation, told him of Miss Wilmot and a crowned snake—and the stench she had known there—and Mr. Berringer's curious collapse….

'How is this Mr. Berringer?' he asked suddenly.

'That was Dr. Rockbotham you saw with me,' Tighe answered. 'He said there was no change. But he didn't give me a very clear idea of what was wrong. He said something about an intermittent suspension of the conscious vital faculties, but it was all very obscure.'

'Well,' Anthony said, as they reached the road leading to the station, 'I don't think I'll come back with you. A little silent meditation, I fancy, is what I need.' He looked seriously at his companion. 'And you?'

'I am going to look at my butterflies, and recollect everything we saw,' Mr. Tighe answered. 'It's the only thing I can do. I was always certain they were true.'

He shook hands and walked quickly away. Anthony stood and watched him. 'And what in God's own most holy name,' he asked himself, 'does the man mean by that? But he's believed it all along anyhow. O darling, O Damaris my dear, whatever will you do if one day you find out that Abelard was true?'

Half sadly he shook his head after Mr. Tighe's retreating figure, and then wandered off towards the station.

CHAPTER IV

THE TWO CAMPS

But that evening Anthony, lying in a large chair, contemplated Quentin with almost equal bewilderment. For he had never known his friend so disturbed, so almost hysterical with—but what it was with Anthony could not understand. The window of their common sitting-room looked out westward over the houses of Shepherd's Bush, and every now and then Quentin would look at it, with such anxiety and distress that Anthony found himself expecting he knew not what to enter—a butterfly or a lion perhaps, he thought absurdly. A winged lion—Venice—Saint Mark. Perhaps Saint Mark was riding about over London on a winged lion, though why Quentin should be so worried about Saint Mark he couldn't think. The lion they had seen (if they had) wasn't winged, or hadn't seemed to be. Somewhere Anthony vaguely remembered to have seen a picture of people riding on winged lions—some Bible illustration, he thought, Daniel or the Apocalypse. He had forgotten what they were doing, but he had a general vague memory of swords and terrible faces, and a general vague idea that it all had something to do with wasting the earth.

Quentin went back to the window, and, standing by one corner, looked out. Anthony picked up a box of matches, and, opening it by accident upside down, dropped a number on the floor. Quentin leapt round.

'What was that?' he asked sharply.

'Me,' said Anthony. 'Sorry; it was pure lazy stupidity.'

'Sorry,' said Quentin in turn. 'I seem all on edge to-night.'

'I thought you weren't very happy,' Anthony said affectionately. 'What's … if there's anything, I mean, that I can do….'

Quentin came back and dropped into a chair. 'I don't know what's got me,' he said. 'It all began with that lioness. Silly of me to feel it like that. But a lioness *is* a bit unusual. It *was* a lioness, wasn't it?' he asked anxiously.

They had been over this before. And again Anthony, with the best will in the world to say the right thing, found himself hampered by an austere intellectual sincerity. It probably had been, it must have been, a lioness. But it was not the lioness that he had chiefly seen, nor was it a lioness which he had, on the night before, dreamed he had seen stalking over hills and hills and hills, covering continents of unending mountains and great oceans between them, with a stealthy yet dominating stride. In that dream the sky had fallen away before the lion's thrusting shoulders, the sky that somehow changed into the lion, and yet formed a background to its movement; and the sun had sometimes been rolling round and round it, as if it were a yellow ball, and sometimes had been fixed millions of miles away, but fixed as if it had been left like a lump of meat for the great beast; and Anthony had felt an anxious intense desire to run a few millions of miles in order to pull it down and save it from those jaws. Only however fast he ran he couldn't catch up with the lion's much slower movement. He ran much faster than the lion, but he couldn't get wherever it was so quickly, although of course the lion was farther away. But the farther away it was the bigger it was, according to the new rules of perspective, Anthony remembered himself seriously thinking. It had seemed extremely important to know the rules in that very muddled dream.

It had certainly been a lion—in the dream and in the garden. And he could not pretend—not even for Quentin—that the lioness had mattered nearly so much. So he said, 'It was certainly a lioness in the road.'

'And in the garden,' Quentin exclaimed. 'Why, surely yesterday morning you agreed it must have been a lioness in the garden.'

'As a great and wise publisher whom I used to know once said,' Anthony remarked, '"I will believe anything of my past opinions." But honestly—in the garden? I don't suppose it matters one way or the other, and very likely you're right.'

'But what do you think? Don't you think it was a lioness?' Quentin cried. And 'No,' Anthony said obstinately, 'I think it was a lion. I also think,' he added with some haste, 'I must have been wrong, because it couldn't have been. So there we are.'

Quentin shrank back in his chair, and Anthony cursed himself for being such a pig-headed precisian. But still, was it any conceivable good pretending—if the intellect had any authority at all? if there were any place for accuracy? In personal relationships it might, for dear love's sake, sometimes be necessary to lie, so complicated as they often were. But this, so far as Anthony could see, was a mere matter of a line to left or to right upon the wall, and his whole mind revolted at falsehood upon abstract things. It was like an insult to a geometrical pattern. Also he felt that it was up to Quentin—up to him just a little—to deal with this thing. If only he himself knew what his friend feared!

Quentin unintentionally answered his thought. 'I've always been afraid,' he said bitterly, 'at school and at the office and everywhere. And I suppose this damned thing has got me in the same way somehow.'

'The lion?' Anthony asked. Certainly it was a curious world.

'It isn't—it isn't just a lion,' Quentin said. 'Whoever saw a lion come from nowhere? But we did; I know we did, and you said so. It's something else—I don't know what'—he sprang again to his feet—'but it's something else. And it's after me.'

'Look here, old thing,' Anthony said, 'let's talk it out. Good God, shall there be anything known to you or me that we can't talk into comprehension between us? Have a cigarette, and let's be comfortable. It's only nine.'

Quentin smiled rather wanly. 'O let's try,' he said. 'Can you talk Damaris into comprehension?'

The remark was more direct than either of the two usually allowed himself, without an implicit invitation, but Anthony accepted it. 'You've often talked me into a better comprehension of Damaris,' he said.

'Theoretically,' Quentin sneered at himself.

'Well, you can hardly tell that, can you?' Anthony argued. 'If your intellect elucidated Da—— O damn!'

The bell of the front door had suddenly sounded and Quentin shied violently, dropping his cigarette. 'God curse it,' he cried out.

'All right,' Anthony said, 'I'll go. If it's anyone we know I won't let him in, and if it's anyone we don't know I'll keep him out. There! Look after that cigarette!' He disappeared from the room and it was some time before he returned.

When he did so he was in spite of his promise accompanied. A rather short, thickset man, with a firm face and large eyes, was with him.

'I changed my mind, after all,' Anthony said, 'Quentin, this is Mr. Foster of Smetham, and he's come to talk about the lion too. So he was good enough to come up.'

Quentin's habitual politeness, returning from wherever it hid during his intimacy with his friend, controlled him and said and did the usual things. When they were all sitting down, 'And now let's have it,' Anthony said. 'Will you tell Mr. Sabot here what you have told me?'

'I was talking to Miss Tighe this afternoon,' Mr. Foster said; he had a rough deep voice, Quentin thought, 'and she told me that you gentlemen had been there two days ago—at Mr. Berringer's house, I mean—when all this began. So in view of what's happened since, I thought it would do no harm if we compared notes.'

'When you say what's happened since,' Anthony asked, 'you mean the business at the meeting last night? I understood from Miss Tighe that one of the ladies there thought she saw a snake.'

'I think—and she thinks—she *did* see a snake,' Mr. Foster answered. 'As much as Mr. Tighe saw the butterflies this afternoon. You won't deny them?'

'Butterflies?' Quentin asked, as Anthony shook his head, and then, with a slight movement of it invited Mr. Foster to explain.

'Mr. Tighe came in while I was at his house this afternoon,' the visitor said, 'in a very remarkable state of exaltation. He told us—Miss Tighe and myself—that he had been shown that butterflies were really true. Miss Tighe was inclined to be a little impatient, but I prevailed on her to let him tell us—or rather, he insisted on telling us—what he had seen. As far as I could follow, there had been one great butterfly into which the lesser ones had passed. But Mr. Tighe took this to be a justification of his belief in them. He was very highly moved, he quite put us on one side, which is (if I may say so) unusual in so quiet a man as he, and he would do nothing but go to his cabinets and look at the collection of his butterflies. I left him,' Mr. Foster ended abruptly, 'on his knees, apparently praying to them.'

Quentin had been entirely distracted by this tale from his own preoccupation. '*Praying!*' he exclaimed. 'But I don't…. Weren't you with him, Anthony?'

'I was up to a point,' Anthony said. 'I was going to tell you later on, whenever it seemed convenient. Mr. Foster is quite right. It can't possibly have been so, but we saw thousands and thousands of them all flying to one huge fellow in the middle, and then—well, then they weren't there.'

'So Tighe said,' Mr. Foster remarked. 'But why can't it possibly have happened?'

'Because—because it can't,' Anthony said. 'Thousands of butterflies swallowed up in one, indeed!'

'There was Aaron's rod,' Mr. Foster put in, and for a moment perplexed both his hearers. Anthony, recovering first, said: 'What, the one that was turned into a snake and swallowed the other snakes?'

'Exactly,' Mr. Foster answered. 'A snake.'

'But you don't mean that this woman—what was her name?—that this Miss Wilmot saw Aaron's rod, or snake, or what not, do you?' Anthony asked. And yet, Quentin thought, not with such amused scorn as might have been expected; it sounded more like the precise question which the words made it: 'do you mean this?'

'I think the magicians of Pharaoh may have seen Miss Wilmot's snake,' Mr. Foster said, 'and all their shapely wisdom have been swallowed by it, as the butterflies of the fields were taken into that butterfly this afternoon.'

'And to what was Mr. Tighe praying then?' Anthony said, his eyes intently fixed on the other.

'To the gods that he knew,' Mr. Foster said, 'or to such images of them as he had collected to give himself joy.'

'The gods?' Anthony asked.

'That is why I have come here,' Mr. Foster answered, 'to find out what you know of them.'

'Aren't we,' Quentin put in, his voice sounding unnatural to him as he spoke, 'aren't we making a rather absurd fuss over a mistake? We', his gesture included his friend, 'were rather tired. And it was dark. Or almost dark. And we were—we were not frightened: I am not frightened: but we were startled. And the old man fell. And we did not see clearly.' The sentences came out in continuous barks.

Mr. Foster turned so suddenly in his chair that Anthony jumped. 'And will you see clearly?' he demanded, thrusting his body and head forward towards Quentin. 'Will you?'

'No,' Quentin cried back at him. 'I will not. I will see nothing of it, if I can help it. I won't, I tell you! And you can't make me. The lion himself can't make me.'

'The lion!' Mr. Foster said. 'Young man, do you really think to escape, if it is on your track?'

'It isn't on my track, I tell you,' Quentin howled, jumping up. 'How can it be? There isn't any—there never was any. I don't believe in these things. There's London and us and the things we know.'

Anthony interfered. 'That at least is true,' he said, 'There is London and us and what we know. But it can't hurt to find out exactly what we know, can it? I mean, we have always rather agreed about that, haven't we? Look here, Quentin, sit down and let me tell Mr. Foster what we thought—at the time—and for the time—that we saw. And you put me right if I go wrong.'

'Carry on,' Quentin, trembling all over, forced himself to say, turning as he did so to make a pretence of rearranging his chair. Anthony therefore recounted the story of the Tuesday evening and of how on the lawn of that house they had seen, as it seemed, the gigantic form of the lion. He did it as lightly as possible, but at best, in the excited atmosphere of the room, the tale took on the sound of some dark myth made visible to mortal and contemporary eyes. He himself, before he had finished, found himself in the midst of speaking eyeing with mingled alarm, fascination, and hope, the room before him, almost as if at any minute the presence should be manifested there.

'And after that,' Mr. Foster said, 'did you not hear the thunder?'

'Why, yes,' the young men said together.

Mr. Foster made a contemptuous motion with his hand. 'Thunder,' he uttered scornfully. 'That was no thunder; that was the roaring of the lion.'

Quentin seemed to be sitting still by a tremendous effort. Anthony eyed his visitor steadily.

'Tell us what you mean,' he said.

Mr. Foster sat forward. 'You have heard of the owner of the house?' he said. 'Well, Berringer is a very wise man—you must not judge him by all that group who get about him—and he has made it his business to try and see the world of principles from which this world comes. He——'

Anthony's raised hand stopped him. 'The world of principles?'

'He believes—and I believe it too,' Mr. Foster said, 'that this world is created, and all men and women are created, by the entrance of certain great principles into aboriginal matter. We call them by cold names; wisdom and courage and beauty and strength and so on, but actually they are very great and mighty Powers. It may be they are the angels and archangels of which the Christian Church talks—and Miss Damaris Tighe—I do not know. And when That which is behind them intends to put a new soul into matter it disposes them as it will, and by a peculiar mingling of them a child is born; and this is their concern with us, but what is their concern and business among themselves we cannot know. And by this gentle introduction of them, every time in a new and just proportion, mankind is maintained. In the animals they are less mingled, for there each is shown to us in his own becoming shape; those Powers are the archetypes of the beasts, and very much more, but we need not talk of that. Now this world in which they exist is truly a real world, and to see it is a very difficult and dangerous thing, but our master held that it could be done, and that the man was very wise who would consecrate himself to this end as part—and the chief part—of his duty on earth. He did this, and I, as much as I can, have done it.'

'But I haven't done it,' Anthony said. 'And therefore how can that world—if there is one—be seen by me and people like me?'

'As for that,' the other answered, 'there are many people who have disciplined and trained themselves more than they know, but that is not the point now. I know that this man was able sometimes to see into that world, and contemplate the awful and terrible things within it, feeding his soul on such visions; and he could even help others towards seeing it, as he has done me on occasions. But as I told you just now, since these powers exhibit their nature much more singly in the beasts, so there is a peculiar sympathy between the beasts and them. Generally, matter is the separation between all these animals which we know and the powers beyond. But if one of those animals should be brought within the terrific influence of one particular idea—to call it that—very specially felt through a man's intense concentration on it——'

He paused, and Anthony said: 'What then?'

'Why then,' the other said, 'the matter of the beast might be changed into the image of the idea, and this world, following that one, might all be drawn into that other world. I think this is happening.'

'O!' said Anthony, and sat down. Quentin was crouched deeply in his chair, his limbs drawn in, his face hidden in his arms, resting on the arm of the chair. A minute or two went by; then Anthony said—

'It's quite insane, of course; but, if it were true, why a lioness into a lion?'

'Because the temporal and spatial thing may be masculine or feminine, but the immortal being must in itself appear as masculine to us, if masculinity is consonant with its nature,' Mr. Foster answered. 'As, of course, supposing that we could call the lion strength or authority or something like that, it would be. But it is absurd to use such words about these forces, at all.'

'It would be something,' Anthony couldn't help saying, 'to know the pet name of any force one happened to meet.' But he spoke almost as if to prick on his incredulity, and neither he nor the others smiled. A much longer time passed now before anyone spoke: then Anthony asked another question.

'And what about Mr. Berringer himself?'

'We can't yet tell,' Foster said, 'what has happened to him. Myself, for what it's worth, I think he's the focus of the movement; in some way we don't understand. It's through him that this world is passing into that. He and his house are the centre.'

'Is that why everything happens in his garden?' Anthony asked.

'It is why everything *begins* to happen in his garden,' Foster answered. 'But it won't stop there. If I'm right, if all this world is passing into that, then the effects will be seen farther and farther away. Our knowledge will more and more be a knowledge of that and not of this—more and more everything will be received into its original, animals, vegetables, all the world but those individual results of interior Powers which are men.'

Anthony missed part of this. 'I can't believe it,' he said. 'If you're at all right, it would mean destruction. But you can't, you can't be.'

'What did you see in the garden?' Foster demanded. 'You know whether you believe in the shape that was there.'

Quentin looked up and spoke harshly. 'And what of men?' he asked.

'Some men will welcome it,' Foster said. 'As Mr. Tighe has done—as I shall do. And they will be joined to that Power which each of them best serves. Some will disbelieve in it—as I think Damaris Tighe does; but they will find then what they do believe. Some will hate it, and run from it—as you do. I cannot guess what will happen to them, except that they will be hunted. For nothing will escape.'

'Cannot the breach be closed?' Anthony asked.

Mr. Foster laughed a little. 'Are we to govern the principles of creation?' he retorted.

Anthony looked at him thoughtfully, and then said still quietly, 'Well, we don't know till we try, do we?'

Quentin looked anxiously at him. 'Do you think there's a chance?' he exclaimed.

Anthony said slowly, 'You know, Quentin, I'm almost certain that Damaris will dislike it very much indeed. It will interfere with Abelard dreadfully. And of course you may remember that I promised to do everything I could to help her get her degree.'

'Even', Mr. Foster asked sarcastically, 'to ruling the various worlds of creation?'

'Everything,' Anthony answered. 'I don't know why this Mr. Berringer—no, but perhaps it wasn't his fault, which makes it worse—I don't know why this lioness should come upsetting us. You don't care for the notion yourself, Quentin, do you?'

'I hate—I hate it,' Quentin said, controlling himself not unsuccessfully. Anthony looked back at Mr. Foster. 'You get the idea?' he asked.

Their visitor again laughed a little. 'You might as well try and stop daffodils growing,' he said. 'It's the law.'

'If it is,' Anthony agreed, 'that settles it. But, my dear Mr. Foster, I must insist on being allowed to find out. Actually, of course, I feel that all this thesis of yours is, if you'll excuse me, pure bunk. But I've watched some curious things happen, and now you tell me of others. I should hate anything to worry Miss Tighe—seriously; a little worry might be a perfectly good thing for her. And Mr. Sabot doesn't want the lion, and Mr. Sabot and I have done our best for years to assist one another against undue interference.'

'Interference!' Foster said, with another laugh.

'Well, you can hardly call it less, can you?' Anthony asked. 'I gather you're on the side of the lion?'

'I am on the side of the things I have wanted to see,' the other answered, 'and if these Powers destroy the world, I am willing to be destroyed. I have given myself to them.'

'Well, I haven't,' Anthony said, getting up. 'Not yet, anyhow. And Mr. Sabot hasn't, nor Miss Tighe.'

'You fool,' Foster said, 'can you stand against them?'

'If they are part of me, as you tell me, perhaps I might; I don't know,' Anthony answered. 'But if they are, then perhaps the authority which is in me over me shall be in me over them. I'm repeating myself, I beg your pardon.'

Mr. Foster got up, with a not quite good-humoured smile. 'You're like most of the world,' he said, 'you don't know necessity when you see it. Well, I'd better go now. Goodnight, and thank you.' He looked at Quentin and offered him no word.

'Necessity, as no doubt Abelard said,' Anthony remarked, 'is the mother of invention—*invenio*, you know. The question is what shall I *venio in*. We're none of us clear about that, I think.'

He drifted with their visitor to the hall, and returned to find Quentin again restlessly roaming about the room. 'Look here,' he said, 'you go to bed, old thing.'

'But what are you going to do?' Quentin asked wretchedly.

'O lord,' said Anthony, 'how do I know? I'm going to sit and meditate. No, I don't want to talk any more—and it's no use going to Smetham till I've got my ideas clearer. Damaris can fend for herself to-night; at the rate things are going there doesn't seem to be any immediate danger. O lord, what danger can there be? Do go away, and let me think or I shall be no good to anyone. Was ever such a lion-hunt? Goodnight, and God bless you. If you're waking in the morning, I shall probably have gone first, so don't bother about calling me. Goodnight, my dear, don't worry—the young lion and the dragon will we tread underfoot.'

CHAPTER V

SERVILE FEAR

In the morning however it was Anthony who woke Quentin by entering his room before he was up,—it might also be said before he slept, for what sleep he had was rather a sinking into silent terror than into normal repose. Anthony sat down on the bed and took a cigarette from a box on the table.

'Look here,' he said, 'I've been thinking it all over. What about us both going down again for the week end, and having a look round?'

Quentin, taken aback, stared at him, and then, 'Do you think so?' he asked.

'I think we might as well,' Anthony said. 'I should like to see Mr. Tighe again, and find out what he feels, and I should very much like to hear whether anyone else is seeing things. Besides, of course,' he added. 'Damaris. But I'd like it a great deal better if you came too.'

As Quentin said nothing he went on, 'Don't you think you might? It wouldn't be any more tiresome for you there, do you think? And we might, one way or another, get something clear. Do think about it. We've talked about ideas often enough, and we should be able to do something much better if we were together.'

Quentin, a little pale, went on thinking; then he looked at Anthony with a smile. 'Well, we might try,' he said, 'but if the lion is about you *will* have to save me.'

'God knows what I should do!' Anthony answered, 'but you could tell me what you wanted. If I go alone I shall always have to ring you up, and that'll take time. Imagine me among lions and snakes and butterflies and smells, asking everything to wait while I telephoned. Well, that's all right. I think I shall go down to-day—after I've made arrangements at the office. I suppose you can't come till to-morrow? About mid-day or so?'

'If London's still here,' Quentin said, again faintly smiling. 'Let me know where you're staying.'

'I'll ring you up here to-night—say about nine,' Anthony answered. 'I shan't do anything but hang round to-day, and to-morrow we'll see.'

So the arrangement was carried out, and on the Saturday afternoon the two young men wandered out on to the Berringer road, as Anthony called it. Past the Tighe house, past the sedate public-house at the next corner, and the little Baptist chapel almost at the end of the town, out between the hedges, they went, more silent than usual, more intensely alert in feet and eyes. The sun was hot, June was drawing to a rich close.

'And nothing fresh has happened?' Quentin said, after they had for some time exchanged trivialities about nature, the world, philosophy, and art.

'No,' Anthony murmured thoughtfully, 'nothing has happened exactly, unless—I don't really know if it could be called a happening—but Mr. Tighe has given up entomology.'

'But I thought he was so keen!' Quentin exclaimed.

'So he was,' Anthony answered. 'That's what makes it funny. I called on him yesterday—yes, Quentin, I really did call on *him*—and very tactfully asked him…. O this and that and how he felt. He was sitting in the garden looking at the sky. So he said he felt very well, and I asked him if he had been out after butterflies during the day. He said, "O no, I shan't do that again." I suppose I stared or said something or other, because he looked round at me and said, "But I've nothing to do with them now." Then he said, quite sweetly, "I can see now they were only an occupation." I said: didn't he think it might be quite a good idea to have an occupation? and he said: yes, he supposed it might if you needed it, but he didn't. So then he went on looking at the sky and I came away.'

'And Damaris?' Quentin asked.

'O Damaris seemed all right,' Anthony answered evasively. It was true that, in one sense of the words, Damaris *had* seemed all right. She had been in a state of extreme irritation with her father, and indeed with everybody. People had been calling—Mrs. Rockbotham to see her, Mr. Foster to see her father; she could get no peace. Time was going by, and she was continually being interrupted, and she had in consequence lost touch with the precise relationship of the theory of Pythagoras about number with certain sayings attributed to Abelard's master William of Champagne. Nobody seemed to have the least idea of the importance of a correct evaluation of the concentric cultural circles of Hellenic and pre-mediaeval cosmology. And now if her father were going to hang about the house all day! There appeared to have been a most unpleasant scene that morning between them, when Damaris had been compelled to grasp the fact that Mr. Tighe proposed to abandon practical entomology entirely. She had (Anthony had gathered) asked him what he proposed to do—to which he had replied that there was no need to do anything. She had warned him that she herself must not be interrupted—to which again he had said merely: 'No, no, my dear, go on playing, but take care you don't hurt yourself.' At this Damaris had entirely lost her temper—not that she had said so in so many words, but Anthony quite justly interpreted her 'I had to speak pretty plainly to him,' as meaning that.

In consequence he had not been able to do more than hint very vaguely at Mr. Foster's theories. Theories which were interesting in Plato became silly when regarded as having anything to do with actual occurrences. Philosophy was a subject—her subject; and it would have been ridiculous to think of her subject as getting out of hand. Or her father, for that matter; only he was.

Anthony would have been delighted to feel that she was right; she was, of course, right. But he did uneasily feel that she was a little out of touch with philosophy. He had done his best to train his own mind to regard philosophy as something greater and more important than itself. Damaris, who adopted that as an axiom of speech, never seemed to follow it as a maxim of intellectual behaviour. If philosophies could get out of hand … he looked unhappily at the Berringer house as they drew near to it.

But at the gate both he and Quentin exclaimed. The garden was changed. The flowers were withered, the grass was dry and brown; in places the earth showed, hard and cracked. The place looked as if a hot sun had blazed on it for weeks without intermission. Everything living was dead within its borders, and (they noticed) for a little way beyond its borders. The hedges were leafless and brittle; the very air seemed hotter than even the June day could justify. Anthony drew a deep breath.

'My God, how hot it is!' he said.

Quentin touched the gate. 'It *is* hot,' he said. 'I didn't notice it so much when we were walking.'

'No,' Anthony answered. 'I don't, you know, think it was so hot there. This place is beginning'—he had been on the point of saying 'to terrify me,' when he remembered Quentin and changed it into 'to seem quite funny.' His friend however took no notice even of this; he was far too occupied in maintaining an apparently casual demeanour, of which his pallid cheeks, quick breathing, and nervous movements showed the strain. Anthony turned round and leant against the gate with his back to the house.

'It looks quiet and ordinary enough,' he said.

The fields stretched up before them, meadow and cornfield in a gentle slope; along the top of the rising ground lay a series of groups of trees. The road on their left ran straight on for some quarter of a mile, then it swept round towards the right, and itself climbed the hill, which it crossed beyond the last fragments of the scattered wood. The house by which they stood was indeed almost directly in the middle of a circular dip in the countryside. In one of the fields a number of sheep were feeding. Anthony's eyes rested on them.

'They don't seem to have been disturbed,' he said.

'What do you really think about it all?' Quentin asked suddenly. 'It's all nonsense, isn't it?'

Anthony answered thoughtfully. 'I should think it was all nonsense if we hadn't both thought we saw the lion—and if I and Damaris's father hadn't both thought we saw the butterflies. But I really can't see how to get over that.'

'But *is* the world slipping?' Quentin exclaimed. 'Look at it. Is it?'

'No, of course not,' Anthony said. 'But—I don't want to be silly, you know—but, if we were to believe what the Foster fellow said, it wouldn't be that kind of slipping anyhow. It'd be more like something behind coming out into the open. And as I got him, all the more quickly when there are material forms to help it. The lioness was the first chance, and I suppose the butterflies were the next easiest—the next thing at hand.'

'What about birds?' Quentin asked.

'I thought of them,' Anthony said, 'and—look here, we'd better talk it out, so I'll tell you—— It's a minor matter, and I daresay I shouldn't have noticed them, but as a matter of fact, I haven't seen or heard any birds round here at all.'

Quentin took this calmly. 'Well, we don't notice them much, do we?' he said. 'And what about the sheep?'

'The sheep I give you,' Anthony answered. 'Either Foster's mad, or else there must be something to explain that. Perhaps there isn't an Archetypal Sheep.' His voice was steady, and he smiled, but the mild jest fell very flat.

'And what', Quentin asked, 'do you think of doing?'

Anthony turned to face him. 'I think you've probably seen it too,' he said. 'I'm going to do my best to find that lion.'

'Why?' the other asked.

'Because—if it were true—we must meet it,' Anthony said, 'and I will have a word in the meeting.'

'You do believe it,' Quentin said.

'I can't entirely disbelieve it, without refusing to believe in ideas,' Anthony answered, 'and I can't do that. I can't go back on the notion that all these abstractions do mean something important to us. And mayn't they have a way of existing that I didn't know? Haven't we agreed about the importance of ideas often enough?'

'But ideas——' Quentin began, and stopped. 'You're right, of course,' he added. 'If this is so, we must be prepared—if we meant anything.'

'And as we certainly meant something——' Anthony said, relaxing to his former position, 'My God, look!'

Up on the top of the rise the lion was moving. It was passing slowly along among the trees, now a little this side, now hidden by the trunks—or partly hidden. For its gigantic and golden body, its enormous head and terrific mane, were of too vast proportions to be hidden. It moved with a kind of stately ferocity, its eyes fixed in front of it, though every now and then its head turned one way or the other, in an awful ease. Once its eyes seemed to pass over the two young men, but if it saw them it ignored them, and proceeded slowly upon its own path. Half terrified, half attracted, they gazed at it.

Quentin moved suddenly, 'O let's get away!'

Anthony's hand closed on his arm, 'No,' he said, though his voice shook, 'we're going up that road to meet it. Or else I shall never be able to speak of ideas and truths again. Come along.'

'I daren't,' Quentin muttered shrinking.

'But what's lucidity then?' Anthony asked. 'Let's be as quick as we can. For if that is what is in me, then I may be able to control it; and if not——'

'Yes, if not——' Quentin cried out.

'Then we will see what a Service revolver will do,' Anthony answered, putting his hand in the pocket of his loose coat. 'One way or the other. Come on.'

Quentin moved unhappily, but he did not refuse. Their eyes still set on the monster, they left the gate and went on along the road; and up on the ridge it continued its own steady progress. The trees however after a few minutes shut it out of their sight, and even when they came round the curve in the road and began to move up the gentle rise they did not again see it. This added to the strain of expectation they both felt, and as they stepped on Quentin exclaimed suddenly: 'Even if it's what you say, how do you know you were *meant* to see it? We're only men—how should we be meant to look at—these things?'

363

'The face of God….' Anthony murmured. 'Well, even now perhaps I'd as soon die that way as any. But Tighe didn't die when he saw the butterfly, nor we when we saw it before.'

'But it's madness to go like this and *look* for it,' Quentin said. 'I daren't, that's the truth, if you want it. I daren't. I can't.' He stood still trembling violently.

'I don't know that I *dare* exactly,' Anthony said, also pausing. 'But I shall. What the devil's that?'

It was not the form of the lion but the road some little distance in front of them at which he was staring. For across it, almost where it topped the rise and disappeared down the other side, there passed a continuous steady ripple. It seemed to be moving crosswise; wave after gentle wave followed each other from the fields on one side to the fields opposite; they could see the disturbed dust shaken off and up, and settling again only to be again disturbed. The movement did not stop at the roadside, it seemed to pass on into the fields, and be there lost to sight. The two young men stood staring.

'The damn road's moving!' Anthony exclaimed, as if driven to unwilling assent.

Quentin began to laugh, as he had laughed that other evening, hysterically, madly. 'Quite right,' he shrieked in the midst of his laughter, 'quite right, Anthony. The road's moving: didn't you know it would? It's scratching its own back or something. Let's help it, shall we?'

'Don't be a bloody fool,' Anthony cried to him. 'Stop it, Quentin, before I knock you silly.'

'Ha!' said Quentin with another shriek, 'I'll show you what's silly. It isn't us! it's the world! The earth's mad, didn't you know? All mad underneath. It pretends to behave properly, like you and me, but really it's as mad as we are! And now it's beginning to break out. Look, Anthony, we're the first to see the earth going quite, quite mad. That's your bright idea, that's what you're running uphill to see. Wait till you feel it in you!'

He had run a few steps on as he talked, and now paused with his head tossed up, his feet pirouetting, his mouth emitting fresh outbursts of laughter. Anthony felt his own steadiness beginning to give way. He looked up at the sky and the strong afternoon sun—in that at least there was as yet no change. High above him some winged thing went through the air; he could not tell what it was but he felt comforted to see it. He was not entirely alone, it seemed; the pure balance of that distant flight entered into him as if it had been salvation. It was incredible that life should sustain itself by such equipoise, so lightly, so dangerously, but it did, and darted onward to its purpose so. His mind and body rose to the challenging revelation; the bird, whatever it was, disappeared in the blue sky in a moment, and Anthony, curiously calmed, looked back at the earth in front of him. Across the road the movement was still passing, but it seemed smaller, and even while he looked it had ceased. Still and motionless the road stretched in front of him, and though his blood was running cold his eyes were quiet as he turned them on his friend.

Quentin jerked his head. 'You think it's stopped, don't you?' he jeered. 'You great fool, wait, only wait! I haven't told you, but I've known it a long time. I've heard it when I lay awake at night, the earth chuckling away at its imbecile jokes. It's slobbering over us now. O you're going to find out things soon! Wait till it scratches you. Haven't you felt it scratching you when you thought about that woman, you fool? When you can't sleep for thinking of her? and the earth scratches you again? Ho, and you didn't know what it was. But I know.'

Anthony looked at him long and equably. 'You know, Quentin,' he said, 'you *do* have the most marvellous notions. When I think that I really know you I get almost proud. The beauty of it is that for all I know you're right, only if you are there's nothing for us to discuss. And though I don't say there is, I insist on behaving as if there was. Because I will not believe in a world where you and I can't talk.' He came a step nearer and added: 'Will you? It'll be an awful nuisance for me if you do.'

Quentin had stopped pirouetting and was swinging to and fro on his toes. 'Talk!' he said uncertainly. 'What's the good of talking when the earth's mad?'

'It supports the wings in the air,' Anthony answered. 'Come along and support.'

He tucked his arm into his friend's. 'But perhaps for this afternoon——' he began, and paused, arrested by the other's face. Quentin had looked back over his shoulder, and his eyes were growing blind with terror. Sense and intelligence deserted them; Anthony saw and swung round. By the side of the road, almost where the ripple had seemed to pass over, there appeared the creature they had set out to seek. It was larger and mightier than when they had seen it before—and, comparatively close as they now were, they fell back appalled by the mere effluence of strength that issued from it. It was moving like a walled city, like the siege-towers raised against Nineveh or Jerusalem; each terrible paw, as it set it down, sank into the firm ground as if into mud, but was plucked forth without effort; the movement of its mane, whenever it mightily turned its head, sent reverberations of energy through the air, which was shaken into wind by that tossed hair. Anthony's hand rested helplessly on his revolver, but he could not use it—whether this were mortal lion or no, he must take his chance, its being to his exposed being. He had challenged the encounter, and now it was upon him, and all the strength of his body was flowing out of him: he was beginning to tremble and gasp. He no longer had hold of Quentin, nor was indeed aware of him; a faintness was taking him—perhaps this was death, he thought, and then was suddenly recalled to something like consciousness by hearing a shot at his side.

Quentin had snatched the revolver from him and was firing madly at the lion, screaming, 'There! there! there!' as he did so, screaming in a weakness that seemed to lay him appallingly open to the advance of that great god—for it looked no less—whenever it should choose to crush him. The noise sounded as futile as the bullets obviously proved, and the futility of the outrage awoke in Anthony a quick protest.

'Don't!' he cried out, 'you're giving in. That's not the way to rule; that's not within you.' To keep himself steady, to know somehow within himself what was happening, to find the capacity of his manhood even here—some desire of such an obscure nature stirred in him as he spoke. He felt as if he were riding against some terrific wind; he was balancing upon the instinctive powers of his spirit; he did not fight this awful opposition but poised himself within and above it. He heard vaguely the sound of running feet and knew that Quentin had fled, but he himself could not move. It was impossible now to help others; the overbearing pressure was seizing and stifling his breath; and still as the striving force caught him he refused to fall and strove again to overpass it by rising into the balance of adjusted movement. 'If this is in me I reach beyond it,' he cried to himself again, and felt a new-come freedom answer his cry. A memory—of all insane things—awoke in him of the flying he had done in the last year of the war; it seemed as if again he looked down on a wide stretch of land and sea, but no human habitations were there, only forest, and plain, and river, and huge saurians creeping slowly up from the waters, and here and there other giant beasts coming into sight for a moment and then disappearing. Another flying thing went past below him—a hideous shape that was a mockery of the clear air in which he was riding, riding in a machine that, without his control, was now sweeping down towards the ground. He was plunging towards a prehistoric world; a lumbering vastidity went over an open space far in front, and behind it his own world broke again into being through that other. There was a wild minute in which the two were mingled; mammoths and dinotheria wandered among hedges of English fields, and in that confused vision he felt the machine make easy landing, run, and come to a stop. Yet it couldn't have been a machine, for he was no longer in it; he hadn't got out, but he was somehow lying on the ground, drawing deep breaths of mingled terror and gratitude and salvation at last. In a recovered peace he moved, and found that he was actually stretched at the side of the road; he moved again and sat up.

There was no sign of the lion, nor of Quentin. He got to his feet; all the countryside lay still and empty, only high above him a winged something still disported itself in the full blaze of the sun.

CHAPTER VI

MEDITATION OF
MR. ANTHONY DURRANT

When at last, by another road, Anthony returned to Smetham he was very tired. It was not the extra length of the journey that had tired him—he had not at that moment been able to bring himself to go back by Berringer's home—but a shock of wrestling with a great strength. He had taken long to recover his usual equilibrium, and he had been worried over Quentin. But no gazing from the top of the ridge had revealed his friend to him, and there was no sign to show in which direction the fugitive had gone. It was a small comfort to Anthony to remember that he had actually heard the flying feet, for the horrible possibility haunted him that Quentin might … might have been destroyed—shattered or annihilated by the powers which, it seemed, were finding place in the world, or perhaps it would be truer to say (if Foster had been right) into whose dominion the outer world was passing. But the thought of Foster reminded him of another phrase; the man had said something about those who hated and feared it being hunted. Was it possible that such a chase was even now proceeding? that over those sedate hills, and among those quiet cornfields and meadows, a golden majesty was with inexorable speed pursuing Quentin's fearful and lunatic haste? a haste which could find no shelter, nor set any barrier between itself and its fate? The distress of such a thought swelled in Anthony's heart, as, heavily and slowly, he came back to the town. For he, it was evident, could at that time do nothing; he was far too exhausted, and he needed to be alone in order to realize what had happened, and what his next action should be. Besides, always and everywhere, thrusting between even Quentin's need and any possibility of succour, there was Damaris.

He bathed and rested, and ate and drank, and then feeling better went out to smoke and think in the grounds of the hotel. It was still early evening; tennis was going on not far off, but presently everyone would be going in to dinner. Anthony found a deck chair in a remote corner, sat down, lit a cigarette, and began to meditate. He arranged his questions in his mind—six of them:

1. Had it happened?
2. Why had it happened?
3. What was likely to happen now?
4. How was it likely to affect Damaris?
5. What was happening to Quentin?
6. What did he himself propose to do about it all?

Over the first question he spent no time. The things that he had seen had been as real to him as anything that he had ever seen. Besides, Tighe had given up collecting butterflies, and Foster had come and talked with him, and Quentin had run away—all because of various aspects of 'it.' If 'it' hadn't happened, then Quentin had been right and they were all going mad together. The fact that most of Smetham knew nothing about it and wouldn't have believed it was irrelevant. He could act only upon his own experience, and his actions should be, as far as possible, consistent with that experience. 'It' then had happened. But why? or, to put it another way, what was happening? Here he had no hypothesis of his own, and only one of anyone else's—Foster's: that between a world of living principles, existing in its own state of being, and this present world, a breach had been made. The lioness from without, the lion from—within? say within, it meant as much as any other mode of description—had approached each other through the channel of a man's consciousness, and had come together by the natural kinship between the material image and the immaterial idea. And after that first impact others had followed; other principles had found their symbols and possessed them, drawing back into themselves as many of those particular symbols as came immediately within the zone influenced. How far those presences could be seen by men he could not guess; he and Quentin had seen the lion, he and Tighe the butterfly. But Foster had told him how one woman, and only one, had cried out that she had seen a snake, which Foster himself had not seen. What then was the distinction? Pondering over this it occurred to him suddenly that snakes were not as common as butterflies in England, and that only a most unusual chance had loosed a lioness on that country road. Might it not be then that these powers were not visible till they had found their images? not visible at least to ordinary eyes? Why that woman had seen one he did not profess to explain. Nor why, lioness and butterflies being gone, the many sheep he had seen still remained quietly feeding near the house of exodus. He remembered with a shock the strange quiver that had passed across the road that afternoon; was it so certain that he had *not* seen some movement of the snake? If the long undulating body had passed through the earth—if the earth, so to speak, had been charged with that serpentine influence?... All this was beyond him; he could not tell. But, right or wrong, there seemed to him at present no other hypothesis than that of powers loosed into the world; without finally believing it, he accepted it until he should discover more.

And what was likely to happen now? Anthony threw away the end of his cigarette, and sighed. Why did he always ask himself these silly questions? Always intellectualizing, he thought, always trying to find a pattern. Well, and why not? If Foster was right, every man—he himself—was precisely a pattern of these powers. But it wasn't at the moment his own, it was the general pattern he was concerned with. The word supplied a possible answer—the present general pattern of the world was being violently changed into another pattern, perhaps a better one, perhaps not, but anyhow another. And the present pattern looked like being utterly and entirely destroyed, if the world went on passing into that other state. Something had saved him that afternoon, but as he recalled his breathless struggle with overwhelming energy he realized part of the danger that was drawing near. The beauty of butterflies was one thing, but what if these principles drew to their separate selves the elements of which each man was made? Man, it seemed to Anthony, looked like having a thin time. If the animals were swallowed up as Aaron's snake swallowed the snakes of the magicians? Were the other plagues, he wondered, but the permitted domination of some element by its own or another principle? Was that principle—whatever it might be—that knew itself in the frog loosed once in all the palaces of Egypt? and did the life which is in blood enter into and control the waters of the Nile? As perhaps on a later day at Cana ecstasy which is wine entered into lucidity which is water and possessed it? 'Damn!' said Anthony, 'I'm romancing, and anyhow it doesn't matter; it's got nothing to do with what is happening now. It was the lion that began it here and (if they're right) the snake. Is the lion still beginning it?'

He sat up in some excitement. They had seemed to see the shape of the lion moving slowly—and the queer wave in the road had passed almost in the same path but in the opposite direction. Was this the place of entrance?—were those two the guards of the other world, the dwellers on that supernatural threshold, pacing round in widening circles, until slowly the whole world was encompassed? And, in that case, how long before their circle included Smetham—and Damaris?

He was up against his fourth question, and he made himself lean back to look at it quietly. But his heart was beating quickly, and his hands moved restlessly about his chair. How would it affect Damaris? He tried to see her again as she was in her own nature—he tried to think to which of those august powers she was kin; but he could not do it. 'O Damaris darling!' he exclaimed, and felt himself in all a terrible fear for her. If that childish ignorance and concern and childish arrogance and selfishness met these dangers—O then what shelter, what safety, would there be? He wanted to help her, he wanted to stay this new movement till she had understood, and turned to meet it; and if his mind clamoured again with a desire that they should do this together, and together find the right way into or out of this other world—if so far his own self thrust into his otherwise selfless anxiety, it was a momentary accompaniment. But she wouldn't, she would go on thoughtfully playing with the dead pictures of ideas, with names and philosophies, Plato and Pythagoras and Anselm and Abelard, Athens and Alexandria and Paris, not knowing that the living existences to which seers and saints had looked were already in movement to avenge themselves on her. 'O you sweet blasphemer!' Anthony moaned, 'can't you wake?' Gnostic traditions, mediaeval rituals, Aeons and Archangels—they were cards she was playing in her own game. But she didn't know, she didn't understand. It wasn't her fault; it was the fault of her time, her culture, her education—the pseudo-knowledge that affected all the learned, the pseudo-scepticism that infected all the unlearned, in an age of pretence, and she was only pretending as everybody else did in this lost and imbecile century. Well, it was up to him to do something.

But what? He could, he would, go and see her. But what could he do to ensure her safety? Could he get her to London? It would be difficult to persuade her, and if he put it to the touch by attempting to compel her and failed—that would be worse than all. Damaris was still keeping herself at a distance; her feeling for him was still ruled and directed by her feeling for herself. He had the irresistible force all right, but honesty compelled him to admit that she, as an immovable object, was out of its direct line. Besides—London? If this kind of thing was going on, supposing (just for one split second) that Foster's fantastic hypothesis was right, what would be the good of London? Sooner or later London too would slip in and be subject to great animals—the fierceness of the wolf would threaten it from Hampstead, the patience of the tortoise would wait beyond Streatham and Richmond; and between them the elk and the bear would stalk and lumber, drawing the qualities out of mankind, terrifying, hunting down, destroying. He did not know how swiftly the process of absorption was going on—a week might see that golden mane shaken over London from Kensal Rise. London was no good, his thought raced on, no, nor any other place then; no seas or mountains could avail. Still, if he could persuade her to move for a few days—that would give him time to do something. And at that he came up against the renewed memory of Foster's scornful question. Was he really proposing to govern the principles of creation? to attempt to turn back, for the sake of one half-educated woman's personal safety, the movement of the vast originals of all life? How was he, he thought despairingly, to close the breach, he who had that very afternoon been swept almost into death by the effluence from but one visioned greatness? It was hopeless, it was insane, and yet the attempt had to be made.

Besides, there was Quentin. He had small expectation of being of any use to Quentin, but somewhere in this neighbourhood his unhappy friend—if he lived yet—was wandering, and Anthony disliked going off himself while the other's doom remained unknown. And there might be some way—this Berringer now; perhaps something more could be found out about him. If he had opened, might he not close? Or his friends—this infernal group? Some of them might help: they couldn't all want Archetypes coming down on them, not if they were like most of the religious people he had met. They also probably liked their religion taken mild—a pious hope, a devout ejaculation, a general sympathetic sense of a kindly universe—but nothing upsetting or bewildering, no agony, no darkness, no uncreated light. Perhaps he had better go and see some of them—Foster again, or even this Miss Wilmot, or the doctor who was attending Berringer, and whose wife had got Damaris (so she had told him) into this infernal mess. Yes, and then to persuade Damaris to go to London; and to look for Quentin....

And all the while to be quiet and steady, to remember that man was meant to control, to be lord of his own nature, to accept the authority that had been given to Adam over all manner of beasts, as the antique fables reported, and to exercise that authority over the giants and gods which were threatening the world.

Anthony sighed a little and stood up. 'Adam,' he said, 'Adam. Well, I am as much a child of Adam as any. The Red Earth is a little pale perhaps. Let's go and walk in the garden among the beasts of the field which the Lord God hath made. I feel a trifle microcosmic, but if the proportion is in me let these others know it. Let me take the dominion over them—I wish I had any prospect of exercising dominion over Damaris.'

CHAPTER VII

INVESTIGATIONS INTO A
RELIGION

Dr. Rockbotham leaned back and looked at his watch. Mrs. Rockbotham looked at him. Dinner was just over; in a quarter of an hour he had to be in his surgery. The maid entered the room with a card on a salver. Dr. Rockbotham took it.

'Anthony Durrant,' he read out and looked over at his wife enquiringly. She thought and shook her head.

'No,' she began, and then 'O wait a minute! Yes, I believe I do remember. He's one of my cousin's people on *The Two Camps*. I met him there once.'

'He's very anxious to see you, sir,' the maid said.

'But what can he want?' Dr. Rockbotham asked his wife. 'If you know him, Elise, you'd better come along and see him too. I can't give him very long now, and I've had a tiring day. Really, people do come at the most inconvenient times.'

His protest however was only half-serious, and he turned a benign face on Anthony in the drawing-room. 'Mr. Durrant? My wife thinks she remembers you, Mr. Durrant. You're on *The Two Camps*, aren't you? Yes, yes. Well, as you've met there's no need for introductions. Sit down, do. And what can we do for you, Mr. Durrant?'

'I've really only called to ask—if I may—a question about Mr. Berringer,' Anthony said. 'We heard in London that he was very ill, and as he's a person of some importance' (this, he thought guiltily, is the Archetypal Lie) 'I thought I'd run down and enquire. As a matter of fact, there was some sort of idea that he should do a series of articles for us on … on the symbolism of the cosmic myths.'

Mrs. Rockbotham nodded in pleasure. 'I mentioned something of the sort to my cousin once,' she said. 'I'm delighted to find that he followed it up. An excellent idea.'

Anthony's heart sank a little; he foresaw, if the world were not swallowed up, some difficulty in the future. 'We were', he said, 'so sorry to hear he was ill. The housekeeper didn't seem to know much, and as Mr. Tighe—whom you know, I think—mentioned that you were attending him, I ventured….'

'Certainly, certainly,' Dr. Rockbotham said. 'These notorieties, eh? Famous men, and so on. Well, yes, I'm afraid he is ill.'

'Seriously?' Anthony asked.

'O well, seriously——' The doctor paused. 'An affection of the brain, I very much fear. He's more or less in a state of unconsciousness, and of course in such cases it's a little difficult to explain in non-technical language. A nurse has been installed, and I'm keeping a careful watch. If necessary I shall take the responsibility of getting another opinion. You don't, I suppose, know the name or address of any of his friends or his solicitor, do you?'

'I'm afraid not,' Anthony said.

'It's a little difficult position,' Dr. Rockbotham went on. 'His housekeeper knows of no one; of course I haven't looked at his papers yet … if I could get in touch with anyone….'

'If I can do anything——' Anthony offered. 'But I've no personal acquaintance with Mr. Berringer; only a general knowledge of his name.' And that, he thought, only since the day before yesterday. But he wasn't going to stick at trifles now.

'My dear,' said Mrs. Rockbotham, 'perhaps Mr. Durrant would like to see Mr. Berringer.'

'I don't see that Mr. Durrant would gain much by that,' the doctor answered. 'He's lying perfectly still and unconscious. But if,' he went on to the young man, 'I may take it that you represent a widespread concern….'

'I represent,' Anthony said, 'what I believe may be a very widespread concern.' It seemed to him utterly ridiculous to be talking like this, but he couldn't burst out on these two people with his supernatural menagerie. And yet this woman ought to have realized something.

'… don't know that I wouldn't welcome your association,' Dr. Rockbotham concluded. 'We professional men have to be so careful. If you'd care to come out with me to-morrow morning—about twelve——?'

368

'I should be'—no, Anthony felt he couldn't say delighted or pleased at going back to that house— 'honoured.' Honoured! 'What's honour?... Who hath it? he that died o' Wednesday.' 'I shouldn't be a bit surprised if I ended by being he that died o' Wednesday,' he thought grimly.

'Why, that will be capital,' the doctor said, 'and we can see what's best to do. You'll excuse me, won't you? I have to get to the surgery.'

'Don't go, Mr. Durrant,' Mrs. Rockbotham said, as Anthony rose. 'Sit down and tell me how things are with *The Two Camps*.'

Anthony obediently sat down, and told his hostess as much as he thought good for her about the present state of the periodical. He persevered at the same time in bringing the conversation as close as possible to the collapse of Mr. Berringer and the last monthly meeting of the Group. Mrs. Rockbotham was very willing to talk about it.

'Most disconcerting for Miss Tighe,' she said, 'though I must say she behaved very charmingly about it. So good natured. Of course no one had any idea that Dora Wilmot would go off like that.'

'Miss Wilmot is a friend of yours?' Anthony threw in casually.

'We've been connected in a number of things,' Mrs. Rockbotham admitted, 'the social fêtes every summer and this Study Group and the Conservative Committee. I remember she was a great deal of use with the correspondence at the time of the first Winter Lectures we got up to amuse the poorer people. I believe she went to some of them—a good simple soul. But this——!'

'She's belonged to the town for a good while?' Anthony asked.

'Born here,' Mrs. Rockbotham said. 'Lives in the white house at the upper corner of the marketplace—you must have seen it. Just beyond Martin the bookseller's—his assistant was one of our Group too. I suppose Mr. Berringer invited him, though of course he was hardly of the same social class as most of us.'

'Perhaps Mr. Berringer thought that the study of the world of principles——' Anthony allowed a gesture to complete his sentence.

'No doubt,' Mrs. Rockbotham answered. 'Though personally I always think it better and simpler if like sticks to like. It simply distracts one's attention if the man next you rattles his false teeth or can't get up from his chair easily.'

'That', Anthony said, feeling that the confession was due to truth, 'is undeniably so. Perhaps it means that we haven't got very far.'

Mrs. Rockbotham shook her head. 'It's always been so,' she said, 'and I shouldn't myself find I could concentrate nearly so well if Mr. Berringer hadn't shaved for a week. I don't see the smallest use in pretending that it isn't so.'

'Didn't this young man—what did you say his name was?—shave then?' Anthony asked.

'Richardson—yes, of course—I was only illustrating,' the lady said. 'Well, if you must go——' as Anthony stood up firmly. 'If you see Miss Tighe do tell her that I'm still ashamed.'

'I'm sure Miss Tighe wouldn't wish you to be anything of the sort,' Anthony lied with brazen politeness; and, treasuring his two pieces of information, departed. It was at least a small piece of luck that the two places were near together.

From outside the bookseller's he peered cautiously in. A nice looking old gentleman was showing children's books to two ladies; a tall gaunt young man was putting other books into shelves. Anthony hoped that the first gentleman was Mr. Martin, and the other Mr. Richardson. He went in with a quick determined step, and straight up to the young man, who turned to meet him.

'Have you by any chance an edition of St. Ignatius's treatise against the Gnostics?' he asked in a low clear voice.

The young assistant looked gravely back. 'Not for sale, I'm afraid,' he said. 'Nor, if it comes to that, the Gnostic treatises against St. Ignatius.'

'Quite,' Anthony answered. 'Are you Mr. Richardson?'

'Yes,' the other said.

'Then I apologize and all that but I should very much like to talk to you about modern Gnosticism or what appear to be its equivalents,' Anthony said rapidly. 'If you don't mind. I assure you I'm perfectly serious— though I do come from Mrs. Rockbotham. Would you, could you, spare me a little time?'

'Not here very well,' Richardson said. 'But if you could come round to my rooms about half past nine, I should be very glad to discuss anything with you—anything possible.'

'So many things seem to be possible,' Anthony murmured. 'At half past nine, then? And thank you. I'm not really being silly.' He liked the other's equable reception of the intrusion, and the reserved watchfulness of his manner.

'17 Bypath Villas,' Richardson said. 'It's not more than ten minutes away. Along that street, down the second on the right, and then it's the third to the left. No, I'm afraid we haven't it'—this as Mr. Martin, having disposed of his own customers, was drawing near.

'Then,' said Anthony, looking hastily round, with a vague sense of owing a return to the bookseller for the use he had made of the shop, 'I'll have that.' He picked up from a chance shelf of reduced library copies a volume with the title: *Mistresses of Majesty; the lives of seven beautiful women from Agnes Sorel to Mrs. Fitzherbert*. 'But it's not very up-to-date, is it?' he added rather gloomily, as he took his change.

'The morality of the House of Windsor——' Richardson said, and bowed him out.

Tucking the book under his arm in some irritation, Anthony set out for Miss Wilmot's, and found it within a few steps. He rang the bell, and looked despairingly round to see if there were any way of disposing of *Mistresses of Majesty*, but the street-lamps were too bright and the passers-by too many. He was therefore still clutching it when he gave his name to the maid, and asked if Miss Wilmot could see him—'About Mr. Berringer,' he added, thinking that would be as likely as anything to gain her attention.

The maid came back with instructions to show him in at once. He entered a small, neatly-furnished room, and found not only a lady whom he assumed to be Miss Wilmot sitting by the window, but also a gentleman whom he knew to be Mr. Foster standing by her. He bowed gravely to them both.

'Do sit down, Mr. Durrant,' the lady said.

Anthony obeyed, and looked rather thoughtfully at Mr. Foster, whose unexpected presence he felt might hamper his style. It was no use coming as an ignorant inquirer, nor even as a perplexed seeker; he hastily re-arranged his opening.

'So very kind of you to see me, Miss Wilmot,' he began. 'I expect Mr. Foster has told you what I really came to ask. I'm very anxious to find out two things as far as I can—first, what has happened to Mr. Berringer, and secondly, what happened on Wednesday night.'

He studied Miss Wilmot as he spoke, with a feeling that she was somehow different from what he had expected. But so, he thought at the same minute, was Foster. There was something about the man that was more determined—almost more brutal—than had been before; the gaze that met his was almost fierce in its … its arrogance—that was the only word. The woman puzzled him; she was, in the queerest manner, gathered up in her chair—her eyes were half closed—her head every now and then swayed slightly. Nothing seemed to him less like what he had supposed the 'good simple' creature of Mrs. Rockbotham's eulogy would be. But she said: 'And what can *we* tell *you*, Mr. Durrant?' and he wondered if the question was, or was not, inflected with mockery.

'And why should we tell you, Mr. Durrant?' Foster said, sinking his head a little and raising his shoulders, as if the question sprang out of him with a sudden leap.

Anthony, sitting on a chair almost equidistant from both, said, 'It seems more and more to be a matter of general importance.'

'Ha!' Foster said, 'you think that now, do you?'

'I think I never denied it,' Anthony answered. 'But I'm willing to admit that I'm much more inclined to accept your hypothesis than I was.'

'Hypothesis!' Foster deeply exclaimed, and at the same time Miss Wilmot laughed, a little laugh of quiet amusement, which made Anthony move uneasily. Whatever the joke was he hadn't begun to see it. He suspected that he was the joke; well, perhaps he was. Only he said, almost sharply: 'But I believe in my own.'

'And that is?' Miss Wilmot said softly.

'I believe,' Anthony answered, looking straight at her, 'that I must try myself against these things.'

'And if they are in you how will you do it?' she asked, moving her head a little. 'Will you set yourself against yourself? For without us you could not be, and if you struggle against us what shall triumph? Are you quite sure that you have anything which we can't take away? I think though you haven't gone far in your studies, Mr. Anthony Durrant, you would be very wise to ceas-s-se.'

The last word indescribably prolonged itself in the twilight; the sound ran round the walls as if the very room were alive with sibilants. But the noise was lost in the deep voice with which Foster, momently seen more darkly as a hunched shape against the open window, said: 'Very wise.'

Anthony jumped to his feet. 'And what do you mean by that?' he said, staying himself from adding more by an interior warning against rhetoric or futility. So that, as if they waited for more, they did not for a moment answer him, and the three were suspended in expectation. As the pause lengthened Anthony felt a nervous anxiety grow in him, a longing to say something before anything could be said against him, to break into a braggadocio which would betray the weakness it pretended to hide. He bit his lip; his hands behind him drove the edge of *Mistresses of Majesty* into his back; he moved his feet farther apart to take a firmer stand. And then he met Dora Wilmot's eyes.

They were gazing at him as if they were following the helpless scurry of some escaping creature—a rabbit perhaps, and he felt the cunning of his restraint laid open to them. She knew all about him, all his ideas, his intentions, his efforts. His defiance was no subtlety but a mere silliness; his intellect acknowledged a greater power of intellect—or rather a something which passed through intellect. He felt like a student who paused before an expert, and in sheer hopelessness began to relax. The slight movement forward which Foster made escaped him; so did the other's slow raising of his hands till they came up almost level with the shoulders, and the elbows went back and the body crouched a little deeper—all this passed unseen. Anthony knew himself for a fool; he could do nothing; a cold shudder caught his ankles, his knees, and seized his whole body, till in that sudden trembling his hands opened and the book he carried fell with a thud to the floor. The shock of noise went through them all—Dora Wilmot leaned swiftly aside, Foster jerked himself back, and Anthony, violently released, brought his feet together and threw out his arms.

In that movement they were upon him. Quicker than he to recover, swifter than he to realize his escape, drawing more easily on the Powers they knew, they came at him while he still drew the first deep breath of release. The woman slid in one involved movement from the chair in which she had sat half-coiled, and from where she lay on the floor at his feet her arms went up, her hands clutching at his legs, and twisted themselves round his waist. At the same time the man sprang forward and upward, hands seizing Anthony's shoulders, head thrust forward as if in design upon his throat. Anthony was aware of their attack just before it caught him, hardly in time, yet just in time, to throw himself forward to meet it. His rising forearm struck the man's jaw with sufficient force to divert the head whose mouth champed viciously at him, but the woman's fast hold on his body prevented him from shaking himself free of the fingers that drove into his shoulders like claws. He heaved mightily forward, and drove upward again with his forearm, but their bodies were too close for him to get any force into the blow. His foot struck, stumbled, and as he freed and lifted it, trod on a rounded shape that writhed beneath it. All round him in the room were noises of hissing and snarling, and as he staggered aside in the effort to regain his footing the hot breath of one adversary panted into his face, so that it seemed to him as if he struggled in the bottom of some loathly pit where foul creatures fought for their prey. And he was their prey, unless…. He felt himself falling, and cried out; the tightening pressure round his body choked the cry in mid-utterance, and something slid yet higher round his chest. In a tumultuous conflict he crashed to the ground, but sideways, so that as he lay he was able to twist himself face downwards and save his throat. He felt his collar wrenched off and nails tearing at his neck; a twisting weight writhed over him from his shoulders downward. For a second he lay defeated, then all his spirit within him cried out 'No', and thrust itself in that single syllable from his mouth. His arms at least had been freed in his fall; he pressed his hands against the floor and with a terrific effort half raised himself. The man creature, at this abandoning its tearing at his neck, came at him again from one side. Anthony put all the energy he had left into one tremendous outward sweep of his arm, rather as if he flung a great wing sideways. He felt his enemy give before it and heard the crash that marked the collapse of an unstable balance. His own balance was barely maintained, but his hand in its swift return touched the hair of the woman's head, and caught it and fiercely pulled and wrenched till the clasping arms released their hold and for a moment his body was free. In that moment he came to his feet, and lightly as some wheeling bird turned and poised for any new attack. But his enemies lay still, their shining eyes fixed upon him, their hands scrabbling on the floor. The hissing and snarling which all this while had been in his ears ceased gradually; he became aware, as he stepped watchfully backward, of the sedate room in which that horrible struggle had gone on. He took another cautious step away, and bumped into the chair on which he had been sitting, and the jerk restored him to his ordinary self. He looked, and saw Miss Wilmot sitting, half-coiled up, on a rug, and Mr. Foster, her visitor, on one knee near to her, as if he were about to pick up a book that lay not far off. With alert eyes on them Anthony suddenly swooped and lifted it. He remembered what it was without looking.

'I was wrong,' he said aloud, and smiling, 'it's perfectly up-to-date. So sorry to be a nuisance, but I still stick to my own hypothesis. You might think it over. Goodnight, Miss Wilmot, I'll see myself out. Goodnight, Foster, give my love to the lion.'

He backed carefully to the door, opened it, slipped through, and found the maid hovering in the little hall. She gazed at him doubtfully, and he, still rather watchfully, looked back. Then he saw her expression change into entire amazement and remembered his collar.

'O sir!' she exclaimed.

'Quite,' Anthony said. 'But Ephesus, you know——'

'Ephesus, sir?' she asked, more doubtfully still, as he laid his hand on the door.

'My dear,' he said, 'I'm sorry I can't give you the reference, but your mistress will. It was where St. Paul had trouble with the wild beasts. Go and ask her. Goodnight.'

CHAPTER VIII

MARCELLUS VICTORINUS OF
BOLOGNA

In the street he hesitated. He had more or less recovered himself after the struggle, but he felt very strongly that he wasn't ready for any more of the same kind. Suppose Richardson set about him too? On the other hand he had liked Richardson's looks and he was anxious to gather *some* information. So far, what he had was emotional rather than intelligible. He didn't quite see why he should be feeling so cheerful now, but he was. He looked back at those two squatting on the floor not merely with the satisfaction of victory but with an irrational delight that found an additional glee in the small efforts he made to arrange his collar and settle his clothing. The back of his neck was smarting, and his sides were as sore as if a much greater strength than of a mature but small and slight woman had attacked him. But these things did not disturb him. He looked up and down the street and came to a quick decision.

'Come,' he said, 'let us go and see Mr. Richardson. Perhaps he'll turn into a centipede or a ladybird. Like the princess in the *Arabian Nights*. Let's hope I shall remember to tread on him if he does, though if it's anything like the butterfly I shall be simply too terrified to do anything but scramble on to a chair. I wish I could understand something of what's happening. So I do. Is this the right turning? Apparently. But what will be the end of it all?'

Defeated by this question, he was still staring at it as he came to 17 Bypath Villas. Richardson himself opened the door and took him into a kind of study, where he provided chairs, drinks, and cigarettes. Then he stood back and surveyed his visitor. Anthony spoke however before any question could be asked.

'I have', he said, 'been calling on Miss Wilmot. With her Mr. Foster.'

Richardson looked at him thoughtfully. 'Have you though?' he said. 'Which of them was responsible for the collar?'

'Foster,' Anthony answered. 'Miss Wilmot merely tried to squeeze me to death. It was a very pretty five minutes, if it was real. My body tells me it was, but my mind still rebels; what there is left to rebel.'

'I've often wondered whether something of that sort mightn't happen,' the other said, 'if we got where we were supposed to be going. However…. What did you want to ask me?'

Their friendly eyes met, and Anthony smiled a little. Then he again ran over his experiences of the past few days, but this time with more conviction. He had been driven into some kind of action, and now he spoke with the certainty that action gives, expecting yet more action and determined to shape it to his will. Richardson heard him to the end without interruption. Then——

'I suspected something of this on Wednesday night,' he said sharply. 'I suspected it again when I met Foster in the town this afternoon. But I couldn't see how it had begun. Now it's all clear. You're quite right about that, of course.'

'But why should they attack *me*?' Anthony asked. 'Or why should whatever's in them attack me?'

'I've known them for some time,' Richardson answered, 'and though it isn't my business to have more opinions than I can help about other people, still I couldn't help seeing something. They were opposite types—Foster was a strong type and Miss Wilmot a weak. But each of them wanted strength and more strength. I've seen Foster frown when anyone contradicted him, and I've seen Miss Wilmot look at her friend when *she* overruled her, and there wasn't much meekness in either of them. They wanted to get as far as they could all right, but I doubt if it was really to contemplate the principles of life. It was much more likely unconsciously to be in order to use the principles of life.'

'Meekness,' Anthony said meditatively. 'I don't know that I feel very meek myself at present. Ought I?'

'You won't get very much safety out of this effort of yours, if you go prancing about trying to beat these things by yourself,' Richardson answered sardonically. 'My good man, what notice do you suppose any of them are going to take of—I don't know your name.'

Anthony told him. 'But look here,' he said, 'you're contradicting yourself. If they took notice of Foster, why shouldn't they of me?'

'I don't think they *are* taking much notice of him,' answered the other. 'His wishes just happen to fit in with their nature. But presently their nature will overwhelm his wishes. Then we shall see. I should imagine there wouldn't be much of Foster left.'

'Well, what ought one to do? What do you want to do?' Anthony asked.

Richardson leaned forward and picked up from the table a very old bound book and a very fat exercise book. He again settled himself in his chair, and said, looking firmly at Anthony—'This is the *De Angelis* of Marcellus Victorinus of Bologna, published in the year 1514 at Paris, and dedicated to Leo X.'

'Is it?' Anthony said uncertainly.

'Berringer picked it up in Berlin—it's not complete, unfortunately—and lent it to me when he found I was interested to have a shot at translating. There's nothing to show who our Marcellus was, and the book itself, from what he says in the dedication, isn't so much his own as a version of a work by a Greek—Alexander someone—written centuries before "in the time of Your Holiness's august predecessor, Innocent the Second." In the eleven hundreds about the time of Abelard. However, that doesn't matter. What is interesting is that it seems to confirm the idea that there was another view of angels from that ordinarily accepted. Not very orthodox perhaps, but I suppose orthodoxy wasn't the first requisite at the Court of Leo.'

He paused and turned the pages. 'I think I'll read you a few extracts,' he said. 'Most of the dedication is missing; the rest is the usual magniloquence——

'"For it may rightly be said that Your Holiness both roars as a lion and rides as an eagle, bears burdens as an ox, and governs as a man, all in defence of the Apostolic and Roman Church: in this singularly uniting the qualities of those great angels, so that Your Holiness is justly"—his adverbs are all over the place—"to be called the Angel of the Church." Well we can miss that; probably Leo did. The beginning of the text is missing, but on page 17 we get down to it. You'll have to excuse the English; it amused me to do it in a kind of rhetoric—the Latin suggests it.

'"These orders then we have received from antiquity, and according to the vision of seers, who nevertheless reserved something from us, that by the devotion of our hearts and the study of the Sacred Word we might ourselves follow in their footsteps and enlarge the knowledge of those secret things which are laid up in heaven. For by such means the Master in Byzantion"—that's the Greek, of course—"expounded to us certain of the symbols and shapes whereby the Divine Celestials are expressed, but partly in riddles lest evil men work sorcery, not certainly upon those Celestials themselves—for how should the propinquity of the Serene Majesty be subject to such hellish markings and invocations?—but upon that appearance of them which, being separated from the Beatific Vision, is dragon-like flung forth into the void. As it is written: *Michael and his angels fought against the dragon and his angels, and the dragon was cast out.* Which is falsely apprehended by many of the profane vulgar, or indeed not at all, for they...."'

'Half a second,' said Anthony. 'I've a feeling for the profane vulgar. What *is* he talking about?'

'"they,"' Richardson read rapidly, '"suppose that the said dragon is himself a creation and manifest existence, and not rather the power of the Divine Ones arrogated to themselves for sinful purposes by violent men. Now this dragon which is the power of the lion is accompanied also by a ninefold order of spectres, according to the hierarchy of the composed wonders of heaven."'

'The what?' Anthony exclaimed.

'"The composed wonders of heaven,"' Richardson repeated; '"and these spectres being invoked have power upon those who adore them and transform them into their very terrible likeness, destroying them with great moanings; as they do also such as inadvisedly set themselves in the way of such powers, wandering without guide or intelligential knowledge, and being made the prey of the uncontrolled emanations."'

'Do stop a moment,' Anthony said. 'Who *are* the uncontrolled emanations?'

Richardson looked up. 'The idea seems to be that the energies of these orders can exist in separation from the intelligence which is in them in heaven; and that if deliberately or accidentally you invoke the energy without the intelligence, you're likely eventually to be pretty considerably done for.'

'O!' said Anthony. 'And the orders are the original Dionysian nine?'

'Right,' Richardson agreed. 'Well, the next few pages are mostly cursing, and the next few are about the devotion of the Eastern doctor who found it all out. Then we get a little aesthetic theory. "For albeit those who paint upon parchment or in churches or make mosaic work of precious metals have designed these holy Universals in human shape, presenting them as youths of beautiful appearance, clothed in candid vestures, and this for the indoctrination of the vulgar, who are thereby more easily brought to a humble admiration of such essences and dare to invoke them worthily under the protection of the Blessed Triune, yet it is not to be held by the wise that such human masculinities are in any way even a convenient signification of their true nature; nay, these presentations do in some sense darken the true seeker and communicate confusion, and were it not written that we should have respect to the eyes of children and cast no stone of offence in the way of little ones, it would have been better that such errors should have been forbidden by the wisdom of the Church. For what can the painting of a youth show of those Celestial Benedictions, of which the first circle is that of a lion, and the second circle is that of a serpent, and the third circle is——"

'The next eight pages are missing.'

'Damn!' Anthony said heartily. 'Doesn't he tell you anywhere else?'

'He doesn't,' Richardson said. 'When we pick him up again he has got right on to the ninth circle which is that of goodness only knows what and is attributed to the seraphim, and he dithyrambs on about the seraphim without giving any clear view of what they are or what they do or how one knows them. Then he quotes a good many texts about angels in general and becomes almost pious: the sort of thing that Erasmus might have thrown in to placate his enemies the monks. But there's a bit soon after which may interest you—here we are—"written in the Apocalypse. For though these nine zones are divided into a trinity of trinities, yet after another fashion there are four without and four within, and between them is the Glory of the Eagle. For this is he who knows both himself and the others, and is their own knowledge: as it is written *We shall know as we are known*—this is the knowledge of the Heavenly Ones in the place of the Heavenly Ones, and it is called the Virtue of the Celestials."'

He stopped and looked at Anthony. 'Tell me again,' he said, 'how did you seem to escape from the shape this afternoon?'

'As if I were in an aeropl—— O but....' Anthony stopped. Richardson went on reading——

'"As it is written *The Lord brought you out of Egypt on the back of a strong eagle*. And *To the woman were given two wings of a great eagle*." That,' he added, 'is what Marcellus Victorinus of Bologna thought was the key to the situation.' He shut the books and put them down. After a moment he added: 'Not that that's really all,' and picked them up again.

'No', said Anthony, 'don't. Tell me yourself—it'll be simpler for me, and I want to understand.'

'I can't possibly tell you,' Richardson said, 'because I don't understand it myself. Here we are—"But also the Master hid from his pupils certain things concerning the shapes and manifestations of the Celsitudes, and spoke secretly of them. For it is said that he instructed his children in the Lord how that the knowledge of them was of different kinds, and that the days of their creation within this earth were three—that is to say, the fifth, the sixth, and the seventh. And the times in which we now live are the sixth, when man has dominion over the apparitions of the Divine Universals, but there was a time before that when man was but dust in their path, so awful and so fierce were they. As it is written: *let him have dominion* but not *he has it*, and if any have no such dominion and yet seek them out he shall behold them unsubdued, aboriginal, very terrible. But the third day is the Sabbath of the Lord God, and all things have rest." Finally,' Richardson went on, 'this is his colophon—"All these things have I, Marcellus Victorinus, clerk, of the University at Bologna, gathered out of the writings which remain of all that was taught by Alexander of Byzantion, concerning the Holy Angels, their qualities and appearances. And I invoke the power and authority of the Sacred Eagle, beseeching him to cover me with his wings in the time of danger and to bear me upon his wings with joy in the place of the Heavenly Ones, and to show me the balance of all things within the gates of Justice; and I offer prayer to him for all who shall read this book, beseeching them in their turn also to offer prayer for me."'

'And how,' said Anthony after a long pause, 'does one set about finding the Sacred Eagle?'

Richardson said nothing, and after another pause Anthony went on: 'Besides, if this fellow were right, what harm would the Divine Universals do us? I mean, aren't the angels supposed to be rather gentle and helpful and all that?'

'You're doing what Marcellus warned you against,' Richardson said, 'judging them by English pictures. All nightgowns and body and a kind of flacculent sweetness. As in cemeteries, with broken bits of marble. These are Angels—not a bit the same thing. These are the principles of the tiger and the volcano and the flaming suns of space.'

'Yes,' Anthony said, 'I see. Yes. Well, to go back, what does one do about it?'

Richardson shrugged his shoulders. 'I've done all I can,' he uttered, in a more remote voice. 'I've told you what Marcellus said, what he thought was the only safe method of dealing with them. Myself, I think he was right.'

Anthony felt a sudden collapse threaten him. He leaned back in his chair; exhaustion seized on his body, and helplessness on his mind. Belief, against which he had been unconsciously struggling for days, flooded in upon him, as the sense of a great catastrophe will overtake a man who has endured it without realizing it. It was true then—the earth, the world, pleasant or unpleasant, accustomed joys, habitual troubles, was the world no longer. They, this room in which he sat, the people he knew, were all on the point of passing under a new and overwhelming dominion; change was threatening them. He thought of Tighe on his knees before his butterflies; he thought of Foster crouched back like a wild animal, and Dora Wilmot's arm twisting like a serpent under his foot; and beyond them he saw in a cloud of rushing darkness the forms of terror that ruled this new creation—the lion, the soaring butterfly, the shaking ripples of the earth that were themselves the serpent. They grew before his blinded eyes moving to a kind of supernatural measure, dancing in space, intertwining on their unknown passages. And then mightier than all, sweeping down towards him, vast wings outspread, fierce beak lowered, he saw the eagle. It passed through those other forms, and came driving directly down. They still moved in a giant pattern behind it, and then it seemed to sweep them forward within its wings. It came rushing at him; he felt his lower jaw beginning to jerk uncontrollably; his eyes were shut; his heart was swelling till it must, it must, break; he was leaning sideways over his chair. But in that moment he forced himself upright; he forced open his eyes, and saw Richardson leaning against the mantelpiece and the book of Marcellus Victorinus on the table.

'The place, I think,' Richardson was saying, 'is in Berringer's house. You either go or you don't; you either invoke or you don't; you either rule or you don't. But certainly in this present dispensation even the angelic universals were given to the authority of men. So far as man chooses. There is another way.'

———————————————

CHAPTER IX

THE FUGITIVE

Damaris had gone out for a walk, not that she wanted to, but because, as she had rather definitely told her father, it seemed the only way of getting a little peace. In general Damaris associated peace with her study, her books, and her manuscripts rather than with the sky, the hills, and the country roads; and not unjustly, since only a few devout followers of Wordsworth can in fact find more than mere quiet in the country. The absence of noise is not in all cases the same thing as the presence of peace. Wordsworth also found morality there, and no-one is ever likely to find peace without morality of one sort or another. But Damaris had never yet received any kind of impulse from either vernal or autumnal woods to teach her more of moral evil and of good than all her sages. Certainly she had found no particular impulse that way in her sages either, but that was because she was rapidly becoming incapable of recognizing a moral impulse when she saw it, the sages from Pythagoras onwards meaning something quite different from her collocation. Peace to her was not a state to be achieved but a supposed necessary condition of her daily work, and peace therefore, as often happens, evaded her continually. She ingeminated *Peace* so often and so loudly that she inevitably frightened it still farther away, peace itself being (so far as has yet been found) a loveliness only invocable by a kind of sympathetic magic and auto-hypnotism which it never occurred to her to exercise. In a convulsive patience therefore she walked firmly out of the town, and up the rising ground that lay about it.

For the last day or two the centre of gravity of her world seemed slightly to have shifted. This had begun when she had found the attention of her audience diverted on the Wednesday evening, but it had become more marked with Mr. Foster's call on Thursday, and had really shocked her with Anthony's that Saturday morning. Except that it was silly, she would almost have supposed that those two gentlemen had found her father's odd antics more important than her own conversation. They seemed to be looking past her, at some other fact on their horizon; they were preoccupied, they diffused neglect. Her father too—he had been almost patronizing once or twice, infinitely and unconsciously superior. She was liable to find him anywhere about the house or garden—doing nothing, saying nothing, looking nothing; if she spoke to him, which she often did out of mere irritable good nature, he took a moment to collect himself before he replied. She would have been prepared to make allowances for this if he had been engaged upon his butterflies—having at least an understanding of how hobbies affected people, though this particular hobby seemed to her more silly than many. But he wasn't; he just sat or stood about. It was all very well for Mr. Foster to be so profoundly interested—Mr. Foster didn't have to live with him. As for Anthony——

She walked a little faster. Anthony's call had been at a stupid time to begin with, but its purpose—which really did seem to have been to see her father—made it wholly stupid in itself. What *could* Anthony at half-past eleven on Saturday morning want with her father? It annoyed her that she had to take a little care in dealing with Anthony—he was so persistently attached and yet at the same time apt to become troublesomely detached. She disliked the slight feeling of anxiety she had about him—of late she found herself occasionally wondering after each visit whether, when he had gone, he had gone for good. And there was at present simply no other convenient way of getting some of her articles into print. They were good articles of their kind—she and Anthony both knew that—only there weren't very many papers that would care for them. And it did—she half angrily admitted—it did help her, please, encourage, whatever the right word was, to see her name printed at the top of a column. It was a mark and reward of work done and a promise of work and reward to be. It was, in short, an objectivization of Miss Tighe to a point elsewhere at present unobtainable. Probably, though she did not think of this, Abelard, *mutatis mutandis*, felt a similar satisfaction at his lectures, with perhaps less danger owing to the watch that his confessor would have expected Abelard to keep over his conscience.

However, here she was away from them, and a good thing too. For this business of the relation of the Divine Perfection with creation was giving her, as it had given the schoolmen, a little trouble. Plato's Absolute Beauty, she quite saw, was all right because that was not necessarily conscious of the world; but the God of Abelard *was* conscious of the world, and yet that consciousness must not be necessary to Him, for nothing but Himself could be necessary to Him. St. Thomas—only he was later; she didn't want to bring him in, still a short appendix perhaps, bringing the history of the idea up to St. Thomas … just to show that she had read well beyond her subject…. St. Thomas would be a good stopping-place, and she might reasonably not pursue it further. Perhaps the whole thing had better be in an appendix—*On the Knowledge of the World* … no, on *God's Idea of the World from Plato to Aquinas*. Something was wrong with that title, she thought vaguely, but she could alter it presently. The main thing at the moment was to get clear in her mind the various methods by which God was said to know the world. John the Scot had taught that the account of the Creation in Genesis—'let the earth bring forth the living creature after his kind'—referred, not to the making of the earthly animals, but to the formation of the kinds and orders in the Divine Mind before they took on visible and material shapes. Well, now….

She saw on her left a stile, mounted it, sat down, took out her notes on the problem, and set to work on them. Half an hour went by quite pleasantly. At the end of that time she was suddenly startled by hearing a low voice behind her say, 'You oughtn't to be sitting there.'

She twisted round and looked down. From the overgrowth which hid the ditch by the side of the road a head was half-pushed out; two anxious eyes gazed at her. She looked back in mere amazement; the face was that of a young man of her own class; it grew familiar as she stared, and in a minute or two she recognized it. It was a friend of Anthony's who had once or twice been at her house along with her cousin—a Mr. … a Mr. Sabot, of course. But even Damaris's capacity was shocked into helplessness by seeing Mr. Sabot apparently crawling in a rather deep ditch. She sat with her mouth slightly open, her head twisted over her shoulder, still staring.

'I say you oughtn't to be there,' Sabot said more urgently. 'Why don't you hide?'

'Hide?' Damaris repeated.

'It hasn't been here yet,' he whispered loudly. 'Get down before it comes. The only thing is to keep out of sight.'

Damaris got down from the stile, and a final exasperation shook her. She took a step nearer and said sharply: 'What are you doing, Mr. Sabot?'

He thrust himself a little higher and stared carefully all round; then he answered, still in a loud whisper, 'Keeping out of its way.'

'Out of what's way?' Damaris asked irritably. 'Can't you get up and talk sensibly? Come, Mr. Sabot, tell me what you mean at once.'

But with a quick viciousness he snarled at her. 'Don't be such a bloody fool. Get in somewhere. Not here; there's not room for two. Run up the road a bit and make yourself a hole.'

Damaris gaped. This last exclamation of unreason overcame her. It seemed that Mr. Sabot must be completely mad; in which case it was extremely unfair of Anthony not to have told her. Why wasn't Anthony with him? Imagine her being subjected to this sort of thing! She thought of various things to say to Anthony, but they were no good at the moment. He raised himself yet a little higher and caught hold of her skirt.

'I'm trying to help you,' he went on whispering. 'Aren't you Anthony's girl——'

'Certainly not,' Damaris said. 'Let me go, Mr. Sabot. O this is too much!'

'—I knew you when you sat down, but I had to look to see if it was coming. It's been after me, only I dodged it over there and got away. Or perhaps it hasn't come as far, but it will. It'll hunt you too. Not Anthony; Anthony's going to fight it, but you and I can't do that, we're not brave enough. I shouldn't have let you see me, only you're Anthony's girl. Don't stand so high; crouch down a bit.'

'I am *not* Anthony's girl, and I won't crouch down,' Damaris, now utterly furious, cried out. Her stick was out of her reach; she moved one foot back. 'If you don't let me go I'll kick your face. I mean it.'

'No, no,' the other said, 'listen—I tell you you're not safe. It's sure to be along here, but if you crawl along the ditch you may get out of its reach somewhere first. It's too big to get into the ditch. If only it doesn't tread on us!' He began to shake all over with an increasing fear.

'I'm going to kick you,' Damaris cried, paused a moment, jerking her skirt in an effort to free it, and then, failing, kicked. But it was so small a kick, since she was anxious not to lose her balance, that it came considerably short of the white face in the bracken. The hand that held her pulled violently sideways; she staggered, was jerked again, toppled, and came heavily down on her side, lying half in and half out of the ditch against the bank. She was so bruised and shaken that she couldn't, for all her rage, immediately get her breath, and as she lay, the mouth of the hidden man, now not far from her own, went on mouthing its disgusting whispers.

'That's better,' it said, 'a little lower, and you'll be safer still. You ought to be farther away; I wouldn't have you with me if you weren't Anthony's girl. But now you are here get right down and we'll pull the bracken over. Have you heard it yet? They say it was roaring at first, but it's been quite quiet to-day. It goes round in a circle, you know; at least part of it does—the other part's looking for me. Only I got out of the circle. We must try and keep out; we're pretty safe then. Have you felt the earth shake? I'm rather afraid in case that heaves us right up under its paws. Come in, can't you? I swear I'll leave you to it if you don't—only Anthony said he'd promised to help you get your degree and I should like to please Anthony. Come in, blast you! I'm not going to be hunted for you.'

What nightmare this could be Damaris didn't know. She was struggling and wrestling with the horrible creature, who was grabbing and pulling her farther down into the ditch. As she fought with him she screamed for help. At the sound he stopped pulling at her, and, still holding tight, listened. For a minute there was no sound, then as if in answer there came to them the noise of that remote thunder. At this Quentin giving gasps of terror let her go, even tried to push her away, then desisted and himself burrowed still deeper—'I knew it, I knew it,' he babbled softly. 'O God! O God! Get away, you bitch! O you've told it.' He had almost disappeared and she heard the soft frenzied mutterings coming up to her for a moment before they died away, as the shaking fronds showed where below them he was trying to wriggle and push himself along the ditch. Damaris, with an almost equal violence of movement, scrambled out of it, and up again to her stile, where, stick in hand, she turned.

But there was no sign of his following her, and round the bend of the hedge she could not see him or his trail. Panting and horrified she leant against the stile. All her earlier irritations were swallowed up in her furious anger; she wanted to kill. All the indifferences, the negligences, the inattentions, that she had felt as insults ached almost physically in her. Her acquaintances, her father, Anthony—O to tear, to trample them. O this world of imbeciles! Her eyes caught the papers of her notes which had fallen from her hands and she bent, watchfully, to pick them up, then she went back to the stile and glanced across it. As she did so, she felt her footing uncertain; the earth seemed to rock and subside and rise under her. Could she be going to faint? Shutting her eyes she sat down on the step of the stile, and even that seemed to be swaying gently. For some few moments the apparent movement went through her, then it gently ceased. Slowly she opened her eyes, slowly stood up, and leaned against the top bar to recover herself fully. Far off in the sky she saw a winged shape, a bird of sorts—very large it must be, she thought indolently, to be visible, so high as it seemed, and seemed huge even to her. But it flew off or she lost sight of it, and, with a deep breath or two, she pulled and settled her clothing into order, and, crossing the road, took another footpath back to the town, where for the rest of the day she concentrated, even more fiercely than usual, on her work.

Yet her night was disturbed: not merely by the less frequent but still recurring thunder, but by a trouble within. The seclusion in which, more or less successfully, she attempted to live, was so arranged that she was normally ignorant of its conditions. The habitual disposition towards unrighteousness which it involved was at best defended, at worst unnoticed. It was very rarely that her omissions were crystallized in a commission which by that very rarity became noticeable, and as she turned and shifted, and dozed and woke, she found herself accused wherever her thoughts fled by the distracted face in the bracken. It looked towards her and from the mouth she heard the phrases with which she was acquainted: the long wrangles of the early scholastics about universals, a sentence or two from Augustine, a statement from Porphyry … it was Quentin Sabot who uttered them. A couple of lines from one of Abelard's own hymns especially rang in her ears as such things will.

in re verit
on in sche

until her maddened mind produced (incorrectly) as a translation:

h is always in th

377

Quentin's face went on looking at her and repeating this couplet until she could have cried with weariness and misery.

For she was miserable; also she was afraid. She wasn't—no, she certainly wasn't Anthony's girl, but he was Anthony's friend. And if her relations with Anthony had any truth at all, then she was committed to at least such an amount of care for Anthony's wishes as he would have given to hers. For any mightier gift, for any understanding of that state in which she might profoundly and nobly love merely because opportunity for love was offered, she was not asked. She had taken—she knew she had taken, and she had, even by that measure, failed. She produced excuses, reasons, apologies even, and then as she argued there was that distracted face again, and from the distracted mouth came the singing doggerel:

'h is always in th

in the ...

Est in re veritas—but that was all about religion and metaphysics; it was from a hymn for Lauds on Sunday. What had it to do with Quentin Sabot in a ditch? Anthony would be angry with her? Anthony had no right … Anthony couldn't expect … Anthony oughtn't to demand…. All that was very well, but she realized that it hadn't much to do with Anthony. He might not demand or expect or claim, but he would undoubtedly *be*. *Est in re veritas*—O damn, damn!

She ought to be superior to all that. What was the phrase in the *Phaedrus*?—'the soul of the philosopher alone has wings.' She ought to be rising above … above helping anyone in a ditch, above speaking in goodwill to the friend of her friend, above trying to bring peace to the face that now pursued her.—No, she ought, in fairness to Anthony, to have done something. 'I was wrong,' she said, almost irritably, and with a fierce determination not to admit it to Anthony.

She met him therefore when the next morning—Sunday morning of all times—he appeared again, with a destructive fire. As he had been preparing every kind of flag of truce as he came along, under cover of which his diplomacy was to attempt her removal to London, this at first threw him into complete disorder, more especially as he could not for the moment understand what had provoked this fresh battle. She was asking, he at last made out, why he didn't look after his friend better, and at that he broke through her talk.

'Have you seen him then?' he asked sharply. 'Where? when? No, don't chatter; tell me.'

Damaris told him—in general terms. 'It was an extraordinarily unpleasant time,' she said. 'I do think, Anthony, you oughtn't to have let him go off by himself, if that's the state he's in.'

Anthony looked at her, and then took a turn through the room. Before his eyes, as he looked, she had seemed to change; the thought of Quentin, cast off, kicked at, by her outraged anger, hurt him profoundly, and the sombre eyes with which he surveyed her saw a different and nastier Damaris. Yet he had known it all along—only that she should treat him as she did was part of the joke of things, that she should treat Quentin so seemed somehow so much worse. But of course it wasn't worse; it was the same Damaris. Those whom he loved were at war. But Love itself wasn't and couldn't be at war. He loved her, and she had persecuted his friend. But he loved them both, and therefore there was no taking of sides. Love itself never could take sides. His heart ached in him, but as he came back to her his eyes were smiling, even though his face had been struck by pain.

'*O quanta qualia*,' he murmured, pausing near her. 'Those something sabbaths the blessed ones see. Dearest, you'll be like the fellow in the New Testament; you'll meet Abelard one day and he'll stare at you and say he never knew you. I suppose you know you've been a pig.'

'Don't talk to me like that,' Damaris said, and in the contention of emotions within her added absurdly, 'It was a great shock to me.'

'You've got a worse shock than that coming to you,' he answered.

'Why do you always talk as if I didn't know anything?' she asked, opening another attack on more favourable ground; and added, to distract him still further, 'And then you expect me to marry you.'

'I don't expect anything at all,' he said, 'not from anybody. Least of all from you. If you were going to marry me, if you weren't shut up, I should have knocked your damn silly head off your shoulders. But as it is—no. Only the sooner you leave off expecting, the better you're likely to be. Will you come to London?'

Damaris almost gaped, the question was so sudden. 'Will I—will I what?' she exclaimed. 'Why on earth should I go to London?'

'Quentin—God's mercy save him now!—offered you a hole in a ditch … I offer you London,' Anthony said. 'The reason is that the princes of heaven are in the world and you're not used to them. No, stop a minute, and let me tell you. In your own language, you owe me that.'

He paused to choose his words. 'Something has driven Quentin into panic and hiding; something has turned your father away from his hobby to inaction and contemplation; something frightened you all at Berringer's house the other night; something has obsessed Foster and your friend Miss Wilmot till they attacked me yesterday evening; yes, they did—I am not mad, most noble Festa; something is sounding in the world like thunder——'

'Attacked you! What nonsense!' Damaris cried.

'—and you can stop and meet it if you choose. Or you can come to London for a few days' grace at least.'

'If this is a joke——' she began.

'If it is,' he answered, 'all your philosophers and schoolmen were mad together. And your life's work is no more than the comparison of different scribblings in the cells of a lunatic asylum.'

She stood up, staring at him. 'If this is your way of getting back on me,' she said, 'because I didn't do what you think I ought to for your insane friend——'

'What I think is of no matter,' he answered. 'Have I pretended it was? It's the thing that matters: the truth is in the thing. Heart's dearest, listen—the things you study are true, and the philosophers you read knew it. The universals are abroad in the world, and what are you going to do about it? Besides write about them.'

'Do you seriously mean to tell me?' she said, 'that Power is walking about on the earth? Just Power?'

'Yes,' he answered, and though she added before she could stop herself, 'Don't you even know what a philosophic universal is?' he said no more. For his energy sank within, carrying her, presenting, agonizing for her, holding the Divine Eagle by the wings that its perfect balance might redeem them, holding both her and Quentin in his own thought that they all might live together in the strong and lovely knowledge which was philosophy. So that he did not notice at first that she was saying coldly. 'Perhaps you'd better go now.'

When this penetrated his mind, he made a last effort. 'But the things I just spoke of—at least they're true,' he said. 'Your father *has* given up butterflies; you *were* startled; Quentin *has* been driven almost mad. What do you suppose did it? Come away for a day or two—just till we can find out. Ah do! If'—he hesitated—'if you'—he compelled himself to go on—'if you owe me anything, do this to please me.'

Damaris paused. She did not know that one of the crises of her life had arrived, nor did she recognize in its full deceptiveness the temptation that rose in her. But she paused uncertain whether to pretend that in effect she did not owe him anything, or to admit that she did. On the very point of taking hypocritical refuge in the fact that her papers were good papers she paused, and merely answered instead: 'I don't see any reason to go to London, thank you.' She was to see that cold angry phrase as the beginning of her salvation.

He shrugged and was silent. He couldn't go on appealing; he could not yet compel. He couldn't think of anything more to do or say, yet he hated to leave her. He wondered what Marcellus Victorinus would have done in this quandary. Rockbotham would be expecting him soon....

Well, that way was the only one that lay open; he would take that way. He couldn't quite see what was to be gained by looking at the adept, but that possibility—and no other—had been presented to him. He would go. He gave his hand to Damaris.

'Goodbye, then,' he said. 'Don't be too angry with me—not for a week anyhow. After that....'

'I don't understand you a bit,' she said, and then made a handsome concession—after all, she *did* owe him something, and he *was* upset over Quentin—'but I think you're trying to be kind.... I'm sorry about your friend—perhaps if it hadn't been so sudden.... You see, I was preoccupied with that bothering business of the Divine Perfection.... Anthony, you're hurting my hand!'

'I understand that it can be a trouble,' he said. 'O Almighty Christ! Goodbye. We may meet at Philippi yet.' And then he went.

CHAPTER X

THE PIT IN THE HOUSE

The conversation between Anthony and Dr. Rockbotham in the car on the way to Berringer's house was of the politest and chattiest kind, interspersed with moments of seriousness. They began by discussing the curious meteorological conditions, agreeing that such frequent repetitions of thunder without lightning or rain were very unusual.

'Some kind of electrical nucleus, I suppose,' the doctor said, 'though why the discharge should be audible but not visible, I don't know.'

'I noticed it when I was down on Thursday,' Anthony remarked, 'and again yesterday. It seems to be louder when we get out of the town; inside it's much less.'

'Deadened by the ordinary noises, I expect,' the doctor said, 'Very upsetting for some of my patients—the nervous ones, you know. Even quite steady people are affected in the funniest way sometimes. Now my wife, for instance,—nobody less nervous than she is, you'll agree—yet when she came in this morning—there's an old servant of ours she generally calls on every Sunday morning when it's fine and she's not busy—she had an extraordinary tale of a kind of small earthquake.'

'Earthquake!' Anthony exclaimed.

'She declared the ground shifted under her,' the doctor went on. 'She was crossing the allotments just round by the railway bridge at the time, and she very nearly fell on a lot of cabbages; in fact she did stumble among them—rather hurt her foot, which was how it cropped up. Of course I wouldn't say there couldn't have been a slight shock, but I was about the town at the time, and I didn't notice anything. You didn't either, I suppose?'

'Nothing at all,' Anthony said.

'No, I thought not,' the doctor said. 'The heat too—do you feel it? It's going to be a very trying summer.'

Anthony, lying back in the car, with a grim look on his face, said, 'It is going to be a very trying summer.'

'You don't like this heat?' the doctor asked. And 'I don't like *this* heat,' Anthony with perfect truth replied.

'Well, we don't all of us. I don't mind it myself,' the doctor said. 'It's the winter I don't care for. A doctor's life, you know; all sorts of weather and all sorts of people. Especially the people; I sometimes say I'd as soon be doctor to a zoo.'

'Talking of zoos, did they ever catch the lioness that got loose round here the other day?' Anthony asked.

'Now that was a funny thing,' the other answered. 'We heard all sorts of rumours on the Tuesday night, but there's been no more news. They think it must have gone in the other direction and they've been following it that way, I believe. Of course people are a bit shy of coming out of the town by night, but that's sheer funk. These imprisoned creatures are very timorous, you know. Supposing there ever *was* a lioness at all. The show itself moved on the next day, and when I saw the Chief Inspector on Friday he was inclined to laugh at the idea.'

'Was he?' Anthony said. 'He must be a brave man.'

'As I said to him,' the doctor went on, 'I'd rather laugh at the idea than the thing. So would anybody, I expect.'

He paused, but Anthony had no wish to answer. He felt a constriction at his heart as he listened; 'the idea' meant to him a spasm of fear, and he was aware that he existed unhappily between two states of knowledge, between the world around him, the pleasant ordinary world in which one laughed at or discussed ideas, and a looming unseen world where ideas—or something, something living and terrible, passed on its own business, overthrowing minds, wrecking lives, and scattering destruction as it went. There already was the house, silent and secret, in which perhaps potentialities beyond all knowledge waited or shaped themselves. Need he get out of the car—as he was doing? open the gate—enter the garden? Couldn't he get back now, on some excuse or none, before the door opened and they had to go in to where that old man, as he remembered him, lay in his terrible passivity? What new monstrosity, what beast of indescribable might or beauty, was even now perhaps dragging itself down the stairs? What behemoth would come lumbering through the hall?

Actually the only behemoth, and though she was fat she was hardly that, was the housekeeper. She let them in, she conversed with the doctor; she ushered them up the stairs, to where at the top the male nurse waited. Anthony followed, and, his heart full of Quentin and Damaris, aspired to that knowledge which should give them both security and peace. He remembered the sentences over which he had brooded half the night. 'The first circle is of the lion; the second circle is of the serpent; the third circle—' O what, what was the third? what sinister fate centuries ago had so mutilated that volume of angelical lore as to forbid his discovery now? 'The wings of an eagle'—well, if that was what was needed, then, so far as he could, he would enter into that circle of the eagle which was the—what had the sentence said?—'The knowledge of the Celestials in the place of the Celestials.'

'And God help us all,' he added to himself, as he came into the bedroom.

He stood aside while the doctor, leaning over the bed, made his examination. There had, the nurse's report told them, been no change; still silent and motionless the adept lay before them. Anthony walked over to the bed while the doctor spoke to the nurse, and looked at the body. The eyes were open but unseeing; he gazed into them, and went on gazing. Here perhaps, could he reach it, the secret lay; he leaned closer, seeking half-unconsciously, to penetrate it. For a moment he could have fancied that they flickered into life, but not common life; that a dangerous vitality threatened him. Threaten? he leaned nearer again—'the knowledge of

380

the Celestials in the place of the Celestials.' Quentin—Damaris. He could not avoid the challenge that had momently gleamed from those eyes; it had vanished, but he intensely expected its return. He forgot the doctor; he forgot Berringer; he forgot everything but those open unresponsive eyes in which lurked the presage of defeat or victory. What moved, what gleamed, what shone at him there? What was opening?

'Quite comatose, poor fellow!' a voice close by him gibbered suddenly.

'Er—yes,' said Anthony, and pulled himself upright. He could have sworn that the slightest film passed over the eyes, and reluctantly he turned his own away. But they were dazzled with the strain; he could not see the room very clearly; there seemed to be dark openings everywhere—the top of the jug on the washstand, the mirror of the dressing-table, the black handle of the grey painted door, all these were holes in things, entrances and exits perhaps, like rabbit holes in a bank from which something might rapidly issue. He heard the dull voice say again: 'Shall we go downstairs?' and found himself walking cautiously across the room. As he came near the door he couldn't resist a backward glance—and the head had turned surely, and the eyes were watching him? No—it was still quiet on the pillow, but over beyond it the dressing-table mirror showed an oval blackness. He looked at it steadily, then he became aware that he was standing by the door right in the doctor's way; with a murmur of apology he seized the handle and opened it.

'It makes it so awkward,' Dr. Rockbotham said, passing through, with a little bow of acknowledgement, 'when there is no easy way of——'

Anthony followed, shutting the door after him, and as he turned to step along the landing, found that he stood on a landing indeed but no more that of the simple house into which he had so recently come. It was a ledge rather than a landing, and though below him he saw the shadowy forms of staircase and hall, yet below him and below these there fell great cliffs, bottomless, or having the bottom hidden by flooding darkness. He was standing above a vast pit, the walls of which swept away from him on either side till they closed again opposite him, and some sort of huge circle was complete. He looked down with—he was vaguely aware—a surprising freedom from fear; and presently he turned his eyes upward, half-expecting to see that same great wall extending incalculably high above his head. So indeed it did, but there was a difference, for above it leaned outward, and far away he saw a cloudy white circle of what seemed the sky. He would have known it for the sky only that it was in motion; it was continually passing into the wall of the abyss, so that a pale vibration was for ever surging in and around and down those cliffs, as if a steady landslide slipped ever downwards in waves of movement, which at last were lost to sight somewhere in the darkness below. He half put his hand out to touch the wall behind him and then desisted, for such effort would assuredly be vain. It was to the distance and the space that his attention was invited—more, he began to feel, than his attention, even his will and his action. The persistent faint shadow of the staircase distracted him; it hung on the side of the pit and the hall to which it led seemed to be part of the cliff. But he didn't want to look at that—his awaking concentration passed deeper, expecting something, waiting for something, perhaps that wind which he felt beginning to blow. It was very gentle at first, and it was blowing round him and outwards, forcing him, as it grew stronger, towards the brink of the ledge. There came upon him an impulse to resist, to press back, to cling to his footing on this tiny break in the smooth sweep of the cliff, to preserve himself in his own niche of safety. But as still that strength increased, he would not yield to such a desire; a greater thing than that was possible—it was for him to know, urgently for him to know, what that other thing might be. He was standing on the very edge, and the wind was rising into driving might, and a dizziness caught him; he could not resist—why then, to yield, to throw himself outward on the strength that was driving through him as well as around him, to be one with that power, to be blown on it and yet to be part of it—nothing could oppose or bear up against it and him in it. Yet on the edge he pressed himself back; not so, not so, was his passage to be achieved—it was for him to rise above that strength of wind; whether he went down or up it must be by great volition, and it was for such volition that he sought within him. But as he steadied himself there slid a doubt into his mind; what and how could he will? He was thinking faster than he had ever done, and questions rose out of nothing and followed each other—what was *to will*? Will was determination to choose—what was choice? How could there be choice, unless there was preference, and if there was preference there was no choice, for it was not possible to choose against that preferring nature which was his being? yet being consisted in choice, for only by taking and doing this and not that could being know itself, could it indeed be; to be then consisted precisely in making an inevitable choice, and all that was left was to know the choice, yet even then was the chosen thing the same as the nature that chose, and if not.... So swiftly the questions followed each other that he seemed to be standing in flashing coils of subtlety, an infinite ring of vivid intellect and more than intellect, for these questions were not of the mind alone but absorbed into themselves physical passion and twined through all his nature on an unceasing and serpentine journey.

And still all round the walls of the abyss that shaking landslide went on, veiling the dark background with waves of moving pallor within it, and faint colour grew in dark and light, and immense ripples shook themselves down or up, and swifter and swifter those coils of enormous movement went by. By a violent action of the will he questioned, Anthony again drew himself back both from safety and from abandonment, and paused in expectation of what new danger should arise.

His eyes went upward and beheld the sky, and against that sky, as if descending from an immense distance within it, came a winged form. High at first and lifted up, it came down in lessening spirals, until it hovered in mid-air opposite him, and then drove towards the other side of the abyss, and came round again, and hovered, facing him. It was a giant of the eagle kind; and its eyes, even from that remote distance, burned at him with so piercing a gaze that he shut his own and stepped back against the wall behind him. He had heard of drowning men who had seen their whole life in the instant before death, and in a like simultaneous presentation he was aware of his own: of innumerable actions—many foolish, some evil; many beautiful, some holy. And as if he read the history of another soul he saw running through all the passionate desire for intellectual and spiritual truth and honesty, saw it often blinded and thwarted, often denied and outraged, but always it rose again and soared in his spirit, itself like an eagle, and always he followed it in the way that it and he had gone together. The sight of his denials burned through him: his whole being grew one fiery shame, and while he endured to know even this because things were so and not otherwise, because to refuse to know himself as he was would have been a final outrage, a last attempt at flight from the Power that challenged him and in consequence an entire destruction by it—while he endured, the fire fell away from him and he himself was mysteriously rushing over the abyss. He was riding in the void, flying without wings, securely existing by movement and balance among the dangers of that other world. He was poised in a vibration of peace, carried within some auguster passage. The myriad passage of the butterflies recurred to his consciousness, and with an inrush of surpassing happiness he knew that he was himself offering himself to the state he had so long desired. Triumphant over the twin guardians of that place of realities, escaped from the lion and the serpent, he grew into his proper office, and felt the flickers of prophecy pass through him, of the things of knowledge that were to be. Borne now between the rush of gigantic wings he went upward and again swept down; and the cliffs of the abyss had vanished, for he moved now amid sudden shapes and looming powers. Patterned upon the darkness he saw the forms—the strength of the lion and the subtlety of the crowned serpent, and the loveliness of the butterfly and the swiftness of the horse—and other shapes whose meaning he did not understand. They were there only as he passed, hints and expressions of lasting things, but not by such mortal types did the Divine Ones exist in their own blessedness. He knew, and submitted; this world was not yet open to him, nor was his service upon earth completed. And as he adored those beautiful, serene, and terrible manifestations, they vanished from around him. He was no more in movement; he was standing again on his ledge; a rush of mighty wings went outward from him, and the darkness of the walls in which it was lost swept towards him on all sides. A noise of hollow echoes came to him, and he was aware of his own limbs making abrupt and jerky movements. He saw a barrier by him, and laid his hand on it in the dizziness that attacked him. This passed and he came to himself.

'—discovering where his relations live—if any,' Dr. Rockbotham said, shaking his head, and beginning the descent of the stairs.

'Quite,' said Anthony, following him slowly down and into one of the rooms on the ground floor. He wasn't sorry to sit down; the doctor meanwhile wandering round rather restlessly. He was saying something but Anthony was incapable of knowing what, or what his own voice at intervals said in answer. What on earth had happened on the landing? Had he fainted? Surely not, or the doctor would have noticed it—people generally did notice when other people fainted. But he felt very breathless, and yet quite keen. Damaris—something or other was necessary for Damaris. No hurry; it would be clear soon what he was to do. Quentin too—if Quentin had only held out, he would be safe yet. And then the end.

Apparently during this settling of his inner faculties he had been saying the right things, for the doctor was now standing at the French windows looking quite satisfied.

'Very good,' Anthony said, and stood up.

'Yes,' Dr. Rockbotham answered, 'I think that'll be best. After all, as things are, there's no immediate hurry.'

'None at all,' Anthony agreed, and rather wondered why. It was certain that there wasn't, not for whatever Rockbotham was talking about; the things about which there was, if not hurry, at least a necessity for speed, were quite other. But for a knowledge of them he must wait on the Immortals.

'Well, shall we go?' the doctor said, and they began to move towards the door. As Anthony stood up however his eyes caught—he paused to look and it had gone—a sudden point of flame flickering in a corner of the ceiling. He stepped forward, his eyes still fixed on the spot, and again he saw a little rapid tongue of fire burn down the whole corner of the room from ceiling to floor. It swept down and vanished, and he saw the wallpaper unsinged behind it. He shifted his gaze, glancing round the room, as he took in the floor he saw another flame spring up all round his foot as he put it down, and then that also was gone. The doctor, just in front of him, was passing through the doorway, and as he did so a thin line of fire flamed along doorposts and lintel so that Rockbotham stood for a moment in an arch of fire; he went on, and it had disappeared. Anthony followed him into the hall; there also as he went the sudden little flames peered out and vanished—one curled momently round the umbrella-stand, one spread itself in a light glow over the lid of a huge chest that stood there, one broke in a rosy flower of fire right in the middle of the wall and then folded itself up and faded. Anthony caught up with the doctor, and opened his lips to speak, but before he could do so a sudden sharp pain struck into his side, near his heart, as if the beak of a great bird had wounded him. He gasped involuntarily, and the doctor looked round.

'Did you speak?' he asked.

Down the open doorway in front, where the housekeeper was holding the door for them, fell a rain of fiery sparks, and then a curtain of leaping flames, pointing upward and falling downward, as if some burning thing had been dropped. The housekeeper was looking through it at the garden; the pain stabbed again at Anthony's heart. He shook his head with an articulate murmur, as the doctor nodded goodbye to the woman, and as Anthony, silent, followed his example, the sharp injury ceased, and a throb of relief and content took its place. In the virtue of that healing silence he got into the car and sat down.

'The thunder's still sounding,' the doctor said as they started.

'Is it?' Anthony said. It did not strike him as particularly curious that he could not hear it, though with a certain amusement he reflected that if the servants of the Immortals were blind and deaf to the sights and sounds ordinary people noticed it might be slightly inconvenient. Perhaps that, in the past, was why so many of them came to violent and painful ends. But the thunder—which was not thunder, he knew, but the utterance of the guardian of the angelical world—he certainly could not hear. He almost felt as if he might if he gave his whole attention to it, but why give his whole attention to it, unless it would please anyone very much? And he didn't think Dr. Rockbotham was interested enough to want that.

During the ride he looked at the country. Things were not yet clear to him; but communication was going on within him. As they ran past the first few scattered houses of the town, he thought he saw once more the shape of the lion, but he noticed it with awe certainly but now with no fear. The strength that had once overthrown him had now no power upon him; he was within it, and under the protection of another of the great Ideas, that Wisdom which knew the rest and itself also, the very tradition of the Ideas and the Angelicals being but a feather dropped from its everlasting and effectual wing.

Dr. Rockbotham said: 'Did you happen to try and lift his hand?'

'No,' Anthony said.

'Curious, very curious,' the doctor ran on. 'It's almost impossible, so heavy, so impossible to move. I've never known a case quite like this. If there's no change to-morrow I shall certainly get another opinion.'

How could one move the gate of the universals? pull up the columns through which they passed? But Rockbotham was a good man; he was serving to the best of his power, innocent, devoted, mild, surrendered to the intention of some one of these Authorities which had yet not become manifest. He would go safely among these outer wonders until the place of goodness was reached, and then—if that assumption were still proceeding—be gently received into his ruling Idea. Happy were those who found so simple and easy a passing! For others, for those who were given up to the dragon and not to the angel, it might be a more difficult way. From such destruction at least he believed Damaris to be, by her very ignorance and unmalicious childishness, secure.

He refused an invitation to lunch, parted from his companion at the door of his hotel, and after a solitary meal went to his room, and there fell asleep. He slept without disturbance and without dreams till late in the evening, and woke at peace. In the same inner quiet he rose, changed, and set out for Richardson's. What took him there he could hardly tell, and did not indeed trouble to inquire. In that profound sleep something seemed to have been lost; the little goblin of self-consciousness which always, deride it as he would, and derision in fact only nourished and magnified it, danced a saraband in his mind—that goblin had faded and was gone. He moved, though he did not know it, with a new simplicity, and his very walk through the streets had in it a quality of intention which it had never before possessed. He rang in the same way, with no doubt whether Richardson was at home; if Richardson had not been at home he would not have been there, he knew. When he was admitted he shook hands with a joyous smile.

Richardson, when they were settled, sat back and studied him. Anthony, at amused leisure, noticed this and waited for the other to speak.

At last—'You're there then?' Richardson said.

'There?' Anthony asked. 'If you mean the house, I've been there.'

'Do you know how bright your eyes are?' the other irrelevantly asked.

Anthony broke into a laugh, the first time he had laughed wholeheartedly for several days. 'Well, that's jolly!' he said. 'I hope they'll impress Damaris that way.' But he offered no explanation of the name and Richardson courteously ignored it. Instead, he said, thoughtfully, 'So you've been to the house? And what do you know of things now?'

Anthony found himself a little unwilling to speak, not because he mistrusted Richardson, but because to recount his own experience would take them no farther. It was no use saying to another soul, 'I did—I saw—I was—this, that, or the other,' because what applied to him couldn't apply to anyone else, not to anyone else at all in the whole community of mankind. Some more general, some ceremonial utterance was needed. Now, if ever, he needed the ritual of words arranged and shaped for that end. He saw the *De Angelis* on the table, leaned forward, and picked it up, looking over at Richardson as he did so.

'How can *I* tell you?' he said. 'We don't know Victorinus; let's see if he can be the mouthpiece of the gods. Shall I?'

'Do as you like,' the other answered. 'Perhaps you're right; if the symbols are there ready why bother to make fresh?'

Anthony considered this for a few seconds, as if it held some meaning of which he was uncertain. But presently he opened the book, and slowly turned the pages, reading aloud a sentence here and there, and translating as he read. To a certain extent he had always kept up his own Latin, but it was not merely that knowledge which now enabled him to understand so easily the antique habit of that tongue; his perseverance did but open the way to a larger certainty.

'"As it is written *Where wast thou when I laid the foundations of the world?* and this is the place of the foundations, out of which there arise all kinds of men compact of powers; and therefore was it that when the Lord would rebuke Job he demanded of him concerning the said foundations, saying *Doth the eagle mount up at thy command?* and *She dwelleth on the crag of the rock and the strong place.*"…

'"But the names that are given are of one kind, as when it is said among the wise that there is strength or beauty, or humility, meaning that certain men are strong or beautiful or humble, which certain heretics wrenched to their destruction, saying that these names were no more than words used for many like things and had in themselves no meaning; and the shapes which are seen are of another, as the lion and the eagle and the unicorn and the lamb…. Nor is either made sufficient, but as a foreknowledge of the revelation that shall be."…

'"Also they have power in death, and woe unto him that is given up to them and torn aside between them, having no authority over the Mighty Ones because he is cast out from salvation and hath never governed them in himself"….

'"For there is a mystery of the earth and the air, and of the water and the air, and the Divine Ones manifest themselves in both according to their natures; so that the circle of the lion is that of leviathan, and of the others accordingly: as it is written *There is one flesh of beasts and another of fish*: and *They that go down to the sea in ships these see the works of the Lord and his wonders in the great deep….*"'

Anthony stopped reading, and Richardson said briefly: 'But there is something beyond them all.'

'It may be,' the other said, 'and that I suppose we shall discover in time. Meanwhile——'

'There is no meanwhile at all,' Richardson interrupted. 'I think that this fellow was quite right, and I believe you've seen and known something. But for myself I will go straight to the end.'

Anthony swayed the book slowly in his hand. 'Isn't there an order,' he said, 'in everything? If one has to find balance, and a kind of movement in balance … I mean, to act here where we are….'

'But I don't want to act where we are,' the other cried out sharply. 'Why should one act?'

'Other people, perhaps,' Anthony almost shyly suggested. 'If by any chance….'

He stopped abruptly, and listened. Then he stood up, put down the book, and said, 'Open the window.' The words were not exactly a command nor a request; they came to Richardson rather as a statement of something he was about to do; they passed on into the outer world a thing which was already preordained. But though he moved to obey he was already too late; Anthony had crossed the room, pushed the window up, and was leaning out. Richardson came up behind him and also listened.

The Sunday evening was very quiet. A few noises, wheels, footsteps, a door shutting, broke the stillness, and from some distance off the last hymn of the evening service at some church. That died away, and for a few minutes there was utter silence. In that silence there came to Anthony, distant but shrill, the sound of a woman's terrified scream. He pulled himself back, shut the window, said to Richardson, 'I'm sorry, I must go. That was Damaris,' and moved with extreme lightness and extreme quickness to the front door, gathering his hat and stick in one movement as he passed. Richardson called out something which he did not catch; he waved his hand, took a leap down the steps, and ran along the street at top speed.

He was happily aware, as he went, of how easy, how lovely, it was to run like this; he was, more deeply and even more happily, aware that the moment for which he had long waited was come. But he was not aware of himself as bringing any help; it was his business to run because by that some sort of help could reach Damaris; what, he could no more tell than he could tell what danger had threatened her and had wrung from her that scream which some interior faculty of his soul had caught. He came to the corner and turned it.

Richardson, startled out of his contemplations by Anthony's movement, had at first hesitated, and then, half-involuntarily, followed, as if drawn in the other's train. But when he in turn came to the corner he stopped. He saw Anthony before him but he saw something else too.

In the middle of the street there was a horse and cart. Or there had been. It had been jogging along peacefully enough when suddenly its sleeping driver felt the reins torn from his hand, heard a crash and a rending, awoke from his doze, and saw the horse tearing itself free of cart and harness. Its white coat gleamed silver; it grew larger and burst the leather bands that held it; it tossed its head, and the absurd blinkers fell off; it swept its tail round and the shafts snapped and fell. The horse made one final plunge and stood free. The frightened driver, cursing, began to clamber out of the cart. As he did so, he saw a young man running down the street at a tremendous speed, and shouted to him to get hold of the horse's head. The young man swerved, apparently to obey, came up to the horse, leapt with the full force of his run, and with one hand to its neck so sat astride. The driver, half way between his seat and the ground, cried out again with greater oaths, and fell gapingly silent. For the young man, now settling himself, turned the horse with his heel and both against the sinking sun faced the terrified man. They were, he dimly realized, startlingly magnificent; they loomed before him, and then the horse was in motion and they were both flying down the street.

From the corner Richardson, standing still, watched them go, seeing, for the first time in this new world of appearances, the union of high powers for high ends. Where they were going he could not tell, but they went with glory scattered about them and the noise of music. There seemed to him, as he watched, to be not one horse but many horses charging away from him down the street, herds from the pampas and the steppes, a thundering army, riotous and untamed. Here and there amid those tossing manes he saw riders, but their shape and aspect he could not see, only far off beyond that wild expanse of haunches and backs and necks, he saw Anthony, sitting easily upright, leading them, directing them, by virtue of the steed he rode. Down that provincial street all the horses of the world seemed pouring, but he realized that what he saw was only the reflection of the single Idea. One form, and only one, was galloping away from him, these other myriads were its symbols and exhalations. They were not there, not yet, how uneasily soever in stables and streets the horses of that neighbourhood stirred and stamped, and already kicked at gates and carts in order to break free. They were not yet there, although far away on Eastern and Western plains, the uneasy herds started, and threw up their heads and snuffled at the air, and whinnied, and broke into quick charges, feeling already upon the wind the message of that which they were. 'The huntsmen in Persia' soothed their steeds; Chinese squadrons on the march or at bivouac were thrown into disorder; the grooms of the Son of Heaven in Tokio and Kioto ran in alarm to their charges. Out on the Pacific other keepers watched anxiously in scattered ships the restless stamping of sea-borne steeds; farmers in America left their work, and small Mexican figures whispered together as they felt the frenzy rising in many a corral. But the premonition passed, and the wild gallop faded from Richardson's eyes as the distant Anthony wheeled into another road. He sighed and turned and went back to his rooms, while his own thoughts went out again in a perpetual aspiration beyond even the Celestials to That which created the Celestials.

In a spirit of less devotion, but shattered by—for him—wilder and less tolerable vision, the abandoned driver was leaning against his broken cart, holding it with the intensity almost of madness, and crying out perpetually—'My God! O my God!'

———————

CHAPTER XI

**THE CONVERSION OF
DAMARIS TIGHE**

385

It was not the least among the vexations which interfered with Damaris Tighe's exposition of culture that building had begun at the back of her house. For years, indeed ever since they had come to live at Smetham, their garden had looked out over a lane and fields beyond. But quite recently the fields had been bought as a desirable building estate, and a number of villas were to be put up—villas in which it seemed probable that a very different class of people would live from collators of MSS. and students of philosophy. Or so Damaris, who knew very little about people, assumed. They would play tennis, not for an amusement but for a business; they would give parties on lawns; they would talk the jargon of motor-cars and wireless and the gossip of commerce and love. And they would shut her in on every side.

Some of them would be pleasant enough, perhaps here and there one of them would almost have a mind. But even so it probably wouldn't be the kind that would be any use to her. If it were, she could very well make use of a little help in copying and arranging and so on. But probably that was too much to hope for.

It was going on for eight on that Sunday evening when Damaris shut her books and reluctantly decided that she would call her father to supper. If he would have any; he had been eating less and less for the last day or two, and had entirely declined the cold chicken they had had for lunch, contenting himself with a little fruit. Damaris had decided that he must be ill, and she proposed to tell him at supper that she would send for the doctor on Monday. More trouble, she thought; he was probably going to have influenza, and that would mean more work for the maid, and possibly more dislocation of her already dislocated hours. Perhaps she could get him to go away for a few days; if he was going to be ill he had better be ill in a seaside hotel than at home. It would be more convenient for her, and make no particular difference to him. People could be ill anywhere, and they couldn't study bygone cultures anywhere, nor accurately plot out the graph of human thought. There was to be a graph of human thought as an appendix—three graphs actually, from B.C. 500 to A.D. 1200, showing respectively the relation of official thought, cultural thought, and popular thought to the ideas of personalized and depersonalized supernatural powers. By looking at the graph it would be quite easy to see what attitude an Athenian citizen of the age of Thucydides, an Alexandrian friend of Plotinus, or a Burgundian peasant of the Middle Ages had towards this personification. All the graphs had additional little curves running out from them, marked with certain great names. Eusebius of Caesarea who had identified Platonic ideas with the thoughts of the Christian God had one; so had Synesius of Cyrene—only she had mislaid her note on Synesius, and couldn't at the moment remember why he was distinguished in that way; so had William of Occam, Albert, and of course Abelard. Personification was in itself evidence of a rather low cultural state; she had called it somewhere 'The mind's habit of consoling itself with ideographs'. As education developed so a sense of abstraction grew up, and it became more possible to believe that the North Wind was a passage of air, and not an individual, or that St. Michael was a low-class synonym for—probably for just warfare, and justice pure and simple. Which was why he weighed the souls of mankind at Chartres. It was a good graph, and she was proud of it. There would be six appendices in all, but this and the new one on the Creation would be the most important.

She settled her papers. As she did so the air was suddenly shaken by a number of heavy thuds, accompanied by a rain of minor noises. Things at a distance were falling—a great number of things. She went quickly over to the window, and saw to her great astonishment that the newly built houses opposite her were falling in. Falling right down, rather: she stood and stared. The whole row of houses was in a state of increasing collapse. Some were already almost down, and the one nearest her even as she looked began to waver. It sagged inward, a row of bricks came slipping out of the wall, and dropped bumping to the earth. The chimney pots fairly dissolved; it was as if the whole strength of the house was melting. Damaris shrugged; she had said often enough how shameful all this modern jerry-building was, and here was her statement absolutely proved. She remained looking at it in a state of mild complacency. This inefficiency was disgusting; the thing had no backbone to it—no … no … for a moment she fought a consciousness of the word 'guts' and substituted 'real knowledge'. It was after all the reality of one's knowledge that mattered. She *knew*—a sudden terrific crash as the roof fell in distracted and for a moment deafened her. She turned back into the room. 'It's fortunate,' she thought idly, 'that there was no one living in them.'

It was five minutes to eight. She thought abruptly, as she very often did, 'O I must, I must get it.' Doctor of Philosophy—how hard she had worked for it! The … O the smell!

In full strength it took her, so violently that she stepped backward and made an involuntary gesture outward. The horror of it nearly made her faint. It must, she thought, be something to do with these new houses; some corrupt material had been used. The smell was corruption. Something would have to be done; the Council Surveyor must be called in. Perhaps it wouldn't be so bad downstairs. Her window faced the fallen houses; the dining-room looked the other way. She would go down and see.

As she moved the sunlight that was over her papers, except for the light shadow that she herself cast, was totally obscured. A heavy blackness obliterated it in an instant; the papers, the table, all that part of the room lay in gloom. The change was so immediate that even Damaris's attention was caught, and, still wrinkling her nose at that appalling smell, she glanced half round to see what dark cloud had suddenly filled the sky. And then she did come much nearer to fainting than ever before in her life.

Outside the window something was … was. That was the only certainty her startled senses conveyed. There was a terrific beak protruding through the open window into the room, there was the most appalling body she had ever conceived possible; there were two huge flapping wings; there were two horrible red eyes. And there was the smell. Damaris stood stock still, gasping at it, thinking desperately, 'I'm dreaming.' The beastly apparition remained. It seemed to be perched there, on the window-sill or the pear-tree or something. Its eyes held her; its wings moved, as if uncertainly opening; its whole repulsive body shook and stirred: its beak—not three yards distant—jerked at her, as if the thing were stabbing; then it opened. She had a vision of great teeth; incapable of thought, she stumbled backward against the table, and remained fixed. Something in her said, 'It can't be'; something else said; 'It is'. She'd been overworking; that must be it. It was … it was like spots before the eyes. It wasn't; it was detestably different. It—O God, the thing was moving. It was coming … it wasn't … it was, it was coming in. She couldn't see how; whether the window broke or melted or what, but it was certainly nearer. The beak was not much more than a yard off now; the huge leathern-like wings were opening out within the room, or partly within it. She couldn't in the fœtid darkness which was spreading round her see which was room and which was horror, but she flung herself wildly back, scrambling and scrabbling somehow across her table. Her papers went flying before her, her books, her pen—everything fell from it as Damaris Tighe, unconscious of her work for the first time for years, got herself on to the table, and pushed herself somehow across it. The thing stayed still watching her; only the wings furled and unfurled themselves slowly, as if there were no hurry—no hurry at all, about what it had to do. She was half on her feet again, crouching, sliding, getting sideways towards the door, feeling for the handle, praying wildly to Anthony, to her father, to Abelard and Pythagoras, to Anthony again. If only Anthony were here! She got hold of the handle; of course that beak, those eyes, that *smell*—O that sickening and stupendous *smell!*—were all dreams. She was asleep; in a minute she would be outside the door, then she would wake up. In a few seconds. The little red eyes gleamed greed at her. She *was* outside; she banged the door.

On the landing she leaned against the banisters, and dimly considered pulling herself together. For the first time in her life she wanted somebody very badly, somebody—but Anthony for choice. Only Anthony had been driven away that morning. Her father then. Only her father was separated from her. Somebody, *somebody* to break this awful loneliness that had settled on her, this loneliness in which the memory of that horror was her only companion. O somebody … somebody. 'I'm being silly,' she thought. What was that idea of pulling herself together? And … and what was that other noise? She looked up.

Over the skylight above her head she saw something dragged, and knew it for an edge of those wings. There was a noise of scratching; a crash; more scratching or what sounded like scratching. The wing disappeared; came back; went again. And again she saw the beak, thrusting down through the open skylight, stabbing, questing. All bonds of habit broken, mad and fearful of madness, she screamed out and flung herself down the stairs. 'Father!' she cried, 'Father!' and found him standing before her in the hall.

He was looking at her with that utter detachment which had come on him—not so much looking as allowing her, rather reluctantly, to be visible to him. She caught his arm, staggering, and babbling nonsense. Only sometimes she paused and clung, in frightened tears, in terror, in anguish. She didn't dare look round; she looked at him; he would know, he would see, he would do something; and she herself could do nothing at all. But in some two or three minutes she ceased, for there crept into her exhausted consciousness the thought that all this was vain. He was still looking at her, from a placid detachment, and all he said was, 'Yes, yes. Well, I was afraid you might get hurt,' and the very words cost him an effort, so that there seemed to be great silences betwixt them. Then as if relieved of her presence his eyes went blank, his voice changed. 'Ah!' he murmured, 'Ah!' and sighed happily, and pushed at her as if she were hindering him, pushed her away, back into the corruption that was growing round her in the dreadful odour which renewed itself, and was attacking her with a vehemence which made it seem the very body of the creature of her terror.

As he pushed her she loosed hold. It was some stranger who went by, and up the stairs—she gave another wild scream as he did so—a half warning, only he took no notice. He went from her, lost in the contemplation which held him, going away with his memories and his knowledge thick over and around him, abandoned by and abandoning everything but the pure certainty of beauty which he had seen. She dared not go that way; she screamed once more, and took a desperate little run. But her feet didn't seem to move easily; they were sticking, sinking; she had to pull them out of the floor, or the ground, the damp marshy ground they were toiling through. She looked down; the floor was half floor and half bog, squelchy green spreading under her in patches, which widened and joined themselves, and she was being held by them as she moved.

She looked up and saw the shape of the walls and ceiling but now spectral and growing fainter against a wide open space, a vast plain, stretching emptily away to where at the horizon a heavy and inflamed sky sank to meet it. The house was no more than a shadowy diagram; all the solidity had vanished, and a mere arrangement of lines showed against the wild background. She saw it, and yet did not feel it as altogether unknown, she had somewhere been acquainted with that desolate plain. Right in front of her, beyond the framework of the front door, was the gleam of water. She dragged her feet from the mire and tried to get firmer footing, while her mind sought to remember the name of the place. She had never seen it, yet she knew—O very well she knew it, and the figure that was coming towards her across it from far away, a tiny figure, so distant was it, but human. As she gazed she heard another sound above, and looked up to see the earlier horror flying round in circles high over her. There she stood on the edge of a swampy pool, with the pterodactyl wheeling round in the sky, and one remote companion. She couldn't be frightened more; her dulled mind, as she stood there helplessly, returned to that approaching form, and there again she thought she recognized something familiar in its movement. It came on quickly; it was a man wrapped in a kind of large cloak, bareheaded, bald—no, not bald, but with a head shaved in a tonsure. Her remote memory woke—it was a mediaeval priest; he came on towards her still more quickly, and then, though his face was strange, she knew him with a quick certainty. It was—it was Peter Abelard himself, Abelard, mature, but still filled with youth because of the high intensity of his philosophical passion, and he was singing as he came: singing the words that he had himself composed, and which a voice of her own past had spoken to her but lately:

ianta

‡

la Sa

Against that angry sky he came on, in that empty land his voice rang out in joy, and she tried to move; she ran a few steps forward, and made an effort to speak. Her voice failed; she heard herself making grotesque noises in her throat, and suddenly over him there fell the ominous shadow of the pterodactyl. Only for a few seconds, then it passed on, and he emerged from it, and his face was towards her, but now it had changed. Now it was like a vile corpse, and yet still it was uttering things: it croaked at her in answer to her own croakings, strange and meaningless words. *Individualiter, essentialiter, categoricorum, differentia substantialis*—croak, croak, croak. He was coming towards her, and she was trying to run away; and now the blackness had fallen on them both, and the horrid presence of that other filthy being had swept down. She shrieked and stumbled and fell and it caught her.

Something touched her face: something swept her arm; something enveloped and weighed against her heart. Her eyes were shut; she had no power to look again. Her brain was dazed; she had no power to think. Her mouth was panting horribly; and from it, wrenched by a physical power from a physical consciousness, there came one last and feeble and continuous effort to call Anthony. 'An … An … A … A … A …' she was saying, and the effort became mere gasps as she shook and shrank. There was something which could save her—something if that something would come. She lay in a heap and the great flap of great wings beat over her, and she felt them pressing her, and something had hurt her head. 'A … A … A …' she went on moaning, and claws pressed the back of her neck, dreadful, horrible claws. The smell was working within her; in some way it was Abelard. It was Abelard, and the wings lifted and again caught her. She was on her face on the marshy ground, and she was being forced over. As well as she could she hid herself, but it was all in vain. There was nothing round her but a hideous and vile corruption, nothing, nothing except a vibration that went rhythmically through her, as if—almost from somewhere within her—a horse were galloping. And then she heard her name.

It wasn't cried aloud; it was spoken as normally as it had been spoken a hundred times in that place,—that state of knowledge. When she heard it she felt herself straining to hear it again, and did, but this time with a note of command in it, so that in a hasty obedience she opened her eyes. That was what, by nothing but her name speeded on music, she had been bidden to do. She obeyed; not easily, but she obeyed.

Anthony was standing near her, and behind him was the brightness of a sky lovely in a summer sunset. His arm was stretched out towards her, and she felt the weight upon her lifting. He called to her by her name, and she answered with his own, with the name on which she had cried for help, but hardly murmured now, so spent was she. Nevertheless as she breathed it she felt herself free, and then there was the shade of wings in the air, and another flying thing sailed into sight, and floated slowly down to his shoulder. There, eagle-plumaged, eagle-beaked, eagle-eyed, it rested; he raised his hand, and as if in an august leniency it allowed itself to be caressed. His eyes, as he leaned his head aside, full of love and loving laughter, rested on hers. She received with joy both love and laughter; there went out from him, and from the Augustitude upon his shoulder, a knowledge of safety would she but take it, and freely and humbly she let it enter her being. The thing she had rejected and yet used gathered and expanded round him as if a glory attended him. He looked down at her, and though she longed for him to gather her and let her feel more closely the high protection of his power, she was content to wait upon his will. As she made that motion of assent she felt the wildness of the desolate plain shut out. A covering formed over them and hid the sky; shelter was restored, and when at last he moved and came to her, and she half-raised herself to meet him, her hand touched the mat at the dining-room door, and she knew she was lying again in her own house. As he moved the eagle-form left his shoulder, swept up and round, passed her and disappeared in the shadows of the room. But she had no time for that fantastic dream; she looked at her cousin, and felt that either she or he had changed. There was in him something which shook her with a fear, but with a fear very different from that which she had felt but now. This was power and intelligence; this was command. He came over to her, stretching out his hands, and said as he took hers: 'You were only just in time, weren't you, dearest?'

'Yes,' she said, and got to her feet, holding tightly to his grasp. He put his arm round her, and took her to a chair, and stood for awhile in front of her silent. She said suddenly: 'What was it?'

He looked at her gravely. 'I wonder what you'll say if I tell you,' he said.

'I shall believe you,' she answered simply. 'Anthony, I'm … I'm sorry.'

The laughter broke out again in his eyes. 'And why are you sorry, my cousin?' he asked.

'I've behaved very badly,' Damaris said. To tell him seemed to her more important than anything else in the world could be, even the vanished monstrosity.

Anthony took her hand again, and kissed it. 'And *how* have you behaved badly, my cousin?' he asked.

'I've tried to make use of you,' Damaris said, beginning to blush. 'I've been … I've been….'

'… the first-born of Lilith, who is illusion, and Samael the Accursed,' Anthony finished. 'Yes, darling. But that doesn't matter between us. It isn't that which you saw.'

'What was it?' Damaris asked shuddering and looking round in a renewed servile fear. Even as she did so he released his hand from hers and stepped back, so that, as she moved hastily to catch hold of him again, he was beyond her reach, and as he spoke there was a sternness in his voice.

'You saw what you know,' he said, 'and because it's the only thing you know you saw it like that. You've been told about it often enough; you've been warned and warned again. You've had it whispered to you and shouted at you—but you wouldn't stop or think or believe. And what you wouldn't hear about you've seen, and if you're still capable of thanking God you'd better do it now. You, with your chatter about this and the other, your plottings and plannings, and your little diagrams, and your neat tables—what did you think you would make of the agonies and joys of the masters? O I know such things must be: we must shape to ourselves the patterns in what they said—man must use his mind. But you've done more than use it, you've loved it for your own. You've loved it and you've lost it. And pray God you've lost it before it was too late, before it decayed in you and sent up that stink which you smelt, or before the knowledge of life turned to the knowledge of death. Somewhere in you there was something that loved truth, and if ever you studied anything you'd better study that now. For perhaps you won't get another chance.'

She put out her hand for his. 'But tell me,' she said, 'I don't understand. What ought I to do? How can that thing … that horrible thing … what do you mean? Anthony, tell me. I know I've tried to use you….'

'You've tried to use something else than me,' Anthony said more gently, but he did not take her hand. 'And it's up to you to stop. Or not.'

'I'll try to stop if you think I ought to,' Damaris said. 'But what did I see?'

'I'll tell you,' he said, 'if you want me to. Do you want me to?'

She gripped him suddenly. 'Why did you come to me?' she exclaimed, and he answered simply, 'Because I heard you call.'

'Tell me,' she said, and he began, going over the tale as it had been known to him. But he spoke now neither with the irritation nor with the amusement which she had felt in him of old; his voice convinced her of what he said, and the authority that was in it directed and encouraged even while it awed and warned her. He neither doubted nor permitted her to doubt; the whole gospel—morals and mythology at once—entered into and possessed her. When he came to speak of Quentin's flight she trembled a little as she sat and tried to move her hand away. But Anthony, standing above her and looking out towards the darkening eastern sky, did not release it; half a chain and half a caress, his own retained hers by the same compulsion that she heard in his voice, and he exposed her to the knowledge of what she had done. Merciless and merciful, he held her; pitiful and unpitying, he subordinated her to the complete realization of herself and her past.

'So,' he ended at last, 'we can't tell what will happen. But I don't think,' he added, his voice lightening, 'that there is much time left before it does. I shall know presently what I have to do.'

After a long silence she said, 'Do you know, Anthony, I think perhaps I ought….' She paused.

'Ought?' he asked.

'Ought to go and look for your friend.'

He considered it gravely. 'I had expected to do it myself,' he said, 'but I don't feel that I ought…. There's some other thing…. Why will you go?'

'It's either that or Abelard,' she said, smiling faintly. 'My father doesn't want me.'

'No,' he answered. 'I think your father's almost dead already. I thought so when he let me in just now—before I found you lying on the floor.'

She shuddered again. 'O darling, it was dreadful when he pushed me away,' she said, and he answered again, looking down on her, tender and stern at once: 'And you—if it comes to pushing away?'

In such conversation, question and answer exchanged between them while Damaris searched her heart, and the dark places where the images of obscene profanations dwelt, they stayed for a long time. They did not hear the noise where, at the back of the house, a crowd surged and pushed and stared and laughed and talked round the fallen houses, and told one another how here a hoarding and there a fence had also given way, and how funny it was. Nor did they interrupt above them the trance that was increasing upon her father where he lay stretched on his bed, content now not even to move, and aware only of the vision of living colour that possessed him, as the beauty to which he had offered himself accepted inevitably that surrender, and softly gathered him into itself. In the town the living outposts of the invasion awaited it—Richardson and Foster and Dora Wilmot—each after their kind. Beyond the town change was proceeding; in a great circle round that solitary house there was no living thing but a few men and women, unconscious yet of the doom. Birds and insects and animals had all vanished—all but the sheep; they alone in their field seemed to know nothing of the Angels of that other world. And even among these Principles and Dominations perhaps none but that Virtue which Anthony had encountered in the pit and which in its earthly image had deigned to be with him that night when he came to dissipate the fear of that other image which was yet itself to the challenge of the presumptuous and erring mind—none but that Virtue understood, in its soaring comprehension, the safety in which the sheep still lived, or from what yet deeper distance of spirit was to arise the Innocence which everlastingly formed and maintained them.

CHAPTER XII

THE TRIUMPH OF THE ANGELICALS

Richardson, returning towards his rooms, decided suddenly not to enter them.

The sweep and wonder of his vision were still with him; his body still palpitated with the echo of those charging hooves, though within him his spirit desired a further end. He longed to approach that other end with the speed of the racing herd but to such an approach the intoxication of that sight was alien; he subdued himself harshly. Visions and auditions had nothing to do with the final surrender, which was—for him—a thing to be achieved wholly in itself, and (it seemed) without reference to any natural or supernatural event. A lonely life had but emphasized, as the exterior life will, the interior method which he pursued. Even his connexion with Berringer had been but a part of a distraction necessary and right to relieve the rigour of his duty, and to keep him in spiritual health, but not part of that duty. Chance, assisted by his personal tastes, had given him a job among books, and as far as possible he read in those books of the many ways which are always the Way. But not by books or by phrases, not by images or symbols or myths, did he himself follow it. He abstracted himself continually from sense and from thought, attempting always a return to an interior nothingness where that which is itself no thing might communicate its sole essential being.

So separating himself from the memory of the horses, so concentrated on the Nothing of his desires, he walked for some time along the streets until he experienced the easily recognized symptoms of temporary interior exhaustion. Obedient to those symptoms he relaxed and murmured to himself, as was his habit at such conclusions, the phrases from that Dionysius with whom Damaris had been concerned—'He hath not power, nor is He power; He liveth not, nor is He life; neither is He of the things that are or are not, nor is there for Him any word or name or thought, for He is neither darkness nor light, neither error nor truth.' As he ended he began again to look round him. He was standing half way down a street in one of the rather poorer parts of the town—where the lower middle-class were slightly more obviously lower. A tobacconist close by was shutting up for the night; the two recognized each other and nodded.

'Funny business about the telephones,' the tobacconist said.

'I hadn't heard,' Richardson answered casually but politely. 'What was it?'

The tobacconist paused in his task. 'All down, so they say,' he explained. 'I had occasion to want to speak to my brother in London—my wife thought she'd run up to-morrow by the cheap train—and the Exchange girl told me I couldn't get through! Couldn't get a trunk call through on Sunday night! All nonsense it sounded to me, and so I told her, and she as good as told me not to be a fool—the lines were down. They've sent out repair gangs, it seems; I had old Mr. Hoskins in—you know him, I expect; the grandfather, I mean; comes in for his quarter-pound every Sunday evening as regularly as the sun … well, I ought to say moon, oughtn't I? at this time of day, but one gets into a habit of speaking.'

'One does,' Richardson murmured in the pause. 'Unless one is careful.'

'So he told me,' the tobacconist resumed, 'that the poles have fallen down—all along the roads—all smashed to bits they are, he said, and the wires all fused and broken. Most extraordinary thing I ever heard of. Old Hoskins, he thought it must have been the wind, but then as I said to him: "Where's the wind?" Now my belief is that it's got something to do with all that thunder we've been having the last few days—this electricity's a funny thing. Don't you think that's more likely now, sir?'

Richardson nodded; then seeing that he was expected to speak, said,

'It's certain, I should think, to have something to do with the thunder.'

'And as for hoardings and fences I hear they're down in a lot of places. Funny thing altogether.'

'Very funny,' Richardson answered. 'Awkward if the houses follow suit.'

The tobacconist gaped at him for a moment. 'O I don't think that's likely,' he began slowly, but looking up at his own first floor with the beginnings of a fearful anxiety. 'I mean houses are rather different to hoardings, aren't they?'

'Houses that have been lived in, perhaps,' Richardson acknowledged, also looking thoughtfully upwards. 'Yes, perhaps. There maybe an infiltration of human existence….' He ceased and seemed to await a decision.

'Yes,' the tobacconist said, recovering faith. 'Human beings make all the difference, don't they? A little bit of furniture works wonders in an empty house. Why, when we moved in here, I said to my wife about a room where there was nothing had been put but a chair that had got a leg broken—my fault it was—in the shifting—not a carpet down there wasn't, nothing but that bit of chair, and I said to her: "It looks like home already." Just the difference between a room and four walls and a floor.'

'Is there any?' Richardson asked. 'Yes, of course, I see what you mean.' But his spirit cried out that there was in fact no difference; they were alike shape and form and so far temptations to the soul which so long sought refuge in such exterior patterns from the state in which no such patterns were to be found or desired. He felt the contrast so sharply that he could endure no more talk; he forced himself to say, with as little abruptness as possible, 'Ah, well, I daresay we shall hear more about it in the morning,' nodded a goodnight and crossed the road.

As he reached the other side he saw before him a church. It was a small, old, rather ugly Wesleyan church; the doors were open because of the heat, and apparently the service was not yet over. Richardson, casually attracted, looked at his watch: nearly nine. He paused on the pavement and looked in. It must, he thought, be some kind of after-service, and, after a few moments' search the notice-board confirmed the idea. On the third Sunday in the month there was apparently the Breaking of Bread. It must, he thought, be a rather out-of-date place; most of the Nonconforming Churches had adopted the words 'Holy Communion'. Besides, this building still called itself 'Zion', which was surely a rather old-fashioned title. But perhaps he was wrong; he didn't pretend to be an expert in ecclesiology. All that sort of thing was very well for the minds that could use it; he couldn't use it, neither the small dull gatherings of the Evangelicals or the large gaudy assemblies of the Catholics. 'The flight of the alone to the Alone.' But no doubt this was proper to them—if it increased their speed upon the Way. Speed, speed, and always speed! His mind remembered that wild careering herd; so, and swifter than so, he desired the Return. He seemed to hear the beating hooves again, and while for a moment he attended to that interior echo something huge and rapid drove past him and into the church. Certainly he had felt it, though there was nothing visible, but he had felt the movement of a body and heard the sound of hooves. Within him his chief concern renewed itself in a burst of imperious ardour; he burned towards the—no, not fire; no, not darkness; no words, no thought, nothing but … nothing but … well, *but*— that which was when all other 'buts' had been removed, and all hindrances abolished. For a moment he felt a premonition; something wholly new and exquisite touched him and was gone.

He was standing in front of the church and looking into it. There didn't seem to be many there; one or two figures were moving at the upper end; a few more were scattered about the small building. They were seated as if waiting—perhaps for the Breaking of Bread; and as he gazed a gleam of extreme brightness struck through the building and vanished, for the lights within had flashed upon something moving that caught and reflected their radiance in one shining curve as if a sword had been swung right across the church. Blinded by its intensity he took a step back, then he recovered and looked again. This time—and his spirit livened again with his habitual desire—he saw it. It was standing at the other end of Zion; it was something like a horse in shape and size, but of a dazzling whiteness, and from the middle of its forehead there grew a single horn. He recognized the myth of poems and pictures; he saw the Divine Unicorn gently sustaining itself in that obscure and remote settlement of the faithful. He recognized the myth, but he recognized something else too, only he could not put a name to it. The thing moved, pure and stately, a few paces down the aisle, and as it did so he was transported within himself a million miles upon his way. It moved with the beauty of swiftness, however small the distance was that it went; it lowered and tossed its head, and again that gleaming horn caught all the light in Zion, and gathered it, and flashed it back in a dazzling curve of purity. As the brightness passed he saw that within they were still intent upon the service; the deacons were bearing the Bread of the Communion to the few who were there, and as they did so it seemed to the watcher that the unicorn moved its head gently in the direction of each, nay, that some eidolon of itself, though it remained unchanged in the centre, went very swiftly to each, and then he lost sight of the images. Only now he was aware—and only aware—of a sensation of rushing speed passing through his being; it was not for him to adore the unicorn; he was the unicorn. He and those within, and others—who and when and where he did not know, but others—a great multitude whom no man could number—they went swiftly, they were hastening to an end. And again the shining horn flung back the earthly lights around it, and in that reflection the seeker knew himself speeding to his doom. So slow, so slow, the Way had seemed; so swiftly, so swiftly, through aeons and universes, the Principle, the Angel of man's concern, went onwards in unfailing strength. Yet it had not moved; it stood there still, showing itself, as if in a moment's dream, to the fellows of devotion, so that each beheld and supposing it to be a second's fantasy determined not to speak of it. But pure and high the ardour burned in every soul, as Zion shone in Zion, and time hastened to its conclusion in them. The minister gave out a hymn; the voices began it; the great beast of revelation that stood there moved again, and as Richardson unconsciously moved also he felt his arm caught from behind.

Startled and constraining himself, he turned his head. Behind him, a little to his left, clutching his arm, and staring at him with fierce bloodshot eyes, stood Foster. For a few seconds Richardson did not take in the fact; the two remained staring. Then, he could not have told why, he broke into a little laugh; Foster snarled at him, and the hand that was on the other's arm seemed to clutch and drag at it. Richardson took a step or two backward, his eyes going once more to the aisle as he did so. But this time he could see nothing unusual; indeed, he felt doubtful already of what he had seen, only he knew that there was working within him a swiftness more than he had ever dreamed. The hesitations and sloths that had often hampered him had vanished; he looked at Foster from a distance, down a precipice from the forest of the unicorn to the plain of the lion.

Foster said, 'It's here.'

'It's always here,' the younger man answered, 'but we have to go a long way to find it.'

'Have you got the strength?' Foster asked. He was speaking thickly and with difficulty; the voice blurred itself in the middle of the sentence, and the last word came out almost booming. His face was red, and his shoulders heaving; when he ceased to speak Richardson noticed that his breath was coming in great pants, as if he were struggling against some oppression at his heart. The sight brought back the other's attention; he looked at Foster and gently disengaged himself, saying quietly, 'What's the strength to you or me? was that what we went in to it for? Speed now, and at that only the right speed.'

'Speed enough too,' Foster answered deeply. 'Speed to hunt, strength to kill. Are you for them or are you like that other jackanapes that thought he could stand in the way—in the way of the lion?' The voice rose into a roar and he scrabbled with his feet on the pavement.

Richardson, now completely watchful, said, 'It seems that you're with them entirely now.'

'I'm looking for him,' Foster said, 'for him, and'—he began to snarl, 'and—and others. There's—ah! ah!— there's a man in my off—off—office,' he barely achieved the word, 'that I hate, I hate his face, I'll look after him. The strength'll be on him. Look, look for him, I'll look.'

He turned his eyes about him; his mouth opened and his lips curled back over his teeth. Then he seemed to make an effort towards control, and began to mutter something to himself. 'Not too much yet, lord god!' Richardson heard. 'Slowly, lord, slowly! I'll make sacrifice—the blood of the sacrifice,' and at that a sudden impatient anger caught the young man.

'Fool,' he cried out, 'there's only one sacrifice, and the God of gods makes it, not you.'

Foster did not seem to hear, and Richardson almost at once regretted the outburst. Something in it offended him; it was a pit laid for the silver hooves of an immaculate and solitary virtue that was galloping away, away in the cool light of the stars, amid rivers of chastity, to gardens high up among the snows. There—

there—it would find its lair and sleep alone among the trees of Eden before man had fallen and…. Images, images, he caught his mind back, abolishing them; beyond images, beyond any created shape or invented fable lay the union of the end. He was lost in his intensity and woke to awareness again to hear Foster saying,

'… the chosen. The chosen are few. Even the woman … if I knew … knew. The gods know; the gods are here. Here!'

The word went in a roar up the street. Richardson heard a startled exclamation behind him. He looked round—the worshippers were coming out of Zion, and one of them, an old gentleman with his wife, had jumped violently at the noise. A dismayed voice exclaimed, 'Really, really!' A more indignant feminine voice said, 'Disgusting! It's enough to deafen anyone.'

But the bleating of an innocent mortality had no effect on the possessed being before them. He glared round him, then he threw up his head, and began to sniff softly and horribly, as if he were seeking to find a trail. The old gentleman stared, then he said to Richardson, in a voice not quite steady, 'Ill, is he?'

'O if he's ill,' the old lady said in a tone of pity. 'Would he like to come in and sit down for a few minutes? We live close by.'

'Yes, do,' the old gentleman added. 'A little rest—when my wife comes over faint——— Well, Martha dear, you *do* sometimes come over faint.'

'There's ways of being bad besides coming over faint' the old lady, now rather pink, but still sweetly anxious to help, said. 'Do come in.'

'Thank you very much indeed,' Richardson said gravely, 'but I'm afraid it wouldn't help.' And then, by an irresistible impulse, 'I hope you had a happy service?'

They both looked at him with delight. 'Now that's very kind,' the old gentleman said, 'Thank you, sir, it was a very beautiful service.'

'Beautiful,' the old lady said. She hesitated, fumbling with her umbrella, then, taking sudden courage, she took a step towards Richardson and went on, 'You'll excuse me, sir, I know it's old-fashioned, and you quite a stranger, but—are you saved?'

Richardson answered her as seriously as she had spoken, 'I believe salvation is for all who will have it,' he said, 'and I will have it by the only possible means.'

'Ah that's good, that's good,' the old gentleman said. 'Bless God for it, young man.'

'I know you'll pardon me, sir,' the old lady added, 'you being a stranger as I said, and strangers often not liking to talk about it. Though what else there is to talk about….'

'What indeed?' Richardson agreed, and again through the evening there struck upon his ears the noise of galloping hooves, and for a moment the whole earth upon which he stood seemed to be a charging beast upon which he rode, faster than ever his own haste could carry him. But the sound, if it were a sound, struck at the same time on that other creature, half-transfigured, who stood in front of him still. It sprang up, it bellowed out some half-formed word, then it broke off and went leaping down the street; and amazed or meditative the three watched it go.

'Dear me,' the old lady said: and the old gentleman, 'He's behaving very strangely, isn't he?'

Richardson nodded. 'Very strangely, I'm afraid, but—' he sought a phrase at once mutually comprehensible, comforting, and true—'but he's in the hands of God.'

'Still——' the old gentleman said dubiously. But there was nothing to be done, so they parted and went their way, leaving Richardson standing by the now closed church. The other members of the congregation had come out during the brief conversation and gone. He considered vaguely what to do. And then he remembered Dora Wilmot.

He had spoken of her to Anthony the day before as one of those who desired the power of the Immortals, the virtue of the things that they sought, not for that virtue's sake, not even for the sake of fresh and greater experiences, but merely that their old experience might be more satisfactory to them. Foster wanted to be stronger than those with whom he came in contact; he had made himself a place for the lion and it seemed the lion was taking possession of its habitation; its roar echoing in the wilderness and the dry places of the soul. Dora Wilmot had never dreamed of such brutal government; but once Richardson had caught the expression in her eyes as she handed a cup of coffee to Mrs. Rockbotham, and any quiet little supper with the—probably slandered—children of the Lord Alexander VI would have seemed to him preferable. And if there had entered into her some subtlety from that world, what was happening to her? or, perhaps more important, what was she doing? It occurred to him that he might go and see; almost at the same time it occurred to him, as he still watched the old lady stepping down the street beside her husband, that he might perhaps—not stop her but offer her an alternative course, if it seemed possible or desirable. After all, that old lady had wanted to be kind, even if she reduced indescribable complexities of experience to an epigram. His own solitary life had rather left him without any formed habit of being kind, he reflected: perhaps he was a little too much inclined to concentrate on an end which was (all the authorities assured him) largely dependent on the way. Anthony Durrant had gone charging off to some unknown Damaris. Berringer had been kind to him. Very well, he would go and see if the road of the unicorn led through the house of Dora Wilmot.

When he arrived there he was, after inquiry, shown in to the room where Anthony had fought with the beasts. Miss Wilmot, thin and sedate, was at her writing table. Several little sealed envelopes lay in a pile at one side: she put down her pen as he entered. They looked at one another with doubt masked by courtesy, and exchanged a few trifling remarks. Then Richardson said, 'And what do you make of it all, Miss Wilmot?'

She answered softly. 'Have you seen Mr. Foster?'

'Yes,' Richardson admitted. 'But only just now. That must be my excuse for calling so late.' On the Day of Judgment, if there were another, one would probably say things like that, he thought. But he went on swiftly. 'And, to tell you the truth, I don't much like Mr. Foster at the moment.'

'I shouldn't expect you to,' she said. 'For you … he … we aren't meaning….' She was almost stammering, as if she were trying to say several things at once, but under his eyes she made an effort to be collected. Her eyes, nevertheless, went on shooting from side to side, and her restless arms twisted themselves together and again untwisted as she sat.

'You aren't meaning——?'

'We wouldn't … we shouldn't … find it likely … that you….' Suddenly she gave a little tortured scream. 'O!' she cried, 'O! I can't keep up! it keeps dividing! There's too many things to think of!'

He got up and went nearer to her, very watchful. But with an unusual note of pity in his voice he said, 'Need you think of them?'

'O yes….' she breathed, 'yes-s-s. There's the wretch-ch of a Rockbotham, I've done hers-s, and Mrs. Jacquelin, I've done hers. Such a nice, nic-c-ce one, and I'm s-scribbling this-s to the one that s-spoke, the Damaris creature—but sh-she's strange, s-so I had to s-see what was bes-st.'

She looked up at him malevolently as he stood over her, and with the end of her tongue moistened her lips. Then her eyes changed again and terror came into them, and in a voice from which the dreadful sibilance had departed she cried out, 'My head, my head! There's too much to see, there's so many ways of doing it! I can't think.'

Richardson laid his hand on hers. 'There is one thing very certain,' he said with firm clearness, 'the way to the Maker of the Gods.'

She looked sly. 'Will he help me to show old Mother Rockbotham what her husband might be like?' she said. 'Or old Jackie what that nephew of hers is doing?' Her eyes went to the sealed letters. 'They didn't think much of me,' she said. 'I could sit here and do their work. But I'm getting my turn now. If only I could see them reading their letters.'

Richardson gathered both her hands, as they lay on the writing table into one of his, and almost released them again as he did so. They were clammy-cold and they wriggled horribly in his grasp. But he held them while he leant quickly across and caught up the little pile of letters; then he released them and sprang back. 'What devilry have you been up to?' he asked her harshly. 'What are these letters you're so proud of?'

'I was afraid at first,' she said, 'but he told me—Foster told me—they would help us, strength and subtlety he said. And … and … O my head! my head!'

She tried to stand up and could not; she writhed in her chair; but her eyes were fixed on him, and their immediate pain changed as his met them into malice and fear. He ripped a letter open and glanced at it, and as he did so she slithered down and began to wriggle towards him across the floor. He had time only for the first few sentences, and a hasty glance at the middle and the end, but they told him all he needed to know. The letter was to Mrs. Rockbotham; it opened with sympathetic phrases of sorrow, then it went on, with a careful and subtle art he had no time then to admire, to bite with stored venom at the heart. The doctor was … he was … for the moment Richardson did not grasp what he was; some evil was suggested, or something that would seem evil to the reader—perversion and cruelty, was it? 'Take care of yourself,' one sentence began, and the thing wasn't signed—yes, it was: 'From a Sister in Trouble.' He crumpled it in his hand and leapt aside as a hand touched his ankle, then he ran for the door and shouted for the maid. When she showed herself, 'Telephone for the doctor,' he called, 'your mistress is ill.' Then thrusting the letters in his pocket he went back into the room.

She was where he had left her, but a dreadful change was coming over her. Her body was writhing into curves and knots where she lay, as if cramps convulsed her. Her mouth was open, but she could not scream; her hands were clutching at her twisted throat. In her wide eyes there was now no malice, only an agony, and gradually all her body and head were drawn up backwards from the floor by an invisible force, so that from the hips she remained rigidly upright and her legs lay stretched straight out behind her upon the ground, as if a serpent in human shape raised itself before him. The sight drove him backwards; he turned his face away, and prayed with all his strength to the Maker of the Celestials. From that refuge he looked again, and saw her convulsed and convulsed with spasms of anguish. But now the very colour of her skin was changing; it became blotched and blurred with black and yellow and green, nor only that but it seemed distended about her. The face rounded out till it was perfectly smooth, with no hollows or depressions, and from her nostrils and her mouth something was thrusting out. In and out of her neck and hands another skin was forming, over or under her own—he could not distinguish which, but growing through it, here a coating, there an underveiling. Another and an inhuman tongue was flickering out over a human face, and the legs were twisted and thrown from side to side as if something prisoned in them were attempting to escape. For all that lower violence her body did not fall, nor indeed, but for a slight swaying, did it much move. Her arms were interlocked in front of her, the extreme ends of her fingers touched the ground between her thighs. But they too were drawn inwards; the stuff of her dress was rending in places; and wherever it rent and hung aside he could see that other curiously-toned skin shining behind it. A black shadow was on her face; a huge shape was emerging from it, from her, growing larger and larger as the Domination she had invoked freed itself from the will and the mind and the body that had given it a place where it could find the earth for its immaterialization. No longer a woman but a serpent indeed surged before him in the darkening room, bursting and breaking from the woman's shape behind it. It curved and twined itself in its last achievements of liberty; there came through the silence that had accompanied that transmutation a sound as if some slight thing had dropped to the floor, and the Angelic energy was wholly free.

It was free. It glided a little forward, and its head turned slowly from side to side. Richardson stood up and faced it. The subtle eyes gazed at him, without hostility, without friendship, remote and alien. He looked back, wordlessly calling on the Maker and End of all created energies. Images poured through his brain in an unceasing riot; questions such as Anthony had recounted to him propounded themselves; there seemed to be a million things he might do, and he did none of them. He remembered the Will beyond all the makings; then with a tremendous effort he shut out even that troublesome idea of the Will—an invented word, a mortal thought—and, as far as he could, was not before what was. It had mercy on him; he saw the great snake begin to move again, and then he fainted right away.

When he came to himself he found Dr. Rockbotham in the room, and other people, people who were carrying something out. The doctor, as soon as he discovered that the young man was conscious, came over to him, and was at first discreetly cheerful. But in a few minutes he allowed himself to relax, and said very seriously, 'What happened?'

'God knows,' Richardson said, and paused. Then he added, 'What was she like?'

Dr. Rockbotham shook his head and—even he—shuddered. 'Dreadful,' he said. 'I suppose there'll have to be a post-mortem—and I hate the idea. I never want to see it again.'

'God help her,' Richardson said sincerely, 'wherever, after death, she is. It was a dreadful chance that brought her to it. There are enough of her kind about, but the others get off scot-free.'

But his thoughts were elsewhere. He looked round the room; there was no sign of the Power he had seen. The window was wide open at the bottom, and the garden lay beyond—perhaps it had passed upon its way. The end of everything was surely very near. He got to his feet.

'But you must tell me something,' the doctor said. 'I was wondering if I ought to call in the police.'

Richardson looked at him, and mentally refused to speak. The Gods who had come to man he felt he might have to meet, but he simply couldn't explain. He uttered a few words explaining that he had been seized with faintness—which the doctor already knew—and felt he must get home. Somehow he escaped. In the street he remembered the old lady. 'Certainly,' he said to himself grimly, 'there *are* other ways of feeling bad besides coming over faint.'

CHAPTER XIII

THE BURNING HOUSE

Smetham next morning found itself more than a little agitated. It was, to begin with, on one side cut off from the outer world; the telephones and telegraphs were down. Even the railway line had been interfered with; fortunately on that side it was a very small railway, a mere branch line. But still, at a certain point the lines had simply disappeared, had apparently just crumbled into dust. The point happened to be about five yards long when it was first discovered, and by the time the railway gang got to it, it was rather more than six. There was a good deal of difficulty too about mending it—though the news of this did not reach the town till later; none of the usual appliances were reliable; they seemed to have none of their proper strength. Steel bent; wood snapped; hammers went awry, for their weight lightened even between the upward swing and the blow. It was all most unusual and very disconcerting; and those whose business or pleasure took them to the station where they found that the little train remained the whole day were thoroughly upset.

But there were others who were disturbed too. The collapse of the houses behind the Tighes' home was only part of a disturbance that affected a complete arc of the town. In that arc all dissociated buildings had been affected—by wind, by thunder, by a local earthquake, nobody knew how; sheds and garages were found to be broken down and ruinous. Hoardings were down, poles and posts—everything that was not largely used by man and that had not received into it, as matter will, over a long period, part of his more intimate life. The destruction therefore, consistent with its own laws, was inconsistent to uninstructed eyes. A shed where two small boys found continual pleasure in playing and working was left standing; a very much finer summer-house which no-one had wanted or used was found so broken up that it was not much more than a heap of splinters. Strength, though no-one realized it, was being withdrawn from the works of man, for the earth was more and more passing into the circle round the solitary house, and as it passed the Principle of Strength re-assumed all of itself which had been used in human labours. Anthony Durrant, at breakfast in the Station Hotel, heard of this and that piece of destruction, and saw it in the light of that greater knowledge which he had received since, in the abyss, he had accepted the challenge of the Eagle. This was the first circle, the extreme outward change which the entrance of man's world into that other world was producing. Over the coffee and his first cigarette he asked himself what other change was imminent. When everything was drawn farther, into the second circle—silly words, but they had to be used—when Subtlety which was the Serpent began to draw into itself the subtleties of man? A tremor went through him, but he sat on, constraining himself gravely to contemplate the possible result. For the principle of subtlety was double—instinctive and intellectual, and if man's intellect began to fail, or at least all unprepared and undefended intellect, what dreadful fatuity would take its place! He had a vision of the town full of a crowd of expressionless gaping mindless creatures, physical and mental energy passing out of them. Yet since man was meant to be the balance and pattern of all the Ideas—ah, but he was *meant* to be! Was he? Setting aside any who had deliberately abandoned themselves to their own desires instead of the passion for truth, for reality, such as those with whom he had fought, still there were those who had unconsciously become lost in one pursuit, such as Mr. Tighe, or who had studied reality for their own purposes—such as Damaris had been. She had been saved by a terrible experience, and by the chance of (he found himself bound to admit it as an unimportant fact) his own devotion to her. But of the others?

He left the problem. He had his own business to attend to. Damaris, whatever her faults, had never been a fool—outside one particular folly—and in the long talk that they had had on the previous evening she had grown more and more clear that her business was to go out into the lanes and fields and see if she could find Quentin. His breath came a little quicker; his body shook for a moment, as he considered her making this adventure in a countryside where such Powers were to be experienced. But he overcame this natural fear. If Damaris felt it to be her duty, a necessity of her new life, she had better go. In every way it would be wiser and greater than for her to crouch over her books again while transmutation was proceeding. These crises of the soul produced their own capacities, and though too often the capacity faded as the crisis passed, it was better to make use of it at once than to find reasons for neglecting it. He had himself half-intended to search for his friend—at first alone, and then in company with Damaris, but another place, though not another quest, had presented itself to him. As he thought of Quentin he found his mind recurring continually to the rooms they shared, to the long discussions, the immortal evenings, experienced reality, eternal knowledge. Even from the ordinary point of view, it was at least possible that the distracted Quentin might have tried to get back to the place he knew so well, perhaps by train if his habits still had power on him, perhaps on foot if they had not. It was at least as likely that Quentin would be there as anywhere, taking refuge amid dear familiarities from his intolerable fear. But Anthony felt that this possibility was not the real reason of his own decision. He felt that there rather than elsewhere could he best serve his friend; his nature go out to him, and his will be ready. For there, in so far as place mattered at all, was the place of the Principle that had held them together—something that, he hoped, was stronger than the lion and subtler than the serpent and more lovely than butterflies, something perhaps that held even the Ideas in their places and made a tender mockery even of the Angelicals. There his being would have the best possibility of knowing where that other being was; and in his new-found union with Damaris the possibility was increased. It was for her to prove her own new courage and purpose—he could not help her there; except by accepting it. But if her search went among—not the fields alone but those things which moved in the fields, and if he attended, under the protection of the Eagle, in—not their rooms alone but the place that held their rooms, might not some success be granted, and Quentin be brought safely from the chaos that had fallen on him? And even.... But the further thought eluded him; some greater possibility flickered in his mind and was gone. Well, that could wait: there was order even in the Divine Hierarchies, and his first business was to catch the earliest possible train to London.

He failed in this because Richardson telephoned just as he was getting up from the breakfast table, and afterwards came immediately round to see him. The tales they each had to recount made no alteration in either of their purposes. Anthony was still clear that he had to go to London and Richardson—smiling a little ironically—proposed to go as usual to his bookshop. They were both in very different ways too far practised in self-discipline and intellectual control not to be content in any crisis, even the most fantastic, to deal as adequately as possible with the next moment. The next moment clearly invited each of them to a definite job, and each of them immediately responded. They shook hands and parted at the door of the hotel, two young men separating pleasantly for the week's work, two princely seekers after holiness dividing to their lonely individual labours. But as they shook hands they were, each of them, intensely aware of sound and movement in the air about them, though one seemed rather to welcome and one to refuse it; and those who passed either of them in the street threw more than one glance at the intent and noble figure that went vigilantly on its way.

Among those who passed Richardson was Mr. Berringer's housekeeper. She had spent the Sunday night in Smetham, rather against the will of the male nurse whom Dr. Rockbotham had engaged. But the doctor himself had given her permission when he had been at *The Joinings* on the Sunday morning, after asking Lorrigan, which was the nurse's name, whether that wouldn't be all right. The question so obviously was one of those which the Latin grammar states are introduced by the word 'nonne' that the doctor had hardly waited for the affirmative answer which 'nonne' expects. What, as a matter of fact, Lorrigan had said sounded itself more like 'nonne' than any English word had a right to do. He rather disapproved of having to get his own breakfast, but later on the sight of the supper which the housekeeper had put ready placated him, and they parted on the best of terms, condoling with each other over the increasing heat. Once or twice indeed, after she had gone, Lorrigan thought he had smelt something burning, and had gone round to investigate. But everything had seemed all right.

It was certainly very hot. Standing at the door of the house for a few minutes before going upstairs to the bed that had been made up for him in Berringer's room, Lorrigan thought to himself that it was partly due to the position of the house. It lay in a much deeper hollow than he had realized, and yet he had known the road well enough for seven or eight years, ever since he had come to Smetham. He had often been along it on his motor-cycle, and he had always thought of it as mounting just past the house in a gentle rise to the slightly higher ridge where the trees were. But to-night as he stood there, looking out, it seemed very different. The ridge looked higher, and much steeper; indeed, all round the house the ground was much higher than he remembered. He looked along the road in the direction of the climbing road, and thought lazily, 'It does climb too.' For a wild moment the house and Mr. Berringer and he all seemed very deep, almost at the bottom of a pit, with the ground going up about them like walls. There had been less thunder this last day or two, which was fortunate, for it was a creepy house he was in—and he rather wished the housekeeper had not gone. Talk was a useful thing; it kept one steady, he thought, unconsciously repeating Anthony's 'It supports the wings in the air' of the previous day. And there were all sorts of little shiverings and quiverings and flickers—once or twice it had been exactly like a little flame at the edge of his eyes. Patients who felt shiverings and quiverings and saw flames and flashes he was more or less used to. He had once been male nurse for three years to an old gentleman who had a recurring belief that he had been responsible for the Great Fire of London, and who had in consequence at those times fits of deep melancholy and remorse at the deaths he had caused, accompanied by a spasmodic terror of being himself cut off by the Fire. Lorrigan's own view had been that this gentleman ought to have been put away, but the family couldn't bring themselves to such extreme measures, so he was relegated to the Dower House and Lorrigan, and books on the higher mathematics in which he was an acknowledged authority. But with all his drawbacks he had been, at his best, a pleasant gentleman, and the house had been away among the South Downs, where everything was much less oppressive. Lorrigan sighed, and went to bed.

In the morning it was, if anything, worse. The sun was blazing down, and nobody came along the road. It had never been a busy road, but it had not, when he had been along it, ever seemed so deserted as it was now. He waited impatiently for Mrs. Portman's return.

397

She came about half-past eleven, full of the rumours that were going about the town. When he heard of the fall of the telephones Lorrigan went off to try their own, and found indeed that he could not get a reply from the Exchange at Smetham. He came back to her rather gloomily, and interrupted her repetition of her story to ask if she could smell burning. 'It's getting a very peculiar house, this,' he said. 'The old man upstairs—well, I don't mind him; I'm used to them. But all this smell of fire, and things breaking down…. And dreams. I don't know when I've dreamt as badly as I did last night. It was a regular nightmare. All animals—you wouldn't believe, Mrs. Portman; I might have been to the Zoo. There was a great lion walking round everywhere…. I couldn't get past him—you know how it is in dreams….'

'Why,' said Mrs. Portman, 'would you believe it, that's what my daughter's little girl was talking about this morning. Out in the garden before breakfast she was, and came running in to say that there must be a circus come to Smetham, for she'd just seen a big lion go by the end of the garden. She couldn't talk of anything else all breakfast time till her mother shut her up, her father not being very well. He's a policeman, you know, and he'd been on night duty, and came in all dazed this morning. Couldn't talk of anything but how lovely something was.'

'There's not much that's all that lovely,' Mr. Lorrigan said pessimistically.

'O I don't know,' Mrs. Portman answered. 'I like a bit of colour round myself, but I'm not in it with Jack. He ought to've been a painter instead of a policeman, the things he sees in trees and sunsets. I tell him he wouldn't notice a murder right before his eyes if there was a sunset there too.'

'Sunsets have their place,' said Lorrigan. 'Not that I've ever seen much in a sunset myself. My Bessie did an essay on sunsets the other day at school, and the things that child put in! I've not seen all those colours in a sunset—not for forty years. And anyhow I don't hold with teaching children to do too much sky gazing; there's other things that's more important.'

'That's so,' Mrs. Portman said, 'and if I was going to buy a picture it'd be one of those that have got more to them than just a lot of different colours. I like a picture to have a story in it, something that you can enjoy. I've got one upstairs that belonged to my mother—*The Last Days of King Charles the First*, and I'm sure it used to make me cry to look at it, all so natural with the little children and everything. I tell you, Mr. Lorrigan, I like a picture that makes me feel something.'

'I don't care for pictures much, anyhow,' Lorrigan answered. 'Though, of course, a good lifelike bit of work…. One of the best I ever saw was the sign of an inn out the other side of the town—that was a lion too: the *Red Lion*, and anything more natural I never saw. I wonder if I got thinking of it last night.'

'I expect so,' Mrs. Portman said. 'Lor', isn't it close, Mr. Lorrigan? I could do with a cup of tea after that walk. Will you have a cup too?'

'Well, I don't mind,' Mr. Lorrigan agreed. 'I'll just have another look at Mr. Berringer while you get your hat off, and then take a turn in the garden till it's ready.'

'Do,' Mrs. Portman said, and went off to her room. In a few minutes she was downstairs again, and went across to light the gas and put on the kettle for her tea. It would have needed Anthony's purged eyes to see then what neither she in the kitchen nor Lorrigan in the garden could see—the multiplicity of intellectual flame that was leaping and twining all over the house. Some new passion was spreading out through earthly things, another Energy pressed onwards to the moment in which, concerned upon its own business, it should yet take the opportunity of whatever opening into matter might be afforded to it. Mrs. Portman picked up a box of matches, and as the invisible fire arched itself round and over her paused in amused remembrance of her granddaughter's chatter about the lion. Then she opened it, took out a match, struck it——

In the garden Lorrigan was strolling from the gate back towards the house. A wave of heat struck him, a terrific burst of fire blinded him. He reeled back, shouting incoherently, with his hands to his eyes. When he could open them again, after that violent shock, he saw before him the whole house blazing to heaven. This was no fire spreading from room to room, though his first thought was that the curtains had caught. But from the road to which he had fled, looking dazedly back, he saw not flames breaking out from doors or windows, but now a pillar, now a nest of fire. It soared, it sank, it spread outwards and curved back inwards; the heat and light of the burning struck and hurt him, and he went stumbling further along the road to escape it. 'What's happened?' he thought stupidly. 'What's she done? Christ, the whole place is alight!' The roar of the fire beat in his ears; he covered them with his hands and blinked out over the fields. And then he remembered his charge.

He faced round, feeling that he ought to do something. But it was evident, even to his ruining intelligence, that nothing could be done. No one could live in that destructive ferocity of flame; both his patient and Mrs. Portman must already have perished. He had better get hold of somebody; the fire brigade, the police—and the telephones were down. Lorrigan felt like crying, his helplessness was so obvious and extreme. It wasn't more than ten minutes since he had been talking to Mrs. Portman in that kitchen about pictures and lions and zoos, and now she and her master were burnt to death, and the house was falling in…. 'O God….' he exclaimed, 'don't let her come out,' for he had had a moment's dreadful fear of some burning creature rushing out of that fiery splendour. 'O God, kill her, kill her,' he thought unintentionally, 'and then put it out.' But God went on concerning Himself with his Deity and that seemed to imply the continuation of the fire.

It was some time later that Lorrigan came racing into the town, and a shorter time later still that the fire-brigade, and Dr. Rockbotham, and a number of other people were assembled round the house. So fierce was the heat that they were all kept at a good distance, and the efforts that were made to approach the house closely all failed. The hoses were turned on; streams of water were dashed against the fire. By this time it had been burning for the best part of an hour, and if anything it seemed more violent than before. 'You shouldn't have left him, Lorrigan,' Dr. Rockbotham exclaimed, quite unjustly, in the excitement of the moment.

'No,' said Lorrigan, also excited. 'I suppose I ought to have sat by him and been burnt up too. I suppose you pay me for that, don't you? I suppose….'

The doctor looked at him sharply. 'Now steady, steady,' he said. 'Of course, you couldn't tell. I didn't intend to blame you. I only meant that….' He stopped, aware that he had as a fact meant to blame the nurse, and then resumed, 'There, I apologize if I hurt you.'

But Lorrigan's usual equanimity had vanished. 'Coming to me and telling me I ought to have stopped there!' he said. 'What d'you mean, hey? What d'you mean?' He caught the doctor's arm, and shook it fiercely.

'Leave go at once,' Rockbotham exclaimed, shaken out of his usual benignity. 'How dare you touch me? Leave go!'

In the general surging of the crowd in the road a new little vortex formed around the two of them.

'Now then, Jack,' a voice said, 'don't you be silly.'

'Ah,' said another voice, 'it's all very fine, blaming a man for not letting himself be burnt! There's too many treat us that way!'

The doctor looked round. It was a mixed crowd, and part of it wasn't very nice. Loafers and bullies from Smetham had been attracted by the blaze. Lorrigan still held his arm; another man drove an elbow, as if accidentally, into his side. 'Take care,' the doctor exclaimed.

Immediately a sudden fierceness awoke in them. They jolted, thrust, hit at him. His hat was knocked off, and his glasses. He called out. Others in the crowd heard him, looked round, saw what was happening, and came pushing in on one side or the other. In less than five minutes after Rockbotham's first remark nothing less than a free fight was going on. It was not, perhaps, a serious fight, but it shook the doctor very greatly. People were grunting and snarling at each other all round him; they were behaving, he thought disgustedly, like animals. A couple of constables intervened, and the row quietened down. But though the crowd turned its attention again to the fire the panting and grunting remained, as if indeed some animal rather than human nature was then dominating its members. And over everything went up the roar of the fire.

An hour, two hours, went by. Still the hoses were directed towards the blaze; still the torrents of water fell on it. But when three hours were past, and more—when the afternoon was almost done—when the crowd had changed and multiplied and lessened and multiplied again—still the house burned. At least, presumably it was the house. The Captain of the Fire Brigade talked with the Police-Inspector, who suggested that there might be a store of chemicals somewhere in the cellars. Hadn't Mr. Berringer been a scientific man?

'I suppose it must be something like that,' the Captain said. 'But it seems very odd.'

'It's odd how the flames hide the house,' the Inspector answered. 'Generally you can see the walls except for a minute or two here and there. But here you can't see anything but the fire. And that looks more like a great nest than anything.'

'With a bird in it, I suppose,' the Captain answered, looking irritably at the blaze, and then at his watch. 'Why, it's been going on for five hours and it's as bad as ever.'

'Ah well, I daresay you'll get it under soon,' the Inspector said encouragingly, and moved off.

But when night fell, that violent and glorious catastrophe was still visible over the countryside. It was burning up through the earth; indeed, the Captain found himself thinking occasionally that it was actually burning the earth. For as the hours passed, the base of that fiery pillar expanded, and by midnight the perplexed firemen found that its extreme circle had reached on one side to the middle of the garden, the flames seeming to rise from the ground as if the withered grass and the dry hard ground beneath broke into fire of their own accord. The increasing heat drove the workers back, such of them as were left. For a few had been overcome, and one had been almost blinded by an unexpected outbreak of crimson light, and the idle watchers had disappeared. Not merely night and weariness had drawn these off, but a vague rumour an echo of which reached the Captain himself from the mouth of one of his men. 'Did you hear they're shutting up in the town?'

'What d'you mean—shutting up?' the Captain asked.

'All the pubs are closing, they say,' the man said. 'There's animals going about the streets'—and he added another 'they say.'

'It sounds as if it was time the pubs closed,' the Captain muttered. 'Don't talk that blasted rubbish to me. For Christ's sake look what you're doing.'

Yet his incredulity would have ceased could he have seen the town as it lay there away behind him. The doors were shut, the streets were empty, a terrified populace hid in dark houses behind such protection as they could find. For now here and now there, first one and then another wayfarer had seen forms and images, and fled in terror. Certain courageous folk had heard the rumours, and mocked at them, and gone out, but by midnight these too had come rushing home, and the streets were given up to the moonlight, while all one side of the heavens was filled with the glow of the burning. Under that distant glow, and passing from the moon to the dark and from the dark to the moon, there went all night the subdued sound of mighty creatures. Sceptical eyes looked out from occasional windows, and beheld them: the enormous bulk of the Lion, the coiling smoothness of the Serpent, even, very rarely, the careering figure of the Unicorn. And above them went the never-resting flight of the Eagle, or, if indeed it rested, then it was at some moment when, soaring into its own dominion, it found a nest exalted beyond human sight in the vast mountains of the creation natural to it, where it might repose and contemplate its aeonian wisdom. There among the Andes and Himalayas of the soul, it sank to rest; thence again, so swiftly it renewed its youth, it swept out, and passing upon its holy business, cast from its wings the darkness which is both mortal night and night of the mind. It knew, since it knew all things, the faint sounds of the lesser world that was more and more passing into the place of the Angelicals, but what to it were those sounds, however full of distress they might be? For, as the quivering human creatures knew, the destruction was spreading. It was no longer only neglected sheds and empty houses, posts and palisades, that were falling. An inhabited house crashed in ruins, and screams and moans broke through the night. A little after, in another part of the town, a second fell; and then a third. In the double fear that, even through those barred and shuttered houses, began to spread, there was hinted panic. Men came out to help and caught sight of something and fled, except only those who saw the silver horn and heard the silver hooves of the Angel of their Return; they only, free from fear, toiled to rescue their fellows.

All others, crouched in darkness, waited in terror for death.

CHAPTER XIV

THE HUNTING OF QUENTIN

Damaris, on that Monday morning, was conscious as she ate her breakfast of one surprising truth. She had, as a matter of fact, almost finished before the consciousness of it came upon her, though the fact itself had been with her since she woke. She sat staring at the last bit of toast on her plate, as she realised that, very surprisingly, she wasn't worrying. Until that moment it had never seemed to her that she did worry very much; other things worried her, but that was different. It was not she who fretted; it was she who was fretted. It occurred to her suddenly that of all the follies of which she had been guilty, and they seemed to have been many and stupendous, none had ever been greater than that. She had always regarded herself as an unchangeable fact, attacked and besieged by a troublesome world. But she could as easily be, indeed at the moment she was, a changeable fact, beautifully concerned with a troubled world. She had been worrying all her life about herself, and now she wasn't worrying any more. It was not perhaps possible for her then to realize that this was because she herself didn't—for the moment—exist for herself. There being for Damaris—in that moment—no Damaris, there was no Damaris for Damaris to worry about. However soon that lucid integrity might become clouded and that renewed innocence inevitably stained, it did then exist. All this she did not perhaps realize, but she did definitely feel the marvellous release. She still wanted to get on with her work—if she could, if she could approach it with this new sense that her subjects were less important than her subjects' subject, that her arrangements were very tentative presentations of the experiences of great minds and souls. But her work was less important than her immediate task. She ate the toast and stood up pensively. Here she was, abandoning Abelard—Abelard … the word had a new sound. She saw the brilliant young tonsured clerk, the crowds in the growing University, the developing intellect

400

and culture; she felt the rush and tumult—almost physically she felt it—of the students pouring to hear him, because they were burning to listen, to learn, to…. To learn. Damaris twiddled a fork on the table, and felt herself blushing. 'The credulous piety….' she bit her lip. No, Abelard, St. Bernard, St. Thomas—no, they were not merely the highest form in a school of which she was the district inspector. No, intellect might make patterns but itself it was a burning passion, a passion stronger even than that other love of Peter Abelard for Heloise, the Canon's niece, which had always seemed to her a pity—a pity not merely for Abelard himself but in general. To learn. Well, she wasn't past learning, thank God. If it had all got to be redone, it should be redone. Anything should be done that fitted in with Anthony and the sunlight and freedom from worry and that stranger thing which she dimly realised had been the central desire of centuries of labour. But to-morrow. To-day there was Quentin.

She went into the kitchen and made herself some sandwiches, considerably to the maid's astonishment. She even attempted a little conversation, but she was feeling so shy that it was not altogether a success. The maid, she realised, was very much on her guard. That was the kind of world that Damaris Tighe had hitherto insisted on making all round her, a world where people were watchful and hostile. She looked at it humbly while she finished the sandwiches; then she went upstairs to her father.

He hadn't come down to breakfast for the last two days, and the tray that had been taken up to him stood on a table by the bed. But it was with a shock that she realized that he had not even undressed. He had lain down the night before, and though she called out good night to him she had not gone in. For here again was the opposition she had created, and she felt shy and distressed about it. But not worried—not nearly as worried over this far more serious thing as she had done so lately about his apparent disturbance of her work. Or what she chose to think a disturbance. No, not worried. If this also had to be done again, well, it had to be done, that was all. There seemed to be quite a lot that looked like having to be done over again. Everything perhaps except—she realized it as she crossed the room—except Anthony. But she had treated Anthony as she had these others. Well, it was a pity, but something was present there which touched even that iniquity with laughter and holy delight and sweet irony, so that—if Anthony would—they might smile at it together. In a delicate gratitude she came to her father.

He was lying with his eyes shut, motionless. The breakfast tray was untouched. She leaned over him, touched him, spoke to him, and very slowly he opened his eyes, but they did not seem to see her. They did not seem to see anything; their vision was awfully withdrawn. Damaris sank down by the bed, looking at him in fear, but it was with nothing of the same fear as she had experienced on the previous night. She was in the presence of some process which she did not understand, and of which she stood in awe, but she was not merely afraid of it. 'Father,' she said softly, and a flicker of recognition came into his eyes. He moved his lips; she leant nearer. 'Glory,' he said, 'glory,' and ceased. 'Can I do anything?' she asked still softly, and added with a rush of willingness to serve, 'anything at all?' He moved his hand a little and she took it in her own; after a little he said, and she only just caught the words: 'You weren't hurt?'

'Not much,' she answered. 'You and Anthony helped me.'

There was another long pause, then he uttered—'Not me; Anthony knows.—I saw he knew—when he came.—I don't know—much. Only—this. You'll go—your way.'

'I shall go,' she said, and as she spoke she saw him for what seemed the first time. The absurd little man, of whom she had been ashamed, with whom she had been so irritated, on whom she had so often loosed her disguised contempt, was transfigured. He became beautiful before her; he lay there, in all his ridiculous modern clothes, and neither he nor they were at all ridiculous. The colours and tints harmonized perfectly; the slight movements he made were exquisitely proportioned and gracious; the worship that glowed full in his eyes lifted him into the company of the gods he seemed to see. Beauty adored beauty; and lay absorbed in its contemplation. Tears came into her eyes as, from a great distance, she looked at that transfiguration. He was upon his way, and she must follow hers. She felt the call within her; if she could not serve him then she must do what she could do. There was another in greater need, and salvation must be communicated or it would be lost. She might, the day before, have left him as she was about to leave him now, but then it would have been in order, grudging him even those few minutes of attention, to dash back to herself. She thought of it and was ashamed; very faintly there came to her upon the air the slightest memory of the odour of corruption. She kissed him and stood up. He smiled a little, and murmured: 'Don't—get hurt,—goodbye.' She kissed him again, pressed his hand, saw his eyes again close, and went.

It occurred to her, as she changed her shoes, that the maid would think she certainly ought to stop at home. Damaris shook her head helplessly: that, she supposed, was the maid's business. She could hardly expect to have the most favourable construction put on her own words and actions, but what had got to be done had got to be. Anyhow, in this case the maid was wrong. Standing up, Damaris realized that interpretations nearly always are wrong; interpretations in the nature of things being peculiarly personal and limited. The act was personal but infinite, the reasoned meaning was personal and finite. Interpretation of infinity by the finite was pretty certain to be wrong. The thought threw a light on her occupation with philosophies. Philosophy to Plato, to Abelard, to St. Thomas, was an act—the love of wisdom; to her——

But all that was to come. Love or wisdom, her act awaited her. She ran lightly down the stairs.

Neither love nor wisdom had suggested either to her or to Anthony when they had been talking whereabouts in the neighbourhood Quentin was likely to be found. Both of them indeed realized that he might not be in the neighbourhood at all. Only then, if his brain were still functioning he would probably make for the rooms in London; and if not, if fright had possessed him entirely, well, then, he might be anywhere. He might, of course, be dead, overwhelmed by the strength of the Lion, or driven by his fear to destruction. But this Anthony had doubted, on what seemed to Damaris the perfectly satisfactory grounds that, if Quentin were dead, he himself would not still feel the necessity of finding him. 'It's more important even than he is,' Anthony had said, frowning, 'or let's say as important. There are two things muddled up— Quentin's one, and I'm not clear what the other is. But we shall be.'

'We?' she asked.

'We,' he answered. 'Darling, that's why—that's partly why—I think you're right to go.'

On the whole then Damaris saw no better idea than to go out to where she had had her first encounter with the young man, and then—then go whichever way suggested itself. She swung along, keeping a sharp look-out as she went; but within her her soul kept another watch, and her eyes, as they searched the hedges, were prepared both for Quentin and for some other sight. She could not tell whether the incredible visions that had manifested would show themselves to her; she did not desire but neither would she avoid them. She permitted herself to savour, to enjoy, the sensation of trust and dependence, and was astonished to find how comforting it was. It was quite impossible for her to balance and equate great Ideas, but if there were among them one whose nature was precisely that balance, and therefore the freedom of assured movement, then she would give herself to it, whether in looking up references about Pythagoras or looking out for Quentin along country roads. The one thing she had no longer to do was to look after herself. There was something that knew—that was philosophy. Philosophy, then, she mused as she went along, was not so much an act as a being, and it was upon those eagle wings that all her masters had travelled. And Sophia itself—Holy Wisdom—but she was content not to inquire more; she would find that out when she had practised loving it a little longer. She had wasted a lot of time, she thought, and found herself whistling softly as her mind recalled the headings of her papers—*The Eidola and the Angeli, Platonic Tradition at the Court of Charlemagne*—'Damaristic tradition at the Court of Damaris'—she laughed out. How right Anthony had been!

She had come to Saturday's meeting-place. There was the stile; there was the ditch; there she had gone sprawling. In a sudden appreciation she went round to the exact spot where Quentin had pulled her down, and stepping into the ditch sat down where she had fallen. Quentin in his wildness had yet kept some thought for others; he had wished to help her because she was his friend's friend—because she was Anthony's girl. Well, if Anthony's girl could now be any use to him, who in his madness had been greater than she in her sanity, here she was! She sat for a moment attentive, then she sprang to her feet. Far and fast there came to her the sound of something galloping. That sound had echoed through her last night when Anthony came to her, and now she heard it again. She ran up to the stile, looked all round, saw nothing, and jumped up on the step to see better. At a good distance away, down the steep slope beneath her, she saw *The Joinings*. Her eyes dwelled on it thoughtfully and then very high in the air above it she saw again such a shape as had sat on Anthony's shoulder when he came to her, exalted in the secure knowledge of its nature over the offices of its peers—the idea of wisdom, the image of philosophy, the temporal extension of divine science. She stood gazing, and forgetful of her immediate business; and she was taught her duty on the instant. In the old unhappy days she had been left to herself—loving herself she was abandoned to herself. But in loving others, or seeking to love others, the great Angelicals took her in their charge. The noise of hooves rang on the road behind her; a terrific blow, as she turned, caught her shoulder and sent her flying into the hedge, and as she fell she saw a form which seemed like a silver horse, but of whose nature Richardson could have told her truer things, go galloping across the field. 'Idiot!' she exclaimed cheerfully to herself, then, bruised, scratched, and aching, scrambled up, back to the stile and over it. She would follow as far as she could; perhaps this was a guide, and if not, then as well this way as any other. But how stupid of her, she thought as she tried to run, to be caught gaping like that when she had a job to do. They were a little severe, these new masters of hers. Anthony had told her of the sudden stab in his side that had warned him to be silent, and she supposed the bruise on her shoulder was to teach her to be alert. No doubt she needed it. Certainly there had been an invasion of the court of Damaris, and it was no easy conqueror that sat upon her relinquished throne.

She jumped over another stile, came into a wide meadow, and paused. The galloping form had vanished. And now what? The question was answered almost before she had framed it. There were running along the farther edge of the meadow, two figures—the first certainly a man; the second—the second a man too, she supposed, only she couldn't make out whether it were going on two feet or four; sometimes one and sometimes the other, it seemed. But that didn't matter; it was the first figure to which she looked, for she knew within her that it was Quentin.

She began to run towards them across the meadow, forgetting her shoulder. It was an empty meadow, at least almost empty: there was a single white splodge, a sheep or a lamb or something in the middle, moving gently about. But the two figures were running much quicker than she could; she paused, anxiously waiting to see which way they would go. If there were a gate at the bottom…. But apparently there was not; for Quentin turned at the corner and came driving up the side. There was, she could see, no way out from that point till he reached the stile by which she had entered; she went back to it, and waited. They were going terribly fast, both of them, and as they drew nearer she stared at them in horror and pity, though not—no, never again—in fear. For Quentin, though he was running, had already passed, it seemed to her, any state in which a man could be, and live. He was almost naked, he was torn and bleeding all over, especially his feet, which appeared to her no longer feet but broken and shapeless masses of bloody flesh. His arms were tossing frenziedly, his hands dangling from them as they were flung about; his face was inhuman with terror and anguish. The dreadful noise that came to her as he drew near was his breath wrenched from the very extreme of existence; his eyes were sightless, and one cheek was horribly bitten and gnawed. She ran out to meet him, tears on her face for very distress of love, and held out her hands, and called him by both his names: 'Quentin! Quentin! Mr. Sabot! Quentin!' He did not hear or see her; he rushed on, past her, past the stile, round the meadow; and while she cried to him the second form was near her. It too was going swiftly; but it still seemed to be rather leaping than running. Its clothing also was part gone and part disordered; but its boots were on its feet, and its arms not tossing but held close to it, with crooked fingers. The face was as inhuman as that other, but while that was man blasted this was man brutalized. It was a snarling animal, and it was snuffling and snorting with open mouth. Yet she had a dreadful feeling of recognition; she could find no name for it, but somewhere it had had a name, somewhere in her own past it also had had a past, and that past was appallingly kindred to the horror she had seen on the evening before. All this she took in as it came up to her, and sprang forward, greatly adventuring, to check or distract or fight it. Vainly; as she moved a wind poured from its passage and flung her backward till she reeled against the stile. There was strength in and about the man, if it were a man, that drove her from him; or the beast, if it were a beast, for as again she went forward and looked after him, he had lost his upright position, and was leaping clumsily forward, if not actually on all fours, yet so bent and thrust forward that he seemed altogether more animal than human. She ran out into the meadow, and paused; the chase was now going down the fourth side. Since she could not prevent the pursuit she might perhaps aid the pursued. But how? how?

Willing to do all but uncertain what to do, she watched, and then became aware of some other thing in her line of vision. It was the solitary lamb that was gently moving towards her, gently and slowly. She looked at it, and across the meadow there passed suddenly the shadow of the flying eagle, cast over her and proceeding from her towards the lamb. Moved by a quick hope she followed it; the beast, more slowly, advanced to meet her. They came together, and the innocence that sprang in her knew a greater innocence and harmlessness in it; she dropped to her knees, and put a hand on its back. So kneeling, she looked again at that terrible hunt, which, though she did not then know it, had already been going on for several hours. It had been close after midnight when, wandering out of the town upon his greedy pursuit of prey, the creature that had been Foster had startled Quentin from uneasy sleep in the bracken, had scented and trailed him, and once, when Quentin had stumbled and fallen, had come up with and worried him. But the extreme madness of fear had given Quentin strength enough to make one wild struggle, and he had escaped. After that, through the night and the dawn and the early morning, the hunt had gone on, through lanes and woods and fields, now swiftly, now slowly. Sometimes after crossing a small river or among thick trees the driven wretch had had a few minutes respite, but always sooner or later the inevitable snuffling and trampling had drawn near, and again the flight had begun. Quentin now was beginning to run merely round and round; only as he fled along the meadow side once more, something came crying to what function of his brain was left. Damaris, kneeling by the lamb, went on calling—calling one name alone, steadily, clearly, entreatingly—'Quentin! Quentin! Quentin!' She saw his head turn a little, and renewed her effort. He wavered; the creature behind was almost on him. He broke inward across the meadow, and still the voice of Damaris sounded to guide him, though what she was to do when he came she did not know. He came; he was with them; right before her he flung his arms wide once more and fell, and she threw herself forward over his body to protect and guard it with her own. At the feet of the lamb they lay, and the pursuing creature gave vent to something that was both laugh and snarl, and paused, and very softly began to creep round them before he sprang. Damaris thought of several things at once—Anthony and the Eagle and her father, but all of them vanished in the flood of simplicity that suddenly took her. For some reason she knew assuredly that the thing would not hurt her; its hate and its power divided and passed round her. She leaned over Quentin, looking into his sightless eyes, searching him with no purpose but to find what secret of life still throve in him and, for what she could, to nourish it. And by them both, frisking in the sunlight, the lamb jumped and ran and rested and gave itself up to joy.

The other creature continued its uneasy perambulation. As it went circling round them it uttered little noises of effort and pain. Sometimes it made a sudden abrupt rush inward, but every rush was diverted from its intended prey; it was, against its will, drawn aside, and thrust back into its own path. The lamb took no notice of it whatever; Damaris glanced up at it occasionally, but with a serene absent-mindedness; Quentin lay still, his hand in the woman's while with her other she tried, with her handkerchief and a fragment torn from her dress, to wipe away the drying blood from his face. But suddenly there pierced through this passion of goodwill a long and dreadful howl. She looked up, the thing that had pursued them was farther away, and was, apparently by some interior power, being drawn still farther. It was retreating, slowly and grotesquely, and she saw as she looked that under it the grass was all leaning one way as if blown by a wind. With that wind the creature was struggling; it was lifted a little, and hung absurdly in the air, an inch or two off the ground, then it fell and sprawled full length and twisted and howled. She looked over her shoulder; the lamb was cropping the grass. She looked at Quentin; repose was coming back into his face, and with it that beauty of innocence which is seen in unhappy mankind only in sleep and death and love and transmuting sanctity—the place of the lamb in the place of the lion.

Within that farther place Damaris rested. But without, that which had once been the intelligent and respected Mr. Foster struggled to control the strength which he could no longer control. For a few days he had, even with the Idea, exercised some kind of domination upon the Idea, but as the earth, and he with it, slipped more deeply into that other state of being, his poor personal desire could no longer govern or separate. That which was in him rushed to mingle with that which was without. The power of the Lion came upon him in a great wind, and the breath of his spirit fled to meet it. Strangled and twisted he was lifted and carried on the wind; he was flung into the air, and carelessly dropped back on to the earth. As he fell for that last time he saw the Lion upon him. The giant head loomed over him; the great paw struck his chest and thrust him down. Immense pressure enclosed and crushed him; in a dreadful pain he ceased to be.

Damaris, glancing up with a start of recollection from the Lamb and Quentin, looked round for their enemy. It was not for some minutes that she saw, away in the meadow, crushed and trodden flat, and driven by that treading right into the earth, the body of a man.

Even then it was to her no more than a fact. She stood up and looked again to be certain, then she turned her perplexed attention to Quentin. It was by no means clear to her that if she left him he would not go rushing off again, yet she could not get him to the town without help. She paused uncertainly; then she decided at least to try. She bent down and slipped her arm under his shoulders; with something of an effort she half raised him.

He seemed to be vaguely conscious; murmuring encouragement she got him to his feet, and, moving very slowly, managed to make him take an uncertain step forward. It pierced her heart to persist in his using those terrible bleeding feet; she had drawn one arm over her shoulders, and as much as possible relieved them of his weight. Even so the pain troubled his wandering mind, and his body moaned under its suffering. But this she had to ignore. Very, very slowly, they crossed the meadow and reached the stile, and as they did so he came to himself enough to understand something of what was happening. So concentrated was she on this concern that she did not notice the blaze that broke out from the house in the distance below; she had to get him over the stile.

It was by then midday. She would have left him then, had she dared and could she, to find some car, but he would not let her go. Her efforts at explanation he understood but rejected; she was to keep with him, he made clear, and he would do his best to get along. So, all through that long hot afternoon, both the man and the woman retraced their steps along the hard country road—Quentin from his flight, Damaris from her seclusion—and came at last to the house where, as twilight began to fall, her father drew his last breath in final surrender to the beauty that had possessed him.

———————————————

CHAPTER XV

THE PLACE OF FRIENDSHIP

Anthony opened the door of the flat and went quickly into it. He called out as he did so, not that he had much hope of an answer, even if Quentin were there. But instinctively his voice went before him, desiring to cry out to that wilderness of spirit, to proclaim the making straight of the highway of God. No other replied.

He went into each room, and even looked behind chairs and inside a deep cupboard or two and under tables and beds. The agonized fugitive might so easily have tried to hide himself in such an absurd refuge. But he had not; after a very few minutes Anthony was compelled to admit that the flat was untenanted. He came back into their common lounge and sat down. Quentin wasn't here; then he was still in flight—or helpless, or dead. The first possibility of the two which had been in Anthony's mind—that of finding his friend—had proved useless; the second and less defined—the hinted discovery in this house of friendship of a means of being of use to the troubled world—remained. He lay back in his chair and let his eyes wander round the room.

The traces of their common occupation lay before him, rather tidier at this hour of the morning than they generally were, because the woman who looked after the flat had obviously only just 'been round it' and gone. She had been broken of her original habit of putting everything straight, of thrusting papers away in drawers and pushing books back on to shelves—any book on any shelf, so that Spinoza and Mr. T. S. Eliot might jostle, which would have been quite suitable, but then also Milton might neighbour a study in Minoan origins, which was merely inconvenient, or Mr. Gerard Hopkins shoulder Mr. Gilbert Frankau, which was silly. So books and papers—and even pipes—still lay on tables, and Quentin's fountain-pen upon a pile of letter-paper. There were the pictures, most of them signs of some memory—this of a common holiday, that of a common friend, that again of a birthday or even of a prolonged argument. A little reproduction of Landseer's *Monarch of the Glen* was the sign of the last. Anthony had forgotten for the moment what the terrific discussion had really been about, though he knew in general terms that it was on the nature of art and had arisen out of a review of his own in *The Two Camps*. But he remembered how Quentin had won a perfectly devastating triumph, and how the next day he had himself searched several picture shops to find the Landseer and had triumphantly presented it to Quentin that evening as a commemoration of the battle and in illustration of the other's principles. Or so he swore it was, though Quentin had rampantly denied it; but they had hung the thing up in mutual laughter, derision, and joy. Anthony's eyes left it reluctantly, and went on glancing round the room.

The moments of their past showed themselves multitudinously to him as he looked. In that chair Quentin had sat sprawled on a winter evening, while he himself, pacing up and down the warm unlit room, had delivered a long monologue on Damaris; in yonder corner he had himself crouched with books scattered round him while they disputed which 'chorus ending from Euripides' might conceivably have been in Browning's mind. Quentin had a fantastic passion for discovering impossible suitabilities. By the window they had both leaned one evening, while they talked of the exact kind of authority which reposed in moments of exalted experience and how far they each sought to obey it. In another chair they had once seated an uneasy canvasser before a general election, and plied him with questions and epigrams about the nature of the State, and whether a dictatorship was consistent with the English political genius. By the table they had once nearly quarrelled; near the fireplace they had read immortal verse from a new illustrated edition of *Macbeth* which had come to Anthony for review, and had been propped up on the mantelpiece for admiration. Light and amusing, poignant and awful, the different hours of friendship came to him, each full of that suggestion of significance which hours of the kind mysteriously hold—a suggestion which demands definitely either to be accepted as truth or rejected as illusion. Anthony had long since determined on which side his own choice lay; he had accepted those exchanges, so far as mortal frailty could, as being of the nature of final and eternal being. Though they did not last, their importance did; though any friendship might be shattered, no strife and no separation could deny the truth within it: all immortality could but more clearly reveal what in those moments had been.

More certainly than ever he now believed. He reaccepted what they offered; he reaccepted *them*, knowing from of old that this, which seems so simple, is one of the hardest tasks laid before mankind. Hard, for the reality is so evasive; self-consciousness, egotism, heaviness, solemnity, carelessness, even an over-personal fondness, continually miss it. He could do nothing but indicate to that fleeting truth his willingness to be at its service. It accepted him in turn; it renewed within him its work of illumination. He felt how some moving power bore Quentin and himself within it, and so bearing them passed onward through time. Or perhaps it *was* Time; in that they were related, and outside that there was only … whatever 'the perfect and simultaneous possession of everlasting life' might be. The phrase, he remembered, came from St. Thomas; perhaps Damaris would once have quoted it in a footnote.

He sat on, from recollection passing to reflection, from reflection to obedience, from obedience into a trance of attention. As he had dreamed, if it were a dream, that he rose on powerful wings through the air of the spiritual abyss, so now he felt again the power between Quentin and himself active in its own place. Within that power the presence of his friend grew more defined to him, and the room in which he sat was but the visible extension of an immortal state. He loved; yet not he, but Love living in him. Quentin was surely there, in the room, leaning by the window as he had so often leaned, and Anthony instinctively rose and went across, as he had so often gone across, to join him. If, when he reached it, there was no mortal form, there was yet a reception of him into something that had been and still was, his movement freed it to make a movement of its own. He stood and looked out of the window upon the world.

It presented itself to him in an apparition of strength. How firmly the houses were set within the ground! with what decision each row of bricks lay level upon the row beneath! Spires and towers and chimneys thrust into the sky, and slender as they were, it was an energetic slenderness. The trees were drawing up strength and displaying it, and the sunlight communicated strength. The noises that came to him from the streets resolved themselves into a litany of energy. Matter was directed by and inspired with this first and necessary virtue, and through the vast spaces of the sky potential energy expanded in an azure wonder.

But the sounds that came to him though they reached him as a choric hymn, sounding almost like the subdued and harmonious thunder of the lion's roar, were yet many. A subtlety of music held them together, and the strength whose epiphany was before him was also subtilized into its complex existence. Neither virtue could exist without the other: the slender spires were a token of that unison. What intelligence, what cunning, what practice, had gone to build them! Even the chimneys—ways for smoke, improvements on the mere holes by which the accidents of fire dispersed—and fire itself, all signs of man's invention! He, as he stood there, was an incredibly subtle creation, nerves, sinews, bones, muscle, skin and flesh, heart and a thousand organs and vessels. They were his strength, yet his strength parcelled and ordered according to many curious divisions, even as by a similar process of infinite change the few clouds that floated in the sky were transmuted from and into rivers and seas. The seas, the world itself, was a mass of subtle life, existing only by means of those two vast Principles—and the stars beyond the world. For through space the serpentine imagination coiled and uncoiled in a myriad shapes, at each moment so and not otherwise, and the next moment entirely different and yet so and not otherwise again.

The Lion and the Serpent—but what arose between them, the first visitant from the world of abstract knowledge, the blue of the sky, the red of the bricks, the slenderness of the spires? 'The world was created by number,' someone had said—Pythagoras, of course. Dear Damaris! But when Number came to man, it was shown, not merely in pure intellectual proportions, which were no doubt more like its own august nature— No, they weren't; why were mathematics more after its nature than butterflies? Beauty went with strength and subtlety, and made haste to emotion as to mind, to sense as to spirit. One and indivisible, those three mighty Splendours yet offered themselves each to other—and had a fourth property also, and that was speed.

He stood there, looking out, and as if from some point high in space he beheld the world turning on its axis and at the same time rushing forward. So also he looked on created things and saw them moving rapidly upon their own concerns yet also moving forward in a unity. Within the sunlight he could almost have believed that a herd of wild horses came charging towards him across 'the savannahs of the blue', only they were not a herd and not coming towards him; they were single and going from him, or would have been had he not been following at a similar speed. And now the trance deepened upon him, and what had before been half deliberate thought was now dream or vision—and, as if for the last time, he felt the choice offered him once more. Moments of love were either reality or illusion; the instant knowledge required his similar decision. He made it at once, and the sunlight grew brighter still and flowed through and around him. Quentin was leaning on the other side of the window, or whatever opening it was, in whatever world, through which the light poured, and more than light. For the light changed as he remembered again that it was not Quentin but the thing that was between him and Quentin, the thing that went with speed, and yet, speeding, was already at its goal, the thing that was for ever new and for ever old—*tam antiqua, tam nova*, that issued from its own ardent nest in its own perpetually-renovated beauty, a rosy glow, a living body, the wonder of earthly love. The movement of the Eagle was the measure of truth, but the birth of some other being was the life of truth, some other royal creature that rose from fire and plunged into fire, momently consumed, momently reborn. Such was the inmost life of the universe, infinitely destroyed, infinitely recreated, breaking from its continual death into continual life, instinct with strength and subtlety and beauty and speed. But the blazing Phoenix lived and swept again to its nest of fire, and as it sank all those other Virtues went with it, themselves still, yet changed. The outer was with the inner; the inner with the outer. All of them rose in the Phoenix and a pattern of stars shone round its head, for the interfused Virtues made a pattern of worlds and stayed, and all the worlds lived and brought forth living creatures to cry out one moment for joy and then be swallowed in the Return. Ephemera of eternity, they broke into being, and Quentin who stood opposite him was one of them, and Damaris was another, and the song of joy filled them and swept them down as it pulsed for sheer gladness into silence again. But the red glow was changing; a soft white light was substituting itself, in the midst of which there grew the form of a Lamb. It stood quietly, and by it he saw Quentin lying on the ground and Damaris leaning over him. They were in some open place, and around them in circling haste went the Lion, and circling within its path, but in the opposite direction, leapt the Lamb. He saw the concentric and complementary paths only for a moment, for his attention rested on a point between Damaris and Quentin, a point that was speeding infinitely away from them, so that his own gaze passed between, and they were on each side of him, and then they were not. The point hung in remote space.

It hung, and after many centuries it opened out, floating nearer, and within it was the earth itself. That which had been but a point resolved itself into a web of speeding and interwoven colours of so many tones that he could but recognize one here and there. He saw a golden Lion against that background, and again a Butterfly of sprinkled azure, and a crimson Phoenix and a white Lamb, and others which he could not know, so swift were the transmutations. But always the earth—already he could distinguish it, with masses of piling waters heaped back from the dry land between—was in the very forefront of whatever creature showed itself. Presently it hid them altogether, hid even the web of colour, though very dimly within it he could still see the pulsations of the glories. They were not to be denied; they thrust out from it; darkened and in strange shapes. If he had been among them—some million-year old memory woke in his brain—*when* he had been among them, with undeveloped brain and hardly lit spirit, they had gone about him as terrifying enemies—the pterodactyl and the dinosaur, Behemoth and Leviathan. It was not until man began to know them by the spiritual intellect that they were minimized to his outer sight; it was to those who were in process of degrading intellect and spirit that, mentally or actually, they appeared again, in those old, huge, and violent shapes. When the holy imagination could behold them in forms yet nearer their true selves, even the present animal appearances would disappear; the Angelicals would be known as Angelicals, and in the idea of Man all ideas would be at one: then man would know himself. For then the Lion would not be without the Lamb. It was the Lamb of which he was again aware, aware vaguely of Damaris and Quentin somewhere at hand. His thought returned to his friend. Was Quentin to be exposed already to the full blast of those energies? what were Damaris and he doing but trying to redeem him from them? Nay, what else had he been trying to do for Damaris herself? Some dispensation of the Mercy had used him for that purpose, to moderate, by the assumption of his natural mind into living knowledge, the danger that threatened his lover and his friend.

His friend. The many moments of joy and deep content which their room had held had in them something of the nature of holy innocence. There had been something in them which was imparted, by Love to love, and which had willed to save them now. Much was possible to a man in solitude; perhaps the final transmutations and achievements in the zones on the yonder side of the central Knowledge were possible only to the spirit in solitude. But some things were possible only to a man in companionship, and of these the most important was balance. No mind was so good that it did not need another mind to counter and equal it, and to save it from conceit and blindness and bigotry and folly. Only in such a balance could humility be found, humility which was a lucid speed to welcome lucidity whenever and wherever it presented itself. How much he owed to Quentin! how much—not pride but delight urged the admission—Quentin owed to him! Balance—and movement in balance, as an eagle sails up on the wind—this was the truth of life, and beauty in life.

But if so—and unconsciously he turned now from the window and wandered back through that place of friendship to the chair he most commonly used—if so, what of the world of men under this visitation? He thought first of Damaris's father, but also of the struggle in Dora Wilmot's house. One was in some sense beautiful—the other had been horrible; but even that first entire submission and absorption, was it quite the perfect end? This abandonment, awe-inspiring as it had been, surely lacked something; would the great classic poets have desired it for a conclusion? If man was perfectly to know.... And if Mr. Tighe had subordinated himself to one Idea, were not those others in process of being subordinated, each by an Idea to itself? And for others still, what awaited them but thunder, earthquake, terror, chaos—the destruction of patterns and the blasting of purposes?

Unthinkingly he put out his hand to the cigarette box which Quentin had given him one Christmas; given both of them, as he had himself pointed out, in remarking on the superior nature of his own present, which had been a neat kind of pocket-book and therefore an entirely personal gift. But Quentin had maintained that the cigarette box, as being of greater good to a greater number, had been nearer to the ideal perfection of giving. 'For,' he had argued, 'to give to you a means by which you can give to others, is better than to give a merely private thing.'

'But,' Anthony had persisted, 'in so far as you are one of those others—and likely to be the most persistent—you give to yourself and therefore altogether deprive the act of the principle of giving;' to which Quentin had retorted that he was included only as one of a number, and that the wise man would not deprive others of good because he himself might be a gainer. 'Otherwise what about all martyrs, missionaries, and philanthropists?' And so the comedy had been played to its end.

The comedy—but this was no comedy; the fierceness of the Lion was no comedy, nor any of those other apparitions, unless the Lamb … The Lion and the Lamb—and a little child shall lead them. Lead them where? Even a little child was in its own mind presumably leading them somewhere. Or perhaps not, perhaps a little child would be content just to lead. The Lion and the Lamb—if this were the restored balance? Friendship—love—had something in it at once strong and innocent, leonine and lamblike. By friendship, by love, these great Virtues became delicately known. Apart from such love and friendship they were merely destructive and helpless; man was never meant to be subjected to them, unless by the offering up of his being to 'divine Philosophy.' In that very chair he had been mocked by Foster for hoping to rule the principles of creation, and he had answered that he had promised to do *everything* to help Damaris. How far such a profound intention sufficed to rule those principles he did not know—more perhaps than man normally thought. The balance in things—the Lion and the Lamb, the Serpent and the Phoenix, the Horse and the Unicorn: ideas as they were visualized and imagined—if these could be led … if….

He could not clearly understand what suggestion was being made to him. But an intense apprehension of the danger in which many besides Quentin were grew within him, a danger brought about by the disorder which had been introduced. He could not honestly say that in any sense he loved these others, unless indeed love were partly a process of willing good to them. That he was determined to do, and perhaps this willing of good meant restoration. By order man ascended; what was it that St. Francis had written? 'Set Love in order, thou that lovest Me.' First for Quentin and then for all the rest.

So gradually abandoning himself to the purpose of the great Power that lived in him, he sat on. If the Eagle was to be served, the Eagle must show him how to serve. In this place of friendship, among the expositions and symbols of friendship, he was filled with the intention of friendship. Quentin was not here, but here they had been received by the knowledge of good, by comparison with which only could evil be known. Friendship was one, but friends were many; the idea was one, but its epiphanies many. One winged creature—but many, many flights of birds. The sparrows in the garden outside his window—and the brown thrushes that sought in it sometimes—the blackbird and the starling—the pigeons of the Guildhall and the gulls of the Thames—the pelicans of St. James and the ridiculous penguins of the Zoo—herons in shallow waters—owls screaming by night—nightingales, skylarks, robin redbreasts—a kingfisher out beyond Maidenhead—doves and crows—ravens—the hooded falcons of pageantry—pheasants—peacocks magnificently scornful—migrating swallows of October—migrating—migrating—birds of paradise—parrots shrieking in the jungles of India—vultures tearing the bodies in the sands of Africa—Flight after flight went by. He knew them in the spiritual intellect, and beheld by their fashioned material bodies the mercy which hid in matter the else overwhelming ardours; man was not yet capable of naked vision. The breach between mankind and the angelicals must be closed again; 'a little child should lead them'—back. The lion should lie down with the lamb. Separately they had issued—strength divorced from innocence, fierceness from joy. They must go back together; somehow they must be called. Adam, long since—so the fable ran—standing in Eden had named the Celestials which were brought into existence before him. Their names—how should Anthony Durrant know their names, or by what title to summon again the lion and the serpent? Yet even in Anthony Durrant the nature of Adam lived. In Adam there had been perfect balance, perfect proportion: in Anthony——?

He was lying back, very still, in his chair. His desire went inwards, through a universe of peace, and hovered, as if on aquiline pinions, over the moment when man knew and named the powers of which he was made. Vast landscapes opened beneath him; laughter rang up towards him. Among the forests he saw a great glade, and in the glade wandered a solitary lamb. It was alone—for a moment or for many years; and then from the trees there came forth a human figure and stood also in the sun. With its appearance a mighty movement everywhere began. A morning of Light was on the earth; the hippopotamus lumbered from the river, the boar charged from the forest, the great apes swung down to the ground before a figure of strength and beauty, the young and glorious archetype of humanity. A voice, crying out in song, went through the air of Eden, a voice that swept up as the eagle, and with every call renewed its youth. All music was the scattered echo of that voice; all poetry was the approach of the fallen understanding to that unfallen meaning. All things were named—all but man himself; then the sleep fell upon the Adam, and in that first sleep he strove to utter his name, and as he strove he was divided and woke to find humanity doubled. The name of mankind was in neither voice but in both; the knowledge of the name and its utterance was in the perpetual interchange of love. Whoever denied that austere godhead, wherever and however it appeared—its presence, its austerity, its divinity—refused the name of man.

The echo of that high spiritual mastery sounded through the inmost being of the child of Adam who lay tranced and attentive. His memory could not bear the task of holding the sounds, but it was not memory's business. The great affair of the naming was present within him, eternal, now as much as then, and at any future hour as much as now. There floated from that singing rapture of man's knowledge of man a last note which rose through his whole being, and as it came brought with it a cloud. 'A mist went up and covered the face of the earth.' His faculties relaxed; his attention was gently released. He blinked once or twice, moved, saw, recognized, and drowsily smiled at the Landseer; then his head dropped down, and he was received, until his energies were renewed, into such a sleep as possessed our father when he awaited the discovery of himself.

CHAPTER XVI

THE NAMING OF THE BEASTS

The railway station at Smetham lay some half-mile out of the actual town, though it was connected by a row of houses and shops. The staff, therefore, though they soon heard whispers of strange things in the town, were still at work when Anthony, late in the evening, returned. He had spent the afternoon at his rooms in solitude and meditation and had then, rather to his own surprise, determined suddenly to go and have a good dinner. After this he had made his way to King's Cross, and got out of the train at Smetham about half past nine. His room at the hotel was still kept for him but he wanted first of all to see Damaris. From the station, however, he telephoned to the hotel to know if there were any messages. He was told that a gentleman was at that very moment waiting for him.

'Ask the gentleman to speak,' Anthony said, and in a minute heard Richardson's voice.

'Hallo,' it said, 'That you, Durrant?'

'Rather,' Anthony answered. 'How are things with you?'

'I don't know that they are,' the voice said. 'Things, I mean. There seem a good many fewer, and anyhow I want to push one of them off on to you.'

'Sweet of you,' said Anthony cheerfully. 'What particular?'

'I don't quite know,' Richardson said, 'what may happen, though I know what, by God's extreme mercy, I hope. But there's this book of Berringer's—you know, *Marcellus noster*—it seems the kind of thing that might be more useful to you than to me, if anyone comes through at all....'

'O we're all coming through,' Anthony interrupted. 'Business as usual. Premises will be reopened to-morrow with improvements of all kinds. But not, I fear, under entirely new management. The old isn't better, but it can't be shifted yet.'

'Can't it?' the other voice said, grimly. 'Well, never mind. You think things will be restored, do you?'

'The way of the world,' Anthony said. 'We shall jolly well have to go on making the best of both. "Vague half-believers"—not but what Arnold himself was a bit vague.'

'O stop this cultural chat,' Richardson broke in, but not ill-naturedly. 'I want to give you this book.'

'But why?' Anthony asked. 'Wasn't it you it was lent to?'

'It was,' Richardson said, 'but I have to be about my Father's business, and it's the only thing I've got that I ought to do anything with. Where are you? And what are you doing?'

'I'm at the station,' Anthony told him, 'and I'm going straight to Miss Tighe. You might come and meet me, if you've time. Where is the necessity taking you?'

There was a brief silence as if Richardson was considering; then he said, 'Very well, I will. Don't walk too quickly. I'm in rather a hurry and I don't want to miss you.'

'Right,' said Anthony. 'I'll walk like a—like the opposite of the Divine Horse till I see you. Unless the necessity drives me.' And he hung up.

That strange impulse however, to which in the serious and gay humour that possessed him he had given the name of the necessity, allowed him to wander slowly down the station road, till he saw Richardson walking swiftly along to meet him; then he quickened his own steps. They looked at each other curiously.

'And so,' Richardson said at last, 'you think that the common things will return?'

'I'm quite certain of it,' Anthony said. 'Won't He have mercy on all that He's made?'

The other shook his head, and then suddenly smiled. 'Well, if you and they like it that way, there's no more to be said,' he answered. 'Myself, I think you're only wasting time on the images.'

'Well, who made the images?' Anthony asked. 'You sound like a mediaeval monk commenting on marriage. Don't be so stuck-up over your old way, whatever it is. What actually is it?'

Richardson pointed to the sky. 'Do you see the light of that fire?' he asked. 'Yes, there. Berringer's house has been burning all day.'

'I know, I saw it.'

'I'm going out there,' Richardson said and stopped.

'But—I'm not saying you're wrong—but why?' Anthony asked. 'Isn't fire an image too?'

'That perhaps,' the other answered. 'But all this——' he touched his clothes and himself, and his eyes grew dark with a sudden passion of desire—'has to go somehow; and if the fire that will destroy the world is here already, it isn't I that will keep from it.'

Anthony looked at him a little ruefully. 'I'm sorry,' he said. 'I'd hoped we might have talked more. And—you know best—but you're quite sure you're right? I can't see but what the images have their place. *Ex umbris* perhaps, but the noon has to drive the shadows away naturally, hasn't it?'

The other shrugged. 'O I know,' he said. 'It's all been argued a hundred times, Jansenist and Jesuit, the monk and the married man, mystic and sacramentalist. But all I know is that I must make for the End when and as soon as I see it. Perhaps that's why I am alone. But since that's so—I'd like you, if you will, and if restoration comes, to give this book back to Berringer if he's alive, and to keep it if he isn't. What,' he added, 'what you call alive.'

Anthony took the little parcel. 'I will do it,' he said. 'But I only call it alive because the images must communicate, and communication is such a jolly thing. However, I'm keeping you and I mustn't do that … as we sacramentalists say.'

They shook hands. Then Anthony broke out again. 'I do wish you weren't—No; no, I don't. Go with God.'

'Go with God,' the other's more sombre voice answered. They stood for a moment, then they stepped apart, their hands went up in mutual courteous farewell, and they went their separate ways.

No-one saw the young bookseller's assistant again; no-one thought of him, except his employer and his landlady, and each of them, grumbling first, afterwards filled his place and forgot him. Alone and unnoticed he went along the country road to his secret end. Only Anthony, as he went swiftly to Damaris, commended the other's soul to the Maker and Destroyer of images.

Damaris herself opened the door to him when he came. She was about to speak when he prevented her by saying happily: 'So you found him?' 'He's asleep upstairs now,' she answered. 'And you?' He pulled her closer to him. 'Why, that I'll tell you presently,' he said. 'Tell me first. How beautifully you seem to do your job!'

'The doctor's here,' she said. 'I managed to get him round earlier in the day, and he said he'd come again before night. Come and see him.'

'Is it Rockbotham?' Anthony asked, moving with her up the stairs. 'He's a good creature.'

'I used to think he was rather a dull sort of fool,' Damaris said. 'But to-day he was quite strong and wise. O Anthony,'—she checked at the door of the bedroom—'don't hate me, will you?'

'When I hate you,' he answered, 'the place of the angels will be desolate and our necessity will forget itself.'

'What is our necessity?' she asked, looking up at him as they passed.

'It's just to be, I suppose,' Anthony answered slowly. 'I mean, the simpler one is the nearer one is to loving. If the pattern's arranged in me, what can I do but let myself be the pattern? I can see to it that I don't hate, but after that Love must do his own business. But let's go on now, may we? And talk of this another day.'

'Tell me just one thing first,' Damaris said. 'Do you think—I've been wondering this afternoon—do you think it's wrong of me to work at Abelard?'

'Darling, how can intelligence be wrong?' he answered. 'I should think you knew more about him than anyone else in the world, and it's a perfectly sound idea to make a beautiful thing of what you know. So long as you don't neglect me in order to do it.'

'And is that being impersonal?' she mocked him.

'Why, yes,' he said, 'for that's your job too. And all your job is impersonal and one. Or personal and one—it doesn't matter which you say. They're only debating words really. Come on, let's go in.'

As Anthony looked at Dr. Rockbotham he felt that Damaris was right. The first glance had been for his friend, but Quentin seemed to be sleeping quietly, and the doctor was on the point of coming towards the door. He had never been a particularly notable figure until now, but now indeed, in the hackneyed but convincing phrase, Anthony saw him for the first time. The lines of his face were unaltered, but it was moulded in a great strength and confidence; the eyes were deep and wise; the mouth closed firmly as if on the oath of Hippocrates—the seal of silence and the knowledge of discretion. 'Aesculapius,' Anthony thought to himself, and remembered the snake that was the symbol of Aesculapius. 'We sneer at medicine,' he thought, 'but after all we *do* know more—not much, but a little. We sneer at progress, but we do, in a way, progress: the gods haven't abandoned man.' For a moment he dreamed of a white-robed bearded figure, with a great serpent coiled by him, where in some remote temple of Epidaurus or Pergamus the child of Phoebus Apollo laboured to heal men by the art that he had learned from the twy-formed Cheiron, the master of herbs. Zeus had destroyed him by lightning at last, since by his wisdom the dead were recalled to life, and the sacred order of the world was in danger of being broken. But the serpent-wreathed rod was still outstretched and still the servants of the art were sent out by their father on missions of health. He shook hands gravely, as if in ritual.

'I think he'll do very well,' the doctor was saying, and the vowels of the simple words came to Anthony's ears heavy with the harmonies of Greek. 'Exhaustion—absolute exhaustion: he must have been struck by a kind of panic. But sleep, and quiet, and food, will put him right. The proper kind of food.'

'Ah that!' Anthony exclaimed.

'But whether you can manage him here for a day or two,' the doctor went on to Damaris, 'in the circumstances. He could of course be moved——'

'I don't think there's any need,' she answered, and then in answer to Anthony's eyebrows, 'My father died this afternoon.'

Anthony nodded; it was no more than he had expected.

'There isn't any need to sit up with him,' the doctor went on, 'and twenty-four hours' entire rest would make a great difference. Still, it's perhaps rather hard on you, Miss Tighe——'

Damaris put out her hand. 'Ah, no!' she said. 'Certainly he must be here. He is Anthony's friend and mine. I am very, very glad he is here,' and her other hand caught Anthony's and with an intense pressure told him all that that sentence meant of restoration and joy.

After a little more conversation the doctor went, and Damaris and Anthony looked at each other in the hall.

'I won't say I'm sorry about your father,' he said. 'I think he had ended his business,' and as she smiled in a profound assent, he went on, 'and now I must get on with mine.'

She looked at him anxiously, but said nothing for a minute, while he waited: then she asked, 'You will let me come—wherever it is?'

'Come,' he said, and held out his hand, and so without any delay, they went out of the front door and along the street together. The town was caught in the terror; the street lay empty before them. A profound stillness was all round them, except that in some house near at hand a baby was wailing. The sound was the only audible sign of humanity; it was humanity. All man's courage and knowledge came to this in the end—Damaris listening remembered having read somewhere that the god who had given his name to the building which was the home of the greatest bishop in the world, the centre of the Roman Church, the shrine (it was said) of infallible authority, was Vaticanus, and the office of Vaticanus was to preside over the new-born child's first cry. That was all; that was all that the Vatican itself could do, and all that the Vatican held. Here the spirit of man could but reach that far—and as she pondered it, the thunder crashed out again. What she had called thunder, but it was clearer now; it was the roar of a living creature. She heard it, and heard it answered. At her side Anthony had paused, thrown up his head, and sent out another cry upon the night. It was an incomprehensible call, and it broke out right in the midst of that other reverberating roar and checked and silenced it. It was a sound as of a single word, but not English, nor Latin, nor Greek. Hebrew it might have been or something older than Hebrew, some incantation whereby the prediluvian magicians had controlled contentions among spirits, or the language in which our father Adam named the beasts of the garden. The roar ceased on the moment, and then as at Anthony's movement they began again to walk on, there rose about them a little breeze. It was very light, hardly more than a ruffling of the air, but it stirred her hair, and breathed on her face, and even gently shook the light silk sleeves of her frock. She stole a glance at Anthony, and met his eyes. He was smiling and she broke into an answering smile. But it was not until they had gone some way farther that she spoke.

'Where are we going?' she said.

'I think we are going to the field where you found Quentin,' he answered. 'Do you remember what you saw there?'

She nodded. 'And——?' she said, waiting for him to go on. But he did not, only after some minutes he said softly. 'It was good of you to look for Quentin.'

'Good!' she exclaimed. 'Good! O Anthony!'

'Well, so it was,' he answered. 'Or good in you. How accurate one has to be with one's prepositions! Perhaps it was a preposition wrong that set the whole world awry.'

'It was,' she said, 'a preposition that helped to divide the Church.'

'Sweetest of theologians,' he answered, 'I will make it my chief business always to be accurate in my prepositions about you. It shall be good *in* you always, and good *of* you never.'

'Not even for a treat?' she asked.

'O for a treat,' he answered, 'you shall be the good in itself, the rose-garden of the saints. Will you meet me there to-morrow evening?'

'So soon?' she said. 'Will the saints expect me?'

'Image of sanctity,' he answered, 'they will look in you as a mirror to see the glory of God that is about them, by so much will your soul be clearer than theirs.'

'I suppose that's what you mean by a treat,' she said. 'It sounds to me like several at once.'

'But for a treat to me you must believe it,' he said, 'for as long as it takes your finger to mark the line of life on your hand.'

'Supposing I believed it too long?' she said, half-seriously.

'Why for fear of that,' he answered, 'you will remember that what is seen in you is present in all, and that the beauty of every other living creature is as bright as yours.'

'And that,' she said, 'sounds like the morning after the party.'

'It is the present given at the party,' he said, 'and perhaps what the party itself was for.'

They were out of the town, and coming to the stile where Damaris had been twice with Quentin. The time had seemed very quick, but the happiness that beat in her breast had shortened it, she supposed, or else the wind that, stronger now, seemed to carry them along. By the stile they paused and looked over and down the sloping fields beyond; and Damaris suddenly saw and recollected the great glow in the sky, and away below them the tree of fire that burned in the place of the house. She had entirely forgotten it as she came along the road with Anthony, and now she realized that it was beneath the reflection of that terrible thing that their interchange of laughing truths had gone on. So joyous they had been; so awful were the dangers that surrounded them. Her breath came quicker; she looked at Anthony, and saw his face had changed from tenderness to high authority. He dropped her hand and turned to the stile. For a moment she flinched.

'Ah must you go?' she cried. She knew somehow that she would not; she must stay there. Less practised than he, immature in doctrine and deed, she had her place on the hither side of the work. He did not seem to hear her; lightly he laid his hand on the stile and vaulted over, and as her eyes followed him she exclaimed again at what she saw. It was almost dark, and the shadows were confusing, for the fire below did not seem to cast a light on the land, but it seemed to her that the land was changed. It fell away very steeply beneath her, in an open glade, round which on either side trees grew; not the trees of English hedges, but mightier and taller growths. She saw palms waving, and other immense things shaken by the strength of the swiftly rising wind. Huge and shining leaves were tossed in the air; the high grass of the dark glade itself was swept this way and that by the same energy. The glade ran right down to the bottom of the steep descent, and there in its centre was the fire that surged in the shape of a tree—no, it *was* a tree, one of two that grew there, side by side, and otherwise alone. The one at which she had been gazing was still vivid with fiery colour; by it grew a dark mass in which no tone or hint of colour showed. Far above the ground the boughs and foliage interlaced, golden light and heavy blackness were intermingled. But while she looked, the figure of Anthony came between her and the trees, if indeed it were still Anthony, and yet she knew it was. But he was different; he seemed gigantic in the uncertain light, and he was passing with huge strides down the glade. As he moved it seemed to her that he was wearing not clothes but skins, as in some old picture Adam might have fared forth from Paradise. He went on till he was about half-way down the glade, and then he stood still. About him the wind had become a terrific storm; it soared and rushed through the great trees on either hand, yet over it she heard his voice crying. He had stood still, and turned a little, and upon one mighty shoulder there perched a huge bird—at least, it seemed like a bird, and as he called it spread its wings and again closed them. She dimly remembered some other similar motion, and suddenly recaptured it—so the loathsome thing of her own experience had perched outside the windows of her mind, so it had threatened and almost beaten down her life. From such a bestial knowledge she had been barely saved; with a full pulse of gratitude she offered herself, in her own small place, to divine Wisdom.

412

Anthony—Adam—whatever giant stood before her between the trees of an aboriginal forest—was calling as he had called in the streets of the town. But now he uttered not one word but many, pausing between each, and again giving to each the same strong summons. He called and he commanded; nature lay expectant about him. She was aware then that the forest all round was in movement; living creatures showed themselves on its edge, or hurried through the grass. At each word that he cried, new life gathered, and still the litany of invocation and command went on. By the names that were the Ideas he called them, and the Ideas who are the Principles of everlasting creation heard him, the Principles of everlasting creation who are the Cherubim and Seraphim of the Eternal. In their animal manifestations, duly obedient to the single animal who was lord of the animals, they came. She saw the horse pushing its head over his shoulder; she saw the serpent rearing itself and lightly coiling round his body. Only, but now motionless, the eagle sat on his shoulder, observant of all things, as philosophical knowledge studies the natures and activities of men.

They were returning, summoned by the authority of man from their incursion into the world of man. She thought of the town behind her from which the terror was now withdrawing; she thought of the world which had not known what was approaching and now might sleep on in peace. She thought of Quentin and of her father, the one rescued from his fear, the other absorbed by his content. And as she thought, crouched by the stile that seemed as if it were the way into the Garden, only unguarded for this single night by the fire which was its central heart—as she crouched and thought, she wondered with a sharp pain if he who had gone from her was ever to return. Was she to lose that others might gain? was she to be deprived of her lover that Quentin Sabot might be saved from madness? Where anyhow was Anthony? What was this nightmare in which she was held? Out of a sepulchre of death the old Damaris rushed up into the new; anger began to swell within her. Either this was all a horrid dream or else Anthony had lured her into some insane midnight expedition. It was always the same—no-one ever considered her; no-one thought about her. Her father had died at a most inconvenient moment; there would be all the business of what small capital he had. No-one, no-one, ever considered her, and the work she was trying unselfishly to do as a contribution to the history of philosophical thought.

Something, however, still held. As, in the renewed and full pseudo-realization of what she was and what she was doing by her work—hers, hers, the darling hers!—she moved to rise (even in a nightmare she needn't crouch), something for one second held her down. It held her—that slender ligature of unrealized devotion—for the second that the old hateful things took to flood her and a little to recede. The years of selfish toil had had at any rate this good—they had been years of toil; she had not easily abandoned any search because of difficulty, and that habit of intention, by its own power of good, offered her salvation then. The full flood receded; she remembered herself, and her young soul struggled to reach the bright shore beyond the gloomy waters that tossed it. The thing that was the opposite of the pterodactyl, the thing that had been the purpose of the search of Abelard, the thing that was Anthony and yet wasn't Anthony—that. She knew it; as she did so she felt her own name called, and cried out in agony 'Yes, yes.' If Anthony must go, then he must go. He—it—knew; she didn't. Her limbs were released; she sprang up, the older energies renewed almost to fierceness in her determination to discover that other thing. She would be savage with herself, royal in daring, a lioness in hunger and in the hunt. Of that thing itself, she knew little but that it was blessed, innocent and joyous; it was a marvel of white knowledge, as much of earth as any tender creature of the fields, yet bound to its heavenly origin by hypostatic union of experience. A fierce conquest, an innocent obedience—these were to be her signs.

The sound of her name still echoed through her spirit when, recovered from her inner struggle, she looked again upon the glade of the garden where the image of Adam named the beasts, and naming ruled them. But now he was farther from her, nearer to those twin mysterious trees in the centre. Among the shapes that pressed about him she could not at first well discern one from another, but as she leaned and strained to see she beheld them gathering into two companies. There fell over the whole scene a strange and lovely clearness, shed from the wings of a soaring wonder that left the shoulder where it had reposed and flew, scattering light. The intermingled foliage of the trees of knowledge and of life—if indeed they were separate—received it; amid those branches the eagle which was the living act of science sank and rested. But far below the human figure stood and on either side of it were the shapes of the lion and the lamb. His hand rested on the head of the one; the other paused by him. In and for that exalted moment all acts of peace that then had being through the world were deepened and knew their own nature more clearly; away in villages and towns such spirits as the country doctor in Smetham received a measure of content in their work. Friendships grew closer; intentions of love possessed their right fulfilment. Terrors of malice and envy and jealousy faded; disordered beauty everywhere recognized again the sacred laws that governed it. Man dreamed of himself in the place of his creation.

The vision passed from them, and from the woman who watched as Eve might have watched the movements of her companion. He looked on the beasts and seemed to speak to them, and slowly they withdrew. Slowly, each after its own habit, they moved along the glade, and suddenly the lamb was lost to her sight under the massed heaviness of those trees from which they had come. On the very edge of the mystery the lion looked back, half turned towards the way it had gone. Its eyes met those of the man who faced it, but he came no farther. His just concern was still with the world of men and women, and with his gaze he bade the angelical pass back and close the breach. It broke into one final roar—the woman heard and trembled, and heard the roar cease as the Adam answered and quelled it with the sound of its own name. She saw it turn again and move away, and on the very instant the human figure itself turned and at full speed ran towards her. The earth shook under her; from the place of the trees there broke again the pillar of flame, as if between the sky and earth a fiery sword were shaken, itself 'with dreadful faces thronged and fiery arms'. The guard that protected earth was set again; the interposition of the Mercy veiled the destroying energies from the weakness of men.

———————————

One of the firemen who, late at night, and ignorant of the aspect under which Damaris from the ridge beheld that supernaturally deepened valley, still attempted to subdue the fire which raged in the house, said afterwards, when his wife spoke to him of the wild rumours that had till midnight possessed the town, that he also had thought that he saw, as he faced the ridge, a great shape of a lion leap from the field straight into the flames. It was directly afterwards that their prolonged efforts were unexpectedly successful; the fire dwindled, sank, and in a short time expired. It was the same man who had thought that, earlier in the evening, he had seen a young man slip past his comrades towards the pyre, but since he had seen no more of him he concluded it could not have been so. The house itself, and the bodies of the owner and the housekeeper, had been reduced to the finest ash; there was, when the fire died out, nothing but a layer of ash spread over the earth. It was, in short, one of the worst fires he had ever known, and the heat and blaze had at moments evidently dazed him.

But Damaris, when from the glade that behind him became once more nothing but the English fields she received the flying figure of Anthony, did not think she had been dazed. He leapt the stile, stretching out his hand to her as she came, and she caught it, and was swung across the road before he could stop himself. Panting from his rush he smiled at her, panting from her intense vigil she breathed all herself back. Then their hands fell apart, and after a little they began to walk slowly on.

In a minute he looked at her. 'I say, you're not cold, are you?' he asked. 'I wish you'd got a coat or something.'

'It's not very far,' she answered. 'No, I'm not cold.'

THE END

War in Heaven

Chapter One

THE PRELUDE

The telephone bell was ringing wildly, but without result, since there was no-one in the room but the corpse.

A few moments later there was. Lionel Rackstraw, strolling back from lunch, heard in the corridor the sound of the bell in his room, and, entering at a run, took up the receiver. He remarked, as he did so, the boots and trousered legs sticking out from the large knee-hole table at which he worked, but the telephone had established the first claim on his attention.

"Yes," he said, "yes…. No, not before the 17th…. No, who cares what he wants?… No, who wants to know?… Oh, Mr. Persimmons. Oh, tell him the 17th…. Yes…. Yes, I'll send a set down."

He put the receiver down and looked back at the boots. It occurred to him that someone was probably doing something to the telephone; people did, he knew, at various times drift in on him for such purposes. But they usually looked round or said something; and this fellow must have heard him talking. He bent down towards the boots.

"Shall you be long?" he said into the space between the legs and the central top drawer; and then, as there was no answer, he walked away, dropped hat and gloves and book on to their shelf, strolled back to his desk, picked up some papers and read them, put them back, and, peering again into the dark hole, said more impatiently, "Shall you be long?"

No voice replied; not even when, touching the extended foot with his own, he repeated the question. Rather reluctantly he went round to the other side of the table, which was still darker, and, trying to make out the head of the intruder, said almost loudly: "Hallo! hallo! What's the idea?" Then, as nothing happened, he stood up and went on to himself: "Damn it all, is he dead?" and thought at once that he might be.

That dead bodies did not usually lie round in one of the rooms of a publisher's offices in London about half-past two in the afternoon was a certainty that formed now an enormous and cynical background to the fantastic possibility. He half looked at the door which he had closed behind him, and then attempted the same sort of interior recovery with which he had often thrown off the knowledge that at any moment during his absence his wife *might* be involved in some street accident, some skidding bus or swerving lorry. These things happened—a small and unpleasant, if invisible, deity who lived in a corner of his top shelves had reminded him—these things happened, and even *now* perhaps…. People had been crushed against their own front doors; there had been a doctor in Gower Street. Of course, it was all untrue. But this time, as he moved to touch the protruding feet, he wondered if it were.

The foot he touched apparently conveyed no information to the stranger's mind, and Lionel gave up the attempt. He went out and crossed the corridor to another office, whose occupant, spread over a table, was marking sentences in newspaper cuttings.

"Mornington," Lionel said, "there's a man in my room under the table, and I can't get him to take any notice. Will you come across? He looks," he added in a rush of realism, "for all the world as if he was dead."

"How fortunate!" Mornington said, gathering himself off the table. "If he were alive and had got under your table and wouldn't take any notice I should be afraid you'd annoyed him somehow. I think that's rather a pleasant notion," he went on as they crossed the corridor, "a sort of modern *King's Threshold*—get under the table of the man who's insulted you and simply sulk there. Not, I think, starve—that's for more romantic ages than ours—but take a case filled with sandwiches and a thermos…. What's the plural of thermos?…" He stared at the feet, and then, going up to the desk, went down on one knee and put a hand over the disappearing leg. Then he looked up at Lionel.

"Something wrong," he said sharply. "Go and ask Dalling to come here." He dropped to both knees and peered under the table.

Lionel ran down the corridor in the other direction, and returned in a few minutes with a short man of about forty-five, whose face showed more curiosity than anxiety. Mornington was already making efforts to get the body from under the table.

"He must be dead," he said abruptly to the others as they came in. "What an incredible business! Go round the other side, Dalling; the buttons have caught in the table or something; see if you can get them loose."

"Hadn't we better leave it for the police?" Dalling asked. "I thought you weren't supposed to move bodies."

"How the devil do I know whether it is a body?" Mornington asked. "Not but what you may be right." He made investigations between the trouser-leg and the boot, and then stood up rather suddenly. "It's a body right enough," he said. "Is Persimmons in?"

"No," said Dalling; "he won't be back till four."

"Well, we shall have to get busy ourselves, then. Will you get on to the police-station? And, Rackstraw, you'd better drift about in the corridor and stop people coming in, or Plumpton will be earning half a guinea by telling the *Evening News*."

Plumpton, however, had no opportunity of learning what was concealed behind the door against which Lionel for the next quarter of an hour or so leant, his eyes fixed on a long letter which he had caught up from his desk as a pretext for silence if anyone passed him. Dalling went downstairs and out to the front door, a complicated glass arrangement which reflected every part of itself so many times that many arrivals were necessary before visitors could discover which panels swung back to the retail sales-room, which to a waiting-room for authors and others desiring interviews with the remoter staff, and which to a corridor leading direct to the stairs. It was here that he welcomed the police and the doctor, who arrived simultaneously, and going up the stairs to the first floor he explained the situation.

At the top of these stairs was a broad and deep landing, from which another flight ran backwards on the left-hand to the second floor. Opposite the stairs, across the landing, was the private room of Mr. Stephen Persimmons, the head of the business since his father's retirement some seven years before. On either side the landing narrowed to a corridor which ran for some distance left and right and gave access to various rooms occupied by Rackstraw, Mornington, Dalling, and others. On the right this corridor ended in a door which gave entrance to Plumpton's room. On the left the other section, in which Lionel's room was the last on the right hand, led to a staircase to the basement. On its way, however, this staircase passed and issued on a side door through which the visitor came out into a short, covered court, having a blank wall opposite, which connected the streets at the front and the back of the building. It would therefore have been easy for anyone to obtain access to Lionel's room in order, as the inspector in charge remarked pleasantly to Mornington, "to be strangled."

For the dead man had, as was evident when the police got the body clear, been murdered so. Lionel, in obedience to the official request to see if he could recognize the corpse, took one glance at the purple face and starting eyes, and with a choked negative retreated. Mornington, with a more contemplative, and Dalling with a more curious, interest, both in turn considered and denied any knowledge of the stranger. He was a little man, in the usual not very fresh clothes of the lower middle class; his bowler hat had been crushed in under the desk; his pockets contained nothing but a cheap watch, a few coppers, and some silver—papers he appeared to have none. Around his neck was a piece of stout cord, deeply embedded in the flesh.

So much the clerks heard before the police with their proceedings retired into cloud and drove the civilians into other rooms. Almost as soon, either by the telephone or some other means, news of the discovery reached Fleet Street, and reporters came pushing through the crowd that began to gather immediately the police were seen to enter the building. The news of the discovered corpse was communicated to them officially, and for the rest they were left to choose as they would among the rumours flying through the crowd, which varied from vivid accounts of the actual murder and several different descriptions of the murderer to a report that the whole of the staff were under arrest and the police had had to wade ankle-deep through the blood in the basement.

To such a distraction Mr. Persimmons himself returned from a meeting of the Publishers' Association about four o'clock, and was immediately annexed by Inspector Colquhoun, who had taken the investigation in charge. Stephen Persimmons was rather a small man, with a mild face apt to take on a harassed and anxious appearance on slight cause. With much more reason he looked anxious now, as he sat opposite the inspector in his own room. He had recognized the body as little as any of his staff had, and it was about them rather than it that the inspector was anxious to gain particulars.

"This Rackstraw, now," Colquhoun was saying: "it was his room the body was found in. Has he been with you long?"

"Oh, years," Mr. Persimmons answered; "most of them have. All the people on this floor—and nearly all the rest. They've been here longer than me, most of them. You see, I came in just three years before my father retired—that's seven years ago, and three's ten."

"And Rackstraw was here before that?"

"Oh, yes, certainly."

"Do you know anything of him?" the inspector pressed. "His address, now?"

"Dalling has all that," the unhappy Persimmons said. "He has all the particulars about the staff. I remember Rackstraw being married a few years ago."

"And what does he do here?" Colquhoun went on.

"Oh, he does a good deal of putting books through, paper and type and binding, and so on. He rather looks after the fiction side. I've taken up fiction a good deal since my father went; that's why the business has expanded so. We've got two of the best selling people to-day—Mrs. Clyde and John Bastable."

"Mrs. Clyde," the inspector brooded. "Didn't she write *The Comet and the Star*?"

"That's the woman. We sold ninety thousand," Persimmons answered.

"And what are your other lines?"

"Well, my father used to do, in fact he began with, what you might call occult stuff. Mesmerism and astrology and histories of great sorcerers, and that sort of thing. It didn't really pay very well."

"And does Mr. Rackstraw look after that too?" asked Colquhoun.

"Well, some of it," the publisher answered. "But of course, in a place like this things aren't exactly divided just—just exactly. Mornington, now, Mornington looks after some books. Under me, of course," he added hastily. "And then he does a good deal of the publicity, the advertisements, you know. And he does the reviews."

"What, writes them?" the inspector asked.

"Certainly not," said the publisher, shocked. "Reads them and chooses passages to quote. Writes them! Really, inspector!"

"And how long has Mr. Mornington been here?" Colquhoun went on.

"Oh, years and years. I tell you they all came before I did."

"I understand Mr. Rackstraw was out a long time at lunch to-day, with one of your authors. Would that be all right?"

"I daresay he was," Persimmons said, "if he said so."

"You don't *know* that he was?" asked Colquhoun. "He didn't tell you?"

"Really, inspector," the worried Persimmons said again, "do you think my staff ask me for an hour off when they want to see an author? I give them their work and they do it."

"Sir Giles Tumulty," the inspector said. "You know him?"

"We're publishing his last book, *Historical Vestiges of Sacred Vessels in Folklore*. The explorer and antiquarian, you know. Rackstraw's had a lot of trouble with his illustrations, but he told me yesterday he thought he'd got them through. Yes, I can quite believe he went up to see him. But you can find out from Sir Giles, can't you?"

"What I'm getting at," the inspector said, "is this. If any of your people are out, is there anything to prevent anyone getting into any of their rooms? There's a front way and a back way in and nobody on watch anywhere."

"There's a girl in the waiting-room," Persimmons objected.

"A girl!" the inspector answered. "Reading a novel when she's not talking to anyone. She'd be a lot of good. Besides, there's a corridor to the staircase alongside the waiting-room. And at the back there's no-one."

"Well, one doesn't expect strangers to drop in casually," the publisher said unhappily. "I believe they do lock their doors sometimes, if they have to go out and have to leave a lot of papers all spread out."

"And leave the key in, I suppose?" Colquhoun said sarcastically.

"Of course," Persimmons answered. "Suppose I wanted something. Besides, it's not to keep anyone out; it's only just to save trouble and warn anyone going in to be careful, so to speak; it hardly ever happens. Besides——"

Colquhoun cut him short. "What people mean by asking for a Government of business men, I don't know," he said. "I was a Conservative from boyhood, and I'm stauncher every year the more I see of business. There's nothing to prevent anyone coming in."

"But they don't," said Persimmons.

"But they have," said Colquhoun. "It's the unexpected that happens. Are you a religious man, Mr. Persimmons?"

"Well, not—not exactly religious," the publisher said hesitatingly. "Not what you'd call religious unpleasantly, I mean. But what——"

"Nor am I," the inspector said. "And I don't get the chance to go to church much. But I've been twice with my wife to a Sunday evening service at her Wesleyan Church in the last few months, and it's a remarkable thing, Mr. Persimmons, we had the same piece read from the Bible each time. It ended up—'And what I say unto you I say unto all, Watch.' It seemed to me fairly meant for the public. 'What I say unto you,' that's us in the police, 'I say unto all, Watch.' If there was more of that there'd be fewer undiscovered murders. Well, I'll go and see Mr. Dalling. Good day, Mr. Persimmons."

Chapter Two

THE EVENING IN THREE HOMES

I

Adrian Rackstraw opened the oven, put the chicken carefully inside, and shut the door. Then he went back to the table, and realized suddenly that he had forgotten to buy the potatoes which were to accompany it. With a disturbed exclamation, he picked up the basket that lay in a corner, put on his hat, and set out on the new errand. He considered for a moment as he reached the garden gate to which of the two shops at which Mrs. Rackstraw indifferently supplied her needs he should go, and, deciding on the nearest, ran hastily down the road. At the shop, "Three potatoes," he said in a low, rather worried voice.

"Yes, sir," the man answered. "Five shillings, please."

Adrian paid him, put the potatoes in the basket, and started back home. But as at the corner he waited for the trams to go by and leave a clear crossing, his eye was caught by the railway station on his left. He looked at it for a minute or two in considerable doubt; then, changing his mind on the importance of vegetables, went back to the shop, left his basket with orders that the potatoes should be sent at once, and hurried back to the station. Once in the train, he saw bridges and tunnels succeed one another in exciting succession as the engine, satisfactorily fastened to coal-truck and carriages, went rushing along the Brighton line. But, before it reached its destination, his mother, entering the room with her usual swiftness, caught the station with her foot and sent it flying across the kitchen floor. Her immediate flood of apologies placated Adrian, however, and he left the train stranded some miles outside Brighton in order to assist her in preparing the food for dinner. She sat down on a chair for a moment, and he broke in again hastily.

"Oh, Mummie, don't sit down there, that's my table," he said.

"Darling, I'm so sorry," Barbara Rackstraw answered. "Had you got anything on it?"

"Well, I was going to put the dinner things," Adrian explained. "I'll just see if the chicken's cooked. Oh, it's lovely!"

"How nice!" Barbara said abstractedly. "Is it a large chicken?"

"Not a very large one," Adrian admitted. "There's enough for me and you and my Bath auntie."

"Oh," said Barbara, startled, "is your Bath auntie here?"

"Well, she may be coming," said Adrian. "Mummie, why do I have a Bath auntie?"

"Because a baby grew up into your Bath auntie, darling," his mother said. "Unintentional but satisfactory, as far as it goes. Adrian, do you think your father will like cold sausages? Because there doesn't seem to be anything else much."

"I don't want any cold sausages," Adrian said hurriedly.

"No, my angel, but it's the twenty-seventh of the month, and there's never any money then," Barbara said. "And here he is, anyhow."

Lionel, in spite of the shock that he had received in the afternoon, found himself, rather to his own surprise, curiously free from the actual ghost of it. His memory had obligingly lost the face of the dead man, and it was not until he came through the streets of Tooting that he began to understand that its effect was at once more natural and more profound than he had expected. His usual sense of the fantastic and dangerous possibilities of life, a sense which dwelled persistently in a remote corner of his mind, never showing itself in full, but stirring in the absurd alarm which shook him if his wife were ever late for an appointment—this sense now escaped from his keeping, and, instead of being too hidden, became too universal to be seized. The faces he saw, the words he heard existed in an enormous void, in which he himself—reduced to a face and voice, without deeper existence—hung for a moment, grotesque and timid. There had been for an hour some attempt to re-establish the work of the office, and he had initialled, before he left, a few memoranda which were brought to him. The "L. R." of his signature seemed now to grow balloon-like and huge about him, volleying about his face at the same time that they turned within and around him in a slimy tangle. At similar, if less terrifying, moments, in other days, he had found that a concentration upon his wife had helped to steady and free him, but when this evening he made this attempt he found even in her only a flying figure with a face turned from him, whom he dreaded though he hastened to overtake. As he put his key in the lock he was aware that the thought of Adrian had joined the mad dance of possible deceptions, and it was with a desperate and machine-like courage that he entered to dare whatever horror awaited him.

Nor did the ordinary interchange of greetings do much to disperse the cloud. It occurred to him even as he smiled at Barbara that perhaps another lover had not long left the house; it occurred to him even as he watched Adrian finding pictures of trains in the evening paper that a wild possibility—for a story perhaps; not, surely not, as truth—might be that of a child whose brain was that of the normal man of forty while all his appearance was that of four. An infant prodigy? No, but a prodigy who for some horrible reason of his own concealed his prodigiousness until the moment he expected should arrive. And when they left him to his evening meal, while Barbara engaged herself in putting Adrian to bed, a hundred memories of historical or fictitious crimes entered his mind in which the victim had been carefully poisoned under the shelter of a peaceful and happy domesticity. And not that alone or chiefly; it was not the possibility of administered poison that occupied him, but the question whether all food, and all other things also, were not in themselves poisonous. Fruit, he thought, might be; was there not in the nature of things some venom which nourished while it tormented, so that the very air he breathed did but enable him to endure for a longer time the spiritual malevolence of the world?

Possessed by such dreams, he sat listless and alone until Barbara returned and settled herself down to the evening paper. The event of the afternoon occupied, he knew, the front page. He found himself incapable of speaking of it; he awaited the moment when her indolent eyes should find it. But that would not be, and indeed was not, till she had looked through the whole paper, delaying over remote paragraphs he had never noticed, and extracting interest from the mere superfluous folly of mankind. She turned the pages casually, glanced at the heading, glanced at the column, dropped the paper over the arm of her chair, and took up a cigarette.

"He's beginning to make quite recognizable letters," she said. "He made quite a good K this afternoon."

This, Lionel thought despairingly, was an example of the malevolence of the universe; he had given it, and her, every chance. Did she never read the paper? Must he talk of it himself, and himself renew the dreadful memories in open speech?

"Did you see," he said, "what happened at our place this afternoon?"

"No," said Barbara, surprised; and then, breaking off, "Darling, you look so ill. Do you feel ill?"

"I'm not quite the thing," Lionel admitted. "You'll see why, in there." He indicated the discarded *Star*.

Barbara picked it up. "Where?" she asked. "'Murder in City publishing house.' That wasn't yours, I suppose? Lionel, it was! Good heavens, where?"

"In my office," Lionel answered, wondering whether some other corpse wasn't hidden behind the chair in which she sat. Of course, they had found that one this afternoon, but mightn't there be a body that other people couldn't find, couldn't even see? Barbara herself now: mightn't she be really lying there dead? and this that seemed to sit there opposite him merely a projection of his own memories of a thousand evenings when she had sat so? What mightn't be true, in this terrifying and obscene universe?

Barbara's voice—or the voice of the apparent Barbara—broke in. "But, dearest," she said, "how dreadful for you! Why didn't you tell me? You must have had a horrible time." She dropped the paper again and hurled herself on to her knees beside him.

He caught her hand in his own, and felt as if his body at least was sane, whatever his mind might be. After all, the universe had produced Barbara. And Adrian, who, though a nuisance, was at least delimited and real in his own fashion. The fantastic child of his dream, evil and cruel and vigilant, couldn't at the same time have Adrian's temper and Adrian's indefatigable interest in things. Even devils couldn't be normal children at the same time. He brought his wife's wrist to his cheek, and the touch subdued the rising hysteria within him. "It was rather a loathsome business," he said, and put out his other hand for the cigarettes.

II

Mornington had on various occasions argued with Lionel whether pessimism was always the result of a too romantic, even a too sentimental, view of the world; and a slightly scornful mind pointed out to him, while he ate a solitary meal in his rooms that evening, that the shock which he undoubtedly had felt was the result of not expecting people to murder other people. "Whereas they naturally do," he said to himself. "The normal thing with an unpleasant intrusion is to try and exclude it—human or not. So silly not to be prepared for these things. Some people, as De Quincey said, have a natural aptitude for being murdered. To kill or to be killed is a perfectly reasonable thing. And I will not let it stop me taking those lists round to the Vicar's."

He got up, collected the papers which he had been analysing for reports on parochial finance, and went off to the Vicarage of St. Cyprian's, which was only a quarter of an hour from his home. He disliked himself for doing work that he disliked, but he had never been able to refuse help to any of his friends; and the Vicar might be numbered among them. Mornington suspected his Christianity of being the inevitable result of having moved for some time as a youth of eighteen in circles which were, in a rather detached and superior way, opposed to it; but it was a religion which enabled him to despise himself and everyone else without despising the universe, thus allowing him at once in argument or conversation the advantages of the pessimist and the optimist. It was because the Vicar, a hard-worked practical priest, had been driven by stress of experience to some similar standpoint that the two occasionally found one another congenial.

That evening, however, he found a visitor at the Vicarage, a round, dapper little cleric in gaiters, who was smoking a cigar and turning over the pages of a manuscript. The Vicar pulled Mornington into the study where they were sitting.

"My dear fellow," he said, "come in, come in. We've been talking about you. Let me introduce the Archdeacon of Castra Parvulorum—Mr. Mornington. What a dreadful business this is at your office! Did you have anything to do with it?"

Mornington saluted the Archdeacon, who took off his eye-glasses and bowed back. "Dreadful," he said, tentatively Mornington thought; rather as if he wasn't quite sure what the other wanted him to say, and was anxious to accommodate himself to what was expected. "Yes, dreadful!"

"Well," Mornington answered, rebelling against this double sympathy, "of course, it was a vast nuisance. It disturbed the whole place. And I forgot to send the copy for our advertisement in the *Bookman*—so we shan't get in this month. That's the really annoying part. I hate being defeated by a murder. And it wasn't even in my own room."

"Ah, that's the trade way of looking at it," the Vicar said. "You'll have some coffee? But this poor fellow … is it known at all who he was?"

"Nary a know," Mornington answered brightly. "The police have the body as the clue, and that's all. Rather large, and inconvenient to lug about, and of course only available for a few days. Nature, you know. But it's the *Bookman* that annoys me—you wouldn't believe how much."

"Oh, come, not really!" the Vicar protested. "You wouldn't compare the importance of an advertisement with a murder."

"I think Mr. Mornington's quite right," the Archdeacon said. "After all, one shouldn't be put out of one's stride by anything phenomenal and accidental. The just man wouldn't be."

"But, still, a *murder*——" the Vicar protested.

The Archdeacon shrugged. "Murders or mice, the principle's the same," he answered. "To-morrow is too late, I suppose?"

"Quite," Mornington answered. "But I needn't worry you with my phenomenal and specialist troubles."

"As a matter of fact," the Archdeacon went on placidly, "we were talking about your firm at first rather differently." He pointed with his glasses to the manuscript on the table, and looked coyly at Mornington. "I dare say you can guess," he added.

Mornington tried to look pleased, and said in a voice that almost cracked with doubt: "Books?"

"A book," the Vicar said. "The Archdeacon's been giving a series of addresses on Christianity and the League of Nations, and he's made them into a little volume which ought to have a good sale. So, of course, I thought of you."

"Thank you so much," Mornington answered. "And you'll excuse me asking—but is the Archdeacon prepared to back his fancy? Will he pay if necessary?"

The Archdeacon shook his head. "I couldn't do that, Mr. Mornington," he said. "It doesn't seem to me quite moral, so to speak. You know how they say a book is like a child. One has a ridiculous liking for one's own child—quite ridiculous. And that's all right. But seriously to think it's better than other children, to *push* it, to 'back' its being better, as you said—that seems to me so silly as to be almost wicked." He shook his head sadly at the manuscript.

"On the general principle I don't agree with you," Mornington said. "If your ideas are better than others' you ought to push them. I've no patience with our modern democratic modesty. How do you know the publisher you send it to is a better judge than you are? And, if he rejects it, what do you do?"

"If I send it to all the publishers," the Archdeacon answered, "and they all reject it, I think I should believe them. *Securus iudicat*, you know."

"But it doesn't," Mornington said. "Not by any manner of means. The *orbis terrarum* has to be taught its business by the more intelligent people. It has never yet received a new idea into its chaotic mind unless imposed by force, and generally by the sword."

He picked up the MS. and turned over the pages. "'The Protocol and the Pact,'" he read aloud, "'as Stages in Man's Consciousness.' 'Qualities and Nationalities.' 'Modes of Knowledge in Christ and Their Correspondences in Mankind.' 'Is the League of Nations Representative?'"

"I gather," he said, looking up, "that this is at once specialist and popular. I don't for a moment suppose we shall take it, but I should like to have a look at it. May I carry it off now?"

"I think I'd like to keep it over the week-end," the Archdeacon answered. "There's a point or two I want to think over and a little Greek I want to check. Perhaps I might bring it down to you on Monday or Tuesday?"

"Do," Mornington said. "Of course, I shan't decide. It'll go to one of our political readers, who won't, I should think from the chapter-headings, even begin to understand it. But bring it along by all means. Persimmons' list is the most muddled-up thing in London. *Foxy Flossie's Flirtations* and *Notes on Black Magic Considered Philosophically*. But that, of course, is his father, so there's some excuse."

"I thought you told me the elder Mr. Persimmons had retired," the Vicar said.

"He is the Evening Star," Mornington answered. "He cuts the glory from the grey, as it were. But he pops in a good deal so as to do it. He hovers on the horizon perpetually, and about once a fortnight lightens from the east to the west, or at least to Persimmons' private office. A nice enough creature—with a perverse inclination towards the occult."

"I'm afraid," the Vicar said gloomily, "this interest in what they call the occult is growing. It's a result of the lack of true religion in these days and a wrong curiosity."

"Oh, wrong, do you think?" Mornington asked. "Would you say any kind of curiosity was wrong? What about Job?"

"Job?" the Archdeacon asked.

"Well, sir, I always understood that where Job scored over the three friends was in feeling a natural curiosity why all those unfortunate things happened to him. They simply put up with it, but he, so to speak, asked God what He thought He was doing."

The Vicar shook his head. "He was told he couldn't understand."

"He was taunted with not being able to understand—which isn't quite the same thing," Mornington answered. "As a mere argument there's something lacking perhaps, in saying to a man who's lost his money and his house and his family and is sitting on the dustbin, all over boils, 'Look at the hippopotamus.'"

"Job seemed to be impressed," the Archdeacon said mildly.

"Yes," Mornington admitted. "He was certainly a perfect fool, in one meaning or other of the words." He got up to go, and added: "Then I shall see you in the City before you go back to … Castra Parvulorum, was it? What a jolly name!"

"Unfortunately it isn't generally called that," the Archdeacon said. "It's called in directories and so on, and by the inhabitants, Fardles. By Grimm's Law."

"Grimm's Law?" Mornington asked, astonished. "Wasn't he the man who wrote the fairy tales for the *parvuli*? But why did he make a law about it? And why did anyone take any notice?"

"I understand it was something to do with Indo-European sounds," the Archdeacon answered. "The Castra was dropped, and in *parvulorum* the p became f and the v became d. And Grimm discovered what had happened. But I try and keep the old name as well as I can. It's not far from London. They say Cæsar gave it the name because his soldiers caught a lot of British children there, and he sent them back to their own people."

"Then I don't see why Grimm should have interfered," Mornington said, shaking hands. "Fardles … it sounds like an essay by Maurice Hewlett. Castra Parvulorum … it sounds like … it sounds like Rome. Well, good night, sir. Good night, Vicar. No, don't come to the door."

III

Actually at the moment when Mornington was speaking of him the elder Mr. Persimmons was sitting in a comfortable chair in an Ealing flat, listening to his son's account of the afternoon's adventure. He was a large man, and he lay back watching Stephen with amused eyes, as the younger man grew more and more agitated over the incredible facts.

"I'm so afraid it'll be bad for business," he ended abruptly.

The other sighed a little and looked at the fire. "Business," he said. "Oh, I shouldn't worry about business. If they want your books, they'll buy your books." He paused a little, and added: "I called in to see you to-day, but you were out."

"Did you?" his son said. "They didn't tell me."

"Just as well," Mr. Persimmons answered, "because you needn't know now. You won't be called at the inquest. Only, if anybody ever asks you, say you'll ask me and find out. I tell you because I want to know what you are doing and saying."

Stephen was looking out of the window, and a minute went by before he spoke. Then he said absently, "What did you want? Anything important?"

"I wanted to talk about the balance sheet," his father answered. "There are a few points I don't quite understand. And I still incline to think the proportion of novels is too high. It fritters money away, merely using it to produce more novels of the same kind. I want a definite proportion established between that and the other kind of book. You could quite well have produced my *Intensive Mastery* instead of that appalling balderdash about Flossie. Stephen, are you listening?"

"Yes," Stephen said half-angrily.

"I don't believe you mean to produce my book," his father went on equably. "Did you read it?"

"Yes," Stephen said again, and came back into the room. "I don't know about it. I told you I didn't quite like it—I don't think other people would. Of course, I know there's a great demand for that sort of psycho-analytic book, but I didn't feel at all sure——" He stopped doubtfully.

"If you ever felt quite sure, Stephen," the older man said, "I should lose a great deal of pleasure. What was it you didn't feel quite sure about this time?"

"Well, all the examples—and the stories," Stephen answered vaguely. "They're all right, I suppose, but they seemed so—funny."

"*Funny Stories I Have Read*, by Stephen Persimmons," his father gibed. "They weren't stories, Stephen. They were scientific examples."

"But they were all about torture," the other answered. "There was a dreadful one about—oh, horrible! I don't believe it would sell."

"It will sell right enough," his father said. "You're not a scientist, Stephen."

"And the diagrams and all that," his son went on. "It'd cost a great deal to produce."

"Well, you shall do as you like," Persimmons answered. "But, if you don't produce it by Christmas, I'll print it privately. That will cost a lot more money, Stephen. And anything else I write. If there are many more it'll make a nasty hole in my accounts. And there won't be any sale then, because I shall give them away. And burn what are over. Make up your mind over the week-end. I'll come down next week to hear what you decide. All a gamble, Stephen, and you don't like to bet except on a certainty, do you? You know, if I could afford it, I should enjoy ruining you, Stephen. But that, Stephen——"

"For God's sake, don't keep on calling me Stephen like that," the wretched publisher said. "I believe you like worrying me."

"But that," his father went on placidly, "wasn't the only reason I came to see you to-day. I wanted to kill a man, and your place seemed to me as good as any and better than most. So it was, it seems."

Stephen Persimmons stared at the large, heavy body opposite lying back in its chair, and said, "You're worrying me … aren't you?"

"I may be," the other said, "but facts, I've noticed, do worry you, Stephen. They worried your mother into that lunatic asylum. A dreadful tragedy, Stephen—to be cut off from one's wife like that. I hope nothing of the sort will ever happen to you. Here am I comparatively young—and I should like another child, Stephen. Yes, Stephen, I should like another child. There'd be someone else to leave the money to; someone else with an interest in the business. And I should know better what to do. Now, when you were born, Stephen——"

"Oh, God Almighty," his son cried, "don't talk to me like that. What do you mean—you wanted to kill a man?"

"Mean?" the father asked. "Why, that. I hadn't thought of it till the day before, really—yesterday, so it was; when Sir Giles Tumulty told me Rackstraw was coming to see him—and then it only just crossed my mind. But when we got there, it was all so clear and empty. A risk, of course, but not much. Ask him to wait there while I get the money, and shut the door without going out. Done in a minute, Stephen, I assure you. He was an undersized creature, too."

Stephen found himself unable to ask any more questions. Did his father mean it or not? It would be like the old man to torment him: but if he had? Would it be a way of release?

"Well, first, Stephen," the voice struck in, "you can't and won't be sure. And it wouldn't look well to denounce your father on chance. Your mother *is* in a lunatic asylum, you know. And, secondly, my last will—— I made it a week or two ago—leaves all my money to found a settlement in East London. Very awkward for you, Stephen, if it all had to be withdrawn. But you won't, you won't. If anyone asks you, say you weren't told, but you know I wanted to talk to you about the balance sheet. I'll come in next week to do it."

Stephen got to his feet. "I think you want to drive me mad too," he said. "O God, if I only knew!"

"You know me," his father said. "Do you think I should worry about strangling you, Stephen, if I wanted to? As, of course, I might. But it's getting late. You know, Stephen, you brood too much; I've always said so. You keep your troubles to yourself and brood over them. Why not have a good frank talk with one of your clerks—that fellow Rackstraw, say? But you always were a secretive fellow. Perhaps it's as well, perhaps it's as well. And you haven't got a wife. Now, can you hang me or can't you?" The door shut behind his son, but he went on still aloud. "The wizards were burned, they went to be burned, they hurried. Is there a need still? Must the wizard be an outcast like the saint? Or am I only tired? I want another child. And I want the Graal."

He lay back in his chair, contemplating remote possibilities and the passage of the days immediately before him.

Chapter Three

THE ARCHDEACON IN THE CITY

The inquest was held on the Monday, with the formal result of a verdict of "Murder by a person or persons unknown," and the psychological result of emphasizing the states of mind of the three chief sufferers within themselves. The world certified itself as being, to Lionel more fantastic, to Mornington more despicable, to Stephen Persimmons more harassing. To the young girl who lived in the waiting-room and was interrogated by the coroner, it became, on the contrary, more exciting and delightful than ever; although she had no information to give—having, on her own account, been engaged all the while so closely indexing letter-books that she had not observed anyone enter or depart by the passage at the side of her office.

On the Tuesday, however, being, perhaps naturally, more watchful, she remarked towards the end of the day, three, or rather four, visitors. The offices shut at six, and about half-past four the elder Mr. Persimmons, giving her an amiable smile, passed heavily along the corridor and up to his son's room. At about a quarter past five Barbara Rackstraw, with Adrian, shone in the entrance—as she did normally some three or four times a year—and also disappeared up the stairs. And somewhere between the two a polite, chubby, and gaitered clergyman hovered at the door of the waiting-room and asked her tentatively if Mr. Mornington were in. Him she committed to the care of a passing office-boy, and returned to her indexing.

Gregory Persimmons, a little to his son's surprise and greatly to his relief, appeared to have shaken off the mood of tantalizing amusement which had possessed him on the previous Friday. He discussed various financial points in the balance sheet as if he were concerned only with ordinary business concerns. He congratulated his son on the result of the inquest as likely to close the whole matter except in what he thought the unlikely result of the police discovering the murderer; and when he brought up the subject of *Intensive Mastery* he did it with no suggestion that anything but the most normal hesitation had ever held Stephen back from enthusiastic acceptance. In the sudden relief from mental neuralgia thus granted him, Stephen found himself promising to have the book out before Christmas—it was then early summer—and even going so far as to promise estimates during the next week and discuss the price at which it might reasonably appear. Towards the end of an hour's conversation Gregory said, "By the way, I saw Tumulty yesterday, and he asked me to make sure that he was in time to cut a paragraph out of his book. He sent Rackstraw a postcard, but perhaps I might just make sure it got here all right. May I go along, Stephen?"

"Do," Stephen said. "I'll sign these letters and be ready by the time you're back." And, as his father went out with a nod, he thought to himself: "He couldn't possibly want to go into that office again if he'd really killed a man there. It's just his way of pulling my leg. Rather hellish, but I suppose it doesn't seem so to him."

Lionel, tormented with a more profound and widely spread neuralgia than his employer's, had by pressure of work been prevented from dwelling on it that day. Soon after his arrival Mornington had broken into the office to ask if he could have a set of proofs of Sir Giles Tumulty's book on *Vessels of Folklore*. "I've got an Archdeacon coming to see me," he said—"don't bow—and an Archdeacon ought to be interested in folklore, don't you think? I always used to feel that Archdeacons were a kind of surviving folklore themselves—they seem pre-Christian and almost prehistoric: a lingering and bi-sexual tradition. Besides, publicity, you know. Don't Archdeacons charge? 'Charge, Archdeacons, charge! On, Castra Parvulorum, on!' were the last words of Mornington.'"

"I wish they were!" Lionel said. "There are the proofs, on that shelf: take them and go! take them all."

"I don't want them all. Business, business. We can't have murders and Bank Holidays every day."

He routed out the proofs and departed; and when by the afternoon post an almost indecipherable postcard from Sir Giles asked for the removal of a short paragraph on page 218, Lionel did not think of making the alteration on the borrowed set. He marked the paragraph for deletion on the proofs he was about to return for Press, cursing Sir Giles a little for the correction—which, however, as it came at the end of a whole division of the book, would cause no serious inconvenience—and much more for his handwriting. A sentence beginning—he at last made out—"It has been suggested to me" immediately became totally illegible, and only recovered meaning towards the end, where the figures 218 rode like a monumental Pharaoh over the diminutive abbreviations which surrounded it. But the instruction was comprehensible, if the reason for it was not, and Lionel dispatched the proofs to the printer.

When, later on, the Archdeacon arrived, Mornington greeted him with real and false warmth mingled. He liked the clergyman, but he disliked manuscripts, and a manuscript on the League of Nations promised him some hours' boredom. For, in spite of his disclaimer, he knew he would have to skim the book at least, before he obtained further opinions, and the League of Nations lay almost in the nadir of all the despicable things in the world. It seemed to him so entire and immense a contradiction of aristocracy that it drove him into a positive hunger for mental authority imposed by force. He desired to see Plato and his like ruling with power, and remembered with longing the fierce inquisition of the *Laws*. However, he welcomed the Archdeacon without showing this, and settled down to chat about the book.

"Good evening, Mr.—Archdeacon," he said rapidly, suddenly remembering that he didn't know the other's name, and at the same moment that it would no doubt be on the manuscript and that he would look at it immediately. "Good of you to come. Come in and sit down."

The Archdeacon, with an agreeable smile, complied, and, as he laid the parcel on the desk, said: "I feel a little remorseful now, Mr. Mornington. Or I should if I didn't realize that this is your business."

"That," Mornington said, laughing, "is a clear, cool, lucid, diabolical way of looking at it. If you could manage to feel a little remorse I should feel almost tender—an unusual feeling towards a manuscript."

"The relation between an author and a publisher," the Archdeacon remarked, "always seems to me to partake a little of the nature of a duel, an abstract, impersonal duel. There is no feeling about it——"

"Oh, isn't there?" Mornington interjected. "Ask Persimmons; ask our authors."

"Is there?" the Archdeacon asked. "You astonish me." He looked at the parcel, of which he still held the string. "Do you know," he said thoughtfully, "I don't *think* I have any feeling particularly about it. Whether you publish it or not, whether anyone publishes it or not, doesn't matter much. I think it might matter if I made no attempt to get it published, for I honestly think the ideas are sound. But with that very small necessary activity my responsibility ends."

"You take it very placidly," Mornington answered, smiling. "Most of our authors feel they have written the most important book of the century."

"Ah, don't misunderstand me," the Archdeacon said. "I might think that myself—I don't, but I might. It wouldn't make any difference to my attitude towards it. No book of ideas can matter so supremely as that. 'An infant crying in the night,' you know. What else was Aristotle?"

"Well, it makes it much pleasanter for us," Mornington said again. "I gather it's all one to you whether we take it or leave it?"

"Entirely," the Archdeacon answered, and pushed the bundle towards him. "I should, inevitably, be interested in your reasons so far as they bear stating."

"With this detachment," the other answered, undoing the parcel, "I wonder you make any reservation. Could any abominable reason shatter such a celestial calm?"

The Archdeacon twiddled his thumbs. "Man is weak," he said sincerely, "and I indeed am the chief of sinners. But I also am in the hands of God, and what can it matter how foolish my own words are or how truly I am told of them? Pooh, Mr. Mornington, you must have a very conceited set of authors."

"Talking about authors," Mornington went on, "I thought you might be interested in looking at the proofs of this book we've got in hand." And he passed over Sir Giles's *Sacred Vessels*.

The Archdeacon took them. "It's good work, is it?" he asked.

"I haven't had time to read it," the other said, "But there's one article on the Graal that ought to attract you." He glanced sideways at the first page of the MS., and read "*Christianity and the League of Nations*, by Julian Davenant, Archdeacon of Castra Parvulorum." "Well, thank God I know his name now," he reflected.

Meanwhile the third visitor, with her small companion, had penetrated to Lionel's room. They had come to the City to buy Adrian a birthday present, and, having succeeded, had gone on according to plan to the office. This arrangement—as such arrangements by such people tend to be—had been made two or three weeks earlier, and the crisis of the previous Friday had made Lionel only the more anxious to see if Barbara's presence would in any way cleanse the room from the slime that seemed still to carpet it. He had been a little doubtful whether she herself would bear the neighbourhood, but, either because in effect the murder had meant little to her or because she guessed something of her husband's feelings, she had made no difficulty, had indeed assumed that the visit was still to be paid. Adrian's persistent interest in the date-stamp presented itself for those few minutes to Lionel as a solid reality amid the fantasies his mind made haste to induce. But Barbara's own presence was too much in the nature of a defiance to make him entirely happy. He kissed her as she sat on his table, with a sense of almost heroic challenge; neither he nor she were ignorant, and their ignoring of the subject was a too clear simulation of the ignorance they did not possess. But Adrian's ignorance was something positive. Lionel felt that a dead body beneath the desk would have been to this small and intent being something not so much unpleasant as dull and unnecessary; it might have got in the way of the movements of his body, but not of his mind. This was what he needed; his unsteady thought needed weighting, but with what, he asked himself, of all the shadows of obscenity that moved through the place of shadows which was the world—with which of all these could he weight it? From date-stamp to waste-paper basket, from basket to files, from files to telephone Adrian pursued his investigations; and Lionel was on the point of giving an exhibition of telephoning by ringing up Mornington, when the door opened and Gregory Persimmons appeared.

"I beg your pardon," he said, stopping on the threshold, "I really beg your pardon, Rackstraw."

"Come in, sir," Lionel said, getting up. "It's only my wife."

"I've met Mrs. Rackstraw before," Persimmons said, shaking hands. "But not, I think, this young man." He moved slowly in Adrian's direction.

"Adrian," Barbara said, "come and shake hands."

The child politely obeyed, as Persimmons, dropping on one knee, welcomed him with a grave and detached courtesy equal to his own. But when he stood up again he kept his eyes fixed on Adrian, even while saying to Barbara, "What a delightful child!"

"He is rather a pet," Barbara murmured. "But, of course, an awful nuisance."

"They always are," Persimmons said. "But they have their compensations. I've always been glad I had a son. Training them is a wonderful experience."

"Adrian trains himself, I'm afraid," Barbara answered, a little embarrassed. "But we shall certainly have to begin to teach him soon."

"Yes," Gregory said, his eyes still on Adrian. "It's a dreadful business, teaching them what's wrong. It has to be done all the same, and he's too fine a child to waste. I beg your pardon again—but I do think children are so wonderful, and when one meets the grown-ups one feels they've so often been wasted." He smiled at Barbara. "Look at your husband; look at me!" he said. "We were babies once."

"Well," Barbara said, smiling back, "I wouldn't say that Lionel had been altogether wasted. Nor you, Mr. Persimmons."

He bowed a little, but shook his head, then turned to Lionel. "All I came for, Rackstraw," he said, "was to say that I saw Tumulty yesterday, and he was rather anxious whether you could read a postcard he sent you about his book."

"Only just," Lionel answered, "but I managed. He wanted a paragraph knocked out."

"And you got it in time to make the correction?" Gregory asked again.

"Behold the proof," Lionel said, "*in* the proof. It goes off to-night." He held the sheet out to the other man, who took it with a word of thanks and glanced at the red-ink line. "That's it," he said, "the last paragraph on page 218." He stood for a moment reading it through.

In the room across the corridor the Archdeacon turned over page 217 and read on.

"It seems probable therefore," the book ran, "if we consider these evidences, and the hypothetical scheme which has been adduced, not altogether unreasonably, to account for the facts which we have—a scheme which may be destroyed in the future by discovery of some further fact, but till then may not unjustifiably be considered to hold the field—it seems probable that the reputed Graal may be so far definitely traced and its wanderings followed as to permit us to say that it rests at present in the parish church of Fardles."

"Dear me!" the Archdeacon said; and, "Yes, that was the paragraph," said Mr. Gregory Persimmons; and for a moment there was silence in both offices.

The Archdeacon was considering that he had, in fact, never been able to find out anything about a certain rarely used chalice at Fardles. A year or two before the decease of the last Vicar a very much more important person in the neighbourhood had died—Sir John Horatio Sykes-Martindale, K.V.O., D.S.O., and various other things. In memory of the staunch churchmanship of this great and good man, his widow had presented a complete set of altar fittings and altar plate to the parish church, which was then doing its best with antique but uncorresponding paten and chalice. These were discarded in favour of the new gift, and when the Archdeacon succeeded to the rectory and archdeaconry he followed his predecessor's custom. He had at different times examined the old chalice carefully, and had shown it to some of his friends, but he had had no reason to make any special investigation, nor indeed would it have been easy to do so. The new suggestion, however, gave it a fresh interest. He was about to call Mornington's attention to the paragraph, then he changed his mind. There would be plenty of time when the book was out: lots of people—far too many—would hear about it then, and he might have to deal with a very complicated situation. So many people, he reflected, put an altogether undue importance on these exterior and material things. The Archbishop might write—and Archæological Societies—and perhaps Psychical Research people: one never knew. Better keep quiet and consider.

"I should like," he said aloud, "to have a copy of this book when it comes out. Could you have one sent to me, Mr. Mornington?"

"Oh, but I didn't show it to you for that reason," Mornington answered. "I only thought it might amuse you."

"It interests me very deeply," the Archdeacon agreed. "In one sense, of course, the Graal is unimportant—it is a symbol less near Reality now than any chalice of consecrated wine. But it is conceivable that the Graal absorbed, as material things will, something of the high intensity of the moment when it was used, and of its adventures through the centuries. In that sense I should be glad, and even eager," he added precisely, "to study its history."

"Well, as you like," Mornington answered. "So long as I'm not luring or bullying you into putting money into poor dear Persimmons's pocket."

"No one less, I assure you," the Archdeacon said, as he got up to go. "Besides, why should one let oneself be lured or bullied?"

"Especially by a publisher's clerk," Mornington added, smiling. "Well, we'll write to you as soon as possible, Mr. Davenant. In about forty days, I should think. It would be Lent to most authors, but I gather it won't be more than the usual Sundays after Trinity to you."

The Archdeacon shook his head gravely. "One is very weak, Mr. Mornington," he said. "While I would do good, and so on, you know. I shall wonder what will happen, although it's silly, of course, very silly. Good-bye and thank you."

Mornington opened the door for him and followed him out into the corridor. As they went along it they saw a group, consisting of Gregory and the Rackstraws outside Stephen Persimmons's room at the top of the stairs, and heard Gregory say to Barbara, "Yes, Mrs. Rackstraw, I'm sure that's the best way. You can't teach them what to want and go for because you don't know their minds. But you can teach them what *not* to do—just a few simple rules about what's wrong. Be afraid to do wrong—that's what I used to tell Stephen."

"*Le malheureux!*" Mornington murmured as he bowed to the group, and let his smile change from one of respect to Gregory to one of friendliness for Barbara. The Archdeacon's foot was poised doubtfully for a moment over the first stair. But, if he had been inclined to go back, he changed his mind and went on towards the front door, with the other in attendance.

"Yes," Barbara said, distracted by Mornington's passing, "yes, I expect you're right."

"I suppose," Gregory remarked, changing the conversation, "that you've settled your holiday plans by now. Where are you going?"

"Well, sir," Lionel said, "we weren't going away this year at all. But Adrian had a slight attack of measles a month or so ago, so we decided we ought to, just to put him thoroughly right. Only every place is booked up and we don't seem able to get anything."

"I don't want to seem intrusive," Gregory said hesitatingly, "but, if you really want a place, there's a cottage—not a very grand one—down near where I live. It's on my grounds actually, and it's quite empty just now … if it's any good to you."

"But, Mr. Persimmons, how charming of you!" Barbara cried. "That would be delightful and just the thing. Where do you live, by the way?"

"I've just taken a place in the country," Gregory answered, "in Hertfordshire, near a little village called Fardles. Indeed, I've only just moved in. It belonged to a Lady Sykes-Martindale, but she's been advised to go to Egypt for her health, and I took the house. So it's quite new to me. Adrian and I could explore it together."

"How splendid!" Barbara said. "But are you quite sure, Mr. Persimmons? I did want to get away, but we were giving up hope. Are you quite sure we shan't be intruding?"

"Not if you will let me see something of you there," Gregory assured her. "And, if Adrian liked me enough," he smiled at the boy, "you and your husband——" A motion of his hand threw England open to their excursions.

"It's very good of you, sir," Lionel began.

"Nonsense, nonsense," the other answered. "There's the cottage and here are you. I'll write about it. When do you go, Rackstraw? July? I'll write in a week or two, then. And now I must go and look at more figures. Good night, Mrs. Rackstraw. I shall see you again in five weeks or so. Good night, Adrian." He bowed down to shake the small hand. "Good night, Rackstraw. I'm delighted you'll come." He waved his hand generally and departed.

"What a divine creature!" Barbara said, going down the stairs. "Adrian darling, we're really going away. Would you like to go into the country?"

"Where is the country?" Adrian said.

"Oh—out there," Barbara said. "Away from the streets. With fields and cows."

"I don't like cows," Adrian said coldly.

"I daresay you won't see any," Lionel put in. "It does seem rather fortunate, Barbara."

"I think it's perfectly splendid," Barbara said joyously.

"Can I take my new train?" Adrian asked. And, in a whirl of assurances that he should take anything he liked or needed or had the slightest inclination to take, they came out into the hot June evening.

———————

Chapter Four

THE FIRST ATTEMPT ON THE GRAAL

The Archdeacon of Castra Parvulorum returned to Fardles and his rectory on the next morning, for a few days' clearing up before he went on his holiday. After he had spent an hour or two in his study, he got up suddenly, and, going out of the house, took the private path that led through his garden and the churchyard to the small Norman Church. The memory of the article he had read in Mornington's office had grown more dominating as he returned to the place where, if Sir Giles Tumulty were right, the Graal, neglected and overlooked, stood in his sacristy. No-one had ever seen the Archdeacon excited, not even when, in the days of his youth, he had assisted his friends to break up a recruiting meeting in the days of the Boer War; and even now he yielded to himself as he might have yielded to a friend's importunities, and went along the path rather with an air of humouring a pleasant but persistent visitor than with any eagerness of his own.

The church stood open, as it always did, from the early celebration till dusk. The verger was at the moment engaged on the Archdeacon's roses, and, since Fardles lay off the main road, it was rarely that it was visited by strangers. Fardles itself indeed lay a little way distant from the church, the nearest houses being about a quarter of a mile off and the main street of the village beginning another quarter of a mile beyond them. The railway station formed the third corner of an equilateral triangle, with the village and the church at the angles of its base. On the other side of the base a similar triangle was formed by the grounds of the late Sir John Horatio Sykes-Martindale's house. The house itself—Cully, as it was called, to the Archdeacon's secret and serious delight, and without any distress to the naturally ignorant Sir John—lay in the middle of its grounds; an enormous overbuilt place, of no particular age and no particular period. And beyond it, towards the apex of this second triangle, lay the empty cottage of which Mr. Gregory Persimmons had spoken to Lionel.

The Archdeacon went into the church and passed on into the sacristy. He unlocked and opened the tall and antique chest in which the sacred vessels were kept, lifted one of them out, and, carrying it back into the church, set it upon the altar. Then he stood and looked at it carefully.

It was old enough, that appeared certain; it was plain enough too, almost severe. The drinking cup itself was some six inches in depth, with a stem in proportion, and a small pedestal which was carried by slowly narrowing work up some distance of the stem. The whole was about fifteen or sixteen inches high. There were, so far as the Archdeacon could see, no markings, no ornamentation, except for a single line, about half an inch below the rim. It was made of silver, so far as he could tell, slightly dented here and there, but still apparently good for a considerable amount of use. It stood there on the altar, as it had done so many mornings, until the grief of Lady Sykes-Martindale had enriched the late Vicar's sacristy with a new gold chalice. And the Archdeacon stood and considered it.

Of course, the thing was not impossible. He did not remember Sir Giles's article accurately enough to know the stages by which the archæologist had traced the Graal from Jerusalem to Fardles; here a general tradition, there a local rumour, a printed paragraph or an unpublished MS., even the remnants of an old tapestry or a carving in a remote Town Hall. He could see clearly that it might all be nothing but a fantasy of peculiar neatness, and he attached little importance to the vessel itself. But he was conscious that a great many people might attach a good deal of importance to it if there were any truth in the story. If it were the Graal, what would they want to do with it? He considered with pleasure that at least it was in the hands of the officials of the Church, and that there were some things that even officials of the Church could not do. They could not, for example, sell it to a millionaire. But why, the Archdeacon asked himself, should he object to it being sold to a millionaire?

He was about to restore the vessel to the sacristy when he asked himself this question, and stayed for a moment or two with it in his hands. Then he changed his mind, went and locked the door of the cabinet, and came back to the altar. "Ah, fair sweet Lord," he said half-aloud, "let me keep this Thy vessel, if it be Thy vessel; for love's sake, fair Lord, if Thou hast held it in Thy hands, let me take it into mine. And, if not, let me be courteous still to it for Thy sake, courteous Lord; since this might well have been that, and that was touched by Thee." He smiled a little, took up the chalice, and went back to the Rectory.

There he passed straight to his own pleasant bedroom and opened an inner door which led to a small room, once perhaps a dressing-room. It was furnished now with a pallet-bed, a hard chair or two, a table, and a kneeling-desk. On one otherwise empty wall a crucifix hung; a small shelf in one corner held a few books, and there were one or two more on the table. The window in one of the pair of shorter walls looked out over the graveyard towards the church. The Archdeacon went across to the mantelshelf, set down his burden, looked at it for a minute or two, murmured a prayer, and went down to lunch.

After lunch he walked for a little while in his garden. His *locum tenens*, a rather elderly clergyman whom the Archdeacon thoroughly disliked, but who needed the money that the temporary post would bring him, was not due till the next day. The Archdeacon felt a pang, slight but definite, at the idea that this tall, lean, harassed, talkative, and inefficient priest would sit in his chair and sleep in his bed; not so much that they were his chair and his bed as that it seemed a shame that such ready and pleasant things should be subjected to the invasion of human futility. He put out his hand and touched a flower, then withdrew it. "I am becoming sentimental," he thought to himself. "How do I know that a chair is full of goodwill, or a bed anxious to please? They may be, but they mayn't. Their life is hidden with Christ in God. Oh, give thanks to the God of all gods," he sang softly, "for His mercy endureth for ever."

"Mr. Davenant?" said a voice at his back.

The Archdeacon, a little startled, turned. A large man whose face he dimly remembered was looking over the garden gate.

"Er—yes," he said vaguely, "that is, yes. I am Mr. Davenant."

"Mr. Archdeacon, I suppose I ought to say," the other went on agreeably. "I knew I was wrong as soon as I'd spoken."

"Not at all," the Archdeacon answered. "You wanted to see me? Come in, won't you?" He opened the gate for the stranger, who, as he entered, uttered a word of thanks and went on: "Well, I did, rather. My name is Persimmons, Gregory Persimmons. I've just bought Cully, you know, so we shall be neighbours. But I understand from the village talk that you're going away to-morrow, and I didn't come to-day merely for a neighbourly call."

"Whatever the reason——" the Archdeacon murmured. "Shall we go inside or would you rather sit down over there?" He indicated a garden-seat among the flowers.

"Oh, here, by all means," Persimmons said. "Thank you." He accepted a cigarette. "Well the fact is, Mr. Archdeacon, I have come as a beggar and yet not a beggar. I have come to beg for another and pay for myself."

The Archdeacon put a finger to his glasses. The word Persimmons had taken him back to the previous day's visit to Mornington; and he was asking himself whether this was the voice that had been offering advice on how to train children. There was something about this last sentence also that offended him.

"I know a priest," Persimmons proceeded, "who is in bad need of some altar furniture, especially the sacred vessels, for a new mission church he's starting. Now, I was talking to one and another down here—the grocer's an ardent churchman, I find. And one of your choir-boys, and so on—as one does. And I gathered— you'll tell me if I'm wrong—that you had an extra chalice here which you didn't often use. So I wondered, as you have the set that Lady Sykes-Martindale gave, whether you'd consider letting me have it at a reasonable price, for my friend."

"I see," the Archdeacon said. "Yes, quite. I see what you mean. But, if you'll forgive me asking, Mr. Persimmons, surely a new chalice would be better than a—shall I say, second-hand one?" He threw a deprecating smile at Gregory and loosed an inner secret smile to Christ at the epithet.

"My friend," Persimmons said, leaning comfortably back and lazily smoking, "my friend hates new furniture for an altar. He has some kind of theory about stored power and concentrated sanctity which I, not being a theologian, don't profess to understand. But the result of it is that he infinitely prefers things that have been used for many years in the past. Perhaps you know the feeling?"

"Yes, I know the feeling," the Archdeacon said. "But in this instance I'm afraid it can't be rewarded. I'm afraid the chalice is not to be parted with."

"It's natural you should say that," the other answered, "for I expect I've put it clumsily, Mr. Archdeacon. But I hope you'll think it over. Of course, I know I'm a stranger, but I want to feel part of the life here, and I thought if I could send out a—a sort of magnetic thrill by buying that chalice for my friend … and I'd be glad to buy another for you if you wanted it replaced … I thought … I don't know … I thought …"

His voice died away, and he sat looking half-wistfully out over the garden, the portrait of a retired townsman trying to find a niche for himself in new surroundings, shy but good-hearted, earnest if a little clumsy, and trying not to touch too roughly upon subjects which he seemed to regard with a certain ignorant alarm. The Archdeacon shot a glance at him, and after a minute's silence shook his head. "No," he said, "I'm sorry, Mr. Persimmons, but that chalice is not for sale. But perhaps I can do something for you. Over in your direction, some eight miles beyond you, there's a church which I think has exactly the kind of thing you want. I know that recently they had an altar set up in their Lady Chapel, replaced the vessels at the High Altar, and bought fresh ones for the other two. If the Vicar hasn't given his old ones away yet, he's the very man for you—and he hadn't a week ago, because I was over there. I'll give you a note of introduction to him if you like—he's a nice fellow; he's one of the old Rushforths, you know: they're a side branch of the Herberts. A good old Anglican family, one might say. His Christian name's Herbert—a very pleasant fellow. Devoted to the Church, too. Fasts in Lent and all that kind of thing, I believe; and they do say he hears confessions—but I don't want to take any notice of that unless I'm driven to. It wouldn't matter, of course, I couldn't do anything—that's the great charm of being an Archdeacon, one never can. But there's a certain prestige and so on, and I don't want to throw that, for what it's worth, against him. Herbert Rushforth, yes, I'll certainly give you a note. Or, even better—I have to go out that way—probably—possibly—this evening, and I'll call on him and ask him myself. And, if he has them still, he'll be delighted for you to have them; you needn't mind in the least—he's extremely well-to-do. He'll want to leave them at Cully to-morrow, and perhaps he will. Even if you don't want to take them over personally, as, of course, you may, he could have them sent to your friend. Where did you say his church was?" The Archdeacon, a fountain-pen in his hand, a slip of paper on his knee, looked pleasantly and inquiringly at Mr. Persimmons, and all round them the flowers gently stirred.

Mr. Persimmons was a little taken aback. There had not appeared to him to be any conceivable reason why the Archdeacon should refuse to part with the old chalice, and if by any chance there had been any difficulty he had still expected to be able to obtain sight of it, to see what it looked like and where it was kept. He found himself at the moment almost, it seemed, on the other side of the county from Fardles, and he did not immediately see any way of getting back. He thought for a moment of making his imaginary clerical friend a native of Fardles, in order to give him a special delight in things that came from there, but that was too risky.

"Oh, well," he said, "if you don't mind, I think I won't give you his name. He might be rather ashamed of not being able to buy the necessary things. That was why, I thought, if you and I could just quietly settle it together, without bringing other people in, it would be so much better. A clergyman doesn't like to admit that he's poor, does he? And that was why——"

Damnation! he thought, he was repeating himself. But the Archdeacon's fantastic round face and gold glasses were watching him with a grave attention, and where but now had been a steady flow of words there was an awful silence. "Well," he said, with an effort at a leap across the void, "I'm sorry you can't let me have it."

"But I'm offering it to you," the Archdeacon said. "You didn't want the Fardles chalice *particularly*, did you?"

"Only as coming from the place where I was going to live," Persimmons said, and added suddenly: "It just seemed to me as if, as I was leaving my friend myself, I was sending him something better instead, something greater and stronger and more friendly."

"But you were talking about a chalice," the Archdeacon objected perplexedly. "How do you mean, Mr. Persimmons—finer and stronger and so on?"

"I meant the chalice," Gregory answered. "Surely that——"

The Archdeacon laughed good-naturedly and shook his head. "Oh, no," he said, "no. Not the chalice alone. Why, if it were the Holy Graal itself," he added thoughtfully, replacing the cap on his fountain-pen and putting it away, "you could hardly say that about it." He stood up, a little disappointed at not having noticed any self-consciousness about the other when he had mentioned the Graal. "Well," he said, "I must apologise, but you will understand I have some work to do; I'm going to-morrow, as you say. Will you forgive me? And shall I speak to Rushforth?"

"If you will be so good," Persimmons answered. "Or, no, don't let me take up your time. I will go and see him, if I may mention your name? Yes, I assure you I would rather. Good afternoon, Mr. Archdeacon."

"Good afternoon," the Archdeacon said. "I shall see you often when I return, I hope."

He accompanied his visitor to the gate, chatting amicably. But when Persimmons had gone he walked slowly back towards the house, considering the discussion thoughtfully. Was there a needy mission church? and was his visitor to be its benefactor? And the chalice? It seemed possible, and even likely, in this fantastic dream of a ridiculous antiquary, that the Graal of so many romances and so long a quest, of Lancelot and Galahad and dim maidens moving in antique pageants of heraldry and symbolism and religion, the desire of Camelot, the messenger of Sarras, the relic of Jerusalem, should be resting neglected in an English village. "Fardles," he thought, "Castra Parvulorum, the camp of the children: where else should the Child Himself rest?" He re-entered the Rectory, singing again to himself: "Who alone doeth marvellous things; for his mercy endureth for ever."

It was the custom of the parish that there should be a daily celebration at seven, at which occasionally in summer a small congregation assembled. Before this, at about a quarter to seven, the Archdeacon was in the habit of saying Morning Prayer publicly, as he was required to do by the rubrics. Once a week, on Thursday mornings, he was assisted by the sexton; on the other mornings he assisted himself. As, however, the sexton with growing frequency overslept himself, the Archdeacon preferred to keep the key of the church himself, and it was with this in his hand that he came to the west door about half-past six the next morning. At the door, however, he stopped, astonished. For it hung open and wrenched from the lock, wrenched and broken and pushed back against the other wall. The Archdeacon stared at it, went closer and surveyed it, and then hastened into the church. A few minutes gave him the extent of the damage. The two boxes, for the Poor and for the Church, that were fixed not far from the font, had also been opened, and their contents, if they had any, looted; the candlesticks on the altar had been thrown over, the candles in them broken and smashed, and the frontal pulled away and torn. In the sacristy the lock of the cabinet had been forced and the gold chalice which commemorated the late Sir John had disappeared, together with the gold paten. On the white-washed wall had been scrawled a few markings—"Phallic," the Archdeacon murmured, with a faint smile. He came back to the front door in time to see the sexton at the gate of the churchyard, and, judiciously lingering on the footpath beyond, two spasmodically devout ladies of the parish. He waved to them all to hurry, and when they arrived informed them equably of the situation.

"But, Mr. Archdeacon——" Mrs. Major cried.

"But, Mr. Davenant——" Miss Willoughby, who, as being older, both in years and length of Fardles citizenship, than most of the ladies of the neighbourhood, permitted herself to use the personal name. And "Who can have done it?" they both concluded.

"Ah!" the Archdeacon said benignantly. "A curious business, isn't it?"

"Isn't it sacrilege?" said Mrs. Major.

"Was it a tramp?" asked Miss Willoughby.

"What we want is Towlow," the sexton said firmly. "Towlow isn't at all bad at finding things out, though, being a Wesleyan Methodist, as he calls himself, he can't be expected to want to find out these bloody murderers. I'll go and get him, shall I, sir?"

"How fortunate my brother's staying with me," Mrs. Major cried out. "He's in the Navy, you know, and quite used to crime. He even sat on a court-martial once."

Miss Willoughby, out of a wider experience, knew better than to commit herself at once. She watched the Archdeacon's eyes, and, as she saw them glaze at these two suggestions, ventured a remote and disapproving "H'm, h'm!" Even the nicest clergymen, she knew, were apt to have unexpected fads about religion.

"No," the Archdeacon said, "I don't think we'll ask Towlow. And though, of course, I can't object to your brother looking at these damaged doors, Mrs. Major, I shouldn't like him to want to make an arrest. Sacrilege is hardly a thing a priest can prosecute for—not, anyhow, in a present-day court."

"But——" Mrs. Major and the sexton began.

"The immediate thing," the Archdeacon flowed on, "is the celebration, don't you think? Jessamine"—this to the sexton—"will you move those candlesticks and get as much of the grease off as you can? Mrs. Major, will you put the frontal straight? Miss Willoughby, will you do what you can to set the other ornaments right? Thank you, thank you. Fortunately the other chalice is at the rectory; I will go and get it." Then he paused a moment. "And perhaps," he said gravely, "as these two boxes have been robbed, we may take the advantage to restore something." He moved from one box to the other, dropping in coins, and a little reluctantly the two ladies imitated him. Jessamine was already at the altar.

As the Archdeacon walked up to the house he allowed himself to consider the possibilities. The breaking open of the west door pointed to a more serious attack than that of a casual tramp; tramps didn't carry such instruments as this success must have necessitated. But, if a tramp were not the burglar, then the money in the boxes had not been the aim. The gold chalice, then? Possible, possible: or the other chalice, the one of whose reputed history, except for that quarter of an hour in Mornington's room, he would have known nothing—could that be the aim? After all, the man who wrote the book—what was his name?—might have mentioned it, mentioned it to anyone, to a collector, to a millionaire, to a frenzied materialist. But one wouldn't expect them to try burglary at once. He saw in the distance the garden-seat where he had sat in talk the previous afternoon. And had they? Or had they tried purchase? Persimmons—Stephen Persimmons, publisher—*Christianity and the League of Nations*—a mission church in need—sacrilege—phallic scrawls.

He came into the inner room where he had looked at the chalice before he went out that morning, and as he came in it seemed to meet him in sound. A note of gay and happy music seemed to ring for a moment in his ears as he paused in the entrance. It was gone, if it had been there, and gravely he genuflected in front of the vessel and lifted it from its place. Carrying it as he had so often lifted its types and companions, he became again as in all those liturgies a part of that he sustained; he radiated from that centre and was but the last means of its progress in mortality. Of this sense of instrumentality he recognized, none the less, the component parts—the ritual movement, the priestly office, the mere pleasure in ordered, traditional, and almost universal movement. "Neither is this Thou," he said aloud, and, coming to the garden door, looked round him. In the hall the clock struck seven; he heard his housekeeper moving upstairs; as he came out into the garden he saw on the road a few men on their way to work. Then suddenly he saw another man leaning over the gate as Persimmons had leant the previous afternoon; only this was not Persimmons, though a man not unlike him in general height and build. The man opened the gate and came into the garden, though not directly in the path to the churchyard gate, and on the sudden the Archdeacon stopped.

"Excuse me, mister," a voice said, "but is this the way to Fardles?" He pointed down the road.

"That is the way, yes," the Archdeacon answered. "Keep to the right all the way."

"Ah, thankee," the stranger said. "I've been walking almost all night—nowhere to go and no money to go with." He was standing a few yards off. "Excuse me coming in like this, but seeing a gentleman——"

"Do you want something to eat?" the Archdeacon asked.

"Ah, that's it," said the other, eyeing him and the chalice curiously. "Reckon you've never been twenty-four hours without a bite or sup." He took another step forward.

"If you go round to the kitchen you shall be given some food," the Archdeacon said firmly. "I am on my way to the church and cannot stop. If you want to see me I will talk to you when I come back." He lifted the chalice and went on down the path and through the churchyard.

The Mysteries celebrated, he returned, still carefully carrying the chalice, and set it out of sight in a cupboard in the breakfast-room. When his housekeeper came in with coffee he asked after the stranger.

"Oh yes, sir, he came round," she said, "and I gave him some food. But he didn't eat much, to my thinking, and he was off again in ten minutes. Those folk don't want breakfast, money's what they're after. He wouldn't stop to see you, not after I told him you might get him a job. Money, that's what he wanted, not a job, nor breakfast, either."

But the Archdeacon absurdly continued to doubt this. He had felt, all through the short conversation in the garden, that it was not himself, but the vessel that the stranger had been studying—and that not with any present recognition, but as if he were impressing it on his memory. His train went at half-past nine; it was now half-past eight. But the train was out of the question; he had to explain the state of the church to the *locum tenens*; he had to go over to Rushforth, not now for Persimmons, but for his own needs. And, above all, he had to decide what to do with that old, slightly dented chalice that was hidden in the cupboard of the breakfast-room of an English rectory.

The first thing that occurred to him was the bank; the second was the Bishop. But the nearest bank was five miles off; and the Bishop was probably thirty-five, at the cathedral city. He might be anywhere, being a young and energetic and modern Bishop, who organized the diocese from railway stations, and platforms at public meetings before and after speaking, and public telephone-boxes, and so on. The Archdeacon foresaw some difficulty in explaining the matter. To walk straight in, and put down the chalice, and say: "This is the Holy Graal. I believe it to be so because of a paragraph in some proofs, a man who tried to buy it for a mission church and said that children ought to be taught not to do wrong, a burglary at my church, and another man who asked the way to Fardles"—would a young, energetic, modern Bishop believe it? The Archdeacon liked the Bishop very much, but he did not believe him to be patient or credulous.

The bank first then, and Rushforth next. And, in a day or two, the Bishop. Or rather first a telegram to Scotland. He sat down to write it, meaning to dispatch it from the station when he took the train to town. Then he spent some time in looking out a leather case which would hold the chalice, and had indeed been used for some such purpose before. He ensconced the Graal—if it were the Graal—therein, left a message with his housekeeper that he would be back some time in the afternoon, and by just after nine was fitting his hat on in the hall.

There came a knock at the door. The housekeeper came to open it. The Archdeacon, looking over his shoulder, saw the stranger who had invaded his garden that morning standing outside.

"Excuse me, ma'am," the stranger said, "but is the reverend gentleman in? Ah, to be sure, there he is. You see, sir, I didn't want to worry you over your breakfast, so I went for a bit of a walk. But I hope you haven't forgotten what you said about helping me to find work. It's work I want, sir, not idleness."

"You didn't seem that keen on it when you were talking to *me* about it," the housekeeper interjected.

"I didn't want to forestall his reverence," the stranger said. "But anything that he could do I'd be truly grateful for."

"What's your name?" the Archdeacon asked.

"Kedgett," the other answered, "Samuel Kedgett. I served in the war, sir, and here——"

"Quite," the Archdeacon answered. "Well, Mr. Kedgett, I'm sorry I can't stop now; I have to go to town most unexpectedly. Call"—he changed "this evening" into "to-morrow morning"—"and I'll see what can be done."

"Thank you, sir," the other said, with a sudden alertness. "I'll be there. Good-bye, sir." He was out of the porch and down the garden path before his hearers were clear that he was going.

"What a jumpy creature!" the housekeeper said. "Dear me, sir, I hope you're not going to give him work here. I couldn't stand a man like that."

"No," the Archdeacon said absently, "no, of course, you couldn't. Well, good-bye, Mrs. Lucksparrow. Explain to Mr. Batesby when he comes, won't you? I shall be back in the afternoon probably."

Along the country lane on the other side of the churchyard there was little to be seen beyond the fields and pleasant slopes of the country twenty miles out of North London. The Archdeacon walked along, meditating, and occasionally turning his head to look over his shoulder. Not that he seriously expected to be attacked but he did feel that there was something going on of which he had no clear understanding. "How vainly men themselves amaze," he quoted, and allowed himself to be distracted by trying to complete the couplet with some allusion to the high vessel. He produced at last, as he came to a space where four roads met and as he went on through what was called a wood, but was not much more than a copse—he produced as a result:

> *ᵒ vainly men themselves*

> *with this chalice, to theiᵣ*

and heard a motor-car coming towards him in the distance. It was coming very quietly from the direction of the station, and in a few minutes it came round the curve of the road. He saw someone stand up in it and apparently beckon to him, quickened his steps, heard a faint voice calling: "Archdeacon! Archdeacon!" felt a sudden crash on the back of his head, and entered unconsciousness.

The car drew up by him. "Quick, Ludding, the case," Mr. Persimmons said to the man who had slipped from the wood in the Archdeacon's rear. He caught it to him, opened it, took out the chalice, and set it in another case which stood on the seat by him. Then he gave the empty one back to Ludding. "Keep that till I tell you to throw it away," he said. "And now help me lift the poor fellow in. You have a fine judgement, Ludding. Just in the right place. You didn't hit *too* hard, I suppose! We don't want to attract attention. A little more this way, that's it. We have some brandy, I think. I will get in with him." He did so, moving the case which held the Graal. "Can you put that with the petrol-tin, Ludding? Good! Now drive on carefully till we come to the cross-roads."

When, in a few moments, they were there, "Now throw the case into the ditch," Persimmons went on, "over by that clump, I think. Excellent, Ludding, excellent. And now round up to the Rectory, and then you

432

shall go on to the village or even the nearest town for a doctor. We must do all we can for the Archdeacon, Ludding. I suppose he was attacked by the same tramp that broke into the church. I think perhaps we ought to let the police know. All right; go on."

Chapter Five

THE CHEMIST'S SHOP

For some three weeks the Archdeacon was in retirement, broken only by the useful fidelity of Mrs. Lucksparrow and the intrusive charity of Mr. Batesby, who, having arrived at the Rectory for one reason, was naturally asked to remain for another. As soon as the invalid was allowed to receive visitors, Mr. Batesby carried the hint of the New Testament, "I was sick and ye visited me" to an extreme which made nonsense of the equally authoritative injunction to be "wise as serpents." He was encouraged by the feeling which both the doctor and Mrs. Lucksparrow had that it was fortunate another member of the profession should be at hand, and by the success with which the Archdeacon, dizzy and yet equable, concealed his own feelings when his visitor, chatting of Prayer Book Revision, parish councils, and Tithe Acts, imparted to them a high eternal flavour which savoured of Deity Itself. Each day after he had gone the Archdeacon found himself inclined to brood on the profound wisdom of that phrase in the Athanasian Creed which teaches the faithful that "not by conversion of the Godhead into flesh, but by taking of the manhood into God" are salvation and the Divine End achieved. That the subjects of their conversation should be taken into God was normal and proper; what else, the Archdeacon wondered, could one do with parish councils? But his goodwill could not refrain from feeling that to Mr. Batesby they were opportunities for converting the Godhead rather firmly and finally into flesh. "The dear flesh," he murmured, thinking ruefully of the way his own had been treated.

In London the tracing of the murderer seemed, so far as Stephen Persimmons and his people could understand, to be a slow business. Descriptions of the murdered man had been circulated without result. There had been no papers—with the exception, crammed into the corner of one pocket, of the torn half of a printed bill inviting the attendance of outsiders at a mission service to be held at some (the name was torn) Wesleyan church. The clothes of the dead man were not of the sort that yield clues—such as had any marks, collars and boots, were like thousands of others sold every day in London. There were, of course, certain minor peculiarities about the body, but these, though useful for recognition, were of no help towards identification.

Investigations undertaken among the vanmen, office boys, and others who had been about the two streets and the covered way about the time when the corpse entered the building resulted in the discovery of eleven who had noticed nothing, five who had seen him enter alone (three by the front and two by the side door), one who had seen him in company with an old lady, one with a young lad, three with a man about his own age and style, and one who had a clear memory of his getting out of a taxi, from which a clean-shaven or bearded head had emerged to give a final message and which had then been driven off. But no further success awaited investigations among taxi-drivers, and the story was eventually dismissed as a fantasy.

Mornington suspected that a certain examination into the circumstances of the members of the staff had taken place, but, if so, he quoted to his employer from Flecker, "the surveillance had been discreet." Discreet or not, it produced no results, any more than the interview with Sir Giles Tumulty that Inspector Colquhoun secured.

"Rackstraw?" Sir Giles had said impatiently, screwing round from his writing-desk a small, brown wrinkled face toward the inspector, "yes, he came to lunch. Why not?"

"No reason at all, sir," the inspector said, "I only wanted to be sure. And when did he leave you—if you remember?"

"About half-past two," Sir Giles said. "Is that what he ought to have done? I'll say two, if you like, if it'll help you catch him. Only, if you do, you must arrange for me to see the hanging."

"If he left at half-past two, that's all I want to know," the inspector said. "Did you happen to mention to anyone that he was coming?"

"Yes," said Sir Giles, "I told the Prime Minister, the Professor of Comparative Etymology at King's College, and the cook downstairs. Why the hell do you ask me these silly questions? Do you suppose I run round telling all my friends that a loathsome little publisher's clerk is going to muck his food about at my table?"

"If you felt like that," the inspector said, holding down his anger, "I wonder you asked him to lunch."

"I asked him to lunch because I'd rather him foul my table than my time," Tumulty answered. "I had to waste an hour over him because he didn't understand a few simple things about my illustrations, and I saved it by working it in with lunch. I expect he charged overtime for it, so that he'd be two shillings to the good, one saved on his food and another extra pay. I should think he could get a woman for that one night. How much do you have to pay, policeman?"

The inspector at the moment felt merely that Sir Giles must be mad; it wasn't till hours afterwards that he became slowly convinced that the question was meant as an insult beyond reach of pardon or vengeance. At the time he stared blankly and said soberly: "I'm a married man, sir."

"You mean you get her for nothing?" Sir Giles asked. "Two can live as cheaply as one, and your extras thrown in? Optimistic, I'm afraid. Well, I'm sorry, but I have to go to the Foreign Office. Come and chat in the taxi; that's what your London taxis are for. When I want a nice long talk with anyone I get in one at Westminster Abbey after lunch and tell him to go to the Nelson Column. We nearly always get there for tea. Oh, good-bye, policeman. Come again some day."

The immediate result of this conversation was to cause Colquhoun to suspect Rackstraw more grievously than before. But no amount of investigation could prove the tale of the lunch unreliable or connect him in any way with an unexplained disappearance or even with any semi-criminal attitude towards the law. He owed no money; he seemed to do nothing but work and stop at home, and his connection with Sir Giles, which was the most suspicious thing about him, was limited apparently to the production of *Sacred Vessels in Folklore*. The inspector even went the length of procuring secretly through Stephen Persimmons an advance copy of this, and reading it through, but without any result.

Another of the advance copies Mornington had sent personally to the Archdeacon, and a few days before the official publication, and some four weeks after the archidiaconal visit to the publishing house he had a letter in reply.

DEAR MR. MORNINGTON, the Archdeacon wrote, I have to thank you very much for the early copy of *Sacred Vessels* which you were good enough to send me. It is a book of great interest, so far as anything intellectual can be, and especially to a clergyman; who has, so to speak, a professional interest in anything sacred, and especially to anything which has a bearing on Christian tradition—I mean, of course, Sir Giles Tumulty's study of the possible history of the Holy Graal.

There is one point upon which I should like information if you are able to give it to me—if it is not a private matter. This article on the Graal contained, when I glanced through it in the proofs you showed me, a concluding paragraph which definitely fixed the possibility (within the limitations imposed by the very nature of Sir Giles's research) of the Graal being identified with a particular chalice in a particular church. I have read the article as it now stands with the greatest care, but I cannot find any such paragraph. Could you tell me (1) whether the paragraph was in fact deleted, (2) whether, if so, the reason was any grave doubt of the identification, (3) whether it would be permissible for me to get into touch with Sir Giles Tumulty on the subject?

Please forgive me troubling you so much on a matter which has only become accidentally known to me through your kindness. I am a little ashamed of my own curiosity, but perhaps my profession excuses it in general and in particular.

I hope, if you are ever in or near Castra Parvulorum, you will make a special point of calling at the Rectory. I have one or two early editions—one of the *Ascent of Mount Carmel*—which might interest you.

Yours most sincerely,
JULIAN DAVENANT.

"Bless him," Mornington said to himself as, coiled curiously round his chair, he read the letter, "bless him and damn him! I suppose Lionel will know." He dropped the letter on his desk, and was opening another, when Stephen Persimmons came into the office. After a few sentences had been exchanged, Stephen said: "When do you go for your holidays, Mornington?"

"I was going at the end of August—for some of them, anyhow," Mornington answered—"if that fits in all right. It fitted in when I fixed it. But I'm only walking a little, so, if there's any need, I can easily alter it."

"The fact is," Stephen went on, "I've been asked to go with some people I know to the South of France at the beginning of August, and I might stop six weeks or so if things didn't call me back. But I like you to be here while I'm away."

"The beginning of August—six weeks—" Mornington murmured, "and it's the fifth of July now. Well, sir, I'll go before or after, whichever you like. Rackstraw goes next Friday, and he'll be back by the end of the month."

"Are you sure it's convenient?" Stephen asked.

"Entirely," the other said. "I shall walk as long as I feel like it, and stop when and where I feel like it. And I can walk in July as well as in September. Anyhow, I'm only taking ten days or a fortnight now. I have to go to my mother in Cornwall in October for the rest."

"Well, what about now, then?" said Stephen.

"Now, then," Mornington answered. "Or at least Friday week, shall we say? Unless, of course, I'm arrested. I feel that's always possible. Didn't I see the inspector calling on you the other day, sir?"

"You did, blast him!" Stephen broke out. "Why that wretched creature got huddled up here I can't imagine. It's killing me, Mornington, all this worry!" He got up and wandered round the office.

Behind his back his lieutenant raised surprised eyebrows. It was a nuisance, of course, but, as Stephen Persimmons had for alibi the statement of every other reputable publisher in London, this agitation seemed excessive. It might be the murder in general, but why *worry*? Stephen was always reasonably decent to the staff, but to worry over whether any of them had committed a murder seemed to point to a degree of personal interest which surprised him.

"I know," he said sympathetically. "You feel you'd like to murder the fellow just for having *been* murdered. Some people always muddle their engagements. Probably he had arranged to be done in at a tea-shop or somewhere like that—he was just that kind of fellow—and then got mixed and came here first. Has the inspector any kind of clue? The body, by now, is past inspecting."

"I don't believe he knows anything, but one can't be sure," Persimmons answered. "And, of course, if he does it needn't—" He became unhappily silent.

Mornington uncoiled himself and got up. "Are you sure you wouldn't like to go away now for a week or two, sir?" he said. "It's rather knocked you over, I expect."

"No," Stephen said, drifting to the door. "No, I can't go away now. I simply can't. We'll leave it at that then." He disappeared.

"We seem to be leaving it at a very undefined that," Mornington thought to himself, as he went back to his letters. "Stephen never was what the deceased would probably have called 'brainy'. But he seems rather cloudy even for him."

Later in the day he replied to the camp of the children.

MY DEAR MR. ARCHDEACON,—The fact is that the paragraph you refer to was cut out by Sir Giles Tumulty at the last moment. This puts us in a mild fix, because I suppose technically proofs in a publisher's office are private, till the book is published. And after, for that matter. I am given to understand by the people here who have met him that he is the nearest to a compound of a malevolent hyena and an especially venomous cobra that ever appeared in London, and I shrink therefore from officially confirming your remembrance of that paragraph. But you *were* here, and you saw the proofs, and, if you could conceal the unimportant fact that we showed them to you, write to Sir Giles by all means.

This sounds as if I were proposing an immorality. But it only means that, while I can't officially say 'Write,' I am reluctant to say 'Don't write.' Your tact will no doubt discover the wise road. Personally, I hope you'll find out.

Thank you for your invitation. I may conceivably turn up one day before the month ends.

Did you have a pleasant time in Scotland?

Yours very sincerely,
K. H. MORNINGTON.

At the moment when this letter was being dictated Sir Giles had, in fact, a visitor from Fardles sitting with him; not the Archdeacon, but Mr. Gregory Persimmons. They were speaking in subdued tones, both of them rather greedily, as if they each wanted something from the other, and the subject of their conversation might have eluded Mornington, had he heard it, for a considerable time. When Gregory had been shown in, Sir Giles got up quickly from his table.

"Well?" he said.

Gregory came across to him, saying: "Oh, I've got it—a little more trouble than I thought, but I've got it. But I don't quite like doing anything with it…. In fact, I'm not quite sure what it's best to do."

Sir Giles pushed a chair towards him. "You don't think," he said. "What do you want to do?" He sat down again as he spoke, his little eager eyes fixed on the other, with a controlled but excited interest. Persimmons met them with a sly anxiety in his own.

"I want something else first," he said. "I want that address."

"Pooh," Sir Giles said, "that won't help you. Tell me more about this other thing first. Do you notice anything about it? How does it affect you?"

Gregory considered. "Not at all, I think," he said. "It's just an ordinary piece of work—with a curious smell about it sometimes."

"Smell?" Sir Giles said. "Smell? What sort of smell?"

"Well," Persimmons answered, "it's more like ammonia than anything else; a sort of pungency. But I only notice it sometimes."

"I knew a cannibal chief in Nigeria who said the same thing," Sir Giles said musingly. "Not about that, of course, and not ammonia. It was a traditional taboo of the tribe—the dried head of a witch-doctor that was supposed to be a good omen to his people. He said it smelt like the fire that burned the uneaten offal of their enemies. Curious—the same notion of cleansing."

Gregory sniggered. "It'll take Him a good deal of ammonia to clean things out," he said. "But it'd be like Him to use ammonia and the Bible and that kind of thing."

Sir Giles switched back to the subject. "And what are you going to do with it?" he asked alertly.

Gregory eyed him. "Never mind," he said. "Or, rather, why do you want to know?"

"Because I like knowing these things," Sir Giles answered. "After all, I saved it for you when you asked me, on condition that you told me about your adventures, or let me see them for myself. You're going mad, you know, Persimmons, and I like watching you."

"Mad?" Gregory said, with another snigger. "You don't go mad this way. People like my wife go mad, and Stephen. But I've got something that doesn't go mad. I'm getting everything so." He stretched out both arms and pressed them downwards with an immense gesture of weight, as if pushing the universe before and below him. "But I want the ointment."

"Better leave it alone," Sir Giles said tantalizingly. "It's tricky stuff, Persimmons. A Jew in Beyrout tried it and didn't get back. Filthy beast he looked, all naked and screaming that he couldn't find his way. That was four years ago, and he's screaming the same thing still, unless he's dead. And there was another fellow in Valparaiso who got too far to be heard screaming; he died pretty soon, because he'd forgotten even how to eat and drink. They tried forcible feeding, I fancy, but it wasn't a success: he was just continually sick. Better leave it alone, Persimmons."

"I tell you I'm perfectly safe," Gregory said. "You promised, Tumulty, you promised."

"My lord God," Sir Giles said, "what does that matter? I don't care whether I promised or not; I don't care whether you want it or not; I only wonder whether I shall get more satisfaction from——" He broke off. "All right," he said, "I'll give you the address—94, Lord Mayor Street, Finchley Road. Somewhere near Tally Ho Corner, I think. Quite respectable and all that. The man in Valparaiso was a solicitor. It's in the middle classes one finds these things easiest. The lower classes haven't got the money or the time or the intelligence, and the upper classes haven't got the power or intelligence."

Gregory was writing the address down, nodding to himself as he did so; then he looked at a clock, which stood on the writing-table, pleasantly clutched in a dried black hand set in gold. "I shall have time to-day," he said. "I'll go at once. I suppose he'll sell it me? Yes, of course he will, I can see to that."

"It'll save you some time and energy," Sir Giles said, "if you mention me. He's a Greek of sorts—I've forgotten his name. But he doesn't keep tons of it, you know. Now, look here, Persimmons. This is two things you have got out of me, and I've had nothing in return. You'd better ask me down to wherever you hatch gargoyles. I can't come till after Monday because I'm speaking at University College then. I'll come next Wednesday. What's the station? Fardles? Send me a card to tell me the best afternoon train and have it met."

Gregory promised in general terms to do this, and as quickly as he could got away. An hour after he had hunted out Lord Mayor Street.

It was not actually quite so respectable as Sir Giles had given him to understand. It had been once, no doubt, and was now half-way to another kind of respectability, being in the disreputable valley between two heights of decency. There were a sufficient number of sufficiently dirty children playing in the road to destroy privacy without achieving publicity: squalor was leering from the windows and not yet contending frankly and vainly with grossness. It was one of those sudden terraces of slime which hang over the pit of hell, and for which beastliness is too dignified a name. But the slime was still only oozing over it, and a thin cloud of musty pretence expanded over the depths below.

At one end of the road three shops huddled together in the thickest slime; a grocer's at the corner, flying the last standard of respectability in an appeal towards the Finchley Road some couple of yards away—like Roland's horn crying to Charlemagne. At the far end of the street a public house signalized the gathering of another code of decency and morals which might in time transform the intervening decay. Next to the grocer's was a sweet-shop, on which the dingy white letters ADBU OC A appeared like a charm, and whose window displayed bars of chocolate even more degradingly sensual than the ordinary kind. Next to this was the last shop, a chemist's. Its window had apparently been broken some time since and very badly mended with glass which must have been dirty when it was made, suggesting a kind of hypostatic union between clearness and dinginess. Nor, since the breakage, had the occupant, it seemed, troubled to re-dress the window; a few packets of soap and tooth-paste masked their own purpose by their appearance. Persimmons pushed open the door and, first looking to see that the shop was empty, went quietly in.

A young man was lounging behind the counter, but he did no more than look indolently at his customer. Persimmons tried to close the door and failed, until the other said "Push it at the bottom with your foot," when he succeeded, for the door shut with an unexpected crash. Gregory came to the counter and looked at the shopman. He might be Greek, as Sir Giles had said, he might be anything, and the name over the door had been indecipherable. The two looked at one another silently.

At last Persimmons said: "You keep some rather out of the way drugs and things, don't you?"

The other answered wearily: "Out of the way? I don't know what you mean—out of the way? Nothing's out of the way."

"Out of the ordinary way," Gregory said quickly and softly, "the way everyone goes."

"They go nowhere," the Greek said.

"But I go," Persimmons answered, with the same swiftness as before. "You have something for me."

"What I have is for buyers," the other said, "all I have is for buyers. What do you want and what will you pay?"

"I think I have paid a price," Gregory said, "but what more you ask you shall have."

"Who sent you here?" the Greek asked.

"Sir Giles Tumulty," said Gregory, "and others. But the others I cannot name. They say"—his voice began to tremble—"that you have an ointment."

"I have many precious things." The answer came out of an entire weariness which seemed to take from the adjective all its meaning. "But some of them are not for sale except to buyers."

"I have bought everything." Gregory leaned forward. "The time has come for me to receive."

Still the other made no movement. "The ointment is rich and scarce and strange," he said. "How do I know that you are worth a gift? And what will my master say if I mistake?"

"I cannot prove myself to you," Gregory answered. "That I know of it—is not that enough?"

"It is not enough," the other said. "But I have a friendship for all who are in the way. And priceless things are without any price. If you are not worth the gift, the gift is worth nothing to you. Have you ever used the ointment?"

"Never," Gregory said; "but it is time, I am sure it is time."

"You think so, do you?" the Greek said slowly. "There comes a time when there is nothing left but time—nothing. Take it if you like."

Still with the minimum of movement, he put out his hand, opened a drawer in the counter, and pushed on to it a little cardboard box, rather greasy and dented here and there. "Take it," he said. "It will only give you a headache if you are not in the way."

Gregory caught up the box and hesitated. "Do you want money?" he asked.

"It is a gift, but not a gift," the other answered. "Give me what you will for a sign."

Gregory put some silver on the counter and backed toward the door. But the same difficulty that had met him in closing it now held it fast. He pulled and pushed and struggled with it, and the Greek watched him with a faint smile. Outside it had begun to rain.

Chapter Six

THE SABBATH

"I met Mr. Persimmons in the village to-day," Mr. Batesby said to the Archdeacon. "He asked after you very pleasantly, although he's sent every day to inquire. It was he that saw you lying in the road, you know, and brought you here in his car. It must be a great thing for you to have a sympathetic neighbour at the big house; there's so often friction in these small parishes."

"Yes," the Archdeacon said.

"We had quite a long chat," the other went on. "He isn't exactly a Christian, unfortunately, but he has a great admiration for the Church. He thinks it's doing a wonderful work—especially in education. He takes a great interest in education; he calls it the star of the future. He thinks morals are more important than dogma, and of course I agree with him."

"Did you say 'of course I agree' or 'of course I agreed'?" the Archdeacon asked. "Or both?"

"I mean I thought the same thing," Mr. Batesby explained. He had noticed a certain denseness in the Archdeacon on other occasions. "Conduct is much the biggest thing in life, I feel. 'He can't be wrong whose life is for the best; we needs must love the higher when we see Him.' And he gave me five pounds towards the Sunday School Fund."

"There isn't," the Archdeacon said, slightly roused, "a Sunday School Fund at Fardles."

"Oh, well!" Mr. Batesby considered. "I daresay he'd be willing for it to go to almost anything *active*. He was very keen, and I agr—thought just the same, on getting things *done*. He thinks that the Church ought to be a means of progress. He quoted something about not going to sleep till we found a pleasant Jerusalem in the green land of England. I was greatly struck. An idealist, that's what I should call him. England needs idealists to-day."

"I think we had better return the money," the Archdeacon said. "If he isn't a Christian——"

"Oh, but he is," Mr. Batesby protested. "In effect, that is. He thinks Christ was the second greatest man the earth has produced."

"Who was the first?" the Archdeacon asked.

Mr. Batesby paused again for a moment. "Do you know, I forgot to ask?" he said. "But it shows a sympathetic spirit, doesn't it? After all, the second greatest——! That goes a long way. Little children, love one another—if five pounds helps us to teach them that in the schools. I'm sure mine want a complete new set of Bible pictures."

There was a pause. The two priests were sitting after dinner in the garden of the Rectory. The Archdeacon, with inner thoughts for meditation, was devoting a superficial mind to Mr. Batesby, who on his side was devoting his energies to providing his host with cheerful conversation. The Archdeacon knew this, and knew too that his guest and substitute would rather have been talking about his own views on the ornaments rubric than about the parishioners. He wished he would. He was feeling rather tired, and it was an effort to pay attention to anything which he did not know by heart. Mr. Batesby's ecclesiastical views he did—and thought them incredibly silly—but he thought his own were probably that too. One had views for convenience' sake, but how anyone could think they mattered. Except, of course, that even silly views …

A car went by on the road and a hand was waved from it. To Gregory Persimmons the sight of the two priests was infinitely pleasurable. He had met them both and summed them up. He could, he felt, knock the Archdeacon on the head whenever he chose, and the other hadn't got a head to be knocked. It was all very pleasant and satisfactory. There had been a moment, a few days ago, in that little shop when he couldn't get out, and there seemed suddenly no reason why he should get out, as if he had been utterly and finally betrayed into being there for ever—he had felt almost in a panic. He had known that feeling once or twice before, at odd times; but there was no need to recall it now. To-night, to-night, something else was to happen. To-night he would know what it all was of which he had read in his books, and heard—heard from people who had funnily come into his life and then disappeared. Long ago, as a boy, he remembered reading about the Sabbath, but he had been told that it wasn't true. His father had been a Victorian Rationalist. The Archdeacon, he thought, was exceedingly Victorian too. His heart beating in an exalted anticipation, he drove on to Cully.

Mr. Batesby was asleep that night, and the Archdeacon was, in a Victorian way, engaged in his prayers, when Gregory Persimmons stood up alone in his room. It was a little after midnight, and, as he glanced out of the window, he saw a clear sky with a few stars and the full moon contemplating him. Slowly, very slowly, he undressed, looking forward to he knew not what, and then—being entirely naked—he took from a table the small greasy box of ointment and opened it. It was a pinkish ointment, very much the colour of the skin, and at first he thought it had no smell. But in a few minutes, as it lay exposed to the air, there arose from it a faint odour which grew stronger, and presently filled the whole room, not overpoweringly, but with a convenient and irresistible assurance. He paused for a moment, inhaling it, and finding in it the promise of some complete decay. It brought to him an assurance of his own temporal achievement of his power to enter into those lives which he touched and twist them out of their security into a sliding destruction. Five pounds here, a clever jeer there—it was all easy. Everyone had some security, and he had only to be patient to find and destroy it. His father, when he had grown old and had had a good deal of trouble, had been inclined to wonder whether there was anything in religion. And they had talked of it; he remembered those talks. He had—it had been his first real experiment—he had suggested very carefully and delicately, to that senile and uneasy mind, that there probably was a God, but a God of terrible jealousy; God had driven Judas, who betrayed Him, to hang himself; and driven the Jews who denied Him to exile in all lands. And Peter, his father had said, Peter was forgiven. He had stood thinking of that, and then had hesitated that, yes, no doubt Peter was forgiven, unless God had taken a terrible revenge and used Peter to set up all that mystery of evil which was Antichrist and Torquemada and Smithfield and the Roman See. Before the carefully sketched picture of an infinite, absorbing, and mocking vengeance, his father had shivered and grown silent. And had thereafter died, trying not to believe in God lest he should know himself damned.

Gregory smiled, and touched the ointment with his fingers. It seemed almost to suck itself upward round them as he did so. He disengaged his fingers and began the anointing. From the feet upwards in prolonged and rhythmic movements his hands moved backward and forward over his skin, he bowed and rose again, and again. The inclinations gradually ceased as the anointing hands grew higher—around the knees, the hips, the breast. Against his body the pink smears showed brightly for a moment, and then were mingled with and lost in the natural colour of the flesh. All the while his voice kept up a slow crooning, to the sound of which he moved, pronouncing as in an incantation of rounded and liquid syllables what seemed hierarchic titles. He touched his temples and his forehead with both hands, and so for a moment stayed.

His voice grew deeper and charged with more intensity, though the sound was not noticeably quicker, as he began the second anointing. But now it was only the chosen parts that he touched—the soles of the feet, the palms of the hands, the inner side of the fingers, the ears and eyelids, the environs of nose and mouth, the secret organs. Over all these again and again he moved his hands, and again ceased and paused, and the intensity died from his voice.

For the third anointing was purely ritual. He marked various figures upon his body—a cross upon either sole, a cross inverted from brow to foot, and over all his form the pentagon reversed of magic. While he did so his voice rose in a solemn chant which entered with a strange power through those anointed ears, and flowed through his body as did the new faint light that seemed to shine through his closed eyelids. Light and sound were married in premonitions of approaching experience; his voice quivered upon the air and stopped. Then with an effort he moved uncertainly towards his bed, and stretched himself on it, his face towards the closed window and the enlarging moon. Silent and grotesque he lay, and the secret processes of the night began.

If it had been possible for any stranger to enter that locked room in the middle of his journeying they would have found his body lying there still. By no broomstick flight over the lanes of England did Gregory Persimmons attend the Witches' Sabbath, nor did he dance with other sorcerers upon some blasted heath before a goat-headed manifestation of the Accursed. But scattered far over the face of the earth, though not so far in the swiftness of interior passage, those abandoned spirits answered one another that night; and That beyond them (which some have held to be but the precipitation and tendency of their own natures, and others for the equal and perpetual co-inheritor of power and immortality with Good)—That beyond them felt them and shook and replied, sustained and nourished and controlled.

After Gregory had laid himself upon the bed he made the usual attempt at excluding from the attention all his surroundings. But to-night the powerful ointment worked so swiftly upon him, stealing through all his flesh with a delicious venom and writhing itself into his blood and heart, that he had scarcely come to rest before the world was shut out. He was being made one with something beyond his consciousness; he accepted the union in a deep sigh of pleasure.

When it had approached a climax it ceased suddenly. There passed through him a sense of lightness and airy motion; his body seemed to float upwards, so unconscious had it become of the bed on which it rested. He knew now that he must begin to exercise his own intention, and in a depth beyond thought he did so. He commanded and directed himself towards the central power which awaited him. Images floated past him; for his mind, rising as it were out of the faintness which had overcome it, now began to change his experiences into such sounds and shapes as it knew; so that he at once experienced and expressed experience to himself intellectually, and could not generally separate the two. At this beginning, for example, as he lay given up to that sensation of swift and easy motion towards some still hidden moment of exquisite and destructive delight, it seemed to him that at a great distance he heard faint and lovely voices, speaking to him or to each other, and that out of him in turn went a single note of answering glee.

And now he was descending; lower and lower, into a darker and more heavy atmosphere. His intention checked his flight, and it declined almost into stillness; night was about him, and more than night, a heaviness which was like that felt in a crowd, a pressure and intent expectation of relief. As to the mind of a man in prayer might come sudden reminders of great sanctities in other places and other periods, so now to him came the consciousness, not in detail, but as achievements, of far-off masteries of things, multitudinous dedications consummating themselves in That which was already on its way. But that his body was held in a trance by the effect of the ointment, the smell of which had long since become part of his apprehension, he would have turned his head one way or the other to see or speak to those unseen companions.

Suddenly, as in an excited crowd a man may one minute be speaking and shouting to those near him, and the next, part of the general movement directed and controlled by that to which he contributes, there rose within him the sense of a vast and rapid flow, of which he was part, rushing and palpitating with desire. He desired—the heat about his heart grew stronger—to give himself out, to be one with something that should submit to him and from which he should yet draw nourishment; but something beyond imagination, stupendous. He was hungry—but not for food; he was thirsty—but not for drink; he was filled with passion—but not for flesh. He expanded in the rush of an ancient desire; he longed to be married to the whole universe for a bride. His father appeared before him, senile and shivering; his wife, bewildered and broken; his son, harassed and distressed. These were his marriages, these his bridals. The bridal dance was beginning; they and he and innumerable others were moving to the wild rhythm of that aboriginal longing. Beneath all the little cares and whims of mankind the tides of that ocean swung, and those who had harnessed them and those who had been destroyed by them were mingled in one victorious catastrophe. His spirit was dancing with his peers, and yet still something in his being held back and was not melted.

There was something—from his depths he cried to his mortal mind to recall it and pass on the message— some final thing that was needed still; some offering by which he might pierce beyond this black drunkenness and achieve a higher reward. What was the sacrifice, what the oblation that was greater than the wandering and unhappy souls whose ruin he had achieved? Heat as from an immense pyre beat upon him, beat upon him with a demand for something more; he absorbed it, and yet, his ignorance striking him with fear, shrunk from its ardent passions. It was not heat only, it was sound also, a rising tumult, acclamation of shrieking voices, thunder of terrible approach. It came, it came, ecstasy of perfect mastery, marriage in hell, he who was Satan wedded to that beside which was Satan. And yet one little thing was needed and he had it not—he was an outcast for want of that one thing. He forced his interior mind to stillness for a moment only, and in that moment recollection came.

From the shadowy and forgotten world the memory of the child Adrian floated into him, and he knew that this was what was needed. All gods had their missionaries, and this god also who was himself and not himself demanded neophytes. Deeply into himself he drew that memory; he gathered up its freshness and offered it to the secret and infernal powers. Adrian was the desirable sacrifice, an unknowing initiate, a fated candidate. To this purpose the man lying still and silent on the bed, or caught up before some vast interior throne where the masters and husbands and possessors of the universe danced and saw immortal life decay before their subtle power, dedicated himself. The wraith of the child drifted into the midst of the dance, and at the moment when Adrian far away in London stirred in his sleep with a moan a like moan broke out in another chamber. For the last experience was upon the accepted devotee; there passed through him a wave of intense cold, and in every chosen spot where the ointment had been twice applied the cold concentrated and increased. Nailed, as it were, through feet and hands and head and genitals, he passed utterly into a pang that was an ecstasy beyond his dreams. He was divorced now from the universe; he was one with a rejection of all courteous and lovely things; by the oblation of the child he was made one with that which is beyond childhood and age and time—the reflection and negation of the eternity of God. He existed supernaturally, and in Hell....

When the dissolution of this union and the return began, he knew it as an overwhelming storm. Heat and cold, the interior and exterior world, images and wraiths, sounds and odours, warred together within him. Chaos broke upon him; he felt himself whirled away into an infinite desolation of anarchy. He strove to concentrate, now on that which was within, now on some detail of the room which was already spectrally apparent to him; but fast as he did so it was gone. Panic seized him; he would have screamed, but to scream would be to be lost. And then again the image of Adrian floated before him, and he knew that much was yet to be done. With that image in his heart, he rose slowly and through many mists to the surface of consciousness, and as it faded gradually to a name and a thought he knew that the Sabbath was over and the return accomplished.

"He's very restless," Barbara said to Lionel. "I wonder if the scone upset him. There, darling, there!"

"He's probably dreaming of going away," Lionel answered softly. "I hope he won't take a dislike to the place or Persimmons or anything."

"Hush, sweetheart," Barbara murmured. "All's well. All's well."

Chapter Seven

ADRIAN

The Archdeacon, as he considered matters, found himself confronted by several dilemmas. As, for example: (1) Was the stolen chalice the Holy Graal or not? (2) Had it or had it not been taken from him on the supposition that it was? (3) Had Mr. Persimmons anything to do with the supposition or with the removal? (4) Ought he or ought he not to take an active interest in retrieving it? (5) If so, what steps ought he to take?

He felt that, so far as the property itself was concerned, he was very willing to let it slip—Graal or no Graal. But he admitted that, if by any ridiculous chance Mr. Persimmons had had to do with its removal, he should have liked the suspicions he already entertained to be clear. On the other hand, it was impossible to call in the police; he had a strong objection to using the forces of the State to recover property. Besides, the whole thing would then be likely to become public.

He was revolving these things in his mind as he strolled down the village one evening in the week after the Rackstraws had occupied the cottage on the other side of Cully. Except that Barbara, in a rush of grateful devotion, had come to the early Eucharist on the Sunday morning, and he had noticed her as a stranger, the Archdeacon knew nothing of their arrival. He had been diplomatically manœuvred by Mr. Batesby into inviting him to stop another week or two. Mr. Batesby thought the Archdeacon ought to go for a holiday; the Archdeacon thought that he would not trouble at present. For he felt curiously reluctant to leave the neighbourhood of Cully and perhaps of the Graal.

As he came to the village he heard a voice calling him and looked up. Coming towards him was Gregory Persimmons, with a stranger. Gregory waved his hand again as they came up.

"My dear Archdeacon," he said, shaking hands warmly, "I'm delighted to see you about again. Quite recovered, I hope? You ought to go away for a few weeks."

"I owe you many thanks," the Archdeacon answered politely, "not only for rescuing me from the road and taking me to the Rectory, but for so kindly and so often inquiring after me. It has really been very thoughtful of you." He substituted "thoughtful" for "kind" at the last minute with an eye on truth.

"Not a bit, not a bit," Persimmons said. "So glad you're better. Have you met Sir Giles Tumulty by any chance? Sir Giles, 'meet' the Archdeacon of Fardles, as they say elsewhere."

"I hear you have been set on by tramps," Sir Giles said, as they shook hands. "Many about here?"

As the Archdeacon began to reply, Barbara Rackstraw came along the road with Adrian on their way home, and Persimmons, with a word of apology, skipped aside to meet them. The Archdeacon slurred over the subject of tramps, and proceeded casually: "I have just been reading your last book, Sir Giles. Most interesting." He became indefinitely more pompous, a slight clericalism seemed to increase in him, "But, you know, that article on the Graal—most interesting, most interesting. And you think, er—m'm, you think *true*?"

"True?" Sir Giles said, "true? What do you mean—true? It's an historical study. You might as well ask whether a book on the Casket Letters was true."

441

"Umph, yes," the Archdeacon answered, exuding ecclesiasticism. "To be sure, yes. Quite, quite. But, Sir Giles, as we happen to have met so pleasantly, I have a confession—yes, a confession to make, and a question to ask. You'll forgive me both, I'm sure."

Sir Giles in unconcealed and intense boredom stared at the road. Persimmons, Adrian's hand in his, was walking slowly from them, chatting to Barbara. The Archdeacon went on talking, but the next thing that Sir Giles really heard was—"and it seemed most interesting. But it was my fault entirely, only, as I've kept it *quite* secret, I hope you won't mind. And, if you could tell me—in strict confidence, affecting me as it does—why you cut that last paragraph out, it would of course be a very generous act on your part, though I quite realize I have no right to ask it."

His voice ceased, but by this time Sir Giles was alert. The last paragraph cut out? There was only one last paragraph he had cut out lately. And how did this country clergyman know? His fault entirely, was it? He shook a reluctant head at the Archdeacon. "I'm rather sorry you've seen it," he said. "But there's no harm done, of course. After all, being your church, you have a kind of claim! But, as far as cutting it out——" He raised his voice. "Persimmons! Persimmons!"

The Archdeacon threw a hand out. "Sir Giles, Sir Giles, he is talking to a lady."

"Lady be damned," said Sir Giles. "A country wench, I suppose, or a county wench—it doesn't signify, anyhow. Persimmons!"

Gregory made his farewells to Barbara and Adrian near a turn in the road and returned. "Yes?" he said. "Why such particular excitement?"

Sir Giles grinned. "What do you think?" he said. "The Archdeacon saw that paragraph you made me cut out. So he knew it was his church the Graal was in. And it was Persimmons," he added to the priest, "who wanted it taken out. He pretended the evidence wasn't good enough, but that was all nonsense. Evidence good enough for anybody."

From the turn in the road Adrian shouted a final good-bye, and Gregory, remembering his work, turned and waved before he answered. Then he smiled at the Archdeacon, who was looking at him also with a smile. Sir Giles grinned happily, and a bicyclist who passed at the moment reflected bitterly on the easy and joyous time which such people had in the world.

"Dear me," the Archdeacon said. "And was that the cause of the needy mission church, Mr. Persimmons?"

"Well," Persimmons said, "I'm afraid it was. I have been something of a collector in my time, and—once I understood from Sir Giles what your old chalice might be—I couldn't resist it."

"It must be a wonderful thing to be a collector," the Archdeacon answered gravely. "Apparently you may be seized any time with a passion for anything. Have you a large collection of chalices, Mr. Persimmons?"

"None at all, since I didn't get *that*," Gregory answered. "To think it's in the hands of some thief now, or a pawnbroker perhaps. Have you put the police on the track yet, Archdeacon?"

"No," the Archdeacon answered. "I don't think the police would find it. The police sergeant here believes in letting his children run more or less wild, and I feel sure he wouldn't understand my clues. Well, good-day, Sir Giles. Good-day, Mr. Persimmons."

"Oh, but look here," Gregory said, "don't go yet. Come up to Cully and have a look at some of my things. You don't bear malice, I'm sure, since I didn't succeed in cheating you."

"I will come with pleasure," the Archdeacon said. "Collections are always so delightful, don't you think? All things from all men, so to speak." And, half under his breath, as they turned towards Cully, he sang to himself, "Oh, give thanks unto the Lord, for He is gracious; for His mercy endureth for ever."

"I beg your pardon?" Gregory asked at the same moment that Sir Giles said, "Eh?"

"Nothing, nothing," the Archdeacon said hastily. "Merely an improvisation. The fine weather, I suppose." He almost smirked at the others, with gaiety in his heart and curving his usually sedate lips. Gregory remembered the way in which the priest's monologue had carried him half over the county, and began almost seriously to consider whether he were not half-witted. Sir Giles, on the other hand, began to feel more interest than hitherto. He glanced aside at Gregory, caught his slight air of bewilderment, and grinned to himself. It appeared that his country visit might be of even more interest than he supposed. He always sought out—at home and abroad—these unusual extremists in religion; they wandered in a borderland, whatever their creed, of metaphysics, mysticism, and insanity which was a peculiarly fascinating spectacle. He had himself an utter disbelief in God and devil, but he found these anthropomorphic conceptions interesting, and to push or delay any devotee upon the path was entertainment to a mind too swiftly bored. The existence and transmission of the magical ointment had become gradually known to him during his wanderings. Of its elements and concoction he knew little; they seemed to be a professional mystery reserved to some remoter circle than he had yet touched. But the semi-delirium which it induced in expectant minds was undoubted, and whenever chance made him acquainted with suitable subjects and he could, without too much trouble to himself, introduce the method, he made haste to do so. Subjects were infrequent; it required a particularly urgent and sadistic nature; he was not at all sure that Persimmons was strong enough. However, it was done now, and he must gain what satisfaction he could from the result.

Of the Graal he thought similarly. That the chalice of Fardles was the Graal he had little doubt; the evidence was circumstantial, but good. He regretted only that the process of time had prevented him from studying its origin, its first user, and his circle, at close quarters. "All martyrs are masochists," he thought, "but crucifixion is a violent form." Yet, given in the Jew's mind the delusion that he loved the world, what else was the Passion but masochism? And the passion of the communicant was, of course, a corresponding sadism. Religion was bound to be one of the two; in extreme cases both. The question was, which was the Archdeacon?

The Archdeacon, ignorant that this question was being asked, strolled happily on between his two acquaintances, and with them turned up the drive to Cully. He promised himself opportunities of making clear to Persimmons that he guessed very clearly who had the Graal. He wished that in the early stages of his recovery he had not let out to Mr. Batesby that he had been robbed of the chalice. Mr. Batesby had, of course, passed the information on. If only it were still a secret! But why should anyone want it so much, he wondered. Collecting—well, collecting perhaps.

"Do you collect anything in particular, Mr. Persimmons?" he asked. "Or merely any unconsidered trifles?"

"I have a few interesting old books," Gregory said. "And a few old vestments and so on. I once took an interest in ecclesiology. But of late I have rather concentrated on old Chinese work—masks, for instance."

"Masks are always interesting," the Archdeacon said. "The Chinese mask, I think, has no beard?"

"None of mine have—long mustachios, but no beard," answered Gregory.

"False beards," the Archdeacon went on, "are never really satisfactory. A few weeks ago a man called to see me in what I suspect to have been a false beard, I can't imagine why. It seems such a curious thing to wear."

"I believe that many priesthoods make it a part of their convention not to wear beards," Gregory said conversationally. "Now what is the reason of that?"

"Obvious enough," Sir Giles put in. "They have dedicated their manhood to the god—they no longer possess virility. They are feminine to the god and dead to the world. Every priest is a kind of a corpse-woman … if you'll excuse me," he added after a pause to the Archdeacon, who said handsomely: "I wish it were more largely true."

"Not *every* priest," Persimmons said. "There are virile religions, adorations of power and strength."

"To adore strength is to confess weakness," Sir Giles said. "To *be* power is *not* to adore it. The very weakest only dream of being powerful. Look at the mystics."

"Don't, this evening," Gregory said to the Archdeacon, laughing. "Come in and look at some of my treasures."

Cully was a large, rambling house, with "the latest modern improvements". Gregory took his companions up a very fine staircase into a gallery from which his own rooms opened out. In the hall itself were a few noticeable things—a suit of armour, a Greek head, a curious box or two from the Minoan excavations, a cabinet of old china. The gallery was hung with the Chinese masks of which Gregory had spoken, and, having examined them on their way, the visitors were brought at last into their host's sitting-room. It was lined with books, and contained several cabinets and cases; a few prints hung on the walls.

"I suppose," Sir Giles said, glancing round him, "if you had succeeded in cheating the Archdeacon out of the Graal, you'd have kept it in here."

"Here or hereabouts," Gregory said. "The trouble is that in the alterations which earlier inhabitants of the house made the old chapel was converted, at least the upper part of it, into these rooms—my sitting-room, my bedroom, my bathroom, and so on. So far as I can understand, the bathroom—or what is almost the bathroom—- is just over where the altar stood; so that to restore the chalice to its most suitable position would be almost impossible."

"As a matter of manners," the Archdeacon admitted, "perhaps. But surely not more so than achieving it—if I may say so—by throwing dust in the eyes of its keeper. No, I don't speak personally, Mr. Persimmons; I allude only to an example of comparative morals."

"What upsets the comparison," Sir Giles said, "is that in the one case you have a strong personal lust and action deflected in consequence. But in the second action is—comparatively—free."

"I shouldn't have thought that any action was freer than any other," the Archdeacon said as he followed Gregory across the room. "Man is free to know his destiny, but not free to evade his destiny."

"But he can choose his destiny," Gregory answered, taking a book from the shelves. "He may decide what star or what god he will follow."

"If you spell destiny and god with capital letters—no," the Archdeacon said. "All destinies and all gods bring him to One, but he chooses how to know *Him*."

"He may defy and deny him for ever," Gregory said, with a gesture.

"You can defy and deny the air you breathe or the water you drink," the Archdeacon answered comfortably. "But if you do you die. The difference in the parallels is that in the other case, though you come nearer and nearer to it, you never quite die. Almost—you are in the death-agony—but never quite."

Sir Giles interrupted the discussion. "I'm going to revise my last Monday's lecture," he said. "I know the orthodox creed and the orthodox revolt by heart. I don't quite know how the Archdeacon would put it, but I know your *apologia* inside out, Persimmons. I heard it put very well by a wealthy Persian once. I've got a note of it somewhere. What time do you dine in this bloody hole of yours?" he threw over his shoulder as he went towards the door.

"Half-past seven," Gregory called, and turned back to exhibit more of his possessions. These now were rare books, early editions, and bibliographical curiosities in which the Archdeacon took a definite and even specialized interest. The two bent over volume after volume, confirming and commenting, their earlier hostility quiescent, and a pleasant sense of intellectual intimacy established. After the examination had gone on for some time Gregory took from a drawer a morocco case in which was a thin square pamphlet. He drew it out and held it towards the priest. "Now this," he said, "may interest you. Look at the initials."

The Archdeacon took it carefully. It was a copy of the old pre-Shakespearean *King Leir*, stained and frayed. But on the front was scrawled towards the top and just against the title the two letters "W.S." and just under them in a precise, careful hand "J.M."

"Good heavens!" the Archdeacon exclaimed. "Do you mean——?"

"Ah, that's the point," Gregory said. "Is it or isn't it? There's very little doubt of the J.M. I've compared it with the King's College MS., and it's exact. But the W.S. is another matter. One daren't believe it! Alone—perhaps, but both together! And yet, why not? After all, it's very likely Shakespeare didn't take all his books back to Stratford, especially when he'd written a better play himself. And he may have known Milton the scrivener. *We* don't know."

There was a soft tap at the door. "Come in," Gregory called, and the door opened to show a man standing on the threshold.

"Excuse me, sir," he said, "but you're wanted on the telephone. A Mr. Adrian, I understood, sir."

"Damn!" Gregory said. "I forgot I told him to ring me up. It's a child staying near here," he went on, "who was frightfully interested in the telephone, so … And the telephone's in the hall."

"Please, please," the Archdeacon said. "Don't disappoint him, I shall be quite happy here." His eyes were on the books on the table. But so were Gregory's. He had heard and seen the interest the Archdeacon felt, and one or two of these treasures were small, compact things. Yet to disappoint Adrian might throw him back there. He moved to the door and caught the arm of the man who stood there.

"Ludding," he whispered, "keep your eye on him. Don't let him put anything in his pocket. Do something about the room till I get back."

"He may recognize me, sir," the man said doubtfully.

"Then look through the crack in the door, but watch him whatever you do. I shall only be two or three minutes." He went swiftly along the gallery and down the stairs, and Ludding softly manipulated the door till he was able to take in the leaning figure at the table.

The Archdeacon's eyes were on the books, but his attention was on the gallery. He heard Persimmons go, guessed the other was watching, and leaned still more awkwardly forward. Then suddenly he made a grotesque noise, dragged out his handkerchief, put it to his mouth, and rushed out of the room. Ludding, leaping back from the door as he came, received him with a stare.

"I'm going to be sick," the Archdeacon gurgled, leaning forward. "Where's the … Ouch!" He ended with a convulsive choke.

"Here, sir." Ludding ran and threw open a door. The Archdeacon shot by him, banged it, looked round. In a corner behind the door the Graal lay on its side. He caught it up and considered, looking at the window. For him to carry it off, he recognized, was impossible; he would be knocked on the head again before he got home, if he ever did get home. There were only two possibilities, to leave it where it was or to throw it out of the window. He made a loud, hideous noise for Ludding's benefit and peered out. Terrace and lawns below, grounds and plantations beyond, but all the Cully domain. Could he by any chance recover it if he threw it out? But Persimmons would be bound to guess what had happened. He would search too, with the advantages all on his side. The Archdeacon preferred to keep the advantages and leave the Graal. After all, he would know and the other wouldn't. Certainty and uncertainty—certainty for him.

"Ouch," he said loudly, laid down the chalice where he had found it, and said in his heart: "Fair sweet Destiny, draw all men to the most happy knowledge of Thee." He leant against the wall for a minute till he heard a soft whispering outside, then he pulled the chain loudly, opened the door, and came rather staggeringly out. As he did so, Ludding slipped past him into the little room.

"My dear Archdeacon!" Gregory cried sympathetically. "I'm so sorry." But his eyes went hurrying past the other, after Ludding, and for the moment while the servant was absent he stood between his guest and the stairs. Ludding was out almost immediately, and behind the priest's back nodded at his master. Gregory, with a little sigh, looked directly at the Archdeacon, who looked as sorry for himself as his inexperience could contrive.

"It's the screwing myself up," he said faintly. "It's nothing; my stomach's a weak thing, Mr. Persimmons. But I think perhaps I had better be getting home."

"Bring the car round, Ludding," Gregory said. "Yes, I insist. Are you sure you won't stop here a little while?"

"No, really, really," the Archdeacon said, his reluctance sounding like weakness. "I'll just get out into the air."

"Do," Gregory exclaimed. "Take my arm." And with murmurs and distressed ejaculations and gentle protests the two dropped to the hall.

It was later in the evening, when dinner was over and the two were alone, that Gregory told Sir Giles of the incident. "It may have been true," he said doubtfully, "but I didn't quite like it. But he hadn't touched the Cup. I went back to see."

"He'll know it's there," Sir Giles explained.

"He may know it as much as he likes," Gregory answered. "I'll get a whole pedigree for that Cup. Stephen gave it to me, I think. It's his word against half a dozen I can arrange for, if he makes a fuss. And a clergyman accusing his Good Samaritan of theft because he's got a chalice which the clergyman, after a knock on the head, thinks he recognizes. Oh, no, Tumulty, it wouldn't do."

"What should you have done if he'd taken it?" Sir Giles asked.

"Taken it back. I saw that when I was coming upstairs after that beastly baby had been taken away from the telephone," Gregory said spitefully. "Violence—real violence—wouldn't have been necessary. Taken it back and written to the Chief Constable."

"Who'd have wanted it traced, probably," said Sir Giles. "And would have found out about that damned book. Who was the accursed imbecile who let him see it?"

"Some fool at my son's," Gregory said. "But I'll have the pedigree all right. Don't worry, Tumulty."

"Don't worry!" Sir Giles cried. "Who the hell are you talking to, Persimmons? Don't worry! Me worry over your bastard murders, indeed. The thing that'll keep you safe is that no-one with more brains than a gutter-bred snipe like that Archdeacon would think your collection of middle-class platitudes worth adding to. Chinese masks—you might be a Jew financier. And, anyhow, what do you want to do with the thing?"

"Ah, now that's important," Gregory said. "I didn't quite know at first, but I do now. I'm going to talk to the child."

"Ungh?" Sir Giles asked.

"Say it's what we think it is, it's been as near the other centre as anything in this world can get," Gregory went on. "And it's been kept pretty deep down in that world all the time. It's close to the place where all things meet and all souls—anyhow, their souls. And I can get at that baby there—the real baby—and make the thing easy up here. Not at first altogether perhaps, but I shall do it. I shall make the offering there when he agrees—till we go to the Sabbath together."

"You do talk pretty, Persimmons," Sir Giles said. "You believe that this damn Graal is more use than that coffee-cup?"

"I think it is the great chalice of their initiation," Gregory answered. "And I think we can use it—I and my people. I can meet Adrian there and separate and draw and convert him. It's got power in it; it's a gate. But anyone can use the power, and a gate is for coming out as well as going in."

"Pretty, pretty," Sir Giles murmured, his head on one side. "And when does your blessed child bleat out through the gate of the fold? Don't forget I want to see."

"You won't see anything; you'll be horribly bored," Gregory sneered.

"I shall see you," Sir Giles said, with a sweet mildness. "And I shan't be bored. I saw something like it in Brazil. But there they killed a slave. Are you going to kill Ludding, by any chance?"

"Don't be a fool," Gregory said. "Well, come, if you like. I don't mind, all this cleverness of yours is such universes away that it won't interfere. Only I warn you, absolutely nothing'll happen."

"Don't die, that's all I ask," Sir Giles said. "In Brazil one of them did, and it might be more difficult to bribe the police here."

They went from the dining-room to a small room next to Gregory's bedroom, which he unlocked with a key he carried on his own chain. There appeared in it only a cabinet in one corner, two or three cushions dropped beside it, and a low pedestal of wood in the centre on which lay an oblong slab of stone. On this slab stood two candlesticks; around the pedestal, at a good distance, had been drawn a white circle, in which at one point was a small gap. Before he entered the room Gregory had fetched the Graal from its corner; he passed through the gap, set it upright on the slab between the candlesticks, and turned to Sir Giles.

"You'd better sit down at once," he said, "and I should recommend you to keep within the circle. There are curious forces released sometimes on these occasions."

"I know all about that," Sir Giles said, as he brought two of the cushions into the circle, also taking care to pass through the gap. "I saw a man once in Ispahan who looked as if he'd been unable to breathe once he got outside. Atmospheric disturbances, but *why*? Why does your purely subjective industry disturb the air? Well, never mind. I won't say a word more." He settled himself comfortably on his cushions over against one of the shorter sides of the pedestal. Gregory went over to the cabinet, and there first changed from the clothes he was wearing into a white cassock, marked with esoteric signs. He then brought from it an antique vessel, from which he poured what was apparently wine into the Graal till it all but brimmed. He brought also a short rod and laid it on the slab in front of the Graal; he arranged and lit at what appeared to be the back of the altar a chafing-dish containing herbs and powders, scattered other powders upon it, and came back to the front of the altar. Lastly, with great care, he brought to it from the cabinet a parchment inscribed with names and writings, and a small paper from which he let fall on to the wine in the Graal what appeared to Sir Giles to be a few short hairs.

He considered the arrangements, went back and closed the cabinet, re-entered the circle, took the rod from the altar, and, bending down, with a strong concentration of countenance, closed the gap, drawing the rod slowly as if with an effort against the path of the sun. He came to the front of the altar, and immersed himself in a profound silence.

Sir Giles, curled upon the cushions, watched him intently, noting every change in his face and the growing remoteness of his eyes. Almost an hour had passed before those eyes, seeming to stir of their own volition, lowered themselves from the darkness of the room to the Graal standing in the steady light of the two candles. Very slowly he stretched his hands over the chalice and began to speak. Sir Giles, straining his ears, caught only an occasional phrase. "Pater Noster, qui fuisti in cælis … per te omnipotentem in sæcula sæculorum. … hoc est calix, hoc est sanguis tuus infernorum … in te regnum mortis, in te delectatio corruptionis, in te via et vita scientiæ maleficæ … qui non es initio, qui eris in sempiternum. Amen." He took up the rod from the altar, still moving with extreme slowness and, resting it on the edge of the chalice, allowed it to touch the surface of the wine; his eyes followed its length and rested also there. "De corpore, de mente … mitte animum in simulacro … per potestatem tuam in omnibus … animum Adriani cujus nomen scripsi in sanguine meo dimitte in sanguine tuo … Adrianum oblationem pro me et pro seipsum … nomen tuum." The rod moved in magical symbols upon the wine. "De Cujus corpore hæc sunt … O Pastor, O Pater, O Nox et Lux infernorum et domus rejectionis."

The vibrating voice ceased, and it seemed to Sir Giles that the faintest of mists hung for a moment over the chalice and was dissolved; then, more urgently and in a lower tone the voice began again, but the phrases the listener caught were now far between. "… Adrianum filium tuum, ovem tuam … et omnia opera mea et sua … tu cujus sum et cujus erit … dimitte … dimitte." It paused again, and then in a murmur through which the whole force of the celebrant seemed to pass, it came again. "Adrian, Adrian, Adrian…."

Faint, but certain, the mist rose again from the wine; and Sir Giles, absorbedly drinking in the spectacle, saw Gregory's eyes light up with recognition. He seemed without moving to draw near the altar and the chalice and the mist, his face was bent toward it; he spoke, carefully, quietly, and in English. "Adrian, it is I who speak, image to image, through this shadow of thee to thee. Adrian, well met. Know me again, O soul, and know me thy friend and master. In the world of flesh know me, in the world of shadows, and in the world of our lord. Many times I shall shape thine image thus, O child, my sacrifice and my oblation, and thou shalt come, more swiftly and more truly thou, when I desire thee. Image of Adrian, dissolve and return to Adrian, and may his soul and body, whence thou hast come, receive this message that thou bearest. I, dimissus es."

The mist faded again; the priest of these mysteries sank upon his knees. He laid the rod on the altar; he stretched out both hands and took the chalice into them; he lifted it to his lips and drank the consecrated wine. "Hic in me et ego in hoc et Tu, Pastor et Dominus, in utrisque." He remained absorbed.

The candles had burned half an inch more towards their sockets before, very wearily, he arose and extinguished them. Then he broke the circle, and slowly, in reverse order, laid away the magical implements. He took the Graal and set it inverted on the floor. He took off his cassock and put on—in a fantastic culmination—the dinner-jacket he had been wearing. Then he turned to Sir Giles. "Do what you will," he said. "I am going to sleep."

———————————

Chapter Eight

FARDLES

"I have read," said Kenneth Mornington, standing in the station of a small village some seven miles across country from Fardles, "that Paris dominates France. I wish London dominated England in the matter of weather."

Further letters exchanged between him and the Archdeacon had led to an agreement that he should spend the first Sunday of his holiday at the Rectory, arriving for lunch on the Saturday. The Saturday morning in London had been brilliant, and he had thought it would be pleasanter to walk along the chord of the monstrous arc which the railway made. But it had grown dull as the train left the London suburbs, and even as he jumped from his compartment the first drops of rain began to fall. By the time he had reached the outer exit they had grown to a steady drizzle, and the train had left the station.

Kenneth turned up his collar and set out; the way at least was known to him. "But why," he said, "do I always get out at the wrong times? If I had gone on I should have had to sit at Fardles station for an hour and a half, but I should have been dry. It is this sheep-like imitation of Adam which annoys me. Adam got out at the wrong time. But he was made to by the railway authorities. I will write," he thought, and took to a footpath, "the diary of a man who always got out at the wrong time, beginning with a Cæsarean operation. "And let the angel whom thou still hast served Tell thee Macduff was from his mother's womb Untimely ripped." *A Modern Macduff*, one might call it. And death? He might die inopportunely, before the one in advance had been moved on, so that all the angels on the line of his spiritual progress found themselves crowded with two souls instead of the one they were prepared for. "Agitation in Heaven. Excursionist unable to return. Trains to Paradise overcrowded. Strange scenes at the stations. Seraph Michael says rules to be enforced." Stations … stages … it sounds like Theosophy. Am I a Theosophist? Oh, Lord, it's worse than ever; I can't walk to a strange Rectory through seven miles of this."

In a distance he discerned a shed by the side of the road, broke into a run, and, reaching it, took shelter with a bound which landed him in a shallow puddle lying just within the dark entrance. "Oh, damn and blast!" he cried with a great voice. "Why was this bloody world created?"

"As a sewer for the stars," a voice in front of him said. "Alternatively, to know God and to glorify Him for ever."

Kenneth peered into the shed, and found that there was sitting on a heap of stones at the back a young man of about his own age, with a lean, long face, and a blob of white on his knee which turned out in a few minutes to be a writing-pad.

"Quite," Kenneth said. "The two answers are not, of course, necessarily alternative. They might be con—con—consanguineous? contemporaneous? consubstantial? What *is* the word I want?"

"Contemptible, concomitant, conditional, consequential, congruous, connectible, concupiscent, contaminable, considerable," the stranger offered him. "The last is, I admit, weak."

"The question was considerable," Kenneth answered. "You no doubt are considering it? You are even writing the answer down?"

"A commentary upon it," the other said. "But consanguineous was the word I wanted, or its brother." He wrote.

Kenneth sat down on the same heap of stones and watched till the writing was finished, then he said: "Circumstances almost suggest, don't you think, that I might hear the context—if it's what it looks?"

"Context—there's another," the stranger said. "Contextual—— 'And that contextual meaning flows Through all our manuscripts of rose.' Rose—Persia—Hafix—Ispahan. Perhaps rose is a little ordinary. 'And that contextual meaning streams Through all our manuscripts of dreams.'"

"Oh, no, no," Mornington broke in firmly. "That's far too minor. Perhaps something modern—'And that impotent contextual meaning stinks In all our manuscripts, of no matter what coloured inks.' Better be modern than minor."

"I agree," the other said. "But a man must fulfil his destiny, even to minority. Shall I 'think the complete universe must be Subject to such a rag of it as me?'"

He was interrupted by Kenneth kicking the earth with his heels and crying: "At last! at last! 'Terror of darkness! O thou king of flames!' I didn't think there was another living man who knew George Chapman."

The stranger caught his arm. "Can you?" he said, made a gesture with his free hand, and began, Mornington's voice joining in after the first few words:

> *at with thy music-footed horse do*
>
> *lear light out of crystal on dark e*
> *url'st instructive fire about the w*

The conversation for the next ten minutes became a duet, and it was only at the end that Kenneth said with a sigh: "'I have lived long enough, having seen one thing.' But before I die—the context of consanguineous?"

The stranger picked up his manuscript and read:

> *w does thy single heart poss*
> *ible mode of happiness*
> *iet and in busyness!*
>
> *fundities of utter peace*
> *eir own vehemence release*
> *igh rippling toils that never*
>
> *of those ripples' changing n*
> *ignorant at heart, dost broc*
> *most solemn quietude.*
>
> *is idleness and industry*
> *n that laden heart of thee*
> *their rich consanguinity."*

"Yes," Kenneth murmured, "yes. A little minor, but rather beautiful."

"The faults, or rather the follies, are sufficiently obvious," the stranger said. "Yet I flatter myself it reflects the lady."

"You have printed?" Kenneth asked seriously, for they were now discussing important things, and in answer the other jumped to his feet and stood before him. "I have printed," he said, "and you are the only man—besides the publisher—who knows about it."

"Really?" Mornington asked.

"Yes," said the stranger. "You will understand the horrible position I'm in if I tell you my name. I am Aubrey Duncan Peregrine Mary de Lisle D'Estrange, Duke of the North Ridings, Marquis of Craigmullen and Plessing, Earl and Viscount, Count of the Holy Roman Empire, Knight of the Sword and Cape, and several other ridiculous fantasies."

Mornington pinched his lip. "Yes, I see," he said. "That must make it difficult to do anything with poetry."

"Difficult," the other said, with almost a shout. "It makes it impossible."

"Oh well, come," Kenneth said; "impossible? You can publish, and the reviews at least won't flatter you."

"It isn't the *reviews*," the Duke said. "It's just chatting with people and being the fellow who's written a book or two—not very good books, but *his* books, and being able to quote things, and so on. How can I quote things to the people who come to see *me*? How can I ask the Bishop what he thinks of my stuff or tell him what I think of his? What will the Earl my cousin say about the Sitwells?"

"No, quite," Mornington answered, and for a few minutes the two young men looked at one another. Then the Duke grinned. "It's so *silly*," he said. "I really do care about poetry, and I think some of my stuff might be almost possible. But I can never find it anywhere to live for more than a few days."

"Anonymity?" Kenneth asked. "But that wouldn't help."

"Look here," the Duke said suddenly, "are you going anywhere in particular? No? Why not come up to the house with me and stop a few days?"

Mornington shook his head regretfully. "I have promised to stop with the Archdeacon of Fardles over the week-end," he said.

"Well, after then?" the Duke urged. "Do, for God's sake come and talk Chapman and Blunden with me. Look here, come up now, and I'll run you over to Fardles in the car, and on Monday morning I'll come and fetch you."

Kenneth assented to this, though he refused to leave his shelter. But within some half an hour the Duke had brought his car to the front of the shed and they were on the way to Fardles. As they drew near the village, approaching it from the cottage side of Cully, they passed another car in a side turning, in which Mornington seemed to see, as he was carried past, the faces of Gregory Persimmons and Adrian Rackstraw. But he was in a long controversy with the Duke on the merits of the Laureate's new prosody, and though he wondered a little, the incident made hardly any impression on his mind.

The Archdeacon, it appeared, knew the Duke; the Duke was rather detachedly acquainted with the Archdeacon. The detachment was perhaps due to the fact, which had emerged from the few minutes' conversation the three had together, that the Duke of the North Ridings was a Roman Catholic (hence the Sword and Cape), so far as his obsession with poetry and his own misfortunes left him leisure to be anything. But he promised to come to lunch on Monday, and disappeared.

"I forgot Batesby," the Archdeacon said suddenly to Mornington, as the car drove off. "Dear me! I'm afraid the Duke and he won't like one another. Batesby's dreadfully keen on Reunion; he has a scheme of his own for it—an admirable scheme, I'm certain, if only he could get other people to see it in the same way."

"I should have thought the same thing was—officially—true of the Duke," Mornington said as they entered the house.

"But only because he's part of an institution," the Archdeacon said, "and one can more easily believe that institutions are supernatural than that individuals are. And an institution can believe in itself and can wait, whereas an individual can't. Batesby can't afford to wait; he might die."

At lunch Mornington had Mr. Batesby's scheme of Reunion explained at length by its originator. It was highly complicated and, so far as Kenneth could understand, involved everyone believing that God was opposed to Communism and in favour of election as the only sound method of government. The Archdeacon remarked that discovering the constitution of the Catholic Church was a much pleasanter game than tennis, to which he had been invited that afternoon.

"Though they know I don't play," he added plaintively. "So I was glad you were coming, and I had an excuse."

"How do you get exercise?" Kenneth asked idly.

"Well, actually, I go in for fencing," the Archdeacon said, smiling. "I used to love it as a boy romantically, and since I have outgrown romance I keep it up prosaically."

The constitution of the Catholic Church occupied the lunch so fully that not until Mr. Batesby had gone away to supervise the Lads' Christian Cricket Club in his own parish, some ten miles off, did Kenneth see an opportunity of talking to his host about *Christianity and the League of Nations*. And even then, when they were settled in the garden, he found that by the accident of conversation the priest was already chatting about the deleted paragraph of *Sacred Vessels in Folklore*.

"Who?" he asked suddenly, arrested by a name.

"Persimmons," the Archdeacon answered. "I wonder if he had anything to do with your firm. I seem to remember seeing him the day I called on you."

"But if it's the man who's taken a house near here called Mullins or Juggins or something, of *course* he's something to do with our firm," Mornington cried. "He's Stephen's father; he used to *be* the firm. Does he live at Buggins?"

"He lives at Cully," the Archdeacon said, "which may be what you mean."

"But how do you know he wanted the paragraph out?" Kenneth demanded.

"Because Sir Giles told me so—confirmed by the fact that he tried to cheat me out of the Graal, and the other fact that he eventually had me knocked on the head and took it," answered the Archdeacon.

Kenneth looked at him, looked at the garden, looked across at the church. "I am not mad," he murmured, "'My pulse doth temperately keep time.' … Yes, it does. 'These are the thingummybobs, you are my what d'ye call it.' But that a retired publisher should knock an Archdeacon on the head …"

The Archdeacon flowed into the whole story, and ended with his exit from Cully. Mornington, listening, felt the story to be fantastic and ridiculous, and would have given himself up to incredulity, had it not been for the notion of the Graal itself. This, which to some would have been the extreme fantasy, was to him the easiest thing to believe. For he approached the idea of the sacred vessel, not as did Sir Giles, through antiquity and savage folklore, nor as did the Archdeacon, through a sense of religious depths in which the mere temporary use of a particular vessel seemed a small thing, but through exalted poetry and the high romantic tradition in literature. This living light had shone for so long in his mind upon the idea of the Graal that it was by now a familiar thing—Tennyson and Hawker and Malory and older writers still had made it familiar, and its familiarity created for it a kind of potentiality. To deny it would be to deny his own past. But this emotional testimony to the possibility of its existence had an intellectual support. Kenneth knew—his publicity work had made clear to him—the very high reputation Sir Giles had among the learned; a hundred humble reviews had shown him that. And if the thing were possible, and if the thing were likely…. But still, Gregory Persimmons…. He looked back at the Archdeacon.

"You're sure you saw it?" he asked. "Have you gone to the police?"

"No," the Archdeacon said. "If you don't think I saw it, would the police be likely to?"

"I do, I do," Kenneth said hastily. "But why should he want it?"

"I haven't any idea," the priest answered. "That's what baffles me too. Why should anyone want anything as much as that? And certainly why should anyone want the Graal—if it is the Graal? He talked to me about being a collector, which makes me pretty sure he isn't."

Kenneth got up and walked up and down. There was a silence for a few minutes, then the Archdeacon said: "However, we needn't worry over it. What about me and the League of Nations?"

"Yes," Kenneth said absently, sitting down again. "Oh, well, Stephen simply leapt at it. I read it, and I told him about it, and I suggested sending it to one of our tame experts—only I couldn't decide between the political expert and the theological. At least, I was going to suggest it, but I didn't have time. 'By an Archdeacon? By an orthodox Archdeacon? Oh, take it, take it by all means, by all manner of means.' He positively tangoed at it."

"This is very gratifying," the Archdeacon answered, "and the haste is unexpected."

"Stephen," Kenneth went on, "has a weakness for clerical books; I've noticed it before. Fiction is our stand-by, of course; but he takes all the manuscripts by clergymen that he decently can. I think he's a little shy of some parts of our list, and likes to counterbalance them. We used to do a lot of occult stuff; a particular kind of occult. The standard work on the Black Mass and that sort of thing. That was before Stephen himself really got going, but he feels vaguely responsible, I've no doubt."

"Who ran it then?" the Archdeacon asked idly.

"Gregory," Mornington answered. He stopped suddenly, and the two looked at one another.

"Oh, it's all nonsense," Mornington broke out. "The Black Mass, indeed!"

"The Black Mass is all nonsense, of course," the Archdeacon said; "but nonsense, after all, does exist. And minds can get drunk with nonsense."

"Do you really mean," Mornington asked, "that a London publisher sold his soul to the devil and signed it away in his own blood and that sort of thing? Because I'm damned if I can see him doing it. Lots of people are interested in magic, without doing secret incantations under the new moon with the aid of dead men's grease."

"You keep harping on the London publisher," the other said. "If a London publisher has a soul—which you're bound to admit—he can sell it if he likes: not to the devil, but to himself. Why not?" He considered. "I think perhaps, after all, I ought to try and recover that chalice. There are decencies. There is a way of behaving in these things. And the Graal, if it is the Graal," he went on, unusually moved, "was not meant for the greedy orgies of a delirious tomtit."

"Tomtit!" Mornington cried. "If it could be true, he wouldn't be a tomtit. He'd be a vulture."

"Well, never mind," the priest said. "The question is, can I do anything at once? I've half a mind to go and take it."

"Look here," said Mornington, "let me go and see him first. Stephen thought it would look well if I called, being down here. And let me talk to Lionel Rackstraw." He spoke almost crossly. "Once a silly idea like this gets into one's mind, one can't see anything else. I think you're wrong."

"I don't see, then, what good you're going to do," the Archdeacon said. "If I'm mad——"

"Wrong, I said," Kenneth put in.

"Wrong because being hit on the head has affected my mind and my eyes—which is almost the same thing as being mad. If I'm demented, anyhow—you won't be any more clear about it after a chat with Mr. Persimmons on whatever he does chat about. Nor with Mr. Rackstraw, whoever he may be."

Kenneth explained briefly. "So, you see, he's really been a very decent fellow over the cottage," he concluded.

"My dear man," the Archdeacon said, "if you had tea with him and he gave you the last crumpet, it wouldn't prove anything unless he badly wanted the crumpet, and not much even then. He might want something else more."

This, however, was a point of view to which Kenneth, when that evening he walked over to the cottage, found Lionel not very willing to agree. Gregory, so far as the Rackstraws were concerned, had been nothing but an advantage. He had lent them the cottage; he had sent a maid down from Cully to save Barbara trouble; he had occupied Adrian for hours together with the motor and other amusements, until the child was very willing for his parents to go off on more or less extensive walks while he played with his new friend. And Lionel saw no reason to associate himself actively—even in sympathy—with the archidiaconal crusade; more especially since Mornington himself was torn between scepticism and sympathy.

"In any case," he said, "I don't know what you want me to *do*. Anyone that will take Adrian off my hands for a little while can knock all the Archdeacons in the country on the head so far as I am concerned."

"I don't want you to do anything," Kenneth answered, "except discuss it."

"Well, we're going up to tea at Cully to-morrow," Lionel said. "I can talk about it there, if you like."

Kenneth arrived at Cully on the Sunday afternoon, after having heard the Archdeacon preach a sermon in the morning on "*Thou shall not covet thy neighbour's house*," in which, having identified "thy neighbour" with God and touched lightly on the text "*Mine are the cattle upon a thousand hills*," he went off into a fantastic exhortation upon the thesis that the only thing left to covet was "thy neighbour" Himself. "Not His creation, not His manifestations, not even His qualities, but Him," the Archdeacon ended. "This should be our covetousness and our desire; for this only no greed is too great, as this only can satisfy the greatest greed. The whole universe is His house, the soul of thy mortal neighbour is His wife, thou thyself art His servant and thy body His maid—a myriad oxen, a myriad asses, subsist in the high inorganic creation. Him only thou shalt covet with all thy heart, with all thy mind, with all thy soul, and with all thy strength. And now to God Almighty, the Father, the Son, and the Holy Ghost, be ascribed, as is most justly due, all honour ..." The congregation searched for sixpences.

Lionel, Barbara, and Adrian were with Persimmons and Sir Giles on the terrace behind the house when Kenneth arrived, and had already spoken of his probable visit. Gregory welcomed him pleasantly enough, as one of the staff who had originally worked under him. But Kenneth's mind was already in a slight daze, for, as he had been conducted by the maid through the hall, he had seen on a bracket about the height of his head from the ground, in a corner near the garden door, an antique cup which struck him forcibly as being very like the one the Archdeacon had described to him. It seemed impossible that, if the priest's absurd suspicions were right, Persimmons should so flaunt the theft before the world—unless, indeed, it were done merely to create the impression of impossibility. "There is no possible idea," Kenneth thought as he came on to the terrace, "to which the mind of man can't supply some damned alternative or other. Yet one must act. How are you, Mr. Persimmons? You'll excuse this call, I know."

The conversation rippled gently round the spring publishing season and books in general, with backwaters of attention in which Adrian immersed himself.

It approached, gently and unobserved by the two young men, the question of corrections in proof, and it was then that Sir Giles, who had until then preserved a sardonic and almost complete silence, said suddenly: "What I want to know is, whether proofs are or are not private?"

"I suppose they are, technically," Lionel said lazily, watching Adrian. "Subject to the discretion of the publisher."

"Subject to the discretion of the devil," Sir Giles said. "What do you say, Persimmons?"

"I should say yes," Gregory answered. "At least till they are passed for press."

"I ask," Sir Giles said pointedly, "because my last proofs were shown to an outsider before the book was published. And if one of these gentlemen was responsible I want to know why."

"My dear Tumulty, it doesn't matter," Gregory in a quiet, soothing tone put in. "I asked you not to mention it, you know."

"I know you did," Sir Giles answered, "and I said—that I felt I ought to. After all, a man has a right to know why a mad clergyman is allowed to read paragraphs of his book which he afterwards cancels. I tell you, Persimmons, we haven't seen the last of your ... Archdeacon yet."

It was evident that Barbara's presence was causing Sir Giles acute difficulty in the expression of his feelings. But this was unknown to Kenneth, who, realizing suddenly what the other was talking about, said, leaning forward in his chair, "I'm afraid that's my fault, Sir Giles. It was I showed the Archdeacon your proofs. I'm extremely sorry if it's inconvenienced you, but I don't think I agree that proofs are so entirely private as you suggest. Something must be allowed to a publisher's need for publicity, and perhaps something for the mere accidents of a publishing house. There was no special stipulation about privacy for your book."

"I made no stipulation," Sir Giles answered, staring hostilely at Kenneth, "because I didn't for an instant suppose I should find it being read in convocation before my final corrections were made."

"Really, really, Tumulty," Gregory said. "It's unfortunate, as it's turned out, but I'm sure Mornington would be the first to deplore a slight excess of zeal, a slight error of judgement, shall we say?"

"Error of judgement?" Sir Giles snarled. "It's more like a breach of common honesty."

Kenneth came to his feet. "I admit no error in judgement," he said haughtily. "I was entirely within my rights. What is the misfortune you complain of, Mr. Persimmons?" He moved so as to turn his back on Sir Giles.

"I don't complain," Gregory answered hastily. "It's just one of those things that happen. But the Archdeacon, owing to your zeal, my dear Mornington, has been trying to saddle me with the responsibility for the loss of this chalice Sir Giles was writing about. I do wish he'd never seen the proofs. I think you must admit they ought to be treated as private."

"It's exactly like reading out a private letter from the steps of St. Paul's," Sir Giles added. "A man who does it ought to be flung into the gutter to starve."

"Now, now, Tumulty," Gregory put in, as the enraged Kenneth wheeled round, and Barbara and Lionel hastily stood up, "it's not as bad as that. I think perhaps strict commercial morality would mean strict privacy, but perhaps we take a rather austere view. The younger generation is looser, you know—less tied—less dogmatic, shall we say?"

"Less honest, you mean," Sir Giles said. "However, it's your affair more than mine, after all."

"Let's say no more about it," Gregory said handsomely.

"But I will say more about it," Kenneth cried out. "Do you expect me to be called a thief and a liar and I don't know what, because I did a perfectly right thing, and then be forgiven for it? I beg your pardon, Barbara, but I can't stand it, and I won't."

"You can't help it," Sir Giles said, grinning. "What will you do? We've both forgiven you, my fine fellow, and there it stops."

Kenneth stamped his foot in anger. "I'll have an apology," he said. "Sir Giles, what is the importance of this beastly book of yours?"

Barbara moved forward and slipped her arm in his. "Kenneth dear," she murmured; and then to Gregory, "Mr. Persimmons, I don't quite know what all this is about, but couldn't we do without forgiving one another?" She smiled at Sir Giles. "Sir Giles has had to forgive so many people, I expect, in different parts of the world, that he might spare us this time."

Lionel came to her help. "It's my fault more than Mornington's," he said. "I was supposed to be looking after the proofs, and I let an uncorrected set out of my keeping. It's me you must slang, Sir Giles."

"In the firm is one thing," Sir Giles said obstinately, "one risks that. But an outsider, and a clergyman, and a mad clergyman—no."

"Mad clergyman be——" Kenneth began, and was silenced by Barbara's appealing, "But what *is* it all about? Can you tell me, Mr. Persimmons?"

"I can even show you," Gregory said pleasantly. "As a matter of fact, Adrian's seen it already. We had a game with it this morning. It's a question of identifying an old chalice." He led the way into the hall, and paused before the bracket. "There you are," he said, "that's mine. I got it from a Greek, who got it from one of his countrymen who fled before the Turkish recovery in Asia Minor. It comes, through Smyrna, from Ephesus. Old enough and interesting, but as for being the Graal—— Unfortunately, after the Archdeacon had read this paragraph about which we've all been behaving so badly, three things happened. I did ask him if he had a chalice to spare for a friend of mine who has a very poor parish; thieves made an attempt on the church over there; and the Archdeacon was knocked on the head by a tramp. He seems to think that this proves conclusively that I was the tramp and that this is his missing chalice. At least, he says it's missing."

"How do you mean, sir—says it's missing?" Lionel asked.

"Well, honestly—I dare say it's mere pique—but we none of us really *know* the Archdeacon, do we?" Gregory asked. "And some of the clergy aren't above turning an honest penny by supplying American millionaires with curios. But it looks bad if it does happen to come out—so if the thing *can* disappear by means of a tramp or an unknown neighbour ..."

There was a moment's pause, then Kenneth said, "Really, sir, if you *knew* the Archdeacon ..."

"Quite right," Gregory answered. "Oh, my dear fellow, I'm being unjust to him, no doubt. But a man doesn't expect his parish priest practically to accuse him of highway robbery. I shouldn't be surprised if I heard from the police next. Probably the best thing would be to offer him this one to replace the one he says he's—I mean the one he's lost. But I don't think I'm quite Christian enough for that."

"And how did you play with it this morning?" Barbara asked, smiling at Adrian.

"Ah, that is a secret game, isn't it, Adrian?" Gregory answered merrily. "*Our* secret game. Isn't it, Adrian?"

"It's hidden," Adrian said seriously. "It's hidden pictures. But you mustn't know what, Mummie, must she?" He appealed to Gregory.

"Certainly not," Gregory said.

"Certainly not," Adrian repeated. "They're my hidden pictures."

"So they shall be, darling," Barbara said. "Please forgive me. Well, Mr. Persimmons, I suppose we ought to be going. Thank you for a charming afternoon. You're making this a very pleasant holiday."

Sir Giles had dropped away when they had entered the hall, and the farewells were thus robbed of their awkwardness; although Gregory detained Kenneth in order to say, "I think I can put it right with Tumulty, although he was very angry at first. Talked of appealing to my son and getting you dismissed, you know."

"Getting me what?" Kenneth cried.

"Well, you know what my son is," Gregory said confidentially. "Efficient and all that—but you've known him in business, Mornington, and you know what he is. Rather easily influenced, I'm afraid. And Sir Giles is a good name for his list."

"A very good name," Kenneth admitted, feeling less heated and more chilly than he had done. It was true—Stephen Persimmons was weak, and would be terrified of losing Sir Giles. And he had before now been guilty of dismissing people in a fit of hysterical anger.

"But I've no doubt it's all right," Gregory went on, watching the other closely, "no doubt at all. Let me know if anything goes wrong. I've a great regard for you, Mornington, and a word, perhaps ... And keep the Archdeacon quiet, if you can. It would be worth your while."

He waved his hand and turned back into the house, and Kenneth, considerably more disturbed than before, walked slowly back to the Rectory.

Chapter Nine

THE FLIGHT OF THE DUKE OF THE NORTH RIDINGS

When the Duke's car arrived outside the Rectory about twelve on the Monday, its driver saw at the gates another car, at the wheel of which sat a policeman whom he recognized.

"Hallo, Puttenham," he said. "Is the Chief Constable here then?"

"Inside, your Grace," Constable Puttenham answered, saluting. "Making inquiries about the outrage, I believe."

The Duke, rather annoyed, looked at the Rectory. He disliked the Chief Constable, who had taken up the business of protecting people, developed it into a hobby, and was rapidly making it a mania and a nuisance—at least, so it appeared to the Duke. He remembered now that at a dinner at his own house some few days before the Chief Constable had held forth at great length on a lack of readiness in the public to assist the police, as exemplified by the failure of the Archdeacon of Fardles to report to them one case of sacrilege and one of personal assault. It had been objected that the Archdeacon had been confined to his bed for some time, but now that he had preached again the Chief Constable had obviously determined to see what his personal investigation and exhortation could do. The Duke hesitated for a moment, but it occurred to him that Mornington might welcome the opportunity of escaping, and he strolled slowly up to the door. Introduced into the study, he found the Chief Constable in a high state of argumentative irritation, Mornington irrationally scornful of everything, and the Archdeacon—for all he could see—much as usual.

"How do, Ridings," the Chief Constable said, after the priest had greeted his visitor. "Perhaps you may help me to talk sense. The Archdeacon here says he's lost a chalice, and won't help the proper authorities to look for it."

"But I don't want them to look for it," the Archdeacon said, "if you mean the police. You asked me if I knew what the hypothetical tramp or tramps were looking for, and I said yes—the old chalice that used to be here. You asked me if it had disappeared, and I said yes. But I don't want you to look for it."

The Duke began to feel that there might be something satisfying about even an Anglican priest. There were few things he himself would like less than to have the Chief Constable looking for anything he had lost. But robbery was robbery, and though, of course, a priest who wasn't a priest could have no real use for a chalice, still, a chalice was a chalice, and, anyhow, the Chief Constable was sure to go on looking for it, so why not let him? But he didn't say this; he merely nodded and glanced at Mornington.

"I suppose you want to find it?" the Chief Constable said laboriously.

"I don't—you must excuse me, but you drive me to it," the Archdeacon answered. "I don't want the police to find it. First, because I don't care for the Church to make use of the secular arm; secondly, because it would make the whole thing undesirably public; thirdly, because I know where it is; and fourthly, because they couldn't prove it was there."

"Well, sir," Kenneth said sharply, "then, if it can't be proved, we oughtn't to throw accusations about."

"Precisely what I am *not* doing," the Archdeacon answered, crossing his legs. "I don't accuse anyone. I only say I know where it is."

"And where is it?" the Chief Constable asked. "And how do you know it is there?"

"First," the Archdeacon said, "in the possession of Mr. Persimmons of Cully—probably on a bracket in his hall, but I'm not certain of that. Secondly, by a combination of directions arising out of the education of children, books of black magic, a cancelled paragraph in some proofs, an attempt to cheat me, the place where the Cup was kept, a motor-car, a reported threat, and a few other things."

The Chief Constable was still blinking over the sudden introduction of Mr. Persimmons of Cully, and it was the Duke who asked, "But if you have all these clues, what's the uncertainty—in your own mind?" he added suddenly, as he also became aware of the improbability of a country householder knocking an Archdeacon on the head in order to steal his chalice.

"There is no uncertainty in my own mind," the priest answered. "But the police would not be able to find a motive."

"We of course can," Kenneth said scornfully.

"We—if you say we—can," the Archdeacon said, "for we know what it was, and we know that many kinds of religion are possible to men."

"You are sure now that it was—it?" Kenneth answered.

"No," the priest answered, "but I have decided in my own mind that I will believe that. No-one can possibly do more than decide what to believe."

"Do I understand, Mr. Archdeacon," the Chief Constable asked, "that you accuse Mr. Persimmons of stealing this chalice? And why should he want to steal a chalice? And if he did, would he be likely to keep it in his hall?"

"There is always the *Purloined Letter*," the Duke murmured thoughtfully. "But even there the letter wasn't pinned up openly on a notice-board. Couldn't we go and see?"

"That is what I was going to suggest," said the Chief Constable. He stood up cheerfully. "I quite understand about your anxiety over the loss of this chalice"—Kenneth cackled suddenly and walked to the window. "Anyone would be anxious about a chalice of, I understand, great antiquarian interest. But I feel so certain you're mistaken in this … idea about Mr. Persimmons that I can't help feeling that a meeting perhaps, and a little study of his chalice, and so on…. And then you must give us a free hand." He looked almost hopefully at the priest. "If you could spare us half an hour now, say?"

"I can't possibly move from here," the Archdeacon said, "without a clear understanding that I don't accuse Mr. Persimmons in any legal or official sense at all. I will come with you if you like, because I can't refuse a not-immoral call from the Chief Magistrate"—the Chief Constable looked gratified—"and, as I have no reason to consider Mr. Persimmons's feelings—I really haven't," he added aside to Kenneth, who had turned to face the room again—"I should like, as a matter of curiosity, to see if it's another chalice or if it's mine. But that's all."

"I quite understand," the Chief Constable said sunnily. "Ridings, are you coming? Mr.——?" He hesitated uncertainly. The Duke looked at Kenneth, who said: "I think I ought to go; it won't take long. Would you mind waiting a few minutes?"

"I'll take you to the gate," the Duke said, "and wait for you there—then we'll go straight on."

Between the Archdeacon and the Chief Constable in their car the only conversation was a brief one upon the weather; in that which preceded them, Mornington, in answer to the Duke's inquiries, sketched the situation as he understood it.

"And what do you think yourself?" the Duke asked.

Mornington grimaced. "Certum quia impossibile," he said. "If I must come down on one side or the other, I fall on the Archdeacon's. Especially since yesterday," he said resentfully. "But it's all insane. Persimmons's explanation is perfectly satisfactory—and yet it just isn't. The paragraph and the Cup were both there—and now they both aren't."

"Well," the Duke said, "if I can help annoy the Chief Constable, tell me. He once told me that poetry wasn't practical."

At the gates of Cully the cars stopped. "Will you come in, Ridings?" the Chief Constable asked.

"No," the Duke said; "what have I to do with these things? Don't be longer than you can help catechizing and analysing and the rest of it." He watched them out of sight, took a writing-pad from his pocket, and settled down to work on a drama in the Greek style upon the Great War and the fall of the German Empire. The classic form appeared to him capable at once of squeezing the last drop of intensity out of the action and of presenting at once the broadest and most minute effects. The scene was an open space behind the German lines in France; the time was in March 1918; the chorus consisted of French women from the occupied territory; and the *deus ex machina* was represented by a highly formalized St. Denis, whom the Duke was engaged in making as much like Phœbus Apollo as he could. He turned to the god's opening monologue.

> *of those habitable fields whicı*
> *vept by fire nor venomous witı*
> *eing disposed by …*

He brooded over whether to say Zeus or God.

Meanwhile, Gregory received his guests with cold politeness, to which a much warmer courtesy was opposed by the Archdeacon. "It isn't my fault that we're here," the priest said, when he had introduced the Chief Constable. "Colonel Conyers insisted on coming. He's looking for the chalice that was stolen."

"It certainly isn't my wish," the irritated Colonel said, finding himself already in a false position. "The Archdeacon gave me to understand that he believed the chalice had somehow got into Cully, and I thought if that was cleared up we should all know better where we were."

"I suppose," Gregory said, "that it was Mr. Mornington who told you I had a chalice here."

"You remember I saw it myself," the Archdeacon said. "It was the position then that made me feel sure it was the … it was an important one. You people are so humorous." He shook his head, and hummed under his breath: "Oh, give thanks to the God of all gods …"

Colonel Conyers looked from one to the other. "I don't quite follow all this," he said a trifle impatiently.

"'For his'—it doesn't at all matter—'mercy endureth for ever,'" the Archdeacon concluded, with a genial smile. He seemed to be rising moment by moment into a kind of delirious delight. His eyes moved from one to the other, changing from mere laughter as he looked at the Colonel into an impish and teasing mischief for Persimmons, and showing a feeling of real affection as they rested on Kenneth, between whom and himself there had appeared the beginnings of a definite attraction and friendship. Gregory looked at him with a certain perplexity. He understood Sir Giles's insolent rudeness, though he despised it as Giles despised his own affectation of smoothness. But he saw no reason in the Archdeacon's amusement, and began to wonder seriously whether Ludding's blow had affected his mind. He glanced over at Mornington—there at least he had power, and understood his power. Then he looked at the Chief Constable and waited. So for a minute or two they all stood in silence, which the Colonel at last broke.

"I thought," he began, rather pointedly addressing himself to Persimmons, "that if you would show us this chalice of yours it would convince the Archdeacon that it wasn't his."

"With pleasure," Gregory answered, going towards the bracket and followed by the others. "Here it is. Do you want to know the full history? I had it——" he began, repeating what Kenneth had heard the previous day.

Colonel Conyers looked at the priest. "Well?" he said.

The Archdeacon looked, and grew serious. His spirit felt its own unreasonable gaiety opening into a wider joy; its dance became a more vital but therefore a vaster thing. Faintly again he heard the sound of music, but now not from without, or indeed from within, from some non-spatial, non-temporal, non-personal existence. It was music, but not yet music, or if music, then the music of movement itself—sound produced, not by things, but in the nature of things. He looked, and looked again, and felt himself part of a moving river flowing towards some narrow channel on a ripple of which the Graal was as a gleam of supernatural light. "Yes," he said softly, "it is the Cup."

Gregory shrugged, and looked at the Chief Constable. "I will give you the address of the man from whom I bought it," he said, "and you can make what inquiries you like—if you think it necessary."

The Colonel pursed his lips, and said in a lowered voice, "I will tell you if it's necessary. But I'm not sure the identification is sufficiently valuable. I understand the Archdeacon had an accident to his head some time ago."

"Unfortunately, it was I who found him lying in the road and brought him home, and I think that's confused the idea of robbery *with* me," Gregory continued, also in a subdued voice. "It's very unfortunate, and rather embarrassing for me. I don't want to appear un-neighbourly, and if it goes on I shall have to think about selling the house. He's an old resident, and I'm a new one, and, of course, people would rather believe him. If I gave him this chalice—but I should be sorry to part with it. I like old things, but I don't like them enough to half kill a clergyman to get them. I'm in your hands, Colonel. What do you advise?"

The Colonel considered. Kenneth had walked a little distance away, so as not to appear to overhear their talk; the Archdeacon was still gazing at the chalice as if in a trance. But now he was conscious of some slight movement on his own part towards which he was impelled; he knew the signs of that approaching direction, and awaited it serenely. By long practice he had accustomed himself in any circumstances—in company or alone, at work or at rest, in speech or in silence—to withdraw into that place where action is created. The cause of all action there disposed itself according to that Will which was its nature, and, so disposing itself, moved him easily as a part of its own accommodation to the changing wills of men, so that at any time and at all times its own perfection was maintained, now known in endurance, now in beauty, now in wisdom, now in joy. There was no smallest hesitation which it would not solve, nor greatest anxiety which it did not make lucid. In that light other things took on a new aspect, and the form of Gregory, where he stood a few steps away, seemed to swell into larger dimensions. But this enlargement was as unreal as it was huge; the sentences which he had altered a few days back on denying and defying Destiny boomed like unmeaning echoes across creation. Nothing but Destiny could defy Destiny; all else which sought to do so was pomposity so extreme as to become merely silly. It was a useless attempt at usurpation, useless and yet slightly displeasing, as pomposity always is. In the universe, as in Fardles, pomposity was bad manners; from its bracket the Graal shuddered forward in a movement of innocent distaste. The same motion that seemed to touch it touched the Archdeacon also; they came together and were familiarly one. And the Archdeacon, realizing with his whole mind what had happened, turned with unexpected fleetness and ran for the hall door.

Everyone else ran also. The Colonel, having made up his mind, had drawn Gregory a few steps away, and was telling him what he advised. Neither of them had seen, as Kenneth did, the unexpected yet gentle movement with which the Archdeacon seemed suddenly to reach up, take hold of the Cup, and begin to run. But they heard the first step, and rushed. Kenneth, who was nearer the door, was passed by the priest before he could move; then he also took to his heels. The Archdeacon, practised on his feet in many fencing bouts, flew out of the door and down the drive, and Gregory and the Colonel both lost breath—the first yelling for Ludding, the second shouting after the priest. Kenneth only, in as good condition, younger and with longer legs, overtook the fugitive half-way to the gates. Up to that moment he had still been sceptical and undetermined in his mind; but he knew, as he came level, that, right or wrong, it was impossible for him to lay a detaining hand upon his friend, and as he felt the decision taken his own gaiety returned. He ran on in advance, reached the gate and threw it open, reached the Duke's car in three strides, and opened that door also.

The Duke had been writing poetry; Constable Puttenham had been asleep in the August sun. But the Duke, hesitating over a word, had been staring at the gate, and saw the returning guests before the distant shouts had done more than pleasantly mingle with the constable's dreams.

"Drive like hell," Kenneth said to the Duke as the Archdeacon reached the car, and himself jumped up by the driver's side. The constable, awaking to cries of "Puttenham" from the Colonel rushing round the curve of the drive, sat bolt upright. "Stop him, Puttenham," the Colonel yelled. But the bewildered policeman saw no-one to stop. He saw the Archdeacon settling down in the car, and Mornington by the Duke's side. He saw the other car begin to move, but who it was he was to stop was by no means clear—it couldn't be the Duke. Nevertheless, the ducal car was the only thing in sight—unless it was Gregory Persimmons; he by now had reached the gate in advance of the shouting Colonel. The constable ran for him, and met him. "Not me, you everlasting ape!" Gregory howled at him. "The car, you baboon, the car!" "The Archdeacon," the Colonel bellowed. "Stop the Archdeacon!" The constable left Gregory and began to run after the car, which by now had got fairly started. "Stop, God blast you!" the Colonel yelled again. "Come back, you fool!" The constable, in one entire maze, stopped and came back, to find Gregory and the Colonel scrambling into their own car. "Drive like hell," the Colonel said; "we may catch him."

"After the Duke, sir?" the bewildered constable asked.

"After that damned black-coated hypocrite," the Colonel shouted, still in a stentorian voice, so that the Archdeacon, a quarter of a mile away, unconsciously turned to protest. "I'll unfrock him—I'll have him in the dock!"

"*Drive*," Gregory said, looking unpleasantly at the constable, and the constable drove.

So through the English roads the Graal was borne away in the care of a Duke, an Archdeacon, and a publisher's clerk, pursued by a country householder, the Chief Constable of a county, and a perplexed policeman. And these things also perhaps the angels desired to look into.

At least the Duke of the North Ridings did. After a few moments he said to Mornington, "I suppose you know what we're doing?"

"We're carrying the San Graal," Mornington said. "Lancelot and Pelleas and Pellinore—no, that's not right—Bors and Percivale and Galahad. The Archdeacon's Galahad, and you can be Percivale: you're not married, are you? And I'm Bors—but I'm not married either, and Bors was. It doesn't matter; you must be Percivale, because you're a poet. And Bors was an ordinary workaday fellow like me. On, on to Sarras!" He looked back over his shoulder. "Sarras!" he cried to the car behind. "We shall meet at Carbonek!"

"What in God's name are you singing about?" the Duke asked.

Mornington was about to reply when the Archdeacon, leaning forward, said with a slight formality: "I couldn't take advantage of your kindness, my lord, unless you knew the circumstances. I don't want to rush you …"

"Really?" the Duke said, manipulating a corner. "Oh, really? Well, I'm not objecting, but—damn that dog!—there seems to be a slight rush somewhere. Perhaps it's the people behind. Mornington, stop laughing and tell me where I'm to drive to."

"But, indeed," the Archdeacon protested, "I'd rather you put me down than——"

"No, look here," Kenneth said, pulling himself together, "it's all right really. Honestly, Ridings. The Archdeacon *has* got the Graal there."

"The Graal?" the Duke said, and again, in a voice that rejected the idea still more strongly, "The Graal?"

"The Graal," Kenneth assured him. "Malory—Tennyson—Chrétien de Troyes—Miss Jessie Weston. *From Romance to Reality*, or whatever she called it. That's what's happening, anyhow. I give you my word, Ridings, that it's really serious."

The Duke spared him a glance. An hour's conversation on literature between two ardent minds with a common devotion to a neglected poet is a miraculous road to intimacy. Mornington went on explaining as quietly and as clearly as was possible, and at last the Duke said, shrugging his shoulders, "Well, if you say so…. But where are we going?"

Kenneth looked back at the Archdeacon, then changed his mind and said, "Where *are* we going now, anyhow?"

"London as straight as we can," the Duke answered.

"Humph!" said Kenneth. "I suppose you've got a house there?"

"Of sorts," the Duke answered.

"Well, let's go there, and we can tell you the whole thing in full. Unless they telephone to the police on the way?" Over his shoulder he offered the Archdeacon the question.

"I don't think he'll do that," the priest said. "He wants it kept quiet too."

"They can't stop us without arresting us," the Duke said thoughtfully, "if I refuse to stop."

"Arrest of the Duke of the North Ridings and the Archdeacon of Fardles. Strange story. Is the Holy Graal in England? Evidence by a retired publisher. By God, Ridings, they daren't stop us!" Kenneth cried, as the magnitude of the possibilities of publicity became clear to him.

"London, then," the Duke said, and gave himself up to his destiny.

Kenneth glanced back at the pursuing car. "The Archdeacon's lost his Rectory," he thought, "and I've lost my job, and the Duke's near losing his reputation. But poor old Gregory's lost the Graal—and Giles Tumulty will lose his nerve if I ever get a chance at him," he added, remembering the previous afternoon.

In the pursuing car the same thought of publicity entered the minds of its occupants, and first of Gregory. He was therefore in time to check the impulse of Colonel Conyers towards the station telephone by pointing out to him the dimensions of the scandal which might result. "In the courts it's bound at best to be a drawn battle; I may recover the chalice, but a lot of people will believe the Archdeacon—all the clerical party. Whereas, if we can only get hold of the Duke and explain matters, it's quite likely he'll see how strong my case is. Is he a great friend of the Archdeacon's?"

"I didn't know they even knew each other," the Chief Constable said. "The Duke's a Roman Catholic; all his family are. He's in with the Norfolks, too; his mother was a Howard. It makes this freak of his all the more surprising. That damned clergyman must have bamboozled him somehow."

As they rushed on, however, Gregory began to recover his poise; the Duke was the only unknown quantity in the allied opposition, and he found it impossible to believe that the Duke was unpersuadable. He had other resources after all; there was Sir Giles, who had a good deal of curious knowledge of hidden circles, for it was at his advice that a visit had been paid on the Saturday to the Greek in the chemist's shop. Sir Giles had insisted that a pedigree could be more easily and more certainly created there than by a reliance on the less effective Stephen. With this, and the police if necessary behind him, he smiled at the car in front, which maintained a steady space between them. It escaped, as a white hart of heaven, before the pursuing hounds— escaped for a while, but hardly, and with little hope. The teeth were gnashing behind at it; already the blood showed here and there on the white coat; already the pursuer felt the taste in his mouth. Mornington should suffer; that was clear; and the Archdeacon—but how was not yet clear. And the Graal should be withdrawn again into the seclusion of a frozen sanctuary.

They approached London, still with the distance varyingly, but on the whole steadily, maintained; they entered it, and ran down towards the West End. The Duke kept the car at as great a speed as possible, and stopped it at a house in Grosvenor Square. Mornington sprang out and opened the door for the Archdeacon, who got out, still holding the Graal, and the three ran to the front door, which opened before them. The Duke pushed the other two in, and, with his arms in theirs, led them on through the hall, saying over his shoulder as he did so, "If anyone calls, Thwaites, I am not at home."

"Very good, your Grace," the footman said, and went calmly to the door as footsteps sounded before it.

"Ridings, Ridings!" the Colonel called, and found his way blocked as the Duke and his friends disappeared in the indistinct shadows.

"His Grace is not at home, sir," the footman said.

"Damn it, man, I saw him!" the Colonel cried.

"I am sorry, sir, but his Grace is not at home."

"I am the Chief Constable of Hertfordshire," Colonel Conyers raged. "I represent the police."

"I am sorry, sir, but his Grace is not at home."

Gregory touched the Colonel's arm. "It's no use," he said. "We must write, or I must call presently."

"It's perfectly monstrous," the Colonel cursed. "The whole thing's insane and ridiculous. Look here, my man, I want to see the Duke on important business."

"I am sorry, sir, but his Grace is not at home."

"Come with me," Gregory said. "Let's make sure of my right first and enforce it afterwards."

"You'll hear more of this," the Colonel said threateningly. "It's no use standing there and telling me these lies. Tell Ridings I'm going to have an explanation, and the sooner he lets me hear from him the better. I've never been treated like this before in my whole life."

"I'm sorry, sir, but his Grace——"

The Colonel flung away, and Gregory went with him. The footman closed the door, and, hearing the bell, went to the library.

"Have they gone?" the Duke asked.

"Yes, your Grace. One of the gentlemen seemed rather annoyed. He asked you to write to him explaining."

The three looked at one another. "Very well, Thwaites," the Duke said. "I'm not at home to anyone till after lunch, and see that we have something to eat as soon as possible." Then, as the servant left the room, he sat down and turned to the priest. "And now," he said, "let's hear about this Graal."

Chapter Ten

THE SECOND ATTEMPT ON THE GRAAL

Inspector Colquhoun, summing up the situation of the Persimmons investigations, found himself inclining towards three trails, though he was conscious of only one, and that the remnants of the Wesleyan mission bill. The prospects of this fragment producing anything were of the slightest, but he would have done what could be done sooner had he not been engaged in checking and investigating the movements of the staff of Persimmons. His particular attention was by now unconsciously fixed on two subjects—Lionel Rackstraw and Stephen Persimmons. For the first Sir Giles was responsible; for the second, absurdly enough, the adequacy of the alibi. Where few had anything like a sufficient testimony to their occupation during the whole of one particular hour, it was inevitable that the inspector should regard, first with satisfaction but later almost with hostility, the one man whose time was sufficiently vouched for by almost an excess of evidence. His training forbade this lurking hostility to enter his active mind; consciously he ruled out Stephen, unconsciously he lay in ambushed expectation. The alibi, in spite of himself, annoyed him by its perfection, and clamoured, as a mere work of art, to be demolished. He regarded Stephen as the notorious Athenian did Aristides.

Unconscious, however, of this impassioned frenzy, the inspector spent an hour or more going through the files of the *Methodist Recorder* and investigating the archives of the Methodist Bookroom. He found that during the few weeks preceding the murder three missions had been held in London at Wesleyan churches— at Ealing, at East Ham, and near Victoria. He achieved also a list of some seven churches in the country which fitted his demands—ranging from Manchester to Canterbury. He expected no result from this investigation, which, indeed, he undertook merely to satisfy a restless conscience; it might be worth while asking the various ministers whether they had heard of any unexpected disappearance in their districts, but the chance was small. The inspector thought it more than likely that the disappearance had been explained and arranged for, and his mind returned slowly to a sullen hatred of Sir Giles and a sullen satisfaction with Stephen Persimmons as he rode back on a bus to his home.

The two emotions working with him led, however, to an unexpected if apparently unprofitable piece of news. For they drove him to a third interview with Stephen, ostensibly to collect a few more details about the staff and the premises, actually to mortify his heart again by the sight of the one man who could not have committed the murder. The conversation turned at last on Sir Giles, and Stephen happened to say, while explaining which of his books the firm had published and why, "But of course he knows my father better than me. Indeed, he's staying with him now."

At the moment the inspector thought nothing of this; but that night, as he lay half asleep and half awake, the two names which had haunted him arose like a double star in his sky. He felt them like a taunt; he bore them like a martyrdom; he considered them like a defiance. A remote thought, as from the departed day of common sense, insisted still: "Fool, it's his father, his father, his father." A nearer fantasy of dream answered: "He and his father—the name's the same. Substitution—disguise—family life—vendettas—vengeance— ventriloquism …" It lost itself in sleep.

The next evening he spent in writing a report on the case, and part of the afternoon in being examined upon it by an Assistant Commissioner, who appeared to be a little irritated by the hopelessness of the investigation up to that date.

"You haven't any ideas about it, inspector?" he asked.

"Very few, sir," the inspector answered. "There must obviously be a personal motive; and I think it must have been premeditated by someone who knew this Rackstraw wasn't going to be there at the time. But till I know who or what the man was, I can't get my hands on the murderer. I'm having inquiries made in the Wesleyan districts—one of them's near where I live, out by Victoria, and I've told my wife to keep her ears open. She goes to church. But the man's just as likely as not to have been a stranger to the district, just passing or lodging there for a week or so."

The Assistant Commissioner grunted. "Well," he said, "let me know what happens. It's a bad thing, these undiscovered murders. Yes, I know, but they oughtn't to happen. All right."

The inspector saluted and went out, passing on his way Colonel Conyers, who, having been landed in London, was making use of the afternoon to dispose of certain official business. Having settled this, he lingered to ask whether the Duke of the North Ridings was known to Scotland Yard, but discovered that, with the exception of one summons for having ridden a bicycle without a light and one for assault on Boat Race Night, nothing evil was to be discovered. Nor of the Archdeacon of Fardles. Nor of Mr. Gregory Persimmons. Nor of Dmitri Lavrodopoulos, chemist.

"This is all very curious, Colonel," the Assistant Commissioner said. "What's the idea?"

"Nothing official," Conyers answered. "I won't go into it all now. But if ever you hear anything about any of those names, you might let me know. Good-bye."

"Stop a moment, Colonel," said the other. "I think I ought to know why you want to know about this Gregory Persimmons. Nothing against him, but we've come across his name in another connection."

"Well …" the Colonel hesitated. He had included Gregory's name in his inquiries from habit and nothing else; if you were investigating, even in the most casual way, you included everybody and everything in your investigations; and if a case had arisen in which his own wife had played some unimportant part, the Colonel would have been capable of putting her name down on the list for inquiries to be made regarding her life and circumstances. He had paid a visit with Gregory to the shop in Lord Mayor Street, where the Greek, as weary and motionless as ever, had confirmed Persimmons's statement. Yes, he had sold the chalice; he had had it from another Greek, a friend of his who was now living in Athens but had visited London two or three months before; yes, he had a receipt for the money he had himself paid; yes, he had given Mr. Persimmons a receipt; the chalice had come from near Ephesus, and had been brought to Smyrna in the flight before the Turkish advance.

It all seemed quite right. The Colonel felt that Mr. Persimmons was being very harshly dealt with, and he looked now at the Assistant Commissioner with a slight indignation.

"A very nice fellow," he said. "I don't want to go into the story, because at present we want it kept quiet. I think the Archdeacon has gone mad, and if the Duke hadn't behaved in the most unjustifiable manner the whole thing would have been settled by now."

"It all sounds very thrilling," the Assistant Commissioner said. "Do tell me. We don't usually get cases with Dukes and Archdeacons in. The Dukes are usually in the divorce court and the Archdeacons in the ecclesiastical."

He was nevertheless slightly disappointed with the story. There seemed to be no remotest connection between the loss of the chalice and the murder in the publishing office except the name of Persimmons. Still, he wondered what Persimmons had been doing while the murder was going on. But that was a month or more ago; it would be very difficult to find out. The Assistant Commissioner had never ceased to wonder at the way in which many people always seemed to be quite certain what they were doing at four in the afternoon of the ninth of December when they were being examined at half-past eleven on the morning of the twenty-fifth of January. He turned the page of the reports in the file before him.

"You didn't meet Sir Giles Tumulty by any chance?" he asked. "Or Mr. Lionel Rackstraw?"

"I did not," the Colonel said.

"Or Mr. Kenneth Mornington?"

"There was a Mr. Mornington—or some name like it—with the Archdeacon," the Chief Constable said. "But I didn't really catch his name when he was introduced, so I didn't mention it. It may have been Mornington. He ran away with the Duke."

"Very funny," the other murmured. "A chalice, too—such a funny thing to run away with. Ephesus, you say? I wonder if any particular chalice came from Ephesus." He made a note. "All right, Colonel; we'll remember the names."

About the same time the allies in Grosvenor Square separated. There had been some discussion after lunch what the next move should be. The Duke inclined to ask Sir Giles definitely whether he identified this chalice with the Graal. But he had not met the antiquarian, and neither the Archdeacon nor Mornington thought it likely that Sir Giles would do more than cause them as much embarrassment as possible. The Archdeacon was inclined to put the Graal in safe keeping in the bank; the Duke, half convinced of its authenticity, felt that this would be improper. He, like Kenneth, attached a good deal more importance than the Archdeacon to the actual vessel. "It will be quite safe here," he said; "I'll put it in a private safe upstairs and get Thwaites to keep an eye on it. And you'd better stop here too for the present." This, however, the Archdeacon was reluctant to do; his place, he felt, was in his parish, which Mr. Batesby would soon be compelled to leave for his own. He consented, however, to stop for a couple of nights, in case any further move should be made by their opponents.

Kenneth's plan for that afternoon was definite. He intended to go down to the publishing offices on two errands; first, to forestall Gregory Persimmons if that power behind the throne should attempt to influence the throne in the matter of the proofs; and secondly, to obtain a set of the uncorrected proofs containing the paragraph that had caused the trouble, and, if possible, Sir Giles's postcard. He felt that it might be useful in the future to have both these in his possession. For Kenneth, not being more or less above the law like the Duke, or outside it like the Archdeacon, had a distinct feeling that, though it might be good fun to steal your own property under the nose of the police, the police were still likely to maintain an interest in it. Besides, he had never read the paragraph itself, and he very much wanted to.

On arrival at the offices, therefore, he slipped in by the side entrance, reached Lionel's office without passing anyone of sufficient eminence to inquire what had caused this visit, and searched for and found the proofs he desired. Then, going on to his own room, he rang up the central filing office. "I want," he said, "the file of Tumulty's *Sacred Vessels* at once. Will you send it down?" In a few minutes it arrived; he stopped the boy who brought it. "Is Mr. Persimmons in?" he asked. "Find out, will you?"

While the boy was gone on this errand, Kenneth looked through the correspondence. But it consisted wholly of business-like letters, a little violent on Sir Giles's part, a little stiff on Lionel's. There was no special reference to the article on the Graal as far as he could see, beyond the question of illustrations; certainly no reference to black magic. He abstracted the last postcard, took a copy of the book itself from his shelves, and by the time the boy had returned was ready for Stephen.

Mr. Persimmons was in. Mornington went along the corridor, tapped, and entered. Stephen looked up in surprise. "What brings you here?" he asked. "I thought you'd be away till to-morrow week."

"So I am, sir," Mornington said. "But I wanted to see you rather particularly. I called on Mr. Gregory Persimmons yesterday, and I'm not altogether easy about our interview."

Stephen stood up hurriedly and came nearer. "What happened?" he said anxiously. "What's the trouble?"

Kenneth explained, with a certain tact. He didn't blame Gregory at all, but he made it clear that Sir Giles and Gregory between them wanted blood, and that after the morning's chase Gregory was likely to want it more than ever; and he hinted as well as he could that he expected Stephen to stand up for the staff. Unfortunately, the prospect seemed to cause Stephen a good deal of uneasiness. With a directness unusual in him he pressed the central question.

"Do you mean," he said, "that my father will want me to get rid of you?"

"I think it is possible," Kenneth answered. "If ever a man wanted the tongue of his dog to be red with my blood it was Giles Tumulty. That's the kind of fellow he is."

"Oh, Giles Tumulty!" Stephen said. "I don't dismiss my people to please Giles Tumulty."

"He's a source of revenue," Kenneth pointed out. "And Mr. Gregory Persimmons will probably be rather annoyed himself."

"My dear Mornington," Stephen said, looking at the papers on his table, "my father wouldn't dream of interfering … either with me or with the staff—especially any of his old staff." He heard his own voice so unconvincingly that he walked over to the window and looked out. He felt his possession—his business and occupation and security—beginning to quiver around him as he considered the foreboded threat. He knew that he was incapable of standing up against his father's determination, but he knew also that the determination would not have to be called into play; the easier method of threatening his financial stability would be used. His father, Stephen had long felt, never put forward more power than was sufficient to achieve his object; it was the vaster force in reserve which helped to create that sense of laziness emanating from the elder Persimmons, as a man who pushes a book across with a finger seems more indolent than one who picks it up and lays it down in a new place. But an attack on Mornington roused alarm in Stephen on every side. His subordinate was as far indispensable to the business as anyone ever is; he was personally sympathetic, and Stephen was very unwilling to undergo the contempt which he felt the other would show for him if he yielded. Of the more obvious disadvantages of dismissal to Kenneth, Stephen in this bird's-eye view of the situation took little heed; "I can always get him another job," he thought, and returned to his own troubles.

Kenneth in these few minutes' silence realized that he would have to fight for his own hand, with the Graal (figuratively) in it.

"Well," he said, "I've told you about it, sir, so that if anything is said you may know our point of view."

"Our," said Gregory's voice behind him, "meaning the Archdeacon and your other friend, I suppose?"

Stephen jumped round. Kenneth looked over his shoulder. "Hallo," the publisher said, "I … I didn't expect you."

Gregory looked disappointed. "Tut, tut!" he said. "Now I hoped you always did. I hoped you were always listening for my step. And I think you are. I think you expect me every moment of the day. A pleasant thought, that. However, I only came down now to put a private telephone call through." He laid his hat and gloves on the table. Kenneth was unable to resist the impulse.

"A new hat, I'm afraid, Mr. Persimmons," he said. "And new gloves. The Chief Constable, of course, had them."

Gregory, sitting down, looked sideways at him. "Yes," he said, "we shall have to economize somehow. Expenses are dreadfully heavy. I want to go through the salary list with you in a few minutes, Stephen."

"I'll send for it," Stephen said, with a nervous smile.

"Oh, I don't think you need," Gregory answered. "Only a few items; perhaps only one to-day. In fact, we could settle it now—I mean Mr. Kenneth Mornington's item. Don't you think we pay him too much?"

"Ha, ha!" Stephen said, with a twisted grin. "What do you say, Mornington?"

Kenneth said nothing, and Gregory in a moment or two went on, "That is immaterial; in fact, the salary itself is immaterial. He is to be dismissed as a dishonest employee."

"Really——" Stephen said. "Father, you can't talk like that, especially when he's here."

461

"On the contrary," Kenneth said, "he can quite easily talk like that. It's a little like Sir Giles certainly, but your father, if I may say so, sir, never had much originality. Charming, no doubt, as a man, but as a publisher—third rate. And as for dishonesty …"

Gregory allowed himself to smile. "That," he said, "is vulgar abuse. Stephen, pay him if you'd rather and get rid of him."

"There is such a thing as wrongful dismissal," Kenneth remarked.

"My dear fellow," Gregory said, "we're reducing our staff in consequence of my returning to an active business life … did you speak, Stephen?… and you suffer. And your present employer and I between us can make it precious difficult for you to get another job. However, you can always sponge on the Duke or your clerical friend. Stephen …"

"I won't," Stephen said; "the thing's ridiculous. Just because you two have quarrelled …"

"Mr. Stephen Persimmons featuring the bluff employer," his father murmured. He got up, went over to the publisher, and began whispering in his ear, following him as he took a few steps and halted again. Kenneth had an impulse to say that he resigned, and another to knock Gregory down and trample on him. He stared at him, and felt a new anger rising above the personal indignation he had felt before. He wanted to smash; he wanted to strangle Gregory and push him also underneath Lionel's desk; for the sake of destroying he desired to destroy. The contempt he had always felt leapt fierce and raging in him; till now it had always dwelt in a secret house of his own; if anything, calming his momentary irritations. But now it and anger were one. He took a blind step forward, heard Stephen exclaim, and Gregory loose a high cackle of delight. "God, he likes it!" he thought to himself, and pulled madly at his emotions. "Sweet Jesus," he began, and found that he was speaking aloud.

Gregory was in front of him. "Sweet Jesus," his voice said jeeringly. "Sweet filth, sweet nothing!" Kenneth struck out, missed, felt himself struck in turn, heard a high voice laughing at him, was caught and freed himself, then was caught by half a dozen hands, and recovered at last to find himself held by two or three clerks, Stephen shuddering against the wall, and Gregory opposite him, sitting in his son's chair.

"Take him away and throw him down the steps," Gregory said; and, though it was not done literally, it was effectively. Still clutching the proofs of *Sacred Vessels*, Kenneth came dazedly into the street and walked slowly back to Grosvenor Square.

When he reached it, he found the Duke and the Archdeacon were both out, and Thwaites on guard in the Duke's private room. The Duke returned to dinner, at which he found Kenneth a poor companion. The Archdeacon returned considerably later, having been detained on ecclesiastical business first ("I had to come up anyhow," he explained, "this afternoon, so Mr. Persimmons didn't really disarrange me"), and secondly by a vain search for the Bishop.

The three went to the Duke's room for coffee, which however, was neglected while Kenneth repeated the incidents of the afternoon. The removal of the proofs, which was a mild satisfaction, led to the employment question, on which both his hearers, more moved, began to babble of secretaries, and from that to an account of the riot. When Kenneth came to repeat, apologetically, Gregory's cries, the Duke was startled into a horrified disgust; the Archdeacon smiled a little.

"I'm sorry you let yourself go so," he said. "We *must* be careful not to get like him."

"Sorry?" the Duke cried. "After that vile blasphemy? I wish I could have got near enough to have torn his throat out."

"Oh, really, really," the Archdeacon protested. "Let us leave that kind of thing to Mr. Persimmons."

"To insult God——" the Duke began.

"How can you insult God?" the Archdeacon asked. "About as much as you can pull His nose. For Kenneth to have knocked Mr. Persimmons down for calling him dishonest would have been natural—a venial sin, at most; for him to have done it in order to avenge God would have been silly; but for him to have got into a blurred state of furious madness is a great deal too like Mr. Persimmons's passions to please me. And I am not at all clear that Mr. Persimmons doesn't know it. We *must* keep calm. *His* mind's calm enough."

"At least," Mornington said, "we're pretty certain now." And with the word they all turned and looked at the Graal which the Duke, when they entered, had withdrawn from the safe. In a minute the Duke, crossing himself, knelt down before it. Kenneth followed his example. The Archdeacon stood up.

Under the concentrated attention the vessel itself seemed to shine and expand. In each of them differently the spirit was moved and exalted—most perhaps in the Duke. He was aware of a sense of the adoration of kings—the great tradition of his house stirred within him. The memories of proscribed and martyred priests awoke; masses said swiftly and in the midst of the fearful breathing of a small group of the faithful; the ninth Duke who had served the Roman Pontiff at his private mass; the Roman Order he himself wore; the fidelity of his family to the Faith under the anger of Henry and the cold suspicion of Elizabeth; the duels fought in

462

Richmond Park by the thirteenth Duke in defence of the honour of our Lady, when he met and killed three antagonists consecutively—all these things, not so formulated but certainly there, drew his mind into a vivid consciousness of all the royal and sacerdotal figures of the world adoring before this consecrated shrine. "Jhesu, Rex et Sacerdos," he prayed....

Kenneth trembled in a more fantastic vision. This, then, was the thing from which the awful romances sprang, and the symbolism of a thousand tales. He saw the chivalry of England riding on its quest—but not a historical chivalry; and, though it was this they sought, it was some less material vision that they found. But this had rested in dreadful and holy hands; the Prince Immanuel had so held it, and the Apostolic chivalry had banded themselves about him. Half in dream, half in vision, he saw a grave young God communicating to a rapt companionship the mysterious symbol of unity. They took oaths beyond human consciousness; they accepted vows plighted for them at the beginning of time. Liturgical and romantic names melted into one cycle—Lancelot, Peter, Joseph, Percivale, Judas, Mordred, Arthur, John Bar-Zebedee, Galahad—and into these were caught up the names of their makers—Hawker and Tennyson, John, Malory and the mediævals. They rose, they gleamed and flamed about the Divine hero, and their readers too—he also, least of all these. He was caught in the dream of Tennyson; together they rose on the throbbing verse.

> *down the long beam stole the Hol*
>
> *~ed with beatings in it.*

He heard Malory's words—"the history of the Sangreal, the whiche is a story cronycled for one of the truest and the holyest that is in thys world"—"the deadly flesh began to behold the spiritual things"—"fair lord, commend me to Sir Lancelot my father." The single tidings came to him across romantic hills; he answered with the devotion of a romantic and abandoned heart.

The Archdeacon found no such help in the remembrances of kings or poets. He looked at the rapt faces of the young men; he looked at the vessel before him. "Neither is this Thou," he breathed; and answered, "Yet this also is Thou." He considered, in this, the chalice offered at every altar, and was aware again of a general movement of all things towards a narrow channel. Of all material things still discoverable in the world the Graal had been nearest to the Divine and Universal Heart. Sky and sea and land were moving, not towards that vessel, but towards all it symbolized and had held. The consecration at the Mysteries was for him no miraculous change; he had never dreamed of the heavenly courts attending Christ upon the altar. But in accord with the desire of the Church expressed in the ritual of the Church the Sacred Elements seemed to him to open upon the Divine Nature, upon Bethlehem and Calvary and Olivet, as that itself opened upon the Centre of all. And through that gate, upon those tides of retirement, creation moved. Never so clearly as now had he felt that movement proceeding, but his mind nevertheless knew no other vision than that of a thousand dutifully celebrated Mysteries in his priestly life; so and not otherwise all things return to God.

When their separate devotions ceased, they looked at one another gravely. "There's one thing," the Duke said. "It must never be left unwatched. We must have an arranged order—people whom we can trust."

"*Intelligent* people whom we can trust," the Archdeacon said.

"In fact, an Order," Kenneth murmured. "A new Table."

"A new Table!" the Duke cried. "And a Mass every morning." He stopped short and looked at the Archdeacon.

"Quite so," the priest said, not in answer to the remark.

The Duke hesitated a moment, then he said politely, "I don't want to seem rude, sir, but you see that since, quite by chance, it has come into my charge, I must preserve it for ... for ..."

"But, Ridings," Kenneth said in a slightly alert voice, "it isn't in your charge. It belongs to the Archdeacon."

"My dear fellow," the Duke impatiently answered, "the sacred and glorious Graal can't *belong*. And obviously it is in my charge. I don't want to press my rights and those of my Church, but equally I don't want them abused or overlooked."

"Rights?" Kenneth asked. "It is in the hands of a priest."

"That," the Duke answered, "is for the Holy See to say. As it has done."

The two young men looked at one another hostilely. The Archdeacon broke in.

"Oh, children, children," he said. "Did either of you ever hear of Cully or Mr. Gregory Persimmons? It being (legally, my dear Duke) my property, I should like Mr. Persimmons not to get hold of it until I know a little more about him. But, on the other hand, I will promise not to hurt anyone's feeling by using it prematurely for schismatic Mysteries. A liqueur glass would do as well." Kenneth grinned; the Duke acknowledged the promise with a bow, and rather obviously ignored the last remark.

It was already very late; midnight had been passed by almost an hour. The Archdeacon looked at his watch and at his host. But the Duke had returned to his earlier idea.

"If we three can share the watch till morning," he said, "I will bring Thwaites in; he is one of our people. And there are certain others. It is one o'clock now—say, one to seven; six hours. Archdeacon, which watch will you take?"

The Archdeacon felt that a passion for relics had its inconveniences, but he hadn't the heart to check its ardour. "I will take the middle, if you like," he said, normally accepting the least pleasant; "that will be three to five."

"Mornington?"

"Whichever you like," Kenneth answered. "The morning?"

"Very well," the Duke said. "Then I will watch now."

They were at the door of the room, and, as they exchanged temporary good nights, the Archdeacon glanced back at the sacred vessel. He seemed to blink at it for a moment, then he took a step or two back into the room, and gazed at it attentively. The two young men looked at him, at it, at each other. Suddenly the priest made a sudden run across the room and took the Graal up in his hands.

It seemed to move in them like something alive. He felt as if a continuous slight shifting of all the particles that composed it were proceeding, and that blurring of its edges which had first caught his eyes was now even more marked. Close as he held it, he felt strangely uncertain exactly where the edge was, exactly how deep the cup was, how long the stem. He touched the edge, and it seemed to have a curious softness, to give under his finger. The shape did not yield to his grasp, but it suggested that it was about to do so. It quivered, it trembled; now here, now there, its thickness accumulated or faded; now it seemed to take the shape of his fingers, now to harden and resist them. The Archdeacon gripped it more firmly, and, keeping his eyes on it, turned to face the others.

"Something is going on," he said, almost harshly. "I do not know what. It may be that God is dissolving it but I think there is devilry. Make yourselves paths for the Will of God."

"But what is it?" the Duke said amazedly. "What harm can come to it here? What can they do to its hurt?"

"Pray," the Archdeacon cried out, "pray, in the name of God. They are praying against Him to-night."

It crossed Kenneth's mind, as he sank to his knees, that if God could not be insulted, neither could He be defied, nor in that case the procession and retrogression of the universe disturbed by the subject motion of its atoms. But he saw, running out like avenues, a thousand metaphysical questions, and they disappeared in the excitement of his spirit.

"Against what shall we pray?" the Duke cried.

"Against nothing," the Archdeacon said. "Pray that He who made the universe may sustain the universe, that in all things there may be delight in the justice of His will."

A profound silence followed, out of the heart of which there arose presently a common consciousness of effort. The interior energy of the priest laid hold on the less trained powers of his companions and directed them to its own intense concentration. Fumbling in the dark for something to oppose, they were, each in secrecy, subdued from that realm of opposition and translated to a place where their business was only to repose. They existed knit together, as it were, in a living tower built up round the sacred vessel, and through all the stones of that tower its common life flowed. Yet to all their apprehensions, and especially to the priest's, which was the most vivid and least distracted, this life received and resisted an impact from without. The tower was indeed a tower of defence, though it offered no aggression, and resisted whatever there was to be resisted merely by its own immovable calm. Once or twice it seemed to the Duke as if he heard a soft footprint behind him just within the room, but he was held too firmly still even to turn his head. Once or twice on Kenneth there intruded a sudden vision of something other than this passivity; a taunt, unspoken but mocking, moved just beyond his consciousness, a taunt which was not his, but arose somehow out of him. Sudden phrases he had used in the past attacked him—"the world can't judge"; "man chooses between mania and folly"; "what a fool Stephen is." In the midst of these the memory of the saying about every idle word obtruded itself; he began to justify them to himself, and to argue in his own mind. Little by little he became more and more conscious of his past casual contempt, and more disposed to direct a certain regretful attention to it. The priest felt the defence weaken; he did not know the cause, but the result was there; the Graal shook in his hands. He plunged deeper into the abysmal darkness of divinity, and as he did so heard, far above, his own voice crying "Pray!" Kenneth heard, and knew his weakness; he abolished his memories, and, so far as was possible, surrendered himself to be only what he was meant to be. Yet the attack went on: to one a footstep, a whisper, a slight faint touch; to another a gentle laugh, a mockery, a reminder; to the third a spiritual pressure which not he but that which was he resisted. The Graal vibrated still to that pressure, more strongly when it was accentuated, less and less as the stillness within and amidst the three was perfected. Dimly he knew at what end the attack aimed; some disintegrating force was being loosed at the vessel—not conquest, but destruction, was the purpose, and chaos the eventual hope. Dimly he saw that, though the spirit of Gregory formed the apex of that attack, the attack itself came from regions behind Gregory. He saw, uncertainly but sufficiently defined, the radiations that encompassed the Graal and the fine arrows of energy that were expended against it. Unimportant as the vessel in itself might be, it was yet an accidental storehouse of power that could be used, and to dissipate this material centre was the purpose of the war. But through the three concentrated souls flowed reserves of the power which the vessel itself retained; and gradually to the priest it seemed, as in so many celebrations, as if the Graal itself was the centre—yet no longer the Graal, but a greater than the Graal. Silence and knowledge were communicated to him as if from an invisible celebrant; he held the Cup no longer as a priest, but as if he set his hands on that which was itself at once the Mystery and the Master of the Mystery. But this consciousness faded almost before it was realized; his supernatural mind returned into his natural, leaving only the certainty that for the time at least the attack was ended. Rigid and hard in his hands, the Graal reflected only the lights of the Duke's study; he sighed and relaxed his hold, glancing at his two companions. The Duke stood up suddenly and glanced round him. Kenneth rose more slowly, his face covered with a certain brooding melancholy. The Archdeacon set the Graal down on the table.

"It is done," he said. "Whatever it was has exhausted itself for the time. Let us go and rest."

"I thought I heard someone here," the Duke said, still looking round him. "Is it safe to leave it?"

"I think it is quite safe," the Archdeacon said.

"But what has happened?" the Duke asked again.

"Let us talk to-morrow," the priest said very wearily. "The Graal will guard itself to-night."

Chapter Eleven

THE OINTMENT

The afternoon which had preceded the supernatural effort to destroy the Graal had been made use of by Mr. Gregory Persimmons to pay two visits. The first had been with the Chief Constable of Hertfordshire to the shop in Lord Mayor Street. But after the visit was made and the information acquired Colonel Conyers and he had parted in the Finchley Road, the Colonel to go to Scotland Yard in a chance taxi, he ostensibly for the Tube at Golder's Green. Once the Colonel had disappeared, however, Gregory returned as swiftly as possible to the shop.

The Greek had resumed his everlasting immobility, but, though he said nothing, his eyes lightened a little as he saw the other again come in.

"Do you know what has happened?" Gregory asked in that subdued tone to which the place seemed to compel its visitors.

"It seems they have recovered it," the Greek said and looked askew at a much older man who had just come into the shop from a small back room. The new-comer was smaller than the Greek, and much smaller than Gregory; his movements were swift and his repose alert. His bearded face was that of a Jew.

"You heard?" the Greek said.

"I heard," the stranger answered. He looked angrily at Gregory. "How long have you known this?" he asked, with a note of fierceness.

"Known—known what?" Gregory said, involuntarily falling back a step. "Known that they had it? Why, he only took it this morning."

"Known that it was—that," the other said. "What time we have wasted!" He stepped up to the Greek and seized him by the arm. "But it isn't too late," he said. "We can do it to-night."

The Greek turned his head a little. "We can do it if you like," he acquiesced. "If it is worth while."

"Worth while!" the Jew snapped at him. "Of course it is worth while. It is a stronghold of power, and we can tear it to less than dust. I do not understand you, Dmitri."

"It doesn't matter," Dmitri answered. "You will understand one day. There will be nothing else to understand."

The other began to speak, but Gregory, whom his last words had brought suddenly back to the dirty discoloured counter, said suddenly, but still with that subdued voice, "What do you mean? Tear it to dust? Do you mean *that*? What are you going to do?"

The others looked over at him, the Jew scornfully, the other with a faint amusement. The Greek said, "Manasseh and I are going to destroy the Cup."

"Destroy it!" Gregory mouthed at them. "*Destroy* it! But there are a hundred things to do with it. It can be used and used again. I have made the child see visions in it; it has power."

"Because it has power," the Jew answered, leaning over the counter and whispering fiercely, "it must be destroyed. Don't you understand that yet? They build and we destroy. That's what levels us; that's what stops them. One day we shall destroy the world. What can you do with it that is so good as that? Are we babies to look to see what will happen to-morrow or where a lost treasure is or whether a man has a gluttonous heart? To destroy this is to ruin another of their houses, and another step towards the hour when we shall breathe against the heavens and they shall fall. The only use in anything for us is that it may be destroyed."

Before the passion in his tones Gregory again fell back. But he made another effort.

"But can't we use it to destroy *them*?" he asked. "See, I have called up a child's soul by it and it answered me. Let me keep it a little while to do a work with it."

"That's the treachery," the Jew answered. "Keep it for this, keep it for that. Destroy it, I tell you; while you keep anything for a reason you are not wholly ours. It shall tremble and fade and vanish into nothingness to-night."

Gregory looked at the Greek, who looked back impassively. The Jew went on muttering. At last Dmitri, putting out a slow hand, touched him, and the other with a little angry tremor fell silent. Then the Greek said, looking past them, "It is all one; in the end it is all one. You do not believe each other and neither of you will believe me. But in the end there is nothing at all but you and that which goes by. You will be sick at heart because there is nothing, nothing but a passing, and in the midst of the passing a weariness that is you. All things shall grow fainter, all desire cease in that sickness and the void that is about it. And this, even for me, is when I have only looked into the bottomless pit. For my spirit is still held in a place of material things. But when the body is drawn into the spirit, and at last they fall, then you shall know what the end of desire and destruction is. I will do what you will while you will, for the time comes when no man shall work."

Manasseh sneered at him. "When I knew you first," he said, "you did great things in the house of our God. Will you go and kneel before the Cup and weep for what you have done?"

"I have no tears and no desire," the Greek said. "I am weary beyond all mortal weariness and my heart is sick and my eyes blind with the sight of the nothing through which we fall. Say what you will do and I will do it, for even now I have power that is not yours."

"I will bring this thing into atoms and less than atoms," Manasseh answered. "I will cause it to be as if it had never been. I will send power against it and it shall pass from all knowledge and be nothing but a memory."

"So," the Greek said. "And you?" he asked Gregory.

"I will help you, then," Gregory answered, a little sullenly, "if it must be done."

"No, you shall not help us," Manasseh said sharply, "for in your heart you desire it still."

"Let him that desires to possess seek to possess," the Greek commanded, "and him that desires to destroy seek to destroy. Let each of you work in his own way, until an end comes; and I who will help the one to possess will help the other to destroy, for possession and destruction are both evil and are one. But alas for the day when none shall possess your souls and they only of all things that you have known cannot be destroyed for ever."

He stood upright. "Go," he said to Gregory, "and set your traps. Come," to Manasseh, "and we will think of these things."

But Manasseh delayed a moment. "Tell me," he said to Gregory, "of what size and shape is the Cup?"

Gregory nodded towards the Greek. "I brought the book up last Saturday with the drawing in," he said. "You can see it there. But why should I try to recover it if you are going to destroy it?"

The Greek answered him. "Because no one knows what the future may bring to your trap; because till you prepare yourself to possess you cannot possess. Because destruction is not yet accomplished."

Gregory brooding doubtfully, turned, and went slowly out of the shop.

He went on to his son's office, and there, inflamed with a certain impotent rage at the destruction threatened to that which he had spent some pains to procure, eased it by doing all he could to destroy

Kenneth's security. After which he banished Stephen from the room, and talked for some time on the telephone to Ludding at Cully.

It was in pursuance of the instructions then received that Ludding the next morning strolled down to the Rectory. In a neat chauffeur's uniform, clean-shaved and alert, he presented so different an appearance from that of the bearded tramp who had called on the Archdeacon a month earlier that Mrs. Lucksparrow, even had the time been shorter, would not have recognized him. He had come down, it appeared, on a message from Mr. Persimmons to the Archdeacon.

"The Archdeacon isn't at home," Mrs. Lucksparrow said. "I'm sure I'm sorry you've had your trouble for nothing."

"No trouble, ma'am," Ludding answered; "indeed, as things have turned out, it's given me more pleasure than if he had been." His bow pointed the remark.

"Well," said Mrs. Lucksparrow, "I won't deny but what it's a pleasure to see someone to speak to, we being rather out of the way here—except for clergymen and tramps; and naturally the clergy don't come and talk to me, not but what some of them are nice enough in their way. Why, we've had the Bishop here before now, and a straightforward, pleasant-speaking gentleman too, though a bit on the hurried side, always wanting to get on somewhere else and do the next thing. I don't hold with it myself, not so much of it. What's done too quick has to be done twice my mother used to say, and she had eleven children and two husbands, though most of them was before I was born, being the youngest. Many's the time she's said to me, 'Lucy, my girl, you've never dusted that room yet, I'll be bound.'"

She stopped abruptly, a habit arising from a natural fear which possessed her when in attendance on the Archdeacon and his clerical visitors that she might be talking too much. But the sudden silence substituted for a gentle flow of words was apt to disconcert strangers, who found themselves expected to answer before they had any idea they had finished listening. Ludding was caught so now, and had to say in some haste, "Well, I'd rather trust you than a Bishop, Mrs. Lucksparrow."

"Oh, no," the housekeeper answered, "I don't think you should say that, Mr. Ludding, for they're meant to teach us, though there, again, my schoolmistress used to say, 'Take your time, girls, take your time,' though mostly over maps."

"Yes," Ludding said, prepared this time. "And I suppose you don't know when the Archdeacon will be back. I expect he takes *his* time." He laughed gently. "If he was married I expect he'd have to be back sooner."

"If he was married," Mrs. Lucksparrow said, "he wouldn't do a lot he does now. He's brought women home before now—well, it's not right to talk of it, Mr. Ludding, for fear of giving him a bad name, though he meant them nothing but good, little as they deserved it; and sometimes he never goes to bed at all, up in the church all night, when he thinks I'm asleep. If it wasn't that he can't eat pork I'd think he wasn't human, for I like a bit of pork, and it comes hard never being able to have it, for, of course, two joints is what I couldn't think of, and it's bad enough never daring to mention it or I believe it'd slip out, and then he'd go and buy a pig and have it sent home, all for a chop or two, but as for coming back, that I couldn't say, with only a telegram to say detained to-night, meaning yesterday—though, if it was anyone dying or anything, there's Mr. Batesby here."

"It wasn't really important," Ludding said, "only that Mr. Persimmons thought he'd like some fruit and flowers for the Harvest Festival, and wanted to know when it was likely to be."

"Second Sunday in September," Mrs. Lucksparrow said, "at least it was last year. But there *is* Mr. Batesby, and he'd know if anyone did, outside the Archdeacon."

Ludding looked over his shoulder to see Mr. Batesby emerging from the churchyard gate in the company of a stranger, a young man in a light grey suit and soft hat who was strolling carelessly by the priest's side. Mrs. Lucksparrow looked also, and said suddenly: "Why, it's a Chinaman; he's got those squinting eyes the Chinaman had when he stopped with the Archdeacon two years ago," rather as if there was only one Chinaman in the world. Ludding, however, as the two came nearer, doubted Mrs. Lucksparrow's accuracy; there seemed nothing Chinese about this stranger's full face—it was perhaps a little dark, a kind of Indian, the chauffeur thought vaguely.

"Shrines," Mr. Batesby was saying, "shrines of rest and peace, that's what our country churches ought to be, and are, most of them. Steeped in quiet, church and churchyard—all asleep, beautifully asleep. And all round them the gentle village life, simple, homely souls. Some people want incense and lights and all that— but I say it's out of tune, it's the wrong atmosphere. True religion is an inward thing. It's so true, isn't it? 'the Kingdom of God is *within* you.' Just to remember that—*within you*."

"It cometh not by observation," the stranger said gravely.

"True, true," Mr. Batesby assented. "So what do we want with candles?"

They reached the door, and he looked inquiringly at Ludding, who explained his errand, and added that he was sorry the Archdeacon wasn't at home and was it known when he would be back?

Mr. Batesby shook his head. "Not to a day or two," he said. "Gone on good works, no doubt. 'Make hay while the sun shineth, for the night cometh,'" and then, feeling dimly uncertain of this quotation, went on hastily, "We must all do what we can, mustn't we? Each in our small corner. Little enough, no doubt, just a car"—he looked at Ludding—"or a kitchen"—he looked at Mrs. Lucksparrow—"or—something," he ended, looking at the stranger, who nodded seriously, but offered no enlightenment for a moment. Then, as if in pity at Mr. Batesby's slightly obvious disappointment, he said, "I have been a traveller."

"Ah, yes, to be sure," the priest answered. "A broadening life, no doubt. Well, well, I venture to think you have seen nothing better than this in all your travels." He indicated church and garden and fields. "Not, of course, that the serpent isn't here too. The old serpent. But we crush his head."

"And your heels?" the stranger asked. Mr. Batesby took a moment to grasp this, and then said, gently smiling. "Yes, yes, not always unstung, I fear. Why, the Archdeacon here was assaulted only a few weeks ago in broad daylight. Scandalous. If it hadn't been for a good neighbour of ours, I don't know what might have happened. Why, you were there too, Ludding, weren't you?"

"Were you?" the stranger asked, looking him in the face.

"I was," Ludding said, almost sullenly, "if it's any business of yours."

"I think perhaps it may be," the stranger said softly. "I have come a long journey because I think it may be." He turned to Mr. Batesby. "Good day. I am obliged to you," he said, and turned back to Ludding. "Walk with me," he went on casually. "I have a question to ask you."

"Look here," the chauffeur said, moving after him, "who the hell do you think you are, asking me questions? If you want——"

"It is a very simple question," the stranger said. "Where does your master live?"

"Anyone will tell you," Ludding answered reluctantly and almost as if explaining to himself why he spoke. "At Cully over there. But he isn't there now."

"He is perhaps in London with the Archdeacon?" the stranger asked. "No, don't lie; it doesn't matter. I will go up to the house."

"He isn't there, I tell you," Ludding said, standing still as if he had been dismissed. "What the devil's the good of going to the house? We don't want Chinks hanging round up there, or any other kind of nigger. D'ye hear me? Leave it alone, can't you? Here, I'm talking to you, God blind you! You let Mr. Persimmons alone!" As the stranger drew farther away his voice became louder and his words more violent, so that Inspector Colquhoun, who was allowing himself a few days in the village, partly out of his holiday, partly in a kind of desperate wonder whether Cully would yield any suggestions, came round a turn in the road on his way from the station to see a man standing still and shouting after an already remote figure.

"Anything wrong?" he asked involuntarily.

Ludding turned round furiously. "Yes," he said, "you're wrong. Who asked you to blink your fat eyes at me, you flat-nosed, fat-bellied louse?"

The inspector considered the uniform. "You take care, my man," he said.

"Christ Almighty!" Ludding yelled at him, "if you don't get off I'll smash your——"

Colquhoun stepped nearer. "Say another word to me," he said, "you jumping beer-barrel, and I'll knock you into the middle of Gehenna!" The prospect of being able to repay someone connected with a Persimmons for all that he had gone through was almost delightful. Nevertheless, he hardly expected the chauffeur to make such an immediate rush for him as he did. He defended himself with strength enough to make aggression an imperceptible sequence, and succeeded in drawing Ludding to one side of the road, until he unexpectedly crashed into the ditch behind him. Colquhoun stepped back a pace. "Come out if you like," he said, "and let me knock you into it again."

It was upon the chauffeur scrambling furiously out of the ditch that Mr. Gregory Persimmons looked when he in turn, a little later than the inspector, being a slower walker, came along the road from the station. He had paid his visit to Lord Mayor Street that morning, to find Manasseh almost beside himself with enraged disappointment, and only too anxious to take any steps for recovering the Graal. The Greek had taken little part in their discussion; the effort of the night had left him so exhausted physically that he was lying back in a chair with closed eyes, and only now and then threw a suggestion to the others. Gregory's chief difficulty was to insist on maintaining the friendly relations with the Rackstraws that were essential to his designs on Adrian, and might, he recognized, already have been endangered by the break with Mornington. This, however, he hoped to arrange; judicious explanations and promises might do much, and Adrian's own liking for him was a strong card to play. At last he had compelled Manasseh to see his aim, and then a fresh proposal had been made. Manasseh with the Greek would concern themselves with securing the Graal, and

Gregory was to get hold of Adrian within the next few days. "Then," Manasseh said, "we can take the hidden road to the East."

"The hidden road?" Gregory asked.

Manasseh smiled knowingly. "Ah," he said, "you've a lot to learn yet. Ask your friend Sir Giles; he knows about it, I expect. Ask him if he's ever been to the furniture shop in Amsterdam or the picture dealer in Zurich. Ask him if he knows the boat-builder in Constantinople and the Armenian ferry. You are only on the edge of things here in London. The vortex of destruction is in the East. I have seen a house fall to fragments before a thought and men die in agony because the Will overcame them. Bring the child and come, and we will go into the high places of our god."

In the subtle companionship that existed between them Gregory felt the hope in his heart expand. "In three days from now I will be with you," he said. "By Friday night I will bring the child here."

With this purpose and a plan formed in his mind, he had returned to Fardles, to find his chauffeur struggling out of the ditch in the face of a contemptuous enemy.

When Ludding saw his employer he came to the road with a final effort and paused rather ridiculously. The inspector saw the hesitation, and looked round at Gregory, realizing that the odds were in favour of its being Gregory. He took the initiative.

"Mr. Persimmons?" he asked.

"I am Mr. Persimmons," Gregory answered mildly.

"I suspect this man is your chauffeur," the inspector said, and, as Gregory nodded, went on, "I'm sorry to have been obliged to knock him down. I found him shouting out in the roadway, and when I asked if anything was wrong he was first grossly rude and then attacked me. But I don't think he's hurt."

"Hurt," Ludding broke out, and was checked by Gregory's lifted hand. "I'm sorry," Persimmons said. "If by any chance it should happen again, pray knock him down again."

"No offence intended to you, sir," the inspector said. He thought for a moment whether he would make an attempt to enter into conversation with the other, but decided against it; he wanted, so far as he had a clear wish, to pick up opinion in the village first. So, with a casual inclination of the head, he started off down the road.

Persimmons looked at Ludding. "And now perhaps you will explain," he said. "Dear me, Ludding, you are letting this temper grow on you. You must try and control it. Why, you might be attacking *me* next; mightn't you?" He moved a little nearer. "Answer me, you swine, mightn't you?"

"I don't know why I hit him, sir," Ludding said unhappily. "It was the other man who irritated me."

"The other man: what other man?" Persimmons asked. "Are you blind or drunk, you fool?"

Ludding made an effort to pull himself together. "It was a young man, sir, in a grey suit. Asked after you and where you lived, and went off up to Cully. He made me see red, sir, and I was shouting after him when this fellow came up."

"A young man," Gregory said, "wanting to see *me*? This is very curious. And you didn't know him, Ludding?"

"Never seen him before, sir," Ludding answered. "He looked rather like an Indian, I thought."

Gregory's mind flew to what Manasseh had said of the hidden way to the East; was this anything to do with it? What possibilities, what vistas, might be opened! Whatever throne existed there, an end to that path he had followed so long and so painfully, would it not welcome him, coming with the Graal in one hand and the child for initiation in the other? He quickened his steps. "Let us see this young man," he said, and hastened on to Cully.

Followed by Ludding, he came to the gates and up the drive, down which he had rushed twenty-four hours before. As he rounded the turn from which Colonel Conyers had shouted at the constable, he met the stranger face to face, and all three of them stood still.

Gregory's first impression was that Ludding had been merely romancing when he spoke of the stranger being an Indian; the face that confronted him was surely as European as his own. There was something strange about it, but it was a strangeness rather of expression than of race, a high, contained glance that observed an unimportant world. The eyes took him in and neglected him at once, and together with him took in the whole of the surroundings and dismissed them also as of small worth. One hand carried gloves and walking-stick; the other, raised to the level of the face, moved lazily forward now and then as if to wave away some sort of slight unpleasantness, and every now and then also nostrils were wrinkled a little as if at some remote but objectionable smell that floated in the air. He had the appearance of being engaged upon a tiresome but necessary business, and this was enhanced as he paused on the drive and allowed his glance to dwell on Gregory.

"You want me?" Persimmons said, and the instant that he spoke became conscious that he actively disliked the stranger, with a hostility that surprised him with its own virulence. It stood out in his inner world as distinctly as the stranger himself in the full sunlight of the outer; and he knew for almost the first time what Manasseh felt in his rage for utter destruction. His fingers twitched to tear the clothes off his enemy and to break and pound him into a mass of flesh and bone, but he knew nothing of that external sign, for his being was absorbed in a more profound lust. It aimed itself in a thrust of passion which should wholly blot the other out of existence, and again its young opponent's upraised and open hand moved gently forward and downward, as if, like the Angel by the walls of Dis, he put aside the thick and noisome atmosphere of his surroundings.

"No," he said coldly, "I do not think I want you."

"What are you doing here, then?" Gregory asked thickly. "Why are you wandering about my house?"

"I am studying the map," the stranger said, "and I find this a centre marked on it."

"My servants shall throw you out," Gregory cried. "I do not allow trespassers."

"You have no servants," the other said; "you have only slaves and shadows. And only slaves can trespass, and they only among shadows."

"You are mad," Gregory cried again. "Why have you come to my house?"

"I have not entered your house," the stranger answered, "for the time is not yet. But it is not that which you should fear—it is the day when you shall enter mine."

Ludding, encouraged by his master's presence, took a step forward. The stranger threw him a glance and he stopped. His anger was so intense, however, that it drove him into speech.

"Who are you—coming here and talking like this?" he said. "Who the hell are you?"

"Yes," Gregory said, "tell us your name. You have damaged my property—you shall pay for it."

The other moved his hand outward again and smiled. "My name is John," he said, "and you know some, I think, that know me."

Gregory thought of his enemies. "That pestilent priest, perhaps?" he sneered, "or the popinjay of a Duke? Are these your friends? Or is the Duke too vulgar for you? What kings have you in the house of which you brag?"

"Seventy kings have eaten at my table," the stranger said. "You say well, for I myself am king and priest and sib to all priests and kings."

He dropped his hand and moved leisurely forward. Gregory inevitably stepped out of his direct path. As he passed Ludding the chauffeur put a hand out towards his shoulder. But he didn't somehow lay hold, and with an equal serenity of gait the stranger went on and at length passed out of the gates. Gregory, pulsating with anger too bitter for words, turned sharply and went on to the house. And the chauffeur, cursing himself, drifted slowly to the garage.

By the afternoon, however, Gregory had recovered his balance, or, rather, his intention. Whether the stranger was a wandering lunatic or whether he had some real link with the three fools who had carried off the Graal he did not know; and, anyhow, it did not matter. His immediate business was with the Rackstraws, and an hour before tea he went down towards the cottage to find them.

They were a little distance from it among some trees. Barbara was reading Mr. Wodehouse's latest Jeeves book, and Lionel, stretched on the ground, was telling Adrian the adventures of Odysseus the wise, the far-travelled. The story broke off when Gregory appeared.

"Have you been to London?" Adrian asked.

"Darling——" Barbara murmured.

"Well, Jessie said he had, Mummie," Adrian protested. Jessie was the maid from Cully.

"Jessie was perfectly right," Gregory answered. "I have been to London, and I have come back. In London, Adrian, they have large trains and many soldiers." He paused.

"I have a large train in London," Adrian soliloquised. "It has a guard's van with luggage in."

"I saw a train," Gregory said, "which belongs to your London train. It asked to be taken to Adrian because it belonged to him."

"What, another train? A train I haven't seen?" Adrian asked, large-eyed.

"A train you haven't seen, but it belongs to you," Gregory answered seriously. "Everything belongs to you, Adrian. You are the Lord of the World—if you like. One day, if you like, I will give you the world."

"After this week I could almost believe that, Mr. Persimmons," Barbara said. "What would you do with the world, Adrian?"

Adrian considered. "I would put it in my train," he said. "Where is the train I haven't seen?" he asked Gregory.

"Up at the big house," Gregory answered. "Let's all go up there to tea, shall we? And after tea you shall see the train. It's gone to sleep now, and it won't be awake till after tea," he explained gravely.

Adrian took his hand. "Shall we go?" he said, and pulled anxiously to lead the way.

"Let us go," Gregory assented, and looked back laughing over his shoulder. "Will you come?" he cried.

Barbara stretched out her hands, and Lionel pulled her to her feet. "I just want to shimmer up, like Jeeves, not walk," she said. "Do you like Jeeves, Mr. Persimmons?"

"Jeeves?" Gregory asked. "I don't think I know it or him or them."

"Oh, you must," Barbara cried. "When I get back to London I'll send you a set."

"It's a book, or a man in a book," Lionel interrupted. "Barbara adores it."

"Well, so do you," Barbara said. "You always snigger when you read him."

"That is the weakness of the flesh," Lionel said. "One shouldn't snigger over Jeeves any more than one should snivel over *Othello*. Perfect art is beyond these easy emotions. I think Jeeves—the whole book, preferably with the illustrations—one of the final classic perfections of our time. It attains absolute being. Jeeves and his employer are one and yet diverse. It is the Don Quixote of the twentieth century."

"I must certainly read it," Gregory said, laughing. "Tell me more about it while we have tea."

After the meal the four of them climbed to the gallery and Mr. Persimmons's room, where the train was marvellously arrayed and arranged. Adrian gave himself up to it, with Barbara assisting. Gregory took Lionel over to the bookcases. Presently, however, they were recalled by calls from the train, and found that somewhere in the complicated mechanism a hitch had occurred. Gregory examined it, turning the engine over in his hands; then he said: "I think I see what the fault is." He fiddled with it for a minute or two, then he looked at Barbara with a smile. "Would you mind holding it, Mrs. Rackstraw?" he asked. "I just can't get the right bit past the screw with one hand."

Barbara took it willingly, and Gregory pushed and thrust at the mechanism for a minute or two. Then he altered the position of his left hand so that it lay lightly over Barbara's fingers and thrust again with his right. There was a slip, a jangle, an oath from Gregory, a light shriek from Barbara, an exclamation from Lionel; then the engine had dropped to the floor, while the men stared at a long scratch on the inside of Barbara's wrist and lower arm from which the blood was already oozing.

"My dear Mrs. Rackstraw, I am so sorry," Gregory exclaimed. "Do please forgive me. Does it hurt you much?"

"Heavens, no!" Barbara said. "Lend me your handkerchief, Lionel, mine isn't big enough. Don't worry, Mr. Persimmons, it'll be all right in a few minutes if I just do it up."

"Oh, but you must put something on it," Gregory said. "Look here, I've got some ointment here—only a patent medicine, I admit; I forget what they call it—not Zam-buk, but something like it. Anyhow, it works rather well." He had gone across to a drawer, and now produced a small round wooden box, which he held out to Barbara. "And there's some rag somewhere; ah, here it is."

Barbara wrinkled her nose as she took the box. "What a funny smell!" she said. "Thank you so much. But I've got vaseline at home."

"Don't wait," Gregory said, "put some on now and do it up." He turned to Adrian. "Still," he said, "I put the engine right. But it oughtn't to have had a sharp edge like that. I must take it back next time I'm in town."

Half an hour slipped away. Then Lionel, turning by accident to put a book down on the table, saw his wife's face.

"Barbara," he said suddenly, "do you feel ill?"

She was lying back in her chair, and as he spoke she looked across at him, at first unrecognizingly. Then she said, speaking dizzily: "Lionel, Lionel, is that you? I'm fainting or something; I don't know where I am! Lionel!"

Lionel was across the room and by her side, even as Gregory, who was sitting on the floor by Adrian, rose to his feet. Persimmons glanced at his guest, went across and pressed the bell, and returned. Rackstraw was speaking as quietly as he could, to soothe her. But she sat up suddenly and began to scream, her eyes blind to everything round her, her hands thrusting away from her. "Lionel! Lionel! Oh, God! Oh, God! Lionel!"

Lionel threw a look towards Gregory. "Adrian!" he said. Gregory turned to the child, who, startled and horrified, was beginning to cry, picked him up with murmured consolations and encouragements, and went quickly to meet Ludding at the door.

"Mrs. Rackstraw is ill," he said. "Telephone to the doctor; and then come back. I may want you. He'll be here as quickly if you telephone as if you go down in the car, won't he? Hurry!"

Ludding vanished, and Gregory, going with Adrian into the next room, produced a parcel of curious shape, which he presented to the child. But Adrian heard, even through the closed doors, the spasmodic shrieks that came from the next room, and clung despairingly to Gregory. Then amid the cries they heard movements and footsteps, a chair falling, and Lionel's voice on a quick note of command. Adrian began to scream in alarm, and Ludding, on his return from the telephone, was sent to find the maid Jessie, between whom and Adrian a pleasant friendship had ripened. She carried him off to her own quarters, and Gregory ran into the next room.

There Barbara had collapsed again into a seat, in which she was writhing and twisting, at intervals crying out still for Lionel.

"But, my darling, I'm here," he said, tortured beyond any of his own visionary fears. "Can't you see me? Can't you feel me?" He took her hands.

By the long alliance of their bodies, knit by innumerable light touches of impatience or of delight, some kind of bridge seemed to be established. Barbara's hands closed on his, and her voice grew into a frenzy of appeal. "Save me, Lionel, save me! I can't see you. Come to me, Lionel!"

Lionel looked back at Gregory. "What on earth's happened?" he said in a low voice. "Can't we do anything?"

"I've sent for the doctor," Gregory answered in equally subdued tones. "We can't do anything but hang on till he comes. Adrian's with Jessie. Try her with the child's name."

Barbara had relapsed again into comparative silence, though her frame was shuddering and trembling in the moment's exhaustion. Gregory, from behind Lionel, considered her thoughtfully. The operation of the ointment would have, he supposed, some sort of parallel to his own experience. But where in him, it had released and excited his directing purpose to a fuller consummation, in Barbara Rackstraw, who probably drifted through the world like most people, "neither for God nor for his enemies," it was more likely simply to define and energize the one side, without giving it entire separation and control. All with which he had felt himself one would be to Barbara an invader, a conqueror, perhaps even an infernal lover; she would feel it in her body, her blood, her mind, her soul. Unless indeed she also *became* that, though since without her definite intention, so without her definite control. Then, instead of calling for Lionel, would she shriek at him? How funny! He picked up the box of ointment and dropped it into his pocket; there was another more harmless box in the drawer, if inquiries were made.

Almost another quarter of an hour had passed since the crisis had begun. Gregory saw no necessity for it ever to end. In himself the ointment had been a means to a certain progress and return, but Barbara had no will to either, and might, it seemed to him, exist for ever in this divided anguish of war. He wondered very much what the doctor would say.

Suddenly Barbara moved and stood up. Her voice began again its despairing appeals to God and Lionel, but her limbs began to dispose themselves in the preliminary motions of a dance. Gently at first, then more and more swiftly, her feet leapt upon the carpet; her arms tossed themselves in time to unheard music. Lionel made an effort to stop her, throwing one arm round her waist and catching her hands with the other; before his movement was complete she broke his hold and sent him staggering across the room. Gregory's heart beat high; this then was the outer sign of the inner dance he had himself known: the ointment had helped him to seal his body while his soul entered ecstasy. But here the ointment gave the body helpless to the driving energy of the Adversary, and only through the screaming mouth a memory that was not conquered cried out to her lover and to her God.

Gregory heard a movement outside the door; there was a tap. But he was too absorbed to speak. Then the door opened and the village doctor stood in the opening. At the same moment, as if she had waited for it, Barbara, still moving in that wild dance, threw up her hand and, carelessly and unconsciously tore open her light frock and underwear from the breast downwards. It hung, a moment, ripped and rent, from the girdle that caught it together; then it fell lower, and she shook her legs free without checking the movement of the dance.

Even Gregory was not very clear afterwards what had then happened. It had needed the three of them to bring her into some sort of subordination, and to bind her with such material as could be obtained. The doctor's next act was to inject morphia, a proceeding which Gregory watched with considerable pleasure, having his own views on what result this was likely to bring about. She was carried into one of the spare rooms at Cully, and Lionel took up his station there also. "They'll put another bed in presently," Gregory told him. "And my man Ludding will sleep in the next room, so if you want anything ask him. Good heavens, it's not seven yet! Now, about Adrian…. He shall sleep in my room if he likes, that will distract him, and he'll feel important. Hush, hush, my dear fellow, we must all do what we can. The doctor's coming in again later."

The doctor indeed, after asking a few questions, and looking at the box of harmless ointment, had been glad to get away and think over this unusual patient. Gregory, having made inquiries, found that Adrian was out in the gardens with Jessie, and strolled out to find them, just preventing himself from whistling cheerfully in case Lionel should hear. It occurred to him that it would be pleasant before the child went to bed to see if anything could be discovered about the stranger who had disturbed him earlier, but whom, warm with his present satisfaction, he was inclined to neglect. Still….

He suggested, therefore, to Adrian—who had allowed himself to be persuaded how delightful it would be to sleep in his uncle's own room, and that his mother had better be left alone that evening—that another game at hidden pictures would be pleasant. The cup they had used before was not, it seemed, possible, but there were other means.

Installed therefore on a chair in front of a table bearing a shining black disc arranged in a sloping position, Adrian said anxiously:

"Now ask me what I can see."

Gregory leant back in his chair opposite, fixed his eyes on Adrian, made an image of the stranger in his mind, and said slowly: "Can you see a tall man, with a grey suit on, and a soft hat?" He imposed the image on the child's mind.

With hardly any hesitation Adrian answered: "Oh, yes, I can see him. He's on a horse, and ever so many other people are all round him on horses, with long, long sticks. They're all riding along. Oh, it's gone."

Gregory frowned a little. A cavalry regiment? Was his visitor merely a lieutenant in the Lancers? He concentrated more than ever. "What is he doing now?" he asked.

"He's sitting on cushions," Adrian poured out raptly. "And there's a man in red and a man in brown. They're both kneeling down. Oh, they're giving him a piece of paper. Now he's smiling, now they're going. It's gone again," he ended in a tone of high delight.

Gregory brooded over this for some minutes. "Where does he come from?" he asked. "Can you see water or trains?"

"No," said Adrian immediately, "but I can see a lot of funny houses and a lot of churches too. He's coming out of one of the churches. He's got a beautiful, beautiful coat on! And a crown! and there are a lot of people coming out with him, and they've all got crowns and swords! and flags! Now he's on a horse and there are candles all round him and funny things going round in the air and smoke. Oh, it's gone."

Gregory, as delicately and as soon as possible, broke off the proceedings. There was something here he didn't understand. He sent Adrian off to bed with promises of pleasant amusements the next day, and himself, after a short visit to Lionel, went out again into the grounds to await the doctor's second call. Barbara, it seemed, was lying still; he wondered what exactly was happening. If the morphia was controlling her limbs, what about the energy that had wrung them? If it couldn't work outward, was it working inward? Was the inner being that was Barbara being driven deeper and deeper into that flow of desire which was the unity and compulsion of man? What an unusual experience for a charming young housewife of the twentieth century! And perhaps she also would not be able to return.

Chapter Twelve

THE THIRD ATTEMPT ON THE GRAAL

Lionel Rackstraw leant by the open window and looked out over the garden. Behind him Barbara lay, in stillness and apparent sleep; below him at some distance Mr. Gregory Persimmons contemplated the moon. In an ordinary state of mind Lionel might have contemplated it too, as a fantasy less terrible than the sun, which appeared to him often as an ironical heat drawing out of the earth the noxious phantoms it bred therein. But the phantoms of his mind were lost in the horrible, and yet phantasmal, evil that had befallen him; his worst dreams were, if not truer than they had always been—that they could not be—at least more effectual and more omnipotent. The last barricade which material things offered had fallen; the beloved was destroyed, and the home of his repose broken open by the malice of invisible powers. Had she been false, had she left him for another—that would have been tolerable; probably, when he considered himself, he had always felt it. What was there about him to hold, in the calm of intense passion, that impetuous and adorable nature? But this unpredictable madness, without, so far as could be known, cause or explanation, this was the overwhelming of humanity by the spectral forces that mocked humanity. He gathered himself together in a persistent and hopeless patience.

He took out his case and lit a cigarette mechanically. She, he supposed, would never smoke cigarettes again, or, if she did, it would never be the same. At the same time, that question of ways and means which is never far from the minds of the vast majority of the English at any moment, which poisons their sorrows and modifies their joys, which insists on being settled before any experience can be properly tasted, and, if unsatisfactorily settled (as it most frequently is), turns love and death into dancing parodies of themselves, which ruins personal relationship and abstract thought and pleasant hours—this question presented itself also to him. What about money? what about Adrian? what about their home? what about the future? He couldn't look after Adrian; he couldn't afford to keep Barbara *and* a housekeeper; besides, he couldn't, he supposed, have a housekeeper to live in the same house with Adrian and himself—unless she were old enough. And how did you get old housekeepers, and what did you pay them? Barbara might get better, but obviously after such an attack she couldn't for a long time be left alone with Adrian; and if she didn't get better? She had an aunt somewhere in Scotland—a strong Calvinistic Methodist; Lionel cursed as he thought of Adrian growing up in a Calvinistic household. Not, his irony reminded him, that he wasn't something of a Calvinist himself, with his feeling about the universe; but his kind of Calvinism wouldn't want to proselytize Adrian, and the aunt's would. He himself had no available relations—and his friends? Well, friends were all very well, but you couldn't dump a child on your friends indefinitely. Besides, his best friends—Kenneth, for instance—hadn't the conveniences. What a world!

Mr. Persimmons, turning from the moon, looked up at the house, saw him, waved a hand, and walked towards the door. It crossed Lionel's mind that it would be very satisfactory if Adrian could stop at Cully. It was no use his saying that he had no right to think of it; his fancy insisted on thinking of it, and was still doing so when Gregory, entering softly, joined him at the window.

"All quiet?" he asked in a low voice.

"All quiet," Lionel answered bitterly.

"It occurred to me," Gregory said—"I don't know, of course—but it occurred to me that you might be worrying over the boy. You won't, will you? There's no need. He can stop with me, here or in London, as long as ever you like. He likes me and I like him."

"It's very kind of you," Lionel said, feeling at once that this would solve a problem, and yet that the solving it would leave him with nothing but the horror of things to deal with. Even such a worrying question as what to do with Adrian was a slight change of torment. But that, he reflected sombrely, was selfish. Selfish, good heavens, selfish! And, after a long pause he said again, "It's very kind of you."

"Not a bit," Gregory answered. "I should even—in a sense—like it. And you must be free. It's most unfortunate. It seems sometimes as if there was an adverse fate in things—lying in ambush."

"Ambush?" Lionel asked, relieved yet irritated at being made to talk. What did people like Gregory know of adverse fate? "Not much ambush, I think. It's pretty obvious, once one's had a glimpse of the world."

Religion normally has a mildly stupefying effect on the minds of its disciples, and this Gregory had not altogether escaped. He had thought it would give him half an hour's pleasant relaxation to worry Lionel, and he had not realized that Lionel was, even in his usual state, beyond this. He went on accordingly: "There seems a hitch in the way things work. Happiness is always just round the corner."

"No hitch, surely," Lionel said. "The whole scheme of things is malign and omnipotent. That *is* the way they work. 'There is none that doeth good—no, not one.'"

"It depends perhaps on one's definition of good," Gregory answered. "There is at least satisfaction and delight."

"There is no satisfaction and no delight that has not treachery within it," Lionel said. "There is always Judas; the name of the world that none has dared to speak is Judas."

Gregory turned his head to see better the young face from which this summary of life issued. He felt perplexed and uncertain; he had expected a door and found an iron barrier.

"But," he said doubtfully, "had Judas himself no delight? There is an old story that there is rapture in the worship of treachery and malice and cruelty and sin."

"Pooh," Lionel said contemptuously; "it is the ordinary religion disguised; it is the church-going clerk's religion. Satanism is the clerk at the brothel. Audacious little middle-class cock-sparrow!"

"You are talking wildly," Gregory said a little angrily. "I have met people who have made me sure that there is a rapture of iniquity."

"There is a rapture of anything, if you come to that," Lionel answered; "drink or gambling or poetry or love or (I suppose) satanism. But the one certainty is that the traitor is always and everywhere present in evil and good alike, and all is horrible in the end."

"There is a way to delight in horror," Gregory said.

"There is no way to delight in the horrible," Lionel answered. "Let us pray only that immortality is a dream. But I don't suppose it is," he added coldly.

A silence fell upon them, and Gregory was suddenly conscious that he felt a trifle sick. He felt dizzy; he shut his eyes and leant against the wall to save himself lurching. Lionel's face, as it looked out over the garden, frightened him; it was like a rock seen very far off. He opened his eyes and studied it again, then he glanced back over his shoulder at Barbara lying on the bed. This was Cully; Adrian was asleep in *his* room; *he* had overthrown Barbara's mind. And now he was driven against something else, something immovable, something that affected him as if he had found himself suddenly in a deep pit of smooth rock. Lionel, who had been pursuing his own thoughts, began to speak suddenly, in the high voice of incantation with which he was given to quoting poetry,

> ιich way I fly is hell, myself am
> n the lowest deep a lower deep
> ʒaping to devour me opens wide
> hich the hell I suffer seems a heː

Gregory stamped his foot, and managed to change it into a mere shifting of position. After all, he wasn't going to quarrel with Lionel just now, though if he had time he would smash him into splinters. A clerk at a brothel!

"Well," he said, "there's just one thing I should like to say. If the doctor doesn't seem much good when he comes, I have been thinking that I know an old man in London who's seen some curious things and has funny bits of knowledge. I'll get him on the telephone to-morrow and ask him to come down. He mayn't be any good, but he may."

"It's really very kind of you," Lionel said. "But how can anyone do anything?"

"Well, we shall see," Gregory answered cheerfully. "Hallo, there *is* the doctor. And Sir Giles. Shall we go and meet them?"

Sir Giles, who had been out all day on an antiquarian visit, had run into the doctor at the gates. They walked up the drive a little distance apart, and at the door he made to annex Persimmons, who, however, put him aside till he had spoken with the doctor. A new examination of the patient brought no new light. The doctor, who refused to stay for the night, but promised to call again in the morning, went off. Lionel returned to his vigil, and Gregory, having patted him on the shoulder, and said cheerfully, "Well, well, don't despair. We'll ring up old Manasseh first thing," went off with Sir Giles to his own room.

"What's the idea?" Tumulty asked. "And who is old Manasseh, anyhow?"

"Ah, you don't know everyone yet," Gregory answered in high glee. "Pity you weren't here; you'd have liked to see how Mrs. Rackstraw went on. Quite unusual, for an English lady. Unusual for an English doctor, too. Did you think he was a bit bewildered, Tumulty? But you'll meet Manasseh in the morning."

"Coming down, is he?" Sir Giles asked. "Well, there's someone else down here too."

"Yes," Gregory said. "The masquerading fellow in grey? Now, if you can tell me who *he* is——"

"I knew you'd go mad," Sir Giles said, with satisfaction. "What fellow in grey? I don't know what hell's clothes he was wearing, something from his own suburban tape-twister, I expect."

"Why suburban?" Gregory asked. "He didn't look to me like the suburbs. And what did he mean by his name being John?"

"His name may be Beelzebub," Sir Giles answered, "but the man is that lump-cheeked inspector who's trying to find out who committed the murder. *He's* down here."

Gregory stared. "What, *that*?" he said. "Why, I thought they'd dropped all that. There's absolutely nothing to show—— What does he want here?"

"Probably either me or you," Sir Giles answered. "Well, I told you at the beginning, Persimmons, I'm going to damn well see to it he doesn't have *me*. I don't care what insane May dance you get up to, but I'm not going to be dragged in. If the police are after you, they can have you for all I care. I'm leaving to-morrow, and I'm off to Baghdad next week. And, if he asks me anything, I shall tell him."

"Tell him that you told me you were going to ask Rackstraw to have lunch with you, so that the room——" Gregory began.

"Tell him you've been waking up in the night shrieking 'blood, blood,' if it's necessary," Sir Giles said. "The English police are corrupt enough, of course, but the trouble is one doesn't know *where* they're corrupt, and you may hit on the wrong man. Besides, I'll see that lurching sewer-rat in Hinnom before I spend good money on him."

"You're making a ridiculous fuss," Gregory said. "You don't really think he's got evidence?"

"I don't care a curse," Sir Giles answered. "You're not interesting enough to run any risks for, Persimmons; you're merely an overgrown hobbledehoy stealing beer—the drainings in other people's pots. And I'm not going to have to poison myself for you. And now who's this reptile in grey you're bleating about?"

Gregory had grown used to neglecting half of Sir Giles's conversation, but for a moment he remembered Lionel's remark earlier in the evening, and looked nastily across at the other. However, he pulled himself in, and said carelessly, "Oh, a mad fellow we met in the drive. Talked like a clergyman and said he knew seventy kings."

"Only seventy?" Sir Giles asked. "No other introduction?"

"I didn't like him," Gregory admitted, "and he made Ludding foam at the mouth. But he wasn't doing anything except wander about the drive. He mentioned he was a priest and king himself." He dropped his voice and came a little nearer. "I wondered at first whether he was anything to do with—the shop. You know what I mean. But somehow he didn't fit in."

Sir Giles sat erect. "Priest and king," he said, half sceptically. "You're sure you're not mad, Persimmons?" He stood up sharply. "And his name was John?" he asked intently.

"He said so," Gregory answered. "But John what?"

Sir Giles walked to the window and looked out, then he came back and looked with increasing doubt at Gregory. "Look here," he said, "you take my advice and leave that damned bit of silver gilt trumpery alone. Ludding told me about your all going off after it. You may be up against something funnier than you think, Master Gregory."

"But who *is* he?" Gregory asked impatiently yet anxiously. "What's he got to do with the—the Graal?"

"I'm not going to tell you," Sir Giles said flatly. "I never knew any good come of trying to pretend things mightn't be when they might. I've heard tales—lies, very likely—but tales. Out about Samarcand I heard them and down in Delhi too—and it wasn't the Dalai Lama either that made the richest man in Bengal give all he had to the temples and become a fakir. I don't believe in God yet, but I wonder sometimes whether men haven't got the idea of God from that fellow—if it's the same one."

"What have I to do with God?" Gregory said.

"I don't know whether the Graal belongs to him or he belongs to the Graal," Sir Giles went on, unheeding. "But you can trace it up to a certain point and you can trace it back from a certain point, and someone had it in between. And if it was he, you'd better go and ask the Archdeacon to pray for you—if he will."

"Will you tell me who he is?" Gregory asked.

"No, I won't," Sir Giles said. "I've seen too much to chatter about him. You drop it, while there's time."

"I suppose it's Jesus Christ come to look for His own property?" Gregory sneered.

"Jesus Christ is dead or in heaven or owned by the clergy," Sir Giles answered. "But they say this man is what he told you—he is king and priest and his name is John. They say so. I don't know, and I tell you I funk it." He looked at the open window again.

"Well, run then," Gregory said. "But I and my great lord will know him and meet him."

"So you may, for me," Sir Giles answered, and with no more words disappeared to his own room.

The child Adrian slept long and peacefully, and only his angel, in another state of the created universe, knew what his dreams were. But, except for him and the servants, the night was, for those in Cully, empty of sleep. Lionel lay on the couch that had been hastily made up, watching and listening for any movement from his wife. How far she slept none could tell. She lay motionless, but Lionel doubted, when he was near her, whether it were more than a superimposed and compulsory immobility. Her eyes were shut, but her breath trembled as if some interior haste shook it, and every now and then there issued from her lips a faint and barely perceptible moan, faint but profound. Lionel brooded over this companion of his way, torn apart into the depths of some jungle whose terror he could not begin to conceive. He himself would have been, to however small an extent, prepared; but that Barbara, with her innocent concentration on window-curtains and the novels of Mr. Wodehouse and Adrian's meals, should be plunged into it, was a fatality against which even his pessimism felt the temptation to rebel.

Not far from his room Sir Giles also lay wakeful, considering episodes and adventures of his past. Brutal with himself no less than with others, he did not attempt to hide from himself that the new arrivals in the village caused him some anxiety. He had known, in his exploration of that zone of madness which encloses humanity, certain events which had been referred by those who had spoken of them to a mysterious power whose habitation was unknown and whose interference was deadly. Once indeed, in a midnight assembly in Beyrout, he had, he thought, dimly seen him; there had been panic and death, and in the midst of the shrinking and alarmed magicians a half-visible presence, clouded and angry and destructive. At the time he had thought that he also had been affected by a general hallucination, but he knew that hallucination was a word which, in these things, meant no more than that certain things seemed to be. Whether they were or not … He promised himself again to leave England as soon as possible, and to leave Cully certainly to-morrow.

Gregory, after some consideration, had dismissed Sir Giles's warnings as, on the whole, silly. Things were going very well; by the next night he hoped that both the Graal and Adrian would be, for a while, in his hands or those of his friends. Of all those who lay awake under those midnight stars he was the only one who had a naturally religious spirit; to him only the unknown beyond man's life presented itself as alive with hierarchical presences arrayed in rising orders to the central throne. To him alone sacraments were living realities; the ointment and the Black Mass, the ritual and order of worship. He beyond any of them demanded a response from the darkness; a rush of ardent faith believed that it came; and in full dependence on that faith acted and influenced his circumstances. Prayer was natural to him as it was not to Sir Giles or Lionel, or, indeed, to Barbara, and to the mind of the devotee the god graciously assented. Conversion was natural to him, and propaganda, and the sacrifice both of himself and others, if that god demanded it. He adored as he lay in vigil, and from that adoration issued the calm strength of a supernatural union. As the morning broke he smiled happily on the serene world around him.

Sir Giles took himself off after breakfast, leaving his small amount of luggage to be sent on. Gregory and Lionel left Ludding to call them if Barbara moved—a nurse was to arrive later—and went to the telephone in the hall. There, after some trouble, Gregory got through to his desired number and, Lionel gathered, to the unknown Manasseh. He explained the circumstances briefly, urging the other to take the next train to Fardles.

"What?" he asked in a moment. "Yes, Cully—near Fardles…. Well, anything in reason, anything, indeed…. What? I don't understand…. Yes, I know you did, but … No, but the point is, that I haven't … Yes, though I don't know how you knew…. But I can't…. Oh, nonsense!… No, but look here, Manasseh, this is serious; the patient's had some sort of fit or something…. But you can't mean it. … Oh, well, I suppose so…. But, Manasseh…. But you wouldn't … No, stop …"

He put the receiver back slowly and turned very gravely to Lionel. "This is terrible," he said. "You know that chalice I had? Well, I knew Manasseh wanted it. He thinks he can cure Mrs. Rackstraw, and he offers to try, *if* I'll give him the chalice."

"Oh, well," Lionel said insincerely, "if he wants that—I suppose it's very valuable? Too valuable for me to buy, I mean?"

"My dear fellow," Gregory said, "you should have it without a second thought. Do you suppose I should set a miserable chalice against your wife's health? I like and admire her far too much. But I haven't got it. Don't you remember I told you yesterday—but we've been through a good deal since then—the Archdeacon's bolted with it. He insists that it is his, though Colonel Conyers is quite satisfied that it isn't, and I really think the police might be allowed to judge. He and Kenneth Mornington and a neighbour of mine bolted with it— out of my own house, if you please! And now, when I'd give anything for it, I can't get hold of it." He stamped his foot in the apparent anger of frustrated desire.

The little violence seemed to break Lionel's calm. He caught Gregory's arm. "But must your friend have that?" he cried. "Won't anything else in heaven or hell please him? Will he let Babs die in agony because he wants a damned wine-cup? Try him again, try him again!"

Gregory shook his head. "He'll ring us up in an hour," he said, "in case we can promise it to him. That'll give him time to catch the best morning train to Fardles. But what can I do? I know the Archdeacon and Mornington have taken it to the Duke's house. But they're all very angry with me, and how can I ask them for it?" He looked up suddenly. "But what about you?" he said, almost with excitement. "You know Mornington well enough—I daren't even speak to him; there was a row about that book yesterday at the office, and he misunderstood something I said. He's rather—well, quick to take offence, you know. But he knows your wife, and he might be able to influence that Archdeacon; they're very thick. Get on the 'phone to him and try. Try, try anything to save her now."

He wheeled round to the telephone and explained what he wanted to the local Exchange; then the two of them waited together. "Manasseh's a hard man," Gregory went on. "I've known him cure people in a marvellous way for nothing at all, but if he's asked for anything he never makes any compromise. And he doesn't always succeed, of course, but he does almost always. He works through the mind largely—though he knows about certain healing drugs he brought from the East. No English doctor would look at them or him, naturally, but I've never known an English doctor succeed where he failed. Understand, Rackstraw, if you can get the Archdeacon to see that he's wrong, or to give up the chalice *without* seeing that he's wrong, it's yours absolutely. But don't waste time arguing. I know it's no good my arguing with Manasseh, and I don't think it's much good your arguing with the Archdeacon. Tell Mornington the whole thing, and get him to see it's life or death—or worse than life or death. Beg him to bring it down here at once and we'll have it for Manasseh when he comes. There you are; thank God they've been quick."

In a torrent of passionate appeal Lionel poured out his agony through the absurd little instrument. At the other end Kenneth stood listening and horrified in the Duke's study; the Duke himself and the Archdeacon waited a little distance "But what's the matter with Babs?" Kenneth asked. "I don't understand."

"Nobody understands," Lionel answered desperately. "She seems to have gone mad—shrieking, dancing—I can't tell you. Can you do it? Kenneth, for the sake of your Christ! After all, it's only a chalice—your friend can't want it all that much!"

"*Your* friend seems to want it all that much," Kenneth said, and bit his lips with annoyance. "No, sorry, Lionel, sorry. Look here, hold on—no, of course, you can't hold on. But I must find the Archdeacon and tell him." He held up a hand to stop the priest's movement. "Tell me, what's Babs doing now?"

"Lying down with morphia in her to keep her quiet," Lionel answered. "But she's *not* quiet, I know she's not quiet, she's in hell. Oh, hurry, Kenneth, hurry."

Considerably shaken, Mornington turned from the telephone to the others. "It's Barbara Rackstraw," he said, paused a moment to explain to the Duke, and went on. "Gregory's been doing something to her, I expect; Lionel doesn't know what's the matter, but she seems to have gone mad. And that—creature has got a doctor up his sleeve who can put her right, he thinks, but he wants *that*——" He nodded at the Graal, which stood exposed in their midst, and went over the situation again at more length to make the problem clear.

Even the Archdeacon looked serious. The Duke was horrified, yet perplexed. "But what can we do?" he asked, quite innocently.

"Well," Kenneth said restrainedly, "Lionel's notion seemed to be that we might give him the Graal."

"Good God!" the Duke said. "Give him the Graal! Give him *that*—when we know that's what he's after!"

Kenneth did not answer at once, then he said slowly: "Barbara's a nice thing; I don't like to think of Barbara being hurt."

"But what's a woman's life—what are any of our lives—compared to *this*?" the Duke cried.

"No," Kenneth said, unsatisfied, "no…. But Barbara…. Besides, it isn't her life, it's her reason."

"I am the more sorry," the Duke answered. "But this thing is more than the whole world."

Kenneth looked at the Archdeacon. "Well, it's yours to decide," he said.

During the previous day it had become evident in Grosvenor Square that a common spiritual concern does not mean a common intellectual agreement. The Duke had risen, the morning after the attack on the Graal, with quite a number of ideas in his mind. The immediate and chief of these had been the removal of the Graal itself to Rome, and its safe custody there. He urged these on his allies at breakfast, and by sheer force of simple confidence in his proposal had very nearly succeeded. The Archdeacon was perfectly ready to admit that Rome, both as a City and a Church, had advantages. It had the habit of relics, the higher way of mind and the lower business organization to deal with them. Rome was as convenient as Westminster, and the Apostolic See more traditional than Canterbury. But he felt that even this relic was not perhaps so important as Rome would inevitably tend to make it. And he felt his own manners concerned. "It would rather feel like stealing my grandmother's lustres from my mother to give to my aunt," he explained diffidently, noted the Duke's sudden stiffening, and went on hastily: "Besides, I am a man under authority. It isn't for me to settle. The Bishop or the Archbishop, I suppose."

"The Judicial Committee of the Privy Council is the final voice of authority still, isn't it?" the Duke pointedly asked. "I know Southend is a Jew and one or two others are notorious polygamists—unofficially."

"The Privy Council, as everybody knows, has no jurisdiction …" Mornington began.

"There we go again," the Archdeacon complained. "But, anyhow, so far as the suggestion is concerned, mere movement in space and time isn't likely to achieve much. It couldn't solve the problem, though it might delay it."

"Well, what do you propose to do?" the Duke asked.

"I don't know that I really thought of doing anything," the Archdeacon answered. "It would be quite safe here wouldn't it? Or we might simply put it in a dispatch-case and take it to the Left Luggage office at Paddington or somewhere. No," he added hastily, "that's not quite true. But you staunch churchpeople always make me feel like an atheist. Frankly, I think the Bishop ought to know—but he's away till next week. So's the Archbishop. And then there are the police. It's all very difficult."

There certainly were the police. Colonel Conyers made a call that morning; the Assistant Commissioner made a point of having tea with the Duchess, who was the Duke's aunt, that afternoon. The Duke was at his most regal (ducal is too insignificant a word) with both. Neither of them were in a position to give wings to a colossal scandal by taking action unless forced to it by Mr. Persimmons, and Mr. Persimmons had returned to Cully, after reiterating to the Colonel his wish that public action should not be taken. To the Assistant Commissioner the Duke intimated that further attacks on the vessel had taken place.

"What, burglars?" the other said.

"Not burglars," the Duke answered darkly. "More like black magic."

"Really?" the Assistant Commissioner said, slightly bewildered. "Oh, quite, quite. Er—did anything *happen*?"

"They tried to destroy It by *willing* against It," the Duke said. "But by the grace of God they didn't succeed."

"Ah … willing," the other said vaguely. "Yes, I know a lot can be done that way. Though Baudouin is rather against it, I believe. You—you didn't *see* anything?"

"I thought I heard someone," the Duke answered. "And the Archdeacon felt It soften in his hands."

"Oh, the Archdeacon!" the Assistant Commissioner said, and left it at that.

The whole day, in short, had been exceedingly unsatisfactory to the allies. The Duke and Mornington, in their respective hours of vigil before the sacred vessel, had endeavoured unconsciously to recapture some of their previous emotion. But the Graal stood like any other chalice, as dull as the furniture about it. Only the Archdeacon, and he much more faintly, was conscious of that steady movement of creation flowing towards and through the narrow channel of its destiny. And now when, on the next morning, he found himself confronted with this need for an unexpected decision he felt that he had not really any doubt what he would do. Still—"'Wise as serpents'," he said, "Let us be serpentine. Let us go to Cully and see Mrs. Rackstraw, and perhaps meet this very obstinate doctor."

The Duke looked very troubled. "But can you even hesitate?" he asked. "Is anything worth such a sacrifice? Isn't it sacrilege and apostasy even to think of it?"

"I do not think of it," the Archdeacon said. "There is no use in thinking of it and weighing one thing against another. When the time comes He shall dispose as He will, or rather He shall be as He will, as He is."

"Does He will Gregory Persimmons?" Kenneth said wryly.

"Certainly He wills him," the Archdeacon said, "since He wills that Persimmons shall be whatever he seems to choose. That is not technically correct perhaps, but it is that which I believe and feel and know."

"He wills evil, then?" Kenneth said.

"'Shall there be evil in the City and I the Lord have not done it?'" the Archdeacon quoted. "But I feel certain He wills us to get down to Fardles. And of the rest we will talk later."

Neither Kenneth nor the Duke accused the priest of evading the issue, for both of them felt he was speaking from a world of experience into which they had hardly entered. They fell back on the simpler idea that agony and evil were displeasing to God, but that He permitted them, and indeed Kenneth, at any rate, found it necessary, while he telephoned to Lionel their decision to come to Cully, and even on the way there, to keep this firmly in his mind as a counterbalance to the anxiety that he felt. For never before had he been confronted with the fact that certain strong and effective minds were ready and willing to inflict pain with or without a cause. He was becoming frightened of Gregory, and he naturally and inevitably therefore decided that Gregory was displeasing to God. It was his only defence; in such a crisis "if God did not exist it would be necessary to invent Him."

Yet this, even up to the moment when they all met in the hall at Cully, Lionel had refrained from doing. That the universe was displeasing to him did not prove that a god existed who could save him from the universe. But the universe seemed sometimes to relax a little, to permit a little grace to be wrung from it; and he thought it barely possible that such small grace might be granted now. It was undignified to be so greedy, but it was for Barbara—he excused himself to his own scornful mind.

Manasseh had arrived before the other three, and had spent the interval chatting with Gregory in the hall. Persimmons had begged Lionel so earnestly not to make any attempt to moderate his terms, and had seemed to have such a belief in and such a respect for his skill and obstinacy, that Lionel had easily fallen in with the suggestion. Cully had been placed so entirely at his disposal; the chalice itself had been—or was to be—his to yield to Manasseh; his anxiety about Adrian had been reduced; lastly, the possibility of a cure for Barbara had been so wholly Gregory's idea that prudence as well as gratitude demanded so much. He remained therefore, rather to the annoyance of the nurse, who had come by the same train as Manasseh, in Barbara's room, wondering whether the occasional flicker of movement he seemed to discern in her was real or only the suggestion of his own hope or fear.

Manasseh chatted with Gregory, and as the two paced the hall their sympathy with Lionel and Barbara seemed considerably lightened. "It only needs two things," Gregory said. "You must be firm when the other people come, and you ought to be able to do something to make Rackstraw think his wife is getting over it."

"Trust me to be firm," Manasseh answered. "As for the other—I think I can do that too. I've got some stuff that will send her into the heaviest sleep she's ever known; morphia's nothing to it. And it'll last for forty-eight hours or so. By then we can be away."

"I wonder if we've done wisely, after all," Gregory said. "But I don't altogether trust the way things are shaping here. They carry heavy guns, with the Duke—and Tumulty tells me the police haven't dropped that killing yet."

"What—Pattison?" Manasseh asked in surprise. "But Dmitri told me that he thought you'd managed that very well. He was sent to you, wasn't he?"

"He was sent from within," Gregory said. "It was made clear to me that I must kill, and he happened to be getting difficult. He did a pretty little piece of forgery for me once and played up well. But a few months ago he came across a Wesleyan mission-preacher and began to get troublesome. I was going to send him to Canada—but the other chance seemed too good to lose. So it was that."

Manasseh looked at him approvingly. "You will find soon," he said, "that possession is nothing besides destruction. We will go together to the East, and take the child and the Cup with us. And we will leave this madness behind us—and perhaps something else. We will talk with Dmitri. I should like to leave a memory of us with that priest."

There was a ring at the front door. Ludding, who had been told to be in attendance, came through to open it. At the other end of the hall Gregory and Manasseh turned to meet their guests, and Ludding, almost achieving irony, cried out in the voice of a herald: "The Duke of the North Ridings, the Archdeacon of Fardles, Mr. Mornington."

They entered, the Archdeacon carrying a small case, from which Persimmons carefully kept his eyes averted. They entered, and he said to Ludding: "Ask Mr. Rackstraw to come down." Then, as the man went away, he went on: "It is better that Mr. Rackstraw, and Dr. Manasseh here, and you should settle what is to be done. I have given over to Mr. Rackstraw all my interest in the chalice."

The Archdeacon bowed formally and looked at Manasseh. Immediately afterwards Lionel came down the stairs to join them, nodded to Kenneth, and was introduced by Gregory to Manasseh. Then Persimmons went on: "I'll leave you to discuss it for a few minutes. But one way or another the thing should be settled at once." He turned away up the stairs and along the corridor from which Lionel had come.

He went, indeed, straight to the room where Barbara lay, chatted for a moment or two with the nurse, who was about to dress the wound, and then went over to the bed, where he paused to look down on her.

"Poor dear," he said thoughtfully, "and on her holiday, and in such glorious weather!"

"It seems to make it worse somehow, doesn't it, sir?" the nurse said, Mr. Persimmons of Cully being obviously an important personage. Gregory shook his head and sighed. "Yes," he said, "it's very sad, very. And we have fine country here, too. You know it—no? Oh, you must. In your breaks you'll use my car as much as you want, won't you? Now, over there," he went on, drowning the nurse's hesitating thanks, "they say you can almost see the top of the spire of Norwich Cathedral."

"Norwich!" the nurse said, surprised and turning to look out of the window.

"They say!" Gregory said, half-laughing, and running his finger down the long, unhealed wound twice and again. "But I admit I've never seen it. However, I mustn't delay you now. Perhaps you'll let me take you for a run one afternoon."

He smiled, nodded, left the room, and strolled back along the corridor to the top of the stairs.

"… moral decency demands it," the Duke was saying. "I am not concerned with all that," Manasseh answered, more truthfully than any but Gregory knew. "I have told you that from what Mr. Persimmons has told me I am sure I can heal Mrs. Rackstraw. But I must have my price. Unless I have it I will not act."

"There are English doctors," the Duke said coldly.

"Yes," Manasseh said, "you have tried one. Well, as you like …"

Gregory frowned. It was the Duke again, he supposed. But he himself dared not interfere; that would probably make matters worse, for he was suspect to all save Lionel. Well, he would have Adrian, anyhow; the other must be tried for again. But another five minutes might make a difference; he hoped Manasseh wouldn't rush things. Lionel and Kenneth were speaking together; the Archdeacon was imperceptibly drawn in, and the other two awaited their decision.

"I cannot buy it," Lionel broke out; "I have no possible excuse for asking for it. I ought not to have told you even. But I have told you, and there is an end to it."

"No, but, Lionel——" Kenneth began.

"Mr. Rackstraw," the Archdeacon interrupted, "the end to it is very simple. For myself, I would not have delayed so long. I would give up any relic, however wonderful, to save anyone an hour's neuralgia—man depends too much on these things. But, having friends, I felt only——"

He stopped. For from above the shrieks that had shaken Cully the previous night had suddenly begun again. The nurse came flying to the stairs, crying, "She's up, and I can't hold her. Help! help!" But almost at the same instant Barbara was there too, her face wild with an appalling fear, her arms wide and clutching, her voice shrieking incomprehensible things, of which the group in the hall caught only the wild words: "The edge! the edge!" and then again, "I can't stop! The edge, the edge!" Gregory sprang as if to check her; she was past him and rushing down the stairs. Lionel and Kenneth met her as she came, and were flung aside by the irresistible energy that held her. The Duke, horrified, took an unintentional step back and crashed into the Archdeacon, so that Manasseh ran forward alone towards the foot of the stairs. The voice now was beyond description terrible, and still she cried, "The edge, the edge!" and still was hurled blindly forward. And then, at the very height of the agonizing moment, when it seemed that some immediate destruction must rend her whole being, of a sudden the voice faltered and stopped. As Manasseh closed upon her she paused, stumbled, and in one long gentle movement seemed to collapse towards the floor. He had her before she reached it, but, as his eyes momentarily met Gregory's, there appeared in them a great perplexity. In a second or two they were all around her; Lionel and Kenneth moved with her to one of the long seats scattered about the hall and laid her gently down, and Manasseh bent over her. She seemed, as she lay there, almost as if asleep; asleep in that half-repose, half-collapse, which follows prolonged strain. A few tears crept from her closed eyes; her body shook a little, but as if from the mere after-effects of agony, not in the stiff spasms of agony itself. Manasseh straightened himself, and looked round at the others. "I think it is over," he said. "It will need time and patience, but the will is caught and brought back. Her mind will now be safe—now or presently, I cannot tell to a few days. There may be another slighter outbreak, but I do not think so." He drew a small bottle from his pocket. "Give her two drops of this—not more—in a wineglass of water when she wakes, and once every twelve hours afterwards. I will come down again the day after to-morrow."

Kenneth giggled hysterically. Manasseh's speech had an insane likeness to any doctor concluding a visit. Of course, doctors *were* all the same, but the Archdeacon's black case, the anguish they had seen in Barbara's face, seemed to demand a more exalted conclusion. His giggle passed unnoticed, however, for the Archdeacon was holding the case out to Manasseh. "This is what you wanted, I think," he said, paused a moment, and added as he turned to the door, "But no bargain yet brought anyone near to the Graal or to the heart of its Lord." He bowed slightly to Manasseh and slightly to Persimmons and walked out.

On the steps he waited for his friends. They followed him at once, the Duke taking no notice of anyone, Kenneth with a murmur to Lionel; and the three looked at each other. "Well," the Archdeacon said, "I shall go back to the Rectory. Will you come with me or what?"

"No," the Duke said. "Our trust has been ended. I go back to the Castle. Will you come with me for a night or two, Mornington, as you meant to?"

Kenneth considered. He would have to see about getting a job, but a day or two first could do no harm. And if by any wild chance the Duke should really want a secretary …. But he tried to suppress the idea. "I think I will," he said. "I should like to hang round till I knew Barbara was well again."

"I don't see that we can do anything if she isn't," the Duke said. "We've lost all our assets."

"Assets?" the Archdeacon asked. "'The sacred and glorious Graal'? Oh, really, my dear Duke!"

The Duke looked a little embarrassed; his remark had been really irritable, not judicial. But he said stubbornly: "We could have pretended to bargain, at least."

They had begun walking down the drive, and the Archdeacon made no answer for a minute or two. Then he said, "I will not bargain any more for anything, if I can help it. How can one bargain for anything that is worth while? And what else is worth bargaining for?"

"If one bargained for nothing, would everything be worth while?" Kenneth said, but more as a dream than a question.

They came to the gates and paused; then the Archdeacon said cheerfully to Kenneth, "Well, if you run over to see Mrs. Rackstraw in the next day or two, you'll look in on me? I must relieve Batesby—and the parish," he added as an afterthought.

"Certainly I will," Kenneth said, shaking hands. The Duke followed suit, saying a little sadly, "I suppose this is the end."

"I wouldn't be too sure of that," the Archdeacon answered. "If I were Manasseh, I shouldn't trust the Graal too far. But he probably thinks it important."

By the way he was clutching the case, he probably did. Gregory and Lionel, not wanting to disturb Barbara's profound sleep, inserted pillows and cushions under and round her, and then, while Lionel sat down close at hand, Gregory walked over to Manasseh.

"You did that very well," he said softly. "Or—didn't you do it?"

481

Manasseh hesitated; then, his face a little troubled, he answered, "No; and that's what makes me wonder. I thought I could do it one way or another, but she stopped first. I could have drowned her knowledge, and instead she seemed to know something else. It was as if she found everything all right, even on the very edge of the pit."

"'He shall give His angels charge over her,'" Gregory said. "Perhaps He managed it in time. They've usually been rather late. My wife, and Stephen, and even poor dear Pattison. But it doesn't matter."

"No," Manasseh said, and then suddenly, "But I don't like her getting away. She was on the very edge of destruction; she might have been torn to bits *there*—and she wasn't. Is she really safe? Can we try the ointment again?"

"No, we can't," Gregory said. "Don't be a fool. You've got the Cup, take it with you, and, unless something hinders me, I'll be with you to-night. To-morrow certainly, but I think to-night. You won't do anything till I come?"

"No," Manasseh answered. "You shall bring the child and we will talk with Dmitri. We win."

"Praise to our lord," Gregory said. But Manasseh smiled and shook his head. "He is the last mystery," he murmured, "and all destruction is his own destroying of himself."

Chapter Thirteen

CONVERSATIONS OF THE YOUNG MAN IN GREY

When Sir Giles reached the station that morning he met a young man in grey just issuing from the booking-office. He stopped on the pavement and surveyed him. The stranger returned his gaze with a look of considerable interest.

"Are you running away, Sir Giles?" he said rather loudly.

"No," Sir Giles said at once. "Are you Persimmons's bugbear?"

"No," the stranger answered; "yours, much more truly. I like to watch you running."

"I am *not* running," Sir Giles almost shouted. "I was going to-day anyhow, and I have told Persimmons a thousand times I won't be dragged into his Boxing Day glee parties. And, anyhow, he's getting a bore.... Haven't I met you before?"

"Once or twice," the stranger said. "We shall meet again, no doubt. I like to watch your mind working. So long as you don't make yourself too much of a nuisance."

Sir Giles's overpowering curiosity, freed from other desires, thrust him forward. "And who are you?"

"I will tell you, if you like," the stranger said, smiling, "for at least you are really curious. I am Prester John, I am the Graal and the Keeper of the Graal. All enchantment has been stolen from me, and to me the Vessel itself shall return."

Sir Giles stepped back. "Nonsense!" he said. "Prester John, indeed! However, it's not my affair. You don't seem to have kept the Graal very well." He stepped towards the station, but paused as he heard the stranger's voice behind him.

"This is the second time we have met, Giles Tumulty," it said. "I warn you that one day when you meet me you shall find me too like yourself to please you. It is a joyous thing to study the movements of men as you study insects under a stone, but you shall run a weary race when I and the heavens watch you and laugh at you and tease you to go a way that you would not. Then you shall scrabble in the universe as an ant against the smoothness of the inner side of the Graal, and none shall pick you out or deliver you for ever. There is a place in the pit where I shall be found, but there is no place for you who do not enter the pit, though you thrust others in."

During the high tones that had been used at the beginning of their conversation Sir Giles had glanced once or twice at a porter who was lounging near. But the porter had not seemed to take any notice, and even now, while this warning sounded through the bright morning air, he still leant idly against the station wall. Sir Giles, while the stranger was still speaking, went up to him. "What platform for the London train?" he said sharply, and the porter answered at once, "Over the bridge, sir." Sir Giles looked at him hard, but there was no suggestion of anything unusual on the man's face, though the stern voice still rang on. Tumulty shivered a little, and thought to himself, "I must be imagining it; Persimmons is wrecking my nerve." An ant scrabbling in an empty chalice—a foul idea! He looked back as he entered the booking-office; the stranger was strolling away down the station entrance.

Prester John, if it was he indeed, passed on down the country roads till he came near the Rectory, having timed himself so well that he met Mr. Batesby emerging. The clergyman recognized at once his companion of the day before, and greeted him amiably. "Still staying here?" he said. "Well, you couldn't do better. 'Through pleasures and palaces though we may roam, there's no place like home.' Though, strictly speaking, I expect Fardles isn't your home. But a church is our home everywhere—in England, of course I mean. I suppose you don't find the churches abroad really *homely*."

"It depends," the young man said, "on one's idea of a home. Not like an English home perhaps."

"No," Mr. Batesby said, "they haven't, I gather, a proper sense of the family. Didn't one of the poets say that Heaven lies about us in our family? And where else, indeed?"

"What then," the stranger asked, "do you mean by the Kingdom of Heaven?"

"Well, we have to *understand*," Mr. Batesby said. As Ludding had increased in brutality, and Gregory in hatred, so, in conversation with the stranger, Mr. Batesby's superior protectiveness seemed to increase; he became more than ever a guide and guard to his fellows, and the Teaching Church seemed to walk, a little nervously and dragging its feet, in the dust behind him. "We have to *understand*. Of course, some take it to mean the Church—but that's very narrow. I tell my young people in confirmation classes the Kingdom of Heaven is all good men—and women, of course … and women. Just that. Simple perhaps, but helpful."

"And good men," the other said, "are——?"

"Oh, well, good men, one knows good men," Mr. Batesby said. "By their fruits, you know. They do not kill. They do not commit adultery. They are just kind and honest and thrifty and hard-working, and so on. Good—after all, one feels goodness."

"The Kingdom of Heaven is to be felt among the honest and industrious?" the stranger asked. "And yet it's true. The Church is indeed marvellously protected from error."

"Yes," Mr. Batesby agreed. "The Faith once delivered. We can't go wrong if we stick to the old paths. What was good enough for St. Paul is good enough for me."

"When he fell to the ground beyond Damascus and was blinded?" the stranger asked. "Or when he persecuted the Christians in Jerusalem? Or when he taught them in Macedonia?"

"Ah, it was the same Paul all the time," Mr. Batesby rather triumphantly answered. "Just as it's the same me. I can grow older, but I don't change."

"So that when the Son of Man cometh He shall find faith upon the earth? It was beyond His expectation," the stranger said.

"The five righteous in Sodom," Mr. Batesby reminded him.

"There were not five righteous in Sodom," the young man said. "O Jerusalem, Jerusalem!…"

"Well, not strictly perhaps," Mr. Batesby allowed, a little hurt, but recovering himself. "But a parable has to be *applied*, hasn't it? We mustn't take it too literally, too much in the foot of the letter, as the French so wittily say. More witty than moral the French, I'm afraid."

So conversing, they walked on till they came to the village, where, at the inn door, Inspector Colquhoun was regarding it pensively. He looked unrecognizingly at them as they approached. But the stranger stopped and smiled at him in greeting.

"Why, inspector," he said, "what are you doing down here?"

The inspector looked at him critically. "I've no doubt it's your business," he said, "but I'm quite sure it's mine. I don't seem to remember your face."

"Oh, many a time!" the stranger said lightly; "but I won't ask you any questions. Mr. Batesby … do you know Inspector Colquhoun? Inspector, this is Mr. Batesby, who is looking after the parish for the time being."

The two others murmured inaudibly, and the stranger went on, "You ought to have a kindness for one another, for on you two the universe reposes. Movement and stability, aspiration and order …"

"Yes," Mr. Batesby broke in, "I've often thought something like that. In fact, I remember once in one of my sermons I said that the police were as necessary for the Ten Commandments as the Church was. More so nowadays, when there's so little respect for the law."

"There never was much that I could ever hear of," the inspector said, willing to spend a quarter of an hour chatting to the local clergyman. "No, I don't think things are much worse."

"No, not in one way," Mr. Batesby said. "Man had fallen just as far twenty or thirty years ago as he has to-day. But the war made a great difference. Men nowadays don't seem so willing to be *taught*."

"Ah, there you have me, sir," the inspector answered. "I don't have much to do with teaching them, only with those who won't be taught. And I've seen some of them look pretty white," he added viciously.

"Ah, a guilty conscience," Mr. Batesby said. "Yes—guilt makes the heavy head to bend, the saddened heart to sob, and happy they who ere their end can feel remorseful throb. Love casteth out perfect fear. Nothing is sadder, I think, than to see a man or woman *afraid*."

"It doesn't do to trust to it." The inspector shook his head. "It may drive them almost silly any moment, and make them dangerous. I've known a little whipper-snapper fairly gouge a policeman's eyes out."

"Really?" Mr. Batesby said. "Dear me, how sad! I don't think I know what fear is—temperamentally. Of course, an accident …"

"You have never been afraid of anyone?" the stranger said, his voice floating through the air as if issuing from it.

"Yes," the inspector said, "and pretty often."

"Not, I think, afraid *of* anyone," Mr. Batesby said, mysteriously accentuating the preposition. "Of course, every priest has unpleasant experiences. Once, I remember, I was making a call on a farmer and a pig got into the room, and we couldn't get it to go away. And there are callers."

"Callers are the devil—I mean, the devil of a nuisance," the inspector remarked.

"You see, *you* can get rid of them," the clergyman said. "But *we* have to be patient. 'Offend not one of these little ones, lest a millstone is hanged about his neck.' Patience, sympathy, help. A word in season bringeth forth his fruit gladly."

The air stirred about him to the question. "And do these cause you fear?"

"Oh, not fear! by no means fear!" Mr. Batesby said. "Though, of course, sometimes one has to be firm. To pull them together. To try and give them a backbone. I have known some poor specimens. I remember meeting one not far from here. He looked almost sick and yellow, and I did what I could to hearten him up."

"Why was he looking so bad?" the inspector asked.

"Well, it was a funny story," Mr. Batesby said, looking meditatively through the stranger, who was leaning against the inn wall, "and I didn't quite understand it all. Of course, I saw what was wrong with him at once. Hysteria. I was very firm with him. I said, 'Get a hold on yourself.' He'd been talking to a Wesleyan."

Mr. Batesby paused long enough for the inspector to say, with a slight frown, "I'm almost a Wesleyan myself," gave him a pleasant smile as if he had been waiting for this, and went on: "Quite, quite, and very fine preachers many of them are. But a little unbalanced sometimes—emotional, you know. Too much emotion doesn't do, does it? Like poetry and all that, not stern enough. Thought, intelligence, brain—that's what helps. Well, this man had been saved—he called it saved, and there he was as nervous as could be."

"What was he nervous about if he'd been saved?" the inspector asked idly.

Mr. Batesby smiled again. "It seems funny to say it in cold blood," he said, "but, do you know, he was quite sure he was going to be killed? He didn't know how, he didn't know who, he didn't know when. He'd just been saved at a Wesleyan mission hall and he was going to be killed by the devil. So I heartened him up."

The inspector had come together with a jerk; the young stranger was less energetic and less observable than the flowers in the inn garden behind him.

"Who was this man?" the inspector said. "Did you hear any more of him?"

"Nothing much," Mr. Batesby said. "I rather gathered that he'd been employed somewhere near here and was going to Canada, but he wasn't very clear. It was over in my own church that I actually met him, not at Fardles. So I lent him a little book—two, as a matter of fact. One was called *Present Helps* and one was *The Sand and the Rock*. I must have given away hundreds of them. He sent them back to me a week or two after from London."

"Did he write a letter with them?" the inspector asked.

"Well, he did, in fact," Mr. Batesby said. "A touching little note—very touching. It shows how ideas get hold of people. I believe I've got it somewhere." He felt in his pocket, and from a number of papers extracted a folded letter. "Here we are," he said.

REVEREND SIR,—I return you your books, which you very kindly lent me. I've no doubt they're quite right, but they don't seem to mean the precious Blood. They don't help me when the devil comes. He'll kill me one day, but my blessed Saviour will have me then, I know, but I daren't think of it. I hope he won't hurt me much. It's quite right, I'm not grumbling. I've asked for it all. And Jesus will save me at last.

Thank you for the books, which I return herewith. I've not read them both all as I'm rather worried.

I am,
Reverend sir,

"A nice letter," Mr. Batesby said. "But of course, the devil——!"

"Excuse me, sir," the inspector said, "but is there any address on that letter?"

"Yes," said Mr. Batesby, slightly surprised; "227 Thobblehurst Road, Victoria, S.W."

"Thank you, sir; and the date?"

"May 27th," Mr. Batesby said, staring.

"Humph," the inspector said. "And to think it's within two doors of my own house! A small man, you said, sir?"

"Rather small," Mr. Batesby said. "Oh, decidedly rather small. Rather unintelligent-looking, you know. But did you know him, then?"

"I think I met him once or twice," the inspector said. "If I should want to ask you any more questions, shall you be here?"

"I shall be at my own parish, over there: Ridings, at the Vicarage. The Duke's house is in it you know, in the parish—Ridings Castle. I'm sorry he's a Papist, though in a sense he was born blind."

"Humph," the inspector said again. "Well, I must get off. Good-bye, sir." He fled into the inn.

Against the grey wall Mr. Batesby saw the young stranger's grey figure. "How silent you are," he said. "Thinking, yes, thinking no doubt."

"I was thinking that even a sparrow has its ghost," the other said, "and that all things work together."

"For good," Mr. Batesby concluded.

"For God," the other substituted, and moved away.

In Ridings Castle that afternoon the Duke and Kenneth endeavoured to talk poetry. But both of them were distracted—the Duke by the memory of the Graal and Kenneth by the thought of Barbara; and conversation after conversation either dropped or led them wanderingly back to these subjects. Never, Kenneth thought, had he supposed that so much of English literature was occupied either with the Graal or with madness. Before them at every turn moved the Arthurian chivalry or Tom o' Bedlam. And at last, about tea-time, they both seemed to give up the attempt and fell into a silence, which lasted until Kenneth said rather hesitatingly, "I should like to know how Barbara's getting along."

The Duke shrugged. "Naturally," he said, "but I don't see how you can. You can hardly call at Cully and ask Persimmons."

"What I should like to do would be to run across Rackstraw privately," Kenneth answered. "I've half a mind just to go and hang round a little while on the chance. He might come out for a walk, mightn't he?"

"He might," the Duke said. "I shouldn't, myself, leave my wife, if I had one, alone with Mr. Gregory. But your friend seems to like him."

"I think you're a little unfair," Mornington said. "After all, Lionel hasn't known what we have. He doesn't even know that I've been kicked out of the office."

The Duke, with an effort, said, "I expect I am. But when I think of his getting his foul paws on the Cup, I—I could murder your Archdeacon."

There was another silence, then he went on: "And even now I'm not satisfied. After all, what exactly did this doctor *do*? From what I could see, he hadn't reached her when she fainted."

Kenneth looked up swiftly. "That's what I've been wondering about," he said. "Only it's easy to be deceived. But I was on the stairs above her, and he seemed to be a couple of yards off when she—— she didn't exactly faint, at least it was more like sinking down quite quietly *first*. I suppose she fainted afterwards."

"Well, then," the Duke cried, "will you tell me why we let the Archdeacon give them the Graal?"

"I suppose we'd promised it to him if he would take on the case," Kenneth said doubtfully, "and he'd agreed to."

"But that is exactly what we hadn't," the Duke cried again, knocking a pile of Elizabethan dramatists off the table as he turned, "exactly. I remember perfectly well. The Archdeacon was just going to when we heard her screaming. But he wasn't speaking to the doctor, he was talking to your friend. And even so, he hadn't said more than that he wouldn't have delayed so long *if*—something or other."

"By God, that's right," Kenneth said staring. "But, if it hadn't been promised him and if he didn't help Barbara, what——?"

"Precisely," the Duke said. "What's he doing with it?"

There was another short pause.

485

"In another sense," Kenneth said, "what's he doing with it? Is he with Persimmons? Is it all a put-up job? Or will Persimmons and he fight for it? No, that's not likely. Then it must have been all arranged."

"Well, what about getting it back?" the Duke asked.

"Yes," Kenneth said doubtfully. "More easily said than done, don't you think? We don't even know where this doctor comes from or went to. Unless——" He hesitated.

"Unless?" the Duke asked.

"Unless—when the Chief Constable was talking to Persimmons on Monday—the day before yesterday, by heaven!—I couldn't help hearing something of what they said, and Gregory gave him an address. I remembered it because it was so absurd—3 Lord Mayor's Street, in London somewhere. But I don't quite know what we can do about it. We can't go there and just ask for it."

"Can't we?" the Duke said. "Can't we, indeed? We can go and see what sort of place it is, and whether this Doctor Manasseh hangs out there. And, if he does, we can tell him It belongs to us, and if he makes any objection we can take It. We—at least the Archdeacon—did it before."

"He'll bring the police in," Kenneth demurred. "He must—this time."

"And if he does?" the Duke asked. "Let me get the Graal in my hands for time enough to get it over to Thwaites or someone, and It shall be in Rome before the police can guess what's happening. And there are no extradition treaties yet with the Vatican."

"I suppose there aren't," Kenneth said, arrested by this idea. "What a frightful joke! But what about us?"

"We should be sent to prison for burglary perhaps—'first offenders' and all that sort of thing. And the Bishops ought to rally—and yours too. I should leave a statement for the Cardinal-Archbishop of Westminster. My father is supposed to have had something to do—indirectly—with getting him the Hat."

"But it probably won't be there!" Kenneth objected again.

"Then we're no worse off; they won't distrust us more, and they certainly won't call in the police," the Duke answered. "Of course, if it's still at Cully … Perhaps your friend might know. Look here, Mornington, let's go over and see if we can drop across him." He jumped up and went to the door.

Rather to relieve their irritation than because they wanted to, they set out to walk, after the Duke had flung abroad a general warning that he might have to go to London that night, and came at last to where a private road entered the grounds of Cully and, a little farther on, passed near the cottage of the Rackstraws. Nothing, as the Duke pointed out, was more natural than that Kenneth should wish to see his friend or should hesitate to call at the front doors of Cully. But, as they passed the private road, they saw Lionel and Barbara in the lane before them.

"Hallo," Kenneth said, "this is surprising and delightful. I didn't expect you to be rambling round like this. Is all well again?"

"I'm rather tired and rather lazy," Barbara said happily. "But otherwise I'm very comfortable, thank you."

"The devil you are!" Kenneth said, staring at her, with a smile. "I expected you to be in bed at least."

"I seem to have slept on cushions in Mr. Persimmons's hall till about four, but I woke up feeling quite normal," Barbara answered. "But what a business!" She spoke lightly, but her face grew whiter as she referred to it.

"It's all over, anyhow," Lionel said hastily. "I shall screw another's week's holiday out of Stephen, Kenneth, and we'll go to the seaside or something for a few days—without Adrian."

"What's going to happen to Adrian?" Kenneth asked.

"He's going to stop here," Lionel answered. "He's got very fond of one of the maids here, and he adores Gregory, and his motors and telephones and Chinese masks and things."

"And Gregory's willing to have him?" Kenneth asked.

"Loves him, he says," Lionel answered. "Good luck to them both. I don't want another twenty-four hours like the last. Of course, we must see this doctor fellow again first; that will be the day after to-morrow."

"Do you really think it was he that helped you, Babs?" Kenneth said.

Lionel looked at his wife. "Well, Babs doesn't know," he said, "not being in a state then to notice such things. And *I* don't know. If it wasn't him, what was it? And yet he was some way off and didn't seem to have a chance to do anything."

"I can't tell you anything," Barbara said gravely, "for I don't know. There was nothing but a darkness of the most dreadful pressure—and the edge of the pit I was falling towards. Nothing could stop me and just as I fell—no, it's all right, Lionel; I don't mind this part—just as I fell I was entirely all right. I fell into safety. I was just quite happy. I can't tell you—it was just being swallowed up by peace. And like—I don't know— like recognizing someone; when one says, "Oh, joy! there's—" someone or other. I knew him at once."

The three young men considered her gravely. After a minute she went on: "So that now to look back on it's like having had a tooth out, unpleasant but small. I don't mind talking of it. But when I was there it seemed as if things so wicked I could never have thought of them had got their claws into me."

"*You* could never have thought of them!" Lionel scoffed tenderly.

She smiled at him, and then, as she leaned against the gate of the Cully grounds she unconsciously stretched her arms out along the top bar on either side. So, her feet close together, her palms turned upward, her face towards the evening sky, she seemed to hang remote, till Kenneth said sharply, "Don't, Babs; you look as if you were crucified."

She brought her eyes down to meet his without otherwise moving, then, looking past him, she came together suddenly, took a step forward, and cried out: "Oh, joy! it's——" and stopped, laughing and embarrassed.

Her companions looked round in surprise. Behind them, as they stood clustered by the gate, stood an ordinary looking young man smiling recognition at Barbara. She blushed as she shook hands, but, with her usual swiftness, raced into an apology. "It's extraordinarily silly, but I *can't* remember your name. But I'm so pleased you're here. Do forgive me and tell me."

"My name is John," the other said, "though I don't think you ever heard it. But we've certainly met several times."

"I know, I know," Barbara said. "Stop a moment and I shall remember. It was … it was just before I was married, surely…. No, since then, too. Somewhere only the other day. How stupid! Lionel, can't you help?" She turned a face crimson with surprise, delight, and shame to her husband.

But Lionel shook his head firmly. "I do seem to have seen you before," he said to the stranger, "but I haven't the ghost of a notion where."

"It really doesn't matter," the other said. "To be remembered is the chief thing. I think I have met these other gentlemen too."

"It's too absurd," Kenneth said, laughing outright, "but for a minute when I saw you I thought you were a priest I'd seen somewhere. But I couldn't at all fix where, so I suppose I haven't."

"It was certainly in church somewhere," the stranger said, and glanced at the Duke.

"At Oriel," the Duke said, "—in—whose rooms was it? But not lately, I think."

"Not so very much lately," answered the other. "But you haven't quite forgotten me, I'm glad to see."

"I don't understand it at all," Barbara, still flushed and excited, answered. "I feel as if it were only to-day. You weren't at … the house, were you?" she asked doubtfully.

The stranger smiled back. "I know Mr. Persimmons, and he will know me better soon. But don't worry. How's Adrian?"

"Very well, thank you," Lionel said; and rather hesitatingly looked at Barbara. "Babs, don't you think you ought to get back? My wife's not been very well," he added to the stranger, "and I don't want her to get at all excited. You understand, I'm certain."

The young man smiled again. "I understand very well indeed," he answered. "But there is no more danger for her here. Believe certainly that this universe also carries its salvation in its heart." He looked at Barbara. "We have met in places that shall not easily be forgotten," he said, "before you were married, and since, and to-day also. Sleep securely to-night, the gates of hell have no more power over you. And you, my lord Duke, because you have loved the thing that is mine, this also shall save you in the end. Only remember that in your heart as well as your house you shall keep vigil and prayer till the Master of the Graal shall come." He came a step nearer to Kenneth. "But for you I have no message," he said, "except the message of the Graal—*'Surely I come quickly*. To-night thou shalt be with Me in Paradise.'"

He moved backward, and, as they involuntarily glanced at each other, seemed to step aside, so that no one was quite certain which way he had gone. Or, rather, Lionel and the Duke were not certain. Barbara was gazing at Kenneth with rapt eyes. "It was he that was at the edge of the pit to-day," she breathed. "To-night! O Kenneth!"

Kenneth stood silent for a minute or two, then he said only: "Well, good night, Babs," as she gave him both her hands. "Good night, Lionel: I should certainly screw an extra week out of Stephen." He laid his hand on the Duke's arm. "Shall we go straight on to London?" he asked.

The evening had grown darker before the Archdeacon, wandering alone in his garden, saw at the gate the figure of the priest-king. He had been standing still for a moment looking out towards the road, and to his absent eyes it seemed almost as if the form had shaped itself from the sky and the fields and road about it. He came down to it and paused, and words sounded in his mind, but whether from without or from within he no more knew than whether this presence had moved along the road or come forth from the universe which it expressed. "'The time is at hand,'" it said; "'I will keep the passover with my disciples.'"

"Ah, fair sweet lord, Thou knowest," he answered aloud.

"I am a messenger only," the voice, if voice it were, uttered, "but I am the precursor of the things that are to be. I am John and I am Galahad and I am Mary; I am the Bearer of the Holy One, the Graal, and the keeper of the Graal. I have kept it always, whether I dwelt in the remote places of the world and kings rode after me or whether I removed to the farther parts of man's mind. All magic and all holiness is through me, and though men stole the Graal from me ages since I have been with it for ever. Brother and friend, the night of His coming is at hand."

"I have watched many nights," the Archdeacon answered, "and behold His mercy endureth for ever."

"Also I have watched with you," the voice said, "yet not I, but He that sent me. You shall watch yet through a deeper night, and after that I will come to this place on the second morning from now, and I will begin the mysteries of my Lord, and thereafter He shall do what He will, and you shall see the end of these things. Only be strong and of a good courage."

The form was gone. The Archdeacon looked out over the countryside, and his lips moved in their accustomed psalm.

Chapter Fourteen

THE BIBLE OF MRS. HIPPY

As the inspector was carried back to London in the first available train, he found himself slipping from side to side on the smooth ice of his uncertain mind. Impartially he considered that this sudden return was likely to be as futile as any other attempt he had made at solving the problem of the murder. But, on the other hand, there could not be many rather undersized men in the neighbourhood of London who within the last two months had been intimately connected with Wesleyan Methodism and with death. When Mr. Batesby had spoken that morning it had seemed as if two streams of things—actual events and his own meditations—had flowed gently together; as if not he, but Life were solving the problem in the natural process of the world. He reminded himself now that such a simplicity was unlikely; explanations did not lucidly arise from mere accidents and present themselves as all but an ordered whole. He dimly remembered Mrs. Hippy, the occupant of the house next but two to his own; he remembered that she was an acquaintance of his wife, who had gone with her to certain bazaars, sales of work, and even church services. If she had had a lodger who had disappeared, why hadn't his wife mentioned it before? It was such a failure on the part of his intimates that the inspector always expected, he told himself, and always found.

His wife was staying with her mother, so the inspector lunched near King's Cross, and then went on to 227 Thobblehurst Road. Mrs. Hippy came to the door, and appeared delighted to see him. "Why, come in, inspector," she said. "I thought Mrs. Colquhoun said you were going away."

"So I did," the inspector said, following her to the drawing-room, as it was solemnly called, which looked on to the street. "But I had some inquiries to make which brought me back."

"Really?" Mrs. Hippy said, rather absently. "Inspector, can you think of a fish in two syllables?"

"A fish?" the inspector said vaguely. "Walrus? salmon? mackerel? No, that's three."

"It might *count* as two perhaps," Mrs. Hippy answered. "Why did the por-poise? Because it saw the mack-reel."

"Eh?" the inspector said. "What's the idea exactly?"

Mrs. Hippy, plunging at a number of papers on the chesterfield, produced an effort in bright green and gold, entitled in red *Puzzles and Riddles: a Magazine for All*. "They're offering a prize," she said, "for the best ten questions and answers of that sort. They say it's one of the best ways, but rather out of date. But I think they're splendid. Look, I've done four. Why does the shoe-lace?"

She paused, got no answer, and said delightedly, "Because the button-holes. The next——"

"Good! Splendid!" the inspector cried. "Splendid, Mrs. Hippy. I suppose they'll print them all if you win. And you're sure to. You'd be good at cross-word puzzles. But I won't disturb you long. I only came to ask if you could tell me anything about a fellow named Pattison you had stopping here."

"Mr. Pattison?" Mrs. Hippy said, opening her eyes. "Why, do you want to arrest him? I don't know where he is; he left me a month ago."

488

"Where did he go to? Can you tell me that?" Colquhoun asked.

"Canada," Mrs. Hippy answered. "At least, he said he was going to. But he was a funny creature altogether. Not sociable, if you understand. Dull, heavy, so to speak. I lent him all the old numbers of this"—she waved *Puzzles and Riddles*, "but he didn't work out a single one, though I told him the easiest. And he spoilt my Bible, scribbling all over it. My mother's Bible too—not the one I take to church. But there, it always seems to be like that when you try and help. People don't deserve it, and that's a fact."

"Perhaps you won't mind helping *me*, all the same," the inspector said. "Could I see the Bible? And did you *know* that he was going to Canada?"

"Not to say *know*," Mrs. Hippy said, looking longingly at the competition. "He *said* he was going; and one morning he wished me good-bye and said he'd send me a postcard. But he never has done."

Further interrogation made it clear that her knowledge was of the slightest. She sometimes let two rooms, furnished, to a single gentleman, and the late Mr. Pattison, arriving at Victoria one day and seeing the card in her window, had taken them, with solemn assurances of respectability and a month's rent in advance. He had seemed to be rather worried, though what about Mrs. Hippy had never understood. He had come to the Wesleyan Church she herself attended several times, but it had not seemed to calm his distress. He had borrowed a Bible from her, and had scribbled everywhere in it. Finally he had told her that he would be leaving for Canada shortly, and had departed one morning, carrying a suitcase and bidding her a final farewell.

As the rooms had been thoroughly "done out" and were now empty, awaiting the arrival of Mrs. Hippy's married sister, the inspector went through them with care and without success. He then withdrew with the Bible to his own deserted house and gave himself up to its study.

The scribbling seemed entirely haphazard. It was everywhere—on the fly-leaves, in the margins, and here and there right across the pages themselves. It consisted largely of fragmentary prayers, ejaculations, and even texts. A phrase which occurred on the printed page would be rewritten and underscored in the margin; and this seemed to have been done especially with such phrases as record or assert the Mercy and Compassion of God. Sometimes this repetition would be varied by a wild "I believe, I believe" scrawled against a verse, by an "He saves," or a "God is love." On the other hand, certain verses were marked by a line and a question-mark. "Depart from me, ye cursed," was heavily lined; so was "he that is filthy, let him be filthy still"; so was "I have delivered him over to Satan." The sayings about the unpardonable sin were scratched heavily out; so was "He will have mercy on whom He will have mercy." In the midst of these fantastic scrawls there appeared here and there a carefully written comment. Against "God shall be all in all" was written in a small, sedate hand: "Lies," and against "reconciling the world to Himself" appeared, similarly, "Not true."

The fly-leaves, the back of the New Testament half-title, and the spaces between the various books were occupied with longer jottings. The first of these seemed to be a kind of discussion. It was not easy to decipher, but it appeared to be a summing up of the promises of salvation and an *argumentum ad hominem* at the end. But the very end was the words, heavily printed: "I am damned."

This sort of thing, whatever religious mania it suggested, was not of much use to the inspector. It brought him no nearer to discovery why the murdered man, if Mr. Pattison were he, had got himself murdered. Farther on, however, he found himself, at the end of Deuteronomy, confronted with the single word: "Gregory." Nothing followed, but it raised his hopes wonderfully. Still, it was one thing to read "Gregory" and another to prove that Gregory had slain the writer. He went on turning the pages.

At the end of Job there was a whole sentence. "He won't let me go and Jesus won't get me away." This might be Gregory or it might, as the inspector suspected, be meant for the devil. Well, if Mr. Pattison and the devil were on those terms, all wasn't lost yet.

Between two of the minor prophets was scrawled: "I saw her to-day; so she is out"; after which there was a blank, till, on the back, of the half-title of the "New Testament of our Lord and Saviour Jesus Christ," there came this longer note:

"I will put it all down. I am James Montgomery Pattison. I am forty-six years old, and I know that the devil will kill me soon. I have done his will against my wishes too long and I cannot get away from him now. When I heard Mr. Macdermott preach I thought my heart was opened and the Lord had come to me and saved me, and I testified to my master, who was a worse sinner than I. But he has me too fast and I cannot escape. I have served him and the devil together for twenty-four years, since he caught me robbing him. I have done forgery and worse. I have stood by and seen him swear the woman I seduced into prison for soliciting him; and now I cannot get free. He is going to kill me; it is in his eyes and face." There came an outburst of appeals to God and to Christ, and the record resumed. "He had Louise put into prison to torture me. It was him all through." There was a blank space, and then, written in the steady, sedate hand, "I have gone back to him altogether, and he will kill me. This is what comes of God."

On the very last page of the book, enclosed in a correct panel, with decorative curves flowing round it, was printed in clearly and precisely: "Mr. Gregory Persimmons, Cully, Nr. Fardles, Hertfordshire."

The inspector shut the book and went into the kitchen to make himself tea.

Chapter Fifteen

'TO-NIGHT THOU SHALT BE WITH ME IN PARADISE'

Lord Mayor's Street in the evening seemed always, if by any chance it could, to attract and contain such mist as might be about. A faint vapour made the air dim, especially round the three shops, and caused passers-by to remark regularly either that the evening was a bit misty or that the evenings were drawing in or that there might be something of a fog by the morning. But for Gregory Persimmons, as he came swiftly into it about nine o'clock on the same day, the chemist's shop rode London like a howdah on the back of an elephant, the symbol and shelter of the prince that ruled the armies of the air. He reached the door, which was still ajar, pushed it open, entered, and closed it after him.

The shop was dark, after the street light a few paces away outside, but the gleam of a light came from the inner room. For the first time since Gregory had known it the Greek was not there, but as he hesitated a voice sounded from within.

"Is that you, Gregory?" Manasseh called.

"It is I," Gregory answered, crossed the shop, and went in.

The room was bare and dirty. On a table under the window and exactly opposite the door in to the shop, the Graal stood exposed, under the light of a single electric bulb which hung without a shade from the middle of the ceiling. There were no pictures and no books; a few chairs stood about, and in one corner was a high closed cabinet. A dilapidated carpet covered the floor.

The Greek was sitting in a chair on the left of the Graal. Manasseh had apparently been walking up and down, but he stood still as Gregory came in, and looked at him anxiously. "Well," he said, "have you brought the child?"

"Not to-night," Persimmons said. "I thought it better not. You or someone else, Manasseh, have worked wonders. She's almost well again, and wanted to see him. So I promised she should to-morrow, and he's coming to London with me to-morrow afternoon to go to—I forget where he is to go to. It doesn't matter. When do we leave England?"

"The day after," Manasseh said. "I'm supposed to go down and see the woman again that morning. But as things are I don't know …"

"Send them a wire in the morning," Gregory suggested. "'Detained till this afternoon.' We shall be at Harwich by then."

"I don't know why you're so keen on the child," Manasseh said morosely. "You won't have him—interfered with at all, even to make the journey easier?"

"The journey will be all right," Gregory said. "Jessie's coming too. Jessie is the girl who looks after him. It's quite safe—she doesn't know exactly, but she *will* come. She's got no relations near at hand; she's a sensuous little bitch, and she has her wanton eyes on Mr. Persimmons of Cully. She'll hope to be compromised; I know her. And she knows she may have to go on a journey, but not where or why."

Manasseh nodded. "But why take him?" he insisted.

"Because I owe him for a debt to the Sabbath," Gregory answered. "Because we haven't often the chance of such a pure and entire oblation. It's wonderful the way he's taken to me, and I think we shall make him a lord of power before we have done. Isn't that worth more than sending him silly? And Jessie can be dropped anywhere if she's inconvenient." He walked across to the table. "And what about you?" he asked. "Do we take this with us, or do you still want to destroy it now?"

"No," Manasseh said. "I have thought of it, and we will take it. There may be something in what you said."

"What I said?" Gregory asked, whistling softly as he surveyed the Cup.

"We may be able to use it for destruction—to destroy *through* it," Manasseh said. "I have dreamt that we might learn to destroy earth and heaven through it, or at least all intelligible experience of them among men. It is death as well as life, and who knows how far death may go? They talk of their Masses, you talk of your Black Mass, but there may be such a Mass of Death said with this as shall blast the world for ever. But you and I are not great enough for that."

Gregory answered softly, "I think you may be right, Manasseh. Bear with me, for I am young in these things. I know the current of desire in which all things move, and I have guided it a little as I will. But I see there are deeper things below." He looked at the Greek. "And what do you say," he asked, "who are older than we?"

The Greek answered, his eyes fixed on the Graal: "All things are indivisible and one. You cannot wholly destroy and you cannot wholly live, but you can change mightily and for ever as any of our reckoning goes. Even I cannot see down infinity. Make it agreeable to your lusts while the power is yours, for there are secret ways down which it may pass even now and you shall not hold it."

Gregory smiled, and filliped the Graal with a finger. "Do you know," he said, "I should like to annoy the Archdeacon a little." He stood still suddenly and cried out: "And there is a way by which it may be done. I have tried it, and I know. This is the circle of all souls, and I will gather them and marry them as I please. I will bring them from this world and from another and I will bind the lost with the living till the living itself be lost."

Manasseh moved nearer to him. "Tell me," he said; "you have a great thought."

"I have a thought that is pleasant to my mind," Gregory said, "and this is what we will do. There went out from among us lately by my act a weak, wretched, unhappy soul that sought to find its god and in its last days returned to me and was utterly mine. It was willing to die when I slew it, and in the shadows it waits still upon my command. We will draw this back, and we will marry it to this priest, body and soul, so that he shall live with it by day and by night, and come indeed in the end to know not which is he. And let us see then if he will war against us for the Graal."

"This you can do if you will," Manasseh said, "for I have seen spirits recalled, though not by means of the Graal. But can you bind it so closely to the priest?"

"Assuredly you can," the Greek said, "if you have the conditions. But they are exact. You must have that body here into which you will bring that soul in contact—I do not know if it could be done at a distance, but I do not think it has been done, and I am sure you have no time to try. And you must have that soul at your command, and I think you have. And you must have a means of passage, and you have it in this Cup. And you must have a very strong desire, and this you have, both of you, for this is at once possession and destruction. And you are the better for knowing the worst, and this I do, and I will set my power with yours if you choose."

"We must have the body here," Gregory said. "But—will he come?"

"I do not see why he should not come if he is asked," the Greek said. "Cannot Manasseh bring him with some tale of the woman?"

"To-morrow night is the last night we can be sure of having in England," Manasseh answered, "if we wish to escape with both the Graal and the child. But he might come for that."

They were silent, standing or sitting around the Cup, where it seemed to await their decision in a helpless bondage. They were still silent some minutes later when a sudden knock sounded on the door of the shop. Gregory started, and both he and Manasseh glanced inquiringly at the Greek, who said casually: "It may be someone for medicine or it may be they have followed Gregory. Go you, Manasseh. If they ask for me, tell them I am away from home to-night; and if for Gregory, tell them he is not here."

Manasseh obeyed, pulling the door to behind him. Gregory smiled at the Greek. "Do you really give them medicine?" he asked.

The Greek shrugged his shoulders. "Why not?" he said. "I don't poison ants; they may as well live as die. But there are not many who will come."

They heard Manasseh cross the shop and open the door, then several exclamations at once in different voices. Then a gay voice, at the sound of which Gregory started and looked round, said: "Why, if it isn't the doctor himself! Now this is fortunate. My dear doctor, we've been talking about you all day. Let's see, were you properly introduced to the Duke? No, oh, no, don't shut the door. No, I beg you. We've come all the way from Fardles—Castra Parvulorum, you know; the camp of the children—to ask you a question—two questions. Is Gregory here by any chance? That's not one of them. No, really—sorry to push, but … Thank you ever so much; you can shut it now."

Under this rush of talk had sounded Manasseh's exclamatory protests and the scuffle of feet. Gregory put out a hand to the Graal, but the Greek made a motion with his hand and checked him. "How many are there?" he asked softly. Gregory tiptoed to the narrow opening and peeped through. "Two, I think," he whispered, returning. "Mornington and the Duke. I can't see or hear anyone else. Hadn't we better move that?"

The Greek turned a face of sudden malignity on him. "Fool," he said, "will you always run from your enemies?" He stood up as he spoke and began to move the few chairs noiselessly back against the wall.

In the shop, Mornington was plying Manasseh with conversation. "We felt so curious about the Graal," he said, "and to tell you the truth, so curious about what you'd done to Barbara Rackstraw, that we simply had to come and ask you about it. The Duke's done nothing but rave about it ever since. Unrecognized genius, you know—Mrs. Eddy, Sir Herbert Barker. You took the Graal, so you must have done something. Manasseh is an honourable man." He stopped suddenly and sniffed. "I'm sure you've got Gregory here," he said. "It smells like a dung-heap. You don't mind me going in?"

Manasseh apparently had jumped in his way. There was a slight scuffle, then Kenneth said pleasantly: "Hold him, Ridings. Bring him along too and let's look round."

The Greek stooped down, took hold of the carpet, wrenched it from the occasional nail that held it down, and flung it to one side of the room. The floor beneath was marked with what looked like chalk in two broad parallel lines running from about two-thirds of the depth of the room to the two posts of the communicating door. At the end of the room these two lines were joined by a complicated diagram, which Gregory seemed to recognize, for he caught his breath and said: "Will it hold him?"

The Greek threw a cushion on the floor between the diagram and the table on which the Graal stood, and sank down on it. "This is our protection," he said. "Call to Manasseh that he does not enter, for this is the way of death. I have charged these barriers with power, and they shall wither whoever comes between them. Open the door, stand aside, and be still."

Gregory went to the door and drew it open by reaching to the top till the handle came within reach; he seized it and pulled it back till the whole entrance lay open between the equal lines. The Greek peered forward into the little dark shop, and saw dimly Kenneth's figure opposite him at the same time that Kenneth saw the Graal.

"My dear Ridings, he's been admiring it," Mornington said. "The workmanship, probably. It was Ephesus, I fancy, that the dear delightful Gregory told us it came from. There's a gentleman here sitting on the floor who may be the carrier. Hobson, you know, and John what-you-may-call-him in that very disastrous Christmas thing of Dickens's. Or perhaps they've been having their favourite food. The Graal, I remember, in a charming way always provided you with that. What is yours, doctor? Something Eastern, no doubt. Rice? What a horrible thing to waste the Graal on!"

He had come to the doorway as he spoke, and drew a revolver from his pocket. "The Duke's really," he went on. "One of those little domestic utensils you can pick up for almost nothing at a sale. Have you got him, Ridings? There seems to be a pavement-artist somewhere in this establishment; the most original little sketches adorn the floor."

"Take care," the Duke's voice cried. "There is hell near us now."

"I think it very likely," Kenneth said, "but you can't expect me to think much of hell if Gregory is one of its kings." He took two or three swift steps into the room, flung a quick glance behind him lest he should be attacked from the wall he passed, and, even as he did so, staggered and put his hand to his heart. The Duke heard him gasp, and, still clutching Manasseh, pushed forward, to see what was happening. Kenneth had reeled to one of the white lines and was stumbling blindly, now forward, now backward, drawing deep choking breaths. The Greek had thrust his face out, and as the Duke saw it in the full light he gave a little gasp of dismay. For the face that he saw looked at him from a great distance and yet was itself that distance. It was white and staring and sick with a horrible sickness; he shut his eyes before this evil. All the gorgeous colours and pomps of sin of which he had been so often warned had disappeared; the war between good and evil existed no longer, for the thing beneath the Graal was not fighting but vomiting. Once he realized that his eyes were closed he forced himself to open them, saw Kenneth almost fall across the space between the lines, and called to him. Then he flung Manasseh from him to the floor, cried out on God and the Mother of God, and sprang forward; but as he reached the doorway he felt his strength oozing from him. Hollows opened within him; he clutched at the doorpost, and, as he touched it, seemed to feel this also drag him sideways and downward. He crashed to the floor while Kenneth, gathering all his life's energy together, forced himself two steps nearer his aim, moaned as even that energy failed, dropped to his knees, and at last, choking and twisting, fell dead on the diagram before the Greek.

Manasseh had got to his feet, but he remained leaning against the door of the shop as Gregory against the wall of the inner room. The Duke, unable to move, lay prostrate across the threshold. So, as they watched, they saw the body of the dead man shiver and lift itself a little, as if moved by a strong wind. Gradually there appeared, rising from it, a kind of dark cloud, which floated upwards and outwards on all sides, and was at last so thick that the form itself could no longer be discerned. Manasseh watched with eyes of triumph. But Gregory was curiously shaken, for he, less instructed in the high ways of magic, recoiled, not from the destruction of his enemy, but from the elements which accompanied it. He shrank from the face of the sorcerer; like the Duke, he found himself in a state for which he had not been prepared and at which he trembled in horror. A sickness crept within him; was this the end of victory and lordship and the Sabbath, and this the consummation of the promises and of desire? The sudden action had precipitated him down a thousand spirals of the slow descent, and he hung above the everlasting void. He sought to keep his eyes fixed on the symbol of triumph, the dark cloud that streamed upward from floor to ceiling in front of him, but they were drawn back still to the face which dominated it and him.

Slowly, as they watched, the pillar of cloud began to sink, withdrawing into itself. The colour of it seemed to change also, from a dense black to a smoky and then to an ordinary grey. Quicker and quicker it fell, hovered for a few minutes, and at last collapsed entirely. There remained, in the place where the body had been, nothing but a spreading heap of dust.

The Duke, defeated in mind and body, and with too young a soul to dare the tempest, made yet some effort to assert the cause in which he believed. He raised himself on one hand as he lay and cried out in the great Latin he loved—loved rather perhaps as literature than as religion, but still as a strength more ancient and more enduring than himself. "Profiscere, anima Christiana," he stammered, "de hoc mundo, in nomine Patris...."

"Be silent, you!" Manasseh snarled, and, with one of those grotesque movements which attend on all crises, took from the counter a small bottle as the nearest missile and flung it. It smashed on the floor, and the Greek's eyes moved toward it and came to rest on the Duke. He stood up with an effort, and motioned to Gregory to draw the carpet again over the magnetized passage of death. When this was done, the three gathered round the Duke, who half rose to his feet and was overthrown again by the touch of the Greek's hand.

"Will you not destroy him also?" Manasseh asked, half greedily, half timidly.

The Greek slowly shook his head. "I am very weary," he said, "and the strength is gone from the figure. If that other had not despised us, I do not know whether I should have won. And, since he is here, unless you will kill him yourself, you should use him for what you desire to do."

"How can we use him?" Gregory asked, meditatively prodding the Duke with his foot, his momentary fear gone.

"Let him write and tell this priest whom you hate that he and the Graal are here—and that which was the other—and that he must come quickly to free them."

"But will he write?" Gregory asked.

"Certainly he will write," the Greek said, "or one of us will write with his hand."

"Do you write then," Manasseh said, "for you are the greatest among us."

"I will do it if you wish," the Greek said. "Lift him partly up, and give me pencil and paper."

As Gregory tore a page from his pocket-book, Manasseh dragged and pushed at the Duke till he sat at last leaning against the door. The Greek knelt down beside him, put one arm round his shoulders, and laid the right hand over his. To the Duke it seemed as if an enormous cloud of darkness had descended upon him, in the midst of which some unknown strength moved him at its will. In the conflict of his inner being with this tyranny the control of his body was lost; the battle was not in that outer region, but in a more central place. Ignorant and helpless, his hand wrote as the Greek's controlling mind bade, though the handwriting was his own.

"Come, if you can by any means," the letter ran, "for That and we are here. The bearer of this will tell you as much as he will, but believe him if he says that without you there is an end to all.—Ridings."

The Greek released the Duke and rose. Gregory took the note, read it, and shook his head. "I do not think he will be deceived," he said doubtfully.

"But what can he——" Manasseh began, but the Greek silenced him with a gesture and said, "He will do what he must do. There is more than we and he which moves about us now. I think he will come, for I think that the battle is joined, and till that which is with us or that which is with them is loosened it cannot end. Take care of your ways to-morrow."

"And who is to be the bearer?" Gregory asked.

"That you shall be," the Greek said.

"But how much shall I tell him?" Gregory asked again uncertainly.

The Greek turned upon him. "Fool," he said, "I tell you you cannot choose. You will do and say what is meant for you, and so will he. And to-morrow there shall be an end."

Chapter Sixteen

THE SEARCH FOR THE HOUSE

Tea, tobacco, meditation, and sleep brought the inspector no nearer a solution of his problem. On the assumption that J. M. Pattison was the murdered man, there had still appeared no reason why Gregory Persimmons should have murdered him. It was true that so far he knew nothing of their relations. If Pattison had been blackmailing Persimmons now—but then why the scribblings in the Bible? Some ancient vengeance, he rather desperately wondered, some unreasoning hate? But he could not get away from a feeling that, even so, it was the wrong way round. Small nonentities did sometimes murder squires, bankers, or peers, but it was not normal that a squire should murder a small nonentity. Besides, religious mania seemed to come into it somewhere. But whether Mr. Persimmons or the deceased was affected by it, or both of them, the inspector could not decide. And why the devil? Why, in God's name, the devil? The inspector's view of the devil was roughly that the devil was something in which children believed, but which was generally known not to exist, certainly not as taking any active part in the affairs of the world; these, generally speaking, were run by three parties—the police, criminals, and the ordinary public. The inspector tended to see these last two classes as one; all specialists tend so to consider humanity as divided into themselves and the mass to be affected. Doctors see it in the two sections of themselves and patients potential or actual; clerics in themselves and disciples; poets in themselves and readers (or non-readers; but that is the mere wickedness of mankind); explorers in themselves and stay-at-homes; and so on. The inspector, however, was driven by the definitions of law to admit that the public was not as a whole and altogether criminal, and he inevitably tended to consider it more likely that Mr. Pattison should be guilty than that Mr. Persimmons should be. Only someone had strangled Mr. Pattison, and Mr. Pattison's own expectation seemed to point direct to Mr. Persimmons.

Colquhoun went over in his mind the incidents which had led him to this point—his failure to connect anyone directly with the crime, his irritation with Stephen Persimmons and Lionel Rackstraw, his anger with Sir Giles, his discovery of Gregory's connection with Stephen and Sir Giles, his not very hopeful descent on Fardles. His conflict with Ludding had relieved, but not enlightened him. He came to the events of the morning and the way in which the young stranger had recognized him. Of course, more people knew Tom Fool … no doubt, but he had a feeling that he knew the face. He thought of it vaguely, as Mrs. Lucksparrow and Ludding had done, as a foreigner's. The Duke had thought of it in connection with the high friendships of his Oxford days; Kenneth as related to his intelligence of the Church and its order; Sir Giles had seen it with equal curiosity and fear—but this was almost purely intellectual, and did not suggest the revival of some past vivid experience. Gregory and the Archdeacon had answered to it more passionately, as somehow symbolical of a mode of real existence; as Barbara had recognized in it at once the safety and peace which had succoured her in the house of the infernal things. Nor, had Gregory remembered it—but the crisis of Kenneth's death had put it out of his mind—was it without significance that the Greek had seemed to feel a power moving under and through the activities of his opponents.

But these things were not known to Colquhoun, who, nevertheless, found himself trying to recollect who the stranger was. He had met foreigners enough in his life, and he was driven at last to believe that it must have been on a visit of the Infanta of Spain some time before that their meeting had taken place; he had interviewed enough members of the Spanish police then for more than one face to have been seen and since forgotten, till chance rediscovered it. Chance also had directed the conversation with Mr. Batesby to fear and his past experiences, and so to the appeal of the late James Montgomery Pattison. At least, chance and the stranger between them, for it had been he who had asked the occasional helming question. He tried to consider whether this stranger could have had anything to do with the murder, but found himself foiled; when his mind brought the assumed Spaniard into relation with any other being one of them faded and was gone. It was chance, of course; and chance had done him a good turn—up to a point, anyhow.

He took his troubles to the Assistant Commissioner the next morning, who listened to his report carefully, and seemed disposed to make further inquiries. "On Monday," he said, "Colonel Conyers mentioned Gregory Persimmons to me as having taken part with him in a curious little chase after a chalice which had been more or less stolen by the Duke of the North Ridings and the Archdeacon of Fardles. This Persimmons assured us he wouldn't prosecute, and that made it very difficult for us to move. But I went to tea with the Duchess on Tuesday and had a chat with the Duke."

"And did he admit that he'd stolen it?" the astonished inspector asked.

"Well, he seemed to think it really belonged to the Archdeacon," the Assistant Commissioner answered, "but he was rather stiff about it, told me he had reason to believe that the most serious attempts were being made to obtain possession of it, and even talked of magic."

"Talked of *what*?" the inspector asked, more bewildered than before.

"Magic," the chief said. "*The Arabian Nights*, inspector, and people being turned into puppy-dogs. All rubbish, of course, but he must have had *something* in his mind—and connected with Persimmons apparently. I had Professor Ribblestone-Ridley tell me what's known about Ephesian chalices, but it didn't help much. There seem to be four or five fairly celebrated chalices that come from round there, but they're all in the possession of American millionaires, except one which was at Kieff. I did wonder whether it was that—a lot of these Russian valuables are drifting over here. But I still don't see why the Duke should have bolted with it, or why Persimmons should have refused to get it back. Unless Persimmons *had* stolen it. Could the deceased Pattison have been mixed up in some unsavoury business of getting it over?"

"Bolsheviks, sir?" the inspector asked, with a grin.

"I know, I know," the Assistant Commissioner said. "Still, 'wolf,' you know … there *are* Bolshevik affairs of the kind."

"I suppose it's possible," Colquhoun allowed. "But, then, did Pattison mean the Bolsheviks by the devil?"

His chief shook his head. "Religion plays the deuce with a man's sanity," he said regretfully. "Your clergyman told you he thought he was saved, and in that state there's nothing people won't say or do."

"It might be one of the American chalices," the inspector submitted.

"It might," the other said. "But we should have been warned of the theft from New York, probably. It might also be the Holy Graal, which Ribblestone-Ridley says, according to some traditions, came from Ephesus."

"The Holy Graal," the inspector said doubtfully. "Hadn't that something to do with the Pope?"

"It's supposed to be the cup Christ used at the Last Supper—so I suppose you might say so," the Assistant Commissioner answered almost as doubtfully. "However, as that Cup, if it ever existed, isn't likely to exist *now*, we needn't really worry about that. No, Colquhoun, I lean to Kieff. I wonder whether the Duke would tell me anything." He looked at the inspector. "Would you like to go and ask him?" he finished.

"Well, sir, I'd rather you did," Colquhoun said. "I like to have some hold on people when what I'm asking them is as vague as all that—it seems to help things on."

The Assistant Commissioner looked at the telephone. "I wonder," he said. "We don't know much, do we? A chalice and a Bible and a clergyman. What an infernally religious case this is getting! And an Archdeacon on the outskirts.

"Perhaps Persimmons has killed the Archdeacon by now," he added hopefully as he took off the receiver.

The Duke, it appeared, when he got through to the butler, was not in London. He had been up for two nights, but had returned to the country on Wednesday—yesterday—morning. He had been accompanied (this when it was understood who was inquiring) by the Archdeacon of Fardles and a Mr. Mornington. They had both returned with the Duke. Should Mr. Thwaites be called to the telephone? Mr. Thwaites was—no, not his Grace's secretary; no, nor his Grace's valet; a sort of general utility man to his Grace, in the best sense, of course.

The Commissioner hesitated, but he didn't want to seem to be asking questions about the Duke, and decided to try Ridings Castle first. He asked for the trunk call, and sat back to wait for it.

"It all seems to be mixed up together, sir," Colquhoun said. "There was a Mr. Mornington at those publishing offices; it may be another man, of course—but there's a Persimmons and a Mornington there, and a Persimmons and a Mornington here."

"And a Bible all written over with Persimmons there, and a chalice that Persimmons stole or had stolen here," the other said. "Yes. It's odd. And a corpse there. We only want a corpse here to make a nice even pattern."

Scotland Yard not being usually kept waiting for its trunk calls, they had not broken the few minutes' silence by any further remarks before the housekeeper at Castle Ridings had been notified that she was wanted at the telephone. No, the Duke was not in the country. He and Mr. Mornington had left for London last night. By train—the car had been away for a day for some minor repairs. No, nothing was known of his Grace's return. He had said he should be at Grosvenor Square. What had the Duke's movements been yesterday? He and Mr. Mornington had arrived, unexpectedly, for lunch. They had gone out walking in the afternoon, and the Duke had said they might not be back. Where had they gone? She did not know; she had heard the Duke say something about a Mrs. Rackstraw to Mr. Mornington after he had told her they might not be back. Yes, Rackstraw. Could she give any message?

The Assistant Commissioner rang off and looked at the inspector, who was in a state of some excitement.

"That *damned* Rackstraw," he said. "He's always coming in. He lunches out with Sir Giles Tumulty and a man gets killed in his room. The Duke goes out to call on his wife and the Duke disappears."

"I wonder if we've got the other corpse," his chief said. "I think, Colquhoun, we might go and see what this Thwaites fellow can tell us. It's all right, no doubt, but I don't seem quite to like it."

Thwaites, when at Grosvenor Square he was summoned to the presence, seemed at first, if not recalcitrant, at least reluctant. He disclaimed any knowledge of the Duke's whereabouts; he thought his Grace would not be at all pleased if they were brought into publicity. Why? Well, he had an idea that his Grace wished for privacy. Yes, he admitted gradually, he *had* seen a chalice in the Duke's possession on Monday. Considering that on the Monday night he had been awakened to watch in front of it after the other three had retired, content to believe the Archdeacon's assertion that the attack had failed, this was a restrained way of putting it. But it had been indicated to him that the Duke desired secrecy, and secrecy Thwaites was trying to maintain. But he became anxious when he heard of the disappearance, or at least of the non-appearance, of his master and admitted more than he altogether meant. He admitted that the chalice was not now in London; the Duke and his friends had taken it with them on the Wednesday. This was Thursday, he pointed out, to himself as well as the visitors, so the Duke's absence had not yet lasted for much over twelve hours—not so very long.

"Say four o'clock to twelve-twenty," the inspector said.

"Well, not twenty-four," Thwaites answered. "Only a night, you might say. Not so long but what, if his Grace was busy with something, he mightn't easily be away."

"Does the Duke often stay away without warning?" the Assistant Commissioner asked.

Not often, Thwaites admitted, but it had been known. He had gone for a sort of a joy-ride once and not been back for the whole twenty-four hours. Still, his Grace had been very anxious about something, something private, he didn't know what, but something to do with the chalice, on the Monday and Tuesday.

The Duchess, Thwaites thought, had not been told, since the Duke was not much in the habit of telling his aunt anything; and he very strongly dissuaded the visitors from making any inquiries there. Her Grace, he hinted, was a notorious chatterbox, and the incidents they were investigating would be discussed in a thousand drawing-rooms. If inquiry must be made, let it be conducted by the police along their own channels.

It was, however, exactly the method of conducting it which was annoying the Assistant Commissioner. He exhorted Thwaites to let him know immediately the Duke returned, or if news of him arrived, and to report to him by telephone every two hours if the Duke had not returned. He then withdrew with the inspector.

"Well," he said when they were in the street again, "I think you'd better go back to Fardles, Colquhoun, and see if you find out anything there. You might, in the circumstances, have a chat with the Archdeacon, and keep an eye on Persimmons's movements. I'll send another man down to help you. There's only one other thing that occurs to me. When Colonel Conyers was up on Monday he asked about the Duke and the Archdeacon and the others, and also about some North London Greek who had got Persimmons this accursed chalice. I'll put a man on to*him*. Ring me up later and tell me what's happened."

Towards evening the Assistant Commissioner received three telephone reports. The first was Thwaites, with the usual "Nothing has happened, sir. His Grace has not returned and we have received no information." This time, however, he added, "The Duchess is becoming anxious, sir. She is talking of consulting the police. Shall I put her through to you, sir?"

"No, for God's sake," the Commissioner said hastily. "Tell her something, anything you like. Tell her to ring up the nearest police station…. No, she won't do that as she knows me. All right, Thwaites, put her through."

The Duchess was put through, and the Commissioner extracted from her what he really wanted—permission to investigate. He then pretended to be cut off.

It was some minutes later that he received a call from Colquhoun.

"The Archdeacon isn't here, sir," the inspector reported. "He left for London just before lunch, about when we were at the Duke's. They don't know when he'll be back. Mr. Persimmons also left, just after lunch. I must have passed him in the train. Rackstraw is here and his wife, in a cottage in Persimmons's grounds. They apparently have a small boy, but he's been taken to London by a maid of Persimmons'. I knew Rackstraw was in it somehow."

"Family man, Persimmons," the Assistant Commissioner said. "Pity you couldn't have let us know he was coming, and I really think we'd have had him covered."

"Well, sir, both he and the Archdeacon were away before I got down here," the inspector said forbearingly. "Shall I come back?"

"No, I think not," his chief said. "Stop to-day, anyhow, and let me hear to-morrow if there's anything fresh. I've sent Pewitt to Finchley Road, but he's not reported yet. It's all pure chance. We really don't know what we're looking for."

"I thought we were trying to find out why Persimmons murdered Pattison, sir," the inspector answered.

"I suppose we are," his chief said, "but we seem rather like sparrows hopping round Persimmons on the chance of a crumb. Well, carry on; see if you can pick one up and let us guzzle it to-morrow. Good-bye."

He sat back, lit a cigarette, and turned to other work, till, somewhere about half-past eight, Pewitt also rang up. Pewitt was a young fellow who was being tried on the mere mechanics of this kind of work, and he had been sent up to the Finchley Road not more than two hours earlier, having been engaged on another job for most of the day. His voice now sounded depressed and worried.

"Pewitt speaking," he said, when the Commissioner had announced himself. "I'm—I'm in rather a hole, sir. I—we—can't find the house."

"Can't *what*?" his chief asked.

"Can't find the house, sir," Pewitt repeated. "I know it sounds silly, but it's the simple truth. It doesn't seem to be there."

The Assistant Commissioner blinked at the telephone. "Are you mad or merely idiotic, Pewitt?" he asked. "I did think you'd got the brains of a peewit, anyhow, if not much more. Have you lost the address I gave you or what?"

"No, sir," Pewitt said, "I've got the address all right—Lord Mayor's Street. It was a chemist's, you said. But there doesn't seem to be a chemist's there. Of course, the fog makes it difficult, but still, I don't *think* it is there."

"The fog?" the Commissioner said.

"It's very thick up here in North London," Pewitt answered, "very thick indeed."

"Are you sure you're in the right street?" his chief asked.

"Certain, sir. The constable on duty is here too. He seems to remember the shop, sir, but he can't find it, either. All we can find, sir, is——"

"Stop a minute," the Commissioner interrupted. He rang his bell and sent for a Directory; then, having found it, he went on. "Now go ahead. Where do you begin?"

"George Giddings, grocer."

"Right."

"Samuel Murchison, confectioner."

"Right."

"Mrs. Thorogood, apartments."

"Damn it, man," the Commissioner exploded, "you've just gone straight over it. Dmitri Lavrodopoulos, chemist."

"But it *isn't*, sir," Pewitt said unhappily. "The fog's very thick, but we couldn't have missed a whole shop."

"But Colonel Conyers has *been* there," the Commissioner shouted, "been there and talked with this infernal fellow. Good God above, it must be there! You're drunk, Pewitt."

"I feel as if I was, sir," the mournful voice said, "groping about in this, but I'm not. I've looked at the Directory myself, sir, and it's all right there. But it's not all right here. The house has simply disappeared."

"That must have been what just flew past the window," the other said bitterly. "Look here, Pewitt, I'm coming up myself. And God help you and your friend the constable if I find that house, for I'll tear you limb from limb and roast you and eat you. And God help me if I don't," he said, putting back the receiver, "for if houses disappear as well as Dukes, this'll be no world for me."

It took him much longer than he expected to reach Lord Mayor's Street. As his taxi climbed north, he found himself entering into what was at first a faint mist, and later, before he reached Tally Ho Corner, an increasing fog. Indeed, after a while the taxi-driver refused to go any farther, and the Assistant Commissioner proceeded slowly on foot. He knew the Finchley Road generally and vaguely, and after a long time and many risks at last drew near his aim. At what he hoped was the corner of Lord Mayor's Street he ran directly into a stationary figure.

"What the hell——" he began. "Sorry, sir. Oh, it's you, Pewitt. Damnation, man, why don't you shout instead of knocking me down? All right, all right. But standing at the corner of the street won't find the house, you know. Where's the constable? Why don't you keep together? Oh, he's here, is he! Couldn't even one of you look for the house instead of holding a revival meeting at the street corner? Now for God's sake don't apologize or I shall have to begin too, and we shall look like a ring of chimpanzees at the Zoo. I know as well as you do that I'm in a vile temper. Come along and let's have a look. Where's the grocer's?"

He was shown it. Then, he first, Pewitt second, and the constable last, they edged along the houses, their torches turned on the windows. "That's the grocer's," the Commissioner went on. "And here—this blasted fog's thicker than ever—is the end of the grocer's, I suppose; at least it's the end of a window. Then this must be the confectioner's. I believe I saw a cake; the blind's only half down. And here's a door, the confectioner's door. Didn't you think of doing it this way, Pewitt?"

"Yes, sir," Pewitt said, "the constable and I have done it about seventeen times."

The Assistant Commissioner, neglecting this answer, pushed ahead. "And this is the end of the confectioner's second window," he said triumphantly. "And here's a bit of wall … more wall … and here—here's a gate." He stopped uncertainly.

"Yes, sir," Pewitt said; "that's Mrs. Thorogood's gate. We called there, sir, but she's an old lady and rather deaf, and some of her lodgers are on their holiday and some haven't got home from work yet. And we couldn't quite get her to understand what we were talking about. We tried again a little while ago, but she wouldn't even come to the door."

The Assistant Commissioner looked at the gate, or rather, at the fog, for the gate was invisible. So was the constable; he could just discern a thicker blot that was Pewitt. He felt the gate—undoubtedly it was just that. He stood still and recalled to his mind the page he had studied in the Directory. Yes, between Murchison the confectioner and Mrs. Thorogood, apartments, it leapt to his eye, Dmitri Lavrodopoulos, chemist.

"Have you tried the confectioner?" he asked.

"Well, sir, he wouldn't do more than talk out of the first-floor window," Pewitt said, "but we did try him. He said he knew what kind of people went round knocking at doors in the fog. He swore he'd got two windows, and he said the chemist was next door. But somehow we couldn't just find next door."

"It must be round some corner," the Assistant Commissioner said; and "Yes, sir, no doubt it must be round some corner," Pewitt answered.

The other felt as if something was beginning to crack. Everything seemed disappearing. The Duke had not come home, nor Mornington, whoever he might be; the Archdeacon and Gregory Persimmons had left home. And now a whole house seemed to have been swallowed up. He went slowly back to the corner, followed by his subordinates, then he tried again—very slowly and crouched right against the windows. On either side of the confectioner's door was a strip of glass without blinds, and he dimly discerned in each window, within an inch and a half of his nose, scones and buns and jam-tarts. Certainly the farther one no more than the first belonged to a chemist. And yet for the second time, as he pushed beyond it, he felt the rough wall under his fingers and then the iron gate.

The Directory and Colonel Conyers must both be wrong, he thought; there could be no other explanation. Lavrodopoulos must have left, and the shop been taken over by the confectioner. But it was on Monday Colonel Conyers had called, and this was only Thursday. Besides, the confectioner had said that the chemist's was next door. He felt the wall again; it ought to be there.

"What do you make of it, Pewitt?" he asked.

Out of the fog Pewitt answered: "I don't like it, sir," he said. "I dare say it's a mistake, but I don't like that. It isn't natural."

"I suppose you think the devil has carried it off," the Assistant Commissioner said, and thought automatically of the Bible he had studied that morning. He struck impatiently at the wall. "Damn it, the shop must be there," he said. But the shop was not there.

Suddenly, as they stood there in a close group, the grounds beneath them seemed to shift and quiver. Pewitt and the constable cried out; the Assistant Commissioner jumped aside. It shook again. "Good God," he cried, "what in the name of the seven devils is happening to the world? Are you there, Pewitt?" for his movement had separated them. He heard some sort of reply, but knew himself alone and felt suddenly afraid. Again the earth throbbed below him; then from nowhere a great blast of cool wind struck his face. So violent was it that he reeled and almost fell; then, as he regained his poise, he saw that the fog was dissolving around him. A strange man was standing in front of him; behind him the windows of a chemist's shop came abruptly into being. The stranger came up to him. "I am Gregory Persimmons," he said, "and I wish to give myself up to the police for murder."

————————————

Chapter Seventeen

THE MARRIAGE OF THE LIVING
AND THE DEAD

While Inspector Colquhoun had been discussing the Pattison murder with his chief that morning, the Archdeacon of Castra Parvulorum had been working at parish business in his study. He hoped, though he did not much expect, that Mornington would call on him in the course of the day, and he certainly proposed to himself to walk over to the Rackstraws' cottage and hear how the patient was progressing. The suspicions which Mornington and the Duke had felt on the previous day had not occurred to him, partly because he had accepted the episode as finished for him until some new demand should bring him again into action, but more still because he had been prevented by the Duke's collision with him from seeing what had happened. He supposed that the new doctor had been able to soothe Barbara either by will-power or drugs, and, though the doctor's mania for possession of the Graal appeared to him as bad-mannered as Gregory's, that was not, after all, his affair. The conversation of the previous night he kept and pondered in his heart, but here, again, it was not his business to display activity, but to wait on the Mover of all things. He went on making notes about the Sunday school register; the Sunday school was a burden to him, but the mothers of the village expected it, and the Archdeacon felt bound to supply the need. He occasionally quoted to himself "*Feed my lambs*," but a profound doubt of the proper application of the text haunted him; and he was far from certain that the food which was supplied to them even in the Sunday school at Fardles was that which Christ had intended. However, this also, he thought to himself, the Divine Redeemer would purify and make good.

Mrs. Lucksparrow appeared at the door. "Mr. Persimmons has called, sir," she said, "and would like to see you for a few minutes, if you can spare the time. About the Harvest Festival, I think it is," she added in a lower tone.

"Really?" the Archdeacon asked in surprise, and then again, in a slightly different voice, "Really!" Mr. Persimmons's manners, he thought, were becoming almost intolerable. He got up and went to interview his visitor in the hall.

"So sorry to trouble you, Mr. Archdeacon," Gregory said, smiling, "but I was asked to deliver this note to you personally. To make sure you got it and to see if there is any answer."

The Archdeacon, glinting rather like a small, frosty pool, took it and opened it. He read it once; he read it twice; he looked up to find Gregory staring out through the front door. He looked down, read it a third time, and stood pondering.

"'Sihon, King of the Amorites,'" he hummed abstractedly, "'and Og, the King of Basan: for His mercy endureth for ever.' You know what is in this note, Mr. Persimmons?"

"I'm afraid I do," Gregory answered charmingly. "The circumstances …"

"Yes," the Archdeacon said meditatively, "yes. Naturally."

"Naturally?" Gregory asked, rather as if making conversation.

"Well, I don't mean to be rude," the Archdeacon said, "but, in the first place, if it's true, you would probably know; in the second, you probably wrote it; and, in the third, you probably and naturally would read other people's letters anyhow. Yes, well, thank you so much."

"You don't want to put any questions?" Gregory asked.

"No," the Archdeacon answered, "I don't think so. I've no means of checking you, have I? And I should never dream of relying on people who made a practice of defying God—in any real sense. They'd be almost bound to lose all sense of proportion."

"Well," Gregory said, "you must do as you will. But I can tell you that what is written there is true. We have them in our power and we can slay them in a moment."

"That will save them a good deal of trouble, won't it?" the Archdeacon said. "Are you sure they want me to interfere? 'To die now. 'Twere now to be most happy.'"

"Ah, you talk," Gregory said, unreasonably enraged. "But do you think either of those young men wants to die? Or to see the vessel for which they die made into an instrument of power and destruction?"

"I would tell you what I am going to do if I knew," the Archdeacon answered, "but I do not know. You are forgetting, however, to tell me where I shall come if I come."

Gregory recovered himself, gave the address, reached the door, remarked on the beauty of the garden, and disappeared. The Archdeacon went back to his study, shut the door, and gave himself up to interior silence and direction.

Gregory went on to Cully. The slight passage at arms with the priest had given him real delight, but as he walked he was conscious of renewed alarms stirring in his being: alarms not so much of fear as of doubt. He found that by chance he was now in touch with two or three persons who found no satisfaction in desire and possession and power. No power of destruction seemed to satisfy Manasseh's hunger; no richness of treasure to arouse the Archdeacon's. And as he moved in these unaccustomed regions he felt that what was lacking was delight. It had delighted him in the past to overbear and torment; but Manasseh's greed had never found content. And delight was far too small a word for the peace in which the Archdeacon moved; a sky of serenity overarched Gregory when he thought of the priest against which his own arrows were shot in vain. He saw it running from the east to the west; he saw below it, in the midst of a flat circle of emptiness, the face of the Greek spewing out venom. Absurdly enough, he felt himself angered by the mere uselessness of this; it was something of the same irritation which he had expressed to his son on the proportion of capital expended on the worst kind of popular novel. Enjoyment was all very well, but enjoyment oughtn't to be merely wasteful. It annoyed him as his father had annoyed him by wasting emotions and strength in mere stupid, senile worry. Adrian must be taught the uselessness of that—power was the purpose of spiritual things, and Satan the lord of power. He turned in at the gates of Cully, and saw before him the window where he had talked with Adrian's father. "A clerk in a brothel," he thought suddenly; but even the clerk desired power. And then, in a sudden desperation, he saw that unchanging serenity of sky, and even the flames of the Sabbath leapt uselessly miles below it. Here he had met the young stranger: "only slaves can trespass, and they only among shadows." But he was not a slave—that sky mocked him as the boast swelled. Slaves, slaves, it sounded, and his foot in the hall echoed the word again in his ear.

He inquired for Jessie and the boy; they were in the grounds, and he went out to find them, looking also for Lionel and Barbara. But these he did not meet, although he eventually discovered the others. Adrian, apparently resting, was telling himself a complicated and interminable story; Jessie was looking into a small stream and pondering her own thoughts—Gregory smiled to think what they probably were. He very nearly addressed her as "Mrs. Persimmons," remembering that she probably knew nothing of his wife in the asylum, but refrained.

Barbara, it seemed, was as well as ever; she had spent an hour with Adrian before Mr. Rackstraw had made her go away. Then they—Jessie and Adrian—had come out into the grounds, and there had met a strange gentleman who had talked and played with Adrian for a little while. Gregory raised his eyebrows at this, and Jessie explained that she had not approved, but had not been able to prevent it, especially since Adrian had welcomed him so warmly that she had supposed them to be old friends.

"But what was he doing in the grounds?" Gregory asked.

"I don't know, sir," Jessie answered; "he seemed to know them, and he told me he knew you."

Gregory suspected that this was the only cause of her frankness, but it was hardly worth troubling to rebuke her. Within a week Jessie might find herself only too anxious to make friends with strangers in Vienna or Adrianople, or somewhere farther east.

"What was he like?" he said.

"Oh, quite young, sir, and rather foreign-looking, and dressed all in grey. He and the boy seemed to be talking a foreign language half the time."

Gregory stood still abruptly, and then began to walk on again. What had Sir Giles said about this stranger? And who was it the stranger reminded him of? The Archdeacon, of course; they both had something of that same remote serenity, that provoking, overruling detachment. In the rush of the previous day's excitement he had forgotten to consult Manasseh; that would be remedied before night. But the talk of a foreign language disturbed him a little, lest Adrian should have a closer and more intimate friend than himself or than he had known. If there were anything in Sir Giles's babblings…. He gathered himself together and turned sharply to Jessie.

"We shall go to London," he said, "I and Adrian and you to look after Adrian, directly after lunch. To-morrow we may go abroad for a little. It's sudden, but it can't be helped. And it's not to be chattered about. See to it."

It chanced therefore that, by the time Inspector Colquhoun had finished making inquiries of Mrs. Lucksparrow at the Rectory, Gregory, with Adrian and Jessie, had reached Lord Mayor's Street. The shop was closed, but Manasseh admitted them, and Jessie was shown, first the kitchen and afterwards the small upstairs room where she and Adrian were to sleep. She was not shown the cellar, where the Duke of the North Ridings lay bound, and she and Adrian were rushed swiftly through the back room, where the Archdeacon was looking pensively out of the window. He glanced at them as they went through, but neither face conveyed anything to his mind. Gregory had provided Adrian with two or three new toys, but it was intimated to Jessie that the sooner he was put to bed the better, and that she had better stay with him, as it was a strange room, lest he woke and was afraid.

The captives thus disposed of, Gregory went back to his friends, who were in the shop. The Archdeacon had left off looking out of the window and was reading the *Revelations* of Lady Julian close by it.

"He has come, then," Gregory said.

"He has come," Manasseh answered; "didn't you expect *him*?"

"I didn't know," Gregory said. "He didn't seem at all sure this morning. And I don't know why he has come."

"He has come," the Greek said, "for the same reason that we are here—because in the whole world of Being everything makes haste to its doom. Are you determined and prepared for what you will do?"

Gregory looked back through the half-open door. "I have considered it for many hours," he said. "I am determined and prepared."

"Why, then, should we delay?" the Greek said. "I have hidden this house in a cloud and drawn it in to our hearts so that it shall not be entered from without till the work is done."

Gregory involuntarily looked towards the window, and saw a thick darkness rising above it, a darkness not merely foglike, as it seemed to those without, but shot with all kinds of colour and movement as if some living nature were throbbing about them. The Greek turned and went into the inner room, and the other followed him. There the darkness was already gathering, so that the Archdeacon had ceased to read and was waiting for whatever was to follow. All that day, since he had talked with Gregory in the morning, he had been conscious that the power to which he had slowly taught himself to live in obedience was gradually withdrawing and abandoning him. Steadily and continuously that process went on, till now, as he faced his enemies, he felt the interior loss which had attacked him at other stages of his pilgrimage grow into a final overwhelming desolation. He said to himself again, as he so often said, "This also is Thou," for desolation as well as abundance was but a means of knowing That which was All. But he felt extraordinarily lonely in the darkness of the small room, with Persimmons and Manasseh and the unknown third gazing at him from the door.

The Greek moved slowly forward, considered for a moment, and then said: "Do you know why you have come here?"

"I have come because God willed it," the Archdeacon said. "Why did you send for me?"

"For a thing that is to be done," the Greek said, "and you shall help in the doing." As he spoke, Manasseh caught the priest's arm with a little crow of greedy satisfaction, and Gregory laid hold of his other shoulder.

"You shall help in the doing of it," the Greek said, smiling for the first time since Gregory had known him, with a sudden and swift convulsion. "Take him and bind him and lay him down."

It was quickly done; the Archdeacon was unable to resist, not so much because of the greater strength of his opponents as because that interior withdrawal of energy had now touched his body and he was weakening every moment. He was stretched on the ground, and Manasseh tore at his clothes till his breast was bare. Then the Greek lifted the Graal from the table by the window and set it on the priest, and still the darkness increased and moved and swirled around them. The Archdeacon heard voices above him, heard Gregory say: "Are there no markings and ceremonies?" and the Greek answer: "We are retired beyond such things; there is only one instrument, and that is the blood with which I have filled the cup; there is only one safeguard, in the purpose of our wills. For your part, remember the man you slew; keep his image in your mind and let it be imposed on this man's being. For through this Manasseh and I will work."

The darkness closed entirely over, and as the Archdeacon lay he knew for a while nothing but the waste of an obscure night. Then there became known to him within it three separate points of existence and energy about him, from each of which issued a shaft of directed power. He was aware that these shafts were not yet aimed directly at him; he was aware also of a difference in their nature. For that which was nearest him was also the least certain; it shook and faltered; it was more like anger as he had known it among men, red and variable and mortal. This anger was the effluence of a similar centre, a centre which was known on that earth they had left as Gregory Persimmons, and trembled still with desires natural to man. So far as in him lay, the Archdeacon presented himself to that spirit and profession as a means whereby the satisfaction of all desire might meet it; not by such passions was hell finally peopled and the last rejection found.

But this procession was not alone; it was controlled and directed by mightier powers. From another centre there issued a different force, and this, the victim realized, it would need all his present strength to meet. There impinged upon him the knowledge of all hateful and separating and deathly things: madness and tormenting disease and the vengeance of gods. This was the hunger with which creation preys upon itself, a supernatural famine that has no relish except for the poisons that waste it. This was the second death that cannot die, and it ran actively through that world of immortalities on a hungry mission of death. What that mission was he did not yet know; the beam played somewhere above him and disappeared where a central darkness hid the Graal. But he knew that the mission would be presently revealed, and he asserted by a spiritual act the perfection of all manner of birth.

Even as he did so the act itself quivered and almost died. For the third stream of energy passed over him, and its very passage shook the centre of his being from its roots. This was no longer mission or desire, search or propaganda or hunger; this was rejection absolute. No mortal mind could conceive a desire which was not based on a natural and right desire; even the hunger for death was but a perversion of the death which precedes all holy birth. But of every conceivable and inconceivable desire this was the negation. This was desire itself sick, but not unto death; rejection which tore all things asunder and swept them with it in its fall through the abyss. He felt himself sinking even in the indirect rush of its passage; here, if anywhere, the foundation of the universe must hold them firm, for otherwise he and the universe were ruining together for ever. But that foundation, if it existed, had separated itself from him; he cried desperately to God and God did not hear him. The three intermingling currents passed on their way, and, fainting and helpless, he awaited the further end.

There came for a little a relief. He was dimly aware again for some moments of external things—a breath above him, the slight feeling of the Cup upon his breast, the pressure of the cords that held his arms to his sides. Then slowly and very gently these departed again and he felt himself being directed towards—he did not know what. But he was, as it were, moving. He was passing to a preordained tryst; he was meeting something, and he grew dreadfully afraid. Marriage awaited him, and the darkness above him took shape and he knew that another existence was present, an existence that hated and strove against this tryst as much as he hated and strove against it, but which was driven as he was remorselessly driven. Nearer and nearer, through ages of time, they were brought; desire and death and utter rejection gathered their victims from the various worlds and drew them into union. His body became aware again of the Graal, and from the Graal itself the visitation came. He felt that no longer the Graal but a human being was there; he saw a weak, anxious, and harassed face look on him despairingly. He saw it float about him, and his very consciousness, which had taken in all these things up to then, began to feel them differently. Some entry was being forced into that which was he; in that Vessel which had held the Blood which is the potentiality of all he and this other were to be wrecked in each other for ever. Then this knowledge itself was withdrawn and no function of his being recorded any more.

It was at this moment, when he had been driven beyond consciousness, that the masters of the work above him concentrated their utmost resources for the purpose they had in hand. The Graal vibrated before them in the intensity of their power.

In obedience to the Greek's direction, Gregory had concentrated his consciousness upon that being whom he had, not so very long ago, slain; partly for safety, partly for mere amusement, partly as an offering to his god. He set before himself the thought of the wretched man's whole life, from the moment when the discovery of small thefts had put him in his power, through his years of service and torment, through the last effort towards freedom, through the last deliberate return. Pattison had returned to his death and had died, obeying minutely all the orders that had been given him; clean and unmarked linen, no papers, his few belongings left in a bag at some Tube station, and the ticket destroyed—he had seen that all was done under the fascination of his master's law. And now that law was to do something more with him; it searched for him in the place of shadows where his uncertain spirit wandered; it explored the night beyond death to recover him thence. Gregory held the knowledge of the man's soul fast in his mind, and from his own solitary wanderings in the abyss that soul began to return to its lord. Upward now, his image began to rise, as some few days since the wraith of the child Adrian had floated, but even more swiftly by virtue of the triple call. A fantastic bubble of tinged cloud seemed to appear, moving upward from the Graal, and the bubble thickened and became mist and shaped itself into a form and face. The Graal was dimly visible in a faint green light, through which and over which the recalled spirit took on a mortal covering. Gregory involuntarily smiled at the appeal on the face that was momentarily visible, and renewed his effort to offer up both the captives in sacrifice to the tremendous power he adored. Slowly the strength of the three prevailed. Little by little that shadow sank and spread itself over the motionless form on the floor, little by little it flowed round it and into it. Gregory, almost exhausted with the effort, would have ceased, contented, as the last faint coils of mist faded from the light that shone, like a light of decay, from the Graal. But the knowledge and energy of his companions insisted, in the continuous force they expended, that nothing but a mental haunting, a perpetual obsession, had yet been achieved. Something further yet was needed for the final and perfect marriage of these two victims; and in an instant something further came.

The faint glow round the Vessel faded and vanished; and all the moving darkness of the room seemed to direct itself towards and to emerge from that thickest core of night which beat in the Cup, as if its very heart were beating there. One moment only they heard and felt that throbbing heart, and then suddenly from it there broke a terrific and golden light; blast upon blast of trumpets shook the air; the Graal blazed with fiery tumult before them; and its essence, as at last that essence was touched, awoke in its own triumphant and blinding power. None could tell whether light and trumpets were indeed there; but something was there—something which, as it caught and returned upon them the energies they had put forth, seemed also to bestride the prostrate figure on the floor. The Graal was lifted or was itself no more—they could not tell; they were flung back before this lifting and visible form. He over whom it stood returned also from the depths; he looked up and saw it flaming through the scattering night, and heard a litany which changed as it smote his ears from the chant of an unknown tongue into the familiar and cherished maxims of his natural mind.

"Let them give thanks whom the Lord hath redeemed," a great voice sang, and from all about it, striking into light and sound at once, the answer came: "for His mercy endureth for ever."

"And delivered out of the snare of the enemy," it sang again; and again an infinite chorus crashed: "for His mercy endureth for ever."

He moved his arms and the cords that held them snapped; he half arose as the Graal, or he that was the Graal, moved forward and upward. All sense of the horrible intrusion into his nature and essence had gone. He saw somewhere for a moment near him the face he had seemed to see before, but it was free and happy and adoring; he saw Kenneth somewhere and lost him again, and again all round him the litany wheeled like fire:

"He hath destroyed great nations: for His mercy endureth for ever:

"And overthrown mighty kings: for His mercy endureth for ever."

He was on his feet, and before him the room, cleared of light and darkness, showed its usual bare dirtiness. In front of him was the figure of the priest-king, the Graal lifted in his hands. Beyond lay the others—Gregory prostrate on his face, Manasseh shaking and writhing on his back, the Greek crouched half back on his heels.

"I am John," a voice sounded, "and I am the prophecy of the things that are to be and are. You who have sought the centre of the Graal, behold through me that which you seek, receive from me that which you are. He that is righteous, let him be righteous still; he that is filthy, let him be filthy still. I am rejection to him that hath sought rejection; I am destruction to him that hath wrought destruction; I am sacrifice to him that hath offered sacrifice. Friend to my friends and lover to my lovers, I will quit all things, for I am myself and I am He that sent me. This war is ended and another follows quickly. Do that which you must while the time is with you."

The Archdeacon saw Gregory drag himself slowly to his feet; Manasseh was lying still; the Greek crouched lower still on the floor.

"Gregory Persimmons," the voice went on, "they wait for you close at hand. Can a man sacrifice his brother or make agreement with any god for him? Die, then, as this other has died, and there shall be agreement with you also in the end, for you have sought me and no other."

Gregory turned dully to the door and moved towards it. The priest-king turned to the Archdeacon and held the Graal out to him. "Brother and friend," he said, "the rest is in your charge. One of your friends is below, the other is with me. Take your friend and this Cup and return, and I will come to you to-morrow."

The Archdeacon took the Graal with his usual sedateness. It was as tarnished as it had been when he last saw it. He glanced at the figures on the floor; he looked again at the high face of the priest-king, glimmering in the natural dusk; then, gravely and a little daintily, he went out towards the cellars.

In the room above, the maid Jessie was awakened by what seemed the light of a shaded lamp. She saw the stranger with whom Adrian had played that morning standing by her. "Come," he said, "your master is in the hands of the police, and we return to Fardles to-night. Do not disturb yourself about the child; he will not wake." He gathered the sleeping Adrian in his arms, wrapped some dark covering round him, added: "Come; I shall wait for you at the doors," and left the room.

How Jessie got back to Cully she was never very clear. She had a vague impression of moving through country lanes, and supposed it must have been in a motor, though, as she afterwards said, to her most intimate friend, "I was so sleepy it might have been an angel, for all I knew. And a mercy the police got Mr. Persimmons in time, for I don't know that I'd have said 'No' if he'd asked me."

"You'd have had the house and a good bit of money, even so," her friend elliptically said.

"What, and be the wife of a man that's been hung?" Jessie said indignantly, "to say nothing of his being a murderer. Thank you for nothing, Lizzie; that's not the kind of girl I am. Why, it'd be no better than selling yourself for money."

Chapter Eighteen

CASTRA PARVULORUM

The Duke of the North Ridings had spent the night at the Rectory, and both he and the Archdeacon had slept soundly, though it was rather late before they got to bed. They had caught the last train to the nearest junction, which was five miles off; and both in the train and on the walk the Archdeacon had been mildly bothered by the Graal. He had caught up a sheet of paper from the shop when they left it, with some notion of not being a cause of blasphemy to the ungodly by carrying an unveiled chalice, but he had never been able to arrange it successfully, and its ends kept waving about and disclosing the Cup. A cheerful and slightly drunk excursionist in the train had found this a theme for continual merriment at the general expense of the clergy and the Church, and something he had said had caused the Archdeacon to wonder whether perhaps he were being a stumbling-block to one of those little ones who had not yet attained detachment. However, he recovered his usual equilibrium during the walk, and negatived successfully the Duke's feeling that they ought to keep a common vigil.

"I'm extremely sleepy," he said apologetically, but firmly. "After all, it's been rather a tiring day, and—as someone said—I will meet my God with an unclouded mind."

"Doctor Johnson," the Duke unthinkingly supplied the unnecessary information, and then smiled. "I expect you're right," he said. "He gave us sleep also."

"For His mercy endureth for ever," the Archdeacon quite sincerely answered; and they parted for the night.

Barbara awoke early that morning in her cottage; she had taken a dislike to sleeping at Cully, and, without disturbing the sleeping Lionel, wandered out of doors. The first person she saw was Adrian playing on the grass with the young man she had tried to recognize on an earlier day, and she ran over to them with exclamations. Adrian, fresh and energetic, hurled himself at her with tumultuous shrieks of greeting and information, and she looked laughingly to the stranger for an explanation.

"Gregory Persimmons has been arrested," he said, "on his own confession, for murder; and, as I was there, I brought your son back at once. He's slept very well, and we've been playing out here since he woke."

Barbara, holding Adrian with one hand, pushed her hair back with the other, the long scar showing as she moved her wrist. "That's very nice of you," she said. "But Mr. Persimmons! What a dreadful thing!"

"Do you really think so, Mrs. Rackstraw?" the other asked, smiling.

Barbara blushed, and then looked grave. "No," she said. "Well, at least, somehow I don't feel surprised. Since I met you, I haven't felt quite the same about Mr. Persimmons."

"You may feel the same now," Prester John answered, and was interrupted by Adrian.

"Hush, darling!" his mother said. "Go to church? Yes, if you like. I'm afraid," she added, blushing rather more deeply as she looked at the stranger again, "that we don't go as regularly as we should."

"It is a means," he answered, "one of the means. But perhaps the best for most, and for some almost the only one. I do not say that it matters greatly, but the means cannot both be and not be. If you do not use it, it is a pity to bother about it; if you do, it is a pity not to use it."

"Yes," Barbara said doubtfully. "Lionel was rather badgered into it as a boy, and he almost dislikes it now, and so …"

"One's foes are always in one's own household," the other answered, with a rather mournful smile. But, as Barbara glanced at him, suspecting a remoter meaning, he went on. "But this morning Adrian is to serve me in the church over there."

"Serve!" Barbara said, aghast. "But he can't do it. He's only four, and he knows nothing about it, and——"

"He can do all I need, Mrs. Rackstraw," her friend said, and was drowned again by Adrian's "Mum-*mie*! and we've been playing cricket, and will you come and play after breakfast?"

"I thought we were to go to church, darling," Barbara answered.

"Oh, after church too," Adrian said. "And will you come?" he asked the stranger.

The answer was delayed by his seeing Lionel wander out of the cottage in pyjamas, to whom he rushed away still full of the importance and immediacy of life. The other two came after him to the door.

Lionel received with a certain shock the news of Gregory's surrender, but it was a shock produced merely by its suddenness. His eyes dropped to Adrian with a certain questioning dread, as if he were wondering what similar fate in after-life already predestined that innocent and ignorant head. And as Barbara, murmuring of breakfast, or at least of some sort of coffee and biscuits before they went over to the church, disappeared into the cottage with her son, the stranger said to Lionel, "Yet he may escape."

Lionel looked up. "Oh, yes," he said vaguely, though he felt the fantasy, as he stood alone with the other, take sharp form within his mind. "Oh, yes—that, but something awaits him surely of ruin and of despair."

"It may be," the stranger said, "but perhaps a happy ruin and a fortunate despair. These things are not evil in themselves, and I think you fear them overmuch."

"I fear all things," Lionel answered, "and I do not understand how it is that men do not fear them more. In the town it is bad enough, but there one is deafened and blinded by people and things. But here everything is so still and meditative, and I am afraid of what those meditations are."

"Is there, then, nothing pleasant in life?" Prester John said.

Lionel answered, almost savagely, "Can't you see that when life is most pleasant one suspects it most? Unless one can drug oneself with the moment and forget."

"I do not think you drug yourself much," the stranger said, smiling. "Are you sure you do not love your fears?"

"No," Lionel said; "I am not sure of anything. I do think I love to feel them though I loathe them, but I do not know why."

"Because so chiefly you feel yourself alive," the other said, "separated from them and hostile and tormented, but alive in heart and brain. You desire death! Your very desire witnesses how passionately you feel these things and how strongly you live."

Lionel smiled a little. "*Heautontimoroumenos?*" he asked doubtfully.

"No, not that," the stranger answered. "But you are afraid of losing yourself in the fantasies of daily life, and you think that these pains will save you. But I bring the desire of all men, and what will you ask of me?"

"Annihilation," Lionel answered. "I have not asked for life, and I should be content now to know that soon I should not be. Do you think I desire the heaven they talk of?"

"Death you shall have at least," the other said. "But God only gives, and He has only Himself to give, and He, even He, can give it only in those conditions which are Himself. Wait but a few years, and He shall give you the death you desire. But do not grudge too much if you find that death and heaven are one." He pointed towards Cully. "This man desired greatly the God of all sacrifice and sacrifice itself, and he finds Him now. But you shall find another way, for the door that opens on annihilation opens only on the annihilation which is God."

He walked away across the glade, and when Lionel saw him again it was in the church built above the spot where, tradition said, Caesar had restored the children to their mothers.

The Duke of the North Ridings, rather more than obedient to the strict etiquette of his Church, was leaning against the door-post; the Archdeacon was in his stall. As the other members of that small and curiously drawn congregation came in, Adrian broke from his mother's hand and ran up the aisle on small, hasty feet to where, by the altar, Prester John turned to receive him. To Barbara and the Duke, accustomed to liturgical vestments, the priest-king seemed to be clothed in the chasuble of tradition; to Lionel he seemed to stand, pure and naked, in the high sunlight of the morning; what he seemed to the child none then or ever knew. He sank on one knee to meet him, opened his arms to Adrian's rush, and then, after a moment during which they seemed to confer, drew him gently to the credence table at the side. There Adrian, grave and content, plumped himself down on a hassock for a seat, and the priest-king returned to the front of the altar.

The sacristan was away down in the village, but suddenly above them they heard the noise of a bell, only higher and more remote and more clear than any bell they had heard before, as if the very idea of sound made itself felt in those notes, and withdrew and ceased. The priest-king spread out his hands and brought them together, and there was a movement throughout the church, as if a hundred watchers had stirred and drawn breath at the beginning of the Mysteries. The Duke leaned a little forward in perplexity; he saw the forms with which he was acquainted, but here and there, only always just to one side or in some corner, he seemed to see other forms. They had vanished in a moment, yet they had been there. He had caught certain of the faces which he knew in the great gallery of his ancestors in the Castle, and other faces more antique and foreign than these, a turbaned head, a helmed and armoured shape, outlandish robes, and the glint of many crowns. They had vanished, and he saw Adrian plunge to his feet and go to the celebrant's side. And clear and awful to his ears their voices floated.

The voices were clear, but what they said was hidden. To him by the door, as to Barbara kneeling by a chair, there issued sometimes a familiar phrase. "Introibo," he thought he heard, and could have believed that the child's voice answered, "Ad Deum qui lætificat juventutem meam." But he looked in vain for the motions of the Confession; while he looked the priest-king was up the steps by the altar, though he had not seen him go, and about the church rang the *Christe eleison* and died.

Barbara, less adept at ritual, caught only a sentence of the Collect—"to Whom all hearts be open, all desires known"—and then was happily distracted by the sedate movements of her child, till of a sudden the words of the Lesson recaptured her: "And God said: Let us make man, in Our image, after Our likeness ... in the image of God created He him, male and female created He them." The very sound inclined her ever so slightly towards her husband; her hand went out and found his, and so linked they watched till the end. And the priest-king's voice closed on the Gospel: "Behold, I make all things new."

But the Archdeacon, hearing all these words, trembled a little as he knelt. The thoughts with which he approached the Mysteries faded; the Mysteries themselves faded. He distinguished no longer word from act; he was in the presence, he was part of the Act which far away issued in those faint words, "Let us make man"—creation rose and flowed out and wheeled to its august return—"in Our image, after Our likeness"—the great pronouns were the sound of that return. Faster and faster all things moved through that narrow channel he had before seen and now himself seemed to be entering and beyond it they issued again into similar but different existence—themselves still, yet infused and made one in an undreamed perfection. The sunlight—the very sun itself—was moving on through the upright form before the altar, and darkness and light together were pouring through it, and with them all things that were. He saw, standing at the very edge of that channel, the small figure of Adrian, and then he himself had passed the boy and was entering upon the final stage of the Way. Everything was veiled; the voice of the priest-king was the sound of creation's movement; he awaited the exodus that was to be.

Everything was veiled, but not so entirely that he did not hear from somewhere behind him, in space or in experience, the Duke's voice saying, "Et cum spiritu tuo," or a call from in front, "Lift up your hearts," or again, from behind, Barbara's voice crying, "We lift them up unto the Lord," or, in a higher and more tremendous summons, "Let us give thanks unto the Lord," and, amid the tumult of song that broke out, Lionel's own voice joining in the answer, "It is meet and right so to do."

"It is very meet, right ..." the priest-king said; the three heard it, and heard no more intelligible words. They saw Adrian moving up and about; they saw his grave and happy face as he turned to some motion of his Lord's; they saw him go back and sit down again on his hassock, cuddling his knees, glance down at his mother, and turn to watch the event. For now the unknown sounds were pealing steadily on; all separate beings, save where the hands of the lovers lingered in a final clasp, were concentrated on that high motionless Figure—motionless, for in Him all motions awaited His movement to be loosed, and still He did not move. All sound ceased; all things entered into an intense suspension of being; nothing was anywhere at all but He.

He stood; He moved His hands. As if in benediction He moved them, and at once the golden halo that had hung all this while over the Graal dissolved and dilated into spreading colour; and at once life leapt in all those who watched, and filled and flooded and exalted them. "Let us make man," He sang, "in Our image, after Our likeness," and all the church of visible and invisible presences answered with a roar: "In the image of God created He him: male and female created He them." All things began again to be. At a great distance Lionel and Barbara and the Duke saw beyond Him, as He lifted up the Graal, the moving universe of stars, and then one flying planet, and then fields and rooms and a thousand remembered places, and all in light and darkness and peace.

He seemed to hold the Graal no more; the divine colour that had moved in that vision of creation swathed Him as a close-bound robe. Beyond Him the church was again visible, and silence succeeded to the flying music that had accompanied vision. Like the centre of that silence, they heard His voice calling as if He called a name. He had not turned; still He faced the altar, and thrice He called and was still. The Archdeacon stood up suddenly in his stall; then he came sedately from it, and turned in the middle of the chancel to face the three who watched. He smiled at them, and made a motion of farewell with his hand; then he turned and went up to the sanctuary. At the same moment Adrian, as if in obedience to some command, scrambled to his feet and came down towards his mother. At the gate of the sanctuary the two met; the child paused and raised his face; gravely they exchanged the kiss of peace. Before Adrian had reached Barbara the other began to mount the steps of the altar, and as he set his foot on the first sank gently to the ground.

On the instant, as they gazed, the church, but for them and the prostrate form, was empty. The sunlight shone upon an altar as bare as the pavement before it; without violence, without parting, the Graal and its Lord were gone.

They knelt and prayed, and only stirred at last when, with the natural boredom of childhood, Adrian said in a minute to his mother: "Shall we go home now?" The words dissolved as by a predestined act the forces that held them. Barbara stood up, looked once at Lionel, smiled at Adrian, and went with him out of the church. The Duke came up the aisle.

"Will you tell his people or shall I?" he asked Lionel, and Lionel answered with an equal normality, "As you like. I will stay here, if you will go."

"Very well," the Duke said, and paused, looking at the body. Then he said, smiling at Lionel, "I suppose they will say he had a weak heart."

"Yes," Lionel answered, "I expect they will." He felt suddenly the joy of the fantasy rise in his mind; he walked to the door and watched the Duke crossing the churchyard, and waited till beyond the hedge he saw Mr. Batesby hurrying to the church. Then he went out to meet him.

"Dear, dear," Mr. Batesby said, "how truly distressing! 'In the midst of life' … The Archdeacon too…. Cut down like a palm-tree and thrust into the oven…. No doubt the knock on the head affected it rather much."

THE END

507

Made in the USA
Coppell, TX
03 July 2023

18739917R00280

TO BE HONEST

VOICES ON DONALD TRUMP'S MUSLIM BAN

Edited by
Sarah Beth Kaufman, William G. Christ, and Habiba Noor

ELECTION
2016